Guide to Canadian English Usage

GUIDE TO CANADIAN ENGLISH USAGE

SECOND EDITION

MARGERY FEE & JANICE McALPINE

Strathy Language Unit
Queen's University

OXFORD
UNIVERSITY PRESS

OXFORD
UNIVERSITY PRESS

70 Wynford Drive, Don Mills, Ontario M3C 1J9
www.oup.com/ca

Oxford University Press is a department of the University of Oxford.
It furthers the University's objective of excellence in research, scholarship,
and education by publishing worldwide in

Oxford New York

Auckland Cape Town Dar es Salaam Hong Kong Karachi
Kuala Lumpur Madrid Melbourne Mexico City Nairobi
New Delhi Shanghai Taipei Toronto

With offices in

Argentina Austria Brazil Chile Czech Republic France Greece
Guatemala Hungary Italy Japan Poland Portugal Singapore
South Korea Switzerland Thailand Turkey Ukraine Vietnam

Oxford is a trade mark of Oxford University Press
in the UK and in certain other countries

Published in Canada
by Oxford University Press

Library and Archives Canada Cataloguing in Publication

Fee, Margery, 1948-
Guide to Canadian English usage / Margery Fee and Janice
McAlpine. -- 2nd ed.

Includes bibliographical references.
ISBN 978-0-19-542602-1

1. English language--Canada--Usage. 2. Canadianisms
(English)--Dictionaries. 3. English language--Canada--Dictionaries.
I. McAlpine, Janice II. Title.

PE3235.F44 2007   428.00971'03   C2007-901003-2

Cover and Text Design: Brett Miller

1 2 3 4—10 09 08 07
This book is printed on permanent (acid-free) paper ∞.
Printed in Canada

Contents

Introduction to the Second Edition

Between the first edition and this one, the panda ate, shot, and left. Lynne Truss's book about punctuation, the title of which echoes that brief narrative, became a runaway best-seller. The popularity of usage guides is remarkable: H.W. Fowler's *Modern English Usage* is estimated to have sold half-a-million copies between its first publication in 1926 and 1957 and is still in print in its own right, as well as in the most recent revision (1996) by Robert Burchfield (see Bex). Deborah Cameron argues that the strong public interest in the regulation of language is worth study in itself. The title of her book *Verbal Hygiene* refers to the metaphors of purity that pervade discussions of language. Although non-standard language varieties may suit the purposes of people engaging in social transactions, strong beliefs in the importance of a correct or pure language cannot simply be dismissed.

Linguists often regard attempts to regulate or 'purify' language as misguided, while the public regards linguists as permissive and untrustworthy on matters of usage. This is because the job of a linguist is to describe accurately what speakers and writers do (the 'descriptive' approach), whereas English teachers, editors, and many 'usage experts' want instead to establish and promote a set of rules about how best to speak and write (the 'prescriptive' approach). The task of writing a helpful guide to Canadian usage belongs somewhere between these two schools of practice. We describe how the language is used and also give advice on how to adhere to established conventions.

Usage guides deal only with that limited set of items that are currently the subject of public debate. Their goal is to help people produce better written language. Yet as Jaclyn Rea points out, 'because the recycling of handbooks and style guides presupposes an ideal *and* a general failure to attain this ideal (their *raison d'être*), these texts endlessly reproduce [a] promise of perfectibility' (124). Knowing perfection is impossible, we aim more modestly to base our advice on real examples drawn from Canadian English written texts—describing what Canadian writers do, explaining what others have said they should do, and only then offering advice of our own.

To base advice on real examples was expensive and difficult before 1997, when the first edition appeared; it is much simpler now, only a decade later. When Margery Fee arrived in 1987 at the Strathy Language Unit, Queen's University, where most of the research for this book was done, the unit possessed an external hard drive the size of a bread box that had cost as much as a Volkswagen Beetle, and we used a scanner that cost as much as four Beetles. Corpora at that time rarely exceeded one million words. With diligent labour and uses of the scanner not imagined by the manufacturer, we collected the Strathy Language Corpus of 12 million words (with additional newspaper text) on which the previous edition was largely based. Now the corpus has around 50 million words, including new text categories such as Internet news. Indeed, the Internet was barely a presence in 1997 (the term was defined in a resolution of the US Federal Networking Council in 1995).

One visible result of technological change is that we have cut many examples that were cited to emphasize the importance of basing usage advice on examples from real language, something that made our guide unusual in 1997. In the interests of adding new entries and providing new illustrative sentences for difficult distinctions, we have cut many less important examples in this edition.

Since the last edition, English has been on the move: some speak of 'englishes', highlighting the many national and international varieties around the world and their distance from an origin in England. The codifying of Standard English and the entrenchment of attendant beliefs about the language involved the production of many books, dictionaries, grammars, usage guides, writing textbooks, spellers, and language textbooks: Standard English was, and is still, a huge worldwide business (Pennycook).

During the rise of Standard English, colonialism flourished and children all over the world were encouraged to see British English (or the standard languages of the colonizers) as the prestige language, the model language, and in many cases, the only language of civilization. In some cases this lesson was and still is enforced, as in Canada, by the refusal or failure to provide children any education in their native languages, whether Aboriginal or immigrant, even though this would not harm their achievement of literacy or of other languages (see Skutnabb and Philippson). For generations, the ability to speak more than one language was often seen as suspect in all but academic experts, interpreters, diplomats, and language teachers: for everyone else the model was monolingual and 'proper'. As a result of this belief, we are at a point in history where the majority of the world's Indigenous languages are vanishing (see Abley, Crystal, Dalby, Nettle, and Romaine). In Canada, only three of the Aboriginal languages with living speakers—Cree, Ojibway, and Inuktitut—have a sufficient number of speakers and a sufficient number of children learning the language as a first language to be regarded as safe from extinction. Recent moves in Canada to fund Aboriginal language revitalization and the prevalence of French immersion reflect a new, if belated, appreciation of language variety and multi-lingualism.

The global movement of peoples has produced what Evelyn Nien-ming Chi'en calls 'weird english', not just as a temporary phenomenon of language learners, but also as a permanent feature of our language environment, including literature and literary theory: 'In the later twentieth century and the early twenty-first, literary authors are performing the act of weirding English on a political level; they are daring to transcribe their communities and thus build identities' (4). Such writers as Derek Walcott, Salman Rushdie, Toni Morrison, and Thomas King use the full resources of the many englishes and other languages available to them to show readers the cultural richness masked or rejected by overly rigid language attitudes. Postcolonial literary art has certainly challenged the dominance of Standard English.

Not only have English speakers been on the move in the last decade but so has language study. The use of searchable databases such as the one used to produce this book has underpinned not only recently published usage guides and dictionaries but also grammars. For example, *The Longman Grammar of Spoken and Written English* uses a 40-million-word corpus to compare American and British conversation, fiction, academic prose, and newspaper writing, revealing each of these four 'registers' as distinctive: no longer is published, formal written English the model for a monolithic Standard English. Clearly, the Standard takes different shapes in different contexts.

In the past, unproven ideas about 'the Standard' have often been used to forward certain social interests at the expense of others. Knowing this, we do not describe the misuse of the conventions of punctuation in some students' writing as 'a crime against civilization', although we do point out the mistakes. What interests us far more is that these apprentice writers have interesting ideas to convey, and manage to support their arguments well. They should be encouraged to turn to the task of writing seriously and enthusiastically, rather than be discouraged because they cannot punctuate a restrictive clause correctly. But when they ask, 'Does spelling count?' we tell them that in writing, as in life, everything counts. For academic writers, as for writers in a wide variety of fields (business, journalism, education, etc.), correctness in both content and expression is vital. In many fields, reviewing others' writing is an important tool of collaboration, where writers count on their co-writers and editors to save them from embarrassing mistakes or misunderstandings. People readily submit their work to others for editing and believe that it is important to strive to write as well as possible. Language standardization may have been used as a tool of social oppression, but it has also been the vehicle of broad collaboration and communication. We are right to treat usage both warily and seriously.

Margery Fee and Janice McAlpine

Works Cited

Abley, Mark. *Spoken Here: Travels among Threatened Languages*. Toronto: Random House, 2003.

Bex, Tony. 'Representations of English in Twentieth-Century Britain: Fowler, Gowers and Partridge'. *Standard English: The Widening Debate*. Ed. Tony Bex and Richard J. Watts. London: Routledge, 1999. 89–109.

Biber, Douglas, Stig Johansson, Geoffrey Leech, Susan Conrad, and Edward Finegan. *Longman Grammar of Spoken and Written English*. London: Longman, 1999.

Cameron, Deborah. *Verbal Hygiene*. London: Routledge, 1995.

Ch'ien, Evelyn Nien-ming. *Weird English*. Cambridge, MA: Harvard UP, 2004.

Crystal, David. *Language Death*. Cambridge: Cambridge UP, 2000.

Dalby, Andrew. *Language in Danger*. London: Penguin, 2002.

Nettle, Daniel and Suzanne Romaine. *Vanishing Voices: The Extinction of the World's Languages*. New York: Oxford UP, 2000.

Pennycook, Alastair. *English and the Discourses of Colonialism*. London: Routledge, 1998.

Rea, Jaclyn Marie. 'Ideologies of Language: Authority, Consensus and Commonsense in Canadian Talk about Usage'. PhD Dissertation, Simon Fraser University, 2006.

Skutnabb-Kangas, Tove and Robert Phillipson, ed. *Linguistic Human Rights: Overcoming Linguistic Discrimination*. Berlin: Mouton de Gruyter, 1995.

Truss, Lynn. *Eats, Shoots & Leaves: The Zero Tolerance Approach to Punctuation*. New York: Gotham, 2003.

Introduction to the First Edition

'Spelling flame' is a new term for an old phenomenon: outraged arguments about correct language usage. When someone criticizes the spelling or grammar, rather than the argument, of another participant in a discussion group on the Internet, the resulting torrent of acrimonious messages—the spelling flame—often derails the original discussion completely. One reason for the strong emotions that swirl around language use, even in the age of spell-checkers, is that people feel their identity is reflected in their language.

Lynn Johnston, whose cartoon strip *For Better or for Worse* is syndicated all over North America, has never pretended that the family she depicts lives south of the border: 'I refuse to spell *racquet* as *racket*. I want it to be Canadian' ('Michael Goes to Western'). In Margaret Laurence's novel *The Diviners*, Morag's daughter Piquette asks, 'Are there coyotes in these woods, Mum?' The answer is delivered 'with ludicrous pride and snappishness': '*We* say *kiy-oot*,' Morag replies, 'Only John Wayne says *coy-oh-tee*' (Laurence, 416). When Margaret Atwood received a medal recently in New York, Robert MacNeil (co-author of *The Story of English*) said as he introduced her: 'She makes me feel my Canadianness. . . . Her characters misbehave on chesterfields, not sofas.'[1] Here spelling, pronunciation, and word choice are all attached to national identity and seen as distinctively Canadian. Perhaps Canadians are particularly snappish about these issues because other people—even many Canadians—assume that their English is identical to American English.[2]

In fact, it is not: Canadian English is a variety of English in its own right. In the past, however, Canadians seeking information or advice on their language had to look to either British or American dictionaries and usage guides, neither of which reflected the distinctiveness of Canadian English. The *Guide to Canadian English Usage* differs from those other usage guides in two important ways: its comments and advice are based on evidence drawn from a corpus of 12 million words of contemporary Canadian writing, supplemented by some 650 million words of Canadian newspaper and magazine text,[3] and it is written from a Canadian perspective.

The idea of using evidence drawn from published writing is far from new in lexicography. Samuel Johnson used 114,000 quotations to support his definitions (Bryson, 154; see also Reddick). When James A.H. Murray was made editor of what was to become the *Oxford English Dictionary* (*OED*) in 1879, he inherited a huge pile of slips of paper, each bearing a quotation illustrating the use of an English word (Murray, 139), and the first edition of the *OED* contained 1,827,306 illustrative quotations (Willinsky, 50). Philip Gove, editor of *Merriam-Webster's Third New International Dictionary* (1961), inherited a collection of over one-and-a-half million citation slips (Morton, 95), and his completed dictionary contained over 100,000 quotations, with an equal number of verbal illustrations (Morton, 101).

The principle that generalizations about the usage of words should be based on evidence was followed by H.W. Fowler and his brother E.G. Fowler in their first book on usage, *The King's English*, published in 1906. H.W. Fowler's name became synonymous with correct usage as his *Modern English Usage*, first published in 1926, went into printing after printing. Although certainly not above displays of arbitrary personal opinion (if the opinion of someone with such a formidable intellect can ever be described as arbitrary), Fowler frequently quoted examples gleaned from newspapers and supported his points with citations from the *OED*. Subsequent usage commentators have often been far more indebted to the *OED*, Fowler, and *Webster's Third* than they can bring themselves to reveal. Indeed, those without a collection of examples often purvey a set of prescriptions based on personal opinion cobbled together with ideas lifted from the works of their predecessors.

When J.R. Strathy left the Department of English at Queen's University an endowment to promote the use of correct English in Canada and to produce a usage guide for Canadians, the computer corpus was a fairly new research tool for language study. Strathy's generosity permitted W.C. Lougheed, who became the first director of the Strathy Language Unit in 1981, to invest in equipment and begin to compile the computer equivalent of Murray's millions of paper slips.[4] At that time the model for language corpora was the Brown Corpus, a one-million-word database compiled at Brown University by W. Nelson Francis and Henry Kučera. It consisted of 2,000-word samples randomly selected from texts, all published in 1961, of different genres (fiction, history, literary criticism, science, etc.), different degrees of formality (popular magazines and books, newspapers, academic articles and books), and different styles. By the time collection for the Strathy Corpus began, advances in computer technology had made it possible to store much larger samples. The Strathy Corpus of Canadian English currently contains 12 million words of complete texts (rather than 2,000-word samples) based on the categories used for the Brown Corpus but with the addition to its subject categories of feminism and computing. The use of the Brown Corpus as a model ensures a variety of genres, subject matter, contexts, styles, and degrees of formality.[5] The Strathy Corpus has been supplemented by CD-ROMs containing some 600 million words of newspaper text from across Canada and 50 million words of the newsmagazine *Maclean's* (March 1988–Dec. 1991). This corpus allowed us to check our initial list of usage problems, compiled from a wide range of usage guides, old and new, against actual usage. (In addition, a few examples were selected from sources not in the database: all sources are noted on pp. 639–53.)

No clear definition of a 'usage problem' is possible, because usage problems are so various and because different usage guides cover different issues. We have excluded from this guide most of the issues that could be resolved by looking at a good desk dictionary, but many dictionaries are weak on matters of specifically Canadian interest; thus we have included a few 'dictionary' entries on items of this kind.[6] In addition we have included entries on a number of questions that might be answered by looking at a dictionary, because our evidence suggests that writers generally don't bother to look these particular items up. We have not included information that is more usefully found in an encyclopedia, except where it is necessary in explaining a usage issue. Nor do we address the many issues of written convention that are normally covered in book publishers' or newspaper style guides, although we do discuss such broad issues as capitalization and punctuation. Finally, like most usage guides, this one is designed for readers for whom English is either a first language or a language in which they have been educated: issues unlikely to trouble the fluent speaker are not discussed.

The pronunciations given here are mainly for rare words or those that are sometimes pronounced in ways stigmatized as non-standard, dialectal, or 'un-Canadian'. Here we must point out that the information available on the norms of Canadian pronunciation is limited. Only R.J. Gregg's sociolinguistic survey of 300 Vancouver English-speakers and H.B. Woods' survey of 100 Ottawa English-speakers can be called comprehensive, and we cannot assume that the pronunciations common in Vancouver and Ottawa are necessarily the most common ones across the country. Although we relied on Canadian sources where we could, sometimes our suggested pronunciations are based on less than solid evidence. We hope that in future revisions of this guide our ability to describe Canadian pronunciation will have improved.

In checking the usage problems discussed in other guides against our corpus, we discovered that some supposed problems in fact caused writers no trouble at all; these we usually dropped from our list. We also discovered some problems we hadn't expected to find; these were added. Sometimes we found that a well-known usage 'rule' was consistently 'broken' by most writers, including the famous and the well educated, and these we retained for discussion. The words 'rule' and 'broken' are enclosed in quotation marks here because, although there are rules of grammar that are followed without difficulty by all adult native speakers, whatever their education, the reason that most of the issues addressed by usage guides have become topics is, in fact, that no clear 'rules' exist to deal with them: they are issues with which educated writers may have trouble or where usage is a matter of debate. Many questions arise in areas where change is occurring in speech; since writing is usually more public and more formal, the conventions surrounding it are far slower to shift.

That some usage distinctions are not followed, however, even by well-known writers, does not mean that those who believe strongly in them can simply be ignored. 'The CBC Language Guide' (a database that provides pronunciation advice for CBC radio and television announcers), *The Globe and Mail Style Book*, and *The Canadian Press Stylebook* all make it clear that listeners and readers frequently react so strongly to what they consider sloppy or incorrect use of language that they write, fax, e-mail, and phone their objections directly to the source. Debates about usage, often highly combative, are a staple of Letters to the Editor pages. In other words, beliefs about the 'correct' use of language do have a social reality. Most people who work with words, written or spoken, can remember motions overturned or proposals condemned because of disputes over usage. It is all very well to say that the 'rule' about split infinitives is nonsensical because it is based on a faulty analogy with the Latin infinitive, which can't be split because it is a single word. But if your employer or English professor believes that split infinitives are not acceptable, you may suffer the consequences. And even in less crucial circumstances, there is no point in distracting readers: they should be thinking about your argument rather than reacting against your usage. A writer who follows convention may be more persuasive, more credible, and more easily understood than one who flouts it. Yet as the entries in this guide reveal, there are few, if any, usage 'rules' that are consistently followed by professional writers. Usage conventions arise precisely in areas where choice is possible, and though usage guides are expected to approve one choice as 'correct' and the others as 'incorrect', sloppy, or vulgar, this guide—perhaps to the frustration of some readers—is more likely to lay out the possibilities and to discuss the contexts where different choices might be effective.

The history of canonical usage items, such as the split infinitive, is treated comprehensively by *Webster's Dictionary of English Usage*, which tracks down the origins of particular strictures in old guides and manuals and places them in the context of actual contemporary usage. The condemnation of the 'double negative', for example, began with the English grammarian Robert Lowth in 1762; the condemnation of *hopefully* as a sentence adverb (as in 'Hopefully, we will win') can be traced back only to 1964—because, apparently, it was rarely used in this way before the 1960s.

Sometimes, as in the case of *hopefully*, a usage is condemned simply because it is new. Although *hopefully* is only one of a large group of words used in much the same way (e.g. *curiously, admittedly, happily, mercifully*), it is the one that has been singled out for attention. Sidney Greenbaum, in *Good English and the Grammarian*, quotes several extremely negative comments about this use of *hopefully* from the *Harper Dictionary of Contemporary Usage* (e.g., 'It is barbaric, illiterate, offensive, damnable, and inexcusable') and remarks: 'most of us would agree that their vehemence is disproportionate to the offence' (11). The vehemence appears to originate in the fear that a whole set of values, including what is often called 'respect for the language', is in danger. Lapses in usage provide social commentators with what they see as symptoms of a wide range of moral failings.

This use of language as a moral barometer dates to the eighteenth century, when English was being standardized by grammars and dictionaries. In *From Old English to Standard English*, Dennis Freeborn notes that 'the contrasts between the *refined* language of the classically educated class and the *vulgar* language of the common people' were believed to mirror 'equal differences in intellectual capabilities, and also in virtue or morality' (191). Thus several petitions to Parliament, calling for electoral reform, were rejected on the grounds that their language was insufficiently 'decent and respectful' (191). Objections to language usage often camouflage judgments based on class, ethnicity, or political affiliation.

Every generation believes, it seems, that English is going downhill, that younger speakers and writers are careless with words, and that the result can only be bad. As Tony Crowley points out in *Standard English and the Politics of Language*, those who promote 'such reactionary nostalgia' do so in order to 'berate whatever it is at present that they find unpalatable' (272). James Sledd and Wilma R. Ebbitt, in *Dictionaries and That Dictionary*, collected a set of readings on the mixed reception of *Webster's Third New International Dictionary*, published in 1961. Most of the attacks on this dictionary were directed at the decision to reduce the number of usage labels, such as 'slang' and 'vulgar', and to use quotations from the speech of ordinary Americans to support its definitions. Herbert C. Morton's book on this controversy situates the battle in the Cold War polemics of the time. Philip B. Gove, the editor of *Webster's Third*, commented: 'There's no divine sanction in language. It's an instrument of the people who use it' (Sledd and Ebbitt, 57). Many reviewers and editorialists (including some in Canada) responded as if Gove had declared himself a godless Communist, ready to lead the masses into revolution against sacred traditions.

What these reviewers and editorialists didn't realize is that usage shifts in every generation, so that anyone reaching forty will likely notice that the following generation is using unfamiliar words and expressions, or using old ones in new ways. Many words and usages once condemned as unacceptable are now part of the general vocabulary, while other perfectly acceptable expressions have fallen out of use. Jean Aitchison concludes in *Language Change: Progress or Decay?* that although language changes all the time, 'there is no evidence that language is either progressing or decaying' (221).

Even Fowler (625) was well aware of the inevitability of language change:

> What grammarians say should be has perhaps less influence on what shall be than even the more modest of them realize; usage evolves itself undisturbed by their likes and dislikes. And yet the temptation to show how better use might have been made of the material to hand is sometimes irresistible.

These remarks come from Fowler's entry on 'that/which', where he admits he is making a distinction that (which?) many writers do not follow.

But this brings us to one of the most controversial questions raised by differences in usage. If even Fowler admits that usage produces conventions, not the other way around, who decides what is acceptable? If we find that a usage described by many commentators as unacceptable or even incorrect is widespread—and not just in the much-maligned sports pages, but in news, editorials, books, and magazines—and we describe it as acceptable, those who have been taught something different will simply see us as wrong. So we make it clear that no one need abandon a cherished distinction just because the majority has: what those who hold fast to such distinctions should not do, however, is berate others for sloppy usage and set themselves up as experts.

But, this group may reply, surely professional writers, English teachers, and other experts on language can provide the best guidance on how English should be used. And some dictionaries and guides do rely on the opinions of a 'usage panel' of professors and professional writers (for example, the *American Heritage Dictionary* and its companion usage guide, the *Harper Dictionary of Contemporary Usage*). However, as Thomas Creswell's *Usage in Dictionaries and Dictionaries of Usage* points out, dictionaries, usage guides, and usage panels rarely agree on how objectionable certain usages are, why certain usages are problematic, or even which usages constitute problems. Walter E. Meyers compared the usage glossaries of 50 American handbooks of freshman composition published from 1980 to 1990. He found that even the best of them were 'out-of-date, constricted by obsolete theories, and intensely derivative' (343); and almost half of all the items discussed in the 50 books appeared in only one glossary. This 'should warn us', Meyers concludes, 'that glossaries of usage reflect mainly the personal quirks and crochets of the compilers' (342). If even the experts disagree, how useful are their opinions? The temptation is to define as expert those who agree on a specific set of 'correct' usages. But the studies done by Creswell and others show that in fact this definition would not identify the best educated, the most professional, or the most acclaimed writers. If a standard of correct usage excludes a large percentage of writers whose words appear before the public weekly, daily, and even hourly, whose books appear on bestseller lists or win prizes, what is the point of defining their usage as unacceptable? Unacceptable to whom? Only to a small group of self-constituted language experts. And we know that, as Fowler said, what becomes standard usage does not depend on what experts think, but on what becomes standard usage.

A favourite pastime of language experts is to catch their colleagues breaking their own 'rules': Bill Bryson, in *The Mother Tongue: English and How It Got that Way*, offers many examples of slips by such luminaries as Fowler, Robert Burchfield (editor of the supplements to the *OED* and *The New Fowler's Modern English Usage*), and Robert McCrum (one of the authors of *The Story of English*, which accompanied a popular BBC-TV series on English). His point is that language changes and that the opinions of experts often bear little or no relation to actual contemporary usage—even their own. So experts on usage do not even practise what they preach, and many of their favourite strictures are simply rendered irrelevant by language change. Steven Pinker's comment on these experts is the vehement response of the linguist to the popular 'language experts' or what he calls, following William Safire, 'language mavens':

> Most of the prescriptive rules of the language mavens make no sense on any level.
> They are bits of folklore that originated for screwball reasons several hundred years
> ago and have perpetuated themselves ever since. For as long as they have existed,
> speakers have flouted them, spawning identical plaints about the imminent decline

of the language century after century. All the best writers in English at all periods, including Shakespeare and most of the mavens themselves, have been among the flagrant flouters (373).

Well then. Does all this mean that anything goes? Absolutely not. There are language norms that can be discovered by looking at real language. Speakers and writers know that adhering to the language norms of particular social groups or genres of writing is important if their work is to be found acceptable by the audiences it is intended for. If, as Pinker suggests, usage 'rules' serve 'as shibboleths, differentiating the elite from the rabble' (374), those who wish to speak to the elite must take them into account. Usage guides in the computer age, however, will have to present more information than they did in the past. They will have to tell their readers not only what previous guides have said but also what relation those commentaries bear to actual usage. The result is an attempt both to describe and to advise, in such a way as to make it clear to readers that both the description and the advice may well be quite different in the next edition of the guide. Now that computers permit us to tap into large quantities of language and catch it in the act of change—something that was impossible until the late 1980s—we cannot pretend that what usage guides often refer to as 'careful writers' all write alike, or that they all write the same way decade after decade. Thus we have decided that while a usage guide should provide advice (that's why people buy guides), it should also present enough information for readers to make up their own minds about particular issues.

What makes this guide Canadian? It is written from a Canadian perspective: it is not intended primarily for American or British readers, with a few Canadian entries tacked on. At times, of course, Canadian usage is quite like either American or British usage, or both. But this does not mean that Canadian usage is simply whatever can be clearly distinguished from the other two. Canadian usage includes all the ways in which English is used in Canada—it is not just a footnote to the ways English is used in other places. Much debate has taken place over whether Canadian English is a branch of American English or a branch of British English. This model, which parallels the model of imperial centre and colonial periphery, has recently been replaced by one that treats all varieties of English used at a national level as equal and therefore as producing their own standards, rather than deriving them from British English. Even regional varieties of English are seen as producing standards (see, for example, the entry on Quebec English). English, then, no longer 'belongs' to the English but, as Sidney Greenbaum points out in 'Whose English?', is now claimed as well by the much larger group of first-language English-speakers outside Great Britain.

However, this is not to say that one can ignore the strong influence of British and American English in Canada, often resulting from the way textbooks and dictionaries have been used in schools (which varies from province to province). Canadians inherit a strong British tradition, particularly in government, law, the military, education, and publishing, yet at the same time are heavily influenced by American media and American ideas in all fields of knowledge. In fact, Canadian usage is marked by its frequent retention of both 'British' and 'American' spellings, punctuation conventions, and diction, and therefore Canadians have a larger number of variants to argue about (is it *honour* or *honor*? do you *protest something* or *protest against something*? should you pronounce *hostile* to rhyme with *reptile* or *hostel*?).

A further complication arises if we imply that the Canadian writing in our database is Canadian in some definitive sense. Even though the texts in our primary database were published in Canada, and even though we have attempted to ensure that they were written by Canadians, what emerges at the end of the publication process does not necessarily reflect the writer's own usage. Publishers vary in their choice of style guides and dictionaries, and copy editors are not necessarily Canadian. Much of the material in newspapers comes from foreign wire services. Although we have tried to exclude material that is obviously *not* Canadian, we have no way of knowing where most of the writers in the database were born or educated: Canadian magazines, journals, and newspapers routinely publish work by writers from outside Canada. And even those who were educated in Canada read and hear English from outside Canada's borders every day of their lives. As I.W.V. Pringle points out, 'to include everything [as Canadian English] to which one has access in Canada is obviously too broad, but to restrict oneself to the English of Canadians born and bred is certainly too narrow' (27). If Canadians are concerned about the distinctiveness of things Canadian, including Canadian English, it is in part because approximately 20 million English-speaking Canadians live next door to some 275 million English-speaking Americans: hence the constant fear that Canadian English, along with the rest of English-Canadian culture, will disappear under the onslaught of American culture. Thus one often finds a particular spelling or pronunciation or usage touted as 'the' Canadian spelling, pronunciation, or usage, with the implication that those who don't adhere to it are disloyal sellouts. Nevertheless, the feature that may be most distinctive about Canadian English writers and readers is their calm acceptance, even in the same sentence, of both American and British forms. *Editing Canadian English* (Burton et al.), a guide for Canadian book editors, points out that many Canadian writers and editors use both *-re* spellings (*centre, theatre, metre,* etc.) and *-or* spellings (*honor, glamor,* etc.), even though the former are classified as British and the latter as American. After recommending that editors not mix *within* a category (i.e., if you write *honour,* then you should also write *glamour*), they conclude: 'it seems that mixing *between* categories not only is acceptable, but may well constitute the "Canadian style"' (7). This conclusion may be deeply shocking to the many people who believe that, say, only British spellings are truly Canadian, or that the CBC's pronunciation of a word should set the Canadian standard. The idea that there is only one way to write or speak that can be called Canadian derives from a wider attitude that has been called the 'myth of uniform correctness'. This is the belief that where two or more ways of spelling, pronouncing, or using a word exist, only one can be correct. In fact, several variants, all quite acceptable, often coexist in standard Englishes.

The compilers of the Strathy Corpus took care to ensure variety both of style and of levels of formality by including published books, journals, magazines, and newspapers. Because the time and effort taken by writers and editors before publication vary greatly, with books usually receiving the most editorial attention and newspapers the least, the latter often serve as a good source of bad examples. Perhaps for this reason, or because of the informality of newspaper writing, usage writers routinely attack the English found in newspapers. However, it must be remembered that informal English is still standard English, and a writer who cannot vary his or her style from formal to informal cannot really be considered competent. Journalists work to extremely tight deadlines, and their writing receives little or no editing, so it is hardly surprising that newspapers provide countless examples of questionable usage. Yet many of the best writers in the country write for newspapers, and newspaper style guides are clear evidence of journalists' desire to find answers to their questions about language. James Murray used quotations from newspapers in the *OED*, even though his advisers at Oxford objected, because often he could not otherwise give an account of the history of a word. He told the Philological Society in 1884 that he found the criticism of newspaper writing 'by far the silliest that the Dictionary has elicited' and looked to a future 'when this criticism will be pointed out as a most remarkable instance of the inability of men to acknowledge contemporary facts and read the signs of the times' (Murray, 223). In this guide, too, the only examples we could find for certain usage items came from newspapers. In part this reflects the preponderance of newspaper text available to us. In addition, however, newspapers and newspaper style guides are always at the forefront in suggesting alternatives when particular groups of readers find certain usages offensive. (Wheelchair users don't like being described as 'wheelchair-bound', and astronauts who are also women don't like being called 'lady astronauts'.) Newspaper readers are quick to react, and since newspapers depend on subscriptions for their survival, they are far more likely than book publishers to be up to date on what is acceptable to their readers.

This last set of usage items, where usages that offend particular groups are being replaced by more acceptable terms, is finally more important than many others. As David Crystal points out in *Who Cares about English Usage?* (116):

> If by magic everyone were to stop using split infinitives tomorrow, what actually would have been achieved? My argument is: nothing—and something might even have been lost. . . . On the other hand, certain usage topics have brought to light real problems of a linguistic or social kind where unthinking language can lead to misunderstanding, disaccord, open hostility. These matters are certainly worth getting upset about, for they affect the way we live.

We hope, then, that this guide will help writers communicate in ways that avoid causing confusion, annoyance, or offence; we also hope that if we ourselves confuse, annoy, or offend, our readers will be kind enough to let us know so that we may improve subsequent editions.

Margery Fee
University of British Columbia
April 1997

Notes

1   I thank Jack Chambers for this example.

2   For more on Canadian English, see Bailey and Görlach, and 'Canadian English' and related entries in McArthur.

3   Two important usage guides quote examples and draw conclusions from a corpus. Pam Peters' *Cambridge Australian English Style Guide* (Cambridge: Cambridge University Press, 1995) uses the one-million word Australian Corpus of English; and *Collins COBUILD English Usage* (London: HarperCollins, 1992), aimed mainly at speakers of English as a second language, is based on the Collins Birmingham University International Language Database, nearly 200 million words of spoken and written English. Other important guides use citations to exemplify their points, including *Webster's Dictionary of English Usage* (Springield, MA: Merriam-Webster, 1989) and *The Oxford Guide to English Usage* (2nd edn), E.S.C. Weiner and Andrew Delahunty (Oxford: Clarendon Press, 1993). Note that the term *corpus* is used in linguistics and lexicography to refer to a set of data that has been carefully selected to reveal certain aspects of language. The main Strathy Corpus is based on such a selection, but since we are not performing statistical analyses, we have not attempted to ensure that each category is represented by an equal number

of words. Any generalizations we made across genres were based on the Corpus alone, and did not include the 650 million extra words of newspaper and magazine text that we found a useful source of examples.

4 See W.C. Lougheed, 'Towards a National Corpus on a Micro', *Literary and Linguistic Computing* 2.4 (1987): 207–12.

5 The International Corpus of English project, originated by Sidney Greenbaum at University College, London, is producing a set of parallel million-word corpora of over twenty national varieties of world English, including Canadian English. The Canadian corpus is being compiled by a team led by Nancy Belmore of Concordia University. It contains samples of spoken and written English based on different criteria from the Brown Corpus categories, including samples of unpublished writing such as personal and business letters and student essays and examinations. See Greenbaum, 'ICE'.

6 Several dictionaries do cover Canadian English well, including two that appeared too recently to be included in our reference list below: the recently published *ITP Nelson Canadian Dictionary of the English Language* (Toronto: Nelson, 1996) and the revised and expanded *Gage Canadian Dictionary* (Toronto: Gage, 1997). *The Canadian Oxford Dictionary* is forthcoming in 1998.

Works Cited

Aitchison, Jean. *Language Change: Progress or Decay?* 2nd edn. Cambridge: Cambridge University Press, 1991.

Bailey, Richard W., and M. Görlach, eds. 'The English Language in Canada'. *English as a World Language*. Ann Arbor: University of Michigan Press, 1982: 134–76.

Bryson, Bill. *The Mother Tongue: English and How It Got that Way*. New York: Morrow, 1990.

Buckley, Peter, ed. *CP Stylebook: A Guide for Writers and Editors*. Rev. edn. Toronto: Canadian Press, 1993.

Burton, Lydia, et al. *Editing Canadian English*. Prepared for the Freelance Editors' Association of Canada. Vancouver: Douglas and McIntyre, 1987.

'The CBC Language Guide'. CBC, 1995. (Not commercially available.)

Creswell, Thomas J. *Usage in Dictionaries and Dictionaries of Usage*. Publications of the American Dialect Society, nos 63–4. April–Nov. 1975.

Crowley, Tony. *Standard English and the Politics of Language*. Urbana: University of Illinois Press, 1990.

Crystal, David. *Who Cares about English Usage?* Harmondsworth, UK: Penguin, 1984.

Fowler, H.W. *Fowler's Dictionary of Modern English Usage*. 2nd edn. Ed. Ernest Gowers. Oxford: Oxford University Press, 1965.

Francis, W. Nelson, and Henry Kučera. *Frequency Analysis of English Usage: Lexicon and Grammar*. Boston: Houghton Mifflin, 1982.

Freeborn, Dennis. *From Old English to Standard English*. Ottawa: University of Ottawa Press, 1992.

Greenbaum, Sidney. *Good English and the Grammarian*. London: Longman, 1988.

———. 'ICE: The International Corpus of English'. *English Today* 28 (1991): 3–7.

———. 'Whose English?'. *The State of the Language*. Ed. Christopher Ricks and Leonard Michaels. Berkeley: University of California Press, 1990.

Gregg, R.J. 'An Urban Dialect Survey of the English Spoken in Vancouver: Final Report to the Social Sciences and Humanities Research Council'. Unpublished ms. 1984.

Laurence, Margaret. *The Diviners*. Toronto: McClelland and Stewart, Bantam, 1975.

McArthur, Tom, ed. *The Oxford Companion to the English Language*. Oxford: Oxford University Press, 1992.

McCrum, Robert, William Cran, and Robert MacNeil. *The Story of English*. London: Faber, BBC Publications, 1986.

McFarlane, J.A., and Warren Clements. *The Globe and Mail Style Book*. Rev. edn. Toronto: Globe and Mail, 1993.

Meyers, Walter E. 'Usage Glossaries in Current College Handbooks'. *American Speech* 66.4 (1991): 341–58.

'Michael Goes to Western'. *University Affairs*. Aug.–Sept. 1996: 5.

Morton, Herbert C. *The Story of Webster's Third: Philip Gove's Controversial Dictionary and Its Critics*. Cambridge: Cambridge University Press, 1994.

Murray, K.M. Elisabeth. *Caught in the Web of Words: James Murray and the Oxford English Dictionary*. Oxford: Oxford University Press, 1979.

Pinker, Steven. 'The Language Mavens'. *The Language Instinct: How the Mind Creates Language*. New York: HarperPerennial, 1995: 370–403.

Pringle, I.W.V. 'The Complexity of the Concept of Standard'. *In Search of the Standard in Canadian English*. Ed. W.C. Lougheed. Occasional Paper Number 1. Strathy Language Unit, Queen's University. Kingston: Strathy Language Unit, 1986.

Reddick, Allen. *The Making of Johnson's Dictionary, 1746–1773*. Cambridge: Cambridge University Press, 1990.

Sledd, James, and Wilma R. Ebbitt, eds. *Dictionaries and That Dictionary: A Casebook on the Aims of Lexicographers and the Targets of Reviewers*. Chicago: Scott Foresman, 1962.

Weiner, E.S.C., and Andrew Delahunty. *The Oxford Guide to English Usage*. Oxford: Clarendon Press, 1993.

Willinsky, John. *Empire of Words: The Reign of the OED*. Princeton, NJ: Princeton University Press, 1994.

Woods, H.B. 'A Socio-dialectology Survey of the English Spoken in Ottawa: A Study of Sociological Variation in Canadian English'. Ph.D. dissertation. University of British Columbia, 1979.

Acknowledgements

A great many people and organizations provided funding, moral support, advice, and information—so many that we cannot name them all. We could not have accomplished such a large and varied project without them, however, and we are most grateful. The mistakes and inaccuracies that remain, which we hope are few, are ours.

We gratefully acknowledge the help of the following:
J.R. Strathy, whose generous bequest has funded the project since 1982 and will provide for regular revision;

The Department of English and the Faculty of Arts at Queen's University, many of whose members have devoted time and energy to the Strathy Language Unit, particularly George M. Logan; thanks are also due to Stella Gartland, Roberta Hamilton, Peter Sabor, Paul Stevens, and Laureen Snider;

The first director of the Strathy Language Unit, W.C. Lougheed, and Duncan Robertson, the late Helen MacDonald, and Phillip W. Rogers, for laying the foundations of the project;

The Social Sciences and Humanities Research Council of Canada, whose Major Research Grant supported much of the work on the guide, 1989–92;

The Advisory Committee of the Strathy Language Unit: J.K. Chambers (University of Toronto), Sandra Clarke (Memorial University of Newfoundland), the late A.M. Kinloch (University of New Brunswick), Leslie Monkman (Queen's University), T.K. Pratt (University of Prince Edward Island), D.O. Spettigue (Queen's University), and the late H.J. Warkentyne (University of Victoria);

Michael Morrow and E.S.C. Weiner (Oxford University Press, UK), and Katherine Barber (Oxford University Press Canada); Laurel Brinton (University of British Columbia), Pam Peters (Macquarie University, Australia), Lil Rodman (University of British Columbia), Patricia A. Shaw (University of British Columbia), and the late Günter Voss (Kiel University) for advice on particular entries; and the late Charlotte Fee, for proofreading;

All of the authors and publishers who allowed their works to be copied into the Strathy Corpus of Canadian English; InfoGlobe and Dennis Ablett of Southam Electronic Publishing, who provided CD-ROMs for the project.

Production of the Guide and Corpus
Administration and copy coordination: Linda Garrison.

Research and writing: Carla Douglas, Sue Dreier, Susan Fisher, Peter Lapp, Heather McKend, Irwin Streight, Sandra Terry, Kathy Vanderlinden.

Acknowledgements

Assistance with scanning and editing corpus texts, checking quotations, proofreading: Dorothy Adero, Anne Archer, Katie Baldwin, Jeffrey Bratt, Melanie Clare, Terri Gurnsey, Bonnie Hall, Robert Inkoom, Patricia Marois, Shuguang Qi, Tammy Reinhardt, Kurt Reinhardt, Jennifer Tinline.

We are also greatly indebted to Sally Livingston, whose editorial skills contributed immeasurably to the final form of the book.

Acknowledgements for the second edition
Members of our advisory committee:

> Katherine Barber (Oxford University Press)
> Laurel Brinton (University of British Columbia)
> J.K. Chambers (University of Toronto)
> Sandra Clarke (Memorial University of Newfoundland)
> Warren Clements (*Globe and Mail*)
> Pamela Grant-Russell (Université de Sherbrooke)
> Patricia Shaw (University of British Columbia)
> Patti Tasko (Canadian Press)

Additional thanks to: Leslie Monkman (Queen's University), Strathy Professor of English Language and Literature; Matthias Meyer (Christian-Albrechts-Universität, Keil); W.J. Kirwin (English Language Research Centre, Memorial University of Newfoundland); and the students in Laurel Brinton's English Usage and Usage Guides course at UBC, and all the readers of the first edition of this usage guide who took the time to write to us with helpful suggestions.

Production team: Wade Guyitt, chief editorial assistant; Jane Roy, researcher; Bonnie Hall, proofreader.

Notes on Format

The entries are in alphabetical order, with cross-references to related entries. The first edition of this usage guide contained an index, which linked specific words and phrases mentioned within entries to main entry headings. In this second edition, cross-references in the body of the text fulfill this function (e.g., **well**   see ADJECTIVES AND ADVERBS; **fisher**   see JOB TITLES).

Examples   All quoted example sentences have been checked for accuracy. A few quotations for the second edition have been taken from undated documents posted to websites; these we have dated with the month and year we accessed the source. Many new citations have been gathered from the electronic editions of journals, magazines, and newspapers that are also published in print. Page numbers for quotations from articles in electronic publications are often references to the first page of the article or to the whole range of pages for the article rather than to the exact page on which the quotation appears in the print version of the publication.

Occasionally we found a quotation that beautifully illustrated an issue in question but that contained other usages (usually of punctuation, hyphenation, or capitalization) that did not conform to our recommendations in other entries; in these cases we sometimes silently edited the quotation. That is, to avoid confusion, we have revised minor features of some quotations, but never the specific features under discussion in a particular entry. These features are always quoted accurately and, if they do not accord with our recommendations, the problems are noted in the comments, enclosed in parentheses, directly after the quotation. The complete list of example sources can be found on pp. 639–53.

Newspapers   Since newspapers rarely use accents or italics, we frequently make no comment on the absence of these features in examples taken from newspapers, even though in other kinds of writing they might be recommended. Note also that, although levels of formality may vary widely even within a single newspaper, we usually regard newspapers as informal, and comment accordingly.

Pronunciations   Our decision to represent pronunciation by spelling out sounds or using rhyming words, rather than using the International Phonetic Alphabet (IPA), is inconsistent with the practice of major dictionaries. However, we believe that many dictionary users find IPA pronunciations difficult to interpret. Dictionaries usually indicate stress with a diacritical mark at the beginning or end of a stressed syllable. We mark stress by using capital letters; for example, the pronunciation of *artiste* is given as *ar TEEST*.

Brackets   Square brackets around a word or phrase in a heading or cross-reference (e.g., **[could of]**) indicate that it is non-standard.

A

a, an   *A* precedes words that begin with a consonant and *an* precedes those that begin with a vowel. This rule works by pronunciation rather than by spelling. The initial letters in the words *one*, *European*, and *united* are the vowels *o*, *e*, and *u*, but the initial sounds are consonants (*w* or *y*). Thus these words are preceded by *a*, not *an*: 'a one-sided argument', 'a European', 'a union'. When the consonant *h* is sounded at the beginning of a word, the word is preceded by *a*: 'a hutch', 'a house'. When it is silent, as in *heir*, *honest*, *honour*, *hour*, and, for some speakers, *herb*, the word is preceded by *an*.

With the names of letters and abbreviations, the choice of *a* or *an* depends on how they would be read aloud: 'an *a*' but 'a *b*'; 'a Master's' but 'an M.A.'; 'a Hudson's Bay Company trading post' but 'an HBC clerk'. Similarly, figures are preceded by *a* or *an* according to how they are pronounced: 'a 3-speed bike' but 'an 11-kilogram cat'.

One oddity remains. Though Canadians pronounce the *h* in words such as *habitual, hallucinatory, harmonious, historical, holistic*, and *hysterical*, they sometimes precede these words with *an* in formal writing. In British English in the past, the initial *h* was pronounced weakly or not at all in words with an unstressed first syllable, so *an* was generally used before these words. Canadians borrowed this practice, even when they pronounced the *h*. Now the British too are pronouncing the *h* in these words, and British usage guides are recommending against the unnecessary *an*. It is probably time for Canadians to let it go too.

> With more than 12,000 artifacts on display, the Huron County Pioneer Museum is truly an unique, educational and enjoyable place to visit.
> *Leisure Life* 1988: 97

(Here '*a* unique' is correct; the writer followed the *an*-before-a-vowel rule without trying the phrase out loud.)

> It could be an historic step toward realizing the vision of the people, or it could bring two powerful forces into direct conflict.
> *Catholic New Times* 16 Jan. 2005: 7

(Here '*a* historic' is recommended.)

See also HERB; THE, A, AN.

a-, an-   When the prefix *a-* (before vowels or *h*) or *an-* (before other consonants) is added to a word, it indicates the absence of the state or quality named. Thus, *achromatic* describes something without colour; *apathy* refers to a lack of feeling; and *anarchy* means without rule. Many words with the *a-/an-* prefix derive from Greek, and some have stems (-*pathy*, -*archy*) that do not stand alone as words in English. There are also, however, more recent coinages with stand-alone English adjectives: *ahistorical, amoral, asocial, asexual, atypical*.

There are two ways in which these words are misinterpreted. The *a-/an-* prefix is sometimes thought to indicate the contrary rather than the absence of the quality named (see ANTISOCIAL, ASOCIAL; IMMORAL, AMORAL), and, rarely, the prefix is thought not to alter the basic sense of the adjective, by analogy with words like *another* or *awake*.

> Remarkably, the central region of gray matter was aneural and contained only a tenuous meshwork of glial fibers and large extracellular spaces.
> *Canadian Journal of Physiology and Pharmacology* 82.8/9 (2004): 628

(*Aneural* means without nerves.)

See also ANTISOCIAL, ASOCIAL, UNSOCIABLE; IMMORAL, AMORAL, NON-MORAL, UNMORAL.

abbreviation, contraction, suspension, acronym, initialism   Abbreviations are common and appropriate in scientific, technical, and business writing, and indeed in writing for any specialized audience familiar with a particular set of abbreviations. Abbreviations are also acceptable in tables and lists where space is limited, as long as they are familiar or a key is provided. Anyone writing for a general audience, however, should be careful not to use an unfamiliar abbreviation without a full reference or explanation. The most efficient way to introduce the abbreviation to the reader is to place it in parentheses after the first use of the full form and use the abbreviation thereafter: 'the Prime Minister's Office (PMO)'. Although usage guides often warn against the use of abbreviations in formal writing, it is unnecessary to avoid those that are never spelled out or are better known than their long forms; for example, *Ms.*, *Mr.*, *DNA*, *AIDS*, *BMW*, *URL*. And even in formal writing it is better to use an abbreviation than to repeat a long title over and over again.

A true abbreviation is defined as a shortened form in which the first letter(s) of a word are used to stand for the whole; for example, *p.* for *page*, *co.* for *company*, *Sept.* for *September*. Canadians normally use a period after such abbreviations.

A shortened form made by omitting letters in the middle of a word (as in the abbreviation for *manager*, *mgr.*) is usually called a suspension in North America and a contraction in Great Britain. Canadians normally use a period after suspensions too, with the notable exceptions of the French *Mlle* (for *Mademoiselle*) and *Mme* (for *Madame*). In British usage, suspensions (contractions) are not followed by periods, on the reasoning that the final letter of the complete word is included in the shortened form. *Editing Canadian English 1987*, a guide for Canadian book editors, lays out the convention of using no periods after contractions and notes that the practice is common in Canadian government publications. But this convention is far from widespread. Further, differentiating between contractions and true abbreviations leads to some odd-looking mixes: 'Asst Prof. Linda Wentzell'. In this guide we have chosen to use periods with both true abbreviations and suspensions, although not with acronyms.

An acronym is a pronounceable word formed from the first letter or letters of words in a phrase or name: for example, *CIDA* (*SEE da*), for Canadian International Development Agency; *NORAD* (*NOR ad*), for North American Aerospace Defence Command; *CUPE* (*KEWP ee*), for Canadian Union of Public Employees; and *CEGEP* (*SAY zhep*), for College d'enseignement général et professionel. A few acronyms have become full-fledged words, written in lower case, such as *radar* (radio detecting and ranging) and *scuba* (self contained underwater breathing apparatus). Generally, acronyms are written in capital letters without periods. Some widely used acronyms, such as *NATO*, *UNICEF*, and *AIDS*, are occasionally treated as proper nouns and appear with only initial capital letters: *Nato*, *Unicef*, *Aids*. Some acronyms are composed of capital and lower-case letters, with the lower-case letters representing grammatical words (e.g., *of*, *the*); thus the abbreviation for the Museum of Modern Art in New York may be written *MoMA*.

An initialism is formed from the first letters in a phrase or name, but—unlike acronyms—initialisms are usually pronounced letter by letter: *NHL* (*en aitch ell*); *RCMP* (*are see em pee*); *CBC* (*see bee see*). Some initialisms, though they look unpronounceable, are treated like acronyms: for example, *SSHRCC*, an initialism for Social Sciences and Humanities Research Council of Canada, is pronounced *SHIRK*.

Like acronyms, initialisms are usually written in capital letters without periods (MP, UN, USA). Formerly, style guides recommended the use of periods in two-letter abbreviations of place names (B.C., N.B., U.S.) and in abbreviations of academic degrees (B.Sc., M.A., Ph.D.). The more recent trend, however—accelerated by the introduction of the two-letter postal abbreviations, which never include periods—is towards dropping the periods in all such abbreviations (NS, NB; BA, LLD) unless tradition or consistency requires them.

Some categories of abbreviation never take periods, no matter what style the editor or writer chooses:

• SI units (*kg*, *L*; see APPENDIX II)
• abbreviations for points of the compass: N, S, E, SSW

- chemical symbols (*Fe, N*)
- post office abbreviations for the names of the provinces (*BC, ON*; see POSTAL ADDRESSES; APPENDIX I)

Abbreviation, as well as referring to the forms discussed above, is the general term for any type of shortened form of a word or phrase. Forms such as *bike, hippo,* and *phone* are usually called clipped words. Forms combining two words into one, such as *brunch* (breakfast and lunch), *Oxbridge* (Oxford and Cambridge), *permafrost* (permanent and frost), and *Agribition* (agriculture and exhibition), are usually called blends or portmanteau words. As with all abbreviations, the question arises of whether these are appropriate in formal writing. The newer and more unfamiliar a clipped form or a blend is, the more likely it is to be condemned. For forms such as *didn't* and *can't*, see CONTRACTIONS.

See also HIV, HIV VIRUS; MISS, MR., MRS.; MS.; OXBRIDGE; SOCIAL CREDIT; STANDARD TIME; APPENDIX I, APPENDIX II.

abdomen   see BELLY

abduct   see KIDNAP

Abenaki, Wabanaki   These names are not equivalent. The *Abenaki* (or *Abnaki*) are an Aboriginal people whose traditional territory spreads across Quebec, Vermont, Maine and New Hampshire. They are one of five Algonquian groups in this area (the others are the Penobscot, Maliseet, Passamaquoddy, and Mi'kmaq) who collectively once referred to themselves as the *Wabanaki*. Although the Wabanaki Confederacy officially disbanded in 1862, it survives in the strong relation among the groups. Any of these five peoples may sometimes still refer to themselves as Wabanaki.

> The word arrived via Canadian French from an Algonquian language, probably Mikmaq or Abenaki, the author says.
> *Ottawa Citizen* 19 March 2006: B8

> As a young girl she helped her grandparents—Wabanaki Indians living on the Odanak reserve near Sorel—fashion moccasins, clothing and neck-laces from leather.
> *Gazette* (Montreal) 27 Sept. 2004: B3

(Odanak is an Abenaki reserve; these 'Wabanaki Indians' are specifically Abenaki.)

> Alma Brooks, a Maliseet representative of the Wabanaki Medicine Lodge, said sexual abuse and substance abuse have become 'a mechanism to survive the pain, hopelessness and powerlessness.'
> *Toronto Star* 20 May 1992: A11

(This Wabanaki representative is Maliseet, not Abenaki.)

See also ABORIGINAL PEOPLE(S); MALISEET; APPENDIX III.

-able, -(at)able   Verbs with two syllables ending in *-ate* are transformed into adjectives by dropping the final *e* and adding *-able*: for example, *debatable, dictatable, inflatable,* and *translatable*. Note, however, the exception of *placate/placable*.

Verbs with *more* than two syllables ending in *-ate* are transformed into adjectives by replacing *-ate* with *-able*: *allocate, allocable; calculate, calculable; communicate, communicable; demonstrate, demonstrable; educate, educable; imitate, imitable; manipulate, manipulable. Communicatable, demonstratable, educatable,* and so on, are nonstandard.

See also -ABLE, -(E)ABLE; -ABLE, -IBLE; INIMICAL, INIMITABLE.

-able, -(e)able   A silent *e* following the letter *c* or *g* must be retained before the suffix *-able*: *changeable, faceable, manageable, peaceable, traceable*. But in other cases when *-able* is added to a word of one syllable, *e* may be dropped or retained. British writers tend to retain it and American writers to drop it. Canadians prefer *saleable* to *salable*, but usually drop the *e* in *livable* and *movable*; the pairs *likeable/likable* and *sizeable/sizable* are used with about equal frequency.

> And it's small enough to be managable by a single person.
> *Times-Colonist* (Victoria) 19 Jan. 2002: F3

(The correct spelling is *manageable.*)

See also -ABLE, -(AT)ABLE; -ABLE, -IBLE; -E.

-able, -ible   The suffix *-able/-ible* means 'that can be', 'that may be', or 'that must be': thus something flexible can be flexed, something returnable may be returned, and something payable must be paid. It also means 'subject to', as in *dutiable*; 'in accordance with' as in *fashionable;* and 'tending to', as in *perishable* and *profitable*. There is no difference in meaning or pronunciation between the variants *-able* and *-ible*. They do, however, present a spelling challenge.

Newly coined words always end in *-able*: *microwavable, recyclable*. Generally, any word that can be negated with the prefix *un-* ends in *-able*: *uncomfortable, unpresentable, unreadable, unworkable*. Most words ending in *-ible* are negated with the Latin prefix *in-* (or its variants *il-, im-, ir-*) rather than *un-*: *inaccessible, incomprehensible, illegible, implausible, irresponsible*. Unfortunately, not all words negated with *in-* and its variants end in *-ible*; some end in *-able*: *ineducable, inexcusable, inimitable, irreparable*. When in doubt about *-ible* and *-able*, it is best to consult a dictionary.

The summit of Haleakala is accessable by car and is a popular tourist sight.
Vancouver Sun 24 April 1992: A17

(The correct spelling is accessible.)

See also -ABLE, -(AT)ABLE; -ABLE, -(E)ABLE.

able-bodyism   see -ISM

able to be   Many stylists object to the construction *able to be*, as in 'The data will be able to be analysed more efficiently'. They argue that the adjective *able*, which suggests an active ability, should not be used to introduce a passive verb. The disputed structure can be avoided by using *can* or *could* or, in the future tense, an impersonal construction: 'The data can be analysed . . .'; 'The data could be analysed . . .'; 'It will be possible to analyse the data . . .'.

. . . this venture fell far short of being able to be considered a total success.
Computer Dealer News 21 March 1991: 47

(This sentence might be rephrased: 'this venture could by no means be considered . . .'.)

abolition, abolishment   *Abolition* is the more common word for putting an end to a custom or institution, but *abolishment* is also correct. A writer may choose one word over the other to avoid unintentional rhymes: for example, 'the abolition of Prohibition'.

Abolition is familiar because of its specific association with the abolitionist political movement, which ended slavery in Britain in 1833 and in the United States in 1865.

abominable snowman   see SASQUATCH

aboriginal, Aboriginal, Aborigine   From the Latin meaning 'from the beginning', *aboriginal* can refer to anything indigenous, including people. In Australia *Aboriginal* and *Aborigine* evolved to refer specifically to the Indigenous people of that country, and now are capitalized to indicate this use.

Most Australian authorities, including the Aborigines, prefer *Aborigine(s)* for the noun. *Aboriginal* is used as an adjective. More and more Aborigines are using terms derived from their own languages to describe themselves: for example, Nyoongah in Western Australia and Koori in New South Wales and Victoria.

In 1982 the Canadian *Constitution Act* (section 35, Part II) introduced the phrase 'the aboriginal peoples of Canada'. Before that date, most Canadians associated the word *aboriginal* only with the Australian context. Now *aboriginal* (only as an adjective) is used to refer to Native people of Canada in phrases such as 'Aboriginal rights' and 'Aboriginal people'. And now the Canadian government capitalizes the word *Aboriginal* to accord with the general practice of capitalizing words for broad geographic, ethnic, and linguistic groups. This capitalization is recommended, although lower-case *aboriginal* is more common in journalism.

When the aborigines sighted Captain Cook's ships,

they ignored them because they knew such things could not exist.
Margaret Atwood *Life Before Man* 1979: 10

(Here *Aborigines* should be capitalized.)

One problem identified across aboriginal communities is the lack of qualified nurses.
The Aboriginal Nurse 18.1 (2003): 12

(*Aboriginal* should be capitalized in reference to Native people of Canada.)

See also ABORIGINAL PEOPLE(S); CAPITAL LETTERS; NATIVE.

Aboriginal people(s), Native people(s), Indigenous people(s), Status Indian, Registered Indian, Treaty Indian, Non-Status Indian, First Nations, First Peoples, Amerindian As the political identity and constitutional status of Indians, Métis, and Inuit in Canada evolve, so do the terms that refer to them. The Canadian *Constitution Act* of 1982 referred to Indians, Métis, and Inuit under the general rubric *aboriginal peoples*. The Federal Terminology Council (2003) makes the following recommendations with respect to general references to Aboriginal people(s) in Canada. *Aboriginal* and *Native* should be capitalized to parallel other broad ethnic, linguistic, and geographic designations such as *Asian*, *Hispanic*, and *Nordic*. *Aboriginal* and *Native* should be used as adjectives only, as in 'Aboriginal peoples' and 'Native peoples' (*not* 'Aboriginals', 'Natives'). The adjective *Aboriginal* is now preferable to *Native*, which is losing currency. *Indigenous* should be capitalized in the term *Indigenous peoples*, which is often used, for example by the United Nations, to refer to Aboriginal groups worldwide.

Aboriginal people prefer to be identified with the land rather than being discussed in terms that invoke earlier colonial concepts of them as 'wards of the state': 'Aboriginal people(s) of Canada', 'Native people(s) in Canada', 'Indigenous people(s) in Canada' (*not* 'Aboriginal Canadians', 'Native Canadians', 'Indigenous Canadians', or 'Canada's Aboriginal peoples', etc.). *People*, in these phrases, can mean either a group of individuals ('The Aboriginal people

present at the meeting discussed the issue'), the entire body of Aboriginal persons ('Aboriginal people today are fully aware of their changing position with respect to the state'), or a particular group that shares ancestry, language, and sometimes geographical territory ('The Haida are an Aboriginal people'). *Peoples*, plural, always refers to a number of such groups, not a number of individuals.

According to the *Indian Act* (1985), *Registered Indians* (also known as *Status Indians*) are those who are registered—or entitled to be registered—with the government under the specifications of the Act. *Treaty Indians* are those who belong to groups that signed treaties with the Crown, most of whom are also Satus Indians. The many people of Aboriginal ancestry who do not fall into these categories are called *Non-Status Indians*. These terms describe legal categories and, as such, in formal writing, should be capitalized. In common use, they have been supplanted by *First Nations peoples*.

No official definition of the term *First Nation(s)* exists. It can refer broadly to all Status and Non-Status Indians but often has a more limited reference, as it does in the name of the Assembly of First Nations, a national organization that represents the more than 600 bands of Status Indians recognized by the federal government. Many of these bands now call themselves *First Nations*. In this use, the word *Nation* may refer to a group who live in a particular reserve community and who may be descended from a variety of historical Indigenous nations, such as Cree, Ojibwa, Algonquin, or Odawa. Both *First Nation* and *First Nations* (plural) are acceptable modifiers: 'First Nation community', 'First Nations people', 'First Nations students'.

Many First Nations are abandoning the names given to them by Europeans and returning to their names for themselves in their heritage languages: e.g., Anishnabe (*a nish NAW bee*) instead of Ojibwa, Siksika instead of Blackfoot. Others are respelling their names to better represent pronunciations: e.g., Mi'kmaq instead of Micmac. Often these new names and spellings are unfamiliar to a general audience. Thus, for now, it will help the reader if both the old name and the new name are mentioned.

Generally, whether the name is old or new, it serves as an adjective ('Haida canoe'), a singular noun ('One Haida voted against the move'), and a plural ('The Haida are demonstrating against increased logging'). Exceptions include *Inuit* (adjective or plural noun; the singular is *Inuk*), and *Mi'kmaq* (adjective or plural noun; the singular is *Mi'kmaw*) and *Algonquin, Cree, Huron,* and *Mohawk,* which are usually pluralized with an *s*.

Although *Indian* may have declined in general use because it is thought to reflect Columbus's mistaken idea that he had landed in India in 1492, it is common in the usage of many First Nations people and embedded in legislation that is still in effect. Further, it is the only clear way to distinguish among the three most general categories of Aboriginal people: Indians, Métis, and Inuit.

First Peoples, as distinct from *First Nations*, is an umbrella term that covers all Aboriginal people: Indians of whatever status, Métis, and Inuit.

The term *Amerindian* includes all the Aboriginal peoples of Canada as well as the rest of North America, Central America, and South America.

Native protesters from the Tyendinaga territory have moved their protest from the CN Rail tracks near Shannonville to Caledonia, Ont.
Whig-Standard (Kingston) 24 April 2006: 3

(In formal writing and newspapers, the adjective *Aboriginal* is gradually displacing *Native*. Note, however, the effect of context: the phrase 'Native protestors' is still far more common in newspapers than 'Aboriginal protestors'.)

There were roughly 3,500 registered Indians living in Newfoundland and Labrador at the beginning of 2003, according to Indian and Northern Affairs Canada.
Telegram (St. John's) 12 March 2004: A1

(In formal writing, *Registered Indian,* a legal designation, should be capitalized.)

The confederacy believes the [Assembly of First Nations] and Ottawa are trying to lump treaty Indians in with other aboriginal groups, failing to recognize the 'unique' rights of bands that signed treaties with Ottawa about 125 years ago.
Calgary Herald 3 Feb. 1994: B3

(*Aboriginal* should be capitalized and, in formal writing, so should the legal designation *Treaty Indian.*)

The Great Dying [from European diseases] reduced the population of Amerindians from 20% of the human species to just 3% in one century.
Toronto Sun 16 Oct. 1994: M6

See also ABENAKI; ALGONQUIN; ATHABASCAN; BLACK-FOOT; CARRIER; CHIPEWYAN; CREE; DENE; GITXSAN; HAIDA; INNU; INUIT; IROQUOIS; KITCHENUHMAYKOOSIB INNINUWUG; KOOTENAY; KWAKIUTL; MALISEET; MÉTIS; MI'KMAQ; NATIVE; NISGA'A; NLAKA'PAMUX; NUNAVUT; NUU-CHAH-NULTH; NUXALK; ODAWA; OJIBWA(Y); RESERVE, RESERVATION; SECWEPEMC; SLAVEY; STL'ATL'IMX; TSUU T'INA; APPENDIX III.

abortion, pro-life, pro-choice, anti-abortion   In the debate over legal access to abortion, activists commonly call themselves *pro-life* (i.e., anti-abortion), or *pro-choice* (i.e., in favour of a woman's right to choose to have an abortion). Both sides dispute the other's choice of label. Pro-choice groups claim that pro-life groups' concern with life ends at birth, while pro-life groups claim that pro-choice groups' concern with choice excludes the unborn. Writers aiming for a balanced discussion should certainly avoid the terms *anti-choice* and *anti-life*, which are negative and partisan. *Pro-abortion* should also be avoided, since many supporters of the pro-choice movement view abortion as always regrettable. The *Globe and Mail Style Book* (1995) recommends using *anti-abortion* and *pro-choice* as the most accurate and least offensive of these politically charged labels. The *Canadian Press Stylebook* (rev. ed. 2004) allows people and groups in the news to describe *themselves* as *pro-choice* or *pro-life*, but recommends to news writers the phrases *abortion-rights advocates* and *opponents of abortion*. Obviously, those involved in the debate will continue to use the terms they feel are most persuasive.

Anti-abortion and pro-choice forces squared off at UBC Wednesday....
'British Columbia' *CBC News* website 25 Feb. 2000

The women's and pro-choice movements will be

concentrating serious efforts over the coming months to prevent the Tory anti-choice bill from passing.
Our Times March 1990: 20

(*Anti-abortion* would be a less partisan choice than *anti-choice*.)

I find this anti-life feminist agenda an offence to my womanhood, and to common sense.
Calgary Herald 8 Oct. 2005: A31

(An unbiased news writer would avoid the term *anti-life*, which appears here in a letter to the editor.)

abridgement, abridgment   see -E

abrogate, arrogate   To *abrogate* something is to repeal, abolish, or do away with it. To *arrogate* something to (*or unto*) yourself, such as a privilege, power, or desirable characteristic, is to claim it for yourself without justification. To arrogate a characteristic, good or bad, to others is to ascribe it to them without reason.

'Unless we abrogate the free trade agreement there is no possible way that Canada can survive as a country.'
Vancouver Sun 14 April 1992: B8

'I do not feel you should arrogate to yourself the right to determine the degree of impairment,' he wrote, 'in spite of a medical certificate furnished by a qualified doctor in which he recommends that a handicapped sticker be issued.'
Gazette (Montreal) 24 Nov. 1992: C6

absent   *Absent* has been used as a preposition meaning *in the absence of* or *without* since early in the twentieth century. From American legal writing it spread to Canadian legal writing and journalism. It is not a familiar usage in Britain. Some commentators consider the preposition *absent* a legalism, unsuitable for general formal writing.

Absent clear and compelling national security reasons, the state may commandeer them only with our explicit consent.
Toronto Star 30 Dec. 1992: A17

See also FUNCTIONAL SHIFT.

absolute adjectives   see COMPLETE; PERFECT; UNIQUE

absolute comparatives   When advertisers promise 'whiter washes', direct you to 'better bookstores', or offer 'higher interest rates', they are using absolute comparatives. An absolute comparative is a comparative construction (formed with either -*er* or *more*) not followed by *than*: that is, with no explicit basis of comparison. This structure annoys some language commentators who consider it intentionally imprecise. The claim of 'higher interest rates', for example, is so vague (higher than in 1962?) that it cannot be challenged. Commentators have also criticized particular absolute comparatives as snobbish ('better homes') or euphemistic ('older people' sounds less old than 'old people'). In spite of the criticism that absolute comparatives have drawn, they are not grammatically incorrect and cannot be avoided altogether. In fact, in everyday usage they are far more common than explicit comparisons: absolute comparatives that are not evasive or snobbish tend to go unnoticed.

In smaller schools, multigrade classes seem likely to increase. . . .
Education Canada Summer 1989: 10

Shorter plants have higher rates of alternative pathway respiration.
Arctic 41.1 (1988): 1

[Hull] provides a welcome alternative to the prim correctness of some of the region's 'better' neighborhoods.
Ottawa Citizen 5 Dec. 1992: F2

(Here, as the quotation marks indicate, the absolute comparative did not go unnoticed.)

academe, academia, academy, academic
Academe, academia and *the academy* are all used to refer to the world of scholarship and higher learning. Fowler objected to *academe* in this sense because in his view the word was a reference to Academus, a hero of Greek mythology. Plato founded his famous school near the olive grove sacred to Academus, and this school became known as the *Academia*. The *Dictionary*

of Contemporary American Usage, while accepting *academe* as an anglicized variant of *academia*, advises that it be used only in reference to Plato's Academy. Shakespeare, however, initiated a poetic tradition of using *academe* to mean a place of learning, and in this has proved more influential than any language commentator: *academe* is now commonly used to mean the academic world. It is usually pronounced *a ka DEEM*.

Academe and *academia* (pronounced *a ka DEEM ya*) are often used facetiously or pejoratively. Likewise, the adjective *academic* has both a neutral meaning (having to do with scholarship or the university) and a pejorative one (of no practical import).

> It is a story, in many ways, of failure—of women restricted by simple prejudice to the periphery of academe. . . .
> *Queen's Quarterly* 92.1 (1985): 20

> Any conflict he had felt back in East St. Louis about where his musical future lay had been resolved by the head-to-head confrontation of the jazz clubs and academe.
> Jack Chambers *Milestones* 1983: 33

> I escaped from academia and bypassed journalism—which was the other career I considered. . . .
> Margaret Atwood *Second Words* 1982: 216

> The university and its personnel are part of the dominant social order and the work that was produced and taught within the academy on the relations between men and women . . . was deeply embedded in that assumed order.
> *Queen's Quarterly* 92.1 (1985): 9

> 'The community has banquets to give out awards to athletes but we do nothing as a community for academic achievement.'
> *Toronto Star* 28 Dec. 1992: A21

> The debate between the advocates of a 'presidential' and 'parliamentary' system is therefore not just of academic interest to the West. It will probably determine whether the new Russia becomes more or less easy to live with.
> *Toronto Star* 10 April 1992: A27

Acadia, Acadian, Cajun   *L'Acadie* or, in English, *Acadia* was the name given to the first permanent French settlement in North America. It ranged over the present-day provinces of New Brunswick, Nova Scotia, and Prince Edward Island, as well as the Magdalen Islands and parts of the Gaspé and Maine. Maritimers descended from these first French settlers are called *Acadians*. *Acadian* also refers to the dialect of French spoken in the Maritimes. The distinctive pronunciations and vocabulary of this dialect reveal that the original settlers came from south of the Loire River in France. (The majority of Quebec settlers came from north of the Loire.)

The British assumed control of Acadia in 1713 and in 1755 began to deport the Acadians, fearing their disloyalty in the ongoing wars between England and France. Many of the expelled Acadians settled in Louisiana, which was a French territory at the time. Some exiles later returned to Acadia and, together with fugitives who had escaped the British round-up, resettled the area. For generations, the Acadian community lacked both civil rights and French-language institutions.

By the mid-1800s the descendants of Acadians who had remained in Louisiana were known as *Cajuns*, an anglicized version of the French *Acadiens*. Though *Cajun* and *Acadian* are related terms, they are not synonymous. The two cultures diverged over the centuries. Cajun French was influenced by Spanish and the Creole French of the Caribbean. It is now a dialect in imminent danger of extinction. Cajun cuisine and music, on the other hand, are thriving.

> 'The older people didn't talk much about their life in Acadia because they saw the deportation as a humiliation.'
> *Gazette* (Montreal) 5 Dec. 1992: B1

> As in her earlier novels and plays, Maillet reveals the down-to-earth character of Acadian oral culture.
> *Ottawa Citizen* 28 Nov. 1992: n.p.

> Prime Minister Brian Mulroney's crack during the referendum campaign that Quebecers don't want to end up becoming Cajuns, dancing and playing banjos in Louisiana, didn't sit well with the Acadian community, which could mount a strong argument that Cajun musicians have generated

more widespread awareness of the French fact in North America than all of Quebec's intellectuals and political poseurs combined.
Gazette (Montreal) 5 Dec. 1992: B1

See also BLACK, AFRICADIAN; FRANCOPHONE; QUEBE-CER.

a cappella *A cappella*, which means without instrumental accompaniment, is both an adverb ('sang a cappella') and an adjective ('an a cappella group'). The phrase is often mis-spelled. Note that *a* is written as a separate word and that cappella has two *p*'s and two *l*'s. Like many musical terms, *a cappella* ('in chapel style') is a borrowing from Italian, but this bor-rowing is no longer considered foreign and thus does not require italicization.

accede see -CEED, -CEDE, -SEDE

accent, dialect, variety, dialectal An *accent* is a way of pronouncing the language ('a foreign accent', 'a Southern accent', 'a South African accent'). Accents are relative: Canadians think Americans have accents, while Americans think Canadians do. Although there is no such thing as unaccented speech, speakers whose accent is the most widely accepted and presti-gious are sometimes described as having no accent.

A *dialect* is a regional or social form of a lan-guage (e.g., Jamaican English, Ottawa Valley English, uneducated English, Standard English) characterized by distinctive features of pronun-ciation, grammar, and vocabulary. Just as all speakers of a language speak with an accent, all speak a dialect. Speakers of the standard form of a language seldom think of themselves as speak-ing dialect, but in fact they are speaking the dialect with the highest level of social approval. This technical definition of *dialect* is at odds with popular usage. Thus as a way of avoiding the often pejorative implications of the term *dialect,* some writers employ the more neutrally perceived synonym *variety*: 'international vari-eties of English'.

Because Standard English is used worldwide, it exists in many national standard dialects or varieties. Educated English speakers from around the globe all use the same grammar, and largely the same vocabulary, but their accents (or, technically speaking, phonological systems) are traceable to specific regions (South Africa, India, Australia, etc.). Some English speakers are bidialectal, that is, speakers of two dialects: they might, for example, speak both Newfoundland Vernacular English and Standard Canadian English, or both Jamaican English and Standard British English. Adult learners of new languages or new dialects usually have difficulty master-ing a new accent, even when their speech is grammatical and fluent in other respects. Most of those who learn new dialects or languages after late childhood are stuck with the accent of their first variety or language.

The adjective form of *dialect* is *dialectal*. *Dialectic* has to do with logical disputation.

See also DIALECTIC(S), DIALECTICAL; LINGUA FRANCA; PIDGIN, CREOLE; STANDARD ENGLISH, STANDARD.

accents see DIACRITICAL MARKS

accept *Accept* followed by an infinitive and used to mean agree ('Will they accept to come a day earlier?') is a non-standard usage, probably influenced by French. In Standard English *accept* is followed by the *-ing* form of a verb: 'They don't accept eating meat'.

> Will governments of other countries accept to host such centers?
> *Canadian Issues* March 2004: 14

(The usual expression is 'agree to host'; this example is from a Montreal-based magazine, and may be influenced by French.)

> Let's not accept dying on the job as an economic necessity.
> *CAUT Bulletin* 51.5 (May 2004): A3

See also QUEBEC ENGLISH.

access see FUNCTIONAL SHIFT

accidentally, incidentally Because the *-al-* in *accidentally* and *incidentally* is seldom pro-nounced, these adverbs are often misspelled *accidently* and *incidently*. It may help to remember that adverbs are formed from adjectives; hence the adverb ending *-ly* is being added to the adjectives *accidental* and *incidental*, not the nouns *accident* and *incident*.

One dictionary, *Merriam-Webster's*, now lists *accidently* as a standard spelling variant. However, no other dictionary has followed suit, and usage guides uniformly recommend against this spelling.

acclamation, acclaim   In Canada, to be elected *by acclamation* or to *be acclaimed* means to win an election by default because no one else ran. These meanings of *acclamation* and *acclaim* are unique to Canadian English. In Britain and the United States the same expressions refer to winning in a vote decided by cheers and shouts rather than by ballots.

The noun *acclaim* means public approval. In British and American English, the loud and enthusiastic applause of a live audience is usually called *acclamation*. However, Canadians prefer to use *acclaim* in this context as well, reserving *acclamation* for its special political sense.

When the time came for MPs to cast their votes, all candidates who had previously declared interest in the job dropped their names from the ballot, which made Milliken the Speaker by acclamation.
Whig-Standard (Kingston) 4 April 2006: 1

(This is the specialized Canadian sense of *by acclamation*: there was no contest.)

Mayor Lorna Jackson is back for her fourth term on council. She was acclaimed when her only competitor . . . dropped out of the race in early October.
Toronto Star 17 Oct. 1991: NY4

But it was the awesome performances by the American team that drew the acclaim of the full-house crowd of approximately 7,000.
Gazette (Montreal) 6 March 1989: C1

(Here *acclaim* means applause; British and American English speakers would likely say *acclamation*.)

acclimatize, acclimate   To *acclimatize* or *acclimate* (pronounced *AK li mate* or *a KLIME ut*)

is to adjust to a new environment. Both words are acceptable. *Acclimatize* is more common. *Acclimate* is mainly restricted to Canada and the United States.

. . . we were whisked away to a valley 750 metres down, to acclimatize and sip more cups of the Incas' coca remedy.
Times-Colonist (Victoria): 1 Oct. 2005: C1

This process, known as 'hardening off,' gradually acclimates the plants to outdoor conditions.
Edmonton Journal 19 May 1994: C2

accommodate, accommodation   *The words accommodate* and *accommodation* are frequently misspelled with one *m*. These words are related etymologically to *commodious*, 'roomy'—a point that may help with spelling.

accompanied by, accompanied with   *Accompanied with* was more common in the mid-seventeenth century. *Accompanied by* is more common today, and some commentators insist that only *by* is correct. Several language commentators have, however, noted a subtle pattern in contemporary usage. People are usually described as being accompanied *by* other people ('Children must be accompanied by adults'), while things are often described as being accompanied *with* other things ('When the blouse is accompanied with a jacket, it looks very professional'). The *Canadian Oxford Dictionary* lists both prepositions after *accompany* without comment.

A singular noun linked by the phrase *accompanied by* or *with* to another noun (singular or plural) should be followed by a singular verb: 'The poached halibut accompanied with braised radishes is delicious'.

Potential subjects were only excluded if they were accompanied by small children or employed at the store.
Journal of Nutrition Education 33.1 (2001): 24–30

Each submission must be accompanied with an application form.
Telegram (St. John's) 16 Feb. 2001: A11

See also AGREEMENT, GRAMMATICAL.

accordion   Whether it refers to the musical instrument or to something pleated and collapsible, the word *accordion* should be spelled *-ion* (not *-ian*). It may help to know that the ending of *accordion* is probably borrowed from another musical word: *clarion*.

accredit   *Accredited* does not mean acclaimed. To *accredit* means to lend credence to or endorse. Evidence that accredits a theory supports it. Professionals and organizations that are accredited are officially recognized or certified by a regulating body. Diplomats accredited to a certain country are official envoys to that country.

A second accepted meaning of *accredit* is to attribute. A quotation may be accredited to a source, or an effect to a cause.

The publisher's claim that the book was vetted by the Israeli military censor serves to simultaneously accredit the background data and explain the few stilted passages.
Toronto Star 8 Aug. 1992: K15

After all, . . . you don't need to be accredited to sit on a board.
Canadian Business 1–14 March 2004

Canada will then accredit a Canadian representative to Eritrea who will work from the embassy in Addis Ababa.
Ottawa Citizen 21 April 1993: A2

This lateness has been a characteristic of the comet in its past seven revolutions. It is accredited to non-gravitational forces acting on it. . . .
Queen's Quarterly 92.2 (1985): 285

Twenty-two years later he produced Success Story, a highly accredited film about insect survival.
Spectator (Hamilton) 30 Sept. 1994: T3

(Here *acclaimed* or *regarded* should replace *accredited*.)

accused   see ALLEGED

ache   Words derived from *ache*, including *achy*, *achier*, and *aching*, are often misspelled.

Many of the originals have become 'too old, too bent and too achey' to turn out.
Calgary Herald 23 July 1992: N1

(The correct spelling is *achy*.)

See also -Y, -EY.

achieve   see -IE-, -EI-

Achilles' heel   An *Achilles' heel* is a point of vulnerability or a weakness. According to Greek mythology, when Achilles was an infant, his mother dipped him into the River Styx to make him invulnerable; however, since she held him by the heel, it did not go into the water and so remained unprotected. As Homer's *Iliad* recounts, Paris killed Achilles by shooting an arrow into his heel, after learning that it was his only vulnerable spot.

While dictionaries generally include the apostrophe following *Achilles*, some style guides do not, and usage is divided. *Achilles' heel* is more common in formal writing, but *Achilles heel* is also correct. The spelling to be avoided is *Achille's heel*: the *s* is part of Achilles' name.

You found my Achilles' heel.
Howard Engel *Murder Sees the Light* 1981: 65

Goaltending remains the Wings' Achilles heel in post-season.
Edmonton Journal 16 April 1994: F5

While the IOC has approved all of Quebec's other 63 event sites, choosing a site for the Olympic downhill race has proved an Achille's heel.
Calgary Herald 14 Nov. 1994: A2

(The apostrophe should follow the *s* in *Achilles*.)

See also POSSESSIVE.

acknowledgement, acknowledgment   see -E

acme   see EPITOME

acq-   see AQ

acreage   see -E

acronym   see ABBREVIATION

actor, actress   see JOB TITLES

actually   see QUEBEC ENGLISH

acute   see CHRONIC

ad   see ADVERTISEMENT

AD, BC, CE, BCE, BP, century   *AD* is an abbreviation of the Latin phrase *anno Domini*, 'in the year of the (our) Lord'. It is used to distinguish years after the birth of Christ from years before, which are labelled *BC* ('Before Christ'). Most style guides recommend placing *BC* after the year ('55 BC') and *AD* before it ('AD 1511'), to conform to the complete phrase: '55 (years) before Christ'; 'in the year of the (our) Lord 1511'. However, in informal writing *AD* is common in either position.

Some scholars have begun to use *CE* ('Common Era') and *BCE* ('Before Common Era') instead of *AD* and *BC*. Although the dating system itself is not changed—the Common Era commences with the birth of Christ—the use of *CE* and *BCE* removes the explicit Christian reference from the modern Western calendar. These alternative abbreviations are still uncommon enough to require an explanation.

Geologists and other scientists commonly use the international *BP* ('Before Present') dating system to refer to times in the far past, determined, for example, by carbon dating. The present is defined by convention as 1950—12,000 BP is only approximately 12,000 years ago—but the dates referred to are usually not accurate enough to be affected by this.

Most publications (except newspapers) print all these abbreviations in small capital letters (AD, BC, etc.). The use of periods (A.D. *or* AD) is a matter of style (see ABBREVIATIONS).

The 1800s are the nineteenth century, the 1900s, the twentieth century, and now we are in the twenty-first century. Since the first century began with AD 1 (not AD 100), the ordinal that names a century is always one ahead of the hundreds figure in the date.

> Caesar Augustus issued decrees in 28 B.C. and 8 B.C., and again in 14 A.D.
> *Daily News* (Halifax) 12 Dec. 1993: 42

(In formal writing, *AD* is usually placed before the year.)

> Ratio data . . . showed three lower and two higher-than-present timberline phases since 1600 BP,

> with timberline at its lowest elevation c. 500 BP.
> *The Canadian Geographer* Spring 1989: 84

(The equivalent dates in traditional style are AD 350 and c. AD 1450 respectively.)

See also DATES; MILLENNIUM; NUMBERS, DECIMAL POINTS AND COMMAS WITH.

adaptation, adaption   *Adaptation* and *adaption* are variants: either is acceptable in any sense, but *adaption* is used far less frequently.

> After long adaptation to land conditions, slugs are unable to tolerate deep water and most species will drown if immersed in water.
> *Ottawa Citizen* 3 Sept. 1994: J4

> The TV adaption of Timothy Findley's play Elizabeth Rex reigned at the ACTRA awards in Toronto Friday Night.
> *Toronto Star* 22 Feb. 2004: D3

adapter, adaptor   Canadians use either *adapter* or *adaptor* to refer to a person who rewrites material for a different audience or medium, or to a gadget that makes equipment compatible. American and British dictionaries also list either spelling for either meaning. The *-er* spelling is more common in Canada and the United States, the *-or* spelling in Britain.

See also -ER, -OR

addendum, addenda   see PLURALS

addresses   see COMMA; POSTAL ADDRESSES

ad feminam   see AD HOMINEM

ad hoc   *Ad hoc* is a Latin phrase meaning 'for this'. An ad hoc committee is one that is set up for a special purpose, as opposed to an administrative committee set up to deal with recurrent issues.

The phrase *ad hoc* is sometimes used disparagingly to describe a style of management marked by lack of forethought, which consists entirely of reacting to crises. This style is also described by the noun *ad hockery* (sometimes hyphenated and sometimes spelled without the *k*). *Ad hock-*

ery is a facetious coinage, as yet restricted to informal use.

> For many years judges have headed an array of ad hoc commissions of inquiry, ranging from the Gouzenko spy affair to the Dubin inquiry into drugs in sport.
> Andrew Heard *Canadian Constitutional Conventions* 1991: 134

> Young adults who grow up without a demanding science curriculum cannot be said to have educated opinions, and ad hoc Google searches will never compensate for general ignorance.
> *Times-Colonist* (Victoria) 16 April 2006: D10

> So when objections arose, or assumptions proved faulty, ad-hockery took over, with politicians making alternative plans with little regard for their rationality.
> *Ottawa Citizen* 4 Nov. 1991: A8

See also LATIN PHRASES.

ad hominem, ad feminam   *Ad hominem* is a Latin phrase meaning literally 'to the man'. It is used to label a type of fallacious argument that defames an opponent instead of addressing the points he or she is raising. In formal writing the phrase requires italics.

Ad hominem entered the English language in the sixteenth century, when the use of masculine pronouns and nouns as generic forms, referring to either men or women, was unquestioned. The phrase *ad feminam*, 'to the woman', is a twentieth-century feminist coinage.

> Many of the articles in the book have consisted mainly of ad hominem attacks on Cote himself that scarcely address the substance of what he's actually written.
> *Gazette* (Montreal) 8 Dec. 1990: B3

> Argumentum ad Hominem: 'John is a drunkard; therefore, he is wrong about disarmament.'
> *Globe and Mail* (Toronto) 7 Sept. 1985: P6

> As for my critics—spite isn't an argument, and ad feminam taunts do not advance your cause.
> *Toronto Star* 20 May 2001: 2

See also LATIN PHRASES.

adieu   see ADO

ad infinitum   *Ad infinitum* (pronounced *AD in fi NITE um*) is a Latin phrase meaning 'without limit' or 'endlessly'; it does not mean 'taken to an extreme'.

> At the opposite extreme is the belief that the miracles of modern science may be able to stave off every single thing that goes wrong with us, lengthening our lifespan ad infinitum.
> *Toronto Sun* 16 Feb. 1994: S10

> As has been repeated ad infinitum, the 27-year-old left-winger is going through the worst of his nine seasons as a pro.
> *Gazette* (Montreal) 21 March 1992: C2

> It's the modern, corporate, high-tech world ad infinitum. A world where people make lots of money and are plugged in, but have no time.
> *Canadian Speeches* April 1994: 34

(Here *ad infinitum* is inappropriate; 'taken to the extreme' would be better.)

> Women live longer than men, so Canada Pension Plan premiums should be higher for women if this argument is to be taken ad infinitum.
> *Toronto Star* 3 May 1993: A20

(Here *ad infinitum* is inappropriate; 'to the logical extreme' would be better.)

See also LATIN PHRASES.

adjectives and adverbs   Adjectives are words such as *green*, *calm*, *cultural*, and *defective*. They modify—that is, they describe or particularize—nouns: '*green* bananas', 'a *calm* day', 'a *cultural* pursuit', 'the *defective* switch'.

Adverbs—words such as *well*, *too*, *fairly*, and *remarkably*—serve many functions. They modify verbs ('He eats *well* '), adjectives ('*too* cold'), other adverbs ('*fairly* well'), and whole sentences ('*Remarkably*, he wasn't hurt'). For a discussion of adverbs that modify whole sentences—including *hopefully*—see SENTENCE ADVERBS.

The vast majority of adverbs are formed by adding *-ly* to an adjective: *brazen*, *brazenly*; *exceptional*, *exceptionally*; *merciful*, *mercifully*. Yet many of the most frequently used adverbs do not fit this pattern: *already, ever, here, late, often, together, very*. And not every word that ends in *-ly* is an adverb: a handful are adjectives, including *friendly, lovely, scholarly, stately,* and *ugly*. See FRIENDLY on the subject of turning this type of adjective into an adverb.

It is non-standard to use an adjective to modify a verb, as in 'He throws good'. For those who don't normally use adjectives adverbially, a sentence like 'They treat you decent' represents a dialect shift for a casual or insouciant effect. Concern for adhering to the standard can lead people to try to correct and in fact 'overcorrect' their normal usage. Linguists call this phenomenon hypercorrection. With respect to adverbs, this commonly occurs in one of two ways. The first consists in adding a superfluous *-ly* to common words that function as both adverbs and adjectives: 'Open widely'; 'Go easily on them'. In these contexts, *wide* and *easy* are correct.

The second type of hypercorrection consists in changing adjectives to adverbs because they follow verbs: 'I feel badly'; 'We all looked ridiculously in the new uniforms'. The modifier following a verb does not always have to be an adverb. It should be an adverb if it modifies the action of the verb: 'They sang dreadfully'. However, *be, become,* and *seem,* and in some cases other verbs such as *feel, look,* and *sound,* denote no action but instead describe the state of the subject of the sentence. Such verbs are correctly followed by adjectives.

They seem happy.

They play happily for hours.

We got wise.

We chose wisely.

He felt bad about the mix-up.

He dresses badly.

I feel good about the interview.

I wasn't feeling well.

Note that *well* is both an adverb ('They danced well') and an adjective meaning in good health, in good shape: 'I am well'; 'All is well'. Whether—or when—it is acceptable to place an adverb between the function word *to* and a verb, as in 'to really understand', or 'to totally change', is a question that has vexed usage commentators for over two centuries. This issue is discussed under SPLIT INFINITIVE.

See also ABSOLUTE COMPARATIVES; ADVERBS WITHOUT -LY; ATTRIBUTIVE NOUNS; BAD, BADLY; COMPARISONS; HYPERCORRECTION; MISPLACED MODIFIERS; REAL, REALLY.

adjudication   see CONCILIATION

admit   see DOUBLING THE FINAL CONSONANT

admittance, admission   These words are sometimes interchangeable. However, *admittance* is more common in reference to physical entry; signs restricting access to an area say 'No Admittance'. *Admission* more often refers to (the price of) entrance to an entertainment (the phrase *no admission* usually means 'no entrance fee', not 'no entry'). Acceptance into a school or club is usually called *admission*. An acknowledgement of a failure, guilty secret, or problem is always an *admission*, never an *admittance*.

> But two high-profile foes of NAFTA—Maude Barlow and Tony Clarke—were outside after being refused admittance.
> *Daily News* (Halifax) 22 May 1993: 18

> The Haitian singer Sadia alone would be worth the price of admission, if indeed there were an admission price.
> *Gazette* (Montreal) 6 April 2006: D5

> There's no admission and things get under way at 7 p.m.
> *Calgary Herald* 14 Dec. 1993: A14

> Basically each inn provides lectures for law students and examines candidates for admission to the bar [certification to practise law].
> *Globe and Mail* (Toronto) 1 Nov. 1986: F5

> Despite suggestions to the contrary, UTS is a public school in which any student who meets the entrance criteria can gain admittance.
> *Toronto Star* 15 June 1993: A7

(In this context *admission* is more common.)

But there was no admission of mistakes by management.
Toronto Star 19 June 1993: B1

(Here *admittance* is not possible.)

ad nauseam *Ad nauseam* is a Latin phrase meaning to a tedious extreme—literally, 'to the point of nausea'. It is often misspelled *ad nauseum*.

The boast 'we are strong' was repeated by the speaker ad nauseam.
Henry M. Rosenthal and S. Cathy Berson, eds.
Canadian Jewish Outlook Anthology 1988: 37

See also LATIN PHRASES.

ado, adieu *Ado* means fuss or activity and most often occurs in the phrases 'much ado about nothing' (after the title of a Shakespearean play) and 'without further ado'.

Adieu is a French borrowing meaning good-bye (literally, *á Dieu*, 'to God'), most commonly used in English with the verb *to bid*: 'I bid you adieu'. The plural is *adieus* or *adieux*.

Adieu is often pronounced *a DYOO* or *a DYUH*, but it may also be pronounced exactly like the word *ado*, which probably contributes to the confusion of this pair.

At the crest of the hill rising from the valley, bid adieu to Kingston, as South Frontenac Township welcomes you.
Kingston Life Magazine Fall 2003: 92

Without further adieu then, here are 10 suggestions from a slightly different point of view.
Star-Phoenix (Saskatoon) 10 Feb. 2003: C7

(*Ado* is the word required here.)

See also PLURALS, REGULAR, IRREGULAR, FOREIGN.

adopted, adoptive Children are *adopted*; their new parents are *adoptive*. While it is considered wrong to substitute *adopted* for *adoptive*, as in 'adopted parents', it is acceptable to use *adoptive* to mean *adopted*, as in 'adoptive child' or 'adoptive country'. This latter usage is more common in British than Canadian English.

Adopted children, however happy they may be in their adoptive families, may yearn at some point to know more about their birth parents. . . .
Globe and Mail (Toronto) 4 Dec. 1985: A6

The Ontario Society for the Prevention of Cruelty to Animals is looking for adoptive owners.
Toronto Star 30 June 1994: NY6

Before meeting his long-lost brother, Lussier met with his brother's adopted parents and they were stunned at the resemblance to their son.
Daily News (Halifax) 16 Oct. 1992: 40

(The word required here is *adoptive*.)

Blue started the search for her mother when she was 18, but she didn't make any progress until last year, after rules for adoptive children seeking their birth parents were changed.
Daily News (Halifax) 23 Aug. 2002: 5

(Either *adoptive* or *adopted* is acceptable here.)

His birth country boycotted the Olympics in 1984 and his adoptive country didn't rush through citizenship to get him on the team for Seoul four years later.
Gazette (Montreal) 28 July 1992: C3

adult movies see EUPHEMISM

advance, advancement *Advance* is the more general word, referring to any type of movement forward or upward: 'The advance (*not* the advancement) of the snail was slow'. An improvement on a previous state of affairs is usually called an *advance* ('advances in eye surgery'); *advancement* is sometimes used in the same sense, but not all dictionaries list this meaning for it.

Advancement is generally reserved for two meanings: moving to a better position on the job or in society ('advancement through the ranks') or active promotion of a cause ('the advancement of women in sport'). In a narrowing of the latter sense, *advancement* is now frequently a euphemism for institutional fundraising.

The story recounts the relentless advance of raccoon rabies over the last two decades from Florida, then Virginia, and north until it now rages in raccoon populations only 20 kilometers from the Canadian border. . . .
Ottawa Citizen 1 Sept. 1994: B1

Laing said the increase in counterfeiting can be attributed to advances in technology.
Calgary Herald 30 April 2006: A14

[Adult illiterates] work at low paying seasonal or service jobs where the opportunity for advancement and support from the employer is extremely limited. . . .
Briarpatch April 1990: 5

Research independence is critical to the advancement of science.
Telegram (St. John's) 9 April 2006: B6

Jon Dellandrea, the school's vice-president in charge of advancement, maintained the cost of the project would run too high.
National Post 1 Oct. 2004: S1

(Here *advancement* means fundraising.)

'The new line is the most significant advancement in battery technology Sears has brought to its DieHard line in 27 years.'
Calgary Herald 30 Dec. 1994: E3

(Here *advance* would be better.)

See also EUPHEMISM.

advance agent, advance man   see JOB TITLES

adverbs   see ADJECTIVES AND ADVERBS; ADVERBS WITHOUT -LY; SENTENCE ADVERBS

adverbs without -ly   Most adverbs end in *-ly*: *coarsely*, *foolishly*, *happily*, *jauntily*, *rudely*, etc. However, some English adverbs—many of them common words that have been in the language for a long time—have a form identical to the adjective, including *cheap*, *clean*, *clear*, *close*, *deep*, *easy*, *flat*, *high*, *quick*, *right*, *slow*, and *wrong*. These adverbs are often called 'flat adverbs' or 'zero adverbs'. Most flat adverbs also have an *-ly* form.

The flat form is often found in common idioms: 'get rich quick', 'come clean', 'go easy', 'steer clear', 'come close', 'turn wide', 'aim high', 'go wrong', 'live right'. The *-ly* form is more likely to appear in formal contexts: 'resolved the issue quickly', 'was wrongly accused', 'propagated widely'. This may explain why some usage guides recommend against using the flat forms where an *-ly* form exists. However, in some contexts, an *-ly* form sounds odd ('took the turn widely'); in others, it changes the sense ('They sang flat/flatly').

See also ADJECTIVES AND ADVERBS; CHEAP; SLOW.

adverse, averse   *Adverse* means unfavourable, harmful, or opposed, as in 'adverse weather', 'adverse publicity', or 'an adverse decision'. To be *averse* to something means to dislike the idea of it; not to be averse to something means not to object to it, at least in principle. Usage commentators are divided over whether it is acceptable to say that someone is (or is not) *adverse* to something. Some commentators maintain that *adverse* is simply the wrong word in this context. Others claim that a distinction of sense can be made: someone averse to something dislikes it, while someone adverse to something is opposed to it. If such a fine distinction of sense is made in formal Canadian writing, we have not seen it: in formal writing, people are not described as adverse to things. In informal writing, therefore, it is most likely that the disputed use of *adverse* is simply a confusion with *averse*.

...so far the Ministry of Defence has rejected all synthetic substitutes as inferior in wet weather and other adverse conditions.
Calgary Herald 28 April 2006: A11

But Sifton himself was not averse to hiring political rascals if they did the job.
Pierre Berton *The Promised Land* 1984: 12

Don't misunderstand. I'm not averse to glamor, to short skirts and lacy underthings.
Gazette (Montreal) 18 Nov. 1994: A3

'I'm not adverse to other needlework forms,' confided Miller.
Ottawa Citizen 11 Jan. 2006: E1

(Here *averse* is recommended.)

The survey also found that people aren't adverse to a stronger regional government.
Vancouver Sun 13 Nov. 1990: B2

(Here *averse* is recommended.)

advertise   see -IZE, -ISE, -YZE, -YSE

advertisement, ad, advert   *Advertisement* is the standard spelling in Canada, Britain, and the United States. *Advertizement* is an uncommon variant spelling even in North America, where *-ize* endings are generally preferred.

In Canada and the United States, *ad vur TIZE ment* is the predominant pronunciation, but *ad VUR tiss ment*—which is how the British say the word—is also common. It is likely this second pronunciation that leads to the fairly common misspelling *advertisment.*

The short form *ad* has become a standard word, but not a formal one. In British English *advertisement* has two short forms: *ad* and *advert. Advert* is quite uncommon in Canada.

See also -IZE, -ISE, -YZE, -YSE.

advice, advise   The noun *advice*, as in 'good advice', is often misspelled *advise. Advise*, as in 'I advise caution', is the correct spelling for the verb.

> As for flavour-enhancers, my advice is to go easy.
> *Gazette* (Montreal) 12 April 2006: D1

> 'We want to advise people to go to other local hospitals in an emergency.'
> *Gazette* (Montreal) 26 Nov. 1992: G1

> 'I'll sit down at Christmas and talk to some people and listen to their advise.'
> *Daily News* (Halifax) 19 Nov. 1992: 67

(The noun is spelled with a *c—advice.*)

See also -CE, -SE.

adviser, advisor   Canadian writers use *adviser* more frequently than *advisor*. The newer *-or* ending has probably developed because it is close to the adjective form *advisory*, or perhaps by analogy with *supervisor*. Canadian, American, and British dictionaries and sundry usage guides all list both spellings.

See also -ER, -OR.

-ae-, -oe-, -e-   The two-letter combinations *ae* and *oe* are found in words derived from Latin or Greek, such as *aesthetic* and *oestrogen*. Both *ae* and *oe* are pronounced either as a long *e*, as in *weed*, or as a short *e*, as in *wed*. For many words either pronunciation is acceptable.

American spelling convention is generally to replace these two-letter forms with *e*, except in proper names such as Aeschylus and Oedipus. British convention is generally to retain them, and Canadian usage is somewhere in between.

Alternative Spellings
Canadian preference is marked *

aeon	eon*
aegis*	egis
amoeba*	ameba
caesarean*	cesarean
diarrhoea	diarrhea*
encyclopaedia	encyclopedia*
faeces	feces*
foetid	fetid*
haemophilia	hemophilia*
haemorrhage	hemorrhage*
mediaeval	medieval*
oesophagus	esophagus*
oestrogen	estrogen*
palaeolithic	paleolithic*

Canadian journalists tend to follow American spelling conventions, using *fetus, esthetic,* and *anemia,* while the spellings most common in books and academic papers are *foetus, aesthetic,* and *anaemia.* Although some might feel that Canadians should be persuaded to aim for consistency in their treatment of these words and others like them, it is precisely this mix of British and American English that is the hallmark of Canadian English.

Formerly, *ae* and *oe* were printed as linked characters (**æ, œ**) called *ligatures.*

See also CAESAREAN, CAESARIAN; DIPHTHONG, DIGRAPH, LIGATURE; SPELLING, CANADIAN.

aegis, egis   In Greek mythology, *aegis* referred to the breastplate of Zeus or Athena and came to symbolize divine protection. In contemporary usage, *aegis* (pronounced *EE jiss*) usually means protection in the weaker sense of administration or sponsorship. *Aegis* is sometimes spelled *egis* in the United States.

. . . the system of feudalism was born primarily to give life a measure of security and normality under the aegis of a feudal landlord.
J.E. Smyth et al. *The Law and Business Administration in Canada* 1987: 9

He is one of the 22 volunteers from the Neighborhood Helpers Project operating under the aegis of the Downtown Eastside Seniors' Centre. . . .
Vancouver Sun 27 June 1994: C4

Perhaps filing this one under the aegis of 'mistress' is unfair.
Gazette (Montreal) 5 June 1994: C3

(Here *aegis* has been confused with *heading* or *category*.)

See also -AE-, -OE-, -E-; AUSPICES.

aeon   see -AE-, -OE-, -E-

aesthetic   see -AE-, -OE-, -E-

affect, effect, affectation   If something *affects* something, then it has an *effect* on it. Here *affect* is a verb meaning to have some influence on something or to modify it, and *effect* is a noun referring to the result of an action: 'Drinking affects your driving'; 'A slower reaction time is one effect of drinking'.

The verb *effect* means to bring about and can mean something quite different from the verb *affect*, so it is important not to confuse the spellings:

John's visit to the spa effected [brought about] his recovery. (Here he is cured.)

John's visit to the spa affected [helped or hindered] his recovery. (Here he may be better or worse.)

To *affect* may also mean to pretend to have or feel something: 'Some Canadians affect a British accent'. A manner of speaking or dressing, a habit, or an accessory that strikes others as put on or pretentious is described as an *affectation*.

The noun *affect* is a psychological term mean-

ing emotion or feeling. The plural noun *effects*, almost always occurring in the phrase 'personal effects', means belongings.

'Pressure doesn't affect him.'
Toronto Star 30 June 1994: D1

'It's negatively effected virtually every business in Timmins and northeastern Ontario.'
Sudbury Star 1 May 2004: D12

(Here *affected* is required.)

'Laughter has a positive effect on the cardiovascular system. . .'.
Ottawa Citizen 23 Apr. 2006: A6

Winter has arrived with an icy fury, bringing with it one of the season's worst dangers—the wind chill affect that can turn a cold day into a killer.
Province (Vancouver) 31 Dec. 1990: 45

(Here *effect* is required.)

The apparent futility of a time-consuming and expensive process is underlined by the fact that MPs themselves frequently bemoan their inability to effect real changes in legislation.
A. Paul Pross *Group Politics and Public Policy* 2nd ed. 1992: 77

She affects dramatic shifts of accent, posture, complexion and hair color, and her characters appear to be as much a triumph of alchemy as of acting.
Maclean's 28 July 1986: 36

William has produced his pipe, an affectation he by and large reserves for company.
Margaret Atwood *Life Before Man* 1979: 138

Excuse my lack of affect, I'm male: In movies that featured human characters, the preponderance of males with plugged-up passions was impossible to ignore this year.
Calgary Herald 2 Jan. 1994: C1

Paris Hilton's diaries, along with photos of her in various stages of undress, are among a trove of personal affects that have found their way into the hands of a broker aiming to sell them.
Ottawa Citizen 4 Feb. 2006: F8

(The spelling should be 'personal *effects*'.)

affidavit   see EVIDENCE

affirmative action   see EQUALITY

afflict, inflict   *Afflict* is used with the prepositions *by* and *with*; *inflict* is followed by *on* or *upon*. *Inflict* is sometimes mistakenly substituted for *afflict*: 'She was inflicted with Lou Gehrig's disease'. Generally, things afflict people ('Sorrow afflicted the girl') while people inflict things on each other ('He inflicted a beating on the rebel').

Depression afflicts women roughly three times as often as men.
Globe and Mail (Toronto) 16 March 1985: M8

Gravelle ministers to those afflicted with AIDS and HIV.
Ottawa Citizen 23 Dec. 1994: A1

The commissioners were divided on whether the law should permit parents to inflict corporal punishment on children. . . .
Globe and Mail (Toronto) 5 March 1985: P1

About 80 per cent of the veterans in the Mewburn are inflicted with some type of dementia or Alzheimer's disease.
Edmonton Journal 10 Nov. 2005: B3

(Here *afflicted* is the word required.)

affront, effrontery   To *affront* is to offend; an *affront* is an open or intentional insult. *Effrontery* is shameless audacity or barefaced impudence. Because they sound alike and their meanings are similar, *affront* and *effrontery* are sometimes confused—and *effrontery* is often misspelled with an initial *a*.

This is a callous, insensitive affront to those who risked their lives defending our country.
Ottawa Citizen 30 March 1994: A10

They're offended, affronted, ticked off, vexed, irritated, galled and riled by the English they read and hear.
Vancouver Sun 9 April 1994: D9

As national chairman [of the CCF], Prof. Scott wrote a letter saying: 'You have barred your letter columns and your news columns to the CCF and now you have the effrontery to accuse it of silence which is an admission of guilt.'
Globe and Mail (Toronto) 1 Feb. 1985: M4

. . . worse than all of that is the affrontery of the secretary of defence, Mr. Weinberger, who takes it

upon himself to tell us what kind of weapons should be placed on Canadian soil, while the presidential press secretary doesn't even know the name of the Canadian minister of defence.
Henry M. Rosenthal and S. Cathy Berson, eds. *Canadian Jewish Outlook Anthology* 1988: 327

(The correct spelling is *effrontery*.)

What is most disturbing about both these incidents is the affrontery to my right to be on the street at the time of my choosing, and the fear that accompanies being approached by anyone in a threatening manner.
Ottawa Citizen 14 Nov. 1992: A11

(The word required here is *affront*.)

Afghan, Afghani   According to some dictionaries, the adjective for things related to Afghanistan is *Afghan* ('Afghan election', 'Afghan cuisine'), and a person from Afghanistan is 'an *Afghan*'. Canadians, however, also use *Afghani* for the adjective or the people. *Afghani*, a direct borrowing from Pashto, the language of Afghanistan, is also listed in British and American English dictionaries, but only as the name of the country's currency.

After 14 years in Canada, she sees herself as both Canadian and Afghani, and well positioned to act as an interpreter between the two cultures in these troubled times.
Ottawa Citizen 30 April 2005: I3

So, will the Afghan government jump at the chance to legitimize an industry that employs as many as 2.3 million Afghanis and that brings in 12 to 13 per cent of the country's wealth?
Vancouver Sun 15 Nov. 2005: A15

(Here *Afghan* is used as an adjective and *Afghanis* as a noun for the people.)

'The Afghans themselves get paid pennies for [artifacts],' Tarzi said. 'But the pieces themselves are worth a fortune.'. . . Now they are in the hands of the Afghani government, ready to be displayed in the museum once again.
Toronto Star 9 Jan. 2006: A3

(Here *Afghans* is used as a noun for the people and *Afghani* as an adjective.)

Rahim gets 50,000 Afghanis for the work—about $1,000.
Gazette (Montreal) 7 May 2006: A12

aficionado   *Aficionado* is derived from the Spanish verb *aficionar*, 'to become fond of'. In Spanish the word originally referred to bull-fighting enthusiasts, but in both Spanish and English it broadened to encompass devotees and fans of every kind.

Sometimes *aficionado* is misspelled *afficionado,* perhaps because of the double *f* in words like *affinity* and *affection*. The plural is *aficionados*.

aforementioned, aforesaid, said   *Aforementioned*, *aforesaid*, and *said* in general prose are criticized as hackneyed legalisms. Some critics object to their use even in legal and business writing. Usually a word such as *the*, *these*, or *those* followed by the noun is sufficient to alert the reader to a second mention of something that has already been specified.

Because they are strongly associated with the law, the words *aforementioned*, *aforesaid*, and *said* are often used to indicate mock seriousness and to generate humour. This type of humour is not, of course, to everyone's taste.

> Gray, who is fluent in all the aforementioned languages, charges between $2,000 and $6,000 to subtitle a film.
> *Gazette* (Montreal) 26 Aug. 1990: D3

(Here 'in all *these* languages' would be better.)

> The aforesaid anchor sets a TV precedent when he uses a term for a male appendage usually frowned on in polite company (the term and the appendage).
> *Ottawa Citizen* 12 May 1990: D6

Africadian, African Canadian, African-American   see BLACK; HYPHENATION

after   see AFTERWARD(S)

aftermath   *Aftermath* means either the consequences of an event or the period immediately following it. The word has acquired a connotation of unpleasantness, and is most often used in contexts of trauma such as wars, natural disasters, and economic upheavals.

> In the aftermath of the Second World War, Germany lost considerable territory to Poland and the Soviet Union.
> *Vancouver Sun* 14 Feb. 1990: A3

> Like flies hovering over dead corpses, politicians of every stripe exploited the murders. The aftermath was almost as depressing as the event itself.
> *Fuse Magazine* 13.4 (1990): 8

> Engel belonged to the generation of writers who made their debut in the heady aftermath of Expo 67 and the nationalism generated by the country's centennial.
> *Globe and Mail* (Toronto) 18 Feb. 1985: S13

(Here *afterglow* or *wake* might be better; in a positive context, *aftermath* suggests irony.)

afterward(s), after, afterword   *Afterwards* is more common than *afterward* in Canadian writing. Both forms are used in Canada and the United States; *afterwards* is usual in Britain.

The use of *after* as an adverb synonymous with *afterwards* grates on the ears of some critics. They do not object to *shortly after* or *for hours after* but to *after* standing alone, as in 'We went for pizza *after*'. This usage is rare in published Canadian writing, formal or informal, but is common and acceptable in spoken Canadian English.

Occasionally *afterward* is confused with *afterword*, a commentary appended at the end of a book.

> In the hospital, and afterwards in the institution, Caroline would not talk or even move.
> Margaret Atwood *Life Before Man* 1979: 76

> Soon afterward he came to see her mother.
> Constance Beresford-Howe *Night Studies* 1985: 152

> I was a commanding officer of a recruiting centre in Rimouski, responsible for eastern Quebec recruiting, and after went on to DND headquarters as recruiting staff for officer production.
> Proceedings of the Standing Senate Committee on National Security and Defence Issue 10: 2 Feb. 2005

(Common in spoken English, this use of *after* to mean *afterwards* is generally avoided in writing.)

As explained in the afterward of the Kids Can Press edition of the poem, the mock-heroic ballad was written in nonsense verse.
Telegram (St. John's) 28 Nov. 2004: B4

(The proper word here is *afterword*.)

See also ONLY; FOREWORD, PREFACE; -WARD(S).

age, aged   see -ED; MAJORITY; SENIOR CITIZEN

ageing, ageism   see AGING; -ISM

agenda, agendum, hidden agenda   In Latin, *agenda* is a plural noun meaning 'things to do'. In English, it has long been treated as a singular noun referring to the list of things to be dealt with at a meeting. The plural is *agendas*. Use of the Latin singular *agendum* to mean an item on an agenda is obsolete: the usual phrase is *agenda item* or *item on the agenda*.

Since the 1950s, *agenda* has also referred to an underlying motivation or plan, which is sometimes veiled or unconscious: 'a political agenda', 'a hidden agenda'. This use, initially criticized, is now well established.

The United Nations charter clearly says that the Security Council has to be ready to meet in an emergency at all times; an item on the agenda may be suspended only long enough to allow for consultation.
George Ignatieff *The Making of a Peacemonger* 1987: 97

Large foreign firms dominate the resource industry and therefore set the agenda for most resource development in the North.
Robert M. Bone *The Geography of the Canadian North* 1992: 140

. . . we pursue our own individual or neighborhood agendas at the expense of the larger public interest.
Vancouver Sun 17 Nov. 1990: B2

Smith's many detractors claim he has a hidden agenda to eventually force an amalgamation between the most successful CFL franchises and the NFL.
Toronto Star 5 June 1994: C12

See also PLURALS, REGULAR, IRREGULAR, FOREIGN.

aggravate, aggravation   To *aggravate* can mean either to make something worse or to exasperate someone. The first meaning is fully accepted. Although the second sense, to annoy, dates back to as early as 1611, it is still disputed by some language commentators. In Canadian writing, the verb *aggravate* usually means to make worse, while the noun and present participle, *aggravation* and *aggravating*, usually mean annoyance and annoying respectively. There seems to be no reason to avoid the 'new' meaning of *aggravate* even in formal writing. What is more important for contemporary writers is to be aware of the older sense of the word: the legal term 'aggravated assault', for example, refers to a very serious assault, not to one where the victim has provoked or angered (i.e., 'aggravated') the assailant.

. . . a doctor who offers to give free aid to an injured person and negligently aggravates the person's injuries will be liable for damages.
J.E. Smyth et al. *The Law and Business Administration in Canada* 1987: 153

(Here *aggravates* means 'makes worse'.)

Authorities at the prison fear the smell could aggravate prisoners and cause disturbances. . . .
Vancouver Sun 21 Sept. 1990: A18

(Here *aggravate* means irritate.)

Another source of aggravation and personal embarrassment was the Canadian government's ambivalent attitude towards South Africa's policy of racial discrimination. . . .
George Ignatieff *The Making of a Peacemonger* 1987: 239

(Here *aggravation* means annoyance or irritation.)

The sounds are evident in every part of my house and are most annoying, aggravating and disturbing.
Ottawa Citizen 21 April 2006: F8

(Here *aggravating* means irritating.)

See also ASSAULT, BATTERY.

aggressive, assertive   *Aggressive* and *assertive* both mean forceful, but only *aggressive* suggests combativeness. Context determines whether the connotations of *aggressive* are negative or positive. Generally, *aggressive* is positive when it describes athletes, sports teams, or corporations, but decidedly negative when it describes children, countries, and animals. The connotation varies when *aggressive* is applied to women.

Aggressive is often misspelled with one *g*.

> Scientists . . . tested several groups of rats in a series of experiments and found the drug caused subordinate males to become more assertive although they did not become aggressive.
> *Daily News* (Halifax) 4 Dec. 1994: 37

> Dr. Minde's team works on the theory that what is missing in overly aggressive children is the quality of empathy.
> *Globe and Mail* (Toronto) 3 Jan. 1985: P17

> Organizers have also tried to confine females to those sports believed to enhance traditional concepts of 'femininity,' such as swimming, tennis and gymnastics, and to devise 'girls' rules' to discourage the ambitious and aggressive play expected of boys and men.
> *Queen's Quarterly* 94.1 (1987): 120

> Girls are becoming more aggressive, they're playing harder, playing more like boys: Aggressive basketball, tough defence.
> *Whig-Standard* (Kingston) 13 Oct. 1995: 27

(Here *aggressive* is desirable.)

See also CONNOTATION(S), DENOTATION, CONNOTE, DENOTE.

aging, ageing, agism, ageism   The *e* is optional in these words. The spellings preferred in Canada are *aging* (without *e*) and *ageism* (with *e*).

See also GERIATRICS, GERONTOLOGY, GERIATRIC; INCLUSIVE LANGUAGE; SENIOR CITIZEN, SENIOR, AGED, ELDERLY, PENSIONER.

agnostic   see ATHEIST

agreement, grammatical   What is traditionally discussed under the rubric of *grammatical agreement* is number: that is, whether nouns, pronouns, and verbs should be singular or plural. 'He are right' violates number agreement because the subject of the sentence is singular while the verb is plural. But this is not a mistake a native speaker would make. This entry deals with types of subjects of sentences that native speakers sometimes have difficulty classifying as singular or plural. At the end of the entry many individual problem words and phrases are cross-referenced.

Compound subjects—subjects containing two or more elements linked by the word *and*—are plural and should be followed by plural verbs: 'Glazed paper and opaque glass are now collected'; 'A map and compass were issued'. There are a few exceptions to this rule, however.

When the two elements of a compound subject refer to the same person or thing, a singular verb is used: 'My coiffeuse and financial counsellor is getting out of mortgage funds'.

When the elements of a compound subject are to be considered serially, the verb is singular: 'Her writing speaks to us in the way Al Purdy's, Dennis Lee's, and Earle Birney's does'.

When two singular elements joined by *and* constitute a fixed expression, the verb is singular: 'A gin and tonic sounds great'.

Finally, when two singular elements of a compound subject are seen as a unit, the verb is singular: 'Your health and safety is our first concern'; 'The breadth and depth of the investigation was unprecedented'. However, more idiosyncratic applications of this principle are likely to draw notice and criticism. In formal contexts, if you aren't sure whether a compound subject constitutes one thing or two, it's better to use a plural verb.

Elements joined to the subject of the sentence by prepositions are not, strictly speaking, part of the subject, and do not affect the number of the verb: 'Robin and a partner are buying the Canadian rights', but 'Robin, with a partner, is buying the Canadian rights'. This issue is discussed further under TOGETHER WITH, AS WELL AS, IN ADDITION TO.

A subject consisting of singular elements joined by the word *or* takes a singular verb: 'A passbook or monthly statement is issued'; 'Soup or salad comes with the special'.

When *or* has little disjunctive force—that is,

when *and* could be substituted for *or* without changing the meaning of the sentence—a plural verb is sometimes used: 'Chocolate or hazelnut are my favourite flavours'; 'Life or death were the same to him'. In formal contexts, however, this usage is questionable; it can be avoided either by changing *or* to *and* or by making the verb singular.

When *or* links singular and plural elements, the verb agrees in number with the nearest element: 'Both sides or only one side is finished'; 'One side or both sides are finished'. This issue is discussed further under EITHER and NEITHER.

The verb *to be* should agree in number with the subject that precedes it, not the complement that follows it: 'Committee reports are (*not* is) the next item of business'; 'The next item of business is (*not* are) committee reports'.

When phrases or clauses intervene between the bare subject of a sentence and the verb, errors of subject–verb agreement are fairly common. People lose sight of the true subject and make the verb agree with the immediately preceding noun. The following are correct: 'Parts of their story are (*not* is) true'; 'The literary merit of these works was (*not* were) never discussed'.

Plural measures of money, time, weight, etc., take a singular verb if they are considered as a unit:

'Sixty dollars was taken from the till.'

'Two weeks is not enough time.'

'Four metres of cloth make four skirts.'
(Four individual metres.)

'Four metres of cloth is not enough.'
(A total of four for a single project.)

In Canadian English, collective nouns are usually followed by singular verbs, but sometimes plural verbs are also possible: 'The crew is (*or* are) experienced'; 'Pat's family doesn't (or *don't*) get along'. See COLLECTIVE NOUNS.

Many usage problems involving number result from a tension in English grammar between formal and notional agreement. According to the principle of formal agreement, a noun or pronoun is inherently singular or plural and should be treated as such consistent-ly. According to the principle of notional agreement, many nouns and pronouns are either singular or plural depending on the idea in the speaker's mind. For example, the word *family* may be singular or plural depending on whether the speaker is thinking of a unit or a group of individuals. These two contrary principles of agreement are at work in the sentence 'Everyone says they like it'. In form, the pronoun *everyone* is singular. And, in accordance with the principle of formal agreement, the verb *says* is singular. Notionally, however, *everyone* represents a group, and, in accordance with the principle of notional agreement, the personal pronoun that substitutes for *everyone*—*they*—is plural. A traditional grammarian would rewrite the sentence: 'Everyone says he likes it'. But to most English-speakers the corrected sentence would have an entirely different meaning. Adjusting the whole sentence to conform to the principle of notional agreement yields no better result: 'Everyone say they like it' is consistently plural but certainly not English. What this discussion illustrates is that the principles of formal and notional agreement which operate in English cannot be used to solve usage problems, but only to clarify them. In many questions of number agreement, convention is the only arbiter.

Regarding the difficult question of which personal pronoun to use with *everyone*, *anyone*, and *someone*, see EVERYONE.

As the previous chapter demonstrates, the meaning and social construction of abortion has been subject to ongoing political struggle.
Janine Brodie, Shelley A.M. Gavigan, and Jane Jenson *The Politics of Abortion* 1992: 70

(Notional agreement overrides formal agreement in this sentence, and few readers would likely notice or quibble.)

Support and advice about coping with change is often much more helpful.
Wendy Reynolds and Vera Madden *Drug Wise* 1992: 16

(Here again notional agreement determines the number of the verb, though readers who regard 'support and advice about coping with change' as two separate things may quibble.)

No bone marrow or liver toxicity were observed.
Rites March 1990: 9

(Here was should replace *were*.)

I certainly do not think that government aid or subsidies is the answer.
Mennonite Brethren Herald 4 April 1986: 8

(Here, to agree with the plural 'subsidies', *is* should be replaced by *are*.)

Finally, Kagan's list of hopes that parents have for their children do not seem to jive with the literature or my own experience.
Ottawa Citizen 30 Sept. 1994: B4

(Since the subject of the sentence is 'Kagan's list', the verb should be the singular *does*. The plural *do* reflects the influence of the intervening plural nouns.)

See also ANY; ANYONE; BETWEEN; BUT ME; CASE; EACH; EVERY; MORE THAN ONE; NONE; ONE OF THE . . . IF NOT THE; ONE OF THOSE THINGS; POSSESSIVE; POSSESSIVE WITH GERUND; THERE IS, THERE ARE.

agriculturalist, agriculturist   see -IST, -ALIST

ahead   see DATES, AHEAD, BACK

a hold, ahold   see HOLD

AIDS, Aids   see ABBREVIATION

ain't, aren't I   *Ain't* has a long and complicated history; it derives from *an't*, a contraction that appeared first in published writing in the late seventeenth century. The first citation for *ain't* is 1778; it was quickly singled out for criticism and since then has become almost a grammatical taboo. Though it is still common in rural and working-class dialects, educated speakers never use *ain't* unless they are sure that people will understand they know better.

Ain't may well have attracted negative notice because it serves as a sort of generic contraction, doing away with distinctions between different persons and even between *be* and *have*. That is, in nonstandard contemporary English *ain't* can replace *am not* ('I ain't done'); *aren't* ('You ain't invited'); *isn't* ('She ain't well'); and *hasn't* or *haven't* ('I ain't seen him').

Many commentators have noted with regret that the successful suppression of *ain't* created a gap in Standard English, which now has no fully accepted contraction of *am I not*. Although *amn't I* was used by speakers of Irish English, it was not adopted by speakers of Standard British English when *ain't I* fell from favour. *Aren't I* entered Canadian and American English from British English early in the twentieth century. In British English, since *r* is not pronounced after a vowel, *aren't* is merely a different way of spelling *an't* (an obsolete contraction of either *are not* or *am not*). In Canadian English, however, the *r* in *aren't* is pronounced; the connection with *are* is audible. Though *aren't I* is widely used in Canada, it is often uttered with misgivings about the patent incongruity of *I* and *are*. The alternative, the uncontracted *am I not*, often seems too stuffy for its context. Nevertheless, most Canadians use *am I not* in writing, and some prefer it to *aren't I* in speech.

We see that the economists who said there ain't no such thing as a free lunch, in the early 70's, were not wrong.
City Magazine 10.1 (Spring 1988): 39

(Here *ain't* is used in an expression of folk wisdom.)

'I ain't got that kinda money, you know that,' he said.
Canadian Fiction Magazine 64 (1988): 92

(Sometimes *ain't* is used to indicate the socio-economic status of fictional characters.)

One of the questions repeatedly posed to editor Jack about this anthology is, 'Why aren't I in it?'
Vancouver Sun 3 May 2003: D19

Am I not misunderstanding the devotion to duty and the self-denying attitude which makes so many worthy people cut down on the time and energy they give to their private life, so that they may more vigorously serve mankind?
Robertson Davies *One Half of Robertson Davies* 1978: 71

See also CONTRACTIONS.

air force   see CANADIAN ARMED FORCES

a.k.a., aka   see PSEUDONYM

à la   Originally French, à *la* means in the style or manner of. Writing 'sideburns *à la* Elvis' is more economical than 'sideburns in the style of Elvis' and avoids the complications of 'sideburns like Elvis's' or 'Elvis-style sideburns'.

À la is frequently used with reference to cookery, as in 'chicken *à la* king'. *À la mode* means fashionable or in style, unless it is preceded by the word *pie*: pie *à la mode* is served with ice cream.

À la is seldom found in formal writing, and in informal writing it often appears without an accent. Retaining the accent and using italics, however, make this brief foreign phrase more readable.

> If you cannot stomach the *tripe à la parisienne*, veal kidneys in porto sauce, or sweetbreads in heavy cream and calvados, there is simpler fare. . . .
> Alan Tucker, ed. *The Penguin Guide to Canada* 1991: 549

> Recommended Friday night is Picket Fences (CFRN), another quirky drama a la Northern Exposure. . . .
> *Edmonton Journal* 13 Sept. 1992: n.p.

> He has embraced the concept of sustainable development and in the most recent throne speech presented himself, *a la* George Bush, as an environmentalist.
> *NeWest Review* Oct.–Nov. 1989: 5

See also A LA CARTE.

à la carte, table d'hôte   These expressions are borrowed from French. When you dine *à la carte* ('by the bill of fare'), you select your meal from a menu on which each dish is priced separately. A *table d'hôte* (literally, 'host's table') meal is a fixed meal—usually limited choices are offered—at a fixed price. The expressions *table d'hôte* (pronounced TA bluh DOTE) and *à la carte* often lose their accents on restaurant menus. In formal writing, the accents are required.

> Not so very long ago, restaurant critics would nearly always choose a la carte on a first visit in order to get the true measure of a restaurant's capabilities. The daily table d'hôte menu, there to satisfy economy-minded regulars, was usually unimaginative and a dumping ground for the regular menu's excesses.
> *Gazette* (Montreal) 3 March 1989: C13

> Besides the tasting menu, Bonaparte's offerings include a wide choice of bourgeois French fare . . . either a la carte, or the three-course table d'hote. . . .
> *Gazette* (Montreal) 15 April 2006: H5

See also À LA.

albeit   *Albeit* means 'if only' or 'though admittedly'. Some guides describe it as antiquated or overly formal, but its common use in newspapers and popular magazines belies that criticism.

> Parody and burlesque are, it seems to me, inherently cynical, albeit in a mild way.
> Margaret Atwood *Second Words* 1982: 181

> There were unanticipated—albeit minor—problems in serving the 120 passengers aboard each 737.
> *Edmonton Journal* 28 Feb. 2006: E1

> Still, Epstein plans on one day travelling back to Africa for humanitarian work, albeit with a larger charity rather than a small school.
> *Toronto Star* 2 May 2006: D1

Alberta   see APPENDIX I

Albertan   see NAMES OF RESIDENTS OF CITIES AND PROVINCES

alderman   see JOB TITLES

Algonquin, Algonkin, Algonquian, Algonkian   The Aboriginal communities along the Ottawa River between Ontario and Quebec are called *Algonquin* (pronounced al GONE kwin) or *Algonkin* (pronounced al GONE kin). The names of many Aboriginal peoples are already plural and should not be doubly pluralized by adding *s*; however, *Algonquins* is an exception (*Globe and Mail Style Book*). Algonquins also refer to themselves as Anissinapek or Anishinabeg.

Algonquin (or *Algonkin*) is also the language of

the Algonquin nation (though not all Algonquins speak it). Algonquin is a dialect of Ojibway. Although their languages are related, the Algonquins and the Ojibwa (or Anishnabe) are separate Aboriginal nations.

Algonquian or *Algonkian* (pronounced *al GONE kee un* or *al GONE kwee un*) designates a large language family, which includes Algonquin and also Cree, Ojibway, and Mi'kmaq—the most widely-spoken Aboriginal languages in Canada. Algonquin-speakers form only a small subgroup of the many Algonquian-speakers across Canada from British Columbia to the Atlantic provinces, so it is important not to confuse the two words.

> The Algonquins of Golden Lake are managing their own hunters and fishers, and have even instituted their own ban on killing wolves in their traditional territories.
> *Alternatives Journal* 2002: 9

> At his gravesite, a young Algonkin lady sang a haunting song in honor of Don's life. . . .
> *Ottawa Citizen* 11 Dec. 1993: A9

> They called themselves the People of the Dawnland, the Abenaki in their distinct Algonquian language.
> *Gazette* (Montreal) 19 Feb. 1993: A2

> On a flat expanse of rock . . . are hundreds of carvings of symbolic shapes and figures which archeologists say were probably carved by Algonkian-speaking Indians between 500 and 1,000 years ago.
> *Gazette* (Montreal) 2 June 1993: C2

> Bradley also seems to find comfort in the support of David Kelley, an expert on the Maya, yet he gives no indication Kelley has any knowledge of the Algonkians of Eastern Canada.
> *Ottawa Citizen* 10 July 2000: A11

(Here either *Algonquins* or *Algonquian-speaking people* would be clearer.)

See also ABORIGINAL PEOPLE(S); OJIBWA(Y); APPENDIX III.

alias see PSEUDONYM

alibi In legal terms, an alibi is a plea or proof of having been elsewhere when a crime was committed. In fact, the Latin word *alibi* means 'elsewhere'. In general English, however, *alibi* refers more broadly to an excuse of any type, including a concocted one. Some commentators dispute this broader meaning, but it is common in informal usage.

> If you want to know what I was doing between then and finding the body, I'm going to be hard-pressed to give you an alibi for the hours from eleven to eight in the morning.
> Howard Engel *Murder Sees the Light* 1984: 61

> He was in custody for seven hours, without shoes, and released after he and his wife gave matching alibi statements.
> *Daily News* (Halifax) 23 June 1994: n.p.

> No alibis, no excuses, no scandals, just well-earned medals.
> *Sudbury Star* 28 Feb. 2006: A11

> One ex-principal says it's not uncommon for the modern parent to immediately look for either an excuse or an alibi for his child's misbehavior.
> *Ottawa Citizen* 13 Sept. 1994: B4

alight, alit To *alight* means to climb down from a horse or vehicle or to touch down from the sky. To *alight on* means to come upon by chance or to happen to notice. *Alighted* is the usual past tense and past participle; *alit* is poetic.

Alight is also an adjective meaning lighted ('Every window was alight'), glowing ('Their faces were alight'), or on fire ('They poured gasoline on it and set it alight').

Occasionally people substitute *alit* for *alight* ('a single window alit') or use *alit* to mean *lit up* ('Her eyes alit with pleasure'). These uses are nonstandard.

> Fretful babies didn't cry, normally spirited children stood obediently by their parents, teenagers alighted from their bicycles and hung their heads. . . .
> *Toronto Star* 23 June 1994: A6

> Then the eye looks deeper into the scene and alights on another of Montreal's unique views.
> Alan Tucker, ed. *The Penguin Guide to Canada* 1991: 145

At dusk the sky will be alight with a pyrotechnic extravaganza, with each burst synchronized to music.
Toronto Star 30 June 1994: NY4

He set the next mound of chaff alight.
Geoffrey Ursell *Perdue, or, How the West Was Lost* 1984: 70

. . . but his eyes alit when the Olympic flame came in and the cauldron was ignited. The message I saw in his eyes was that peace can ride on a hockey puck and bobsleds can carry dreams.
Calgary Herald 9 Feb. 1992: E9

(Either *lit up* or *came alight* is required here.)

See also LIGHT.

-alist   see -IST

alit   see ALIGHT

all, all of   *Of* is required between *all* and a non-possessive pronoun such as *me, you, which, us, them,* and *it*: 'I went out with all of them'. *Of* is not required between *all* and a noun phrase ('all [of] the computers'), and many commentators consider it both unnecessary and informal.

The disputed *of* is more common in Canadian and American English than British English. The famous comment on the impossibility of fooling 'all of the people all of the time' is attributed to Abraham Lincoln. In the full quotation, '*all of* the people' parallels '*some of* the time', and including *of* in both phrases creates balance. Thus, *all of* is a stylistic option that is sometimes determined simply by rhythm or cadence.

All of can suggest each and every ('She walked around the church blowing out all of the votive candles'), while *all* without *of* suggests an undifferentiated whole ('One switch controls all the lights'). *All of* also has a special idiomatic meaning. In the sentence 'He said we'd have an hour, but he gave us all of thirty-six minutes', *all of* means only or no more than.

All of preceding a noun phrase was first noticed by language commentators in the nineteenth century, when it was considered a mere variant without semantic distinction. Since then *all of* has differentiated itself subtly from *all,* with the result that the single word is not always the better alternative.

All of us came to this project with multiple and overlapping motivations.
BC Studies 140 (Winter 2003/2004): 91

(Here *all of* is necessary because *us* is a non-possessive pronoun.)

What he wants is a Canada that works for all the people.
Vancouver Sun 31 Oct. 2001: A22

(Here *all* or *all of* is correct, but *all* emphasizes the unity of the people.)

All of the people infected are from Saskatchewan.
Leader-Post (Regina) 19 Aug. 2003: n.p.

(Here *all* or *all of* is correct, but *all of* suggests a group of individuals.)

It took Canada all of 63 seconds to open the scoring.
CBC News Online 3 May 2005

(Here *all of* means 'a mere'; *all* would have a different meaning.)

all around   see ALL-ROUND

all but   see SPLIT INFINITIVE

alleged, accused   The news media make liberal use of the words *alleged* and *accused* in crime reporting, partly in fairness to people wrongly accused, partly to avoid defamation suits. But many language commentators object to phrases such as 'alleged arsonist', 'accused murderer', and 'alleged drug dealer' because these phrases apply a criminal label to a person who has not been convicted of a crime.

Some commentators prefer *alleged* to *accused* in this context because they think that *alleged* lends a more tentative quality to the noun that follows. Other commentators find *alleged* a worse choice on grammatical grounds: you can accuse a person, but you can't allege a person. Therefore 'accused murderer' is possible, but 'alleged murderer' is ungrammatical. Most commentators agree that it is better to allege only actions: 'the alleged malpractice'; 'the youth alleged to have set the fire'. The disputed noun phrases, though fairly common in crime reporting, are not established in other types of writing, including more formal legal writing.

A final note: reporters are sometimes overzealous in applying the word *alleged*. Someone under investigation for a crime is a real suspect, not an 'alleged suspect'. A sexual assault may be described as an 'alleged assault' until it is proved, but there is no reason to refer to a break-in or a shooting as *alleged* if there is no doubt that it took place.

Accused murderer F——M—— is innocent, says a woman who says she is her sister.
Daily News (Halifax) 16 June 1994: n.p.

('F——M——, who has been accused of murder' would be better.)

Accused arsonist A——E——admitted Thursday he initially lied to police. . . .
Calgary Herald 2 Dec. 2005: B3

('A——E——, accused of having set the fire,' would be better.)

The alleged attacker had checked out of the hotel earlier in the day.
Ottawa Citizen 4 March 1994: B7

('The man alleged to have committed the attack' would be better.)

How did the alleged suspect, who barely knew how to drive, according to a former roommate, activate the vehicle's complicated keyless ignition system?
Toronto Star 1 Apr. 2006: B5

(A *suspect* is merely someone under investigation; the modifier *alleged* is unnecessary.)

Police said the alleged break-in occurred Dec. 6.
Gazette (Montreal) 23 Dec. 2004: A12

(Here *alleged* should be omitted, since the break-in is unquestioned.)

See also SUSPECTED.

alleluia   see HALLELUJAH

allied   see ALLY

allocable   see -ABLE, -(AT)ABLE

allophone   see FRANCOPHONE; QUEBEC ENGLISH

all ready, already   *All ready* means either completely ready ('Your room is all ready') or each one ready ('Are you all ready, or is someone missing?'). *Already* is an adverb meaning before now (It's already done') or as early as this ('Are they here already?').

all right, alright   *All right* is standard for all uses. The one-word spelling *alright* is considered incorrect by most commentators. However, it appears in print often enough that some dictionaries recognize it as a variant. Sometimes it seems to function as a visual cue indicating relaxed speech.

The government through lotteries is promoting the philosophy that it is all right not to work, if we can get out of it by living off the earnings of others.
Mennonite Brethren Herald 4 April 1986: 7

If a woman wants to do flower painting or crewel work or writing in her spare time, that's all right with us; you can do it at home, in between taking care of your family, as long as it doesn't interfere with the serious business of life, which is your husband's.
Margaret Atwood *Second Words* 1982: 341

It is spectacular alright, but the pacing leading up to it is off.
Vancouver Sun 6 Jan. 2006: C6

(The more widely accepted spelling is *all right*.)

'Alright, since you're so free, you be the one to lead us into the future.'
David Williams *Eye of the Father* 1985: 146

(The more widely accepted spelling is *all right*.)

all-round, all-around   Canadian writers use the adjective *all-round* ('best all-round player') slightly more often than *all-around*. Only *all-round* is standard in British English; *all-around* is the more common variant in American English. Either form should be hyphenated.

all together, altogether   *All together* means every one together, or in a group or whole: 'They were finally all together'. *Altogether* means on the whole or all told ('Altogether, we had a good time') or completely or entirely ('That is an altogether different story').

> But the character which holds it all together and gives the book weight is Sponge himself. . . .
> Robertson Davies *A Voice from the Attic* 1960: 148

> In fact, Riffs is a curious and not altogether satisfactory mixture of the two.
> *Toronto Star* 13 Nov. 1993: J14

> . . . it is said to have been committed under circumstances which either justified it altogether, or reduced the crime to manslaughter.
> William Teatero *John Anderson: Fugitive Slave* 1986: 53

> '. . . they are a huge multi-cultural mix and this event helps bring them altogether like no other.'
> *Calgary Herald* 13 Sept. 2003: B1

(Here *all together* is required.)

allude, elude, allusive, elusive   To *allude to* something is to make an indirect reference to it or to mention it in passing. To *elude* something is to keep out of its path; if something eludes you, it remains beyond your reach. Writing that is *allusive* refers obliquely to other texts; if a piece of writing is described as *elusive*, its meaning is difficult to understand.

> During his speech, [he] alluded to a few questionable operators promising potential franchise owners pie-in-the-sky.
> *Toronto Star* 30 Oct. 1993: C2

> The Black population of Brant and Norfolk counties sheltered him, and he eluded his pursuers for months.
> William Teatero *John Anderson: Fugitive Slave* 1986: 24

> . . . these students are able to master skills and knowledge that have previously alluded them. . . .
> 'Alberta Initiative for School Improvement' Alberta Government website 2006

(The word needed here is *eluded*.)

> Gold's poems are allusive (references to Mayakovsky, Frank O'Hara and Charles Ives pepper the volume) and sophisticated, but their intelligence does not impair their sensuality. . . .
> *Gazette* (Montreal) 25 Sept. 1993: J2

> The meaning of Ducharme's novels is elusive.
> Ben-Z. Shek *French-Canadian & Québécois Novels* 1991: 75

See also ELUSIVE, ILLUSORY, ELUSORY, ILLUSIVE.

ally, allied   *Ally* is both a noun and a verb. The noun is stressed on the first syllable (*AL eye*), the verb on the second (*a LIE*). When the adjective *allied* follows the verb *to be*, the second syllable is usually stressed: 'They were allied (*a LIED*) during the Second World War'. When it precedes a noun, the first syllable is usually stressed: 'Allied (*AL eyed*) Forces'. Both *allied to* and *allied with* are acceptable.

almost   see MOST; PRACTICALLY

alongside, alongside of   Canadian writers use *alongside* almost exclusively. *Alongside of*, the older form, is rare in writing but acceptable.

> While leading the canoe alongside a wide ledge, I happened to glance at the rock below my feet.
> *Up Here* Jan.–Feb. 1990: 48

a lot, lots, [alot]   *A lot* and *lots* function both as adverbs ('We eat out a lot/lots') and as nouns ('A lot/Lots of us are going'). The question is often raised whether these uses are appropriate to formal writing. Certainly they are far less common in formal writing than in speech. However, most usage guides stop short of calling them inappropriate. Some writers prefer to use expressions with more serious connotations, such as *a great deal* or *a good number*, in formal writing. Others like the conversational tone of *a lot* and *lots*.

For many years now *a lot* has been appearing in unpublished writings as one word—*alot*—and this spelling is beginning to creep into newspapers. *A lot* may eventually become an accepted spelling, following the precedents of *amiss*, *apiece*, and *awhile*, which were all originally written as two words. But for now *alot* should be avoided. Dictionaries don't list it, and many people consider its use a mark of illiteracy.

> 'That's a lot of goals.'
> *Toronto Star* 1 Jan. 1994: F4

However, they all like lots of sun—which is often a tall order in city yards.
Toronto Star 4 May 2006: J3

Geller's 'Young Offenders in Conflict with the Law' summarizes a lot of fuzzy literature with the statement that the criminal justice system treats adolescent women's sexual behavior harshly while largely ignoring their criminal behavior, and does the reverse for adolescent males.
Canadian Journal of Sociology 14.2 (1989): 255

The Bible, of course, contains blasphemy, torture, rape, sodomy, orgies, murder, lying and lots of other unpleasant things. It also contains the Sermon on the Mount, which would mean a lot less without its setting.
Margaret Atwood *Second Words* 1982: 354

An easily accessible parking space makes alot of sense—but free? No way.
Gazette (Montreal) 3 Oct. 1993: B3

(The correct spelling is *a lot*.)

My mother used to make icebox cookies alot, often adding chopped walnuts to the dough. . . .
Ottawa Citizen 1 June 1994: F1

(The correct spelling is *a lot*.)

aloud, out loud Some commentators consider *aloud* more acceptable than *out loud*. *Aloud* is the older and more common of these two expressions, but either is fine at any level of formality.

In my day at Gage, and that is not so very long ago, when we proofread, we proofread aloud, and we proofread aloud to another person.
W.C. Lougheed, ed. *In Search of the Standard in Canadian English* 1986: 133

On this couch . . . visiting poets and painters sat . . . two or three abreast, listening to poetry being read out loud by one of them. . . .
Miriam Waddington *Apartment Seven* 1989: 4

alphabetical order There are two systems for alphabetizing lists that contain both single words and phrases. Occasionally, this means that people don't find the heading they are looking for in an index or a reference work, because it is not where they expect it to be.

The first system is called 'word-by-word'. Alphabetization is interrupted by word breaks. Thus, in the example that follows, all the entries beginning with the word *black* alone precede those where *black-* is a combining form:

> black Loyalists
> black settlement
> Blackfoot
> blackrobes
> blacksmithing

In the second system, called 'letter-by-letter', word breaks are ignored. The same list of items looks like this:

> Blackfoot
> black Loyalists
> blackrobes
> black settlement
> blacksmithing

Dictionaries and reference books are almost always compiled on the letter-by-letter principle, and this one is no exception. One very good reason for this is that readers may not know ahead of time whether there will be a word break in the item they are looking up. In the lists below, the usual letter-by-letter arrangement can be compared with word-by-word alphabetization:

letter-by-letter	*word-by-word*
bookend	book in
book in	book learning
booking	book value
book learning	bookend
bookstore	booking
book value	bookstore

The letter-by-letter system is the one now generally recommended by style books. In the letter-by-letter system, commas may or may not be ignored. That is, alphabetization may proceed across commas, or commas may serve as points of interruption, like word breaks in the word-by-word system. Interrupting alphabetization at commas is usually preferable. For example, in the list of headings below, it allows all the people named White to be grouped together. If the commas were disregarded, *white paper* and *White Pass* would appear in the middle of this list:

White, James

White, Nancy

White, Robert

White, Thomas

white paper

White Pass

A few other conventions of alphabetization follow. An initial *the*, *a*, or *an* is ignored in the alphabetization of titles. Titles beginning with the word *this*, however, are alphabetized under *this*. Names beginning with *St.* (e.g., 'St. Lawrence College') are often alphabetized as if the word *Saint* were spelled out. However, since this convention is not built into software for alphabetizing, more recent indexing guides are recommending against it. Acronyms are sometimes alphabetized as if written in full—a practice that is not recommended when the acronym is far better known than the words it stands for (*UNICEF*, *NATO*). Numbers may be alphabetized as if they were written in words: thus '24 Sussex Drive' would be listed under T (for 'twenty-four'). Alternatively, when there are many numbers in an alphabetical list—for example, when a listing of city streets contains many numbered streets—all the numbers may appear in numerical order before the *a*'s.

In alphabetizing people's names, especially in a multicultural environment, distinguishing which part of the name is the surname can be difficult. Unfortunately, there are no completely reliable rules. In some cases, you cannot be sure without asking the person.

In Canada, surname particles—which are relatively uncommon—are usually considered part of the surname and alphabetized accordingly:

de la Roche, Mazo

De Mille, James

Van Herk, Aritha

In most European countries, however, surnames with particles are alphabetized according to the main part of the name; the particle is inverted with the first name:

Beauvoir, Simone de

Beethoven, Ludwig van

Gaulle, Charles de

Gogh, Vincent van

In Canadian indexes, for ease of reference, it is probably best to list names containing particles in both styles.

See also THE, A, AN; CHINESE NAME, FAMILY NAMES.

Alpine   see SCANDINAVIAN

already   see ADJECTIVES AND ADVERBS; ALL READY

alright   see ALL RIGHT

also, as well   The adverbs *also* and *as well* mark elements within sentences as additions:

The boys who were out of high school were also *out of work.*

He criticized *their methodology* as well.

She directed the choir and also *composed for* it.

In all varieties of English, *also* is acceptable at the beginning of an inverted sentence, that is, one in which the verb precedes the subject:

Also affected were the families of the victims.

Only in Canadian English, however, are *also* and *as well* frequently used at the beginning of sentences as connecting adverbs to introduce the whole sentence as an additional point:

As well, they will be responsible for emergency care.

Also, a firm may establish a probationary period.

In British and American English, *as well* is so seldom used in this way that it has escaped the attention of commentators. The use of *also* as a connecting adverb, on the other hand, has been noticed and condemned by a series of British and American stylists. Robert Burchfield, for example, in *The New Fowler's Modern English Usage*, calls this use 'a marked feature of uneducated speech'. Burchfield's claim is rebutted by Pam Peters, who, having done a frequency analysis of all the types of discourse in the British National Corpus, reports that *also* occurs most often as a connecting adverb in academic writing (*The Cambridge Guide to English Usage*). The debate over this contentious sentence connector is not really about grammatical acceptability; it is about style. That some writers choose not to use *also* in this way as a sentence adverb does not make it wrong for others to do so.

Also and *as well* are well established connecting adverbs in every variety of Canadian writing, and Canadians who are writing for a Canadian audience need not have any qualms about using them. Canadians writing for an international audience may (or may not) want to substitute sentence adverbs with wider international acceptance, such as *in addition* or *furthermore*.

Also, a pack of Bernardo's favourite cigarettes was found in Bain's bloodstained car.
CBC News online 21 Sept. 2004

Also, there were complaints that club bouncers were not properly handling problem patrons and were becoming involved in disturbances.
Vancouver Liquor Licensing Commission report, City of Vancouver website 3 Nov. 1995

As well, it may take two or three years for a case to come to trial, thereby delaying the time between asset seizure and forfeiture.
Juristat: Canadian Centre for Justice Statistics 22.10 (2002)

As well, we offer many workshops to meet a wide variety of student needs.
Concordia University *Online Study Skills Help* 1998

See also SENTENCE ADVERBS.

alter, altar To *alter* means to change or modify something. A piece of clothing is altered or adjusted for a better fit. An *altar* is a raised place or table used in religious ceremonies.

She was an active member of the alter guild in the All Saints Cathedral, Halifax. . . .
Daily News (Halifax) 19 April 1994: 37

(The correct spelling here is *altar*.)

alter ego *Alter ego* is a Latin phrase that means 'second self'. Cicero used the expression to refer to a close and trusted friend. In English that meaning is still possible today, but it is fairly uncommon. An alter ego is more likely to be the hidden side of someone's personality or a fictional character as brought to life by an author or an actor.

Smart . . . was Sifton's alter ego. The two men were contemporaries—Smart was just a year older—and had grown up in Brandon politics together.
Pierre Berton *The Promised Land* 1984: 11

(This is the older meaning of *alter ego*).

His interior alter ego, 'Unborn Twin,' eggs him on to acts of derring-do.
Gazette (Montreal) 22 April 2006: J10

Over the course of a life, and some 470 books, Asimov came to regard [fictional character] Hari Seldon as his alter ego.
Calgary Herald 29 May 1993: D11

See also LATIN PHRASES.

alternate, alternative An *alternate* is a back-up person, as for a delegate, a jury, or an Olympic team. An *alternative* is an option: 'What alternative did we have?'

The adjective *alternate* refers to every second one ('alternate Saturdays') or to two things that succeed each other by turns ('alternate sun and clouds'). The adjective *alternative* refers to something available as an option ('alternative route'), to something that can be substituted if necessary ('alternative telephone number'), or to something non-traditional ('alternative school', 'alternative medicine', 'alternative newspaper').

Two usage issues are associated with these

two words. The first is whether there can be more than two alternatives. This question was raised in the last half of the nineteenth century because the Latin word *alter*, from which *alternative* is derived, means the other of two. Fortunately, this issue has been laid to rest. Contemporary commentators unanimously consider it pedantry to reject 'We have three alternatives'.

The second issue is whether the adjective *alternate* can be used as a synonym of *alternative*, as in 'alternate plan', 'alternate date', or 'alternate music'. This use of the adjective is obviously closely related to the meaning of the noun *alternate* and is well enough established to be recorded by all dictionaries. Nevertheless, since many commentators still consider it a mistake, it is not recommended in formal writing.

Stephanie and Peter are designated team members, while Victoria is an alternate.
Calgary Herald 18 June 1994: B1

As governor general, he charmed Canadians with alternate displays of flawless decorum and engaging informality.
Maclean's 19 Aug. 1991: A17

On alternate weeks another doctor comes in from out of town.
Ottawa Citizen 28 Feb. 1993: A7

Iskandar said the town is studying several options to dispose of its snow, including using the St. Charles St. site, but he refused to describe the alternatives.
Gazette (Montreal) 30 June 1993: G1

(The use of *alternatives* to describe several options is common and acceptable.)

When they tried an alternative route, raging winds forced them to retreat to Alert.
Maclean's 11 Nov. 1991: A24

Motorists are reminded to allow extra time to reach their destination and to take alternate routes when possible.
Sudbury Star 6 Aug. 2005: A3

(This use of *alternate* is common but criticized.)

Available on board the Golden Odyssey is an alternate menu for those on low-cholesterol or low-sodium diets.
Torch: University of Victoria Alumni Magazine Spring 1990: 16

(This use of *alternate* is common but criticized.)

Alternately, use a more natural interface, like a binary keyboard.
National Post (Toronto) 8 April 2006: A18

(Here *alternatively* would be better.)

although, though   *Although* and *though* are interchangeable as conjunctions: 'Although/though John is very conservative in his politics, his taste in clothes is quite radical'. Some usage guides suggest that *although* is more appropriate in formal writing. Canadian writers seem to be guided by other considerations. They use both words at all levels of formality, and often in the same piece of writing.

What a man considers indecent is an important clue to his character, and although there are exceptions, it has been my experience that book collectors have strange opinions on this subject, and few of them lack a book or two which they think they should conceal.
Robertson Davies *A Voice from the Attic* 1960: 264

They were not often needed for direct attendance upon the Royal Household, though the Bug Catcher once captured a single bedbug in the chamber of Princess Charlotte, with her fascinated assistance.
Robertson Davies *A Voice from the Attic* 1960: 126

P.K. Page's *The Metal and the Flower* . . . got the Governor-General's Medal, and deserved it, although my opinion of the practice of giving a medal to any poet over the age of ten is not high.
Northrop Frye *The Bush Garden* 1972: 39

. . . and only Riel remains to haunt the later period of it, though he is a formidable figure enough, rather like what a combination of John Brown and Vanzetti would be in the American conscience.
Northrop Frye *The Bush Garden* 1972: 224

See also SENTENCES, SENTENCE FRAGMENT, RUN-ON SENTENCE, COMMA SPLICE.

altogether   see ALL TOGETHER

altos   see -OS, -OES

alumnus, alumna, alumni, alumnae
These words referring to the graduates of a university are among the few Latin terms in popular use for which there are no regular English plurals. *Alumnus* is used of a male graduate, *alumna* of a female graduate, and the plurals are *alumni* and *alumnae* respectively. *Alumni* has long been established as the term for a mixed group, but literally this usage refers only to men. *Alumnae and alumni, alumni/ae, former students*, and *graduates* are all recommended as non-sexist alternatives. *Alums* (pronounced *a LUMZ*), a clipped form popular in the United States, is another gender-neutral alternative.

The term *alumni/-ae* is also often applied to former employees, former members of a group, former summer campers, etc. In literal translation, *alumni/-ae* are foster children.

The Latin plural endings *-ae* and *-i* can both be pronounced in English to rhyme with either *eye* or *see*. The more common pronunciations of *alumni* and *alumnae*, which serve to distinguish the two words, are *ah LUM nye* for the masculine plural and *ah LUM nee* for the feminine.

> All former alumni invited.
> Gazette (Montreal) 20 April 2006: F16

(*Former* is redundant here unless *alumni* is replaced with *students*.)

> An alumnus of St. Pat's and St. Lawrence, Pierre is now studying at Glendon Campus of York University in Toronto.
> Chronicle-Telegraph (Quebec) 14 Aug. 1991: 13

> The Queen's University student and Canadian Idol alumna, who sang her way to sixth place on the second season of the popular talent show, is the new Canadian Idol roving reporter.
> Whig-Standard (Kingston) 15 April 2006: 4

> Avi Lewis, Daniel Richler and Laurie Brown are other alumni who moved to CBC programs.
> Star-Phoenix (Saskatoon) 15 Nov. 2004: D2

(Here *alumni* refers to both sexes.)

> This, of course, has promoted an esprit de corps, one easily passed from generation to generation as students turned into alumni and alumnae, and as graduates sent their children down to Queen's.
> Frederick Gibson Queen's University 2 (1983): 433

See also PLURALS; SEXIST LANGUAGE.

am   see ADJECTIVES AND ADVERBS; AGREEMENT, GRAMMATICAL; AIN'T, AREN'T I

a.m.   see TIME

a mari usque ad mare   *A Mari Usque Ad Mare*, the Latin motto affixed to the Canadian coat of arms, is a quotation from the Bible (Psalm 72: 8). It is officially translated 'From Sea to Sea' or 'D'un océan à l'autre'. 'From sea to shining sea', another phrase that Canadians often use, originates in the American song 'America the Beautiful'.

In formal writing, the Latin motto should be italicized; initial capitals are optional. Note the different spellings of *mari* and *mare*.

> The essential element in the national sense of unity is the east-west feeling, developed historically along the St. Lawrence–Great Lakes axis, and expressed in the national motto, *a mari usque ad mare*.
> Northrop Frye *The Bush Garden* 1971: iii

See also DOMINION OF CANADA.

amateur   In sports, an amateur athlete is differentiated from a professional one on the basis not of skill but of money: an amateur does not compete for money nor earn a livelihood from sports, whereas a professional does. In other contexts, *amateur* usually implies a lack of skill or seriousness; used in this way, the word may be synonymous with either *bungler* or *dilettante*.

Amateur is etymologically linked to the Latin for lover. An 'amateur of the arts', for example, can be someone with a cultivated appreciation of the arts. This usage, fairly common in the nineteenth century, is becoming rare—at least outside Quebec. There the English word *amateur* retains this older meaning because the most common meaning of the French word *amateur* is fan. (See QUEBEC ENGLISH.)

Pronunciations of *amateur* vary considerably. Most Canadians say *AM a cher*, but the last syllable may also be pronounced *ter, tour,* or *chure*.

> The Player agrees that during the term of this contract he . . . will not play for or be directly or indirectly employed by or interested in any other ama-

teur or professional hockey club.
J.E. Smyth et al. *The Law and Business Administration in Canada* 1987: 185

Even an amateur could clearly spot it, thanks to the infrared camera.
Truck News 24.9 (2004): 33

The difference between the amateur autobiographer and the professional man of letters is that the former is concerned with self-approval, the latter with self-revelation.
Robertson Davies *A Voice from the Attic* 1960: 298

It is not for one who is an amateur of lexicography to offer authoritative pronouncements on the role of the dictionary in Canadian English.
W.C. Lougheed, ed. *In Search of the Standard in Canadian English* 1986: 48

(Here *amateur* combines the senses of devotee and dilettante.)

A keen amateur who has read and reread all 60 of the [Sherlock Holmes] adventures, de Freitas said he won't call them 'stories' because he maintains they are true.
Gazette (Montreal) 10 June 1993: G5

(In Quebec English *amateur* often means fan.)

See also DILETTANTE; QUEBEC ENGLISH.

amazement   see -E

ambiguous, ambivalent, equivocal   *Ambiguous* usually refers to external things, *ambivalent* to mental states. A sign, word, or expression that can be understood in two or more ways at the same time is *ambiguous*. A person who experiences opposing feelings or attitudes simultaneously is *ambivalent*.
Equivocal has several meanings. It can mean either ambiguous or ambivalent. A statement that reveals its author's ambivalence may be described as *equivocal*. Sometimes *equivocal* implies deception, contrived ambiguity, or pretended ambivalence. (The related verb to *equivocate* means to conceal the truth through ambiguity.) Occasionally *equivocal* means morally questionable or of dubious value.

Some issues were dealt with explicitly, others were left vague and ambiguous, leaving room for vari-

ous interpretations.
Queen's Quarterly 94.3 (1987): 563

The French, in their accounts of the period, display a marked ambivalence toward the Indians, depicting them as noble on the one hand and savage on the other—a stereotype that was unquestioningly accepted by later historians.
Saturday Night July 1986: 50

The government's ambivalent policy with regard to South Africa—condemning apartheid out of one corner of its mouth and encouraging improved trade relations out of the other—was a case in point.
George Ignatieff *The Making of a Peacemonger* 1987: 245

(Normally a policy would be described as *ambiguous* rather than *ambivalent*. Because Ignatieff goes on to personify the policy by giving it a 'mouth', *ambivalent* works here.)

Equivocal words are assigned the meaning that makes the contract enforceable, if at all possible.
J.E. Smyth et al. *The Law and Business Administration in Canada* 1987: 268

(Here *equivocal* means ambiguous.)

All females want to give feminists substantial promotions up the influence hierarchy. Male respondents are far more equivocal on that score.
Neil Nevitte and Roger Gibbins *New Elites in Old States* 1990: 144

(Here *equivocal* means ambivalent.)

Whitehorn is equivocal. 'No one bore more responsibility,' he writes, 'but perhaps no one worked harder.'
Ottawa Citizen 11 Sept. 1994: B3

He said Mr. Miller has been vague and equivocal about the issue during the election campaign, apparently hoping to create the impression that he would consider changing the current policy.
Globe and Mail (Toronto) May 2 1985: P8

(Here *equivocal* implies deliberate deceit.)

Other reasons listed as causes for censorship are: Ministers of religion in equivocal situations, blasphemous incidents, objectionable prison scenes, hospital incidents treated flippantly. . . .
Toronto Star 1 Sept. 1992: A10

(Here *equivocal* means morally questionable.)

The one sister in Terre Haute reappears to provide equivocal support in A Visit Home.
Gazette (Montreal) 20 Feb. 1993: K1

(Here *equivocal* means of dubious value.)

See also LIE, EQUIVOCATE; UNEQUIVOCAL.

ameba see -AE-, -OE-, -E-

ameliorate   *Ameliorate* is related to the Latin *melior*, 'better'. Basing their argument on this relationship, some usage commentators have stated that *ameliorate* should be used only in contexts where *improve* or (*make*) *better* could be substituted. In this view, to *ameliorate* does not mean to reduce or relieve; one does not ameliorate hardship or pain, although one may alleviate or relieve it.

In this case, as in many, English usage has ignored Latin etymology, and the advice of these commentators can also be safely ignored. Today a negative complement, such as 'hardship' or 'pain', follows *ameliorate* far more often than not. Dictionaries have made allowances for what is now the predominant usage by including both definitions: to improve and to make more tolerable, more bearable.

In the face of the mounting opposition of the common people, the oligarchy of nobles and rich merchants sometimes ameliorated the material lot of the people.
Irving M. Zeitlin and Robert J. Brym *The Social Condition of Humanity* 1991: 309

Clay soils can also be ameliorated with generous applications of organic matter such as compost, well-rotted manure or peat moss.
TLC . . . for plants Summer 1991: 26

Researchers from Oxford University will try to discover how beliefs are formed and whether they can ameliorate suffering.
Daily News (Halifax) 20 Feb. 2005: YOU13

(Some authorities dispute this usage.)

Enhanced legislative influence in the policy process ameliorates the tension between our spatial and sectoral systems of representation, but it does little to ensure that all interests in Canadian society have an equal opportunity to contribute to public decision-making.
A. Paul Pross *Group Politics and Public Policy* 2nd ed. 1992: 257

(Some authorities dispute this usage.)

Will an extra 5,000 peacekeepers ameliorate the danger?
Calgary Herald 12 Sept. 1992: A4

(Some authorities dispute this usage.)

See also QUEBEC ENGLISH.

amenable   The word *amenable* is usually followed by *to*. The correct verb form after *amenable to* is the *ing* form ('amenable to sharing'), not the infinitive ('amenable to share').

One of the most common meanings of *amenable* is willing to accept: 'They were amenable to sharing the cost of the freight'. Another common meaning is responsive: 'Most strains of tuberculosis are amenable to treatment'. In formal writing, *amenable to* sometimes means open to a particular type of testing or judgment.

When *amenable* is not followed by *to*, it means easily influenced or pliable. Increasingly, however, people are using the word to mean pleasing or congenial, probably because they associate *amenable* with the unrelated word *amenity*, 'something that makes life more pleasant'. Note that 'pleasing' is not yet widely accepted as a sense of *amenable*.

The second syllable of *amenable* may be pronounced either *MEN* or *MEAN*.

Certainly today's reporters are less amenable to the notion that before, during and after military action it's somehow disloyal to question the interpretation of the facts by government and the armed forces.
Ottawa Citizen 24 June 1992: A10

. . . neurosurgeon James Drake similarly relies on a customized industrial robot for excising brain tumors in gravely ill children. Inner ears and prostates are also proving amenable to robotic assistance.
Ottawa Citizen 2 Aug. 1992: F1

Levin says they're amenable to passing on as much information as possible.
Ottawa Citizen 31 Oct. 1992: I1

Eskenazi is more than amenable to shoot the breeze in the aisle and discourse on the Muppets and children's movies. . . .
Gazette (Montreal) 10 Dec. 1992: F5

(Here the *-ing* form is required: 'amenable to *shooting* the breeze . . . and *discoursing*'.)

Freud found the tenacity with which religious beliefs are held to be psychologically remarkable. Though they are not amenable to rational or empirical proof, people cling to them anyway.
Irving M. Zeitlin and Robert J. Brym *The Social Condition of Humanity* 1991: 214

(Here *amenable* means open to a certain kind of testing.)

The problem for his patrons was that he turned out to be exactly what they said he was. . . . It remains to be seen whether his successor, Ali Kafi, will prove more amenable.
Calgary Herald 4 July 1992: B3

(Here *amenable* means manageable, easily influenced.)

Well that's my report for today. Now that it's done, I can return to more amenable surroundings, like the Ogilvy book shop.
Gazette (Montreal) 17 June 1992: A2

(Here *congenial* would be a better choice.)

Austen, Texas, the technology triangle of North Carolina, and San Jose, California, have more amenable climates than Ottawa's.
Ottawa Citizen 26 Jan. 2006: C4

(Here *pleasant* would be a better choice.)

Smith, who presented a detailed business plan for the league to the governors, said the concept of the cap is amenable to all teams.
Ottawa Citizen 30 April 1992: H6

(The word *amenable* means 'willing to accept', not 'acceptable'. Either 'the cap is acceptable to all teams' or 'all teams are amenable to the cap' would be better here.)

amend, emend, amendment, emendation

Both *amend* and *emend* mean to revise, correct, or improve, but they are used in different contexts. *Amend* is appropriate in a broader range of contexts than *emend*; it is often used to refer to the revision of laws, motions, statutes, bills, or official documents.

Emend is used more narrowly, referring most often to the scholarly editing of texts or the rewriting of musical scores. *Amendments* are made to laws, while *emendations* are made to texts and musical scores.

The Government introduced a bill yesterday to amend more than 50 federal statutes that the Justice Department believes are in clear violation of the Charter of Rights and Freedoms.
Globe and Mail (Toronto) 1 Feb. 1985: P1

Amend soil with well-rotted compost or mushroom manure.
Vancouver Sun 31 Dec. 1994: E5

Pettle also attends rehearsals and does on-the-spot rewrites and emendations, she says.
Toronto Star 20 Nov. 2003: G12

(Pettle is a playwright.)

American, America, the United States, the Americas

In Canada, *American* is used almost exclusively in reference to the United States and its citizens. Several American usage guides state that Canadians resent the appropriation of *American* by the United States. Whether or not this is so, many Canadians do resent being called *American*—something quite different—because they assume they are being mistaken for US citizens. People who call Canadian travellers *American* may be using a short form for *North American*—a common usage in Britain and Europe—or they may be unable to distinguish Canadian and American accents.

Canadians seldom refer to the United States as *America*, although this usage is quite common around the world. Canadians say *the United States* or, informally, *the States*. The full name, 'the United States of America', and the long abbreviation, *USA*, are uncommon even in writing. But the short abbreviation *US* is used frequently as an adjective in both formal and informal writing. *US* usually refers to things associated with government ('US Army', 'US dollar') as opposed to culture ('American dream', 'American film industry'). Sometimes *US* is used when *American* might have a broader, continental reference: 'the US market'.

Political trends in the 1990s, such as the creation of world trading blocs and the international solidarity movement among Indigenous peoples, have raised Canadians' awareness of Canada as a country in the Americas. *The Americas* refers to the whole of North, Central, and South America, including the West Indies.

> A city with clean subways, no graffiti and fans so polite that they didn't even boo the American national anthem even though the folks from the Big Apple had booed theirs after it was sung by a singer who couldn't remember the words.
> *Globe and Mail* (Toronto) 19 Oct. 1985: E3

> 'A Canadian,' Arthur L. Phelps has said, 'is one who is increasingly aware of being American in the continental sense without being American in the national sense.'
> Carl F. Klinck, ed. *Literary History of Canada* 1 (1976): 139

> I am nonplussed for an answer, searching among the nebulosities of our national life, until I think of America, as we allow the citizens of the United States to name their fragments of the continent.
> George Woodcock *The New Romans* Ed. A.W. Purdy 1968: 75

(This use of *America* is uncommon in Canada.)

> 'Mexico wants help to become the hub, the economic downtown of the Americas.'
> *Toronto Star* 28 June 1994: D1

> Ruptures is a literary quarterly published in Montreal by Edgard Gousse, an immigrant from Haiti with the vision of uniting in one magazine the four languages (English, French, Spanish and Portuguese) of the 'three Americas' (North, Central and South).
> *Gazette* (Montreal) 25 June 1994: H3

Amerindian   see ABORIGINAL PEOPLE(S)

amid, amidst, among, amongst   *Amid* is used in Canadian writing far more often than *amidst*; either is correct. Although several guides have suggested that these words are bookish or quaint, both are quite common in Canada.

Some commentators suggest that *amid(st)* should be used with singular nouns ('amid the controversy'), while *among* should be used with plural nouns ('among the items'). This distinction is fanciful. The only real grammatical restriction is on *among*, which cannot be used with singular nouns ('among the controversy' would not be acceptable). However, *among* can be used with singular nouns that can be seen as notionally plural, such as *crowd* ('He walked among the crowd') or *grass* ('We found the beads among the grass'). *Among* is far more common than *amongst*. A few commentators call *amongst* old-fashioned, but that judgment is not borne out by Canadian usage.

> . . . amid the nudges, winks, outrageous opinions and good humor is a foundation of useful information.
> *Province* (Vancouver) 23 Dec. 1990: 71

> The two men were led away amid a further exchange of invective, and business at the shop returned to normal.
> J.E. Smyth et al. *The Law and Business Administration in Canada* 1987: 96

> Amidst all the controversy his remarks caused, Berger resigned from the bench.
> Andrew Heard *Canadian Constitutional Conventions* 1991: 131

> 'AIDS was first identified amongst homosexual males in large urban centres and subsequently amongst prostitutes and drug addicts.'
> Daniel Gawthrop *Affirmation: The AIDS Odyssey of Dr. Peter* 1994: 63

See also AGREEMENT, GRAMMATICAL; BETWEEN, AMONG.

amoeba   see -AE-, -OE-, -E-

amok, amuck   *Amok* is the more common spelling. *Amuck* is a variant used more often in Britain than Canada or the United States. According to most dictionaries, to *run amok* means to run about in a homicidal rage or to go berserk. These are the meanings closest to the word's Malay origins, and, with allowances for figurative uses, the most common meanings in Canadian English. However, *run amok* and *go amok* are also used today to mean go too far or go wrong. Perhaps folk etymology is at work here: people may be associating *amuck* with *muck* and getting off the track. In any case, a few dictionaries have begun to list these newer, nonviolent meanings.

> Suffering from what the doctors called 'delusions of persecution and disease phobia', he'd run amok, jumped through a large window and run bleeding and screaming down the street.
> Max Braithwaite *The Night We Stole the Mountie's Car* 1971: 159

> This is yet another example of an amateur sports bureaucracy run amok.
> *Gazette* (Montreal) 12 Feb. 1994: C3

> Crown attorney Michael Leshner professed to be 'appalled' by the idea and called it 'human rights gone amok.'
> *Daily News* (Halifax) 17 Nov. 1994: 26

See also FOLK ETYMOLOGY.

among, amongst   see AMID; BETWEEN, AMONG

amoral   see IMMORAL

ampere   see APPENDIX II

ampersand   An *ampersand* (pronounced *AM per sand*) is the symbol &. In published writing, the ampersand is not freely substituted for *and*. It is used as a space-saving device in tables, notes, and parenthetical documentation; it is used in business names (e.g., Fitzhenry & Whiteside), if that is the practice of the business; and it is used in certain abbreviations such as 'R & D' (research and development), 'R & B' (rhythm and blues), and 'B & B' (bed and breakfast). Note that the spaces are sometimes omitted in abbreviations containing an ampersand: 'R&B', 'B&B'. Either style is acceptable if used consistently.

Long before it was used in English, the ampersand stood for *et* (the Latin word 'and'); thus, until the twentieth century, the Latin abbreviation *etc.* was often written &c. Though the symbol & is centuries older, its name was not coined until the nineteenth century. *Ampersand* is a distortion of the phrase 'and *per se* and', which means '& by itself is and'. Perhaps this name distinguished the symbol & from &c., 'etcetera'.

> 'This Philosophy both speculative & active is not only to be found in ye volume of nature but also in ye sacred scriptures, as in Genesis, Job, Psalms, Isaiah & others.'
> *Queen's Quarterly* 95.1 (1988): 34

(In contemporary formal writing, & cannot be freely substituted for *and*.)

See also ETC.; PER SE.

amuck   see AMOK

an   see A

an-   see A-, AN-

anachronism, anachronistic   An *anachronism* is a person, thing, event, or custom placed outside its proper historical period. A motorcycle, for example, would be anachronistic in a painting of the Red River uprising. It is acceptable to use *anachronism* to refer to something outdated or old-fashioned, but *anachronism* or *anachronistic* should not be used to describe something that is simply out of place or contradictory.

> . . . what stands out is the anachronism that has Theudebert I, dead in 548, react to a Langobard invasion that occurred in 568.
> *Canadian Journal of History* 14.1 (1989): 94

> He has rejected allegations that [the United Nations] has become an expensive anachronism, too vulnerable to political opportunists to be of much further value.
> *Globe and Mail* (Toronto) 9 March 1985: P5

(Here *anachronism* means something belonging to a bygone era.)

> The wider stuff, usually in silky, limp textures, is all over the place in long skirts cut in circles: take down the curtains, mother, I'm going out tonight. They look plain curious by day, but Italians love anachronisms in dress, so they make the point even clearer by adding a tough-looking biker's jacket in black leather. . . .
> *Globe and Mail* (Toronto) 19 March 1985: F1

(A better word here would be *incongruities*.)

anaemia see -AE-, -OE-, -E-

analog, analogue Most Canadian writers use *analog* as a technical adjective meaning 'as opposed to digital' ('analog radiography') and *analogue* as a general-purpose noun for something that is similar to or functions in the same way as something else. However, either spelling is acceptable for either use; both spellings are listed in British and American dictionaries.

This watch's crystal encrusted face cover flips up to reveal an analog watch.
Toronto Star 11 Dec. 2004: L1

In 1952, working under Harold Urey at the University of Chicago, Miller created a laboratory analogue of the young Earth.
Vancouver Sun 25 March 2006: C4

analogous, similar Both *analogous* and *similar* are adjectives used to describe things that have a resemblance but are not identical. *Analogous* is usually found in technical and academic contexts and refers to things that work the same way or serve the same purpose, though they may differ in many respects. *Similar* is a more general word and, unlike *analogous*, can be modified by words such as *very*, *almost*, and *somewhat* to indicate the degree of resemblance. Where a preposition is needed, both words are followed by *to*.
The *g* in *analogous* is pronounced as in *go*.

Logging is seen as a practice analogous to farming, from the 'harvesting of crops' to the creation of 'plantations.'
Vancouver Sun 23 June 1990: B6

Rather than being a 'colony of settlement' Canada might have been a 'colony of conquest' analogous to those of Asia and Africa.
Wallace Clement and Glen Williams, eds. *The New Canadian Political Economy* 1989: 135

More, they were practical farmers with years of experience under conditions very similar to those on the northern plains.
Pierre Berton *The Promised Land* 1984: 175–6

analyse, analyze see -IZE, -ISE, -YZE, -YSE

-ance, -ant, -ence, -ent Although the *-ance/-*

ant and *-ence/-ent* suffixes are pronounced the same way, they are not interchangeable. The *Cambridge Guide to English Usage* provides some useful spelling guidelines.

If the word can take an *-ation* ending, it requires an *a* ending: think of *signification/significance/significant*.

If the word can take an *-ential* ending, it requires an *e* ending: think of *confidential/confidence/confident*, *consequential/consequence/consequent*, and *reverential/reverence/reverent*.

If the word ends in *-ate* as a verb, it retains the *a* in other forms: think of *dominate/dominance/dominant*, *luxuriate/luxuriance/luxuriant*, and *tolerate/tolerance/tolerant*.

Unfortunately, a great many other words look as if they should be spelled consistently but are not. *Assistance* and *resistance*, for example, use *a* endings, while *insistence*, *persistence*, and *subsistence* use *e*. When in doubt, it is best to consult a dictionary. A very few words can be spelled either way, and fewer still take on different meanings depending on which ending is used. For these cases, see the individual entries cross-referenced below.

This is just one of the differances aside from cost you need to consider before deciding which policy makes more sense for you.
Province (Vancouver) 18 Sept. 2002: A37

(The correct spelling is *differences*, with an *e*; compare *differEntial*.)

There is zero tolerence for infractions that reduce the natural flow of the game.
Daily News (Halifax) 3 Sept. 2006: 54

(The correct spelling is *tolerAnce*, with an *a*; compare *tolerAte*.)

So far, that view has met resistence from Russia and France.
Daily News (Halifax) 5 Oct. 2002: 11

(The correct spelling is *resistance*; no general rule can help with this one.)

See also CONFIDANT, CONFIDANTE, CONFIDENT; DEPENDENT, DEPENDANT, INDEPENDENT; DESCENDANT, ANCESTOR, DESCENDENT.

ancestor see DESCENDANT

anchor, anchorman see JOB TITLES

and Despite school-day admonitions, there is nothing wrong with beginning a sentence with *and*. When *and* joins two clauses within a sentence, it is generally preceded by a comma, unless the clauses are quite short. A comma is optional before the *and* that precedes the last item in a list: 'hockey, basketball(,) and soccer' (see COMMA). When the subject of a sentence consists of two elements linked by *and*, a plural verb is required (see AGREEMENT, GRAMMATICAL).

And who wants to take that risk?
Ken Dryden *The Game* 1983: 230

And there was something else in his motive.
Jack Batten *Robinette* 1984: 82

And indeed, the content, if taken seriously, is disturbing, even frightening.
Miriam Waddington *Apartment Seven* 1989: 104

See also AMPERSAND; AND/OR; COMMA.

and/or Most commentators reject the combined form *and/or* except in business writing. For some, the reason is aesthetic: they don't like the virgule. Others find *and/or* clumsy in a sentence and argue that *and* or *or* alone usually suffices to carry the meaning: if greater precision is required, the phrase 'A or B or both' can be used. This phrase should be followed by a plural verb: 'Either a pickaxe or a shovel or both *are* required'.

And/or was first used in legal writing, but now even legal style guides recommend against it; too many court battles have been fought over the exact meaning of 'A, B, and/or C'.

Analysts of South African society, so often preoccupied with issues of race and/or class, have tended to take the state for granted as an agency of other social forces.
Queen's Quarterly 92.1 (1985): 226

(Here *or* is not needed; *and* alone would be preferable.)

It seems to me dangerous to talk about 'Canadian' patterns of sensibility in the work of people who entered and/or entered-and-left the country at a developmentally late stage of their lives.
Margaret Atwood *Second Words* 1982: 142

(Here *or* alone would be less confusing and would not alter the meaning.)

Where there is an unconditional contract for the sale of specific goods in a deliverable state, the property in the goods passes to the buyer when the contract is made, and it is immaterial whether the time of payment or the time of delivery or both is postponed.
J.E. Smyth et al. *The Law and Business Administration in Canada* 1987: 385

(Since *both* is plural, '*are* postponed' is required.)

See also AGREEMENT, GRAMMATICAL.

anemia see -AE-, -OE-, -E-

anemone see CATASTROPHE, CATASTROPHES

anesthetist, anesthesiologist An anesthetist (pronounced *a NEES thuh tist* or *a NES thuh tist*) is any medical person who administers anesthetics. An anesthesiologist is a doctor specializing in anesthesiology, which is the study of anesthetics, their effects, how to administer them, etc. Alternative, though uncommon, spellings of these words are *anaesthetist* and *anaesthesiologist*.

See also -AE-, -OE-, -E-.

Anglo-Celtic see CELT

Anglo-Irish, Anglophile see FRANCOPHONE

anglophone see FRANCOPHONE; QUEBEC ENGLISH

Anglo-Saxon see OLD ENGLISH

animator see FACILITATE, FACILITATOR; QUEBEC ENGLISH

Anishnabe see OJIBWA(Y)

anniversary *Anniversary* is derived from the Latin for 'the year turned'; hence some commentators disapprove of expressions such as 'our six-month anniversary'. Most people are aware that an anniversary is supposed to come but once a year, and the first uses of the word to refer to shorter time periods were probably playful. However, the extended meaning is now established in newspaper writing in serious contexts. Eventually the new meaning may gain full acceptance because there is no other word for a recurrent date. But so far most dictionaries don't list the meaning, nor is it used in formal writing.

> Israeli authorities saw the Friday prayers as a serious test of Palestinians' mood on the one-week anniversary of the Hebron massacre.
> *Toronto Star* 5 March 1994: A2

> The novel opens in Vancouver at a gathering of Gail's family and friends to commemorate the six-month anniversary of her death.
> *Vancouver Sun* 22 April 2006: F15

Annunciation   see ENUNCIATION

anoint   *Anoint* is frequently misspelled with two *n*'s.

another, more   Some commentators object to following the adjective *another* with a number, as in 'another fifty copies'. *Another*, they say, means *one* more or *a* different, and should be reserved for use with singular nouns: 'another round', 'another story'. *More*, the word generally used with plural nouns, is the appropriate word to use with a plural noun preceded by a number: 'fifty more copies', 'two more people to see'. However, this rule is breached continually not only in speech but also in formal writing.

> When the doors were not opened for another 15 minutes, tempers flared and there was much pushing and shoving.
> William Teatero *John Anderson: Fugitive Slave* 1986: 76

> Another $10,000 raised in a head-shaving event will also be donated in April, Cancer Awareness Month.
> *Vancouver Sun* 10 Apr. 2006: F5

See also EACH OTHER, ONE ANOTHER.

-ant   see -ANCE, -ANT, -ENCE, -ENT

antagonist, protagonist   An *antagonist* is a rival, opponent, or opposing force, someone or something that acts against—*ant(i)*—another.

Some classically educated language commentators, including Fowler, could not abide the use of the plural *protagonists* to refer to the main characters in a play, film, or novel. Ancient Greek plays had only one leading actor, who alone was referred to as the *protagonist*. However, as the *OED* points out in a usage note, restricting the number of protagonists to one makes sense only in reference to ancient Greek drama.

In the nineteenth century, the meaning of *protagonist* broadened to include a prominent figure in a real-life drama or a celebrated champion of a cause. By the 1920s this meaning had broadened once again so that *protagonist* could mean simply supporter, proponent, or advocate, as in 'My brother has become an ardent protagonist of animal rights'. With this last shift, the whole notion of a protagonist as a leading figure is lost. Many commentators dispute this use because it is apparently based on the misconception that if antagonists are *against* something or someone, then protagonists must be *for* something or someone. In fact, the *pro-* in *protagonist* is not the Latin prefix meaning 'for'. *Protagonist* begins with the Greek prefix *prot(o)-*, meaning 'first' (also found in the English word *prototype*).

Some dictionaries list the disputed meaning, supporter or proponent, and some don't. In Canadian English, the disputed meaning is very rare, not used at all in formal writing, and probably best avoided. In British English, the disputed meaning has become the most common meaning, which has led some commentators to accept it, albeit with misgivings.

> Eventually Maude and Mavor became such bitter antagonists that in their respective books on the Doukhobor migration they scarcely mentioned one another.
> Pierre Berton *The Promised Land* 1984: 72

> While Thomas and Eric are the protagonists of Favorite Son, the philosophers are the adults, especially the Vietnamese nanny.
> *Calgary Herald* 29 Apr. 2006: F4

(This use of *protagonists*, plural, is now accepted.) The Liberal Party tells itself a story in which it is the protagonist of Canada, the builder and preserver of Canadian unity.
Calgary Herald 10 Feb. 2006: A28

(Here *protagonist* means champion.)

I applaud Peter March . . . for shedding some shadow on the 'absolute light' shone by environmental protagonists.
Daily News (Halifax) 20 Oct. 1996: 22

(Here *activists* would be a better choice.)

ante- see ANTI-

anthem see O CANADA

anti-, ante- *Anti-,* meaning against or opposed to, is an extremely prolific combining form. New compounds formed with the prefix are usually hyphenated, while established words rarely are, unless the first letter following the prefix is *i* (*anti-intellectual*) or a capital (*anti-American*).

Anti- also has a second meaning, which sometimes confuses people: 'false' or 'reversing conventional expectations', as in *anticlimax* or *antihero*. An anticlimax is no climax at all and an antihero is a very unheroic protagonist.

The prefix *ante-* means before or in front of. Most *ante-* words are well established and not hyphenated: *antebellum, antechamber, antedate, antenatal, anteroom*. New words tend to be formed with the prefix *pre-* rather than *ante-*: 'preseason', 'prepackaged'. One might expect *antipasto*, a pre-meal appetizer, to be spelled *ante-*, but the word and the spelling come directly from Italian. Both *anti-* and *ante-* are usually pronounced *AN tee*. In American English *anti-* is sometimes pronounced *AN tie*, a pronunciation used occasionally in Canada.

. . . it is hardly consistent with the aims of the current government, which has shown itself to be heartless, anti-people, and pro-Big Business.
Toronto Star 1 July 1992: A12

(As a new coinage, *anti-people* is hyphenated.)

Using industrial materials like corrugated card-board and aluminum beading, Harding constructs anti-art sculptures that walk a funny line between poignancy and banality.
Vancouver Sun 18 Dec. 1993: D7

(Here *anti-* means completely unconventional.)

There can be little doubt that Hailey ransacked Crawford's article in order to find some of the words that Davis speaks in the *Playboy* interview, rather than vice versa, not only because Crawford's article ante-dates Hailey's, but also because of textual evidence.
Jack Chambers *Milestones* 1983: ix

(The word *antedates*, meaning precedes, does not require a hyphen.)

antebellum, antechamber, antedate, antenatal see ANTI-, ANTE-

anti-abortion see ABORTION

anticlimax, antihero, antipasto see ANTI-, ANTE-

antiseptic see SEPSIS

antisocial, asocial, unsociable The word *antisocial* usually describes destructive and violent behaviour. *Asocial* behaviour is not motivated by antagonism towards society or its members, but rather reveals an ignorance of or inattention to social conventions; however, *asocial* is commonly used as a synonym for *antisocial*. Although both words are used occasionally to describe shy or reserved behaviour, a more neutral alternative is *unsociable*.

Boys are especially vulnerable to antisocial acting out of problems when exposed to a violent father figure in the home. . . .
Mennonite Brethren Herald 7 March 1986: 5

'. . . are you concerned that we are going to become asocial animals all sitting in front of our computers living completely on the Internet and not ever being able to relate to one another?'
CBC News [transcript] 20 Sept. 1994

In the script, Nielson arrives at her posting a reclusive and unsociable person, but learns to open up and depend on the others in the little icebound community.
Calgary Herald 2 Jan. 2004: E8

See also ANTI-, ANTE-.

antithesis, antitheses see PLURALS, REGULAR, IRREGULAR, FOREIGN

antivenin, antivenom *Antivenin* is the original and proper name for an antiserum given to counteract the poisons transmitted by snake and spider bites. *Antivenom* is a popular coinage, likely motivated by the unfamiliarity of the technical word *venin* (which refers to any of several toxic compounds contained in venom). The popular and erroneous form of the word is easier to understand.

While a number of authorities have embraced *antivenom*, many prefer *antivenin,* and Canadian usage is split between the two variants. The best course of action is to write for your audience. While specialists will appreciate the correct term, the prime consideration in labelling a product that nonspecialists might need to use is ensuring that its purpose is clear. For a similar linguistic dilemma, where proper usage and public safety hang in the balance, see FLAMMABLE, INFLAMMABLE.

> A better understanding of what snake venoms are—and how snakes cooked them up over eons of evolution—promises better antivenins for future snakebite victims.
> *Edmonton Journal* 20 March 2005: D9

> When sailing, antivenom should be kept in a refrigerator, taking care that the temperature doesn't rise over the recommended storage temperature stated on the package of the vial.
> *Journal of Travel Medicine* 8.6 (2001): 309

> (Here, appropriately, the less approved but more recognizable word is used.)

See also FLAMMABLE, INFLAMMABLE, NON-FLAMMABLE, NON-INFLAMMABLE, INFLAMMATORY; FOLK ETYMOLOGY.

antler, horn Deer, reindeer, and moose have *antlers*, which are shed and regrown each year. Cattle, goats, sheep, and antelope have *horns*, which are not shed and which do not grow back if they are cut off. Antlers are branched, while horns usually are not. Antlers are found only on males in species of deer other than reindeer (both sexes of which carry antlers), whereas horns are borne by both males and females.

See also MOOSE, CARIBOU, REINDEER, ELK, WAPITI, RED DEER.

antonym see SYNONYM

anxious, eager The primary meaning of *anxious* is worried or uneasy. In addition, *anxious* is often used to mean eager or desirous. Some language commentators still condemn this use, even though it is common and can be traced back to as early as 1742. Since the 'eager' meaning of *anxious* is well established in formal Canadian writing, there is no need to avoid using it.

> Students get out of school and are anxious to have careers.
> *Vancouver Sun* 6 May 2006: C4

> (Here *anxious* means eager.)

any The pronoun *any* is used with both singular and plural verbs: 'Was any found?'; 'Were any needed?'

The adverb *any* usually modifies adjectives or other adverbs: 'any hotter', 'any less'. In Canada and the United States, informal usage permits it to stand alone in sentences such as 'You're not helping any'. This usage is considered odd and questionable in Britain.

Sometimes the adjective *any* and a singular noun are used with the plural pronoun *their*: 'Any member can bring their friends'. This usage is long-established, and the fact that it is non-sexist recommends it. However, some authorities still regard it as a violation of grammatical agreement, and thus it is not completely acceptable in formal writing (see the full discussion of this issue in EVERYONE).

> Is any of us so completely just, or merely so sobersided, that he can take the name 'Samuel Smiles' quite seriously?
> Robertson Davies *A Voice from the Attic* 1960: 42

> 'Are any of the opinions you express the result of

adjudged cases?'
William Teatero *John Anderson: Fugitive Slave* 1986: 148

See also AGREEMENT, GRAMMATICAL.

anybody else   see ELSE

anymore, any more   *Anymore* meaning any longer is usually written as one word: 'The falcons did not return anymore'. *Any more* as in 'I don't want any more, thank you' or 'Is that any more reasonable?' is written as two words. *Anymore* (one word) refers to time, *any more* (two words), to quantity or extent.

Not very many people know how to design a pysanka anymore.
Canadian Collector 21 (1986): 53

. . . a poet may talk forever about forests and prairies and snow and the Land of the North and not be any more Canadian than he will be Australian if he writes a sonnet on a kangaroo.
Northrop Frye *The Bush Garden* 1971: 131

The country we lived in was presented to us in our schools as colourless, dull and without much historical conflict to speak of, except for a few massacres, and nobody did *that* any more.
Margaret Atwood *Second Words* 1982: 378

(In this use, the recommended spelling is one word, *anymore*.)

'We'll be saying to the legislative committee on Monday, "Don't shove anymore of this debt onto us, we can't take it",' said MacKinnon.
Toronto Star 2 March 2002: A6

(When referring to quantity or extent, the correct form is *any more*.)

anyone, any one   The pronoun meaning any person is always written as one word: 'Anyone could have made that mistake'. If the word *single* can be inserted between *any* and *one* or can replace *one*, then the two-word spelling *any one* is correct: 'Any one of these candidates could do the job'; 'You can't blame any one person for that'.

Regarding the use of the plural pronoun *their* after *anyone*, see EVERYONE.

A month later, without telling anyone, he left for the United States.
The Beaver Feb.–Mar. 1990: 27

It could be any one of them talking.
Ottawa Citizen 7 Jan. 2006: E2

anyplace   see -WHERE, -PLACE

any time, anytime   *Any time* should always be written as two words after *at*: 'He could be called in at any time'. Similarly, the two-word form is required when it means 'any amount of time': 'She never has any time for herself'. In fact, the two-word form is correct in all situations, and one way to avoid difficulty is simply to write *any time* every time. However, *anytime* is common and acceptable in informal contexts in both Canadian and American English when it is used as an adverb meaning at any time: 'Drop in anytime'. *Anytime* is also commonly used as a conjunction meaning whenever: 'Anytime there's trouble, the police are at our door'.

'On the reserve, I'm used to going into everybody's house anytime.'
Province (Vancouver) 29 Nov. 1990: 83

Think of fibre optics and the imminent demise of the postal system; think of satellite transmission, ready and able to beam anything anywhere any time.
Margaret Atwood *Second Words* 1982: 390

(Here *anytime* would also be correct.)

'Anytime they have trouble with our community they try to define and divide it.'
Gazette (Montreal) 29 Oct. 1990: A3

(The use of *anytime* as a conjunction meaning whenever is informal.)

'The girls have never given up at anytime during the season and as they gain confidence and learn about each other, they will only improve.'
Windsor Star 2 May 2006: D4

(After *at*, the correct spelling is *any time*.)

At least two members—Gordy Mathews and Sue Leonard—haven't wasted anytime.
Province (Vancouver) 31 Oct. 1990: 56

(*Any time* is required here.)

anyway, anyways   *Anyway* is standard. Although *anyways* is common in informal speech, it is consistently labelled non-standard and should be avoided in writing.

> Anyways, the McGillicuddys and all the folks of the village feel better once they've vented their spleen on the politicians every morning.
> *Vancouver Sun* 8 Dec. 1990: B4

(Here, in a humour piece, the writer is imitating stereotypical rural speech.)

apartment   see SUITE

apex   see EPITOME

apogee, zenith, nadir   An *apogee* (pronounced *APP o jee*) is literally the farthest point from the earth or a planet in the orbit of a satellite; the *zenith* (pronounced *ZEE nith* or *ZEN ith*) is the point in the heavens directly above an observer. Both terms are used figuratively to mean either the high point or the furthest reach.

The *nadir* (pronounced *NAY der* or *NAY deer*) is the opposite of the zenith; it's the part of the celestial sphere directly below an observer. *Nadir* is used figuratively to mean the low point.

> Football reaches its apogee as the thermometer hits its nadir.
> *Calgary Herald* 23 Feb. 1993: A5

> The slap shot . . . produced glamorous new stars, most especially Bobby Hull and Frank Mahovlich, and a glamorous new image. This was the league's competitive and commercial zenith.
> Ken Dryden *The Game* 1983: 222

> And when things are at their nadir and the reasons for which you wrote your book appear to have come completely unbuckled from the result . . . you can always tell yourself that the pursuit of literature is a significant human activity.
> Margaret Atwood *Second Words* 1982: 406

apology, apologia   An *apology* is an expression of regret for having offended or hurt someone. An *apologia* (pronounced *app uh LOW jyuh*) is a statement defending and explaining a way of life, a system of belief, an institution, etc. An apologia may also be called an *apology*.

> Chris Cobb's vacuous apologia for Alan King's execrable May 13 cartoon . . . is probably one of the most twisted pieces of sophistry I have ever had the misfortune of attempting to decipher.
> *Ottawa Citizen* 20 May 1993: A14

(Here *apologia* means defence.)

> At the time of its release, the painstakingly researched document . . . elicited much public comment and a contrite apologia from police administrators. Police Chief William McCormack vowed that the mistakes made in the handling of internal affairs complaints would not be repeated.
> *Toronto Star* 15 Jan. 1993: A7

(An *apologia* is never an admission of guilt; *apology* is the word required here.)

> Julius Grey's latest apology for the legal status quo [exacerbates] the apprehensions of the Anglophone community.
> *Gazette* (Montreal) 21 June 1994: B2

(Here *apology* or *apologia* is appropriate.)

a posteriori   *A posteriori* (pronounced *AY*, or *AH, po steer ee OR eye*) is a Latin phrase that means 'by inductive reasoning'. Inductive reasoning is reasoning from observable effects to probable causes, as in 'The stove is off, yet the burner is hot. A posteriori, the burner was on recently.'

> It seems unfair to put *The Pegnitz Junction* and *Survival in Auschwitz* side by side: any memoir authored by a survivor is bound to have an authenticity and power that the fiction of an *a posteriori* observer cannot match.
> Janice Kulyk Keefer *Reading Mavis Gallant* 1989: 177–8

See also A PRIORI; LATIN PHRASES.

apostrophe   The *apostrophe* has two main uses: to mark a missing letter in a contraction (*ne'er*, *don't*) and to indicate the possessive case. Occasionally it is used to form plurals with odd lexical items, when the plural otherwise would be hard to read: 'I got five A's'; 'Dot your i's and cross your t's'; 'Mind your p's and q's'.

Note that the apostrophe is not the mark of an ordinary plural: 'No Dogs (*not* Dog's or Dogs') Allowed'.

The apostrophe was once commonly used with numbers ('the 1960's'), but now it is not required: 'the 1990s'.

> The RT100 is a mid-size package of 97cc's, with styling from the YZ series.
> *Canadian Biker Magazine* Feb. 1990: 16

> One of the most fun motorcycle do's I attended in 1989 involved people who have never owned or ridden a motorcycle.
> *Canadian Biker Magazine* Feb. 1990: 8

See also CATASTROPHE; CONTRACTIONS; ITS, IT'S; POSSESSIVE.

appal, appall, appalling   see -L, -LL

apparatus   see -US

apparent   Some commentators dislike the expression 'died of an apparent heart attack', pointing out rather facetiously that only real heart attacks are fatal. Less controversial, if slightly longer, expressions that make the same point are 'The man died, apparently of a heart attack' and 'The man died from what appeared to be a heart attack'.

> Twenty-nine rescuers, firefighters and plant workers died later from radiation poisoning and burns and another person died of an apparent heart attack.
> *Guardian* (Charlottetown) 26 Apr. 2006: B7

(Substituting 'died of *what appeared to be* a heart attack' here would avoid criticism.)

appeal   In law, to *appeal* is to ask that a case be referred to a higher court for review. The 'CBC Language Guide' states that one appeals a case; one does not appeal *against* a decision. General Canadian usage does not follow this distinction, however. People are described as appealing cases, rulings, convictions, and decisions as well as appealing *against* convictions, rulings, and decisions with about equal frequency. 'Appeal against' is common in Great Britain (Garner, *Dictionary of Modern Legal Usage*), while 'appeal a decision, ruling (etc.)' is common in the United States.

Appeals are allowed or dismissed in Canada and Great Britain; in the United States they are affirmed or reversed (Garner).

> Gibbings said the commission may yet decide to appeal the case.
> *Leader-Post* (Regina) 11 April 2006: A5

> . . . he plans to appeal both the conviction and the sentence, handed down late last week.
> *Edmonton Journal* 28 Nov. 1994: A3

> Salem and Bedi had separately appealed against their deportation from Portugal, arguing that they would not get a fair trial in India.
> *Winnipeg Free Press* 30 Sept. 2006: C10

> Three judges of the Nova Scotia Court of Appeal dismissed the appeal of [one man], but partly allowed the appeal of [another].
> *Daily News* (Halifax) 3 May 1994: n.p.

> For that reason, the Crown's appeal is allowed and a new trial is ordered, Cameron said.
> *Leader-Post* (Regina) 14 March 2003: F3

appear   see DUE TO

appear   *Appear* can mean either to become visible or to give a certain impression. When *appear* is followed by an infinitive ('He appeared to help'), its meaning is ambiguous. Substituting *arrive* or *seem* for *appear* will clarify the sense.

> But the Montreal native appeared to help as Pittsburgh rebounded from a 7-2 humiliation in Hartford 24 hours earlier.
> *Calgary Herald* 4 Jan. 1994: D4

(Here either or both senses of *appear* could be intended: the player in question *arrived* from the minor leagues and *seemed* to help his new team.)

appendix, appendices   see PLURALS

appetizer   see ENTRÉE

appraise, apprise, apprize   *Appraise* means evaluate: 'Real estate agents appraise houses'. *Apprise* is a formal synonym of *inform*: 'I apprised her of her rights'. *Apprise* is often used in the passive: 'We were not apprised of all the facts when we made that decision'. Although some dictionaries equate 'to be apprised of' with 'to be aware of', there is a subtle difference in emphasis: if you say you are not apprised of all the relevant facts, you are placing the blame on others for not having told you.

Apprize is an obsolete synonym of *appraise* and *esteem* or a misspelling of *apprise*.

> Elizabeth quickly appraises her clothes: jeans again.
> Margaret Atwood *Life Before Man* 1979: 134

> 'I sent Father Emanuel . . . to Rome for this special course so all the members of the committee might be apprised of the latest thinking and scholarship. . . '.
> *Edmonton Journal* 8 Jan. 2006: A2

apprehend, comprehend   Both words can mean understand, but their emphases differ: to *apprehend* something is to perceive or discern it, or to expect it with fear; to *comprehend* something is to have a thorough intellectual grasp of it.

> Other freelancers will immediately apprehend tax difficulties with depreciable business-use property that also serves for decidedly non-business candle-lit dinners. Any accountants in the audience, please write.
> *Globe and Mail* (Toronto) 2 March 1985: H4

> (Here freelancers can *apprehend* problems that they need an accountant to help them *comprehend*.)

> The judge said C—— lacked the capacity to comprehend what was happening, and give consent.
> *Calgary Herald* 21 Dec. 1993: B4

apprise, apprize   see APPRAISE

approbation, opprobrium   *Approbation*, from the Latin *approbare*, 'to praise', is a formal word for praise, approval, or favourable opinion. *Opprobrium*, from the Latin *opprobare*, 'to reproach', is a state of public disgrace following some conduct considered shameful, or the contempt and criticism directed at someone in this state. Some writers mistakenly use *approbation* as if it were negative.

> There are great numbers of people to whom the act of reading a book—any sort of book—is wondrous; they speak of the reader in the tone of warm approbation which they use otherwise when referring to pregnant women, or the newly dead.
> Robertson Davies *A Voice from the Attic* 1960: 253

> Yet, like Jackson, who left office shortly before his economic policies saddled his successor, Martin Van Buren, with a nasty economic depression following the Panic of 1837, Reagan seemed at every turn to escape major personal opprobrium.
> *Queen's Quarterly* 95.4 (1988): 802

> Yes, the apartheid government of South Africa was at least partially brought down via international boycotts and approbation.
> *Leader-Post* (Regina) 14 Feb. 2006: B7

> (The word required here is *opprobrium*.)

April Fool's Day   see NEW YEAR'S DAY

a priori   *A priori* (pronounced *AY pry OR eye* or *AH pree OR ee*) is a Latin phrase that means 'by deductive reasoning'. Deductive reasoning proceeds from something known, or assumed, to a necessary conclusion: 'It's raining, and I forgot to bring in the clothes. They're going to be soaked.' Some a priori arguments are purely theoretical. Though they unfold logically, they start from an untested hypothesis. Thus *a priori* is sometimes used negatively to mean not based in real experience.

> The United States, being founded on a revolution and a written constitution, has introduced a deductive or a priori pattern into its cultural life that tends to define an American way of life and mark it off from anti-American heresies.
> Northrop Frye *The Bush Garden* 1971: 218

> Hence Marx was trying to provide not a suprahistorical, a priori system but a historical-sociological method of inquiry.
> Irving M. Zeitlin and Robert J. Brym *The Social Condition of Humanity* 1991: 91

> Why must we accept, a priori, a definition of Canada and Canadianism supplied by people like Ford?
> *Calgary Herald* 18 Oct. 1993: A5

See also A POSTERIORI; LATIN PHRASES.

apropos The adjective *apropos* (pronounced *A pruh PO*), often followed by *to*, means pertinent, appropriate, or opportune.

Apropos of—or, less commonly, *apropos* alone—is a preposition meaning with regard to or concerning: 'apropos of our discussion', 'apropos our discussion'.

Occasionally *apropos* is used as an adverb to introduce a sentence, in which case it means by the way or on that topic.

While à *propos* is two words in the original French, in English it is written as one word with no accent.

Written 1600 years ago, it has never been more apropos.
Catholic Register 16 Aug. 1986: 2

'There's a constant search to make it more realistic, more apropos to what's going on on the street.'
Calgary Herald 12 Oct. 2004: D14

And apropos the rent we pay when abroad, what about reporting on our housing expenses, mortgage forfeiture or damage costs if we don't find the right tenants for our homes here?
Ottawa Citizen 12 May 1994: A10

(In this context *apropos of* is more common, but *apropos* alone is also correct.)

Apropos, having heard the Prime Minister on this subject several times, I am convinced there is no pride of authorship with regard to the accord.
Toronto Star 28 March 1990: A27

(Here *apropos* means by the way.)

And so I take this opportunity to . . . ask you to look inward—how a propos for the holidays, n'est-ce pas?
Gazette (Montreal) 28 Dec. 2000: C14

(The English spelling is *apropos*.)

apt see LIABLE

aq-, acq- Spelling mistakes are frequent in words beginning with *aq-* and *acq-*. Derivatives of the Latin word *aqua*, 'water', such as *aquamarine*, *aquarium*, *aquatic*, *aqueduct*, and *aqueous*, all begin with *aq-*, as does *aquiline*, meaning eagle-like. These are the only common words that begin with the letters *aq-*.

Acquaint, acquiesce, acquire, acquit, and derived words begin with *acq-*. These words contain the Latin prefix *ac-*, 'to' (also occurring in *accede, acclimatize*), which is a phonetic variant of *ad-* (*administer, adjoin*).

She enrols in school today and a week later leaves for the world acquatic championships in Rome.
Edmonton Journal 22 Aug. 1994: D4

(The correct spelling is *aquatic*.)

They aquire their commercial value after they've been cut and polished overseas.
National Post 2 July 2003: FP8

(The correct spelling is *acquire*.)

Arabic, Arab, Arabian *Arabic* is the language associated with Islam, a religion that originated in the Arabian peninsula (the southwest corner of Asia bounded by the Red Sea and the Persian Gulf) in the seventh century AD and spread through the Middle East and North Africa.

Arab is a loose term for the people living in countries that have in common the Arabic language and the Islamic tradition, including Arabic-speakers in Algeria, Egypt, Iraq, Jordan, Kuwait, Mauritania, Morocco, Oman, Palestine, Qatar, Saudi Arabia, Sudan, Syria, Tunisia, and the United Arab Emirates. Some people also consider Iranians 'Arab', though most Iranians speak Farsi (Persian). And some people would call Lebanon an Arab country, though much of the population is Christian. The terms *Arab* and *Muslim*, though related, cannot be equated (see ISLAM).

For contemporary ethnic, political, or cultural references, the adjectives *Arabic* and *Arab* should be preferred to *Arabian*, which is obsolete in these contexts. In current English, *Arabian* is used either to evoke the exotic image of the East that captured the European imagination in the eighteenth century with the translation of *The Thousand and One Nights* or to refer to the Arabian Peninsula as a geographic region, as in 'Arabian deserts', 'Arabian fauna', 'Arabian horse'.

Fluent in English, French, Italian and Arabic, she graduated from the American University in Cairo. . . .
Gazette (Montreal) 7 March 1989: C1

Its last shreds of support in the Arab world would vanish.
Guardian (Charlottetown) 19 April 2006: A6

One of the best of many North African restaurants to open in recent years, Chez Fatma is decorated Arabian style complete with tented ceiling and Arabic music.
Gazette (Montreal) 4 March 1989: T4

See also ISLAM.

arbitration   see CONCILIATION

arbitrator, arbiter   According to most dictionaries, *arbitrator* and *arbiter* are synonyms for a person chosen to decide a dispute. In practice, *arbitrator* is generally reserved for a judge in legal disputes, such as labour disputes or child-custody battles, whereas *arbiter* refers to judges of other issues, especially matters of style and taste.

Dates with an arbitrator have been scheduled, after two days of bargaining on potential wage increases at the airline went nowhere.
Province (Vancouver) 7 May 2006: A26

Despite the concerns and efforts, it is the viewer that remains the ultimate arbiter of Canadian and U.S. telecasting.
Globe and Mail (Toronto) 28 Aug. 1985: B5

. . . he associates value-judgements with class superiority—arguing that a critic who evaluates is an arbiter of taste. . . .
Queen's Quarterly 92.2 (1985): 382

arc, arch   Both words are used as verbs as well as nouns. To trace a curved path through the air is to *arc* or to *arch*. The past and present participles of *arc* are *arced* and *arcing*, rhyming with *barked* and *barking*.

Atlantis rose from its seaside pad at 9:56 a.m. and pierced a low deck of clouds as it arced over the Atlantic Ocean.
Gazette (Montreal) 1 Aug. 1992: A12

Starting near the foul line, Jordan . . . drove to his right, the ball rolling off his fingers ever so softly as it arched toward the net.
Leader-Post (Regina) 17 April 2003: C9

archaisms   *Archaisms* are words and expressions, such as *quoth, runneth, 'twas, methinks, thee, whosoever,* and *verily,* that are no longer current and have a strong air of the past about them. But they have not been discarded. They are common in legal and liturgical language—where they make the weight of tradition felt—and they are used for humorous, poetic, and historical effects.

See also DERRING-DO; HITHER, THITHER, WHITHER; QUOTH; YE.

Archbishop, Archdeacon   see RELIGIOUS TITLES

archetype, prototype, stereotype   In the seventeenth century, an *archetype* was an ideal version of something or a standard pattern from which copies were made. Since the early twentieth century, however, *archetype* (pronounced *ARK e type*) has been closely associated with the theories of the psychoanalyst Carl Jung. Jung used the term *archetype* to refer to those ideas, images, and symbols that he believed to be pervasive in human experience, forming part of what he called the 'collective unconscious'. Northrop Frye adapted the term to literary criticism, where he used it to mean an image or symbol that recurs so often that it becomes conventional.

Prototype is close in meaning to the seventeenth-century meaning of *archetype*. In design and manufacturing, a trial model of a car, for example, is called a prototype. Another meaning of *prototype* is the most typical example of a category: thus a robin is a prototype of the bird, while the earth-bound ostrich is not.

A *stereotype* is a fixed, simplistic—usually negative—image of a group that is applied unthinkingly to individuals. The usual adjective forms of these nouns are *archetypal* (pronounced *ark e TYPE ul*), *prototypical*, and *stereotypical*. None of these adjectives should be used to mean *typical*.

Rather than attempt a direct translation of Hearn's observations, Nakajima uses them as a springboard for her own exploration of mythical archetypes and rituals, helping them transcend their specific cultural roots to achieve a universal resonance.
Toronto Star 30 Oct. 1992: C14

Like the archetypal daisy pushing through asphalt, kids can refuse to be crushed by life.
Vancouver Sun 11 Dec. 1992: D6

Nearly five years and 5,000 prototypes later, he came up with a centrifugally forced machine with no bag.
Gazette (Montreal) 25 March 2006: H2

'But I do gravitate to forms and experiences that seem to be prototypical of their kind, that seem, somehow or other, to be imbued with an essence.'
Vancouver Sun 14 May 1995: D5

The typical family farm in Saskatchewan could one day look quite different from the stereotypical image of rolling wheat or barley fields.
Star-Phoenix (Saskatoon) 22 March 2006: C10

The stereotypical image of the Indian still exists within the business community, and contributes to the low number of natives in the workforce. . . .
Calgary Herald 7 Dec. 1992: B1

. . . what is archetypal of political correctness among media sophisticates is a failure to appreciate [that] the aversion to homosexual practices is strong and deeply seated in Canada.
Toronto Sun 28 Oct. 1994: 11

(The word required here is *typical*.)

See also INCLUSIVE LANGUAGE.

archives, archive   Large institutional collections of various types of records and documents valued for historical purposes are usually called *archives*, plural, as is the building in which the collection is housed. Either a singular or a plural verb is acceptable with *archives*: 'Where is (*or* are) the archives?'

Sometimes a collection of one specific type of material or a small, personal collection is called an *archive*, singular.

A Crown corporation, The Rooms is a cultural centre which houses the provincial art gallery,

museum and archives.
Telegram (St. John's) 29 July 2005: A4

One of my wife's musical sources was in the church archive of a small town.
Ottawa Citizen 1 Oct. 1990: A11

Arctic, arctic   The two common pronunciations of this word, *AR tik* and *ARK tik*, both reflect its etymology. *Arctic* is derived from the Greek word *arktikos*, 'bear', the name of the constellation of the northern sky (Ursa Major). In the 1400s, the English spelling of the word was *artic*, influenced by Old French *artique*. In the 1600s, however, Classical scholars became aware that the original Greek word contained an additional *c* or *k*, and they corrected the spelling to *arctic*. Many Canadians say *AR tik*, especially in informal speech, but *ARK tik* is the recommended pronunciation.

Arctic is usually capitalized when it refers specifically to the region bounded by the Arctic Circle ('the Arctic', 'Arctic tundra') and uncapitalized when it refers to extreme cold ('arctic gear', 'arctic blast').

The two ships, the Erebus and the Terror, reached the Canadian Arctic, only to be repeatedly trapped in ice.
Calgary Herald 30 June 1994: A8

You tromp down the low embankment, your legs sinking in snow up to your shins, and then enter the arctic embrace of the woods.
Canadian Fiction 97/98 (2000): 115

are   see ADJECTIVES AND ADVERBS; AGREEMENT, GRAMMATICAL; AIN'T, AREN'T I

aren't   see AIN'T; CONTRACTIONS

argot   see COLLOQUIAL

argument   see -E

armed forces   see CANADIAN ARMED FORCES

armoury, armory, armo(u)ries   In Canadian and American English, *armoury* and *armory* are alternative spellings for a stockpile of weapons or a place where weapons are stored. *Armory* is the usual spelling in the United States; both spellings are common in Canada.

In Canadian English, the building where the militia trains is often referred to in the plural as the *armo(u)ries*. In American English, the local headquarters of the military reserve is the *armory*, singular.

In British English *armory* and *armoury* are two different words. *Armory* is a synonym of *heraldry*, the art of designing and assigning coats of arms, while an *armoury* is a stockpile of weapons or a place where weapons are kept.

> And, on Saturday night, there will be period dances at the Lansdowne Park Coliseum and the armouries in Hull.
> *Ottawa Citizen* 1 June 1994: B3

See also SPELLING, CANADIAN.

army   see CANADIAN ARMED FORCES

around, round   The use of *around* to mean approximately ('around fifty') is common in speech and informal writing. However, this expression is rare in formal writing.

In most contexts where Canadians and Americans say *around* ('around the corner', 'turn around'), British speakers are more likely to say *round*, but both variants are used on both sides of the Atlantic.

> Around three percentage points were added to banks' prime loans, one-year mortgages and other short-term credits.
> *Toronto Star* 30 March 1994: C2

See also ALL-ROUND, ALL-AROUND.

arrogate   see ABROGATE

artful   see ARTISTIC

article   see A, AN; THE, A, AN; entry in Glossary

artificial, synthetic   Any product or situation that humans manufacture or contrive to resemble something natural can be called *artifi-*

cial: 'artificial flowers', 'an artificial island', 'an artificial scarcity'.

Synthetic has a narrower meaning. Synthetic products are specifically those created through the process of synthesis: that is, by combining chemical elements. Nylon and plastic, for example, are synthetic materials. By extension, any unnatural conglomeration can be called *synthetic*.

Both *artificial* and *synthetic* may refer to insincere or affected human behaviour, but *artificial* is far more common in this sense.

Synthetic does not have connotations of artificiality when it refers to a person's thinking; synthetic thinking is comprehensive, capable of linking and consolidating diverse ideas.

> He had lost a leg in World War I, and though he managed remarkably well with an artificial leg, he always carried a spare in case of trouble.
> George Ignatieff *The Making of a Peacemonger* 1987: 66

> The material, a synthetic blend that's a trade secret, has been used for over 20 years in medical devices, according to the manufacturer.
> *Horizons* 17.3 (2004): 22

> Watching this week's world figure skating championships in Moscow, one wonders why the scriptwriters went to such artificial lengths.
> *Toronto Star* 18 Mar. 2005: D3

> . . . Müller had not the same comprehensive synthetic grasp of the whole field as Darwin had, so that his work had nothing like the rounded completeness of Darwin's, which renders it capable of being easily held and visualized in a single view.
> R.A. Wilson *The Birth of Language* 1937: 29

See also ERSATZ.

artillery   see GUN

artist, artiste, artisan   An *artist* is someone who creates or performs works of art in music, painting, sculpture, literature, drama, dance, etc. The word *artist* almost always has positive connotations, implying great creativity and skill. It is sometimes applied approvingly to people who have remarkable talent in a field not generally considered to be art, such as cooking, clothing design, or hairdressing.

Artiste (pronounced *ar TEEST*) the French variant of the word *artist*, can be applied to singers and dancers without insult. But in other contexts *artiste* is usually derogatory: it's applied to people whose artistic sensibility is difficult to bear, or to artists whose pretensions are thought to overshadow their talents.

An *artisan* is a skilled craftsperson such as a weaver, a potter, a woodcarver, or a cabinetmaker. Artisans produce useful objects, which is what generally distinguishes them from artists.

> He was a great, creative jazz artist.
> Jack Chambers *Milestones* 1983: 88

> The Toronto-based artiste is best known as a singer/songwriter who turns out quirky, diverse albums like last year's Bombazine, which earned her a Juno nomination for best new solo artist.
> *Ottawa Citizen* 5 May 1994: C2

> I'm very glad when I see artists of any kind getting involved in social action. It's too easy to say, 'I'm an artiste. I don't have anything to do with anything that isn't my ah-t.'
> *Vancouver Sun* 22 April 1990: C5

(Here *artiste* has negative connotations.)

> After one experience with a temperamental artiste who chased him from the kitchen, Mirvish says he brought his parking lot attendant into the restaurant and had him trained as a cook.
> *Financial Post* 17 March 1989: 17

(Here *artiste* has negative connotations.)

> If handmade bracelets, brooches, necklaces and earrings are on your Christmas list, it's probably worth a visit to see the work of Toronto artisan Donna Polichuk.
> *Ottawa Citizen* 1 Dec. 1994: G4

See also ARTISTIC; ARTS.

artistic, artful, arty, artsy People who are *artistic* have a talent or affinity for art, while people who are *artful* are cunning, sometimes even deceitful. In reference to a creative endeavour, *artistic* means tasteful or successful, while *artful* means ingenious in design.

Arty and *artsy* are informal, sometimes disparaging adjectives. They always suggest a self-conscious connection to the arts, and sometimes they imply pretentiousness or triteness.

> I don't know who I got it from; neither of my parents was artistic, yet even as a child of ten I was drawing.
> *Saturday Night* March 1986: 34

> Like an artful politician, Farrell dodged many questions he didn't care to answer.
> *Toronto Star* 16 May 1995: B6

> [She] bought a pleated Issey Miyake 'because it was so sculptural and artistic looking.'
> *Calgary Herald* 14 June 1994: B10

> *Green Water, Green Sky* is composed of four self-contained sections linked by an artful fluidity of narrative line.
> Janice Kulyk Keefer *Reading Mavis Gallant* 1989: 80

> 'Bands I hate the most are ones that put out those serious, black-and-white, arty press photos with shadows, where everyone's looking in a different direction, and they've all got perfect haircuts.'
> *Ottawa Citizen* 19 Oct. 1990: D3

> We also meet . . . Broadway Bob (Steve Buscemi), who owns an artsy restaurant where one table is 'practically reserved for post-minimalists.'
> *Vancouver Sun* 5 May 2006: D3

See also ARTIST; ARTS.

arts, visual arts, performing arts, performance art, fine arts, liberal arts *The arts* include drawing, painting, photography, cinema, sculpture, music, literature, drama, and dance. The *visual arts* are drawing, painting, and sculpture. The traditional *performing arts* are dance, music, and drama. *Performance art* is an avant-garde mixture of drama and visual elements such as sculpture or video. The term *fine art(s)* is used to distinguish artistic work produced only to be contemplated from crafts and commercial art.

In a university setting, the creative arts are usually called *fine arts* to distinguish them from the humanities and social sciences (literature, languages, history, sociology, psychology, etc.), which are called *arts*. Canadians often use the terms *arts* and *liberal arts* as synonyms. In the United States, *liberal arts* has a slightly different meaning: it refers not only to arts but also to pure sciences, as opposed to professional studies such as engineering, medicine, and business.

> Recently, Saskatoon artist Cindy Baker set up shop in the Lounge for her Fashion Plate performance art experiment, whereby audience members chose fabrics and designs to build her an outfit.
> *Ottawa Citizen* 8 April 2006: L5

> She . . . soon realized that her talents did not lie in fine art, and switched to fashion design.
> Ann Davis *Somewhere Waiting* 1991: 4

> He had studied painting at the University of Wisconsin at Madison and graduated with a degree in Fine Arts before joining the faculty of the Manitoba School of Art in 1973.
> *Queen's Quarterly* 98.1 (1991): 11

> In January, some U of S professors and students held rallies to protest what they believe is the [neglect] of the university's liberal arts programs compared to the boost given to science and technology . . .
> *Star-Phoenix* (Saskatoon) 10 March 2005: A4

(In Canadian usage, the term *liberal arts* doesn't usually include the sciences.)

> Liberal arts refers to studies that impart general knowledge, rather than a vocation.
> *Edmonton Journal* 31 May 1994: B8

(Here the speaker is an American university teacher.)

See also ARTIST; ARTISTIC.

artsy, arty   see ARTISTIC

as   The use of *as* instead of *that* as a conjunction or a relative pronoun is a regionalism, obsolete in Standard English: 'She says as she's your cousin'; 'Folks as went on the appointed day got tickets'.

See also AS, WHILE, BECAUSE; AS . . . AS, SO . . . AS; AS BEST; AS FAR AS; AS GOOD AS OR BETTER THAN; BEING AS; EQUALLY; LIKE, AS; SEEING AS; THAN; TOGETHER WITH, AS WELL AS, IN ADDITION TO.

as, while, because   *As* frequently means while or when: 'Please sign the register as you go out'. Much less often it means because or

since: 'We stayed as we had no choice'. Some commentators object to the use of *as* to mean because, but all dictionaries recognize it as standard.

Generally, commentators who disapprove of the causal use of *as* think that it creates ambiguity. In the sentence 'She left as the speeches were about to begin', for example, *as* could refer to either the timing or the cause of her departure. Certainly in this sentence it would be better to replace *as* with *just as* or *because*. But this is a made-up and rather unlikely example. In actual usage, *as* often serves a useful purpose by combining the ideas of 'while' and 'because' in just those contexts where the two strands of meaning cannot be separated.

> Janet comes into the kitchen as he's sliding the casserole dish into the oven.
> Margaret Atwood *Life Before Man* 1979: 8

(Here *as* means while.)

> And as this is true of all of a person's central desires, our understanding of them can be remarkably fragile.
> *Canadian Journal of Philosophy* 31.4 (2004): 107–136

(Here *as* means because.)

> As the reporter listened, nodding, writing, offering no argument in return, Larouche grew more and more sure of himself, and gradually more angry.
> Ken Dryden *The Game* 1983: 144

(Here *as* means while—and possibly *because*.)

> As government expanded and the role of the bureaucracy in policy formation became more pronounced, restrained behind-the-scenes lobbying became the norm.
> A. Paul Pross *Group Politics and Public Policy* 2nd ed. 1992: 82

(Here again *as* combines the notions of while and because.)

as . . . as, so . . . as   'Sarah is not *as* tall as Katie' and 'Sarah is not *so* tall as Katie' are both correct. In the past, some usage guides insisted on *so* in negative comparisons. *Not so . . . as* was the usual construction until the twentieth century; now, however, it is much less common than *not as . . . as*.

Even so, the question about possible Reformation influence on the history of Ukraine is not as strange as at first it might appear.
Journal of Ukrainian Studies 28.1 (2003): 105

It is not so easy as it seems.
Ken Dryden *The Game* 1983: 178

See also COMMA; THAN.

as best, as well as [as best as]   *As best* in 'I will manage as best I can' is a fixed expression meaning 'as well as'. Either 'as best I can' or 'as well as I can' is standard but the blend 'as best *as* I can' is not.

. . . the graceless, neglected Lucie gets through the weekend as best she can. . . .
Janice Kulyk Keefer *Reading Mavis Gallant* 1989: 69

Is it any wonder then that the English literary community has finally taken it upon itself to nourish itself as well as it can?
Canadian Fiction Magazine 63 (1988): 5

'My job is managing the resources I have as best as possible.'
Gazette (Montreal) 2 March 1989: G5

(The standard phrasing is either 'as well as possible', or 'as best I can'.)

'At that point, I told him I would look into it as best as I could,' the officer told the hearing.
Edmonton Journal 29 March 2006: B3

(The standard phrasing is either 'as best I could' or 'as well as I could'.)

aseptic   see SEPSIS

asexual   see A-, AN-

as far as   *As far as* is becoming established in spoken English as a preposition meaning 'with regard to'. In other words, people are using 'as far as his attitude' instead of 'as far as his attitude is concerned (*or* goes)' or 'as for his attitude'. At present this usage is limited to speech and informal writing, and most commentators disapprove of it in writing.

Christian Europeans indulged in a series of crusades, military invasions, to the Holy Land but the result, as far as geographic knowledge was concerned, was minimal.
William Norton *Human Geography* 1992: 14

'But as far as drawing the final picture, that's up to me.'
Gazette (Montreal) 11 June 1994: H5

(Here 'as far as drawing the final picture *goes*', or 'as *for* drawing. . .' would be more widely accepted.)

Canadian coach Currie Chapman said Percy still is in the thick of things as far as winning another medal.
Calgary Herald 21 Feb. 1988: OA6

(Here 'as far as winning . . . *is concerned*', or 'as far as winning . . . *goes*' would be more widely accepted.)

See also WORDINESS, VARIATION.

as follows, [as follow]   The invariable form of the phrase indicating that information is to come is *as follows* (a shortened form of '*as* it *follows*'): 'The details are as follows: . . .'. *As follows* usually precedes a colon. The first word after the colon is always lower case unless the colon is introducing a quotation or a series of related sentences.

Bridget described her mornings as follows: My husband had already left for work by about six in the morning, so I had to get the two kids up, fed breakfast, their lunches made, myself showered and fed. I had to take my eighteen month old to a neighbor, I had to drive my son to a daycare center, and then arrive at work by eight o'clock so I could teach.
Canadian Journal of Higher Education 34.1 (2004): 1

(Here *as follows* introduces a series of related sentences; therefore the first word after the colon, *My*, is capitalized.)

See also COLON.

as good as or better than   In speech, people quite often omit the second *as* in 'as good as or better than'. Some usage guides defend 'as good or better than' as idiomatic, but most criticize it as an example of faulty parallelism: that is, although the word *than* fits after *better*, 'as good than' is ungrammatical. In writing, it is probably safest to include the second *as* in 'as good as or better than', 'as bad as or worse than', 'as great as if not greater than', etc.

> . . . but members of the classics department could hardly have sympathized entirely with the view that if one must study old languages the claims of Sanskrit were as good as or better than those of Greek or Latin.
> Hilda Neatby *Queen's University* 1 (1978): 174

> Health care is just as good if not better than in Ontario. . . .
> *Canadian Business* 27 Oct. 2003

(The second *as* should be included: 'as good *as* if not better than'.)

See also EQUALLY; PARALLELISM.

as how   see BEING AS; SEEING AS

Asia, South Asia, Southeast Asia, Far East
Europe and Asia are considered separate continents, even though they form a continuous land mass. Tradition separates them in the north at the Ural mountains. To the south, the dividing line is the Caucasus mountains, between the Black and Caspian seas. Turkey and the countries of the Middle East are considered part of Asia, as is the island of Cyprus. At the eastern end of the continent, the large islands of Java, Borneo, and Sumatra and the smaller islands near them are considered part of Asia, while New Guinea is associated with Australia.

South Asia is a common term for the countries of the Indian subcontinent, separated from the north by the Himalayas, including India, Pakistan, Sri Lanka, Nepal, Bhutan, and Bangladesh. The peoples of this area can be referred to as South Asians.

Southeast Asia includes the countries of Burma, Cambodia, Thailand, Malaysia, Singapore, Vietnam, Laos, Indonesia, and the Philippines.

The *Far East* includes China, Japan, North and South Korea, and Taiwan.

See also INDIAN.

as me, as I   see THAN

asocial   see ANTISOCIAL

asphalt   The first and often the only pronunciation given in dictionaries for *asphalt* is ASS *fault*. However, ASH *fault* is also widely heard. In fact, the 'Survey of Vancouver English' (1984) found it to be twice as common as ASS *fault*. Some people who say ASH *fault* may mistakenly think that ashes are an ingredient in this tarry paving material; others may simply be trying not to sound rude.

aspic   see JELLO

as regards   see IN REGARD[S] TO

assault, battery   In general usage, the word *assault* suggests physical violence, unless it is clearly a figure of speech: 'His tie was an assault on good taste'. The legal meaning of *assault* is somewhat different. An assault may not be particularly violent, and the charge of assault includes gestures that threaten violence as well as forcible physical contact.

Assault-related criminal charges include *aggravated assault*, in which the intention is to cause serious physical harm but not death; *common assault*, in which the physical harm—or the threat of physical harm—is less serious; *assault with a weapon*; and *sexual assault*, in which the intention is to violate a person's sexual integrity.

In civil law, which deals with legal actions between individuals, such as suits for damages, the offences of *assault* and *battery* are distinguished. These offences usually, but not invariably, occur together. *Assault* involves causing someone to fear that he or she will be harmed. Thus an assault can occur whether or not there was any physical contact and whether or not the defendant had any intention of carrying out the threats. Physically harming someone is *battery*. It is possible for one assault to incur both criminal charges and a civil action.

> Police said they charged [one man] with assault because he admitted at the scene having beaten [another man].
> *Globe and Mail* (Toronto) 1 Jan. 1985: P1

(Here *assault* is a criminal charge.)

The suit charges [him] with assault and battery, intentional shooting and intentional infliction of emotional pain. . . .
Globe and Mail (Toronto) 30 Jan. 1985: P11

(Here *assault* and *battery* are offences named in a civil action.)

See also AGGRAVATE, AGGRAVATION.

assay, essay The verbs *assay* and *essay* are usually pronounced with the stress on the second syllable: *a SAY, eh SAY*. Both verbs mean to try. Contemporary writers use *assay* to mean try in the sense of test or evaluate, and *essay* to mean try in the sense of attempt. *Assay* is used most often in scientific and medical writing. To *assay* a blood sample or a mineral ore is to determine the concentration of particular factors or ingredients. The verb *essay*, as in 'I will essay to improve', is now uncommon enough in everyday language that most dictionaries label it formal or literary.

The company says it has extracted a 9,100-tonne bulk sample and assayed the ore. . . . Assay results are still preliminary.
Calgary Herald 15 Sept. 1994: E6

Like prospectors seeking the faintest glimmer of gold, they fanned out across the nation's heartland last week to assay the national soul.
Maclean's 18 Feb. 1991: A22

Fostering an exchange of ideas, presenting new perspectives, essaying new approaches to issues— these are defining qualities of documentary film-making.
Daily News (Halifax) 21 Nov. 1992: 15

. . . when the immortal Bjorn Borg assayed a comeback at Monte Carlo, some young players actually laughed when the racket Borg brought out was a wooden Donnay model he had won numerous Wimbledon and French Open titles with barely a decade ago.
Maclean's 3 June 1991: A57

(The 'attempted' sense is spelled *essayed*.)

assertive see AGGRESSIVE

as such The phrase *as such* means 'in itself': 'The author's main subject is not geology as such but geologists'. A second standard meaning of *as such* is 'being so': in the sentences below *as such* refers to a particular preceding adjective or noun phrase (italicized).

They have made their studies *openly available* and as such open to independent scrutiny.

I became *part of his future* and accepted my life as such.

As such is criticized when it occurs at the beginning of a sentence or clause. In this position, it means 'therefore' or 'this being so' and relates to the whole of the preceding statement. While this use is far too common in academic writing to be labelled nonstandard, it is often awkward, particularly after the conjunction *and*.

Several of the chemicals in wood residue leachate are found at levels equal to or higher than that of raw municipal sewage. As such, wood residue leachate has the potential to harm the environment. . . .
'Fact Sheet' Ontario Ministry of the Environment website June 2006

(The use of *as such* to mean 'therefore' has been criticized but is very common in formal and academic writing.)

Poor parenting and violence cuts across all socio-economic levels of the community and as such, empathy needs to be fostered in all children.
Orbit: OISE/UT's Magazine for Schools 34.2 (2004): 39

(Readers may expect *as such* to refer to 'poor parenting and violence'. Replacing *as such* with *thus* or *therefore* would improve this sentence.)

assure see INSURE

asterisk The star-shaped *asterisk* (*) is often used in short, informal texts to mark a footnote. Linguists use this symbol to mark a hypothetical, reconstructed form in an ancient language or a rule-breaking utterance in a contemporary language: for example, '*Run they'. A line of asterisks can mark a long omission in quoted material (although style guides now recommend a line of periods). In a work of fiction, a line of asterisks may signal an abrupt shift in the narrative.

Asterisk is sometimes misspelled *asterick* or *asterix*. The standard pronunciation is *ASS tuh risk*.

as well   see ALSO, AS WELL

as well as   see AS BEST; TOGETHER WITH

-(at)able   see -ABLE

Athabascan, Athapaskan, Athabaskan, Na-Dene   *Athabascan* is derived from the Cree word for the territory drained by the Athabasca River. *Athabasca(n)* is the spelling most common in place names. *Athapaskan* or, less commonly, *Athabaskan* is the name of a family of Aboriginal languages. There are about fifteen different Athapaskan languages, including Chipewyan and Dogrib. They are spoken by some 12,000 people in Canada in a subarctic area that runs through northern and central BC and subarctic Yukon and Northwest Territories. Many speakers of Athapaskan languages identify themselves as belonging to the Dene Nation of the Mackenzie River Valley and the Barren Grounds in the Northwest Territories. Many linguists now refer to the Athapaskan language group as *Na-Dene*.

See also ABORIGINAL PEOPLE(S); CHIPEWYAN; DENE; APPENDIX III.

atheist, agnostic, heathen, pagan, infidel, gentile   An *atheist* does not believe in the existence of God, while an *agnostic* isn't sure. The Victorian scientist T. H. Huxley coined the term *agnostic* from the Greek *agnostos*, meaning unknowable.

Heathen is a word that monotheists (people who believe in one God, e.g., Christians, Muslims, and Jews) have applied to polytheistic peoples. The word *heathen* has fallen from favour in contemporary usage because it connotes backwardness and ignorance.

The Greeks and Romans of antiquity were never referred to as *heathens*, though they were polytheistic. They were and are called *pagans*. In contemporary usage, some orthodox Christians use *pagan* as a blanket term for non-Christians—a usage that many non-Christians find offensive. On the other hand, some people who have pointedly rejected the major established religions in favour of pre-Christian traditions, such as wicca, happily call themselves *pagans*.

Infidel means non-believer and is used to describe someone who does not follow the prevailing religion of the country. Historically, Christians have used the word to mean Muslims, while Muslims have used it to refer to Christians and Jews. Contemporary fundamentalist Muslims also use the word for Muslim critics of the religious state.

Gentile, often capitalized, is a biblical word meaning people of other nations, that is, non-Jews. In contemporary English it's also used by Muslims to mean non-Muslim, and by Mormons to mean non-Mormon.

In my own education, it was my philosophy don at Oxford, an avowed atheist, who taught me most about one's absolute duty to pursue the truth above all else.
Toronto Star 26 Jan. 2003

My personal choice of inscription will be 'A militant agnostic. Gone to the great perhaps.'
Toronto Sun 15 Sept. 1994: 12

Studies probing oral history now uncover reports from the few early missionaries to remote South Pacific islands who took time to listen and record 'heathen' tradition, before displacing it with the gospel.
Canadian Baptist Feb. 1986: 63

But that's where Valentine's Day has its roots—in ancient Rome and the pagan festival of Lupercalia.
Toronto Star 14 Feb. 1994: E1

As a teenager, Adler visited churches and synagogues but finally found the right religion for herself in 1971, joining the neo-pagan movement.
Calgary Herald 16 May 1992: E10

Thousands of Muslim fundamentalists, demanding [that] a feminist writer be put to death as a blaspheming infidel, clashed with opponents and

police Thursday in the streets of Bangladesh's capital.
Gazette (Montreal) 2 July 1994: A12

This book tells the story of what may be called the major 'race riot' of Canadian history, in which hundreds if not thousands of Jewish and Gentile Torontonians fought on the streets of Toronto on the night of August 16, 1933.
Canadian Journal of Sociology 14.2 (1989): 239

athlete, athletics   Sometimes people insert an extra syllable in a word to make it easier to pronounce. *Athlete* is one of those words. The standard pronunciation has two syllables: *ATH leet*. The three-syllable pronunciation, *A thuh leet*, is common but often derided.

Athletics has two meanings in Canadian English. It can refer to sports and fitness activities in general or to track and field in particular. The former is the common American usage; the latter, the common British usage.

Athletics can be followed by either a singular or a plural verb: 'Athletics is (*or* are) important to her'.

Chris Newman, convener of athletics for the HIAC, said the high school hockey schedule is slated to begin in early December.
Spectator (Hamilton) 28 Sept. 1994: D3

(Here *athletics* refers to all sports.)

Tom McIllfaterick of the Canadian Sport Council said it appears single-sport federations, such as Athletics Canada and Basketball Canada, lost five to 10 percent of their budgets. . . .
Edmonton Journal 1 Oct. 1994: H8

(Here *athletics* means track and field.)

See also MISPRONUNCIATION AND PRONUNCIATION SHIFTS, EPENTHESIS, METATHESIS.

Atikamekw   see INNU

Atlantic provinces, Atlantic Canada, Maritime provinces, Maritimes, maritime   The Atlantic provinces are New Brunswick, Prince Edward Island, Nova Scotia, and Newfoundland and Labrador; the whole region is called *Atlantic Canada*. The terms

Maritime provinces and *Maritimes* refer only to New Brunswick, Prince Edward Island, and Nova Scotia.

This distinction is important to the people of eastern Canada. Culturally and economically, Newfoundland developed independently of the Maritime provinces because it was a colony of Britain until joining Canada in 1949. Newfoundlanders and Maritimers take pride in their distinctive histories.

Maritime(s) is capitalized when it designates the Canadian region, uncapitalized when it refers generally to the sea, seafaring, and coastal regions ('maritime law').

Pulling keepers off 35 lights in B.C., 32 in Newfoundland and three in the Maritimes may save $7 million a year.
Spectator (Hamilton) 14 July 1994: A8

He repeats a thoughtful judgement on the conduct of most of the maritime fur traders.
B.C. Historical News 37.1 (2004): 12–17

at-sign   see E-MAIL ADDRESSES

attorney, attorney at law   see LAWYER

attributive nouns, false titles   Attributive nouns are nouns used in front of other nouns as modifiers: '*coffee* shop', '*football* coach', '*college* dictionary'. They are extremely common and generally unobjectionable. However, some commentators have taken exception to 'false titles': that is, strings of attributive nouns placed in front of people's names to identify them ('former world record holder Jim Ryun', 'jazz legend Oscar Peterson', 'Barriefield home owner Cynthia Harvey'). False titles (as opposed to genuine titles, such as '*Father* Boyle', '*Prime Minister* Campbell') are a hallmark of journalistic writing. They are useful because they convey information quickly and economically, and thus they're unlikely to disappear from reporting. But false titles are rarely found in other styles of writing. In literary, academic, and even conversational prose, the same information tends to be presented in a phrase or clause *following* the person's name: 'Jim Ryun, who held the world record . . .'.

That would be former Motley Crue drummer Tommy Lee, with whom she resolved an ugly custody battle in January.
Daily News (Halifax): 22 Oct. 2003: 30

(The sentence could be rewritten 'That would be Tommy Lee, the former drummer for Motley Crue, with whom . . .'.)

See also FUNCTIONAL SHIFT.

atypical   see A-, AN-

au   *Au*, which rhymes with *go*, occurs in phrases borrowed from French, such as *au courant*, 'up to date' or 'in the know', *au contraire*, 'on the contrary', *au naturel*, 'naked' or 'unadorned', and *au fond*, 'fundamentally'. These phrases are more common in breezy journalism than in formal prose, and some critics consider them pretentious.

Au is also frequently used in phrases describing styles of cooking: *au gratin* (topped with breadcrumbs or grated cheese), *au vin* (braised in wine), *au poivre* (coated with crushed peppercorns), etc.

'Our people are very much au courant,' Gentes-Ham said. 'They know that if the industry standard is a profit margin of 20 per cent and the taxpayer claims 10, then something is wrong.'
Ottawa Citizen 18 April 1994: A10

Au contraire: scientific communication is evolving quickly, and NRC Research Press is evolving with it.
Environmental Reviews 12.3 (2004): iii

Among desserts was a rich, dark, nutted chocolate mousse cake and good profiteroles au chocolat.
Gazette (Montreal) 26 Nov. 1994: T10

audible to the ear   see WORDINESS, VARIATION

audience, spectators, congregation
Audience is derived from the Latin for 'hear', and until the mid-nineteenth century referred exclusively to listeners. Today, though, the word *audience* can refer to the people addressed by almost any form of art or entertainment: a speech, play, concert, book, radio or television program, podcast, or painting.

Spectator is derived from the Latin for 'view', and although *audience* has become detached from its etymological connection with hearing, *spectator* retains its connection to seeing. It would seem odd, for example, to refer to the audience of a violin recital as spectators; rock concerts, however, with their emphasis on the visual, do have spectators. The people attending sports events are usually called spectators, while movies are viewed by spectators or audiences.

Congregation is used to describe those who assemble for a common and usually serious purpose: in particular, religious worship, but also political meetings, academic ceremonies, and so on.

This attention to detail makes the book accessible to an audience with little previous knowledge of northern Quebec and Inuit education.
Alberta Journal of Educational Research 50.2 (2004): 209–211

This is a North American phenomenon that has caused numerous problems for the art gallery audience and often in the art galleries themselves.
Queen's Quarterly 94 (1987): 561

The Puritans suppressed this sport, according to Macaulay, not because it gave pain to the bear but because it gave pleasure to the spectators.
Northrop Frye *The Educated Imagination* 1963: 41

'In a [television] series like Blanche, you know that 3 million people are glued to their television sets, but you still can't feel that special audience reaction the way you can by taking in your movie with 900 spectators.'
Gazette (Montreal) 10 Sept. 1994: C7

This is the first congregation of first ministers since Mr. Mulroney's Conservatives swept the Liberals out of office.
Globe and Mail (Toronto) 14 Feb. 1985: P7

audit   see FUNCTIONAL SHIFT

auger, augur   An *auger* is a tool for boring holes, or a spinning spiral channel inside a tube used to move grain, snow, etc. An *augur* was a Roman soothsayer. To *augur* means to bode and survives mainly in the phrases 'augur well' and 'augur ill'. The verb is often misspelled *auger*.

Kirchner's inaugural remarks, cabinet appoint-

ments, military purge and promises to clear the corrupt, right-wing Supreme Court judges auger well for the future of the country.
Canadian Dimension 37.4 (2003): 28

(The correct spelling is *augur*.)

aught   see NAUGHT

aunt   Outside the Maritimes, most Canadians pronounce *aunt* the same as *ant*, but Maritimers often rhyme *aunt* with *font*.

auspice, auspices, auspicious   An *auspice* is a sign, usually a favourable one. This meaning is now rare, although it survives in the adjective *auspicious*, which describes something that promises future success. The plural noun *auspices* is used almost exclusively in the phrase 'under the auspices of', which means under the protection of or sponsored by.

It was not an auspicious start.
Queen's Quarterly 110.1 (2003): 82

. . . family planning under the auspices of international organizations or individual countries in the developed sector runs counter to the best interests of people in the less developed world.
Queen's Quarterly 92.2 (1985): 254

See also AEGIS.

author   The use of *author* as a verb, as in 'She authored two books', is often criticized by commentators who maintain that books are *written*, not *authored*. Dictionaries, however, consider the verb *author* standard, and it is certainly acceptable in contexts where the verb *write* doesn't fit well.

A much bleaker voice authored her poems.
Margaret Atwood *Second Words* 1982: 288

(Here *wrote* would sound odd with *voice*.)

Allaire . . . authored the ultra-nationalist platform the Quebec Liberal party rejected when it supported the Charlottetown constitutional accord last year.
Toronto Star 5 Nov. 1993: A1

Picking up a provincial bronze medal in the national final examinations authored by the Canadian Institute of Chartered Accountants of Canada was Carri Clark. . . .
Calgary Herald 17 Dec. 1993: C6

Wilson has authored 11 books, including The Leaving, which won the 1991 Dartmouth Book Award for fiction.
Daily News (Halifax) 13 Nov. 1993: 22

(Here *written* is recommended.)

See also FUNCTIONAL SHIFT.

authoritarian, authoritative   An *authoritarian* person is overbearing, domineering, or tyrannical, while an *authoritative* one acts decisively and commands respect. Thus people look for *authoritativeness*, not *authoritarianism*, in their leaders. An *authoritative* text is either an edition of a classic that scholars consider reliable or a widely respected contemporary treatment of a subject.

'They talk about democracy but it is a disguise for their authoritarian ambitions.'
Ottawa Citizen 26 March 1994: B2

It is crucial, however, that the activities be supervised with strong authoritative guidance from an adult so that the situation does not provide further opportunities for victimization.
Alberta Counsellor 28.1 (2003): 27–31

Smart collectors of china don't buy so much as a bud vase before buying an authoritative reference on pottery and porcelain marks.
Vancouver Sun 25 June 1994: H6

His opposition to an elected legislature brought him into conflict with the reform movement . . . demanding an end to the authoritative rule exercised by the governor.
Telegram (St. John's) 6 June 2005: A7

(The word required here is *authoritarian*.)

automate   see BACK-FORMATION

autoroute   see ROAD

autumn, fall   In general, Canadian writers prefer *fall* to *autumn*, especially in the catalogue of seasons: spring, summer, fall, winter. *Autumn* is more common than *fall* in Canadian literary writing and in British English. Although the names of the seasons were once routinely capitalized, today they usually are not.

avant-garde, vanguard   *Avant-garde*, a term applied to jarring new styles in the arts and the innovative artists who introduce them, is often misspelled *avante-garde*. It may help to remember that the word before the hyphen is the French preposition *avant*, 'before'. *Avant-garde* is pronounced *A VON gard* or *A VONT gard*.

Interestingly, the expression *avant-garde* was borrowed twice from French. The first time, in the late fifteenth century, it was borrowed for its literal, military meaning (an advance guard or unit of soldiers that goes ahead of the main body of an army) and anglicized as *vanguard*. Today the expressions *vanguard* and *in the vanguard* are often used figuratively in political contexts.

> The Fifth Generation is an avant-garde group of Chinese film-makers who use the increasing artistic freedom to tackle subjects long considered taboo, such as sexuality, pacifism and capitalism.
> *Ottawa Citizen* 30 Dec. 1992: B10

> The European Community is a strong proponent of global environmental reform with Holland, Denmark and Germany in the vanguard.
> *Calgary Herald* 1 June 1992: A7

avenge, revenge   *Avenge* suggests seeing justice done, while *revenge* suggests getting even. To *avenge* usually means to seek retribution for an injustice done to someone else. The object of the verb can be either the person who has been wronged or the wrong itself: 'She avenged her sister' *or* 'She avenged her sister's murder'. To *revenge yourself* is to retaliate against someone who has harmed you.

However, not every act carried out on someone else's behalf seems impartial, and not every act carried out on one's own behalf seems base, which is probably why people also use the expressions *revenge someone else* and *avenge oneself*. Some commentators dislike these variants, but they are too common to be considered non-standard.

> Shiite militants have vowed to avenge the kidnapping.
> *Calgary Herald* 25 May 1994: A5

> And the scene from Titus Andronicus in which the hero revenges himself on Queen Tamora by serving up her two sons baked in a pie is dinner theatre of quite a different order.
> *Telegram* (St. John's) 24 Aug. 2001: B1

> There are also subplots as tangled as an Elizabethan maze—husbands spying on wives, servants revenging on masters, conspiring tavern owners. . . .
> *Province* (Vancouver) 24 June 1990: 82

(Here the idiom requires that *revenging* be followed by *themselves*.)

> There are two separate but linked stories—one about high society, the other about a journalist's quest to revenge his murdered daughter. . . .
> *Ottawa Citizen* 12 May 1990: D6

(Some commentators would recommend *avenge* here.)

average, mean, median   What in ordinary usage is called the *average* of a group of numbers is in mathematical usage called the *mean* or *arithmetic mean*. For example, in a group of seven people aged 12, 20, 27, 30, 43, 55, and 65, the *average* or *mean* age, 36, is obtained by dividing the sum of all the values in the group (the sum of the ages, 252) by the number of values in the group (the number of people, seven).

The *median*—which, confusingly, is sometimes also referred to as an *average*—is the middle value in a series of values arranged in order of size. In the example above, which lists an odd number of ages, the median age is 30 because there are equal numbers of people above and below the age of 30. In an even-numbered series of values, the median is the mean, or average, of the middle two values: for example, in the series 3, 4, 6, 92, the median is 5 (the mean, or average, of 4 and 6).

> . . . median incomes give a more accurate view of real earnings than average incomes because a wel-

fare recipient or billionaire living in a community could wildly alter averages.
Calgary Herald 23 July 1994: B1

(Here *average*, meaning 'mean', and *median* are contrasted.)

averse   see ADVERSE

avocation   see VOCATION

avow   see VOUCH

awful, awfully, awesome   Today the most common sense of *awful* is extremely bad or unpleasant ('awful food', 'awful weather'). The adverb *awfully* is most often used as an informal equivalent of *very*: 'She's awfully helpful'. *Awesome,* when used to mean 'great', is slang. While these common uses have been criticized for straying from the seventeenth-century meanings of *awful* and *awesome*—inspiring fear or awe—they are firmly established in the language.

Many adjectives and adverbs describing strong feelings have undergone the same kind of transformation as *awful(ly)* and *awesome*. For example, *dreadful, horrible, shocking*, and *terrible* can all be used to describe handwriting, and a person can be called *dreadfully, horribly, shamefully, shockingly*, or *terribly* late. Despite such hyperbolic uses, none of these words has lost the power to evoke intense emotion in serious contexts: 'dreadful devastation', 'terrible anger', 'horribly disfigured'.

When dinner came, the food was so awful he forgot one misery and replaced it with another.
Pierre Berton *The Promised Land* 1984: 114

In this funny and terrifying sculpture, banality achieves an awful apotheosis.
Vancouver Sun 18 June 1994: D15

(Here 'an awful apotheosis' means something like a terrible perfection.)

'The perogies are so awesome,' she said.
Whig-Standard (Kingston) 14 Jun. 2005: 3

(Here *awesome* is slang for great.)

He was greeted with an awesome sight: a 91-year-old three-masted barque, complete with 27 sails and 200 ropes.
Ottawa Citizen 17 Oct. 2005: C3

(Here *awesome* means awe-inspiring.)

awhile, a while   *Awhile* is an adverb. The one-word spelling is appropriate only where the phrase 'for a while' could be substituted: 'We chatted awhile'. The two-word spelling *a while* is appropriate for other uses: for example, after the prepositions *for, in*, or *after*, or before the word *ago*. This is the distinction that most usage guides uphold, although some accept *a while* as a variant spelling of the adverb.

Hensall has an attractive downtown that offers a variety of shops. Stop and rest awhile.
Leisure Life 1988: 36

You'd think I'd guess correctly once in awhile.
Star-Phoenix (Saskatoon) 8 April 2006

(Here a while is required.)

See also A LOT, LOTS, [ALOT].

AWOL, AWL   *AWOL*, an acronym pronounced *AY WALL*, means absent without leave. It was coined in the United States during the First World War to describe an unauthorized absence from military duty. *AWL* is the equivalent acronym in common use in the Canadian military. Unfortunately, *AWL* is also sometimes used in to mean absent *with* leave, which means this abbreviation is ambiguous and should be explained at first mention.

AWOL is the form of the acronym that has passed into casual speech and writing to describe civilians shirking work or duty. In a very informal use, *AWOL* sometimes describes *things* that are missing.

It took the army a while to discover that it had a bombardier gone AWL—absent without leave.
Legion Magazine Jan.–Feb. 2005: n.p.

Failure to produce a 'chit' during the week following the missed parade will result in the Nominal Roll/Attendance being changed to reflect an Absent Without Leave (AWOL) notation for the missed parade. A properly formatted 'chit' should

be forwarded to the AdminO by the SWO for filing upon receipt to ensure that the Nominal Role reflects the Absent With Leave (AWL) notation.
'Standing Orders 222 Shuswap' Department of National Defence website 1 Sept. 2005

(Here *AWOL,* meaning absent without leave, is contrasted to *AWL,* absent with leave.)

He is famously elusive and, even after signing on for a movie, has a habit of going AWOL just before shooting is due to start.
National Post 30 Jan. 2004: PM6

. . . the young quartet's sophomore effort . . . adds

an element of spunk 'n' funk that was AWOL the first time around.
Spectator (Hamilton) 8 Sept. 1994: n.p.

(Here *AWOL* means missing or lacking, a very informal meaning.)

axe, ax   *Axe* is the more common spelling in Canada, although *ax* is used occasionally. American writers prefer *ax*, but also use *axe*. The British use only *axe*.

axis, axes   see PLURALS

B

BA   see ABBREVIATION

baby bonus   *Baby bonus*, like *pogey*, is a Canadianism. In 1945 the federal government established the Family Allowance, a national family subsidy that, in the late 1950s, was informally dubbed the *baby bonus*. Since then this informal term has been applied to various federal and provincial child subsidy programs, including those that replaced monthly cheques with income tax credits.

Since Mikhail was born, his mother, Mary Anne, has been contributing his baby bonus cheques (now called the child tax benefit) to . . . an 'informal in-trust account.'
Edmonton Journal 13 April 1994: C6

True, the more children you have in Quebec the higher your rewards from the baby bonus fund, much of which is supplied by Ottawa.
Financial Post 20 April 1994: 3

Only a naif would assume that all of this new variant of the old baby bonus will actually get spent on child care, or indeed on children.
Toronto Star 21 April 2006: A17

See also CANADIANISMS AND CANADIAN PRONUNCIATIONS; POGEY.

baby boomer   see GENERATION

babysit   see BACK-FORMATION

baccalaureate, International Baccalaureate   A *baccalaureate* is a university bachelor's degree. The International Baccalaureate, commonly abbreviated as *IB*, is a prescribed program of pre-university studies and a set of examinations leading to a diploma that qualifies students for higher education in any one of several countries.
Some Canadian universities give university credits for IB courses.

The Department of French and Faculty of Education jointly offer a post-baccalaureate diploma in French and education, comprising a set of organized courses for practising or future teachers of French.
Department of French, Simon Fraser University website 2004–5

(A bachelor's degree is a prerequisite for this post-baccalaureate diploma program.)

The University of Waterloo recognizes that the completion of the I.B. Diploma is an excellent academic preparation for success at the university level of studies.
Admissions, University of Waterloo website May 2006

(The International Baccalaureate or IB diploma is a pre-university qualification.)

The University of Calgary awards a full year (five full-course-equivalents) for the completed IB Diploma.
Admissions, University of Calgary website May 2006

See also PERK, PERQUISITE, PREREQUISITE.

Bach see GERMAN WORDS, PRONUNCIATION OF

bachelor, ba(t)ch There is no *t* in *bachelor*, whether it refers to an unmarried man, a university degree, or a one-room apartment.

Batch with a *t* is an accepted spelling variant of the informal verb *bach*, meaning lead the life of a bachelor: 'Sean's baching (*or* batching) it while Melissa's away'.

bacillus, bacilli see PLURALS

back see DATES, AHEAD, BACK; RE-

back-formation Adding suffixes and prefixes to existing words is a common way of forming new words in English. *Revision*, for example, which dates from the early seventeenth century, is derived from *revise*, which dates from the mid-sixteenth century. *Back-formation* is the reverse of this common process of word creation: a new word is formed, when a suffix or prefix—or what appears to be a suffix or prefix—is removed from an existing word. For example, *televise* (coined circa 1927) is a back-formation from *television* (1907).

While new words formed by adding suffixes and prefixes often enter the language unnoticed, back-formations tend to attract attention. Some back-formations are humorous coinages that never lose their note of jocularity: *ept*, from *inept*, *couth*, from *uncouth*, and *gruntled*, from *disgruntled*. Some back-formations gain full acceptance fairly quickly: *automate*, from *automation*; *babysit*, from *babysitter*; *diagnose*, from *diagnosis*; and *escalate*, from *escalation*. But others continue to raise the hackles of commentators many years after they were coined. Still sometimes criticized are *emote* (c. 1917), from *emotion*; *enthuse* (c. 1827), from *enthusiasm*; *laze* (c. 1592), from *lazy*; *liaise* (c. 1928), from *liaison*; *sculpt* (c. 1864), from *sculptor*; and *surveil* (c. 1949), from *surveillance*.

A few back-formations have been formed by removing what only appeared to be a suffix. For example, the verbs *grovel* (1593) and *sidle* (1697) were created from *grovelling* and *sidling*, which people took to be the *-ing* forms of verbs. In fact, *grovelling* and *sidling* were directional adverbs (meaning 'face downwards' and 'sideways', respectively) with the *-ling* ending comparable to the *-long* ending in the adjectives *sidelong* and *oblong*. A contemporary example of the same phenomenon is the word *kudo*, a singular created by dropping the *-s* from *kudos*. *Kudos*, a Greek loan word meaning glory, is not in fact a plural. While *grovel* and *sidle* have long been accepted as standard words, *kudo* is not, because many people still recognize it as a back-formation based on a misconception.

The rally, organized by Margaret Atwood and Erika Ritter, will bring together the beautiful people of the word to orate, recite, sing, incant . . . against free trade.
Gazette (Montreal) 14 Nov. 1987: B3

(Here the deliberate use of the back-formations *orate* and *incant* creates a humorously irreverent tone.)

See also BICEPS, TRICEPS; BONA FIDES; BURGLE; COMMENTATE; EMOTE; ENTHUSE; KUDOS; LIAISON, LIAISE; ORATE; PREMISE, PREMISES; SCULPTURE, SCULPT.

backhanded compliment, left-handed compliment A *backhanded* or, less commonly, a *left-handed* compliment is one of two things: a criticism that, given its source, can be taken as a compliment, or a compliment that can also be viewed—and may have been intended—as an insult.

Although I sympathize deeply with Laurence in her current plight, I think that . . . it may be a back-handed compliment that the more reactionary elements of society find her work 'dirty and disgusting.'
Globe and Mail (Toronto) 9 March 1985: M12

(Note that dictionaries spell *backhanded* without a hyphen.)

'After the game, he said that I'd be the perfect quarterback for the CFL. . . . I thought it was a backhanded compliment.'
Gazette (Montreal) 12 May 1994: E1

See also COMPLIMENT, COMPLEMENT, SUPPLEMENT.

back of, in back of   In a survey of Canadian English-speakers (*Modern Canadian English Usage*, 1974), about one in six reported that they would say 'back of the house' or 'in back of the house' rather than 'behind the house'. But while the compound preposition *in front of* troubles no one, *in back of* and *back of* are contentious. British commentators tend to reject these expressions—or label them Americanisms—while American commentators staunchly defend them as standard. *Back of* and *in back of* are used by Canadian writers in informal contexts, especially sports writing; *behind* is used in formal prose.

The Oilers beat Calgary 4-1 last night and are now just three points back of third-place Vancouver. . .
Province (Vancouver) 28 Dec. 1990: 42

Driving into Dornhoefer, Robinson hit him so hard that the Flyer's body dented a section of boards, leaving it an inch or so in back of where it had been just moments before.
Ken Dryden *The Game* 1983: 95

back up, back-up   see PHRASAL VERBS

backward(s)   see -WARD(S)

backwoods   see FOREST

bacterium, bacteria   *Bacterium* is the singular of *bacteria*. It is common only in scientific writing, where it refers either to a strain of bacteria or to a lone micro-organism.

Bacteria is the Latin plural form. In formal and scientific writing, it is always treated as plural and used with a plural verb: 'These bacteria are clearly visible when stained'.

In everyday English, *bacteria* is also used as a singular noun meaning a strain of bacteria: 'They said it was a bacteria, not a virus'. This singular use has generated a double plural: *bacterias*. *Bacterias*, meaning strains of bacteria, is fairly common in journalism, but not suitable for technical or formal writing.

Once a bacterium possessing the desired DNA segment—or gene—is located, it can be removed from the broth.
Queen's Quarterly 97.4 (1990): 606

(Here *bacterium* refers to one microbe.)

Though wine is a 'living thing', where bacteria thrive, only those bacteria harmless to humans seem to survive in wine.
Bon Vivant Nov. 1981: 12

(Here *bacteria*, meaning strains of bacteria, is plural.)

Bt is a stomach poison, derived from a natural bacteria that kills the budworm after the poison has been eaten.
Globe and Mail (Toronto) 18 March 1985: M4

(In newspaper writing, *bacteria* is often a singular noun, meaning a strain of bacteria.)

'The electrical charge . . . inactivates all the viruses and bacterias. . .'.
Edmonton Journal 4 May 2006: E1

(The speaker quoted by this newspaper uses the informal double plural *bacterias*; in formal writing, *bacteria* would be better.)

See also FLU; PLURALS, REGULAR, IRREGULAR, FOREIGN.

badly, bad   The adverb *badly* modifies action verbs and participles: 'play badly', 'behave badly', 'badly suited', 'badly made'. In informal speech, *bad* often replaces *badly*: 'He's hurt bad'; 'We didn't do bad'. However, *bad* is seldom used as an adverb in writing, and it is not accepted unless it is seen as a deliberately folksy touch.

The verb *feel*, except when it means touch, is a linking verb, followed by adjectives, not adverbs: 'feel strong', 'feel hopeful', 'feel sad'. Thus commentators have disparaged the use of the adverb *badly* in the phrase 'feel badly'. Some commentators call it a hypercorrection; others, a genteelism acceptable in conversation. In any case, in writing, 'feel bad' is more widely accepted and far more common.

Mine is badly done and incomplete.
Canadian Fiction Magazine 64 (1988): 25

'Sometimes you do well, sometimes you do bad, and here I have not done as well as I had hoped.'
Vancouver Sun 13 Jan. 1992: D4

(In writing, 'do badly' is recommended.)

Sexual violence can make you feel bad, dirty, ugly, crazy or different.
Jennifer Jones *Making the Links* 1992: 3

Don't feel badly if you've never heard of it.
Edmonton Journal 19 Aug. 2003 E1

(In writing, 'feel bad' is recommended.)

See also ADJECTIVES AND ADVERBS; HYPERCORRECTION; WORSE.

bail out, bale   In Canadian and American English, to *bail out* is to dip water out of a boat, to make an emergency exit from an aircraft, to assist someone in an emergency, or to guarantee security for the release of a person held in custody. To *bale* is to bundle and bind hay, cloth, etc.

In British English, *bale* means bundle and bind, but is also the preferred spelling for all the 'bail' meanings above except the last, to guarantee security for a person in custody.

Both have failed to clean out patronage, and both emerged red-faced from attempts to bail out financial institutions.
Saturday Night April 1986: 16

Newspapers, cardboard, etc. are each baled separately, ready for shipment.
Vancouver Sun 11 June 1994: A3

bait   see BATE

baklava, Balaklava, balaclava   *Baklava*

(pronounced *BAK luh vuh* or *bak luh VAH*) is a rich Greek dessert made of flaky pastry, honey, and nuts. *Balaklava* (*ba luh KLA vah*) is a Crimean seaport and the site of the 1854 battle that inspired Tennyson's poem 'The Charge of the Light Brigade'. A *balaclava* is a woollen head and neck covering in the style of those worn by the Crimean soldiers.

The spellings *baclava*, *Balaclava* (with a *c*) and *balaklava* (with a *k*) are less common but also correct for the dessert, seaport, and hat, respectively.

bale   see BAIL OUT

baleful, baneful   *Baleful* and *baneful* both mean harmful, but *baleful* usually refers to looks or portents that threaten harm ('a baleful glance', 'a baleful indication'), while *baneful*, a less common word, refers to agents or results that actually are harmful ('a baneful role', 'baneful effects'). In some contexts either word is possible: 'a baleful (*or* baneful) influence'. Note that *baleful* does not mean woebegone.

. . . cinematographer Robert Elswit catches the baleful grandeur of Montana's looming mountains, turning the jagged landscape into a silent conspirator.
Toronto Star 30 Sept. 1994: C6

'Jean Chretien is playing in this fiscal matter the same baneful role he had in the constitutional debate, that of a destroyer disrespectful of democratic forms.'
Gazette (Montreal) 28 Sept. 1995: B3

Political correctness is widely seen as a baleful American import.
Gazette (Montreal) 14 Nov. 1993: B4

(Here *baneful* could also be appropriate.)

A harp seal stares at the camera with its baleful brown eyes; the seals are tame enough to pat.
Ottawa Citizen 21 Feb. 1987: G1

(Here *baleful* is inappropriate; perhaps *woeful* was intended.)

Balkan   see BALTIC

[ball out]   see BAWL

baloney   see BOLOGNA

Baltic, Balkan   The Baltic and the Balkans are both maritime regions of Europe. The Baltic countries are those, in *northern* Europe, with access to the Baltic Sea: Denmark, Estonia, Finland, Germany, Latvia, Lithuania, Poland, Russia, and Sweden. The Balkan region is in *southeastern* Europe, extending into Albania, Bosnia and Herzegovina, Bulgaria, Croatia, Greece, Macedonia, Serbia and Montenegro, and Turkey.

A story about Canada's Vimy memorial in France, on page A6 of Sunday's editions, erroneously referred to instability in the Baltic region. The reference should have been to the Balkan region. *Ottawa Citizen* 10 Aug. 1999: A2

baneful   see BALEFUL

bank, credit union, caisse populaire, trust company   Canadians often use *bank* as a generic term to refer to a bank, credit union, caisse populaire, or trust company—in other words, any financial institution that receives deposits, provides chequing, and offers loans. In fact, though, Canada has only six chartered banks—the Bank of Montreal, the Canadian Imperial Bank of Commerce (CIBC), the Bank of Nova Scotia, the Royal Bank, the Toronto Dominion Bank (TD Canada Trust), and the National Bank of Canada. Foreign-owned banks (e.g., the Hongkong Bank of Canada) are now allowed to operate in Canada, but the amount of business they can do in this country is restricted by law. Banks are owned by stockholders to whom their profits accrue.

Credit unions differ from banks in being cooperatives, which means that their profits are shared equally and jointly by all depositors. Members (i.e., depositors) can also borrow from the assets of the credit union. Some credit unions are public; others are associated with trade unions or other employee groups.

Caisse populaire (pronounced *KESS pop yoo LAIR*) is the French term for credit union. In Quebec there is a strong province-wide network of community Caisses Populaires Desjardins—note the *s* at the end of *populaire* in the plural—named after their founder, Alphonse Desjardins.

The original purpose of *trust companies* was to manage assets placed in trust by judicial order or through the terms of a will. Now, however, banks are also allowed to act in this capacity, and trust companies, which originally could not provide chequing services, now offer chequing accounts. Thus banks and trust companies are becoming more and more alike from the point of view of the individual customer; however, large corporate accounts are still handled only by the chartered banks.

barbarisms   In the past, some usage commentators educated in the Classics suggested that new English words should not mix Latin, Greek, and English elements. Words that fail this test include *television*, combining Greek *tele-*, 'far', and Latin *visio(n-)*; *speedometer*, combining English *speed* and Latin *metr-*; and *bureaucrat*, in which *-eau-* does double duty as the end of the word *bureau* and the beginning of the suffix *-ocrat*. Such supposedly malformed words were labelled *barbarisms*. Fowler, in the first edition of *Modern English Usage* (1926), went so far as to suggest that the 'barbarism' *electrocution* 'jars the unhappy latinist's nerves much more cruelly than the operation denoted jars those of the victim'. Perhaps predictably, the idea that English coinages should be subject to the rules of Latin and Greek word formation has not survived the de-emphasizing of the Classics in school curricula.

See also LATIN PHRASES, FOREIGN PHRASES; PARAPLEGIC, QUADRIPLEGIC.

barbiturate   *Barbiturate* (a class of drugs derived from barbituric acid) is often misspelled without the second *r*—*barbituate*—and often mispronounced *bar BIT choo it*. The accepted pronunciations are *bar BIT chuh rit* and *BAR bi TYOO rit*.

bare   see BEAR

barely   see EVER; HARDLY

baroque, rococo Both *baroque* and *rococo* (often misspelled *rococco*) refer to artistic styles characterized by a rich profusion of details. In popular usage, *baroque* may suggest bewildering complexity, flamboyance, or a touch of the grotesque. *Rococo* (pronounced *ruh CO co* or, less often, *RO cuh CO*) suggests elaborate ornamentation.

Baroque and *Rococo* are often capitalized when they refer to specific historical periods, as opposed to styles loosely associated with them. *Baroque* designates a period in the seventeenth and early eighteenth centuries when European taste in art, architecture, music, and literature favoured an elaborate, decorous, and highly decorative style. In music during this period the orchestra and opera became established, and composers such as Bach, Handel, Scarlatti, Verdi, and Vivaldi flourished. *Rococo* is an even more ornamental style that developed near the end of the Baroque period, from approximately 1720 to 1780. In the visual arts it is characterized by curly decorative motifs such as scrolls and shells.

Boyle has been compared with absurdist and experimental writers like John Barth and Thomas Pynchon, but these stories are not as formally inventive, baroque or convoluted as Barth's or Pynchon's more challenging work.
Gazette (Montreal) 4 June 1994: 13

U.S. soprano Jennifer Casey Cabot is a wonderful Donna Elvira, her voice generous, abundant, suitably rococo in its curves and gilt-on-cream colors.
Vancouver Sun 21 March 1994: C3

UNSCOP ended up recommending a more clearcut, surgical form of partition, without the rococo details of the Rand plan.
Globe and Mail (Toronto) 21 Dec. 1985: D22

Caccini's tender Baroque aria 'Amarilli' after intermission was only a token nod in the direction of better music. . . .
Queen's Quarterly 94.2 (1987): 351

The garden arrangement is mounted on a mirrored pink and gilded porcelain rococo stand that Chilton first noticed stashed away in a drawer at the ROM years ago.
Toronto Star 13 Sept. 1992: E5

(Capitalizing *rococo* here would indicate that the porcelain piece actually dated from the Rococo period.)

Barrens, Barrenlands see TUNDRA

barrister see LAWYER

bases *Bases* is the plural of both *base* ('round the bases') and *basis* ('the bases on which these decisions were made'). The plural of *basis* is pronounced *BAY seez*.

See also PLURALS, REGULAR, IRREGULAR, FOREIGN.

basically see PUBLICLY

bass *Bass* has two meanings and two pronunciations. When it refers to a fish, it is pronounced to rhyme with *pass*. When it refers to the lowest musical range ('He sings bass'; 'She plays the double bass'), it is pronounced like *base*.

Take the 14-pound, two-ounce largemouth bass reportedly caught in Stoney Lake in 1948. . . .
Toronto Star 14 Oct. 1992: F8

By 2:15 the streets pulsate with the deep bass of car stereos cranked to the hilt.
Ottawa Citizen 4 Aug. 1992: A1

basset hound see DALMATION

batch see BACHELOR

bate, bait In the phrase 'with bated breath' the adjective is often misspelled as *baited*. To *bate*, a variant form of *abate*, means to hold back or reduce. To wait with bated breath is to hold one's breath with interest or anxiety. The phrase is a cliché, now most often used humorously. *Bait* comes from the Middle English and Old Norse for 'hunt'. To *bait* means to entice or lure, or to goad or torment.

It is an understatement to say that I awaited the decisions of my final choices with bated breath. As a matter of fact, my breath was so baited at times that I forgot to exhale.
Whig-Standard (Kingston) 29 March 2006: 8

(Bated is spelled correctly in the first sentence but misspelled in the second.)

You'll be surprised what you can accomplish if you refuse to be baited or put on the defensive.
Daily News (Halifax) 12 Aug. 2004: 32

bath, bathe, breath, breathe, cloth, clothe, teeth, teethe, wreath, wreathe In all cases, the shorter form (lacking the *e*) is the noun, while the longer form (with the *e*) is the verb. Thus, to *bathe* is to take or give a *bath*; to *breathe* is to take a *breath*; to *clothe* yourself is to cover yourself with *cloth* (in the form of *clothes*, unless you are on the way to a toga party); to *teethe* is to develop *teeth*; and to *wreathe* is to surround as if with a *wreath*. In the noun forms, *-th* is pronounced as in *thin*, while, in the verb forms, *-th-* is pronounced as in *these*.

In Canadian English, *bath,* pronounced like the noun, is an alternative form of the verb *bathe*. Canadians rarely use the verb *bathe*, as the British do, to mean take a swim.

Most of us . . . wonder why—just when we are sitting down to eat, bathe the kids, put in a load of laundry, finish that report—these people are bothering us.
Kingston This Week 10 May 2006: n.p.

Fahra Razak holds her three-year-old son Adnan as she baths him outside their tent. . . .
Windsor Star 29 Oct. 2005: A13

See also LOATH, LOATHE.

bathroom   see EUPHEMISM

battery   see ASSAULT; COLLECTIVE NOUNS

Bauhaus   see GERMAN WORDS, PRONUNCIATION OF

bawl, bawl out, [ball out]   To *bawl* means to cry loudly and uncontrollably. To *bawl* somebody *out* means to chastise them aggressively and thoroughly. The phrase is sometimes misspelled *ball out*.

'I'm going to go home and bawl my eyes out,' she said, 'but you better believe they're going to have

a force to reckon with these next four years.'
Maclean's 117.36–37 (2004): 68

In one incident his father, the coach, marched onto the field ready to bawl him out for not paying attention to the play, only to stop and admire the picture he'd scrawled in the dirt with his foot.
Star-Phoenix (Saskatoon) 19 July 2005: A1

BC, BCE   see ABBREVIATIONS; AD

BCer   see NAMES OF RESIDENTS OF CITIES AND PROVINCES

be   see ADJECTIVES AND ADVERBS; AGREEMENT, GRAMMATICAL; AIN'T

bear, bare   'She bears the scars on her arms' means that she lives with their presence. 'She bares the scars on her arms' means that she displays them. *Baring*, meaning revealing what is usually kept under wraps, is often misspelled *bearing*.

The Toronto Argonauts' Blue Thunder dance team rolled into Ottawa for Grey Cup this week, and 20 women dressed in midriff-bearing blue silk and silver go-go boots are hard to miss.
Ottawa Citizen 20 Nov. 2004: E6

(*Midriff-baring* is the appropriate spelling.)

See also BEAR, PANDA, KOALA; BORNE, BORN, BOURNE.

bear, bearish   see BULL, BEAR, BULLISH, BEARISH

bear, panda, koala   Though they look like bears, pandas and koalas do not belong to the bear family (Ursidae). In formal writing they should not be referred to as 'panda bears' or 'koala bears'.

See also GRISLY, GRIZZLY.

beat, beaten   The past tense of *beat* is *beat* and the usual past participle is *beaten*: 'The Sydenham team beat us last night, which means we've been beaten twice so far this season'.

Beat is listed as a variant past participle in some dictionaries, but not all. It's very common in speech ('We've been beat fair and square') but some commentators consider this use uneducated. In writing, it is safer to use *beaten* unless you are aiming for a conversational tone.

> Party members who sat out the federal election in Ontario—every New Democratic MP was beaten—are prepared to sit out the next provincial vote, too.
> *Toronto Star* 26 Nov. 1993: A1

> 'We got beat by the weather this year,' the chilled, wet and weary golfer said stoically. . . .
> *Daily News* (Halifax) 23 June 2003: 32

(In writing, the usual past participle is *beaten*.)

beau, beaux, beaus, belle   *Beau*, from the French word meaning handsome, has been labelled old-fashioned when used to mean admirer, sweetheart, or boyfriend. However, it appears fairly often in Canadian writing. The French form is masculine and thus the word usually refers to men only; but a gender-neutral use of *beau* has also developed. The plural is usually the French form, *beaux*, but *beaus* is acceptable. Both plural forms are pronounced *BOZE*.

The feminine equivalent of *beau* in French is *belle*, which has also come into English as a noun; it means 'the woman most admired for beauty', as in 'She was the belle of the ball'.

> . . . she married a couple of times (the first at 16, to a childhood beau) and has a 7-year-old daughter, Jessica.
> *Globe and Mail* (Toronto) 28 May 1985: F2

> Sleek lines, towering acrylic windows and the posh atmosphere make it the perfect place to take your beau.
> *Ottawa Citizen* 24 Dec. 2004: G5

(Here gender is not specified.)

> A comedy about the manners and mores of Manhattan debutantes and their beaux may sound as relevant as learning how to mix the perfect dry martini. . . .
> *Vancouver Sun* 5 Oct. 1990: C4

(Less formal but also acceptable is the plural *beaus*.)

> She plunges right into her mother's most personal diaries and exposes the young Belle of Berlin's dalliances with an array of men and women.
> *Gazette* (Montreal) 4 Oct. 1993: C5

See also PLURALS, REGULAR, IRREGULAR, FOREIGN.

because   One of the most widely known maxims of prescriptive grammar is 'Never begin a sentence with *because*.' Yet grammatically there is nothing wrong with sentences beginning with *because*, and Canadian writers, including some noted stylists, don't avoid them. The 'rule' was probably devised in the classroom as a way to keep students from writing sentence fragments beginning with *because* when answering questions.

Some objections have been made to sentences in which a clause beginning with *because* is the subject of the sentence: 'Because they don't listen to classical music does not mean they are culturally impoverished'. This construction is informal, and though common in speech, it is much less common in writing. In formal writing, 'That they don't listen . . .' or 'The fact that they don't listen . . .' is recommended.

When *because* follows a negative clause, as in 'They didn't join the union because they feared for their safety', ambiguity results. In this example, either fear prevented them from joining the union or it was something other than safety issues that compelled them to join. Intonation disambiguates these two possible meanings in speech. In writing, however, it's best to rephrase: either 'Because they feared for their safety, they didn't join the union' or 'Fear for their safety was not the reason they joined . . .'.

> Because I am a Canadian, my outlook may possess some novelty for readers in the United States, for my country sees not only the greater part of the books produced in yours, but those published in Great Britain as well—not to speak of our own books.
> Robertson Davies *A Voice from the Attic* 1960: 3

> Because the United States is the most powerful centre of this civilization, we often say, when referring to its uniformity, that the world is becoming Americanized.
> Northrop Frye *The Bush Garden* 1971: 247

'Just because someone's decided to get into sea kayaking doesn't mean that he or she is environmentally aware.'
Vancouver Sun 24 June 1994: B4

(In formal writing, 'That' alone or 'The fact that . . .' would be preferable to 'Just because. . .'.)

See also AS, WHILE; FACT THAT; REASON IS BECAUSE; SENTENCES, SENTENCE FRAGMENT, RUN-ON SENTENCE, COMMA SPLICE.

beck and call, [beckon call]   see MISHEARD EXPRESSIONS

become   see ADJECTIVES AND ADVERBS

beer   *Beer* is a mass noun pluralized only when it refers to varieties of beer ('beers with a high malt content') or is measured out in pints or bottles ('a few beers'). In Canadian English, *beer* has become a common alternative to the plural *beers* when drinks are being counted: 'I usually have two or three beer at the game'. It is odd for an irregular plural form to develop, and this one, which occurs even in edited prose, seems to be confined to Canadian English. Some speculate that the unmarked plural for *beer* has been patterned on *deer* (plural *deer*). Certainly, both entities figure prominently in the Canadian psyche.

They'd guzzle a few cold beer to take the edge off the day's work before heading back to the motel in Milligan to clean up.
Canadian Fiction Magazine 64 (1988): 97

Boyde has nights she comes home and isn't sure if she won or lost, and she hasn't had more than one or two beer.
Telegram (St. John's) 11 Jan. 2006: B1

See also PLURALS, REGULAR, IRREGULAR, FOREIGN.

Beethoven   see GERMAN WORDS, PRONUNCIATION OF

begin   see DOUBLING THE FINAL CONSONANT

begrudge   see ENVY

beg the question   The expression *beg the question* leads a double life. Usually, it means invite or raise the question. The phrase functions as a rhetorical bridge introducing a question that seems highly pertinent or obvious. In the field of philosophy, however, *begging the question* has a very different meaning: it refers to the logical fallacy of arguing in a circle. If you draw a conclusion from an unproved premise—claiming the truth of your conclusion because you have *assumed* the truth of your premise—you have begged the question. Here is an example:

Putting money for childcare directly into the hands of ordinary Canadians will create new daycare spaces. More daycare spaces will be available once a childcare allowance is instituted.

The second statement follows reasonably from the first. The logical problem is that the first statement remains unproved.

The philosophical meaning of *beg the question* is the older one, dating from the late sixteenth century. The newer meaning—now a century old—is frequently criticized because it is assumed that people who use the newer meaning are ignorant of the older one. Three factors weigh in favour of accepting the 'new' meaning. First, it represents a perfectly reasonable interpretation of the sequence of words *beg the question;* second, the coexistence of the newer and older meanings has not created ambiguity since the two meanings are used in recognizably different contexts; and, third, the newer meaning is by far the more common one in published writing at all levels of formality.

Some major dictionaries, such as the British *Concise Oxford Dictionary* and the American *Merriam-Webster Collegiate Dictionary*, list both meanings of *beg the question* without comment. In other words, the 'new', long-disputed meaning of *beg the question* has become standard.

. . .whatever the problem, it's bound to be expensive, which begs the question: Do mechanics also get special training in how to break bad news?
Toronto Star 25 Feb. 2006: G18

(*Begs the question* now usually means invites the question.)

Ultimately, the film begs the question: under what circumstances could narration offer salvation?
Canadian Journal of Film Studies 12.1 (Spring 2003): 16

'To say that a man is insane because he does not appreciate the insanity of his acts and is thus insane is to beg the question.'
Province (Vancouver) 7 March 1990: 6

(Here beg the question means argue in a circle.)

See also FOLK ETYMOLOGY; VICIOUS CIRCLE, VICIOUS CYCLE.

behalf, on behalf of, on the part of, in behalf of An action taken *on behalf of* a group is done for them. An action taken *on the part of* a group is done by them. *On behalf of* means as a representative of or in the interest of. *On the part of* means by or among. People often use *on behalf of* instead of *on the part of*: 'There seemed to be an unwillingness on behalf of the survivors to talk about the event'. This use is non-standard.
In behalf of is rare in Canadian English; it is used interchangeably with *on behalf of* in American English.

. . . I proposed a toast on behalf of the visiting Canadians to the Khrushchevs, 'our gracious hosts'.
George Ignatieff *The Making of a Peacemonger* 1987: 143

Running parallel to the concerted movement of women graduates for a women's residence was a growing interest on the part of men students in obtaining a social centre of their own.
Frederick Gibson *Queen's University* 2 (1983): 27

Rev. Gael Matheson has alleged that the gender bias on behalf of the Presbytery of Prince Edward Island led to her getting unfair treatment. . . .
Guardian (Charlottetown) 2 May 2006: A3

(The alleged bias is by, not for, the Presbytery. The expression required here is *on the part of*.)

behavior, behaviour see -OUR, -OR

behest 'At the behest of Elizabeth' or 'at Elizabeth's behest' means because Elizabeth asked. A *behest* is an urgent prompting, something between a request and a command. The expression *at the behest of* is sometimes mistakenly used to mean subject to or under the control of.

The guilt or innocence of a criminal defendant cannot be made less by reason of the fact that the criminal act was done at the behest of another.
Gazette (Montreal) 5 March 1989: B3

In continuing to assume that judging art is entirely subjective, whimsical or at the behest of some community consensus, we do it a disservice.
Calgary Herald 4 June 1994: A6

(Here 'subject to' would be better.)

behoove, behooved, behove What *behooves* you is what it is necessary or fitting that you do. The most common construction begins with *it*: 'It behooves the Senate to consult more widely'. *Behoove* rhymes with *move*; the past tense is *behooved*.
In Britain *behoove* is spelled *behove* and pronounced to rhyme with *rove*.

. . . the NBA wouldn't be coming here if it didn't think it could make money. So it behooves the league to make some concessions.
Toronto Star 20 Dec. 1993: A20

Despite the motion's failure, it behooved us to annul it at the following meeting so as to keep our record clean.
Gazette (Montreal) 21 Sept. 1994: B2

being as, being as how, being that, seeing as how These constructions are inappropriate except in writing that imitates very informal speech. *Because, since,* and *considering that* are more widely accepted substitutes. For example, 'Being as how he was going downtown, he offered to drive her' could be rephrased as 'Since he was going downtown . . .'; 'I wanted to go to the beach, being that it was finally sunny' as 'Because it was finally sunny . . .'; and 'Seeing as how we are friends . . .' as 'Since we are friends . . .'.

See also SEEING AS.

belabour, labour   To go over and over the same point in a boring or ineffectual fashion is either to *belabour* or to *labour* it. Canadians favour *belabour* in this context. British commentators prefer *labour* because, in British English, *belabour* is still often used in the older sense, 'beat vigorously'.

> I could go on, but why belabour the point?
> *Whig-Standard* (Kingston) 27 June 2000: 6

> 'I don't have to labor that point.'
> *Globe and Mail* (Toronto) 7 March 1985: P18

See also -OUR, -OR.

belated, late   *Belated* and *late* are synonyms in that both refer to something that happens after the usual or appropriate time. However, *belated* often adds the connotation of reproach or regret.

> His was one of several wartime appointments made in a belated attempt to appease public opinion.
> George Ignatieff *The Making of a Peacemonger* 1987: 11

> (Here *belated* suggests reproach on the part of the writer.)

> So I offer my belated appreciation through this letter to him. . . .
> *Ottawa Citizen* 11 Nov. 1999: A17

> (And here *belated* suggests a pang of regret at the delay.)

See also LATE, THE.

belie   The truth can *belie*, or give the lie to, a false impression. A false appearance can *belie*, or disguise, the truth. Hopes can be *belied*—that is, left unfulfilled—by the way things turn out. In each of these correct usages, *belie* implies a contradiction or reversal.

Occasionally *belie* is used like *betray* to mean simply show: 'His pallor belied his fear'. This usage should be avoided.

> Face Off has been created to belie the notion that Canadian information telecasts are bland.
> *Gazette* (Montreal) 18 Sept. 1994: F4

> But Avvy Go's modest demeanor belies the powerful impact she's having in Toronto's legal and social justice circles.
> *Toronto Star* 11 Dec. 1994: C1

> 'Trade! Trade! Find out where I'm going.' The remarks were in jest, but they belied a player's anxiety.
> *Calgary Herald* 18 Aug. 1994: C4

> (Here *betrayed* or *revealed* would be more appropriate.)

beliefs   see -F, -V-

believe   see DON'T THINK; -IE-, -EI-

Bella Bella   see KWAKIUTL

Bella Coola   see NUXALK

belle   see BEAU

belly, abdomen, stomach, tummy, guts
Belly has been labelled too vulgar and *abdomen* (pronounced with the stress on either the first or the second syllable) too clinical for general use. Nevertheless, both words are used in serious non-medical Canadian prose for the part of the human body between the chest and the thighs, including the stomach, intestines, and internal reproductive organs. *Stomach* is also used, especially in spoken English, for this portion of the anatomy ('The horse kicked him in the stomach'). Of course, more precisely, the stomach is an organ of digestion.

Most dictionaries describe *tummy* as a childish pronunciation of *stomach*, and many usage guides deplore its use by adults.

Guts meaning courage and determination is slang but very common in informal writing. *Guts* or *gut* can also mean intestines.

> Martha punches him in the face, then begins kicking him in the shins. She's hampered by the long skirt of her dress, so she slugs him, aiming for the belly, hitting him in the rib cage.
> Margaret Atwood *Life Before Man* 1979: 95

> One man was shot in the left leg, another in the

right arm and a third in the abdomen.
Gazette (Montreal) 9 Dec. 1994: A3

beloved   see -ED

benchmark, hallmark   A *benchmark* is literally a mark cut in a bench or board as a reference for measurement. Figuratively, it can refer to the standard by which any subsequent achievement will be measured: 'This research sets a benchmark in the field'.

A *hallmark* was originally a stamp certifying the standard of gold, silver, or platinum in a product, after Goldsmiths' Hall in London, England, where such stamps were applied. Today, *hallmark* indicates the distinctive or signature aspect of an object, person, or activity: 'Creativity is the hallmark of a great chef'.

Benchmark is sometimes used incorrectly to mean *hallmark*; remember that a benchmark measures future accomplishments while a hallmark defines past ones.

Hallmark, with a capital letter, is sometimes used in informal writing to mean trite or sentimental: 'a Hallmark portrait of the ideal family'.

What must Canadian manufacturers do to become the world's benchmark for delivering customer value and increasing productivity while sustaining profitable business growth?
Plant 63.10 (2004): 62

Today, a formal code of ethics is the hallmark of professionalism. . . .
Canadian Appraiser 47.3 (2003): 31

Such 'hopeful inquiry' was a benchmark of the Nova Scotian educators' approach.
Canadian Journal for the Study of Adult Education 16.2 (2002)

(Because 'hopeful inquiry' is a defining feature, *hallmark* is the better word here.)

If you are in the woods, or a field, on the shore, you can think Hallmark-card thoughts about the cycle of life. . . .
Daily News (Halifax) 20 Jan. 2002: 17

benefactor, beneficiary   A *benefactor* is someone who gives help, especially financial help, to an organization or an individual, while a *beneficiary* is someone who benefits or will benefit from something. The people who receive a donation or who profit from a situation are sometimes mistakenly referred to as 'the benefactors'.

He will also have to persuade the university's corporate and private benefactors to fund any potential expansion.
Ottawa Citizen 10 Sept. 2005: E1

The main beneficiaries of the law will be small and medium companies, which often can't afford to go to court to get protection from their creditors. . . .
Daily News (Halifax) 24 June 1992: 24

 . . . the Argo offence was inept as usual and the Lions, 3-8, were the benefactors.
Edmonton Journal 20 Sept. 1992: B1

(The Lions benefited: they were the *beneficiaries*, not the *benefactors*.)

beneficent, benevolent, munificent, benign   There is some overlap in the meaning of these adjectives. *Beneficent* means beneficial or, when used of a person, disposed to good deeds. *Benevolent* means kindly or full of good will. *Munificent* (pronounced *myoo NIF i sunt*) means grandly generous and is applied to both people and things. *Benign* means gentle or innocuous. Specifically in the medical context, a *benign* tumour is non-cancerous; it may be nonetheless dangerous.

 . . . one of the most beneficent technological discoveries ever made [is] penicillin. . . .
Queen's Quarterly 93.1 (1986): 92

In theory, that decision left room for an angel to come to the rescue, a beneficent someone who would resurrect the magazine as it was intended to be. . . .
Vancouver Sun 26 June 1993: C4

Marx was little concerned with humanity in the mythical 'original state of nature'; yet he did assume that, once freed from the corrupting influence of a class society, people would be benevolent toward their fellows.
J.E. Smyth et al. *The Law and Business Administration in Canada* 1987: 10

So it is, too, with the munificent pensions that MPs enjoy after six years.
Gazette (Montreal) 3 Nov. 1993: B3

His face was alert, yet there was a benign quality about him which reminded me of a medieval monk.
George Ignatieff *The Making of a Peacemonger* 1987: 130

Dr. David Doty, the ear, nose and throat specialist treating Kurchaba, said the tumour, attached to the inner ear, is benign. But it's still dangerous because eventually it will pressure the brain.
Times-Colonist (Victoria) 8 Jan. 1999: A1

beneficiary   see BENEFACTOR

benevolent, benign   see BENEFICENT

bereaved, bereft   The verb *bereave* has two past participles: *bereaved* and *bereft*. *Bereaved* is the form commonly used before a noun ('the bereaved parents') while *bereft* is used after a verb ('were bereft'). *Bereaved* almost always refers to the loss of a loved one; *bereft* commonly refers to other kinds of loss.

What good is causing more pain, a bereaved father asks, when you know first-hand the awful feeling of having lost a loved one?
Toronto Star 21 Oct. 2005: C9

But when the puck drops for Game 1 on Sunday . . . the series will be utterly bereft of the cultural baggage that has made the Edmonton-Calgary matchups magical.
Edmonton Journal 4 May 2006: A1

See also -T, -ED.

Berkeley   see DERBY

Bernese mountain dog   see DALMATION

beseech, beseeched, besought   The past tense and past participle of *beseech* may be either *beseeched* or *besought*: 'I beseeched *or* besought her to help me, just as she had beseeched *or* besought me earlier'. *Beseeched* is more common.

'Stop. Stop. Stop,' they beseeched in horror.
Vancouver Sun 15 Nov. 1990: B1

That's why they were invited—and repeatedly besought—to participate in multi-party talks on electoral and constitutional reforms.
Toronto Star 17 April 1994: C2

best   see OPTIMUM

bestiality   *Bestiality* is sometimes misspelled *beastiality*. This misspelling reflects a pronunciation, *BEECE tee al uh tee*, that is now well established in Canada and the United States. The only pronunciation that British dictionaries list is *BESS tee al uh tee*.

A subscription to Playboy, or some similar non-electronic form of titillation, would probably prove more erotic than FreeNet discussions on spanking, beastiality and breasts.
Ottawa Citizen 7 Oct. 1994: A12

(The correct spelling is *bestiality*.)

bestow   A gift, a talent, or an honour is bestowed *on* or *upon* a person. To say that a person is 'bestowed with' a thing is non-standard; one might say instead 'awarded' or 'provided with'.

It gives you information and, in subtle ways, information bestows confidence on the person who has it.
Daily News (Halifax) 21 Sept. 1992: 17

It was not long before his followers bestowed upon him the title der Fuehrer (the leader).
Irving M. Zeitlin and Robert J. Brym *The Social Condition of Humanity* 1991: 238

They gather, beginning at about 5:30 p.m., at a square in the city's financial district and are bestowed with an impressive array of literature and other goodies before the ride sets off.
Toronto Star 3 Dec. 1994: E6

(Here *provided with* would be better.)

bête noire   A *bête noire*, from the French meaning black beast, is a thing or person feared or disliked intensely. *Bête noir* is a misspelling; *noire* always ends in *e* to agree with the feminine noun *bête.* The plural, *bêtes noires* (both words end in *s*), is pronounced the same as the singular: *BET NWAR.* In formal writing this phrase should be italicized and its accent should be retained.

> We all have our betes noires. Mine was always mathematics.
> *Gazette* (Montreal) 19 Dec. 1993: A3

(In formal writing, *bêtes noires* would be italicized and would retain its accent.)

better, had better *Had better* is an idiom meaning *ought to:* 'You had better see for yourself'. In speech the word *had* is often dropped ('You better go'); in writing, however, *had* (or the contraction *'d*) should be included.

> 'We'd better go back inside.'
> *Calgary Herald* 16 May 1994: A3

better stores see ABSOLUTE COMPARATIVES

better than Some usage guides recommend against the use of *better than* to mean *more than,* as in 'We spent better than three hours in bumper-to-bumper traffic'. *More,* as in this case, is not always better. However, the usage is idiomatic and widespread. Though uncommon in formal writing, it is accepted in informal contexts.

> Skip Morris has been, for better than two decades, one of the top North American rod builders.
> *Atlantic Salmon Journal* Autumn (1990): 17

See also AS GOOD AS OR BETTER THAN.

between, among Many writers believe that *between* must never be used in reference to relationships involving more than two things or people. However, *between* can be used with more than two items in some contexts. In a sentence describing a relationship or difference between each of the pairs in a group of three or more items, *between* is in fact the appropriate choice. For example, in 'They discussed the issue of trade between Canada, Mexico, and the U.S.', *among* would not work.

Among is the better word to use when discussing relationships that are general or collective: 'The organization aims to encourage equal distribution of food among nations'.

In some contexts either preposition is acceptable.

> One of the things I've always admired about Shakespeare was that he distinguished between an African, an Ethiope and a Moor.
> *Toronto Star* 1 Jan. 1994: F4

> I have been a green card holder in California since 1966 but work between there, New York and Toronto.
> *Toronto Star* 1 Jan. 1994: H8

(Here *among* would not be possible.)

> . . . St. Laurent believed that most Canadians wanted their country to contribute to world peace and better understanding among nations.
> George Ignatieff *The Making of a Peacemonger* 1987: 108

> . . . Station 7 at Parliament and Dundas Sts. had the most calls overall, split between three trucks.
> *Toronto Star* 1 Jan. 1994: A4

(Here *among* is recommended.)

See also BETWEEN EACH.

between . . . and *And* is the word normally used to link items after *between. Between . . . or* (as in 'The choice is between you or me') and *between . . . to* (as in 'Between five to ten per cent are flawed') are not accepted in formal writing.

> . . . the Toronto Globe had daily, tri-weekly and weekly editions that together sold between 20,000 and 25,000 copies and were read religiously throughout the province.
> William Teatero John Anderson: *Fugitive Slave* 1986: 47

> Yet their albums sell between 10,000 to 20,000 copies.
> *Queen's Quarterly* 95.2 (1988): 299

(Here either *between* should be deleted or *to* should be changed to *and.*)

From Regina's perspective, cheering for the Moose Jaw Warriors or Vancouver Giants is like a choice between kissing your sister or being escorted to the prom by your mother.
Leader-Post (Regina) 6 May 2006: C1

(Here *or* should be changed to *and*: 'between kissing your sister and being escorted . . .'. Alternatively, *between* could be deleted and *of* inserted: ' . . . like having a choice of kissing your sister or being escorted. . .'.)

between a rock and a hard place   see SCYLLA AND CHARYBDIS

between each, between every   Some commentators disapprove of *each* or *every* following *between*, as in 'Between each sentence, she paused', or 'Between every play-off game, he went through the same ritual'. They argue that *between* requires a plural or compound object ('between jobs', 'between a rock and a hard place'), while the noun that follows *each* or *every* ('between every meal') is singular. Commentators who accept the usage consider it idiomatic and note that the noun following *each* or *every*, though grammatically singular, is notionally plural in meaning (see AGREEMENT, GRAMMATICAL).

Given how common *between each* is at all levels of writing—and how difficult it sometimes is to paraphrase—it seems quite defensible as an idiom. *Between every* is less common and seems to be avoided in formal writing.

There are three knots between each bead.
Maclean's 2 Oct. 1989: A62

Still, a large number of those in the crowd applauded between every movement of both pieces.
Vancouver Sun 25 Aug. 1990: D4

See also AGREEMENT, GRAMMATICAL; BETWEEN, AMONG.

between Scylla and Charybdis   see SCYLLA AND CHARYBDIS

between you and me   *Between you and me* is correct, though *between you and I* is often heard.

I is the subject form of the first-person pronoun; *me* is the object form. After a preposition (*between*, *about*, *after*, etc.), it is the object form that is required. No one is confused when only one pronoun follows a preposition: 'after me', *not* 'after I'. The general trend toward the use of subjective pronouns in object position is discussed in CASE.

The difference between you and your government is much bigger than the difference between you and me.
Toronto Star 7 May 2006: H10

'Between you and I, a nitwit wouldn't propose something like that.'
Vancouver Sun 24 July 1990: D1

(The accepted form is *between you and me*.)

See also CASE; HYPERCORRECTION; PRONOUNS BETWEEN LINKED VERBS.

biannual, bimonthly, biweekly, biennial
Biannual means twice per year. *Bimonthly* and *biweekly* mean every two months and every two weeks. However, *biannual* is often used mistakenly to mean every two years, and twice per month and twice per week are secondary definitions of *bimonthly* and *biweekly*, according to most dictionaries. In short, there is so much confusion around these terms that it's best to avoid them altogether.

Biennial means occurring every two years. Plants with a two-year life cycle are called *biennials*.

The CSA puts out a bimonthly magazine which reviews specific stocks and offers investment advice.
Toronto Star 26 April 1992: H1

(Since *bimonthly* is ambiguous, it would be better to specify either 'twice a month' or 'six times a year'.)

The backdrop was the New Democratic Party's biennial convention.
Toronto Star 1 Dec. 1994: A31

(The convention is held every two years.)

bias   see DOUBLING THE FINAL CONSONANT

bias-free writing see INCLUSIVE LANGUAGE

Bible, bible see SACRED WRITINGS

biceps, triceps, quadriceps, forceps *Biceps*, *triceps*, and *quadriceps* are muscles in the arms and the legs. The prefixes *bi-*, *tri-*, and *quadri-* describe not muscle groups but single muscles with multiple (two, three, and four) heads or attachments. Thus the words *biceps*, *triceps*, and *quadriceps* are singular: 'a rock-hard biceps', 'a torn quadriceps'.

Because *biceps*, *triceps*, and *quadriceps* end in *-s*, they look plural and have come to be used as plural forms: 'Both quadriceps were strained'. The word *biceps* has, in addition, two Latin plurals (*bicepses* and *bicipites*), but these rather daunting forms are rarely used. In formal writing, *biceps*, *triceps*, and *quadriceps* are the established forms for both singular and plural use.

The vexed question is the appropriate singular form in informal contexts. The use of *biceps* as a plural led—by the process of back-formation—to a new singular form: *bicep*. While the *s*-less forms *bicep*, *tricep*, and *quadricep* are all very common in informal writing such as sports journalism, they are not well accepted by authorities. The *Canadian Oxford Dictionary*, for example, lists *bicep* but cautions that *biceps* is the standard singular. Writers who fear censure should avoid the *s*-less singular forms even in informal contexts. But writers whose greater fear is sounding pedantic can rest assured that 'a bicep' is the majority informal usage.

The word *forceps*, like *scissors* or *tongs*, is a plural noun, requiring a plural verb: 'Forceps were used to deliver the baby.'

> . . . Kim Johnsson snapped a shot that struck a lunging Belfour on the right bicep before bouncing off the right post and out.
> *CBC Sports* CBC website 16 April 2003

(In journalism, the singular form is usually *bicep*.)

> Walter wore a red baseball cap for the trip; between the back of it and the top of his jacket collar his bristly neck bulged out like a biceps.
> Margaret Atwood *The Blind Assassin* 2000: 289

(In this novel the more formal singular, *biceps*, is used.)

See also BACK-FORMATION; NUMBER PREFIXES, GREEK AND LATIN; PLURALS, REGULAR, IRREGULAR, FOREIGN.

bid When the verb *bid* means to make an offer, the past tense and past participle are *bid*. When it means to command, the past tense is usually *bade*, and the past participle is usually *bid* or *bidden*. When the verb *bid* is followed by a greeting, the past tense and past participle are usually *bade*: 'She bade her friends farewell'. *Bade* is usually pronounced like *bad*, or sometimes to rhyme with *made*.

> His company had bid to build only the second one, due for delivery in 1993.
> *Vancouver Sun* 8 Sept. 1990: H1

> The light bade him lift his eyes to the heavens, where the Big Dipper blazed in the sky above.
> *Queen's Quarterly* 95.1 (1988): 171

> Now Sigfrid goes as she is bid to her bedroom.
> David Williams *Eye of the Father* 1985: 118

> Brian Mulroney has sacrificed his personal credibility—and, in my opinion, honor—by failing to find the time to say 'Godspeed' to the people he has bidden to voyage to the gulf.
> *Gazette* (Montreal) 5 Sept. 1990: B2

> With a mournful blast of its whistle, The Canadian pulled out of Ottawa for the last time Sunday as about 300 protesters bade farewell to a victim of the VIA cuts.
> *Ottawa Citizen* 15 Jan. 1990: A4

biennial see BIANNUAL

bigfoot see SASQUATCH

big shot see COLLOQUIAL

bike see ABBREVIATION

bilateral see UNILATERAL

billion, trillion, milliard In Canadian, American, and international scientific English, *billion* means a thousand million (1,000,000,000) and *trillion* means a million million (1,000,000,000,000). In British English *billion* was formerly used for a million million (what everyone else called a *trillion*) and *milliard* for a thousand million (what everyone else called a *billion*). Now, however, British usage is shifting toward the international norm, and *billion*, in current British government reports, newspapers, and financial bulletins, means a thousand million. Yet, in everyday usage, the shift in meaning is not complete, and some speakers of British English feel obliged to avoid the word *billion* or qualify it: 'an English billion' or 'an American billion'.

bimonthly   see BIANNUAL

binomial   see SPECIES, GENUS

birth name   see MAIDEN NAME

bisexual   see GAY

Bishop   see RELIGIOUS TITLES

bison, buffalo   In scientific terms, *buffalo* are large mammals indigenous to Africa and India, while *bison* are similar species indigenous to Europe and North America. In the past, North American bison were commonly called *buffalo*. Now the more precise term *bison* is more common in general use, but *buffalo* is still perfectly acceptable where confusion isn't likely to result. The *Dictionary of Canadianisms* lists nearly 70 historical compounds using *buffalo*, including 'buffalo robe' and 'buffalo wallow' (a pit made by wallowing buffalo). *Buffalo* has two plurals, *buffalo* and *buffaloes*; the plural of *bison* is always *bison*.

Occasionally *buffalo* is used informally as a verb meaning to baffle or intimidate.

> As recently as two centuries ago, 60 million mangy wood and plains bison roamed the west. . . . So effective was the slaughter that by 1893 there were fewer than 500 wood bison left.
> *Globe and Mail* (Toronto) 23 Nov. 1985: A8

> At the Mountain Lake Bison Range near Owen Sound, visitors can watch the buffalo grazing in the pasture.
> *Globe and Mail* (Toronto) 23 Oct. 1985: C6

> In brief, don't be buffaloed by the stories about the federal government off-loading its debt problems on the doorsteps of the provinces. . . . The reports of provincial pain are . . . without statistical support.
> *Ottawa Citizen* 24 Feb. 1990: A3

bite, bit, bitten   The past tense of *bite* is *bit* and the usual past participle is *bitten* ('has bitten', 'were bitten', 'got bitten'). *Bit* is a variant past participle, rare in Canadian writing, though not uncommon in speech.

> A 50-year-old Pointe Claire man was bitten by a mixed Labrador and German shepherd dog. . . .
> *Gazette* (Montreal) 15 Nov. 1990: I4

> 'I got bit by a poodle a while back and nobody wrote about how dangerous they are.'
> *Ottawa Citizen* 3 July 1994: A8

(In formal writing *bitten* is recommended.)

biweekly   see BIANNUAL

black, coloured, Negro, white, African Canadian, Africadian   As a term for people of African descent, *black* is common and widely accepted in Canada. This term replaced the now obsolete *coloured* and *Negro* in the 1960s. Some writers capitalize it to designate an ethnic group with a shared culture and common goals. *Black* is always capitalized in expressions such as Black English, Black Power, and Black Muslim. The opposite term, *white*, is normally not capitalized, because it does not designate a particular cultural or ethnic group. If you choose to capitalize *black* and not *white*, you should probably explain the reasons for this decision to the reader, who may find the inconsistency puzzling or annoying.

The term *African Canadian*, which parallels *African American*, has slowly gained popularity in Canada. Many Canadians of African ancestry are recent immigrants and prefer to use more specific terms, such as *Nigerian Canadian* or *Jamaican Canadian*. Since the black population in Canada is far more culturally heterogeneous than its counterpart in the United States, writers using *African Canadian* or *black* should be aware that these collective terms may obscure important cultural differences.

Africadian, from *African* and *Acadian*, is a term coined by the Canadian poet and critic George Elliott Clarke for those of African descent who live in the Atlantic provinces. Many Canadians are descended from the 3500 free blacks (escaped slaves and Loyalist soldiers) and the 2000 slaves belonging to Loyalists who came north to Nova Scotia and New Brunswick after the American Revolution.

> Today, blacks in the Sudbury area are active through several means, including the Afro-Heritage Association and a local chapter of the Congress of Black Women.
> *Sudbury Star* 27 Feb. 2006: A3

> I use the term 'Africadian', a word I have minted from 'Africa' and 'Acadia' (the old name for Nova Scotia and New Brunswick), to denote the Black populations of the Maritimes and especially of Nova Scotia.
> George Elliott Clarke *Fire on the Water* 1991: n.p.

See also CAPITAL LETTERS; RACE; VISIBLE MINORITY.

Blackfoot, Siksika The Blackfoot Aboriginal group lives in southern Alberta and Montana. In Canada, *Blackfoot* is singular or plural, while in the United States, the plural form is *Blackfeet*. The name is thought to refer to the dark moccasins the group wore. It is a direct translation of *Siksika*, the name of one nation in the Blackfoot Confederacy and of the Blackfoot language (in the Algonquian family).

> In 1977, MacDonald assigned him a documentary on how the Blackfoot on the Siksika reserve east of Calgary felt about the 100-year anniversary of Treaty 7.
> *Edmonton Journal* 9 April 2006: E6

See also ABORIGINAL PEOPLE(S); ALGONQUIN, ALGONKIN, ALGONQUIAN, ALGONKIAN; APPENDIX III.

blatant, flagrant, patent *Blatant* and *flagrant* are both adjectives commonly used to describe conspicuous transgressions. *Blatant* suggests that no attempt was made to conceal the offence, while *flagrant* suggests that the offence far exceeds the bounds of acceptable behaviour. In many contexts either word is appropriate.

Neither word should be used to mean simply obvious, as in 'a blatant cry for help'. In neutral contexts *patent* (pronounced *PAY tunt*), which means manifest or obvious, without the negative connotations, would be a fairly formal alternative. *Obvious* and *manifest* are also possible substitutes.

> In one of the more blatant cases of corruption, a team of Chinese archeologists from Changsha, central China, recently opened their own antique shop and sold 5,000 pieces of porcelain and jade before being found out by tax auditors.
> *Toronto Star* 20 Nov. 1994: A14

> Players who commit two flagrant fouls in a game will be ejected.
> *Ottawa Citizen* 1 Nov. 1994: C3

> '[The referee] was out of position the whole night. He also took a goal away from us, which was a blatant goal. . . .'
> *Vancouver Sun* 17 Feb. 1990: H3

(A better choice here would be *obvious*.)

blend   see ABBREVIATION

blessed   see -ED

bleu, rouge   *Bleu* is the equivalent in Canadian French of the English label *Tory* for a member of the Conservative Party, the traditional colour of which is blue. The radical reformers who opposed the Conservatives in Quebec during the 1850s and 1860s were known as the 'Parti rouge'; this party merged with the Liberals after Confederation, and red became the Liberal Party colour. Thus, a *rouge* is a Liberal Party member. In current English usage, *rouge* and *bleu* are not capitalized whether they are used as adjectives or as nouns. These terms should be italicized in formal writing.

> He has always defined himself as a 'bleu' (Quebec's slang for conservatives)—but contrasts the 'bleu' tradition with the 'rouge' (liberal) tradition as the difference between a humanist approach and a technocratic approach.
> *Globe and Mail* (Toronto) 27 Sept. 1985: P8

The Liberals' present difficulties should not hide three enormous advantages: the historic rouge vote in Quebec, the ability to raise money from corporations and the non-ideological, brokerage nature of Canadian politics.
Globe and Mail (Toronto) 23 Jan. 1985: P6

Not wanting to be left out of a possible Harper victory, Quebecers quickly cobbled together a new potential outcome, one that might see Conservatives winning five or six old bleu strongholds in the Beauce or Quebec City.
Daily News (Halifax) 17 Jan. 2006: 13

See also CONSERVATIVE; GRIT.

bloc, block   A *bloc* is a group of people or regions sharing a common political, military, or economic interest. Sometimes the term refers to a formal alliance: 'the European trading bloc'. *Block* is the correct spelling for a cube ('building block'), an obstruction ('writer's block'), or a quantity of things regarded as a unit ('a block of theatre tickets').

The hard fact remains that the people who write books do not constitute a powerful voting bloc.
Ottawa Citizen 20 Dec. 1990: A15

The vast majority of part-time workers fall within provincial bounds, but the federal labor jurisdiction covers a large bloc of part-time workers in the banking field.
Globe and Mail (Toronto) 3 June 1985: B11

DiMonte's 'quarter-hour average' (defined by the BBM as the average number of listeners tuned to a 15-minute bloc of a radio program) is 57,100. . . .
Gazette (Montreal) 3 March 1989: C1

(The correct spelling in this context is *block*.)

blond, blonde   In French, *blond* is the masculine form and *blonde* the feminine. In Canadian English, the adjective is spelled either way when it refers to a thing ('a blond *or* blonde wood finish'), but *blond* is more common in this context.

When people or their features are described, *blond* generally refers to men and boys and *blonde* to women and girls. Some usage guides consider *blonde* unacceptable in references to men, but none objects to *blond* for women

because gender-neutral usage favours one unmarked spelling for both sexes.

The demeaning phrase 'dumb blond(e)' has given the noun *blond(e)* negative connotations, although not in Quebec. In Quebec French—and perhaps also Quebec English—*blonde*, which rhymes with *phoned*, means 'girlfriend' (of any hair colour).

Bowen Island Brewery's Blonde Ale's the best new beer here in years.
Vancouver Sun 31 Dec. 1994: D6

(Things can be described as *blonde or blond*.)

His accomplice is 6 feet tall, with short blonde spiked hair.
Toronto Star 22 Dec. 1994: OS6

(Here, in reference to a man, *blond* is recommended.)

See also BRUNETTE; QUEBEC ENGLISH; SEXIST LANGUAGE.

blue language   see PURPLE PROSE

Bluenose, herring choker   *Bluenose*, or sometimes *Bluenoser*, is a jocular label applied to Nova Scotians. The origin of this nickname is obscure, but it long precedes the naming of the famous schooner pictured on the Canadian dime.

A *herring choker* is any Maritimer, but especially one from New Brunswick.

Sobey was a hard-working, tough, shrewd Bluenose who kept his ear to the ground, his shoulder to the wheel and his eye on the main chance.
Globe and Mail (Toronto) 30 Aug. 1985: P101

HERRING CHOKERS: . . . Janice Seeley . . . wants to hear from former students, teachers and trustees of Waasis, Bunkerville, Rusagonis, and South-West Rusagonis schools [in New Brunswick].
Vancouver Sun 20 April 1992: B1

bluff   see FOREST

bluntly   see SENTENCE ADVERBS

blush, flush, hot flash To *blush* and to *flush* both mean to become red in the face. While blushing is always linked to embarrassment, flushing can have various causes: anger, pride, exertion, sickness, and so on.

Spells of feeling intensely hot experienced by women at menopause are called *hot flashes* or, less often, *hot flushes*. *Hot flush* is the more common term in Britain.

> I blushed at my confession, but I had begun and so I went on.
> *Ottawa Citizen* 17 Nov. 1992: C10

> Birdie flushed with pleasure, then grimaced.
> David Williams *Eye of the Father* 1985: 56

> Once outside, she shivered in the chill, washed air, but it cooled her flushed face and refreshed her.
> Constance Beresford-Howe *Night Studies* 1985: 220

> Many women are confused about the pros and cons of taking estrogen to relieve menopausal symptoms, such as hot flashes. . . .
> *Chatelaine* April 1986: 32

> The 45-year-old University of Ottawa health economist and author got hot flushes in airplanes.
> *Ottawa Citizen* 4 Aug. 1992: E1

BMW see ABBREVIATION

BNA Act see CONSTITUTION

board see COLLECTIVE NOUNS

boat, ship A *boat* is a small, usually open vessel used on inland waterways or in coastal areas, whereas a *ship* is a large sea-going vessel. Landlubbers frequently refer to ships as boats and are unlikely to stop, although this may irritate those familiar with nautical terminology. Submarines, even the largest ones, are correctly referred to as boats.

bog see SWAMP

bologna, baloney *Bologna*, the sandwich meat with the poor reputation, is pronounced *buh LONE ee* or *buh LONE uh*. The city in Italy that lent its name to this sausage is pronounced *buh LONE yuh*. Neither should be spelled *balogna*.

Baloney, or sometimes *boloney*, is both an informal spelling of *bologna* and a mild expletive meaning nonsense.

> That claim is 'total baloney,' Morrison said.
> *Daily News* (Halifax) 10 March 1994: 26

Bombay, Mumbai see PLACE NAMES

bona fide, bona fides *Bona fide* is usually pronounced *bone uh FIDE* (and sometimes misspelled *bonified*). *Bona fides* is usually pronounced *bone uh FIDE eez*. These Latin phrases were first used in law to mean 'in good faith' and 'good faith', respectively: 'The offer was made bona fide (in good faith)'; 'The bona fides (good faith) of the trustee was in question.'

Over time, as these phrases came into general use, they acquired new meanings. The adverb phrase *bona fide*, 'in good faith', was re-interpreted as an adjective meaning sincere ('a bona fide offer'), or authentic, accredited ('a bona fide Chippendale', 'a bona fide member'). This use is now both common and accepted. The use of *bona fide* as an adverb has become rare, even in formal writing.

The noun phrase *bona fides* was reinterpreted as a plural because it ends in *s*. *Bona fides* is now commonly used with a plural verb to mean 'credentials' or 'qualifications': 'Her bona fides were impeccable'. This use is disputed: some dictionaries list it but others don't. It's probably best to use only the older meaning of *bona fides*, 'sincerity' or 'good faith', in formal writing. Even in informal writing, use of *bona fides* with a plural verb may be criticized.

> The bride was presented as very much a child of her time, the mildly, even admirably rebellious offspring of a bona fide member of the old Liberal elite.
> *Vancouver Sun* 30 Oct. 1990: A6

> Patsy is that third element in the play that seems more like a vehicle for the exploration of Sydney's and Tawe's relationship . . . than a truly bonified character.
> *Queen's Journal* (Kingston) 8 Feb. 1994: 23

(The correct spelling is *bona fide*; *truly* is redundant.)

'If there are any doubts about the bona fides of the marriage, the applicant is called for an interview,' Iadinardi said.
Toronto Star 26 Dec. 2004: A20

(Here *bona fides* means sincerity.)

A track record in politics, the Quebec civil service and private industry provides the 46-year-old executive with the bona fides to run an organization overseeing operations in 15 locally-managed ports across Canada.
Gazette (Montreal) 17 Aug. 1985: 5

(Here *qualifications* would be better.)

See also BACK-FORMATION; LATIN PHRASES.

bonuses   see -US

bony, [boney]   see -Y, -EY

bookkeeping   see HYPHENATION

bookmark   see COMPUTER TERMS

boomers   see CLICHÉ; GENERATION

bootless, footless   The most obvious meaning of *bootless* is without footwear. However, it also means profitless or unavailing, a sense derived from the Old English *boot*, meaning profit or advantage. This word survives in the expression *to boot*, which means as a bonus, or besides.

Footless has three meanings in Canadian English. The most common meaning, and the only one shared with Standard British English, is without feet, as in 'footless tights'. Canadians and Americans occasionally use *footless* figuratively to mean baseless or insubstantial, as in 'footless plans'. North Americans have also borrowed an informal meaning from Scottish English: awkward or helpless, referring most often to an alcohol-induced state.

If some uppity peasant complained that he never got to hear a cantata or sit for a portrait, a kindly aristocrat would explain that the bootless bumpkin couldn't possibly appreciate art, then have him flogged.
Province (Vancouver) 26 March 1990: 6

Now if only this kind of pragmatism could prevail in the UN General Assembly, where so many of the Third World states support unbalanced and counter-productive resolutions as if to compensate in bootless rhetoric for what they lack in economic and military clout.
Globe and Mail (Toronto) 22 Oct. 1985: A6

But even now, with feature number one under his belt and a pocketful of good notices to boot, Hauka is still having a hard time making headway.
Vancouver Sun 18 June 1993: C1

And in the late 18th and early 19th centuries, hard-bitten Scottish magnates of the fur trade drank themselves footless in Montreal at their Beaver Club dinners.
Financial Post (Toronto) 1 Oct. 1990: 48

bore   see GUN

bored with, bored by, bored of   *Bored with* and *bored by* offend no one. Some stylists object to 'bored *of*', a prepositional choice that was uncommon until recently but is now flourishing in informal speech and writing.

Couttes said he thinks people get bored with bands that put out similar sounding albums year after year.
Calgary Herald 28 Jan. 2003: C13

As the style grew more mannered Evans became bored by it. . . .
Jack Chambers *Milestones I* (1983): 98

I was bored of reading lame-o columns repeating the stale old line that whatever candidate is ahead on Labour Day always wins the election.
National Post (Toronto) 31 Dec. 2001: A14

(*Bored of* is now common in writing, but only at the informal level.)

borne, born, bourn   The verb *bear* has two past participles, *borne* and *born*. *Borne* is used when *bear* means carry or withstand ('They've borne the brunt of it'), and also when it means give birth to ('She had borne him three sons'), unless the construction is passive. In passive constructions, the past participle is *born* ('He was born in 1917'), except when it's followed by *by* ('children borne by teenagers'). In other words, *born* is the past participle for an unattributed birth and *borne* for one in which the mother is given credit.

Bourn (or *bourne*) is an archaic word meaning goal or limit; Hamlet, in his famous soliloquy, refers to death as 'The undiscover'd country from whose bourn / No traveller returns'. This spelling may have affected some writers who intend *borne*.

The system benefits retailers and yet the cost of setting up the tracking system is borne by suppliers.
Gazette (Montreal) 6 Dec. 1994: C1

It can be transfused regardless of blood types and it won't harbour blood-born diseases like HIV and hepatitis.
CBC News [transcript] 23 Nov. 1994: n.p.

(Diseases carried in the blood are *blood-borne*.)

My wife has borne a child.
Gazette (Montreal) 22 Dec. 1994: C4

[Remittance men] were borne of primogeniture inheritance law, which left everything to the first-born. . . .
Vancouver Sun 17 Dec. 1994: D15

(Before *of*, *to*, or any preposition except *by*, the correct spelling is *born*.)

Fears that the federal government wanted [a] rubber stamp for foreclosure-minded bankers have not been bourne out.
Country Guide Nov. 1986: 8

(The correct spelling is *borne*.)

See also BEAR, BARE.

-boro, borough   see -BURGH

borrow   The use of *borrow* to mean lend ('Could you borrow me yours?') is non-standard. The prepositions *off* and *off of* are commonly used after *borrow*: 'We borrowed it off of Joel's parents'. In speech this usage is disputed; in writing it should definitely be avoided. *From* is the preposition required.

The foreman seemed to like him. Borrowed smokes off him all the time, anyway.
NeWest Review Feb.–Mar. 1990: 30

(Here *borrowed . . . off* is an imitation of casual speech; the standard expression is *borrowed . . . from*.)

See also OFF, OFF OF, FROM.

Bosnia and Herzegovina   *Bosnia and Herzegovina* is the name of a single country. This country, formerly a part of Yugoslavia, is homeland to three ethnic groups: Croats, Serbs and Bosniaks (Bosnian Muslims). *Herzegovina* can be pronounced either *HEHR tseh GO vin ah* or *HEHR tseh go VEEN ah*. The CBC uses the former pronunciation.

bosom   see BREAST(S)

botanic, botanical   see -IC, -ICAL

both . . . and   see COMMA; PARALLELISM

bottom line   Usage commentators have taken a distinct dislike to the expression *bottom line*, labeling it overworked business jargon; it is best avoided in formal writing. In informal contexts, however, the expression is quite defensible. Although it has developed several different uses, it has not become—as some critics suggest—a meaningless catch-all.

The top line of a financial statement is gross income. From this line costs are deducted, and on the bottom line net profit or loss is reported. Thus the literal meaning of *bottom line* is financial profit or loss, and this meaning is still current.

In business, the bottom line (i.e., profit) is the key consideration. Thus *bottom line* has also come to be used as a metaphor referring to the most important consideration in other types of endeavour. Extending this meaning, which first appeared in the 1970s, people began to use *bottom line* to refer to what they saw as the essential or relevant point in any situation. Thus the crux of a complex issue or the upshot of a chain of events may be called 'the bottom line'.

A less common and more recent meaning of

bottom line is final bargaining position. This meaning is probably partly derived from the unrelated metaphor 'to draw the line'.

When hyphenated, *bottom-line* is an adjective meaning concerned only with profit or cost.

> In an effort to improve the bottom line, companies are tempted to reduce promotional expenditures or, worse, completely suspend them.
> *Computer Dealer News* 7 March 1991: 49

> Socially and culturally, it remains to be seen whether the current narcissism has run its course and the possibility of a new, more inclusive public ethos might come about where the bottom line for community is something more than the dollar bill.
> *City Magazine* Spring 1988: 40

> 'The bottom line is: what kind of agriculture are we going to have in Canada and who is going to control the production of food?'
> *Briarpatch* Dec. 1989–Jan. 1990: 2

> As business and government realize that they cannot push the arts any further along the road to bottom-line thinking, I believe that we will begin to see a return to—happy days—serious and more generous cultural subsidies.
> *Performing Arts in Canada* Spring 1990: 46

[boughten], store-bought   In some North American dialects, *boughten* is used as an adjective meaning purchased from a store rather than homemade. This usage is generally considered non standard, though it is used in writing representing speech. *Store-bought* is an accepted alternative.

> Storeboughten cookies are looked down upon.
> Margaret Laurence *The Diviners* 1974: 29

> (Here the dialectal *-en* captures the flavour of the speech of the novel's narrator.)

-bound   The combining form *-bound* has two senses: constrained by and going in the direction of.

In the first sense, familiar single-word compounds include *housebound*, *spellbound*, and *stormbound*. Hyphenated combinations include *desk-bound*, *duty-bound*, *honour-bound*, *muscle-bound*, and *root-bound*.

In the second sense, *eastbound*, *southbound*, *inbound*, and *outbound* are established as single words. Most other combinations take a hyphen: 'university-bound'. Proper names are always hyphenated when combined with *bound*: 'Alberta-bound'. Note that some combinations are ambiguous: *snowbound*, for example, could describe either avid skiers or frustrated travellers.

> . . . the reigning doctrines are merely gender-bound and culture-bound parochial theories, with no grip on a reality common to all.
> *Queen's Quarterly* 97.4 (1990): 616

> He said he was reminded of a conversation he had overheard on a Toronto-bound train. . . .
> *The Beaver* Dec. 1989–Jan. 1990: 38

bourgeois,   bourgeoisie,   proletariat
Bourgeois (pronounced *BOOR zhwah* or *boor ZHWAH*) is an adjective meaning middle-class and, occasionally, a noun meaning middle-class person. In Marxist theory the *bourgeoisie*, or middle class, are those who own the means of production, such as factories, and are thus able to exploit the lower social and economic class. The lower class, called the *proletariat*, survives by selling its labour.

Most people in contemporary Canadian society who would call themselves middle-class do not fit the Marxist definition of *bourgeois*. And few Canadian writers, other than historians and Marxist social critics, attempt to use the term as Marx defined it. Instead, *bourgeois* is often used with humour to describe people preoccupied with propriety, position, and comfort.

> The source of Plaskett's popularity is an unrepentantly bourgeois sensibility. His art is about home, hearth, comfort and security.
> *Ottawa Citizen* 3 Oct. 1994: B6

> . . . in all the capitalist democracies the industrial working class has become something other than the revolutionary proletariat that Marx anticipated.
> Irving M. Zeitlin and Robert J. Brym *The Social Condition of Humanity* 1991: 133

bourn   see BORNE

BP   see AD

brace   In informal English *brace*, like *bunch* or *slew*, is sometimes used to mean a considerable number. However, dictionaries have not yet recorded this use, probably because it conflicts with the standard definition of a brace as a pair.

The white, mild-tasting meat of a roasted brace of grouse . . . is often preferred on the table over the dark breasts of waterfowl.
Ottawa Citizen 7 Oct. 1990: B6

(Here *brace* means pair.)

The latest head-turner is a brace of bodyguards. 'It's something different,' said Clayton Heffernan who celebrated his graduation Saturday with two hulking protectors at his side.
Toronto Star 23 June 1992: B1

(Here brace means pair.)

Both works have been recorded dozens of times since, and each new digital assault on the Matterhorn seems to get its brace of ecstatic reviews.
Gazette (Montreal) 17 Feb. 1990: H13

(The use of brace to refer to more than two should be avoided.)

brackets   see PARENTHESES

brain drain   see CLICHÉ

brand names   see TRADEMARKS

bravo   see -OS, -OES

breach, breech, breeches, britches   *Breach* is a verb meaning break through ('breach enemy defences') and a noun meaning rupture or violation. The noun is most often used figuratively to refer to rifts, broken promises, and unfulfilled obligations: 'breach in their friendship', 'breach of etiquette', 'breach of trust'. The idiom 'to step into the breach' means to fill the gap or lend a hand where needed.
   Breech is an obsolete word for buttocks that is still used in the expression 'breech birth'. *Breech* also refers to the back end of a gun barrel.
   Breeches are tight pants fastened below the

knee that are worn now only for some sports, like riding or fencing, or as part of uniforms or period costumes. *Britches* is a North American variant spelling that reflects the most common pronunciation of *breeches*, which also can be pronounced *BREE chiz*.

I have felt that it is well worth insulting the intelligence of some readers if one can do anything to breach the barriers of panic and prejudice in others.
Northrop Frye The Bush Garden 1971: 125

The languid Opposition of Leicester House and the Tories could take heart in the possibility that a breach between king and ministers might afford an alternative to the cultivation of the heir apparent as a road to power.
J.A.W. Gunn Beyond Liberty and Property 1983: 67

[Analysts] wonder whether yesterday's noisy split was a tactic, or a symptom of a breech too wide to mend.
Toronto Star 6 April 1994: A16

(Here the correct spelling is *breach*.)

The 10-member panel . . . proposed that doctors reverse the current trend toward caesareans for breech births, where the baby is born buttocks-first.
Globe and Mail (Toronto) 28 Oct. 1985: A17

Amputated at either end, dull brown and black in color, its breach cracks open with a quick snap of the wrist to admit a single pellet shell.
Toronto Star 13 April 1994: A6

(Shells are inserted in the *breech*, not *breach*, of a gun.)

break-in   see PHRASAL VERBS; BURGLARY

break and enter, breaking and entering   see BURGLARY

break up, break-up, breakup   see PHRASAL VERBS

breast(s), bust, chest, bosom   The most common and least euphemistic name for a woman's mammary glands is *breasts*. *Bust* appears most often in descriptions of clothing and fashion. The upper front part of the male or female body is called the *chest*; *breast* and *bosom* are poetic alternatives.

> His splendid iron bosom, his mountainous biceps, his mouth-watering forearms, that proud tree-trunk neck, those shoulders set square; O, Stallone, what labors you have known!
> *Globe and Mail* (Toronto) 23 May 1985: E3

breath, breathe see BATH

breech, breeches see BREACH

brethren see PLURALS

briefly see SENTENCE ADVERBS

bring, brought, [brung] *Brought* is the standard past tense and past participle of *bring*: 'I brought my lunch'; 'They have brought someone in from the outside'. *Brung* is non-standard.

> 'People all year have brung it up.'
> *Toronto Star* 23 Oct. 1992: B2

(The accepted past participle is *brought*.)

> What was Oscar Goldman's attitude towards the hero who brung 'em over the finish line a winner?
> *Ottawa Citizen* 20 Jan. 1990: F1

(Here *brung* is a deliberate folksy touch.)

bring, take Generally, *bring* indicates a motion towards the speaker or writer; *take*, a motion away from the speaker or writer: 'Please bring me a coffee'; 'Take this upstairs'. Native speakers of English don't often confuse these verbs. But a usage problem arises when the writer shifts his or her point of view without regard for where the reader is likely to be mentally situated, or fails to consider the position and movement of the people or things being described.

> Opposition critics howled indignantly, and South Cayuga residents immediately chartered buses to bring them to a mass demonstration before the Legislature.
> *Harrowsmith* Aug.–Sept. 1985: 32

(Here *bring* may well occur because the sentence starts in the legislature and thus the writer's perspective is situated there, rather than in South Cayuga. However, it would have made sense for the writer to use the residents' point of view: 'South Cayuga residents immediately chartered buses to take them to a mass demonstration'.)

> Mark your calendar, check your kids and bring your shopping list—Canada's largest wine festival is ready once more to educate, entertain and delight.
> *Bon Vivant* Aug.–Sept. 1982: 28

(Depending on the point of view, either *bring* or *take* could work here; *bring* implies that the speaker, at least in spirit, will be at the festival.)

Brit see BRITON

Britain, Great Britain, British Isles, United Kingdom *Britain* and *Great Britain* both refer to the island containing England, Scotland, and Wales. The *British Isles* comprise this island, Ireland, and several other islands, including the Isle of Man, the Isle of Wight, and the Channel Islands. The *United Kingdom* (formally, the United Kingdom of Great Britain and Northern Ireland; informally, the U.K.) is a political entity, comprising England, Scotland, Wales, and Northern Ireland, and excluding the Republic of Ireland. Canadian writers often don't distinguish among these terms.

See also BRITON, BRITISHER; IRELAND; SCOTTISH, SCOTS, SCOTCH.

britches see BREACH

British Columbia see APPENDIX I

British Columbian see NAMES OF RESIDENTS OF CITIES AND PROVINCES

British Isles see BRITAIN

British North America Act see CONSTITUTION; DOMINION OF CANADA.

Briton, Britisher, Brit, Englishman, Englishwoman *Briton*, *Britisher*, and *Brit* are all used to refer to citizens of the United Kingdom. However, most British people prefer to be identified more specifically as English, Scottish, Welsh, or Northern Irish, or, where the noun is required, as Englishmen and Englishwomen, Scotsmen and Scotswomen, and so on.

> Another unheralded Briton, Michael Lankester, will be on the podium, in front of the commercially attractive Montreal Symphony Orchestra.
> *Gazette* (Montreal) 1 Sept. 1990: D7

> Britisher Wally Herbert, himself no slouch in Arctic exploration, presents a meticulous history of self-service gone berserk.
> *Ottawa Citizen* 6 Oct. 1990: J6

> Montrealer Alfred Baumgarten, who was born in Saxony, was the first non-Brit to serve as president of the Hunt Club.
> *Gazette* (Montreal) 14 Sept. 1990: D9

> He can rely on Northern Irish allies to bolster his slim majority of 14 seats.
> *Calgary Herald* 27 Nov. 1994: A10

> Our age has seen the utter decay of the funny Welshman, and the rise to a rivalry in eminence of the Witty Irishman and the Pawky Scot. . . .
> Robertson Davies *A Voice from the Attic* 1960: 210

See also BRITAIN, GREAT BRITAIN, BRITISH ISLES, UNITED KINGDOM; IRELAND, EIRE, ULSTER, NORTHERN IRELAND; SCOTTISH, SCOTS, SCOTCH.

broach, brooch   *Broach* is an uncommon noun meaning a skewer or spit. To *broach* something, like a cask, is to punch a hole in it to gain access to the contents; to *broach* a subject is to bring it up for discussion. A *brooch* is an ornamental pin. *Broach* rhymes with *coach*; *brooch* rhymes with *coach* or *pooch*.

> He did not broach the politically sensitive question of reducing federal support for pensioners in order to help needy children.
> *Vancouver Sun* 14 Oct. 1994: A19

> There was also a little red Santa brooch.
> *Toronto Star* 1 Jan. 1994: A2

> A public relations fellow with flowing black curls wore a dashing red tunic, broach at the throat,

with a gold chain drooping from the shoulder.
> *Globe and Mail* (Toronto) 14 March 1985: M1

(The correct spelling is *brooch*.)

broadcast   see CAST

broke   To be *broke* is to have no money. Some commentators label the expression slang, but in fact it is common in fairly formal writing. More formal synonyms such as *destitute* and *impoverished* suggest a more extensive loss of money, possessions, and social standing; being broke is usually only a temporary state, though often a recurrent one.

> . . . O.M. Helgerson was so broke in 1908 he almost had to pawn his watch; but in seventeen months he had made $238,403.87.
> Pierre Berton *The Promised Land* 1984: 327

> As Wyrick and Owens have observed . . . , black female offenders 'usually go to jail because they are broke and they often return to jail because they are still broke.'
> Irving M. Zeitlin and Robert J. Brym *The Social Condition of Humanity* 1991: 271

brooch   see BROACH

Brooklynese   see -ESE

brother-in-law   see IN-LAWS

brought   see BRING

browser   see COMPUTER TERMS

brunch   see DINNER

brunette, brunet   *Brunette* is derived from French, which distinguishes between the masculine, *brunet*, and the feminine, *brunette*. Canadian dictionaries list both forms, but the use of *brunet* is largely an American phenomenon; Canadian writers use *brunette* almost exclusively.

Both men and women are called *blond*, but the term *brunette* is applied only to dark-haired white women.

In countless novels written fifty years ago the heroine, having discovered that her husband was deceiving her with the beautiful brunette, crept away to the nursery to weep over her beloved children.
Robertson Davies *One Half of Robertson Davies* 1978: 81

See also BLOND, BLONDE; SEXIST LANGUAGE.

[brung]   see BRING

brusque, brusk   *Brusque*, meaning abrupt and blunt in speech or manner, is pronounced to rhyme with *tusk* in Canada and the United States. British speakers are more likely to pronounce it with the vowel as in *book* or *boot*. *Brusk* is an American spelling variant, rare in Canada and not listed in Canadian or British dictionaries.

Brusque and blunt, Ley was criticized in Hartford for his lack of sensitivity, especially his indelicate handling of the Ron Francis situation.
Vancouver Sun 19 March 1992: D10

buffalo   see BISON; -OS, -OES

bug   *Bug* has developed a number of meanings both as a noun and as a verb, some more acceptable than others in writing.

In North America, *bug* is widely used in informal writing to refer to insects, especially when the creatures are regarded as pests. In zoology, *bug* refers to a particular order of insects (Hemiptera), known as 'true bugs'. In Britain, the term is applied only to bedbugs (which are true bugs).

Any disease-causing micro-organism or unspecified virus may be referred to in informal writing as a *bug*: 'She's home from school with a bug'. When that meaning is extended to a newly developed enthusiasm ('He's caught the windsurfing bug'), the usage is usually considered slang.

Bug meaning defect, especially one computer software or in a mechanical device, is now standard. *Bug* meaning electronic listening device is considered appropriate to journalism, but not more formal writing. Some newspaper style guides distinguish between *tapping* a telephone and *bugging* a room. The conventions of legal writing have not caught up with new communications technologies; the verbs that will describe court-approved surveillance of e-mail, instant messages, and Internet phones are not yet established.

As a verb meaning to annoy or pester, *bug* generally is considered slang, more acceptable in casual speech than in writing.

A great admirer of the new mayor was George Brossard, the insect collector whose collection of butterflies and bugs is the basis of the city's Insectarium.
Gazette (Montreal) 26 Dec. 1994: A3

Doctors in Brantford are calling the virus . . . a 'California A' bug, but Health Ministry officials say they don't know anything about a California A virus and doubt that one exists.
Globe and Mail (Toronto) 24 April 1985: M1

The bite of the gold bug drove me on.
Atlantic Salmon Journal (Autumn 1990): 27

Many bugs in software development emerge from trying to make one type of program work with other programs or new chips.
Ottawa Citizen 22 Dec. 1994: B5

Her home was bugged, her phone tapped.
Vancouver Sun 29 Jan. 1994: A15

'You're bugging Mrs. Harbison and that bothers me'.
Howard Engel *Murder Sees the Light* 1984: 164

bull, bear, bullish, bearish   In the jargon of the stock market, a *bull* buys stocks, anticipating an increase in their value; a *bear* sells stocks, thinking their value may decrease. Thus a *bullish* market is rising and a *bearish* market is falling. Sometimes *bullish* and *bearish* are used more generally to mean optimistic and pessimistic.

[He] is bullish on Canadian stocks for 1995, with expectations of strong earnings growth and dividend increases leading to higher stock prices.
Gazette (Montreal) 31 Dec. 1994: C3

But the strength on the TSE this week isn't fooling . . . the consistently bearish technical analyst. . . .
Toronto Star 16 Dec. 1994: E6

Far from conceding defeat, the man who will lead TVOntario into its 25th year is confident, even bullish, about the network's future.
Ottawa Citizen 27 Dec. 1994: C13

(Here *bullish* means optimistic.)

Same goes for his bearish buddy, Sheldon (Rob Reiner), an anti-establishment gasbag who prides himself on never having had one of his plays produced.
Toronto Star 4 Nov. 1994: D1

(Here *bearish* means pessimistic.)

bum   see BUTTOCKS

bummer   see COLLOQUIAL

buoy, buoyant   In Canada *buoy* is usually pronounced *BOY*, although *BOO ee* (rhymes with *chewy*) is also used in some areas, particularly for the noun. American dictionaries list *BOO ee* as the usual pronunciation; British dictionaries give only the *BOY* pronunciation. In all three varieties of English, the adjective *buoyant* is pronounced *BOY unt*; an alternative American pronunciation is *BOO yent*.
Buoy is sometimes misspelled *bouy*.

High Canadian interest rates are also continuing to bouy the dollar, he added.
Ottawa Citizen 9 Aug. 1990: A1

(The correct spelling is *buoy*.)

bureau, bureaux   see PLURALS

bureaucrat, bureaucratese   see BARBARISMS; -ESE

-burgh, -burg, -borough, -boro   All these suffixes mean 'town'. In North American place names, *-burgh* is usually pronounced like *-burg*: *Pittsburgh*, *Newburgh*. The *-burgh* in *Edinburgh*, on the other hand, is pronounced like the *-borough* in *Scarborough* and *Peterborough*: *BUR ruh*. The suffix *-boro*, as in *Peterboro Petes*, is an informal variant of *-borough*, mainly used in journalism as a space-saver.

burglary, break and enter, breaking and

entering, theft, robbery, larceny   Historically and in Canadian law, *burglary* is defined as the act of breaking into a dwelling, at night, with the intention of committing a serious crime, such as murder, rape, or theft. But in everyday usage *burglary* (often misspelled *burglery*) means breaking into a building with intent to steal (see also BURGLE).

Break and enter, as defined in Canadian law, is entry without lawful justification. The official name of the offence in the Canadian Criminal Code is *break and enter*; however, people commonly refer to it as *breaking and entering* or *break and entry*. Neither forced entry nor theft is a necessary component of this crime. The onus is on the accused to provide an innocent explanation for trespassing. The short form *B and E* is unfamiliar to many law-abiding citizens and should not be used without an explanation.

Theft is a very broad term for stealing that includes shoplifting, fraud, and misappropriation of real estate. A *robbery* is a face-to-face theft that involves intimidation or violence. People and places are *robbed*. Money and valuables are not *robbed* but *stolen* (see also ROB).

Larceny, which means theft of personal property, is a term used more in the United States than in Canada or Britain, where it is not currently codified in law. Some American states distinguish between *petty* and *grand* larceny on the basis of the dollar value of the goods stolen.

. . . a visible, barking dog may serve as a deterrent to someone contemplating burglary in your absence, while a dog locked in a basement is no threat.
Dogs in Canada Special Issue 1986: 111

(Here *burglary* is used in the everyday sense, as a synonym of break and enter.)

Montreal police say a Pierrefonds couple who were robbed Friday night were victims of a break and entry, which is not considered a home invasion since there was no violence.
Gazette (Montreal) 9 May 2006: A6

(Break and entry and breaking and entering are common variants of the legal term break and enter.)

Robbery includes the additional element that the taking must be by force or fear.
J.E. Smyth et al. The Law and Business *Administration in Canada* 1987: 428

Two men armed with a knife robbed three Burnaby men in two different incidents Monday night.
Vancouver Sun 6 May 2006: B3

So far about 13,000 cars have been stolen in B.C. this year. . . . 'Some of these automobiles are worth $20,000 to $30,000 and in the U.S. it's treated as grand larceny.'
Vancouver Sun 22 Dec. 1994: B1

burgle, burglarize The verbs *burgle* and *burglarize* are both in common use in Canada to mean break into a building to steal. *Burgle* is the more common term in Britain; in the United States *burglarize* is more common.

See also BACK-FORMATION; BURGLARY.

Burma, Myanmar see PLACE NAMES

burn see COMPUTER TERMS

burnout see PHRASAL VERBS

burnt see -T, -ED

burst, bust *Burst* is both the past tense and the past participle of *burst*; *bursted* is archaic.

Bust was originally a dialectal variant of *burst*, as *cuss* is of *curse*, but it has developed into a separate word with many meanings that *burst* does not share. For example, to *bust* means to break; *go bust* means go bankrupt; a *bust* is a failure, especially a financial failure. To *get busted* means to be arrested or to be demoted in the military. All these uses of *bust* are slang or informal: they are common in conversation and journalism, but avoided in more formal speech and writing.

. . . the doors burst open and Gerrit Smith strode into the hall amid tumultuous cheering.
William Teatero John Anderson: *Fugitive Slave* 1986: 122

He's got a busted leg, I said.
Canadian Fiction Magazine 64 (1988): 102

Way down south in Memphis, the 50th anniversary of Elvis Presley's birth on Tuesday turned out to be something of a bust.
Globe and Mail (Toronto) 11 Jan. 1985: E7

She was also famous for being regularly busted for running illegal drinking joints.
Province (Vancouver) 31 Oct. 1990: 2

bury Most Canadians pronounce *bury* to rhyme with *hairy*, but for some, it rhymes with *hurry*.

bus, omnibus The plural of *bus* is either *buses* or *busses*. As a verb, to *bus* means to transport by bus or to set tables and clear dishes in a restaurant. The *-ed* form is *bused* or *bussed* and the *-ing* form *busing* or *bussing*. The *-ss-* spellings are all uncommon in Canada, where to *buss* is an old-fashioned synonym of to *kiss*.

In the early nineteenth century, the Latin word *omnibus*, meaning 'for all', came into use in English to refer to vehicles that followed fixed routes and were open to everyone. *Omnibus* was soon shortened to *bus*, and today *omnibus* has only two common uses: an *omnibus bill* is a piece of legislation that covers several different items usually relating to one broad issue; an *omnibus* is a book containing several works by one author or on one subject. The plural is *omnibuses*.

'I hope the buses are still running'.
Canadian Fiction Magazine 63 (1988): 117

There are no busses, no taxis, no local trains.
Vancouver Sun 18 July 1992: B10

(The spelling *busses* is correct but uncommon.)

Last year, all the students were bused to school but this November the board said the busing would stop because the children live within the accepted walking distance of 1.6 kilometres.
Gazette (Montreal) 17 Dec. 1992: G1

The Liberal party of Nova Scotia will discuss at its general meeting in November the problems of bussing voters from one constituency to another to give a candidate additional support.
Daily News (Halifax) 21 Sept. 1992: 3

(The spelling *bussing* is correct but uncommon.)

He read Kant (Macmurray's favourite philosopher) when riding on an omnibus.
Eugene Forsey *A Life on the Fringe* 1990: 36

(The use of *omnibus* to mean bus is now rare.)

As Prime Minister Trudeau put it in the famous debate on the omnibus bill to reform the Criminal Code, 'the state has no business in the bedrooms of the nation.'
Janine Brodie, Shelley A.M. Gavigan, and Jane Jenson
The Politics of Abortion 1992: 40–1

His stories are conveniently packaged in one brick of a book, The Golf Omnibus.
Ottawa Citizen 17 Jan. 2006: A14

bush, bushed   see FOREST

bust   see BREAST(S); BURST

but   It is not ungrammatical and is often stylistically effective to begin a sentence with *but*. But it shouldn't become a habit.

Armed with European weapons, tribal warfare became more bloody. . . . But the real killer in the post-contact period was disease brought to the New World by Europeans.
Robert M. Bone *The Geography of the Canadian North* 1992: 42

But while the choice of theme may have been easy, the theme itself is fantastically difficult.
Northrop Frye *The Bush Garden* 1971: 11

See also COMMA; ONLY, BUT.

but me, but I   When *but* means 'except', it is normally followed by the object form of the pronoun: 'She asked everyone but me'. However, *but I* is also acceptable if a clause follows: 'Nobody but me will know' or 'Nobody but I will know'. Grammarians disagree about whether *but* functions as a preposition ('Nobody except me will know') or as a conjunction introducing an elliptical clause ('Nobody will know—but I will') in such sentences.

He 'has' her in his dreams—she 'has' everyone but him in hers.
Janice Kulyk Keefer *Reading Mavis Gallant* 1989: 124

See also CASE.

butter up   see IDIOMS

buttocks, bum, butt, fanny   The *buttocks* are rarely referred to as such except in the gym or the doctor's office. A host of synonyms substitute for the word in general conversation, including *seat, bottom, behind, backside, rear end, derrière*, and *keister* (*KEE ster*). In Canadian and British English the noun *bum* has two main senses: buttocks and someone who isn't earning his (usually) or her keep. Many Americans use the word only in the latter sense, and will be puzzled by the former. British English-speakers may well be puzzled by *butt*, North American slang for *buttocks*.

Canadians should also note that *fanny*, just another innocuous synonym for *buttocks* in North America, is rude slang for *female genitals* in Britain.

The first knocked her off her bike and mauled her head, while the other mauled her thighs, buttocks and chest.
Vancouver Sun 9 May 1994: A3

'One parent will mean a whack on the bum once in a while.'
Toronto Star 9 April 1994: J1

I got tired of feeling sorry for myself. I said, 'Come on, get off your butt. There are lots of people worse off than you.'
Toronto Star 6 June 1994: A6

The skirts will stop at any number of places on the leg, from just below the fanny to just below the knee.
Vancouver Sun 28 June 1994: C3

(A speaker of British English might be taken aback by this use of *fanny*.)

bylaw, by-law, byelaw   A *bylaw* is a municipal law or a regulation governing an organization; all these spellings of the term are correct. Canadians use *bylaw* and *by-law* with about equal frequency, but *byelaw* is rare. The prefix *by(e)* means 'town'.

See also ORDINANCE.

bypass   see FUNCTIONAL SHIFT

C

c., ca. see CIRCA

-c, -ck- Many but not all words that end in *-c* add *k* before adding the endings *-ed*, *-ing*, *-er*, and *-y*: *mimicked*, *frolicking*, *trafficking*, *picnickers*, *colicky*. This indicates that the *c* is pronounced as *k*. Note that in current English *k* is not added before *-al* (*economical*, *political*); *musickal* is an archaic spelling.

See also ARC; QUEBECER, QUEBECKER.

cacao see COCOA

cactus, cactuses, cacti Most dictionaries give three plural forms of *cactus*: *cactuses*, *cacti*, and *cactus*. The 'correct' form is a prickly issue for some cactus lovers, but there is no definitive answer. *Cactus* is a scholarly Latin term created in the seventeenth century from the Greek word *kaktos*. *Cacti* is its Latin plural; *cactuses* is the regularized English plural. *Cactus* is the scientific name of this genus of plants. All three forms are used in Canadian writing and all are accepted.

See also PLURALS, REGULAR, IRREGULAR, FOREIGN.

Caesar, Caesar salad *Caesar* (pronounced *SEE zur*) is frequently misspelled: note the *a* before the *e*, and the *-ar* ending. *Caesar salad* is apparently not named after Julius Caesar. There are several contenders for the honour; no etymology has been established conclusively.

caesarean, caesarian, cesarean, C-section In the Canadian medical profession, the preferred spelling for the surgical delivery of a baby is *Caesarean* (after Julius Caesar, who is said to have been delivered this way). The same spelling with no capital and the alternative spellings *caesarian* and *cesarean* (favoured in the United States) are also common in general usage. Colloquially, and in medical shorthand, the operation is referred to as a *C-section*.

Anything connected to Julius Caesar or the Caesars may be referred to as *Caesarean* or *Caesarian*.

> Although we Christians have given lip service to the Galilean vision, ironically it has all too often been the Caesarean ideal that has most shaped our thinking and acting.
> 'That We May Know Each Other' United Church of Canada website 2004: 39

See also CAPITAL LETTERS.

caffeine see -IE-, -EI-

cagy, cagey see -Y, -EY

cahoots see COLLABORATION

caisse populaire see BANK; QUEBEC ENGLISH

Cajun see ACADIA

calculable see -ABLE, -(AT)ABLE

caldron see CAULDRON

calèche see QUEBEC ENGLISH

calendar, calender *Calendar*, meaning table of dates, is frequently misspelled *calender*. *Calender* is a separate word with two separate meanings: a machine with rollers used to give paper a glossy finish, or a member of a Sufic order of wandering dervishes.

> Mark your calendars: The annual event that enrages motorists but thrills thousands of cyclists occurs Sunday, June 6.
> *Gazette* (Montreal) 28 Apr. 2004: A5

Soft calender is a paper-making term meaning slightly polished, said Norske spokesman Stu Clugston.
Times-Colonist (Victoria) 23 Apr. 2003: C1

Calgary   Calgarians usually pronounce the name of their city *KAL guh ree* or *KAL gree*. Other Canadians sometimes say *KAL GAIR ee*.

calibre   see GUN

call   see PHONE

callus, callous   The noun referring to a thick, hardened area of skin is spelled *callus* or, often in Canadian English, *callous*. The adjective meaning emotionally hardened or unfeeling is spelled *callous*. The *-ed* form, spelled *callused* or *calloused*, can refer to either hardened skin or hardened emotions. Some usage guides suggest that *callused* be reserved for the physical sense and *calloused* for the emotional one, but writers ignore this distinction.

> Slender, with dark pop-star good looks, in a room of slab-muscled bodies, he looks immature and unused, like a hand without calluses.
> Ken Dryden *The Game* 1983: 144

> Much bad art hides behind Christianity, for to criticize it on purely artistic grounds is to seem callous toward its inspiration. . . .
> Robertson Davies *A Voice from the Attic* 1960: 332

(*Callous* is the only correct spelling for the adjective.)

> I know how easy it would be to dismiss this, callused as we are to things like drug overdoses.
> *Vancouver Sun* 15 Sept. 1994: A3

> Prof. Check cites a 1982 study . . . showing that males who regularly view pornographic materials became 'calloused' or 'desensitized' in their perceptions of female sexuality.
> *Globe and Mail* (Toronto) 9 March 1985: M7

Calvary, cavalry   *Calvary* is the hill near Jerusalem where Jesus was crucified; it is sometimes used figuratively to refer to a period of terrible suffering. The *cavalry* is the part of an army that fights mounted on horseback or, nowadays, from motorized vehicles.

> It appears that a dashing former calvary officer claims he had a three year love affair with the Princess and that she contemplated leaving Prince Charles for him.
> *CTV News* [transcript] 1 Oct. 1994: n.p.

(The word needed here is *cavalry*.)

calves   see -F, -V-

camaraderie, comrade   Note the three *a*'s in *camaraderie*, a word often misspelled. The most common misspelling is *comraderie*, an attempt to parallel the related word *comrade*. *Camaraderie*, meaning fellow feeling, and *camarade*, meaning friend, mate, or fellow soldier, were both borrowed from French. The spelling of *camarade*, a sixteenth-century borrowing, was later influenced by Spanish and became *comrade*; *camaraderie*, which was borrowed later, in the nineteenth century, retained its French spelling. All three of these words, *comrade*, *camarade*, and *camaraderie*, are derived from an obsolete Spanish word meaning 'roommate' or 'tentmate'.

cameos   see -OS, -OES

cameraman   see SEXIST LANGUAGE

Cambodia, Kampuchea, Khmer   Cambodia and Kampuchea are alternative spellings; the former is the traditional and still more common spelling, while the latter is more faithful to the Khmer pronunciation. Khmer, pronounced *kuh MAIR*, is the name of the language of Cambodia and of its main ethnic group.

See also PLACE NAMES.

can   see MAY, CAN

Canada Day   see DOMINION OF CANADA

Canada goose   see CANADA, CANADIAN; CAPITAL LETTERS

Canadian, Canada   *Canadian* is the usual adjective form: *Canadian bacon, Canadian foot-*

ball, Canadian Shield. Canada, however, functions as an adjective in some established names: for example, in familiar names of flora and fauna (*Canada goose, Canada jay, Canada lily, Canada thistle*), and in the names of some boards, corporations, and posts (*Canada Council, Canada Labour Relations, Canada Post, Canada Research Chair*).

In order to make the names of federal government departments similar in both official languages, *Canada* is used as an adjective and placed *after* the noun: *Elections Canada/Élections Canada; Environment Canada/Environnement Canada; Industry Canada/Industrie Canada; Statistics Canada/Statistique Canada*. This usage has spread to the non-profit sector: *Orchestras Canada/Orchestres Canada; Epilepsy Canada/ Épilepsie Canada*.

Canadian Armed Forces

In 1968 the Canadian Army, the Royal Canadian Navy, and the Royal Canadian Air Force were united under the official designation the *Canadian Armed Forces*. The terms *army, navy,* and *air force* are still used in unofficial contexts; the official designations are the *Land Force Command, Maritime Command* and *Air Command*. The *Canadian Armed Forces* are also referred to as the *Canadian Forces* or the *Armed Forces*. Unification ensured a single pay and seniority system throughout the Armed Forces; however, some of the traditional naval ranks are still in use. The *Canadian Press Stylebook* contains a useful list of military titles and abbreviations.

Canadian Bill of Rights, Canadian Charter of Rights and Freedoms

The *Canadian Bill of Rights* and the *Canadian Charter of Rights and Freedoms* are both designed to protect citizens against the state, and minorities against the legislative power of majorities. The Canadian Bill of Rights was enacted in 1960, during John Diefenbaker's tenure as prime minister. It applies to federal law only, because it was not ratified by the provinces, and it is not part of the Canadian Constitution.

The Canadian Charter of Rights and Freedoms became part of the Canadian Constitution when it was amended and patriated in 1982. The Charter of Rights and Freedoms should not be confused with the Bill nor referred to as the 'Canadian Bill of Rights'.

The Canadian Charter of Rights and Freedoms contains what is popularly known as the 'notwithstanding clause'. This clause allows Parliament or a provincial legislature to pass— for a limited period of time—legislation that contravenes the Charter. In other words, if the notwithstanding clause is invoked, a federal or provincial statute may operate 'notwithstanding' (i.e., despite) a provision in the Charter. In 1988 Quebec invoked this clause to permit a French-only sign law, which contravened the Charter's guarantee of freedom of expression.

> Stroud apparently does not know the Charter is part of our Constitution, and is legally superior to the Bill of Rights. At one point he even confuses the two.
> *Daily News* (Halifax) 27 June 1993: 49

> The government has legal advice indicating Quebec could restrict the use of English on signs without resorting to the use of the constitution's notwithstanding clause, the tool it used in 1988 to override the Charter of Rights and Freedoms and ban bilingual signs.
> *Gazette* (Montreal) 25 April 1993: A1

See also CONSTITUTION.

Canadian Heritage

see HERITAGE CANADA

Canadianisms and Canadian pronunciations

Canadianisms are words or meanings peculiar to the English of Canadians. For example, *washroom*, meaning a room equipped with a toilet or toilets, especially in a public building, is a Canadianism. Canadianisms—at least those used right across the country—pose no communication problems when Canadians are dealing with each other, but these expressions can baffle the speakers of other national varieties of English: Britons, Americans, Australians, New Zealanders, South Africans, Indians, Bahamians, and so on. When Canadians leave the country and ask for a *washroom*, they may be directed to a sink or a laundry room. Below are some examples of words and phrases familiar in Canada but little-known elsewhere.

Education
bird course
supply teacher
university calendar

Hockey
rink rat
shinny
stickhandle

Policing
detachment (police
  headquarters)
ghost car (unmarked
  police car)
musical ride

**Product names
  used generically**
javex
gravol
tensor bandage

Weather
Chinook (warm
  winter wind)
humidex
whiteout

Food
butter tart
club sandwich
pepper squash, acorn
  squash

Household
blue box
call display
dish soap

Politics
acclamation (no-contest
  election)
language police (see
  Quebec English)
riding (electoral
  district)

Streets & roads
autoroute
grid road
man drag

Miscellaneous
klicks (kilometres per
  hour)
joe job (menial job)
suck (crybaby)

Canadian English pronunciations are pronunciations common and acceptable only in Canada (which is not to say that these are the pronunciations used by a majority of Canadians). Below are some examples:

aria pronounced like area
claret to rhyme with chalet rather than ferret
genuine to rhyme with wine rather than win
khaki to rhyme with malarkey rather than lackey or hockey

Standard Canadian English is distinct from both Standard British English and Standard American English. Additions to, and divergences from, the English of the motherland, once derided by genteel British visitors to Canada, are now recorded in—and given legiti-macy by—Canadian dictionaries. Generally, as the former colonies of Britain gained political independence, they also gained linguistic self-confidence, resulting in the production of dictionaries reflecting national standards of English, for example, the Canadian Oxford Dictionary, the Dictionary of Jamaican English, the Macquarie Dictionary of Australian English, and the South African Concise Oxford Dictionary.

Canadians who are aware of some of the unique elements of Canadian English are less likely to assume that their usage is wrong when they look in vain for a familiar word, meaning, spelling, or pronunciation in a British or American dictionary. Similarly, they are less likely to assume the speakers of other dialects of English are making a mistake when they use an unfamiliar word or pronunciation.

See also ACCENT, DIALECT, VARIETY; AFTERWARDS, AFTER; ALSO, AS WELL; AWOL, AWL; BABY BONUS; BACK OF; BLEU, ROUGE; BLOND, BLONDE; CALLOUS; CHOMP, CHAMP AT THE BIT; DATES; DIVED, DOVE; DOMINION OF CANADA; ENDORSEMENT, ENDORSATION; FINALIZE; FORCEFUL, FORCIBLE; FORGET, FORGOT, FORGOTTEN; FOREST; GARAGE; GENUINE; GOT, GOTTEN; HAVE GOT, HAVE GOT-TEN; KEEP FROM; KHAKI; HOLIDAY, VACATION; LACK FOR; MARRIAGE; QUEBEC ENGLISH; QUIT; QUITE; REEVE; ROAD; -SELF, -SELVES; SANATORIUM, SANITARIUM; SICK, ILL; SLED; SOUND OUT; SPELLING, CANADIAN; STANDARD ENGLISH, STANDARD; VAN DOOS; VISIT WITH; YOGURT, YOGOURT.

Canadian Shield, Laurentian Shield, Precambrian Shield All three names are correct for the rock formation that covers about forty per cent of Canada's area. Over time, this formation has been marked by the advance and retreat of glaciers. The Shield arcs around Hudson Bay from the Northwest Territories, through northern Saskatchewan and Manitoba and northern and central Ontario and Quebec, to Labrador and Baffin Island; the area is characterized by muskeg, thin soil, expanses of bare rock, and forest cover (in the south), and contains an abundance of lakes and rivers. The same Precambrian rock formation protrudes in Scandinavia, where it is known as the Baltic Shield.

In the heart of the Canadian Shield, a vast sweep of lakes and forest and mostly rock, it was an area

largely unsettled until early this century when rich ore bodies were discovered—nickel and silver mainly to the south and west, gold to the west, iron, lead, zinc, and copper in and around Rouyn—and towns went up as if overnight.
Ken Dryden *The Game* 1983: 67

Hydro's transmission system is also weakened by its location on the Laurentian shield, whose rocky structure resists, rather than absorbs, the geomagnetic voltages.
Gazette (Montreal) 14 March 1990: A6

(*Shield* is usually capitalized.)

Even though most Canadians think the Precambrian shield is a birth control device, territorial integrity (holding on to our northern turf) remains our strongest sustaining myth.
Maclean's 21 Nov. 1988: A49

(*Shield* is usually capitalized.)

cancel out   Several commentators object to the phrase *cancel out* as a wordy synonym for *cancel*. However, *cancel out* conveys ideas not expressed by *cancel*. The phrase *cancel out* is generally used when each of two forces or things acts to offset or neutralize the other. *Cancel out* is also used informally to mean withdraw, as in 'They cancelled out at the last minute'.

Canadians usually double the *-l-* (*cancelled*, *cancelling*), as do the British; however, Americans prefer single-*l* spellings (*canceled*, *canceling*).

Powell went on to a fine career in the Attorney-General's office, but when he looks back on the Ballard case, regret almost cancels out the satisfaction of having won.
Jack Batten *Robinette* 1984: 196

Your uninformed, uncaring, random vote cancels out my carefully considered choice.
Edmonton Journal 14 June 2004: A3

Actress Ann Jillian was originally scheduled to speak about breast cancer, but cancelled out for personal reasons. . . .
Toronto Star 23 March 1993: A3

See also DOUBLING THE FINAL CONSONANT.

candela   see APPENDIX II

candelabrum, candelabra, menorah   The plural of *candelabrum* (a candle-holder with several branches) is either *candelabra* or *candelabrums*. In contemporary usage *candelabra* is also well established as the singular, yielding the plural *candelabras*. Dictionaries list all of these forms.

A *menorah* (pronounced *men OR ah*; plural *menorahs*) is a candelabrum—with seven to nine branches—that is a traditional symbol of Judaism.

Candles are lit in a special eight-branched candelabrum known as a menorah—one candle the first night of Hanukkah, two the second night and so on.
Gazette (Montreal) 12 Dec. 1990: A3

The most outrageous candelabra in this show were designed by Colleen Hussey.
Vancouver Sun 20 Dec. 1990: C15

(Here *candelabra* is plural.)

Use a candelabra to add Gothic drama.
Calgary Herald 17 Dec. 2004: C2

(Here *candelabra* is singular.)

Greene offers a detailed description of how to make pretzel dough and form it into menorahs (candelabras), stars of David, and other shapes appropriate for Chanukah.
Globe and Mail (Toronto) 4 Dec. 1985: E9

(Here *candelabra* or *candelabrums* would also be accepted.)

See also PLURALS, REGULAR, IRREGULAR, FOREIGN.

candidly   see SENTENCE ADVERBS

cannon, canon   The weapon is spelled *cannon*: 'cannon fodder', 'cannonball', 'a loose cannon'. *Canon* is the spelling associated with rules and ecclesiastical sanction: 'the canons of good taste', 'canon law', 'the canon of gospels'. Often people mistakenly use the same spelling for both words, although which spelling that is depends on which word they see more often.

In literary criticism, 'the canon' is that body

of literary works traditionally regarded as most important and worthy of study. This concept has been critiqued to the point that 'the canon' is now rarely seen in print without quotation marks.

> Late yesterday, police loosed water cannons and tear gas on rioting students and activists who rampaged through a McDonald's and attacked storefronts in Paris.
> *Gazette* (Montreal) 19 March 2006: A8

> For as we scan 'the canon' it quickly becomes clear that the questioning of ruling ideas and the breach of tradition are themselves a tradition.
> *Queen's Quarterly* 101.4 (1994): 828

See also ITALICS AND QUOTATION MARKS.

cannot, can not Both *cannot* and *can not* are accepted. The single-word spelling is much more common.

> An important component of their argument was that a law which cannot be enforced is a bad law.
> Janine Brodie, Shelley A.M. Gavigan, and Jane Jenson *The Politics of Abortion* 1992: 40

> We simply can not afford any more delays.
> *Windsor Star* 25 Jan. 2006: A3

(Here the word may have been split in order to make *not* more emphatic.)

cannot help, cannot but, cannot help but These three phrases are all used in Standard English to mean 'to be unable to do otherwise than'. Some commentators have criticized *cannot help but* as an illogical blend of *cannot help* and *cannot but*; logical or not, however, it has become an established idiom over the last fifty years, and is now quite common in formal writing.

> A review of a living poet cannot help being written with one eye on the poet: she will read it, whether it's a good review or not, and she will judge us.
> Margaret Atwood *Second Words* 1982: 307

> . . . for the originals cannot last, and the copies cannot but lose of the life and truth.
> R. A. Wilson *The Birth of Language* 1937: 149

Yet anyone who reads Gallant's work cannot help but come to the conclusion that for her there are two kinds of people: the free and the trapped.
> Janice Kulyk Keefer *Reading Mavis Gallant* 1989: 32

canoeing see -E

canon see CANNON, CANON; RELIGIOUS TITLES

can't see CONTRACTIONS

Cantonese see MANDARIN

Canuck, Johnny Canuck, Janey Canuck
In contemporary usage, *Canuck* (stressed on the last syllable) is a nickname for Canadians generally. However, the term does have a history in Quebec and the northeastern United States of being used in a derogatory way to refer specifically to French Canadians. The origin of the term is obscure; it has been connected to the Iroquoian *kanuchsa*, 'hut'; to the Irish surname *Connaught*, which French Canadians used as a nickname for Irish Canadians; and to the Hawaiian word *kanaka* meaning 'man'. A simpler explanation connects it to the first syllable of *Canada*.

Canuck was first recorded in the mid-1800s. By the turn of the century *Johnny Canuck* was being used to personify Canada in the same way that *John Bull* personifies England and *Uncle Sam* the United States. And by 1901 Emily Murphy, a feminist and the first woman magistrate in the British Empire, had assumed *Janey Canuck* as her pen name. During the Second World War, Leo Bachle created the cartoon character *Johnny Canuck*, who fought the Nazis single-handedly. The major hockey team in Vancouver has been called the *Canucks* since 1946.

> By 1946, almost all of the Canuck soldiers' European and British wives had made their way to Canada.
> *Sudbury Star* 8 May 2006: A7

(Here *Canuck* is simply a synonym for *Canadian*.)

Martin O'Malley writes an interesting column on nomenclature, but I was disappointed that he did

not include the Vancouver Canucks in his 10 worst list. Does he not realize that Canuck is an offensive term to many Canadians? That a Canadian team should bear the name Canucks is one of our lesser national disgraces.
Globe and Mail (Toronto) 21 Jan. 1985: S8

(*Canuck* seems to be a nickname like *Yankee*: it is used both proudly and pejoratively.)

See also YANKEE.

Canute   According to legend, Canute the Great (995–1035), king of Denmark, Norway, and England, once commanded the tide to stop in order to show his sycophantic followers that in fact he was *not* all-powerful. In contemporary popular allusions to the story, Canute's motivation has been altered; he is depicted as a fool vainly trying to defy forces beyond his control. The reader must determine from the context whether an allusion to Canute connotes the wise king or the arrogant fool. Canute is pronounced *kuh NOOT*.

The two symbols come together in the fine opening poem, where the mist is the poet's mortality, like the waves that reminded Canute of the limits of his power.
Northrop Frye *The Bush Garden* 1971: 97

(Frye alludes to the original legend.)

For the court to try to prevent homosexual couples from being treated like conventional families is like King Canute trying to stop the tide.
Vancouver Sun 9 July 1990: A6

(Here the writer alludes to the popular notion that Canute thought he could hold back the tide.)

canvas, canvass   *Canvas* is the usual spelling for the heavy hemp or cotton material used for tents, sails, tote bags, etc. A *canvas* (plural *canvases*) is a piece of canvas prepared for a painting, especially in oils.
   To *canvass* means to approach people systematically to solicit something from them, usually money for a charity, their vote in an election, or their opinion on an issue. A round of canvassing is called a *canvass.*

. . . I went to a boys' camp where we slept under canvas. . . .
Richard Davies and Glen Kirkland, eds. *Dimensions* 1986: 116

Jackson Pollock painted canvases with tubes instead of brushes. . . .
Jack Chambers *Milestones* 1983: 90

Building a course entails clearcutting up to 121 hectares of forest near Cypress Provincial Park. Students in the youth alliance plan to canvass door-to-door against the project.
Vancouver Sun 30 Oct. 1990: A2

Clean canvass tents sit on the shore of a thawing fiord hemmed with mountains.
Ottawa Citizen 22 July 1988: C11

(Here the correct spelling is *canvas*.)

capital, Capitol   *Capital* is the spelling used for capital punishment, capital letters, capital cities, and accumulated money.
   The *Capitol*, capitalized and spelled with an *o*, is the name of the massive domed building that houses Congress in Washington, D.C., and the elevation it is built on is called Capitol Hill. In some American states, the building that houses the legislature is also named the Capitol.
   In antiquity, the Capitol was the Temple of Jupiter, built on the highest of the seven hills of Rome. Capitol Hill was the hub of Roman political life. Thus the name of the American house of government is an allusion to the government of Classical Rome.

The protected harbor was a perfect site for a provincial capital and Simcoe moved his headquarters from Niagara-on-the-Lake.
Toronto Star 1 Jan. 1993: A7

But the Clinton administration must also make sure not to alienate too many Republicans on Capitol Hill.
Ottawa Citizen 10 June 1993: F1

In Virden (oil capitol of Manitoba), it was the first movie in years to play the defunct Derrick Theatre. . . .
Vancouver Sun 20 July 1990: D1

(The correct spelling is *capital.*)

Wisconsin Democrat William Proximire, known on Capital Hill as Senator Scrooge, is not on the

American ballot this week.
Maclean's 14 Nov. 1988: A36

(The correct spelling is *Capitol Hill*.)

capital letters   What to capitalize? Style guides devote scores of pages to this question precisely because the answer is so often a matter of preference. In this entry, the established rules of capitalization are presented first; then some points are discussed where current usage is quite variable.

The first word of a sentence is capitalized unless the sentence is enclosed in dashes or parentheses and contained within another sentence:

> Levi, on the other hand, writes not with detachment—how could that be possible for a survivor of Auschwitz?—but with a dispassionate lucidity that makes his observations all the more devastating.
> Janice Kulyk Keefer *Reading Mavis Gallant* 1989: 178

The first word of a direct quotation is capitalized unless the quotation blends syntactically into the sentence in which it occurs:

> Then the Mountie, shaking his head, remarked, 'And all we wanted was to get their names as the one thousandth car to cross the bridge.'
> Max Braithwaite *The Night We Stole the Mountie's Car* 1971: 74

> Are you telling me that English-speaking Canadians, almost exactly two hundred years later, 'still only grudgingly concede' the right of Claude Jodoin to go to Mass?
> Eugene Forsey *A Life on the Fringe* 1990: 85

When a reporting clause (e.g., 'Mary said') occurs in the middle of a quoted sentence, the second part of the quotation does not begin with a capital:

> 'It was awfully sketchy,' he says, 'and it didn't bring home to the jury the accused's side of the story.'
> Jack Batten *Robinette* 1984: 74

When two full sentences are linked by a colon, the second may or may not begin with a capital. Usually it does not:

The appeals worked: in 1957, the Conservatives came into federal power after twenty-two years as the official opposition.
David V.J. Bell *The Roots of Disunity* 1992: 171

Only the first word of the complimentary close of a letter is capitalized: *Sincerely yours, Yours truly, Best regards, All the best.*

All proper nouns are capitalized, including the names of people, languages, religions, countries and their subdivisions, government departments, and organizations.

Noun–number combinations (things designated by number) begin with a capital letter: *Class 7B, Flight 104, Poll 54, Room 206.*

Popular names of geographic regions are usually capitalized: *the Barrens, the Canadian Shield, the Far North, the Gaspé, the Gaza Strip, the Gold Coast, the Maritimes, the Midwest, the Ottawa Valley, the Pacific Rim, the Panhandle, the Prairies, the Sunshine Coast, the West Coast.*

However, descriptions of geographic regions are not capitalized: *northern Alberta, the coast of Labrador.*

Names, scholarly or popular, given to time periods are capitalized: *the Gay Nineties, the Jurassic (period), the Me Decade, the Middle Ages, the Precambrian (era), the Quiet Revolution, the Renaissance.*

However, time periods without specific names are not capitalized: *the eighteenth century, the seventies.*

Names of months, days of the week, and holidays are capitalized. The names of the seasons used to be capitalized but are no longer.

The words *sun, moon,* and *earth* are not usually capitalized. However, they are capitalized, for consistency, when they appear with the names of other planets: 'Mars has two satellites and Earth has one'.

In binomial scientific names of plants and animals only the first term is capitalized: *Sequoia sempervirens* (redwood), *Parus atricapillus* (chickadee).

Common names of animals are not capitalized: *dachshund, gerbil, palomino, robin.* However, proper nouns in the names of species or breeds usually retain their capitals: *Canada goose, Holstein, Labrador retriever, Pekingese, Siamese cat.*

When words such as *company, department, group, unit,* and *university* form part of a name, they are capitalized: *Sales Department, Health Unit, Laurentian University, Ministry of Education.* Subsequent references to 'the department', 'the unit', 'the university', or 'the ministry' usually are not capitalized. The exception occurs in legal writing, where 'the Company', for example, is used throughout a document to designate a specific company named in the preamble.

In the titles of books and works of art, the first word and last word are capitalized, as are the first word and last word of the subtitle, if there is one. All internal words are also capitalized except for coordinating conjunctions (*and, but, nor, or*), articles (*a, an, the*), and prepositions of fewer than five letters: *A Man Called Intrepid: The Secret War; Memoirs of a Bird in a Gilded Cage; Life Before Man.*

These rules also used to be applied consistently to newspaper headlines, to the titles of articles in magazines and journals, and to headings in books. However, a 'down' style, i.e., a style that uses fewer capital letters is becoming more and more popular. Often now newspapers capitalize only the first word in a headline, and many science journals capitalize only the first word in the title of an academic article. With respect to the finer points of capitalization in titles and bibliographies, professional and academic writers need to consult the style guides of particular publications or disciplines.

Adjectives derived from proper nouns are capitalized when they refer to a specific person or thing: *Roman* (Rome's) *law, Shakespearean* (Shakespeare's) *comedies.*

When such adjectives begin to refer to a type of thing they usually lose their capitals: *quixotic impulses, roman* (vs. italic) *type, venetian blinds.*

But this rule is applied inconsistently. Adjectives of nationality often retain their capital letters, as do adjectives derived from proper nouns in medical terms: *Caesarean section, Dutch oven, Fallopian tubes, Irish coffee, Turkish bath.*

When in doubt about the capitalization of a particular term, you can always look in a dictionary. It's customary to follow the recommendations of one dictionary consistently in a single piece of writing.

Whether the names of people's positions should be capitalized is a matter of some uncertainty. In the past, the names of positions that were considered important were usually capitalized: 'our new Principal' but not 'our new Janitor'. Today the spirit of the times is more egalitarian. The incumbents of very prestigious posts are often referred to in small letters: 'the prime minister', 'the duke', 'the archbishop', 'the president', 'the chief of staff'. Names of high-ranking positions are capitalized consistently only when they are used as titles in front of a person's name:

On most social and economic issues, Canadians know by now where Prime Minister Brian Mulroney stands.
Toronto Star 2 Jan. 1992: A12

He spent four years in Ottawa as an economic advisor to the prime minister and minister of finance.
Toronto Star 2 Jan. 1992: A13

However, the Queen is an exception to this democratizing trend. The word *queen* is always capitalized when it refers to the Queen of England and Canada:

The Rankin Family will be among the guests performing in the presence of the Queen today on Parliament Hill.
Daily News (Halifax) 1 July 1992: 18

But note that the word *queen* is not necessarily capitalized when it refers to the monarch of a foreign country—here, the Queen of the Netherlands:

Shortly before the queen and prime minister arrived, workers were being hoisted by a giant crane to search for bodies and survivors in apartments next to those plowed to bits by the plane.
Toronto Star 5 Oct. 1992: A3

The variable treatment of *queen* illustrates the principle of relativity in capitalization. Names of positions and official bodies are more likely to be capitalized within their own domains. For example, Canadian newspapers refer to the Canadian *Armed Forces* but the U.S. *army.*

Similarly, the in-house newsletter of a corporation or institution is likely to capitalize names of positions (*Vice-President, Personnel Director, Senior Analyst, Trustee*) that would not be capitalized by an outside publication.

Another area where capitalization varies is in the names of races and groups of people. *Black* and *white* usually are written without capitals. *Métis* and *Asian* are capitalized. *Native* and *Aboriginal* are capitalized in Canadian government documents (see ABORIGINAL PEOPLE[S]), though rarely in journalism. Politics can affect people's use of words that identify them. For example, *Black* may be capitalized as a point of pride (just as the word *Loyalist* is often capitalized in Canada), or to designate an ethnic group with a shared culture and common goals. And *Native people* is often capitalized when it parallels *Canadian people*, designating a political entity (see NATIVE).

When capitalization choices seem both arbitrary and sensitive, a writer should aim to be as impartial and consistent as possible. In other words, parallel terms should appear in parallel form in the same piece of writing: *not* 'Anglophone' and 'francophone', 'energy minister' and 'Minister of Finance', 'pope' and 'Dalai Lama', 'Nordic' and 'hispanic'.

See also BLACK; EAST, WEST, NORTH, SOUTH; DALMATIAN, DOG BREEDS; NEW YEAR'S DAY; SACRED WRITINGS; THE, A, AN.

Capitol   see CAPITAL

capitulate   To *capitulate* used to mean to surrender only under specified conditions. However, the idea of conditions has disappeared from the current meaning, which is to yield completely.

> The public authorities reiterate their determination not to capitulate to blackmail/terrorism.
> *Calgary Herald* 18 March 1993: A5

> 'I'm hearing that the schools are capitulating to anti-choicers who don't want anything to do with Planned Parenthood.'
> *Calgary Herald* 28 April 1993: B3

cappuccino   *Cappuccino* is an Italian-style espresso coffee with frothy, steamed milk. Note the correct spelling with two *p*'s followed by *u* and two *c*'s. The plural is *cappuccinos*.

captivate, capture   To *captivate* means to fascinate or enthrall ('The children were captivated by the puppet show') while to *capture* means to seize ('It captured their attention'). 'To captivate someone's interest', like 'to fascinate someone's interest', is redundant. When *attention, interest*, or *fancy* is the object, the verbs *capture* and *catch* are better choices than *captivate*.

> Each gesture threw another thread of a gossamer net of fascination around the men. Jack was particularly captivated.
> *Canadian Fiction Magazine* 64 (1988): 29

> The dancer's 30-minute routine captivates the crowd, including one 6-year-old boy who sits on the stage staring with his mouth open wide, hardly believing what his eyes are seeing.
> *Gazette* (Montreal) 5 March 1989: D2

> Yet today, as an adult, there's little that captures my fancy on that stretch of Bloor St. anymore.
> *Toronto Star* 25 March 2002: A3

> This toy will captivate the interest of tots from 12 to 24 months with its simple sorting activity, working levers and peg people.
> *Vancouver Sun* 7 Dec. 1990: F2

(Here *capture* would be more idiomatic.)

carafes   see -F, -V-

carat, karat, caret   A *carat* is a unit of weight (200 milligrams) used for measuring precious stones.

A *karat* (sometimes also spelled *carat*) is a measurement of the amount of gold in an object: a 24-karat gold ring is pure gold; an 18-karat gold ring is eighteen parts gold to six parts alloy; a 10-karat gold ring is ten parts gold and fourteen parts alloy, and so on.

A *caret* (^) is a wedge-shaped mark used in copy editing to show where something is to be inserted into a text.

> A shipwreck salvor says he has found a 964-carat

emerald off the coast of Florida that he believes was once intended as a gift to Queen Isabella of Spain.
Vancouver Sun 5 April 1993: C8

. . . the 22-karat gold coin was minted for the collectors market, and was limited to 4,500 copies.
Vancouver Sun 30 Jan. 2006: C3

'I've seen 14-carat gold pacifiers worn by teenagers.'
Daily News (Halifax) 13 Feb. 1993: n.p.

(The more common spelling for the gold measure is *karat*.)

carburetor   see SPELLING, CANADIAN

Cardinal   see RELIGIOUS TITLES

care   see COULDN'T CARE LESS

careen, career   People and vehicles that lurch from side to side, bounce, bob, or ricochet are said to *careen*; *careen* is also used figuratively to describe erratic thought and behaviour. To *career* means to move rapidly over a course, often out of control. Some commentators suggest that *careen*, unlike *career*, implies a swaying motion; but this distinction seems artificial, since fast-moving objects are quite likely to sway. In many contexts either word will do.
   In British English the use of these two words is different. The usual British meaning of *careen* is lean or tip over: for example, a boat is careened for caulking or painting. The North American sense, to proceed erratically, is considered a confusion with *career*.

We can hear the bus coming long before it careens around the corner, reggae music blaring through the windows.
Torch: University of Victoria Alumni Magazine Spring 1990: 17

On Sept. 3, with these and other illogical thoughts careening through his mind, Trottier felt physically ill.
Calgary Herald 21 Oct. 1994: C4

He careened from stage left to stage right, from front to back, bouncing around like a super-charged pinball.
Globe and Mail (Toronto) 24 Sept. 1985: E3

Gasps of joy turned to screams of terror yesterday as a Metro zoo monorail train lost power, careered backwards and slammed into another train, injuring 27 people.
Toronto Star 12 July 1994: A1

career-minded, careerwise   see -MINDED, -WISE

carefree, careless   Generally, these two words are distinguished: *carefree* means untroubled, without a care, and *careless* means not vigilant enough, sloppy. In literary usage, however, *careless* is also used as a synonym for *carefree*.

I knew he meant our College quadrangle, for . . . it had been while he knew it a place of sunshine and of the laughter of the careless youths who play croquet there.
Robertson Davies *One Half of Robertson Davies* 1978: 114

(Here *careless* means free of cares.)

caret   see CARAT

carful   see -FUL, CUPFUL, SPOONFUL, TEASPOONFUL

cargo   see -OS, -OES

Caribbean   see WEST INDIES

Cariboo, caribou   Historically, *cariboo* and *caribou* were spelling variants, but in this century they are clearly distinguished. *Cariboo* is the correct spelling for the region of the Cariboo Mountains in southern British Columbia, and for things associated with the gold rush of the 1860s, such as 'Cariboo fever' and the Cariboo Road.
   Caribou is the correct spelling for the North American reindeer (plural *caribou* or, less often, *caribous*), which once ranged from coast to coast in Canada and as far south as Massachusetts; for the Caribou Inuit, who live west of Hudson Bay (so named because until recently they depended on caribou for food, clothing, and shelter); for the twin-engine airplane made by de Havilland; and for the names

of several Canadian towns located outside BC.

In Quebec, *caribou* has two additional meanings, both borrowed from French. It is a beverage made of red wine and whisky, and a hardline sovereigntist. The sovereigntist meaning is not an allusion to the stiff drink. Rather it's an allusion to the thousands of Quebec caribou that drowned while trying to migrate across the flooded Caniapiscau River in 1984. The sovereigntist who pushes for a sovereignty vote regardless of the political climate and the chance of success is likened to the ill-fated and instinct-driven caribou.

> After spending several days touring the city, the more adventurous head to the Island (meaning Vancouver Island), the Southwest, the Cariboo, or the Okanagan.
> Alan Tucker, ed. *The Penguin Guide to Canada* 1991: 570

> Moose, wolves, and caribou populate the northern forests. . . .
> Alan Tucker, ed. *The Penguin Guide to Canada* 1991: 503–4

> If after being raised domestically [wolves] are returned to the wild, they will observe caribous with only casual interest; even when they are hungry it never occurs to them that the caribous are potential prey.
> Irving M. Zeitlin and Robert J. Brym *The Social Condition of Humanity* 1991: 28

(The more common plural is *caribou*.)

> Councillor Ed McMaster of Caribou said he . . . agreed the lobsters shouldn't be taken to New Brunswick for processing.
> *Chronicle-Herald* (Halifax) 14 May 1988: 23

(This *Caribou* is in Nova Scotia.)

> Nowadays, the carnival is very much a family affair, and while you can still buy caribou (and much more refined drinks besides), you have to drink it at the SAQ Bistro.
> *Gazette* (Montreal) 24 Jan. 2004: I1

> The incident inspired the nickname 'caribou' for the PQ hard-liners of the time, who wanted to plunge into a sovereignty referendum the party had little chance of winning. Back then, the caribou were in the minority. Now the herd has grown, and the entire party seems to be made up

> of caribou. . . . The proposed policy could be summed up as 'sovereignty or bust'.
> *Gazette* (Montreal) 21 Aug. 2004: A21

See also MOOSE.

cariole see SLED

carnival, Carnaval *Carnival* is the correct English spelling; *carnaval*, with three *a*'s, is French. The French spelling may be used in English to refer to the annual winter festival in Quebec City (*le Carnaval de Québec*), but only if the word is capitalized.

> . . . Quebec City's winter carnival is the world's third largest outdoor bash, after Rio and New Orleans' Mardi Gras.
> *Calgary Herald* 12 Nov. 1994: F6

> We are reminded of this event, the Carnaval de Quebec, with a 14-cent stamp, issued in 1979.
> *Chronicle-Telegraph* (Quebec City) 14 Aug. 1991: 10

> But they won't upstage Bonhomme, Carnaval's cheerful mascot.
> *Gazette* (Montreal) 21 Oct. 1994: A5

> Caps have Carnaval against Nordiques: Capitals 12; Nordiques 2.
> *Gazette* (Montreal) 7 Feb. 1990: D2

(The choice of *Carnaval* here may well have been a deliberate reference to the festival.)

carousel see MERRY-GO-ROUND

carrier see JOB TITLES

Carrier, Nat'ooten, Wet'suwet'en, Dakelh, Sekani, Tsilhqot'in, Chilcotin The name *Carrier*, which designates an Aboriginal group of the central interior of British Columbia, is still in use (e.g., the Carrier-Sekani Tribal Council in Prince George), although some groups among the Carrier also use Aboriginal names: the *Nat'ooten*, the *Wet'suwet'en* (pronounced *weet SOOH wet an* and occasionally spelled *Wit'suwit'en*), and the southerly *Dakelh* (*DAH kelth*). The languages of these peoples (one of which is called Carrier) belong to the Athapaskan family.

The *Sekani* (*SEK an ee*) are a related people who live to the north of the traditional territory of the Carrier but are associated with them politically.

The *Tsilhqot'in* (*tsil KOAT in*), whose traditional territory is farther to the south, are closely associated with all these groups. Their language is also Athapaskan (Na-Dene). They were formerly called *Chilcotin*.

Chief Jimmy Stillas was an admired leader of the 525 Carrier and Chilcotin Indians of the Ulkatcho reserve.
Vancouver Sun 9 Dec. 1992: A8

Carrier, spoken in north-central B.C., and Halkomelem, spoken in the Lower Mainland, are about as similar as English and Mandarin Chinese.
Vancouver Sun 12 May 1990: R4

She and fellow students—among them, three elders who speak Carrier—studied with six instructors.
Vancouver Sun 9 March 2000: B7

The Carrier-Sekani Tribal Council represents 12 central interior Indian bands.
Vancouver Sun 11 Aug. 1990: A13

The focus on land gained further strength in the court case launched by the Gitksan-Wet'suwet'en of the Smithers area in the early '80s.
Vancouver Sun 4 Oct. 1994: A13

The creation of Williston Lake to feed the turbines of the W.A.C. Bennett Dam in the late 1960s was the start of a 20-year search for a new way of life for the Sekanis, who hunted in the valleys between the Wolverine Mountains in the Omineca Range and the Rockies.
Toronto Star 18 Oct. 1992: B2

(The names of most Aboriginal groups are not made plural with *s*; *Sekani* would be better here.)

See also ABORIGINAL PEOPLE(S); GITXSAN; APPENDIX III.

carryall   see SLED

carry on, carry-on   see IDIOMS; PHRASAL VERBS

carry out   see IDIOMS

carryover   see PHRASAL VERBS

case   In contemporary English, word order is critical to meaning: 'The man held the child' means something quite different from 'The child held the man'. In some languages, including Old English, endings added to *man* and *child* would distinguish between the actor and the acted upon in these sentences, and word order would not be crucial to the meaning. English nouns gradually lost all their case endings except for the possessive case, which is marked in writing with an *s* and an apostrophe or an apostrophe alone: 'John's book,'; 'the students' essays'. For pronouns three cases survive:

subjective	objective	possessive
I	me	my
you	you	your
he	him	his
she	her	her
it	it	its
we	us	our
they	them	their
who	whom	whose

Sometimes writers are unsure whether to use the subjective or the objective case. The subjective (sometimes called the nominative) case is used for the subject of the sentence ('I will'); the objective (sometimes called the accusative) case is used for the direct or indirect object of the sentence ('Try me'; 'Pass me that section') and after prepositions ('before us').

In speech and informal writing, the objective case is commonly used after the verb *be*: 'It's me'. In formal usage, however, the subjective case is required because a pronoun that follows the verb *be* is a subject complement, not an object: 'It is I'; 'This is she'.

The significance of case—or, more precisely, of these forms of the pronouns—is, in fact, shifting, as increasingly tone or level of formality overrides grammatical function in determining pronoun form. For example, the speaker who says, 'Assuredly, it was not I!' (using the subjective case) in the context of a formal meeting may moments later call home and say, 'Honey, it's me!' (using the objective case). Speakers are using subjective personal pronoun forms to indicate formality and objective personal pronoun forms to indicate a more relaxed tone. Within compound objects, where *objective* forms are expected, the use of subjective forms has become very common: 'The news hit *she* and Sylvia hard'; 'This is strictly between you and *I*'. In these contexts, the appeal of the subjective pronoun forms may be an aura of refinement. The corresponding objective forms (*her, me*) seem blunter, more casual, and, thus, to some speakers, less polite: 'The news hit her and Sylvia hard'. With pronouns *who* and *whom*, this tonal polarity is reversed. It is the objective form, *whom,* that is marked as refined ('To whom should I send this?'), while the subjective form, *who,* is casual (Who should I send this to?'). Most language commentators object strenuously to the trend toward using pronoun forms to indicate level of formality or politeness. Grammarians label the use of objective personal pronouns in subject position 'uneducated' and the use of subjective personal pronouns in object positions HYPERCORRECTION. A broader view might allow that a shift is occurring in English whereby tone or level of formality is co-determining pronoun form.

Any shift in the language puts the formal writer in a quandary, and this one is no exception. If you write, 'The committee invited Dr. Cheng and *I* to address the council,' you risk the censure of traditional grammarians. Yet, if you write, 'The committee invited Dr. Cheng and me to address the council,' the objective form *me* may strike some readers as too casual. If, like most editors, you lean toward linguistic conservatism, you will use objective pronoun forms only in object positions.

See also BETWEEN YOU AND ME; HYPERCORRECTION; MYSELF, I, ME; POSSESSIVE; PRONOUNS BETWEEN LINKED VERBS; THAN; WHO, WHOM; WHO'S, WHOSE.

case in point, [case and point]　see MIS-HEARD EXPRESSIONS

casse-croûte　see QUEBEC ENGLISH

cast, broadcast　The past tense and past participle of *cast* are *cast*, whether the verb means to assign dramatic roles ('He cast her as Anne') or to throw ('The die was cast'). Either *broadcast* or *broadcasted* can be used for the past tense and

past participle of the related verb *broadcast*. Canadians favour the irregular form *broadcast*.

> On Tuesday, Al-Jazeera broadcast a video showing Hassan, who is in her 60s, sitting on a couch in an otherwise empty room.
> *CBC Magazine* online 20 Oct. 2004

castrate　see NEUTER

catalogue, catalog　Canadian writers prefer the longer spelling. *Catalogue* is the more common spelling in Britain, *catalog* in the United States.

catalyse, catalyze　see -IZE, -ISE, -YZE, -YSE

catalyst　In chemistry a *catalyst* is a substance that stimulates change in other substances, but that remains unchanged itself. *Catalyst* is also used metaphorically to refer to a person or thing that acts as a spur or precipitates change. The use of *catalyst* as a synonym for *reason* is disputed.

> From last place to a Stanley Cup in four years, it could only happen because, as catalyst and driving force, Orr brought the Bruins along with him.
> Ken Dryden *The Game* 1983: 104

> Her novels and plays are at one and the same time a reflection of, a tribute to, and a catalyst for the Acadians' struggle to survive culturally against great odds.
> Ben-Z. Shek *French-Canadian & Québécois Novels* 1991: 111

> . . . Dormidontov hints getting rid of the Communist-era names was the catalyst for this week's decision to rename every street inside Moscow's Garden Ring, the moving traffic jam that encircles the city centre.
> *Gazette* (Montreal) 13 June 1993: B5

(Here *catalyst* means reason—a use that is disputed.)

catastrophe, catastrophes　Usually, in English, a final *e* is silent, but there are several words borrowed from Greek in which a final *e* is pronounced *ee*, including *anemone, apostrophe, catastrophe, epitome, facsimile, simile,* and *stro-*

phe. Catastrophe and its plural *catastrophes* are sometimes misspelled *catastrophy* and *catastrophies*.

> The federal government must toughen standards for oil tankers before Canada's coasts are hit with an environmental catastrophy. . . .
> *Ottawa Citizen* 2 Nov. 1990: A5

(The correct spelling is *catastrophe*.)

See also EPITOME.

catchup   see KETCHUP

cater-corner(ed)   see KITTY-CORNER

catholic, catholicity, Catholicism   Spelled with a small *c*, *catholic* means universal, or embracing all. The noun corresponding to this meaning is *catholicity*.

With a capital *c*, *Catholic* usually means Roman Catholic, though it can also refer to other Catholic churches, such as the Anglican, Eastern Orthodox, and Philippine Independent, in which an apostolic succession of bishops has been maintained, although the authority of the pope has been rejected. The noun form is *Catholicism*.

> 'Ron has very catholic tastes,' says Ottawa jazz writer James Hale, a longtime friend who writes for Downbeat magazine. 'There's not a lot in jazz that he doesn't like.'
> *Ottawa Citizen* 1 May 2006: C3

> But she has become a star of far more than the opera house—and one of the keys to that has been the deliberate catholicity of her film recording career (she has more than 65 recordings, films and videos on the market.)
> *Vancouver Sun* 5 June 1993: C10

> Protestant extremists retaliated yesterday by shooting and wounding a Catholic driver who was dropping off his child at school.
> *Financial Post* 15 Nov. 1991: 2

> Eling thinks he left St. Anne's—a parish that emphasizes the Catholic side of the Anglican tradition . . . in reasonably good shape.
> *Gazette* (Montreal) 2 Jan. 1993: H8

> He said he sees no conflict between his Catholicism and his biblical research.
> *Toronto Star* 10 April 1993: A2

> There's an evil genius behind this bill. The evil aspect is how it forces separate school systems to choose between a catholicity principle and a monetary interest.
> *Calgary Herald* 21 April 1994: A3

(Here it is a principle of *Catholicism*, not *catholicity*, that is at stake if separate schools accept full public funding.)

catsup   see KETCHUP

catty-corner(ed)   see KITTY-CORNER

cauldron, caldron   Both spellings are correct. Canadian writers prefer *cauldron*. *Cauldron* is more common in Britain, *caldron* in the United States.

caulk   see KHAKI

cavalry   see CALVARY

cave-in   see PHRASAL VERBS

caveat emptor   see LATIN PHRASES

cay   see QUAY

CCF   see NEW DEMOCRATIC PARTY

CE   see AD

-ce, -se   *Defence* is the usual choice for British and Canadian writers, especially in references to law or the military: 'The defence presented evidence'; 'Department of National Defence'. The American spelling *defense* is chosen less often, but is common in reference to sports: 'The team had a good defense'.

Offence follows the same pattern: most Canadian and British writers use *c*; the American spelling is *offense*. Some Canadians may choose *s*, especially for references to sports, and *s* is the usual choice in the phrase 'no offense taken'. Note that other forms, such as *defensible*, *defensive*, and *offensive*, are never spelled with a *c*.

Licence is the usual spelling of the noun ('driver's licence') in Canadian English and *license* of the verb ('is licensed', 'licensed mechanic'), but either spelling is accepted for either part of speech. In British English, the noun is spelled *licence* and the verb *license*. In American English, both the noun and the verb are usually spelled *license*. Note that the derivatives *licensable, licensee, licensor,* and *licensure* are always spelled with an *s*.

Most Canadians spell the noun *practice* and the verb *practise*: 'She has a medical practice downtown'; 'He practises the tuba daily'. However, many Canadians spell the verb with a *c*, and this variant is recommended by some Canadian newspaper style guides. The American spelling is usually *practice* for all forms.

Pretence and *pretense* are both used by Canadians, while British writers prefer the *c* and American writers prefer the *s*.

See also ADVICE, ADVISE; SPELLING, CANADIAN; VICE, VISE.

-ceed, -cede, -sede Only three English words end in *-ceed*: *exceed, proceed,* and *succeed*. The more common ending is *-cede*, as in *accede, concede, intercede, precede, recede,* and *secede*. All these words are derived from the Latin *cedere*, 'to go'. The spelling of *procedure* probably reinforces the tendency to misspell *proceed* as *procede*.

Supersede is the only word that ends in *-sede*. *Supersede* is derived from the Latin words *sedere*, 'to sit', and *super*, 'on top of'.

If 1,000 employees don't leave voluntarily, then the company will procede with layoffs.
Vancouver Sun 1 Nov. 1990: C6

(The correct spelling is *proceed*.)

He learned how to count money and transact business in some of the many Black communities that had become so numerous in Upper Canada in the two decades preceeding the American Civil War.
William Teatero *John Anderson: Fugitive Slave* 1986: 16

(The correct spelling is *preceding*.)

Sadly, there is no reason to hope that final exams will ever be superceded by something better.
Star-Phoenix (Saskatoon) 20 April 2006: A3

(The correct spelling is *supersede*.)

CEGEP see QUEBEC ENGLISH; UNIVERSITY

ceiling see -IE-, -EI-

celebrant, celebrator The original and still current meaning of *celebrant* is one who performs a religious rite, particularly the Christian Eucharist. Some object, therefore, to the use of the word to describe participants in less solemn celebrations. However, *celebrant* is widely used to describe people engaged in private festivities or public revelry. *Celebrator* is an accepted alternative for those objecting to the non-liturgical use of *celebrant*.

At noon, there is a sung eucharist in the ruined nave of the abbey. The celebrant and preacher will be the bishop of Ramsbury.
Canadian Churchman April 1986: 15

Irreverent poet emeritus, reverent celebrant of being alive, Purdy refuses to succumb to emotional or intellectual sclerosis. . . .
Vancouver Sun 7 July 1990: D19

The out-of-control party overflowed onto the street, then to Swan's pub, where the celebrants performed the dance for bewildered patrons.
Times-Colonist (Victoria) 22 Dec. 2005: D6

Provincial Culture Minister Karen Haslam stunned celebrators at an Art Gallery of Ontario open house last night by announcing a $2 million increase to the AGO's operating grant.
Toronto Star 22 Jan. 1993: A1

cellos see -OS, -OES

Celsius, centigrade, Fahrenheit The terms *Celsius* and *centigrade* refer to the same temperature scale, in which zero is the freezing point of water and 100 the point at which water boils. Since 1948, this scale has been officially called *Celsius*, after Anders Celsius (1701–44), its Swedish inventor. This is the scale of the international metric system, adopted by Canada in 1971.

Most Canadians are also familiar with Fahrenheit temperatures because they're still used in cooking and in American weather reports. On the Fahrenheit scale, named after the German physicist Gabriel Fahrenheit (1686–1736), the freezing point of water is 32° F and its boiling point is 212° F.

The abbreviation for degrees Celsius is °C; for degrees Fahrenheit, °F. Newspapers omit the degree symbol (°), probably because it's not a character on the keyboard.

Celt, Celtic, Kelt, Keltic, Anglo-Celtic
Both *Celt* and *Kelt* are correct, but *Celt* is far more common. The initial letter may be pronounced either *k* or *s*, although some object to the *s* pronunciation. The name of the Boston Celtics, an American basketball team, is always pronounced *SELL tics*.

The *Celts* were the first Indo-European people to inhabit Europe and the British Isles. In modern times the term refers to the Irish, Scottish, Welsh, and Cornish people of Britain, as opposed to the English, who are descended from a later group of Indo-European invaders, the Anglo-Saxons. Among the Celtic languages are Irish or Irish Gaelic (formerly referred to as Erse), Cornish, Welsh, and Scottish Gaelic.

In Canada, the umbrella term *Anglo-Celtic* often refers to Canadians of British descent, as opposed to those whose ancestors came from outside the British Isles.

It is often assumed that every region but Ontario has an authentic voice, just as it is assumed that every group but the Celts and Anglo-Saxons have loveable ethnic peculiarities and every city but Toronto has a soul.
Margaret Atwood *Second Words* 1982: 294

Every immigrant who arrived in the West was expected to accept as quickly as possible the Anglo-Celtic Protestant values of his Canadian neighbours.
Pierre Berton *The Promised Land* 1984: 59

A surprise in the Dictionary of Afro-American Slang is the variety of expressions for whiteys like me. Cracker, honkey, kelt, hayeater, paddy and pale all mean the same thing: a white person.
Gazette (Montreal) 10 March 1990: J2

See also WASP.

cement, mortar, concrete *Cement* is a fine grey powder made by burning limestone and clay. Mixed with sand and water, cement makes *mortar*, the paste used to hold bricks in place; when gravel is added to the mixture, the rock-hard substance it sets into is called *concrete*. Technically speaking, finished sidewalks and building foundations are not cement but concrete.

Cement also is used to refer to any paste or gluey substance used to fasten things together. It may be a verb as well as a noun, and is also used figuratively.

The 105 were arrested after a blockade Feb. 7 at the clinic, a windowless cement building located in a quiet residential area.
Gazette (Montreal) 1 March 1989: F12

(Strictly speaking, the building is *concrete*.)

Starting a business isn't going to help cement a marriage.
Calgary Herald 7 Nov. 1994: C1

censor, censorship, censorial, censorious, censure To *censor* means to cut offending sections out of a play, film, letter, exhibition, or publication, etc., or to ban it entirely. The noun is *censorship*; those who exercise it are called *censors* and have *censorial* powers. People who constantly criticize others are described as *censorious*.

Censure is strong disapproval or harsh criticism; a book may be *censured* by critics without being *censored*.

'At one time, the pressures to censor were largely from fundamentalist sectors of the community. Now they are also coming from the feminist sector and minorities. . . .'
Daily News (Halifax) 28 Sept. 1994

Many critics censured Sassafras, Cypress and Indigo for what they described as its deliberately

alienating style.
Toronto Star 24 Dec. 1994: G17

He questioned whether school councils might be allowed to censure library books. . . .
Calgary Herald 4 Dec. 1994: B2

(The word required here is *censor*.)

Eventually the activists made their point, helped by the threat of civil servants' censorious scissors snipping at advertising copy.
Globe and Mail (Toronto) 25 Oct. 1985: n.p.

(Here *censorial* would be more appropriate.)

census   see -US

centigrade   see CELSIUS

centre, center   *Centre* is the British spelling and *center* the American. Generally, Canadian writers use *centre* when referring to a place, such as a shopping mall, a housing complex, or an entertainment or research facility. In the Prairie provinces, however, where spelling tends towards American practice, *center* is more often found for places: for example, the Canadian Plains Research Center, in Regina.

For the meaning *midpoint*, Canadians use *center* or *centre* with equal frequency in all kinds of writing. The same is true of the verb, and all three possible spellings of the present participle are found in Canadian writing: *centering*, *centreing*, and *centring*.

Raymond put the Redmen on the scoreboard 38 seconds into the second on a centering pass from defenceman Bryan Larkin.
Gazette (Montreal) 2 March 1989: B4

The current discussions are centreing on how to realistically present the history of the shuttle and the space station.
Windsor Star 23 Aug. 2003: F3

Above the dinner tables floated clusters of blue and white balloons attached to a block of ice, centring the table. . . .
Gazette (Montreal) 6 March 1989: F3

See also -RE, -ER; SPELLING, CANADIAN.

centre around   *Centre around*, as in 'Discus-

sion centred around job parity', is a widely used idiom. Nevertheless, some authorities have criticized the expression as illogical (because a centre is a point). To avoid criticism, in formal writing you may want to use *centre on*, or an expression such as 'focus on' or 'revolve around'.

Most of these techniques centre around preparing the bird, physically and mentally, for a life in the wild. . . .
Harrowsmith Jun.–Jul. 1985: 58

(Here *revolve around* might be better.)

The 1922 strike . . . was clearly seen by management as centring around the general question of control at the point of production, rather than the narrower racial issue.
Queen's Quarterly 92.1 (1985): 227

(Here *focusing on* might be better.)

centripetal, centrifugal   Forces tending towards the centre of a circle are *centripetal*. Forces tending outwards from the centre of a circle ('fugitive' from the centre) are *centrifugal*. Centripetal force pulls objects into the middle of a whirlpool. Centrifugal force makes it hard to stay on a curved highway ramp at high speeds. In both words the second syllable should be stressed: *sen TRIP it ul*; *sen TRIF yoo gul*.

He describes the provinces as 'quasi-nations,' each struggling to hang on to its autonomy and way of life. As economic forces push them toward integration, pride compels them to resist this centripetal pull.
Toronto Star 25 May 1993: A23

Tarah drops her gloves on the ice to get a better grasp on a friend's hands and they spin until the centrifugal force flings them in separate directions.
Ottawa Citizen 23 March 1993: C3

century   see AD, BC, CE, BCE, BP; HYPHENATION

ceremonial, ceremonious   Objects and occasions for ceremonies are *ceremonial*. *Ceremonious* means ritualistic, or formal and polite.

In Provence, the Occitan dialect is no more than a folkloric prop, fetched from the cultural attic to

furnish the odd ceremonial gathering with a few token phrases.
Gazette (Montreal) 27 June 1993: B1

In its early years, the business of the Royal Trust was conducted in formal and ceremonious ways. . . . Porters, in red uniforms, stood at its door.
Gazette (Montreal) 30 Jan. 1993: B4

More time elapses. The waiter reappears with the ceremonial presentation of the fish platter. The offering is slim and uninspired. . . .
National Post (Toronto)14 Aug. 2004: TO2

(Here *ceremonious* is more apt.)

certainly   see SENTENCE ADVERBS

certainness   see -NESS

cesarean   see CAESAREAN

ceteris paribus   *Ceteris paribus,* a Latin phrase meaning 'all other things being equal', is often pronounced *SET uh riss PAR uh bus,* but options abound for the pronunciation of the first syllable: *KET-, KATE-, SEAT-.*

Theorists in political studies and economics frequently use this qualifying phrase when describing relationships between factors: 'As inflation rises, *ceteris paribus* [if all other relevant factors remain constant], unemployment falls'. In formal writing, this foreign phrase should be italicized.

Political economy theories suggest that a country lacking political stability has an incentive, ceteris paribus, to let its exchange rate float, since it will be difficult for the government to gather support for the unpopular measures that may be required to defend a peg [fixed rate].
Bank of Canada Review (Ottawa) Winter 2002/2003: 17

That is because situations in the world are never *ceteris paribus*; any given situation brings together a web of contextual factors that may or may not be similar to those that were present in the experiment.
Ted S. Palys. Background report for BC Supreme Court, *Little Sister's Book and Art Emporium v. The Queen* 7 Oct.1994

See also LATIN PHRASES; MUTATIS MUTANDIS.

chaff, chafe, chafing dish   The noun *chaff* (rhymes with *laugh*) refers to the husks of seed or grain, or anything considered light and worthless. The verb to *chaff* means to tease good-humouredly.

The verb to *chafe* (rhymes with *safe*) means to rub, often painfully, against skin, or to vex, or to grow irritated. A *chafing dish* is a dish in which food can be cooked or kept warm at table. This device is not new: *chafing dish* has been part of the vocabulary of English since the fifteenth century, when one of the meanings of to *chafe* (from Old French *chaufer*) was to warm.

There, several rings of men surrounded the wheat, and with flails beat the grain loose from the chaff.
Geoffrey Ursell *Perdue, or, How the West Was Lost* 1984: 58

'A lot of it is junk,' admits Rayner of The Women's Bookstore—but a lot of it is anything but, she adds. You learn in time how to separate the wheat from the chaff.
Ottawa Citizen 27 June 1992: B3

Rub off the chafe of Freesia seeds and soak them 24 hours before sowing.
Daily News (Halifax) 8 March 1992: 37

(The word required here is *chaff.*)

As the Cowans made their book tour, they found that the men in television camera crews they worked with would chaff each other about such things as never learning how to operate the dishwasher.
Toronto Star 23 May 1992: J1

Most have a slightly higher crew neckband to conceal the collarbone and prevent chafing at the neck from the jacket.
Ottawa Citizen 19 March 1992: G2

He graduated to writing editorials and investigative features, but soon chafed at the constraints of a daily paper.
Saturday Night Feb. 1986: 10

The wool chaffing my legs made a rash of my pride.
Vancouver Sun 1 Feb. 1992: D4

(The word required here is *chafing.*)

Brides were inundated with chafing dishes, trays,

bowls, pitchers and ice buckets. . . .
Ottawa Citizen 2 May 1992: I16

chair, chairman, chairwoman, chairperson

The use of *chair* to refer to someone in charge of a meeting or group dates from 1658 (*OED*). Recently this gender-neutral word has become far more popular than the gender-marked *chairman* and *chairwoman,* or the longer alternative *chairperson,* which was coined in the 1970s.

> Until recently, he was a member of the board of directors and chair of the finance committee.
> *Rites* Feb. 1990: 5

See also JOB TITLES; METONYMY, SYNECHDOCHE; SEXIST LANGUAGE.

chaise longue, chaise lounge, [chez lounge], lounge chair

A chair you can stretch your legs out on—usually a piece of lawn furniture—is a *chaise longue,* plural *chaise longues* or *chaises longues*. The expression is borrowed from French and means 'long chair'. Since a long chair invites lounging, the French word *longue* was soon confused with the English word *lounge,* and many Canadians call this piece of furniture a *chaise lounge*. Both Canadian and American dictionaries list *chaise lounge* as a variant of *chaise longue*. British dictionaries do not: *chaise longue* is the only form accepted in Britain, where the term is most likely to refer to a piece of indoor furniture, a sofa with only one arm and a back along part of its length.

The confusion does not end there. Some writers now mistakenly use the spelling *chez lounge* for the piece of lawn furniture. This spelling may first have appeared as a pun: Chez Lounge is a common name for a bar. The French word *chez,* which means 'home of' or 'place of', is pronounced *SHAY* (not *SHEZ*).

Happily, the whole issue of the correct form of this expression can be avoided by calling the object in question a *lounge chair*.

> At the far end of her balcony Shier has created a restful nook for herself with a chaise longue hidden from the sight of rows of balconies that prolif-

erate in her neighborhood.
Gazette (Montreal) 4 June 1992: C1

> Her only concession to her growing health problem was a chaise lounge in her dressing room.
> *Daily News* (Halifax) 28 March 1992: 18

> Students enjoyed the new velvety couches, chairs and chez-lounges while sipping flavoured martinis.
> *Queen's Journal* (Kingston) 21 Sept. 2004: 1

(Here *chez-lounges* should be *chaises longues, chaise lounges,* or *lounge chairs*.)

> Picture yourself stretched out on a lounge chair by a sparkling pool in a lush tropical setting and then tell me spring break is only for kids.
> *Gazette* (Montreal) 27 Feb. 1992: G8

See also FOLK ETYMOLOGY.

chalet see QUEBEC ENGLISH

challenged see DISABILITIES

chamois, shammy

A *chamois* (usually pronounced *SHAM ee*) is a very soft, supple piece of leather often used for polishing shoes, cars, or blackboards. The plural (*SHAM eez*) is spelled the same as the singular: *chamois*. *Shammy* is an informal spelling.

Originally, *chamois* were made only from the hide of a goat-like antelope of Europe and Western Asia called the *chamois,* though now they are also made from the skins of other animals and even from cotton. The name of the antelope, and occasionally the name of the leather, is pronounced *sham WAH*.

> A recent tour of several Marks & Spencer stores turned up such fashion steals as a fabulous three-quarter-length, flange-shouldered wool jacket with chamois underlining. . . .
> *Globe and Mail* (Toronto) 20 Aug. 1985: F10

> In a room filled with shammy vendors and encyclopedia salesmen, Starkey throws no pitch, wears no throat mike.
> *Province* (Vancouver) 22 Aug. 1990: 16

champ at the bit see CHOMP

changeable see -ABLE, -(E)ABLE

character, personality, reputation *Character* usually refers to distinctive moral and mental qualities ('a strong character'), *personality* to social relations ('a charming personality'), and *reputation* to society's perception of someone ('She has a reputation for efficiency'). Conceivably, someone with a sterling character might have a boring personality and an undeservedly bad reputation.

Despite objections from some usage commentators, *personality* is now fully established as a synonym for *celebrity*.

Character is informal when used to mean a person with an original or eccentric personality.

Not only was there a celebrity air to it with the lights, the cameras, . . . and the handsome TV personalities, Peter Mansbridge and Brian Stewart—but there was something else in the air, too.
Whig-Standard (Kingston) 11 April 2001: 7

'You just mention his name and they start talking about him. . . . Apparently, he was quite a character.'
Vancouver Sun 11 June 1992: A12

charades, charade The guessing game involving pantomime is called *charades*. In the singular, the term is used figuratively to mean an obvious pretence or grotesque imitation. *Charade* is usually pronounced *sha RAID* in North America and *sha RAHD* in Britain.

The cops are never quite sure that they're not being led astray by a charade cooked up by a truly ingenious and twisted mind.
Times-Colonist (Victoria) 15 May 2005: D10

Still, she doesn't feel like going through the charade of nodding and smiling; not right now.
Margaret Atwood *Life Before Man* 1979: 285

Charter of Rights and Freedoms see CANADIAN BILL OF RIGHTS

Charybdis see SCYLLA

château, châteaux see PLURALS

chauvinism see SEXISM

cheap, cheaply *Cheap* is used in all kinds of Canadian writing to mean inexpensive or low-priced ('cheap parking', 'a cheap airline ticket'); these meanings do not have negative connotations. When applied to goods or accommodations, however, the word may also suggest shoddiness or inferiority. The context should make the connotation clear. Where it doesn't, as in 'They booked us into a cheap hotel', you may want to reword: 'a reasonably priced hotel' or 'a shabby hotel'.

Applied to people, *cheap* is both informal and derogatory, meaning ungenerous or stingy. *Cheap* is also very negative, suggesting unfairness, in the expressions 'cheap shot' and 'cheap trick'.

Cheap commonly precedes words like *price*, *cost*, *rate*, or *rent*, especially in informal writing. But this usage is also commonly criticized and best avoided in formal writing. Commentators argue that it is the item, service, or accommodation that is *cheap*; the cost, rate, or rent is *low*.

Cheap is also used as an adverb, most often in expressions such as 'come cheap', 'buy cheap', and 'get something cheap'. Some writers substitute the regular adverbs form, *cheaply*, in these contexts, but *cheap* is idiomatic and widely accepted.

Unlike most of his contemporaries, Wilson in particular, who had established the prewar plan in expectation of a short, cheap war, Kitchener believed in a long, costly conflict requiring mobilization of the resources of the British Empire.
Canadian Journal of History 14.1 (1989): 55

Try Vivaldi, which has reasonably satisfying Italian food and striking decor, or the Mazurka, a cheap and excellent Polish restaurant. . . .
Alan Tucker, ed. *The Penguin Guide to Canada* 1991: 201

Eventually, nothing else mattered and the company began offering consumers a selection of cheap, shoddy products.
Gazette (Montreal) 8 Dec. 1990: D1

This sounds like a lot, but it's only 2.5 per cent of the government's annual payroll—a cheap price for fairness and justice.
Vancouver Sun 20 March 1990: A17

(In formal writing, *low price* would be better.)

The town bought the power at the cheap 1905 price and sold it to its citizen users at attractive prices that still yielded it a large profit.
J.E. Smyth et al. *The Law and Business Administration in Canada* 1987: 331

(Here some commentators would prefer *low*.)

But it's a thrill that doesn't come cheap.
Vancouver Sun 8 Oct. 1994: A21

Miracles don't come cheaply.
Spectator (Hamilton) 13 June 1994: B2

(Here *cheap* would also be acceptable.)

See also ADVERBS WITHOUT -LY.

cheat see COLLOQUIAL

cheque, check, chequered, checkered
Canadian writers overwhelmingly prefer the spelling *cheque* for the bank draft, although they use *check* for all other senses of the noun ('a thorough check', 'check mark', 'the check for the meal') and verb ('Check it first').

Canadians prefer *checkered* ('a checkered tablecloth') over *chequered*, although both spellings are used.

The British also use *cheque* for a bank draft, but prefer *chequered* for the pattern. Americans rarely use the *-qu-* spellings, preferring *check* for all senses and the adjective *checkered*.

See also SPELLING, CANADIAN.

chest see BREAST(S)

chesterfield, sofa, couch, davenport, divan, settee, settle Canadians have several names for an upholstered piece of furniture with a back and armrests that seats more than two people, or on which one person can recline. *Chesterfield* is a Canadianism that emerged in the 1920s but has been declining in use since the 1970s. Of the 300 informants in the 'Survey of Vancouver English' (1984), 72 per cent gave *chesterfield* as one name for such an object and 30 per cent reported it as the only word they would use. However, age was an important factor in these results, since younger informants overwhelmingly preferred *sofa* or *couch*. Of

these two terms, *couch* has connotations of serviceability and comfort, while *sofa* may suggest a more fashionable piece of furniture.

Davenport, *divan*, *settee*, and *settle* are also used by Canadians, but only rarely. A *settle*, strictly speaking, is a straight-backed wooden bench with armrests and a storage cupboard under the seat.

One by one, tiny babies were brought to the largest chesterfield in the house and plopped down in a row.
Vancouver Sun 23 June 1994: C10

A deep sofa upholstered in exquisite ivory brocade invites visitors to sink into its cushioned depths.
Edmonton Journal 11 May 2006: F1

Some say we should throw our remotes into the recycling bin and go back to the old days, when changing a channel involved walking from couch to set, twisting a knob, and returning, on foot, to couch.
Calgary Herald 26 June 1994: E8

See also CHAISE LONGUE.

Chicana, Chicano see HISPANIC

chief see -F, -V-; -IE-, -EI-

Chilcotin see CARRIER

childish, childlike, infantile, juvenile
The connotations of *childish* are usually negative, while those of *childlike* are usually positive: 'His childish fear of social encounters was the negative side of the childlike simplicity everyone admired'. *Childish* can, of course, be neutral if the person being described is actually a child.

Infantile and *juvenile* are neutral when used of children, especially in scientific, legal, or sociological writing, but are often even more derogatory than *childish* when applied to adults.

Crankiness is an issue when working with child actors (and childish adults, but that's another story).
Gazette (Montreal) 15 May 1994: F1

He has worked for Holland America since 1986, traveling the world, collecting artifacts and satisfy-

ing a curiosity that is quite childlike in its intensity and innocence.
Vancouver Sun 8 July 1993: B5

I looked back to the two apple-cheeked girls in the doorway . . . and I saw that their faces shone with a childish innocence, unabashed as they were by the attention they were provoking from the audience. . . .
Canadian Fiction Magazine 64 (1988): 129

(In this description of children, *childish* is not derogatory.)

Some of them did a good deal to form my own infantile imagination, and I could well have fared worse.
Northrop Frye *The Bush Garden* 1971: 234

(Here *infantile* refers to an early stage of development.)

She also does a wonderful takeoff on a motherly Queen Elizabeth demanding the constitution back from some squabbling, infantile Canadian politicians.
Gazette (Montreal) 13 July 1990: F4

The works include two novels, two books of poetry, a juvenile novel and one book of photography.
Calgary Herald 11 June 1994: A17

(Here *juvenile* means 'written for children' and is neutral.)

We have all seen these juvenile dotards whose boast is that they are just as young as their sons or their grandsons; they do not realize what a pitiful boast that is.
Robertson Davies *One Half of Robertson Davies* 1978: 128

chili, chilly, Chile   In Canadian English, the spicy dish and the hot pepper are spelled *chili*, the adjective meaning cool or unwelcoming is spelled *chilly*, and *Chile* is the South American country.

Canadian dictionaries list only *chilies* as the plural of *chili*, but in fact *chilis*, which parallels *martinis*, *delis*, and *zambonis*, is also quite common.

In the United States, *chile*, the Spanish spelling, is a common alternative to *chili*. In Britain, *chili* is spelled with a double *l*: *chilli* or *chilly*.

Hearty chili is ideal for low-key entertaining.
Chatelaine 78.3 (2005): 144

The new Thai sauce is a flavourful blend of garlic, lemongrass, lime and chilies, and is a great dip for spring rolls and shrimp.
Canadian Grocer Dec. 2003/Jan. 2004

(*Chilies* is the standard plural of *chili*.)

Top half the slices with meat, chiles and cheese and cover with remaining bread slices.
Province (Vancouver) 23 Nov. 2005: B26

(In Canadian English, *Chile* is used only for the country.)

chimera, chimaera   A *chimera* (rarely, *chimaera*) is a Greek mythological monster with a lion's head, a goat's body, and a serpent's tail. By extension, it can be any horrid vision, mere illusion, or unrealizable fantasy. In this century biologists have appropriated the term for organisms containing genetically different tissues, formed by grafting or mutation. The *ch* in *chimera* is pronounced like a *k*, and the *i* can be either long or short: *kih MEAR uh* or *kye MEAR uh*.

Haliburton seems to have believed that the ideal for Nova Scotia would be a combination of American energy and British social structure, but such a chimera, or synthetic monster, is hard to achieve in practice.
Northrop Frye *The Bush Garden* 1971: 218

To get around this, the researchers want to merge DNA from the adult cells of motor neuron disease patients with rabbit eggs, to produce 'chimera' embryos that would provide stem cells that are good genetic models of the disease.
Calgary Herald 13 Jan. 2006: A17

See also -AE-, -OE-, -E-.

China   The official name of mainland or communist China is the People's Republic of China. Hong Kong, which was a British colony for 99 years, reunited politically with the mainland in 1997. Hong Kong is now a 'special administrative region' with economic autonomy within the People's Republic of China. Taiwan, which asserts its independence from the People's Republic of China, is called the Republic of China.

The meeting began with another embarrassing moment for the White House when an announcer referred to China by the formal name for Taiwan— Republic of China. . . .
Toronto Star 21 April 2006: A10

See also CHINESE NAMES, FAMILY NAMES; MANDARIN, CANTONESE; PINYIN

Chinese names, family names   When discussing Chinese names, the terms *first name* and *last name* inevitably lead to confusion, for, in China, a person's family name comes before his or her given name (for example, Mao Zedong's given name was Zedong). The terms *given name* and *family name* are less ambiguous across cultures. Common Chinese family names are monosyllabic (Zhang, Wang, Li, Chen, Zhou, Huang, Wu, Xu, etc.), and, formerly, two-syllable given names (Jinlan, Xiongwei) were the norm. Thus, until recently, it was easy for non-Chinese to guess which part of a Chinese name was the surname—the monosyllable. Currently, however, one-character, one-syllable given names are very popular, making it more difficult to discern the family name. A useful convention for indicating surnames (regardless of name order) is to put them in block letters: Dr. XU Chang.

The practice of putting family names first is not restricted to China. It is common in other countries where Chinese is spoken or where Chinese characters are used, i.e., in Japan, Korea, Vietnam, and Singapore. Family name first is also the norm in Hungary.

In Tibet, Burma, Java, and Iceland, there is no tradition of a family name passed from generation to generation. Also among some Aboriginal groups in Canada, patrilineal family names were not traditional and were adopted only at the behest of government officials.

See also MANDARIN, CANTONESE; PINYIN.

Chinese writing   see PINYIN; MANDARIN

Chipewyan, Chippewa   The *Chipewyan* (pronounced *chip uh WYE un*) are an Aboriginal people whose traditional territories are in northern Manitoba, Saskatchewan, and Alberta and the southern Northwest Territories. *Chipewyan* is also the name of their language, which belongs to the Athapaskan (or Na-Dene) language group. Most Chipewyan now also identify themselves as Dene or as members of the Dene Nation. (*Dene* is a word from their own language, while *Chipewyan* is the name the Cree called them.)

Chipewyan is both singular and plural, like most Aboriginal group names; *Chipewyans* is less common.

Chippewa (pronounced *CHIP uh waw*) and *Ojibwa* are two names for the same Aboriginal people. They speak Ojibway, an Algonquian language, and their traditional territory is in Ontario around the shores of Lake Huron. Although most names designating Aboriginal groups do not need to be pluralized with *s*, *Chippewas* is an exception (*Globe and Mail Style Book*).

Matonabbee and his Chipewyans ranged a vast hunting territory, extending from Hudson Bay to the Arctic Ocean to Great Slave Lake.
Robert M. Bone *The Geography of the Canadian North* 1992: 53–4

(Some writers would avoid *Chipewyans* here by using a phrase like 'Chipewyan hunters'.)

The success of [Samuel Hearne's] amazing journey was due to Chipewyan knowledge of the land and animals.
Robert M. Bone *The Geography of the Canadian North* 1992: 53

The Red Lake reservation was founded in 1889, and unlike other tribes, the Chippewa have kept their land intact and not sold off portions of it.
Edmonton Journal 24 March 2005: B5

The band, members of the Chippewa Nation, have been fighting for 50 years for the return of 2,200 acres of their reserve, expropriated in 1942 for Camp Ipperwash.
Toronto Sun 24 Feb. 1994: 51

See also ABORIGINAL PEOPLE(S); ATHABASCAN; DENE; OJIBWA(Y); APPENDIX III.

chomp, champ at the bit   Canadians who *chomp* at the bit—like a horse—may slightly outnumber those who *champ* at it, but either word is correct in this idiom, which means to be impatient or eager to begin something. *Champ* (rhymes with *damp*) and *chomp* (rhymes with *romp*) are variants; both mean to chew indelicately. *Champ* is the older form, dating from the sixteenth century and surviving in Canadian English only in *champ at the bit*. *Chomp* was a regional form in Britain that crossed the Atlantic to become, by the nineteenth century, the predominant form in Canada and the United States. And now *chomp* is competing with *champ* in Standard British English.

> Unscrupulous car salespeople like nothing more than wide-eyed customers who chomp at the bit to buy a car.
> *Canadian Consumer* March 1986: 5

> People were champing at the bit to play the video gambling games.
> *Toronto Star* 5 Jan. 1992: B1

See also STAMP, STOMP.

choose, chose   Both the present tense and the infinitive form of *choose* are sometimes incorrectly spelled *chose*. This confusion may arise because the rhyming word *lose* is spelled with only one *o*. *Chose* is the past tense.

> Whatever path you choose to building a pension, start soon.
> *Canadian Consumer* Jan. 1985: 14

> Of the 11 players they chose Wednesday, the most promising may be Clark.
> *Calgary Herald* 30 June 1994: C2

> Pro-choice discourse advocates women's right to chose while pro-life advocates the primacy of the right to life of the foetus.
> Janine Brodie, Shelley A. M. Gavigan, and Jane Jenson *The Politics of Abortion* 1992: 70

(The correct spelling is *choose*.)

chord   see CORD

choruses   see -US

Christian name   see FIRST NAME

chronic, acute   The word *chronic* characterizes the duration of an illness, not its severity. A *chronic* illness or problem persists over a long time. An *acute* illness is severe, sudden in onset, and resolved in the short term. Acute- and chronic-care medical facilities are those geared to short- and long-term stays respectively.

> 'They were ready to pay for John's immediate injury, right off the bat, but they won't pay for continuing pain and chronic problems.'
> *Toronto Star* 25 May 1992: A17

> . . . infants and young children infected with hepatitis-B virus rarely manifest an acute symptomatic illness, but commonly become chronically infected with the virus.
> *Gazette* (Montreal) 14 June 1994: B2

> The 87-year-old has been a patient at Kingston General Hospital for nine weeks and has progressed to the point where she no longer requires acute care.
> *Whig-Standard* (Kingston) 28 March 2006: 1

> A partial snapshot of Canada's chronic-care patients suggests those requiring long-term care in hospitals are younger than one might think.
> *Edmonton Journal* 23 March 2006: A8

Churchilliana   see -(I)ANA

cigarette, cigaret   *Cigarette* is the more common spelling, but *cigaret* is not incorrect. It's a chiefly American variant, seldom used by Canadian writers.

cineaste   see FILMMAKER

cinq à sept   see QUEBEC ENGLISH

circa, c., ca.   *Circa* (pronounced *SIR ka*) the Latin word for 'around', is used in front of dates to mean approximately. It is usually abbreviated to *c.* or *ca.* (or *ca* if other contractions do not take periods).

> This is a study of private association in Venice c. 1297 to 1423; the author is interested in how Venetians of various classes interacted with one another.
> *Canadian Journal of History* 14.1 (1989): 97

See also LATIN PHRASES.

circuses   see -US

cite, sight, site   To *cite* means to refer to a source or an example ('She cited four authorities'), or to single out either for praise ('She was cited for good work') or for blame ('He was cited for failing to obey orders').

To *sight* something is to see it. To *set your sights* on something is to aim for it.

A *site* is a location ('historic site', 'construction site'), unless it's a place that tourists must see, and then it may also be a *sight*. To *site* something is to put it in a particular location.

The trusts have been so successful in the United States that three have been cited by the United Nations for special merit awards in 1987.
Vancouver Sun 14 Nov. 1990: B2

The environment ministry cited itself for its failure to clean up the contaminated soils on the former Expo site on False Creek.
Province (Vancouver) 14 Dec. 1990: 42

cities   see NAMES OF RESIDENTS

citizen, national, permanent resident, subject, inhabitant, resident   A *citizen* or *national* of a particular state has obligations to that state and in return receives rights and protection. Anyone born in Canada or to a Canadian citizen living abroad is a Canadian citizen. A *permanent resident*, formerly called a *landed immigrant*, is someone who has been granted admission to Canada as an immigrant. Permanent residents are usually eligible to apply for citizenship after three years.

Nations, such as Britain, that have a monarch as head of state use the word *subject* as well as *citizen*. Canadians were considered *British subjects* until the passing of the Citizenship Act, 1977, when they became *Commonwealth citizens*.

Resident and *inhabitant* are general words for people who live in a certain place, whether they are citizens or not.

See also CIVILIAN; EMIGRANT, IMMIGRANT.

civilian   In war zones the term *civilian* refers to the general public as opposed to members of the armed forces. In peaceful settings *civilian* is also used to distinguish the public from police, firefighters, or any other uniformed group organized along military lines. Sometimes *civilian* refers to anyone outside a specified group, such as a sports team, band, or club, but this extended use is not suitable for formal writing. The phrase 'in civilian clothes' means in street clothes and may be applied to anyone who is out of uniform. Occasionally the term *civilian* is confused with *citizen*.

The fact is that the invention of the airplane destroyed the sanctuary of civilians beyond the range of surface weapons and changed the nature of warfare forever.
Ottawa Citizen 25 June 1994: B7

Civilians and police officers have received dozens of awards for bravery from the Eastern Region Ontario Provincial Police.
Whig-Standard (Kingston) 23 Sept. 2005: 12

(Here civilians are distinguished from police officers.)

Already dressed in civilian clothes, he was spotted nursing a beer in one of the Blue Jay training rooms.
Globe and Mail (Toronto) 17 Oct. 1985: C4

Kimberley civilians aren't buying this march-of-history angle, maybe because they think they can't afford it—and nobody's shown them a better way.
Canadian Heritage Magazine Feb.–Mar. 1986: 27

(The word required here is *citizens*.)

See also CITIZEN.

civilize, civilization   see -IZE, -ISE, -YZE, -YSE

civil law   see COMMON LAW

-ck-   see -C

clad, clothed   Some usage commentators have labeled *clad* (the irregular past participle of *clothe*) as archaic or obsolescent, suggesting *dressed* or the regular form (*clothed*) as alternatives. However, *clad* is used in perfectly ordinary contexts in many different kinds of writing and is quite acceptable. It is often found as part of a compound modifier: 'pyjama-clad', 'kilt-clad', 'fur-clad'.

> Five youths clad in just T-shirts and sweat pants were in hospital yesterday after police found them running around in the snow in -20 C temperatures.
> *Province* (Vancouver) 26 Nov. 1990: 6

> . . . streetcars and buses were full of the kerchiefed heads and pants-clad legs of the country girls who flocked to the city to work in the munitions plants.
> Miriam Waddington *Apartment Seven* 1989: 17–18

clamour, clamber To *clamour* is to cry out insistently, to make your demands heard, while to *clamber* is to climb with effort, sometimes using your hands as well as your feet. Some writers mistakenly use only one of these two words to cover both meanings.

Clamour rhymes with *slammer*, while *clamber* is pronounced either to rhyme with *amber* or exactly like *clamour*. The homophonic pronunciation is not incorrect but it has no doubt contributed to the mistaken lumping together of these two words.

> Party members from the region have long clamoured for restoration of benefits.
> *Sudbury Star* 29 Sept. 2000: A14

> These folks pulverize every human obstacle in their path as they clamber up the corporate ladder.
> *BC Business* April 2004: 38

> The hard rubber soles of many hip and chest waders can be very slippery when you're clamouring over slimy, rocky river bottoms.
> *Outdoor Canada* Summer 2002: 81

(*Clambering* is the word required here.)

> He observes that before the invention of the electric light customers were not clambering for a replacement of coal lamps. . . .
> *Education Canada* Spring 1995: 9

(*Clamouring* is the word required here.)

See also -OUR, -OR.

clandestine The basic meaning of *clandestine*

is secret, although the word strongly connotes illegality and underhandedness.

Clandestine is usually pronounced *clan DESS tin*. Some dictionaries, including the *Canadian Oxford Dictionary*, also list *clan DESS tine* and *CLAN duh stine*.

> Cocaine is prepared in clandestine labs and shipped from hidden airstrips dotting the tropical lowlands of eastern Bolivia near the Brazilian border.
> *Chronicle-Herald* (Halifax) 14 May 1988: 5

> For some reason I can never find a flashlight even though I tend to attempt these things under the cover of darkness, for fear of being watched, perhaps, or out of some sense that I am engaging in clandestine activity.
> *Queen's Quarterly* 96.2 (1989): 237–8

class   see SPECIES

classic, classical, Classical   In the seventeenth century the adjectives *classic* and *classical* were used interchangeably, and even today their uses are not completely differentiated. However, particular uses are commonly associated with each form, as follows.

Classic describes something of high quality and enduring interest, something that has become a benchmark by which similar efforts are judged: 'a classic study'. *Classic* also means absolutely typical: a 'classic case' exhibits all the features you would expect. In fashion and design, 'classic styles' are simple, tasteful, and as close to timeless as fashion gets.

'Classical music' is distinct from the popular music both of the present and of the past. 'Classical dance' is choreographed and performed in accordance with a codified tradition. A 'classical method', in any field, is standard or traditional as opposed to innovative. *Classical* also means having to do with ancient Greece and Rome—the language, literature, art, architecture, jurisprudence, and so on, of that era. In some contexts it isn't clear whether *classical* means ancient or merely traditional; thus it is a good idea to capitalize the adjective if it refers to ancient Greece and Rome.

In spite of the prairie dogma that every man was as good as the next, some were, in Orwell's classic phrase, more equal than others.
Pierre Berton *The Promised Land* 1984: 299

We need more, not fewer, of such dictionaries of usage, a good preparation for the compilation of which is still provided by Leonard Bloomfield's old, but still classical paper 'Secondary and Tertiary Responses to Language'.
W.C. Lougheed, ed. *In Search of the Standard in Canadian English* 1986: 49

(Here *classic* would be the usual choice.)

It was a classic scenario for a spinal injury.
Gazette (Montreal) 29 Dec. 1992: D1

The toolshed, which sometimes doubles as a garage, is a classic bluenose outbuilding and deserves to be immortalized by some magic-realist painter.
Harrowsmith Aug.–Sept. 1985: 14

'My fashions are wearable, classical, and we've already tested women's interest in the collection in Vancouver and it's been very good.'
Vancouver Sun 29 Dec. 1992: C3

(Here *classic* would be the usual choice.)

It is doubtful whether the market system ever worked in the automatic, self-regulating way in which the classical economists conceived of it.
Irving M. Zeitlin and Robert J. Brym *The Social Condition of Humanity* 1991: 77

To look at the range of Professor Kilpatrick's professional interests is to recognize both the vitality of the current renewal of interest in Classical studies and the breadth of vision that such study may yield.
Perspectives: Profiles of Research at Queen's 1986: 26

The book begins with the short chapter 'Aristotle and the Greeks,' then briefly covers the Roman and Late Classic Period.
Queen's Quarterly 94.3 (1987): 592

(The usual choice here would be *Classical*.)

See also BENCHMARK, HALLMARK.

clause　see entry in Glossary

clean　see ADVERBS WITHOUT -LY

cleaner, cleaning lady　see JOB TITLES

clear　see ADVERBS WITHOUT -LY; TRANSPARENT

cleave　Two different words in Old English, with contrary meanings, have curiously evolved into one form in contemporary English: *cleave*. To *cleave* means either to split or to cling. When it means split, the past tense is *clove*, *cleft*, or *cleaved*, and the past participle is *cleft* or *cloven* ('cleft palate', 'cloven hoof'). When it means cling, *cleave* is a regular verb with the past tense and past participle *cleaved*. Both verbs are literary or archaic, though the participles *cleft* and *cloven* are current.

There is some kind of maddening bond between them that I cannot seem to cleave.
Queen's Quarterly 96.2 (1989): 398

(Here to *cleave* means to split.)

Yet, though 'mate of the god of light,' she is also prepared (at least in the life of the mind) to renounce sexual passion, to cleave fully to her art.
Queen's Quarterly 92.2 (1985): 315

(Here *cleave* means cling to.)

Now Monette—hair thinner, frame fleshier though the famous cleft chin is as chiselled and classic as ever—is no longer acting.
Ottawa Citizen 24 July 1994: B1

See also -T, -ED.

cleft　see CLEAVE

clerk　see DERBY; JOB TITLES

clever　*Clever* suggests mental adroitness and the ability to find quick solutions to problems. *Clever* is not always a synonym for *intelligent*. It can be uncomplimentary, implying craftiness or a lack of deep thought.

At first I thought it was just a clever line and then it became more and more profound.
Bruce Meyer and Brian O'Riordan, eds. *In Their Words* 1984: 49

She believes that women should be clever, in a social sense, but that intellect in a woman is a dan-

gerous thing. It threatens the male ego.
Queen's Quarterly 92.1 (1985): 54

cliché   *Cliché* is derived from a French word meaning a printing-block; it almost always retains its acute accent. The adjective is usually *clichéd*, but *cliché'd* and *cliché*—as in French, where *cliché(e)* is both the past participle and the adjective—are also accepted.

The term *cliché* may be applied to ideas, images, or styles of almost any kind. Most often, however, a cliché is an expression that was once fresh but has become flat and trite through overuse. Many different types of expressions, including idioms ('good for nothing'), proverbs ('no smoke without fire'), stock metaphors ('tip of the iceberg'), well-known allusions ('sour grapes'), vogue terms ('boomers'), and fashionable jargon ('mission statement'), have been labelled clichés.

A curious problem with clichés is that, for all their familiarity, they are not always understood. To say that what someone is doing is like 'carrying coals to Newcastle' means that it is a waste of time or it makes no sense in the context. This meaning will be lost on someone who doesn't know that Newcastle (in the north of England) was once a major coal-mining centre. Similarly, people unfamiliar with the Bible may not understand the phrase 'manna from Heaven'; those unfamiliar with the Classics may not understand 'Achilles' heel'; and those unfamiliar with rural life may not understand why you shouldn't 'look a gift horse in the mouth'. (It's not because it might bite you, but because the condition of a horse's teeth reveals its age. Thus to look a gift horse in the mouth is to scrutinize it as you would a used car, checking for defects.) When readers encounter a stock phrase, they may have no idea how to interpret it. This is not to say that writers should eliminate expressions that allude to history, literature, or religion, but rather that they should keep in mind the cultural background of their audience.

Writing that is full of clichés seems devoid of original thinking. Yet, clichés are not without purpose. In speech, these expressions can improve the rhythm or sound of a sentence, or fill in a pause while the speaker thinks ahead. Thus phrases such as 'rack and ruin', 'each and every', and 'hard and fast' survive despite all criticism. Although clichés are both more common and more forgivable in speech than in writing, strenuously avoiding them in either form may lead to a style that is precious or strange. After all, stock expressions may sum up situations that are otherwise difficult to describe concisely ('sour grapes', 'brain drain'), or allude to shared cultural experience ('stiff upper lip'), allowing the argument to go forward succinctly. Many excellent writers use clichés judiciously in their work; these expressions can offer an efficient way of conveying ideas, images, and emotions.

> Pointed hats are a cliché, it seems, and real witches often wear flowers in their hair.
> *Gazette* (Montreal) 30 Oct. 1990: C1

> Their story starts off wobbly at first, like a toddler learning how to walk—the language is a bit awkward, sometimes clichéd. . . .
> *Province* (Vancouver) 24 June 1990: 93

> Just as musicals had their cliché situations, so too did war movies.
> *Gazette* (Montreal) 18 Feb. 1990: D3

(This use of *cliché* as an adjective is accepted, though *clichéd* is more common.)

See also DEAD METAPHOR; IDIOMS.

client   see CUSTOMER

climatic, climactic, climacteric   *Climatic* derives from *climate* and refers to prevailing weather conditions, while *climactic* and *climacteric* derive from *climax*. *Climactic* is an adjective relating to a high point or culmination. *Climacteric* (both a noun and an adjective) is now used mainly to refer to menopause, although it can be used more generally to refer to any major life change.

> You'd think a group from Iceland would have been prepared for the rigors of a North American winter, but the climatic changes of travelling from city to city have laid low the Sugarcubes' singer,

Bjork Gudmundsdottir, in San Francisco with a hoarse throat.
Province (Vancouver) 23 Feb. 1990: P7

(The word required here is *climatic*.)

Wonderfully shot, with tons of fantastical apparitions and surreal backdrops (the climatic scene at the evil temple is a sight to behold), the film unveils unique and amazing special effects.
Vancouver Sun 14 Dec. 1990: E5

(The word required here is *climactic*.)

. . . . artists seem, if they are lucky, to approach and pass a climacteric in middle life which leaves them changed for the better.
Robertson Davies *A Voice from the Attic* 1960: 225

climax   see CLIMATIC; CRESCENDO

clipped words   see ABBREVIATION

clique, coterie   A small, exclusive group within a group (in society, in a school, in a workplace, etc.) is a *clique*. A *coterie* is a group of people united by common interests or pursuits. Although the term *coterie* may connote narrowness, it is not as negative as *clique*, which characterizes a group as snobbish, pretentious, selfish, or hostile to others.
Clique may be pronounced either *CLEEK* or *CLICK*; *CLEEK* is more common and more widely accepted in Canada.

The ruling clique makes self-righteous statements characterizing its critics as 'criminal elements, enemies of the state.'
J.E. Smyth et al. *The Law and Business Administration in Canada* 1987: 38

What about that clique of pretty-but-irritating high school girls who were forever sneering at the underdressed and arguing about who among them were the best best friends?
Vancouver Sun 11 June 1994: D10

Painters and composers deal with arts capable of a higher degree of abstraction, but even they are likely to have their roots in some very restricted coterie in Paris or New York.
Northrop Frye *The Bush Garden* 1971: i

Still, it's building a reputation as an underground club with a coterie of regulars.
Gazette (Montreal) 2 June 1994: E6

clone   *Clone* originated as a biological term for a cell or individual that is genetically identical to another organism from which it has been asexually derived. Now *clone* is a popular metaphor for a nearly exact copy. In the marketplace, *clone* can be a neutral term, but in the arts, where slavish imitation is frowned upon, its tone is definitely disparaging.

Like many other prospective consumers, the Chings were looking at an IBM clone, the type found in 75 to 80 per cent of businesses and homes today.
Toronto Star 21 April 1994: G3

Obviously Gallant did not set out to write stories that would be clones of what The New Yorker was publishing in the late forties and early fifties.
Janice Kulyk Keefer *Reading Mavis Gallant* 1989: 34

close, shut, turn off, turn out   *Close* and *shut* are synonyms (a door or gate can be either closed or shut), but *close* is more often used metaphorically. Bank accounts, speeches, real estate deals, and parks are closed, never shut.
Generally, Canadians *turn off* or *shut off* their electrical appliances and *turn off* or *turn out* their lights, but speakers of English in Quebec may also 'close the lights'. This expression, influenced by similar expressions in French (*fermer la radio*, etc.), should be avoided in writing.

'We have noticed that when we close the lights in the room, the odor disappears.'
Gazette (Montreal) 3 June 1994: A4

('Close the lights' is a regional usage.)

See also ADVERBS WITHOUT -LY.

closed-minded   see -MINDED

cloth, clothe, clothed   see BATH; CLAD

cloven   see CLEAVE

cloverleaf   see -F, -V-

CLSC   see QUEBEC ENGLISH

clump   see FOREST

Co. see ABBREVIATION

coal oil see KEROSENE

coals to Newcastle see CLICHÉ

cocoa, cacao, coca, coco *Cocoa*, a hot chocolate drink or the bitter powder from which it is made, is derived from the seeds of the *cacao* (pronounced *kuh KAY o* or *kuh KAH yo* or *kuh COW*) tree. These seeds are called either *cocoa beans* or *cacao beans*. *Coca* is a South American shrub from which cocaine is derived. A *coco* is a coconut palm tree or a coconut; the adjective *coco* describes things made of the fibres of husks of coconuts. *Cocoanut* is a variant spelling of *coconut*.

> Maybe for a little treat she'd make herself a cup of cocoa, because for no reason that made any sense this early in the fall, she felt cold.
> Constance Beresford-Howe *Night Studies* 1985: 114–15

> Plantations produce such crops as coffee, tea, oil palm, cacao, coconuts, bananas, jute, sisal, hemp, rubber, tobacco, ground nuts, sugar cane, and cotton.
> William Norton *Human Geography* 1992: 260

> Democracy, unlike coca, does not have strong roots [in Peru].
> *Vancouver Sun* 8 April 1992: A10

> Coco and rubber mats are good for scraping off mud and large chunks of dirt, while mats made from carpeting will absorb moisture and attract smaller dirt particles.
> *Vancouver Sun* 12 Sept. 1992: C14

> He saw the frozen chocolate pie, the banana cream pie, and the cocoanut cream pie.
> *NeWest Review* Feb.–Mar. 1990: 31

> (The more common, and more widely accepted, spelling is *coconut*.)

> He retired to his room with a cup of cacao and around midnight a footman found him reading in bed.
> *Ottawa Citizen* 6 Feb. 1992: A11

> (The word wanted here is *cocoa*.)

co-conspirator see COLLABORATION

cod see PLURALS, REGULAR, IRREGULAR, FOREIGN

codeine see -IE-, -EI-

code-switching see QUEBEC ENGLISH

co-ed, coed The term *co-educational* was coined in the late nineteenth century to describe what was then an innovation: educational programs and institutions open to both female and male students. In contemporary British usage, the informal abbreviation *co-ed* (or *coed*) refers to a co-educational school. In North America, by contrast, the noun *co-ed* refers to the female students (never the males) at mixed schools: 'undergraduates and co-eds'. This use, which is sexist and condescending, is now on the decline. In its latest use *co-ed* is a synonym for *mixed*, referring to activities and facilities open to both sexes, as in 'co-ed washrooms' or 'co-ed hockey'. Note that this use, which has nothing to do with education, is quite informal.

> Outside Victoria Hall, a former women's residence at Queen's University, there is a plaque which is signed 'Science 67' and which reads: 'She who is kissed by an engineer while standing by this plaque officially becomes a Queen's co-ed.'
> *Queen's Quarterly* 96.2 (1989): 237

> (This use of the term *co-ed* is now discouraged as sexist and the plaque mysteriously vanished sometime after 1989.)

> A strong believer in the value of fitness, he works out three times a week in a co-ed aerobics class.
> *Catholic Register* 16 Aug. 1986: 21

See also SEXIST LANGUAGE.

coequal, co-equal Official or political equals are sometimes described as *coequal* (or *co-equal*). While this word has sometimes been criticized as a redundancy for *equal*, it has been used in literary and formal contexts since the fourteenth century.

> The world over, that foundation assumption of political science—that all nation-states are sovereign and so are co-equal internationally—is being

stood on its head, shaken and found wanting.
Toronto Star 4 Sept. 1991: A21

After 20 years of intensive effort, in which millions of English-Canadian children have studied French as a coequal official language, . . . Quebec's militant official assault on bilingualism is profoundly disillusioning.
Financial Post 23 Feb. 1989: 14

cohort, crony, cronyism   *Cohort*, derived from the Latin word *cohors*, originally referred to the group of 600 soldiers making up one-tenth of a Roman legion. In the eighteenth century, the English used the word figuratively to refer to any group of people who supported a particular cause. Since *cohorts* meant troops, allies, or supporters of the cause, many people began to assume that a *cohort* was a single comrade-at-arms. Thus *cohort* has come to mean a comrade or companion. British critics tend to object to this last meaning, but *Webster's Dictionary of English Usage* (1989) remarks that it is too firmly established in North America 'to be eradicated by commentators demonstrating their knowledge of Roman military organization'. In sociology, a *cohort* is a group of people sharing similar demographic characteristics; in education, it is group of students who go through the same program together.

While a *cohort* is a comrade or colleague, a *crony* is a close friend. Recently *crony* has developed pejorative connotations of political friendship, and the term *cronyism*, meaning the practice of appointing unqualified friends to public office, has taken a firm hold in journalism.

But I almost put the boots to my old friend and cohort, the redoubtable Pierre Berton, when he asked me on television why all the men in my recent book *Bodily Harm* were wimps.
Margaret Atwood *Second Words* 1982: 424

(British commentators object to this usage.)

These later immigrants may have swelled the urban ghettos where, according to Akenson's argument, only a minority of the earlier cohorts had put down roots.
Canadian Journal of History 14.1 (1989): 121

(This is the sociological sense.)

Why doesn't a prime minister know that it is wrong to appoint his cronies to positions on the public payroll?
Vancouver Sun 10 July 1990: A7

This should be about depth and quality, not politics and cronyism.
National Post 4 Feb. 2006: TO6

coiffure, coiffeur   A *coiffure* (pronounced *kwa FYOOR*) is a hairstyle. A *coiffeur* (*kwa FUR*) is a hairdresser. Both terms are borrowed from French.

In French a female hairdresser is a *coiffeuse*, but in English *coiffeur* is acceptable for both sexes.

Don King, the fight- and self-promoter with a coiffure like an abused Brillo pad, started his campaign through Givens and her mother, Ruth Roper.
Maclean's 27 June 1988: A54

Victoria Louise Flett is only twenty-two years old, a student at the University of Toronto, a tall string-bean of a woman with large hands and feet and straight blond unyielding hair that she bends carelessly behind her ears. So much for her coiffeur.
Carol Shields *The Stone Diaries* 1993: 265

(A *coiffeur* is a hairdresser; the word needed here is *coiffure*, 'hairstyle').

coin   see entry in Glossary

coincident   see SYNCHRONOUS

coincidentally, incidentally   *Coincidentally* introduces a statement about two things happening at the same time—an occurrence that might seem to have been planned, but in fact was not: 'Coincidentally, my brother was driving on the same highway at the same time'. *Incidentally* indicates that a remark is a digression: 'Incidentally, we never got paid for that job'. People often use *coincidentally* where the idea of coincidence is weak or non-existent and the appropriate word is *incidentally*.

Police say the alleged attacker was not stalking T——; he was seeing a friend off at the airport and coincidentally encountered [her].
Ottawa Citizen 27 June 1992: B5

Along narrow la rue Elle (a pun, incidentally, on *la ruelle*, or alley) are 12 up-market boutiques that specialize in European imports.
Alan Tucker, ed. *The Penguin Guide to Canada* 1991: 209

And you not only like it, but prefer it to our old size (which coincidentally you are now reading).
Toronto Star 12 Dec. 1992: D2

(Here *incidentally* would be more appropriate.)

Ottawa won its first game of the season, coincidentally against the Canadiens, and haven't won in 20 games since.
Gazette (Montreal) 22 Nov. 1992: D3

(Here *incidentally* would be more appropriate, since no other mention is made of the Canadiens.)

colicky   see -C-, -CK-

Coliseum   see COLOSSEUM

collaboration, collaborator, collaborationist, quisling, conspiracy, conspirator, coconspirator, collusion, cahoots   *Collaboration* means either working with someone towards a common goal, usually artistic, scientific, or literary, or cooperating traitorously with an enemy. A *collaborator* is either a co-author or a traitor. The term *collaborationist*, coined in the twentieth century, invariably means traitor.

A synonym for *collaborationist* is *quisling*. Vidkun Quisling was a Norwegian politician who collaborated with the Nazis during the Second World War. The name *Quisling* probably would not have entered the English language as a generic label for traitors—it did not become part of French vocabulary—if it had not coincidentally echoed the English suffix *-ling*. Among the meanings of *-ling* are young, small (*duckling, gosling*) and inferior (*hireling, underling*), and in the latter sense it can sometimes have a pejorative connotation. Thus to English ears the name *Quisling* suggested something contemptible.

A *conspiracy* is a secret plan by a group to do something treacherous. In law, a *conspiracy* is an agreement between at least two people to commit a crime. A person involved in a conspiracy is a *conspirator*. The word *co-conspirator*, which

seems redundant, is the standard legal term for defendants charged with the same conspiracy.

Collusion is illegal or immoral cooperation. Usually it is a secret agreement between people that allows them to perpetrate a fraud.

In cahoots means in partnership, usually to pursue questionable activities. This phrase, of uncertain origin, should not be used in formal writing.

Complaints that these Davis/Evans collaborations produced unrhythmic music were due to faulty hearing. . . .
Jack Chambers *Milestones* 1983: 261

More than 50 Israelis have died in the violence and about 300 Palestinians have been killed by fellow Arabs, most on suspicion of collaboration.
Vancouver Sun 6 Dec. 1990: A3

U.S. authorities did formally screen prospective refugees for Nazi connections, but it proved almost impossible to weed out those who hid their collaborationist past.
Globe and Mail (Toronto) 1 June 1985: E17

At best, he is viewed as a misguided soul; at worst, as a paid Israeli quisling determined to trample his own people's claim to international sympathy.
Toronto Star 4 June 2005: A1

'. . . the fact that a co-conspirator and co-accused is acquitted doesn't mean the same thing will happen to another co-accused.'
Gazette (Montreal) 15 Jan. 1994: A3

The historical reason for this special liability was to prevent the practice, once frequent in England, of collusion between carriers and highwaymen, whereby the highwayman would 'rob' the carrier of the shipper's goods and the carrier would plead that it was not his fault that the goods were taken.
J.E. Smyth et al. *The Law and Business Administration in Canada* 1987: 459

The parents—in cahoots with the show's staff—bring their children to the studio under false pretenses.
Gazette (Montreal) 2 Nov. 2005: D2

collateral damage   see EUPHEMISM

collective nouns   A collective noun is a noun that is singular in form even though it refers to a group of persons, objects, or acts: for example, 'a *committee* of concerned citizens', 'the *majority* of the student body', 'the provincial *government*', 'a *fleet* of fishing vessels', 'a *range* of musical styles', 'a *battery* of tests'.

A collective noun can be followed by either a singular or a plural verb depending on whether the writer regards the group as a unified whole or as a collection of individuals: 'The Canadian Olympic rowing team *is* favoured to win'; 'The Olympic rowing team *are* signing autographs'. The *team* is treated as a single unit in the first example and as a collection of individuals in the second.

While most Canadians would say 'The government *is* about to call an election', most speakers of British English would say 'The government *are* . . .'. Words such as *family*, *committee*, *council*, *board*, and *faculty* are more frequently used with plural verbs in British English than in Canadian or American English.

Once the choice has been made to regard a particular collective noun as singular (or plural) in a given context, it is important to be consistent in the use of verbs and pronouns. 'The company *is* planning to market the product soon. *They* will start a national advertising campaign next month': in these sentences, a plural pronoun (*they*) inconsistently follows a singular verb (*is*). Since the verb suggests that the company is being regarded as an entity, the pronoun should be *it*.

The word *number* is a special case. When preceded by *a* it is considered plural: 'A number of us *are* willing to help out'. When preceded by *the* it is considered singular: 'The number of participants *is* not as high as expected'. However, if a singular verb would sound awkward, *number* can always be made plural: 'The *numbers* of participants *are* increasing'.

The government is able to secure the passage of the bulk of its proposed bills. . . .
Andrew Heard *Canadian Constitutional Conventions* 1991: 78

(Here *government* is regarded as singular.)

When the federal government found out about the provincial complex they wanted one too.
Canadian Fiction Magazine 63 (1988): 100

(Here *government* is regarded as plural and followed by *they*.)

His committee were displeased with me, but as they were not paying me anything and I was writing simply out of political loyalty, I could afford to ignore their huffing and puffing.
Robertson Davies *One Half of Robertson Davies* 1978: 9–10

(Here the plural verb *were* is consistent with the pronoun that follows, *they*.)

If you are satisfied that the factoring company is thoroughly professional and that you can work with it, you will complete an application form for approval as one of their clients.
Computer Dealer News 7 March 1991: 56

(Here the writer has slipped, referring to the company first in the singular—*it*—and then in the plural: 'one of *their* clients'.)

See also AGREEMENT, GRAMMATICAL; TRIVIAL, TRIVIA.

collectivity   see QUEBEC ENGLISH

college, collegiate   see UNIVERSITY

collide, collision   Many newspaper style guides state that a car cannot *collide with* or be *in a collision with* a tree, because both objects in a collision must be moving. Contemporary usage, however, does not support this rule. What follows *collide with* may be either stationary or moving. Thus 'The canoe collided with the kayak' and 'The canoe collided with the dock' are both acceptable.

The real constraint on the verb *collide* is that its subject must be in motion ('My toe collided with the coffee table', *not* 'The coffee table collided with my toe')—unless the speaker is intending to be funny. When the subject is compound, both elements must be in motion ('The canoe and the kayak collided', but *not* 'The canoe and the dock collided').

A medical professor whose car collided with a tree after he suffered a cardiac arrest was brought back to life when the impact of the steering wheel against his chest restarted his heart.
National Post (Toronto) 24 March 2006: A19

. . . he missed a curve and demolished the car in a collision with a rock-cut.
J.E. Smyth et al. *The Law and Business Administration in Canada* 1987: 444

colloquial, informal, slang, jargon, argot

Colloquial English is the everyday spoken variety, as opposed to the English of formal writing or prepared speech. Dictionaries once used the label *colloq.* to indicate acceptable informal language, but many people interpreted this label to mean non-standard or slang. Many dictionaries and guides (including this one) now use *informal* to distinguish the casual usage of educated speakers from literary or formal language.

Slang is very casual language that is generally not acceptable in either formal or informal writing. Most slang is ephemeral. It develops as the 'in-language' of a specific group and functions as a code that distinguishes its members from the general population. Teenagers are well-known for coining slang—and discarding old expressions as soon as adults learn them. Some slang does become widely understood and widely used while retaining slang status: for example, *dud*, *big shot*, *bummer*. Other slang words, such as *piano* (a short form of *pianoforte*), *cheat*, and *jaywalk*, eventually become Standard English. Generally, slang should be avoided in writing, unless it is being used to a particular effect, as by fiction writers who use it to represent speech or set a particular tone.

Jargon usually refers to the language—the special terms and the phrasing—peculiar to a profession, occupation, or hobby: 'legal jargon', 'computer jargon', 'social-work jargon'. While initially jargon develops as a way of increasing precision in a field, ultimately it often has just the opposite effect, obscuring simple ideas. Specialist writers in any field need to make a continual effort to use jargon sparingly when writing for a non-specialist audience. Jargon is especially objectionable when used to impress or befuddle the reader.

Argot (pronounced *AR go* or *AR got*) originally referred to the coded language of French thieves. Now it's the general term in French for slang, and in English it's a synonym for *jargon*.

See also -ESE; FORMAL, INFORMAL WRITING; SCIENTIFIC ENGLISH; STANDARD ENGLISH, STANDARD; VERNACULAR.

colloquies   see -Y, -IES

collusion   see COLLABORATION

colon   The colon (:) is used to signal that an explanation, amplification, illustration, or list is to follow. It often serves a transitional function, replacing expressions such as *the reason being, that is, namely,* or *such as*:

> A small ad in a children's magazine set me going: it offered a free stamp.
> Richard Davies and Glen Kirkland, eds. *Dimensions* 1986: 60

> I also thought about me: a little wearied, a little worn, tormented by doubts and feelings and life-long illusions I can no longer reconcile, yet still able to find joy in the game.
> Ken Dryden *The Game* 1983: 3

> Besides its logic and neutral spirit, his argument had exhibited one other quality: brevity.
> Jack Batten *Robinette* 1984: 17

> Ottawa is a small town that breaks easily into three basic chunks: Upper Town, Lower Town, and Sussex Drive.
> Alan Tucker, ed. *The Penguin Guide to Canada* 1991: 301

A list that is grammatically incorporated into a sentence (following *are* or *consists of*, for example) should not be preceded by a colon:

> Cat food segments in order of national ranking are: luxury canned, dry, maintenance canned, semi-moist and cat treats.
> *Western Grocer Magazine* Aug. 1990: 22

(Here the colon should be omitted.)

Occasionally a full sentence following a colon is capitalized, though it needn't be unless it is a quotation, a slogan, or the first in a series of parallel sentences ('The accident raises a number of questions: How did it happen? Who is responsible? How can such accidents be avoided in future?').

A caution: Most Montreal drivers seem to have taken the New York cab drivers' training course.
Alan Tucker, ed. *The Penguin Guide to Canada* 1991: 15

The colon is also used to introduce quotations (especially if they are more than one sentence long); to separate a main title and subtitle (*When the Fat Lady Sings: Opera History as It Ought to Be Taught*); in biblical citations (Ruth 2: 1–4); in scholarly documentation (1993: 54); in time of day (6:55); in ratios (3:1); and in formal correspondence after the salutation ('Dear Sir or Madam:').

See also AS FOLLOWS; QUOTATION; TIME.

colonist, colonial, colonialist, post-colonial, neo-colonial   *Colonists* and *colonials* are people who live in a colony. *Colonists* also may refer more specifically to the people who first settled a colony; these people are also called settlers or pioneers. *Colonialists* usually refers to those who are advocates of the colonial system or those in power in a colony.

The adjective *colonial* may be neutral, as when it refers to an era or style ('colonial architecture'). It may also be negative, implying a lack of culture or sophistication in the colonies or referring to a sense of inferiority on the part of colonials.

The adjective *post-colonial* means after the end of colonial rule. *Post-colonial* (or *postcolonial*) *studies* is an academic field that analyzes the aftermath of imperialism. Some scholars within the field in fact object to the name *post-*colonial on the grounds that colonialism is not over: the *'post-'* is premature. They prefer the terms *neo-colonial* and *neo-colonialism* and see their subject as the study of the persistence of colonial power in new forms.

Almost the entire francophone population of Quebec has therefore descended from about 10,000 original colonists who arrived between 1608 and 1760.
David V.J. Bell *The Roots of Disunity* 1992: 33.

British colonials adopted the style [jodhpurs] while playing polo in India.
Vancouver Sun 30 Aug. 1994: C1

Colonies breed something called 'the colonial mentality', and if you have the colonial mentality you believe that the great good place is always somewhere else.
Margaret Atwood *Second Words* 1982: 382

On the level of language, irony becomes one of the chief characteristics of what Bharati Mukherjee calls 'the step-mother tongue' in which post-colonial writers write, 'implying as it does the responsibility, affection, accident, loss and secretive roots-quest in adoptive family situations.'
Linda Hutcheon *Splitting Images* 1991: 81

coloration   see -OUR, -OR

Colosseum, coliseum   The *Colosseum* is the ancient amphitheatre built in the first century A.D. in Rome, while *coliseum* is a common name for a large building designed for public exhibitions, performances, and sports events in Canada and the United States. The British often use *colosseum* for this sense, although *coliseum* is also found.

The swimming pool, with surrounding walls made of bricks laid unevenly to emulate the Coliseum of Rome (Mr. Guccione's idea), glistens beneath electric simulated candles.
Globe and Mail (Toronto) 7 Nov. 1985: E11

(The correct spelling for the building in Rome is *Colosseum*.)

The Bulldogs got goals from six different players in their last game of the season in front of 7,700 fans at Copps Coliseum.
Toronto Star 16 April 2006: B7

colour, spectrum, primary colour, secondary colour, hue, tint, shade, tone   A gradation of wavelengths of light perceived as bands of *colour* is called a *spectrum*. In the atmosphere, this phenomenon is called a rainbow. Combining all the colours of the rainbow (red, orange, yellow, green, blue, indigo, and violet) produces white light.

Primary colours are colours that can be mixed to produce all the other colours of the spectrum. When mixing beams of light, the usual primaries are red, green, and blue; when mixing pigments, red, yellow, and blue. *Secondary colours* are colours produced by mixing two primaries. Orange, green, and violet are the secondary colours that result from mixing the primary pigments.

In popular use *hue* is a synonym for *colour*; in technical use it refers specifically to the wavelength of a colour. In popular use *tint, shade,* and *tone* all refer to nuances of colours, while in technical use a *tint* is a colour lightened by adding white; a *shade* is a colour darkened by adding black; and a *tone* is either a tint or a shade.

See also -OUR, -OR.

coloured   see BLACK

colourless   see TRANSPARENT

come   The past tense is *came. Come,* as in 'Archie come home for Christmas last year', is nonstandard. 'Come Sunday, it'll all be over', however, is standard; this is an inverted subjunctive construction that exists in current English only in a handful of set expressions such as 'Be that as it may' and 'Perish the thought'.

See also SUBJUNCTIVE.

comfort station   see EUPHEMISM

comic, comical   *Comic* and *comical* both mean funny or amusing; *comic* is the more common, general word. *Comical* usually refers to something that is unintentionally or unexpectedly funny, but this is a tendency rather than a clear distinction of sense. Only *comic* can be used to refer to the genre of comedy: 'Comic conventions differ from tragic conventions'.

comma   The comma is the most often used and probably the most controversial of all punctuation marks. Although there are a few well-established rules governing comma usage, in many cases writers may use commas at their discretion to promote clarity and ease of reading.

The modern trend is to use a minimum of commas. If a sentence seems to require a thicket of commas, it probably needs rewriting.

The comma has so many possible uses that space does not permit listing them all. The following are some of the most common or troublesome constructions.

in compound sentences A comma separates two or more independent clauses joined by a coordinating conjunction—*and, but, or, nor, yet* (meaning *but*), *so* (meaning *therefore*), and *for* (meaning *because*)—unless the clauses are short and closely related:

> Tabitha took a flying leap at the catnip mouse intended for Cuddles, but she missed and landed in the magazine rack.

> The party was a bore and we left early.

Compound sentences are often confused with simple sentences in which a conjunction separates a compound predicate (two verbs with the same subject):

> Tabitha is a clumsy cat, but she has survived so far. (*Compound sentence.*)

> Tabitha is a clumsy cat but has survived so far. (*Compound predicate.*)

In the second example, *but* separates the two verbs *is* and *has survived,* which have the same subject, *Tabitha;* it does not introduce a clause and does not need a comma before it. However, some writers defend this use of the comma in long sentences as a means of breaking them up:

> Tabitha has frequently taken what can only be described as death-defying leaps of faith, but hasn't killed herself yet.

with introductory clauses and phrases A dependent clause (one that cannot stand alone) placed before the main clause is usually followed by a comma:

> If I tell you the truth, will you stay?

A comma may follow an introductory phrase but is often omitted, especially if the phrase is short:

During the surprising summer of 1991, the world witnessed two Russian revolutions in quick succession.

After suffering a series of blows, Sam came into a windfall.

Running for the bus, Marina slipped and fell.

In May she left home for good.

If an adverb phrase (one that modifies a verb) immediately precedes a verb, no comma is used:

Running along the ground was a fine wire.

In the kitchen stood a large china cupboard.

with adjective clauses or phrases following a noun An adjective clause or phrase following a noun is set off by commas if it is non-restrictive (if it adds information not essential to the meaning of the sentence). No commas are used if the clause or phrase is restrictive (if it limits the noun in a way that is necessary to the meaning of the sentence):

That book, which I will leave on the hall table for you, is one of my favourites.
(Non-restrictive, providing additional information.)

The book that is on the hall table is one of my favourites.
(Restrictive, providing necessary information.)

My cat, lying curled up in the corner, seemed to be having an exciting dream.

The cat lying in the corner seems to be having an exciting dream.

If you have trouble deciding whether a clause or phrase is a restrictive or non-restrictive modifier, try the pause test. If it seems natural to pause between the noun and the modifier that follows ('My cat, lying curled up in the corner, . . .'), the modifier is non-restrictive; use commas. If the noun and the modifier that follows are articulated without pause, as if they named a unit ('The-cat-lying-in-the-corner . . .'), then the modifier is restrictive and commas are inappropriate.

with adverb phrases between subject and verb An adverb phrase occurring between the subject and verb is usually set off by commas:

Sam, after suffering a series of blows, came into a sudden windfall.

My cat, without any prompting, has learned to fetch.

Be careful not to put a comma between subject and verb, as in 'Learning how to fetch without prompting, is a sign of great intelligence in a cat'. This comma would seriously perplex the reader. If, on the other hand, you wrote 'Learning how to fetch, without prompting, is a sign of great intelligence in a cat', the punctuation would be acceptable because 'without prompting' would become a parenthetical comment. But note that the meaning of the sentence would shift: in this case, instead of first being taught to fetch with prompting and then figuring out how to fetch on its own, the cat would have learned the whole process—how to fetch—without any prompting.

It is also an error to put a comma between a verb and its complement or object: 'Cuddles ate, her food, Tabitha's food, and the salmon off the counter'.

in a series Commas separate words, phrases, or clauses in a series:

Mix in the dates, raisins, nuts, and seeds.

The cat stretched out, rolled over, and fell asleep.

It is a matter of debate whether to insert the final comma—called a series or serial comma—before the conjunction (as this guide does). Those in favour argue that the series comma prevents ambiguity, while those opposed contend that the conjunction makes it redundant. Both conventions are common, with the series comma somewhat more likely to be used in scholarly and more formal writing and less likely in newspapers and magazines.

Whichever style is chosen, it should be followed consistently within a given text. A decision not to use the series comma, however, does not preclude using it occasionally for greater clarity:

> The boomers' future is likely to include nursing homes run like California spas, art and entertainment aimed at octogenarians, and service professionals of all kinds.

If a series is made up of long or complex phrases or clauses, especially if they include internal punctuation, it is usually best to separate them with semicolons. In this case, a final (series) semicolon is required:

> I am getting a little tired of writing speeches that will be changed beyond recognition, on the spur of the moment, by ill-informed politicians; that will be deemed frivolous, libelous, or anti-family; or worse, that will be ignored altogether.

to enclose parenthetical elements Parenthetical terms such as *indeed, in fact, perhaps, though, nevertheless, of course, naturally, too,* and *oh* are usually set off by commas when they interrupt the flow of thought or call for a pause in reading:

> In fact, I've seen it myself.

> She told me, nevertheless, that there was no such thing.

> There are two sides to everything, of course.

> Oh, I hardly think so.

If such terms don't interrupt the flow of thought or call for a pause, they are usually not set off by commas:

> She told me that the book in fact needs a chapter on constructing a home page.

> Perhaps there have always been two sides.

> He thinks so too.

Parenthetical phrases and clauses are also usually set off by commas:

> Granola, no matter what you think, is not a healthful food.

> In the morning, Mary decided, she would drive into town.

Be sure, though, that the element is in fact parenthetical. If it is essential to the meaning of the sentence, it should not be set off by commas:

> In the morning Mary decided she would drive into town.

Here removing the commas changes the meaning of the sentence. Without commas, the sentence tells us when Mary decided; with them, we don't know when she made her decision, but we know when she will drive into town.

with nouns in apposition A word, phrase, or clause that is in apposition to a noun (a title, name, synonym, or definition that immediately follows the noun and has the same relation as the noun to the rest of the sentence) is set off by commas if it is nonrestrictive but is not set off if it is restrictive:

> His third novel, *No Respite*, caused a stir.

> Asina Timbale won the coveted First Novel Award. Her novel, *Sinister Editors*, caused a stir.

> Her novel *The Stone Diaries* won a Governor General's Literary Award.

In the first example the word *third* identifies which of the author's novels caused a stir, so the title is not essential to the meaning of the sentence; it is nonrestrictive, so commas are used. Similarly, in the second example the context makes it clear that the author has written only one novel; thus the title is not essential and is set off by commas. In the third example, however, the title is essential: it restricts the comment to that particular novel, so no commas are used.

It is a common error to confuse restrictive and non-restrictive appositives. The distinction is important, however, since incorrect usage may convey the wrong meaning:

> In Shakespeare's play, *Hamlet*, Ophelia goes mad.

(Here the punctuation implies that Shakespeare wrote only one play.)

Prime Minister Harper introduced his wife Laureen.

(Here the lack of punctuation implies that Mr. Harper has more than one wife.)

The same rules apply with phrases and clauses:

In the adage 'Absence makes the heart grow fonder', we see the poignant hope of the estranged.

But the adage referred to earlier, 'Absence makes the heart grow fonder', is refuted by 'Out of sight, out of mind'.

In the second example, the words *referred to earlier* indicate that the adage has already been given, so repeating it is not essential but simply courteous; hence commas are used.

In some cases, nouns in apposition could be mistaken for a series:

Antony had three pets, two horses and a goat.

If Antony owns three animals, make that clear by replacing the comma with a colon or a dash. If he owns six animals, it would help to specify the pets (or use the series comma).

with parallel adjectives Use a comma to separate two or more adjectives that modify the same noun if they are parallel. The positions of parallel adjectives can be reversed with no ill effect: 'The happy, breathless children poured into the room' could also be written 'The breathless, happy children. . .'. *Happy* and *breathless* are parallel here, and a comma is needed to separate them. However, in 'The old wooden desk needs refinishing', *old* and *wooden* are not parallel; this sentence could not be written 'The wooden old desk . . .', and so the adjectives are not separated by a comma.

Be careful not to put a comma between the last adjective and the noun or pronoun that follows, as in 'The breathless, happy, children poured into the room'. Over-punctuation of this kind will derail the reader.

with explanatory terms Commas usually set off definitions preceded by *or*:

The leaves were of a russet, or red, colour.

Sheba belonged to the Felis, or cat, family.

The commas in this case distinguish an explanation from a simple choice:

She hasn't decided whether to paint the walls russet or celadon.

with dates and addresses In month–day–year constructions a comma follows the day and the year. Be careful to include the comma following the year; it is often incorrectly omitted.

He met her on July 11, 1987, and never looked back.

In month–year constructions ('August 1991') usage is divided between those who insert a comma after the month and those who don't. The trend is towards omission.

In day–month–year constructions ('28 August 1991'), common in Europe and in some kinds of Canadian publications, no commas are used.

Commas are used to separate parts of an address (though not on an envelope, see POSTAL ADDRESSES). Note the comma following the final element ('Canada') when, as in this case, the sentence continues:

She grew up in Medicine Hat, Alberta, Canada, and would often go on and on about it.

to prevent misreading A comma is sometimes used to clarify meaning or ease reading even when no rule requires it:

Whatever is, is good.

To Ben, Nelson remained an enigma.

She saw who came in, and gasped.

Be careful, however, not to use a comma to rescue a badly structured sentence, as in 'Those that fail, naturally incur public criticism'. Here *naturally* modifies the whole sentence; placed where it is, it may be read at first as modifying *fail*; then the desperate reader may try to attach it to *incur*. The writer has tried to use a comma to solve this problem, instead of restructuring the sentence: 'Naturally, those that fail incur public criticism'.

A comma occurring with parentheses is placed after, not before, them:

> Whatever she said (and I don't know what it was), she couldn't have meant it maliciously.

as the wrong punctuation choice Commas, which indicate the smallest pause or break in thought, are sometimes inadvisedly used where stronger breaks—dashes, colons, semicolons, parentheses, or even periods—are needed:

> She cleared the table and put away the food, she hardly knew what she was doing.
> (*Semicolon or period.*)

> I hope you can stand another example, many couldn't, because here it is.
> (*Dashes or parentheses.*)

A comma should not precede or divide sentence elements connected by correlative conjunctions (*so. . .that, as. . .as, more. . .than, both. . .and, either. . .or, neither. . .nor*). In 'In criminal law, a charge of assault may be laid, not only if an attack occurs, but also if the victim reasonably believes he or she is being threatened with physical harm', the commas between *laid* and *not only* and between *occurs* and *but* should be omitted.

See also DATES; NUMBERS, DECIMAL POINTS AND COMMAS WITH; POSTAL ADDRESSES; QUOTATION, QUOTATION MARKS; SENTENCES, SENTENCE FRAGMENT, RUN-ON SENTENCE, COMMA SPLICE; WHICH, THAT.

comma fault, comma splice   see SENTENCES

command   see QUEBEC ENGLISH

commentate   *Commentate* is a back-formation from *commentator*. It has been criticized as a pretentious and unnecessary synonym for *comment*. Some recent usage guides have defended the word by pointing out that it is used differently from *comment*. While to *comment* means to make remarks, to *commentate* means to act as a commentator, to provide a running commentary on a live event for an audience. It may in fact be the rather vapid nature of much broadcast commentary that irks critics of the word *commentate*; whatever the reason, the word remains stigmatized. Though the noun *commentator* occurs often in formal writing, the verb *commentate* does not.

> Still, the commentators commentated: 'Very early lead . . . very early results . . . too soon to tell . . . only eight votes total there, but still . . . I know it's still early, but . . . Very, very early but is this a trend?'
> *National Post* (Toronto) 3 Oct. 2003: A8

See also BACK-FORMATION.

commiserate   One usually commiserates *with* someone *over* or *about* a problem. Because the Latin prefix *com-* means 'with', commentators used to deplore this usage, arguing that the verb was transitive: 'I commiserate you on your loss'. Usage has passed them by, however, and *commiserate* now often functions grammatically just as *sympathize* does. *Commiserate* may also be used without a preposition if it describes reciprocal action: 'They were disheartened; they commiserated'.

> Barnes commiserated with him, telling the youngster to put the experience out of his mind and go on with his life.
> *Vancouver Sun* 24 Nov. 1994: D3

> Inside the Allendale recreation centre dozens of homeless victims commiserated and asked newcomers for the latest news and weather reports.
> *Globe and Mail* (Toronto) 1 June 1985: M4

commissionaire   see LEGION

committal, commitment   A *committal* is a burial, an involuntary admission to a mental hospital, or a court order sending someone to trial or to prison. A *commitment* is a pledge of one's time or money, a strong feeling of attachment to a vocation, cause, etc., or a sense of obligation or loyalty towards another person.

Note that *committal* (like *committed* and *committing*) is spelled with a double *t*, while *commitment* is not.

> A funeral will be held at Lawrence Park Community Church today at 1:30 p.m. A committal service will be held later in Renfrew.
> *Globe and Mail* (Toronto) 15 Jan. 1985: N11

> Like her music, the characters peopling Mandell's songs are a mixed bunch, from the roll-in-the-hay, no-strings-attached girl of the title track to committal-averse guys.
> *Ottawa Citizen* 8 July 2004: E5

(*Commitment* is the word needed here.)

committed, committing   see COMMITTAL, COMMITMENT

committee   see COLLECTIVE NOUNS

common   see MUTUAL

common law, civil law, bijural, common-law   In Canada, the *common law* is used everywhere except in Quebec, which instead uses the *civil law* derived from the Napoleonic Code and Roman law. The common law originated in England; it is based on the decisions of judges, called precedents, and on custom, rather than on comprehensive written statutes. At the federal level, all legislation must be harmonized with the country's two legal systems, making Canada one of the few *bijural* countries in the world.

Common-law is usually hyphenated when it functions as an adjective, as in 'common-law marriage' or 'common-law spouse'. When *common law* functions as an adverb ('They were living common law'), the phrase should not be hyphenated. Canadian journalism guides recommend against describing relationships as *common-law* when the legal status of a couple's relationship is irrelevant. Thus the use of *common-law* in Canadian journalism is largely restricted to contexts where it is important to clarify that two individuals cohabit as spouses but have not had a religious or civil marriage ceremony.

In Canadian usage, the category *common-law* is not applied only to heterosexual couples. Citizenship and Immigration Canada and Statistics Canada are among the government departments that classify cohabitating same-sex partners who have not legally married as *common-law*.

> Nevertheless, even a strict interpretation of the Statute did not prevent it from thwarting a large number of contracts in the common law courts.
> J.E. Smyth et al. *The Law and Business Administration in Canada* 1987: 254

> Under the law, individuals aged 60 to 64 who are married to or live common law with low-income pensioners can apply for the monthly supplement.
> *Toronto Star* 5 Dec. 1991: A13

> The last census in 2001 referred only to common-law same-sex relationships, before legal challenges in several provinces helped topple the traditional definition of marriage.
> *Vancouver Sun* 18 April 2005: A4

See also MARRIAGE; SPOUSE.

communicable, [communicatable]   see -ABLE, -(AT)ABLE

community college   see UNIVERSITY

comparable, comparative   Things that are *comparable* are similar enough to invite comparison; in colloquial terms, they're in the same league. Things that are *comparative* are either reckoned by comparison ('comparative worth') or systematically investigated through comparison ('comparative literature').

Comparable is usually pronounced with stress on the first syllable: COM *per a* bull. The pronunciation *com* PAIR *a bull* is criticized.

> All are comparable in terms of quality and price.
> Alan Tucker, ed. *The Penguin Guide to Canada* 1991: 494

> Leitch was a respected Canadian company that had been active in mining in Northern Ontario for many years; Texas Gulf was a large and wealthy American corporation and a comparative Johnny-come-lately to Northern Ontario mining.
> Jack Batten *Robinette* 1984: 145

Their successors have had occasional, but hardly comparative, success.
Vancouver Sun 16 Dec. 1992: D13

(The word required here is *comparable*.)

'Hockey is not a sport here. Hockey is a religion. There's no comparative love for a sport . . . in America.'
Province (Vancouver) 7 May 2003: A52

(The word required here is *comparable*.)

See also COMPARISONS.

comparatively   see RELATIVELY

comparisons   Few people have trouble making comparisons with adverbs or adjectives. Occasionally, though, mistakes are made when a writer uses both a comparative ending and either the comparative form with *more* or *most* ('more better', 'most fastest') or a word that is already comparative on its own ('worser'). Although these 'double comparatives' were common in literary writing until the eighteenth century, they are now considered uneducated.

Adjectives and adverbs change form when they are used to make comparisons: 'She runs faster than John'; 'This plant has the greenest leaves of the three'. Adjectives and adverbs of one syllable produce the comparative with the ending *-er* (*faster, sweeter*) and the superlative form with the ending *-est* (*fastest, sweetest*). Adjectives and adverbs with three or more syllables must make the comparative with *more* (*more beautiful, more generous, more gracefully*) and the superlative with *most* (*most beautiful, most generous, most gracefully*).

Two-syllable adjectives vary; some that are acceptable with either comparative endings or *more* and *most* are *clever, common, cruel, honest, pleasant,* and *polite*. Adjectives that end in *-le, -ow,* and *-y* usually make the comparative with endings: *abler, yellower, lovelier*.

Adverbs that end in *-ly* use *more* and *most*: *more slowly, most frequently*.

It is always possible to use *more* and *most* to make comparisons with one- and two-syllable adjectives and adverbs for reasons of style or

idiom: 'a more clear and convincing explanation'.

See also ABSOLUTE COMPARATIVES; COMPLETE; DIFFERENT FROM; LIKE, AS; OFTEN, OFTENER, MORE OFTEN; PERFECT; THAN; UNIQUE; WORSE.

compass points   see EAST, WEST, NORTH, SOUTH

compendium, compendia   see PLURALS, REGULAR, IRREGULAR, FOREIGN

competence, competency   Both variants are acceptable in all senses, including the sense of enough money or property to live on: 'She inherited a competence/competency from her grandmother'. The far more common form is *competence*; *competency* is sometimes used in education ('competency in Spanish') and law ('ordered an assessment of his mental competency').

complaisant, complacent   *Complaisant* (usually pronounced *com PLAYS ent*) means deferential or obliging. *Complacent* (pronounced *com PLACE ent*) means smug, self-satisfied, or dangerously unconcerned.

It also concluded that one reason for his dismissal was that Crowe was 'not sufficiently complaisant, not servile enough in thought and attitude to his administrative superiors.'
Toronto Star 18 July 1993: B1

While Ladner appreciates success, she's too smart to be complacent.
Edmonton Journal 20 April 2006: F4

compleat   Book publishers are largely responsible for reviving the seventeenth-century spelling of *complete*, currently in vogue in titles of handbooks and modelled on the title of Izaak Walton's classic *The Compleat Angler* (1653). *Compleat* is also used humorously in newspaper writing.

But, we hear you ask in anxious chorus, can this jogger seriously consider himself compleat without the latest product of Puma Sportschuhfabriken KG of West Germany—a pair of jogging shoes with a built-in computer?
Globe and Mail (Toronto) 20 April 1985: P6

The central premise of The Compleat Wrks of Wllm Shkspr [sic]—that people of the 21st century are too addicted to video games and Fear Factor to read or sit through some of the greatest works of art in human history—is enough to make a guy want to stab himself, twice if not thrice, with a fake sword.
Edmonton Journal 21 Aug. 2005: B2

complement   see COMPLIMENT

complete   Some usage commentators object to the use of the comparative modifiers *more* and *most* with *complete* on the grounds that *complete* is an absolute adjective and therefore cannot be compared. The same objection is raised against using comparatives with *unique* and *perfect*. In the history of their use, however, these words have been freely modified.

There is little reason to use *more*, *less*, or *most* when *complete* means total or unequivocal, as in 'a complete surprise'; it's hard to imagine a partially complete surprise. But when *complete* is used to mean thorough or comprehensive, as in 'a complete investigation' or 'a complete collection', it is common and accepted at all levels of English to modify the word with the comparative terms *more* and *most*. A keen investigator is likely to do a more complete investigation than a lazy one, and a collector who finds a rare item now enjoys a more complete—or perhaps the most complete—collection.

A complete postglacial pollen profile is needed for a more complete understanding of Holocene paleoclimatic changes.
Canadian Journal of Earth Sciences 26 (1989): 263

Brébeuf is not only the greatest but the most complete Canadian narrative, and brings together into a single pattern all the themes we have been tracing.
Northrop Frye *The Bush Garden* 1971: 153

The winning cookbooks will enter U of G's culinary archives, the most complete collection of Canadian cookbooks in the world.
Edmonton Journal 23 Nov. 2005: F3

See also DESTROY; PERFECT; REPLETE; UNIQUE.

compliment, complement, supplement   To *compliment* someone is to praise him or her; a *compliment* is praise. *Complimentary* tickets are a gift.

Something that *complements* something else completes it or fits harmoniously with it. A *complement* is something that completes a set or pair, or the full number of people or things needed to perform some particular task.

To *supplement* means to add something to a whole, such as a vitamin supplement to a diet or an advertising supplement to a newspaper.

A parody is a compliment; nobody troubles to mock what nobody takes seriously.
Robertson Davies *One Half of Robertson Davies* 1978: 253

The city of Stratford has many other pleasures to complement and round out a visit to the famous Shakespeare Festival.
Leisure Life May 1988: 84

HMCS Huron, with a complement of 280 sailors, will sail Jan. 4 from Victoria. . . .
Vancouver Sun 20 Dec. 1990: A1

We encourage subscribers to use the full complement of safety features, such as hands-free speed dialling and voice activation.
Vancouver Sun 17 Oct. 1990: A12

'I knew . . . my movement background and dance teaching would compliment each other.'
Guardian (Charlottetown) 3 Sept. 2005: C3

(The correct spelling is *complement*.)

That would also be a true four-pillar strategy—one where the pillars are necessarily intertwined and complimentary.
Vancouver Sun 8 May 2003: A10

(The correct spelling is *complementary*.)

See also BACKHANDED COMPLIMENT.

compound subject   see entry in Glossary

comprehend   see APPREHEND

comprehensible, comprehendible   Canadian writers use *comprehensible*. *Comprehendible* is listed as an alternative form of the adjective in American dictionaries.

Rabbior is president of the Canadian Foundation for Economic Education, a non-profit organization that tries to make economics comprehensible to the average person.
Toronto Star 21 Nov. 1994: A21

comprise   A whole comprises its parts. *Comprise* functions grammatically in the same way as the verb *include*. However, after *comprise* all the parts making up the whole are named, while after *include* only some need be mentioned: 'The set comprises twelve volumes'; 'The twelve-volume set includes an index'.

The passive form, *be comprised of*, is disputed, often strenuously, although it is in common use. Usage guides tend to reject this form, probably because it is used with exactly the same meaning as the active form: 'The set is comprised of twelve volumes'. When *comprise* is used in the passive, it becomes grammatically analogous to *compose* rather than *include*.

A second disputed usage, also well established, reverses the subject and object of *comprise* so that the parts comprise the whole, or one part comprises a specified portion of the whole: 'Twelve volumes comprise the set'; 'Prince Edward Island comprises 0.1% of Canadian territory'. This usage is very common.

Thus *comprise* is currently an anomalous and confusing verb. To avoid criticism, it is best to use *comprise* only in the active voice to mean 'consist of'. Where the passive voice seems more appropriate, *is made up of* or *is composed of* can be substituted for *is comprised of*. And where the parts making up a whole are the subject of the sentence, *constitute* or *make up* is a better choice than *comprise*.

The pot still process comprises four stages: malting, mashing, fermentation and distillation.
Bon Vivant Aug.–Sept. 1982: 13

The Quebec Furniture Conciliation Committee comprises one manufacturer and one retailer who are not involved in the dispute and two representatives of the Quebec Consumers' Association. . . .
Canadian Consumer Jan. 1985: 7

Style is comprised of many elements, the major ones being diction, figurative language, sentences, and tone. . . .

Richard Davies and Glen Kirkland, eds. *Dimensions* 1986: 181

(Here *comprises* or *is composed of* is recommended.)

The short, glass wall is comprised of five flat panes that are joined at angles.
Whig-Standard (Kingston) 19 May 2006: 2

(Here *composed of* is recommended.)

Food aid comprised less than one per cent of Canadian grain production in recent years.
Guardian (Charlottetown) 18 Oct. 2004: A7

(Here the 'part', not the 'whole', is the subject: *constituted* is recommended.)

The various statutes comprising our companies and securities legislation now require a disclosure of information. . . .
J.E. Smith et al. *The Law and Business Administration in Canada* 1987: 232

(Again the parts are the subject: *constituting* is recommended.)

comptroller, controller   A *comptroller* is the chief accounting officer of a business or institution. A *controller* is a person or device that directs or regulates something. The spelling *controller* may be substituted for *comptroller*—though the spelling choice of a company or institution should be respected—but the reverse is not true: there are no air traffic comptrollers. *Comptroller* is pronounced just like *controller*.

Comptroller is a variant spelling of *controller* that was introduced around 1500 by scribes who mistakenly assumed that the word was related to the Latin *computare* and the French *compter*, 'to count'. In fact, the prefix in *controller* is derived from the French word *contre*, 'against'. The fourteenth-century controller was a person who kept contre- or counter-rolls, copies of household accounts, against which all expenditures were checked. Thus the word *controller* referred to a financial officer before it had any broader application, and the variant spelling *comptroller* probably survived because it became entrenched as an institutional job title.

As construction of the third apartment building neared completion, the comptroller of Gilman

pressed for payment in full of the account.
J.E. Smyth et al. The Law and Business *Administration in Canada* 1987: 329

She was promoted to controller of the company within five years and vice-president finance within eight years. . . .
Vancouver Sun 3 May 2002: F5

compunction, compulsion To feel no *compunction* about doing or saying something means to feel no shame or guilt about it. To feel no *compulsion* to do something means to feel unpressured or uncompelled to do it.

Goldman felt no compunction about comparing Jagger's influence on his audience with Nazism.
Queen's Quarterly 92.2 (1985): 273

Rarely can a salmon angler, when handed pen and paper, resist the compulsion to tell the world why and when, in his opinion, salmon take flies.
Atlantic Salmon Journal Summer (1990): 20

There is the general assumption that readers can sniff out bad faith—works that aren't generated by the compunction to uncover some deeply felt human truth.
National Post 23 April 2005: WP13

(The word required here is *compulsion*.)

computer terms The last quarter century has seen the advent of the Internet and an overwhelming increase in the use of computers in daily life. Specific words and usages have developed around computer use and culture, and to date they have rarely been mentioned or disambiguated in general usage manuals. This entry discusses some of the more common computer terms, including many which are long established English words that have developed new, parallel meanings in the 'virtual' or computer domain. Probably not since English speakers began exploring the New World have so many words in such short order acquired extended meanings and new referents.

The word *Internet*, which refers to long-distance computer-based media, is overwhelmingly capitalized. Most usage guides recommend the capital, treating the Internet like a place, albeit a virtual one. *Web* is a short form of *World Wide Web*, the system that links documents on the Internet and makes them viewable, but in non-technical use, 'the *Web*' is simply a synonym of the Internet. *World Wide Web* is abbreviated in Internet addresses to *www*, but this lower-case acronym is not common in everyday usage. *Web*, in lower case, is often used to form compounds such as *website*, usually written as one word, and *web page*, usually written as two. *Web-*, with a hyphen, is also used as a prefix attached to participles, as in *web-based* and *web-enabled*. Another prefix that has arisen around computers is *e-*, a shortened form of *electronic*, used to designate things done by computer or on the Internet, as opposed to by traditional means and methods. The single-letter prefix is predominantly lower case and hyphenated (*e-business*, *e-learning*, *e-book* and *e-commerce*); occasionally, it occurs in lower case before a capitalized root (*eBusiness*). (See also E-MAIL.)

Spam is the e-mail equivalent of junk mail, a term which can be used as its synonym. *Spam* can also be used as a verb meaning 'to send junk e-mail'. *E-mail* is sometimes shortened to *mail*, and thus *mail* can now mean to send e-mail. There are three verbs commonly used to describe looking for information on the Internet: *search* means use any search engine, i.e., computer program designed for searching, to find specific information on the Internet or on a website; to *google*, a verb derived from the proprietary name of a specific, highly successful and widely used search engine, means to use Google to find information online; to *surf* means to look at web pages on the Internet without much of a goal in mind. If you wish to visit a website often, you can *bookmark* it, that is, you can save its web address on your *browser*. A *browser* is a program such as Internet Explorer or Netscape that allows you to *visit*—in other words, view—websites. To access a website is to *hit* it, and many websites record the number of times they have been accessed as a number of *hits*. As they operate, browsers record the *history* of your meandering on the Internet, allowing you to re-access previously visited web pages.

Three verbs describe the transfer of information between hard media such as compact discs

(CDs) and computers. To *rip* means to copy a file from its original source and place it in the memory of your computer or in a data storage website. *Rip* is most commonly used of music files. To *burn* is to take files that are already on your computer and copy them by laser onto blank CDs or digital video disks (DVDs). To *write* also means to encode files on a blank disk. Data and programs are stored on the *hard drive* that comes with a computer; *disk drives* are also standard features in computers, into which CDs, DVDs, etc., can be inserted. It is sometimes necessary to compress, or *zip*, data and programs that take up too much *memory*, or space on a computer chip, so they can be stored on a disk or sent easily via e-mail.

Hard drives have a tendency in many computers to *crash*, or fail, stop, or shut off, often resulting in the loss of information. Computer systems can also be *hacked into* meaning someone has gained unauthorized entry (see HACKER, CRACKER). A *firewall* is a protective barrier, specifically, a security program that checks all information received by a computer from a network or the Internet to make sure that it is safe for the computer to handle. One thing a firewall checks for is *viruses,* codes and programs that duplicate themselves when introduced to a computer system, thus spreading from computer to computer, overloading systems and damaging hard drives. Computers also have *menus*, displays of lists of available choices, and *windows*, on-screen displays, often appearing within a frame. Windows can usually be *scrolled*, that is, moved up or down to show more of what they contain.

See also E-MAIL; -ESE; HACKER, CRACKER.

comrade   see CAMARADERIE

concave, convex   *Concave* means hollowed (think of a cave). *Convex* means the opposite, bulging outward.

> Climbing to the top of the castle, up stone steps worn concave over the centuries, takes time but is certainly worth it for the view.
> *Globe and Mail* (Toronto) 2 Nov. 1985: F16

To smooth the caulk in place, try dipping an old spoon into a bowl of soapy water and then gently running the convex side along the bead.
Ottawa Citizen 6 Oct. 1990: C3

concede   see -CEED, -CEDE, -SEDE

conceit   see -IE-, -EI-

concerto   The second syllable of *concerto* is stressed and pronounced CHAIR. The plural is *concertos*, or sometimes, especially in historical references, *concerti* (-*ti* is pronounced -*tee*).

> She has already played most of the major concertos for her instrument.
> *Calgary Herald* 26 Sept. 1992: D14

> Thibaudet is the soloist in . . . the Liszt Concerti Nos. 1 & 2, Hungarian Fantasy and Totentanz. . . .
> *Ottawa Citizen* 4 July 1992: G2

See also -OS, -OES; PLURALS, REGULAR, IRREGULAR, FOREIGN.

concession road   see ROAD

conciliation, mediation, arbitration, judicial determination, adjudication, judgment   These words have special legal meanings. In a labour dispute, if negotiations reach an impasse, *conciliation*, *mediation*, and *arbitration* are steps taken in the formal process of resolving the dispute. The first two facilitate negotiations without imposing a settlement; arbitration, however, is binding. The disputing parties can also decide to have a judge make the binding decision; this process is called *judicial determination*.

In law, *adjudication* generally follows a hearing, while *judgment* follows a trial.

> Labour Minister Jean Corbeil . . . wants the Canadian Union of Postal Workers back at the bargaining table for a second round of conciliation and not on the picket line after 15 months of often-troubled negotiations with Canada Post.
> *Province* (Vancouver) 1 Nov. 1990: 16

> The native concept of justice differs from the Canadian one; it focuses more on mediation and

restitution than on retribution.
Gazette (Montreal) 12 Feb. 1990: B2

He must carry out his obligation, hearing the evidence to the end, before he makes his adjudication.
Province (Vancouver) 4 Jan. 1990: B1

concise, succinct, concision, conciseness
Concise implies that anything inessential has been removed or cut off. *Succinct* suggests compression, so that much is conveyed in few words. In general, however, these words are used synonymously.
Concision and *conciseness* both mean succinctness; either word is acceptable.

It was a commendable accomplishment; the entries are models of concision yet contain an impressive amount of information.
Globe and Mail (Toronto) 7 Sept. 1985: E1

Conciseness helps to win readers.
Financial Post 30 Jan. 1989: 9

concord   see AGREEMENT, GRAMMATICAL

concrete   see CEMENT; CONCRETIZE

concretize   To *concretize* means to make concrete and specific what was nebulous or abstract. Though the word has been criticized as business jargon, it is more often used in academic and essay writing.

Murray Favro's Van Gogh's Room (1973-74) is an installation piece that both concretizes and simulates (in Baudrillard's sense) a simulation—that is, a representation of a real thing.
Linda Hutcheon *Splitting Images* 1991: 24

Further, concretizing our 'free floating' fears of HIV—for example, in the form of visa restrictions—gives credibility to the unreasonable fears of many persons with respect to HIV.
Gazette (Montreal) 22 June 1990: B3

See also -IZE, -ISE; QUEBEC ENGLISH.

concurrent   see SYNCHRONOUS

condemn, contemn   To *condemn* is to express disapproval of, to find guilty, or to sentence to punishment. *Contemn* is a rare verb meaning to despise, scorn, or hold in contempt.

A long procession of clergymen came forward to condemn slavery and to sing the virtues of English liberty.
William Teatero *John Anderson: Fugitive Slave* 1986: 168

Oddly enough, self-made men generally yearn for acceptance from those they contemn, just as academics become misty-eyed in the presence of a bulging bank book.
Globe and Mail (Toronto) 19 June 1985: P6

conditional   see entry in Glossary

confer   see DOUBLING THE FINAL CONSONANT

conference   see QUEBEC ENGLISH

confidant, confidante, confident   A *confidant* is a person who is respected and trusted with intimate information. A *confidant* can be either male or female. Sometimes, because *confidant* is borrowed from French, writers use *confidant* for men and *confidante* for women; *confidante* should be applied only to women. *Confidant* is usually pronounced *con fee DAUNT* or *CON fih DAUNT*.
Confident is the spelling of the adjective meaning self-assured.

Dunning, unlike Richardson, did not have a private fortune, but he was a trusted confidant of many who did.
Frederick Gibson *Queen's University* 2 (1983): 226

Sauvé has, after all, served as a constitutional confidant to her Prime Minister—in her case, three of them.
Toronto Star 28 Oct. 1990: B3

(Here *confidante* would also be acceptable.)

Again, the initial triangle becomes a second when husband exits and his best buddy becomes confidante to each of the women.
United Church Observer June 1986: 53

(The correct spelling here, in reference to a man, is *confidant*.)

confidentially see SENTENCE ADVERBS

confute see REFUTE

congenial, genial According to many usage guides, a *congenial* person is a person one gets along with, someone with similar interests and tastes, while a *genial* person is generally good-natured. This distinction is all but obsolete, however. In contemporary Canadian English, *congenial* and *genial* are used interchangeably to refer to people with a kind, friendly manner, while *congenial* is also used in more formal contexts to mean suited to a particular taste, purpose, mood, etc.

> It would be hard to imagine a man more congenial to Grant in opinion and in temperament.
> Hilda Neatby *Queen's University* 1 (1978): 172

> He enjoyed drinking and had a few scrapes with the law, but overall [he] was considered a congenial person who often regaled friends with tales of his exploits around the world.
> *Gazette* (Montreal) 7 June 1992: A7

> He was a genial, easy-going man who enjoyed a drink, didn't take religion seriously, and was perfectly willing to let his wife take charge.
> Pierre Berton *The Promised Land* 1984: 280

> Speech-making was very much in Fyfe's line, but the role of fund-raiser he found neither familiar nor congenial.
> Frederick Gibson *Queen's University* 2 (1983): 101

> In Britain and New Zealand, the Labour Party 'welfare leaders' found the redistributive consequences of Keynesianism to be particularly congenial to their social democratic goals.
> Neil Nevitte and Roger Gibbins *New Elites in Old States* 1990: 20

congenital, hereditary, genetic A *congenital* disorder is one that dates from birth. It may be a problem caused during the birth process, such as a brain injury, or one that developed in the foetus before birth, such as a heart defect. Sometimes the word *congenital* is used figuratively to describe habits and attitudes so entrenched as to seem inborn. A *hereditary* disorder is one that is passed genetically from generation to generation, such as hemophilia or Tay-Sachs disease. Not all hereditary problems can be called *congenital*, because they do not all appear at birth.

On the other hand, all hereditary problems are *genetic* because they have to do with genes—but not all genetic disorders are hereditary. For example, gene damage caused by radiation can result in sterility, which is obviously not a heritable condition.

> The baby was delivered by caesarean section . . . with a number of congenital defects, the most serious being brain damage.
> *Vancouver Sun* 5 Dec. 1990: A1

> Alison, who is congenitally nervous of horses, was somewhat discomfited to find herself seated beside [the] Master of the Horse.
> George Ignatieff *The Making of a Peacemonger* 1987: 175

> Well, dogs can fall heir to a number of diseases, many of them hereditary. Some seem to occur in particular breeds or in certain types or sizes of canines.
> *Dogs in Canada* Special Issue 1986: 137

congratulate, congratulations *Congratulate* and *congratulations* are occasionally misspelled, *congradulate* and *congradulations*. The association between graduations and congratulations may contribute to this error. The common pronunciations of *congratulate* are *con GRACH yoo late* and *con GRAJ yoo late*.

congregation see AUDIENCE

congress see QUEBEC ENGLISH

conjoined twins, Siamese twins *Conjoined twins* are twins joined at any part of the body, sometimes sharing organs. The term *Siamese twins* comes from the conjoined twins Chang and Eng who were born in Siam (modern-day Thailand) and who became famous touring with P.T. Barnum. *Conjoined twins* is the preferred medical term and that preferred by conjoined twins and their families, many of whom point out that they are not necessarily from Thailand. The term *Siamese twins* is sometimes used metaphorically.

The pair are the 10th set of conjoined twins to be separated at the world-renowned hospital.
Leader-Post (Regina) 20 July 2005: A8

A quite different constructivist reading of the Canada-US narrative would focus on these serial rejections of mutuality that have punctuated the otherwise neat story of convergence and brotherhood, and have reinforced distinct identities in what J. Bartlett Brebner has classically described as a pair of national 'Siamese twins'.
Canadian-American Public Policy 52 (2002):1

conjugal, connubial *Conjugal* (*CON jew gal*) and *connubial* (*con NUBE ee al*) are both formal words referring to the married state. *Conjugal* is far more common, perhaps because it occurs in the legal phrase 'conjugal rights': the rights of married partners to each other's company and affection, including physical intimacy. The word *connubial*, which is often found in the cliché 'connubial bliss', has connotations that are romantic rather than legal.

Orton said courts have 'extended' benefits to disadvantaged groups before, . . . allowing homosexual partners conjugal prison visits. . . .
Vancouver Sun 24 Feb. 1990: H14

The conjugal partner category is for partners— either of opposite sex or same sex—in exceptional circumstances beyond their control that prevent them from qualifying as common-law partners or spouses.
Citizenship and Immigration Canada website 27 Sept. 2005

The trick had always been . . . to behave well, or at least reasonably well, in exchange for parental or connubial love, a job, social position.
Gazette (Montreal) 8 Sept. 1990: K2

conjunction, conjunctive adverbs   see entries in Glossary

connive Derived from the French for 'to close the eyes to' or 'to wink at', to *connive* in its historical sense means to pretend ignorance of wrongdoing. Thus a conniver doesn't actively participate in misbehaviour but condones it through silence and inaction. This meaning is still common in British English, but almost unknown in Canada and the United States.

Since the Second World War, in North America, *connive* has become a synonym for *conspire*: to actively participate with others in secret wrongdoing. This newer meaning has also become established in Britain. *Connive* in its older sense is followed by *at*: 'The secretary connived at the lawyer's misuse of funds'. When it is a synonym for *conspire*, *connive* is often followed by *with* or an infinitive: 'The spy connived with the enemy'; 'They connived to defraud the public.'

The company has also presented several world premieres, including . . . Fred Euringer's Night Noises (about a nineteenth-century nutritionist who connived at the starvation deaths of his own children). . . .
'Our History' Theatre Kingston website 2002

The opposition Labour Party called for the resignation of Defence Minister Michael Heseltine and a junior minister, John Stanley, saying they had connived to mislead Parliament.
Globe and Mail (Toronto) 12 Feb. 1985: P1

The petition also said that the three trial judges connived with prosecutors to acquit the accused, saying that in one instance a judge allegedly passed a note to the defence.
Globe and Mail (Toronto) 20 Nov. 1985: A10

See also COLLABORATION, COLLABORATOR.

connoisseur   A *connoisseur* (pronounced *con uh SER*) is an expert in some particular matter of taste. This word was borrowed from Old French; in modern French it is spelled *connaisseur*. This modern French spelling sometimes leads to misspelling of the English word, especially in Quebec.

He did not consider himself a first-rate judge of plays, but he successfully asserted his claim to be regarded as a great connoisseur of acting, and his many books of collected criticism burn with a splendid and infectious enthusiasm.
Robertson Davies *A Voice from the Attic* 1960: 195

Connaisseurs and collectors tend to sniff at the choice and selection of the music offered by Discus. . . .
Gazette (Montreal) 12 Nov. 1993: F1

(The correct English spelling is *connoisseurs*.)

connotation(s), denotation, connote, denote The *connotations* of *thin* are fairly neutral; those of *lean*, *slender*, and *svelte*, usually positive; and of *skinny*, usually negative. Yet all these words have the same *denotation* or bald meaning: of less than average weight. *Connotations* are the implications of words—the ideas and feelings habitually associated with them. *Denotation* is literal signification. Thesauruses may lead inexperienced writers astray because sometimes they list as synonyms words with the same basic denotation while ignoring their connotations. For example, *Roget's 21st Century Thesaurus* (1992) has after *thin* a long list of words with very different connotations, including *cadaverous*, *delicate*, *fragile*, *lanky*, *lean*, *skeletal*, *skinny*, *slim*, *small*, *spare*, and *spindly*.

The verbs *connote* and *denote* are used less technically and distinguished less carefully than the nouns *connotation* and *denotation*. *Connote* usually means imply or suggest. *Denote* has a range of meanings, including signify, represent, indicate, symbolize, and imply.

He also said the judge had used [a word] 'only in a descriptive and not in any other sense.' Yet linguists say that is impossible: words carry not only denotation, but connotation.
Vancouver Sun 20 Jan. 1990: B4

The suffix '-man' has lost its original masculine denotation and now connotes merely one-who-does-something.
Vancouver Sun 16 April 1990: A9

(Here *denotes* would also be possible.)

The design consists of a stylized open fan created to connote service and luxury.
Globe and Mail (Toronto) 20 Feb. 1985: B9

Barbers, in fact, were more responsible for caring for the wounded than doctors because they had the closest thing to sterile conditions. Hence the red and white barber's pole, denoting red blood and white bandages.
Globe and Mail (Toronto) 20 April 1985: P10

The plume of smoke that surrounded the face of many an author on the back of a dust-jacket was supposed to denote deep contemplation as well as exotic mystery.
Globe and Mail (Toronto) 12 Jan. 1985: E22

(Here *connote* would also be possible.)

See also SYNONYM, ANTONYM, THESAURUS.

connubial see CONJUGAL

conscious, conscience, unconscious, subconscious If a person is *conscious*, he or she is alert, awake, or aware of physical stimuli or mental information ('He was still conscious when the ambulance arrived'; 'I'm conscious of your irritable mood'). The noun *conscience* refers to the capacity people have to assess their actions morally. This adjective and noun are often confused, especially in phrases such as *knocked unconscious* and *guilty conscience*.

Psychologists now use *unconscious*, not *subconscious*, to describe a part of the human psyche below or beyond consciousness. Freud coined the term *subconscious* in his early writings on psychoanalysis; he later refined this concept, delineating the *unconscious* and the *preconscious*, and later still, the id-ego-superego model. Each new set of concepts supplanted the previous in his work, and Freudians are careful to distinguish among these terms.

The general public is less careful and the adjectives *subconscious* and *unconscious* are used interchangeably to describe things that people think, do or feel without full awareness: 'subconscious doubt', 'unconscious desire', 'unconscious gesture'.

In using the nouns *unconscious* and *subconscious*, writers should take care not to imply a distinction ('Look into your subconscious and let your unconscious guide your choice') that they have not explained to their readers. In popular usage, these terms are synonyms; thus, to avoid puzzling your reader, it is usually best to choose one of these terms and stick with it.

So it is with a guilty conscious—but a sense of civic musical duty, goaded on by promises of free booze and loose women—that I will be in attendance as a guest judge at the Regina finals. . . .
Leader-Post (Regina) 21 Nov. 2002: D1

(The intended phrase is *guilty conscience*.)

I have an unconscience reflex to cover my mouth even when I yawn.
CTV Forums Online 8 Nov. 2005

(The intended phrase is *unconscious*.)

See also -IE-, -EI-.

consecutive days in a row   see WORDINESS

consensus   The common phrases *consensus of opinion* and *general consensus* are criticized as redundant, but *Merriam-Webster's* defends them, saying one meaning of *consensus* is unanimity. Certainly, a *consensus of opinion* could be contrasted with a *consensus vote*.

Note that *consensus* is frequently misspelled *concensus*. The word is related to *consent*, not to *census*.

> The general consensus seemed to be that he acted out of compassion. Given this good motive, and their view that death should be a private matter, many Canadians expected [him] to be acquitted.
> *Toronto Star* 22 Nov. 1994: A21

consequently, consequentially, consequential   *Consequently* and *consequentially* both mean therefore. *Consequently* usually implies a direct causal relationship, while *consequentially* suggests that what follows is an indirect result of what precedes. Thus, in Canadian law, the terms *consequential loss* and *consequential damage* refer to secondary damages, which are one stage removed from an initial breach of contract.

In general English, *consequential* means important, significant.

> We found several instances of reviewers identifying an author as a 'housewife' and consequently dismissing anything she has produced (since, in our society, a 'housewife' is viewed as a relatively brainless and talentless creature).
> Margaret Atwood *Second Words* 1982: 198

> More than 30,000 [Loyalists] settled in Nova Scotia, tripling that colony's population and spilling into New Brunswick, which was consequentially established as a separate colony in 1784.

> Neil Nevitte and Roger Gibbins *New Elites in Old States* 1990: 6

> For instance, failure to repair the heating system of a concert hall as promised in time for a performance in midwinter may lead to the cancellation of the program, making the heating contractor liable for the consequential losses due to cancellation, as well as for damage to the building by frozen pipes, since these were foreseeable harms.
> J.E. Smyth *The Law and Business Administration in Canada* 1987: 352

> Mr. Caplan said the media now dominate the political process with their emphasis on personality politics, trivial and staged confrontation . . . and their warped ethic of covering whatever is said as if it were consequential.
> *Globe and Mail* (Toronto) 2 Feb. 1985: M5

Conservative, Tory, Red Tory, Loyalist, United Empire Loyalists   The contemporary *Conservative Party of Canada* represents the merger, in 2003, of the Progressive Conservative Party and the Canadian Alliance (which had in 2000 subsumed the Reform Party). The term *Tory* is well established as an informal name for members and supporters of the Conservatives. *Tory* has a long history in British politics; by 1689 it was associated with a new British political party that favoured conservatism. *Conservative* became the official name of that party in 1830, but *Tory* remains in use to refer to British Conservatives. A *Red Tory* is a member of the Conservative Party who has (or is said to have) liberal or populist leanings.

In American English, *Tory* refers to colonists who remained loyal to Britain and opposed independence at the time of the American Revolution. In Canada, these people are called *Loyalists* or *United Empire Loyalists* (sometimes abbreviated *UEL*).

> To that end, the citizens of Riverview, a Moncton suburb, voted Liberal in last spring's by-election— the first time in thirty-seven years they failed to elect the Tory candidate.
> *Saturday Night* Jan. 1986: 29

> Only on a few social issues does he show any Red Tory instincts, any concern for the disadvantaged.
> *Saturday Night* March 1986: 24

The United Empire Loyalists Heritage Centre on Quinte Isle . . . tells the story of the Loyalist refugees who settled the region in 1784. . . .
Leader-Post (Regina) 19 May 2006: F1

See also BLEU, ROUGE; GRIT, WHIG, LIBERAL.

consider   *Consider* takes a direct object ('consider it') and sometimes a direct object and object complement ('Consider it *done*'; 'I consider them *the best*'). Some commentators object to the word *as* between the object and the complement, preferring, for example, 'Consider me your friend' to 'Consider me as your friend'. Others have noted that *as* sometimes implies an effort of imagination ('Try to consider me as a friend, even though I've been making your life miserable') and that *as* is necessary when it indicates one way among other possibilities of considering something ('When the rental property is considered as a long-term investment . . .').

'Writing is what I like to do, but I don't consider it a career.'
Bruce Meyer and Brian O'Riordan, eds. *In Their Words* 1984: 154

As a Nazi, Goetz refused to consider the thousands of German refugees driven from their homes and country by the Nazis as 'real Germans'.
Canadian Journal of History 14.1 (1989): 74

consist   *Consist* is usually followed by the preposition *of*. In formal writing, *consists in* is sometimes used, especially to describe the basis of an abstraction.

Duress consists in actual or threatened violence or imprisonment as a means of coercing a party to enter into a contract.
J.E. Smyth et al. *The Law and Business Administration in Canada* 1987: 237

consonants, doubling of   see DOUBLING THE FINAL CONSONANT

conspiracy, conspirator   see COLLABORATION

Constitution, British North America Act, BNA Act, Constitution Act   All the acts that make up the formal written part of the Canadian Constitution are called the Constitution Acts, 1867 to 1982. The Constitutional Act (1791) is only one of a series of earlier acts and proclamations, beginning with the Royal Proclamation of 1763, that established Canada as a legal entity. The Canadian Constitution is supplemented by laws having constitutional effect and by unwritten conventions. The British North America Act (abbreviated BNA Act) was passed in 1867 by the British parliament. It created the Dominion of Canada, a federation consisting of the Province of Canada (Ontario and Quebec), New Brunswick, and Nova Scotia, which other provinces joined later. The Act remained a British statute, however, rather than a Canadian one. In 1982, as part of the initiative to patriate the Canadian Constitution—in other words, to bring it under Canadian control—the BNA Act was renamed the Constitution Act, 1867. The Canadian Charter of Rights and Freedoms is part of the Constitution Act, 1982.

See also CANADIAN BILL OF RIGHTS; DOMINION OF CANADA, CANADA DAY; PATRIATE, PATRIATION.

consul   see COUNCIL

consummate   The adjective, which means perfect, complete, unsurpassable, or, when describing a role, highly accomplished, is pronounced *CON sum it* or *con SUM it*. The verb, meaning complete or fulfil, is pronounced *CON suh MATE*. The verb refers to the first act of sexual intercourse in a marriage, which makes the marriage valid in canon law, or to the completion of a business deal or other transaction.

Yet, ironically, Reagan was nothing during his eight years in office if not the consummate product of the consumer culture—and all its deficits, its emphasis upon style and personality, and its demand for instant gratification—that he claimed to abhor.
Queen's Quarterly 95.4 (1988): 798

'She was the consummate mom. She took great pleasure in making sure everyone was comfortable, happy and well-fed.'
Windsor Star 23 May 2006: A1

She insisted on visiting her relatives for long periods and refused to consummate the marriage, not because of a physical complaint but because of a lack of desire.
Jack Batten *Robinette* 1984: 41

After 15 months of negotiations, union organizers have failed to consummate a deal with the network.
Calgary Herald 18 Aug. 2005: A18

contact   see FUNCTIONAL SHIFT

contact clauses   see THAT, OMISSION OF

contagious, infectious   *Contagious* and *infectious* are often used as synonyms in everyday speech and popular writing. In medical terms, however, these words don't mean exactly the same thing, and the distinction is worth maintaining in serious writing. All diseases caused by micro-organisms are infectious (e.g., colds, AIDS, scabies, malaria, and amoebic dysentery). But only those diseases transmitted directly from person to person are contagious. Of the diseases above, colds, AIDS, and scabies are contagious, transmitted by sneezing, sexual contact, and physical contact, but malaria, which is transmitted by a particular type of mosquito—never from human to human—is not contagious, and neither is amoebic dysentery, which is usually contracted by drinking contaminated water.

Both words are acceptable when used figuratively to describe something that spreads from one person to another: *contagious* is used more often than *infectious* when describing something unpleasant.

Now doctors are blaming bacteria for these painful craters in the stomach and upper intestine. Peptic ulcers an infectious disease? That's the controversial theory.
Ottawa Citizen 13 July 1994: B3

Victims catch [Legionnaires'] disease, which is not thought to be contagious, by inhaling minute water droplets in the air from contaminated cooling, air conditioning and hot water systems.
Globe and Mail (Toronto) 4 May 1985: P17

Paris terrorism is contagious.
Globe and Mail (Toronto) 25 June 1985: P7

Father Terry, who said he is basically a happy person, finds joy is infectious. 'If I'm bubbly and joyful it's contagious.'
Catholic Register 16 Aug. 1986: 21

contemn   see CONDEMN

contemporary, contemporaneous   Most dictionaries list 'existing at the same time' as the first meaning of *contemporary*, but since the 1940s its more common meaning has been modern or present-day. *Contemporary with*, as in 'writers contemporary with Chaucer', always means 'existing at the same time as'. The noun *contemporary* refers to a person from the same era or of roughly the same age. In other contexts, however, *contemporary* can be ambiguous. For example, '*contemporary* accounts' could be versions of an event written by historical witnesses or by present-day historians.

Some usage commentators suggest reserving *contemporary* to mean modern or up-to-date and using *contemporaneous* to mean existing at the same time. However, there are two problems with this advice: first, while *contemporaneous* is a useful and unambiguous term, it is quite formal and usually found only in academic writing; second, the word *contemporary* remains ambiguous to the reader. The best advice is to paraphrase *contemporary* in contexts where both meanings are plausible. For example, use 'period costume' or 'modern dress' rather than 'contemporary costume'.

One of the first projects that the Commission undertook was to carry out 'a deep philosophical probe' of Canada's criminal law, leading to the enactment of a comprehensive Criminal Code reflecting contemporary values.
Canadian Bar Review 66.3 (1987): 532

(Here *contemporary* means present-day.)

. . . once I have, so to speak, recovered myself as I used to be, I can look at the town, whose childhood was exactly contemporary with my own, with more understanding.
Richard Davies and Glen Kirkland, eds. *Dimensions* 1986: 139

(Here *contemporary* means existing at the same time.)

Coincidentally, the beginning of this European activity was roughly contemporaneous with a decline of both Chinese and Islamic exploratory activity.
William Norton *Human Geography* 1992: 16

contemptible, contemptuous   *Contemptible* means deserving of contempt; to be *contemptuous* is to feel contempt, to be scornful.

This current liberal attempt to redefine one of the more contemptible aspects of society is most worrying—nay, depressing.
National Post 13 March 2006: A14

A contemptuous Supreme Court of Ontario judge yesterday sent the kingpin of a massive marijuana importing operation to jail for 20 years. . . .
Globe and Mail (Toronto) 11 June 1985: P1

continuance, continuation, continuity
Continuance has two meanings. It may be a formal synonym for duration ('Its continuance was brief'); or it may refer simply to the fact that something continues ('Its continuance was taken for granted'). *Continuation* is also used in this second sense, but more often refers to an addition to something, or a prolonging or renewal of it: 'It's a continuation of his previous novel'. *Continuity* is the quality of connectedness between the parts in a whole or a series. In filmmaking, the person in charge of *continuity* ensures that there are no discrepancies in the details of scenes shot at different times. In radio and television programs, *continuity* is the music or commentary that introduces or links segments.

The green symbolized the continuance of life through the winter and meshed with the Christian belief of eternal life through Christ.
Toronto Star 27 Dec. 1994: A7

The continuation of the revolution depends on keeping the flame lit by Guevara alive.
Queen's Quarterly 92.2 (1985): 392

Sydney lies farther southeast on the highway's continuation around Sydney's Atlantic harbor.
Alan Tucker, ed. *The Penguin Guide to Canada* 1991: 64

To start fermentation, and also to ensure continu-ity of taste and character, must from a previous fermentation is added.
Bon Vivant Feb.–Mar. 1983: 9

continuous(ly), continual(ly)   Something *continuous* goes on without a break: 'Their store is continuously monitored by video camera'. Something *continual* goes on and on but with breaks: 'Their store is continually being robbed'. Almost every usage guide presents this distinction, although many concede that it is widely ignored. In formal writing the distinction should be maintained. Occasionally, however, the choice is debatable: for example, does the population of a city grow continually or continuously?

Instead of continuously heating a huge reservoir of water, a tankless system doesn't start warming it up until you turn on the tap.
Calgary Herald 20 May 2006: H1

With the weight of heavy packs, we continually sank to our knees in oozing, freezing black mud.
Up Here Jan.–Feb. 1990: 48

As an aside, the data presented clearly indicate that men, too, were greatly interested in finding an effective, safe way of avoiding continuous childbearing. . . .
Canadian Journal of Sociology 14.2 (1989): 247

(Here *continual* is recommended.)

contractions   Contractions (*I'm, they're, don't, wouldn't, aren't*, and so on) are appropriate in reported speech, dialogue, personal letters, business letters, and light journalism. They are inappropriate in highly formal writing such as official documents. Commentators agree on this much. The grey area is formal writing such as essays, reports, serious journalism, and serious fiction. *Fowler's* (1965) deemed contractions too chatty—hence grating—in such contexts. However, some modern writing guides say that avoiding contractions altogether results in a stilted style. What is at issue is not just a typographical convention, but how writing 'sounds'. Writing without any contractions has an oratorical tone (*let us not, do not, is it not?*), while writing full of contractions (*there's,* *should've, we'd*) sounds conversational. Most formal writing aims for something between a pontifical and a chummy tone, and thus some contractions are appropriate.

See also ABBREVIATION; AIN'T; [COULD OF]; ITS, IT'S; SHAN'T; THERE IS; YOUR.

contretemps   Dictionaries define a *contretemps*—pronounced *CON truh tah(m)*—as an embarrassing incident or awkward mishap. Recently, though, the word has developed a new meaning: dispute, controversy, or altercation. Although this newer meaning now predominates in Canadian journalism, it's not fully accepted and should be avoided in formal writing.

> Eves downplayed the embarrassing contretemps, saying, 'if I'd have known (he wasn't here), obviously I wouldn't have asked him to stand up. . .'.
> *Calgary Herald* 27 Oct. 2002: A8

(This is an accepted use of the term.)

> Strand happily recalled the occasion when Basham physically defended him during a contretemps with some campus radicals.
> *Financial Post* 21 Sept. 1990: 11

(This use is disputed.)

controller   see COMPTROLLER

convention   see QUEBEC ENGLISH; entry in Glossary

convex   see CONCAVE

conveyer, conveyor   see -ER, -OR

convince, persuade   In current Canadian and American usage these two words are synonyms, but before the 1950s their meanings were more distinct (*Webster's Dictionary of English Usage*). *Convince* was then generally reserved for mental conviction alone, as in 'Joan was convinced of the justice of the measure'. *Persuade* referred to mental conviction followed by action, as in 'Joan was persuaded to donate money to the cause'. Usage commentators sometimes object to the use of *convince* followed by an infinitive, but this structure is now firmly established and unobjectionable.

> The ways of publishers are unfathomable, but I hope someone can convince New Press to bring Reaney's poems out in paperback soon. . . .
> Margaret Atwood *Second Words* 1982: 159

(Here *convince* is directly linked to action.)

> Memories of what happened to the Wehrmacht in Yugoslavia in the Second World War should suffice to persuade foreigners that imposing solutions leads to even more problems in that proud, unforgiving, strong part of the world.
> *Financial Post* 10 Oct. 1991: 15

(Here *persuade* refers solely to mental conviction.)

co-op, cooperate, coordinate   see HYPHEN-ATION

Coordinated Universal Time   see GREEN-WICH MEAN TIME

coordinates   see QUEBEC ENGLISH

cop, cop out   In spoken English, police officers are usually referred to as *cops*. Yet the word *cop* is avoided in news writing and formal prose. At issue is not only the formality of the word, but whether it is respectful to officers of the law. Most newspaper style guides recommend against using *cop* in serious contexts, though it is certainly not a highly pejorative term: the police use it themselves.

Cop was used as an informal verb meaning capture or take by 1704; by 1844, to *cop* meant to arrest. Subsequently, the slang name for those who arrest became *copper*, which was later shortened to *cop* (*copper* is still common in Britain).

The slang expression to *cop out*, meaning to evade responsibility or back down from a promise, is related to *cop* meaning police. *Copping out* was first used in the 1920s to mean confessing to the police in exchange for leniency, i.e., plea bargaining, a process that often involves shifting responsibility to others.

From the dock, where I went to take a fast swim, I couldn't see a cop car in the parking lot, only the regulars frying in the early sun.
Howard Engel *Murder Sees the Light* 1984: 188

(The word *cop* is often used in fiction where everyday speech is represented.)

Constable Joe Marshall of the Ontario Provincial Police would like to ask you to 'Adopt-A-Cop', especially him, to raise funds for Special Olympics.
Whig-Standard (Kingston) 10 May 1994: 13

(Here the police are calling themselves *cops*.)

The provincial police officer shot his killer twice before he was shot to death in Sudbury, Ont.
Ottawa Citizen 28 June 1994: A5

(In this context *cop* would be inappropriate.)

See also POLICE OFFICER.

copse   see FOREST

copyright, copywriter   *Copyright* is the legal right to publish or copy a book, song, video, work of art, etc., and to *copyright* is to assert or secure that exclusive right. Works protected by copyright are described as *copyright* ('copyright books') or *copyrighted* ('copyrighted DVDs'). Some stylists object to the use of *copyrighted* as an adjective when *copyright* serves the same purpose, and, indeed, *copyrighted* is rarely found before a noun in formal Canadian writing. Other commentators defend this use of *copyrighted*—which is common in informal writing—as easier to understand; for the adjective *copyright* usually has a different meaning: 'of or having to do with copyright', as in 'copyright holder' or 'copyright law'. Increasingly common in both formal and informal writing is the phrase *copyright-protected* ('copyright-protected materials'), which is both clear and without detractors.
   Note the spelling: *copyright*, not *copywrite*. A *copywriter* is someone who writes copy: that is, advertising or publicity material.

The Society of Composers, Authors and Music Publishers of Canada (SOCAN) is a not-for-profit organization that collects licensing fees for the public use of copyright-protected music on behalf of its members.
Gazette (Montreal) 15 April 2006: E1

cord, chord   A *cord* is a thick string or thin rope or cable. Cut wood is measured in units called *cords* because stacks of wood were once measured with a length of cord. *Cord* is also the name given the spinal *cord* and vocal *cords*. The spelling *chords* is often found after *vocal*; most North American authorities regard this as an error. British and Australian guides are more likely to see it as an acceptable variant.
   Chord spelled with an *h* refers to music, emotional feeling, or geometry. A musical *chord* is a group of notes sounded together in harmony; to *strike a chord* in someone means to elicit empathy; a geometric *chord* is a straight line between two points on a curve.

'I thought I only had to do these things on Thursdays,' he says, forcing an enormous amount of disdain through those legendary vocal chords.
Ottawa Citizen 18 Feb. 1993: E1

(The more common, and recommended, spelling is *vocal cords*.)

'I think we really struck a cord with women, particularly middle-aged women such as ourselves.'
Ottawa Citizen 14 Jan. 1993: A12

(Here the correct spelling is *chord*.)

core, corps, corpse, corpus   The *core* is the center or essence of something. A *corps* (pronounced CORE) is a specialized military unit or a group of people engaged in a special activity: 'the diplomatic corps', 'the press corps', 'a dance corps'. A *corpse* is a dead body, usually a human body. A *corpus* is a complete collection of writings by a single author, or a collection of texts or recordings having to do with a particular subject of study, usually literary or linguistic. The plural of *corpus* is *corpuses* or *corpora* (pronounced CORP or *uh*).

Louis Bruce in geology and J.A. Gray in physics, holders of the university's two research chairs,

made valuable contributions of their own and trained a corpus of young scientists.
Frederick Gibson *Queen's University* 2 (1983): 322

(In reference to a group of people, the word required is *corps*.)

cork   see KHAKI

corn, grain, maize   The rising price of 'corn' sparked riots in nineteenth-century Britain—not the price of corn on the cob, but the price of wheat and other grains used to make bread. What Canadians call *grain*, Brits call *corn*. What Canadians call *corn*, Brits call *maize*. When Europeans arrived in the Americas, they found a tall, indigenous plant in cultivation by the Aboriginal peoples. It was the New World equivalent of European cereal plants, so British settlers called it 'Indian corn'. That was later shortened to *corn* by English speakers in North America, who began to use the word *grain* to describe the cereal crops brought over from Europe. British speakers, meanwhile, continued to call wheat, barley, oats, etc., *corn* and adopted an Aboriginal word for the New World plant: *maize*.

cornet, coronet   A *cornet*, pronounced *kor NET*, is a brass musical instrument, similar to a trumpet but slightly shorter, wider, and producing a higher sound. In Britain, a *cornet* is also an ice cream cone. The word comes from the Latin *cornu*, meaning 'horn', from which we also get *cornucopia*. *Cornet* is often misspelled *coronet* and mispronounced with three syllables.

A *coronet,* pronounced *kor uh NET*, is a small crown, not usually a sovereign's crown but a woman's headdress made of jewels or flowers; the word is derived from the Old French word for *crown*, from which we also get *corona*. *Coronet* is also a verb, which does not double the *t* in the past tense: 'She coroneted her hair with ribbons'.

The instruments played at the festival include cornets, soprano cornets, flugelhorns, tenor horns, baritones, euphoniums, trombones and tubas.
Star-Phoenix (Saskatoon) 28 April 2005: D1

The woman's hair is a rich brown with reddish

lights—like a chestnut mare—and black combs or a jet coronet hold it in place.
Border Crossings 23.3 (2004): 6-7

He played the coronet, his father the fiddle, his mother the piano and his sister the guitar.
Leader-Post (Regina) 3 Sept. 2005: A15

(Here *coronet* should be *cornet*, the musical instrument.)

corporal, corporeal   The adjectives *corporal* (pronounced *CORP er ul*) and *corporeal* (pronounced *cor POR ee ul*) both mean bodily. *Corporal* is found almost exclusively in the phrase 'corporal punishment'. *Corporeal* is used mainly to indicate that something is physical, substantial, or material in nature, as opposed to spiritual or immaterial.

The new policy will prohibit foster families from using corporal punishment—spanking, hitting, punching or shoving—as a means of discipline. . . .
Globe and Mail (Toronto) 18 Jan. 1985: P1

The dancers . . . appear to enjoy giving the dissonance of the music a corporeal form.
Globe and Mail (Toronto) 10 Jan. 1985: E3

The whole idea of virtuosity is that the mental component is there as well, and the mental ideas are made corporeal through technique.
Globe and Mail (Toronto) 23 April 1985: M11

corporation   see FIRM

corps, corpse, corpus   see CORE

corpus, corpuses, corpora   see PLURALS; -US

cost, costed, cost out   When to *cost* means to have as a price, the past tense and past participle are *cost*: 'That is twice what it cost last week'; 'It had cost him a fortune'. When to *cost* means to calculate or estimate the cost of something, the past tense and past participle are *costed*: 'She costed the print run at $1500'. In Canada and the United States, *cost out* is a common variant of *cost* meaning to calculate the cost of.

. . . they couldn't be costed in the regular way . . . because of the unprecedented nature of the roof.

Only two major cities have tried a retractable dome.
Globe and Mail (Toronto) 22 June 1985: E15

The candidates said the scheme had not been costed out, but there would be a return for the city from long leases on the land.
Vancouver Sun 12 Nov. 1993: C1

cortex, cortices   see PLURALS

coterie   see CLIQUE

couch   see CHESTERFIELD

couldn't care less, could care less   Both phrases mean the same thing: the speaker does not care at all. The far more widely used and approved form is *couldn't care less*. How the reversal *could care less* came to mean the same thing has puzzled word historians. Some speculate that it may have to do with the rhythm of the phrase: dropping the negative particle shifts the emphasis from the grammatical word *couldn't* to the content word *care*, which allows for a more lingeringly sarcastic delivery of the phrase. *Could care less* is often criticized as illogical, and both versions of the phrase are informal.

Above all, I loved the experience of proving myself, of being accepted as one of the boys by teammates who couldn't care less who I was or where I came from.
George Ignatieff *The Making of a Peacemonger* 1987: 46

Rick would have to fight his own battles. And if he got beat up in the process, Harley could care less.
Canadian Fiction Magazine 64 (1988): 66

[could of], [would of], [should of], [might of], eye dialect   *Could of, might of, should of,* and *would of* are non-standard spellings of contractions with *have*: *could've, might've, should've,* and *would've*. In normal speech, *could of* and *could've* sound the same, which is what leads people to make this error. These *of* spellings rarely find their way into print except in fiction, where they may be used to set a certain tone or to suggest laxness of speech. This literary effect is called *eye dialect,*

since its impact is not on the ear—there is no real divergence from the standard pronunciation—but on the eye.

Mind you, father Adrian tried his best to turn things around and to make Ben the boss. And Ben would of let him. But I wasn't having any of that . . . !
Canadian Fiction Magazine 64 (1989): 88

'I should of blasted out the nearest exit.'
Canadian Fiction Magazine 63 (1988): 134

coulee   see SWAMP

council   see COLLECTIVE NOUNS

council, councillor, counsel, counsellor, consul   A *council* is a group of elected representatives of a city, town, village, township, or county. Members of council are called *councillors* (or, rarely, *councilors*). Any advisory or deliberative body, or assembly of such a body, may be called a *council*.

The noun *counsel* means advice; to *counsel* means to give advice. A *counsellor* (or sometimes *counselor*) is a therapist, an adviser, or a supervisor at a children's camp. Lawyers in Canadian court proceedings are occasionally referred to as *counsellors*; more often they are called *counsel* (singular and plural): 'Defence counsel objected'. As in this example, the word is normally used without an article: 'Did he have counsel?' (that is, did he have a lawyer?).

A *consul* is an official appointed by a country to look after its business interests and its citizens in a foreign city.

'I said I wouldn't come,' said Bonnie McKinnon, a newly elected counsellor from the Surrey Electors Team (SET).
Vancouver Sun 29 Nov. 1993: B1

(The correct spelling for a member of a council is *councillor*.)

It is hard to think of someone more likely to give good counsel than Mitchell Sharp.
Gazette (Montreal) 5 Nov. 1993: B2

An employment counsellor based in Courtenay, O'Hara repeatedly saw clients stressed from too much work and others stressed from not having any.
Vancouver Sun 16 Dec. 1993: B6

See also JOB TITLES; LAWYER; SPELLING, CANADIAN.

countable noun see entry in Glossary

counterfeit see -IE-, -EI-

coup de grâce, pièce de résistance
Occasionally people confuse these French expressions. Translated literally, *coup de grâce* means 'mercy blow': the stroke that puts an end to the suffering of an opponent or a wounded animal. In contemporary English usage, however, the expression rarely connotes mercy: a *coup de grâce* is a death blow.

The *pièce de résistance* is the best part or feature of something: the most delicious dish of a meal, the high point in a concert, the best room in a house, and so on. Originally, the *pièce de résistance* was the most substantial dish in a meal, but now the term refers to quality, not quantity.

Coup de grâce is pronounced *coo duh GRASS*; the plural is *coups de grâce*. *Pièce de résistance* is pronounced *pee ESS duh RAY zee stahnce*; the plural is *pièces de résistance*. The plural *s* is not pronounced. Though newspapers don't put these expressions in italics, in formal writing they should be italicized and should retain their accents.

> If France today rejects the Maastricht Treaty it will deal the coup de grace to swift European unification, a process already badly shaken by this week's monetary crisis.
> *Calgary Herald* 20 Sept. 1992: A6

> The piece de resistance of the Canada pavilion is the front courtyard, which extends under the building like a huge cavern and brings a feel of the icy north to a place where summer temperatures can reach 50 degrees Celsius.
> *Vancouver Sun* 18 April 1992: A1

> Wedgewood's coup de grace is two-fold: an open-concept kitchen/breakfast combo overlooking the sunken family room, separated by a solid oak railing.
> *Toronto Star* 1 Feb. 1992: E12

(The expression required here is *pièce de résistance*.)

> Even with a career that includes four feature films to date, Burnett's undisputed coup de grace will likely forever be The Carol Burnett Show, which ran for 11 highly successful seasons on CBS.
> *Calgary Herald* 29 June 1992: A14

(The expression required here is *pièce de résistance*.)

courageous see -E

coureur de bois, voyageur The terms *coureur de bois* (or *coureur des bois*) and *voyageur*, borrowed from Canadian French into English in the eighteenth century, both refer to the European and Métis fur-traders and adventurers who operated across much of the region that is now Canada and the northern United States.

Coureurs de/des bois (*cuh RER duh/day BWAH*), 'runners of the woods', was the term in general use until 1680, when the fur trade in New France was licensed. At that time select coureurs de bois were hired by Montreal merchants and were given the title *voyageur* (*voy a ZHUR*), 'traveller'. These voyageurs travelled the continent in freight canoes, establishing and maintaining trade with Native trappers. *Coureurs de bois* then became the designation for independent, unlicensed traders.

courtly see ADJECTIVES AND ADVERBS; FRIENDLY, FRIENDLILY

cousin In the sixteenth century *cousin* was a general term for relatives outside the immediate family. Nieces and nephews, for example, were often called cousins. In contemporary usage the term is more restricted. Your *cousin*, or *first cousin*, is the son or daughter of your aunt or uncle. Your *second cousin* is the son or daughter of your mother's or father's first cousin. Children of second cousins are *third cousins* to each other. First cousins have the same grandparents, second cousins the same great-grandparents, third cousins the same great-great-grandparents, and so on.

Cousins who are *removed* are of different generations. You and the child of your first cousin are *first cousins once removed*. You and the grandchild of your first cousin are *first cousins twice removed*. To the children of your second cousin, you are a *second cousin once removed*.

Cousin is often used figuratively in current English for things in the same general category and for people related by race or culture.

> We found routers with such expensive gadgets as dust vacuums and electronic controls perform no better than their less expensive cousins. . . .
> *Canadian Consumer* Feb. 1986: 32

> His compatriots . . . would never forget the way their cousins across the Atlantic had come to their assistance during the darkest days of World War II.
> George Ignatieff *The Making of a Peacemonger* 1987: 108

couth   see BACK-FORMATION

cover-up   see PHRASAL VERBS

covet, covetousness   see ENVY

coyote   In North America *coyote* has three pronunciations: *kye OH tee, KYE oat,* or *KYE oot.* The CBC recommends *KYE oat* to its announcers. Some Canadians believe that the two-syllable pronunciations are particularly Canadian, but they are also found in the United States. Other names for the coyote—which is smaller than the wolf, but closely related to it—are brush wolf and prairie wolf.

cracker   see HACKER, CRACKER

cranium, crania   see PLURALS

crash   see COMPUTER TERMS

crazy   see -E

credence, credibility   To give something *credence* (pronounced *CREE dense*) is to believe it, whereas to give or lend something *credibility* is to make it more believable and convincing, or at least to make it appear more reputable.

A *letter of credence* is an official or confidential recommendation or a letter of introduction. A *credibility gap* is a discrepancy between what is presented as truth and what it is possible to believe.

> Any organization can be discredited if one chooses to give credence to the fringe elements within it.
> *Globe and Mail* (Toronto) 30 Jan. 1985: P7

> An audit can give an organization credibility because it shows that its money is properly and professionally handled.
> *Canadian Baptist* Jan. 1986: 55

> Because such international events invariably involve 'official' relations with the supplying countries (and provide representatives of those nations with valuable windows for public relations), they confer upon the Festival a degree of credence.
> *Queen's Quarterly* 95 (1988): 819

(The word required here is *credibility.*)

> Presenting my letters of credence turned out to be an even more interesting experience than I had expected.
> George Ignatieff *The Making of a Peacemonger* 1987: 153

See also CREDIBLE.

credible, incredible, credulous, incredulous, creditable, discreditable   *Credible* means believable. A credible story rings true, and a credible witness seems reliable. *Incredible* can simply mean not credible, not believable, but it usually means far beyond belief ('an incredible tale') or, in informal use, wonderful or great ('an incredible party', 'an incredible amount').

Credulous means gullible or overly disposed to believe ('credulous investors'); *incredulous* means skeptical or shocked and unable to believe something.

Creditable and *discreditable* are applied to actions rather than people. *Creditable* acts are praiseworthy, and *creditable* performances are reasonably good; *discreditable* actions are blameworthy, bringing disrepute.

Of all the surveys done by pollsters, the least cred-

ible is the one claiming to establish that 40 per cent of adults are shy.
Vancouver Sun 26 Nov. 1990: A8

The stories of four women who accuse their brothers of sexually abusing them for 15 years are so horrific and incredible they can't be true, a lawyer said. . . .
Toronto Star 8 Dec. 1993: A14

The sky is an incredible clear blue smudged with white clouds.
Vancouver Sun 15 Dec. 1990: B1

Contrary to the institute's educational philosophy, the purpose of the school system is more than just preparing students to become docile workers, credulous consumers and corporate drones.
Vancouver Sun 23 May 2006: A8

'I honestly can't believe they have sunk that low,' he said. 'I am incredulous.'
Daily News (Halifax) 12 May 1994: n.p.

He clicks his tongue and shakes his head the way Montrealers do when they hear something incredulous.
Canadian Fiction Magazine 63 (1988): 115

(The word required here is *incredible* or *unbelievable*.)

Actor and vocal coach Trish Allen does a creditable job in her debut as a director.
Vancouver Sun 26 March 1994: EA17

'There are other people, equally creditable, who say, "This is death, don't touch it."'
Vancouver Sun 31 March 1994: D1

(Here *credible* is required.)

See also CREDENCE, CREDIBILITY.

Créditiste   see SOCIAL CREDIT

credit union   see BANK

credulous   see CREDIBLE

Cree   The Cree, one of the most populous and far-ranging of the First Nations, generally refer to themselves by names that specify local groups: for example, Ermineskin, Lubicon, Star Blanket, Sunchild. They are also divided into regional groups marked by dialectal and cultur-

al differences: Plains Cree (Alberta and Saskatchewan), Woodlands Cree (Saskatchewan and Manitoba), and Swampy Cree (Manitoba, Ontario, and Quebec). *Cree* is the name of the language of all of these groups; the six Cree dialects are East, Moose, Northern, Plains, Swampy, and Woods. Although most names designating Aboriginal groups are not pluralized by adding *s* ('two Inuit' *not* 'Inuits'), either *Cree* or *Crees* is acceptable (*Globe and Mail Style Book*).

See also ABORIGINAL PEOPLE(S); APPENDIX III.

crematorium, crematoria   see PLURALS

creole   see PIDGIN

crescendo, climax   *Crescendo* (pronounced *kruh SHEN doe*) is an Italian word meaning 'growing'. It was first used in English as a musical term to describe a gradual increase in force or loudness: 'a crescendo of drumbeats'. The plural is *crescendos* or *crescendi*.

Figuratively, a *crescendo* is a progression towards a *climax* or peak: 'A crescendo of complaints preceded the amendment'. *Crescendo* now also refers to the climax itself: 'Tensions reached a crescendo'. This newer meaning is very common and listed in all contemporary dictionaries; nevertheless, it is harshly criticized. If you are thin-skinned, substitute 'reached a climax' for 'reached a crescendo' in formal writing.

. . . the island of Illyria is ultimately a never-never land . . . where the castaway Viola can disguise herself as a boy and enter the court of Duke Orsino where she sets off a crescendo of romantic love and sexual confusion.
Ottawa Citizen 31 May 1994: B6

'You get situations where an employee is not performing, the manager is not able to deal with it and the situation reaches a crescendo.'
National Post 9 May 2006: JV2

cricketana   see -(I)ANA

crippled   see DISABILITIES

crisis, crises see PLURALS

criterion, criteria *Criterion* is the singular and *criteria* is the plural: 'Should academic ability be the only criterion for admission?'; 'Each submission is judged on five criteria'.

> 'Seniors have said we must examine programs where the only criterion (to qualify) is age . . . we must have criteria other than age.'
> *Calgary Herald* 30 Sept. 1993: B2

> While Martyniak says he'll rely on his personal taste for his selections, he'll also have to use the size of individual models as a criteria.
> *Province* (Vancouver) 17 Feb. 2006: A9

(The singular *criterion* is required here.)

> The author suffers a serious credibility loss by first basing her comparisons on an outdated study, and then brazenly adding criterion as she goes along.
> *Vancouver Sun* 17 June 1990: 93

(The plural *criteria* is required here.)

See also PLURALS, REGULAR, IRREGULAR, FOREIGN.

criticize, critique To *criticize* a literary work or artistic performance is to judge its merits as well as its faults. In ordinary use, however, someone who criticizes something is pointing out its faults. The disparaging overtones of *criticize* may have prompted the recent revival of *critique* as a neutral verb meaning to judge. Some commentators have criticized the verb to *critique* as faddish, but since the *OED* cites its use as early as 1751, and it serves a useful purpose, it will probably gain full acceptance.

> The Giraffe Project has also created an array of educational and motivational programs. . . . One of the programs, called Standing Tall, is currently being critiqued by several Vancouver teachers.
> *Vancouver Sun* 25 March 1994: B2

> When you critique the Vancouver Canucks, it's tough to make a case for the defence.
> *Vancouver Sun* 21 Feb. 1990: B6

See also SPELLING, CANADIAN; FUNCTIONAL SHIFT.

crocus, croci see PLURAL

crony see COHORT

cruising see EUPHEMISM

cum *Cum,* which rhymes with *room* or *rum,* is a Latin preposition meaning 'with'. To graduate *cum laude* is to graduate 'with distinction'. *Cum* is often used in journalism to form compound titles (usually hyphenated) for people or things that function in more than one capacity: 'teacher-cum-coach', 'studio-cum-laundry room'. This use, often facetious, is always informal.

> On May 26, 1954, the retired athlete-cum-politician was up to bat in a charity softball game against members of the press on the lawn of Parliament Hill.
> *Toronto Star* 26 May 1994: E1

> At Cut Offs 'n' Jeans, a hair-salon-cum-jean-emporium, Pamela Mannix decorates worn-but-loved jeans in all the right places.
> *Calgary Herald* 8 Feb. 1994: B8

See also LATIN PHRASES.

cupful see -FUL, CUPFUL, SPOONFUL, TEASPOONFUL

curb, kerb Canadians use *curb* for all senses, as do Americans. British writers use *kerb* to refer to the edging at the side of a road, and *curb* for all other senses of both the noun and the verb.

currency see DOLLAR AMOUNTS

curriculum vitae Literally, this Latin phrase means 'the course of a life', but in English usage a *curriculum vitae* is an account of one's qualifications, education, and previous experience that is submitted with applications for professional or academic positions, grants, or scholarships. In most situations the abbreviation *cv* can be used, and thus the plural is not a problem: *cv's.* However, the abbreviation looks a little odd in very formal contexts. The Latin plural of the unabbreviated phrase varies: *curricula vitae,* if you are referring to several versions of one person's *curriculum vitae;* or *curricula vitarum* if you are referring to the cv's of more than one person: 'Please forward curricula vitarum for all four applicants'.

See also APOSTROPHE; RÉSUMÉ; PLURALS, REGULAR, IRREGULAR, FOREIGN.

cursed   see -ED

customer, client, patient, patron   Generally *customers* buy *things*, while *clients* purchase *professional services*, such as those of a lawyer, accountant, architect, or hair stylist. However, *client* is sometimes used in upscale settings as a synonym for *customer*. Someone receiving medical services is a *patient*, but *client* is often used for people seeing a counsellor or psychotherapist. *Patron* is a common synonym for *customer* in the context of theatres, restaurants, and accommodation. A 'patron of the arts' is someone who financially supports arts organizations or buys works of art.

> His father owned a car dealership and during the hockey season gave away hockey sticks to his customers as a promotion.
> Ken Dryden *The Game* 1983: 57

> Depression doctors and lawyers went unpaid, and joined many of their patients and clients in common poverty.
> *Canadian Journal of Sociology* 14.2 (1989): 252

> The program offers individual counselling and group activities for its clients, most of whom range from 65 to 75.
> *Calgary Herald* 26 May 1994: B7

> In one club where he was opening for blues legend Muddy Waters, he was knocked cold by a patron swinging a ketchup bottle.
> *Globe and Mail* (Toronto) 18 Jan 1985: E4

customs   see TAX

cutter   see SLED

cutthroat   see HYPHENATION

cut off one's nose to spite one's face, [cut off one's nose despite one's face]   see MISHEARD EXPRESSIONS

cyclone, hurricane, typhoon, tornado, twister, funnel cloud, waterspout   *Cyclone* is the most general term for a weather system in which winds circle an area of low pressure. A *cyclone* can blow over huge areas with relatively little effect, but if the system is compressed over land, the winds rushing towards the central low-pressure area can literally lift houses.

East of the International Date Line, the most severe cyclonic storms, with winds reaching 120 to 460 kilometres per hour, are called *hurricanes*. Similar storms originating west of the date line are called *typhoons*.

The centre of such a storm is called *the eye*. This centre is quite calm; hence references to 'the eye of the hurricane' should not imply that the eye itself is stormy, even though it is circled by high winds.

Although *tornado* and *cyclone* are sometimes used as if they were synonyms, *tornado* is best reserved for a funnel-shaped column of rotating air that touches the ground in a narrow but very destructive path. A *twister* is small tornado whose damage is limited to 100 metres. Several tornados may be attached to one cyclone, and several twisters to one tornado. If the column of rotating wind does not touch the ground it is called a *funnel cloud*, and if it touches down over water it is called a *water spout*. *Tornado* can be made plural by adding either *-s* or *-es*.

See also MOTHER NATURE.

Czechoslovakia   see SLOVAKIA, SLOVENIA.

D

da see ALPHABETICAL ORDER

dachshund see CAPITAL LETTERS; GERMAN WORDS, PRONUNCIATION

dais, rostrum, podium, lectern A *dais*, *rostrum*, or *podium* is a platform for speakers. Often a *dais* (pronounced *DAY iss* or *DIE iss*) is a raised surface or low stage at the front of a classroom or hall. A *podium* is sometimes a small platform for one person, such as a musical conductor. A *lectern* is a stand with a slanted top to hold a speaker's notes. Especially in North America, *podium* is now commonly used to mean lectern, and although dictionaries list this meaning, some authorities—for whom the etymological connection between *podium* and *podiatry* is especially vivid—cannot accept this use. Be warned.

Rostrum and *podium* each have two plurals: *rostrums* and *rostra*, *podiums* and *podia*.

The dons took their place at High Table . . . [which] stood on a raised dais above the rest of us.
Toronto Star 23 Oct. 1994: A11

Moroccan Prime Minister Mohammed Karim Lamrani announces from the rostrum that his country has agreed to a unilateral cease-fire in its battle with insurgents in the Western Sahara.
Globe and Mail (Toronto) 26 Oct. 1985: A6

A respectful hush ripples through the audience at Montreal's Tudor Hall as Alexander Brott approaches the podium. The maestro raises his baton.
Performing Arts in Canada March 1988: 26

At one point during his speech, Juneau began pounding the podium as he lashed out at what he called an obsession with the distribution aspect of the film and broadcasting industry.
Globe and Mail (Toronto) 13 April 1985: E12

(Some would insist that he is pounding the *lectern*.)

See also PLURALS, REGULAR, IRREGULAR, FOREIGN.

Dakelh see CARRIER

Dalmatian, dog breeds Dalmatians, the people, come from Dalmatia, a region on the east coast of the Adriatic Sea. The breed of dog also comes from Dalmatia, or, at least, it is named for the region. Note the correct spelling for both meanings: the *D* is capitalized and the ending is *-ian* (as in *Canadian*) not *-ion*.

Dog breeders and kennel clubs usually capitalize every word in the name of a breed: Bernese Mountain Dog. Beyond dogdom, however, the names of dog breeds are treated like the common names of other animals, so only proper nouns within the names are capitalized: Bernese mountain dog, Jack Russell terrier, yellow Labrador retriever, Dalmatian, German shepherd, Italian greyhound, Newfoundland dog, Pekingese, basset hound, fox terrier, toy poodle, and so on.

There are some exceptions to this rule. Dictionaries list *vizsla* with no capital, even though this breed is named after a Hungarian town; *lab*, the short form for Labrador frequently appears in print without a capital: 'a black lab'. In these two cases, awareness of the geographic association in the breed name is fading and a proper noun (a place name) is slowly turning into a common noun (a name shared by a group of animals). *Great Dane* is another exception. While the rule to capitalize only the proper noun would suggest *great Dane*, dictionaries capitalize both words. Probably, the similarity of this breed name to proper nouns such as Great War, Great Depression, and Great Spirit has influenced the capitalization as has the need to distinguish 'Great Danes' (the dogs) from 'great Danes' (remarkable Danish people).

See also CAPITALIZATION.

damned with faint praise, [damned with feigned praise] see MISHEARD EXPRESSIONS

dangling modifiers Sometimes part of a sentence, usually an introductory element, does not actually modify any word or clause in the sentence. The detached element of the sentence is called a *dangling modifier*. In some contexts dangling modifiers are barely noticeable; in others they seriously disrupt the sense of the sentence. What follows are some examples of dangling modifiers that should be rewritten, and then a discussion of those contexts where language commentators consider 'dangling' modifiers allowable.

Hard-working volunteer and full-time paramedic, the rewards had been a long time coming.
(*Rewritten*: For Jane Johnson, hard-working volunteer and full-time paramedic, the rewards had been a long time coming.)

Driving through the pass, our muffler fell off.
(*Rewritten*: While we were driving through the pass, our muffler fell off.)

Once taken to pieces, you should carefully clean the rust off the parts.
(*Rewritten*: Once you have taken the mechanism to pieces, carefully clean the rust off the parts.)

At age three, his family moved to the Yukon.
(*Rewritten*: When he was three, his family moved to the Yukon.)

Some contexts permit dangling modifiers. In instructions, for example, the subject of the main clause is not stated, but is commonly understood to be *you*:

To prepare for an audit, [you should] locate all the accounting records, any supporting invoices, payroll records, deposit slips, contracts and other related documents.
Canadian Baptist Jan. 1986: 55

Technically, phrases such as 'taking this into consideration', 'to begin with', 'to sum up', and 'assuming that' all introduce dangling modifiers. But they are used in all kinds of writing and refer implicitly to either the writer or the reader.

Assuming Trixie has all the qualifications of a carefree traveller, there are still certain types of vacations on which Trixie's presence would be a burden, rather than a pleasure.
Dogs in Canada Special Issue 1986: 12

To look back to an earlier precedent, while the European invention of moveable type in the fifteenth century supported the replacement of Latin as the language of literacy, it did so through a strong standardization of Europe's vernacular languages.
W.C. Lougheed, ed. *In Search of the Standard in Canadian English* 1986: 106

To assess the influence of Montesquieu's distinction it may be useful to compare complaints about the state of liberty before and after the appearance of his book.
J.A.W. Gunn *Beyond Liberty and Property* 1983: 240

(This could be rewritten 'To assess the influence of Montesquieu's distinction one may find it useful . . .', but Canadian writers rarely use *one* as a pronoun, even in formal contexts.)

In scientific experimentation, the individual experimenter's identity is downplayed, since it should be irrelevant to the result. Hence the common use of the passive in scientific writing and the frequency of structures such as the following, where the human agent who is the subject of the modifier does not appear in the sentence:

To further define the phenomenon, the fate of the virus populations in whole plants derived from the disk cultures was studied.
Canadian Journal of Botany 67.4 (1989): 985

Legal writers also tend to avoid explicitly stating the human subject in their sentences, either because the identity of this subject remains to be proven or because it is unimportant:

To bring a substituted agreement into existence, a major alteration of the original agreement must be made with the consent of all parties.
J.E. Smyth et al. *The Law and Business Administration in Canada* 1987: 310

See also MISPLACED MODIFIERS; VOICE in the Glossary.

[daring-do] see DERRING-DO

dash A *dash* (—) marks an abrupt break in a sentence; it's often used where a colon is also possible:

> The standard joke now referred to George Brown's reversible coat—orange on one side and green on the other.
> William Teatero *John Anderson: Fugitive Slave* 1986: 21

> He was generous, and was constantly buying John clothes—once he returned from a trip with three button-down, Oxford cloth shirts.
> Daniel Gawthrop *Affirmation* 1994: 19

A pair of dashes, like a pair of commas or parentheses, may be used to set off an aside:

> Sex does not determine your rights—to vote, for example, or to hold property—as it once did.
> *Calgary Herald* 5 April 2006: A16

A comma is always dropped if it coincides with one of a pair of dashes, but an exclamation mark or question mark may be retained inside the second of a pair of dashes:

> The examiner who rebuked him was an old man, who explained courteously and patiently—but oh, the courtesy and patience of Oxford can burn like a refiner's fire!—that the word had no respectable ancestry. . . .
> Robertson Davies *One Half of Robertson Davies* 1978: 12

A dash is often used in front of the name of the person to whom a quotation is attributed:

> The real utopia is a world not to see but to see by.
> —NORTHROP FRYE

Dashes should be used judiciously in formal writing, since too many dashes can make a writer's style seem breathless or choppy.

Formerly, two hyphens with no space before or after were an acceptable alternative to a dash, since most keyboards have no dash key. However, as word processing has become more advanced, readers increasingly expect to see a proper dash, so it is worth the effort to learn how to generate one using your keyboard.

See also COLON; COMMA; PARENTHESES.

data In scientific and academic writing, and even in journalism, *data* is used both as a plural noun with a plural verb ('These data are misleading') and as an uncountable singular noun, like *information*, that takes a singular verb ('This data is misleading'). Most commentators accept both usages. The plural construction is more formal. For consistency, when *data* is treated as a plural noun, subsequent references should be to *they*, not *it*. Like the uncountable noun *information*, *data* is never preceded by a number: one speaks of 'twenty-five pieces of data' rather than 'twenty-five data'. *Datum*, the Latin noun meaning 'thing given' and the singular form of *data*, is very rare even in scientific writing. *Data* is pronounced either *DATT uh* or *DATE uh*.

> This means that when you book a flight to, say, Winnipeg, your data is zapped through a mainframe in Tulsa, Okla.
> *Toronto Star* 31 Dec. 1994: D1

> Salinity and temperature data used in the calculations of the freshwater content of James Bay were obtained during early March and August 1976.
> *Arctic* 41.1 (1988): 8

(Here the verb *were* indicates that *data* is being treated as a plural.)

> Data come from a Statistics Canada survey of about 40,000 Canadian households.
> *Gazette* (Montreal) 21 Dec. 1990: B1

(Here the plural verb *come* indicates that *data* is being treated as a plural.)

> The PN phase showed a reasonable fit to the standard curve, but too little data were derived for the PG and SN phases for one to make a conclusive judgement on these phases.
> *Canadian Journal of Earth Sciences* 26 (1989): 379

(Here *data* is treated as singular and plural simultaneously. The sentence should read either 'too *few* data were. . .' or 'too *little* data was. . .'.)

See also PLURALS, REGULAR, IRREGULAR, FOREIGN.

dates   Two styles of dates are currently used in business correspondence and published writing:

July 1, 1962, was the first day of the strike.

The strike began 1 July 1962.

In the first style, commas precede and follow the year. Many writers omit the second comma, but style guides insist on it. The second style, originally British and now becoming more popular in Canada and the United States, requires no commas. One style should be used consistently throughout one piece of writing.

The informal date style in which a slash separates the day of the month and the year (indicated with two digits) is common in Canada but unfamiliar elsewhere:

It was signed March 12/06.

When we say dates aloud, we use ordinal numbers: 'March 15th', 'December 1st', 'November 2nd'. However, in formal writing, even when the year is not given, dates are usually written as cardinal numbers: 'March 15' *or* '15 March'. An ordinal number may be used in formal writing if it is written as a word: 'The fifteenth of March passed uneventfully'.

The traditional short form for dates ('3/9/96') is ambiguous. In Britain 3/9/96 means 3 September 1996; in the United States it means 9 March 1996. In Canada it could mean either. Fortunately, this short form is being supplanted by an unambiguous computer-style date. In the computer style, four digits are devoted to the year, two to the month, and two to the day in that order (YYYY/MM/DD). Thus 9 March 1996 is rendered 1996/03/09.

Decades, in formal writing, may be referred to either in words or in figures: *the sixties, the thirties, the '50s, the 1930s, the 1860s, the 1780s.* (In an older style, now seldom used, an apostrophe separated the letter *s* from a numeral: *1930's.*) The first and second decades of a century are probably best referred to as such, though they are sometimes referred to as 'the aughts' (see NAUGHT) and 'the teens' respectively.

The redistribution of the sediment provided by the June 28, 1984, event contributed to these changes.
Canadian Journal of Earth Sciences 26 (1989): 336

Tenders must be submitted on or before 3:00 p.m., 4 July 1982.
J.E. Smyth et al. *The Law and Business Administration in Canada* 1987: 225

On January 31, 1991 a tie vote in the Senate of Canada defeated Bill C-43, An Act Respecting Abortion.
Janine Brodie, Shelley A.M. Gavigan, and Jane Jenson *The Politics of Abortion* 1992: 4

(The year should be followed by a comma.)

Burke's speech of 14 June made the same point, with some typical embellishments, when he pointed to the ominous aspect of appealing to the sense of the people.
J.A.W. Gunn *Beyond Liberty and Property* 1983: 282

On December 30th the Winnipeg Art Gallery was opening a show of her work, including her Paris and Tunis pieces. . . .
Ann Davis *Somewhere Waiting* 1991: 227

('December 30', or '30 December', is preferable in formal writing.)

Its success . . . owed something as well to new developments in criticism during the twenties and thirties.
Queen's Quarterly 95.3 (1988): 563

Indeed from the 1920s to the 1950s there was an ongoing battle between the controlling body of the Law Society—the Benchers—and the university-minded academics. . . .
Queen's Quarterly 96.3 (1989): 590

As early as the second decade of the nineteenth century, the economist Sismondi in his *Nouveaux Principes d'Economie Politique* (1819) demonstrated that the poor suffer most from economic crises. . . .
Irving M. Zeitlin and Robert J. Brym *The Social Condition of Humanity* 1991: 77

See also AD, BC; DATES, AHEAD, BACK; NAUGHT, NOUGHT, AUGHT; NEXT, THIS.

dates, ahead, back   The future is ahead of us, the past behind us. On that much English speakers agree. English speakers do not, however, agree about what it means to shift a date or time 'ahead' or 'back'. Does 'ahead' mean further into the future or closer to the present? Does 'back' mean earlier or later? Moving a date 'ahead' often means making it earlier, and moving a date 'back' often means postponing it, but the choice of adverb always depends on how the speaker is conceptualizing the situation. When we move the clock 'ahead' in the spring, for example, we set it an hour *later* (see STANDARD TIME). In reference to time, then, the words 'ahead' (as well as 'forward' and 'up') and 'back' are truly ambiguous. Writers need not avoid these adverbs, but should not expect them to carry a semantic burden. They need to be accompanied by explicit references to dates and times in order to make the meaning clear.

> Waters, who will be sworn in to the Senate this afternoon. . . . had originally intended to be sworn in closer to the end of the month but moved the day ahead so he wouldn't miss the selection process for Senate committee membership.
> *Calgary Herald* 19 June 1990: A7

(Here moving the day 'ahead' means shifting to an *earlier* date.)

> Plamondon suggested the Griffin hearing is to begin Jan. 4, but bowed to requests from counsel to move the date ahead to Jan. 14.
> *Guardian* (Charlottetown) 12 Dec. 1998: A1

(Here moving the date 'ahead' means shifting to a *later* date.)

> Greek sports authorities have postponed by two weeks the judgement on the sprinters for missing doping tests, their lawyer said yesterday. Late evidence . . . has pushed the date back from the end of February.
> *National Post* (Toronto) 1 Mar. 2005: S7

(Here pushing the date 'back' means shifting to a *later* date.)

> Some observers contend that the first dogfight occurred on Aug. 28, 1914. Others attribute it to Aug. 14th. And some push the date back to 1912, when reconnaissance and messenger pilots began shooting small arms at each other.
> *National Post* (Toronto) 27 Jan. 2005: AL8

(Here pushing the date 'back' means assigning an *earlier* date.)

See also NEXT, THIS; STANDARD TIME, DAYLIGHT SAVING(S) TIME.

daughters-in-law see IN-LAWS

davenport see CHESTERFIELD

day see APPENDIX II

daylight time, daylight saving(s) time
see STANDARD TIME

de see ALPHABETICAL ORDER

de-, dis- These prefixes are used before both verbs and nouns to mean undo, do the opposite of, or remove, as in *declassification, delouse, desegregate,* and *disassemble, disillusionment.* Words formed with the *de-* prefix in particular tend to proliferate in the jargon of technology and government: *defragment, de-energize, dehire.* When an established expression exists, such as *unplug,* or *lay off,* it should be chosen over a newer *de-* coinage. When the *de-* prefix is added to a noun or verb beginning with a vowel ('de-emphasize', 'de-ink'), it's usually followed by a hyphen.

> It takes an average of 11 man-hours to destuff a container, compared with only 2.8 hours to process it intact, shipping officials have estimated.
> *Globe and Mail* (Toronto) 25 March 1985: IB5

(Here *unpack* would be better.)

dead metaphor The dial of a clock is its *face,* and a chair stands on *legs;* a potato has *eyes,* a shoe a *tongue,* and an airplane a *nose.* These implied comparisons with parts of the human body no longer strike us as figures of speech. Some metaphors have been in use for so long that they have become *dead metaphors.*

A *dead metaphor* is different from a *live metaphor* in that it no longer evokes a literal image in the reader's or listener's mind. For instance, in the sentence 'They worked hard to *build* support for the campaign', *build* does not call to mind a group of workers equipped with hammers and saws. *Build* has become merely a synonym for *increase*; its once figurative meaning is now one of its dictionary definitions: it is dead as a metaphor. On the other hand, in the sentence 'Snow blanketed the region', the idea of a blanket may well come to mind, which means that *blanket* is still a live metaphor. We tend to use live metaphors consciously, and dead metaphors unconsciously. Occasionally a problem arises when a writer unwittingly uses a dead metaphor along with another figure of speech. The second metaphor may bring the defunct metaphor back to life, resulting in incongruity or unintentional humour: 'They went overboard and we were left high and dry'; 'I offered to give him a hand, though he didn't have a leg to stand on'. To avoid unintentionally resuscitating dead metaphors, it's a good idea to check figurative language carefully.

See also CLICHÉ; MIXED METAPHOR.

deal   The past tense of *deal* is always *dealt*, never *dealed*, except in the expression *wheeled and dealed*.

'Every two or three years he shuffled these cards [themes] and dealt himself a hand that became his next film.'
Vancouver Sun 12 Feb. 1994: D16

The accused, an Ontario man who wheeled and dealed on both sides of the world's longest undefended border, applied to the court to be released on bail.
Calgary Herald 7 June 1992: B5

death knell, [death nail]   see MISHEARD EXPRESSIONS

debacle   A *debacle* is a fiasco or a disaster. Usually the word is spelled without its French accents, but in formal writing it may retain them: *débâcle*. The usual pronunciation is a modified French one: *dih BAHK ul*. The anglicized pronunciation *DEB i kul* is criticized. Although this disputed pronunciation follows the stress pattern of other French loan words such as *miracle* and *spectacle*, these were borrowed early, in the twelfth century, while *debacle* was borrowed much later, in the nineteenth century.

The loan debacle pushed Royal Trust's parent, Royal Trustco Ltd., to the brink of bankruptcy.
Gazette (Montreal) 21 June 1993: C2

. . . Hu Yaobang was dismissed in 1987 for failing to control pro-democracy demonstrations, and Zhao Ziyang fell in 1989 after the debacle on Tiananmen Square.
Gazette (Montreal) 26 May 1993: B3

debar, disbar   To *debar* someone from doing something is to officially prohibit him or her from doing it. Circumstances may also debar, or preclude, someone from doing something, and a person may be debarred (banned) from a place.
Disbar is used only in a particular legal sense. To be disbarred is to be deprived of the right to practise law.

Speaking of staff appointments in his installation address, he said that a man 'may debar himself by his beliefs.'
Frederick Gibson *Queen's University* 2 (1983): 343

A lawyer in those years might borrow twenty-five dollars from his clients' accounts to pay the rent and take food home. He'd be caught and disbarred.
Jack Batten *Robinette* 1984: 34

debark   see EMBARK

debatable   see -ABLE, -(AT)ABLE

debate   see DISCUSS

debus   see EMBARK

début   see PREMIÈRE

DEC   see QUEBEC ENGLISH

decades   see CAPITAL LETTERS; DATES; NAUGHT, NOUGHT, AUGHT.

deceitful, deceptive   People are *deceitful* when they intentionally hide the truth to gain advantage. People are *deceptive* when—intentionally or unintentionally—they create a misleading impression. Appearances and things can also be deceptive: 'The way it looks from the outside is deceptive; inside it's huge'.

'By making deceitful statements to them and by failing to inform them of material facts, J___ D___ and G___ perpetrated a fraud against investors,' the commission alleges.
Vancouver Sun 6 May 2006: A3

Justice Douglas Cunningham called [the defendant] clever, deceitful and fraudulent for duping investors out of $400,000 in two aborted condo developments. . . .
Gazette (Montreal) 1 Oct. 1993: B12

The process that the Liberals are using to reform the social safety net is also very deceptive. While a great deal of effort has been put into making the process seem open, fair and consultative, the real agenda for the reform has been set privately, behind closed doors.
Ottawa Citizen 18 Oct. 1994: A9

She had the manner of a conventional lady bountiful, but that manner was deceptive.
Miriam Waddington *Apartment Seven* 1989: 19

decided, decisive   A *decided* victory is clear, not likely to be mistaken for defeat, while a *decisive* victory is conclusive, turning the balance in the series or finally settling the score. A *decided* person is resolute or firm, while a *decisive* person is capable of making decisions quickly. To some extent, the senses of these words overlap.

We have to face the fact that many students go into engineering with a decided bias against literature, history and philosophy.
Engineering Dimensions May–Jun. 1988: 24

Mr. Attorney General Macdonald has expressed a decided opinion against the fugitive.
William Teatero *John Anderson: Fugitive Slave* 1986: 61

The error led to a 2-on-1 break for the Blues and the decisive goal in a 3-2 Chicago loss.
Gazette (Montreal) 28 Dec. 1993: D3

Chretien won last month's election because he is honest, hard-working, decisive and capable of bringing out the best in people.
Toronto Star 13 Nov. 1993: B1

decimal points   see NUMBERS, DECIMAL POINTS AND COMMAS WITH

decimate   Decimation was a Roman punishment for mutinous military units: one-tenth of an offending unit's members were chosen by lot and executed. Originally, then, to *decimate* meant to kill one in every ten. In current English it means to all but destroy, and it doesn't always suggest intentional destruction: disease or famine can decimate a population.

Decimate has been used to mean massacre or drastically reduce since as early as 1663 (*OED*). This use has been criticized because it doesn't match the original Latin meaning of the word, but as *Webster's Dictionary of English Usage* remarks, 'Most recent usage books recognize that the Latin etymology does not rule the English word.' Anyone who does use *decimate* to mean reduce by one-tenth certainly risks being misunderstood.

The words describe the American General Sherman's plan to decimate the buffalo stocks in order to cripple the native population.
Mark A. Cheetham with Linda Hutcheon *Remembering Postmodernism* 1991: 81

(Here *decimate* means to greatly reduce.)

See also MASSACRE.

decision   The most common idiom is *make a decision*, although we also *come to a decision* or *reach a decision*. Several Canadian style guides warn against *take a decision*, claiming that the expression is a recent import from French (*prendre une décision*). This notion appears to be unfounded, since *take a decision* is used more in Britain, where French exerts little influence, than in Canada. British and American guides do not mention *take a decision* as a problem, and the idiom is listed without comment in several British dictionaries. In Canada it appears most often in newspaper writing and reported speech.

External Affairs Minister Joe Clark . . . urged U.S. Secretary of State James Baker 'to weigh fully the impact the Mack amendment will have on U.S.-owned enterprises in Canada as well as our bilateral relationship before a decision is taken to sign this bill into law.'
Vancouver Sun 3 Nov. 1990: B12

decisive   see DECIDED

deck   see PORCH

declaim   see DECRY

declassification   see DE-, DIS-

decriminalize   see LEGALIZE

decry, descry, declaim, disclaim   To *decry* is to speak out strongly against. To *descry* (pronounced *dis CRY*) is to barely discern or catch sight of. To *declaim* is to speak or recite in a theatrical manner. To *disclaim* is to renounce a legal claim to something, or to disown, disavow, or deny something.

> They are quick to decry the garbage going into our atmosphere and the pollution of large corporations, yet they throw away their newspapers, popcorn and soft-drink containers and, worst of all, cigarette butts are jettisoned from car windows when the ashtray is right at hand.
> *Province* (Vancouver) 1 June 1990: 48

> That the leopard's spots were not changed overnight is indicated . . . by a casual remark in the *Journal* as many as eleven years later that at last 'the law of equal rights' is 'dimly descried'.
> Hilda Neatby *Queen's University* 1 (1978): 196

> But reviewing a dead poet pressures the reviewer into declaiming like Brutus over Caesar's corpse.
> Margaret Atwood *Second Words* 1982: 307

> If [Quebec] intends to preserve its credit rating, it surely is not about to disclaim its fair share of Canada's debt.
> *Toronto Star* 20 Nov. 1990: A20

deduction, induction   In ordinary speech and writing a *deduction* is a conclusion or conjecture inferred from known facts. In logic *deduction* and *induction* refer to opposite types of reasoning. The process of *deduction* starts with a general principle that is used to predict particular cases. The process of *induction* involves examining specific cases in order to reach a general rule or principle that accounts for all of them.

He saw nothing and made the incorrect deduction that there was nothing to see.
Ottawa Citizen 24 March 1993: A11

(Here *deduction* means inference.)

> Deductive reasoning depends upon the acceptance of the initial generalizations as the assumed truth.
> Margot Northey and David B. Knight *Making Sense in Geography and Environmental Studies* 1992: 16

> The quality of knowledge arrived at through inductive reasoning depends upon the representativeness of the specific cases used as the bases for generalization.
> Margot Northey and David B. Knight *Making Sense in Geography and Environmental Studies* 1992: 16

See also A POSTERIORI; A PRIORI.

de-emphasize, de-energize   see DE-, DIS-

deep   see ADVERBS WITHOUT -LY; SLOW

deepness   see -NESS

deep-seated, [deep-seeded]   see MISHEARD EXPRESSIONS

deer   see BEER; MOOSE

defective, deficient, deficit, debt   *Defective* means faulty or flawed. *Deficient* means insufficient or lacking in some particular way.
   A *deficit* is a lack or insufficiency ('cognitive deficit'; 'sleep deficit'), often an amount of money lacking ('We checked the figures, and there is a deficit of four hundred dollars'). In terms of parliamentary budgets, the *deficit* is the shortfall accrued over one fiscal year, while the *debt* is the total of deficits accumulated over time.

> The only sound was a faint rasping buzz from a defective fluorescent tube overhead.
> Constance Beresford-Howe *Night Studies* 1985: 132

> Compost and wood ashes will certainly work, but if the soil is severely depleted or deficient in nutri-

ents, I believe the gardener should follow the rec-ommendations given with the soil analysis.
Harrowsmith Jun.–Jul. 1985: 112

A finance minister who had the determination to abolish the deficit and actually start paying down our accumulated debt.
Whig-Standard (Kingston) 29 April 2006: 8

defence   see -CE, -SE

defendable, defensible   The customary advice is to use *defendable* to describe something which can be physically defended and *defensible* to describe something which can be intellectu-ally defended. A castle wall, for example, is *defendable* against armed attack; an idea or argu-ment, on the other hand, is *defensible* if it can be justified or considered tenable.

In fact, Canadians use both words in either context. While each has a long history, *defend-able* is now the rarer of the two, found less often in formal prose than in speech and informal writing. If you are unsure, choose *defensible*—the more common and easily defensible choice.

Note the difference in spelling of the ending: *defendable* ends with *-able*, *defensible* with *-ible*. Their opposites are *undefendable* and *indefensible* respectively.

Add 80 km/h gusts and Terry realized Chisholm [Alberta] was not defendable, not even with 3,000 men and not just the few dozen on the scene.
Edmonton Journal 2 June 2001: A1

(Here *defendable* means *protectable*; the sentence refers to the physical threat of a forest fire.)

The contracts might have been defendable if the right process had been followed.
Calgary Herald 4 Oct. 2004: A5

(Here, where the battle is not physical, some commentators would recommend *defensible*.)

First of all, the site would be easily defensible in case of aggression from the United States. . . .
Queen's Quarterly 110.2 (2003): 199

(Here, where the defence is physical, some com-mentators recommend *defendable*, but *defensible* is also common and acceptable.)

See also -CE, SE.

defense, defensible, defensive   see -CE, SE; DEFENDABLE

defer, defray   To *defer* an expense is to delay it; to *defray* an expense is to offset it or provide for its payment.

Blencoe said senior citizens, widowed spouses and homeowners with physical disabilities can defer their taxes until they die or sell their homes.
Vancouver Sun 3 April 1992: C11

The funds are being used to help defray costs on the operation of the 15-year-old building.
Guardian (Charlottetown) 16 May 2006: A3

Admission is free, or pay-what-you-can to help defer costs involved.
Toronto Star 7 Dec. 1992: B6

(The word required here is *defray*.)

See also DOUBLING THE FINAL CONSONANT.

deference, deferral, deferment   When to *defer* means to yield respectfully to another's authority or wishes, its noun form is *deference*. When *defer* means postpone, it has two accept-able noun forms: *deferral* and *deferment*. In many financial and institutional contexts, these terms are interchangeable. Literary theorists favour the term *deferral*; draft boards prefer *deferment*.

Although habituation may undermine the defer-ence that bears have towards humans, bear-human incidents resulting in human injury have never been reported at Kulik.
Arctic 57.2 (2004): 160

If your combined household income from all sources is $35,000 or less, you may qualify for deferral of your property tax increase for 2004.
'2004 Property Tax Deferral Program' City of Toronto website 2004

(*Deferral* or *deferment* is appropriate here.)

Stylistically, they cover most of the ground of post-modern country—self-referentiality, deferral, the erotics of narration, even a hoax or two.
Ottawa Citizen 14 Dec. 1985: C2

In expectation of a formal reinstatement of the draft, websites have sprung up advising potential

recruits how to beat the system by obtaining deferments.
Maclean's 30 Aug. 2004: 43-44

See also DEFER, DEFRAY.

deficient see DEFECTIVE

definite, definitive *Definite* means unambiguous, clearly defined, or certain. *Definitive* conveys a sense of finality and means authoritative or decisive. A *definite* plan—one with all its details worked out—might not be the *definitive* plan: that is, the final choice. In some contexts either word is appropriate.

> The answer is a definite 'no', for although no action may be brought on the contract itself, it may affect the legal relations between the parties in several ways.
> J.E. Smyth et al. *The Law and Business Administration in Canada* 1987: 251–2

(Here *definite* means unambiguous.)

> He indicated in an interview Friday that his plans are definite and he will formally announce his plans this upcoming week.
> *Leader-Post* (Regina) 27 Feb. 1988: A4

(Here *definite* means certain.)

> Earlier this month, the bank signed a definitive agreement with Gentra Inc. . . . to buy its international and Canadian operations.
> *Calgary Herald* 30 June 1993: D3

(Here *definitive* means final.)

> Setting definitive standards for hearing damage is difficult, says Whitehead, because sound tolerance varies between individuals.
> *Daily News* (Halifax) 27 June 1993: 34

(Here *definitive* means authoritative, but *definite*, meaning precisely defined, would also be appropriate.)

> I, for one, would appreciate a definitive public statement from the Anglican Church of Canada on Canadian military policy. . . .
> *Canadian Churchman* April 1986: 5

(Here *definitive* means authoritative, but *definite*, meaning unambiguous, would also be appropriate.)

definite article see THE, A, AN.

defray see DEFER

defuse see DIFFUSE

dehire see DE-, DIS-

de-ink see DE-, DIS-

déjà vu *Déjà vu* was borrowed from French at the end of the nineteenth century as a psychological term denoting the illusion of having previously experienced something that is actually being encountered for the first time. In psychology *déjà vu* always refers to an illusory impression. In general usage the expression is sometimes used humorously to imply that a supposedly new experience is in fact tediously predictable. Occasionally *déjà vu* is mistakenly used to mean premonition or expectation.

Déjà vu should retain its two accents, especially in formal writing, but it no longer needs to be italicized as a foreign phrase.

> Checking in with the wilderness volunteer was like deja vu—Jennifer's twin sister, Jeanine, worked this entrance.
> *Toronto Star* 3 Dec. 1994: F20

(Here *deja vu* refers to an illusion. Note that *déjà vu* requires accents in formal writing.)

> A Commons committee has suggested a 'temporary tax' to help pay down the deficit. . . . Déjà vu—income tax was introduced as a 'temporary measure' in 1917.
> *Vancouver Sun* 14 Dec. 1994: A14

(Here *déjà vu* is used humorously.)

> Hilda Gregory, who heads the diocese of New Westminster's 127 Society, has feelings of deja vu about the evictions. 'This is what we knew would happen,' she says.
> *Canadian Churchman* April 1986: 7

(Here something has been foreseen: thus '*expected* the evictions' would be better.)

deke see FEIGN

delay see QUEBEC ENGLISH

delimit   see LIMIT

deliverance, delivery   Both nouns are related to the verb *deliver,* but *deliverance,* which means release or rescue, is only used of things that we can be delivered *from,* such as evil or oppression. *Delivery* refers to getting something to its destination, or to childbirth, or to the style of making a speech.

> It was a hard heart that wasn't lifted with the weekend drama of Nelson Mandela's deliverance.
> *Vancouver Sun* 12 Feb. 1990: A8

> The wealthier *Canadien* merchants consequently returned to France; their less prosperous colleagues stayed, but were allowed neither to take delivery of goods from France nor to establish ties with British trading firms.
> Irving M. Zeitlin and Robert J. Brym *The Social Condition of Humanity* 1991: 166

> The audience was impressed with the delivery but not many were buying the contents of Quebec Premier Jacques Parizeau's speech yesterday.
> *Toronto Star* 23 Nov. 1994: A32

delouse   see DE-, DIS-

delusion, illusion   Both words refer to confused notions or misapprehensions. Strictly speaking, *delusions* are caused by the mind, while illusions originate outside it: 'It's difficult to overcome delusions of inadequacy'; 'The scene gives the illusion of something overhead, and movie-goers ducked lower in their seats as it passed'. *Illusion* is a neutral term, often referring to a misperception that passes quickly: 'an optical illusion'. *Delusion* is a term psychiatrists use to refer to a persistent false belief that contributes to mental or emotional instability. The expression *delusions of grandeur* (always plural) refers to an overblown sense of one's own abilities and importance. In popular usage, *delusion* has pejorative connotations: 'Your delusions, sir, are harmful to the future of this country'.

False beliefs that are widely held in society are described either as *illusions* or *delusions*—*illusions* is a better choice if the negative connotations of *delusion* are unwanted.

> While there have been several definitions of psychosis, symptoms such as delusions and (or) prominent hallucinations are considered to be the defining features for this diagnosis.
> *Canadian Journal of Psychiatry* 49.11 (2004): 713

(Here *delusion* is used in a psychiatric context.)

> Stage illusions, audience participation, original music and humour highlight the show.
> *Star-Phoenix* (Saskatoon) 12 April 2002

(Here an *illusion* is a trick.)

> In any event, once the facade of homogeneity begins to crack it quickly becomes apparent that it was a delusion all along and that diversity is the norm.
> *Education Canada* 44.2 (2004): 4

(Here a pernicious false belief is described as a *delusion.*)

> In Arcand's world, giving up your illusions often seems the only kind of moral heroism possible.
> *Toronto Star* 25 Feb. 2001

(Here a self-protective false belief is described as an *illusion.*)

See also ELUSIVE, ILLUSIVE.

demagogue   see IDEOLOGY

demean   *Demean* is two distinct verbs. The older one—related to the noun *demeanour*—means to behave: 'Always strive to demean yourself in a manner befitting your calling'. This meaning is nearly obsolete. Today writers are more likely to choose a verb such as *behave,* or *conduct,* or *comport.*

The newer verb—related to the adjective *mean,* meaning inferior—dates from the seventeenth century: to *demean oneself* is to lower oneself; to *demean someone* is to disparage him or her; to *demean something* is to debase it. This 'new' verb was criticized as a confusion throughout the eighteenth and nineteenth centuries and labelled uneducated by Fowler. Nevertheless, today it predominates, and it is considered standard by commentators.

> Although Parker . . . was notorious for singling out his young idolators and treating them with cruel

condescension—making them carry his saxophone case, hold doors for him, run trifling errands, and otherwise demean themselves—nothing we know about Davis suggests that he would play that role.
Jack Chambers *Milestones* 1983: 25

Young girls need to attain an outlook on life that empowers women, not one that demeans them.
Whig-Standard (Kingston) 17 Dec. 2005: 9

demi-, demigod, demitasse   see SEMI-

demonstrable, [demonstratable]   see -ABLE, -(AT)ABLE

demonym   see NAMES OF RESIDENTS OF CITIES AND PROVINCES

demoralize   see -IZE, -ISE, -YZE, -YSE

demur, demure   To *demur* is to hesitate or object because one has doubts. *Demure* is an adjective meaning modest or dainty. *Demur* rhymes with *fur*, *demure* with *pure*.

As the name of Sir John A. Macdonald had been suggested for the chancellorship, Cook had demurred a little at accepting the honour.
Hilda Neatby *Queen's University* 1 (1978): 125

At first, she demurred, but then she too said, 'Why not?'
Henry M. Rosenthal and S. Cathy Berson, eds. *Canadian Jewish Outlook Anthology* 1988: 287

Although Krystal says she is always covered in her portraits, others are not so demure.
Toronto Star 15 April 2006: L06

'It's just another form of motivation,' said Pape, demur on dry land.
Gazette (Montreal) 28 March 1992: C1

(Pape is the forceful female coxswain of a men's rowing team; it is the adjective *demure* that is required here.)

But he demures. He talks about priorities and family.
Vancouver Sun 7 Aug. 1992: D1

(The verb is *demurs*.)

Dene, Na-Dene   *Dene* (pronounced *DEN ay*)

an Athapaskan word meaning 'the people', refers to those Aboriginal peoples of the Barren Grounds and the Mackenzie Valley of the Northwest Territories who have been politically represented since 1978 by the Dene Nation (formerly known as the Indian Brotherhood of the Northwest Territories). Strictly speaking, it is redundant to refer to the 'Dene people', since *Dene* already means people. *Dene* is used for both singular and plural.

The Dene call their traditional territories Denendeh (*DEN en DAY*), meaning 'home of the people' (see NUNAVUT).

Most members of the Dene Nation come from groups whose traditional languages are Athapaskan; some, however, come from groups whose traditional language is Cree.

Mr. Erasmus later said he was optimistic the Queen would meet with him, adding he was prepared to travel to Britain to press his case for Denendeh, as the Dene call the land they claim.
Spectator (Hamilton) 22 Aug. 1994: A2

House, 20, plays the rebellious teenager Teevee Tenya on the popular show *North of Sixty*, which depicts a fictional Dene settlement called Lynx River.
Daily News (Halifax) 27 July 1994: 29

Stung, the federal government said it would now negotiate land claim settlements separately with any groups who wished to do so, thereby fracturing the Dene Nation as a political entity that spoke for all the Indians of the Mackenzie Valley.
Toronto Star 31 July 1994: E1

While the Inuit make up about 80 per cent of the Eastern Arctic's population, the West is a mix of several Dene nations, Metis, the Inuvialuit of the Beaufort Sea area and non-native people.
Ottawa Citizen 5 May 1992: A3

See also ABORIGINAL PEOPLE(S); CHIPEWYAN; NUNAVUT, NUNAVUMMIUT, DENENDEH; SLAVEY; APPENDIX III.

Denendeh   see NUNAVUT

Dene-Tha(h)   see SLAVEY

denizen   A *denizen* is an inhabitant. Although

the word is applied figuratively to people who inhabit or frequent a certain place, it should not be used simply to refer to a fan or devotee.

> Earle's words, and those of the other authors, are accompanied by stunning photos of the weird, beautiful denizens of the deep [i.e., fish].
> *Toronto Star* 31 Oct. 1992: H18

> Having been a denizen of Parliament Hill for nearly 40 years, I have few illusions about the place.
> *Ottawa Citizen* 25 Nov. 1994: A12

> 'What's going on in the sports world worth writing about?' asked a disgruntled denizen of the games people play.
> *Daily News* (Halifax) 15 March 1992: 67

(Here *fan* would be appropriate.)

denotation, denote   see CONNOTATION

denounce   see PRONUNCIATION

dépanneur   see QUEBEC ENGLISH

dependent, dependant, independent *Dependent* is an adjective: 'The children are dependent on her for food'; 'dependent family members'. *Dependant* is a noun: 'Her child is her dependant'. Canadian and British writers generally follow this distinction; American writers use *dependent* for both the adjective and the noun.

Some Canadian newspapers follow the American style; style guides for the Montreal *Gazette* and the Toronto *Globe and Mail*, for example, recommend the *-ent* form in all senses. The *Canadian Press Stylebook*, however, recommends the *-ent/-ant* distinction.

Independent is spelled the same whether it is used as an adjective ('an independent act') or as a noun meaning a politician not affiliated with any particular party ('She sits in Parliament as an independent').

> Because the dog sled is their only means of winter transport, they are still in part dependent on subsistence hunting.
> *Arctic* 41.1 (1988): 53

> . . . you can only claim medical expenses for the

child if your child is also claimed as a dependant.
> *Financial Post* 25 Nov. 1991: 14

> Among these preconditions are . . . effective state institutions, a high literacy rate and an economy not dependant on natural resources.
> *Toronto Star* 23 June 2005: A26

(The adjective is spelled *dependent*.)

See also DESCENDANT, DESCENDENT; SEPARATIST.

deplane   see EMBARK

depreciate, deprecate, self-deprecating, self-depreciating   To *depreciate* means to drop in value. If you depreciate a business asset for income tax purposes, you deduct a portion of its original cost from your income over a period of several years. *Depreciate* also means to undervalue or speak disparagingly of. To *deprecate* means to censure or deplore. *Self-deprecating* and *self-depreciating* both mean self-belittling. Some commentators think that *self-depreciating* is the more apt term for this activity, but *self-deprecating* has far more currency in Canadian English. Either word is acceptable.

> Unlike new furniture that depreciates in value from the moment it's unpacked in your living room, antiques increase in value through the years.
> *Vancouver Sun* 13 Nov. 1993: E7

> Certainly a large number of them are members of the educated middle class, conditioned through many years of schooling to depreciate things Canadian.
> Margaret Atwood *Second Words* 1982: 189

> Islam glorified the holy war against unbelievers, but strongly deprecated war between fellow Muslims.
> *Toronto Star* 4 Dec. 1993: H15

> Comedian David Broadfoot . . . warmed up the audience with his own brand of self-deprecating Canadian humor. How many Canadians does it take to change a lightbulb? None. We accept them the way they are.
> *Ottawa Citizen* 30 Nov. 1990: D3

deputy speaker   see SPEAKER

derby, clerk, Berkeley Most Canadians and Americans pronounce the *er* in *derby* and *clerk* like the *ur* in *lurk*. Most British speakers, on the other hand, rhyme *derby* with *Barbie* and *clerk* with *lark*.

The first syllable of *Berkeley*, the American city, rhymes with *lurk*; the first syllable of *Berkeley*, the eighteenth-century British philosopher, rhymes with *lark*.

Other words containing *er*, such as *jerk* and *perk*, rhyme with *lurk* on both sides of the Atlantic.

de rigueur *De rigueur* (pronounced *duh ree GUR*) is borrowed from French and means 'proper' or 'currently considered indispensable'. *De rigueur* is often misspelled without the first *u*, perhaps because several familiar borrowings from French (*auteur, hauteur, provocateur*) end in a consonant followed by *-eur*.

> Alarming revelations are de rigueur in biographies now, it seems.
> *Vancouver Sun* 22 Oct. 1994: D17

> So tans became de rigeur for the leisured classes, a signal that their owners could pursue lives of sailing, golf and lying about on the beach at Corfu.
> *Vancouver Sun* 25 July 1994: A9

(The correct spelling is *de rigueur*.)

derisive, derisory A hundred years ago *derisive* and *derisory* were used interchangeably to mean either expressing derision (mocking) or deserving ridicule (trifling). Today both words are used in the first sense ('derisive *or* derisory laughter'), but only *derisory* is used in the second ('a derisory sum of money').

> When she's at a distance from Auntie Muriel she can think of derisive and vulgar things to say to her, but in her presence she knows she would be mute.
> Margaret Atwood *Life Before Man* 1979: 163

> It's no wonder that the survey was greeted by derisory hoots.
> *Toronto Star* 31 Dec. 1988: M3

> 'Given the very long absence of five years, this argument is diluted to the point of seeming

derisory,' Judge Duranleau ruled.
> *Globe and Mail* (Toronto) 12 June 1985: P3

derring-do, [daring-do] *Derring-do,* which means daring action or a bold willingness to act, is a pseudo-archaism. The phrase has an antique air although it is by no means obsolete or rare. It is an alteration of the Middle English *dorring don*, which means 'daring to do'. Those who have heard this jocular expression but not read it are likely to update the spelling. *Daring-do*, however, is not listed in dictionaries.

> Pity the Canadian writer of spy fiction . . . . whose spy agency, CSIS, has a reputation more for paper-shuffling than derring-do.
> *Gazette* (Montreal) 24 May 2003: I6

See also ARCHAISMS.

descendant, ancestor, descendent Our descendants will live in the future, after us; our ancestors lived in the past. *Descendants* and *ancestors* usually refer to relatives whose lifetimes do not overlap with ours, rather than our children and grandchildren or parents and grandparents. Most Canadian and British usage guides echo an eighteenth-century pronouncement by Samuel Johnson that *descendant* is a noun and *descendent* an adjective. Thus a *descendant* is a person born of a particular family or a thing derived from an earlier model, while *descendent* means moving downward, as in 'a diagonal descendent from left to right'. In reality this distinction may never have been as firmly established as Johnson hoped it would become. The adjective is so rare a word that its correct spelling is debatable. The predominant spelling of the noun in contemporary Canadian English is *descendant*, but *descendent* is common enough that it should be considered an acceptable variant—which is how it is listed in American dictionaries and also in the *New Shorter Oxford English Dictionary*.

> It shows the State Department was mindful that separatist sentiment in Quebec and New Brunswick might spread to descendants of Acadians living in the U.S. northeast.
> *Toronto Star* 30 Dec. 1992: D19

Recording contracts are the direct descendants of film contracts from the 1930s and '40s, which tied an actor or director to a studio indefinitely.
Toronto Star 30 Nov. 1992: B4

In it, the settlers or their descendents would 'come to terms with' their 'own real past' and so live with fewer delusions in less destructive ways.
NeWest Review Feb.–Mar. 1990: 34

Amenartas fled from Africa and gave birth to a son, through whom her story has passed along a line of descendents to Leo Vincey, an Englishman who decides to explore the mystery. . . .
Margaret Atwood *Second Words* 1982: 39

See also DEPENDENT, DEPENDANT.

descry see DECRY

desegregate see DE-, DIS-

desert see DESSERT

desk-bound see -BOUND

despatch see DISPATCH

despite, in spite of, notwithstanding
These three prepositions all mean the same thing. *Despite* is by far the most common. *Notwithstanding* is used mainly in formal academic writing and is sometimes positioned after its object: 'notwithstanding this rebuke' *or* 'this rebuke notwithstanding'.

All three prepositions may be combined with the phrase 'the fact that' to introduce a clause. In most contexts, however, this construction is wordy, and *although* or *even though* is preferable.

Despite the fact that the plaintiff was a widow 78 years of age who had just broken her glasses, the court found her careless in signing a deed she had been unable to read, and thus bound by subsequent dealings in the property transferred in the document.
J.E. Smyth et al. *The Law and Business Administration in Canada* 1987: 221

In spite of the fact that most Canadians assess American English to be inferior, most ESL texts in Canada are American.

W.C. Lougheed, ed. *In Search of the Standard in Canadian English* 1986: 141

Notwithstanding these criticisms, the work should be of interest to the specialist in British military or European diplomatic history as a source for the study of the occupation.
Canadian Journal of History 14.1 (1989): 144

Hall had been trying 'about 20 years' to have a baby and, colic notwithstanding, she's thrilled with motherhood.
Toronto Star 20 Dec. 1993: B11

See also CANADIAN BILL OF RIGHTS, CANADIAN CHARTER OF RIGHTS AND FREEDOMS.

dessert, desert, just deserts The name for a sweet last course of a meal is spelled with a double *s*: *dessert* (*di ZERT*). The name for a sometimes sandy region with very low rainfall is spelled with one *s*: *desert* (*DEZ ert*). *Desert* is also used as an adjective to describe a barren, desolate, or uninhabited area that may not necessarily be a desert in the technical sense: for example, a 'desert island'. Figuratively, a desert is an uninteresting period, subject, or area, as in 'a cultural desert'. The verb *desert* (*di ZERT*) means to abandon or leave. (The related noun for this word is *desertion*.)

The plural noun *deserts* (*di ZERTS*) means what is deserved and survives mainly in the expression *just deserts*: 'Voters know he abused their trust and he'll get his just deserts at the polls'. Because the pronunciation of this word is the same as that of *desserts*, the expression 'just desserts' occasionally appears as a pun on menus, as the name of a restaurant, or in other references to food.

The First Week is gloomy: it envisages sin and its just deserts, death and damnation.
Canadian Journal of Philosophy 19 (1989): 197

. . . if he believes so strongly in the so-called exceptional athlete getting his just desserts, why doesn't he suggest they be paid on a strict 'merit' basis instead of their absurdly high long-term contracts?
Financial Post 23 Feb. 1990: 8

(Here the correct spelling is *deserts*.)

It was a bake sale designed to give the Tories their just desserts.
Vancouver Sun 9 March 1990: 3

(Here *just desserts* is an intentional play on words.)

destabilize   see EUPHEMISM

destroy   To *destroy* a thing is to render it useless or to end its existence; to *destroy* a person is to ruin him or her financially, professionally, or in some other way. Some usage experts criticize 'completely destroyed' as redundant and 'partly destroyed' as a contradiction in terms, but most find no fault with these expressions. Parts of a whole can be destroyed: if a building survives a fire with some rooms ruined and others intact, it could be described as 'partly destroyed', whereas a building razed by fire could be called 'completely destroyed'.

If the goods are only partly destroyed, the contract is not discharged completely; instead the carrier is absolved from liability to the extent that the damage was caused to the goods by an act of God and must deliver them as they are.
J.E. Smyth et al. *The Law and Business Administration in Canada* 1987: 314

Some paintings, including Death of Adonis by Sebastiano del Piombo, a follower of Michelangelo, were completely destroyed. Several statues had their arms and legs chopped off by flying glass.
Calgary Herald 28 May 1993: D9

See also COMPLETE.

determinant   see QUEBEC ENGLISH

detract   see DISTRACT

detrain   see EMBARK

deus ex machina   *Deus ex machina* (usually pronounced *DAY us ex MAK in uh*) is a Latin phrase used in literary criticism. It describes a character or event introduced suddenly and implausibly to resolve a difficulty in the plot. The literal translation of *deus ex machina* is 'god

from a machine'. This phrase is a reference to ancient Greek drama, in which the gods (played by actors suspended from pulleys above the stage) would descend at the end of the play to resolve conflict.

Deus ex machina should be italicized in formal writing.

Shields herself used the term 'deus ex machina' to describe an unlikely scene inserted towards the book's end.
Gazette (Montreal) 28 March 1992: K1

Obstacles arise haphazardly and are often resolved by a convenient deus ex machina. The plot has neither real suspense nor any continuity.
Ottawa Citizen 25 March 1990: E3

See also LATIN PHRASES.

Deutschmark   see GERMAN WORDS, PRONUNCIATION OF

develop, developed, development   *Developed* is often misspelled with a double *p*, and *development* is often misspelled with an *e* after the *p*. In Canada these misspellings may be influenced by the French words *développer* and *développement*.

devil's advocate   Originally, the devil's advocate was a Roman Catholic official appointed to present a case against the proposed canonization of a saint, thus ensuring that the case for canonization would be properly tested. By extension, a devil's advocate is anyone who introduces an unpopular or contradictory view to test—and possibly strengthen—the original view. A devil's advocate does not necessarily believe in the view she or he is defending, although those who play the devil's advocate risk having their arguments mistaken for their true beliefs. A devil's advocate is not simply someone who holds an unpopular view.

Mowat's friends presumably were convinced that there could be no better appointment, but there is no evidence that any one on the board felt the serious obligation at least to play the part of the devil's advocate for any one of the other candidates.
Hilda Neatby *Queen's University* 1 (1978): 68

(Here the role of the *devil's advocate* would be to promote one of the other candidates, making the board look less partial and presumably strengthening the case for Mowat's appointment.)

. . . [Ball] warned Kennedy privately that it would be a tragic blunder to commit U.S. troops to Vietnam. 'Within five years, we'll have 300,000 men in the paddies and jungles and never find them,' Ball recalled saying. . . . During Lyndon Johnson's presidency, Ball was often called the 'Devil's advocate' on Vietnam. . . .
Gazette (Montreal) 28 May 1994: G16

(Ball was not, strictly speaking, a *devil's advocate* because he sincerely believed that U.S. involvement in the war was a mistake.)

dharma   see KARMA

di   see ALPHABETICAL ORDER

diacritical marks, diacritics, diaeresis, accent marks   *Diacritical marks*, *diacritics*, or *accent marks* are added to letters to indicate variations in pronunciation. English uses very few of these, and writers often drop them in borrowed words that have the marks in their original language. For example, while in French *élite* is written with an accent, in English Canadians usually drop it: *elite*. Often the difficulty is technical: many diacritical marks do not survive the journey from the keyboard to the printed page.

A *diaeresis* or *dieresis* (the former spelling is favoured in Britain, the latter in the U.S.) consists of two points set over a vowel; in German this mark is called an *umlaut*. In English it indicates that the vowel so marked is to be pronounced separately rather than run in with another vowel or left silent. Among the few words that are still found with a diaeresis are the proper names *Brontë*, *Noël*, and *Zoë*, and *naïve* and its derivatives. Even these, however, appear without the mark in many publications.

An *accent mark* is sometimes similarly used to indicate that a syllable that is normally not stressed should be pronounced separately (generally in poetry or songs). For example, in the phrase 'my piercèd side, O Thomas see', *pierced* is pronounced with two syllables (*PEER sed*)

rather than the usual one (*PEERST*). This accent may be written in two ways ('piercèd' or 'piercéd').

See also -ED; NAIVE.

diagonal   see SLASH

dialect   see ACCENT

dialect, eye   see [COULD OF]

dialectic(s), dialectical, dialectal   A very general meaning of *dialectic(s)* is discussion and logical analysis. But the term can also refer specifically to one of several philosophical approaches and schools of thought to which it has been applied throughout history, including Socratic dialectics, Hegelian dialectics, and the dialectical materialism of Marx and Engels—the official Communist Party philosophy. What all these philosophies have in common is the resolution of opposites. Thus a *dialectic* is often simply something that encompasses two opposing elements or forces. *Dialectics*, with an *s*, usually refers to the process of examining and discussing contradictory forces with the aim of finding a resolution.

The adjective form of *dialectic* is *dialectical* or, less often, *dialectic*. *Dialectal* is the adjective associated with *dialect*, meaning a regional or class variety of speech.

There are manifold contradictions here, but without dialectic, just the pervasive co-existence of opposites indifferently clashing without combustion or progression.
Queen's Quarterly 96.1 (1989): 107

(Here *dialectic* means resolution of opposites.)

Generating great excitement is charismatic Toby Stephens, 25, as Coriolanus in Shakespeare's fierce dialectic about dictatorship and the power of the masses.
Toronto Star 19 Nov. 1994: J9

(Here *dialectic* refers to an analysis.)

In fact, this is the great dialectical moment of today's history: economics versus ecology. Suzuki

is able to show that the synthesis of an ecologically oriented economy is the wave of the present.
Calgary Herald 16 April 1994: B10

This settlement pattern, with the populace mainly located along the coast-line, raises basic problems not simply logistical for the conduct of dialectal research in Newfoundland. . . .
G.M. Story, W.J. Kirwin, and J.D.A. Widdowson, eds. *Dictionary of Newfoundland English* 2nd ed. 1990: xviii

What can this chap know about the dialectical distinctions between west Texas and east Texas?
Ottawa Citizen 23 June 1994: H12

(The chap referred to is a speech coach; the word required is *dialectal*.)

See also ACCENT, DIALECT, VARIETY.

dialogue, dialog In the early 1960s, *dialogue* came to mean an exchange of ideas and opinions, as in the 'East–West dialogue' that dominated the global politics of that era. Usage commentators called this meaning of *dialogue* faddish, but it has since become established, and *dialogue* is now widely used in Canadian writing to refer to any discussion or exchange of information between parties.

The verb *to dialogue* is not new. The *OED* records it in the works of Shakespeare and also in literary works of the eighteenth and nineteenth centuries. Perhaps the current censure of the verb can be attributed to its overuse by bureaucrats. Although the verb is listed in major American and Canadian dictionaries, usage commentators generally despise it and many Canadian writers avoid it.

Dialogue is the more common spelling in Canadian, British, and American English. *Dialog* is a variant used infrequently in Canada.

If we are to have a serious dialogue about the vital issue of peace between East and West, NATO and the Warsaw Pact must address the fundamental question 'Who is the enemy?'
George Ignatieff *The Making of a Peacemonger* 1987: xi

Their biggest challenge will be to dispel the stereotype image of the conniving salesperson, establish a dialogue and show the consumer the human side of dealership personnel.
Toronto Star 4 Jan. 2003: G06

'I think it's been encouraging,' he says, and then slips into bureaucratese to describe the organizing process: 'We're dialoguing in a non-confrontational way with clients.'
Globe and Mail (Toronto) 11 March 1985: M1

diarrhea, diarrhoea see -AE-, -OE-, -E-

diaspora, Diaspora, Dispersion A *diaspora* (pronounced *dye ASP uh ruh*) is a dispersion, usually forced, of a people from their homeland; *diaspora* may also refer to the people themselves who are living outside their ancestral homeland. The term was first used to refer to the dispersion of the Jews from Palestine, beginning in the eighth century BC. For this meaning it is usually capitalized; in other references no capital is required, though one is sometimes used. *Dispersion*, the English translation of the Greek word *diaspora*, is also sometimes used to refer to the Jewish Diaspora.

A perpetual diaspora of all peoples is the book's thematic underpinning: Individuals wander about the globe, full of longing and sadness, seeking ancestors and cultural roots.
Toronto Star 1 Oct. 1995: H18

The sacrifice is reminiscent of the Jewish Diaspora, whose investment in children and education helped the Jewish faith to flourish in exile over nearly two millennia.
Ottawa Citizen 16 July 1994: A6

(Here *Diaspora* refers to the people themselves.)

This is the first official homecoming for the Acadian diaspora and has attracted people from France, Belgium, Texas, Louisiana, New England, California and from across Canada, where there are more than 1.5 million people of Acadian descent.
Daily News (Halifax) 17 Aug. 1994: 8.

When the state of Israel was established in 1948, it became necessary to find a language that was common to all Jews, despite their many centuries of dispersion. . . .
Gazette (Montreal) 24 Dec. 1994: G2

dice see DIE

dictatable see -ABLE, -(AT)ABLE

diction, enunciation *Diction* may refer either to a writer's choice of words or to the clarity of a speaker's word production. *Enunciation* in this context refers solely to the clarity of the production of words in speech (but see ENUNCIATION, ANNUNCIATION). Usage experts, especially in the United States, have often recommended confining *diction* to the sense of word choice in order to completely differentiate these two words. However, *diction* was used to refer to clarity of speech as early as the mid-eighteenth century (*OED*), and in contemporary English this meaning is both common and accepted.

> The forbidding landscape is not relieved by his fondness for the imagery of dry bones and dead trees, nor by dense tangled diction that all too often makes the reader stop and wonder what the hell he is talking about.
> Northrop Frye *The Bush Garden* 1971: 17

(Here *diction* refers to word choice.)

> Her diction was excellent, though much of what she sang was in Old French and was not entirely intelligible to the likes of me.
> *Ottawa Citizen* 4 Dec. 1994: C7

(Here *diction* means clarity of word production.)

> Genius he may be, but there's a tendency for Van Morrison in live performance to sing as if he has a large wad of cotton batting in his mouth . . . through all the syllables there's that familiar Marlon-Brando-as-Don-Corleone wuff-wuff in the enunciation.
> *Globe and Mail* (Toronto) 29 Aug. 1985: E5

See also ENUNCIATION, ANNUNCIATION.

didn't see ABBREVIATION; CONTRACTIONS

die, dice In the past, gamblers rolled one *die* but two or more *dice*. Increasingly, however, *dice* is used for both the singular and the plural. Most authorities now accept 'one dice' in informal use. The more formal singular *die* survives in the expression 'The die is cast'.

> . . . piece movement is determined by the roll of a die.
> *Ottawa Citizen* 30 July 1994: J2

(Here the formal singular *die* is used.)

> We're willing to bet our financial futures on the roll of a dice.
> *Vancouver Sun* 8 Dec. 1994: D1

(This use of *dice* as singular is informal.)

> 'I'm afraid there are people who have come to the conclusion that the dice are loaded against the poor in the Axworthy reform program.'
> *Gazette* (Montreal) 7 Dec. 1994: A1

Diefenbaker see GERMAN WORDS, PRONUNCIATION OF

die of, die from *Die of* and *die from* are both acceptable. *Die of* is more common, and preferred in formal writing. If the cause of death is indirect, however, *from* must be used: 'The child died from lack of attention'.

> Terry Fox died of osteosarcoma, a form of bone cancer.
> *Queen's Quarterly* 97.2 (1990): 256

> All the others died of natural causes.
> Alan Tucker, ed. *The Penguin Guide to Canada* 1991: 8

diesel see GERMAN WORDS, PRONUNCIATION OF

differ see DOUBLING THE FINAL CONSONANT

different from, different than, different to *Different from* is common in sentences such as 'Your book is different from mine' or 'Ravens are different from crows'. Here a noun follows *from*. Some usage guides suggest that *from* should follow *different* in all cases. However, *different than* is frequently used by Canadian writers in sentences like those above. It is even more common, and more widely accepted, in comparisons where a clause (rather than a noun) follows *than*: 'What happened was different than (what) we had expected'; 'He looks different than he did last week'; 'Hilda is a very different person than she was last year'. To rewrite this last sentence 'Hilda is a very different person from the person she was last year' is no real improvement, since *person* must be repeated.

Different to is a British form regarded as informal (at best) by British commentators; this form is uncommon in Canadian English.

Whether you are using *from* or *than*, it is important to make sure that readers know what is being compared with what.

> Perhaps the most impressive part of listening to the new album is that each tune sounds different from the last. . . .
> *Edmonton Journal* 3 March 2006: G4

> Thus, no share of a given class can be given a different voting power from other shares of the same class.
> J.E. Smyth et al. *The Law and Business Administration in Canada* 1987: 708

> 'A bishop occupies a different role than a priest,' he stressed.
> *Canadian Churchman* April 1986: 6

> 'Fieldwork sometimes produces different results than what you're looking for,' Caldwell said. . . .
> *Edmonton Journal* 13 July 2004: A2

See also VARIOUS DIFFERENT.

differentiate, distinguish, discriminate
All three words mean to recognize or separate on the basis of difference. *Differentiate* is commonly used with the prepositions *from* and *between*. *Distinguish* and *discriminate* are used with a direct object ('distinguish red and green') or with *between*, *from*, and *among* ('distinguish among red, green, and blue').

Discriminate can have either positive or negative connotations. In the positive sense, to *discriminate* is to distinguish subtle differences between similar things: people with this knack, such as connoisseurs of wine, art, food, and fashion, are called *discriminating*. When *discriminate* is used negatively, as in 'This study discriminates against women', it is always followed by *against*, and the related adjective is *discriminatory*.

> It seeks to differentiate between long-term, structural unemployment, often related to simultaneously declining and expanding industries or technological change, and short-term unemployment, attributable, say, to insufficient aggregate demand.
> *Canadian Journal of Sociology* 14.2 (1989): 261

> For it does not enable us to distinguish among the various kinds of social groups we all know about—families, friendship groups, residential communities, formal and complex organizations, etc.—all of which may be regarded, according to the definition, as 'social systems.'
> Irving M. Zeitlin and Robert J. Brym *The Social Condition of Humanity* 1991: 84

> 'And in Alan Wilde we see an effort to discriminate its modes: "mediate irony", "disjunctive irony", and "postmodern" or "suspensive irony" with its yet more radical vision of multiplicity, randomness, contingency, and even absurdity.'
> Linda Hutcheon *Splitting Images* 1991: 90

> (Here, to *discriminate* means to categorize on the basis of subtle distinctions.)

> . . . [Aboriginal peoples] were largely forced to give up their old ways and are unable to enter the Canadian mainstream because white Canadians discriminate against them.
> Irving M. Zeitlin and Robert J. Brym *The Social Condition of Humanity* 1991: 161

difficultness   see -NESS

diffuse, defuse   To *diffuse* means to spread or scatter in all directions. A *diffuse* argument is rambling and unfocused. The verb is pronounced with a final *z* sound: *di FYOOZ*. The adjective has a final *s* sound: *di FYOOSS*.

To *defuse* (pronounced *dee FYOOZ*) means literally to remove a fuse, rendering an explosive or other device harmless. Figuratively, to *defuse* means to counteract a potentially harmful or tense situation. Sometimes the way to defuse a confrontation is to diffuse anger or tension.

> Choose one of the cushion fabrics as side drapes for the window and use creamy white sheers to help diffuse the strong sunlight.
> *Ottawa Citizen* 3 Dec. 1994: I4

> Mr. Rouleau said a referendum wouldn't necessarily defuse the situation and could even make matters worse.
> *Ottawa Citizen* 5 April 2006: C1

> (Only *defuse* is appropriate here.)

Harcourt said the kids-at-risk projects will diffuse the potentially explosive situations many students face and are aimed at helping reduce the drop-out rate.
Vancouver Sun 2 Dec. 1994: B3

('Explosive situations' can't be dispersed; the word required here is *defuse*.)

digraph see DIPHTHONG

dilemma A *dilemma* is a choice between two undesirable alternatives (sometimes called the 'horns of the dilemma'). Often the only thing that makes these alternatives undesirable is their exclusivity: choosing one rules out the other. Now, especially in informal writing, *dilemma* is also used to mean difficulty, problem, or predicament, with no suggestion of choice. Many usage guides still resist this extended sense, however, and it is best avoided in academic and formal writing.

> The government faced a dilemma: it could not allow the demise of close to nineteen hundred souls; neither could it be seen to thwart the religious aspirations of a devout and inoffensive religious sect.
> Pierre Berton *The Promised Land* 1984: 87

> He may find himself in the dilemma that if he does not interfere, the business may fail completely; yet if he chooses to exercise some control in order to save the business, he will incur unlimited liability.
> J.E. Smyth et al. *The Law and Business Administration in Canada* 1987: 665

> A lottery winner's dilemma. Is losing privacy worth 39 million dollars?
> *CTV News* [transcript] 14 Dec. 1994: n.p.

> With this emphasis upon their geographical identity, historians were faced with the dilemma of how to deal with residents of Quebec who were not of French origins.
> *Queen's Quarterly* 92.1 (1985): 88

(This use of *dilemma* is informal; in this academic article, *problem* would be a better choice.)

> Finding a unique gift for a special person is a chore that accompanies the otherwise delightful Christmas season. But Canada's antique shops, auctions and shows offer an easy solution to the dilemma. . . .
> *Canadian Collector* 21 (1986): 1

(This use of *dilemma* is informal.)

See also HOBSON'S CHOICE; SCYLLA AND CHARYBDIS.

dilettante *Dilettante* is derived from the Italian word for 'delight', and in the eighteenth century it was used positively to refer to an admirer or devotee of the fine arts. Now the word is almost always used negatively to describe someone who dabbles in any art or intellectual pursuit in a superficial and unfocused way.

Canadians and Americans usually say *DILL uh taunt*, while the British prefer the Italianate pronunciation *di li TAN tay*. The plural is *dilettantes* or, less commonly, *dilettanti*. A dilettante is *dilettantish* and engages in *dilettantism* or *dilettanteism*.

> It's possible to go to the other extreme, to be a dilettante so bemused by possibilities that one has no convictions or power to act at all.
> Northrop Frye *The Educated Imagination* 1963: 32

> The 1980 election saw resurrected Liberals determined to disprove obituaries that painted the Trudeau years as dilettantish and uninspired.
> *Globe and Mail* (Toronto) 30 March 1985: P6

> My generalism (please do not confuse this with dilettantism because they are not the same) clearly led me to seek the editorship because of the scope it allows for putting this predilection into practice.
> *Queen's Quarterly* 92.2 (1985): 442

dingy, dinghy Note the different spellings: *dingy* (rhymes with *stingy*) means dull or dirty-looking, while *dinghy* (rhymes with *wingy*) refers to a small boat used for pleasure or emergencies. The boat is always spelled with an *h*.

> She'll rent a room, an inexpensive room but not too dingy—nothing a coat of paint won't brighten up.
> Margaret Atwood *The Blind Assassin* 2000: 463

These can range from price points to extra gear . . . or perhaps a dingy for your dream boat.
Canadian Yachting Feb. 2005: 32

(Here *dinghy* is the proper spelling.)

dinner, supper, lunch, luncheon, tea, brunch   In the past, especially in rural settings, Canadians ate up to four meals a day: breakfast, dinner (a large meal at noon), supper (a lighter meal in the evening), and lunch (a light snack late in the evening). The main meal was served at noon to sustain farm workers for an afternoon of heavy labour. Urbanization changed this pattern of cooking and eating. Today, when many people do not go home for a midday meal, the large meal is served in the evening and is called *dinner* or *supper*. The 'Survey of Vancouver English' (1984) indicated that *dinner* is preferred to *supper*, although many informants used either word. Those who do distinguish these words as terms for the evening meal use *dinner* for a hot, substantial meal and *supper* for a quicker cold meal. *Lunch* is now the name of the midday meal, although in Atlantic Canada and the Prairie provinces *lunch* may also refer to a late-night snack.

At one time *luncheon*, not *lunch*, was the usual term for the midday meal. *Lunch* is now established as the preferred form, and *luncheon* usually refers to a formal meal for a group of people gathered for a meeting or entertainment.

Tea in Canada is often an afternoon social event to which guests are invited. In Britain and Australia, especially among working-class speakers, *tea* is the everyday word for dinner.

The term *brunch*, a blend of *breakfast* and *lunch*, was coined by students at Oxford at the end of the nineteenth century and is now fully established in North America.

diphthong, digraph, ligature   *Diphthong* is a linguistic term for a vowel sound that is actually two vowels run together. For example, the vowel sounds in *boy*, *loud*, and *tide* are diphthongs: *oi*, *au*, and *ai* respectively. Traditionally, the *ph* in *diphthong* has been pronounced as in *phone*: *DIF thong*. While this pronunciation is recommended, many dictionaries and usage guides now also list the pronunciation *DIP thong*.

A *digraph* is two letters pronounced as one sound: for example, *ph*, *ch*, *th*, the *ea* in *bead*, or the *ps* in *psychology*.

Ligature is a printer's term for two letters joined together: for example, *æ* in *æsthete* or *œ* in *foetus*. Ligatures occur in English borrowings from Greek. Sometimes ligatures are mistakenly called diphthongs, probably because in the original Greek they represented diphthongs, though in English pronunciation they do not.

See also -AE-, -OE-, -E-; F, PH.

directions   see EAST, WEST, NORTH, SOUTH

dis-   see DE

disabilities   People with disabilities have recently begun to challenge demeaning traditional labels that equate them with their disabilities, as in 'a diabetic', 'an epileptic', 'a Down's child', 'a cripple', 'a mental case', 'an MS-victim', and so on. The handbook *The Canadian Style*, which represents the editorial policy of the Canadian government, supports this point of view and recommends to Canadian editors that they abandon noun labels, such as those above, in favour of descriptive phrases such as 'who has epilepsy', 'who has Down's syndrome', 'whose mobility is impaired by arthritis', 'who uses a wheelchair', 'who has mental health problems', 'who is intellectually impaired', and so on. In recommended usage, a person is always mentioned before his or her disability; a disability is mentioned only if it is relevant to the context; and it is described in neutral terms. Expressions that are disrespectful or pitying ('crazy', 'crippled', 'devastated by', 'stricken with', 'victim of') should be avoided. People 'should be identified by their achievements rather than their limitations' (*Canadian Style* 259).

Most deaf people are not, in fact, mute, so phrases such as 'deaf-mute' and 'deaf and dumb' are inaccurate. In addition, the contemporary connotations of *dumb* render the latter phrase insulting. Instead of saying that someone is unable to speak, indicate how they do communicate: for example, by signing, with a voice synthesizer, with the help of a computer.

'Blind people' is preferred to 'the blind', though 'the deaf' is accepted because those deaf people who sign constitute a language community.

The term *challenged*, as in 'intellectually challenged' or 'physically challenged', is a euphemism that has spawned jokes such as 'vertically challenged' for short people, and 'sartorially challenged' for sloppy dressers; it's not recommended for serious use.

Bergman won the marathon gold medal in the open wheelchair division at the European Open Paralympic championships.
Athletics Canada website 20 Dec. 2005

(The achievement rather than the wheelchair is highlighted.)

Booth, 33, is a student in the social services program at Fraser Valley Community College in Abbotsford. He has had multiple sclerosis since 1982 and has been nearly blind for three years.
Province (Vancouver) 29 Oct. 1990: 50

But it's no toy. MS sufferer Richard Beecroft, of Ottawa, will be riding a custom-built, three-wheeled bicycle like the one he rode on a three-year trek around the world to raise awareness about MS.
Province (Vancouver) 7 Aug. 1990: 53

(Here 'who has multiple sclerosis' would be preferable to 'MS sufferer'.)

Finley, an epileptic who can't work, lost 50 pounds during the period.
Gazette (Montreal) 7 July 1990: A14

(Here 'who has epilepsy' would be preferable.)

Despite being confined to a wheelchair, Jonathan went skiing and mountain climbing last week with the Eastern Seals.
Telegram (St. John's) 15 April 2006: A4

('Despite using a wheelchair' is preferable.)

See also DOWN SYNDROME; INCLUSIVE LANGUAGE.

disaffected, unaffected   *Disaffected* people are unhappy either with society in general or with some particular thing they were once committed to, such as their work, a relationship, an ideal, or an organization. People who are *unaffected* either don't put on airs or don't feel the impact of a change.

Amerindians could become a permanently disaffected group, as happened with the Irish in Great Britain.
Toronto Star 29 Aug. 1992: G10

Disaffected Tories and Liberals are going Green in a way they never have before, according to the data.
Ottawa Citizen 5 June 2005: B3

When I entered his office, I was greeted by an unaffected charming man with an impish glint in his eyes and a shock of red hair.
Chatelaine April 1986: 139

MacEachern said the children were assessed by a school psychologist and a Health Department official, who found them generally unaffected.
Gazette (Montreal) 19 Nov. 1994: A26

(Here the context disambiguates *unaffected*: the children aren't disarmingly sincere; they are untouched by a bad experience.)

disassemble   see DISSEMBLE

disassociate   see DISSOCIATE

disastrous, wondrous, thunderous   All three words are commonly misspelled. Note that the *e* is dropped from *disaster* and *wonder* to form the adjectives *disastrous* and *wondrous*, while in *thunderous* the *e* is retained.

disbar   see DEBAR

disburse   see DISPERSE

disbursement   see DISPERSION

disc, disk *Disc* and *disk* are spelling variants. In the recording industry, *disc* is the usual spelling: *disc jockey, disco, discography, compact disc. Disk* is preferred internationally for disks used in computers (apart from compact discs): *high-density disk, hard disk.* In other contexts *disc* is the more common spelling in Canada and Britain ('slipped a disc', 'an enormous red disc', 'disc-shaped'), while *disk* is preferred in the United States.

disclaim see DECRY

discomfit, discomfiture, discomfort
Discomfit is a verb meaning to disconcert or embarrass; the related noun is *discomfiture. Discomfort* is usually used as a noun meaning physical or mental unease, but it can also be used as a verb meaning to make uncomfortable. *Discomfit* refers only to mental or emotional states, while *discomfort*, although it covers both mental and physical states, is more commonly used of the latter.

> Trying to produce small talk when isolated with Trudeau at a stand-up cocktail reception has proved discomfiting for the most accomplished social lioness.
> *Maclean's* 31 March 1986: 15

> It was a man's duty to see that they were not discomforted by things like trekking in the dark to the outhouse in subzero blizzards.
> *Ottawa Citizen* 11 Sept. 2005: A11

> Hidden away where they didn't embarrass or discomfort anybody, they were society's forgotten people—unseen, unheard, unimportant.
> *Whig-Standard* (Kingston) 28 Oct. 2005: 8

(Here *discomfit*, meaning embarrass or disconcert, would be more precise.)

> To add to my discomforture and embarrassment I have noticed a letter in your paper, Feb. 7, from my daughter. . . .
> *Globe and Mail* (Toronto) 21 Feb. 1985: M11

(Either *discomfiture* or *discomfort* is needed here.)

discreditable see CREDIBLE

discreet, discrete *Discreet* is often misspelled *discrete. Discreet* means tactful, prudent, and circumspect; the related nouns are *discretion* and *discreetness. Discrete* means distinct, separate, or discontinuous, and the related noun is *discreteness.*

> Though Arafat insists on the PLO's right to attack Israeli military targets, his discreet efforts to stop the raids reflect worry that the U.S. might call off talks with the PLO.
> *Gazette* (Montreal) 3 March 1989: A7

> He tackles the unity question not as a discrete problem but within the broader issue of enhancing Canadian justice and international peace.
> *Toronto Star* 26 Feb. 1994: J13

> Finally, I treated the complete picture with what's called a facet filter, a filter that separates a photographic image into discrete patches of color that resemble dabs of paint on a canvas.
> *Gazette* (Montreal) 15 Oct. 1994: J2

> The seventh-inning stretch takes on a new meaning as a less than discrete couple in the SkyDome Hotel are caught copulating by fans that originally thought the entertainment was on the field between the Seattle Mariners and Toronto Blue Jays.
> *Ottawa Citizen* 29 Dec. 1990: C3

(The phrase needed here is 'less than *discreet* couple' although, joined as they are, neither are they entirely discrete.)

discriminate see DIFFERENTIATE

discuss, debate *Discuss about* is non-standard: 'We discussed schools', *not* 'We discussed about schools'. *Discuss* without an object is also non-standard: 'Last night we had a discussion', but *not* 'Last night we discussed'.
Debate is sometimes followed by a preposition, either *about* or *over*: 'They debated about moving again'. Usually, though, it takes a direct object: 'They debated children's rights'. Some

authorities dislike *debate about* and *debate over*, but the prepositions serve the purpose of emphasizing indecision.

> The sessions enabled composers to discuss their common problems, especially of attracting audiences for contemporary concert music.
> *Queen's Quarterly* 94.1 (1987): 177

> So, being a good citizen, I decided to call my elected city representative to discuss about this unnecessary noise.
> *Sudbury Star* 18 Jan. 2006: A11

(Here *about* is unnecessary: 'discuss this unnecessary noise' is preferable.)

> Both were highly regarded on The Street a few years earlier, and listeners inevitably debated their relative merits. . . .
> Jack Chambers *Milestones* 1983: 141

> At Montreal's Jewish General Hospital, the 12-member ethics committee . . . debated for 90 minutes last month over whether to discharge a 48-year-old schizophrenic who wanted to go back to living on the city streets.
> *Maclean's* 1 May 1989: A56

disembark   see EMBARK

disenfranchise, disfranchise   To deprive people of their rights, particularly voting rights, is to *disenfranchise* or *disfranchise* them. Both are correct. Most usage guides recommend the shorter form, *disfranchise*, but Canadian writers overwhelmingly prefer *disenfranchise*.

> With no voice, no vote and little economic clout, young people in Canada are one of the most disenfranchised groups in the country.
> *Toronto Star* 25 May 2006: R14

> Speaking to a subdued crowd of about 100, congress chairman Bernard Finestone said he did not think the Quebec government went out of its way to disfranchise members of Montreal's ethnic communities.
> *Gazette* (Montreal) 17 June 1985: A4

dishevelled, disheveled   *Dishevelled* (pronounced *di SHEV uld*) means untidy. It refers to wayward hair (the root of the word is the Old French word *chevel*, 'hair') or now, more commonly, a generally rumpled personal appearance. Occasionally things in disarray are called dishevelled. *Disheveled* is an alternative spelling, preferred in the United States.

> Her hair was terribly sparse and what there was of it was dishevelled.
> *Canadian Fiction Magazine* 63 (1988): 87

> The roly-poly Klein, who always looks slightly dishevelled—with his tie askew, his shirttail sticking out and his hair mussed up—shrugged off suggestions he doesn't look much like a premier.
> *Vancouver Sun* 28 Dec. 1992: A4

> Yet it could not even put up a decent byelection fight against the Civic Party, a disheveled assemblage with no real leader, program or philosophy of government.
> *Gazette* (Montreal) 4 Nov. 1992: B2

See also DOUBLING THE FINAL CONSONANT; UNKEMPT, UNKEPT.

disillusionment   see DE-, DIS-

disingenuous   see INGENIOUS

disinterested, uninterested, disinterest   *Disinterested* means impartial, without selfish motives or not standing to gain, while *uninterested* means not interested: that is, bored by or incurious about something. A good referee is disinterested but never uninterested in the game.

Disinterested is also used to mean uninterested. All dictionaries list this meaning, but most commentators object strongly to it, fearing that the special sense of *disinterested* will be obscured or lost. Canadian usage provides no grounds for this fear. *Disinterested* is rarely ambiguous in context, and, at least in writing, it is still used far more often to mean impartial than bored. Those who use *disinterested* to mean bored or indifferent are not likely to be misunderstood, but they do run a substantial risk of being criticized; it is best to avoid the disputed usage in formal writing.

Note that the noun *disinterest* can mean either impartiality or lack of interest. Both meanings are accepted.

Uninterested in school, she had begun smoking grass, taking LSD, and hanging around the hippie district of Yorkville.
Ann Davis *Somewhere Waiting* 1991: 249

Since the mediator is disinterested, he can adopt an objective attitude toward the conflict.
Irving M. Zeitlin and Robert J. Brym *The Social Condition of Humanity* 1991: 62

I am no disinterested reviewer of *Still Barred From Prison*. The author is one of my favorite persons.
Henry M. Rosenthal and S. Cathy Berson, eds. *Canadian Jewish Outlook Anthology* 1988: 338

At times, the 120 attending the hour-long question-and-answer luncheon seemed completely disinterested. In fact, at one point there was a lull in the action as no one had a question at the three microphones.
Winnipeg Free Press 17 Nov. 1990: 10

(This use of *disinterested* is disputed.)

That is to say, they conceive of participation in the elective process as a vestigial duty, rather like going to church. . . . Apathy or disinterest of this sort is one of the great privileges of the tiny fraction of the world which calls itself democratic.
Queen's Quarterly 94.4 (1987): 973

(Here *disinterest* means lack of interest.)

disk   see DISC

disk drives   see COMPUTER TERMS

disorganized, unorganized   *Disorganized* and *unorganized* are synonyms meaning lacking system and order. *Unorganized* also has a specialized sense, referring to workers who do not belong to a labour union.

Our impressions of human life are picked up one by one, and remain for most of us loose and disorganized.
Northrop Frye *The Educated Imagination* 1963: 24

. . . Kanata was once a stable, planned suburban community. He says it's now in a period of unorganized growth and intense real-estate speculation.
Ottawa Citizen 12 July 1994: A1

Public opinion surveys consistently indicate that millions of unorganized Canadian workers wish they had a union.
National Post (Toronto) 17 March 2006: FP17

dispassionate, impassive, impassable
Dispassionate means either unswayed by emotions, and thus unbiased and fair, or, sometimes, cold and aloof. *Impassive* means unflinching, not roused to emotion, or not betraying emotion. *Impassable* means impossible to travel over or through.

But more than his formal qualifications, it was his capacity for dispassionate, objective analysis that I found so impressive.
George Ignatieff *The Making of a Peacemonger* 1987: 79

But 'neath the lovely minimalist jazz-pop exterior, her delivery is cold and dispassionate.
Vancouver Sun 17 Feb. 1990: D2

Mr. Justice Eugene Ewaschuk, describing the crime as 'particularly cruel and odious,' sentenced an impassive H—— to life in prison with no opportunity for parole for 14 years.
London Free Press 28 April 1988: B5

It was the dead of winter, school finally closed till spring, with roads impassable for all but poker players.
David Williams *Eye of the Father* 1985: 98

dispatch, despatch   Dictionaries list both spellings. *Dispatch* is far more common; *despatch* first appeared in Johnson's *Dictionary* (1755) and may have been a typographical error, since Johnson used *dispatch* in his own writings.

The verb *dispatch* means to send with haste, or to dispose of some work, or to kill someone. The noun means speed and efficiency (this is an element of all meanings of the noun and the verb) or a report of some kind (e.g., a military report or a news report filed by a correspondent).

By then Secretary General Dag Hammarskjold had become convinced that the only hope of bringing the situation under control was to dispatch an international peace-keeping force to the Congo.
George Ignatieff *The Making of a Peacemonger* 1987: 192

Now they require him to snatch and despatch a KGB executioner in East Germany as a reprisal for breaching the unwritten code of espionage forbidding violence against one another's agents on their home ground.
Globe and Mail (Toronto) 23 Feb. 1985: E15

(Here *despatch* means kill.)

Our diplomats are responsible for the way in which we analyze changing realities in the world, but the Government is accountable for the dispatch with which we respond to those changes.
Globe and Mail (Toronto) 19 Feb. 1985: P9

(Here *dispatch* means speed and efficency.)

The confidential dispatch from Prime Minister Brian Mulroney to the premiers last week included both a request and a warning.
Maclean's 28 July 1986: 12

dispel   *Dispel* is occasionally misspelled *dispell*, probably because similar words, such as *appal*, *enrol*, and *expel*, are correctly spelled with either a single or a double *l* in Canadian English. Note, however, that the past tense and present participle, *dispelled* and *dispelling*, are spelled with a double *l*.

It dispells an erroneous view of them as being tolerant cultural relativists and, instead, portrays them as human beings of their own times, and with their own cultural and personal biases and illusions.
Arctic 41.1 (1988): 86

(The correct spelling is *dispel*.)

See also DOUBLING THE FINAL CONSONANT; SPELLING, CANADIAN.

dispersal   see DISPERSION

disperse, disburse   Unruly crowds are *dispersed* or broken up by police; sums of money are *disbursed* or paid out. To *disperse* also means to spread over a wide area, as in 'The clouds dispersed' or 'The centre disperses information'.

In addition, many Arctic plants depend on the wind to disperse their seeds in winter, when the seed heads are mature and well dried.
Up Here Mar.–Apr. 1990: 42

Where do you get the wisdom you disperse?
Robertson Davies *One Half of Robertson Davies* 1978: 73

So far, CIDA has disbursed about $17,000 for the project, which is being funded to July 31.
Calgary Herald 1 May 2006: A6

Social workers and volunteers make sure rent and food are paid for, and disperse spending money.
Canadian Churchman April 1986: 12

(The word required here is *disburse*.)

See also DISPERSION.

dispersion, dispersal, disbursement, [dispersement]   *Dispersion* and *dispersal* are both accepted nouns derived from *disperse* (to scatter or disseminate). *Disbursement* is derived from *disburse* (to pay out funds). *Dispersement* is an unacceptable hybrid patterned on *disbursement*.

. . . Petro-Canada has agreed to build a new 100-metre stack within two years that will improve the dispersion of pollutants and reduce odor and emissions.
Globe and Mail (Toronto) 5 Dec. 1985: C5

With wind dispersal of seeds, the group has also invaded the islands of Madagascar, Sri Lanka and the Canaries.
TLC . . . for plants Spring 1991: 8

Once the money is collected, no agency will receive less than it has in the past and an audited statement showing the disbursement of funds will now be published in July.
Calgary Herald 6 Feb. 1993: E9

. . . the only way to prevent the displacement and disbursement of destructive minnow species to waters where they could prove harmful to native fish is to completely ban the sale, use and transportation of live minnows province-wide.
Gazette (Montreal) 1 March 1994: D12

(The word required here is either *dispersal* or *dispersion*.)

The exhibition charts the dispersement of the Metis throughout the West, and their inability to find acceptance at conventional employment through a mix of racial intolerance and poor education.
Globe and Mail (Toronto) 24 July 1985: S7

(Either *dispersion* or *dispersal* is required here.)

See also DIASPORA; DISBURSE; DISPERSE.

dispute   see REFUTE

disrespect   *Disrespect* is a noun meaning lack of respect, or discourtesy. In Standard American English it is also a verb meaning to feel or exhibit a lack of respect for. The verb *disrespect* is archaic in British English and informal in Canadian English, where it occurs almost invariably in quoted speech.

'I know how to make a living on the street,' she says, 'and I never hated or disrespected myself for knowing how to.'
Gazette (Montreal) 25 June 1992: C7

Cory, a Grade 11 student at Ernest Manning senior high, chipped in: 'It makes you feel disrespected.'
Calgary Herald 18 June 1992: B1

'There was a point when I wanted to return to Ottawa, but that was before they began disrespecting me as a football player and person,' Allen said, his smile quickly replaced by a very serious look.
Ottawa Citizen 17 June 1992: E2

He accused the ministry of 'creating a welfare program with natural resources' and said a government cull 'disrespects the rights of hunters to exercise abilities and duties.'
Toronto Star 11 Jan. 1992: B7

dissatisfied   see UNSATISFIED

dissemble, disassemble   To *dissemble* is to conceal the truth or hide one's real intentions or feelings. To *disassemble* something is to take it apart in an orderly fashion.

The Australian army may be dissembling when it claims that the 541,000 condoms it bought are for waterproofing guns.
Globe and Mail (Toronto) 23 Oct. 1985: A7

To get to the wheel you may have to disassemble the machine.
Canadian Consumer Jan. 1985: 38

dissociate, disassociate   Both forms are accepted, and both date from the seventeenth century. Some style guides insist on the shorter and more common *dissociate*, perhaps because it has a Latin antecedent (*dissociare*).

dissolvable   see SOLUBLE

distil, distill   see -L, -LL

distinct, distinctive   *Distinct* means separate, different, or clear: 'There are two distinct bacteria on this slide'. *Distinctive* means characteristic or distinguishing or distinguishable: 'His crazy laugh is his most distinctive feature'; 'Her needlework is distinctive'. In some contexts the senses overlap.

In recent Canadian history, the attempt to produce a constitutional accord to which the Quebec government would agree has led to frequent use of the phrase 'distinct society'. One meaning of *distinct*, in both English and French, is separate. Yet the whole point of constitutional negotiations is to allow Quebec to remain in Canada while preserving its cultural difference or *distinctiveness*.

Under the deal, the Ouje-Bougoumou will be recognized as a distinct band. Until now, they had been lumped with the Mistassini Cree, a different group, as a bureaucratic convenience.
Gazette (Montreal) 28 Dec. 1992: B2

(Here *distinct* means separate.)

Kindly note that Dominica and the Dominican Republic are two separate and distinct countries.
Gazette (Montreal) 4 Dec. 1990: B2

Friesen does an excellent job of explaining the political differences of the three Prairie provinces. Like brothers, each has its own distinct personality.
Globe and Mail (Toronto) 5 Jan. 1985: E15

(Here either *distinct* or *distinctive* would work.)

Also because the child actors are always bundled up in snowsuits and tuques, they needed to have distinctive faces so viewers could tell them apart.
Globe and Mail (Toronto) 5 Feb. 1985: P16

(Obviously the children have different or distinct faces; here *distinctive* is the only choice possible, meaning that they have faces that will allow the viewers to distinguish them clearly from one another.)

Can we carve out a truly distinctive society, living under the (often patronizing) gaze of a superpower neighbour?
City Magazine 1988: 11

(Canada is *distinct*—that is, politically separate—from the United States. What is at issue is whether its society is culturally *distinctive*.)

When supporters of Meech Lake assert that 'of course Quebec is a distinct society; we can all see that,' what they really mean is that Quebec is a distinctive society, which it certainly is.
Financial Post 14 Nov. 1989: 14

distinguish   see DIFFERENTIATE

distract, detract   To *distract* someone is to draw his or her attention away from something: 'His partner distracted the security guard'. To *detract from* something is to take away from it or diminish it: 'The squalling detracted from the ceremony'. The phrases 'distract attention' and 'detract attention' have both been used for centuries to mean divert attention, but the latter is less common and is likely to be considered a mistake.

Unnecessary details are eliminated so as not to confuse and distract the driver.
Star-Phoenix (Saskatoon) 19 May 2006: E10

Members of the church also shun publicity. There's a feeling that earthly gratitude might somehow detract from the final reward for service to your fellow man.
Canadian Heritage Feb.–Mar. 1986: 22

The political fallout over the closing of the St. Jean college has detracted attention from the fact that Canada, before this week's budget, already had as

many military colleges as the United States.
Gazette (Montreal) 26 Feb. 1994: B1

(The usual expression is '*distracted* attention'.)

distrust, mistrust   *Distrust* and *mistrust* can be used interchangeably. *Distrust* is more common, both as a noun and as a verb.

Ditidaht   see NUU-CHAH-NULTH

divan   see CHESTERFIELD

dived, dove   *Dived* and *dove* are both accepted in Canadian English as the past tense of *dive*. *Dived* is more common in writing; *dove* is more common in speech, but is also found in all types of writing. *Dove* is rare as a past participle: 'has dived' is recommended. *Dove* is in common use as the past tense form in Canada, the northern United States, and some parts of Britain, but is not used in Standard British English.

Early in the war, when nerves were particularly on edge, an F-16 landed in the middle of an air-attack alert at Canada Dry One and the troops dived for cover.
Maclean's 4 March 1991: A34

Now, unemployment in the Toronto area has dived to 3.2 per cent, while a building boom has created intense demand for skilled labor.
Maclean's 23 May 1988: A26

I folded a towel on the end of the dock and dove into Big Crummock Lake.
Howard Engel *Murder Sees the Light* 1984: 159

The CCB's board and management, the auditors, the government, and the regulators all dove for cover.
Saturday Night July 1986: 47

divide   see WATERSHED

division   see SPECIES

DNA   see ABBREVIATION

do   The plural of the noun *do* is either *do's* or *dos*: 'Do's and Don'ts for Visitors'; 'The food is always wonderful at their dos'. The former is less likely to puzzle the reader.

> One of the most fun motorcycle do's I attended in 1989 involved people who have never owned or ridden a motorcycle.
> *Canadian Biker* Feb. 1990: 8

> The insurance bureau has pamphlets spelling out the Dos and Don'ts of moving.
> *Gazette* (Montreal) 30 June 1994: A4

See also APOSTROPHE; DON'T, DONE.

doctor, Dr.   The honorific *Dr.* is used for medical doctors and people who hold academic doctorates. If the degree MD or PhD (or D Litt, D Ed, Th D, etc.) is listed after the name, the honorific is not used before the name: *Joan Treverton, MD* or *Dr. Joan Treverton*, but not *Dr. Joan Treverton, MD*.

Psychologists and psychiatrists are doctors of two different types: a psychologist has a PhD in psychology and a psychiatrist is a medical specialist. In Canada, licensed practitioners of osteopathy, chiropractic, podiatry, optometry, dentistry, and veterinary medicine may also use the title *Dr.* Outside academic circles it is often assumed that anyone referred to as *Dr. So-and-so* is a medical doctor. Thus, in writing for a general audience, the use of *Dr.* as an academic title should be accompanied by a gloss: '*Dr. So-and-so*, a professor of sociology at Queen's University'.

In Britain, the abbreviation is written *Dr*, without a period at the end. This is the general rule there for abbreviations where the last letter of the abbreviation is the last letter of the full word. This style is becoming more popular in Canada. It is recommended by the authors of *Editing Canadian English* and is now used in Canadian government documents, but *Dr.* with a period is still the usage favoured by the Canadian Press. Both styles are accepted.

See also ABBREVIATION, CONTRACTION, SUSPENSION; JOB TITLES; PSYCHOLOGIST, PSYCHIATRIST.

dog breeds   see DALMATIAN

dogged   see -ED

dollar amounts, currency   A dollar amount at the beginning of a sentence should be written in words ('Fifty thousand dollars was not enough') because beginning a sentence with an Arabic numeral is considered poor style. A small dollar amount, an isolated reference to money, or a round figure is also often written in words ('about twenty dollars'); however, multiple or precise dollar figures should always be presented in Arabic numerals: \$14.79 to \$22.99. Placing a zero before the decimal (\$0.65) helps ensure that amounts below one dollar will not be misread.

Generally, the symbols for dollars (\$) and cents (¢) are used with numerals (10¢), while the words *dollars* and *cents* are used with numbers written as words ('ten cents'). However, very large sums of money are easier to read if presented as combinations of numerals and words: '\$2.41 million'. The dollar sign in front of the numeral makes the word *dollars* redundant: *not* '\$2.41 million dollars'. The use of *K* to mean 'thousand' ('\$100K earners') in a dollar figure is very informal, although it is often seen in newspaper headlines, where it saves space.

Various styles are used to differentiate the dollars of various countries. The following all indicate Canadian currency, for instance: Cdn\$50, Can\$50, C\$50, \$50 Cdn. The International Organization for Standardization (ISO) has developed a system that dispenses with traditional symbols (e.g., \$, £, ¥) and identifies each currency with a three-letter code—for example, American dollars (USD), Australian dollars (AUD), British pounds (GBP), Canadian dollars (CAD), Cayman Islands dollars (KYD), European euros (EUR), and Japanese yen (JPY).

> It retails for \$14.99 CAD, \$12.99 USD.
> *Edmonton Journal* 19 Jan. 2006: F6

> (Many Canadians do not yet associate *CAD* and *USD* with money, so although the dollar signs are technically redundant, they are quite defensible in journalism.)

See also AGREEMENT, GRAMMATICAL; BILLION, TRILLION, MILLIARD; LOONIE, TOONIE; NUMBERS.

-dom A *kingdom* is a king's realm; *freedom* is the state of being free; *x-dom*, in contemporary English, is 'the state of being an *x*' or 'the land of the *x*'s—where the *x*'s reign'. New words formed with *-dom* are often humorous and always informal: *jockdom, moviedom, official-dom, wifedom*.

> She came into my life as I was becoming bored with jockdom and ready to stretch my intellectual wings.
> *Vancouver Sun* 28 May 1994: D13

> If they were too short, you were banished to geek-dom, your 'highwaters' flapping in the wind.
> *Toronto Star* 25 Feb. 1993: F8

> The discovery of oil in commercial quantities the previous summer had set in motion the forces of officialdom.
> *Up Here* Jan.–Feb. 1990: 70

> Downing, the last great champion of dogdom, was sold for $150,000.
> *Globe and Mail* (Toronto) 11 March 1985: S1

domineer, dominate Both *domineer* and *dominate* mean to exercise control over, but their connotations differ. *Domineer*—which most frequently appears as an adjective, *domineering*—is always negative. People who are *domineering* are overbearing and tyrannical in their attempts to control, whereas people who *dominate* sometimes do so without arrogance or self-assertion; they are merely conspicuously successful in a particular setting.

> She had a domineering father who stunted her and wouldn't let her go to college because college was for boys.
> Margaret Atwood *Life Before Man* 1979: 105–6

> In many western settlements, they dominated the first white-collar class: they were the doctors, teachers, bankers and merchants in agricultural communities where the producers were Britons, Irishmen, Germans, French Canadians and, of course, other Ontarians.
> W.C. Lougheed, ed. *In Search of the Standard in Canadian English* 1986: 12

Dominion of Canada, Canada Day The phrase *Dominion of Canada* dates from the making of the *British North American Act* (often shortened to *BNA Act*) of 1867, which joined the colonies of New Brunswick, Nova Scotia, and the Province of Canada (Ontario and Quebec) to create 'One Dominion under the Name of Canada'. While the phrase *Dominion of Canada* was not used in the Act, it did appear in later documents as the official name of the country and came to be thought of popularly as such. The Act came into law on 1 July, a date celebrated annually, first as Dominion Day, then (since 1982) as Canada Day.

According to no less an authority than John A. Macdonald, *Dominion* was chosen (with typical Canadian politeness) to avoid provoking Canada's anti-monarchist American neighbours with *Kingdom*, another proposed title. Suggested by Sir Samuel Leonard Tilley, *Dominion* originates in Psalm 72:8: 'He shall have dominion also from sea to sea, and from the river unto the ends of the earth'. It is also from this line that Canada's official motto is taken (see A MARI USQUE AD MARE). After Canada became a *dominion*, this term was used generically to refer to self-governing countries within the British Empire. Newfoundland, before it joined Canada in 1949, was known as the *Dominion of Newfoundland*. In the latter half of the twentieth century, as Canada began to de-emphasize its historical connection with Britain, the phrase *Dominion of Canada* became less common.

See also A MARI USQUE AD MARE; CONSTITUTION, BRITISH NORTH AMERICA ACT; MAGNA CARTA, MAGNA CHARTA; PATRIATE, PATRIATION; PROVINCES, TERRITORIES.

domino see -OS, -OES

don't, done In some American regional dialects, *doesn't* doesn't exist and *don't* is used in its place: 'She don't drive'; 'It don't seem right'. This usage is obsolete in Britain and considered uneducated in Canada.

The use of *done* instead of *did* as the past tense of *do* ('They done it again') is a non-standard, chiefly North American usage.

The use of *done* with the verb *be* to mean 'finished', as in 'The casting is done', or 'Yes, I'm done, thanks', was criticized in the past; 'I have finished' was considered more genteel. But *be done* is certainly standard in Canadian English today. This construction is mainly used in speech.

See also CONTRACTIONS; DO; DON'T THINK.

don't think   'I don't think I'll be finished in time' usually means 'I think I won't be finished in time'. The other possible interpretation, which requires a heavy stress on *think*, is 'I don't *think* [i.e., I *know*] I'll be finished in time'. Many language commentators have called the more common interpretation of this sentence illogical because the verb *think* is negated even though the negation actually applies to the clause that follows. However, logical or not, sentences like the first one above are perfectly good English.

Linguists call the rule by which negation is shifted from the reported clause ('I won't be finished in time') to the reporting clause ('I think') 'negative-raising'. Other verbs that allow negative-raising include *believe*, *seem*, *expect*, and *suppose*; for example, 'We didn't expect you before three' means 'We expected you, but not before three'. Note that all such verbs report interior states or perceptions. Verbs that describe interactions between people are not amenable to negative-raising: 'I didn't tell them I was coming' means something quite different from 'I told them I wasn't coming'. Though some commentators would restrict negative-raising to informal writing, it is fairly common in formal prose.

W.J. White, then Acting Superintendent of Immigration, didn't think Barr would be successful.
Pierre Berton *The Promised Land* 1984: 109

I don't believe audiences have the same spontaneous and genuine interest in her playing as in the Labèque Sisters'. . . .
Queen's Quarterly 94.3 (1987): 644

Income from student fees could not be expected to cover more than a fraction of the educational costs; actually in the 1920s it covered less than one third.
Frederick Gibson *Queen's University* 2 (1983): 29

dot   see E-MAIL

double entendre   A *double entendre* is a pun, especially a bawdy one. *Double entendre* is standard contemporary English but archaic French (the current French phrase for an ambiguous expression is *phrase à double entente*). *Double entendre* is pronounced either *DUB ul on TAHN druh* or *DOO blon TAHN druh*.

The message is a double entendre on sex and condom use: 'You'd be crazy to do without it.'
Province (Vancouver) 18 Oct. 1990: 59

(Here *it* is a condom or sex or both.)

See also PUN.

double negative   A *double negative* is a construction, such as 'I didn't do nothing', that contains two negative words—here, *didn't* and *nothing*. This sentence has two possible interpretations: either 'I did nothing at all' or 'I chose to act'. In the first interpretation, *didn't* and *nothing* together reinforce the idea of negation. This construction is called the emphatic double negative, and it is strongly disapproved of by teachers and language commentators. In the second interpretation, the two negatives create an understated positive: 'I did something; I *didn't do nothing*'. This construction, called the rhetorical double negative, is standard. When sentences such as 'I didn't do nothing' are spoken, they are never ambiguous: stress and intonation always make the meaning clear.

The traditional explanation for the rejection of the *emphatic* double negative is that it is not logical: logically, two negatives in one sentence cancel each other out, making a positive meaning. If this were actually the way the language worked, then three negatives would make a sentence revert to a negative meaning, and 'We never did nobody no harm' would pass muster as Standard English. Of course it does not, for the basis of the censure of the emphatic double (and triple) negative in English is not logic but convention. The rule that two negatives make a positive was invented by eighteenth-century English grammarians. It is not a rule that exists in French or German, where multiple negatives are standard, nor did it exist in English before the eighteenth century, nor does it exist in many present-day dialects of English. However, in Standard English the rule has been so successfully propagated that, justified or not, it cannot be ignored. The prejudice against the emphatic double negative is very real, and people who use it are perceived as uneducated or ignorant.

Less conspicuous than sentences of the 'didn't do nothing' variety but still non-standard are sentences that combine a negative adverb, such as *scarcely* or *hardly*, and a negated verb ('We didn't hardly have time to start when he stopped us') and sentences where the negation of one clause is repeated in the next ('I wouldn't be surprised if she didn't walk right through that door'). Although some commentators have defended these structures as idiomatic, all agree that they are inappropriate in writing. The accepted versions of these sentences are 'We hardly had time to start when he stopped us' and 'I wouldn't be surprised if she walked right through that door'.

Another form of double negation—this type is without defenders—is the addition of a negative prefix to a word already negated with *-less*. *Regardless* and *relentless* have generated the nonstandard variants *irregardless* and *unrelentless*.

> 'I wouldn't drink nothin' my pa had a hand in making.'
> *Queen's Quarterly* 93.3 (1986): 477

(In fictional dialogue, the emphatic double negative is used to indicate that the speaker is either uneducated or unconcerned with social niceties.)

> And no disrespect to Michael Schumacher, who . . . continued his unrelentless drive toward a seventh drivers' title.
> *Gazette* (Montreal) 16 Aug. 2004: C9

(*Unrelenting* and *relentless* are standard words, but the double negative *unrelentless* is not.)

See also HARDLY; REGARDLESS.

double possessive   Sometimes the possessive is marked by both an *of* phrase and an apostrophe: 'a sweater of Linda's'. This construction is called the double possessive and usually occurs when the 'possessor' is human and has more than one of the 'possessions' in question: for example, 'I borrowed an old hat of my father's'; 'Greed is a fault of John's'. The double possessive is sometimes used to avoid confusion: 'a student of Northrop Frye's' once took a course from him, while 'a student of Northrop Frye' is studying Frye's life, thought, and writing. 'I took my mother's picture' could mean either 'I took a picture of my mother's' or 'I took a picture of my mother'. Although the double possessive has been criticized as inelegant, it is idiomatic and often useful.

> Let us say it is an opera of Benjamin Britten's—*The Turn of the Screw.*
> Robertson Davies *A Voice from the Attic* 1960: 10

See also POSSESSIVE.

doubling the final consonant   When adding an ending to a word that ends in a consonant, sometimes the consonant is doubled and sometimes it is not. There are general rules for when to double and when not to double.

Most one-syllable words that end in a single consonant double it when an ending that begins with a vowel or *y* is added to the word: *big, bigger, biggest; quit, quitter, quitting; sad, sadder, saddest, saddened; stub, stubby; wed, wedded, wedding.*

If the vowel sound of the one-syllable word is written as two letters, the final consonant is not doubled: *boat, boating; green, greener, greenest; soak, soaked, soaking; treat, treated, treating.*

If the word has more than one syllable, the rules become more complicated. If the final syllable has a single vowel, then you must determine which syllable bears the stress. The final consonant is doubled only if the stress falls on the final syllable, as in *admit* (*admitted, admittance, admitting*), *begin* (*beginning, beginner*), and *occur* (*occurred, occurring, occurrence*). If the stress falls on the first syllable, the final consonant stays single: *bias* (*biased, biasing*), *differ* (*differed,* difference), *focus* (*focused, focusing*), *offer* (*offered, offering*). However, some people double the final *s* in *bias* and *focus* before endings (*biassed, focussing*), and this is accepted.

Note that, for some words, the spelling shifts as the stress shifts: *confer* (*conferring, conference*), *defer* (*deferring, deference*), *prefer* (*preferring, preference*), *refer* (*referring, reference*). Thus the rules still hold: double consonants when the stress falls on the second syllable, single when it falls on the first.

There is a general exception to this rule. If the final syllable of a multisyllable word can stand alone as a single word, then the rule that applies to this single word applies to the longer one: *kidnap* (*kidnapped, kidnapper*) and *worship* (*worshipped, worshipper*). A few other words that follow this rule are *eavesdrop, handicap, leapfrog, nonplus, program,* and *zigzag*. About a third of Canadian writers would add *benefit* to this list, writing *benefitted* and *benefitting*, but most use the single-*t* forms.

If the vowel of the second syllable is written with two letters, the final consonant is not doubled: *bemoan, bemoaned, bemoaning; repeat, repeated, repeatable.*

The final consonants *h, w, x,* and *y* are never doubled.

Words that end in *l* are handled differently in the United States and Britain. The American spelling convention follows the rules above for doubling the final consonant. The British tradition favours doubling the *l* before all endings except -*ize*, as in *totalize* Most Canadians follow the British convention: *dispel, dispelled, dispelling; equal, equalled, equalling; model, modelling; signal, signalled, signalling; total, totalled, totalling; travel, travelled, travelling*. Note that *l* is never doubled at the end of a syllable where the vowel sound is written as two letters: *appealing,* not *appealling.*

See also -C, -CK-; FULFIL; -L-, -LL-; SPELLING, CANADIAN; TRANSFERABLE.

doubtful   see DUBIOUS

doubt if   see DOUBT WHETHER

doubtless   *Doubtless* is an adverb: 'Doubtless this was not the first time'. While dictionaries also list *doubtlessly*, the -*ly* form is much less common and is criticized by commentators.

> Haitians, Bosnians and Somalis would doubtless make the same observation.
> *Gazette* (Montreal) 31 Dec. 1993: B1

> It doubtlessly helped that after Larkin moved to Belfast, they always lived in different cities.
> *Calgary Herald* 30 Oct. 1993: C10

(This form is criticized; *doubtless* is recommended.)

doubt whether, doubt if, doubt that   A clause following the verb *doubt* may be introduced by *whether, if, that,* or no conjunction at all: 'I doubt he'll come'. All these constructions are accepted in Canadian English. Some commentators suggest that the conjunction *that* is appropriate only after a negative statement of doubt ('I don't doubt that . . .'; 'We never doubted that . . .'), but Canadian writers do not restrict its use in this way.

> But he doubted whether Imogen Hughes had ever shed a tear in her life.
> Constance Beresford-Howe *Night Studies* 1985: 10

> I now have so much work lined up that I doubt if I would have time to visit your showings. . . .
> J.E. Smyth et al. *The Law and Business Administration in Canada* 1987: 149

> Yet his mother never doubted that both her boys were stolen from her, Wayne as much as Charles, by the curse of her father's life.
> David Williams *Eye of the Father* 1985: 158

> Few doubt that the Meech Lake constitutional paralysis and the post-Meech malaise have adversely affected Canadian federalism.
> Alan Whitehorn *Canadian Socialism* 1992: 244

dove   see DIVED; PIGEON

downfall   *Downfall* usually refers to a sudden fall from prosperity, eminence, or success. It can also refer to the cause of this fall: 'Their downfall was a failure to plan for inflation'. *Downfall* should not, however, be used to refer to a minor drawback or shortcoming that does not lead to failure.

In business writing *downfall* has taken on a new sense synonymous with *downturn*: that is, a sudden drop in value or loss in earnings.

Walesa said the downfall of communism in eastern Europe last fall actually began in August 1980, when he and a government representative signed the Gdansk Accords.
Gazette (Montreal) 1 Sept. 1990: A8

Her downfall was her reluctance to become a Canadian. Quebec Culture Minister Marie Malavoy resigned Friday after admitting she had voted in several elections before obtaining her citizenship.
Calgary Herald 26 Nov. 1994: A8

But the innovative structure of this book is also its greatest downfall.
Calgary Herald 10 Dec. 2005: F5

(Here *shortcoming* would be better.)

downplay, play down   For reasons unknown, usage commentators are especially reluctant to approve of new compound words that begin with adverbs. *Ongoing, upcoming,* and *downplay* have all been disparaged by commentators. The *Globe and Mail Style Book* (1994) goes so far as to call *downplay* 'a non-word'. Other usage guides call it 'journalese'; all commentators recommend *play down* instead. However, *downplay*—which dates from the 1950s—is as widely used in Canadian academic prose as it is in newspaper and magazine writing; *play down* is used far less frequently.

A persisting tendency to downplay the division between usage and convention, as well as the pervasive trend to ignore distinctions among conventions, greatly weakens our understanding of the informal rules shaping the Canadian constitution.
Andrew Heard *Canadian Constitutional Conventions* 1991: 141–2

By ignoring or downplaying questions of domestic labour and the double day of labour, feminist groups seem to have fallen into the 'passive revolutionary' trap of being enticed by the state agenda much more readily than either neo-conservative or anti-feminist groups.
Carl J. Cuneo *Pay Equity* 1990: 150

The maximalist party leadership, downplaying the gravity of the disagreement, appointed a three-man commission. . . .
Canadian Journal of History 14.1 (1989): 24

Because the authority they possessed in the twentieth-century university would, it seemed, be exercised in the classroom, the growing tendency of research-minded scholars to play down the importance of the teaching role was anathema to them.
Queen's Quarterly 95.3 (1988): 556

down style   see CAPITAL LETTERS

Down syndrome, Down's syndrome
Either *Down syndrome* or *Down's syndrome* may be used to refer to the medical condition named after an English physician, J.L.H. Down. (It is caused by a chromosomal abnormality and distinguished by varying degrees of mental disability and a characteristic physical appearance.) The spelling *Down syndrome* is now the more popular choice. Note that the word *syndrome* should not be capitalized. *Mongolism*, a term formerly applied to this condition, is now considered offensive.

When I was five years old we didn't know what DNA did, how many chromosomes humans have, what causes the differences in males and females, or the cause of Down's syndrome.
Queen's Quarterly 93.1 (1986): 86–7

Power, who has Down syndrome, has been swimming since she was 14 and is accomplished, having won numerous ribbons and medals.
Telegram (St. John's) 1 May 2006: A1

Over the years identification of other genetic disorders will surely follow—hemophilia perhaps, or Downs syndrome, or phenylketonuria, or diabetes mellitus.
Gazette (Montreal) 20 April 1990: B2

(Either *Down's* or *Down* would be correct.)

See also DISABILITIES.

downward(s)   see -WARD(S)

Dr.   see DOCTOR; PSYCHOLOGIST, PSYCHIATRIST

draft, draught   Both spellings are pronounced the same way. *Draft* is the more common spelling in Canadian writing for a current of air, beer on tap, or the depth of water needed to float a boat; *draught*, the usual British spelling, is an accepted alternative. *Draft* is the only spelling for a rough version of a document, a written order for payment of funds by a bank, or military conscription.

drama   Canadians and Americans pronounce *drama* either *DRAM uh* or *DRAW muh*; the British say *DRAW muh*.

drank   see DRINK

draught   see DRAFT

dreadful   see AWFUL

dreamt   see -T, -ED

drier   see DRYER

drink, drank, drunk, drunken   In Standard English, the past tense of *drink* is *drank* and the past participle (used after *have*) is *drunk*. Some commentators accept *have drank* in informal speech, but most consider it uneducated.

As adjectives, *drunk* and *drunken* both mean intoxicated. Traditionally, *drunk* was used after a verb such as 'seem' or 'be' ('They were drunk before midnight') and *drunken* before a noun ('Two drunken party-goers passed out on the couch'). Now, however, in Canadian English, both *drunk* and *drunken* are used attributively (i.e., before nouns), and a distinction of sense has developed: *drunken* typically means prone to drinking or habitually intoxicated, while *drunk* simply means inebriated. When *drunken* describes a situation rather than a person, it may imply licentiousness: 'a drunken brawl', 'a drunken encounter'. The informal name for the offence of operating a motor vehicle under the influence of alcohol is *drunk driving* in Canada and the United States, *drink-driving* in Britain.

For one thing, Descartes assures us, his altered state was not the result of inebriation: he had not drunk wine for three months before.
Canadian Journal of Philosophy 19 (1989): 214

Heath said if not for a water-borne bacterium that brings on an ailment known as 'beaver fever', he might have drank some water from side creeks during the first few days of the expedition.
Vancouver Sun 14 Sept. 1990: B1

(The more widely accepted past participle is *drunk*.)

An insane or drunk person is liable for a reasonable price for the necessary goods.
J.E. Smyth et al. *The Law and Business Administration in Canada* 1987: 178

'The Collector of Customs at Winnipeg is a drunken reprobate.'
Pierre Berton *The Promised Land* 1984: 28

(Here *drunken* means habitually intoxicated.)

drought, drouth   A *drought* is a dry spell or, figuratively, a prolonged lack of anything. *Drouth* is an alternative spelling, rare in Canada.

Deliveries to Vancouver are running only slightly ahead of last year, when drought cut grain exports by 30 per cent.
Vancouver Sun 14 Feb. 1990: D10

Skywatchers then suffered a comet drought until 1947, when a fairly impressive celestial visitor navigated the postwar skies.
Terence Dickinson *Halley's Comet* 1985: 36

drunk, drunken   see DRINK

dryer, drier, driest   The noun *dryer,* as in 'clothes dryer', can also be spelled *drier,* but rarely is in Canadian English.

The usual comparative and superlative forms of the adjective *dry* are *drier* and *driest. Dryer* and *dryest* also occur in published Canadian writing, but not all dictionaries record these alternative spellings.

dual, duel   *Dual,* meaning double or two-fold, is sometimes misspelled *duel.* A *duel* is a formal fight arranged between two contestants, or, loosely, any contest involving two groups.

This article has a dual purpose: to present and analyze the legal repercussions of the patient's death, and then to consider the viability of a defence of medical necessity if the case had gone to trial.
Health Law Journal 10 (2002): 1

They took part in a garrison parade, an officer's duel and battles.
Whig-Standard (Kingston) 30 June 2003

The tight trio of guitarist Mike Stand, bassist Jon Taschuk and drummer Bobby James fronted by the duel-engine fury of singer/rappers White and Brian Howes are frequently compared to Fishbone and the Red Hot Chili Peppers.
Toronto Star 5 Oct. 1995: G10

(The correct spelling is *dual-engine*.)

dubious, doubtful   Someone can be either *dubious* or *doubtful* about future prospects. Something can be of *dubious* or *doubtful* value. Both words mean uncertain, skeptical, or questionable, and in these contexts there is little to choose between them. However, 'a *doubtful* starter' inspires uncertainty, while 'a *dubious* character' arouses suspicion and unease. When *dubious* is used attributively (directly before a noun) it often means shady or suspect, a meaning not shared by *doubtful*.

Newspaper editors were plainly dubious about the new comet, having been burned by heavily promoting Kohoutek as 'The Comet of the Century,' then watching as it barely gained naked-eye visibility.
Terence Dickinson *Halley's Comet* 1985: 38

It is doubtful whether the market system ever worked in the automatic, self-regulating way in which the classical economists conceived of it.
Irving M. Zeitlin and Robert J. Brym *The Social Condition of Humanity* 1991: 77

Racial statistics, so-called, have proven to be of little or doubtful significance and value to sociologists.
Richard Davies and Glen Kirkland, eds. *Dimensions* 1986: 123

But driving it [the rate of inflation] to zero has dubious value and enormous economic and human costs.
Gazette (Montreal) 24 July 1993: B5

The dubious bookshops of London offer the strangest assortment, to suit as many tastes as possible.
Robertson Davies *A Voice from the Attic* 1960: 277

dud   see COLLOQUIAL

duel   see DUAL

due to   According to *Webster's Dictionary of English Usage*, 'Due to has entered the folklore of usage.' At issue is whether *due to* is a compound preposition like *because of* and *on account of*, and thus whether it is acceptable in sentences such as 'Due to bad weather, the road was closed'. Certainly this is just how the phrase is often used by educated Canadian, American, and British writers. Nevertheless, this use is criticized, which leaves many writers under a vague pall of unease about the phrase.

Commentators who criticize the prepositional use of *due to* claim that *due* is an adjective, meaning 'attributable', and *to* is the preposition. According to this view, *due to* should not be used in any sentence where 'attributable to' wouldn't also be possible. Thus 'Due to [attributable to] bad weather, the road was closed' is unacceptable, while 'The closure of the road was due to [attributable to] bad weather' is acceptable. The traditional advice is that *due to* is acceptable after a copula verb (*is*, *seems*, *appears to be*, etc.), which links *due* to a particular noun (here, 'closure'), but not acceptable at the beginning of a sentence where it functions as a preposition heading an adverb phrase that modifies the whole sentence.

Of course it is always possible to substitute *because of* or *on account of* for the disputed prepositional use of *due to*. On the other hand, you may well feel justified in ignoring a prescription that is clearly at odds with contemporary educated usage.

His hero's plight is due to the ways of the world, which, Leacock implies, nothing can ever change.
Miriam Waddington *Apartment Seven* 1989: 68

(The use of *due to* after the verb *to be* is undisputed.)

Due to the uncertain distance of that close ap-

proach, the gravitational influence on Halley's orbit is impossible to pin down, making it difficult to determine its precise orbit before 1404 B.C.
Terence Dickinson *Halley's Comet* 1985: 8

(Some commentators disapprove of this prepositional use of *due to*.)

On 24 February, at the end of a meeting of the Arab Cooperation Council, Iraq's president predicted that, due to the decline of Soviet power, the US would exercise hegemonic power in the Middle East for five years.
Queen's Quarterly 97 (1990): 532

(Some commentators disapprove of this prepositional use of *due to*.)

due to the fact that   see WORDINESS

duly   see -E

dumb   see DISABLED

durum, Durham   *Durum* as the name for a kind of wheat is often misspelled *Durham*. This wheat was not named after Lord Durham, who was briefly governor general of Canada, but comes from the Latin word *durus*, 'hard'. Durum is a hard wheat typically used to make pasta.

Returns on amber durum will rise by 9 per cent to $204 a tonne and feed oats will rise by 7 per cent to $107 a tonne.
Globe and Mail (Toronto) 12 Jan. 1985: B4

He has learned his Durham from his barley and can tread conversationally into the realms of

swathing, quotas and fertilizers.
Globe and Mail (Toronto) 26 Aug. 1985: P4

(The correct spelling is *durum*.)

Dutch oven   see CAPITAL LETTERS

duty   see TAX

dwarf   see -F, -V-

dye, dyed, dyeing   The past and present participles of the verb *dye*, meaning to colour or stain, are *dyed* and *dyeing*. *Dyeing* is often misspelled *dying*—which is the present participle of the verb to *die*. And *dyed* is often misspelled *died* in the expression *dyed-in-the-wool*.

Everything it sells in its store is made in Quebec, from the dyeing of the fabric to the cutting and sewing.
Edmonton Journal 25 April 2006: F1

Singer Emmylou Harris says she has no intention of dying her grey hair.
Daily News (Halifax) 17 Feb. 1992: 18

(The correct spelling is *dyeing*.)

It is important to know that she considers herself a dyed-in-the-wool feminist.
Ottawa Citizen 26 Jan. 1992: B3

If you're a died-in-the-wool baseball fan, you can, if you work hard enough, see a game in a different park in a different area of Florida every day.
Gazette (Montreal) 8 Feb. 1992: I5

(The correct spelling is *dyed-in-the-wool*.)

E

e- see COMPUTER TERMS; E-MAIL

-e Usually words that end with a silent *e* drop it when endings beginning with a vowel or *y* are added (*craze, crazy; extreme, extremism; note, notable*) and retain it when endings beginning with a consonant are added: *amazement, extremely, whiteness*. Exceptions:

- keep the *e*: *acreage, mileage*
- drop the *e*: *argument, awful, duly, ninth, truly, wholly*
- Sometimes the *e* is retained to avoid confusion with other words: *dyeing* (to colour, as opposed to *dying*), *lineage* (line of descent, one's family tree, as opposed to *linage*, number of lines), and *singeing* (scorching, as opposed to *singing*).
- Words ending in *-ce* and *-ge* retain the *e* before endings beginning with *a* and *o* to indicate that the consonants are 'soft' (pronounced like *s* and *j*): *peaceable, courageous*.
- If the word ends in *-oe*, the *e* is kept before *-ing*: *canoeing, hoeing, shoeing*.
- If the word ends in *-dge*, Canadian writers vary in their decision to drop the *e*; most drop it (as do Americans) in *judgment* but keep it in *acknowledgement*. Usage with *abridg(e)ment* is mixed.
- In words where Canadians and Americans tend to drop the silent *e* (*aging, livable, lovable*), the British tend to retain it (*ageing, liveable, loveable*). Canadians are evenly divided on keeping the *e* in *likeable/likable*.
- Sometimes adjectives created by adding a *-y* to a noun retain the final *-e*: *homey, pricey*.

See also -ABLE, -(E)ABLE; DYE; -Y,-EY.

-(e)able see -ABLE

each When *each* is the subject of the sentence, it is followed by a singular verb: 'Each is sure she is right'. When *each* acts as an adjective modifying a singular noun subject, the singular verb form is also used: 'Each woman is sure she is right'. Most grammarians insist that when *each* is followed by a phrase beginning with *of*, the verb should remain singular; 'Each of the women is (*not* are) responsible for setting up her own computer'.

Though grammatically *each* is singular, the sense it conveys is often plural, which leads writers to use the plural forms *they* and *their* after it: 'Each brings a lunch and they share'; 'Each has their own strengths'. This usage is very common, but some commentators consider it informal. For more discussion of this point, see EVERYONE.

When *each* acts as an adjective modifying a plural subject, a plural verb always follows: 'They each have their own clientele'. Once disputed, this usage is no longer contentious.

> Each of the three women in *Dawn* has a 'philosophy,' and Angela's is a pure belief in individual immortality.
> Margaret Atwood *Second Words* 1982: 42

(Here the subject *each* correctly takes the singular verb *has* even though a plural noun phrase, *three women*, intervenes.)

See also AGREEMENT, GRAMMATICAL; BETWEEN EACH; EACH AND EVERY; EACH OTHER; EVERYONE.

each and every Many language commentators have warned that *each and every* is both redundant and a cliché. Even so, many good writers use the phrase to focus a sentence, improve its rhythm, or add emphasis.

> We could go into considerable detail tracking the fortunes of each and every group.
> Neil Nevitte and Roger Gibbins *New Elites in Old States* 1990: 141

(Here *each and every* emphasizes the difficulty of the task.)

Language, then, is the vehicle by which the accumulated wisdom and experience of numerous generations is transmitted to each and every one of us.
William Norton *Human Geography* 1992: 14

We learned later that John McAllister was always loaded, since he drank about a half gallon of home-brew each and every day.
Max Braithwaite *The Night We Stole the Mountie's Car* 1971: 55

each other, one another   An old rule states that *each other* refers only to two people, while *one another* refers to three or more. There seems to be little historical precedent or support in modern usage for this rule; writers use either phrase for any number of people.

The possessive form is *each other's*, not *each others'*: 'They read each other's books'.

Several guides warn against using either phrase as the subject of an embedded clause: 'We know what each other likes in a work of art'. This should be rephrased as 'We each know what the other likes in a work of art'.

eager   see ANXIOUS

Early Modern English   see OLD ENGLISH

early on   The phrase *early on* has been criticized as redundant. Although *early* alone can sometimes be substituted for it, *early on* usually conveys a different meaning: at an early stage. Canadian writers use the phrase freely in all kinds of writing.

Early on became common in Britain after the First World War and was criticized mainly by American authorities, but it is now fully established in Canada, Britain, and the United States.

Early on, when President Kennedy had asked the Canadian leader's advice, Pearson had answered that the right American policy would be to get out [of Vietnam] if they could, but to do it while saving face.
Queen's Quarterly 95.1 (1985): 111

(Here *early* could not be substituted for *early on*.)

That was early on, when they were having a good time.
Margaret Atwood *Life Before Man* 1979: 26

(Here too, *early* could not be substituted for *early on*.)

He [B.H. Haggin] had discovered early on that much of the writing about music, performance and events differed from what he heard for himself or discovered by investigation.
Queen's Quarterly 94.3 (1987): 654

(Here *early on* conveys the sense that Haggin was at an early stage in his research.)

earth, planets   *Earth* may be capitalized when it refers to our planet, but the uncapitalized spelling is more common. The other seven planets in our solar system are named after Roman gods, and their names are always capitalized: *Mercury, Venus, Mars, Jupiter, Saturn, Uranus,* and *Neptune, (Pluto has been demoted from planetary status). Earth* should be capitalized for consistency when it appears with any of these names. Although some critics claim that it is unidiomatic and potentially ambiguous to drop *the* before the name of the planet, it is often done ('heaven on earth', 'where on earth'). The context makes it clear whether the reference is to the planet or to soil.

'You train constantly for months and suddenly you're up there above the Earth, seeing the most privileged, most exalted view any human being could hope for.'
Leader-Post (Regina) 27 Feb. 1988: B16

This time around, Halley will be greeted by five spacecraft sent from Earth to view the spectacle close up.
Terence Dickinson *Halley's Comet* 1985: 2

. . . it is hard to imagine any country on earth investing so much of its per capita wealth and energy on the business of governance.
Calgary Herald 29 Dec. 1993: A4

earthen, earthy, earthly   *Earthen* means made of earth or baked clay. *Earthy* describes anything with the characteristics of earth, such as its colour or smell. *Earthy* also describes people, attitudes, etc., that are unpretentious, down to earth, sensuous, or coarse. *Earthly* is the opposite of *other-worldly*; it describes the material or worldly aspects of the human condition. *Earthly* also means 'practical' in some idiomatic expressions: 'Of what earthly good is that?'

> . . . the Peninsula People came here to bury their dead in earthen mounds which can still be seen today; one serpentine mound and eight oval ones.
> *Globe and Mail* (Toronto) 24 Aug. 1985: T2

> Earthy colours—greens, greys, browns—work best.
> *Gazette* (Montreal) 8 May 2005: B8

> 'I write very much from a vulnerable point of view,' says McLachlan, whose earthy humor . . . is so unlike the celestial waif imagery of her songs.
> *Toronto Star* 25 Nov. 1993: WO10

> It was good to take the focus away from the earthly pressures for a while and have time to reflect on spiritual values.
> *Mennonite Brethren Herald* 4 April 1986: 9

earth tremor   see TREMOR

east, west, north, south   Generally, the names of the compass points (*east*, *west*, *north*, *south*), and their derivative adjectives (*northern*, *northward*, *northerly*, *northwest*, etc.), are not capitalized: 'a garden to the east of the house', 'a southern exposure'. They are, however, capitalized in place names, including the informal names of districts: 'the South Shore', 'the Eastern Townships', 'the West End'. They should not be capitalized in mere descriptions of geographic areas: 'fisheries off the south shore', 'species found in eastern North America'. Quite often it is a moot point whether an area is named or merely described, and in these cases capitalization varies.

> Known for her abrasive manner and sharp tongue, she got into vicious battles with the Cree of Northern Quebec over the James Bay hydroelectric projects.
> *Ottawa Citizen* 15 Dec. 1993: A12

> She got into battles with the Cree of northern Quebec over the James Bay hydroelectric projects.
> *Vancouver Sun* 15 Dec. 1993: A8

> The North Toronto couple said they are not aware of any payments made to Morgan's natural mother.
> *Toronto Star* 9 Dec. 1993: A1

> Workers also demonstrated outside Hydro's north Toronto service centre on MacPherson Ave.
> *Toronto Star* 5 Nov. 1993: A2

Canadians usually capitalize '(down) East', '(out) West', and '(up) North', as regions of the country. To western Canadians *east* and *eastern* refer to anything east of the border of Manitoba, but to inhabitants of Ontario and Quebec *east* and *eastern* refer only to the provinces east of Quebec. Unlike the United States, Canada has no region that is routinely called 'the South'. The majority of Canadians live on the southern border of the country, but they do not think of themselves as living in the south because the stereotype of Canada subsumes all of it into the 'True North'. However, those who live in northern Canada refer to the more populated southern regions of the country as 'the South'.

The authors of *Editing Canadian English* recommend capitalizing *Eastern* and *Western* when *Canadian* is omitted, as in 'Eastern fisheries' and 'the Western provinces', while the *Canadian Press Stylebook* recommends *eastern* and *western*. Both styles are common and accepted.

See also CAPITAL LETTERS; NORTHERLY.

eastbound   see -BOUND

East Indian   see INDIAN

easy   see ADJECTIVES AND ADVERBS; ADVERBS WITHOUT -LY

eatable   see EDIBLE

eavesdrop   see DOUBLING THE FINAL CONSONANT

e-book, **eBusiness**, **e-business**, **e-commerce**
see COMPUTER TERMS

echoes   see -OS, -OES

eclectic   *Eclectic*, which means derived from various sources, can have negative, neutral, or positive connotations. It can mean haphazard, diverse, or carefully selected, depending on the context.

> Hawks players used to laugh when they saw Hasek walking around the Stadium dressing room in black socks and white tennis shoes. Eclectic outfits of this nature made the Czech a more amazing sight off the ice than on during his years in Chicago.
> *Toronto Star* 20 Dec. 1993: D2

(Here *eclectic* has negative connotations.)

> From glitz to funk, Queen Street West (University to Bathurst, and slowly spreading) is an eclectic blend of artists, literati, and progressive music clubs.
> Alan Tucker, ed. *The Penguin Guide to Canada* 1991: 365

(Here *eclectic* is neutral.)

> Because his approach to this question has been thoroughly eclectic, his vision is far wider than others in this group.
> Wallace Clement and Glen Williams, eds. *The New Canadian Political Economy* 1989: 127

(Here *eclectic* is positive.)

economic, economical   Generally *economic* means having to do with the economy, or economics, or viability in business terms, while *economical* means thrifty, not wasteful.

The *e* in *economic(al)* is pronounced as in either *bet* or *beet*.

> It is stifling economic growth with too much regulation, he said.
> *Daily News* (Halifax) 1 July 1993: 14

> 'We've got new technology like 3-D seismic and horizontal drilling that's made the Western Sedimentary Basin economic again.'
> *Calgary Herald* 26 Dec. 1993: C14

> It's easier and more economical to perfect one recipe and make multiple batches than it is to prepare half a dozen different items.
> *Calgary Herald* 10 Nov. 1993: B8

> 'Audio-visual documents have a social, political, economical, cultural and artistic value'.
> *Gazette* (Montreal) 21 Dec. 1993: A4

(Here *economic* is required.)

economize   see -IZE, -ISE, -YZE, -YSE

-ed   *Aged, beloved, blessed, cursed, dogged,* and *learned* each have two spoken variants; unfortunately, there is no general rule governing which variant is used in which situation.

The adjective *aged* is pronounced with two syllables when it modifies a human subject: 'an ag*ed* man'. When it is used to refer to something subjected to aging, such as cheese or brandy, it is pronounced as one syllable. The past participle and past tense of the verb are also monosyllabic: 'only for those *aged* 65 and over'; 'It *aged* him'.

The adjective *learned* has two syllables when it refers to someone or something distinguished by or associated with learning: 'a learn*ed* judge'; 'a learn*ed* journal'. When it means simply that something has been learned, it is pronounced with one syllable: 'a *learned* habit'.

Dogged is pronounced with two syllables when an adjective ('dogg*ed* determination'), and with one when a verb ('*dogged* by reporters').

Blessed and *cursed* are usually pronounced as two syllables before a noun ('the bless*ed* martyrs', 'curs*ed* luck'), and as one syllable after a linking verb ('She was *blessed*'; 'They were *cursed*'), but this is by no means a rule. The pronunciations of *blessed* and *cursed* are quite variable. The pronunciation of *beloved* is similar: it usually has three syllables before a noun and two after a linking verb.

Sometimes in poetry an accent is used to ensure that an *-ed* is pronounced as a separate syllable: 'O curs*éd* (*or* curs*èd*) spite'.

See also DIACRITICAL MARKS, DIAERESIS; -T, -ED.

edible, eatable   The adjectives *edible* and *eatable* are interchangeable, although several commentators have tried to distinguish them. They claim that *eatable* refers to food that is reasonably tasty and not spoiled, while *edible* distinguishes something that is not poisonous from something that is. Canadians use *edible* in all senses and *eatable* only rarely. The antonyms are *inedible* and *uneatable*.

The food . . . is barely edible. Lemongrass souffle tarts look like quiche but taste like lemon chiffon pie.
Toronto Star 9 Nov. 2002: J18

Is there any way of telling if the fish are edible by examining them?
Canadian Consumer Jan. 1985: 8

Edinburgh   see -BURGH, -BURG, -BOROUGH, -BORO

Edmontonian   see NAMES OF RESIDENTS OF CITIES AND PROVINCES

educable, [educatable]   see -ABLE, -(AT)ABLE

educationist, educationalist, educator
An *educationist* or *educationalist* is a specialist in the theory and methods of education.

An *educator* is a teacher, an administrator in the field of education, or an educationist. Sometimes those trained to work with very young children are called 'early childhood educators'.

> Other recipients [of the Saskatchewan Award of Merit] are . . . Frederick Gathercole, a retired educationist and community leader. . . .
> *Globe and Mail* (Toronto) 21 Nov. 1985: A3

> Gerald Graham . . . hailed the advent of a principal 'who is not only an administrator but a superb scholar—who is incapable of talking the jargon of the educationalist'. . . .
> Frederick Gibson *Queen's University* 2 (1983): 306

> The number of educators—teachers and administrative staff—rose by almost 20 per cent over that period to about 333,000. . . .
> *Calgary Herald* 20 Dec. 1994: A3

> The course was developed by Donna Wood, an early childhood educator with years of experience working in nursery schools.
> *Globe and Mail* (Toronto) 4 April 1985: CL4

effect   see AFFECT

effective, efficient, (in)effectual, efficacious   *Effective* describes something or someone that has achieved, or will achieve, a goal or purpose: 'That was an effective treatment'; 'She is an effective team leader'. *Effective* also means

taking effect or coming into operation: 'The new law is effective immediately'.

While *effective* emphasizes ends, *efficient* considers the means as well, taking into account the amount of time, effort, money, and resources expended. 'Energy-efficient' and 'fuel-efficient' vehicles and appliances do the job they are meant to do with reduced impact on the pocketbook and the planet. (The term *cost-efficient* would make sense to describe business strategies that will not deplete the company coffers; nevertheless, the term *cost-effective* is much more common.)

Effectual is a synonym of *effective* that in law means valid or binding: 'The agreement was effectual'. While *effectual* is rarely used of people, its opposite, *ineffectual,* often describes people with a lamentable inability to have an impact on anything: 'Her campaign was as ineffectual as she was'.

Efficacious, which means certain to produce the desired result, usually describes medicine or treatments: 'a safe and efficacious treatment'.

> Given that the provision of effective and cost-effective care for patients with heart failure presents a difficult challenge for any health care system, this study has important implications.
> *Canadian Medical Association Journal* 172.2 (2005): 207

> . . . the developer will install a co-generation system, a highly efficient way of producing both heat and electric power simultaneously.
> *National Post* (Toronto) 22 June 2006: PH1

> The currently available vaccines against hepatitis A and hepatitis B are highly efficacious and safe.
> *Journal of Travel Medicine* 8 (2001): S3

See also AFFECT, EFFECT.

effete   *Effete*, pronounced *i* FEET, was first used in the seventeenth century to mean physically depleted and incapable of reproducing, usually in reference to domestic animals. By the beginning of nineteenth century the word was also being applied to people and systems that were intellectually or morally spent. More recently the word has taken on connotations of weakness, decadence, effeminacy, and affectation, and the original meaning of exhaustion has all but disappeared. Although several commentators have objected to this 'semantic drift', the new meaning is firmly established in Canadian usage and is now listed in most dictionaries.

> The image of the Bushman . . . lawless, unwashed and above all virile, composing four-line ballad verses with irrepressible gusto, is set up against a pale straw-man of a nail-gnawing Canadian intellectual, smothered in Englishness, bleating and effete.
> Margaret Atwood *Second Words* 1982: 31

> It set the Prime Minister apart from the effete Easterners who had no conception of pioneer prairie life.
> Pierre Berton *The Promised Land* 1984: 259

> While effete Vancouverites lounge around their upscale billiard-and-cappuccino clubs decadently discussing the works of Euripides, Polyclitus and Kim Campbell, we in the rest of the country spend the winter months engaging in less affected discourse.
> *Vancouver Sun* 5 Feb. 1994: D3

efficacious see EFFECTIVE

effrontery see AFFRONT

e.g. see I.E.

egis see AEGIS

egotist, egoist, ego(t)ism, egocentric, egomaniac The traditional distinction characterizes an *egotist* as conceited and boastful and an *egoist* as self-centred but not necessarily attention-seeking. In Canadian usage, *egoism* and its variants are quite uncommon, and *egotism* often refers to self-interest without boastfulness. *Egocentric* means self-centred and often unaware of or indifferent to the needs of others. An *egomaniac* is exceptionally self-centred and boastful.

> Aw, America, smarten up. You are a world-class egotist. You almost seem to savor slighting your neighbors. . . .
> *Toronto Star* 5 Nov. 1987: A29

> 'I'm the classic egoist, I do this for myself. . . . My motivation has always been self-imposed.'
> *Ottawa Citizen* 27 Nov. 1991: E7

> Blondie, said McLuhan, 'is efficiently masculine, purposive, egotistical and hard, just as Dagwood is ineffectually feminine, altruistic and sensitive.'
> *Vancouver Sun* 12 April 1994: A11

(Blondie is not given to bragging; here *egotistical* is used as a synonym of *egoistic*.)

> We are the egocentric species. We spend most of our time thinking about ourselves—one generation of time, that's all.
> *Vancouver Sun* 7 April 1994: A15

> She was a great medical reformer, an excellent surgeon and something of a rebel, but no egomaniac.
> *Globe and Mail* (Toronto) 2 Nov. 1985: A7

egregious In the sixteenth and seventeenth centuries, *egregious* (pronounced *e GREE juss*) often meant prominent or outstanding. The positive connotations were borrowed from Latin. 'Illustrious' is the translation of Latin *egregius*, formed from *e*, 'out of' and *grex*, 'the herd'. The English word now, however, invariably means outrageous or outstanding in a bad way: 'egregious blunder', 'egregious liar'.

> What do Canadians expect from a major change of government? The correction of outstanding abuses, no doubt, such as the total indulgence of patronage and the egregious waste of taxpayers' money on failing public projects.
> *Globe and Mail* (Toronto) 4 Sept. 1985: P6

> Lunch at the National Arts Centre consisted of egregious sandwiches.
> *Globe and Mail* (Toronto) 28 March 1985: CL2

(They were remarkably bad.)

> 'This is just egregious and offensive,' he says.
> *National Post* (Toronto) 5 July 2002: DO2.

eh? The informal question word *eh* ('You're back Wednesday, eh?') is not unique to Canadian English, but Canadians seem to use it more widely and more often than other English-speakers. *Eh?* can be the equivalent of 'What did you say?', 'Isn't that so?', or 'Are you with me so far?'.

Far from being ashamed of a verbal tic that speakers of other varieties of English have mocked, Canadians have embraced *eh* and use it playfully and punningly, sometimes as shorthand for 'Canadian':

Thanks a latte! (a note affixed to the tip jar in a cappuccino bar)
Heading South, Eh? (a government pamphlet for Canadians wintering in Florida)
Sir John, Eh? (a dramatic biography of Sir John A. Macdonald)

It was intriguing that many tourists who understand formal English will be completely thrown by an English-speaking Canadian's expression. Thus, Rule 1 became: 'Speak slowly and do not use idioms. It is also well to avoid the Canadian "eh?"' *Vancouver Sun* 22 Dec. 1994: A17

At the metaphorical border of Customs and Immigration at Toronto International Airport I was startled to hear an immigration official say, upon checking my passport, 'Vindicated at last, eh?' (The up-turned 'eh' is a species of linguistic dim-witticism to which Canadians are addicted.) Quentin Crisp and John Hofsess *Manners from Heaven: A Divine Guide to Good Behaviour* 1984: n.p.

EI   see POGEY

-ei-   see -IE-

Eire   see IRELAND

either . . . or, neither . . . nor   The first vowel in *either* is pronounced like the vowel in *eel* by most Canadians, but like *eye* by a sizeable minority; many use both pronunciations. The former is more common in the United States, the latter in Great Britain.

Either can be an adjective ('either way', 'either system'), a pronoun ('either will do'), or, in combination with *or*, a conjunction ('Either I'll come myself or I'll send someone else.') When there are more than two alternatives, the adjective or pronoun form of *either* changes to *any*: 'Either of the older two children could help; in fact, any of the kids could do it'. This has led to the argument that *either* should never be used in situations where there are more than two

alternatives. However, when *either . . . or* is used as a conjunction, there are often more than two alternatives: 'Either John, Martha, or David will come to the meeting'. Here changing *either* to *any* also changes the meaning: 'Any of John, Martha, or David will come . . .'. This sentence, unlike the previous one, permits the possibility that one, two, or all three of those named could turn up at the meeting. The previous sentence indicates that only one person will come. Thus the use of *either . . . or* with more than two alternatives is defensible.

In formal writing, care should be taken to observe the rules of grammatical agreement with *either*. The pronoun *either* is singular and takes a singular verb: 'Either is fine with me'. When *of* and a plural noun follow *either*, a plural verb is often used: 'Are either of the applicants here yet?' Nonetheless, in writing *either* should be treated as singular: 'Is either of the applicants here yet?'

Either . . . or is a disjunctive conjunction, which means that the elements it links are considered separately. The formal convention for verb agreement with subjects linked by *either . . . or* is that the verb should agree in person and number with the nearer subject: 'Either several or just one is chosen' *or* 'Either just one or several are chosen'. Since these grammatically correct constructions can sound quite stilted, you may want to avoid them altogether by splitting such sentences into two clauses: 'Either Elizabeth is coming tonight or I am'.

As a point of style in written English, the elements that follow *either* and *or* should be grammatically parallel: for example, 'Put it either on the desk or on the chair' or 'Put it on either the desk or the chair', but *not* 'Put it either on the desk or the chair'. All the comments made with respect to *either . . . or* also apply to *neither . . . nor*.

Furthermore, the independence of the judiciary has to be protected from attempts by either the legislature, the executive, or private parties to direct the outcome of the case.
Andrew Heard *Canadian Constitutional Conventions* 1991: 120

(This is an example of the accepted use of *either* to introduce three alternatives.)

They were interviewed either in person, through focus groups or by telephone.
Rites March 1990: 5

(This is an example of the accepted use of *either* to introduce three alternatives.)

Either additional time to compute the relationship between the principal axis and the XYZ axes or additional time to identify a foreshortened principal axis are plausible accounts of the effect we obtained in Experiment 2.
Canadian Journal of Psychology 44 (1990): 382

(For all their complexity, the two subjects linked by *either . . . or* are both singular. To agree with the nearer subject—'time to identify . . .'—the verb *are* should be replaced by the singular *is*, followed by '*a plausible account*'.)

Since your car is still running, you can shop around for the best price and either have a rebuilt or used transmission installed.
Gazette (Montreal) 4 March 1989: F1

(Since *either* precedes a verb in the original sentence, one is led to expect another verb after *or*. Placing *either* after *have* and adding a second article—'*a used . . .*'—makes the second alternative grammatically parallel to the first: 'have *either* a rebuilt or *a* used transmission installed'.)

The NBA has mandatory counselling for players either convicted of drug offences or players who voluntarily come forward to seek treatment.
Gazette (Montreal) 4 March 1989: C2

(Stylistically, it would be better to place *either* before *players*: 'for *either* players convicted of drug offences or players who . . .'. Alternatively, the second *players* could be omitted.)

See also AGREEMENT, GRAMMATICAL; COMMA; NEITHER; PARALLELISM.

elder, eldest, older, oldest The use of the adjectives *elder* and *eldest* is now largely restricted to ranking the birth order of family members. *Elder* is used when speaking of the first-born of two children and *eldest* for the first-born of three or more children. Some usage commentators recommend *eldest* rather than *oldest* to refer to the first-born of three or more children, but Canadians use either word.

Older and *oldest* may be used of both people and things. *Older* and *younger* are ambiguous when applied to siblings: 'my older brother' may be older than me or older than another brother. *Elder* is never used to make comparisons with *than*, though it may be used with *of*: 'She is older than her brother'; 'She is the elder of two children'.

The noun *elders* refers to older people generally, to particular older people held in high esteem in a community, or to the lay officers of certain churches.

The Jiraneks' eldest of two sons, Martin, was selected by the Washington Capitals in the National Hockey League supplemental draft. . . .
Today's Skater 1991: 63

(The comparative adjective *elder* is used when referring to one of two children.)

Joan Sadleir, the oldest, born in 1932 and the best student among the three daughters . . . recalls: 'I was the only person who was allowed to go into the library at night.'
Jack Batten *Robinette* 1984: 153

Only the elders, traditional leaders of Chechen society, are holding them back from an all-against-all struggle with the Russians, they said.
Toronto Star 31 Dec. 1994: A2

elderly see SENION CITIZEN

e-learning see COMPUTER TERMS

electric, electrical see -IC, -ICAL

electrocution see BARBARISMS

electronic, electronic mail see COMPUTER TERMS; E-MAIL

elegy, eulogy An *elegy* is an expression of mourning for a person, a group, or a way of life that has passed; traditionally, it takes the form of a poem. A *eulogy* is a speech praising a person or action. A funeral oration, however sorrowful, is called a *eulogy* because it praises the deceased. *Eulogy* (pronounced *YOO luh jee*) is preceded by *a*, not *an*.

[The song] 'Men At The Cafe,' on Memory To Steel, is an elegy for the men killed in the Scotia Tower accident of 1987.
Toronto Star 13 Nov. 1994: C3

The final section [of the dance] is a lament, an elegy for people dead of AIDS.
Vancouver Sun 17 Nov. 1994: C1

In an impromptu eulogy, his brother is hard-pressed to rise above the usual graveside platitudes.
Gazette (Montreal) 13 May 2006: J5

'His is the temperament of the pioneer,' Sifton's own newspaper wrote in April, 1905, in a eulogy of the new minister.
Pierre Berton *The Promised Land* 1984: 206

(Here the *eulogy* is in praise of a living man.)

elemental, elementary Both words describe something fundamental: 'elemental *or* elementary foods', 'elemental *or* elementary rights'. However, only *elemental* suggests the uncontrollable power of nature: 'unleashing elemental forces'. Only *elementary* suggests simplicity, or self-evidence: 'elementary precautions'.

We used our first cold frame . . . to provide a transitional home for flat-grown seedlings on the way from the warm and windless environment of our kitchen to the elemental uncertainties of the open garden.
Harrowsmith Aug.–Sept. 1985: 86

The elementary truth that seems to elude the experts again and again . . . is that power is its own reward.
National Post (Toronto) 1 Dec. 2001: A16

elicit, extract, extort, illicit To *elicit* means to draw forth or bring out ('elicit sympathy'); to elicit information from someone implies questioning but no use of force. To *extract* a confession suggests that it was obtained with difficulty, perhaps through accusation, or interrogation, or even torture. To *extort* information or a response from someone implies the use of some form of threat. *Illicit*, the adjective meaning illegal or immoral ('illicit drugs', 'illicit sex') is occasionally confused with its homophone *elicit*.

Spear underlines that they never really know what's going to elicit laughs.
Gazette (Montreal) 13 June 2005: E1

Drapeau extracted an on-air promise from Gaucher that the cost of building the structure would not exceed the money being put up by the province of Quebec.
Globe and Mail (Toronto) 2 Feb. 1985: E6

Hope is Jean-Bertrand Aristide returning to Haiti with the consent of the military—albeit a consent extorted by the United States, which threatened invasion.
Gazette (Montreal) 30 Dec. 1994: B3

The conference is looking at 2008 as the goal for global eradication of elicit drugs.
Vancouver Sun 10 June 1998: A7

(*Illicit* is the word needed here.)

That illicited a comment from Crown counsel Ivan Fernandes to the effect that people in the vending machine business might not see it that way.
Whig-Standard (Kingston) 24 June 1991: 1

(*Elicited* is the word needed here.)

See also HOMOPHONE, HOMOGRAPH, HOMONYM; ILLEGAL, UNLAWFUL, ILLICIT.

elk see MOOSE

ellipsis, ellipses see PLURALS

ellipsis points Some writers use ellipsis points (. . .) humorously to mean 'and so on' or 'Need I say more?' Others use them to link sentences in a continuous stream. Such uses characterize informal writing. In formal and academic writing, ellipsis points are used only to indicate omissions of text within quotations.

Ever since she figured out how to hold a knife between her paws, we've been at her mercy. . .
Living with Bengals a personal weblog 1 Oct. 2005

(This use of ellipsis points is informal.)

See also QUOTATION, QUOTATION MARKS.

elude see ALLUDE

elusive, illusory, illusive   *Elusive* describes things which are difficult to grasp, are perpetually escaping, but actually do exist. *Illusory*, on the other hand, describes things that seem real, but are only illusions. *Illusive* is a rare variant of *illusory*; while it is correct, it tends to be confused with *elusive* and is best avoided.

> But she remains an elusive personality, holed up in her Los Angeles villa until it suits her to emerge. . . .
> *Whig-Standard* (Kingston) 20 Feb. 2002: 27

> Like the empire, the protagonist grasps at illusory riches, and finds that what once appeared solid simply dissolves in his hands and slips through his fingers.
> *Queen's Quarterly* 107.4 (2000): 520

(The riches are not merely difficult to grasp; they are an illusion.)

> And consensus seems as illusive as ever.
> *Queen's Quarterly* 110.4. (2003): ii

(*Elusive* is the word needed here.)

See also ALLUDE, ELUDE, ALLUSIVE, ELUSIVE; DELUSION, ILLUSION.

elves   see -F, -V-

e-mail, email, e-mail addresses   *E-mail* is spelled with or without a hyphen. Eventually, the hyphen will probably be dropped, but for now Canadians prefer it. It distinguishes the prefix meaning 'electronic' (*e-commerce*, *e-book*) from the much older Latin prefix meaning out or from (*emit*, send out; *emigrate*, move from). E-mail addresses are divided into two parts by an at-sign (@). The first part is the name or nickname usually of an individual (the user name); the second part (the domain name) identifies the server, i.e., the computer that sends and receives the individual's mail. The last element in a domain name, always preceded by a dot (.), is a code that places the server in a country (e.g., *.ca* for Canada, *.uk* for United Kingdom, *.au* for Australia) or a class (*.com*—commercial, *.edu*—educational, *.org*—organization). Dots may further subdivide domain names (gov.bc.ca), and either dots or underscores (_) may be included in a user name (Richard.Ford;

annie_tremblay). Note that the user name portion of an e-mail address is case sensitive. Its capitalization should be preserved, although many servers will successfully route mail whether or not this is done.

While commentators initially balked at the plural *e-mails*, meaning e-mail messages, and the verb to *e-mail*, both are now standard usage.

See also COMPUTER TERMS; FUNCTIONAL SHIFT.

embark, debark, disembark, emplane, deplane, entrain, detrain, embus, debus   To *embark*, from the French *embarquer*, originally meant to get on board a boat. Nowadays one can also *embark* on a train, plane, or bus. To *embark* also means to begin a voyage, literal or figurative; thus one can embark for Auckland or embark on a program of fiscal responsibility. The verb *embark* may also be used transitively to mean load or take on: 'The stevedores embarked the cargo'; 'The ship embarked passengers'.

Disembark and *debark* are synonyms, meaning to get off a ship or other public conveyance; *disembark* is more common.

In addition to the generic terms *embark* and *disembark*, parallel terms have arisen to refer to particular modes of transportation. Air travellers are offered assistance 'emplaning' and 'deplaning'. *Entrain* and *detrain* were familiar words during the Second World War, when troops were transported by train. *Embus* and *debus* are in common use in Britain, though not Canada or the United States. *Garner's Modern American Usage* has four words of advice: 'get on', 'get off'.

> Having established myself in my job and in my home, it was now time to embark on the grand plan.
> Max Braithwaite *The Night We Stole the Mountie's Car* 1971: 46

> The station is deserted as the train from which he has just disembarked vanishes in the distance.
> *Canadian Fiction Magazine* 63 (1988): 15

> But once I'd deplaned from the 'Red Eye,' I was able to head straight for the room Trophy Lodge had booked for me in one of Edmonton's finest hotels.
> *Up Here* Jan.–Feb. 1990: 54

By the time the Doukhobors entrained, the commissary cars were loaded with 1,700 two-pound loaves of bread, 1,700 pounds of baked beans . . . and 50 pounds of coffee.
Pierre Berton *The Promised Land* 1984: 76

emcee   see HOST

emend, emendation   see AMEND

Emergency Response Team   see SWAT TEAM

emigrant, immigrant, in-migrate, out-migrate, migrate, migrant   An *emigrant* and an *immigrant* can be the same person, depending on the perspective from which he or she is viewed: an *emigrant* is leaving one country and moving permanently to another, while an *immigrant* is arriving (as indicated by the Latin prefixes *e-*, 'out of', and *im-*, 'in'). Usually people are said to *emigrate from* and *immigrate to*, but this generalization is far from absolute. It is also possible to say that someone who left France for Canada emigrated *to* Canada or immigrated *from* France.

The verbs *in-migrate* and *out-migrate* describe movement from one area to another within the same country; these words are often used by demographers.

The verb *migrate* means to move from one place to another permanently or temporarily, and is often used to refer to the seasonal movements of animals.

The noun *migrant* often refers to people who move for economic reasons. In the United States, where many migrant agricultural workers are illegal immigrants, the term can have negative connotations. In Australia, however, *migrant* is a neutral synonym of *immigrant*.

In the early 1950s, the family had emigrated from Iran to start a carpet importation business in Montreal.
Saturday Night May 1986: 51

He emigrated to England in the sixties and shed his Marxist beliefs.
Canadian Journal of Sociology 14.2 (1989): 264

Before she married her banker suitor and immigrated to Canada, she was one of the first women graduates of Trinity College, Dublin. . . .
Saturday Night Jan. 1986: 24

Children of new immigrants who later become Canadian citizens also get their citizenship automatically, added Lee, who immigrated from Hong Kong to Canada with her family in 1974.
Edmonton Journal 13 May 2006: A6

An influx of new residents and a slowing of out-migration has increased Manitoba's population by 22,000 to about 1,050,000 in the past two years.
Globe and Mail (Toronto) 25 Jan. 1985: R5

But migrants who enter countries illegally to find work get no such special treatment.
Gazette (Montreal) 19 Nov. 1994: B3

See also ÉMIGRÉ.

émigré, exile, refugee, internally displaced person, expatriate   These words all refer to someone who has left his or her native land. *Émigré* often refers to a person who is forced to emigrate because of political activity; it is spelled with an accent over each *e*. The French feminine form *émigrée* is rarely found in English; it should be used only in references to women. An *exile* is someone who has been banished from or has felt compelled to leave his or her native land. A *refugee* is someone who takes refuge, usually in a foreign country, to escape danger or persecution. A distinction is sometimes made between *refugees*, who cross international borders, and *internally displaced persons (IDPs)*, who have been forced out of their homes but remain within the borders of their own country. The words *émigré* and *exile* have literary, diplomatic, and social connotations that are not shared by the more neutral terms *refugee* and *IDP*.

An *expatriate*—derived from the Latin *ex-*, meaning 'out of', and *patria*, 'native country'— is someone who willingly lives in a foreign country without giving up his or her original citizenship.

Ex-patriot, which would correctly refer to someone whose nationalist fervour has abated, is a fairly common misspelling of *expatriate*.

The latter is a work published pseudonymously in Paris (by a Russian émigré living in Istanbul). . . .
Globe and Mail (Toronto) 30 Nov. 1985: E2

And it weaves through the collection of characters 'dreamed' by a troubled Chilean emigree in Janet Hinton's . . . new play.
Edmonton Journal 11 Feb. 1995: F5

(In formal writing, *émigrée* should be written with accents.)

An exile from his native land, an escapee from a Siberian cell, expelled from Switzerland, imprisoned in France, this one-time royal aide and army officer had an international reputation. . . .
Pierre Berton *The Promised Land* 1984: 66

There is no electricity and little food, and the refugees of war are on the run.
CBC News [transcript] 30 Dec. 1994: n.p.

'. . . the pervasive presence of the national security apparatus inspires fear and apprehension among internally displaced persons and their host communities.'
Windsor Star 6 May 2006: D1

Duncan is an expatriate Scot who came to Canada for Expo 67 and never went home.
Gazette (Montreal) 20 Dec. 1994: D7

'It's a very nationalistic market, even when we sell [Canadian art] abroad, it's usually to a Canadian ex-patriot.'
Toronto Star 23 May 1993: G3

(The word required here is *expatriate*.)

See also CITIZEN; EMIGRANT.

eminent   see IMMANENT

emote   *Emote* is an early twentieth-century back-formation from the noun *emotion*; it means to show emotion, especially in acting or as in acting. Commentators warn that this word should not be used in formal prose, but its facetious connotations make such use unlikely.

Now, actors love to show off with hysterics, especially actors like Ellen Burstyn and Marsha Mason (the respective moms), who emote buckets all over their squeaky-clean living rooms.
Globe and Mail (Toronto) 9 Feb. 1985: E3

It would seem that having actors emote furiously behind frozen expressions just doesn't have the resonance it once did.
Toronto Star 2 July 1993: E10

See also BACK-FORMATION.

emotional, emotive   *Emotional* means having to do with the emotions ('emotional problems'), showing or arousing emotion ('an emotional scene'), or susceptible to emotion ('an emotional person'). *Emotive* is a more technical and less common adjective used to describe something that elicits or generates strong emotion: 'emotive language', 'an emotive issue'.

Here the student of Greek will be impressed by Shankman's analysis of the emotive power of Pope's translation, and the student of the eighteenth century may be amazed by the obvious modernity of Pope's technique of psychological portraiture.
Queen's Quarterly 92.2 (1985): 407

According to a poll of senior executives carried out for Report on Business Magazine, the issue of closer Canada–U.S. relations is not the vexed or emotive one it once was.
Globe and Mail (Toronto) 1 March 1985: 120

'I know we are going to have to deal with a huge emotional issue out there,' said the MLA who . . . will lead her team of five Tories through five weeks of public meetings across the province on the youth crime problem.
Calgary Herald 19 June 1994: A5

(Here *emotive* would also be appropriate.)

'We are supposed to be the emotive, irrational founding nation. English Canada is supposed to be the rational one,' says David Cliche, a member of the Parti Quebecois.
Calgary Herald 8 June 1994: A5

(A better choice here would be *emotional*: Quebecers are supposed to feel, rather than elicit, emotion.)

empathy, sympathy, empathetic, empathic   In general usage, *empathy* is the capacity to enter imaginatively into another person's experience, while *sympathy* is a feeling of compassion or like-mindedness. *Empathy* was coined early in the twentieth century as a translation of the German word *Einfühlung* (a technical term in aesthetics). In this now rare sense, *empathy* is the ability to project oneself emotionally into a work of art in order to discover its meaning. The original adjective form of *empathy* was *empathic*, but now *empathetic*, which parallels *sympathetic*, is far more common. Both forms are accepted.

> 'I implore parents and teachers to teach ethnic and racial tolerance,' he said. 'Empathy needs to be cultivated.'
> *Daily News* (Halifax) 29 June 1994: 31

> There is intimacy and a keen empathy among officers when one of their own comes in harm's way.
> *Toronto Star* 20 June 1994: A7

> You cannot, no matter how much sympathy you have for the parties, condone the taking of a life.
> *CTV News* [transcript] 24 Dec. 1994: n.p.

> Anyway, in the last few days there's been a subtle but perceptible shift in public sympathy toward the owners and away from the players, regardless of the sport.
> *Toronto Star* 26 Sept. 1994: E1

> One hopes 'the black experimentress' will turn her attention to other subjects and leave the biography of Canadian poets to more empathetic hands.
> *Ottawa Citizen* 23 Oct. 1994: B3

emplane   see EMBARK

employment equity   see EQUALITY

emulate   In current English, to *emulate* usually means to imitate zealously, to hold up as a model for oneself. But an earlier meaning of the word is still used by some writers: to imitate in order to equal or outdo.

In computer jargon, software or hardware designed to accommodate or reproduce the action or function of a competitor's product is said to *emulate* it.

> The same goes for trainees in the martial arts, who observe the master, then emulate him until they achieve technical perfection.
> *Ottawa Citizen* 29 May 1994: B1

> The White Paper's other main cost savings are of a sort that the whole government should emulate—reducing administrative positions in headquarters to increase the number of soldiers in the field.
> *Vancouver Sun* 3 Dec. 1994: A16

> For all his intellectual powers and inexhaustible curiosity, Coleridge realized that he did not possess the literary gifts of Wordsworth or Percy Bysshe Shelley. . . . [Coleridge's] inability to emulate the best of the Romantic poets pained him until his death in 1834.
> *Maclean's* 16 April 1990: A58

(Here *emulate* means rival or outdo.)

> In look and feel, Toshiba's Mobilphile emulates Apple's popular iPod. . . .
> *AudioWorld Online* 19 Aug. 2003

enamour   Some language commentators insist that the only preposition that should follow *enamoured* is *of*, but *with* is used almost as frequently in Canadian writing, and *by*, although much less common, is also standard. The meanings of *enamour*, to inspire love or liking, and to charm or delight, preclude none of these prepositions.

> Enamoured as she was by the history and folk ways of Tunisia, little wonder that Christiane appropriated for herself the poignant symbol of a caged bird.
> Ann Davis *Somewhere Waiting* 1991: 111

-ence   see -ANCE, -ANT, -ENCE, -ENT

endemic, epidemic, pandemic   All three terms are both adjectives and nouns describing patterns of disease occurrence. *Epidemic* and *endemic* both refer to the occurrence of something in a particular area or among a particular group of people: something *epidemic* is widespread or prevalent there at a particular time, whereas something *endemic* is a constant, though not necessarily widespread, problem. *Pandemic*, a less common word, refers to something that affects a broad population over a very wide area. Thus a 'world-wide epidemic' would be a *pandemic*.

The phrase *endemic to* is used metaphorically to describe a problem associated with a field of activity, profession, etc.: 'a spiritual pride endemic to the ministry'. In this use, *endemic* often suggests prevalence as well as persistence. Perhaps this use leads some writers to mistakenly regard *endemic* as the adjective form of *epidemic*. *Epidemic*, however, is not only a noun; it is also an adjective meaning widespread or rampant.

> 'Rabies is endemic to Southern Ontario and goes in cycles of outbreaks among wildlife, so you might have an epidemic in certain areas at certain times.'
> *Globe and Mail* (Toronto) 16 Dec. 1985: A13

> While some flu pandemics are relatively mild, the 1918 Spanish flu pandemic killed an estimated 50 million people worldwide.
> *Gazette* (Montreal) 24 May 2006: A13

> I also revelled in the psychological warfare that is endemic to sports, and loved to probe a competitor's personality. . . .
> *Queen's Quarterly* 94.1 (1987): 125

> Academic observers of South African politics say the violence today is unique because of its length . . . and its endemic spread throughout the country.
> *Globe and Mail* (Toronto) 25 July 1985: P1

(The word required here is *epidemic*.)

> Since the collapse of the Soviet Union in 1991, theft of lucrative military equipment has become endemic.
> *Ottawa Citizen* 1 June 1994: A6

(The word required here is *epidemic*.)

endorsement, endorsation   In Canadian English, *endorsation* is an acceptable, variant of *endorsement*; *endorsation* is particularly common in British Columbia. Both forms of the word are attested in the historical *Oxford English Dictionary* from the sixteenth through the nineteenth centuries, but, in British and American English, *endorsation* then became obsolete.

> . . . a social stigma against slugabeds—and a corollary endorsement of sleep-sacrifice as a sign of toughness . . . encourages people to underreport their slumber.
> *Now Magazine* (Toronto) 18–24 April 1996: 66

> No one is openly criticizing him for his rapid endorsation of America's ballistic missile shield. 'What's happened to left-wing Liberalism?' *News Analysis and Viewpoint* CBC website 26 Jan. 2004

See also CANADIANISMS.

enervate   The verb *enervate* is often mistakenly used as a synonym for *energize*. In fact, to *enervate* something is to sap it of its strength, to weaken it physically or morally.

> Traffic jams are a way of life for motoring suburbanites. Commuting to work or the cottage, drivers curse the inevitable, enervating snarl, the perpetual postponement.
> *Toronto Star* 2 Oct. 1994: F11

> . . . we Canadians are no longer victim to that enervating sense of uncertainty that derives from self-perceived 'colonial' status. . . .
> *Ottawa Citizen* 17 Sept. 1985: A9

> Bob Rae, leader of the Ontario NDP, said 'It's entirely natural for Canadians to be debating their relationship with the United States. It's been enervating to see people talking about free trade on the streetcars.'
> *Toronto Star* 21 Nov. 1988: A1

(Here *energizing* would make more sense.)

> The nationalist fervor of their parents may be ebbing, but passions are still lively here. These CEGEP-level students at College Jean de Brébeuf are the children of the Parti Québécois: [Raised] on an enervating potion of Quebec nationalism, they have never developed an appetite for their country [Canada].
> *Toronto Star* 12 Oct. 1991: B6

(These young Quebecers are not less fervently nationalistic than their parents, but more so: the word required here is *energizing*.)

English   see OLD ENGLISH; QUEBEC ENGLISH; SCIENTIFIC ENGLISH; STANDARD ENGLISH

Englishman, Englishwoman   see BRITON

enjoin, injunction   To *enjoin* is to command or urge. The usual construction is *enjoin* someone *to* do something, as in 'Sarah enjoined the caucus to re-examine its goals'.

However, *enjoin* may also mean prohibit. This meaning is the usual one in a legal context. If the court *enjoins* a company *from* selling a product, then it issues an *injunction* freezing sales.

Because of its two different meanings, *enjoin* is highly ambiguous when it takes a direct object. For example, if the board of trustees enjoins the sale of a school, has it ordered the sale or prohibited it? To avoid confusion it is best to choose another word altogether, such as *orders* or *vetoes*, in such contexts.

None of them enjoined their followers to act upon the world, for the highest good was a contemplative flight from it.
Irving M. Zeitlin and Robert J. Brym *The Social Condition of Humanity* 1991: 222

Today we learned that CTV has been enjoined from showing an interview with Margaret Trudeau until after her book *Beyond Reason* is published.
Ken Dryden *The Game* 1983: 20

This was in keeping with Korean funeral rites, which enjoin public wailing by bereaved relatives.
Ottawa Citizen 20 July 1994: A9

(Here, without context, *enjoin* is ambiguous; either *require* or *forbid* would be clearer.)

enormity, enormousness   Both words are derived from the Latin *enormis*, meaning irregular, unusual, or immense. *Enormity* was originally used to mean extraordinary wickedness, while *enormousness* meant extraordinary size. Since the late 1700s, *enormity* has also been used to mean great size with no implication of evil. Yet to this day usage experts disagree on whether this substitution of *enormity* for *enormousness* is acceptable. In Canadian writing *enormousness* is not a common word. Canadians use *enormity* to mean either great size or extreme wickedness, or a combination of both.

Undaunted by the enormity of the task before him, he began to select participants from a wide variety of musicians he'd met over many years of professional travel.
Performing Arts in Canada March 1988: 22

(Here *enormity* carries no connotation of evil.)

Similarly, a painting of a mountain must have empty space around it so you can appreciate the enormity of the mountain.
Ottawa Citizen 4 March 1990: A3

There is great interest in the case because of the enormity of the crime, adds Travers, and the curiosity is highlighted by the publication ban on evidence.
Ottawa Citizen 27 Nov. 1994: A8

(Here *enormity* connotes both magnitude and evil.)

The country's enormousness infused the saga of the construction of the Canadian Pacific Railway, its bright silver rails forging across the continent to stitch together a nation.
Toronto Star 23 Dec. 1991: A18

See also -NESS.

enquire, enquiry   see INQUIRE

enrol, enroll, enrolment   see -L, -LL

en route   Major dictionaries list only *en route* (two words), from the French meaning 'on the way'. Although *enroute* is beginning to appear in published prose, until this single-word spelling becomes established, it's best to use the standard form.

ensure   see INSURE

-ent   see -ANCE, -ANT, -ENCE, -ENT

enthral, enthrall, enthralled   see -L, -LL

enthuse   The verb *enthuse* (first *OED* citation, 1827) is newer by two centuries than the noun *enthusiasm* from which it derives. Nineteenth-century language commentators attacked *enthuse* as a back-formation and labelled it 'informal' or 'humorous'. Although some of the first recorded uses of the verb were tongue-in-cheek, *enthuse* is now commonly used, without irony, in all types of writing.

Such a speech could not enthuse an intelligent audience.
Henry M. Rosenthal and S. Cathy Berson, eds. *Canadian Jewish Outlook Anthology* 1988: 38

On average, each survey took about 20 minutes, although in some cases, where respondents enthused over the topic, they ran somewhat longer.
Canadian Geographer 48.2 (2004): 152

But not all are as enthused about the Liberals' approach.
Ottawa Citizen 17 Dec. 1994: A1

See also BACK-FORMATION.

entitle, title   Either word may introduce a title: 'a book entitled (*or* titled) *Elimination Dance*'. Some people mistakenly assume that *entitled* can mean only 'justified in claiming', as in 'Everyone is entitled to a share'.

entomology   see ETYMOLOGY

entrain   see EMBARK

entrée, appetizer   The French word *entrée* was used in English in the eighteenth century to mean a light dish served after the first course of fish and before the main meat dish. It was called an entrée because it marked the entry into the main meal. Over the centuries eating habits have changed and so has the meaning of *entrée*. The *entrée* is often still the second course of a meal, but now it is the main course—at least in most of Canada. Speakers of English in Quebec tend to follow the French usage, in which the *entrée* is the first course, or what most English Canadians call the *appetizer*.

Entrée usually retains its accent in formal writing.

For appetizers, we had one winner (delicious garlic prawns at $6.95) and one loser. . . . My entree was the superbly seasoned . . . rack of lamb. . . .
Vancouver Sun 23 Nov. 1990: P9

The eggplant parmigiana entree might well serve as a main dish and is very good.
Gazette (Montreal) 27 Oct. 1990: T4

(Here *entrée* is used with the meaning common in Quebec English: appetizer.)

See also HORS D'OEUVRE; QUEBEC ENGLISH.

enumerable, innumerable   *Enumerable* means countable, listable; it comes from the word *enumerate*, which means literally to give number to something.

If something is *innumerable*, it, literally or figuratively, cannot be counted: 'The atoms in the universe are innumerable'; 'The spelling mistakes in the report were innumerable and distracting'.

Both words are sometimes misspelled *inumerable*.

A biotech policy must be formulated so that it can be applied to enumerable cases over the long term.
Sudbury Star 10 Nov. 1999: A11

(Here the author means 'too many to be counted': *innumerable* is the word needed here.)

In other words, you must buy a book that you can stand to re-read inumerable times while sounding fairly happy about it.
National Post (Toronto) 8 Dec. 2001: BK6

(The correct spelling is *innumerable* with two *n*'s.)

enunciation, Annunciation   An *enunciation* is a detailed statement of rules or principles or a public declaration. *Enunciation* also means manner of articulation (see DICTION, ENUNCIATION). The comic-strip spellings *gonna* and *wanna* represent not mispronunciation but the lax enunciation that characterizes informal talk.

The term *Annunciation* refers to the angel Gabriel's announcement to the Virgin Mary that she would give birth to Christ (Luke 1: 26–38). Occasionally *annunciation* is also used to refer to any formal announcement.

Discussion of the variety and utility of the approaches taken is warranted, for the clear enunciation of methodology is a crucial issue facing interpretive social science.
Canadian Geographer Spring 1989: 94

. . . doubts about this should have been dispelled in 1968, following the Soviet invasion of Czechoslovakia, by the enunciation of the Brezhnev Doctrine, which proclaims the right of the Soviet Union to intervene in any 'socialist'

country whose government deviates from the Marxist-Leninist path.
Globe and Mail (Toronto) 8 June 1985: E17

One of the angels of Jewish, Christian and Muslim tradition, [Gabriel] is the second of the archangels, angel of the Annunciation, and messenger of God.
Globe and Mail (Toronto) 23 March 1985: M2

See also GONNA; DICTION, ENUNCIATION; IMMACU-LATE CONCEPTION, VIRGIN BIRTH; MISPRONUNCIATION.

envelop, envelope The verb *envelop*, meaning to surround or cover, is spelled with no final *e* and pronounced with the stress on the second syllable: *en VEL up*.

The noun *envelope* is stressed on the initial syllable, which may be pronounced either *EN* or *ON*. The *ON vuh lope* pronunciation is sometimes criticized as affected or pseudo-French; however, it's very common and comes naturally to many English-speakers.

envious, enviable *Envious* means feeling or showing envy, while *enviable* means evoking or apt to evoke envy.

Others who have cast envious glances at the Carlton St. cashbox say it's worth more.
Toronto Star 11 April 1994: B1

He has the rare and enviable knack of making complexities clear, of speaking engagingly without ever talking down.
Vancouver Sun 7 May 1994: D9

'It's an envious situation actually because they already have the patents, the innovation behind them,' Swystun said.
Toronto Star 24 May 2004: D1

(The word required here is *enviable*.)

'Without greater economic growth, Canada's envious quality of life will be endangered.'
Toronto Star 3 May 1994: A18

(The word required here is *enviable*.)

See also ENVY.

environment see ECOLOGY; GREEN

envision, envisage Both these verbs mean to form a mental picture of something, often in

the future. Canadian writers use both words equally in all styles of writing. British writers prefer *envisage*, Americans *envision*. Some commentators attempt to distinguish between these terms, but in current usage all distinctions have vanished. *Envisage* once meant to face squarely or confront, but this sense is now rare.

He said the boys originally envisioned it as a slow Roy Orbison crooner rather than the boppy number we know today.
Times-Colonist (Victoria) 20 May 2006: E5

Obviously the kind of settlement Pearson envisaged could not be negotiated quickly or under the pressure of constant border clashes.
George Ignatieff *The Making of a Peacemonger* 1987: 122

envy, jealousy, covet, begrudge The connotations of *envy* range from mild feelings of rivalry to bitter resentment of another's advantages, possessions, or achievements. *Jealousy* usually implies fairly strong feelings of envy. Its meaning extends beyond that of *envy* in that one can be jealous not only of something someone else owns, controls, or has achieved, but also of one's own relationships, privileges, possessions, etc. In other words, *envy* refers to the perception of oneself as lacking or deprived in relation to someone else, while *jealousy* may refer either to this perception *or* to the feeling that one is likely to suffer a loss at someone else's hands. For example, a jealous husband fears losing the affections of his wife to someone else. *Jealous* and *zealous* are related etymologically; this connection is clear in phrases such as 'a jealously guarded secret', where the senses of *zeal* and *jealousy* combine.

To *covet* means to desire something belonging to someone else, and often suggests a longing that is morally or legally wrong. Sports reporters—playing on these dire connotations—often use *covet* with reference to athletic rivalries. To *begrudge* means to resent another person's good fortune. The noun forms are *covetousness* and *begrudgement*.

Now it goes without saying that people envy the life of scholars—the long summer vacations, the excursions to distant lands.
Canadian Fiction Magazine 63 (1988): 72

What a woman writer is often unprepared for is the unexpected personal attack on her by a jealous male writer. The motivation is envy and covetousness, but the form is often sexual put-down.
Margaret Atwood *Second Words* 1982: 202

As one would expect, a prime source of employment in a critically depressed area is guarded jealously by the people.
Daily Gleaner (Fredericton) 26 April 1988: 4

It is a fact that all ethnic, racial, and social groups, including the very rich, contain individuals who covet and unlawfully take the property of others.
Irving M. Zeitlin and Robert J. Brym *The Social Condition of Humanity* 1991: 274

Of course, the grandpa of them all was Cy Young, for whom the award all pitchers covet was named.
Globe and Mail (Toronto) 23 April 1985: S1

I won't begrudge wealthy Canadians their corporate boxes at GM Place or their private jet junkets to the Super Bowl, if he and his cronies will pay hard-working Canadians a living wage.
Vancouver Sun 18 March 2006: C7

See also ENVIOUS, ENVIABLE.

eon see -AE-, -OE-, -E-

epenthesis see MISPRONUNCIATION AND PRONUNCIATION SHIFTS

epic An *epic* is a long narrative poem that celebrates the achievements of a hero. It is written in a formal style and often expresses the ideals of a nation. *Beowulf*, Homer's *Iliad*, Virgil's *Aeneid*, and Milton's *Paradise Lost* are all epic poems. *Epic* is also used as an adjective to describe long, usually historical movies and novels, or achievements and events unusual in their magnitude and importance. Critics have disparaged these extended uses of *epic*, but they are common and accepted. In literary criticism, where *epic* is used as a technical term, the extended meanings should be avoided.
Epic is often used humorously to mean *huge* or *grandiose*. This usage is always informal.

This synthesis takes place most notably in 'The Pride,' an almost epic long poem which traces the history of western Canada through the defeat and dispersal of the Indians and ends by seeing the current inhabitants—'we' or 'us'—as their metaphorical descendants.
Margaret Atwood *Second Words* 1982: 126

(Here *epic* is a technical term.)

Clark's new epic novel about the life of Freydis, daughter of Erik the Red and sister of Leif the Lucky, reads like a cross between a bodice-ripper and a living-history textbook.
Ottawa Citizen 19 June 1994: B3

. . . Pearson ended up laying his wreath on a ridge which had changed hands many times during the epic World War II struggle for Stalingrad, and where 36,000 identifiable bodies were found when the battle was over.
George Ignatieff *The Making of a Peacemonger* 1987: 140

Forget Paul Henderson's jump for joy after scoring the winning goal of the 1972 Summit Series. . . . The World Cup is here. And that means post-goal celebrations of epic proportions.
Toronto Star 17 June 1994: B9

(This use of *epic* is informal.)

Examples span from the country's first trans-continental railway in the 1880s . . . to the now notorious and epic Dome Petroleum fiasco of the 1980s. . . .
Queen's Quarterly 94.4 (1987): 939

(This use of *epic* is informal.)

See also ODYSSEY.

epicurean, epicure, Epicurean An *epicurean* is especially fond of eating, drinking, and sensual pleasure. An *epicure*—like a gourmet—has refined tastes in food and wine. To some extent these two terms are used interchangeably, but this is the distinction of sense presented in most dictionaries.
When capitalized, *Epicurean* refers to *Epicurus*, the Greek philosopher who taught that pleasure is the highest goal. Epicurus defined pleasure not as sensualism—that interpretation distorts his teachings—but as freedom from anguish, which he associated with a life of moderation and simplicity.

D—— is Ontario's soon-to-be-former deputy health minister . . . and, it seems, enthusiastic epicurean. . . . according to expense claims released

this week by the opposition, [he has] claimed $11,238.94 in meals.
Ottawa Citizen 18 Nov. 1993: A14

Our epicure prides himself on exotic chow from India, Italy, France, Mexico and Thailand. . . . 'Something about the perfumes and flavors,' muses Comeau. . . .
Gazette (Montreal) 7 May 1994: D1

See also GOURMET, GOURMAND.

epidemic   see ENDEMIC

epigram, epigraph, epitaph, epilogue, epithet   An *epigram* is a short, pointed statement in prose or verse. Epigrams are satiric and witty. Frequently, as in this verse by B.K. Sandwell (editor of *Saturday Night*, 1932–51), they are of topical and local, rather than universal, interest:

> Toronto has no social classes.
> Only the Masseys and the masses.

An *epigraph* is an engraved inscription on a building or monument, or a short statement, usually a quotation at the beginning of a book or part of a book. The statue of Sir George-Etienne Cartier in Jeanne-Mance Park, Montreal, includes a carved scroll with the epigraph 'Above Everything, We Are Canadian'. An epigraph may well appear on a tomb, although the usual term for such inscriptions is *epitaph*.

An *epitaph* is a short composition written in memory of a dead person, often engraved on a tombstone. Reginald Fessenden, a pioneer of Canadian radio-communications, is buried in St. Mark's Church, Bermuda. His epitaph reads:

> By His Genius
> Distant Lands Converse
> And Men Sail
> Unafraid Upon the Deep.

An *epilogue* is the final speech of a play or the concluding section of a novel or poem; it is the opposite of a *prologue*.

Finally, an *epithet* is a descriptive expression or phrase attached to someone's name; it is usually an adjective, as in 'Ivan the Terrible' or 'Ethelred the Unready'. Sometimes *epithet*

means a term of abuse: 'They hurled racist epithets'. Some usage commentators object to this use of the word, but it is well established in Canadian writing.

What they had discovered were gardens known as lazy beds, a term derived from 'lazy root,' an English epithet for the potato.
Harrowsmith Jun.–Jul. 1985: 125

A Jewish resident in the surgical clinic . . . at a famous Berlin hospital is making his rounds in the wards when a brutal Nazi patient begins to shout anti-Semitic epithets at him.
Queen's Quarterly 92.1 (1985): 133

epileptic   see DISABILITIES

epilogue   see EPIGRAM

epiphany   *Epiphany* is capitalized when it refers to the Christian festival held on 6 January. At Epiphany some churches celebrate the manifestation of Christ's divinity at his baptism; other churches celebrate the manifestation of Christ to the Magi. An *epiphany* (not capitalized) is an appearance by a deity, or an important revelation, or, in current extended usage, a sudden insight.

In Rome the storm coincided with the traditional arrival of Befana, the old woman who brings Italian children presents for the feast of Epiphany.
Globe and Mail (Toronto) 7 Jan. 1985: P10

But Page holds back before releasing her joyful tears, and the film achieves a magnificent epiphany.
Maclean's 24 Feb. 1986: 65

This remarkable epiphany [the realization that you can see what the weather is like by looking out the window] is the reason that, when Bert Adkins is on the air, you never drive through a rainstorm and listen to a radio report that tells you it's clear out.
Ottawa Citizen 30 Dec. 1993: A1

(Here *epiphany* is ironic.)

epitaph, epithet   see EPIGRAM

epitome, exemplar, acme, apex, pinnacle, paragon, ne plus ultra   An *epitome* (pronounced *uh PIT uh mee*) is a prime example. A person or thing perfectly embodying or representing a quality is said to be 'the epitome' of it. An *exemplar* is someone or something that serves well as an example or model. Thus an inn that is the *epitome* of comfort might also be described as *exemplary* with respect to comfort. *Epitome* and *exemplar* can both refer to negative as well as positive things: 'the epitome of selfishness'; 'an exemplar of the neglected child'. Because *epitome* does not mean highest point or peak, some critics object to the expression 'to reach the epitome'. *Acme*, *apex*, and *pinnacle*, which all mean highest point, are better choices in this context, although *acme* is rarely used in Canadian writing except as part of a company name ('Acme Glass Ltd.', for example). A *paragon* is a model of excellence or perfection (and *paragon* is the name of a perfect diamond of 100 carats or more). The Latin expression *ne plus ultra* refers to the highest or farthest point. Meaning literally 'nothing more beyond', *ne plus ultra* is said to have been inscribed on rocks at the western gate of the Mediterranean as a warning to sailors. This phrase should be italicized in formal writing.

> With chocolate cheesecake brownies, brownies with milk chocolate icing and caramel fudge pecan brownies, she seems to have reached the epitome of this particular craft.
> *Globe and Mail* (Toronto) 11 Dec. 1985: E8

(Here *apex* or *pinnacle* would be a better choice.)

> 'He has all the physical characteristics to play in the CFL,' Hargreaves said. 'But playing in the NFL is the epitome for young athletes.'
> *Globe and Mail* (Toronto) 5 Dec. 1985: D12

(Here *ultimate achievement* would be more appropriate.)

> To me, this was not surprising because generally, I have not found mourning doves to be the epitomy of intelligence.
> *Gazette* (Montreal) 2 June 1990: L3

(The correct spelling is *epitome*.)

> For the time being this may mean quick-fix loans and perhaps exemplary punishment for culpable former politicians.
> *Globe and Mail* (Toronto) 11 Sept. 1985: P7

(Here *exemplary* describes something unpleasant that is meant to serve as an example.)

See also APOGEE; CATASTROPHE; LATIN PHRASES; SINE QUA NON.

epoch The older meaning of *epoch* (pronounced either *EE pock* or like *epic*) is a turning-point in history or the beginning of an era. This sense is now rare. Most writers now use *epoch* as a synonym for *era*: a period of time that is distinct in some way. Most dictionaries list the new meaning; however, some commentators still disparage it.

The older meaning is recalled by the adjective *epoch-making*, which describes highly significant events or achievements, and means literally 'marking the beginning of a new era'.

> Simple though these words may sound, the movement represented a historic epoch in the saga of the Jewish people.
> Henry M. Rosenthal and S. Cathy Berson, eds. *Canadian Jewish Outlook Anthology* 1988: 74

(Here *epoch* is used in the older sense of turning-point.)

> It was the best of times, it was the worst of times, it was the age of wisdom, it was the age of foolishness, it was the epoch of belief, it was the epoch of incredulity—in short, it was the beginning of the Autumn Term, and the year was 1969.
> Robertson Davies *One Half of Robertson Davies* 1978: 107

> In that epoch humans first emerged as food gatherers.
> Irving M. Zeitlin and Robert J. Brym *The Social Condition of Humanity* 1991: 92

(Here *epoch* means era.)

> In 1859 Charles Darwin published his theory of biological evolution in an epoch-making book called *On the Origin of Species by Means of Natural Selection*.
> Irving M. Zeitlin and Robert J. Brym *The Social Condition of Humanity* 1991: 1

(Here *epoch-making* refers to a publication that heralded a new era.)

eponym, eponymous   An *eponym* (pronounced *EPP un im*) is a person's name that has been given to something else, such as a place, institution, discovery, object, invention, or work of literature. Both the person and the thing are called eponyms. Some examples are the sandwich, named after the fourth Earl of Sandwich, who according to the legend, demanded a snack that was easy to eat so that he would not have to leave the card table; the Stetson, the hat taking its name from the American hat-maker J.B. Stetson; the *Bombardier* (a snowmobile, forerunner of the Ski-Doo), named after its Canadian inventor, Armand Bombardier of Valcourt, Quebec.

Anna Karenina is an example of an *eponymous* (rhymes with *synonymous*) novel: 'Anna Karenina is the *eponymous* heroine of Tolstoy's fourth novel'. Titles that merely describe the hero or heroine—e.g., *The Egoist*—are not eponyms. A first album is often named *eponymously*; in other words, its title is simply the name of the singer or group that made it.

> Formerly the host of Variety Tonight, she now has a new show, eponymously called Gabereau.
> *Globe and Mail* (Toronto) 6 July 1985: E1

(The 'she' is radio and television host Vicki Gabereau.)

> What children are to the eponymous heroine of 'Irina'—darling zeros—Linnet's husband is to her, and one is not too sure that the darling part was ever applicable.
> Janice Kulyk Keefer *Reading Mavis Gallant* 1989: 131

(The heroine of the story 'Irina' is named Irina.)

> More than 20 years after their eponymous debut, the Red Hot Chili Peppers remain a commercial juggernaut.
> *Toronto Star* 21 May 2006: C2

(The Red Hot Chili Peppers called their first album *Red Hot Chili Peppers*.)

> For the next two hours, Geraldine Page turns the Countess Aurelia, the eponymous heroine of Jean Giraudoux's 1945 farce The Madwoman of Chaillot, . . . into a theatrical banquet. . . .
> *Globe and Mail* (Toronto) 26 Feb. 1985: M7

(The heroine of *The Madwoman of Chaillot* is not properly called *eponymous*.)

equable, equatable, equitable   Something *equable* is unvarying or steady. The word is most frequently used to describe climatic conditions. Things that are *equatable* (*ee KWAIT uh bul*) can be considered equivalent. *Equitable* (pronounced *ECK wit uh bul*) means fair: an equitable solution or arrangement is one in which all parties are treated justly.

> Its equable climate, the country's balmiest, draws retirees from across Canada, giving Victoria its dichotomous character, the genteel-among-the-great-outdoors aspect.
> Alan Tucker, ed. *The Penguin Guide to Canada* 1991: 562

> In England, where the word [serviette] is used less in any case, it is more or less equatable with a napkin, cloth or paper.
> W.C. Lougheed, ed. *In Search of the Standard in Canadian English* 1986: 59

> The report also suggests that the unions should address non-traditional issues of collective bargaining, such as equitable pay for women, greater worker participation in decision-making, and health and safety issues.
> *Globe and Mail* (Toronto) 27 Feb. 1985: P12

See also EQUALITY, EQUITY.

equal   see DOUBLING THE FINAL CONSONANT

equality, equity, reverse discrimination, affirmative action, employment equity   Where there is *equality*, everyone receives equal shares: one slice of cake for each. The word *equality* is most often used in discussions of unifying, democratic principles such as freedom of speech, freedom from discrimination, the right to vote, the principle of one person, one vote, and so on.

Equity—setting aside legal and investment meanings—refers to the principle whereby everyone receives what is appropriate to his or her requirements, no less and no more: that is, anyone hungry can have a second slice, but those already full require none. *Equity* is usually achieved by reparations, financial or otherwise, to members of a minority group experiencing physical, mental, financial, or social disadvantage. With respect to employment, according to Canada's *Employment Equity Act*, equity demands that no one lacks opportunities to do their best, regardless of what holds them back in other areas of their lives.

Opponents of equity programs consider them instruments of *reverse discrimination*, arguing that to give special assistance to disadvantaged people is to discriminate against everybody else.

The American term *affirmative action* properly refers to the equity legislation of that country specifically. The Canadian government chose a different term for its own program: *employment equity*. Unlike the American program, employment equity does not involve hiring by quota. While some Canadians—and even some Canadian government publications—do use the phrase *affirmative action* to describe all equity-based legislation and practices collectively, the term *affirmative action* should not be used as a synonym for *employment equity* specifically.

We need to remain vigilant and committed to the values of equality and opportunity.
Education Canada 44.2 (2004): 28–31

(Here equality means equal access to rights and privileges.)

The very term 'bullying,' when used to refer to all student behaviour that is inappropriate, masks the equity and human rights issues often at play in such incidents.
Orbit 34.2 (2004): 41–42

(Here the word equity suggests the special vulnerability of some groups of children to peer abuse.)

Governments and even the courts (as a result of the affirmative action provisions in the Charter of Rights and Freedoms) had an obligation to intervene both in the economy and in traditional patterns of behaviour to make it happen.
Queen's Quarterly 111.1 (2004): 67

(In Canada, the term *affirmative action* may be used with a broad reference—as here—but should not be used to describe employment equity programs.)

See also INCLUSIVE LANGUAGE.

equally   Phrases such as 'equally as hard' and 'equally as good' are criticized because *equally as* is redundant. Either *equally* or *as* can stand alone in a comparison: 'Her new play and her previous ones are equally good' *or* 'Her new play is as good as her previous ones'.

In addition, she would compel male academics to take early retirement at age 60, while allowing women to work to age 65—a proposal equally as offensive as the reverse requirement once in place at the university.
London Free Press 6 May 1988: B6

(Here *equally* could be omitted; if emphasis is required, *just* or *every bit* could precede *as*.)

Robinette was almost equally as effective in making points with his cross-examination of a variety of other crown witnesses.
Jack Batten *Robinette* 1984: 86

(Here 'almost *as* effective' or 'almost *equally* effective' would be better.)

For anglers on a tighter budget, there are less costly—but in my opinion equally as enjoyable—ways to visit and fish Ireland. . . .
Atlantic Salmon Journal Summer 1990: 23

(Here the *as* should be dropped.)

See also AS GOOD AS.

equatable   see EQUABLE

equinox, solstice   The *equinox*, from Latin *aequi-*, 'equal' and *nox-*, 'night', is the day of the year when day and night are of equal length, occurring twice per year: the spring equinox is around 22 September and the fall equinox is around 20 March. The *solstice* is the longest or shortest day of the year: the summer solstice is around 22 June and the winter solstice is around 22 December.

equitable   see EQUABLE

equity   see EQUALITY

equivocal   see AMBIGUOUS

equivocate   see LIE

-er, -or   The endings *-er* and *-or* both indicate something or someone (*baker, computer, investigator, radiator*) that performs a function. There is no difference in meaning or pronunciation between these endings, but they do present a spelling challenge. Note that new words tend to be formed with *-er* (*computer*), while *-or* is a historical variant. Many of the words spelled with *-or* fall into one of the following categories: (1) nouns with stems that are not stand-alone English verbs (*author, councillor, juror, tailor, traitor, suitor, victor*); (2) nouns derived from verbs ending in *-ate* (*accelerator, agitator, calculator, dictator, educator, illustrator, investigator, operator, radiator, translator*) or *-ute* (*distributor, executor, prosecutor*); or (3) terms for people acting in legal (or illegal) capacities (*abettor, abductor, conveyor, executor, grantor, mortgagor, prosecutor, solicitor, successor*). A few words (*advisor, adviser; conveyor, conveyer*) have two common spellings.

See also ADVISER, ADVISOR.

err   Most Canadians pronounce *err* like *air*, but the British usually pronounce it to rhyme with *her*.

ersatz   *Ersatz* (pronounced *UR zats* or *AIR zats*) means artificial or imitation, and its connotations are negative. German manufacturers developed many products during the two world wars to replace food and commodities that were in short supply, and the German word for these substitutes was borrowed by the English.

> Once, a Bruce woman had doubtless thought these pieces were elegant, but they were not antiques, and they were not cheerful. They were ersatz Victorian, decidedly lumpy and vaguely funereal.
> *Harrowsmith* Aug.–Sept. 1985: 16

See also ARTIFICIAL.

ERT   see SWAT TEAM

escalate   see BACK-FORMATION

escalation   An *escalation* is a step-by-step increase that seems self-propelled. The phrases 'escalation of international good will' and 'sudden escalation of happiness' sound peculiar, perhaps because *escalation* is almost always linked to worrisome things such as costs, violence, and hostilities.

> One presidential candidate warned that an escalation of tension between Aristide and Lafontant could lead to civil war.
> *Gazette* (Montreal) 16 Dec. 1990: B1

> 'I am nevertheless distressed about this exorbitant escalation of rent for downtown office space,' Mr. Johnston wrote.
> *Globe and Mail* (Toronto) 29 Jan. 1985: P5

-ese   The suffix *-ese* has two functions. It is used to form adjectives referring to a place or its residents (*Chinese, Maltese, Portuguese, Viennese, Vietnamese*) and to create nouns specifying distinctive manners of speaking or writing (*Brooklynese, bureaucratese, journalese*). This second *-ese* is often used in the popular media to produce ad hoc words to describe the jargon of a particular group: for example, *legalese* and *computerese*. Some of the more inventive creations of Canadian writers follow.

> This is indeed a welcome relief to his impeccably written double-starched Doctoralese.
> *Queen's Quarterly* 92.1 (1985): 218

> You didn't know I could talk Architectese, did you? I have always been a good linguist and can pick up a smattering of any language quite quickly.
> Robertson Davies *One Half of Robertson Davies* 1978: 77

> In a world of complexity and ambiguity, Reagan reduced everything to 3 x 5 note cards, single-page briefings, or ghost-written telepromptese.
> *Queen's Quarterly* 95.4 (1988): 802

See also COLLOQUIAL, INFORMAL, SLANG, JARGON.

Eskimo   see INUIT

esophagus   see -AE-, -OE-, -E-

esoteric   see EXOTIC

especial(ly)   see SPECIAL

espresso, expresso   The Italian coffee is properly called *espresso* (*ess PRESS o*). Dictionaries list the variant spelling *expresso*, which reflects a common pronunciation, but some commentators still condemn it. The plural is *espressos*.

> You get the pleasantly odd feeling that it's an extraordinarily permanent set built by a Hollywood movie company for High Noon, and Gary Cooper should be happily swilling expresso on one of its many outdoor restaurant terraces.
> *Globe and Mail* (Toronto) 18 June 1985: S2

(This spelling is quite uncommon in Canada.)

esprit de corps   see FRENCH WORDS, PRONUNCIATION OF

Esquire, Esq., Maître   *Esquire* most often appears as *Esq.* after a man's name in a mailing address. It should not be combined with *Mr.*; either 'Mr. Richard Harris' or 'Richard Harris, Esq.' is correct.

In the medieval period, an esquire was an aspirant knight and a sort of knight's assistant. Later an esquire was part of the landed gentry, ranked just below a knight in the British social hierarchy. Now *Esq.* is appropriate for any man without another title. The British are more likely to use *Esq.*, particularly on formal occasions when titles are de rigueur, than are Canadians.

Canadians do make use of *Esq.* in the legal domain. *Esq.* is used as an honorific for lawyers (nonsexist usage guides recommend using it for both male and female lawyers). The parallel honorific in Quebec English (and Quebec French) for male or female lawyers is Maître. It precedes the name: 'Maître Mireille Goulet'.

> . . . his grandfather, the late J.J. McGill, Esq., sat on the MGH Board of Management from 1919 to 1939.
> *Gazette* (Montreal) 6 Dec. 1990: F4

> G. Ross Davis, Esquire, for appellant.
> *Globe and Mail* (Toronto) 17 Oct. 1985: B11

(This quotation is from the Osgoode Hall court reports, and Davis is a lawyer.)

> The Panel dealt with a complaint sent to the Council in July 2001 by a Quebec lawyer, Maître

> Gilles Doré.
> Media Release, Canadian Judicial Council website 22 July 2002

essay   see ASSAY

esthetic   see -AE-, -OE-, -E-

estrogen   see -AE-, -OE-, -E-; SWAT TEAM

et al.   This phrase is an abbreviation of *et alia*, Latin for 'and others'. Since only the second word is an abbreviation, only one period is required, after *al. Et al.* is most often used in citing a publication that has three or more authors. For example, a 1991 article written by Smith, Jones, and Brown can be referred to as 'Smith et al. 1991'. (Note that both names are always given when a source has only two authors.)

Although etymologically justified, the use of *et al.* to mean 'and other things' has been criticized, as has its use in expository prose. Such uses are often facetious, playing on the scholarly connotations of *et al.* When no humour is intended, *etc.* can be substituted.

> On the broader scale, Hannah grapples with the usual [Woody] Allen issues—love, death, the perfect pastrami sandwich et al.
> *Gazette* (Montreal) 4 March 1989: T3

(Here *et al.* is used facetiously.)

See also ETC.; LATIN PHRASES.

etc.   *Etc.* (pronounced *et SET er ah*) is an abbreviation of the Latin phrase *et cetera*, which means 'and other things'. It is wholly integrated into English, where its meanings include 'and so on', 'and the rest', 'and the like'. *Etc.* generally occurs at the end of a list where the next items are obvious; it allows the writer to avoid boring the reader with too much detail. One valuable point stressed by many guides is that readers should have no trouble deciding what *etc.* is intended to stand for: it should not be used evasively to avoid giving necessary information.

Strunk and White, in their influential guide *The Elements of Style*, summarize the opinion of many commentators: 'In formal writing, *etc.* is a misfit.' But in fact *etc.* is used far more often in academic prose than in magazines and newspapers; there is no need to avoid it in formal writing.

Because the Latin phrase refers to things, not people, some commentators suggest that it should not be used at the end of a list of people, where they prefer 'and others' or even *et al.* However, Canadian writers treat *etc.* as an English word and cannot be expected to use it only in its Latin sense.

In the past, major style guides have insisted that *etc.* be preceded by a comma and, if the sentence continues, followed by one too. Generally, Canadian writers follow this advice. Some writers omit the second comma, and some style guides, following a trend to less punctuation, now endorse this omission.

The practice of using an ampersand to replace *et* ('and')—*&c*—has all but disappeared. *Etc.* need not be italicized.

> The Corporation was to provide and to manage the common services (finance, personnel, security, etc.) of all the museums; the four museum directors were to direct the museum functions (collection, conservation, documentation, exhibition, etc.) in their respective museums.
> *Queen's Quarterly* 94.3 (1987): 556

> Have you had a recent or chronic or major ailment, especially rheumatoid arthritis, anemia, emotional stress that required medications etc.?
> *Globe and Mail* (Toronto) 5 Feb. 1985: F5

(Here *etc.*—at the end of a modifying clause—is ambiguous. It is not clear whether the writer is referring to other ailments or other treatments.)

> He assumes another Canadian tradition, which he thinks of as the other 'half' and which he sees as consisting of people like Richardson, Leacock, MacLennan, Lampman, Livesay, Marriott, Mitchell, Haliburton, Callaghan, etc.
> Margaret Atwood *Second Words* 1982: 146

(Here Atwood uses *etc.* at the end of a list of people.)

See also AMPERSAND; ET AL; LATIN PHRASES.

ethics, ethical   *Ethics* meaning the study and philosophy of moral conduct takes a singular verb: 'Ethics is taught to business students'. *Ethics* as a personal or professional code of conduct takes a plural verb: 'Her professional ethics were impeccable'. *Ethic* also may appear as a singular noun, as in the phrase 'Protestant work ethic'. The established form of the adjective is *ethical*, not *ethic*.

etymology, entomology   *Etymology* is the study of word origins and derivations; *entomology* is the study of insects.

Many arguments about the 'correct' meaning and use of disputed words and expressions are based on etymology. The arguments about words derived from Classical Greek and Latin have been particularly bitter. Since knowledge of these languages was until recently the sign of an educated gentleman, in the past the appeal to etymology often succeeded—at least until the gap between the 'original' sense of the word and established English usage became too large. Now English is spoken and written mostly by people who have never studied the Classical languages, and these arguments cannot be expected to prevail over the actual usage of educated people. For more about these arguments, see ALTER EGO; ANTAGONIST, PROTAGONIST; COMMISERATE; DECIMATE; ET AL.; ETC.; INTERNECINE; KUDOS; SUPERIOR, SENIOR, INFERIOR, JUNIOR, MAJOR, MINOR.

> Jeanne d'Arc's monicker, La Pucelle, bears no relationship to a flea, either etymologically or entomologically, so his flea-bitten argument about fumigation doesn't wash.
> *Globe and Mail* (Toronto) 10 July 1985: P7

> The etymology of the term 'theory' is from the Greek root *thea*, to see.
> *International Journal* 59.4 (2004): 886–92

See also BACK-FORMATION; BARBARISM; FOLK ETYMOLOGY.

eulogy   see ELEGY

euphemism   A *euphemism* is a polite or socially acceptable way of saying something that might be disagreeable or offensive if stated directly. Not surprisingly, English-speakers have developed roundabout or more palatable terms for many things felt to be taboo, terrifying, or disgusting, especially in matters of sex, death, and bodily functions. An abiding Victorian concern for propriety remains in such terms as *washroom*, *bathroom*, and *comfort station*, each a euphemism for *toilet* (itself originally a euphemism). Euphemisms for all manner of sexual matters abound: *making love, having a good time, swinging, cruising*. The common euphemism for *die* is *pass away*.

Most insidious are those euphemisms that attempt to obscure or deny the reality they pretend to describe. Government, military, and business are the greatest offenders, producing such euphemisms as *strategic misrepresentation* for lying; *destabilize* for wage war against; *collateral damage* for civilian deaths in an act of war; *net profits revenue deficiency* for a business loss; and *adult books/movies* for pornography.

Generally the extent to which euphemisms are employed reflects the social climate. Whether a particular euphemism is employed is a matter of taste or ethics.

> High-density suburb is a euphemism for the dusty, box-house, all-black townships skirting the formerly all-white residential preserves—the low-density suburbs—of the lush, gardened inner city.
> *Globe and Mail* (Toronto) 14 Jan. 1985: B12

> Political correctness and euphemism have distorted our perspective and use of language in discussing the reality of war.
> *National Post* (Toronto) 24 May 2006: A19

> They are summoned to sessions of political 're-education.' Sometimes they are beaten, sometimes imprisoned. Sometimes they disappear.
> *Gazette* (Montreal) 5 March 1989: B5

(Here the quotation marks around 're-education' mark it as a euphemism for mental and physical harassment and torture.)

See also INCLUSIVE LANGUAGE.

ever see ADJECTIVES AND ADVERBS; RARELY EVER; SELDOM EVER.

every The adjective *every* precedes a singular noun and is used with a singular verb: 'Every

dog has its day'. The use of a plural verb, as in 'Every one of her pay cheques go straight into the bank', is considered non-standard by most commentators. Regarding the use of *every* with the plural pronoun *their,* see EVERYONE.

See also AGREEMENT, GRAMMATICAL; BETWEEN EACH, BETWEEN EVERY; EACH AND EVERY; EVERYONE.

everybody see EVERYONE

everyday, every day *Everyday* is an adjective meaning typical, ordinary, or daily, as in 'everyday events' or 'everyday clothing'. The two-word phrase *every day* describes *when* something happens: 'She visited him every day'. The two-word spelling should be used whenever *each* could be substituted for *every*: 'It rained every (each) day for a week'.

> Breakfasts could include everyday fare such as instant oatmeal, individually-boxed cereal and pancakes from pre-made batter.
> *Leisure Life* May 1988: 62

> Students are curious about the language they hear every day.
> W.C. Lougheed, ed. *In Search of the Standard in Canadian English* 1986: 83

> The Nomad is not one of your average, every day wading jackets, which normally rely on either wax (as in Barbour garments) or a microporous film (such as Goretex) to protect the wearer against rain.
> *Atlantic Salmon Journal* Autumn 1990: 35

(The adjective *everyday* is needed here.)

> Imagine feeling fulfilled everyday because you have the best job ever.
> *Manitoba Business* 25.7 (2003): 16

(Here *every day* is required.)

everyone, everybody *They* and *their* are the pronouns most commonly used with the indefinite pronouns *everyone, everybody, anyone, anybody, someone, somebody,* and *no one, nobody* ('Everyone does just what they like'; 'Everybody has their problems'), as well as singular nouns modified by adjectives such as *any, each, every,* and *no* ('Every listener has their favourite show'). Although the following comments focus on *everybody* and *everyone*, they apply to all constructions of this kind.

The *everybody . . . they* construction can be found as early as 1530. However, eighteenth-century grammarians decided that it was incorrect. *Everybody*, they said, is a singular pronoun. The verb that follows it is always singular (*does* and *has*, not *do* and *have*, in the examples above), and any pronoun replacing it should be singular. Thus *they* and *their* were rejected and *he* and *his* approved for use with *everyone*: 'Everyone does just what he likes'; 'Everybody has his problems'. Though *he* and *his* are masculine pronouns, they were to be understood to refer to women as well. This usage became standard in formal writing.

For the most part, however, people went on using *they* and *their*. One reason is that *everybody* and *everyone*, though grammatically singular (as evidenced by the singular verbs they take), are notionally plural: that is, these words do not refer to one person, but to people in general. As the *Dictionary of Contemporary American Usage* points out, it is often impossible to use the approved pronoun *he* with *everyone* when the two words are in separate clauses. 'Everyone was at risk, as I tried to tell him' means something quite different from 'Everyone was at risk, as I tried to tell them'.

Another reason *everyone* continued to be used with *they* and *their* is that *they* is gender-neutral, applying equally to men and women. The notion that 'Everyone . . . he' could refer to women always seemed artificial to some people, and today many would label the usage sexist. For this reason most contemporary usage guides approve of the use of *they* and *their* with *everyone*, at least in speech and informal writing. However, they evade the question of what to do in formal writing, for there are many people who still consider the use of *their* with *everyone* unsuitable in formal writing. While it is possible to replace 'everyone . . . his' with 'everyone . . . his or her' (*or* 'his/her'), even handbooks of nonsexist usage generally note that this solution is awkward. Thus they suggest rephrasing the sentence. Often *their* can be omitted with little damage to the sense: 'Everyone has prob-

lems' instead of 'Everyone has their problems'. Alternatively, it may be possible to replace *everyone* with a plural noun or pronoun: 'We all have our problems'; 'Students do just what they like'. Eventually, one hopes, 'everyone . . . their' will regain its good standing in all levels of writing, and evasive tactics such as these will be unnecessary.

Interestingly, Robertson Davies uses the *everyone . . . they* construction when the notion expressed by *everyone* is plural, and *everyone . . . he* when it is singular (see examples below). Perhaps the example of an eminent writer will convert those who feel that *everyone . . . they* has no place in formal writing.

St. Vincent's School would like to thank everyone for their work, interest and presence at the fair.
Chronicle-Telegraph (Quebec City) 22 May 1991: 9

(In speech and informal writing, *everyone . . . their* is accepted.)

That is the ingenious premise for *Hook*, director Steven Spielberg's $79-million attempt to give everybody everything they have always wanted for Christmas: magic.
Maclean's 16 Dec. 1991: A64

'You haven't spoken and treated everybody in such a manner as to convince them that you are now going to do the job.'
Financial Post 9 Dec. 1991: 1

(Here replacing *them* with *him* would change the meaning.)

The pragmatic socialism of Turati had produced nothing and everyone was in a position to judge for himself whether the man in Moscow or the man in Milan had contributed more in terms of socialist literature and revolutionary theory.
Canadian Journal of History 14.1 (1989): 28

(Though once approved, the use of *him* or *himself* with *everyone* is now criticized as sexist.)

Teach everybody to read, and they will read what appeals to them, what accords with their experience and ideal of life.
Robertson Davies *A Voice from the Attic* 1960: 24

(Here the notion expressed by everybody is plural. Since the emphasis is on what will happen when many people learn to read, Davies uses they.)

I struggled, as must everyone who concerns himself with this matter, with the question of nomenclature.
Robertson Davies *A Voice from the Attic* 1960: 274

(Here the notion expressed by *everyone* is singular. Imagining people struggling individually with this question, Davies uses *himself*.)

See also AGREEMENT, GRAMMATICAL; ANY; EACH; -SELF, -SELVES; SEXIST LANGUAGE.

everyplace, everywhere see -WHERE, -PLACE

evidence, testimony, testimonial, affidavit, proof   *Evidence* is the general term for anything that points towards the truth or falsity of something. In a court of law, testimony, test results, and objects could all be presented in evidence.

In law, *testimony* is a formal written or oral statement made by a witness. In more general use, words or actions that bear witness to something are *testimony*: 'The video includes testimonies of youth who have struggled with addiction'; 'His restraint was (a) testimony to his good nature'.

A *testimonial* is either an endorsement of a product ('celebrity testimonials') or a written account of someone's good qualities to be used, for example, in a job search.

An *affidavit* is a sworn document that may be used as testimony in court if the testifier cannot appear in person; affidavits are used, for example, to attest to a defendant's alibi or good character.

Proof is evidence that leaves no room for doubt. Legally, it is what permits a judgment 'beyond a reasonable doubt' in criminal cases, and 'on a balance of probabilities' in civil cases.

In disputes before the courts, written evidence of a contract will aid the judge in determining what the terms are and in resolving a conflict of testimony by the parties, each with a different recollection of the contract.
J.E. Smyth et al. *The Law and Business Administration in Canada* 1987: 245

In his written complaint, Mr. Cornblum noted contradictions between Mr. Greenberg's testimony and information contained in building records.
Globe and Mail (Toronto) 4 Jan. 1985: M6

The 50-year-old woman, who was introduced Wednesday at the YWCA of Calgary's annual general meeting by the pseudonym Sara, delivered powerful and heartfelt testimony about her decades of savage battery.
Calgary Herald 20 April 2006: B6

Tewksbury's revelatory new book, Inside Out: Straight Talk From a Gay Jock, has elicited glowing testimonials from such disparate individuals as Dick Pound, the Canadian IOC member and anti-doping czar, educator Barbara Coloroso. . . .
National Post (Toronto) 22 April 2006: S1

One of the biggest obstacles to the recovery is proving ownership in cases where documentation was lost. . . . One solution is temporary ownership certificates drawn up by aid workers based on testimonials by a village headman or witness.
Toronto Star 26 June 2005: A10

(In this legal context, *testimony* is the word required.)

'All of us were practising Catholics, and we were so wounded by the organization.' Today ODAN . . . acts as a conduit for the cautionary testimonials of thousands of former Opus Dei members and their families throughout North and South America, Europe and Australia.
Ottawa Citizen 30 April 2006: B1

(*Testimonials* are positive; *testimonies* or *testimony* is the word needed here.)

In an affidavit filed in court, H—— said tensions grew over work-related issues and she believed that one board member was besmirching her reputation.
Province (Vancouver) 25 May 2006: A16

If the creditors present convincing proof of the insolvency of their debtor, the court adjudges him bankrupt and appoints a licensed trustee to take charge of his property.
J.E. Smyth et al. *The Law and Business Administration in Canada* 1987: 300

evoke, invoke, evince   To *evoke* is to call forth something, such as an emotion, a memory, or a response, while to *invoke* is to call upon something, usually a higher power or authority.

Thus anger or nostalgia is evoked; God or a law is invoked. To *evince* something is to reveal or demonstrate it: 'Her performance evinced an ability to deal with conflict'.

> Even though the first criticisms . . . evoked anger, the novel [*Maria Chapdelaine*] had many imitators. . . .
> Ben-Z. Shek *French-Canadian & Québécois Novels* 1991: 19

> Cooke invoked rules the NDP wrote to limit debate on government laws.
> *Toronto Sun* 26 Oct. 1992: 42

> He . . . then plunged into an argument that centred on the 'constitutional convention' which the provinces had evoked.
> Jack Batten *Robinette* 1984: 235

(The word required here, in the context of appealing to a legal precedent or other authority, is *invoke*.)

> It has been asserted by solemn scholars that the unappeasable appetite for puns which the Victorians evinced . . . was the dawn of a literary theater, the pun being essentially a literary device.
> Robertson Davies *A Voice from the Attic* 1960: 180

> The quick costume change is an old theatre trick. Nevertheless, it evinced gasps and applause from the capacity audience.
> *Globe and Mail* (Toronto) 21 Feb. 1985: E3

(The word required here is *evoked*, meaning called forth.)

> A painting of a flower could never, according to this line of thought, evince the passionate engagement with the world that a political painting could.
> *Border Crossings* 23.3 (2004): 44–56

(The word required here is *evoke* or *inspire*.)

ex-   see EXH-

exacerbate   The historical meaning of *exacerbate* is to embitter. Although several critics still decry the more general sense, 'to make worse', it is now common in all varieties of writing and attested in most dictionaries.

> As the tensions within the quintet grew, they were exacerbated by Parker's erratic behavior, which caused all the members grief.
> Jack Chambers *Milestones* 1983: 83

> The Canada Council's actions have exacerbated the shortage of talented curators in the institutions.
> *Queen's Quarterly* 94.2 (1987): 557

(Here *exacerbated* means made worse.)

exacting, exact   An *exacting* task requires considerable effort and attention to details; an *exacting* employer is demanding and hard to please; and an *exact* measurement is accurate. The emphasis in the adjective *exacting* is on the demands made and the effort required; *exact* simply means correct and precise. To *exact* something from someone is to demand and obtain it.

> Striking the right combination of responses to these often complicated and very sensitive demands is an exacting business, and researchers must proceed with due caution and deliberation.
> *Alternatives Journal* 27.4 (2001): 53

> He could not provide exact numbers.
> *Calgary Herald* 21 Dec. 1993: D6

> . . . the day he found Evelyn slumped over the peonies she was planting in the front yard . . . [was] a day he could describe in exacting detail right down to the interior colors of the ambulance. . . .
> *Ottawa Citizen* 24 Dec. 1990: A14

(The word required here is *exact*.)

> Sequential releasing was formerly worked out on exacting charts, timing the availability of films from the first-run theatre showings to airline use, small-town distribution, 16mm rental to schools, free television and so on.
> *Globe and Mail* (Toronto) 9 Sept. 1985: S12

(Here 'worked out *exactly* on charts' would make better sense.)

> The ordeal has exacted a toll from [his] family.
> *Calgary Herald* 14 Jan. 1995: A1

See also EXACT SAME.

exact same   Many usage guides note that *exact* is not an adverb and thus should not be used to modify the adjective *same* in the phrase *exact same*. However, *exact same* is idiomatic and accepted in conversation and informal writing. In formal writing *exactly the same* should be used.

My gripe is city transit buses that pull out at the exact same time as they signal—regardless of whether or not there are cars in the lane beside them.
Province (Vancouver) 30 Dec. 1990: 17

See also EXACTING, EXACT.

exalt, exalted, exaltation   see EXULT

exceed   see -CEED, -CEDE, -SEDE

excellent   see PERFECT

exceptionable   see UNEXCEPTIONABLE

excise   To *excise* is to cut out. *Excise* or *excise tax* is a tax or duty levied on goods produced within the country. Sometimes these words are misspelled *exise*.

> In her will, however, she stipulated that this reference be excised in all subsequent printings, and this was done.
> Ben-Z. Shek *French-Canadian & Québécois Novels* 1991: 31

> She . . . worked for Revenue Canada, customs and exise, for several years.
> *Daily News* (Halifax) 27 Feb. 1998: 40

(The correct spelling is *excise*.)

See also TAX.

exclamation mark   The exclamation mark (called an exclamation point in the United States) should be used sparingly in serious writing. An exclamation mark cannot bolster a weak argument or add force to a sentence that lacks it.

For some writers, however, overuse is not the problem. For fear of seeming unsophisticated, they have banished the exclamation mark from their writing, with the result that their readers may be puzzled by the tone of an utterance such as 'How the responsibility weighed on him'. Unless this is part of a title ('How the Responsibility Weighed on Him and Led to his Premature Demise'), it requires an exclamation mark: 'How the responsibility weighed on him!' Sentences are exclamations if they begin with *how*, *what*, or *why* but do not ask a question: 'How tall you've grown!'; 'Why there you are!'; 'What a mistake that was!' Occasionally, sentences in question form may also be exclamations; when 'What did you say?' is an expression of astonishment or a threat, it should be punctuated with an exclamation mark: 'What did you say!' Interjections, such as *hey*, *hi*, *oh*, or *oops*, should be followed by an exclamation mark if they are said in excitement ('Hey! Get out of there!'), by a comma ('Oh, soon, I think') if they are not. Though exclamations are often incomplete sentences, they are not considered ungrammatical: 'If only I'd known!'; 'To think that you were there the whole time!'; 'If it isn't Rob!'

True exclamations can be recognized by their tone. In informal writing, the exclamation mark often tags the content of a non-exclamatory sentence as notable or interesting: 'Bob will be sending Melinda in his place!'; 'One of them was issued in 1944!' This use of the exclamation mark as a graphic equivalent of 'Interesting, eh?' is not suitable for formal writing. It is probably this use that writing guides are trying to forestall when they advise using the exclamation mark sparingly.

Double exclamation marks, strings of exclamation marks, and exclamation marks combined with question marks are found in journalism but never used in formal writing.

> The disquietude has even begun to awaken moral philosophers from the dogmatic slumbers of our moral anthropocentrism. A good thing that!
> *Queen's Quarterly* 92.1 (1985): 209

(An exclamation mark is the appropriate punctuation here; a formal context does not preclude exclamation marks.)

> 'What a prodigious task!'
> W.C. Lougheed, ed. *In Search of the Standard in Canadian English* 1986: 66

> Just the other day I was looking through a box of old souvenirs from my childhood and I spotted some old hockey card wrappers from the mid-1970s and noticed in those days packs sold for 15 cents!
> *Evening Telegram* (St. John's) 25 May 1993: 13

(This use of the exclamation mark is informal.)

See you all there!!!
Chronicle-Telegraph (Quebec City) 6 June 1991: 3

(Using more than one exclamation mark is informal.)

What do you mean it probably will happen to my daughter!?
Evening Telegram (St. John's) 23 May 1993: 15

(Combining a question mark and an exclamation mark is informal.)

See also QUOTATION, QUOTATION MARKS.

executor   see -ER, -OR

exemplar   see EPITOME

exh-, ex-   When the letter *h* follows the prefix *ex-* it is usually silent. *Exhibition, exhilarating,* and *exhort* are often misspelled without *h*, while *exorbitant, exonerate,* and *exuberant,* are often misspelled with an *h* after the prefix *ex-*.

Related words may be helpful in remembering which of these words contain *h*. Spelled with an *h* are *exhibition*, like *inhibition*; *exhilarating*, like *hilarious*; and *exhort*, like *hortatory*. Spelled without an *h* are *exorbitant*, like *orbit*; *exonerate*, like *onerous*; and *exuberant*, like the German *über*, 'over'.

exhaustive, exhausting   *Exhaustive*, which means comprehensive or very thorough, is often confused with *exhausting*, which means very tiring.

'The body remained unidentified for 19 years despite an exhaustive investigation.'
Vancouver Sun 18 Dec. 1993: B6

It's an exhausting process that can take more than eight hours just to travel a metre or two.
Whig-Standard (Kingston) 27 Dec. 2002: 1

Add in a demented Pole named Wojtek Dmochowski doing exhaustive calisthenics to the songs and you've got your full concert experience.
Gazette (Montreal) 15 Nov. 1990: C1

(Here exhausting would be a better choice.)

exhibition, exhilarating, exhort   see EXH-, EX-

exile   see ÉMIGRÉ

exist   see SUBSIST

exonerate, exorbitant   see EXH-, EX-

exotic, esoteric, exoteric   *Exotic* once meant simply foreign, not native. Today, in botany and zoology, *exotic* still means simply not indigenous, but in general use it means strange or unusual, often in a fascinating or beautiful way. *Exotic dancer* is usually a euphemism for stripper.

Esoteric and *exoteric* were originally used to refer to disciples in the Greco-Roman world. The master shared his deepest thoughts with the 'inner circle' of *esoteric* disciples. The *exoteric* disciples were the large group who were given only general knowledge. *Exoteric*, meaning capable of being understood by a general audience, is now rare, but *esoteric*, meaning comprehensible only to those with special knowledge, is fairly common.

More exotic plant species were relegated to conservatories and botanical exhibits.
Canadian Consumer Jan. 1986: 13

A reference work of this kind is meant to be used selectively. Some entries require thorough study, others should be read for the factual information they provide, and a few will prove to be too esoteric for the general reader's interest.
Queen's Quarterly 92.2 (1985): 403

But another Hechler contribution to today's collections is the quantity of elaborate and attractive envelopes he prepared in his flowing handwriting. These covers, to and from many esoteric destinations, now grace some of the best collections.
Globe and Mail (Toronto) 26 Jan. 1985: CL16

(The word required here is *exotic*.)

expatriate   see ÉMIGRÉ

expect   The use of *expect* to mean suppose, as in 'I expect I will', is labelled informal in most dictionaries. Yet it's common in fairly formal Canadian writing. Perhaps it could be more accurately described as having a conversational tone.

When they cut Mary Webster down the next day, she was, to everyone's surprise, not dead. . . . I

expect that if everyone thought she had occult powers before the hanging, they were even more convinced of it afterwards.
Margaret Atwood *Second Words* 1982: 331

'I expect you'd like some breakfast too.' She didn't wait for an answer.
David Williams *Eye of the Father* 1985: 43

I expect you are all familiar with the real significance of the symbol of Aquarius.
Robertson Davies *One Half of Robertson Davies* 1978: 59

See also ANTICIPATE; DON'T THINK

expedient   see EXPEDITIOUS

expedite, [expediate]   To *expedite* means to hasten or streamline a process; this word is often used with reference to bureaucratic or legal procedures. *Expediate* is a non-standard variant, probably influenced by *expedient*. The *OED* records *expediate* as a persistent error; current dictionaries do not list it at all. Though it is not accepted as a word, *expediate* does appear in print occasionally.

Accordingly, once the war was over, Principal Wallace did everything he could, by way of negotiation and pressure, to expedite the discharge of Queen's staff members from the armed services. . . .
Frederick Gibson *Queen's University* 2 (1983): 244

Terrace reveals Plan B, a possible OMB hearing swap with another party to expediate rezoning farmland for an arena.
Ottawa Citizen 7 Dec. 1990: C4

(The correct spelling is *expedite*.)

See also EXPEDITIOUS, EXPEDIENT.

expeditious, expedient   An *expeditious* manner of proceeding is speedy and efficient. An *expedient* course of action serves the purpose well, though it may be morally questionable.

'Funding considerations are not a legitimate reason for [court] cases not being dealt with in an expeditious fashion,' Hall said.
Calgary Herald 5 Nov. 1994: A9

But the darker side of the North, the bureaucratic

decisions made in the 1950s to transport Inuit from their homelands farther north as an expedient way of claiming territory for Canada, isn't mentioned.
Ottawa Citizen 31 Oct. 1993: C6

More important it is a party that has lost the confidence of the Canadian people—and not even the judicious, politically expeditious removal of former leader Kim Campbell will restore that confidence.
Calgary Herald 19 Dec. 1993: A6

(The expression *politically expeditious*—politically speedy—doesn't make sense. If the author did mean to emphasize speed, *expeditious* by itself would be better; otherwise the word required is *expedient*.)

See also EXPEDITE.

expel, expell   see DISPEL

explicit   see IMPLICIT

exploitive, exploitative   These variants are equally acceptable and about equally popular in Canadian English.

exposition   see QUEBEC ENGLISH

ex post facto   *Ex post facto* is a Latin phrase meaning 'after the fact'. An '*ex post facto* analysis' benefits from hindsight; Canadian criminal laws are not enforced *ex post facto*—that is, retroactively. This phrase requires italics in formal writing.

The OPP had claimed, falsely, that the Indians shot at them, but the judge in the trial of the OPP officer who killed George ruled that 'the story of the rifle . . . had been concocted ex post facto in an ill-fated attempt to disguise the fact that an unarmed man was shot'.
Toronto Star 29 Oct. 2000: A2

See also LATIN PHRASES.

expresso   see ESPRESSO

expressway   see ROAD

extemporaneous, impromptu   Both words

mean without preparation. An unrehearsed comment or performance may be called either *extemporaneous* or *impromptu*. A spontaneous action is usually *impromptu*: 'an impromptu visit'. In the context of formal public speaking, an *extemporaneous* speech has received some preparatory attention but is delivered without notes and has not been memorized.

An *impromptu* speech is spontaneous, completely unpremeditated.

> Davis . . . and Hank Jones, a superior accompanist who plays beautifully throughout this session, fashion a long, apparently extemporaneous movement at the end of *Autumn Leaves*. . . .
> Jack Chambers *Milestones* 1983: 275–6

> . . . Esposito is remembered for his remarkable all-round play, for being the emotional heart of his team, the man who made a poignant impromptu speech to the nation on TV after the crushing fourth-game defeat in Vancouver.
> Ken Dryden *The Game* 1983: 103

See also EXTEMPORIZE.

extemporize, temporize   To *extemporize* is to speak off the cuff, to improvise; to *temporize* is to stall or delay purposely.

> 'Julia Duffy comes in every day with the script totally memorized. . . . And so does David—of course David is more apt to extemporize, or improvise.'
> *Vancouver Sun* 23 July 1994: A13

> Their temporizing and backsliding have disappointed many of their supporters. . . .
> *Toronto Star* 4 June 1994: B4

See also EXTEMPORANEOUS.

extort, extract   see ELICIT

extreme   see PERFECT

extremely, extremism   see -E

exuberant   see EXH-, EX-

exult, exultant, exalt, exalted, exulta- **tion, exaltation**   To *exult* is to rejoice (you feel *exultant*). To *exalt* is to raise someone in status (so that he or she enjoys an *exalted* rank) or to fill someone with joy (then he or she is, or feels, *exalted*.) *Exultation* and *exaltation* both suggest rejoicing and elation, but only *exaltation* refers to spiritual uplifting or an elevation of status.

> 'With one second left, we got a goal,' exulted Ray Diabo.
> *Gazette* (Montreal) 22 Nov. 1992: D1

> But beneath the tumbling quiff of hair and behind the guarded amused eyes, [k.d.] Lang is exultant.
> *Calgary Herald* 19 June 1993: D5

> . . . we remain a society which exalts lawyers and looks down on the people who know how to run your basic laser-powered widget buster.
> *Gazette* (Montreal) 16 March 1993: A3

> Yet until recently, the exalted critical status of [Bruno Bettelheim's] The Uses of Enchantment had gone virtually unchallenged.
> *Gazette* (Montreal) 6 June 1992: J1

> 'He said he would be back, he said he would play again and he said he would get drafted,' exalted Jackie Marshall. . . . 'And he's done it!'
> *Daily News* (Halifax) 21 June 1992: 64

(The word required here is *exulted*.)

> Hamilton coach Don Sutherin wasn't going to ruin his feelings of exultation by pondering Hamilton's tenuous playoff situation.
> *Edmonton Journal* 17 Oct. 1994: D2

> Delacroix's Liberty Leading the People shows us the exaltation of righteous struggle.
> *Gazette* (Montreal) 30 April 1994: A1

> Hollywood, in David Gurr's eyes, is the exultation of the average.
> *Calgary Herald* 16 April 1994: B11

(The word required here is *exaltation*, meaning glorification.)

-ey   see -E, -EY

eye dialect   see [COULD OF]

F

f, ph Words derived from Latin, French, Italian, or Old English tend to be spelled with an *f* (*federal, famous, fiasco, fish*). Words containing the digraph *ph* are usually borrowings from Greek (*philosophy, photograph, amphibian*). A very few English words, such as *phantasy/fantasy* and *sulphur/sulfur*, have two standard spellings. The historical *f/ph* spelling variation is being exploited in contemporary English to create new informal words. *Phat* (slang synonym of 'cool' or 'hot'), *phreaking* (hacking into telephone lines to make free calls), and *phishing* (fraudulent solicitation of identity and financial information by e-mail) are examples of recent coinages in which *ph-* replaces an initial *f-*.

See also COMPUTER TERMS; DIPHTHONG, DIGRAPH; FANTASY, PHANTASY; SULPHUR, SULFUR.

-f, -v- A small group of nouns that end with *f* or with *f* followed by a silent *e* (e.g., *knife*) form their plurals in *-ves*: *calf, calves; elf, elves; half, halves; knife, knives; leaf, leaves; life, lives; loaf, loaves; self, selves; sheaf, sheaves; shelf, shelves; thief, thieves; wife, wives; wolf, wolves*. However, many similar words are pluralized in the regular way, simply by adding *s*: *beliefs, carafes, chiefs, handkerchiefs, proofs, roofs, safes, skiffs, staffs*. For a few words, either an *-s* or a *-ves* plural is accepted: *cloverleaf* (the highway junction), *dwarf, hoof, scarf, wharf*.

Generally, new coinages and compounds are pluralized regularly: for example, *low-lifes*. Paintings of flowers, fruit, domestic objects, etc., are called *still lifes*. And Toronto's National Hockey League team is called the *Maple Leafs*, which may account for Canadian writers' tendency to use the unacceptable plural *leafs* for the parts of a plant or the pages in a book.

Once you get a puzzle piece, bring it to the office tower atrium at Harbor Centre, where one of Santa's friendly elfs will fit your puzzle piece into a gigantic jigsaw puzzle.
Province (Vancouver) 7 Dec. 1990: 16

(The accepted plural is *elves*.)

But don't think that just because your cereal box shows sheafs of grain and a wholesome farm-family background, what's in it is healthy.
Ottawa Citizen 14 Feb. 1990: C1

(The accepted plural is *sheaves*.)

A friend recently corrected me for saying roofs. 'Rooves?' I said. 'Rooves with a "v"? Are you mad?'
Telegram (St. John's) 12 June 2003: B3

(*Roofs* is the accepted plural.)

Torontonians Valdine MacLeod and her husband Norman lugged two plastic shopping bags filled with Canadian first editions to the reading, hoping the writers would find time to lay their John Hancocks . . . on the front leafs.
Globe and Mail (Toronto) 8 May 1985: P19

(The accepted plural is *leaves*.)

See also MAPLE LEAF; -SELF, -SELVES.

fabliau, fabliaux see PLURALS

faceable see -ABLE, -(E)ABLE

facile *Facile* usually has negative connotations: a facile remark is glib, a facile argument superficial, and a facile emotion shallow. Occasionally *facile* is used in the positive sense of smooth or easy. The word is pronounced with stress on the first syllable, *FASS-*; the second syllable rhymes with *mile* or *mill*.

Yet this is not to say that Gallant is a dishonest writer, a superficial or facile spinner of verbal webs.
Janice Kulyk Keefer *Reading Mavis Gallant* 1989: 58

Lawren Harris makes it clear that what drove him

and his colleagues out to the northern part of Canada was their distrust of the 'picturesque,' that is, the pictorial subject which suggests a facile or conventional pictorial response.
Northrop Frye *The Bush Garden* 1971: 209

. . . Davis was asleep on the floor, completely unaware of Gillespie's facile manipulation of the trumpet part that had stumped him.
Jack Chambers *Milestones* 1983: 41

(Here *facile* is used in a positive sense.)

facilitate, facilitator To *facilitate* means to help or ease. Several commentators note that things and actions, not people, are facilitated: 'The work of the cook was facilitated by the new microwave oven', *not* 'The cook was facilitated by the new microwave oven'.

In the jargon of social work, a *facilitator* is a person who chairs a meeting or leads a group through a workshop. Thus the verb *facilitate* has developed a new meaning: to lead a group through a meeting. In Quebec English, an *animator* leads a discussion.

See also QUEBEC ENGLISH.

facility *Facilities* are premises, equipment, or services tailored to a particular purpose: 'conference facilities', 'storage facilities'. Some usage guides object to the use of the word *facility* where a more common or precise word exists: for example, 'educational facility' instead of 'school', or 'correctional facility' instead of 'prison'. While *facility* is sometimes used euphemistically or to exaggerate the importance of a structure, it is also used appropriately when there is no common word for what is being described.

Like the first, most of which was shot at Toronto's former Queen Street mental health facility, it will be filmed in Toronto.
Globe and Mail (Toronto) 11 Jan. 1985: E7

(Here *mental health facility* is a euphemism for *psychiatric hospital*.)

He said if he ever had a few million dollars to spare he'd love to build an indoor facility with 12 basketball courts.
Globe and Mail (Toronto) 15 Nov. 1985: D20

(Although the proposed *indoor facility* is a *gym*, the word *gym* would not have suggested the intended size.)

facsimile see CATASTROPHE; FAX

fact see FACT THAT; TRUE FACTS

factious, fractious, factitious Someone who is *factious* (pronounced *FACK shuss*) causes strife by showing loyalty to a faction: a small group within a larger group. Groups with factious members are faction-ridden and frequently engage in factional disputes. *Fractious* (pronounced *FRACK shuss*) means unruly or irritable; since those who are *factious* are often *fractious* as well, these terms are sometimes confused.

The adjective *factitious* (pronounced *fack TISH us*) refers to something that is artificial or contrived.

Supporting the Americans against Lord North, he still reflected that opposition to the war came from factious politicians.
J.A.W. Gunn *Beyond Liberty and Property* 1983: 207

The ever-popular Something True, a French filly with an attitude problem, was fractious at the gate and delayed the start of the race. . . .
Canadian Thoroughbred Jan. 1989: 29

. . . it may seem to some readers that I have raked over a handful of forgotten, or almost forgotten, books of the past century, attributing to them a factitious significance by reading into them what is not there.
Robertson Davies *A Voice from the Attic* 1960: 152

Giving a report on a conference working group on the mutual development of the East Coast's fisheries, Mr. MacLean said the industry is fractious and 'there are four serious splinter groups in New England.'
Globe and Mail (Toronto) 19 June 1985: P5

(The word required here is *factious*.)

As Western Europe continues to integrate, large chunks of Eastern Europe are rapidly disintegrating. Yugoslavia remains mired in a bloody civil war and the former Soviet Union is dissolving into fractious republics.
Financial Post 30 Dec. 1991: 36

(The contrast with an integrating Europe suggest that *factious* is meant here, although either word is possible.)

See also FICTIVE, FICTIONAL, FICTITIOUS.

fact that, the   Phrases containing *the fact that* are almost universally condemned by usage experts on the grounds of wordiness. They recommend replacing 'in spite of the fact that' with *although*; 'in view of the fact that' with *because* or *considering that*; and 'due to the fact that' with *because*. Despite the experts' advice, 'in spite of the fact that' and 'in view of the fact that' are quite common, especially in academic writing. Since eliminating *the fact that* is usually easy and almost always results in improvement, writers should try to cut it. However, there are cases where it is difficult to avoid (for example, where a fact is the focus of attention), and in these cases *the fact that* is defensible.

Wodehouse is a popular writer, and the fact that he is a popular writer has a lot to do with his use of stock plots.
Northrop Frye *The Educated Imagination* 1963: 15

(Here '*the fact that* he is a popular writer' could be replaced by two words: 'his popularity'. Frye may well have deliberately chosen this structure to emphasize the phrase 'a popular writer'.)

. . . . he has somewhat modified this conclusion because of the fact that he did not then take into consideration sufficiently that the war had provoked a temporary speeding-up of the rhythm of economic phenomena. . . .
Queen's Quarterly 96.3 (1989): 616

(Using *of the fact that* after *because* is redundant.)

It is estimated that 24,000 cancer deaths could result. . . . The gravity of this should not be understated, especially in view of the fact that the [Chernobyl] accident was far from unavoidable.
Queen's Quarterly 95.2 (1988): 313–4

(Here *in view of the fact that* could be replaced with *since*.)

This is probably due to the fact that he views . . . religion (or culture) and social structure as distinct ontological entities.
Canadian Journal of Sociology 14.2 (1989): 213

(Here *because* would be a better choice.)

Much was made of the fact that he bought up all the oats in town for 40 cents a bushel and sold them for a dollar when the going rate was only 23 1/2 cents.
Pierre Berton *The Promised Land* 1984: 124

(Here a fact is the focus of attention.)

Meanwhile I was agonizing over the fact that I'd spent the summer trying to read *The Waste Land* and hadn't understood a word of it.
Margaret Atwood *Second Words* 1982: 399

(Here a fact is the focus of attention.)

faculty   see COLLECTIVE NOUNS; UNIVERSITY

faeces   see -AE-, -OE-, -E-

fag, faggot   In Britain *fag* is slang for a cigarette, a tedious chore, or a public-school boy who waits on a senior boy, and a *faggot* (also spelled *fagot*) is a bundle of sticks used for making a fire. However, Canadians would be unlikely to use these words in these senses. In North America *fag* and *faggot* are highly derogatory terms for a gay man.

Indeed, on Oct. 1, 1985, Cockburn took part in a taping for CBC television and accidentally saw program notes describing him as a 'Commie fag sympathizer'.
Maclean's 8 Sept. 1986: 68

See also GAY, LESBIAN, HOMOSEXUAL, BISEXUAL, TRANSGENDERED, QUEER, LGBTQ.

Fahrenheit   see CELSIUS

fail to   *Fail to* usually has overtones of recrimination: 'He failed to complete the assignment'. Using this expression with a non-human subject may create an unintentionally humorous effect: 'The new carpet failed to cheer him up'.
   Some usage guides recommend using *fail to* only in contexts where there is an unsuccessful attempt to do something ('I failed to convince her') or where there is negligence ('They failed to warn the passengers of the additional risk').

But this advice is too restrictive. While it would prevent unintentional humour in sentences such as 'The fire failed to burn down the whole house', it would also rule out the idiomatic use of *fail to* to express a departure from what was expected or hoped for: 'Over a fifteen-year period, the wage gap had failed to narrow'; 'Our tests fail to replicate Hennessy's results'.

> Machiavelli, so often now hailed as a great realist, failed to impress Horsley, who was armed with a new standard for judging insight.
> J.A.W. Gunn *Beyond Liberty and Property* 1983: 37

> Only one tissue, a basidioma of Hebeloma crustuliniforme, failed to yield DNA. . . .We suspect that contaminants present in the tissue coprecipitated with the DNA, preventing rehydration of the DNA in the final solution.
> *Canadian Journal of Botany* 67.4 (1989): 1237

(This use of *failed to* with a non-human subject is idiomatic in the sciences.)

> During the past decade, few issues of the Book Review Index have failed to list at least one of Akenson's works. . . .
> *Canadian Journal of History* 14.1 (1989): 120

(Some critics would object to *fail to* here, since the 'few issues' omitting Akenson cannot be faulted.)

fain   see FEIGN

fair, fare   The adjective *fair* means pleasing, or pretty good, or just and equitable, or light in skin or hair colour. The noun *fair* means exhibition.
The noun *fare* means food or entertainment offered to the public, or the amount one pays to ride a public conveyance. The verb *fare* means to get along or succeed. It is the verb that is most often misspelled.

> Two of the victims are in good condition, one is in fair condition and the child has been released from hospital.
> *Windsor Star* 1 April 2006: A12

> Taxi fares are based on time or distance travelled, said Phillip Seymour of the Calgary taxi commission.
> *Calgary Herald* 20 Dec. 1992: A4

> There's a good selection of light fare for noontime and a few more substantial dishes. . . .
> *Ottawa Citizen* 24 Dec. 1992: C5

> When her mother caught sight of her, she called out, 'Well, my daughter, how did you fare?'
> *Ottawa Citizen* 13 Dec. 1992: F3

> The other Nova Scotia team did not fair as well.
> *Daily News* (Halifax) 7 Nov. 1992: 41

(The correct spelling is *fare*.)

> In contrast, countries such as Scotland, which integrated the subject across the curriculum, faired poorly.
> *Globe and Mail* (Toronto) 23 Oct. 1992: n.p.

(The correct spelling is *fared*.)

fairly   see ADJECTIVES AND ADVERBS

fall   see AUTUMN

fallacy, fallacious   In logic, a *fallacy* is a statement that appears to be sound but is actually faulty. (Two logical fallacies described in this guide are *begging the question* and *ad hominem* argument.)
In ordinary usage, a *fallacy* is a mistaken idea. The adjective *fallacious* usually means deceptive or misguided, and some critics maintain that it should not be used simply to mean erroneous. Most Canadian writers appear to observe this distinction.

> It's a critical fallacy of our times, derived perhaps from psychology or optimistic self-help books, that a writer should 'grow,' 'change,' or 'develop.'
> Margaret Atwood *Second Words* 1982: 621

> However, the fallacy of pegging investment to anticipated leaps in petroleum prices was illustrated all too clearly in the early 1980s.
> *London Free Press* 6 May 1986: B6

> Thus if someone argues that wars accomplish a kind of 'natural selection' among humans, it is easy to see why the argument is fallacious.
> Irving M. Zeitlin and Robert J. Brym *The Social Condition of Humanity* 1991: 27

> 'Such imaginative accounting serves only to produce a most fallacious bottom line.'
> *Gazette* (Montreal) 10 Oct. 1990: A1

(Here, although the bottom line is indeed wrong, the point is that this is not just an inadvertent error, but one intended to mislead.)

Fallopian tubes   see CAPITAL LETTERS

false friends, false cognates   see QUEBEC ENGLISH

falsehood, falsity, falseness   A *falsehood* is an untrue statement. *Falsity*, *falsehood*, and *falseness* all refer to the quality of being untrue. Applied to a statement or belief, these words do not suggest any intent to deceive; applied to a person, however, that is exactly what they imply. *Falsehood* in a person is the habit of lying. *Falsity* once commonly referred to a lover's infidelity—a use that now sounds quaint. *Falseness* in a person is insincerity.

> Consequently he's judged by the truth or falsehood of what he says—either there was such a battle or there wasn't, and if there was he's got the date either right or wrong.
> Northrop Frye *The Educated Imagination* 1963: 24

(Here *falsehood* does not imply intentional deceit.)

> 'To say this won't affect the budget is a falseness,' said Coun. Bill McNulty. 'It will require a tax increase next year.'
> *Vancouver Sun* 14 April 2006: B2

(*Falsehood*, meaning untrue statement, is the word needed here. Probably the speaker avoided the word *falsehood* because it sometimes means lie. Falsehoods, however, are not necessarily lies—not necessarily purposely deceptive.)

> 'When people talk about the issues, they sometimes do so as if they were on TV. . . . Sometimes I had to do an interview several times to get beyond the falseness. . .'.
> *Whig-Standard* (Kingston) 10 March 2006: 30

(Here *falseness* means artificiality.)

false titles   see ATTRIBUTIVE NOUNS

falsity   see FALSEHOOD

family   see COLLECTIVE NOUNS; SPECIES

family names   see CHINESE NAMES

fanatic, fanatical   see -IC, -ICAL

fanny   see BUTTOCKS

fantastically   see PUBLICLY

fantasy, phantasy   *Fantasy* is the usual Canadian spelling for all meanings of the word; *phantasy* is literary or archaic. In British English, however, *phantasy* still has some currency as a medical term for delusions.

> The 'melodrama of the American Dream' involves a fantasy of social mobility doomed to failure.
> *Queen's Quarterly* 97 (1990): 95

> Schoenberg was represented first by his Phantasy for Violin and Piano, Op. 47, with David Zafer, violin, and Sharon Krause, piano.
> *Globe and Mail* (Toronto) 19 Jan. 1985: E10

far away, faraway, far-away   *Far away* is two words except when it's an adjective used directly before a noun. Then the spelling is *faraway* or, less commonly, *far-away*.

> From far away a deep voice rumbled at me.
> *Room of One's Own* June 1990: 80

> He seemed very far away.
> Geoffrey Ursell *Perdue, or, How the West Was Lost* 1984: 144

> . . . it's a testament to his teaching and mentorship abilities that former PhD students—now faculty members at such faraway institutions as the Universities of Illinois and Hong Kong—flew in to attend his retirement party.
> *Beyond Numbers* Feb./March 2004: n.p.

> Russia was not about to expend large sums on a build-up in the distant Pacific or get involved in some far-away adventure of dubious outcome.
> *Queen's Quarterly* 92.1 (1985): 182

fare   see FAIR

Far East   see ASIA

far-sighted   see NEAR-SIGHTED

farther, further In the past *farther* and *further* were used interchangeably both as adverbs ('He went farther *or* further') and as adjectives ('further *or* farther research'). Now *farther* is most often used when literal or figurative distance is implied ('We slid farther'), while *further* is most often used to mean additional ('no further help'). In British English *further* is more common in all senses.

> The analyses of 22 relatively unaltered samples reported in Store *et al.* (1984) and a further 18 that were analysed recently . . . are considered here.
> *Canadian Journal of Earth Sciences* 26 (1989): 408

> St. Hubert MP Pierrette Venne herself suggested that [the proposal] be referred to the party's executive for farther study. . . .
> *Gazette* (Montreal) 4 Nov. 1990: A1

(*Further* is more common in Canadian English when the meaning is 'additional'.)

fascist The Fascists (*Fascisti* in Italian) were an Italian political party that set up a dictatorship under Benito Mussolini in 1922 and joined forces with the Nazis. Fascist policy was racist and ultranationalist. Now the adjective *fascist* is applied to anything or anyone considered dictatorial or undemocratic. Although the term is historically connected to the right, today it is often applied to left-wing groups.

The *sc* in the middle of *fascist* is pronounced *sh*. The word should be capitalized only when referring to the political party.

> *Sun* writers have attacked the Ontario Human Rights Commission for what they see as potentially fascist tendencies. *Sun* writers have argued that non-whites in Canada are, perversely, favoured over whites; and they have condemned organized multiculturalism.
> *Saturday Night* April 1986: 6

fast ADVERBS WITHOUT -LY; SLOW

fatal, fateful A *fatal* event results in death or disaster. A *fateful* event is highly significant, marking a turn of fortune for better or worse. Though both words may be applicable in some contexts, they are not synonyms in current usage.

> The most fatal disease of friendship is gradual decay. . . .
> Richard Davies and Glen Kirkland, eds. *Dimensions* 1986: 22–3

> Then the rookie Liberal MPP got married, and on one fateful day accompanied his wife on a shopping outing. To his horror, he discovered that various products—from women's suits to female deodorant—cost more than their male counterparts! From this barren soil, a human rights crusader was born.
> *National Post* (Toronto) 21 March 2006: A16

> A sustained determination to make the best possible appointments to the academic staff is one means of avoiding a fateful descent into the cosy and second-rate, but it was only one weapon in the armory of Principal Grant.
> Frederick Gibson *Queen's University* 2 (1978): 435

(The use of *fateful* to mean disastrous or ruinous is uncommon; *fatal* would be a better choice.)

father-in-law see IN-LAWS

faucet see TAP

fauna see FLORA

faux amis see QUEBEC ENGLISH

faux pas *Faux pas* (pronounced *FOE PAW*) is an expression borrowed from French. It translates literally as 'false step' and refers to a blunder, especially a social one. The plural is *faux pas* (pronounced *FOE PAWS* or, as in French, *FOE PAW*). *Faux pas* is sometimes hyphenated, though it shouldn't be.

> Suddenly realizing his faux pas, he quickly added: 'Ah! Poor woman.'
> Terence Dickinson *Halley's Comet* 1985: 26

> Those fortunate people got their kicks by pointing out the fashion faux pas of others.
> *Ottawa Citizen* 3 June 1992: C4

> Was she supposed to tell Shireen of these plans, or would this be committing an enormous cultural faux-pas?
> *Ottawa Citizen* 8 March 1992: B4

(The hyphen should be deleted.)

favorite, favourite   see -OUR, -OR

fax, FAQs   Three homophones share the pronunciation *FAX*. A *fax* is a document sent through the public telecommunication system; this noun and the related verb are derived from *facsimile*. *Fax* is also a tongue-in-cheek and very informal spelling of *facts*. The acronym *FAQs*—pronounced either *FAX* or letter by letter—means Frequently Asked Questions.

> After checking the results, he said he faxed them to Mellow the same day.
> *Ottawa Citizen* 11 July 1990: B2

> FAX OF LOVE: Italian porn star-politician Ilona (Cicciolina) Staller and American sculptor Jeff Koons have fallen in love by fax and plan to marry on Valentine's Day.
> *Vancouver Sun* 5 Dec. 1990: A2

(The headline in this example is a pun.)

> You have until September to make your plans for Oktoberfest—www.oktoberfest.de [is] a website that offers helpful tips under Facts & FAQs.
> *Province* (Vancouver) 12 Sept. 2004: C15

See also HOMOPHONE, HOMOGRAPH, HOMONYM.

faze   see PHASE

February   Although teachers encourage their pupils to pronounce both the *r*'s in *February* (*FEB rew air ee*), many—perhaps most—educated Canadians say *FEB yew air ee*, which is analogous to *January* and easier to articulate. Most Canadian, American, and British dictionaries now list both pronunciations without comment.

See also LIBRARY.

feces   see -AE-, -OE-, -E-

feel good, feel bad   see ADJECTIVES AND ADVERBS; BAD, BADLY

feet   see FOOT

feign, feint, deke, fain   *Feign,* pronounced *FAIN,* is a verb meaning pretend, as in 'feign illness'. A *feint* is a pretend blow or delusive move intended to draw an opponent out of position; today this sense is most common in the context of sports. *Feint* is also used as a verb meaning to execute a feint. *Deke* is a slang synonym of *feint;* the word originated in hockey, but is now used more widely.

Fain is an archaic word, now used only for humorous effect. Traditionally, *fain* occurs in two constructions. To be *fain* to do something is to be willing or compelled by circumstances to do it: 'I was fain to take a breath'. The phrase *would fain* means 'would gladly' or 'would rather'.

> 'You have a point, Toma,' said Workun, feigning joviality.
> *NeWest Review* Feb.–Mar. 1990: 23

> Like a big stallion, feinting with fluid crossing strides, he prances languorously right, then left, swinging his body to shield the puck, easing by them.
> Ken Dryden *The Game* 1983: 192

> Four helicopters fly to his appointments, deking here and there to confuse assassins.
> *Globe and Mail* (Toronto) 24 Sept. 1985: P14

> 'The Sentinel represents no particular class, creed or party, and we would fain hope its unassuming pages might interest our many friends of the colony.'
> *Star-Phoenix* (Saskatoon) 17 Oct. 2002: F21

(A quotation from Saskatchewan's first newspaper, 1884.)

> . . . I wondered if James Reginald Pruett Fane, Nationalist supporter of Franco, ex-Catholic, and wartime government employee, was the kind of man Amis would fain have been.
> *Ottawa Citizen* 26 Nov. 1995: C5

(This book reviewer puns on Fane, the name of a character in a novel by Kingsley Amis.)

See also see -IE-, -EI-.

fell swoop   In Shakespeare's play *Macbeth,* MacDuff uses the phrase 'at one fell swoop' to describe how his whole family has been murdered by Macbeth. Here *fell* is used in the now rare sense of cruel or savage; the image recalls a bird of prey suddenly attacking a helpless victim. In contemporary use the phrase refers to things happening all at once, with no connotation of ruthlessness. Canadian writers most often begin the phrase with *in*, but *at* is still common. The expression appears mostly in journalism. Some critics call it a cliché.

> The firm has developed a water filtration system that siphons off a variety of contaminants in one fell swoop, without the need for several filters or heavy doses of chlorine.
> *Province* (Vancouver) 29 April 1990: 44

See also CLICHÉ.

felony   see INDICTABLE OFFENCE

ferment, foment   In brewing or yogourt-making, the verb *ferment* is used to describe the natural process in which bacteria or yeast grows and becomes acidic or alcoholic: 'The grapes are fermenting into wine'. The noun *ferment* refers to the agent of this change: 'We added the yeast as a ferment to initiate the brewing'.

To *foment*, in medieval times, was to apply either a warm poultice or heat alone to the body for restorative purposes. The noun *foment* or *fomentation* was thus a synonym for a poultice: 'We applied a foment to the wound'.

While *ferment* retains its scientific use today, the medieval and literal meaning of *foment* is either listed as archaic in dictionaries or else listed not at all. Due to their similar pronunciations, these words have acquired figurative meanings that have begun to overlap.

Figuratively, *ferment* is used as an intransitive verb to describe a process of change or development: 'The idea had been fermenting for some time'. *Ferment* as a noun thus describes a state of activity or upheaval: 'Society is in ferment'. This makes sense when one considers the literal meaning of *ferment*: change caused by an evolution of constituent elements.

Foment, in contrast, is used figuratively as a transitive verb to meaning to encourage change in something else: 'He is fomenting discord'.

This use makes sense when one remembers that the original meaning of *foment* was to apply heat to something.

Today, in rare cases, *foment* is used figuratively as a noun: 'Society is in foment'. And slightly more often the verb *ferment* is used with an object to mean incite: 'He is fermenting discord'. While commentators denounce the use of *foment* as a noun, they seem increasingly to accept the use of *ferment* as a transitive verb. Indeed, most dictionaries now list *foment*, stir up, as one sense of the verb *ferment*. In conservative usage, however, either trouble *ferments* (on its own) or people *foment* it.

> Naturally, good ideas ferment in spaces that are prepared for them. . . .
> *Convergence* 36.3–4 (2003): 47

(This is the accepted figurative use of *ferment* as an intransitive verb.)

> In the 1540s, when Protestant doctrine began to spread within her borders, Poland was in the grip of intellectual ferment brought on by the Northern Renaissance.
> *Journal of Ukrainian Studies* 28.1 (2003): 105–117

(This is the undisputed figurative use of *ferment* as a noun.)

> Dispatching happiness, when you could have prevented it, foments tragedy.
> *Queen's Quarterly* 108.3 (2001): 450

(This is the accepted figurative use of *foment* as a transitive verb.)

> Don't we risk polarizing the debate, and fomenting ill will where none now exists?
> *Globe and Mail* (Toronto) 6 Sept. 2006: A4

(This is the accepted figurative use of *foment* as a transitive verb.)

> Pope Benedict XVI said yesterday that the media can spread peace but also ferment violence, and called on journalists to exercise responsibility to ensure objective reports that respect human dignity and the common good.
> *Daily News* (Halifax) 9 May 2005: 9

(*Foment* is the safer choice here, although *ferment* is gaining acceptance as a transitive verb.)

fête   see QUEBEC ENGLISH

fetid   see -AE-, -OE-, -E-

fetus   see -AE-, -OE-, -E-

fewer, less   According to most usage guides and writing handbooks, *fewer* refers to a smaller number, while *less* refers to a smaller amount. In other words, *fewer* should be used of things that can be counted ('fewer books', 'fewer students', 'fewer votes') and *less* of things that are regarded as wholes ('less flour', 'less crime', 'less money'). Phrases like *less people* or *less books* are widely regarded as incorrect and should definitely be avoided both in speech and in writing.

In idiomatic structures, however, *less* often occurs with numbers and quantities. For example, the phrase *or less*, rather than the technically correct *or fewer*, often follows countable nouns: '100 words or less', 'two children or less'. The very common phrase *more or less* reinforces this usage to the point that *or fewer* may well sound odd to some people.

Less than is commonly used with quantities of time, money, distance, etc., that, although they are countable, are usually regarded as wholes: 'less than ten dollars', 'less than 40 per cent', 'less than two months', 'less than 400 km'. Note that these quantities are often treated as singular in other ways: 'Ten dollars is enough'; 'Four hundred kilometres is not very far'. In addition, countable nouns often follow the expression *no less than*: 'They had been to Europe no less than five times in two years'.

These structures are idiomatic and very common in all kinds of Canadian writing. It would be pedantic to insist on *fewer* in these structures, although *fewer* is certainly correct.

Other store owners say it's not that there are fewer customers—they're just buying less.
Gazette (Montreal) 18 Dec. 1990: A3

'Obviously, the broader you are the less restrictions you put on them and the better the trustees can do.'
Edmonton Journal 8 Sept. 1992: n.p.

(Here, directly preceding a countable noun, *fewer* would be a better choice.)

Job ranking is feasible in small organizations or businesses with roughly a hundred jobs or fewer.
Carl J. Cuneo *Pay Equity* 1990: 97

(Although this sentence follows the rule, the phrase or fewer is rare in Canadian writing.)

In most jurisdictions, short-term leases, usually for three years or less, need not be registered or even in writing. . .
J.E. Smyth et al. *The Law and Business Administration in Canada* 1987: 589

The remaining 52 percent of all forested land in the province is held by private individuals in parcels of 200 acres or less.
Harrowsmith Jun.–Jul. 1986: 123

All you had to do was state in fifteen words or less why you liked Cleanso Soap.
Max Braithwaite *The Night We Stole the Mountie's Car* 1971: 207

Artisanal families were small nuclear units with two children or less.
Canadian Journal of History 14.1 (1989): 97

Wayne Gretzky became the first player in NHL history to score 50 goals in fewer than 50 games.
Gazette (Montreal) 30 Dec. 1990: D5

While on average each woman must have 2.1 children in order to insure that the population size does not fall, women are now having fewer than 1.7 children on average.
Irving M. Zeitlin and Robert J. Brym *The Social Condition of Humanity* 1991: 181

[Moore] points out that the records cite less than twenty offences, mostly minor in nature, for a detachment of 212 men over four years of rigorous service.
Canadian Journal of History 14.1 (1989): 108

(*Less than* often precedes a number in formal Canadian English.)

In the twenty-seven months from its debut in Baltimore until it became a sextet, the great quintet was disbanded no less than four times. . . .
Jack Chambers *Milestones* 1983: 216

The Newtonian theory which seemed so entrenched proved within less than 250 years to be false, strictly speaking.
Queen's Quarterly 95 (1988): 25

fiber, fibre   see -RE, -ER

fictive, fictional, fictitious All three words have to do with the invented or imaginary, and all three have a secondary meaning: not true, not genuine. In current English, however, they often have distinct applications. *Fictive* refers to the capacity to create stories: 'the fictive imagination'. *Fictional* refers to invented stories and the literary techniques used to write them, while *fictitious* has come to mean false, counterfeit, or feigned.

> As long ago as 1981, New Yorker writer Kennedy Fraser took note of a 'salacious new public interest in the fashion world' and of how this world . . . has been fodder for the fictive mind.
> *Globe and Mail* (Toronto) 16 July 1985: E1

> . . . Oliva concentrates exclusively and superficially on the content of the book, with no consideration of Ellis's fictional techniques.
> *Ottawa Citizen* 15 Oct. 1994: E12

> He did his business at the Tower Bank, where from time to time he filed statements of largely fictitious assets as a basis for increasing loans.
> J.E. Smyth et al. *The Law and Business Administration in Canada* 1987: 242

See also FACTIOUS, FRACTIOUS, FACTITIOUS.

fiddle, violin, fiddler *Fiddle* and *violin* may be used as synonyms, although generally *violin* suggests classical music, symphony orchestras, and string quartets, while *fiddle* suggests barn dances and bluegrass.

Sometimes the instruments used in these different milieux have actual physical differences. The instrument used for classical music is unamplified, and may be strung with three strings made of gut (or a modern substitute) and a single steel string. The instrument used in bluegrass, country, and traditional music may have four steel strings. Some pop musicians use an 'electric violin', an amplified instrument that may have five or more strings and just a skeletal fibreglass frame instead of a wooden body.

In Newfoundland English a *fiddler* is the musician who plays the music for a dance, no matter what instrument is played; it may be a fiddle but it's often an accordion.

fifth estate see FOURTH ESTATE

fight with *Fight with* is ambiguous, meaning either fight alongside or fight against: 'The Serbs fought with the Croats during the Second World War'. Where the context leaves any doubt as to which meaning is intended, it's best to avoid the phrase.

figuratively see LITERALLY

figurehead A *figurehead* on a ship is a carved figure on the prow. By metaphorical extension, a *figurehead* is a leader in name only, without real authority or responsibility. The connotations of this term are pejorative or at least dismissive. The term shouldn't be used when the context is positive.

> They dismiss the current press lord as 'Young Ken,' an immature figurehead whose main accomplishment was to be his father's only son.
> *Maclean's* 14 Oct. 1991: A44

> Prime ministers take more care in choosing Supreme Court justices than they do in picking the governor-general, perhaps because they feel the former are important while the latter is merely a symbol, a figurehead.
> *Vancouver Sun* 23 Oct. 1990: A13

> People who love fine things know that Kenneth Donald McLeish has long been a figurehead among Canada's hardy breed of antique dealers.
> *Canadian Collector* 21 (1986): 12

(Here *leader* would be a better choice.)

> A figurehead of the increasingly popular graphic novel genre, Seth has been published everywhere from The New Yorker to Aimee Mann album covers to the pages of this paper.
> *National Post* (Toronto) 1 Sept. 2005: AL8

(The context is clearly positive: *leader* is a better choice.)

figure of speech see entry in Glossary

filet, fillet *Filet* and *fillet* are spelling variants, and both the French pronunciation (*fi LAY*) and the British (*FILL it*) are acceptable for either spelling. A *filet* or *fillet* is a narrow band or thin slice of anything. To *fillet*—the verb is usually spelled with a double *l*—means to debone a fish or cut meat into thin strips. *Filet mignon*, a particular cut of beef, is always spelled with a single *l* and usually pronounced *FI lay MEE nyaw(n)*. *Filet* (pronounced *fi LAY*) also refers to lace of a particular weave.

> Filet of Sole . . . is a busy concourse at lunch and between 6:00 PM and curtain time.
> Alan Tucker, ed. *The Penguin Guide to Canada* 1991: 354

> Fillets of sage are placed about their heads, ankles, and wrists; a whistle is suspended about the neck; their bodies are rubbed with white clay.
> Pierre Berton *The Promised Land* 1984: 215

> Lloyd had caught me filleting the pickerel and right away knew what kind of fisherman I was.
> Howard Engel *Murder Sees the Light* 1984: 25

Filipino, Filipina see PHILIPPINES; OS, -OES

fill in see IDIOMS

filmmaker, videographer, cineaste A *filmmaker* (*film-maker*, with a hyphen, in British English) is a person who directs or produces films. The medium need not be celluloid. Filmmakers now work with film, video and digital recording techniques. A *videographer* is someone who works with a video camera. Camera operators, people who make a business of recording special events such as weddings, and filmmakers with a declared preference for video are all called videographers. A *cineaste*, pronounced *SIN ay ast or SIN ee ast*, is a film devotee or a filmmaker. In formal writing, Canadians often retain the acute accent in this borrowing from French: *cinéaste*. Americans prefer to anglicize the spelling by dropping the final *e*: *cineast*.

> In *Atanarjuat*, filmmakers Norm Cohn and Zacharias Kunuk combined traditional storytelling with digital technology to create a unique film.
> *Canadian Journal of Communication* 29.1 (2004): 47

> Capt. Stephanie Walker, spokesperson for the Snowbirds, said a videographer often films the

squadron's training for debriefing sessions, where pilots can watch and identify areas that need to be corrected.
> *Leader-Post* (Regina) 14 Dec. 2004: A1

> Even the most self-righteous cineaste in the world would have to agree that after watching a steady run of alternative movies, it's a guilty pleasure to see something mindless, fun and Hollywood.
> *Vancouver Sun* 22 Sept. 2000: H3

See also HYPHENATION.

finalize Many British commentators have scorned *finalize* since it came into general use in the 1920s. It has been called gobbledygook and an unnecessary synonym for *complete*. In fact, though, *finalize* has a special meaning: to put in final form or give final approval to. Deals, plans, and agreements, etc., are all commonly said to be finalized. There seems to be no logical reason to avoid this useful word. Hostility to it can in part be explained by its provenance. The *Oxford English Dictionary* lists citations for *finalize* in Australia and the United States before Great Britain. According to R.W. Burchfield, in *The New Fowler's*, the word 'was for a long time regarded in Britain as an "unwanted Americanism"' (297).

> In the fall of 1976, more than a year after Cameron's arrival, the adoption still hadn't been finalized.
> *Saturday Night* April 1986: 32

> After NATO foreign ministers had finalized the wording of the communiqué, some members of the alliance sought credit for the wording that made the agreement possible.
> *Maclean's* 12 June 1989: A24

> Soon the children will finalize their costumes and come upstairs to display themselves, which is the point of the whole game.
> Margaret Atwood *Life Before Man* 1979: 262

See also -IZE, -ISE.

fine arts see ARTS

fiord see FJORD

firearm see GUN

fireman, firefighter   see JOB TITLES

firewall   see COMPUTER TERMS

firm, corporation   Sometimes *firm* is used loosely to refer to any type of business; properly speaking, however, a *firm* is a commercial partnership of two or more people. Legal, accounting, and consulting partnerships are often firms: 'The firm of Smith and Doe prepared the report'. *Firm*, like other collective nouns, may take a plural verb in British usage, but in North American writing it usually takes a singular verb.

A *corporation* is a business or organization that is recognized as a legal person: that is, a legal entity distinct from its owners and employees.

> The large corporation has replaced the small family firm as the decisive unit of the economy, and government consultation with big business forms a major basis for the formulation of economic policy.
> Irving M. Zeitlin and Robert J. Brym *The Social Condition of Humanity* 1991: 124

> His reputation as a brilliant young lawyer had already been established, and his successful Toronto firm frequently acted as agents for Crown business.
> William Teatero *John Anderson: Fugitive Slave* 1986: 171–2

> It is available only to firms which use the carrier for business travel.
> *Globe and Mail* (Toronto) 5 Jan. 1985: T10

(Some object to the general use of *firm* for any company or business.)

firstly   Although dictionaries list *firstly* as an adverb used in enumerated lists of items, usage commentators do not necessarily approve of it. Some consider it a pretentious or ridiculous substitute for *first*. For others the issue is consistency: *either* 'first', 'second', 'third' *or* 'firstly', 'secondly', 'thirdly'. To steer clear of the shoals of criticism, the safest choice is 'first, second, third'.

first name, given name, Christian name, forename   *First name* and *given name* are the terms commonly used in Canada for the personal name before the surname, the family name. *Given name* is less likely to cause confusion (see CHINESE NAMES). The term *Christian name*, which technically applies to the name given at a Christian baptism, is also sometimes used interchangeably with *first name* or *given name*. The British term *forename* is uncommon in this country.

> First names were rare and reserved for close relatives.
> Miriam Waddington *Apartment Seven* 1989: 2

> Jordan, whose given names were Irving Sydney but who was known only as Duke to musicians and fans alike, came from Brooklyn. . . .
> Jack Chambers *Milestones* 1983: 59

> A few months earlier it would have been inconceivable for her to call my father by his Christian name.
> George Ignatieff *The Making of a Peacemonger* 1987: 31

First Nations, First Peoples   see ABORIGINAL PEOPLE(S)

First World War, World War I, Second World War, World War II   *First World War* and *World War I* are both correct, as are *Second World War* and *World War II*. Many Canadian style guides stipulate one form or the other, but there is no clear Canadian preference. Use one form or the other consistently throughout a single piece of writing.

first-year student, freshman, frosh   A Canadian university student in first year is called a *first-year student*, one in second year is called a *second-year student*, and so on. In the United States, students in successive years of any four-year program—high school, college, or university—are called *freshmen, sophomores, juniors*, and *seniors*. *Freshman* is also used in Canada, but the other American terms are not. *Freshman* is used of either sex, but the fact that it is not gender-neutral may have boosted the popularity of the slang variant *frosh*—used of men and women alike in both the singular and the plural.

Freshman is widely used in newspaper writing to describe male newcomers to sports and politics.

> First-year students did Latin, Greek, and mathematics, second-year students more of the same, and in the third year logic, moral philosophy, and natural philosophy were added.
> Hilda Neatby *Queen's University* 1 (1978): 58

> At the time the proposed shutdown was announced, a majority of third-year and fourth-year students, backed by many teachers, were boycotting the most crucial aspect of their design studies. . . .
> *Saturday Night* May 1986: 14

> Two freshmen, Jennifer Williams, 19, of Mississauga, Ont., and Mike Morse, 19, of Thornhill, Ont., were injured.
> *Globe and Mail* (Toronto) 7 Sept. 1985: P14

> I was a 'frosh,' a freshman at university.
> *Gazette* (Montreal) 4 Oct. 1990: A2

> At the end of a hectic week with much partying, I invited the frosh to listen while I read a poem by Walt Whitman.
> *Ottawa Citizen* 30 Jan. 2006: C4

See also CO-ED; GRADUATE, POSTGRADUATE, POSTDOCTORAL.

fish, fishes   *Fish* and, less commonly, *fishes* are both accepted plural forms of *fish*. Some usage guides suggest using *fishes* for more than one species of fish: 'The piranha is one of the few freshwater fishes that eat flesh'.

> Fish absorb pollutants from the water and their daily diet, storing metals and chemicals in their body tissue, and some fish species are more susceptible to contamination than others.
> *Canadian Consumer* Jan. 1985: 8

> Two pale blue barrettes, shaped like fishes, held back Leah's hair at her temples.
> *Canadian Fiction Magazine* 63 (1988): 44

> In vertebrates, almost all major length variation and heteroplasmy was seen in the fishes, reptiles, and amphibians.
> *Canadian Journal of Zoology* 67.4 (1989): 899

(Here *fishes* refers to various species.)

fisher   see JOB TITLES

fix   see NEUTER

fjord, fiord   Both spellings are correct, and Canadians do not show a marked preference for one or the other. British dictionaries list *fiord* first; American dictionaries, *fjord*. But in Britain and the United States, as in Canada, both spellings are common.

flack, hack, spin doctor   A *flack* is a press agent or public relations person. The word is often used in the same contexts as *hack*, which is a light-hearted or derogatory slang term for journalist. *Hack* can also be used pejoratively to refer to a mediocre or mercenary writer. Someone who gains a position through influence or political connections rather than merit may also be called a *hack*.

   Spin doctor emerged in the 1980s as a synonym—one with slightly more Machiavellian connotations—of *flack*. A spin doctor interprets events for the media in the way that will cast his or her employer in the best light.

> Although he fundamentally disagrees with nearly everything [environmentalists] say, he is willing to debate the issue, instead of hiding behind a public relations flack.
> *Maclean's* 22 April 1991: A41

> But the paper's dotty proprietor mistakenly sends a meek, innocent gardening correspondent named Boot to get the story instead of a seasoned hack.
> *Vancouver Sun* 28 Dec. 1990: TJ24

> The New Democrats charged that the law permitted the cabinet to appoint a political hack as acting commissioner without consulting anybody.
> *Vancouver Sun* 2 Oct. 1990: A8

> Darryl Sutter, the master spin doctor, was somehow able to extract a glimmer of hope from the awful mess. 'I don't like ever getting beat,' mused the Flames skipper, 'but sometimes (a lopsided loss) hits home a little harder for some of our players.'
> *Calgary Herald* 19 March 2006: F3

See also FLAK, FLACK; HACKER, CRACKER.

flagrant   see BLATANT

flair, flare These two homophones are sometimes confused. *Flare*, meaning a blaze of light or a widening (usually in trouser legs or skirts), is used where *flair*, meaning aptitude, talent, or knack, is meant.

> Smillie tells his history with the flare of a good adventure writer.
> *Canadian Churchman* April 1986: 16

(The word required here is *flair*.)

> To provide those guidelines, Goldsmith chooses musicians for her concert series who have a flare for discussing their work.
> *Vancouver Sun* 5 Sept. 1990: C4

(The word required here is *flair*.)

flak, flack During the Second World War, German anti-aircraft fire came to be called *flak*, an acronym for the air defence weapon called the *Fliegerabwehrkanone* in German. In the early 1960s, a figurative use of *flak*, meaning harsh criticism, arose in American slang. The term was frequently spelled *flack*, which is now an accepted variant spelling for this sense. Canadians prefer *flak*. Like its literal counterpart, figurative *flak* is often 'run into', 'encountered', 'caught', or 'taken'.

> He told an audience of about 200 . . . that some UN agencies deserve criticism, but not all should catch flak.
> *Globe and Mail* (Toronto) 19 March 1985: P5

See also FLACK, HACK.

flamingo, flamenco A flamingo is a long-legged pink or scarlet wading bird with a penchant for standing on one leg. The plural is *flamingos* or, less often, *flamingoes*. *Flamenco* (pronounced *fluh MENG ko*) is a vigorous Spanish style of music and dance, involving stamping heels and clicking castanets; the plural is *flamencos*. The word *flamingo* was borrowed from Portuguese, *flamenco* from Spanish. Both words are closely related to the Provençal word *flamenc*, 'flaming' or 'fiery', which aptly describes both the colour of the bird and the spirit of the dance.

> And the *Monitor*, the student newspaper at King's College, of which I am the titular publisher, ran . . . a cutline under a picture that pretended to portray José and Miranda, famed flamingo dancers. . . .
> W.C. Lougheed, ed. *In Search of the Standard in Canadian English* 1986: 90

(The word required was *flamenco*.)

flammable, inflammable, non-flammable, non-inflammable, inflammatory *Flammable* and *inflammable* are synonyms; both words describe things that catch fire easily. *Inflammable* is derived from the Latin *inflammare*, 'to set on fire'. However, with the development of highly combustible synthetic materials, fire officials and insurance underwriters came to fear that people would think the *in*-prefix indicated a negative (i.e., '*not* likely to catch fire'); thus they promoted *flammable* for use on warning labels. Things that won't burn easily or ignite are labelled *non-flammable* or, rarely, *noninflammable*.

Literally, *inflammatory* means causing fire. The word is often used figuratively to mean the opposite of *conciliatory*.

See also ANTIVENIN, ANTIVENOM.

flare see FLAIR

flashback see FUNCTIONAL SHIFT

flat see SUITE

flat adverbs see ADVERBS WITHOUT -LY

flaunt, flout To *flaunt* something is to show it off: 'If you've got it, flaunt it!' To *flout* is to treat laws, rules, or conventions with contemptuous disregard: 'He doesn't just break the rules, he flouts them'. These words not only look and sound alike but also have similar connotations of display and disregard for convention. *Flaunt* is frequently used where *flout* is meant ('She flaunts convention'), though the converse is rare. This confusion is a favourite target of usage commentators.

> These are not fashions for the timid—you must be the flaunt-it type. See-through lace jeans and

blouses, body-hugging stirrup pants, lambada skirts and camisoles, skin-tight leathers (black, naturally), and show-off accessories are the rule.
Alan Tucker, ed. *The Penguin Guide to Canada* 1991: 208

The girls liked to flout convention. Marriage and children were not their calling; art was.
Globe and Mail (Toronto) 26 Oct. 1985: H4

The transnational power of these large companies means they can flaunt environmental and health safeguards at the national and regional levels, all in the name of being compelled by international market forces.
Briarpatch Dec. 1989–Jan. 1990: 31

(The word required here is *flout*.)

Although the correctional service instituted an indoor ban at the end of January 2006, Page says inmates are flaunting it and staff are still constantly surrounded by second-hand smoke.
Whig-Standard (Kingston) 26 May 2006: 8

(The word required here is *flouting*.)

flautist   see FLUTIST, FLAUTIST

flee   Both the past tense and the past participle (the form used after *have*) are *fled*.

. . . many in the crowd fleed early in the performance. . . .
Times-Colonist (Victoria) 28 June 1996:1

(*Fled* is standard.)

fleet   see COLLECTIVE NOUNS

fleur-de-lis   Since 1948 the official flag of Quebec has borne an emblem called the *fleur-de-lis* (literally, 'flower of the lily'), a stylized iris that was part of the royal arms of France before the Revolution. *Fleur-de-lis*, rather than the variant *fleur-de-lys*, is the preferred spelling in Quebec, and the name of the flag, 'the Fleur-de-lis', should be capitalized. In French the phrase is pronounced *flur duh LEECE*, but in English the final *s* sound is often dropped. The plural, *fleurs-de-lis*, may be pronounced *flur duh LEE* or with a *z* sound (*flur duh LEEZ*).

flier   see FLYER

floe, flow   *Floes*, sheets of floating ice, often *flow* or move with the currents, which perhaps creates the spelling confusion. 'Ice floe' is frequently misspelled 'ice flow'. *Flow* is an Old English word, while *floe* did not enter the language until the nineteenth century, perhaps as an alteration of the Norwegian word *flo*, 'layer'.

On March 21, the Greenland began dropping off men on the ice floes.
Telegram (St. John's) 28 Oct. 2001: B1

The author of *The Shadow Boxer* reads from his new book, *Afterlands*, a novel set on an Arctic ice flow.
Calgary Herald 9 Sept. 2005: SW47

(The correct spelling is *floe*.)

floor   see STORY

flora, fauna   *Flora* refers to the plants and *fauna* to the animals of a certain region or period. The rarely used plural forms are *floras* or *florae* and *faunas* or *faunae*. The plural forms are most likely to be used when comparing 'the floras' or 'the faunas' of two different environments. A *flora* is also a systematic description of all the plants of an area.

Each island has unique varieties of flora and fauna that have evolved to meet a particular set of climatic and geological conditions.
Vancouver Sun 12 Feb. 1994: C1

floral, florescence   see FLUORINE

flounder, founder   To *flounder* is to struggle clumsily, while to *founder* is to fail utterly or sink. Something or someone who flounders is still functioning. Drunks flounder; ships founder. This distinction is useful, but in some cases either word is appropriate.

A few months ago, it didn't seem like the Canadiens would make the playoffs at all. After a quick start, the team floundered in January and February, trailing such non-playoff teams as the Boston Bruins and the Toronto Maple Leafs.
Daily News (Halifax) 19 April 2006: 40

A basketball camp, with Phoenix players as men-

tors, started in 2003 but foundered. . . . It will be resurrected with some grant money, she said.
Ottawa Citizen 3 May 2006: C3

A risk attendant on this type of home ownership, however, is that the whole co-operative venture may flounder because of bad management and insolvency: all members are affected equally by the failure. . . .
J.E. Smyth et al. *The Law and Business Administration in Canada* 1987: 578

(In this example the venture fails; thus *founder* would be better.)

The commercial real estate market has also been foundering. Some markets, like Toronto's office rental market, face an oversupply of new construction.
Vancouver Sun 27 July 1990: D9

(Here *floundering* would be better, since complete failure is not yet evident.)

. . . those willing to go further than the flawed surfaces of his prose in search of significant archetypes may well founder in a morass of half-grasped symbols. . . .
Margaret Atwood *Second Words* 1981: 35–6

(Here *flounder* would also make sense, but Atwood is playing on the 'sinking' meaning of *founder*.)

flourish   see FLUORINE

flout   see FLAUNT

flow   see FLOE

flu, virus, bacteria, germ   *Flu* is a shortened form of *influenza* and, strictly speaking, refers to a disease caused by the influenza virus. However, people often use *flu* generally to refer to a cold or any short-lived illness involving fatigue, sore muscles, or nausea. Although a virus is the agent of such ailments, the ailment itself is sometimes called a *virus*: 'She was in bed with a virus'. These extended meanings of *flu* and *virus* are informal, but not likely to cause confusion.

Not all noxious microbes are viruses. Some are *bacteria*: 'Antibiotics can kill bacteria but not viruses'. *Germ* is the general term used to cover both types of micro-organism.

Marianne habitually has lunch with Trish, who's off with the flu.
Margaret Atwood *Life Before Man* 1979: 79

The package of disposable diapers instructs parents to rinse the diapers before placing them in the garbage, but since most parents don't take the time to do this, . . . raw sewage, containing many viruses, [is] sent to landfill sites instead of the sewage treatment plant.
Western Grocer Aug. 1990: 48

(Bacteria are much more likely than viruses to be a problem in sewage; the general term *germs* would be a better choice here.)

See also BACTERIUM, BACTERIA.

fluid, liquid   In scientific terms, a *fluid* is a substance that changes shape readily: that is, either a liquid or a gas. A *liquid* changes shape readily but, unlike a gas, cannot be compressed. In general writing, however, both words are used to refer to liquids and, figuratively, to describe things that flow freely or are not fixed.

. . . convective heat transfer [is] a method of cooling in which energy is transferred from a hot surface to a fluid (either a gas or a liquid) that flows over it.
Perspectives: Profile of Research at Queen's University Dec. 1986: 32

It was a comparable insight that led champions of influence to conclude that government was a fluid process of mutual accommodation, not a static balance of stalemated forces.
J.A.W. Gunn *Beyond Liberty and Property* 1983: 203

In theory, if bonds and shares are to serve the purposes of a capital market they should be readily transferable (that is, 'liquid'). . . .
J.E. Smyth et al. *The Law and Business Administration in Canada* 1987: 687

fluorine, fluoride, fluorescent, florescence   The words *fluorine*, *fluoride*, and *fluorescent* (emitting light in the presence of certain types of light or radiation) are often misspelled with *flour-* at the beginning instead of *fluor-*. *Fluor-* is derived from the Latin verb *fluere*, 'to be in a state of flux'.

Flour- (as in *flourish*) and *flor-* (as in *floral*)

have to do with flowers. *Florescence* means period of flowering.

> . . . light intensity [was] 90 mol: m-2.5-1 from combined florescent and incandescent lamps.
> *Canadian Journal of Botany* 67.4 (1989): 991

(The adjective *florescent* means flowering. The word required here is *fluorescent.*)

flush   see BLUSH

flutist, flautist   Both words mean flute player. *Flautist* (the first syllable rhymes with *hot* or *vow*) is the preferred usage in Britain and is considered by some to be the only acceptable term. According to the *Oxford English Dictionary*, however, *flutist* is actually much older (1603) than *flautist,* which did not appear until 1860 when Nathaniel Hawthorne used it in *The Marble Faun.*

The North American preference is for *flutist*; this is the form of the word various Canadian flute societies use. The *Globe and Mail Style Book* recommends *flutist.*

> A Canadian vibe is present among the long list of musical nominees for this year's Jazz Journalists Association Awards, with Jane Bunnett of Toronto up for flutist of the year and Vancouver cellist Peggy Lee for string player of the year.
> *Globe and Mail* 1 May 2004: R15

> You still know you're in a church, but pulpit and lectern have been moved away, banners and potted plants have been brought in to brighten things up, a grand piano, trumpeter, flautist, bass player all stand ready, all bathed in the hot brightness of television lights.
> *United Church Observer* 49.11 (1986): 50

flyer, flier   Either *flyer* or *flier* is correct for any sense, including flying machines, the people in them, pilots, some insects, most birds, fast passenger trains, and advertising circulars. Canadians prefer *flyer* for all meanings.

> The invitation to the party was among the pile of letters, cards, and flyers inside his door.
> *Queen's Quarterly* 96.2 (1989): 356

> Last year offered white-knuckle flyers good reason

to grip their armrests more tightly.
> *Canadian Consumer* Feb. 1986: 29

> Hudson Bay Co. of Winnipeg puts out a twice-yearly fashion flier called Applause, described . . . as following a 'news magazine format'.
> *Globe and Mail* (Toronto) 16 Jan. 1985: B6

> Edwards . . . served as a sailor and then as a flier in the First World War.
> *Gazette* (Montreal) 11 Feb. 1990: D5

focus   see DOUBLING THE FINAL CONSONANT; PLURALS

foetid   see -AE-, -OE-, -E-

foetus   see -AE-, -OE-, -E-

folk, folks   *Folk* designating traditional art forms or ways—folk art, folk dances, folklore, folk music, folk singers, folk songs, folktales, folkways—is acceptable in all forms of writing.

Folk or *folks* meaning people has warm connotations. Someone who speaks of country folk, old folk, or prairie folk, for instance, is usually thinking of the common characteristics that unite the designated group, and may also be conveying a sense of affection for its members. Where these connotations are not desired, it's better to use the neutral word *people.*

Folks is also an informal word for parents or close family.

> Among Church of Scotland folk in Canada there was much disgust at the spread of this controversy to a country where the rights of patronage did not exist and where there was no real equivalent to the Scottish state church.
> Hilda Neatby *Queen's University* 1 (1978): 45

(Here *folk* is used to underline the unpretentious character of these members of the Church of Scotland.)

> It's motorhomes and fishing tackle that are bringing folks into the Regina Sportsmen's Show.
> *Leader-Post* (Regina) 27 Feb. 1988: A3

(This use of *folks* suits the breezy, informal style of the event itself.)

folk etymology   *Folk etymology* is the process by which the speakers of a language alter the spelling or pronunciation of an unfamiliar word or phrase so that it makes sense to them. For example, in Cree the Canadian jay is called *weskuchanis*. English-speakers borrowed this name, but soon altered it to accord with familiar English words, calling the bird *whisky-john* and *whisky jack*. Similarly, the French borrowing *chaise longue*, 'long chair', was altered to *chaise lounge*—a chair for lounging. Such alterations are likely to be criticized by those aware of the 'true' etymology of the word. Nevertheless, the altered words often become standard over time.

> Or *angishore*, also *angashore*, *angyshore*, an Irish Gaelic borrowing for 'a weak, sickly or unfortunate person deserving pity,' which since an aspirate (h) is frequently pronounced initially in words beginning with vowels, is often pronounced and spelled *hangashore*, and this is turn has been re-interpreted by folk etymology as 'a man regarded as too lazy to fish.'
> W.C. Lougheed, ed. *In Search of the Standard in Canadian English* 1986: 47–8

See also AMOK; ANTIVENIN, ANTIVENOM; CHAISE LONGUE; ETYMOLOGY; FREE REIN; HELPMATE; PARTING SHOT; SLED; TACK, TACT; TOE THE LINE; WHET THE APPETITE; WREAK HAVOC.

follow-through   see PHRASAL VERBS

foment   see FERMENT

foot, feet   The plural of *foot* is *feet*, whether the foot is an extremity or a unit of measurement: 'He always lands on his feet'; 'Your subject should be at least three feet from the camera'.

However, when a measurement in feet functions as an adjective, directly before a noun, the plural *feet* becomes *foot*: 'They built an eight-foot fence'. A hyphen usually appears between the number and the word *foot*. After the verb *be*, either *feet* or *foot* is correct and there is no hyphen: 'The fence was eight foot (*or* eight feet)'.

When describing a person's height in feet and inches it is customary to say either 'Mary is five feet four inches tall' or 'Mary is five foot four'.

When one is four feet high, ten-foot willows are a sufficient cover, and ten acres are a wilderness.
Richard Davies and Glen Kirkland, eds. *Dimensions* 1986: 135

A 40-foot ketch accompanied it to facilitate the shoot.
Photo Life Jul.–Aug. 1991: 13

The mystery merchants . . . are getting nice new signs: ED'S HARDWARE in two-feet-red, and, maybe, *quincaillerie* in six-inch-black at the top left corner, maybe even as big as the phone number.
Canadian Fiction Magazine 63 (1988): 110

(This use of *feet* is not idiomatic: 'two-*foot*-red' would be better.)

There is that 6,000 feet difference from port to peak.
Bon Vivant Nov. 1981: 32

(Here again, the idiom requires *foot*.)

foot-and-mouth disease, hoof-and-mouth disease   Both terms are acceptable in Canada for a contagious viral disease of cattle, affecting their hoofs and mouths. Canadian government agencies prefer *foot-and-mouth disease*, the term in wider use around the world; *hoof-and-mouth disease* is used only in Canada and the United States. Foot-and-mouth disease (FMD) should not be confused with a similar-sounding viral disease that affects humans: hand, foot and mouth disease (HFMD).

football   see SOCCER

footless   see BOOTLESS

footnotes   see IBID.

for   see COMMA; LIKE FOR

fora   see FORUM

for all intents and purposes, [for all intensive purposes]   see MISHEARD EXPRESSIONS

forbear, forbears   see FOREBEARS

forbid   The past tense of *forbid* is *forbade* (usually pronounced *for BAD*) or *forbid*. Only *forbade* is seen in published writing. The past participle is *forbidden* or, rarely, *forbid*.

The construction 'to *forbid* someone *from doing* something' (as in 'I forbid you from taking part') is recorded by the *OED* in citations from as early as 1526 and is quite common in writing at all levels of formality. Nonetheless, it is widely condemned in usage guides and should be avoided by writers with a low tolerance for criticism. The approved constructions are 'to *forbid* someone *to do* something' and 'to *forbid* the *doing of* something'.

'My father, Miles the first, was born six years after the Emancipation and forbade me to play music because the only place a Negro could play then was in barrel houses.'
Jack Chambers *Milestones* 1983: ix–x

. . . workers were forbidden to organize and bargain collectively with factory owners about rates of pay and other working conditions.
J.E. Smyth et al. *The Law and Business Administration in Canada* 1987: 10

. . . in the capacity of an employer in his own right he was forbidden by the Labour Relations Act of British Columbia from participating in union activities.
J.E. Smyth et al. *The Law and Business Administration in Canada* 1987: 519

(This is the disputed construction.)

There are no rules that forbid them from betting on other sports.
Calgary Herald 10 Feb. 2006: A1

(This is the disputed construction.)

forceful, forcible   In Canadian usage, *forceful* is preferred for a figurative use of force ('She presented a forceful argument'), while *forcible* implies the use of physical force ('forcible confinement'). The connotations of *forceful* are often favourable, while those of *forcible* are usually unfavourable. In British English, however, *forcible* is used favourably (and figuratively) in phrases such as 'a forcible reminder', 'a forcible argument', and 'a forcible expression of opinion'. The figurative use of *forcible* may create unintentional humour for Canadian readers.

Direct and simple language always has some force behind it, and the writers of gobbledegook don't want to be forceful; they want to be soothing and reassuring.
Northrop Frye *The Educated Imagination* 1963: 61

Since 1960 3 million black South Africans have been forcibly moved off their land or from their homes in the cities onto the 13 percent of land left for non-white use.
Briarpatch Dec. 1989–Jan. 1990: 24

His professors . . . spoke in warm terms of his 'modest and manly character,' his devotion to philosophic study, his special gift of a clear and forcible English style, and his logical vigour and metaphysical insight.
Hilda Neatby *Queen's University* 1 (1978): 136

(This figurative use of *forcible* is uncommon in Canadian prose.)

forceps   see BICEPS

forebears, forbears, forbear   *Forebears* (the noun is almost always plural) are ancestors, those who have come before. *Forbears* is an uncommon spelling variant. *Forebearers* is an error.

To *forbear* is to hold back, to keep oneself from saying or doing something.

Many of us were baptized and married here, and likely will be buried from here as well—as were our forebears, in some cases three, four, five generations back.
Chronicle Telegraph (Quebec) 3 July 1991: 10

Not that all our forbears were deluded.
Robertson Davies *A Voice from the Attic* 1960: 101

(This spelling is the less usual one.)

The chapter on origin and history is full of references to old drawings and articles on poodles plus some charming pictures of our poodles' forebearers.
Dogs in Canada Aug. 1986: 64

(The correct spelling is *forebears*.)

I cannot forbear from commenting on his rather patronizing remark. . . .
Gazette (Montreal) 21 March 1993: D2

I cannot, though, forebear to mention the omi-

nous pizzicato basses and cellos at the opening of the slow movement, the powerful yet mellow brass, the colourful winds, or the multi-hued richness of the full ensemble.
Times-Colonist (Victoria) 12 Sept. 2005: D4

(Here the spelling should be *forbear*.)

forego   see FORGO

foreign   see -IE-, -EI-

foreign words   see LATIN PHRASES; FRENCH WORDS; GERMAN WORDS; PINYIN

foreman   see SEXIST LANGUAGE

forename   see FIRST NAME

forensic   *Forensic* is derived from the Latin *forum*, the place where court cases were argued, and means legal or having to do with a court of law. It is often used in combination with other words to indicate a legal specialization within a field: 'forensic accounting', 'forensic anthropology', 'forensic chemistry'. *Forensic medicine* is the use of medical knowledge to establish guilt or innocence. *Forensic* is so often used with reference to medical evidence that several dictionaries now list 'pertaining to medical evidence' as one of its senses.

An older meaning of *forensic*, related to the debates held in the Roman Forum, is 'rhetorical' or 'suited to debate'.

He used the services of a team of forensic accountants from the firm of Touche Ross & Co. to analyze every piece of Maple Leaf Gardens paper.
Jack Batten *Robinette* 1984: 193

A forensic toxicologist was of the opinion the chemicals could be dangerous taken in large quantities. . . .
London Free Press 28 April 1988: A2

Forensic evidence presented at the trial indicated that the blood was consistent with Christine's. . . .
Winnipeg Free Press 17 Nov. 1990: 8

(This is the new sense of *forensic* meaning medical.)

By the time John Robinette arrived in the court-

room, the forensic approach to litigation was giving way to a less showy and more measured style.
Jack Batten *Robinette* 1984: 36

(Here *forensic* means rhetorical.)

foreseeable future   This phrase is often condemned as trite. However, it does serve to distinguish the future about which it may be thought possible to make sensible predictions from the future in general. Note that *foreseeable* is often misspelled without its first *e*, as *forseeable*.

Dental anesthetic, delivered by the dreaded needle, will be around for the forseeable future despite a universal longing for alternatives.
Province (Vancouver) 26 Nov. 1990: 43

(The correct spelling is *foreseeable*.)

forest, woods, wood, grove, bluff, backwoods, bush   A large, heavily treed area is usually called a *forest*. *Woods* are less dense or wild than forests. In Britain a grove of trees is called a *wood*, but in Canada this usage is rare (usually literary).

In a 1970s survey of Canadian usage (*Modern Canadian English Usage*, 1974), Canadians were asked what they would call a group of trees. Most chose the term *grove*. *Clump*, the overall second choice, was the preferred term in Alberta, while in Saskatchewan and Manitoba most adults chose the word *bluff*. In the rest of the country, a *bluff* is a cliff. It may be that on the prairies a group of trees is called a *bluff* because a grove of trees on the horizon looks like a rise in the land.

The bush and *the backwoods* are common expressions for remote, unpopulated or sparsely populated areas: 'He had just come out of the bush, where he had lived for six months'. Canadians also use *bush* to refer to any wooded area, for example, in a park, on a farm, or at the edge of a city. In the wilderness, the expression 'to be *bushed*' means to show signs of mental confusion as a result of isolation, but generally Canadians use *bushed* to mean really tired. *Backwoods*, when applied to people, usually has negative connotations; it is more likely to suggest lack of sophistication than hardy self-sufficiency.

Two nights before, shivering in a cottonwood bluff, they had slept in six inches of snow.
Pierre Berton *The Promised Land* 1984: 91

The Cheyenne is the perfect choice for someone who lives or works in the backwoods, where the snowmobile is essential to the transportation of goods and passengers to and from the chalet.
Snowmobile Canada 1991 Buyers Guide: 44

It was the sort of house rich people sometimes have off in the bush where they can go to rough it.
Max Braithwaite *The Night We Stole the Mountie's Car* 1971: 117

After fighting the blaze for seven hours, Beck said he was bushed.
Times-Colonist (Victoria) 29 June 1999: A1

Allison Brewer, a former director of New Brunswick's only private abortion clinic, said Tuesday she is appalled elected politicians have not debated the pending loss of abortion services in the last provincial hospital to regularly perform the procedure. 'It makes us look backwoods,' Brewer said.
Guardian (Charlottetown) 24 May 2006: A9

foreword, preface   Both are introductory statements in a book. A *foreword* is literally something before the main text. The word *preface* is derived from the Latin for 'say before'. Most dictionaries make the distinction that a *preface* is written by the book's author, while a *foreword* is written by someone else (thus it is possible for a book to have both a foreword and a preface), but these words are often used interchangeably.

Foreword is spelled with an *e* and two *o*'s. Occasionally it is misspelled *forward*.

. . . White decided to put some of his disparate short pieces together. The result is an entrancing medley of poems, stories and oral histories garnished with photographs, sketches, maps and a foreword by Barry Broadfoot.
Vancouver Sun 17 Nov. 1990: D19

(Here someone other than the author wrote the foreword.)

Although Clark wrote only a new foreword for *Beyond the Fall of Night*, the book is a roadsign to his past.
Vancouver Sun 13 Oct. 1990: D18

(Here the author himself wrote the foreword.)

See also AFTERWARD(S), AFTER, AFTERWORD.

forfeit   see -IE-, -EI-

for free   Some commentators consider the informal expression *for free* childish, and maintain that *free* by itself will always do: 'They were free (*not* for free)'. There are many contexts, however, in which *for free* is idiomatic ('He'll play for free') and *free* alone is not ('He'll play free'). In formal writing it's best to substitute 'at no cost' or 'without payment' or 'free of charge' for the disputed phrase.

You could get warm for free there.
Constance Beresford-Howe *Night Studies* 1985: 4

The rest of the paper you can have for free.
Province (Vancouver) 27 Dec. 1990: 14

Boris Becker refused to play in the $6 million US Grand Slam Cup tournament because he objected to the obscenely high prize money, but he'll play for free. . . . the German star won't charge for playing in an Adelaide charity event to benefit children with cancer.
Vancouver Sun 28 Dec. 1990: F2

forget, forgot, forgotten   'He had forgot about his ticket' and 'He had forgotten about his ticket' are both acceptable in Canadian English. In British English *forgot* is archaic as a past participle.

And he winked at Alf who had forgot all about his camel humps.
David Williams *Eye of the Father* 1985: 73

forgo, forego   The word meaning to do without or relinquish is spelled either *forgo* or *forego*. The word meaning precede is always spelled with the *e*: 'the foregoing remarks'.

The past tense and past participle of both verbs are patterned on the root verb *go*: *for(e)went, for(e)gone*. In the phrase 'a foregone conclusion', *foregone* means predictable or inevitable.

But the police should have thought about the consequences of credit cards before advising people to forgo cash for plastic.
Gazette (Montreal) 25 Oct. 1990: G2

Several hundred loggers from across Vancouver Island are expected to forego a day's wages to attend a solidarity rally Monday at the Nanaimo courthouse.
Vancouver Sun 3 Nov. 1990: A6

In the light of what has been considered in the foregoing pages, that comment may not seem an overstatement.
Canadian Bar Review 66.3 (1987): 613

Oscar de la Renta forewent his party-boy reputation and offered several muted suits with only velvet trim by way of fanciness.
Globe and Mail (Toronto) 14 May 1985: F1

The bill need only receive approval from the Senate — a forgone conclusion — and royal assent to become law.
Vancouver Sun 29 June 2005: A14

(The spelling here should be *foregone*.)

formal, informal writing   In this book, reference is made to formal and informal writing when a usage is considered generally more appropriate to one level of formality than another; this is not to say that a usage labelled 'informal' should be avoided altogether. There is no firm boundary between formal and informal writing, and some writers will always write more formally than others in similar circumstances. Broadly speaking, however, formal writing is the style found in academic journals, judicial opinions, legal documents, government reports, civic announcements, speeches for ceremonial occasions, submissions or reports to authorities, literary journalism, and letters to people one has never met. It tends to be serious, precise, and impersonal.

Writing in most magazines and newspapers is informal. Informal writing is closer to everyday speech: it does not make use of elevated vocabulary or studied syntax, and it may take a familiar tone with its readers. Friendly correspondence is often more informal still. It may contain slang, abbreviations, vague references, ellipses, sentence fragments, and syntactic U-turns. These features, which would mar formal writing, add immediacy to a personal letter and reflect the shared knowledge of the correspondents.

See also COLLOQUIAL; STANDARD ENGLISH, STANDARD; VERNACULAR.

format   see FUNCTIONAL SHIFT

former, latter   The phrase 'the former' refers to the first of two people or things previously mentioned. 'The latter' refers to the second. The former' and 'the latter' are disputed when they refer to the first and last items in a list longer than two. It is perfectly acceptable to use one of this pair of terms without the other.

I have nothing against universities or creative writing classes; I have attended the former and taught the latter.
Margaret Atwood Second Words 1982: 337

Inside, the Murano—especially the SE—is tastefully attired, with clear instrumentation, . . . power seats, mirrors and sunroof, full leather and a back-up camera. The latter displays the view to the rear through the LCD screen that dominates the centre stack.
Windsor Star 11 April 2006: B4

('The latter' is disputed when it refers to the last item in a list of more than two items. Substituting 'The camera displays . . .' for 'The latter displays . . .' would make this sentence unobjectionable.)

To begin with, the 'managerial revolution' fails to distinguish technicians from managers and the latter, in turn, from other corporate power holders.
Irving M. Zeitlin and Robert J. Brym The Social Condition of Humanity 1991: 125

(The terms *former* and *latter* do not always have to be paired.)

former name   see MAIDEN NAME

formidable   The standard pronunciation of *formidable*, which means inspiring awe or fear, is *FOR mi duh bul*. The alternative pronunciation *for MID uh bul* is accepted in Canada and the United States, but disputed in Britain.

formulae   see PLURALS, REGULAR, IRREGULAR, FOREIGN

forte   *Forte*, meaning a person's strong point, is almost always pronounced *FOR tay* or *for TAY* in North America. Some commentators have recommended the pronunciation *FORT* because the word is not derived from Italian, in which it would be pronounced with two syllables, but from French. Although this one-syllable pronunciation is found in British English, it has not caught on in North America. The most common pronunciation for the musical sense, 'loud', is *FOR tay*.

fortuitous, fortunate   *Fortuitous* is derived from the Latin *fors*, 'chance' or 'luck'. Most dictionaries distinguish between *fortunate*, meaning favoured by fortune, privileged, or prosperous, and *fortuitous*, meaning accidental or by chance, and most usage guides warn against confusing them: a fortuitous event may well have an unfortunate result.

Yet many—perhaps most—writers now use *fortuitous* to mean 'occurring by *lucky* chance'. Not all dictionaries record this narrower sense, but it can't be faulted since it falls within the scope of the older meaning. What should be avoided is the use of *fortuitous* to mean fortunate in a context where happenstance is not involved.

> It is fortuitous and to a large extent arbitrary which persons are detected as being HIV antibody-positive and refused entry [to the country].
> *Gazette* (Montreal) 22 June 1990: B3

(Here *fortuitous* means by chance and is connected to an unfortunate event.)

> Hennessy's involvement with the musical was fortuitous rather than planned.
> *Gazette* (Montreal) 26 July 1990: D10

> The death toll would have been much higher, residents said, but police used loudspeakers to tell townspeople to sleep outside after a 4.7-magnitude quake struck Thursday evening. The warnings proved fortuitous.
> *Daily News* (Halifax) 1 April 2006: 16

(The police warnings were no accident. Thus they proved *fortunate* or *beneficial*, but should not be called *fortuitous*.)

forty, four, fourth, fourteen   *Forty* is the only variant of *four* that omits the *u*; it is some-

times misspelled *fourty*. *Fourth* is sometimes misspelled *forth*.

forty-ninth parallel   The *forty-ninth parallel* divides Canada and the United States from Lake of the Woods on the border of Manitoba and Ontario to just south of Vancouver on the mainland of British Columbia. Although the southern tip of Vancouver Island and most of the populated areas of Eastern Canada are south of the forty-ninth parallel, the term is used loosely to describe the Canada–U.S. border. The phrase is perfectly comprehensible to Canadians, but is best avoided when writing for a wider audience.

> The expansion of *Harrowsmith* demonstrates that, in certain ways, the forty-ninth parallel is irrelevant.
> *Saturday Night* Feb. 1986: 12

> The differences between Canada and America are overstated. . . . The forty-ninth parallel is losing its definition.
> *Edmonton Journal* 10 Dec. 2000: A11

forum, forums, fora   The common plural of forum is the regular one, *forums*, but the Latin plural *fora* is used in some formal and legal contexts.

> Having noticed that experts were looking to Canada as a model for accommodating diversity, the government realized that Canada could benefit by creating high-profile international fora where issues of diversity are discussed.
> *International Journal* 59.4 (2004): 829–52

See also PLURALS, REGULAR, IRREGULAR, FOREIGN.

founder   see FLOUNDER

four, fourth, fourteen   see FORTY

fourth estate, fifth estate   In pre-industrial Europe, society was divided into three 'estates': the nobility, the clergy, and the common people. The press established itself as the *fourth estate* (a fourth political force) when it began to report on parliamentary debates and decisions in the late eighteenth century. In current usage the term *fifth estate* refers to the electronic media of television and radio. This term is familiar to many Canadians as the name of a CBC public affairs show.

> . . . modern historians continue to date the rise of the press as the fourth estate from the effective acknowledgment after 1772 of the press's right to publish parliamentary debates.
> J.A.W. Gunn *Beyond Liberty and Property* 1983: 90

> Demers is a skilled manipulator of the media, Murray suggested, and now that Demers is a member of the fifth estate he has concocted a piece of folklore to make himself look good.
> *Vancouver Sun* 23 Oct. 1990: C2

foxes   see PLURALS

fox terrier   see DALMATION

fractions   see HYPHENATION

fractious   see FACTIOUS

francization, francize   *Francization* (pronounced *fran si ZAY shun*) is the process of assimilating or converting things into French. French-speakers have always *francized* words borrowed from other languages (English *budgetary* became French *budgétaire*), just as English-speakers have anglicized foreign borrowings. However, in the province of Quebec today, francization is not just a spontaneous linguistic process but a legislated policy. The provincial Office de la langue française oversees the creation of technical terms to parallel terminology developing in English and other languages. The Office also oversees the francization of business in Quebec: all large and medium-sized companies operating in the province must use French as their working language and must be certified to that effect. The word *francization* is used as well in reference to policies and programs designed to assimilate immigrants to the province's francophone rather than anglophone population.

The legislated promotion of the French language is a new Canadian sense of *francization*. In earlier British usage the word meant conferral of French national status or acculturation to France.

Francize and *francization*—with *z*—are anglicized spellings of the French words *franciser* and *francisation*. Occasionally in Canadian English the noun is spelled as in French: *francisation*.

> 'The young anglophones that I am in touch with are functionally and operationally bilingual,' said Guilotte, who develops francization programs for large companies in Montreal.
> *Gazette* (Montreal) 8 March 1990: A6

> A coalition of 180 groups supported by the Societe St. Jean Baptiste will demonstrate in front of the Montreal office of Premier Jean Charest this afternoon to protest against budget cuts to francization and integration programs for immigrants that take effect May 3.
> *Gazette* (Montreal) 18 April 2004: A2

> 'But it is only by fostering access to all immigrants to adequate francization services that Quebec will maximize the spinoffs from immigration.'
> *Gazette* (Montreal) 14 Dec. 1990: B3

> The trouble with francization is that it makes it more difficult to remain in blissful ignorance of the mindset of francophone Quebecers. . . .
> *Gazette* (Montreal) 2 May 1991: B3

> . . . the Centre de linguistique de l'entreprise, which helps Quebec businesses 'francize' their operations, or increase the use of French, [reported] that some businesses have to give their francophone employees basic courses in their mother tongue.
> *Gazette* (Montreal) 18 March 1992: B3

See also FRANCOPHONE; QUEBEC ENGLISH.

Franco-   see FRANCOPHONE; QUEBECKER.

francophone, anglophone, allophone   A *francophone* is a French-speaker—in Canada, usually someone whose first language is French. The adjective *francophone* means French-speaking, or French-language, or having to do with the French-speaking population. An *anglophone* is an English-speaker. An *allophone* (from the

Greek for 'other sound') is a Quebecer, often an immigrant, whose first language is neither French nor English. According to the *Canadian Oxford Dictionary*, the term *allophone* does not include speakers of Aboriginal languages, although there is confusion on this point.

Francophone, anglophone, and *allophone* have all been absorbed into Canadian English from Canadian French over the last few decades. Normally, words with the prefixes *Anglo-* and *Franco-,* such as *Anglo-Irish, Anglophile,* or *Franco-Prussian,* are capitalized in English, but in the case of *francophone* and *anglophone* the French convention of writing these words without capitals has been adopted.

Allophone in the sense outlined above is a Canadianism, because it takes its meaning from a particularly Canadian linguistic and political situation. However, *allophone* is also used around the world as a technical term in linguistics.

> That may be why . . . young francophones are now about as likely as young anglophones to complete university.
> Irving M. Zeitlin and Robert J. Brym *The Social Condition of Humanity* 1991: 165

> At least one francophone country artist, Gilles Goddard, a bilingual songwriter and performer from Cornwall, Ontario, has received recognition from the Quebec music industry.
> *Queen's Quarterly* 95 (1988): 297

> This distinction is important to many of the 47 member countries of the francophone summit.
> *Gazette* (Montreal) 9 June 1992: B6

> But that job went to Montreal broadcaster and former anglophone rights activist Royal Orr.
> *Vancouver Sun* 16 Dec. 1992: C5

> But Constas said he does not consider himself an allophone. 'I speak French to my two children,' he said. 'The only thing that isn't French about me is my name.'
> *Gazette* (Montreal) 14 June 1992: A3

> 'The ideal would be for all parents in our school board to understand the spirit of their child's report card.' . . . More than half the parents of children at the CSDM [Commission scolaire de

Montréal] are allophones, Bouchard said.
> *Gazette* (Montreal) 25 May 2006: A8

See also ACADIA; FRANCIZATION; FRANCOPHONIE; QUEBEC ENGLISH; QUEBECER.

Francophonie   The French-speaking nations of the world, considered collectively, are the Francophonie, pronounced *FRANK OH FOE NEE.* Usage regarding the definite article is not settled: some English-Canadian writers retain the French definite article ('la Francophonie'), some opt for *the* ('the Francophonie'), while a few use no article at all: 'The comparison is often drawn between Francophonie and the Commonwealth.' In French, *Francophonie* (capitalized) refers to the organization of member countries, and *francophonie* (lower-case) to the linguistic community of French-speaking people. This distinction is seldom maintained in English.

> La Francophonie is a cultural and linguistic community of more than 170 million people. These people use French to varying degrees in their daily lives. La Francophonie is also an institutional community of 56 states and governments on five continents.
> 'What is La Francophonie?' Canadian International Development Agency website 20 Dec. 2005

See also FRANCOPHONE, ANGLOPHONE, ALLOPHONE.

Franco-Prussian   see FRANCOPHONE

Frankenstein   In Mary Wollstonecraft Shelley's novel *Frankenstein, or The Modern Prometheus* (1818), Frankenstein is the scientist who constructs a man-like monster and eventually perishes in a desperate effort to regain control over the creature. Shelley did not give a name to Frankenstein's creation, but generations of movie-goers believe that Frankenstein is the name of the monster. Those familiar with the book are likely to refer to 'Frankenstein's monster' or 'a Frankenstein monster'; however, the use of *Frankenstein* to mean monster is standard according to the dictionaries.

> April is changeable, and powerful—a time when the life force can be seen creaking back into

action, like Frankenstein's monster lurching up from the lab table.
Toronto Star 2 April 2006: A9

Perhaps, Dyer and the National Film Board think all these things are bogeymen like Frankenstein on late-night movies.
Maclean's 31 March 1986: 9

frankly   see SENTENCE ADVERBS

Fransaskois   see QUEBECKER

Frau, Fräulein   see GERMAN WORDS, PRONUNCIATION OF

free   see FOR FREE

freedom fighter   see GUERRILLA

free gift   see WORDINESS

freelance, freelancer, free-lance, free lance   In Canadian usage, the most common spelling of the verb is *freelance. Freelancer* and *freelance* are alternative forms of the noun. The adjective is spelled *free-lance* or, less commonly, *freelance.* In the Middle Ages, a *free lance* was a mercenary soldier.

After graduation he took his one and only salaried job as a department-store window designer before going on to freelance as a commercial artist for 10 years.
Vancouver Sun 28 Dec. 1990: 17

Such lucrative projects enabled Brittain—who has worked as a freelancer since 1968—to spend time on painstaking, low-budget documentaries for the NFB and the CBC.
Maclean's 28 March 1988: A42

The Hampstead headmaster's son, born in 1882, began his writing career as a freelance for Punch.
Vancouver Sun 22 Dec. 1990: D20

The chilling effect would be all the more noticeable for free-lance and academic researchers who do not have the resources of a corporation behind them.
Ottawa Citizen 1 Nov. 1990: A4

Now he's back as a freelance drummer working

with the best B.C. bands and creating a solo recording career.
Vancouver Sun 10 Aug. 1990: 25

free rein   *Free rein* is a figurative application of the expression for loosening one's grip on a horse's reins, allowing it to go wherever it pleases. Since *rein* and *reign* sound alike, the expression is often misconstrued as *free reign* or anarchy.

Callers yesterday to a Kahnawake open-line radio show said Chateauguay police are not enforcing the law at the highway barricade, but giving free reign to rabble-rousing town residents who are burning effigies on municipal lamp-posts.
Gazette (Montreal) 18 July 1990: A4

(The usual expression is *free rein.*)

Both Chisholme and Christie made it quite clear in their reviews that they regarded literature in which the fancy was given free reign as being inappropriate to a new country.
Carl Ballstadt, ed. *The Search for English Canadian Literature* 1978: xvii

(The usual expression is *free rein.*)

See also FOLK ETYMOLOGY.

freeway   see ROAD

freight   see -IE-, -EI-

French Canadian, French-Canadian   see QUEBECKER

French words, pronunciation of   What follows is a brief guide intended to help with the pronunciation of French words and phrases commonly used in English. Generally, consonants at the ends of words are not pronounced (e.g., *esprit de corps* is pronounced *ess PREE duh CORE*); a single *m* or *n* at the end of a word (and often in the middle) is barely pronounced itself, but affects the sound of the vowel that precedes it. Thus *temps* is pronounced (roughly) *TAH(m)*; *sans, SAH(n)*; and *mont, MOH(n)*. A number of these pronunciations are only approximate, since some French vowel sounds are not found in English.

French Letter(s)	English Sound	Example
á	a (as in bad)	á la (A LA)
â	a (bad)	château (sha TOE), grâce (GRASS)
as	aw (law)	pas (PAW)
au(x)	o (so)	faux (FOE)
é(e)	ay (say)	cliché (klee SHAY), née (NAY)
è	e (bed)	pièce (pee ESS)
ê	e (bed)	bête (BET)
eau(x)	o (so)	beau(x) (BO)
et	ay (say)	gourmet (goor MAY)
eu	uh	bleu (BLUH)
ç	s	garçon (gar SOH[n])
g (before e, i, or y)	zh	rouge (ROOZH), gendarme (zhah[n] DARM)
j	zh	joual (zhoo AL)
o, ô	o (so)	table d'hôte (TA bluh DOTE)
oeu	uh	hors d'oeuvre (or DUH vruh)
oi(s)	wah	noir (NWAR), bourgeois (BOOR ZHWAH), coiffure (kwah FYOOR)
qu	k	clique (KLEEK)

See also À LA; À LA CARTE; TABLE D'HÔTE; AU; BEAU, BEAUX; BÊTE NOIRE; BLEU, ROUGE; BLOC; CLICHÉ; CLIQUE; COIFFURE, COIFFEUR; CONNOISSEUR; CONTRETEMPS; COUP DE GRÂCE, PIÈCE DE RÉSISTANCE; COUREUR DE BOIS, VOYAGEUR; DEBACLE; DÉJÀ VU; DOUBLE ENTENDRE; ÉMIGRÉ; ENTRÉE; FAUX PAS; FLEUR-DE-LIS; FRANCOPHONE; GARAGE; GENDARME; GOURMET; HORS D'OEUVRE(S); JOUAL; LARGESSE; MACABRE; MANQUÉ; MÉTIS; NAIVE; PASTICHE; PÉQUISTE; PREMIÈRE, DÉBUT; QUEBECER; RECONNAISSANCE, RECONNOITRE; REPERTOIRE; RÉSUMÉ; SANS; SAULT; TUQUE; VIS-À-VIS.

freshman   see FIRST-YEAR STUDENT

Freud   see GERMAN WORDS, PRONUNCIATION OF

Freudian slip   see SLIPS OF THE TONGUE

friendly, friendlily   Though *friendly* is listed in dictionaries as both an adjective and an adverb, the adverb use is so rare in contemporary English that it sounds ungrammatical: 'They greeted us friendly'. *Friendlily* first appeared in the seventeenth century as an alternative adverb, but it too is rare, probably because the double ending sounds awkward. The most common way around this difficulty is to recast the sentence to allow the use of the adjective: 'She gave us a friendly smile'; 'They insulted each other in a friendly fashion'.

Friendly is one of several words that entered English before the seventeenth century, at a time when the *-ly* ending was used to create adjectives as well as adverbs. Others include *courtly, homely, kindly, princely, rascally,* and *scholarly.*

They went on hikes with their little picks and kits, and chipped samples off cliffs; then they ate jelly sandwiches and copulated in a friendly way behind clumps of goldenrod and thistles.
Margaret Atwood *Life Before Man* 1979: 111

But even Mrs. Thatcher's Conservative diehards are now beginning to look at the American military presence in a less friendly light.
Canadian Churchman Jun.–Jul. 1986: 9

See also ADJECTIVES AND ADVERBS; -IE-, -EI-.

frolicking   see -C, -CK-

from   see BORROW, OFF, OFF OF, FROM

front-runner   The term *front-runner* was coined early in the twentieth century to refer to a contestant who likes to take the lead at the beginning of a race and force the pace, as opposed to one who likes to come from behind. The idea that the frontrunner was in a strategic position was lost when the term began to be used metaphorically. *Frontrunner* now usually means leading contender or favourite. Though criticized as a debasement, this meaning is too well established to be considered wrong. In fact, the older meaning is now familiar only to runners and horse-racing enthusiasts. Although most dictionaries hyphenate *front-runner*, one- and two-word spellings are not uncommon.

> 'There's no clear frontrunner,' said one Tory constituency president.
> *Calgary Herald* 11 Sept. 1992: A12

(Here *frontrunner* means leader.)

> It was no disgrace to find himself behind such perennial stars as Dizzy Gillespie (second), Roy Eldridge (fourth), and Louis Armstrong (sixth), or even the swing trumpeter Harry James (third), but the other front-runners were about the same age as Davis and had been learning their scales or sitting anonymously in band sections when he was already making innovations.
> Jack Chambers *Milestones* 1983: 175

(Here the *front-runners* are leaders.)

> Emily MacLennan of C.P. Allen, national champion in the under-15 1500m, is the front runner in the intermediate girls category.
> *Daily News* (Halifax) 6 Nov. 1992: 62

(Here *front runner* means favourite.)

> No front-runner has ever won the Mile, and Gulfstream's tight course doesn't favor early speed.
> *Toronto Star* 11 Oct. 1992: G10

(The older meaning of *front-runner* is intended here, in the context of horse racing.)

frosh   see FIRST-YEAR STUDENT

froze, frozen   The use of *froze* as an adjective ('I was half froze') or as a past participle ('We could have froze') is non-standard.

> Michael kept watching the homeless and thinking about . . . how he had read in the newspaper that a street person in Seattle had froze to death in the surprising cold.
> *Province* (Vancouver) 28 Dec. 1990: 14

(Only *frozen* is considered correct after *have* or *had*.)

See also STANDARD ENGLISH, STANDARD.

fuchsia   *Fuchsia* (pronounced *FEW shuh*) is the name of a flower and a colour—an intense purplish red or purplish pink. The word is com-

monly misspelled *fuschia*. The plant was named after the German botanist Leonhard Fuchs; remembering this may help with the spelling.

-ful, cupful, spoonful, teaspoonful   The plural of words ending in *-ful*—*cupful*, *spoonful*, *teaspoonful*, *carful*, *armful*, etc.—is usually formed by adding a final *s*: *cupfuls*, *spoonfuls*, *teaspoonfuls*, *carfuls*, *armfuls*. The variants *cupsful*, *spoonsful*, *teaspoonsful*, *carsful*, and *armsful* are much less common, and are criticized by some authorities.

> With spoonfuls of buffalo stew half-way to their mouths, she and Perdue paused, turned to the kitchen window.
> Geoffrey Ursell *Perdue, or, How the West Was Lost* 1984: 106

> 'I take just two spoonsful of the mixture every day.'
> *Gazette* (Montreal) 23 Sept. 1990: D3

(This usage is less common and less widely accepted.)

See also PLURALS.

fulfil, fulfilment, fulfill, fulfillment   Canadian spelling is about evenly divided between *fulfil* and *fulfilment* (preferred in British English) and *fulfill* and *fulfillment* (preferred in American English). The Canadian Press recommends *fulfil*, so this spelling is dominant in newspapers and in the many magazines that follow the Canadian Press guidelines. Most editors recommend using single or double *l* in both the verb and the noun consistently throughout one document. In other words, use *fulfill* with *fulfillment* and *fulfil* with *fulfilment*. The *l* must be doubled in two forms of the verb: *fulfilling*, *fulfilled*.

While the final *l* in *fulfil(l)* may be either single or double, the first *l* is always single. Thus *fullfil*, with two *l*'s in the first syllable, is a spelling error, as is *fufill*, with none. The latter error reflects a common—and acceptable—pronunciation: *fuh FILL*.

> To Heavysege, a man who, like Jephthah, worships a God who demands fulfilment of a rash vow of

sacrifice even if it involves his own daughter, is really a man in the state of nature. . . .
Northrop Frye *The Bush Garden* 1971: 151

For [Jane] Foster, passing the [fighter-pilot] course was the fulfillment of a life-long dream.
Ottawa Citizen 11 June 1989: A1

. . . the horse was supposed to run in the July 14 Ascot Sophomore at 1 1/8 miles; but because of an oversight his connections did not fullfil all nomination obligations.
Province (Vancouver) 12 Aug. 1990: 99

(The first *l* is always single: either *fulfil* or *fulfill* would be correct.)

See also DOUBLING THE FINAL CONSONANT.

fulsome   *Fulsome* in the phrase 'fulsome praise' means insincere or excessive. This negative meaning is the common one in formal writing. Yet, in informal writing, *fulsome* often means full, abundant or generous, and this very different meaning—which is, in fact, centuries older—is not wrong. Because both meanings are currently in wide use, and because many people are unaware that there are two different meanings, *fulsome* is a word that should probably be avoided.

As party president Gerry St. Germain noted in a fulsome letter, 'you and Mrs. Mulroney have been the glue that has preserved the unity of our party and the focus and effectiveness of our caucus.'
Calgary Herald 26 Feb. 1993: A4

(Here the writer suggests that the letter was *effusive* or *fawning*—excessive in its praise.)

With a net income of $2.22 per common share, the bank was the most profitable in the country. Analysts and competitors were fulsome in their praise.
Saturday Night July 1986: 41

(Here *enthusiastic* could replace *fulsome*.)

'I put it to you that as this case progressed, your allegations became more fulsome and complete because you are fabricating them,' Kaplan told the woman.
Vancouver Sun 27 May 1993: A3

(Here *full* or *detailed* is a better word choice.)

fun   Most dictionaries consider the use of *fun* as an adjective ('We had a fun time') informal. This usage is common in conversation and in the popular media; however, it should be avoided in formal writing. *Fun-filled, enjoyable*, and *entertaining* can all serve as substitutes.

It is common to complain of the brutality of some of our ancestors' fun, though if we think about the jokes of our own time, we may find them equally harsh.
Robertson Davies *A Voice from the Attic* 1960: 205

(In formal writing, *fun* is used only as a noun.)

Next week, the cubs and scouts will be going to Mont St-Sacrement for their winter camp. We have planned a fun weekend of different winter activities. . . .
Chronicle-Telegraph (Quebec City) 27 March 1991: 2

(This use of *fun* is informal.)

See also FUNCTIONAL SHIFT.

functional shift   In language, a functional shift occurs when a word that has commonly been used as one part of speech starts also to be used as another. The most common shift is from a noun to a verb. Recent examples of such shifts are *access, format, parent, impact*, and *scapegoat*, nouns of long standing that are now commonly used as verbs too.

Though this tendency is disparaged by language purists, many English words have made successful functional shifts. These include verbs that have become nouns, such as *streak* and *spiral*, and verb phrases have become compound nouns, such as *flashback, handoff, takeover*, and *wind-up*. Nouns that are now undisputed as verbs include *audit, bypass, contact*, and *index*. Adjectives now also used as nouns include *local* (a local person or thing), *natural* (someone with seemingly innate skills), and *temporary* (or *temp*, an office worker hired for a short time). The Gulf War introduced the military use of *unfriendly* as a noun (*an unfriendly, unfriendlies*) for the enemy. Adjective-to-verb shifts are relatively uncommon, though *short* is now used as a verb meaning to cheat and *green* is used to mean address (or appear to address) environmental issues.

While the English language has considerable tolerance and precedent for such functional shifts, they usually provoke strong opposition for some time before gaining wide acceptance.

> With their new upgrading of Information Access software and hardware this broker looks forward to networking with other customers.
> *Western Grocer* Aug. 1990: 27

(The use of *network* as a verb is still criticized.)

> . . . the major emotions that accompany mating and parenting no longer have to occur within rigid legal and traditional boundaries.
> *Chatelaine* April 1986: 48

(The use of *parent* as a verb was initially scorned.)

> The 'Greening' of the grocery store must continue—for the sake of our planet's future.
> *Western Grocer* Aug. 1990: 34

functionary see QUEBEC ENGLISH

fungus, fungi see PLURALS

funnel cloud see CYCLONE

funny, funnily Usage guides still occasionally warn against the use of *funny* to mean strange, perplexing, or odd. Yet the word is used in these senses almost as often as it is to mean amusing. This usage is perfectly acceptable, except perhaps in very stodgy prose. On the other hand, the use of *funny* as an adverb meaning oddly, as in 'dress funny' or 'talk funny', is quite informal and not recommended for writing that isn't meant to imitate speech. *Funnily* is the accepted adverb; it means either oddly or amusingly.

> In a gutsy, very funny and completely bilingual opening set, Massicotte trashed Ladas ('the only cars on the market that are biodegradable'). . . .
> *Gazette* (Montreal) 18 Nov. 1990: F5

> I happened to glance at the rock below my feet. Funny little lines aroused my curiosity and I bent down for a closer look.
> *Up Here* Jan.–Feb. 1990: 49

> It's funny how so many of those old wives' tales are resurrected as modern medical science.
> *Bon Vivant* Nov. 1981: 12

> For they too were strangers; they too were 'different': they dressed funny and they talked funny and, like so many others who came to the West in those years, they refused to reject the roots of the culture in which they had been nurtured.
> Pierre Berton *The Promised Land* 1984: 145

(This adverbial use of *funny* suggests informal speech.)

> Satire lacerates, but, funnily enough, it also endears politicians to the public and makes them more human than their speeches or TV news sound bites.
> *Toronto Star* 22 Feb. 1993: C5

> Goldman shows us—rapidly, funnily—that those images are real, but that there's a lot more going on behind the scenes.
> *Province* (Vancouver) 6 May 1990: 91

funny money see SOCIAL CREDIT

further see FARTHER

futile see HOSTILE

future see FORESEEABLE

G

G7, G8 see GROUP OF SEVEN

gaff, gaffe A *gaff* is a pole with a hook on the end used for landing big fish, or a spar on a sailboat. The verbal, social, or diplomatic blunder is spelled *gaffe*. A gaffe is almost always embarrassing.

> But, besides that embarrassing gaffe, the dance proceeded relatively unblemished.
> *Globe and Mail* (Toronto) 22 June 1985: E8

> Instead, O'Brien's listing appears on page 1085 in the spot occupied last year by Miroslav Zzub. Bell officials were unable to explain the alphabetical gaff.
> *Ottawa Citizen* 22 Jan. 1990: A2

(The correct spelling is *gaffe*.)

gage see GAUGE

gallery see QUEBEC ENGLISH

galore *Galore* means in abundance, and is placed after the noun it modifies: 'kittens galore'. It conveys a light-hearted tone inappropriate to very serious or melancholy topics or formal prose.

> Complete with television coverage, international recognition and goals galore, the first world championship got under way in the city that claims to be the birthplace of women's ice hockey.
> *Province* (Vancouver) 21 March 1990: 70

> There are mistakes galore of which I will note three only: the number of regular army personnel in 1939, the number of Canadian dead, and the Great War rank of General Andrew McNaughton are all incorrectly stated.
> *National Post* (Toronto) 17 June 2004: A20

(The serious tone of this review is undercut by the use of galore; 'a plethora of mistakes' might be substituted for 'mistakes galore'.)

gambit, gamut see GAUNTLET

gamy, gamey see -Y, -EY

gaol see JAIL

garage Two hundred and forty Vancouverites were interviewed for the 'Survey of Vancouver English' (1984), and among them they produced twenty discernibly different pronunciations of *garage*. The most common Canadian pronunciation is *guh RAHZH*, rhyming with *mirage*. This is also the most popular American pronunciation. The second and third most common Canadian pronunciations are *guh RAJ*, rhyming with *badge*, and *guh RAZH*, in which the vowel sound in *badge* precedes *zh*. These two pronunciations are distinctly Canadian. Americans are more likely to rhyme *garage* with *lodge*. None of these pronunciations is popular in Britain, where the stress falls on the first syllable: *GA rahzh*, *GA rahj*, or *GA rij*, rhyming with *carriage*.

The pronunciation of *garage* is so variable because it was borrowed from French only at the beginning of this century. The British have anglicized the stress pattern so that it matches the pattern of Middle English borrowings such as *courage* and *passage*. North Americans have preserved the French stress pattern, which is also retained in similar words borrowed from French, such as *mirage* and *ménage*. Since *zh* is not a native English sound, there is confusion on both sides of the Atlantic about how to pronounce the final *g* of *garage*, and Canadians specifically have not settled on how to pronounce the *a* that precedes it.

garderie see QUEBEC ENGLISH

garnish, garnishment, garnishee To *garnish* something, especially food, is to decorate

259

it; the decorative items, such as sprigs of parsley or slivers of pimento, are *garnishes* or, rarely, *garnishment*.

In law, *garnishment* is the legal seizure of a portion of someone's salary or property in payment of a debt. The verb is either to *garnish* or to *garnishee*; *garnishee* (pronounced *GAR ni SHEE*) is more common in Canada. In the United States *garnish* is the more common form of the verb because there the debtor who is subject to the process is called 'the garnishee'. *Garnishee* is often mispronounced as if it were spelled *garinshee*.

> They garnish the church with final harvest products such as corn stalks and pumpkins. . . .
> *Globe and Mail* (Toronto) 14 Oct. 1985: A14

> Normal collection procedures, including garnishment of wages and seizure and sale of property, will be used to collect the money, Marshall says.
> *Telegram* (St. John's) 26 March 2006: B1

> If the usual series of written notices and telephone calls proves fruitless, the final recourse is taking a debtor to court. In most cases, an order to garnish the debtor's wages is sought.
> *Ottawa Citizen* 29 Nov. 1990: B1

> . . . unless he eventually receives a discharge from the courts in bankruptcy proceedings, any property he acquires for many years to come may also be seized, and judgment creditors may garnishee his salary or wages.
> J.E. Smyth et al. *The Law and Business Administration in Canada* 1987: 717

Gaspé   see CAPITAL LETTERS

gather together   see TOGETHER

gauge, gage   *Gauge* and *gage* are variants. Both spellings rhyme with *cage*; *gauge* is far more common. To *gauge* something is to measure or estimate it. A *gauge* is a measuring device, or a means of roughly measuring something, or a standard of measure, as in '12-gauge shotgun' or 'narrow-gauge railway'.

See also GUN.

gauntlet, gamut, gambit   A *gauntlet* is a type of glove that covers the wrist and may

extend up the forearm. Gauntlets were originally part of a knight's armour; throwing one to the ground was a formal way of issuing a challenge. The expressions 'throw down the gauntlet', meaning to challenge someone, and 'pick up the gauntlet', meaning to accept the challenge, have their origins in this medieval custom.

The unrelated expression 'to run the gauntlet' comes from a form of military punishment in which a prisoner was forced to walk between two rows of men armed with clubs and other weapons. This punishment, known in Swedish as *gatlopp*, came to be called *gauntlet* in English through a common process whereby a familiar word is substituted for a foreign one. (See FOLK ETYMOLOGY.) *Gantlet* is a chiefly American spelling variant.

A *gamut*, derived from the medieval Latin word for a musical scale, is a range of something. To 'run the gamut' means to move through a range of things, usually from one extreme to another: 'The courses offered ran the gamut from Art to Zoology'. A *gambit* is an opening move in chess in which a player sacrifices a piece in the hope of gaining an advantage later on. By extension, *gambit* is used to mean tactic. This calculated move may or may not involve sacrifice. A gambit can also be an opening remark intended to start a conversation. *Gambit* is sometimes mistakenly substituted for *gamut*.

> A pair of gauntlet gloves completed the uniform.
> Max Braithwaite *The Night We Stole the Mountie's Car* 1971: 124

> . . . recommendations on arms control and disarmament which were being drafted before I left for Geneva in February 1969 reached me in June, presumably after running the gauntlet of interdepartmental brickbats.
> George Ignatieff *The Making of a Peacemonger* 1987: 245

> . . . the views on public interest intervention expressed by these courts run the gamut from enthusiastic endorsement to grave suspicion.
> *Canadian Bar Review* 66.3 (1987): 504

> As an opening gambit he informed me that the Canadian smoked oysters, which were being served as hors d'oeuvres, tasted like cod liver oil and felt like rubber.
> George Ignatieff *The Making of a Peacemonger* 1987: 137

Another type of pain, that from cancer, is regarded as a separate kind, even though cancer covers a whole gambit of diseases which cripple the immune system and leave it vulnerable to other infections, too.
Globe and Mail (Toronto) 27 May 1985: P13

(The word required here is *gamut*.)

gay, lesbian, homosexual, transgendered, transsexual, trans, queer, LGBTQ

Gay, *lesbian*, and *homosexual* are all used as both nouns and adjectives. The words *gay* and *homosexual* may refer to both men and women who prefer same-sex relationships, but sometimes they refer only to men, so it is best to use an inclusive phrase ('lesbians and gays', or 'gay men and lesbians') when reference to both sexes is intended.

The adjective *homosexual* has more clinical connotations than *gay*, and *gay* is often preferred by gays and lesbians themselves. In the seventeenth century, 'gay' men were rakes and 'gay' women were prostitutes. Even at that time, however, *gay* may also have referred to same-sex relationships: historically, in English, several slang words for *prostitute*, such as *queen* and *molly*, have been applied to, and subsequently adopted by, gay men. Nonetheless, it was not until the twentieth century that the 'homosexual' meaning of *gay* was documented in dictionaries.

Transgendered and *transsexual* people feel that their biological sex, the sex they were born into—or, in some cases, the sex that was assigned to them by doctors early in life—does not match their gender identity. *Transgendered* is the broader term, with *transsexual* usually reserved for people who have had or are seeking medical sex reassignment. Some transgendered people do not in fact feel that they belong to the opposite sex but rather that their gender is both male and female or neither. The clipped form *trans* is sometimes used as an umbrella term for transgendered and transsexual. Note the two *s*'s in *transsexual*. This word is often misspelled.

The proliferation and increasing specificity of terms for non-heterosexual and differently gendered people has not escaped the notice of gay, lesbian, bisexual, and trans people themselves. Some call themselves simply *queer*, rehabilitating an old term of abuse and emphasizing solidarity among sexual minorities. The term *queer* has gained currency in academe too, with some universities now offering programs of Queer Studies. The initialism *LGBTQ* (Lesbian, Gay, Bisexual, Transgendered, and Queer)—the final Q is often omitted—is an umbrella term. *LGBTQ* is commonly used to describe events, organizations, initiatives, etc., for all men or women who are not heterosexual or who are transgendered. Some people prefer this initialism to *queer* because it contains an explicit reference to each group.

Never before have we heard a leader of a national party speak about equality for lesbians and gay men to a national television audience.
Rites Feb. 1990: 10

If public washrooms were open to everyone, while at the same time preserving everyone's privacy, then they would be safer for transgendered people.
Whig-Standard (Kingston) 23 May 2006: 5

'You might say teenagers have jumped from the closet to the courtroom,' says Kristopher Wells, a U of A education doctoral student and local queer activist. Now, 'we have a group of out kids who know and want to exercise their rights.'
Edmonton Journal 13 May 2006: D9

Camp Ten Oaks: A one week, sleep-away summer camp for ages 8–17 from LGBTQ (lesbian, gay, bisexual, trans, two spirit, queer) and/or non-traditional families, LGBTQ youth and their allies.
Ottawa Citizen 25 April 2006: E1

(Note the addition to the usual LGBTQ list of *two spirit*, a term used by Aboriginal people in North America to refer to gender-variant people.)

See also COMMON LAW; FAG, FAGGOT; INCLUSIVE LANGUAGE; MARRIAGE; SEXUAL MINORITIES; SEXUAL ORIENTATION

Gay Nineties see CAPITAL LETTERS

Gaza Strip see CAPITAL LETTERS

gel, jell The noun for jelly-like substances ('hair gel', 'energy gel') and for the gelatinous sheets used in theatre lighting, is spelled *gel*.

The verb meaning to become firmer, to take shape, or to begin to work well together is spelled either *gel* or *jell*. Canadians usually spell the verb *gel*.

Gel is a shortened form of *gelatin*, while *jell* is a back-formation from *jelly*. Both of these words, *gelatin* and *jelly*, derive from the Latin word *gelata*, 'frozen, congealed'.

> There the DNA is extracted and set on a gel that allows the strands to be laid out separately.
> *Vancouver Sun* 27 Aug. 2005: A7

> What is clear is that the team failed to gel.
> *Calgary Herald* 27 Feb. 2006: A14

> . . . like all other vegetable oils, biodiesel starts to jell into a solid form at temperatures that are not too practical in a Canadian winter.
> *Gazette* (Montreal) 1 Nov. 2004: E3

See also BACK-FORMATION; JELLO, JELL-O, JELLY, ASPIC.

gendarme, gendarmerie *Gendarme* is borrowed from French and derived from 'gens d'armes', meaning men-at-arms. In France, *gendarmes* are military police officers, members of one branch of the armed forces, whose duties include internal defence and law enforcement in rural areas. *Gendarmerie* refers either to a corps of police officers (as in the French name of the Royal Canadian Mounted Police, la Gendarmerie royale du Canada) or to the headquarters of the force.

Since gendarmes are not municipal police, some usage commentators disapprove of English-speaking writers who use the term generally for any French-speaking police officer. But Canadian writers do use the term in this way, especially in humorous contexts. The loose English use of *gendarme* is not a problem unless the context requires a precise term.

> At that time, the French Government sent in an emergency gendarme corps from Paris to restore order.
> *Globe and Mail* (Toronto) 28 Feb. 1985: P11

> It can be found in U.S. overall strategy for the Middle East, which casts Israel in the role of *gendarme* enforcing 'stability' on the area and its oil supplies.
> Henry M. Rosenthal and S. Cathy Berson, eds. *Canadian Jewish Outlook Anthology* 1988: 169

> City-operated and private parking lots are jammed throughout the tourist season [in Quebec City] . . . and the local gendarmerie takes a dim view of violators in no-parking zones.
> Alan Tucker, ed. *The Penguin Guide to Canada* 1991: 280

gender, sex In some languages nouns are grouped into *genders*: categories labelled masculine, feminine, and sometimes neuter. Gender may determine word endings and agreement with other words. Gender is not necessarily tied to sex: for example, in German the word for 'girl' is neuter, while inanimate objects may be feminine or masculine. In English, with a few exceptions, nouns are not gendered, and the gender of English pronouns (*he*, *she*, *it*, etc.) corresponds to biological sex, or the lack of it. There is a convention of using feminine pronouns to refer to ships and cars in English, but that practice has been labelled sexist and may be on the wane.

Some commentators condemn the use of *gender* except as a grammatical term. However, many people today use *gender* as a synonym for *sex*. And these two terms are distinguished by many academic writers who use *gender* to refer to the roles and characteristics associated with men and women by society and *sex* to refer to characteristics that can be classified as anatomical, genetic, or biological; this distinction can be a useful one.

> In their daily speech they abandoned some basic rules of Old English grammar, giving us our wonderfully simple adjectives, with no inflectional endings, and our natural, gender-free nouns.
> *Saturday Night* March 1986: 43

> Most respondents view sex pre-selection—tests used to select the gender of a child—as the technology with the strongest potential for abuse.
> *Ottawa Citizen* 19 Sept. 1990: A14

(Here *sex* and *gender* are used as synonyms.)

Authorities on women were usually men. They were assumed to possess that knowledge, like all other knowledge, by virtue of gender.
Margaret Atwood Second Words 1982: 216

Playing to traditional gender roles, the bulk of the car commercials played to classic male insecurities, and a need for 'power under the hood,' while just about every cleaning product featured a hard-working woman.
Vancouver Sun 29 April 2006: F13

(Here *gender* refers to cultural expectations linked to sex.)

gender-neutral　see INCLUSIVE LANGUAGE; JOB TITLES; SEXIST LANGUAGE

genera　see PLURALS; -US

generation, baby boomer　How long is a generation? According to most dictionaries, the average age difference between parents and children defines the length of a generation, and that is usually reckoned at thirty years. However, the word *generation* is also commonly used to describe a set of people born about the same time, who share childhood memories and youthful experiences and who reach adulthood in the same social and economic climate. In this sense, a generation may span as little as a decade.

People have no trouble deciding on the start date of the generation popularly known as the *baby boomers*: 1945–46, just after the Second World War. There is no consensus, however, on when the temper of the times changed. The cut-off year for this generation is usually placed in the period 1960 to 1966, when the birth control pill became widely available in North America.

The term *first-generation* is used to refer both to the first generation to arrive in Canada ('first-generation immigrant') and to the first generation to be born in Canada. This makes expressions such as 'second-generation Canadian' ambiguous unless they are qualified somehow.

After eleven generations am I still a Frenchman, rather than a North American? Are my children, who are half-Scottish, to be listed as French because three hundred years ago one of my ancestors was Huguenot?
Richard Davies and Glen Kirkland, eds. Dimensions 1986: 123–4

The new darlings of advertising and Network Row are people in their 20s—the group that advertisers have dubbed the baby-bust generation. . . .
Gazette (Montreal) 28 June 1992: F2

. . . the values of the first-generation immigrants make them even more difficult to break away from than your average Canadian-born, out-of-it parents.
Spectator (Hamilton) 6 Oct. 1995: C6

I am a third generation Canadian and very much a product of my culture.
Vancouver Sun 1 April 1995: D3

(Here 'third generation' may mean either the third generation to be born in Canada or the second.)

genetic　see CONGENITAL

genial　see CONGENIAL

genie, Genie, genius　A *genie* (plural *genii* or *genies*) is a magical spirit. A *Genie* (plural *Genies*) is an award presented by the Academy of Canadian Cinema and Television. A *genius* (plural *geniuses*) is a person whose intellectual or creative gifts are considered extraordinary.

Sometimes a spirit is called a *genius*, as in 'the genius of the place'; the plural is *genii*. Occasionally, *genius* in the sense of gifted person is pluralized *genii*.

When the boards were torn from the doors and windows of New Westminster's Paramount Theatre in 1988, a century of entertainment ghosts rose up from the dust, the dirt, the shame, and the shadows over Columbia Street, like genies released from a lamp.
Province (Vancouver) 19 Oct. 1990: 32

In the beginning, the Soviet president probably didn't know that the genii he released would take on lives of their own outside his control.
Ottawa Citizen 16 Oct. 1990: A10

A Canada-France co-production, The Triplets of Belleville was nominated for a pair of 2004 Oscars but qualified under the rules for the 2005 Genies.
Calgary Herald 22 March 2005: C2

The great mathematical geniuses often do their best work in early life, like most of the great lyrical poets.
Northrop Frye *The Educated Imagination* 1963: 54

genitive   see POSSESSIVE

genius   see GENIE

genocide   see HOLOCAUST

gentile   see ATHEIST

genuine   The British and the Americans pronounce *genuine* the same way: *JEN yoo in*. The pronunciation *JEN yoo wine*—very common and unstigmatized in Canada—is considered a vulgarism in both the United States and Britain.

genus   see SPECIES; PLURALS; -US

geographic, geographical   see -IC, -ICAL

gerbil   see CAPITAL LETTERS

geriatrics, gerontology, geriatric   *Geriatrics* is a branch of medicine that deals with the diseases of the aged and aging, while *gerontology* is the study of the processes and problems of aging. *Geriatrics*, like *obstetrics* and *ethics*, is treated as a singular.

The adjective *geriatric* means relating to the elderly. *Geriatric* is sometimes used facetiously to describe anything decrepit or run-down; some may find this use insensitive.

. . . take your dog in for a geriatric check-up (heart, kidneys, etc.) while he's still 'middle-aged' and there's time to make changes in diet or treatment which will ease and extend the later years.
Dogs in Canada Special Issue 1986: 66

But David MacDonald, Canada's African aid co-ordinator, described the UN as an 'infant' rather than the 'geriatric institution' it is often thought to be.
Globe and Mail (Toronto) 7 March 1985: P1

See also INCLUSIVE LANGUAGE.

germ   see FLU

German shepherd   see DALMATIAN

German words, pronunciation of
German words—unlike English words—tend to be pronounced exactly as they are spelled. But the relationships between letter combinations and sounds are not always the same in English and German. The following chart may aid in the pronunciation of German loan words and names.

German spelling	English sound	Example
au	ow (*how*)	Frau, Bauhaus
aü, eu	oy (*boy*)	Fraülein, Freud, Deutschmark
ch	ck*	dachshund
ee	ay (*pay*)	Beethoven
ei	I	Heinz, stein, Reich
ie	ee (*see*)	diesel, Diefenbaker
j	y	Johann, jaeger
sch	sh	Schiller, schnapps, schnitzel
tsch	ch	kitsch, Deutschmark
w	v	Wagner, Weltanschauung
z	ts	Mozart, Nazi

*-*ch*- in words borrowed from German is often pronounced as if it were spelled *ck*. But for words such as *Bach* and *Mach*, where -*ch* appears at the end of the word, a more German pronunciation results if the -*ch* is pronounced as an exaggerated version of the English initial *h*, as in *help*, *hurt*, etc.

gerontology   see GERIATRICS

gerund   see POSSESSIVE BEFORE GERUND; entry in Glossary

gesture, gesticulation   A *gesture* is a movement, especially of the hands, used to express or amplify one's meaning. *Gesture* (noun and verb) can also refer to any action undertaken to indicate one's intentions or to show politeness. *Gesticulation* is the use of physical gestures, usually in an excited, energetic, or theatrical way. *Gesticulation* is used both as an uncountable noun ('a lot of gesticulation') and as a countable one ('wild gesticulations'). The *g* sound in all these words is soft, that is, pronounced like *j*.

He extends one hand toward the door handle and reaches his other hand out . . . in a grand, biblical gesture to the eight school trustees ranged around him.
Province (Vancouver) 6 Dec. 1990: 14

Restaurant staff borrowed the Quebec flag and raised it Tuesday beside the Canadian flag as a friendly gesture to their guests. . . .
Province (Vancouver) 29 June 1990: 54

Carving out his thoughts with constant gesticulation, he speaks with the strength and confidence of a stage actor.
Maclean's 21 Oct. 1991: A34

One girl did a sort of half-knee bob while her left hand made wild gesticulations around the upper half of her body.
Catholic Register 23 Aug. 1986: E4

get Sometimes *get* is used in place of *be* in passive constructions: for example, 'They got hurt' rather than 'They were hurt'. Some language commentators have called this construction ugly and unnecessary. However, the *OED* includes citations of the passive use of *get* from as early as 1652, and the structure has its special uses.

First, the *be* structure sometimes leaves it unclear whether an ongoing state or a single event is being described. For example, 'Most of their stock was stolen' could mean either that they routinely offered stolen goods for sale or that they had had a break-in. The *get* passive unambiguously describes an event: 'Most of their stock got stolen'. Second, only the *get* passive can be combined with the emphatic *do*: 'Merchandise does get stolen!'

The *get* passive is quite legitimate but generally informal. In academic writing it is used only when the regular passive would be stilted or ambiguous.

Just because we get elected doesn't mean we get up the next day with any special wisdom.
Saturday Night Feb. 1986: 23

I know people are going to get killed.
Saturday Night July 1986: 14

Sometimes, of course, metaphors got mixed, for it cannot have been easy to proclaim a faith fash-

ioned for rulers from the modest station of an insecure subject.
J.A.W. Gunn *Beyond Liberty and Property* 1983: 163

Sukhomlin also got involved in a furious polemic with the Menshevik Georgii Plekhanov. . . .
Canadian Journal of History 14.1 (1989): 19

See also GOT, GOTTEN.

get by see IDIOMS

ghetto, ghettoize In sixteenth-century Venice, the *ghetto* was the area where Jewish people were forced to live. Confining the Jews to a certain quarter was common practice in European cities at the time, and was justified on the grounds that their religion would contaminate the Christian faith. Since the 1900s, any area to which a minority group is restricted by official policy, by poverty, or by racism has been termed a *ghetto*. More recently, *ghetto* has been used figuratively to stress limitations or restrictions on economic and social forms of mobility, as in 'job ghetto' or 'ghetto mentality'. And, more recently still, it has been without negative connotations to describe voluntarily formed communities: 'student ghetto', 'gay ghetto'. This neutral use was criticized as insensitive to the harsh historical reality of ghettos, and it may in fact be in decline.

Although some desk dictionaries do not list the verb *ghettoize*, meaning restrict to a (literal or figurative) ghetto, this verb is perfectly acceptable and current in Canadian writing. Interestingly, the *OED's* earliest quotations for *ghettoization* and *ghettoize* come from Canadian sources: the *Jewish Standard* (Toronto, 1939) and the *Canadian Jewish Chronicle* (1939).

Ghettos is the more common plural of the noun, but *ghettoes* is also accepted.

It is therefore clear that crime in the ghetto is rooted in blocked economic opportunities and in racial discrimination.
Irving M. Zeitlin and Robert J. Brym *The Social Condition of Humanity* 1991: 271

He criticizes them for knee-jerk reactions, overblown rhetoric, and a ghetto mentality which

suggests that all those who are not for them are against them.
The Beaver Feb.–Mar. 1990: 59

I began to get worried about the possibility of a new ghetto: women's books reviewed only by women, men's books reviewed only by men, with a corresponding split in the readership.
Margaret Atwood *Second Words* 1982: 106

Rue St-Denis is Montreal's boulevard St Michel, the *quartier Latin*, a Francophone student ghetto of bookstores, cafes, boutiques, restaurants, smoky jazz clubs, cinemas, and theaters.
Alan Tucker, ed. *The Penguin Guide to Canada* 1991: 165

And how did Church and Wellesley come to be known as the Gay Village? Ten years ago, I interviewed Kid-in-the-Hall Scott Thompson's fabulously gay writing partner, Paul Bellini, about life in gay Toronto. He referred to his stomping grounds with acidic pride as The Ghetto.
Toronto Star 23 Jan. 2005: A4

The people at the society have done much to break the old stigma of jazz, seen for so long as an art form ghettoized to late-night hours in smoky clubs in neighborhoods decent folks are afraid to enter.
Vancouver Sun 21 June 1990: F16

And while more women are in the workforce, many are still in low-paying female job ghettos.
Vancouver Sun 19 Oct. 1990: D11

gibe   see JIBE

gift, free   see WORDINESS

gift horse   see CLICHÉ

giga   see APPENDIX II

gipsy   see GYPSY

Gitxsan, Gitksan   Both names are in use for the Aboriginal group whose traditional territory is along the Skeena River and in the Bulkley Valley in northwestern British Columbia. *Gitxsan*, however, is more popular and seems to be preferred by this First Nation. *Gitksan* (GIT ksan), is sometimes misspelled *Gitskan*.

Gitxsan or *Gitksan* is used for both singular and plural. Their language, also Gitksan (or Gitxsan or Gitxsen) belongs to the Tsimshian family. It is similar to the nearby Nisga'a, and both languages are sometimes referred to collectively as *Nass-Gitksan*.

In the Gitskan-Wet'suwet'en case, Chief Justice Allan McEachern reject[ed] present-day aboriginal title and the right to self-government.
Vancouver Sun 15 Dec. 1994: SR1

(The correct spelling is *Gitksan*.)

See also ABORIGINAL PEOPLE(S); CARRIER; APPENDIX III.

give   The past tense is *gave*. The use of *give* as the past tense, as in 'She give me this puzzle and helped me put it together', is non-standard.

He give me a blank look. His cheekbones were sharp enough to puncture my lies.
David Williams *Eye of the Father* 1985: 37

(*Give* marks the dialect of this character as nonstandard.)

See also STANDARD ENGLISH, STANDARD.

given name   see FIRST NAME

gladiolus, gladiola   Some writers, botanists, and gardeners cringe when a *gladiolus* is called a *gladiola*. The form *gladiola* for a single flower appeared because people, hearing *gladiolus* as *gladiolas*, thought it was a regular English plural and dropped the *s* to form a singular. Thus *gladiolus* is the technically correct singular form, but *gladiola* is acceptable in informal, non-technical contexts.

The preferred plural in formal and technical writing is *gladioli*. However, in everyday speech Canadians tend to avoid pluralizing the word, either by saying 'gladiolus plants' or by using the informal short form *glads*. Canadians also use *gladiolus* as a collective noun: 'I planted gladiolus'. The regularized plural *gladioluses*, though acceptable, is seldom used.

But women still baked pies, boiled jam and steamed bread for the cooking contests and com-

peted to see who could grow the tallest gladiola.
Gazette (Montreal) 1 Sept. 1990: 15

(In informal writing *gladiola* is acceptable.)

Larger gladioli are attractive cutting flowers, but I particularly like the butterfly gladiolus.
Vancouver Sun 5 May 1990: C8

Late-blooming tubers such as dahlias, gladiolas and canna lilies . . . will also provide some interest in late September and early October.
Gazette (Montreal) 13 Sept. 1990: D3

(Here, in a gardening column, *gladioli* would be more appropriate.)

Glads can be planted as soon as the digging is good.
Ottawa Citizen 17 May 1990: G7

Ferncliff Gardens [offers a] massive selection of dahlias, gladiolus, irises, and peonies.
Province (Vancouver) 8 Nov. 1990: 103

(Here *gladiolus* is used as a collective noun.)

When can gladioli bulbs be planted and how deep should they be?
Ottawa Citizen 17 May 1990: G7

(The correct form here, where the noun is being used as an adjective, is *gladiolus*; saying *gladioli bulbs* is like saying *tulips bulbs*.)

See also PLURALS, REGULAR, IRREGULAR, FOREIGN.

glamorous see -OUR, -OR

glance, glimpse To *glance* at something is to look at it purposely but briefly. To *glimpse* something is to catch sight of it, to see it briefly or partially. With *glance* the emphasis is on the person looking and the action; with *glimpse* the emphasis is on the thing seen. Thus the sentences 'I glimpsed at my watch' and 'I caught a glance of Beth's face' are unidiomatic.

When I glanced back again, only her face was visible.
Queen's Quarterly 94.1 (1987): 52

At last I saw a clearing forming in the distance, and when I got there I could glimpse water spread out ahead through the trees.
Howard Engel *Murder Sees the Light* 1984: 116

global see QUEBEC ENGLISH

Gloucester, Worcester, Worcestershire, shire *Gloucester* and *Worcester* are pronounced with only two syllables. *Gloucester* rhymes with *roster*. Some people rhyme *Worcester* with *rooster—WOO ster*. More commonly, though, the first vowel is pronounced like the *oo* in *wood*.

Worcestershire is the name of an English county and of a spicy steak sauce. The *-shire* in *Worcestershire* (and the other shires) is usually rhymed with *hear* or *sure*, not *sire*. However, the word *shire* by itself does rhyme with *sire*.

glutton see GOURMET

go see GO, LIKE, SAY; GO, WENT; GO AND; GOES WITHOUT SAYING; GO MISSING; GONNA

go, like, say The substitution of *go* or *be like* for *say* in recounting conversations is slang ('I go, "Can I come in?" and he's like, "No problem"'). In Standard English, these descriptions of conversations would use *say* in the past tense ('I said, "Can I come in?" and he said, "No problem"'). These replacements for *say* are currently popular among teenagers and young adults and reviled by many older people. *Go* meaning say was first noticed by language commentators in the 1970s. The *OED* connects the new slang meaning of *go* to one of its standard meanings, to emit a characteristic sound, as in 'The sheep goes baaa'. The use of *be like* for *say* (linguists call this use 'quotative like') is but one of many new uses of *like* that seem to have spread rapidly from California around the English-speaking world. In Standard English, *like* is a preposition ('It works like a charm') and an adjective ('like minds'). In the casual conversation of many young people, it is also an adverb meaning nearly ('I like died') or a discourse particle, similar to *um*, indicating hedging and hesitation ('I like forgot') or emphasis ('We were like upstairs: we never heard a thing').

'So I go, "Where's the restaurant?" And he goes, "Find it yourself".'
Ottawa Citizen 23 Dec. 1990: F3

Two weeks later you overhear her whining to a friend. 'So, then he goes, "We're o-ver".'
Ottawa Citizen 2 Sept. 1990: F5

'My mom and dad were like, "You can do the movie as long as you don't smoke!"'
Windsor Star 23 Nov. 2005: E7

'So I'm like, give me a break.' Get over it. Life is moving on.
Edmonton Journal 19 Feb. 2004: F1

See also FUNCTIONAL SHIFT.

go, went, gone   In Standard English the past tense of *go* is *went*: 'She went'. The past participle is *gone*: 'She has gone'. 'She has went' is non-standard.

See also STANDARD ENGLISH, STANDARD

go and   'To go *and* check the mail' means 'to go *to* check the mail'. Using *and* after *go* is idiomatic and correct, though *go to* is more common in writing. *Go and* has a special meaning not shared by *go to*: to blunder or make a mistake, as in 'Now you've gone and done it!' *Go*, with or without *and*, is also sometimes used to intensify the verb that follows it: 'Go jump in the lake'.

'And what kind of a mess have you gone and made this time?' Dora snapped at Nadia.
Canadian Fiction Magazine 63 (1988): 82

She's gone and saved the lucky bastard.
Robert Kroetsch *Badlands* 1975: 69

gobbledygook, gobbledegook   *Gobbledygook* is the original spelling, but *gobbledegook* is also standard for unintelligible speech, writing, or ideas. An American Congressman named Maury Maverick coined the term in 1944 to refer specifically to governmental and bureaucratic reports, which often use complex grammar, indirect phrasing, and inflated vocabulary. As some politicians know, the effect of gobbledygook is to leave people confused or numbed. *Bafflegab* is a synonym.

Some ministers stumbled, while others showed they had taken a remarkably firm grip on government gobbledegook. Here, for instance, is how the chairman of Management Board, Elinor Caplan, replied to a question on reviewing programs announced by the Miller cabinet: 'Let me assure the leader of the Opposition that this Government is reviewing carefully and with a sense of sensitivity the commitments made to ensure that the review will be undertaken in a co-ordinated and efficient manner and that we will be proceeding clearly in the immediate future to determine which, if any, of the commitments we will be undertaking.'
Globe and Mail (Toronto) 11 July 1985: P7

See also COLLOQUIAL, INFORMAL, SLANG, JARGON; WORDINESS, VARIATION.

God, god   *God* is capitalized when the word refers to the supreme being of any monotheistic religion. This practice usually, though not always, extends to expletives: 'Good God, when did he get back?' References to deities in religions that have more than one god are not capitalized: 'the gods of the ancient Greeks'.

Capitalized pronouns and adjectives relating to the Christian God are beginning to disappear, although their use is still sometimes preferred in religious writing.

I prayed to God that if I died in Toronto He would be good enough to take care that this last event in my life should happen on a Saturday to save me from one Toronto Sunday.
Henry M. Rosenthal and S. Cathy Berson, eds. *Canadian Jewish Outlook Anthology* 1988: 345

'For god's sake, look at yourself, Karen.'
David Williams *Eye of the Father* 1985: 149

See also HINDU, HINDUISM; ISLAM; RELIGION; SACRED WRITINGS; SIKH.

God Save the Queen   see O CANADA

goes without saying, needless to say   Some argue that both these phrases are nonsensical, since if something goes without saying, it shouldn't be said. Both phrases, however, are idiomatic and common. Like the adverbs *obviously* and *naturally*, they function to suggest without lengthy explanation that a statement is (or should be) self-evident.

It goes without saying that there is considerable variation in the degree to which different men exercise control over different women.
Carl J. Cuneo *Pay Equity* 1990: 196

This fact, needless to say, poses a serious challenge to our conclusions.
Canadian Journal of Philosophy 19 (1989): 220

See also OF COURSE.

Gold Coast   see CAPITAL LETTERS

Goldwynism   see MALAPROPISM

go missing   To *go missing*, meaning to disappear, is informal. Although the expression is common in speech and in the popular press, in formal writing the verb *disappear* is preferable. Some speakers of American English are unfamiliar with this phrase and find it humorous.

Indeed, a spokesman for Lloyd's of London noted that in 1984 insurance companies had paid out $385 million to the owners of satellites which had gone missing in space or malfunctioned after being launched.
Maclean's 10 Feb. 1986: 30

The area where the little girl went missing is about 60 kilometres southwest of Winnipeg.
Leader-Post (Regina) 29 May 2006: A2

gone   see GO, WENT

gonna   *Gonna* is a slang contraction of the phrase 'going to'. The construction is generally used to express an intention or expectation: 'She's gonna work hard all summer'; 'He's gonna be sorry'. *Gonna* is never used for 'going to' in the sense of moving towards a destination: 'I'm going to (*not* gonna) Halifax'. When *gonna* appears in Canadian journalism and fiction, it is meant to imitate very casual speech. It is inappropriate in other contexts and should be used sparingly; most dictionaries do not list it.

'I told his secretary, "Look, I'm gonna be there tomorrow morning and if I have to, I'm going to sit down on his doorstep until he talks to us".'
Globe and Mail (Toronto) 4 March 1985: P13

The policeman stepped closer and said, 'Are you goin' peaceful, or am I gonna put handcuffs on you?'
Jack Chambers *Milestones* 1983: 314

When I decided I was gonna marry that man I knew what I had to do.
Canadian Fiction Magazine 64 (1988): 87

good   see ADJECTIVES AND ADVERBS; AS GOOD AS OR BETTER THAN

goodbye, good-bye, goodby, good-by   All these spellings are standard, but Canadian writers overwhelmingly prefer *goodbye*.

good for nothing   see CLICHÉ

google   see COMPUTER TERMS

go on about   see IDIOMS

go out (with)   see PHRASAL VERBS

gormandize   see GOURMET

got, gotten   Canadians use both *got* and *gotten* as the past participle of *get*: 'I had got *or* gotten a lot done by then'. Both past participles are also used in the United States, while in British dictionaries only *got* is listed. Before 1800, both *got* and *gotten* were in common use in Britain, but after that date *gotten* became obsolete; *Fowler's* (1965) called *gotten* archaic and affected. In North America *gotten* has never become obsolete and certainly could not be condemned on the grounds of affectation. Nonetheless, some North American usage guides, influenced by British ones, have condemned *gotten*. While Canadians in general have ignored this unwarranted censure, academics have taken it to heart. *Gotten*, common in every other type of writing, is rare in academic prose.

The difference may be that had I been a husband and failed, I might have got away with it.
Queen's Quarterly 96.2 (1989): 232

Soon, I had gotten as much line out as I was going to, which wasn't a lot.
Atlantic Salmon Journal Autumn 1990: 43

Mostly we have gotten what we wanted.
Ken Dryden *The Game* 1983: 110

See also GET; HAVE GOT, HAVE GOTTEN; HAVE GOT TO.

gourmet, gourmand, glutton, gormandize Many commentators maintain that a *gourmet* is a connoisseur of fine food and wine, while a *gourmand*, though appreciative of quality, is more interested in quantity. However, *gourmand* is often used interchangeably with *gourmet*. Unlike *gourmand*, *glutton* always has pejorative connotations of greed and excess.

Gourmet is used more often as an adjective than as a noun, describing such things as menus, restaurants, or specialty food shops. To *gormandize* is to eat either voraciously or discerningly.

Gourmets from across the globe trek to John Tovey's Miller Howe Hotel here as if it were mecca.
Bon Vivant Aug.–Sept. 1982: 7

First off, no self-respecting Japanese gourmand would even set foot in a new sushi bar without being taken there by a regular and formally introduced to the head chef.
Globe and Mail (Toronto) 6 April 1985: M8

(Some commentators would insist on *gourmet* here.)

What a gourmand for love and punishment he was. . . .
Canadian Fiction Magazine 64 (1988): 80

(Here *gourmand* replaces *glutton* in a play on the idiomatic expression 'glutton for punishment'.)

In this atmosphere, gourmandizing does not easily thrive. When was the last time you ate haute with The Beach Boys on tap?
Globe and Mail (Toronto) 5 Sept. 1985: S6

(The correct spelling is *gormandize*.)

See also EPICUREAN.

government *Government* is often incorrectly spelled without the first *n*. Correctly spelled, *government* contains the word *govern*.

See also COLLECTIVE NOUNS.

governor-elect see ELECT

governor general see HEAD OF STATE

graduate, be graduated, graduand From one perspective, a university or other institution graduates students: 'Queen's graduated a record number of students in English this year'. This perspective produces 'Mary Smith was graduated from Queen's', which sounds slightly old-fashioned but is still fairly common. From another perspective, however, students graduate *from* a university. This perspective produces 'Mary Smith graduated from Queen's', which is more common nowadays. Both of these forms are accepted. However, the construction 'Mary Smith graduated Queen's' is both rare and disputed.

Those who are about to receive a degree in a graduation ceremony or convocation are sometimes referred to as *graduands*; once the degree is conferred, they become *graduates*.

He refers to Mr. Miller as a used-car salesman. Mr. Miller was graduated from McGill University with a science degree in chemical engineering.
Globe and Mail (Toronto) 22 Feb. 1985: P7

Joe Zuken graduated with distinction from the Winnipeg Peretz Shule.
Henry M. Rosenthal and S. Cathy Berson, eds. *Canadian Jewish Outlook Anthology* 1988: 375

I have often heard an honorary graduand, whose achievements had been amply rehearsed in the speech in which he was presented to the Chancellor, go over the whole of that ground again, explaining in detail how he took every step in his distinguished, and wearisomely long, career.
Robertson Davies *One Half of Robertson Davies* 1978: 54

See also GRADUATE, POSTGRADUATE, POSTDOCTORAL.

graduate, postgraduate, postdoctoral In Canada *graduate* is more often used than *postgraduate* to refer to students who have completed a first university degree and are pursuing a program of study leading to an advanced degree. British and Australian writers use *postgraduate* more often in this context. American dictionaries note that in the United States *postgraduate* may refer to studies following high school as well as university, while *graduate* refers mainly to studies beyond the first university degree.

Postdoctoral refers to research and study beyond a doctoral degree (e.g., a PhD). Many Canadians write *post-doctoral* and *post-graduate*, though major dictionaries do not hyphenate these words.

> He emphasized the importance of liberal and humane studies, rather than science; the importance of undergraduate education, as opposed to graduate studies. . . .
> Frederick Gibson *Queen's University* 2 (1983): 428

> After four years of undergraduate and three years of postgraduate study, my husband entered a four-year medical program at the University of B.C.
> *Vancouver Sun* 5 Nov. 1990: A7

> (In Canada *graduate* is more common than *postgraduate* in reference to studies carried out after completion of an undergraduate degree.)

> The new research . . . will require a systems analyst, a good computer and a post-doctoral fellow with expertise in mineral deposits.
> *Torch: University of Victoria Alumni Magazine* Spring 1990: 11

See also GRADUATE, BE GRADUATED, GRADUAND.

graffiti, graffito *Graffiti*, a borrowing from Italian, is often misspelled with a double *t*. *Graffiti* is used as a mass noun with a singular verb ('Is graffiti art or vandalism?') or, less commonly, as plural noun ('There are even sloppy graffiti painted on it'). In Italian, *graffiti* is a plural noun; the Italian singular form, *graffito*, is sometimes used in English to refer to a single piece of graffiti. The verb *graffiti*, meaning to mark with graffiti ('caught graffitiing the bridge') or to write as graffiti ('graffitied slogans'), is pronounced exactly like the noun.

> This decaying graffito is a metaphor for the state of justice in Guatemala.
> *Independent Voice* (Kingston) July/August 2005

> I walk through the still graffitied streets of Quebec

City, and then hop a boat across the wide mouth of the St. Lawrence River to Levis.
> *Now* (Toronto) 17–23 May 2001

See also PLURALS, REGULAR, IRREGULAR, FOREIGN.

grain see CORN

grammatical agreement see AGREEMENT, GRAMMATICAL

grammatical terms Grammatical terms used within entries are explained in a Glossary at the end of this book.

Grammatical categories that have usage issues associated with them (e.g., adjectives vs. adverbs) and usage issues with traditional grammatical labels (e.g. split infinitive) are dealt with in the main body of the book in the entries listed below.

See also ADJECTIVES AND ADVERBS; ADVERBS WITHOUT -LY; AGREEMENT, GRAMMATICAL; BACK-FORMATION; CASE; FUNCTIONAL SHIFT; GENDER, SEX; NEGATIVE-RAISING; PHRASAL VERBS; PLURALS, REGULAR, IRREGULAR, FOREIGN; POSSESSIVE; POSSESSIVE BEFORE GERUND; PREPOSITION AT END; PRONOUN WITH POSSESSIVE ANTECEDENT; SENTENCE ADVERBS; SPLIT INFINITIVE.

grand, grandiose Sometimes the adjective *grand* hints at pretension, but often it conveys a very positive impression. *Grandiose* always describes something overambitious, inflated, or pretentious.

> He does not appear to be interested in the big conceptual effect or the grand gesture.
> *Globe and Mail* (Toronto) 3 Jan. 1985: E4

> In an era when professional historians lament the difficulty the lay public faces in engaging with much that contemporary historians write, Ambrose's work is a refreshingly accessible narrative, written in the grand style. . . .
> *Queen's Quarterly* 95.4 (1988): 808

> Even as the boom collapsed several Western cities were still contemplating grandiose schemes designed to enhance their prestige.
> Pierre Berton *The Promised Land* 1984: 343

> The urge to erect grandiose, egotistical monuments has long been a French characteristic. Louis

XIV's immense seventeenth century palace at Versailles is one obvious example, as is the Eiffel Tower, built in 1889 to commemorate the centenary of the French Revolution.
Globe and Mail (Toronto) 16 Oct. 1985: A7

grand-aunt, grand-uncle   see GREAT-AUNT

grantor   see -ER, -OR

grapple   The verb *grapple*, meaning to take hold of, or grip, or wrestle, is used both literally and figuratively. In literal use *grapple* sometimes takes a direct object. When used figuratively, however, *grapple* almost always takes a preposition: usually *with*, but occasionally *for* or *over*.

Muscular linemen grapple ferociously, the ball dips gracefully to earth and the pass connects.
Globe and Mail (Toronto) 17 Oct. 1985: E1

Travel agents must grapple with mountains of ever-changing information.
Canadian Consumer Jan. 1986: 34

. . . of all the civil servants grappling for job tenure in the department only a minute percentage are of native ancestry.
Globe and Mail (Toronto) 8 May 1985: P6

grateful, gratified   Usually one is *grateful to* benefactors *for* their help; one is *gratified by* an event or experience, or *gratified that* something has happened.

So, with unintentional sexual messages rampant even in the least likely places, I, for one, am grateful to those who vigilantly expose them.
Harrowsmith Oct.–Nov. 1985: 18

Ray Goldman, one of 15 Canadian fish dealers who tested Dallas as a market, was gratified by the interest Texans showed in some traditionally underutilized varieties.
Globe and Mail (Toronto) 6 April 1985: P6

He was gratified that the CBC purchased the script for a series on Canadian history and gave it a first-class production.
Globe and Mail (Toronto) 31 Oct. 1985: E13

Grimes said he was gratified for the support, and will stick around as leader.
Telegram (St. John's) 8 Nov. 2004: A1

(Usually it is either '*grateful* for' or '*gratified by*'.)

gratis   see PERSONA NON GRATA

gratuitous, gratuitously   *Gratuitous* usually means unnecessary, unwarranted, unsolicited, or unjustified. It can also mean free, but this older meaning is rare. *Gratuitously*, the adverb, is used commonly to mean either 'unnecessarily' or 'without charge'. From the common phrase 'gratuitous violence' some people have mistakenly inferred that *gratuitous* means explicit or graphic.

In Canada, parents, players, teachers, and government leaders have contributed to the effort to eliminate the gratuitous violence of ice hockey.
Queen's Quarterly 94.1 (1987): 127

Saving people from drowning was not Joe Vincent's job, but he did it anyway. It was a voluntary, gratuitous service.
Gazette (Montreal) 16 June 1990: B2

(This usage may be influenced by the French *gratuit*, 'free' or 'without charge'.)

In the meantime, it was agreed that all available facilities should be given to the medical faculty gratuitously.
Hilda Neatby *Queen's University* 1 (1978): 73

(Here *gratuitously* means without charge.)

Even the doctor in the white lab coat delivers her graphic message that there are only three ways to contract AIDS in a way that is easily understood without being gratuitous.
Vancouver Sun 4 April 1990: A11

(Here *gratuitous* is mistakenly used to mean explicit or graphic.)

graveness   see -NESS

gray   see GREY

great-aunt, great-uncle, grand-aunt, grand-uncle   Your parents' aunts and uncles are your *great-aunts* and *great-uncles*. The children of your nieces and nephews are your *great-nieces* and *great-nephews*. These four relationships are also called *grand-aunt*, *grand-uncle*, *grand-niece* and *grand-nephew*, although much less commonly. Some genealogists recommend the exclusive use of the less common terms because they parallel *grandparent* and *grandchild* in designating relationships two generations apart. While this recommendation is logical, it is also largely unheeded.

These relationship terms are usually hyphenated, which makes the adjective, *great-* or *grand-*, unambiguously a kinship designator. When capitalized before a name, the adjectives are not ambiguous, and the hyphen is usually omitted.

> Ontario's adoption legislation defines a 'relative' for the purpose of adoption as 'the child's grandparent, great-uncle, great-aunt, uncle or aunt, whether by blood, marriage or adoption'.
> Ontario Ministry of Child and Youth Services website 25 Nov. 2005

> Nelly remembers her Great Uncle Ferdinand well—though she points out that his wife Adele, Klimt's most celebrated subject, died before she was born.
> *Province* (Vancouver) 22 Jan. 2006: B2.

(Here 'Great Uncle' is used as a title; it is capitalized and not hyphenated.)

Great Britain   see BRITAIN

Great Dane   see DALMATIAN

Grecian, Greek   see HELLENIC; NUMBER PREFIXES, GREEK AND LATIN

Green, green   The Green Party, a political party formed in Germany that focuses on environmental issues, and Greenpeace, an environmental activist group formed in Canada, both originated in the 1970s. Members of the Green Party, which has spread to other countries from Germany, are called *Greens* (capitalized). Since the 1970s, *green* (uncapitalized) has been used to describe anything or anyone that protects the environment, or claims to do so. *Green* is also used as a verb in the same contexts.

> . . . institutions such as the Green Party have achieved for the social and political reformer and

visionary a more established and politically influential status.
> *Queen's Quarterly* 94.1 (1987): 10

> This is the politics of personal awareness and commitment which McConkey espouses, and is increasingly reflected in the emerging paradigm of 'green consciousness', which seems to be taking root and beginning to thrive on a global scale.
> *City Magazine* 10.1 (1988): 41

> Naturally, retailers are eager to obtain information on how well green products are selling, particularly with industry surveys indicating that consumers will not only pay more for green products but also switch to a supermarket that provides them.
> *Western Grocer* Aug. 1990: 34

> The Australia New Zealand Bank has been 'greened' and is seen as a model of corporate environmental responsibility.
> *Ottawa Citizen* 29 April 1990: C6

> The more I ponder, the more I feel that better use of our existing infrastructure could go a long way toward greening up our rush-hour traffic blues.
> *Vancouver Sun* 17 May 1990: A17

See also FUNCTIONAL SHIFT.

green paper, white paper   A *green paper* is a preliminary report prepared by the government to promote debate on an issue in the House of Commons before legislation is drafted. A *white paper* outlines proposed legislation in what the government hopes is its near-final form. These terms are also used in the United Kingdom. Several newspaper style guides recommend capitalizing these names only in the formal title of a document, but most journalists capitalize them in all uses; this is probably a good policy to follow when writing for an audience not familiar with the terms.

> Instead of creating the socialist Swedish model, the NDP's recently published Green Paper on Rent Controls will lead to a New York-style rent control system.
> *Financial Post* 12 April 1991: 10

> Ten days ago, Mr. Parizeau's successor, Yves Duhaime, released the white paper, a 380-page document entitled White Paper on the Personal Tax and Transfer Systems.
> *Globe and Mail* (Toronto) 19 Jan. 1985: P8

A White Paper produced by the federal government in 1969 proposed eliminating the special legal status of Indians.
Queen's Quarterly 94.3 (1987): 674

Greenwich Mean Time, Coordinated Universal Time, UTC   In 1985 the task of operating the atomic clocks that keep the world's time passed from the Royal Observatory near Greenwich, England, to the International Bureau of Weights and Measures in Paris. Since then, *Greenwich* (pronounced *GREN itch*) *Mean Time* has also been known as *Coordinated Universal Time*, abbreviated internationally as UTC.

The Globe reports each day the temperatures in various cities around the larger globe. It is curious and tantalizing that these temperatures are taken at noon, Greenwich Mean Time. One would think that the maximum temperature of the day, or the temperature at noon local time, would be of more general interest.
Globe and Mail (Toronto) 2 Jan. 1985: P6

See also STANDARD TIME.

grey, gray   Canadian writers spell this word *grey* more often than *gray*. *Grey* is also the most common British spelling; the American spelling is *gray*.

However you spell the colour, you have no choice with certain proper names:

grey	*gray*
Grey Cup	*Gray's Anatomy*
Grey Nuns	Gray's 'Elegy Written in a
Earl Grey tea	Country Churchyard'
Greyhound bus	Gray's Inn (the English
Grey Owl (the writer)	law society)

grievance, grievous, grieve   Both *grievance* and *grievous* are often misspelled with the *e* before the *i*. *Grievous* is pronounced *GREE vus*. Sometimes it is mispronounced with an extra syllable, which leads to the misspelling *grievious*.

To *grieve* is to feel grief. Recently the verb has developed a new meaning: to lodge a formal complaint in the workplace.

What's consistent in all these accounts is the sense of grievance, defensiveness and fear among both blacks and whites.
Toronto Star 30 May 1992: J12

. . . the court convicted Col. Y— M— of causing greivous bodily harm and behaving in a manner inappropriate for an officer.
Financial Post 24 April 1991: 2

(The correct spelling is *grievous*.)

Since there is no collective agreement in effect, such an employee cannot grieve a discharge.
Toronto Star 3 Aug. 1992: C1

grisly, grizzly   *Grisly* means horrible or disgusting. *Grizzly* means grey or grey-haired. The 'grizzly bear' gets its name from the appearance of its fur, which ranges from black to brown to blond, but which is always grizzled—flecked with white or grey—on the flanks, back, and shoulders. Although some dictionaries list *grizzly* as a variant of *grisly*, most do not. This distinction is worth keeping.

And this is a book that gives us a clear if grisly view of the various forms of class terror practiced by masters against slaves—progressive mutilation, dismemberment, beheadings, starvation in cages. . . .
Queen's Quarterly 92.1 (1985): 195

Our conversation, in spite of its grizzly subject matter [instruments of torture], was integrating Des and his friend into the group. . . .
Howard Engel *Murder Sees the Light* 1984: 82

(The standard spelling is *grisly*.)

When painted on a large scale, the same subjects tend to be as intimidatingly theatrical as the grizzly scene of David holding Goliath's head painted by Giambattista Tiepolo.
Ottawa Citizen 10 March 1990: C4

(The standard spelling is *grisly*.)

Grit, Whig, Liberal   Members of the Liberal Party of Canada and its provincial counterparts are informally referred to as *Grits*. The name dates from the 1840s, when a radical reform party in Upper Canada was called the *Clear Grits*. In 1870 this party joined with reformers from Quebec to form the Liberal Party.

Since *grit* is abrasive, some feel the nickname is derogatory. However *clear grit* (meaning pure grit) was an expression of praise in the 1840s, acknowledging tenacity. The term is now used neutrally.

Whig is an old British term for members of the political party that favoured political reform and opposed conservatism. The Whigs changed their name to *Liberals* in the mid-1800s. *Whig* is not used as a nickname for the Liberals in Canadian politics, although the term survives in the name of the Kingston, Ontario, newspaper, the *Whig-Standard*.

His parents were Conservative farmers and doctrinaire Methodists. But a single speech by the great Liberal orator Edward Blake turned Dafoe into a Grit. . . .
Pierre Berton *The Promised Land* 1984: 34

In the past, Raina has run provincially for the Liberals in his native eastern Ontario and has been involved in other Grit campaigns.
Now Magazine 3–9 Nov. 1986: 13

See also BLEU, ROUGE; CONSERVATIVE.

grizzly   see GRISLY

Group of Seven, G7, G8   The *Group of Seven* was a group of Canadian artists whose work challenged the nineteenth-century values that still dominated the Canadian art world in the first decades of the twentieth century. The seven original members, based in Toronto, were Franklin Carmichael, Lawren Harris, A.Y. Jackson, Frank Johnston (who later changed his first name to Franz), Arthur Lismer, J.E.H. MacDonald, and F.H. Varley. A.J. Casson replaced Frank Johnston in 1926. In an attempt to broaden the national perspective of the group, Edwin Holgate of Montreal was invited to join in 1930, and a Winnipegger, L.L. Fitzgerald, joined in 1932. The group existed officially between 1920 and 1933. Tom Thomson painted with several members of the group but died in 1917, three years before it was formally established.

The term *Group of Seven* has also been used for an economic and political coalition of the seven leading industrialized countries: Canada, France, Germany, Italy, Japan, the United Kingdom, and the United States. This name was often shortened to G7. Unlike the artistic group, however, the G7 changed its name when it accepted a new member. With the entry of the Russian Federation, the G7 became the G8.

grove   see FOREST

grovel   see BACK-FORMATION

grow   Some commentators have objected to phrases such as 'grow smaller', 'grow thinner', and 'grow narrower', because *grow* suggests adding to or increasing in size. This argument ignores the commonly accepted use of *grow* to mean become, which is found in all types of writing.

The verb *grow* has developed a new transitive use in the financial and business domain: 'grow your money', 'grow our market share'. Although people have long grown crops and flowers, until recently they expected their money and their businesses (at least, grammatically) to grow by themselves. Despite the misgivings of some commentators, the new transitive sense is very well established in financial journalism.

The past tense is *grew* and the past participle is *grown*. Sometimes the incorrect past tense *growed* is used for humorous effect. 'I 'spect I just growed' is an allusion to Harriet Beecher Stowe's novel *Uncle Tom's Cabin*; it's the answer the character Topsy gives when she's asked where she came from.

Looking in through the reflections, it's tempting to contemplate a world which grows smaller and more dangerous as we feed our illusions.
Vancouver Sun 19 Sept. 1990: A13

But the window for deep interest-rate reductions is rapidly growing narrower.
Ottawa Citizen 14 Sept. 1990: A1

The important issue will be finding someone smart and experienced who can help you grow the company to the next stage.
Ottawa Citizen 4 March 2006: D10

Like Topsy, the phenomenon just growed.
Gazette (Montreal) 16 Nov. 1990: B7

gruntled   see BACK-FORMATION

guarantee, guaranty, warranty   Canadian writers use the spelling *guarantee* for both the noun and the verb, despite the traditional recommendation in style guides that *guarantee* be used as the verb form and *guaranty* as the noun. In Canada, *guaranty* is most commonly seen in the names of various financial or insurance companies.

An assurance by a seller to a buyer that goods or services will be satisfactory is a *guarantee* or a *warranty*. Both words are thought to derive from the same Germanic word meaning guarantor; however, they were borrowed at different times, *guaranty* from Old French and *warranty* from Old Norman French, which accounts for the different spellings. In current writing, Canadians prefer *warranty* for this sense, as in 'The toaster is under warranty for one year'.

That the process involved federal-provincial negotiation was itself almost enough to guarantee failure.
Queen's Quarterly 94.3 (1987): 667

A guarantee is a promise to pay only if the debtor defaults: 'If he does not pay you, I will.'
J.E. Smyth et al. *The Law and Business Administration in Canada* 1987: 246

Mr. Johnson said Quebec supports Article 23 in the Constitution, which guarantees access to education in either official language wherever numbers warrant, but he added that Article 23 alone is not a sufficient guaranty of minority rights.
Globe and Mail (Toronto) 27 May 1985: P5

(This writer makes the traditional distinction in spelling, using -*ee* for the verb and -*y* for the noun.)

He said artificial trees, which range from $99 to $199, come with a 10-year guaranty. . . .
Financial Post 19 Dec. 1989: 4

(Here *guaranty* is not incorrect, but *warranty* is the more common term.)

Car companies will have to double the warranty on emission-control equipment and make avail-

able to California as many as one million cars that run on alternative fuels.
Ottawa Citizen 16 Nov. 1990: A7

guard of honour   In the Canadian military, personnel assigned to ceremonial duty form a *guard of honour. Honor guard* is the equivalent American term.

Then, after a short pause, the guard of honour slowly lowered the casket into the tomb, as many veterans wept openly. . . .
Ottawa Citizen 29 May 2000: A1

guerrilla, guerilla, insurgent, freedom fighter, terrorist   Canadian writers use *guerrilla* (pronounced like *gorilla*) far more often than *guerilla*, but both spellings are accepted. The word, taken from the Spanish for 'little war', dates from the Napoleonic Wars. Guerrilla warfare is usually carried out by irregular, independent forces acting against superior forces, and involves hit-and-run attacks or ambushes rather than large-scale confrontation. *Guerrilla* is a fairly neutral term for forces opposing a government, as is *insurgent.*

Freedom fighter has been in common use since the Second World War, when it referred to regular or irregular forces that used guerrilla tactics to resist Nazi occupation. Those who support the political aims of a particular group of guerrillas, and who view their violence as justified, might well describe them as *freedom fighters*. Yet, as the saying goes, 'One person's *freedom fighter* [or now *martyr*] is another person's *terrorist.*'

The term *terrorist* dates from the post-revolutionary Reign of Terror in France. Most dictionaries define *terrorism* as the systematic use of terror to intimidate; it is commonly understood to refer to the use of violence or threats of violence, especially against civilians, to further a political cause.

The Canadian Press advises journalists whenever possible to avoid politically charged terms such as *terrorist* and to label the perpetrators of violence by their actions, for example, 'the hostage takers' or 'the bombers'.

The peace plan calls for the gradual removal of all foreign military advisers and bases in Central

America, an end to support of guerrilla armies, and respect for self-determination and territorial sovereignty.
Maclean's 24 Feb. 1986: 44

Actually, the October Crisis doesn't really mean all that much today, except to the family of the man who died at the hands of a few tragically inept, muddle-headed romantics playing at urban guerrilla.
Gazette (Montreal) 6 Oct. 1990: B3

This account comes from The Martyrs of the Land of the Two Rivers, a collection of 430 biographies of insurgents who are connected by conviction, if not organization, to a global jihad symbolized by al-Qaeda.
National Post (Toronto) 12 Oct. 2005: A19

Ignored as well are U.S. President Ronald Reagan's 'freedom fighters,' whose terrorist activities in Nicaragua have resulted in the deaths of more than 5,000 civilians, and who have been condemned as the 'worst human rights violators in Latin America'. . . .
Globe and Mail (Toronto) 13 Feb. 1985: P6

(Here the quotation marks around *freedom fighters* indicate that the writer does not agree with giving this label to this group.)

See also REBELLION, REVOLUTION, REVOLT.

guest   see INVITED GUEST

guilty, not guilty   see PLEAD GUILTY

gun, small arms, firearm, artillery, shot, calibre, bore, gauge   *Gun* is a broad term, covering everything from handguns to cannons. *Small arms*, or *firearms*, can be carried by one person; these are guns with a calibre (the internal diameter of the barrel) of less than 20 mm. *Artillery* includes both guns and missiles; this is a useful general term for large-calibre weapons.

The *calibre* of rifles and pistols (which both fire bullets) may be expressed in millimetres: 'a 9 mm rifle'. But traditionally it is expressed as decimals of inches: 'a .22-calibre rifle' or 'a .45-calibre pistol'. In references to shotguns (which fire pellets or *shot*), *calibre* is usually called *bore*:

'a .410 bore shotgun'. Shotguns are also measured by *gauge*. The gauge of shotgun pellets indicates the number of them that amount to a pound. Thus shot for a 12-gauge shotgun (12 pellets to a pound) is bigger than shot for a 20-gauge shotgun (20 pellets to a pound), as are the shotguns themselves.

See also GAUGE; ORDINANCE, ORDNANCE.

gunwale, gunnel   Either spelling of this word, meaning the top edge of the side of a boat, is correct. Canadians use *gunwale* far more frequently. Both are pronounced to rhyme with *tunnel*.

And now I was up to the gunwales in Big Crummock Lake.
Howard Engel *Murder Sees the Light* 1984: 137

guts   see BELLY

guttural   *Guttural* is sometimes misspelled with -*er*- instead of -*ur*-. The term is derived from the Latin *guttur*, 'gullet' or 'throat'. A guttural sound comes from the throat, not the gutter.

Dropping my lower E string to a D gave me that bizarre, gutteral sound.
Ottawa Citizen 29 June 1990: D3

(The correct spelling is *guttural*.)

gybe   see JIBE

gym, gymnasium   *Gym*, the shortened version of *gymnasium*, is labelled informal by some dictionaries. However, *gym* is used far more frequently than *gymnasium* in all but quite formal Canadian writing.

Occasionally *gymnasium* refers not to a room for sports but to a German secondary school. For this meaning only, the pronunciation is *gim NAW zee um*, with a hard *g*, as in *get*.

After the lecture and a short warm-up in the gym, we move out to the track.
Imperial Oil Review Spring 1988: 15

The house is a converted Russian Orthodox

church, with four storeys and a gymnasium in the basement.
Jack Chambers *Milestones* 1983: 298

Their children were grown and had graduated from a gymnasium and the boys prepared to enter their father's business.
Henry M. Rosenthal and S. Cathy Berson, eds. *Canadian Jewish Outlook Anthology* 1988: 62

gym shoes   see RUNNING SHOES

gypsy, gipsy, Gypsy   Canadian, British, and American dictionaries all list the spelling *gypsy* first. *Gipsy* is an uncommon variant. *Gypsy* should be capitalized in reference to the ethnic group whose language is Romany.

The verb *to gyp*, meaning to swindle or short-change, is now considered a slur on Gypsies.

Every evening, groups gather at candle-lit tables to the sound of a gypsy violinist.
Vancouver Sun 29 Dec. 1990: A3

See also WELCH, WELSH.

H

h-   Canadians, like Americans, pronounce *herb* either *URB* or *HURB* and *human* either *HYOO mun* or *YOO mun*. In Standard British English both words are always pronounced with an initial *h* sound. *Heir, honest, honourable, hour,* and related words are pronounced without an initial *h* sound by English-speakers everywhere.

Canadians generally pronounce the *h* in *historical*, but often write 'an historical' (see A, AN).

Because of the heavy stress on the first syllable of the words *vehicle* and *vehement*, the *h* that follows is not pronounced. However, the *h* is pronounced in the adjective *vehicular* because the main stress is on the second syllable: *vee HICK yoo ler*.

See also HERB.

habeas corpus   *Habeas corpus* is the legal right, now recognized in the Canadian Charter of Rights and Freedoms, of a person who has been arrested to question his or her detention. In the tradition of *habeas corpus*, police bring detainees before a judge in a timely manner and charge them with a specific crime. This safeguard prevents a government from detaining its political foes without trial.

Habeas corpus is Latin phrase meaning 'you shall have the body': in other words, the arrestee will be brought into court. This phrase is not usually italicized. The first word is pronounced *HAY bee us*. Common spelling errors are *habeUs,* with a *u* instead of an *a,* and *haPeus,* with a *p* instead of a *b*.

The cabinet was looking at either the War Measures Act—which would allow arrest without warrant and suspend habeas corpus—or amendments to the Criminal Code which would allow the arrest of suspected FLQ members.
Guardian (Charlottetown) 24 April 2001: A8

See also CANADIAN BILL OF RIGHTS, CANADIAN CHARTER OF RIGHTS AND FREEDOMS; LATIN PHRASES.

habitual   see A, AN

hack   see FLACK

hacker, cracker   In the eyes of the public, a *hacker* is an ignoble computer user. The media and law enforcement officials reinforce this view by using the term *hacker* to describe people engaged in computing activity for nefarious purposes. In the computer world, however, the term *hacker* is often used differently to refer to any person who enjoys programming computers and does so with exceptional skill.

In the mid-1980s, in order to put an end to the public's equation of hacking with criminality, *hackers* (i.e., adept programmers) coined the term *crackers*—probably on analogy to *safecrackers*—to describe people who used computers to steal, destroy, or alter information. While this distinction is worth noting, the term *cracker* has yet to catch on widely.

'Dozens of people collaborated spontaneously, motivated by loyalty, friendship, or the love of craftsmanship. . . . We were hackers, creating something for the sheer joy of making it work.'
National Post (Toronto) 15 Sept. 2005: WK1

(Here *hacker* is used to refer to those who use ingenuity to solve computing problems; no illegality is implied.)

A computer hacker has gained access to more than eight million account numbers by breaking into the records of a company that processes transactions for retailers.
CBC News Online 18 Feb. 2003

(Here a *hacker* is a criminal.)

Most routers include a firewall that prevents Internet crackers from accessing your computer.
Toronto Star 17 Jan. 2005: D2

(This writer refers to a criminal programmer as a *cracker*.)

had better   see BETTER

[had have], would have   'If I had been there' and 'Had I been there' are standard constructions. 'If I had have been there' and 'If I would have been there' are non-standard.

Sentences that deal with what will or might happen under certain circumstances are called conditional sentences. These present facts ('If you heat a gas, it expands'), possibilities ('If I were there, that wouldn't happen'), or counterfactual possibilities in the past ('If I had been there, that wouldn't have happened'). The tenses in clauses such as 'If I had have been there' and 'If I would have been there', intended to describe counter-factual conditions in the past, are non-standard. Note that *had have* is always unacceptable—grammarians call this spurious tense the 'plupluperfect'—while *would have* is correct in the clause that follows the *if*-clause. It is non-standard only when it is inserted into the *if*-clause as well.

The non-standard constructions are common in informal speech, where they often go unnoticed because the verbs are contracted. People often say 'If I had've been there' or 'If I had've known'. When they are used in writing, however, these constructions are condemned. Doubly stigmatized in writing are the clauses 'If I had of been there' and 'If I would of been there', where *'ve*, the contraction of the spurious *have*, is confused with *of*—a word that sounds the same.

The non-standard *had have* construction is certainly not an innovation; there is evidence that it existed as early as the fifteenth century. All in all, it may be more accurate to describe these aberrant tenses as colloquial usages of long standing that have never been accepted in writing or formal speech.

'If a strong stand had of been made when the cuts were first announced perhaps they might have been able to do something.'
Chronicle-Herald (Halifax) 12 Jan. 1990: B1

(Here *of* should be omitted: 'If a strong stand *had been* made' is the standard construction.)

See also COLLOQUIAL; [COULD OF]; IF I WERE YOU; SUBJUNCTIVE.

haemophilia   see -AE-, -OE-, -E-

Haida   The *Haida* (singular and plural) are a group of Native people who live on the Queen Charlotte Islands, off the coast of British Columbia. Their distinct language is also called *Haida*. Their traditional territory is called *Haida Gwaii*, and they are renowned for their wood carvings (canoes, totem poles, longhouses) and paintings.

See also ABORIGINAL PEOPLE(S); APPENDIX III.

hail   see HALE

hairbrained   see HAREBRAINED

Haisla   see KWAKIUTL

halcyon, halcyon days   *Halcyon* (pronounced *HAL see un*) is an adjective meaning calm or peaceful; today it is also used to describe any period of happiness and prosperity. The word comes from Greek mythology: after Alcyone and her husband were turned into sea birds called *halcyons*, her father, the god of wind, decreed that the seas would be calm for two weeks each year around the winter solstice, so that the halcyons could breed in their floating nest. These fourteen days of calm and happiness were called the *halcyon days*.

In contexts where achievement is being emphasized rather than happiness, *heyday* is a more appropriate expression than *halcyon days*.

Back in the halcyon days of the Toronto Maple Leafs, when Punch Imlach's teams were winning Stanley Cups, the team practised every day during the playoffs.
Globe and Mail (Toronto) 9 May 1985: M11

(Here *heyday* would be more appropriate.)

See also HEYDAY, SALAD DAYS.

hale, hail   *Hale* means robust or healthy, and is most often used in the phrase 'hale and hearty'. The verb *hale*, meaning to haul or compel ('He was haled into court'), is nearly obsolete.

All other senses of the word are spelled *hail*: 'She hailed a taxi'; 'rain turning to hail'; 'a hail of bullets'. The expression 'hail fellow well met' describes someone friendly and easy to get along with.

The hale Michener is honorary 'master' of The Masters Games for mature athletes. . . .
Globe and Mail (Toronto) 23 April 1985: M9

half, half-   To 'cut something *in half*' is idiomatic even though logically two *halves* result.

'A half dozen' and 'half a dozen' are both acceptable, but 'a half a dozen' should not be used in writing.

When *half* is used as the subject of a sentence, the verb that follows may be singular or plural, depending on the sense (see COLLECTIVE NOUNS): 'Half (of) the delegates is not enough'; 'Half (of) the delegates are undecided'.

With a *half-brother* or *half-sister* you share one biological parent (see STEP-, HALF-).

See also AGREEMENT, GRAMMATICAL; COLLECTIVE NOUNS; STEP-, HALF-.

half-breed   see MÉTIS

half-mast, half-staff   Some usage commentators argue that a flag partly lowered to honour the dead should be said to be at *half-mast* only when it is on a ship, and at *half-staff* when it is on land. However, while *half-mast* is the usual expression for such a flag on a ship, *half-mast* and *half-staff* are both in common use for flags on land, and both terms are perfectly acceptable. The two-word spellings *half mast* and *half staff* are fairly common, but most dictionaries hyphenate these terms.

Quebec, which had greeted the new Constitution five years earlier with flags at half-mast, was triumphant.
Financial Post 24 April 1989: 1

As we entered the city, I did not see a single flag at any location, be it government, commercial or personal, that was not at half-staff.
Windsor Star 18 May 2006: A9

Haligonian   see NAMES OF RESIDENTS

hallelujah, alleluia   *Hallelujah* and *alleluia* are the most common spellings used to render in English the Hebrew word meaning 'Praise the Lord'. The word is used in Christian liturgy and songs, and sometimes as a spontaneous exclamation of joy or gratitude.

There are plenty of songs, frequent cries of 'hallelujah' and 'praise the Lord,' hand-wavings and stern admonitions to follow the scriptural words of Jesus.
Globe and Mail (Toronto) 31 Aug. 1985: P13

'Alleluia,' responds Louise. 'Let's give him a load of

hand-clapping.'
Calgary Herald 28 May 1994: C6

Halley's comet   The British astronomer after whom this comet is named was Edmund Halley (1656–1742); *Halley* is pronounced with an *a* as in either *hall* or *hat*. Halley did not discover this comet, which has been on record since 239 BC, but was the first to accurately predict its return.

Halley's comet is often misspelled or mispronounced *Hailey's comet*, an error that has probably been reinforced by the name of a popular rock and roll band of the 1950s: Bill Hailey and the Comets.

> Halley's comet is practically the only one whose name is not that of its discoverer.
> *Queen's Quarterly* 92.2 (1985): 284

hallmark   see BENCHMARK

hallucination   see A, AN

halves   see -F, -V-; HALF, HALF-

Hambletonian   see NAMES OF RESIDENTS OF CITIES AND PROVINCES

handicap   see DISABILITY; DOUBLING THE FINAL CONSONANT

handiwork   *Handiwork* is often misspelled *handywork*, an understandable mistake. While *-y* often changes to an *-i-* before a suffix (*grumpy* becomes *grumpiness*), a final *-y* does not typically change to *-i-* when two words combine in a compound: *handyman, ready-made, bellyflop*. *Handiwork* breaks this pattern because it is not, in fact, a combination of *handy* and *work*. It derives from Old English *handgeweorc*, 'work of the hands'; *geweorc* (or *iwork*) is a collective form of the noun *work*. Thus, the older and still current meaning of *handiwork* is work attributable to someone ('God's handiwork', 'definitely her handiwork'), while the newer use—which dates from the sixteenth century—contrasts head work and work done with the hands ('repairs and general handiwork').

See also FOLK ETYMOLOGY; YE.

handkerchiefs   see -F, -V-

handoff, handout   see FUNCTIONAL SHIFT; PHRASAL VERBS

hangar   see HANGER

hanged, hung   *Hanged* is standard as both the past tense and the past participle of *hang* in the sense of execution: 'They hanged him'; 'He was hanged'. *Hung* is the past tense and past participle of *hang* in all other senses: 'Is the wash hung out?' Canadians still make this traditional distinction in writing, although *hung* in the sense of executed is very common in speech. Some commentators will accept this usage in informal contexts, but it is best avoided in writing.

> Canada's last executions took place in 1962, when two men were hanged in Toronto.
> *Globe and Mail* (Toronto) 4 Feb. 1985: S13

> They were the last of 700 to be hanged in Canada. . . . 'We have lots of inquiries about where they are buried,' says [the] manager of Prospect Cemetery. 'I guess it's because they were the last two men hung.'
> *Globe and Mail* (Toronto) 21 Jan. 1985: P17

(This example includes both the standard written and the common spoken usage.)

hanger, hangar   Clothes hang on *hangers*; airplanes are kept in *hangars*.

> But the ballroom is as big as an airplane hangar. . . .
> *Saturday Night* April 1986: 60

hara-kiri, seppuku   *Hara-kiri* is the correct spelling for the Japanese ritual suicide by disembowelment, practised by Samurai warriors in disgrace. It is correctly pronounced *hah rah KEER ee*, though often, especially in facetious use, it is misspelled and mispronounced *hari-kari* (*HAIR ee KAIR ee*). In fact, *hara-kiri* is Japanese slang that literally means 'belly-cutting'; the Japanese themselves prefer the term *seppuku* for the ritual. Since *hara-kiri* has a venerable history in Japanese culture, facetious figurative use of the term may give offence.

. . . it is a complex movie made in Japan in Japanese by an American director about a novelist who killed himself by committing seppuku (hara-kiri) at the age of 45.
Globe and Mail (Toronto) 16 May 1985: E1

The palate, weary of comparing Chateau Jolys' sweet Jurancon with Inniskillin's Vidal beere-nauslese, could commit hara-kiri with innumerable gourmet salad dressings, dusty crackers and chocolate dainties.
Globe and Mail (Toronto) 23 Oct. 1985: F2

(This is the facetious use.)

harass, harassment, sexual harassment
Harass is spelled with only one *r*—unlike *embarrass*, which is spelled with two. Some Canadians pronounce *harass* and *harassment* with stress on the second syllable, while others stress the first. Either is correct; commentators are divided in their recommendations. Many British commentators recommend that the stress be placed on the first syllable, so that *harass* sounds like the surname *Harris*; nonetheless, in Britain as in North America, younger, educated speakers are more likely to say *huh RASS*. To *harass* means to annoy, wear down, or attack someone persistently. *Sexual harassment* is one particular type of harassment; it consists of persistent and unwelcome sexual commentary or sexual advances, or ongoing disparagement of a person's sex.

> Collection agencies—accused from time to time of using high pressure tactics and harassment to collect outstanding debts—are also subject to similar registration requirements.
> J.E. Smyth et al. *The Law and Business Administration in Canada* 1987: 414

> Gretzky . . . didn't even get a shot on goal as Tikkanen hooked, tripped, hounded and harrassed him.
> *Province* (Vancouver) 19 April 1990: 72

(The correct spelling is harassed.)

harbinger In the twelfth century a *harbinger* was a person who provided lodging for an army; later the term came to refer to a person who went ahead of the army to find lodging. Now a harbinger is anything that announces or indicates the arrival of something else. The *g* is soft, pronounced as in *passenger*.

What better harbinger of summer than the perennial return of gardening magazines?
Ottawa Citizen 14 May 2006: C3

hard drive see COMPUTER TERMS

hardly, barely, scarcely *Hardly*, *barely*, and *scarcely* all mean by a small margin or with difficulty. Critics argue that when these words are used in conjunction with other negative words, such as *not* or *without*, they form a double negative. Constructions like 'I can't hardly walk' and 'She didn't scarcely try' may be found in speech, but Canadian writers generally avoid them, preferring 'I can hardly walk' and 'She scarcely tried'.

A few commentators state that these words, when used in the sense of 'only just', may be followed by *when* or *before*, but not by *than*. For example, 'I had scarcely made it to my seat when the movie started' and 'I had scarcely made it to my seat before the movie started' are acceptable, but 'I had scarcely made it to my seat than the movie started' is not.

These disparaged constructions in which *hardly*, *barely*, and *scarcely* are followed by *than* may be influenced by the expression *no sooner . . . than*, in which *than* is standard and *when* is criticized. See NO SOONER.

When a sentence begins with one of these adverbs, the subject and verb that follow it change positions: 'Scarcely had I opened the letter when the doorbell rang'.

> The 1950s had scarcely opened before educational authorities in the United States were predicting . . . an explosion in American university enrolments [in the 1960s].
> Frederick Gibson *Queen's University* 2 (1983): 313

> Scarcely were our words committed to print than McDonald's Canada announced that it would indeed switch from foam containers to cardboard.
> *Vancouver Sun* 5 Nov. 1990: A6

(Replacing *than* with *when* or *before* would forestall any criticism.)

See also DOUBLE NEGATIVE; EVER; NO SOONER.

hardy, hearty *Hardy* and *hearty* can both be

used as synonyms for *healthy* or *robust*. However, they cannot be used interchangeably in the sense of resistant to hardship, which is the primary definition of *hardy*, or to mean nourishing, which is one sense of *hearty*. Thus a *hardy* plant is one that can withstand harsh conditions and a *hearty* meal is a nutritious and plentiful one. The similar pronunciations of these words may explain their occasional misuse.

Now my mother may be slender, but she has a hardy constitution, got from climbing over fences with an easel on her back. . . .
Queen's Quarterly 96 (1989): 399

Fritz's beef, as it turned out, was hardy fare, piquantly seasoned. . . .
Gazette (Montreal) 18 April 1990: D1

(The word required here is *hearty*.)

. . . more than 24,000 hearty souls braved Boston's inclement winter weather to attend NetWorld last month.
Computer Dealer News 7 March 1991: 1

(A *hearty soul* is a person full of good cheer; a *hardy soul* is someone able to withstand harsh conditions, such as Boston's 'inclement winter weather'.)

harebrained [hairbrained]   The accepted spelling is *harebrained*, referring to a foolish, flighty person who has no more sense than a hare. *Hairbrained* is an alternative spelling that dates from the sixteenth century but is listed in only one major current dictionary. Most dictionaries do not hyphenate *harebrained*, although it often appears that way in print.

When it comes to harebrained schemes, those who want to save Canada are just as guilty as those who want to destroy it.
Maclean's 22 April 1991: A11

Of all the hair-brained promotions the Saskatchewan government has come up with, this one takes the prize.
Leader-Post (Regina) 16 Dec. 2005: B8

(The correct spelling is *harebrained*.)

hark, harken, heark, hearken, hark(en) back, heark(en) back   *Hark* and *heark*,

harken and *hearken* all mean listen carefully, as in 'Hark! The herald angels sing'.

To *hark back*—and, increasingly, to *harken* (or *hearken*) *back*—is to revert to a topic or to suggest an earlier time. *Hark back* was originally used as a call to hunting hounds telling them to retrace their steps.

Looking toward the future, I would like to hark back to the suggestions I have already made for new research plans.
W.C. Lougheed ed. *In Search of the Standard in Canadian English* 1986: 167

The idea of individuals walking in a city on a mission carrying a candle harkens back to medieval times.
Globe and Mail (Toronto) 1 Jan. 1985: M1

. . . the parents who had come of age during the Depression hearkened back to the stern rigors of that childhood.
Globe and Mail (Toronto) 26 April 1985: P6

harmonious   see A, AN

Hatter   see NAMES OF RESIDENTS OF CITIES AND PROVINCES

have got, have gotten   Most Canadians and Americans make a distinction of sense: 'She's got a laptop' means she owns one, while 'She's gotten a laptop' means she's just acquired one. This distinction of sense can't be made in Standard British English, where the past participle *gotten* is archaic.

See also GOT, GOTTEN; HAVE GOT TO.

have got to   Commentators have condemned the use of *have got to* meaning be compelled to, recommending *must* or *have to* instead: that is, 'I must (*or* have to) go' rather than 'I have got to go'. However, *Webster's Dictionary of English Usage* notes that Otto Jesperson collected many examples of *have got to* from a range of important British writers, among them Dickens, Trollope, and Shaw, and its authors add a list of their own that includes William Faulkner and several American presidents. In other words, it is not necessary to avoid *have got to*.

See also GOT; HAVE GOT.

have the heart to   see IDIOMS

he, him, his   see CASE; EVERYONE; GENDER

head of state, governor general, lieu-tenant-governor   In Canada the prime minister is the head of government, but the Queen is the head of state. When the Queen is not on Canadian soil, the head of state is the governor general. The lieutenant-governors, appointed by the governor general on the advice of the prime minister, represent the Crown in each province.

Canadians in general show no sign of establishing a clear preference regarding hyphenation of the terms *governor general* and *lieutenant-governor*. However, the Department of the Secretary of State recommends hyphenating only *lieutenant-governor*. *Governor* is the main noun in both of these titles, and thus it is the word pluralized: *governors general, lieutenant-governors*.

Both *Governor General* and *Lieutenant-Governor* should be capitalized when they are used directly in front of an incumbent's name: 'Lieutenant-Governor Barbara Hagerman'. References to 'the governor general' or 'past Lieutenant-Governors' are sometimes capitalized, sometimes not, according to the editorial policy of individual publications.

The sweeping legal powers of the Governor General are transferred by convention to the Cabinet.
Andrew Heard *Canadian Constitutional Conventions* 1991: 1–2

The Governor-General's speech got a standing ovation.
Daily News (Halifax) 28 May 2006: 12

(Government publications do not hyphenate *governor general*.)

When the provincial environment minister visited the Daily Bread Food Bank yesterday, she heard five would-be lieutenants-governor give their versions of the Throne Speech to the Legislature.
Toronto Star 21 April 1992: A6

(The correct plural is *lieutenant-governors*.)

See also CAPITAL LETTERS; HONOURABLE; LIEUTENANT.

headquarters, headquarter   *Headquarters*, the noun meaning an administrative centre for business or military operations, is both the singular and the plural form: 'One headquarters is enough; two headquarters are too many'. *Headquarters* meaning management is usually treated as a singular: 'Headquarters is sending out conflicting statements'.

Some usage guides classify the verb *headquarter*, meaning either to have headquarters or to establish headquarters, as jargon. It is used extensively in business and financial contexts, but is not yet found in other types of writing.

Nortel's transmission group world headquarters is situated in Edmonton.
Globe and Mail (Toronto) 29 March 1985: P42

The headquarters for many of Washington's leading lobbyists are located in the modern office buildings lining K Street, a few blocks north of the White House.
Maclean's 24 Feb. 1986: 19

. . . Shamian Island [was once] headquarter for the opium trade. . . .
Vancouver Sun 1 June 1990: G1

(The noun always ends in *s: headquarters*.)

. . . headquartered in Montreal, the firm is growing rapidly.
Western Grocer May–June 1990: 84

Current clientele ranges from V-P Dan Quayle to leading Saudi families who headquarter here for their shopping sprees.
Financial Post 1 May 1991: 62

See also FUNCTIONAL SHIFT.

health care, healthcare, health-care   The two-word spelling, *health care*, is most common in Canada, but *healthcare*, the one-word spelling, is also very common and has been adopted by many professional organizations and journals. Both spellings are used as nouns ('*improved* health care/healthcare') and adjectives ('healthcare/health care *dollars*'). The hyphenated form *health-care*, somewhat less common, should be used only as an adjective: 'health-care workers'.

See also HYPHENATION.

healthful, healthy *Healthful* has one meaning: conducive to good health ('a healthful climate'). *Healthy* has two: possessing good health ('a healthy person') and conducive to good health ('a healthy breakfast'). Although the use of *healthy* in the second sense has been criticized, most authorities now accept it.

> Fruit and vegetables all qualify as healthful, but a few merit 'super' status because of their larger amounts of vitamins and minerals.
> *Gazette* (Montreal) 1 March 1989: C1

> Grocery store owners are getting this confused message from consumers who say they want healthy food but continue to eat out and buy snack food.
> *Province* (Vancouver) 13 June 1990: 48

health-minded see -MINDED

heart to, have the see IDIOMS

heark, hearken, heark(en) back see HARK

heart-rending To *rend* means to tear or break; something *heart-rending* arouses deep distress and figuratively rends the heart. Some dictionaries omit the hyphen: *heartrending*. *Heart-rendering* is a mistaken (sometimes humorous) form, influenced by the more familiar verb *render*.

> Everybody loves a story about horses and kids, and there's no finer story around than the classic sentimental tale of a Victorian girl's heartrending search for her missing colt.
> *Gazette* (Montreal) 1 Sept. 1990: T48

> Bishop Matthews not only ministered to the condemned man, but also to his mother, and referred to the experience as the most 'horrible, heart-rending time you can imagine.'
> *Canadian Churchman* Jun.–Jul. 1986: 17

> Canadian peacekeepers who have served in Croatia are bringing home memories of war both horrific and heartrendering.
> *Edmonton Journal* 11 Sept. 1995: A2

(The *-er-* should be dropped.)

hearty see HARDY

heathen see ATHEIST

heave, heaved, hove The past tense of *heave* is *heaved*. The nautical expressions *hove into sight* ('came into view') and *hove to* ('came or brought to a stop') retain the otherwise archaic past tense *hove*; these expressions are sometimes used figuratively.

> And much to her surprise, friends heaved a huge sigh of relief, glad to have the old Nancy back.
> *Vancouver Sun* 15 Sept. 1990: C1

> In school, we sat up straight and stopped flicking inkballs as soon as 'sir' hove into sight.
> *Vancouver Sun* 20 Oct. 1990: B5

Hebrew see JEW

hectare see APPENDIX II

hegemony *Hegemony* is domination, especially the domination of one political state over another; the word is often used figuratively. Pronunciation varies, but the *g* is usually pronounced like a *j*. The stress may fall on the second syllable (*heh JEH muh nee*) or on the first (*HEDGE eh moh nee*).

> . . . the British and French . . . would presumably oppose any border settlement that threatened their naval hegemony in the Pacific.
> George Ignatieff *The Making of a Peacemonger* 1987: 5

> ' . . . education for women poses a threat to male hegemony in the family; a threat to male dominance that few male egos can withstand.'
> *Briarpatch* April 1990: 7

height see -IE-, -EI-

Heiltsuk see KWAKIUTL

heinous *Heinous*, meaning, wicked and abominable, is pronounced *HAY niss* or *HEE niss*, but be aware that not all dictionaries record the latter pronunciation. In the more widely accepted pronunciation, *hein-* rhymes with the similarly spelled *vein* and *rein*.

Heinz see GERMAN WORDS, PRONUNCIATION OF

heir, heir apparent, heir presumptive In popular usage, an *heir* may be someone who is going to inherit something: 'Her uncle has made her his heir.' In law, an *heir* is not an heir until inheritance takes place, because even if someone is named as in a will, others (especially spouses and children) may have prior rights.

Heir apparent and *heir presumptive* are technical terms arising from the British system of primogeniture, whereby estates and titles pass to the closest male relative (usually the eldest son). In this system, an *heir apparent* is someone who will definitely inherit as long as he survives the relevant relative (usually his father). Some mistakenly think that the *heir apparent* is only 'apparently' the heir, but the word *apparent* here carries an older sense: manifest or unquestionable. An *heir presumptive*, however, will inherit only as long as no one else is born who is more closely related to the title-holder.

Heir and *heir apparent* are both used figuratively. An *heir apparent* is cultivated as a successor; an 'apparent heir' is the person most likely to take over.

As heirs to a family fortune valued at about $435 million, Paul Desmarais Jr., 31, and his brother Andre, 29, are among Canada's wealthiest businessmen.
Maclean's 24 Feb. 1986: 46

As heir apparent, this Prince of Wales sees confidential cabinet papers and he is well informed about day-to-day political issues.
Maclean's 14 Nov. 1988: A40

The still-youthful premier has no apparent heir and thus leaves a political vacuum that Quebec's separatists . . . hope to fill.
Daily News (Halifax) 19 Sept. 1993: 19

Marois said Bloc Quebecois Leader Lucien Bouchard, heir apparent to retiring Premier Jacques Parizeau, knows about the proposal. . . .
Calgary Herald 13 Dec. 1995: A15

See also A, AN; PRESUMPTIVE.

Hellenic, Hellene, Hellenist, Hellenistic, Grecian, Greek *Hellenic* is an adjective formed from the Greek word for Greece, *Hellas*; it's applied to both ancient and modern Greece.

A *Hellene* is either a modern or an ancient Greek. A *Hellenist* is an expert on Greek language or culture, or, in ancient history, a non-Greek, especially a Jew, who adopted the Greek language and customs. *Hellenistic* refers to the period between the death of Alexander the Great and the reign of Augustus (the fourth to the first century BC).

Grecian usually describes something in the style of or pertaining to ancient Greece as opposed to something from Greece today: 'a Grecian pillar', but 'a Greek wine'.

Music and dance by the Hellenic Community Dancers complement the cuisine.
Star-Phoenix (Saskatoon) 19 Aug. 2004: B1

Rexroth, invoking the shade of Walter Pater, declares: 'H.D.'s Greece was a land that never was' and, more recently, David Perkins suggests that 'her "Greece" was typically Romantic and literary, a Hellenic world distilled from Shelley, Keats, Byron, Arnold. . .' .
Queen's Quarterly 92.2 (1985): 312

It includes Late Minoan III tomb artifacts, Hellenistic sculpture, Roman glass and ancient coins dating back to Ptolemy.
Globe and Mail (Toronto) 19 Oct. 1985: G17

It is, very briefly, about a German barbarian living in an early but vague period of history who is domesticated by a Grecian maiden called Parthenia.
Robertson Davies *A Voice from the Attic* 1960: 181

'You stand on a terrace flanked by a row of unreal Grecian columns.'
Margaret Atwood *Second Words* 1982: 241

helpmate, helpmeet *Helpmate* derives from the older and now rarer word *helpmeet*. *Helpmeet* first arose in seventeenth-century writing from an aural misinterpretation of a passage from the King James Bible, in which God considers the creation of 'an help meet for' Adam (Genesis 2: 18). The *help* in the reference was Eve; *meet* was an adjective meaning suitable, but it became part of a new noun, *helpmeet*, meaning wife or partner. By the eighteenth century the term coexisted with *helpmate*, which became the standard form in the nineteenth century. No one is sure why the *-mate* form developed. The most common explanation is that it is a product of folk etymology: the meaning of *meet* was lost and the substitution of *mate* made more sense.

Today *helpmate* refers to any helpful companion, but especially to a wife or husband. Wives are more likely to be called *helpmates* and cast in the supporting role. For this reason, guides to non-sexist language suggest avoiding the word unless it is applied equally to men.

> Carole Longpre, the pair's trainer and foster mother, is preparing the monkeys for use as companions and helpmates to severely disabled people.
> *Ottawa Citizen* 4 March 1990: A5

> Liberal Leader John Turner and his anti-free trade helpmates on the left, the NDP, behaved as though the Marines had just stormed the border at Buffalo.
> *Ottawa Citizen* 10 April 1987: A2

> There is no stinting, however, when it comes to the great love of his life and helpmate in every way, Nancy.
> *Vancouver Sun* 8 Dec. 1990: D20

(This traditional use of *helpmate* has been criticized as sexist.)

See also FOLK ETYMOLOGY; SEXIST LANGUAGE.

hemi-, hemisphere see SEMI

hemophilia   see -AE-, -OE-, -E-

he or she   see SEXIST LANGUAGE

her   see CASE; EVERYONE; GENDER

herb   Canadians pronounce *herb URB* or *HURB*, with or without an audible *h*. Written Canadian English reflects this practice: both 'a herb' and 'an herb' are used. Most Americans do not pronounce the *h*. In Standard British English, the *h* in *herb* is always pronounced. Because *herb* was derived from the Old French word *erbe*, the *h* was initially not pronounced, nor was it written except by Latinists. However, nineteenth-century British usage writers, aware of the word's Latin antecedent, *herba*, recommended pronouncing the *h*.

> A neighbour of ours, Doreen Kapala, tends a gem of a lakeside garden, that features . . . a herb bed around a sundial. . . .
> *Harrowsmith* Aug.–Sept. 1985: 86

> It is not easy to decide how important an herb garden would have been in a town the size of Kingston.
> *The Beaver* Dec. 1989–Jan. 1990: 15

See also H-.

here   see ADJECTIVES AND ADVERBS

hereditary   see CONGENITAL

Heritage Canada, Canadian Heritage
Heritage Canada is a charitable foundation created in 1973 by the federal government to help protect and promote historic sites and architecturally significant buildings, as well as scenic and wilderness areas in Canada. Canadian Heritage is the federal government department concerned with arts and culture, multiculturalism, citizenship, youth, and sports. Because the foundation works closely with the department of Canadian Heritage, and because so many federal departments and agencies are named Something-Or-Other Canada (e.g., Health Canada, Parks Canada), these two bodies are often confused.

> Although elementary and secondary education is a provincial responsibility, Heritage Canada transfers funds to the provinces to support minority language rights and English or French immersion programs.
> Rianne Mahon *School-Aged Children Across Canada* 2001: 19

(The writer means to refer to the federal department—Canadian Heritage—not the non-governmental organization, Heritage Canada.)

See also CANADA.

heroes   see -OS, -OES

heroism, heroics   Most usage guides and dictionaries distinguish between the noun *heroism*, which suggests courage and nobility, and the noun *heroics* (always plural), which is used pejoratively to mean flamboyant behaviour or language, or unnecessary gallantry.

> We read about the heroism of Grace Darling in saving shipwrecked mariners off the coast of Scotland. . . .
> Robertson Davies *One Half of Robertson Davies* 1978: 282

> Professor Barton Bernstein, one of a Stanford, Calif., team studying medical ethics, voiced concern about the 'bravado, foolhardiness and heroics' associated with heart surgery.
> *Globe and Mail* (Toronto) 14 March 1985: P7

> The two occupants managed to escape from the cockpit just before the explosion and one witness said only the pilot's heroics prevented death.
> *Province* (Vancouver) 13 Nov. 1990: 20

(The word required here is *heroism*.)

herring choker   see BLUENOSE

hers   see ITS

herstory, history   In the 1970s, American feminists coined the word *herstory* to refer to past events recounted by women rather than by men or from a female rather than a male perspective. Although *history* is not etymologically derived from 'his story', as the formation of *herstory* implies, it does come from Greek *histor*, 'a wise or learned man', and *herstory* effectively drew attention to the traditionally male-dominated viewpoint of history. Little used now beyond feminist circles, the word is not listed in the *Canadian Oxford Dictionary*.

> It is as if, in Patricia Smart's words, writing 'son histoire à elle' (herstory)—as opposed to 'son histoire à lui' (his(s)tory)—will offset the pessimism encoded there.
> Ben-Z. Shek *French-Canadian & Québécois Novels* 1991: 92

heterosexism   see -ISM

heyday, salad days   *Heyday* means the period of greatest success, fame, or prosperity. It is sometimes misspelled *heydey*.

The expression *salad days* suggests youth, enthusiasm, and inexperience. It comes from a speech in Shakespeare's *Antony and Cleopatra*, in which Cleopatra refers to 'My salad days, when I was green in judgement' (1.5.73). Although the expression has been condemned by usage guides as a cliché, overuse has not made the meaning transparent. It is often used in contexts where *heyday* would be more appropriate.

> Mildred certainly qualifies as a donor—in her heyday as a 4-year-old, she produced almost 23,000 pounds of milk in a 305-day lactation period. . . .
> *Harrowsmith* Oct.–Nov. 1985: 36

> Politicians in southwest Montreal, a district whose industrial heydey was 60 years ago and centred around the Lachine Canal, are long on promises and plans to raise their community out from under a chronic depression.
> *Gazette* (Montreal) 31 Oct. 1990: A4

(The correct spelling is *heyday*.)

> So we find, as we begin at last to face the facts of life, that serious thought is a harder exercise than we expected in our salad days of innocence.
> *Vancouver Sun* 2 March 1991: B4

> In his salad days, Foreman was one of boxing's most powerful punchers.
> *Financial Post* 12 Jan. 1990: 39

(From the context, it appears that the writer is reflecting on a time when the famous boxer was in his prime, not on a period of inexperience or 'greenness' in the profession; in this case, *heyday* is the word required.)

See also HALCYON, HALCYON DAYS.

hiatus   see -US

hiccup, hiccough   The spelling *hiccup* is preferred over the rare variant *hiccough*, although both are found in dictionaries. Both versions are pronounced to rhyme with *pickup*. Some dictionaries and usage guides insist on the spellings *hiccuped* and *hiccuping* for the inflected forms; others insist on *hiccupped* and *hiccupping*; and still others recognize both spellings.

See also DOUBLING THE FINAL CONSONANT.

hidden agenda   see AGENDA

high   see ADVERBS WITHOUT -LY

high-minded   see -MINDED

highway   see ROAD

hindrance   see OBSTACLE

Hindu, Hinduism, Hindi, Urdu, Hindustan, Hindustani   A *Hindu* follows the traditions of *Hinduism*, the religion of the majority of the people of India and Sri Lanka. In the past *Hindu* was used to refer to any native of India. However, since many Indians are Muslim, Sikh, Buddhist, Christian, etc., this usage should be avoided. *Hindi* is one of the most widely spoken languages of India and one of the country's official languages. *Urdu* is one of the official languages of Pakistan. Urdu and Hindi are mutually intelligible, but are distinguished on sociopolitical grounds.

Hindustan refers to the northern section of India; a *Hindustani* is someone from that area. *Hindustani* is also the related adjective and the name of a language of northern India closely related to both Hindi and Urdu.

> We notice that 'Canadian' in this poem means French Canadian habitant: O'Grady no more thinks of himself as Canadian than an Anglo-Indian colonel would think of himself as Hindu. Northrop Frye *The Bush Garden* 1971: 165

(Frye used *Hindu* to mean *Indian* in this piece published in 1956. This usage is now dated.)

See also INDIAN; SACRED WRITINGS.

hippo, hippopotamuses   see ABBREVIATION; -OS, -OES; -US

Hispanic, Latin American, Latino, Latina, Chicano, Chicana, Mexican American, Tex-Mex   *Hispanic* means 'Spanish-speaking' and is the broadest term available to describe Spanish-speaking peoples and cultures in both Europe and the Americas. In American usage it often refers specifically to those of Spanish-language background within the United States: for example, the communities of Cuban immigrants in Miami, Puerto Ricans in New York City, and Mexicans and descendants of early Spanish settlers in California and the American Southwest. Occasionally *Hispanic* is mistakenly applied to those with language backgrounds other than Spanish, such as Portuguese speakers in Brazil and speakers of Indigenous languages in Central and South America.

The term *Latin American* applies to all Central and South American speakers of Romance languages and thus includes Portuguese-speakers from Brazil and French-speakers from French Guiana. *Latinos* are Latin Americans or people of Latin American descent living in the United States. The singular *Latino* can be used of both men and women, although *Latina* is also used to refer to women.

Chicano (plural *Chicanos*) is an altered, shortened form of the Mexican Spanish word for Mexican, *Mexicano*. The initial *Ch-* is usually pronounced in English like the *ch-* in *cheek*. In the early twentieth century, American-born Hispanics used the term sometimes insultingly to refer to more recent immigrants from Mexico. *Chicano* later came to be used pejoratively by those outside the community to describe all Mexican Americans. However, during the American civil-rights movement of the 1960s, *Chicano* was reclaimed by politicized Mexican Americans and used with pride to designate their Spanish, Mexican, and American cultural heritages. The feminine form *Chicana* came into popular use in English around 1960. Today some dislike the word *Chicano* because of its political flavour and prefer *Mexican American*.

In use since the 1940s, *Tex-Mex* is a slang reference to language and cultural traditions that combine Texan and Mexican influences. In Canada *Tex-Mex* is used mostly to describe a style of cooking.

> Otherwise, Thalia says, the fashion sensibility of Hispanics isn't that different from anyone else. *Calgary Herald* 2 Aug. 2005: C7

> It appears to be the slice-of-life story of a 37-year-

old Chicana welfare recipient named Consuelo, whose past history we are given in the first few pages of the book.
Margaret Atwood *Second Words* 1982: 272

[hisself], [theirselves] *Himself* and *themselves* are standard. *Hisself* and *theirselves* are highly stigmatized dialect forms. Presumably the non-standard forms persist because they follow the pattern of the other reflexive pronouns (*myself, yourself, ourselves*) in adding *-self* or *-selves* to a possessive adjective (*my-, your-, our-*). Standard forms are not always products of logic.

'Man needs somethin' to keep his mind off of hisself,' he said, peeking out from under his flattop hat minutes before Lyle fired the opening pitch.
Toronto Star 11 May 1992: C4

(Here and below *hisself* has been preserved to illustrate the speaker's dialect.)

The music stops abruptly . . . and one of them says, 'Man, the cat's cutting hisself.'
Jack Chambers *Milestones* 1983: 192

And like teachers, serious and gentle-voiced, the marshals (what they called theirselves) was slipping, sliding up and down the row, lighting candles here and there.
Queen's Quarterly 94.1 (1987): 95

(*Themselves* is standard.)

See also -SELF, -SELVES.

historical, historic The adjective *historical* means having to do with the past ('historical novel') or the study of the past ('historical approach'). The adjective *historic* is used to describe events that are significant for a whole society ('historic breakthrough'), the places they occurred ('historic site'), as well as places that preserve heritage architecture ('historic Old Quebec').

Interchanging these adjectives was perfectly acceptable in the nineteenth century and is still fairly common today. However, it makes sense to follow the contemporary trend towards distinguishing them.

In this tame historical romance about French Canada in 1661, Bishop Laval was portrayed as a bigot.
Fraser Sutherland *The Monthly Epic* 1992: 146

The Baptist Union of South Africa took historic action at its annual assembly in October when it urged South African President Botha to lead in abolishing evil apartheid.
Canadian Baptist Feb. 1986: 53

The Downtown Development Corporation . . . of St. John's and Main Street Canada have signed a three-year, $185,000 agreement aimed at breathing new life into the Newfoundland capital's downtown, particularly the historic Water Street area.
Canadian Heritage Magazine Feb.–Mar. 1986: 10

When he came to realize the deep flaws in the historic record of Indian activities, Trigger . . . scoured all contemporary accounts for the names of individual Hurons. . . .
Saturday Night July 1986: 50

(Here *historical* is recommended.)

An innocent comment opened the door for Prime Minister Brian Mulroney to turn on his legendary Irish charm and break the ice at Sunday's historical meeting with aboriginal leaders.
Ottawa Citizen 29 June 1992: A3

(Here *historic* is recommended.)

See also A, AN; -IC, ICAL; PRESENT TENSE, HISTORICAL PRESENT.

history see COMPUTER TERMS; HERSTORY; PAST HISTORY

hither, thither, whither *Hither, thither,* and *whither* are old-fashioned words now used for comic or rhetorical effect. *Hither* means to this place; *thither* means to that place; *whither* means to which place, to whatever place, or to what end. In other words, *hither, thither,* and *whither* mean here, there, and where, respectively, with the emphasis on movement to or towards. *Whither* is sometimes misspelled *wither*.

Some days, say Spruce Lake oldtimers, you can hardly hear yourself think for the float planes buzzing hither and yon.
Vancouver Sun 20 Feb. 1992: D6

Thither I repaired one afternoon when school was

out, and came home lugging a four-pound gong of the kind they used to place on the outside of school walls to ring in the children from recess.
Richard Davies and Glen Kirkland, eds. *Dimensions* 1986: 118

Whither go the flowers, so goes mankind.
Ottawa Citizen 12 April 1992: B2

A poster in the halls announced that he was giving a talk on 'Whether the United Nations Now.'. . . it should have been 'whither,' but Sulzner had got it wrong over the phone from New York.
Saturday Night May 1986: 36–7

Wither no man knoweth.
Toronto Star 13 May 1992: A7

(The correct spelling is *whither*.)

See also ARCHAISMS; HITHERTO.

hitherto   *Hitherto* means up to this time, or until now. Some usage guides warn against using *hitherto* to mean up to *then*, up to a moment in the past. But this advice seems pedantic. *Hitherto* is used far more often in reference to a past moment than to the present. *Thitherto*, expressly meaning 'until then', is obsolete.

Perhaps the most significant finding of our 1983–86 field work was the discovery of Nearctic species not hitherto recorded in the Thule district, namely, the sandhill crane and the Canada goose.
Arctic 41.1 (1988): 57

. . . a hitherto unpublished essay by Roger North (d. 1734), arguing for the supremacy of the Crown, also appeared in that year.
J.A.W. Gunn *Beyond Liberty and Property* 1983: 174

'He was continually discovering new, hitherto unknown, properties of natural objects.'
Irving M. Zeitlin and Robert J. Brym *The Social Condition of Humanity* 1991: 9

See also HITHER, THITHER, WHITHER.

hits   see COMPUTER TERMS

HIV, HIV virus   The acronym *HIV* means human immunodeficiency virus. Thus, the phrase 'HIV virus', which repeats *virus*, has been roundly criticized as a redundancy. Redundancy, however, should not be eliminated at the expense of clarity. A lay audience may be unaware of the word-by-word meaning of a technical acronym. The phrase 'HIV virus' appears often in the press and in health promotion literature, and, in such contexts, is appropriate. In literature written for the specialist, the redundant phrase is rare.

When the HIV virus enters your body, it must enter a cell to live and reproduce.
'T-cell count (CD4 count)' *Plain and Simple Fact Sheets* Canadian AIDS Treatment Information Exchange website April 2003

These considerations of the genetic diversity of the HIV and its potential consequence on drug resistance are of paramount significance in treating non-B HIV.
Clinical and Investigative Medicine 24.1 (2004): 56

See also ABBREVIATION, CONTRACTION, SUSPENSION, ACRONYM, INITIALISM.

HMCS   The definite article often precedes the name of a ship ('the *Titanic*') but should not precede the designation for a Canadian Navy vessel: HMCS. *HMCS* stands for Her Majesty's Canadian Ship, and '*the* Her Majesty's Canadian Ship' is ungrammatical. In formal writing, the names of ships are italicized, but HMCS is not.

HMCS Summerside, a naval coastal defence vessel, returns to its namesake port on July 14.
Guardian (Charlottetown) 8 March 2006: A5

See also ABBREVIATION, CONTRACTION, SUSPENSION, ACRONYM, INITIALISM.

hoard   see HORDE

Hobson's choice   This expression, although it seems to imply a choice, actually means no choice at all; modern equivalents are 'my way or the highway' and 'take it or leave it'. Thomas Hobson (d. 1631) rented out horses in Cambridge. So that each horse would get regular exercise, he required that his customers take the most rested one. Students at Cambridge

University, including John Milton, immortalized him in various comic verses, and so his name entered the language. Language commentators often make a point of distinguishing between 'Hobson's choice' and 'a dilemma'—the need to make a choice between unpalatable alternatives. However, Hobson's customers might also be said to have faced a dilemma: take a horse they didn't like, or walk.

> . . . Mr. Bourassa represents Hobson's choice for many anglophone voters—they do not want Mr. Bourassa again, but they do not want the PQ.
> *Globe and Mail* (Toronto) 9 Nov. 1985: A4

> Apple was faced with a Hobson's choice. Either leap to a new chip or be left behind by more powerful processors from competing hardware manufacturers.
> *Daily News* (Halifax) 19 Dec. 1994: 19

See also DILEMMA; SCYLLA AND CHARYBDIS.

hoeing   see -E

hoi polloi   Literally translated from the Classical Greek, *hoi polloi* means 'the many', that is, the common people as opposed to the elite. In English usage the phrase is the equivalent of 'the masses'; it is often used in humorous contexts.

Some people mistakenly use *hoi polloi* to refer to the people at the top rather than the bottom of the social ladder. Perhaps this confusion stems from the similar sound of the expressions *hoi polloi* and *hoity-toity*, which means condescending or haughty.

Because *hoi* is the Greek definite article, some usage experts have argued that to say 'the hoi polloi' is the equivalent of saying 'the the many'. While some writers do omit the English *the*, it is neither necessary nor idiomatic to do so.

> On a trip to the Soviet Union one of the flight attendants heard from a pal of his in first class that the richest man in the U.S. was on her plane. She went back into tourist to spread the news to the hoi polloi.
> *Financial Post* 4 Oct. 1991: 11

> It was interested in taxation and the maximization of revenue, not in the social security of hoi polloi.
> *Canadian Journal of History* 24.1 (1989): 90

(Here the writer has dropped the English article.)

> Every label has been given a chance to show off, whether in a free-standing boutique all its own (Gucci) or spotlit areas in the menswear department (Armani, Klein). But while the names may be distinctly hoi polloi, the displays are not forbidding.
> *Globe and Mail* (Toronto) 20 Dec. 1985: D14

(The writer has mistakenly used *hoi polloi* to refer to the elite of the fashion world.)

hold, a hold, ahold   The phrase 'get hold of' is acceptable in writing as well as in speech. But the variant 'get *a* hold of', though often heard in speech, is inappropriate in formal writing. Some consider the fused spelling *ahold* (which parallels *aside*, *ahead*, etc.) even less acceptable than *a hold*.

> As a result I was dispatched to 10 Downing Street with instructions to get hold of the highest placed person possible and make sure the Canadian division received appropriate mention.
> George Ignatieff *The Making of a Peacemonger* 1987: 72

> Sigfrid looks up through her tears, struggling to get hold of herself.
> David Williams *Eye of the Father* 1985: 112

> 'The other side of the lawsuit might get ahold of it. . . .'
> *Vancouver Sun* 23 Aug. 1990: A10

('Get a hold' is common in speech, but the spelling should be two words: *a hold*.)

holiday, vacation, holidays   A one-day break from work is *a holiday* in Canada, the United States, and Britain. Such days may be called 'public', 'civic', 'general', or 'statutory' holidays. When the reference is to a longer break, *vacation* and *holiday(s)* are used differently in Britain and North America.

Canadians and Americans use *vacation*, *holiday*, or *holidays* to refer to any extended break from school, work, or regular routine. However, *vacation* is more often used to refer to the summer break, while *the holidays* is more often used of the week or so that many people take off between Christmas and New Year's. Similarly, the *vacation season* usually means summer, while the *holiday season* usually means the Christmas season. In the context of labour law, *holidays* are statutory one-day breaks, while a *vacation* is an employee's annual break, usually of two weeks or more.

In Britain, the term *vacation* is generally reserved for periods when institutions such as Parliament, universities and schools, or the law courts are officially not in session. Otherwise a break from work or the usual routine is called a *holiday* or *holidays*.

> . . . compared with production workers, the 'new working class' enjoys a number of significant advantages: more paid holidays, more frequent and longer paid vacations. . . .
> Irving M. Zeitlin and Robert J. Brym *The Social Condition of Humanity* 1991: 131

> But some of them could also work for others, and they were prepared for long hours, few holidays, and no vacations.
> Pierre Berton *The Promised Land* 1984: 165

> . . . spending the holidays without your mother or father, husband or wife is still daunting.
> *Province* (Vancouver) 29 Dec. 1990: B2

(Here *holidays* refers to the festive season.)

> . . . university students are eager for holiday jobs, and few of them seem to know that in the beginning, university vacations were made long so that students could spend them in reading which would augment their formal studies.
> Robertson Davies *A Voice from the Attic* 1960: 34

(Davies uses both *holiday* and *vacation* to refer to the long summer break.)

See also NEW YEAR'S DAY.

holistic   see A, AN

holocaust, genocide   *Holocaust* is derived from a Greek word for burnt sacrifice and now usually means a great destruction of life, especially when fire is involved. 'The Holocaust', usually capitalized, refers to the systematic exe-

cution of millions of Jews by the Nazis in the Second World War.

Genocide is a twentieth-century term for the planned extermination of a cultural or racial group. The Holocaust was an attempted genocide of the Jewish people.

> This rooting for the home team by Canadian film writers—an admitted relief after the holocaust of the tax shelter—is not provincialism.
> *Performing Arts in Canada* July 1988: 16

(Using *holocaust* facetiously may give offence; *disaster* would be preferable here.)

> According to documents displayed at the former prison, preserved as a genocide museum, about 12,500 people were held and tortured at the site.
> *Gazette* (Montreal) 22 May 2006: A1

> He likened the placement of Indian and Métis children in white homes outside Manitoba to 'cultural genocide.'
> *Saturday Night* April 1986: 35

See also DECIMATE.

Holstein   see CAPITAL LETTERS

home in on, [hone in on]   The standard expression for finding a target is *home in on*, as in 'homing pigeon', not *hone in on*. Since to *hone* means to sharpen, *honing in*, sharpening the focus, is an understandable reinterpretation of the phrase (see FOLK ETYMOLOGY).

> One project homed in on Revenue Canada employees who were claiming rental losses on their own returns.
> *Financial Post* 25 March 1991: 13

> Once in the soil, the nematodes seek out targets by homing in on their heat and carbon dioxide emissions.
> *Gazette* (Montreal) 28 June 1990: F4

> In one method, the broth is laced with radioactivated RNA molecules which hone in on the desired DNA strip and mark it.
> *Queen's Quarterly* 97.4 (1990): 606

(The standard expression is *home in on*.)

See also FOLK ETYMOLOGY; MISHEARD EXPRESSIONS.

homely see FRIENDLY, FRIENDLILY

homophone, homograph, homonym
Homophones are words that sound the same but have different meanings: for example, *pair* and *pear*. *Homographs* are words that are spelled the same but have unrelated meanings: for example, *rest* (repose) and *rest* (remainder). *Homonym* is the general term for words that are pronounced or spelled the same.

homosexual see GAY

homy, homey see -Y, -EY

[hone in on] see HOME IN ON

honestly see SENTENCE ADVERBS

honorarium, **honorary** see -OUR, -OR

honor guard see GUARD OF HONOUR

honorific see -OUR, -OR

honour see A, AN

honourable, honorable   Canadians use both spellings. *Honourable* is more common.

Though members of Parliament and the provincial legislatures are often referred to as 'honourable' members (note that the spelling for this sense normally requires the *u*), this is not an official designation. Officially, in Canada, cabinet ministers, senators, the Speaker of the House, Supreme and Federal Court judges, and the lieutenant-governors of the provinces are called *the Honourable* for life. Provincial cabinet ministers, Speakers of the provincial legislatures, and provincial court judges above the level of district judge are also called *the Honourable*, but only during their terms of office. Governors general, prime ministers, and chief justices of Canada are called *the Right Honourable* for life.

The abbreviated forms *the Hon.* and *the Right Hon.* are also correct and quite common, even in formal writing, but they should appear before a person's name, not before a position.

Right may be abbreviated to *Rt.* in informal writing.

> . . . after the trustees' meeting Principal Mackintosh addressed himself to the Hon. W.M. Nickle, Kingston's representative in the provincial legislature. . . .
> Frederick Gibson *Queen's University* 2 (1983): 382

> The federal government's immediate response was to appoint a high-ranking judge (the Honourable Willard Estey of the Supreme Court) to investigate the bank failures. . . .
> *Queen's Quarterly* 94.4 (1987): 935–6

> But not a Canadian among them—not even the Rt. Hon. Pierre Trudeau, who is usually considered to have achieved emeritus status in the 'most eligible' category in North America.
> *Ottawa Citizen* 9 Sept. 1990: A10

(The abbreviation *Rt. Hon.* is appropriate here before a name.)

> Many of the honorable senators in the Red Chamber wear their title with pride and a touch of pomposity.
> *Ottawa Citizen* 16 Dec. 1990: A1

(Since *honorable* here is the honorific, it should be spelled *honourable*.)

> Another Hon. Senator glared at his Conservative adversaries across the aisle, drew a mighty breath, and expressed his displeasure at the parliamentary process by blowing on a kazoo.
> *Ottawa Citizen* 6 Oct. 1990: A1

(The capital letters and abbreviation are appropriate only before a person's name: the form required here is *honourable senator*.)

See also -OUR, -OR.

honour-bound see -BOUND

hoof see -F, -V-

hoof-and-mouth disease see FOOT-AND-MOUTH DISEASE

hopefully see SENTENCE ADVERBS

horde, hoard   A *horde* is a swarm or a gang, or a nomadic clan; a *hoard* is a quantity of treasure, food, or other valuables. To *hoard* something is to gather and store a hoard of it.

'They were troubled by the hordes of mosquitoes.'
Geoffrey Ursell *Perdue, or, How the West Was Lost* 1984: 37

Facing more than a dozen TV cameras, a thicket of microphones, and a horde of reporters, [he] was grilled on whether police had checked the room where the body was found.
Province (Vancouver) 25 Oct. 1990: 46

It is a fascinating treasure hoard, displayed with taste and clarity.
Globe and Mail (Toronto) 15 May 1985: P15

But if Spector was irritated, I was pugnacious—a primitive Canadian, I told him, one of those nationalists who still believes that we should hoard our resources.
Saturday Night May 1986: 30

Smith says souvenir sales are already more than $200,000 above the expected horde of $750,000.
Vancouver Sun 27 July 1990: D3

(The correct spelling for this sense is *hoard*. However, *take* or *income* might work better here, since *hoard* implies something saved up and stored away.)

horn   see ANTLER

horrible   see AWFUL

hors d'oeuvre, hors d'oeuvres   *Hors d'oeuvre* are finger foods or small appetizers served before a meal or at a cocktail party. The word comes from the French phrase meaning outside the meal (literally, 'outside the work'). In French *hors d'oeuvre* is both the singular and the plural form, but English-speakers sometimes add an *s* to form the plural: *hors d'oeuvres*. Both spellings are accepted. The phrase is commonly pronounced *or DURV(Z)*.

The hors d'oeuvre were a mixture of Canadian and Chinese.
Globe and Mail (Toronto) 18 Jan. 1985: M6

The seminar will be followed by cocktails and hors d'oeuvres. . . .
Computer Dealer News 7 March 1991: 8

horticulturalist, horticulturist   see -IST, -ALIST

host, emcee   Non-sexist usage guides suggest using the noun *host* for men or women and avoiding the gender-marked *hostess*.

The use of *host* as a verb, as in 'host a party' or 'host an event' was initially criticized but is now standard.

The verb *emcee*, from the abbreviation for 'master of ceremonies' (*MC*), is still labelled slang by many dictionaries.

Early in 1972, I was invited to appear on a late-night talk show called Appelez-moi Lise. It was hosted by a bright, dynamic woman named Lise Payette, at the time the most popular TV personality in Quebec. . . .
Ken Dryden *The Game* 1983: 26

The evening will be emceed by radio announcer Robert Gillet.
Chronicle-Telegraph (Quebec City) 5 June 1991: 6

(In more formal writing, *emcee* could be paraphrased: 'Radio announcer Robert Gillet *will be the master of ceremonies* for the evening.')

See also FUNCTIONAL SHIFT; SEXIST LANGUAGE.

hostess   see HOST

hostile, futile   Many Canadians rhyme *hostile* and *futile* with *reptile*. Most Americans, on the other hand, pronounce *hostile* like *hostel* and rhyme *futile* with *brutal*. In the past, Canadian border guards used words like these in a test to distinguish Canadian and American citizens. Today such a test would be less useful because increasing numbers of Canadians are adopting the American pronunciations.

hot flash   see BLUSH

hour   see A, AN; APPENDIX II

housebound   see -BOUND

housecleaner   see JOB TITLES

hove   see HEAVE

how come   *How come* meaning 'why' occurs in speech and written dialogue, but it is too casual for formal writing.

'How come my contract says I'm so rich and this check says I'm not?' he wonders, knowing the answer.
Ken Dryden *The Game* 1983: 152

When someone asks you, live, on air, how come you're such a pessimist and why you don't have happier endings, you can think to yourself, 'Because I'm writing in the ironic mode, thick-head.'
Margaret Atwood *Second Words* 1982: 406

How come, one boy said after a wistful silence, we're so backward here in North Dakota?
David Williams *Eye of the Father* 1985: 74

If Wayne Gretzky is so great, how come he can't keep his hockey sweater on right?
Vancouver Sun 17 Feb. 1990: D2

however   see SEMICOLON

Hudson Bay, Hudson's Bay   The large body of water and the small Saskatchewan town are both spelled *Hudson Bay*. The *Hudson's* Bay Company, established in 1670, is Canada's old-est incorporated company. These spellings are frequently confused.

At hand, for the creative process, they had the assembled resources of the Hudson's Bay Company Archives: the historic portraits, maps and documents, the drawings of James Isham, the water-colours of William Richards—the mixed-blood Company servants whose work gave life to the day-to-day journals of events at the forts on Hudson Bay in the 1770s.
The Beaver Feb.–Mar. 1990: 50

(In this example both spellings are correct.)

Throughout the 40's, the disease spread south on both sides of Hudson's Bay, and in the early 50's raced across Alberta and the prairies in the coyote population.
Perspectives: Profiles of Research at Queen's University 1986: 8

(The correct spelling here is *Hudson Bay*.)

In the late 1800s the Hudson Bay Company had begun weaving imitation sashes on looms.
Canadian Collector 21.4 (1986): 33

(The spelling of the company's name is *Hudson's Bay*.)

hue   see COLOUR

human, humane, inhumane, inhuman, non-human, unhuman   A long tradition in usage maintains that *human* is an adjective, as in 'the human touch', and not a noun, as in 'The ability to speak distinguishes humans from animals'. Canadian writers use *human* as a noun in all kinds of writing, however, and this usage is perfectly acceptable.

Human, when not simply a descriptive term, as in 'human tissue', means characterized by typically human sympathies and foibles: 'It's only human to long for company'. *Human* can also have the negative connotations of 'human error'. *Humane*, on the other hand, is invariably positive: a humane person shows compassion for the suffering of others, human or animal. 'Humane killing' is the killing of animals in a way that minimizes suffering.

Inhumane is the opposite of compassionate; *inhuman* is a more negative synonym meaning unfeeling or cruel and brutal. However, *inhu-man* can also mean lacking human qualities: 'He displayed an inhuman perfection'. Even in phrases like this one, where cruelty and brutali-ty are not implied, *inhuman* usually has nega-tive connotations. *Non-human* usually means not human in the biological sense only. *Unhuman*, meaning inhuman, superhuman, or non-human, is very rare in Canadian English.

. . . it's especially hard to write about communica-tion between cats and humans in any way that isn't whimsical.
Margaret Atwood *Second Words* 1982: 275

Suitable cats are placed for adoption while those that 'display aggressive behavior' or 'illness' are euthanized 'by approved humane methods.'
Daily News (Halifax) 8 Dec. 1993: n.p.

Some are subjected to particularly inhumane treatment, imprisoned for years in cells reserved for those sentenced to death.
Fuse Magazine 13.4 (1990): 40

Of course slavery was nowhere regarded in the ancient Greek world as fundamentally immoral or inhuman.
Irving M. Zeitlin and Robert J. Brym *The Social Condition of Humanity* 1991: 310

In *Maria Chapdelaine* the forest is constantly seen as a threat, described always in sombre, hostile, inhuman terms, while high value is placed on its reduction and clearing.
Ben-Z. Shek *French-Canadian & Québécois Novels* 1991: 22–3

I, on the other hand, consider a bed made as long as there's nothing non-human living in it.
Toronto Star 11 Sept. 1993: J1

Most of the rest [of the 22 million vertebrate animals killed annually for research and education] are dogs, cats and non-human primates.
Daily News (Halifax) 1 Aug. 1993: 21

human beings, humankind   see SEXIST LANGUAGE

humanitarian, humanitarianism, humanist, humanism, humanities   A *humanitarian* is someone who is concerned with the welfare of humanity; the beliefs or practices of such a person are called *humanitarianism*. Usually these words imply a practical involvement in helping others through activities such as social work or philanthropy. The senses of *humanitarian* and *humanitarianism* overlap with the meanings of the terms *humanist* and *humanism*, but these latter words have a much wider range of senses.

Humanism frequently refers to a philosophical stance that stresses the importance of the human over the supernatural or the divine. It may refer to the belief that human problems can be solved through reason. Often a *humanist* is contrasted with a religious believer: a secular humanist may believe that Christ was an exceptional human being, but does not accept his divinity. The movement among scholars and artists during the Renaissance from a purely Christian focus to an interest in Latin and Greek culture is called *Humanism*; its founders and exponents are called *Humanists*. Both words are capitalized because they refer to a particular historical movement and a specific group of people. In academic contexts, *humanist* is occasionally used to refer to the study of the *humanities*: that is, the branches of learning associated with human culture, such as art history, history, literature, languages, and philosophy (see also ARTS).

Donor fatigue and the demands of other crises have largely dried up humanitarian aid from the international community.
Toronto Star 28 May 2006: A15

The Victorian humanists who called for a lessening of the harshness of prison life made the point that the infliction of unnecessary suffering debases and brutalizes the society that condones it.
Richard Davies and Glen Kirkland, eds. *Dimensions* 1986: 67

He aroused all our liberal, humanist, do-gooder, middle-class guilt.
Gazette (Montreal) 16 Dec. 1993: A2

Chenevert's humanism is restricted to abstract beings suffering in distant parts of the world—he finds it difficult to relate to people around him.
Ben-Z. Shek *French-Canadian & Québécois Novels* 1991: 38

In postmodern art today, it might be said that the humanist interest in 'the moral' has been transcoded into an interest in 'the political'.
Linda Hutcheon *Splitting Images* 1991: 152

'True-blue' humanists, on the other hand, reject the authority of God and believe that they are sufficient in themselves.
Canadian Baptist Feb. 1986: 14

'The material I am writing tries to show that humanists can live a life that is fully moral without following a special dogma or tenets of a specific religion.'
Toronto Star 24 July 1993: H14

See also ARTS, VISUAL ARTS, LIBERAL ARTS.

humorist, humorous   see -OUR, -OR

hung   see HANGED

hurdle, hurl   see HURTLE

hurricane   see CYCLONE

hurtle, hurl, hurdle   To *hurtle* is to move with great speed. To *hurl* is to fling violently or throw down. Insults and invective are figuratively hurled, and a speeding train hurtles along. To *hurdle* means to leap or overcome a barrier.

> An ICBM is a three-part rocket that can hurtle across the world in half an hour or less.
> *Saturday Night* Jan. 1986: 14

> 'She started hurtling insults at me.'
> *Globe and Mail* (Toronto) 4 May 1985: M1

(The word required here is *hurling*.)

> The searing heat of the detonation scorched the shirt of a farmer standing on his porch 40 miles away. Seconds later a deafening shock wave hurled him to the ground, knocking him unconscious.
> Terence Dickinson *Halley's Comet* 1985: 61

> He sat beside the constable and across from the jailer, and he watched the flat white fields hurling past the window.
> William Teatero *John Anderson: Fugitive Slave* 1986: 144

(The word required here is *hurtling*.)

> He vaults the low iron railing of the cement porch, hurdles the short hedge onto the neighbors' lawn.
> Margaret Atwood *Life Before Man* 1979: 265

hush   see ONOMATOPOEIA

hyper-, hypo-, hyper   The prefix *hyper-* means above, beyond, or excessively; the prefix *hypo-* means below, under, or insufficiently. Thus someone with a high fever is *hyperthermic*, whereas someone suffering from exposure to severe cold is *hypothermic*.

Since the 1970s, *hyper* has come into common use among North Americans as an adjective describing tense or excessively active people. *Hyper* in this sense is probably an abbreviation of *hyperactive*. It is listed in some North American dictionaries, always as slang; in formal writing *excitable* or *nervous* would be a better choice.

> Hence hyperrealism: that which is more realistic than the realistic.
> *Queen's Quarterly* 96.1 (1989): 105

> 'At night [the temperature] really drops and you can get hypothermic.'
> *Ottawa Citizen* 2 Sept. 1990: B7

> Most of the time Curtis is hyper, grabbing at the air with her hands when she talks, as if reaching for the centre of attention.
> *Province* (Vancouver) 16 March 1990: P4

hyperbole, hyperbola, hyperbolic   *Hyperbole* (pronounced *high PER buh lee*) is a figure of speech, the use of exaggeration for emphasis and rhetorical effect: 'He invested a fortune in lottery tickets'. A *hyperbola* is a geometric curve. *Hyperbolic*, the adjective for both nouns, is pronounced *high per BAWL ic*.

hypercorrection   This is the name for the 'overcorrect' pronunciations and grammatical structures that result when people, fearing their usage is not up to par, attempt to produce a standard form or structure and instead produce a nonstandard one. A speaker of Cockney English, for example, who typically does not pronounce the *h* at the beginning of words (saying '*art* for *heart*), when attempting to produce Standard English often adds an *h* even to words that don't have one (saying *harm* for *arm*). In the American television comedy *All in the Family*, Archie Bunker's pronunciation of *toilet* as *terlet* reflects an attempt to correct a particularly stigmatized pronunciation associated with Brooklyn, which produces, for example, *toity-toid* instead of *thirty-third*. Archie's attempt to correct this nonstandard pronunciation (by substituting *er* for *oi* wherever it occurs) takes the correction too far.

The same linguistic insecurity can also affect highly educated speakers. Many speakers of Standard English now say *between you and I. I* sounds more refined than *me,* but *me* is traditionally correct (see CASE).

See also ADJECTIVES AND ADVERBS; BAD, BADLY; BETWEEN YOU AND ME; CASE; PRONOUNS BETWEEN LINKED VERBS; WHO, WHOM.

hyperthermic, hypothermic   see HYPER-, HYPO-, HYPER

hyphenation   Hyphens have two major functions. The first is to indicate that a word has been divided at the end of a line. The general principle to follow is to insert the hyphen where it will least distract the reader, usually at a syllable break (which can be checked in a dictionary).

The second use of hyphens is to combine discrete verbal elements into a single unit of meaning. For example, in the sentence 'I went to a few more-highly recommended restaurants' the hyphen indicates that the speaker visited some less-highly recommended restaurants before moving on to the better establishments. Without the hyphen this sentence would suggest that the speaker visited *only* highly recommended places. Generally speaking, hyphens are inserted to prevent ambiguity or make reading easier.

Hyphens often follow prefixes in new words ('*non-stick* cookware') or words coined for an occasion ('my *pre-trip* checklist'). The more familiar a word becomes, the less likely it is to be spelled with a hyphen. Canadian and American writers are quicker to drop these hyphens (e.g., in words such as *nonprofit* and *predate*) than the British (*non-profit, pre-date*). Canadians are also less likely than the British to spell compound words with a hyphen, often preferring an open compound (such as *bear hug, slave driver*) or a solid word (*northeast, newlywed*) to a hyphenated British spelling (*bear-hug, slave-driver, north-east, newly-wed*). Given that hyphens are more common in British than in North American writing, Canadians who routinely use a British dictionary may want to shift to one that reflects North American practice for hyphenation.

It is not always possible to use a dictionary to settle a hyphenation problem. Some words are too new to be in the dictionary, and some combinations, such as 'more-highly recommended restaurants' in the example above, will never appear in a dictionary because they are linked to a particular context. Editors and usage guides have developed some useful general guidelines for cases where dictionaries fail. Hyphens are normally used in the following contexts:

• after a prefix preceding a numeral ('mid-1900') or a capital letter ('un-Canadian')

• where dropping the hyphen would produce a word with another meaning ('*co-op* housing', not '*coop* housing'; '*re-cover* the footstool' not '*recover* the footstool')

• in a compound consisting of multiple elements ('non-German-speaking visitor', 'mid-twentieth-century scholarship')

• in a phrase describing age, length, etc. ('six-year-old child', '12-foot-high fence')

• between double vowels (*anti-intellectual, re-examine, multi-entry, pre-issue*) or identical consonants (*non-national*); however, note that many familiar words with double vowels or consonants (these will be found in a dictionary) do not require a hyphen (e.g., *cooperate, coordinate, bookkeeping, cutthroat, nighttime*)

• after paired prefixes where the first stands alone, as in 'nineteenth- and twentieth-century scholarship' or 'pre- and post-operative care'

• in spelled-out fractions ('three-quarter length', 'one-fifth reduction', 'four and one-quarter'), unless the denominator already contains a hyphen ('one thirty-second'); note that when fractions are written as numerals, a slash, not a hyphen, is used to separate the numerator and denominator (3/4).

Many multi-word modifiers that are not hyphenated when they follow a verb *are* hyphenated if they directly precede a noun:

He is completely burned out. / He's a burned-out executive.

This schedule is out of date. / An out-of-date schedule is useless.

Similarly, noun phrases that are not normally hyphenated often *are* hyphenated when used attributively (i.e., in front of another noun):

My son is in day care. / He goes to a day-care centre.

They support law and order. / They ran on a law-and-order platform.

Nouns designating ethnicity, such as *French Canadian* or *African American* (as in 'His mother was a French Canadian, his father an African American') are hyphenated when they are used as adjectives: 'French-Canadian literature', 'African-American history'.

There are several contexts where writers are tempted to insert unnecessary hyphens. Hyphens are *not* required in the following contexts:

• in an adjectival phrase consisting of a foreign phrase ('ad hoc decision', 'in camera meeting')—unless the foreign phrase is hyphenated in the original language ('laissez-faire policy')

• after an *-ly* adverb modifying a past participle ('politically charged situation', 'newly coined words'); it is only irregular adverbs that might be mistaken for adjectives that are joined to past participles by hyphens ('the best-known case', 'much-used material').

Phrasal verbs should not be hyphenated or written as one word unless they are being used as adjectives or nouns (see PHRASAL VERBS):

They turn out to every game.

They expected a better turnout.

He sugars off when the weather is right.

Sugaring-off season brings visitors.

See also DASH; PHRASAL VERBS; PREFIX, SUFFIX; RE-; SEMI-; SLASH.

hypo-   see HYPER

hypocrisy, idiosyncrasy   Note that both of these words end in *-sy*, not *-cy*.

hypothesis, hypotheses   see PLURALS

hysterical   see A, AN

I

I   see CASE; MYSELF; PRESENT WRITER

-(i)ana   The suffix *-(i)ana* is used to form a collective noun meaning 'things associated with' the place, person, pastime, or period in the root word. It usually refers to books or memorabilia. *Canadiana* is a familiar example. In addition, the *OED* includes *Africana, Churchilliana, cricketana, Shakespeariana* (also spelled *Shakespear-eana*), *Victoriana*, and *Walpoliana*.

ibid., op. cit.   *Ibid.* is an abbreviation of *ibidem*, Latin for 'in the same place', and *op. cit.* is an abbreviation of *opere citato*, Latin for 'in the work cited'. Both these abbreviations were designed to reduce the length of footnotes, which helped typesetters save both time and page space. Now many modern scholarly pub-

lishers have turned to endnotes rather than footnotes, a practice that permits longer notes and reduces the need for abbreviations. Most disciplines have one or more recognized styles for articles published in scholarly journals. Typically, references to books or articles by other writers are placed directly in the running text, enclosed in parentheses, while endnotes are reserved for comments of some substance. The *Chicago Manual of Style* (15th ed.) is the style guide used by many scholarly book editors.

See also LATIN PHRASES, FOREIGN PHRASES.

-ible   see -ABLE

-ic, -ical   Many *-ic/-ical* adjective pairs are

essentially interchangeable, including *botanic/ botanical, electric/electrical, fanatic/fanatical, geographic/geographical, ironic/ironical*. Other pairs are partially or completely differentiated (see CLASSIC, CLASSICAL; COMIC, COMICAL; ECONOMIC, ECONOMICAL; HISTORIC, HISTORICAL; MYTHOLOGICAL, MYTHIC; POLITIC, POLITICAL).

-ic, -ically   see PUBLICLY

ice cream, ice water, iced tea, ice
Canadians write *ice cream* and *ice water*, but still prefer *iced tea* to *ice tea*. Originally, the dessert and water were also termed *iced*, since these products are not made of ice; rather, ice is used to cool them. The *-ed* ending began to disappear in the eighteenth century.

In Britain if you ask for 'an ice' you will be offered iced sweets such as ice cream, sherbet, or frozen fruit juice.

> We've told them a million times that it's not ice cream, it's iced cream.
> W.C. Lougheed, ed. *In Search of the Standard in Canadian English* 1986: 78

(*Ice cream* is standard in Canadian English.)

> Iced tea is synonymous with warm summer months and tea companies have worked hard to cash in on the traditional image of someone drinking a tall, frosted glass of lemon-flavoured iced tea on a sweltering July day.
> *Western Grocer* May–Jun. 1990: 29

See also SKIM MILK, SKIMMED MILK, WHIP CREAM, WHIPPED CREAM.

ideology, ideological, ideologue   *Ideology* is frequently used to refer to a set of political beliefs that determines the actions of a particular party or group. Although the term can be used neutrally or positively, it is generally applied to beliefs that, in the speaker's view, are held dogmatically or distort reality. Supporters of both the left and the right have accused their opponents of adhering to ideology in the negative sense.

Marxist theory holds that widespread systems of beliefs—ideologies—are designed to justify and preserve the power of a dominant class, and that they serve that end by representing social structures as natural and inevitable.

Ideologue, like *demagogue*, is almost always a negative term. An *ideologue* is a person who promotes a particular—implicitly false—ideology.

> Rogin argues that cultural historians must take film seriously, both because political groups use the medium as an instrument of control and change, and because cinema can reveal important clues to the mind-set and ideology of these groups.
> *Queen's Quarterly* 95.4 (1988): 807

> If the Liberal party is seen as bereft of an ideology, it is precisely because its core values of inclusion, openness, moderation and tolerance are the values of Canada itself.
> *Star-Phoenix* (Saskatoon) 16 Feb. 2006: A10

(Here *ideology* is used positively to mean political principles.)

> Above all, our evaluation should move beyond ideology to a concrete, pragmatic and enlightened assessment of our interest.
> *Globe and Mail* (Toronto) 28 May 1991: P7

(Here *ideology* is used negatively.)

> Yet, when a Canadian journalist reports the purges, repressions and doubletalk, well, he or she becomes a fascist right-wing ideologue.
> *Maclean's* 19 Sept. 1988: A9

idioms   An *idiom* is a phrase, such as 'have the heart to' or 'be on top of', that can't be interpreted literally. English, like all languages, has many idioms. Though generally they pose no special problem for the native speaker, they often mystify the language learner.

The meaning of an idiom is a metaphorical extension of its literal, or word-for-word, meaning. When we learn the meaning of an unfamiliar idiom we file it away just as we would that of a new word. Because they are items of vocabulary, idioms are inflexible. With even a slight change of wording, idioms often devolve into literal speech. 'He's spreading me with butter' does not mean the same thing as 'He's buttering me up'. Nor does 'Don't take your shirt off' have the same meaning as 'Keep your shirt on'.

Phrasal verbs form a special class of idiom in English. These are verbs with prepositional particles attached to them that alter their meaning. 'Look out', for example, is a phrasal verb in 'Look out for the car!' while it is two independent words in 'Look out over the water'. 'Look up' is a phrasal verb in 'Look up their phone number', but not in 'Look up, so I can take your picture'. Other examples of phrasal verbs are *carry on, carry out, fill in, get by, go on about, put up with*, and *take off*. Phrasal verbs are so common in English that native speakers may not realize how much trouble they can pose for non-native speakers.

Idioms, including phrasal verbs, need not (indeed cannot) be avoided. However, if you are writing for an audience that may have trouble comprehending idioms, it's a good idea to repeat your central points in several different ways.

See also CLICHÉ; PHRASAL VERBS.

idiosyncrasy   see HYPOCRISY

idiot savant   see SAVANT

i.e., e.g.   An abbreviation of the Latin phrase *id est, i.e.* means 'that is'; *e.g.* is an abbreviation of *exempli gratia*, meaning 'for example'. The meanings of these two abbreviations are different: *i.e.* introduces a paraphrase or further explanation, while *e.g.* introduces an example. Both of these abbreviations require *two* periods because they abbreviate two words.

Although *Fowler's* (1965) suggested that these abbreviations should appear only in notes, and the *Chicago Manual of Style* confines them to notes and parenthetical comments, they appear increasingly in running text in works of all kinds. Most guides recommend that *i.e.* and *e.g.* be preceded and followed by commas. They need not be italicized.

The feminist and pro-choice movement's call for reproductive rights rests on the fundamental liberal principles of 'bodily integrity' (i.e., citizens have a right to make decisions about their own bodies free from state interference) and 'individual conscience' (i.e., women are autonomous, rational, and moral agents capable of exercising choice).
Janine Brodie, Shelley A.M. Gavigan, and Jane Jenson *The Politics of Abortion* 1992: 72

The names [for dogs] should be two syllables, but should not sound like commands (e.g. down, sit, stay) or other animals (e.g. bear, cougar, moose).
Edmonton Journal 2 May 2006: A6

If industrial production is stopped (e.g., by a strike) every member of society feels the consequences.
Irving M. Zeitlin and Robert J. Brym *The Social Condition of Humanity* 1991: 149

. . . Carsten lacked those silly misconceptions [held] by some travellers (i.e., all Canadians live in igloos, all Aussies wrestle alligators in their spare time).
Calgary Herald 21 July 1995: B4

(Here *i.e.* should be replaced by *e.g.*)

See also LATIN PHRASES.

-ie-, -ei-   Most writers know the rule: *i* before *e* (*achieve, believe, chief, relieve*) except after *c* (*ceiling, conceit, receive*), but there are exceptions: *caffeine, codeine, either, leisure, neither, protein, seize, sheik, weird*. And there are many instances where the rule does not apply.

First, the rule does not apply if the *i* and the *e* are pronounced separately, as in *science*, or if the *c* is sounded like *sh*, as in *conscience, species*, and *sufficient*.

Second, the rule does not apply if the sound is a long *a*. A long *a* sound is spelled *ei*: *feign, freight, inveigle, neighbour, rein, reign, veil, vein, weigh*. In fact, any vowel sound other than the long *e* sound (as in *achieve, believe*, etc.) is usually spelled *ei*: *height; counterfeit, forfeit* (but *mischief*); *heir, their; foreign, sovereign* (but *friend*— because a *friend* is a friend to the *end*).

See also WEIRD.

-ies   see -Y

if, whether   The most common meaning of *if* is 'in the case that': 'If you see them, say hello'. *If* also means 'whether': 'Ask if I can come'. Sentences in which *if* could have either meaning ('Let us know if you are coming') should be avoided. Depending on which meaning is intended, this sentence should be rephrased: either 'If you are coming, let us know' or 'Let us know whether you are coming'.

When either *if* or *whether* is possible, the usual choice in formal writing is *whether*.

When *if* means 'whether', it should not be followed by the subjunctive: 'He asked if I was (*not* were) aware of the implications'.

> And when they ask if you want a medium hot salsa or the 'dangerous stuff' they're not kidding about the latter.
> Alan Tucker, ed. *The Penguin Guide to Canada* 1991: 190

(This use of *if* meaning 'whether' is common in speech and informal writing.)

> It remains to be seen whether this abnormal biochemistry is a cause of Alzheimer's, or an effect. . . .
> *Queen's Quarterly* 92.1 (1985): 155

See also IF I WERE YOU; SUBJUNCTIVE.

if I were you   Sometimes *were* displaces the usual past tense in a clause introduced by *if*:

> If I made all the arrangements, would you come? / If I were to make all the arrangements, would you come?

> If she was eligible, she would apply. / If she were eligible, she would apply.

The use of *were* indicates that the condition named in the *if*-clause is purely hypothetical, or highly unlikely. The clause containing *were* is said to be in the subjunctive mood. Note that the subjunctive *were* is a stylistic option, not a grammatical necessity—with one exception: in formal writing and speech, Canadians never use the phrase 'If I was you'. The subjunctive 'If I were you' is the norm. In British English 'If I was you' is viewed more tolerantly.

See also SUBJUNCTIVE.

ignorant   see ILLITERATE

-ile   see HOSTILE

ilk   'Of that ilk' now means 'of that sort or type'. In Scotland an older meaning—'of the same place, estate, or name'—has been retained, mainly in the names of landed families. Thus 'Moffatt of that ilk' means someone named Moffatt whose lands are in a place called Moffatt. Some commentators would restrict *ilk* meaning sort or kind to informal contexts, but Canadian writers use the expression in all kinds of writing.

> Peregrine will be known as the Moncreiffe of That Ilk, a . . . title in which the word Ilk means 'the same.' The title means Moncreiffe of Moncreiffe.
> *Globe and Mail* (Toronto) 28 Feb. 1985: P16

> Kristin and Tay John are both figures of this sort, demigods, with unusual births and strange attributes; like satyrs and their ilk, they are bridges joining the human world, the natural world and the supranatural world.
> Margaret Atwood *Second Words* 1982: 240

> 'This is typical of scammers and virus writers and people of that ilk, who will take advantage of any way to exploit an unsuspecting, innocent user of the Internet,' said Ross.
> *Vancouver Sun* 18 Jan. 2005: D3

ill   see SICK

illegal, unlawful, illicit   *Illegal*, *unlawful*, and *illicit* are all used to mean contrary to law. *Illegal* is most common in general writing that describes acts contravening the law of the land. However, the Canadian Criminal Code uses *lawful* and *unlawful* almost exclusively; thus this word occurs frequently in the press in such fixed phrases as 'unlawful confinement', 'unlawful assembly', and 'unlawful possession'.

Illicit usually describes things or activities that are illegal under certain circumstances ('illicit drugs', 'illicit trade') or are not approved of under certain circumstances ('illicit sex').

Burglary, as a criminal offence, consists in the unlawful entry of premises with or without force. . . .
J.E. Smyth et al. *The Law and Business Administration in Canada* 1987: 428

The illicit arms trade is a major concern for Canadian officials.
Maclean's 28 July 1986: 8

Watching *Home Alone* is as boring as babysitting a child you don't like, in a house with an empty fridge, no TV, not even a medical book or dirty magazine for a few illicit adolescent thrills.
Vancouver Sun 16 Nov. 1990: D4

See also ELICIT, ILLICIT.

illegible   see -ABLE, -IBLE; UNREADABLE

illicit   see ELICIT; ILLEGAL

illiterate, illiteracy, innumerate, ignorant   An *illiterate* person does not know how to read or write. Someone who is 'functionally illiterate' cannot read or write well enough to cope with everyday tasks such as reading directions, looking up telephone numbers, or filling out application forms. By extension, *illiterate* can be used to describe a person who does not possess the rudiments of a specified subject: 'Computer illiterates are becoming a rarity on campus'.

Usage guides may use the term *illiteracy* to label a usage that they condemn. This use is rather hyperbolic considering that the examples so labelled are often from newspapers, and their perpetrators are not only literate but make their living by writing.

Innumerate is the term for those lacking adequate skills in arithmetic or knowledge of mathematics and science.

Ignorant means lacking in knowledge either generally or in a particular subject area. Although to be called ignorant is insulting, to be deemed ignorant of some specific area of knowledge is not necessarily an insult: 'They were ignorant of military protocol'; 'I claimed ignorance of the missing chocolate'.

Informally, *ignorant* has come to mean rude and obnoxious.

He was illiterate, and 'his principal object in marrying was to have a wife who was able to read his parts to him'; he must have been a quick study and she must have been a good wife, for he occasionally acted two brand-new parts on two successive days.
Robertson Davies *A Voice from the Attic* 1960: 208

If you're illiterate or innumerate in a society where the fastest growing group in the workforce is the technical and professional class, you're in big trouble.
Ottawa Citizen 24 Oct. 1990: A11

Our children probably never pined for home versions of video-arcade games, nor did we worry that our children were becoming computer illiterates, space-age versions of the village idiot.
Canadian Consumer Jan. 1986: 11

I'm sure that the dictionary definition of 'ignorant' gives you license to use the word in your Feb. 22 headline, 'Finding 12 ignorant jurors for North was a trial in itself,' but surely colloquial usage would give you pause. 'Finding 12 jurors ignorant of North . . .' would have been a lot better.
Gazette (Montreal) 1 March 1989: B2

In recent days, I've heard some fellow citizens making rude and ignorant comments about Premier Lorne Calvert.
Star-Phoenix (Saskatoon) 24 Oct. 2003: A16

(Here *ignorant* means ill mannered.)

illusion   see DELUSION

illusive, illusory   see ELUSIVE

I'm   see CONTRACTION

imaginary, imaginative   Something *imaginary* exists only in the mind, while something *imaginative* demonstrates the creative powers of the mind. Thus a child's 'imaginary friend' is not real, while an 'imaginative friend' is one full of fanciful and intriguing ideas. Both words are applied to works of art: an imaginative (creative) work may evoke an imaginary world. The term *imaginative literature* is sometimes used to distinguish literary writing from other kinds of writing that are also referred to as literature. For example, social scientists use *literature* to refer to all the published material on a particular topic ('a review of the literature on drug abuse'), and groups attempting to attract support use it to refer to their promotional material ('We have some literature you might like to read').

> Here society is seen as controlled by certain anxieties, real or imaginary, which are designed to repress or sublimate human impulses toward a greater freedom.
> Northrop Frye *The Bush Garden* 1971: 230

> When Dan Stone was three, he introduced his imaginary frog, Cricket, to the family.
> *Edmonton Journal* 1 April 2006: B9

> The idea of possessing the means and the milieu for a life devoted entirely to imaginative creation is extremely attractive, especially to the story-telling sort of talent.
> Robertson Davies *A Voice from the Attic* 1960: 304

> The Romantic poets . . . elevated *imaginative* literature to a status far above other kinds of writing. . . .
> *Queen's Quarterly* 95 (1988): 557

Imam   see RELIGIOUS TITLES

imbue, instil, infuse, inculcate   These near synonyms are now most often used figuratively. But because of their different literal senses, they are followed by different prepositions, and this is where the usage difficulties arise. *Imbue*, literally to soak or dye, is usually followed by *with*; *instil*, literally to introduce drop by drop, is usually followed by *in* or *into*; *infuse*, literally to steep in or pour into, may be followed by *with* or *into*. *Inculcate*, originally meaning to press in with the heel, may be followed by *in*, *into*, or *upon*. Objections have been raised to *imbue into*, *instil with*, and *inculcate with*. As the literal meanings fade from use, these objections will doubtless fade as well, but until then it is safest to use the prepositions that are conventionally found with each word.

Instill is the common spelling in the United States and Canada; *instil* is usual in Britain. *Instilled* and *instilling* always have two *l*'s.

> The Seabird band is one of about 100 B.C. bands in charge of its own education. That means the band can imbue its young with a respect for their heritage. . . .
> *Vancouver Sun* 8 Sept. 1990: A7

> These are the largest and oldest trees in the world, and their age and size imbue this forest with a solemnity so deep it seems to many visitors spiritual.
> *Vancouver Sun* 16 June 1990: A1

> Contrary to the industrious image of overseas Chinese, the work ethic does not seem necessarily imbued into modern mainland China—as it is . . . in modern Japan.
> *Globe and Mail* (Toronto) 26 Dec. 1985: A7

(The sentence could be rewritten: '. . . modern mainland China does not necessarily seem *imbued with* the work ethic—as modern Japan is'; or '. . . the work ethic does not necessarily seem to have been *instilled into* [or *inculcated in*] modern mainland China. . .'.)

> 'Munich has never really become a big city,' says August Everding, a 'Prussian' who for two decades has instilled his ebullient spirit into the city's opera and theatre.
> *Globe and Mail* (Toronto) 9 Feb. 1985: T12

> Even when the dance catapults into the ridiculous, she manages to instill the whole thing with some moments of calm—a difficult feat considering the bustling variety of dance styles in the play.
> *Globe and Mail* (Toronto) 30 Jan. 1985: M9

(Since the 'moments of calm' are intermittent, a more appropriate verb might be *introduce*: '. . . she manages to introduce some moments of calm. . .'.)

> In his new role as chairman of the Metro Toronto Board of Police Commissioners, he talks wistfully of infusing fresh talent into the corporation.
> *Globe and Mail* (Toronto) 4 May 1985: M1

> Children generally don't have much money, but bankers want to inculcate a savings ethic in them early.
> *Globe and Mail* (Toronto) 30 Dec. 1985: B1

imitable   see -ABLE, -(AT)ABLE

immaculate   see IMMACULATE CONCEPTION; IMPECCABLE

Immaculate Conception, virgin birth
Immaculate means pure, without spot or stain.

immanent, imminent, eminent, pre-eminent

The term *Immaculate Conception* (usually capitalized because it is the official name of a dogma) does not, as is popularly thought, refer to the special circumstances of Jesus Christ's conception (i.e., that he was fathered by the Holy Spirit). Rather, it refers to a Roman Catholic dogma, dating from 1854, according to which Mary, in preparation for her role as the Mother of God, was born without original sin.

The expression *virgin birth* is the popular name of the doctrine that Christ was born of a mother who was a virgin; because it is not an official term, it is not capitalized.

See also ENUNCIATION, ANNUNCIATION.

immanent, imminent, eminent, pre-eminent

Immanent means inherent or existing within; the word is usually found in theological, philosophical, and psychological writing. *Imminent* means impending or likely to happen in the very near future. *Eminent* means outstanding or prominent. *Pre-eminent* and *eminent* are sometimes used interchangeably, although *pre-eminent* carries the sense of most distinguished, and excelling above all others: an eminent lawyer is not necessarily the pre-eminent, or most distinguished, lawyer in town.

> At the root of the problem, writes Sennett, was a 19th century secularism 'based on the code of the immanent, rather than the transcendent. Immediate sensation, immediate fact, immediate feeling, were no longer to be fitted into a pre-existent [religious] scheme in order to be understood.'
> *Ottawa Citizen* 26 Nov. 1994: B6

> My stay in Bulgaria came to an abrupt end when I was informed by the British legation in Sofia that war was imminent and that, with my name, I would be well advised to leave the country as quickly as possible.
> George Ignatieff *The Making of a Peacemonger* 1987: 53

> Philip said talk of an immanent deal was premature. 'I do not see it completed in two days', said Philip.
> *Financial Post* 31 Oct. 1991: 3

(The correct spelling is *imminent*.)

Eminent ancestors make one's causes and programs respectable; disreputable ancestors taint and disgrace.
Canadian Journal of History 14.1 (1989): 10

. . . given the claim that the king was pre-eminent within British government, it seems probable that he was the supreme power who was to be obeyed. . . .
J.A.W. Gunn *Beyond Liberty and Property* 1983: 182

immigrant   see EMIGRANT

immigrant, landed   see CITIZEN

imminent   see IMMANENT

immoral, amoral, non-moral, unmoral

Many usage guides caution readers to distinguish between *immoral*, meaning contravening accepted standards of morality, and *amoral*, meaning lying beyond the sphere in which moral judgments apply. This distinction reserves *immoral* for those capable of understanding morality—that is, responsible adult human beings, as opposed to children, other animals, or forces of nature.

In practice, however, *immoral* tends to be used specifically of behaviour that violates sexual conventions, while *amoral* often refers to other kinds of moral transgressions—the kinds of things that in a more religious age might have been called *evil*. *Amoral* is often used with the implication that the people in question are acting as if they were beyond the range of moral judgment or had no concept of the prevailing standards of morality. These uses seem acceptable for most audiences.

Because of the ambiguity that may attach to the use of *amoral*, some people writing on ethics or philosophy use *non-moral* or *unmoral* to refer to those matters outside the scope of moral judgment.

> Peter De Vries in *The Tunnel of Love* has brilliantly caricatured an editor who sets out on an adulterous path for which he has no talent and small appetite, in order to show that he can be as immoral as any of the creative men with whom his work associates him.
> Robertson Davies *A Voice from the Attic* 1960: 315

'We consider it is amoral to use the hostages for political ends,' he told the joint news conference.
. . .
Ottawa Citizen 29 Oct. 1990: A1

(The speaker thinks that the behaviour of the hostage-takers is evil; thus most usage guides would recommend *immoral* here.)

He believes American individualism is an amoral creed leading to a selfish, Hobbesian state of nature, and that our sense of collective rights and of shared social responsibilities makes a better model for the future.
Saturday Night July 1986: 51

(Here many usage guides would recommend *immoral*.)

It's called 'realpolitik'. That's the term for a hard-nosed, amoral attitude toward the rest of the world.
Province (Vancouver) 20 March 1990: 31

It casts moral values as obligations and makes them overriding. Its effect is to leave no room for non-moral considerations.
Canadian Journal of Philosophy 19 (1989): 298

immunization, vaccination, inoculation

In current medical usage, *immunization* and *vaccination* are synonymous and are preferred to *inoculation*, which is considered an outmoded term. However, *inoculation* is still the word most likely to be used in a figurative sense.

The frequent misspelling *innoculate* is probably influenced by the double *n* in the similar but etymologically unrelated word *innocuous*.

The students also learn how immunization with vaccines has helped prevent a wide range of human diseases around the world.
Toronto Star 20 Jan. 1994: NY2

I am afraid we were never able to innoculate him with the Queen's spirit.
Frederick Gibson *Queen's University* 2 (1983): 131

(The accepted spelling is *inoculate*.)

Through education, it is possible to inoculate against these dangers, Ganor argues.
Edmonton Journal 11 Nov. 2001: D6

impact

The verb to *impact* is by no means new. It's been used for centuries in its literal sense, to hit or compress; this use, however, is relatively

rare except in dentistry: 'impacted wisdom tooth'. The figurative use of *impact* to mean affect or influence became popular in business writing in the 1980s: 'Our earnings were negatively impacted by the recession'. Some commentators still consider this use jargon, and you may want to avoid it in general writing.

The Berkeley team announced their findings as evidence that an asteroid had impacted the Earth 65 million years ago, causing the extinction holocaust.
Terence Dickinson *Halley's Comet* 1985: 64

Fortunately the errors would not impact greatly upon ice seamanship.
Arctic 41.1 (1988): 85

(This sentence could be rewritten: '. . . would not greatly *affect* ice seamanship'.)

See also FUNCTIONAL SHIFT.

impassable, impassive   see DISPASSIONATE

impeach, impeachment

Impeach has two main senses: to censure or criticize someone for wrongdoing and to remove someone from office for misconduct. Although some commentators insist that only the first sense is acceptable, it is less common than the second.

'They've begun with a parade of witnesses to systematically impeach the prosecution witnesses,' said Michael Cardoza, a former prosecutor following the trial.
National Post (Toronto) 10 May 2005: A18

(Here the witnesses for the prosecution are being criticized, not removed from office.)

'I don't recall Mulroney speaking forcefully against Quebec's sign law here. I don't want to impeach his motives, but given the strong nationalist feelings in his own Quebec caucus, he probably doesn't dare to.'
Ottawa Citizen 10 Feb. 1990: B7

(Here *impeach* means criticize.)

There should be a way for citizens to impeach a mayor or council.
Whig-Standard (Kingston) 1 April 2006: 7

(Here *impeach* means remove from office.)

It is also the time to develop an impeachment process to recall and depose legally a government that acts illegally.
Ottawa Citizen 27 Sept. 1990: A14

(Here *impeachment* refers to removal from office.)

impeccable, immaculate   *Impeccable* is derived from the Latin meaning 'not sinning'; *peccadillo*, 'a trifling sin', is derived from the same root. Some usage guides would restrict *impeccable* to descriptions of people or their behaviour, presumably because only people or their behaviour can be described as 'sinless' or—extending this meaning beyond the religious sphere—'exemplary' or 'faultless': 'Gertrude spoke impeccable French'.

Impeccable is also, however, quite commonly used to describe things such as clothes, decor, and design. In such contexts it means either unerringly tasteful or flawlessly clean and tidy. Although some commentators have suggested that writers are confusing *impeccable* (faultlessly clean) and *immaculate* (spotless), the meanings are now too close to quibble about.

Nevertheless, British authorities went on placing unquestioning faith in traitors such as Philby, Maclean, and Blunt whose impeccable family and school credentials provided a perfect camouflage for their subversive activities.
George Ignatieff *The Making of a Peacemonger* 1987: 64–5

Her sound was clear, her articulation impeccable, her approach to the lead part of Mozart's Quartet for Flute and Strings, K. 285 irresistibly fresh and sunny.
Globe and Mail (Toronto) 4 March 1985: S14

Ferre is an acknowledged perfectionist. Every seam, every stitch, every belt, shoe or bracelet is impeccable, precise and original.
Globe and Mail (Toronto) 19 Feb. 1985: F6

As the Act I curtain falls, she is giving birth while the fussy civil servant dashes around his impeccable apartment uttering tiny whoops of consternation.
Globe and Mail (Toronto) 20 Aug. 1985: S8

See also IMMACULATE CONCEPTION; PRISTINE.

impediment   see OBSTACLE

imperial, imperious   Both words involve power, but in different ways. *Imperial* is related to *empire* and implies majesty and authority. *Imperious* is not necessarily used in connection with royalty or politics but describes anything commanding or compelling, and often things or people that are overbearing or menacing.

Imperial is also the name of the Imperial system of measurement, used in Canada until 1971 when the country converted to SI—the *Système international d'unités*—more commonly known as *metric*.

This led to imperial rivalries, first between the British and the French and then between the British and the Americans.
Journal of Eastern Townships Studies 23 (2003): 27–40

(Here the author is commenting on the political structure of the rivalries; *imperial* is correct.)

In stunned silence, we watch as he seats himself on his throne and casts an imperious glare upon us.
English Quarterly 34.1–2 (2002)

(Here the throne suggests an *imperial* setting, yet the emphasis is on the sternness of the gaze; *imperious* is correct.)

See also MEASUREMENT, SI, METRIC SYSTEM; APPENDIX II.

impetus   see -US

impinge, infringe   Both *impinge* and *infringe* can be used to mean encroach on, but they are generally distinguished in usage. *Impinge* is most often used to mean have an effect on someone or something; this effect may be neutral or negative. *Infringe* denotes a transgression of some kind, a violation of a boundary, a law, an oath, or personal freedom. Although *infringe* is sometimes used without a preposition ('to infringe copyright law'), both words usually take a preposition: either *upon* or, much more commonly, *on*.

Speakers of Canadian English cannot avoid being

aware of two other existing standards which impinge on them, namely the British and the American. . . .
W.C. Lougheed, ed. *In Search of the Standard in Canadian English* 1986: 163

To those people, the environmental problems lacked urgency because they would be long dead before the effects could seriously impinge on their lives.
Toronto Star 7 Aug. 2005: C24

But the judge said the inquiry provides adequate opportunities for examination to the defence and does not infringe on Mr. B——'s rights.
Globe and Mail (Toronto) 3 April 1985: M3

Now the laws passed by parliament are subject to review by non-elected courts, which have the power to strike down any laws they believe infringe the rights and freedoms contained in the charter.
Catholic Register 16 Aug. 1986: 7

The court held that this impinged freedom of speech, and this was such an unreasonable decision as to be outside of the board's jurisdiction.
Globe and Mail (Toronto) 24 June 1985: B11

(The verb *impinge* is normally followed by *on* or *upon*. However, in this case the verb itself might be better changed: in the context of a violation of rights, *infringe* is the usual choice.)

implausible   see -ABLE, -IBLE

implicit, explicit   *Implicit* means inherent or contained within: 'a flaw implicit in the design'. It often refers to a message indirectly expressed by (i.e., contained within) another message: 'The implicit message was that we were to do nothing'.

Explicit means clear or open to view. In this sense it may refer specifically, and somewhat euphemistically, to nudity or sex: 'explicit photos'. *Explicit* also means directly and unambiguously stated: 'I had explicit instructions'.

Implicit in the decision to open the centres is the belief that industry and government can work together.
Globe and Mail (Toronto) 1 March 1985: R4

Since South African law forbids the advocacy of economic boycotts, Bishop Tutu's carefully chosen words amount to implicit encouragement of

Canadian trade unions and church activists who call for disinvestment.
Globe and Mail (Toronto) 18 Jan. 1985: P7

Police said a man was arrested after a woman in suburban Etobicoke complained that sexually explicit scenes suddenly appeared on her television set. . . .
Calgary Herald 30 Dec. 1994: B7

She said children learn through explicit instruction, demonstration, modeling and opportunity to practice.
Guardian (Charlottetown) 30 Aug. 2003: A1

imply, infer   To *imply* something is to hint at it without stating it directly. To *infer* something is to gather it or deduce it from what one hears or observes. *Imply* refers to the transmitting of an idea, *infer* to the receiving of one. Some writers use *infer* to mean *imply*, and some dictionaries record this usage; however, it is not generally accepted.

'. . . people have tried to identify me with a certain period, particularly some hostile critics who imply that my work is obsolete.'
Now Magazine (Toronto) Nov. 1988: 25

To make things worse . . . people were returning to New York full of news about young trumpeters coming along for whom Davis, they implied, was no match.
Jack Chambers *Milestones* 1983: 165

Cadieux was wrong when he said I had 'implied' lack of coordination. I had spelled it out to the best of my ability. . . .
George Ignatieff *The Making of a Peacemonger* 1987: 245

Today astronomers only infer the nature of the heart of a comet. No one knows for sure precisely what it is.
Terence Dickinson *Halley's Comet* 1985: 3

. . . the political success of one party or another gives only a slender basis for inferring the state of the public mind.
J.A.W. Gunn *Beyond Liberty and Property* 1983: 122

Senior prosecutor James Jardine contends the nine items, if taken as a whole, infer R—— had access to the main components from which the bomb was made.
Vancouver Sun 6 Dec. 1990: D1

(The word required here is *imply*.)

imply, insinuate To *imply* or *insinuate* something is to suggest it indirectly, without coming right out and saying it. What is *implied* may be positive or negative; however, only negative things are *insinuated*. A second meaning of *insinuate* is to move something, often oneself, gradually and stealthily into a desirable position: 'He insinuated himself into the front row'. When *insinuate* is used figuratively in this sense, it overlaps with *ingratiate*: 'She insinuated herself into their affections' or 'She ingratiated herself with them'. An insinuating person is deviously self-promoting; an insinuating remark hints at something improper or negative.

Insinuate must take a direct object. In other words, one cannot say 'Robin is insinuating again'. Whatever the intended meaning—hinting at improprieties or slithering into place—Robin must be insinuating *something*. Moreover, in contemporary English *insinuate* in the sense of suggest requires a human agent: only people, not objects or circumstances, can insinuate things. The sentence 'The flag on his balcony insinuates his politics' would have been perfectly acceptable in the eighteenth century. Today, however, the use of *insinuate* to mean signify is obsolete.

I've implied that the writer functions in his or her society as a kind of soothsayer, a truth teller; that writing is not mere self-expression but a view of society and the world at large, and that the novel is a moral instrument.
Margaret Atwood *Second Words* 1982: 353

In a number of famous recent cases, judges insinuated that women who stayed out late, dated more than one man or separated from husbands without prior consent had somehow 'provoked' their own rape, murder or beating.
Briarpatch Dec. 1989–Jan. 1990: 23

But what I take exception to is the government's continuous attempt to test our level of intelligence by insinuating that the country is soundly managed.
Ottawa Citizen 14 Feb. 1990: A9

(The picture the government is painting is positive, not negative; thus *implying* would be more appropriate here.)

Robert Stanfield warned of the dangers to democracy when otherwise legitimate lobby groups are able to insinuate themselves directly into the political process.
Vancouver Sun 17 Dec. 1990: A11

He was insinuating and over-familiar.
Vancouver Sun 17 April 1990: A11

(The verb *insinuate* requires an object; *ingratiating* might be a better choice here.)

See also IMPLY, INFER; INGRATIATE.

important see MORE IMPORTANTLY

impractical, impracticable, unpractical A suggestion that is *impractical*, meaning not practical or useful, may also be *impracticable*, meaning impossible to put into practice. But an impracticable suggestion need not be impractical: it may well offer a practical solution to a problem, even though this solution cannot be carried out with the means at hand. Understandably, *impractical* and *impracticable*, a less common word, are sometimes confused, but they are generally well distinguished in usage. Although the form *unpractical* is given in some dictionaries, it is rarely used and is considered archaic.

Spokesperson Steve Taylor said it would be impracticable to check bags, or to install airport-style metal detectors and X-ray machines in a subway network that carries three million passengers a day or a bus system that carries some six million daily.
Star-Phoenix (Saskatoon) 22 July 2005: C15

Cream is great in coffee, but for today's smaller families and single-person households, the 250 mL carton can be impracticable. Some of the cream in an opened carton may spoil before it gets used.
Country Guide Nov. 1986: 27

(The context makes clear that the word required is *impractical*.)

There were many dead ends . . . in our search for the fireweed nectar that summer. Sometimes, patches of fireweed would add up to only a handful of plants, or the roads were steep and bridges

washed out so that further travel was impractical.
Harrowsmith Oct.–Nov. 1985: 51

(When a bridge is missing, travelling further on a road is not just *impractical*, not sensible, but *impracticable*, not possible.)

With a 20-game schedule for each team, travelling to each club for games would be unpractical, so the conference plays its schedule by way of four tournaments between early January and March. . . .
Globe and Mail (Toronto) 7 Jan. 1985: S5

(Though it can be found in some dictionaries, *unpractical* is almost never used; the preferred negative form is *impractical*.)

impromptu   see EXTEMPORANEOUS

impugn, impute   To *impugn* (pronounced *im PYOON*) something is to challenge or discredit it; to *impute* (*im PYOOT*) something to someone is to ascribe a quality (usually negative) to him or her. To *impugn* Stan's motives is to challenge them; to *impute* selfish motives to Stan is to accuse him of selfishness.

At Rafferty-Alameda, environmentalists managed to impugn provincial jurisdiction on division-of-powers grounds.
NeWest Review Dec. 1989–Jan. 1990: 6

He began to impugn and attack the character of the prime minister and the integrity of the government.
Ottawa Citizen 12 Dec. 1985: A9

Can such words, imputing sin and guilt, be justified?
Globe and Mail (Toronto) 16 April 1985: P7

Feet firmly planted on the high road, Weingarten refuses to impute unkind motives to the province.
Calgary Herald 23 Nov. 2003: B1

impunity   *Impunity* is freedom from punishment or reprisal; 'with impunity' means without punishment. The slang equivalent of doing something with impunity is 'getting away with' it.

'Mass marketing fraudsters think they can use modern technology to operate from anywhere in the world with impunity.'
Calgary Herald 24 May 2006: B1

impute   see IMPUGN

in, into   The primary function of the preposition *in* is to indicate location ('Your socks are in the laundry basket') or state or condition ('She is in good spirits'). A secondary use of *in* is with verbs indicating motion, and it is this use that sometimes meets with objections. While there is no difference of meaning in the sentences 'I went in the house' and 'I went into the house', some usage commentators argue that *into* is preferable because it more strongly suggests the idea of entering something. In addition, because *in* can also indicate location, there are contexts with verbs suggesting motion in which *into* must be used in order to avoid confusion: 'The furniture was moved out of his room into the garage'. However, to make a rule that only *into* should be used with verbs of motion would be pedantic and would mean ignoring the idiomatic uses of *in* in such expressions as 'Go jump in a lake' or 'Throw it in the garbage'. In brief, *into* is usually used with verbs of motion, but it is not considered a serious infraction to use *in* instead when there is no possibility of ambiguity. Most writers seem to choose the one that best fits the rhythm of the sentence.

'Just Do It' has been credited with everything from pulling couch potatoes into the gym to giving women the courage to leave abusive husbands.
Ottawa Citizen 7 Aug. 1994: B4

The eight-year-old tried to jump and fell in the water.
Ottawa Citizen 17 March 1990: A21

It's an effective way to beat the dilemma of 'whether to watch television or go in the whirlpool.'
Edmonton Journal 19 Sept. 1992: E1

See also INTO, IN TO.

in-, un-   Among pairs of negated words beginning with either *in-* or *un-* (for example, *inarguable* and *unarguable*) are some that have no clearly predominant form. Thus in the following pairs, the form is a matter of personal choice:

inarguable, unarguable
inessential, unessential
inharmonious, unharmonious
insupportable, unsupportable
insusceptible, unsusceptible

Among the following pairs, both forms are acceptable, but the italicized word is slightly more common in Canada:

inadvisable, unadvisable
inalterable, *unalterable*
indecipherable, undecipherable
insubstantial, unsubstantial

In the following pairs, one option is best avoided because it has become so rare that it is likely to be considered a mistake by many. The italicized word indicates the recommended usage in Canada:

incommunicative, *uncommunicative*
inconsolable, unconsolable
indescribable, undescribable
indistinguishable, undistinguishable
inescapable, unescapable
insurmountable, unsurmountable

In rare cases, the choice of prefix determines the meaning of the word itself. For more about these instances, see the individual entries listed below.

With this film he has dramatically opened a wider dialogue, helping to make the inarguable into the debatable.
Telegram (St. John's) 13 Jan. 2006: B2

(*Unarguable* is equally common and correct.)

The trip is available year-round, although the excessively hot climate in July makes the tour unadvisable during that month.
National Post (Toronto) 23 Nov. 2002: PT2

(*Unadvisable* is common, although *inadvisable* occurs even more frequently.)

Most of the characters . . . are incommunicative loners.
National Post (Toronto) 22 Nov. 2003: RB8

(*Incommunicative* is correct but rare.)

See also HUMAN, HUMANE, INHUMANE, INHUMAN, NON-HUMAN, UNHUMAN; IMMORAL, AMORAL, NON-MORAL, UNMORAL; IMPRACTICAL, IMPRACTICABLE, UNPRACTICAL; UNSANITARY, INSANITARY.

in absentia   *In absentia* is a Latin expression that means in someone's absence. It is generally used in formal circumstances: at university convocations, where degrees are conferred *in absentia* on members of the graduating class who are not present; and in courts of law, where rulings are made *in absentia* if the defendant is not present. *In absentia* should be italicized in formal writing.

He was convicted in absentia by a Dutch court after he fled the country.
Financial Post 23 Oct. 1991: 2

He returned to Canada on a brief visit in 1894, and the following April Queen's was the first university anywhere to award him an honorary degree, a doctorate of laws conferred *in absentia*.
Queen's Quarterly 92 (1985): 224

See also LATIN PHRASES, FOREIGN PHRASES.

inaccessible   see -ABLE, -IBLE

in addition to   see TOGETHER WITH

inasmuch as   see INSOFAR AS

in back of   see BACK OF

in behalf of   see BEHALF

inbound   see -BOUND

in camera   This Latin phrase entered legal English in the late nineteenth century with the meaning 'in the judge's chambers' as opposed to 'in open court'. Now, both in law and more widely, *in camera* refers to legal proceedings or formal meetings held behind closed doors. The usual justification for in camera proceedings is that they deal with prejudicial or confidential matters. *In camera* need not be italicized, nor should it be hyphenated even when it is used as an adjective, as in 'an in camera hearing'.

> In June, after weeks of investigation in camera, the royal commission submitted its report, a document of more than 600 pages containing information so damaging that the commissioners recommended it not be published.
> Frederick Gibson *Queen's University* 2 (1983): 275–7

> No date has been set for the appeal of the in camera ruling, which Blanchard has argued violates freedom of the press guarantees in the Canadian Charter of Rights and Freedoms.
> *Gazette* (Montreal) 12 Jan. 1990: A4

> . . . he wanted an in-camera hearing with the public banned.
> *Vancouver Sun* 21 Dec. 1990: A8

> (Latin phrases such as *in camera* do not take hyphens.)

See also LATIN PHRASES.

inchoate The use of *inchoate* to mean 'in chaos' is well-established, even in formal writing, although *chaos* and *inchoate* are unrelated etymologically. *Chaos*, which means 'total confusion', was the ancient Greek word for the infinite void that preceded the creation of the ordered universe, the *cosmos*. *Inchoate* (pronounced *in KO ate*, *in KO it*, or *IN ko it*) means just beginning, early, or undeveloped and is derived from the Latin *incohare*, 'to begin'. This original meaning of *inchoate* is uncommon but still in use, especially in legal contexts.

Some dictionaries present the new meaning as a logical extension of the old—i.e., something 'formless' is 'not yet fully developed'—but it is more likely that the shift in meaning occurred as a result of the resemblance between the words *inchoate* and *chaos*. Whenever a language development appears to be based on a misconception—in this case, a faulty derivation—usage-guide writers rush in. In this instance, however, the new meaning was well entrenched before the attack was even mounted.

> But he does believe he is tapping into an inchoate feeling that something has gone wrong in the land.
> *Toronto Star* 10 Oct. 1994: A13

> (Here *inchoate* means not yet fully formed.)

> . . . learning Mandarin was easy for a person who had spent years at the agonizing task of memorizing material that presented itself as an inchoate jumble of characters.
> *Globe and Mail* (Toronto) 2 Nov. 1985: B1

> (Here *inchoate* means *chaotic*.)

> This equates inner-city blight and unemployment with inchoate anger and mindless violence.
> *Globe and Mail* (Toronto) 8 June 1985: S1

> (Here *inchoate* means formless.)

incidence see INCIDENTS

incidentally see ACCIDENTALLY; COINCIDENTALLY

incidents, incidence *Incidents* is the plural of *incident*: 'We hope to prevent any more incidents of that nature'. *Incidence* is the rate at which something occurs, or the fact or scope of its occurrence: 'The incidence of HIV infection among street children is appalling'.

> It's normal procedure for an outside force to investigate incidents in another police force, such as shootings and serious complaints from the public.
> *Ottawa Citizen* 28 Dec. 1992: B2

> Although the characters and incidents in the two-part series were fictitious, the story was inspired by recent events in Newfoundland.
> *Daily News* (Halifax) 30 Dec. 1992: 8

> Large doses of vitamin C don't seem to decrease the incidence of the common cold, but they may have an effect on symptoms and severity.
> *Ottawa Citizen* 30 Dec. 1992: A16

> Obviously we should . . . provide more services for women who are victims of violence, but this will not reduce the incidents of violence against women.
> *Gazette* (Montreal) 28 Dec. 1992: B3

> (The word required here is *incidence*.)

> He was part of the Police Association of Nova Scotia's critical incidence stress debriefing team that helps firefighters, police officers, health care workers and draegermen.
> *Daily News* (Halifax): 25 Nov. 1992: 1

> (The word required here is *incidents*.)

See also PRECEDENCE, PRECEDENTS.

include see COMPRISE

inclusive language The legacy of the American civil rights movement—a heightened awareness and intolerance of discrimination against minorities—has not faded. Rather, with each passing decade, the battle against social bias has become more far-reaching and insistent, to the point where many people complain, both in jest and in earnest, about the zeitgeist of political correctness. Politically correct vocabulary can be off-putting when it seems vague, euphemistic, or transitory. But there is something worth pursuing at the heart of the inclusive language movement: a humane impulse to widen the scope of a writer's identification with other people. In other words, inclusiveness is not about pussyfooting around people's differences in age, in sex or sexuality, in race, religion, or cultural background. Neither is it about aggrandizing minority status and discounting disability. It is about writing with empathy and respect. It requires that we see others with differences as more like us than unlike, as inhabitants of our world rather than outsiders, and—when the prospect does not defy logic—as potential readers rather than merely subject matter.

The entries listed below discuss particular issues and word choices relevant to the goal of writing inclusively.

See also AGEISM; ARCHETYPES, PROTOTYPE, STEREOTYPE; DISABILITIES; GAY, LESBIAN, BISEXUAL, TRANSGENDERED; JOB TITLES; PLACE NAMES; RACE; SEXIST LANGUAGE.

incomprehensible see -ABLE, -IBLE

incredible, incredulous see CREDIBLE

inculcate see IMBUE

incumbent, present incumbent, incumbent on (upon) The term *the incumbent* usually refers to the person who currently holds an office. However, an incumbent is simply someone who holds or has held office, whether in the present or in the past. Thus the usual prescription against *present incumbent* as a tautology is unfounded.

When *incumbent* is used as an adjective, it is usually in a phrase implying that something is someone's duty or responsibility and is followed by either *on* or *upon*: 'It is incumbent on (*or* upon) her to respond'.

One more appointment was that of Adam Shortt, one of the most famous of Queen's early professors and the first incumbent of the Sir John A. Macdonald Chair of Political and Economic Science founded in 1899.
Hilda Neatby *Queen's University* 1 (1978): 180

(Here *first incumbent* means the first one to hold the office.)

The larger the corporation, the more difficult it is to dislodge an incumbent board of directors, but there have been a number of instances of dissatisfied shareholders' turning out the entire board of directors. . . .
J.E. Smyth et al. *The Law and Business Administration in Canada* 1987: 708

(Here *incumbent* is used as an adjective meaning existing or currently acting.)

St. Gregory the Illuminator was elected as the first Supreme Patriarch and Catholicos of the Armenian Church, thus establishing the long and continuous line of Catholicoi up to the present incumbent, His Holiness Vazken I. . . .
Globe and Mail (Toronto) 2 Nov. 1985: F19

At some stage, therefore, it will be incumbent on the Supreme Court to settle such outstanding questions.
Canadian Bar Review 66.3 (1987): 613

indeed see COMMA

independantiste, independentist see SEPARATIST

independent see DEPENDENT

index see FUNCTIONAL SHIFT

Indian, East Indian, Indo-Canadian, South Asian, West Indian   *Indian* is the name given to citizens of the Republic of India or to those whose ancestors came from India. Although the term *East Indian* is sometimes used by Canadians, it echoes the name of the British East India Company (which colonized India) and is sometimes disliked by contemporary Indians. Canadians whose ancestors came from India often refer to themselves as *Indo-Canadian*. The phrases *Indian Canadian* and *Canadian Indian* are easily confused and neither is recommended.

Those from the Indian subcontinent who are not citizens of India should not be referred to as Indian, but as Sri Lankan, Bangladeshi, Nepalese, Pakistani, or Bhutanese. If a general term for people from the Indian subcontinent is needed, *South Asian* is now preferred.

It is said that when Christopher Columbus touched land on his westward voyage from Spain in 1492, he thought he had reached India and thus gave the name *Indian* to the Indigenous inhabitants of the Caribbean (also known as Caribs). The term was subsequently extended to the Indigenous peoples of North, Central, and South America. The use of *Indian* has lately declined in Canada as a label for First Nations people (see ABORIGINAL PEOPLE[S]). However, *Indian* is still a term used in Canadian law and a term used to distinguish among the three broad Aboriginal groups in Canada: Indians, Métis and Inuit.

West Indian is the general term for people who come from the West Indies, of whatever ancestry. Most of the Indigenous people, the Caribs, were killed, died of disease, or fled to mainland South or Central America shortly after contact with Europeans, although a few of their descendants now live in Dominica and St. Vincent. In the West Indies, therefore, *Indian* typically refers not to Indigenous people but to those whose ancestors came from India. (Many indentured labourers were brought to the West Indies from India after slavery was abolished in 1838.) Indians, who today form a large part of the population of Guyana, Trinidad, and Tobago, refer to themselves as *Indo-Caribbean* or *East Indian* when it is necessary to distinguish themselves from the majority of West Indians, who are of African descent.

> And in Calgary's Riley Park, East Indians and Pakistanis dressed in whites play cricket on weekend afternoons.
> *Maclean's* 11 July 1988: A8

(This sentence could be rewritten in two ways: either *East* could be omitted, or *South Asians* could replace the entire phrase 'East Indians and Pakistanis'.)

> Attempts by governments, churches and the general population to change Indians, Metis and Inuit into just another ethnic group in the multicultural mosaic have failed.
> *The Beaver* Feb.–Mar. 1990: 58

> You can satisfy all of these needs by consulting SAWID, a business directory created by Manjeet Singh Atthwal that lists businesses and professional offices owned by members of the South Asian and West Indian community and which is about to go into its second edition.
> *Gazette* (Montreal) 5 Dec. 2005: B1

See also ABORGINAL PEOPLE(S);   ASIA, SOUTH ASIA, SOUTHEAST ASIA; VISIBLE MINORITY; WEST INDIES.

indices   see PLURALS

indict, indite   Both *indict* and *indite* rhyme with *incite*. To *indict* means to charge with a crime or to publicly censure. To *indite* means to write or compose something such as a letter or poem; *indite* is now rare.

> Both . . . later admitted their guilt and were indicted for murder. . . .
> *Gazette* (Montreal) 31 Aug. 1992: A3

> That about summarizes the book; it indicts the entire securities industry as a parasite in a three-piece suit.
> *Vancouver Sun* 26 Oct. 1992: D9

> No matter who pulled the trigger on Arkan, you can be sure that two other indited war criminals, R—— K—— and Gen. R—— M——, are concerned for their own skins.
> *Ottawa Citizen* 25 Jan. 2000: A10

(*Indited* means wrote; *indicted*, meaning charged, is needed here.)

indictable offence, felony, summary offence, misdemeanor In Canadian law, *indictable offence* is the term for a serious crime, such as murder or armed robbery. The comparable American term is *felony*. A less serious crime is called a *summary offence* or *summary conviction offence* in Canada; in American law the equivalent term is *misdemeanor*.

indigenous *Indigenous* means original or belonging to a particular place. For example, the maple tree is indigenous to Canada; the lilac bush, which was brought over by European settlers, is not. The term can be applied not only to plants, animals, and landforms but also to people, practices, and institutions. Confusion may arise when *indigenous* is applied to people, since it can refer to a nation's Aboriginal peoples specifically or to its whole presently established population. In Canada, *Native* and *Aboriginal* are the general terms most often used when referring to Inuit, Indian, and Métis people; however, *Indigenous* is frequently used in reference to the Aboriginal populations of other countries. It is now recommended that *Indigenous* be capitalized when it refers to Aboriginal people; this practice also reduces the possibility of ambiguity.

Point Pelee is one of the four national parks in Ontario. This spectacular haven provides an ideal environment for hundreds of migrating and indigenous species of birds.
Leisure Life 1988: 6

Their region was said to need more indigenous banking services which would be more attentive to local interests.
Queen's Quarterly 94.4 1987: 940

(Here *indigenous* means local.)

In Canada Sotheby's was hardest hit in the early 1980s when the bottom fell out of the indigenous art market. . . .
Canadian Collector 21.2 (1986): 13

(Here *indigenous* means domestic.)

A government policy of accepting refugees, immigrants, etc., does not guarantee acceptance by the indigenous population.
Globe and Mail (Toronto) 18 Jan. 1985: P6

(Here *indigenous* refers to all long-term residents.)

'Responsible trapping as it contributes to the survival of Canada's indigenous culture is acceptable and welcome.'
United Church Observer June 1986: 19

(Here the reference is to Aboriginal people; the recommended spelling is *Indigenous*.)

See ABORIGINAL; ABORIGINAL PEOPLE(S); NATIVE.

indignity, indignities, indignation *Indignity* refers to a lack of dignity, and is more rarely a euphemism for any objectionable act which removes dignity. *Indignities* is the plural of *indignity* in both senses, but suggests the second meaning more often than the first: 'They suffered grave indignities at the hands of their captors'.

Indignation is sometimes mistakenly used to mean *indignity*, but actually refers to anger resulting from it. It is sometimes paired with *righteous*, to indicate a heightened sense of moral correctness.

Some cases have gone beyond the mere difference in treatment of the sexes to look deeper at the indignity caused when a required uniform has no relationship to the job other than to exploit or accentuate the sexuality of the worker.
Law Now 29.3 (2004–05): n.p.

(Here *indignity* means humiliation.)

It can, however, promise . . . that undesirable behaviour is not tolerated, or that any indignity, slight or devastating, will not go unreported.
Ivey Business Journal 68.2 (2003): n.p.

(Here *indignity* refers to an act.)

Though many decades have since gone by, Japanese Canadians continue to live with the injustices and indignities of the past.
Canadian Journal of Sociology 29.3 (2004): 359–88

(Here *indignities* refers to acts.)

Were another person to have taken and displayed the photographs of these women, this would have occasioned the greatest indignity possible.
Journal of Palliative Care 20.3 (2004): 179–84

(Although the pictures might have been an *indignity*, only *indignation* could be occasioned).

These natives have suffered the same indignations as native peoples throughout North America. . . .
Dominion (Montreal) 12 Sept. 2003: n.p.

(The proper word here is *indignities*.)

indirect speech   see QUOTATION; WONDER

indiscriminate, undiscriminating   *Indiscriminate* means not selective ('an indiscriminate reader'), or haphazard ('an indiscriminate collection'), or random ('indiscriminate acts of violence'). *Undiscriminating* suggests a lack of good taste or good judgment. *Indiscriminating* is an uncommon American variant of *undiscriminating*.

Yet necrotizing fasciitis, commonly known as the flesh-eating disease, is a swift, indiscriminate killer, capable of destroying skin, fat and muscle so fast that antibiotics don't stand a chance.
Vancouver Sun 3 Dec. 1994: A12

What virtues has the Western world shown Afghanis, and what restitution has been provided for indiscriminate bombings?
Star-Phoenix (Saskatoon) 18 April 2006: A6

Of all the American culture that slops over the border and is soaked up by undiscriminating Canadians, gun love is perhaps the most noisome.
Vancouver Sun 31 Aug. 1994: A18

indite   see INDICT

individuals   see SEXIST LANGUAGE

Indo-Canadian, Indo-Caribbean   see INDIAN

induction   see DEDUCTION

inedible   see EDIBLE

ineducable   see -ABLE, -IBLE

inequity, iniquity   *Inequity* is unfairness or bias, while *iniquity* is wickedness, sin, or wrong-doing: a 'den of iniquity' is a place of vice or crime.

And he swung at the boxing world—a 'den of inequity'—that refused to let him go, refused to let him stop being the man he didn't want to be.
National Post (Toronto) 13 June 2005: S4

(The word needed here is *iniquity*.)

The iniquity of the language situation was brought home to me in a very personal way about a decade ago.
National Post (Toronto) 4 April 2005: A20

(*Inequity* is the word needed here. The writer is decrying the lack of equal access to English-language education in Quebec.)

See also EQUALITY, EQUITY.

inexcusable   see -ABLE, -IBLE

in fact   see COMMA

infamous   see NOTORIOUS

infantile   see CHILDISH

infectious   see CONTAGIOUS

infer   see IMPLY

infernos   see -OS, -OES

infidel   see ATHEIST

infinitive   see SPLIT INFINITIVE; entry in Glossary

inflammable, inflammatory   see FLAMMABLE

inflatable   see -ABLE, -(AT)ABLE

inflection, inflected form   see entry in Glossary

inflict   see AFFLICT

informal   see COLLOQUIAL; FORMAL

informer, informant, source   Both *informer* and *informant* mean someone who provides information. *Informer* has negative connotations and is the usual choice when describing someone who gives information to police or other officials in exchange for money or favours. *Informant* is either neutral or positive in its connotations; for example, it is the usual term for someone who provides information to a researcher. Journalists usually call their informants *sources*.

> . . . an RCMP informer told of threats he had overheard to kidnap Canadiens players, somehow interpreted as Lafleur and me.
> Ken Dryden *The Game* 1983: 138

> An informant in Arkansas writes to say that the loons and geese wintering in that southern state have gathered their belongings and even now are flying north. . . .
> *Globe and Mail* (Toronto) 14 March 1985: M10

infrastructure   *Infrastructure* was first used in 1927 in reference to the Maginot Line, the defensive fortification built between 1929 and 1934 to defend France's northeastern boundary against German invasion. Although many language critics have criticized *infrastructure* as jargon or gobbledygook, it is now used in all types of writing to mean structural supporting elements. Some critics are wary of this word because of its broad application to everything from social structures to sewers. In contexts where the meaning of *infrastructure* is difficult to deduce, you may need to elaborate.

> It [job searching] can be one of the loneliest activities on earth unless there is emotional support as well as the infrastructure of an office, telephone answering service and secretarial facilities, etc.
> *Queen's Quarterly* 94.4 (1987): 864

> In addition to a large part of the population, the economic infrastructure was almost totally destroyed. Trains, buses, cars, banks, factories, post offices, power plants and a hydroelectric dam were dynamited, as well as schools, hospitals, market buildings, mosques, churches, pagodas, about one million houses and libraries.
> Henry M. Rosenthal and S. Cathy Berson, eds. *Canadian Jewish Outlook Anthology* 1988: 140

> Feminist writers, who began to create their own

institutional infrastructures, treated the feminine condition openly. . . .
> Ben-Z. Shek *French-Canadian & Québécois Novels* 1991: 87

> The mixed-farm economy gave rise to a socioeconomic infrastructure that is notably similar across much of North America, and remarkably enduring.
> *The Canadian Geographer* Spring 1989: 33

infringe   see IMPINGE

infuse   see IMBUE

ingenious, ingenuous, ingénue, disingenuous   Someone with the ability to find original solutions to problems is *ingenious*; such solutions themselves are also called *ingenious*. *Ingenuous* (pronounced *in JEN yoo us*) means frank or innocent, usually to the point of naïveté. The noun *ingénue* (usually pronounced *ahn zhay NOO* or *AN jen NOO*) can refer to an innocent young woman, or an actress playing such a character, or the part itself. Dictionaries list the word both with and without the accent; it need not be italicized. There is no male equivalent for this term.

Disingenuous, the opposite of *ingenuous*, is applied to people, actions, or statements that seem sincere but are in fact insincere or devious.

> And he proudly produced a tiny pocket flashlight set into a plastic heart and attached to a key-ring by some ingenious manufacturer in Taiwan.
> Constance Beresford-Howe *Night Studies* 1985: 165

> Dictionaries of music contain amusing accounts of ingenious machines which were designed to enable people who were not composers to write music.
> Robertson Davies *A Voice from the Attic* 1960: 316

> Its surprises come from its frank and ingenuous stating of things that everybody knows but rarely says.
> *Globe and Mail* (Toronto) 5 Oct. 1985: D14

> In faded jeans and with a student book-bag slung over her shoulder, she still suggests the all-Canadian ingenue.
> *Spectator* (Hamilton) 22 Dec. 1995: E4

Such comments are often written off as melodramatic or disingenuous, but in Wheeler's case, the comment is valid and entirely believable.
Vancouver Sun 3 June 2006: F2

. . . Subaru's disingenuous tribute to Volvo turns on the conceit that Subaru's brakes make it unnecessary for you to crash into concrete walls. The sly suggestion is that Volvo's sturdy frame is necessitated by a shoddy braking system.
Vancouver Sun 24 Nov. 1990: C2

ingratiate   *Ingratiate* is a reflexive verb: in other words, it is always used with a reflexive pronoun (*myself, himself,* etc.) To *ingratiate* oneself means to bring oneself into favour with someone or something else. Other people or things cannot be ingratiated. Thus 'He tried to ingratiate himself with his in-laws by cutting their grass' is idiomatic, but 'He tried to ingratiate his in-laws by cutting their grass', or 'He tried to ingratiate his dog with his in-laws', is not.

Herod's building projects were meant to reflect well on him and his dynasty, to curry favour with the population and to ingratiate himself with Rome.
Ottawa Citizen 15 Dec. 2005: A13

Now free to express their views, Whigs were still at times confined by strategic considerations, wishing to ingratiate the new order with as many fellow citizens as possible.
J.A.W. Gunn *Beyond Liberty and Property* 1983: 147

(This use of *ingratiate* is not idiomatic: 'make the new order appeal to' would be better.)

See also IMPLY; INSINUATE.

inhabitant   see CITIZEN

inhuman, inhumane   see HUMAN

inimical, inimitable, [inimicable]
Inimical means unfriendly. Something inimical to something else is unfavourable or injurious to it. *Inimitable* means defying or surpassing imitation. Although some usage guides accept *inimicable* as a rare but standard variant of *inim-*

ical, contemporary dictionaries do not list this spelling, and it is best avoided.

'Everything from the shameful wages of day-care workers to the isolation of the at-home mother is evidence of how . . . our culture remains inimical to children and to the people raising them.'
Ottawa Citizen 9 Nov. 1992: C1

There is also no doubt that, despite all reassurances to the contrary, such a [treatment] facility would be inimical to the community in which it is situated.
Harrowsmith Aug.–Sept. 1985: 31

One's own distinctive, inimitable style, she suggests, is 'the distillation of a lifetime of reading and listening, of selection and rejection'.
Janice Kulyk Keefer *Reading Mavis Gallant* 1989: 28

Set during World War II in French-ruled Morocco, Casablanca is the story of Rick (the inimitable, genre-defining Humphrey Bogart). . . .
Gazette (Montreal) 9 July 1992: E4

Buthelezi envisages the limitation of federal powers to the extent that they are inimicable to state laws, local control of taxation and a regional police force.
Gazette (Montreal) 10 Dec. 1992: B6

(The accepted spelling is *inimical*.)

See also -ABLE, -(AT)ABLE; -ABLE, -IBLE.

iniquity   see INEQUITY

initialism   see ABBREVIATION

injunction   see ENJOIN

in-laws, mother-in-law   *In-laws* is a generic term meaning relatives by marriage. The plural of *mother-in-law* is *mothers-in-law*, not *mother-in-laws*. This pattern also applies to *brothers-, sisters-,* and *fathers-in-law*.

They must build harmonious family relationships (which often centre on good relations with in-laws), do a heavy stint of housework, support their husbands' careers, and raise fine and talented children.
Canadian Journal of History 14.1 (1989): 153

. . . mothers-in-law drew high marks along with moms who apparently are conjuring up everything from perogies and quiche to Black Forest cake. . . .
Vancouver Sun 24 Oct. 1990: C1

'Sometimes you walk into offices on a sales call, and it's like walking into the Pick N Save of mother-in-laws. Everybody has a daughter, a friend's daughter, a neighbor they want to set you up with.'
Calgary Herald 3 Jan. 1992: A2

(The desirable bachelor quoted here should have used *mothers-in-law*).

in-migrate see EMIGRANT

innocent see PLEAD GUILTY

innocuous see IMMUNIZATION

Innu, Montagnais, Naskapi, Atikamekw
These people have traditionally called themselves *Innu* (more recently, the *Innu Nation*). Those living in Quebec are usually called *Montagnais-Naskapi* (the Montagnais live south of the Naskapi); those in Labrador, *Innu*. *Atikamekw* (sometimes spelled Attikameg) is another name used by some Innu. They are Indian, not Inuit, and live in northeastern Quebec and northern Labrador. Their traditional language, Montagnais-Naskapi, belongs to the Algonquian family.

The Naskapi-Montagnais Innu Association had asked the court to issue an injunction forcing the defence department to stop the controversial flights. . . .
Vancouver Sun 14 April 1990: A16

The Atikamekw and Montagnais claim 550,000 square kilometres of northeastern Quebec and another 150,000 square kilometres in Labrador. . . .
Gazette (Montreal) 22 Oct. 1992: A6

Labrador Innu have staged numerous protests at the base in recent years to express opposition to military training flights by NATO jets.
Calgary Herald 2 Dec. 1992: A6

. . . the Montagnais, who number about 11,000 in Quebec and are known as the Innu in Labrador, are running out of patience.
Toronto Star 24 Nov. 1992: A14

. . . Kashtin, the Quebec Montagnais duo who sing contemporary songs in the Innu language.
Ottawa Citizen 27 June 1991: D5

(Linguists refer to the language of the Innu as Montagnais-Naskapi.)

Flanked by a representative of Quebec's Grand Council of the Cree and the Conseil Atikamekw-Montagnais, [Konrad] Sioui said the forum isn't enough.
Gazette (Montreal) 8 Nov. 1990: A7

See also ABORIGINAL PEOPLE(S); INUIT; APPENDIX III.

innumerable see ENUMERABLE

innumerate see ILLITERATE

inoculation see IMMUNIZATION

input The verb *input*, meaning 'put in', upsets those language commentators who feel that shifting the preposition *in* to the front of the verb is completely unnecessary. Nevertheless, the verb is well established as a technical term in computing ('input data'), electronics, and economics. And Canadians rarely use this verb outside these contexts.

Some also object to the noun *input* meaning opinions or recommendations. This use is well established in the press, but rare in more formal writing.

inquire, enquire, inquiry, enquiry The preferred Canadian and American spelling is *inquire*, though *enquire* is occasionally used for all senses of the word.

British usage once distinguished the verbs *enquire* (seek information) and *inquire* (conduct a formal investigation). This distinction is not upheld in Canada, where *inquire* is widely used as a slightly formal synonym for *ask*.

However, Canadian writers do tend to distinguish the nouns *inquiry* and *enquiry*, preferring the former for legal or formal investigation and the latter for scholarly research or intellectual work.

I felt there was something about this trip I didn't

know and should but, when I obliquely inquired, I was put off with more laughter and leers.
Max Braithwaite *The Night We Stole the Mountie's Car* 1971: 154

. . . when she enquired about her package, a customs agent told her the book was being held to determine whether it was 'suitable' for entry into Canada.
Vancouver Sun 27 Dec. 1990: B1

The inquiry by a Royal Commission in Nova Scotia into the wrongful conviction of Donald Marshall Jr for murder raised the broader question of whether judges can be required to explain their reasons for particular decisions.
Andrew Heard *Canadian Constitutional Conventions* 1991: 126

Until quite recently musical aesthetics has been a monistic field of intellectual enquiry.
Queen's Quarterly 92.1 (1985): 218

in regard[s] to, with regard[s] to, as regards, regarding   Usage commentators are unanimous in their objection to the phrases *in regards to* and *with regards to*, considering them blends of the acceptable phrases *as regards* and *in* or *with regard to*. The disputed phrases occur most frequently in newspapers and magazines in quoted speech and letters to the editor. *With regards to* with an *s* is perfectly acceptable when it means 'with best wishes to'. Some critics consider both *in* and *with regard to* wordy and suggest using *regarding* instead.

'I don't think the committee was as well informed in regard to the recent violations of human rights in the Mohawk issue. . . .'
Gazette (Montreal) 25 Oct. 1990: A1

In regards to Betty Olson's Aug. 28 letter to the editor, I was under the impression that lottery profits were originally meant for hospitals and schools.
Province (Vancouver) 14 Sept. 1990: 56

(The standard expression is 'in regard to'.)

With regard to delays in getting government funding for the 478-unit Whistler athletes village, Fasel said he can't comment until the commission has met Whistler officials next week.
Province (Vancouver) 1 June 2006: A3

. . . the only matter science seems to agree on, with regards to global warming, is that the evidence is inconclusive.
Atlantic Salmon Journal Summer (1990): 5

(The standard expression is 'with regard to'.)

insanitary   see UNSANITARY

inscription   see QUEBEC ENGLISH

insidious, invidious   Something is *insidious* if its slow or subtle progress makes it seem less harmful than it actually is. Something *invidious* is likely to cause ill will because it is, or seems to be, unjust.

Meanwhile poverty, that insidious hired gunman of the state, stalks women daily.
Fuse Magazine 13.4 (1990): 9

Meanwhile, that colourless, invisible bacterial plaque continues to develop and work its way insidiously into the gumline.
Canadian Consumer Feb. 1986: 26

This leaves Canada in the invidious position of earnestly courting a brutal dictatorship, while shunning an emerging liberal democracy.
Calgary Herald 14 Oct. 2005: A28

. . . the authors have lapsed into invidious role stereotyping by identifying a particular workplace with a particular sex.
Canadian Bar Review 66.3 (1987): 670

'The only explanation I can give,' Skelton added, 'is that after the wrecking of the English Department it has been felt that it would be invidious not to wreck the Economics Department also.'
Frederick Gibson *Queen's University* 2 (1983): 57

insinuate   see IMPLY

in situ   *In situ*, 'in place', is a Latin borrowing. It is usually synonymous with *on site* in English, but it also has a special medical meaning: a cancer that has not spread from its original location to other parts of the body is said to be *in situ*. The phrase should be italicized in formal writing. Used as an adjective before a noun, *in situ*, like other Latin phrases, is not hyphenated.

Once there, Galileo will deploy a probe into Jupiter's liquid and gas atmosphere to make in situ measurements of the chemical and physical forces at work.
Vancouver Sun 4 Aug. 1990: B6

Results from transplant studies are often more convincing than in situ studies because they are the product of an experimental rather than an observational approach.
Canadian Journal of Zoology 67.4 (1989): 855

. . . fewer than 100 cases of carcinoma in situ (considered a non-invasive cervical cancer) were reported to the registry.
Globe and Mail (Toronto) 22 Jan. 1985: M2

See also LATIN PHRASES.

insofar as, inasmuch as, [insomuch as]
Insofar and *inasmuch* are written as one word. *Insofar as* means to the extent that and is more common than *inasmuch as*, which usually means since or because, but may also mean to the extent that. *Insomuch as* is an archaic variant of both expressions.

Success, insofar as it appears in modern fiction, is given a wry turn.
Robertson Davies *A Voice from the Attic* 1960: 71

Once developed, a learning system provides student-friendliness inasmuch as it outlines the scope of programs and courses they will undertake and the criteria by which they will be evaluated. . . .
Education Canada Summer (1989): 33–5

insoluble   see SOLUBLE

[insomuch as]   see INSOFAR AS

in spite of   see DESPITE

in spite of the fact that   see WORDINESS

instil, instill   see IMBUE; -L, -LL

insure, ensure, assure   If you *insure* something, such as a house or a car, you take out an insurance policy on it so that you will be compensated in the event of loss, damage, or liabil-

ity. If you *ensure* something, you verify that it is so, or you take steps to make certain that it will happen: 'I ensured that the company was reputable'; 'Our lawyer will ensure that our rights are not violated'. In the past, *insure* and *ensure* were mere spelling variants, but in contemporary Canadian and British English the two spellings usually have these distinct meanings. Many American writers use the spelling *insure* for all senses, but *ensure* is current there too.

One thing can *assure* another thing, meaning make it inevitable: 'Her wealth assured her welcome'. More commonly, *assure* is used with both a personal subject and a personal object: someone *assures* someone of something, meaning someone tells someone that something is certain: 'They assured us of jobs'; 'They assured us that the barking would stop'. A few usage guides treat *ensure* and *assure* as interchangeable. While there are contexts in which either word is correct, there is always a slight difference in meaning between the two. *Ensure* emphasizes action, taking steps, while *assure* emphasizes inevitability, removing doubt.

When one insures his life, he enters into a contract of insurance with an insurance company.
J.E. Smyth et al. *The Law and Business Administration in Canada* 1987: 290

He asked Mr. Timbrell what he would do, as premier, to ensure that 'all people are treated equally' and no one has special rights.
Globe and Mail (Toronto) 16 Jan. 1985: P5

'Quotas in school admissions and job hiring should be used to insure black representation.'
Neil Nevitte and Roger Gibbins *New Elites in Old States* 1990: 110

(The usual Canadian spelling is *ensure*. This sentence is quoted from an American source.)

The recent election of Abraham Lincoln to the presidency seemed to assure the break-up of the American union.
William Teatero *John Anderson: Fugitive Slave* 1986: 75

For one thing, Descartes assures us, his altered state was not the result of inebriation: he had not drunk wine for three months before.
Canadian Journal of Philosophy 19 (1989): 214

intact, [in tact] *Intact* means whole, unbroken: 'The windshield remained intact despite the accident'. *Intact* is sometimes mistakenly spelled as two words: *in tact*. The two-word phrase might legitimately appear in a sentence on good social judgment: 'He surpassed his friends in tact'. Otherwise, it should be kept intact.

> Arrows were often recovered intact rather than broken into numerous pieces, as was common in the dart sample.
> *Arctic* 57.3 (2004): 260–72

> Apparently, interior designers take courses in tact.
> *Calgary Herald* 7 Jan. 2005: SW18

> The art is in making the new parts fit seamlessly into the old ones, while keeping . . . the bone and connective tissues in tact.
> *Vancouver Sun* 14 July 2003: C1

(Here *intact* is the proper spelling.)

integral see MISPRONUNCIATION

intelligent, intellectual, intelligentsia, IQ An *intelligent* person is quick of mind; an *intellectual* person, in addition to being intelligent, enjoys exercising his or her mental abilities. The noun *intellectual* sometimes carries a derogatory connotation of self-conscious superiority and lack of practicality.

The collective noun *intelligentsia* was coined in mid-nineteenth century Russia, where it referred to a reform-minded class of society consisting of educated thinkers. In English it now refers, often derisively, to any group of highly educated people in a society. *Intelligentsia* is pronounced *in tel i JENT see uh* or occasionally *in tel i GENT see uh*, with a hard *g* as in *get*.

IQ (Intelligence Quotient) is a number used as a measure of intelligence and calculated from the score obtained on standard tests that are intended to measure innate intelligence rather than acquired knowledge. Though designed to be universally applicable, IQ tests have been criticized as skewed in favour of those from the dominant social and cultural groups.

Part of that price has been the resignation of literary taste, by the intelligent reading public, into the hands of professionals, of experts, of an intelligentsia.
Robertson Davies A Voice from the Attic 1960: 34

intense, intensive Something may be *intense* (strong, acute, extreme, forceful) without being *intensive* (highly concentrated or focused). Normally, *intense* modifies such things as feelings, colours, and sensations: 'intense anger', 'intense red', 'intense heat'. *Intensive* often modifies processes or regimens: 'intensive farming', 'intensive training', 'intensive study'. In phrases such as 'labour-intensive' and 'capital-intensive' *intensive* means requiring a great deal of.

> So intense were the flames that the workmen did not bother to use the doors; they got out through the windows.
> J.E. Smyth et al. *The Law and Business Administration in Canada* 1987: 430

> His flushed complexion and twitching nose, I was soon to discover, were tell-tale signs of intense annoyance.
> George Ignatieff *The Making of a Peacemonger* 1987: 172

> The latter got the most cursory once-over; the former—especially the Blacks—were subjected to intensive medical examinations, which in some cases were fraudulent.
> Pierre Berton *The Promised Land* 1984: 183

> Feore doesn't feel that his intensive homework for a role should be considered something bizarre.
> *Toronto Star* 27 May 2006: H1

> The psychophysiological effects of wine are increasingly the object of intensive scientific scrutiny—with some mildly startling discoveries.
> *Bon Vivant* Nov. 1981: 13

(Here either word would make sense.)

See also INTENTS AND PURPOSES, TO (FOR) ALL.

intenseness see -NESS

intensifier, intensify see entry in Glossary

intents and purposes, to (for) all The phrase *to* (or *for*) *all intents and purposes* has been criticized as longwinded. It may, however, suit the rhythm of the sentence. Where compression is desired, *in effect* is more succinct. Occasionally people write 'to (*or* for) all intensive purposes', an error that indicates they have probably heard this cliché more often than they have read it.

> For all intents and purposes, a majority government rules with the authority of a dictatorship for up to five years.
> *Vancouver Sun* 19 Oct. 1990: A17

(Here *in effect* could be substituted)

> . . . a peacekeeping force had become more or less a permanent fixture, and the armistice line had evolved, to all intents and purposes, into an international frontier.
> George Ignatieff *The Making of a Peacemonger* 1987: 238

(Here 'had *in effect* evolved' or 'had evolved into a *de facto* international frontier' might be better.)

> 'For all intensive purposes, it hasn't really been seen since 1998.'
> *Daily News* (Halifax) 20 April 2002: 29

(The phrase is *for all intents and purposes*.)

See also MISHEARD EXPRESSIONS.

inter see INTERN

inter-, intra- The prefix *inter-* means between; *intra-* means within. For example, *intercontinental* trade occurs between different continents, whereas *intracontinental* trade occurs within one continent.

> 'The intramural athletic competitions,' reported the director of physical education in 1943, 'have, during the past season, attracted more competitors than ever before.' A year later Principal Wallace noted the same phenomenon: 'There has been a very great increase in the active interest that the individual student has taken in sport during the years when intercollegiate athletics has not been possible.'
> Frederick Gibson *Queen's University* 2 (1983): 187

(The term *intramural* means within the walls of a single institution; *intercollegiate* means between colleges or universities.)

See also HYPHENATION.

intercede see -CEED, -CEDE, -SEDE

interface An *interface* is the surface that forms the boundary between and connects two regions. The word, which dates from the late 1800s, is now often used figuratively. It is also used as a technical term in computing to refer to a device or software that allows information to be passed from one system or program to another. Some object to its appearance as a verb outside the context of computing. Most occurrences of *interface* as a verb in published Canadian texts are in quotations of speech; although *interface* is a perfectly reputable noun, use of the same word as a verb is still disputed.

> [Pheasants] are creatures of the edges, of the interface between woods and meadow, birds that feed in the open spaces but take refuge in the undergrowth of thick brush.
> *Harrowsmith* Jun.–Jul. 1985: 53

> Shah and Parikh represent the new generation of South Asian dancers who perform at the interface of east and west—tradition and innovation.
> *Vancouver Sun* 16 May 1994: C1

> Members also approved a motion to set up a task force to 'make recommendation to the Board of Governors regarding the interface and relationship' between the foundation and its local membership.
> *Canadian Heritage Magazine* Feb.–Mar. 1986: 8

> The product can interface with any type of computer including PCs, laptops and handheld data collectors, printing on whatever surface.
> *Computing Canada* 1 March 1991: 41

> Mr. Mulroney's aide Fred Doucet called Miss MacDonald one of several staff members who 'interface with the children'.
> *Globe and Mail* (Toronto) 20 March 1985: P4

> He was astounded to learn that another man is paid in excess of $200,000 a year to actually run the railroad, with Mr. Smith expected to keep order at the board meetings and 'interface' with the federal government.
> *Vancouver Sun* 2 Jan. 1990: B1

(Here the writer is using quotation marks to distance himself or herself from the verb *interface*.)

See also FUNCTIONAL SHIFT.

intern, inter   To *intern* is to place in detention. To *inter* is to bury.

> By the time the RCMP's two-day sweep of Montreal's Little Italy district was over, 2,400 Italian males—some no older than 16—had been rounded up and 236 of them were interned.
> *Gazette* (Montreal) 10 June 1994: A4

(The reference is to the internment of 'enemy aliens' during the Second World War.)

> John Montagu's life disproves the adage that the evil men do lives after them while the good is oft interred with their bones.
> *Toronto Star* 18 June 1994: L7

> Michiko Ayukawa, a 65-year-old women's historian and PhD candidate who was interred with the rest of her Japanese family in the Second World War, says she spent four decades assimilating, being anglo, living in the suburbs.
> *Times-Colonist* (Victoria) 20 June 1995: C6

(The word required here is *interned*.)

internecine   The adjective *internecine* (pronounced *in tur NEE sign* or *seen*) is used to describe destructive conflict between people one would expect to be allies. Interestingly, this standard current use of the word is at odds with its etymological roots. The word is derived from the Latin verb *internecare*, 'to exterminate or slaughter'. Here *inter-* does not have the usual meaning of between or among; it is a separate prefix used in a number of Latin verbs to denote destruction. Originally, in English, *internecine* was used in its Latin sense to describe murderous, bloody conflict. However, in his *Dictionary of the English Language* (1755) Samuel Johnson defined the word as meaning 'mutually destructive'. Johnson's definition soon gained ground. As Fowler points out, English has many synonyms for *slaughter*, but no word with this particular meaning. Here is a rare instance in which language commentators have given more authority to custom than to etymology.

> The Zulus had abandoned the south and were occupied in internecine wars (in what is now Zimbabwe) which left 1.1 million dead at the hands of their brothers.
> *Globe and Mail* (Toronto) 23 March 1985: P7

> The best thing that could happen out of all the internecine squabbling between standardbred and thoroughbred horsemen over post times would be that the harness people carry out their threat to split from the Ontario Jockey Club.
> *Globe and Mail* (Toronto) 24 Jan. 1985: P22

> Such integration was ordered by the U.S. Securities and Exchange Commission to put an end to the internecine rivalries between regional exchanges—rivalries which have been all too frequent in Canada.
> *Gazette* (Montreal) 3 March 1989: D6

See also INTER-, INTRA-.

Internet   see COMPUTER TERMS

interpretive, interpretative   Both adjectives are accepted, although many critics prefer *interpretative*, arguing that it follows the Latin formation of the word. Canadian writers use the briefer *interpretive* more often.

> Today the restored defense site is a small park, marked with interpretive signs and open free of charge every day from May through mid-October.
> Alan Tucker, ed. *The Penguin Guide to Canada* 1991: 276

> Reading is my theme, and reading is a private, interpretative art.
> Robertson Davies *A Voice from the Attic* 1960: 8

interrogate   see QUEBEC ENGLISH

into, in to   To turn a lost handbag *in to* a police officer is a virtuous act; to turn a lost handbag *into* a police officer would require supernatural powers. In the first phrase, the *in* is part of a phrasal verb, *turn in* (meaning to hand over), and *to* is a preposition whose object is *police officer*. In the second phrase, *into* belongs to the phrasal verb *turn into* (meaning to transform). Writers seldom have any difficulty with expressions such as these. However, if you are suddenly seized by doubt, you can simply look the base verb up in a dictionary: phrasal verbs are usually listed at the end of the definitions.

See also IN, INTO; PHRASAL VERBS.

intonation see entry in Glossary

intra- see INTER-, INTRA-

intrude, obtrude To *intrude* means to thrust in and to *obtrude* means to stick out, but these two verbs are now synonymous in the sense of imposing oneself without warrant or welcome. A distinction of sense is maintained in the adjectives: something *intrusive* is invasive or unwelcome, while something *obtrusive* is noticeable enough to be bothersome.

> An estimated 300 donkeys roam the smallest of the three main U.S. Virgin Islands. They knock over garbage cans, chew up gardens, wake people in the night, intrude on campers. . . .
> *Gazette* (Montreal) 4 March 1989: I14

> Long before TV or the telephone, the privacy of the home in Poe's day was being obtruded upon by the public street light. . . .
> *Globe and Mail* (Toronto) 20 Feb. 1985: P7

> The Tory retreat from a more intrusive government has been dictated in large measure by the harsh imperative of the deficit and the debt, and by the need to keep business competitive.
> *Financial Post* 4 March 1991: 11

> Most of the time the motor is relatively unobtrusive.
> *Financial Post* 7 June 1991: 42

Inuit, Inuk, Inuktitut, Inuvialuit, Eskimo, Inupiat, Inupiaq The Indigenous people of the Canadian Arctic prefer to be called *Inuit* (singular *Inuk*), the word meaning 'the people' in their language, *Inuktitut*. The Inuit Circumpolar Conference formally established the use of *Inuit* in 1977, although Inuit political organizations had used the term earlier. The Inuit of the Mackenzie Delta in the western Arctic call themselves the *Inuvialuit*. The Inuit and Inuvialuit were formerly called *Eskimos*, a word that is thought to be derived from an expression in an Algonquian language meaning 'eaters of raw meat'. The word *Eskimo* is still used in historical references, in the name of Edmonton's Canadian Football League team,

and to refer to one breed of the large northern sled dog popularly known as the husky.

Inuit is sometimes spelled with two *n*'s. The singular form *Inuk*, which refers to one person, is becoming more familiar to English writers. The adjectival use of *Inuit* is acceptable ('Inuit art'), but note that neither *Inuk* nor *Inuit* should be pluralized with an *s*. According to the national organization representing Inuit in Canada, Inuit Tapiriit Kanatami, the preferred use of the noun *Inuit* (meaning 'the people') is without *the* or *people*: 'Inuit (rather than 'the Inuit' or 'the Inuit people') harvested marine mammals in every season'.

The term *Inuit* is not completely accepted in Alaska, where *Eskimo* is still current. Only one of the four linguistic groups in Alaska identifies with the label *Inuit*. This one group may be called Inuit or *Inupiat*; their language is *Inupiaq*. (The three other groups are Central Yupik, Alutiiq or Pacific Yupik, and Siberian Yupik.)

> In general the Inuit are known for their engaging sense of humour, their sharing. . . .
> *Arctic* 41.1 (1988): 76

(*Inuit* without *the* is now preferred.)

> But Robert Aknavigak, an Inuk from Cambridge Bay on the Arctic Ocean, said he was for the Hamilton Tiger Cats because 'I like cheering for the underdog.'
> *Globe and Mail* (Toronto) 25 Nov. 1985: C3

> Of the council's 27 regional members, there are only three women—a black, an Inuit and a Metis—who step outside the usual mold of women and men appointed by the government to the CACSW.
> *Gazette* (Montreal) 28 Dec. 1990: B5

(The accepted singular form is *Inuk*.)

> And yesterday marked the day when George Erasmus, national chief of the Assembly of First Nations, launched his own uphill battle in London to educate West Europeans about the claims of the anti-fur campaign and how it threatens the single most important source of independent income for the majority of Indians, Inuits and Metis in Canada, Alaska and Greenland.
> *Globe and Mail* (Toronto) 4 Oct. 1985: A9

(The preferred plural is *Inuit*.)

Eva Deer does not buy the stereotype of the downtrodden Inuk female.
Vancouver Sun 21 June 1990: 36

(The accepted adjectival form is *Inuit*.)

The fisheries department will change regulations to permit the harvest of bowhead whales, if the hunters are Inuvialuit, the waters Canadian, and the total catch within limits set by the International Whaling Commission for aboriginal subsistence use.
Ottawa Citizen 29 Dec. 1990: A5

The 37 pieces of 'early' Inuit sculpture at the embassy date from the middle of this century, when James Houston and the Canadian Handicrafts Guild began to promote traditional Eskimo carvings.
Ottawa Citizen 29 Aug. 1992: H9

In some parts of Newfoundland, Eskimo dogs—even cross-breeds—are forbidden.
Dogs in Canada 1986: 19

Animal names, previously rendered by phrases such as 'something for doing the act dogs do when pulling a sled' to describe a horse, are now translated by their Inuktitut equivalents.
Ottawa Citizen 7 April 1990: J7

See ABORIGINAL PEOPLE(S); INNU; INUKSHUK, INUKSUK, INUKSUIT; NUNAVUT, NUNAVUMMIUT, DENENDEH; APPENDIX III.

inukshuk, inuksuk, inuksuit   An *inukshuk* (pronounced *i NOOK shook*) is a cairn of stacked stones in the shape of a person, used by Inuit as a guidepost or commemorative marker. Literally, *inuksuk* means 'in the capacity of a person', and this Inuktitut word contains the word for person: *inuk*. Two spelling are acceptable: the more common one with an 'h', *inukshuk*, reinforces the pronunciation, while *inuksuk* preserves the Inuktitut spelling. Either spelling may be pluralized with an 's'. *Inuksuit* is the alternative Inuktitut plural: note the parallel with *Inuit*, the plural form of *Inuk*.

Off to the edge of the tarmac, a sentinel bore quiet witness to the scene. It was a traditional Inuit Inukshuk, a crude stone statue in the shape of a man.
Leader-Post (Regina) 24 April 2006: A1

See also INUIT, INUK, INUKTITUT, INUVIALUIT, ESKIMO, INUPIAT, INUPIAQ.

inveigle, inveigh   To *inveigle* someone is to lure him or her by deception or flattery *into* something. To *inveigh* is to protest or complain bitterly *against* something or someone. *Inveigle* is pronounced *in VAY gul* or *in VEE gul*. *Inveigh* rhymes with *weigh*. These terms are seldom confused, though they are occasionally misused.

She was just strange and impulsive enough to order Dick killed out of pique, and she was unquestionably persuasive enough to inveigle B——— and her father into the plot.
Jack Batten *Robinette* 1984: 66

Abandoning vocal finesse, they mumble those opening dirges of boredom, emptiness and crushed dreams that inveigle so many directors (and, we briefly fear, this one too).
Globe and Mail (Toronto) 23 Feb. 1985: M8

(The verb *inveigle* is always followed by *into* or *to*; perhaps the writer meant *seduce*.)

More surprisingly, the government press in these years inveighed against the 'rabble'. . . .
J.A.W. Gunn *Beyond Liberty and Property* 1983: 102

See also -IE-, -EI-.

invidious   see INSIDIOUS

invite   Usage commentators are unanimous in viewing the noun *invite*, the clipped form of *invitation*, as slang or informal, even though the *OED* reveals that it has been in use for over three centuries. Some words remain informal no matter how long they have been in use; the noun *invite* is largely restricted to breezy journalism.

Whereas one short year ago, buyers and press would cheerfully have killed for an invite, last season's attendance was merely lacklustre. . . .
Globe and Mail (Toronto) 22 Jan. 1985: F6

To add to the confusion, the invite says 'Black Tie Optional or Period Costume.'
Province (Vancouver) 6 Sept. 1990: F23

invited guest Commentators have criticized the phrase *invited guest* as redundant. However, judging from the mail to Dear Abby, many people see themselves as the reluctant hosts of uninvited guests. Thus the expression may be useful in distinguishing between solicited and unsolicited visitors. It's also appropriate in descriptions of events where the general public is welcome or at least permitted, but where some people have received personal invitations.

> But Paul George, an invited guest at the ceremony and the founder of the Western Canada Wilderness Committee, was skeptical. . . .
> *Calgary Herald* 5 Dec. 1992: B10

(Paul George received a special invitation to a public ceremony.)

> On a given night some hundreds of invited guests assembled in Convocation Hall at eight o'clock.
> Hilda Neatby *Queen's University* 1 (1978): 145

(Here the qualifier *invited* indicates that invitations were issued.)

> The great thing about a prom is the fact that . . . all the invited guests know each other well and are of approximately the same age.
> *Ottawa Citizen* 5 May 1994: E1

(Here *invited* could well be omitted.)

in vitro, in vivo *In vitro* and *in vivo* are Latin expressions commonly used in scientific writing to describe the conditions under which an experiment is conducted. Literally, *in vitro* means 'in glass'; *in vivo* means 'in life'. An *in vitro* experiment is carried out in simulated conditions in a laboratory, whereas an *in vivo* test or experiment takes place in a living system, such as an animal or a natural ecosystem. The term 'in vitro fertilization' has become common recently in press reports about reproductive technologies. In this procedure, an egg cell is removed from a woman's body and fertilized in a glass dish in which the necessary chemical and physical conditions are provided to sustain it temporarily until it can be implanted in the uterus. Both terms should be italicized in formal writing.

> . . . the responsible selective mechanism might be directly associated with the changes that occur during the rapid development of plant tissues and organs both in vitro and in vivo.
> *Canadian Journal of Botany* 67.4 (1989): 985

> Today, from the IUD and the pill to artificial insemination and in vitro fertilization, women have better, if not perfect, means of controlling their own fertility.
> *Chatelaine* April 1986: 48

See also LATIN PHRASES, FOREIGN PHRASES.

invoke see EVOKE

inward(s) see -WARD(S)

IQ see INTELLIGENT

Ireland, Irish Republic, Eire, Irish Free State, Northern Ireland, Ulster, Hibernian The island of Ireland has been divided into two political entities since 1920. *Ireland* often refers to the whole island.

The larger southern part of the island officially became the *Republic of Ireland* (less formally, the *Irish Republic*, or just the *Republic*) in 1949, when it withdrew from the British Commonwealth. Sometimes it is still called *Eire*, which was its official name from 1937 to 1949. *Eire* (pronounced *AIR ah* or *IRE ah*) is the Gaelic word for *Ireland*. This name may be chosen to distinguish the Republic from the north, or for its Gaelic flavour, but writers should note that its significance may be lost on Canadian readers. When the southern region was first given the status of a dominion, in 1921, it was called the *Irish Free State*; this name is no longer in use.

The smaller northern section of the island and its name are contested. Unionists, who wish it to remain part of the United Kingdom, refer to it by its official name, *Northern Ireland*, or as 'Ulster'; Republicans, who regard it as an integral part of the Irish Republic, refer to it as 'the North' or 'the six counties'. Before the political division of Ireland in 1949, the northernmost province, Ulster, contained nine counties. Now six of those counties constitute 'the North' or 'Northern Ireland' and the remaining three lie within the boundary of the Republic. When 'Ulster' is mentioned in the Republic, mainly in the context of sports, it refers to the whole of the historical province.

The adjective *Hibernian*, meaning 'of or about Ireland', is derived from the Latin name for the island.

> When the famine in Ireland drove thousands of farmers to Canada, a typhus epidemic broke out.
> *Chronicle-Telegraph* (Quebec) 7 Oct. 1991: 11

(Here *Ireland* refers to the island as a whole.)

> But he personified the aspirations of his compatriots, and somehow he succeeded in preventing Cyprus from becoming another Ireland.
> George Ignatieff *The Making of a Peacemonger* 1987: 216

(Here *Ireland* refers to a divided country.)

> Three members of the Ulster Resistance Movement, a right-wing loyalist paramilitary organization in Northern Ireland, were arrested in Paris for attempting to exchange a surface-to-air missile for South African weapons.
> *Briarpatch* Dec. 1989–Jan. 1990: 26

> To date, the hangup has been not how to arrange self rule, but getting the North's nationalists (Catholics) and unionists (Protestants) to agree to sit down with each other and representatives of the Irish Republic and the British government.
> *Vancouver Sun* 8 Dec. 1990: B8

> Seven years after the Belfast Agreement committed the republican movement in Northern Ireland to pursue political and constitutional change by 'exclusively peaceful and democratic means,' the Provisional IRA yesterday declared a formal end to its armed campaign. . . .
> *National Post* (Toronto) 30 July 2005: A16

> The same kind of play is to be found in McWhirter's other fiction . . . [and] it clearly links McWhirter with his Hibernian roots.
> *Canadian Fiction Magazine* 89 (1994): 42

See also BRITAIN.

iridescent   *Iridescent*, meaning luminous and rainbow-like, is often misspelled with two *r*'s. It

is derived from the Latin word *iris*, 'rainbow'.

Irish bull   see MALAPROPISM

Irish coffee   see CAPITAL LETTERS

Irish Free State, Irish Republic   see IRELAND

ironic, ironical   see -IC, -ICAL

Iroquois, Six Nations, Iroquoian   *Iroquois* originated as the name of a confederacy of Aboriginal groups living in what is now northern New York State; the Iroquois Confederacy was also called the Five Nations (Seneca, Cayuga, Oneida, Onondaga, and Mohawk). When the Tuscarora joined in the early eighteenth century, the Iroquois Confederacy became known as the *Six Nations*. The Six Nations, with the exception of the Oneida, supported the British during the American War of Independence, and after that war many moved north to Canada. Members of the Six Nations may be called Iroquois, although they also identify themselves as Mohawk, Tuscarora, etc.

Iroquoian is the name of a language family: the six different languages of the Six Nations are all Iroquoian. *Iroquoian* is also used as an adjective to refer to members of the Six Nations or their ancestors.

> The Six Nations Confederacy negotiators, who have been a moderating force, flatly rejected proposals Thursday by the federal and provincial governments and allied themselves . . . with the Mohawks trapped in Kanesatake.
> *Vancouver Sun* 7 Sept. 1990: A8

> The spokesman said the Mohawks' Six Nations Iroquois Confederacy passports were accepted by most West European countries.
> *Province* (Vancouver) 25 Oct. 1990: 42

> There is a large variety of native languages, including the major families of Algonkian (Cree, Ojibway), Athapaskan (Dene), Inuktitut (Eskimo), Iroquoian, and others.
> *Queen's Quarterly* 94.3 (1987): 668

> Iroquoian cultural ambassadors promise to add some excitement to the annual Shondecti, or rendezvous, at Midland's living history site, Sainte-

Marie-among-the-Hurons.
Globe and Mail (Toronto) 13 July 1985: T3

See also ABORIGINAL PEOPLE(S); APPENDIX III.

[irregardless]   see REGARDLESS

irreparable   see -ABLE, -IBLE; REPAIRABLE

irrespective   see REGARDLESS

irresponsible   see -ABLE, -IBLE

is   see ADJECTIVES AND ADVERBS; AGREEMENT, GRAM-
MATICAL; AIN'T, AREN'T I

-ise   see -IZE

Islam, Muslim, Moslem, Muhammed, Koran, Qur'an, [Mohammedan], Mecca

Islam, which means 'surrender to God' in Arabic, is the name of one of the major world religions. Its adherents, called *Muslims*, worship Allah and revere Muhammed, his prophet. Their holy book is the *Koran*.

Moslem is an older variant of *Muslim*; the latter is now preferred. *Muhammed* is preferred to *Mohammed* in the United States and Britain, although *Mohammed* is retained in the names of historical figures. Canadians still use *Mohammed* about as often as *Muhammed*. Although *Qur'an*, a variant spelling for *Koran*, is closer to the Arabic, it has not replaced *Koran*.

Mohammedan is a term sometimes used for Muslims; however, since it incorrectly implies that they worship Muhammed, not Allah, it is considered inappropriate.

The terms Arab and Muslim are not synonymous (see ARABIC). Islam has adherents all over the world.

Muslim and *Islamic* are both used as adjectives, *Islamic* most often in reference to religious law.

Mecca, in Saudi Arabia, is the birthplace of Muhammed and the site of religious pilgrimages. Muslims face Mecca (which is not necessarily to the east) when they pray. Some usage guides point out that to use the word *mecca* to refer to sites of more secular pilgrimage—as in 'Las Vegas is a mecca for gamblers'—trivializes Islam.

> Najmuddin Shaikh, ambassador from Pakistan and spokesman for the Islamic nations with representatives in Canada, said there is a general feeling among Muslims that Rushdie's book has made a joke of Islam and created contempt and hatred in the West for followers of the Prophet Mohammed.
> *Gazette* (Montreal) 2 March 1989: B1

> As a relatively nascent population of immigrants and first-generation Canadians, most have come to this country to escape persecution, seek an education and to have a better life—things which most individuals of the Muslim community treasure and appreciate probably more than those who have been here for generations.
> *Toronto Star* 8 June 2006: A25

See also ARABIC, ARAB, ARABIAN; GOD; SACRED WRITINGS.

-ism   The suffix -*ism* has a number of established uses. It identifies an action or practice (*fetishism, snobbism, cannibalism*), a state or condition (*alcoholism, dwarfism, optimism*), a doctrine or belief (*monotheism, Judaism, Darwinism*), or a specific linguistic usage (*Canadianism, euphemism, witticism*).

Recently, a number of new -*isms* have established themselves, modelled on words, such as *racism* and *sexism*, that name a basis of discrimination. These include *able-bodyism* (discrimination against people who are physically disabled), *agism* or *ageism* (discrimination based on age), *lookism* (discrimination on the basis of physical appearance), *heterosexism* (discrimination in favour of heterosexuals, and implicitly against homosexuals), and *speciesism* (discrimination against certain species, usually a reference to human exploitation of animals). This new use of the -*ism* suffix is prolific and appears well-established in informal North American English.

When an -*ism* word is formed from a proper name it retains the initial capital: for example, *Marxism, Mormonism, Platonism.*

Several *-isms* appear frequently in academic and media commentaries on Canadian culture and politics: *biculturalism, bilingualism, federalism, multiculturalism, regionalism.*

> Atwood had risen to speak when everyone else had addressed the meeting sitting down. 'I suffer from heightism,' Atwood explained.
> *Chatelaine* June 1986: 100

> So we've developed laws against such things as racism and sexism. But now we must deal with a new form of discrimination: 'agism.'
> Richard Davies and Glen Kirkland, eds. *Dimensions* 1986: 76

> . . . racism, sexism, homophobia, able-bodyism, ageism—they are all about invasion.
> *Room of One's Own* June 1990: 45

> What Singer has done singularly is to give a name—speciesism—to the flawed intellectual reasoning that sanctions the slaughter of an estimated 10 million animals a day for food and several million a year by experimenters. Speciesism joins two other scourge isms of the 20th century—racism and sexism—as unresolved torments imposed by the powerful on the weak.
> *Vancouver Sun* 9 June 1990: B5

See also -IST, -ALIST.

Israeli, Israelite   see JEW

Issei, Nisei, Sansei, Yonsei   These words, borrowed from Japanese, are plural nouns referring to different generations of people of Japanese descent in North America. The first wave of Japanese immigrants to Canada and the United States in the late nineteenth and early twentieth centuries are referred to as *Issei* (pronounced *EE say*), meaning first-generation. Children born of Issei are known as *Nisei* (*NEE say*). A third generation of Japanese Canadians, born mostly in the 1950s and 1960s of Nisei parents, are called *Sansei* (*SAN say*). Although, according to statistics, more than 90 per cent of the Sansei have married outside the Japanese community, the children of both mixed and unmixed Sansei marriages are called *Yonsei* (*YON say*), fourth-generation. These Japanese

words are always capitalized in Canadian writing; they are understood most widely in areas where many Japanese Canadians live, such as British Columbia.

> Included in this wholesale confiscation was the property of Issei, naturalized Japanese-Canadian veterans of the First World War, 54 of whose names can be found on the Vimy Ridge Memorial and scattered Canadian graves in France as well as the memorial in Stanley Park, Vancouver.
> *Globe and Mail* (Toronto) 20 April 1985: P7

> Every spring, the ranks of San Francisco's 12,500 residents of Japanese descent are swelled by thousands of Nisei, Sansei and Yonsei from all over northern California.
> *Globe and Mail* (Toronto) 13 April 1985: T9

> 'We Issei first-generation Canadians couldn't do the work of the young people, the Nisei second-generation and Sansei third-generation.'
> *Vancouver Sun* 22 March 1990: A15

See also GENERATION.

-ist, -alist   An adherent to an *-ism* can usually be indicated by changing the *-ism* to *-ist*: someone who believes in transcendentalism is a transcendentalist; a person who practises Buddhism is a Buddhist; a proponent of federalism is a federalist. The *-ist* suffix is also used to identify a person with particular qualities or beliefs (*conformist, conventionalist, idealist*), to name someone working in a particular artistic style, area of interest, or discipline (*impressionist, philatelist, physicist*), and to designate someone who is proficient on a musical instrument (*cellist, guitarist, violinist*). Recently the *-ist* ending has come to designate someone who practises a certain type of discrimination, as in *sexist* or *racist*. Note that any final vowel is dropped when combined with *-ist*: *futurist, pianist, propagandist.*

Some words can be formed with either the *-ist* or the *-alist* ending: for example, *agricultur(al)ist, education(al)ist, horticultur(al)ist.* Which form to use in such cases is largely a matter of preference. But see NATURALIST, NATURIST.

Thus the defeat of Menaud following the death of

his son . . . becomes a harsh blow to nature in favour of culture, in this case the agriculturalist, right-wing nationalist ideology.
Ben-Z. Shek *French-Canadian & Québécois Novels* 1991: 23

District agriculturist Bill Smith said yesterday it appears average yield losses in the country could be between $123 and $247 a hectare.
Globe and Mail (Toronto) 24 July 1985: P8

Funds continue to come in . . . and will be used to create an Amelia Hall award for educationists in the festival's Young Company program.
Globe and Mail (Toronto) 8 May 1985: P19

Gerald Graham . . . hailed the advent of a principal 'who is not only an administrator but a superb scholar—who is incapable of talking the jargon of the educationalist'. . . .
Frederick Gibson *Queen's University* 2 (1983): 306

Expert horticulturalist Trevor Cole recommends that imported plants . . . have excess fertilizers flushed out of their soil.
Canadian Consumer Jan. 1986: 14

Mr. Sherk, a horticulturist, is also the president of the new Trillium chapter of The Beer Can Collectors of America. . . .
Globe and Mail (Toronto) 4 May 1985: A3

Sexists violate the principle of equality by favoring the interests of their own sex. Similarly, speciesists allow the interests of their own species to override the greater interests of members of other species.
Vancouver Sun 9 June 1990: B5

See also -ISM; NATURALIST, NATURIST.

is when, is where   Many usage experts describe definitions containing *is when* or *is where* as immature and unsophisticated. The grammatical objection is to following the verb *to be* with an adverb clause rather than a noun phrase or noun clause. In writing, constructions such as 'A strike is when people refuse to work' should not be used except to represent speech. The disputed usage can be avoided by replacing the verb *to be* with *to occur* ('A strike occurs when . . .'), by inserting a noun in front of the adverb clause ('A strike is an occasion when

. . .') or, better yet, by reframing the definition around a different verb ('In a strike people refuse to work'). The disputed construction 'An example of this *is when* . . . ' can simply be replaced by 'for example'.

'Haute Wasp is when you have this tatty carpet that looks like hell but cost a million bucks, and only a few people know it.'
Margaret Atwood *Life Before Man* 1979: 85

(Here *is when* occurs in a fictional conversation.)

A paradigm opportunity is when we meet someone for the first time and can deliberately try to shape our response to that person along different lines than our immediate inclination.
Queen's Quarterly 94.1 (1988): 9

(This sentence could be rewritten by replacing *is* with *arises* or by rewording entirely: 'We are presented with a paradigm opportunity when we meet someone. . .'.)

'Proper maintenance is when the operator knows what to do and does it correctly.'
Gazette (Montreal) 5 March 1989: A1

(This sentence, referring to airplanes, could be reworded: 'They can be properly maintained if the operator knows what to do and does it correctly.')

Italian greyhound   see DALMATIAN

italics and quotation marks   Italics and quotation marks are both means of highlighting certain words in a text. Their different uses are governed by convention.
Italics are used to indicate:

• words that require especially strong emphasis in a sentence:

The Court received exhaustive evidence about the inferior quality of education black children were *in fact* receiving under the purported equality of the dual education system in many states.
J.E. Smyth et al. *The Law and Business Administration in Canada* 1987: 26

• words and letters referred to as such:

Doubling of consonants (especially *l*, as in *marvellous* or in *signalled*) created general confusion.
W.C. Lougheed, ed. *In Search of the Standard in Canadian English* 1986: 128

- foreign words or phrases that have not been fully assimilated into English (*fin de siècle*, *Weltanschauung*):

They agreed that the only sensible solution was to sell the farm, and father was presented more or less with a *fait accompli*.
George Ignatieff *The Making of a Peacemonger* 1987: 39

- Latin scientific names of genera and species (see SPECIES, GENUS):

The deer mouse *Peromyscus maniculatus* occurs throughout North America in a variety of habitats.
Canadian Journal of Zoology 67.4 (1989): 789

- publications, including books, newspapers, magazines, journals, pamphlets, long poems, and long musical works as well as titles of films, plays, and radio or television programs. However, note that the names of sacred books, such as the Koran, the Bible, and the Talmud, and the names of musical works identified only by form and number, such as Beethoven's Symphony no. 7 in A, are *not* italicized:

Dualism has rarely had such a thorough and successful presentation as in *The Strange Case of Dr. Jekyll and Mr. Hyde*, written by Robert Louis Stevenson in 1886.
Robertson Davies *One Half of Robertson Davies* 1978: 236

The Bible and the world were God's revelations and man should have freedom to search both.
Hilda Neatby *Queen's University* 1 (1978): 232

(*Exception*: names of sacred books are not italicized.)

Joyce expects the reader to know, or to have the pleasure of finding out, as does Eliot in the shotgunning plethora of allusions in *The Waste Land*.
Queen's Quarterly 94.2 (1987): 298

And Bruce Hutchison, while editor of the *Vancouver Sun* and Winnipeg *Free Press*, actually

wrote speeches for Lester B. Pearson.
Pierre Berton *The Promised Land* 1984: 39

Such films as *My Beautiful Laundrette*, *El Norte*, and *Smooth Talk*, originally produced for broadcast, . . . can earn added revenues through theatrical release.
Queen's Quarterly 95.2 (1988): 323

Music I Like was an afternoon show in 1976, to which non-musician guests brought along their favourite records (*My Fair Lady*, the *Moonlight Sonata*) and chatted about why they liked them—just ordinary folks like you and me.
Queen's Quarterly 92.1 (1985): 28

However, readers of Mr Schonberg's book will find no mention of Gould's achievements and no warning against his excesses, of which his disfiguration of Beethoven's sonata op. III on records was a good example at the time.
Queen's Quarterly 94.1 (1987): 67

(*Exception*: musical works named by form and number are not italicized.)

- titles of paintings and sculptures:

The cross itself is reminiscent of her own earlier and more overtly emotional abstract paintings like *Constellation of the Great Owl* and *Cross by the Sea* of 1985.
Mark A. Cheetham with Linda Hutcheon *Remembering Postmodernism* 1991: 30

- names of ships and spacecraft:

His father . . . went down with the *Titanic* in 1912.
Pierre Berton *The Promised Land* 1984: 289

When writing by hand or using a word processing system that will not print italics, you may underline. By convention, italics and underlining are considered equivalent.

Quotation marks are conventionally used to indicate:

- words quoted exactly:

Then on July 29, 1976, a reporter from *The Gazette* called me a 'veteran goalie'.
Ken Dryden *The Game* 1983: 13

- the first mention of an unfamiliar word:

Not that domestic service was necessarily hard, for even in a modest household two or three servants might be kept—a nurse, a cook, a housemaid, and possibly also a 'rough girl'. . . .
Robertson Davies *A Voice from the Attic* 1960: 137

- the translation of a foreign word or phrase:

Trompe l'oeil, which is French for 'deceive the eye,' is an eye-fooling painting on a wall, ceiling or floor.
Vancouver Sun 20 Nov. 1993: F3

- titles within publications—that is, titles of chapters, stories, articles, poems, songs, etc., within books, journals, magazines, newspapers, compact discs:

'Goodmorning and Goodbye', published by *Preview* in 1944, has as its only character or centre of consciousness a Jewish refugee living with a Canadian family.
Janice Kulyk Keefer *Reading Mavis Gallant* 1989: 71–2

- words used ironically:

There are a couple of 'good' Indians, too; Pontiac is noble-looking, as befits a chief; Oucanasta and her brother both get points for helping the British.
Margaret Atwood *Second Words* 1982: 139

On signboards and in advertisements, quotation marks are sometimes used for straight emphasis: *"Fresh" Coffee*. In any other context the quotation marks would signal irony—that the coffee was actually less than fresh. This use of quotation marks for emphasis is strongly disparaged by usage commentators, who recommend using more accepted markers of emphasis such as bolding, italicization, or underlining.

Neither italics nor quotation marks are used to highlight names of legal documents or legislative acts:

However, we now have a new, extensive Charter of Rights in the Constitution Act proclaimed April 17, 1982.
J.E. Smyth et al. *The Law and Business Administration in Canada* 1987: 21

In formal writing and in books, these guidelines are followed fairly strictly. Omitting italics or quotation marks is considered a stylistic flaw. Newspapers are less stringent; titles and foreign words are rarely highlighted, although journalists do take care to indicate direct quotations:

Kline would much rather portray Shakespeare's Hamlet, which he's done twice, or the nutty fascist crook in A Fish Called Wanda, which won him an Academy Award, or the lusty Pirate King in the hit Broadway production of The Pirates of Penzance.
Calgary Herald 2 Jan. 1992: B9

(Newspapers rarely use italics. In formal writing, both the film title *A Fish Called Wanda* and the play title *The Pirates of Penzance* would be italicized.)

See also HMCS; LATIN PHRASES; QUOTATION, QUOTATION MARKS; SACRED WRITINGS; SPECIES, GENUS; THE, A, AN.

iterate   see REITERATE

it is I, it's me   see CASE

its, it's   *Its* is both a possessive adjective (like *my, your, his, her, our, their*) and, rarely, a possessive pronoun (like *mine, yours, his, hers, ours, theirs*). Although the apostrophe is normally used to mark possession, it is not used with these words: 'The dog has its bone'; 'We have our amusements; it has its'. People often incorrectly insert an apostrophe: 'This is *it's* collar'. In moments of confusion it may be helpful to remember that *its* is exactly parallel to *his*: if *his* would fit where *its* is being used, no apostrophe is required.

It's with the apostrophe is a contraction of *it is*. If *it is* fits where *its* is being used, an apostrophe is needed.

Sometimes the form *its'* is found; this is never correct.

The money will allow the Banff Centre to revive its arts journalism program, which was dropped due to budget cuts in 1985.
Calgary Herald 21 Feb. 1988: B6

One of her favorite cheeses is ricotta, even though it's not the lowest in fat.
Gazette (Montreal) 3 March 1989: C3

(Here *it's*, meaning *it is*, is correct.)

Bench-bound Expos take heart: relief is on it's way.
Gazette (Montreal) 17 May 1990: E1

(The possessive adjective is *its*.)

See also POSSESSIVE.

-ize, -ise, -yze, -yse   Where there is a choice between *-ize* and *-ise* Canadian writers, like Americans, tend to choose the endings with z. In fact, Canadian, American, *and* British writers all prefer *-ize* for *recognize*, *civilize* and *civilization*, *organize* and *organization*, *realize* and *realization*, and *specialize* and *specialization*. The British preference for *-ise* endings is an innovation rather than a longstanding spelling tradition. In Canada and Britain either spelling is usually considered correct, while in the United States the *-ize* endings are de rigueur.

Note, however, that Canadian, American, and British writers all use *-ise* for *advertise*, *supervise*, and *surprise*. For these words, the spelling with z is not an option.

Only a handful of words end in *-yse* or *-yze*. Canadians prefer the American spellings *catalyze* and *paralyze* to the British *catalyse* and *paralyse*. Canadian usage of *analyse* and *analyze* is almost equal, with more newspaper journalists using *-yze*.

The *-ize* ending is often used to coin new words, and dictionaries list a wide range of meanings for it. Words with this ending have been annoying readers and hearers since as early as 1591, when Thomas Nashe, cited in the *OED*, commented on having been reprehended for making up new words with this ending. Most recently, *finalize* and *prioritize* have been singled out for criticism, even though no one today objects to *demoralize*, *economize*, or *terrorize*.

See also ADVERTISEMENT; FINALIZE; PRIORITIZE; SPELLING, CANADIAN.

J

Jack Russell terrier   see DALMATIAN

jaeger   see GERMAN WORDS, PRONUNCIATIAN OF

jail, gaol   *Jail* and *prison* can be used interchangeably, but in Canada and the United States *jail* usually refers to a place of short-term detention and *prison* to a place where long sentences are served. *Gaol* is a British spelling variant of *jail* with exactly the same pronunciation and meaning. Unless the reference is to a historic place, such as the Reading Gaol (made famous by Oscar Wilde's 'Ballad of Reading Gaol'), *jail* is now the more common spelling even in Britain. *Gaol* survives in some legal references in Canada. It is sometimes misspelled *goal*.

In the mornings, he breathes the antiseptic smell

of jails, the smell of coops, caged flesh, sour air breathed in and out too many times; the smell of boredom and hatred.
Margaret Atwood *Life Before Man* 1979: 251

Motion by the plaintiff for an order directing that the . . . defendant . . . be committed to the common gaol for contempt of the Judgment of the Honourable Mr. Justice Henry dated September 4, 1984.
Globe and Mail (Toronto) 18 Jan. 1985: B4

jamb   Windows, fireplaces, and doors have jambs, that is, vertical sidepieces. Because the *b* is silent, the word is sometimes misspelled *jam*. *Jamb* is derived from the French *jambe*, meaning 'leg'; remembering this may prevent writers from dropping the final *b*.

Dead bolts for doors, reinforced door jams, locks

for sliding glass doors, screws to join top and bottom sashes of double-hung windows; all can present a time-consuming obstacle to burglars.
Vancouver Sun 9 Nov. 1990: E15

(The correct spelling is *jambs*.)

Janey Canuck   see CANUCK

jargon   see COLLOQUIAL

jaywalk   see COLLOQUIAL

jealousy   see ENVY

jeer   In British English *jeer* is used with the preposition *at*: 'The boys jeer at him'. Canadian and American writers also have the option of using *jeer* without a preposition: 'The boys jeered him'. This transitive use of *jeer*, which makes it parallel to its rhyming antonym *cheer*, is more common in journalism than in formal writing.

. . . it was believed that the principal had encouraged Queen's students to jeer at temperance lecturers in Kingston.
Hilda Neatby *Queen's University* 1 (1978): 236

. . . I allowed four goals in a first period against Vancouver, then was jeered by Forum fans the rest of the game.
Ken Dryden *The Game* 1983: 43

Kiniski, 61, retired from the mat two years ago, his days as world heavyweight champion a faint memory even to those who once jeered him as Mean Gene and cheered him as Gentleman Gene.
Province (Vancouver) 3 April 1990: 42

jell   see GEL

jello, Jell-O, jelly, aspic, jam   In North America *jello* (originally a trade name, *Jell-O*) refers to the wobbly dessert known in Britain as *jelly*. On either side of the Atlantic a savoury gelatinous salad made with tomato juice or meat stock is usually called an *aspic*. In Canada, the term *jelly* refers to the clear thickened fruit preserve used as a condiment or spread. The culinary distinction between *jelly* and *jam* is

that *jelly* is made from juice pressed from fruit but contains no bits of fruit, while *jam* contains crushed fruit. Many Canadians, however, use the words *jam* and *jelly* interchangeably.

Chicken-flavoured rice, green beans, hot rolls, jello made this morning—yes, that would please the computer expert.
Room of One's Own June 1990: 59

She picks highbush cranberries for juice and wild raspberries and black currants for jam and jelly. . . .
Harrowsmith Aug.–Sept. 1985: 78

See also GEL, JELL.

jet, jettison   To *jet off* is to fly by jet aircraft or, more loosely, to rush away to more important things. Some writers mistakenly have blended the expressions *jet off* and *jettison*. To *jettison* something is to throw it overboard or, more commonly, to discard or abandon it.

The grand prize winner will jettison off on an exotic trip courtesy of Canadian Travel Abroad.
'Support the ROM' Royal Ontario Museum website 19 Oct. 2006

(The correct expression is *jet off*.)

Jew, [Jewess], Israeli, Israelite, Hebrew, Yiddish   *Jew* and *Jewish* refer to those who, however nominally, adhere to Judaism, or more generally to those of Jewish ancestry who identify with the Jewish people, history, and culture. *Jewess*, like many other feminine forms, is no longer accepted usage.
Israeli refers to all citizens of the state of Israel, who are of various religious and cultural backgrounds. The term *Israeli Jew* distinguishes members of the Jewish majority from other groups.
Israelite designates the historical ancestors of the Jews.
Classical *Hebrew* is the sacred language of Judaism; modern *Hebrew* is the official language of Israel. *Hebrew* is no longer used as an ethnic designation.
Yiddish is a Germanic language that originat-

ed in Eastern Europe in the ninth century. It is written in Hebrew characters, and about fifteen per cent of its vocabulary is Hebrew. Jewish immigrants brought Yiddish to North America, where many of its expressions—such as *kibitz* and *klutz*—have moved into English.

> . . . in the 1950s discriminatory quotas prevented many Jewish students from entering the McGill University medical school. So some Jews left Quebec and went to Swiss medical schools, or they chose rewarding careers in other fields, such as business and law.
> Irving M. Zeitlin and Robert J. Brym *The Social Condition of Humanity* 1991: 172

> In the northern port city of Haifa, about 4,000 Jews and Israeli Arabs marched in the streets holding signs and shouting slogans demanding Israeli withdrawal from the West Bank of the Jordan River and Gaza Strip. . . .
> *Calgary Herald* 14 Feb. 1988: B6

See also KIBITZ, KIBITZER, KIBBUTZ.

jewellery, jewelry, jeweller, jeweler
Canadian writers use the spellings *jewellery* (the common form in Britain), and *jewelry* (the common form in the United States) with about equal frequency. Canadian retailers strongly prefer *jeweller* to *jeweler* (the usual American spelling).

> For women who are always the first with the latest, streamlined gold jewellery with modern geometric edges is a perfect 'thank you.'
> *Province* (Vancouver) 7 Jan. 1990: B11

> The good life for some women also means the ability to buy their own fur coats, jewelry and trips around the world.
> *Bon Vivant* Feb.–Mar. 1983: 16

See also SPELLING, CANADIAN.

jibe, gibe, gybe, jib, jive *Jibe, gibe*, and *gybe* are all pronounced the same way: *JIBE*. The difficulty is in knowing which spelling to use for various meanings. To *jibe* or *gibe* means to tease or taunt; *jibes* or *gibes* are insults. Some usage guides recommend *gibe* for this sense, but Canadian writers use *jibe* about twice as often as

gibe in every type of writing. *Jive* is also found in this sense in informal contexts.

Jibe and *gybe* also are used in a nautical sense. The *jib* is the foresail of a sailing boat. When a sail (or boom) *jibs*, *jibes*, or *gybes*, it swings around suddenly from one side to the other; when a boat *jibs*, *jibes*, or *gybes*, it changes course.

Jibe has another common sense, to be in accord with: 'That story doesn't jibe with my experience'. This use is regarded as informal by some critics. However, it is found in serious journalism and historical writing, and there seems to be no reason to avoid it.

Sometimes *jive* is also used to mean accord with: this usage should probably be reserved for informal contexts.

> He pricked balloons, jeered at the newly rich, attacked the bluestockings, poked fun at boosterism, jibed at humbug and bombast.
> Pierre Berton *The Promised Land* 1984: 265

> 'I've got a long memory when it comes time to appoint Cabinet ministers,' Mr. Turner reportedly gibed. . . .
> *Globe and Mail* (Toronto) 23 Sept. 1985: P5

> Millar's paintings are jam packed with images and texts, dialogue, jokes, puns, double entendres and jibes. . . .
> *Calgary Herald* 11 March 2006: F1

> He was superb at reducing her to weepy incoherence, even though his gibes were repetitive and came by rote.
> *Room of One's Own* June 1990: 4

> 'I distinctly remember playing hockey with other kids and being jived about wearing a kilt and blowing into a bagpipe.'
> *Calgary Herald* 18 July 1994: B4

> (Here, in informal speech, *jived* means teased.)

> When True North One hits the water, it will have its own computer on board that will analyze and record every tack, gybe and mark rounding during a 24-mile race.
> *Globe and Mail* (Toronto) 21 Feb. 1985: M8

> We . . . learned how to jibe in open seas.
> *Vancouver Sun* 7 Nov. 1992: E10

> That many historical facts of 'Old Hickory's' life did

not jibe with the legend did not always matter.
Queen's Quarterly 95.4 (1988): 800

That statement . . . jibes perfectly with everything we know about Davis's disdain for rehearsals and multiple takes.
Jack Chambers *Milestones* 1983: 310

'We just happened to have personalities that gibe, I guess.'
Dogs in Canada Special Issue 1986: 88

(The accepted spelling for this sense is *jibe*.)

That would mean losing, and that doesn't jive with Polischuk.
Star-Phoenix (Saskatoon) 4 July 2003: B1

(The use of *jive* to mean jibe or agree is informal.)

job titles   The sentence 'He is a male nurse' is redundant: the sex of the nurse is identified twice, in the pronoun *he* and in the adjective *male*. Yet the sentence does not seem redundant, because for many people *nurse* is gender-marked 'female'. One goal of non-sexist language reform in English has been to dissociate gender from job titles.

Interestingly, in Quebec French the opposite tack has been taken. The Office de la langue française has overseen the creation of feminine versions of the titles of all traditionally masculine occupations and vice versa. In both languages, the intent of the reform is the same: to promote the idea that every type of work is open to either sex, and to facilitate compliance with the law that forbids discrimination on the basis of sex in job hiring. Though detractors of non-sexist language consider gender-neutral job titles silly, in public or official communications they are now de rigueur. Following is a sample of traditional and non-sexist titles. (Prospective employers and others can obtain more information on this topic from various government publications.)

Traditional	Preferred
actress	actor
advance man	advance agent
alderman	councillor
anchorman	anchor
chairman	chair
cleaning lady	housecleaner, cleaner
fireman	firefighter or (for someone tending a furnace) stationary engineer
mailman, postman	mail carrier, letter carrier
male nurse	nurse
paperboy	carrier
policeman	police officer
salesgirl, saleslady	clerk, sales representative
waitress, waiter	server
weatherman, weathergirl	weather reporter or (for someone compiling reports) meteorologist
woman doctor, lady doctor	doctor
workman	worker

The job title *fisher* deserves a special note. *Fisher* is an archaic term used in the King James translation of the Bible to describe the vocation of Jesus' disciples: 'fishers of men' (Matthew 4:19). The term was revived as a gender-neutral replacement for *fisherman*. While many gender-neutral occupation titles initially evoked derision, most soon ceased to be noticed and settled into the language. *Fisher* is an exception. It never gained popular acceptance, and has been resisted by the women and men who catch fish for a living. Blair Shewchuck, a language columnist for the CBC, offers this usage recommendation: '. . . one logical conclusion is that *fishermen* is the right choice until women in the industry start calling themselves *fisher*' (*Words: Wonder and Woe*, CBC online).

See also CHAIR; SEXIST LANGUAGE; WAITER, WAITRESS.

jockdom   see -DOM

jodhpurs   This word is often misspelled *jodphurs*; the correct pronunciation is *JAWD purs*. The British borrowed the design of these riding breeches, cut loose above the knee and tight on the calf, from Jodhpur, India.

At end of a long day in court, lawyer Susan Mackey can't wait to trade her briefcase for a hard hat and jodphurs.
Ottawa Citizen 8 July 1990: B7

(The correct spelling is *jodhpurs*.)

Johann   see GERMAN WORDS, PRONUNCIATION OF

Johnny Canuck   see CANUCK

joual   *Joual* (pronounced *zhoo AL*) is a non-standard dialect of Quebec French. First found in print in the 1930s, the word is supposed to represent a rural pronunciation of *cheval* ('horse'). *Joual* has been disparaged by some educated Quebeckers because it contains many words borrowed from English and because its speakers (usually rural or working-class) are regarded as ignorant of grammar and sloppy in their pronunciation. However, the term is not always used disparagingly. Since the 1970s many Quebec writers, including the playwright Michel Tremblay, have participated in *le mouvement joualisant*: by choosing to write literature in relaxed Quebec French, they have given legitimacy to *joual* and to the ways in which Quebec French differs from Parisian French.
Joual should be italicized in formal writing.

What had begun as a complaint by Dr. Fabrikant about the instructor smoking . . . degenerated into vitriolic criticism of the teacher's methods and accent, which Dr. Fabrikant characterized as 'joual.'
Gazette (Montreal) 1 June 1994: A8

Beau Dommage gained popularity for songs sung in joual that captured the spirit of Montreal.
Gazette (Montreal) 12 Nov. 1994: C1

joule   see APPENDIX II

journalese   see -ESE

jubilant   The accepted pronunciation of *jubilant* is *JEW bi lunt*. The first two syllables are the same as in *jubilee*. The common pronunciations *JEW byew lunt* and *JEW byew lee unt*, which dictionaries do not list, probably account for spelling errors.

Is Montreal the jubiliant crowds who cram the streets during the jazz festival each summer, or the lone pilgrim mounting the steps of St Joseph's Oratory on her knees?
Gazette (Montreal) 26 May 1990: K4

(The correct spelling is *jubilant*.)

judgment, judgement   Both spellings are found in Canadian writing, but *judgment* (also preferred in the United States) is far more common in all types of writing, including academic, than *judgement* (the spelling preferred in Britain).

The most dangerous physical condition that wind chill causes is hypothermia, the rapid lowering of body temperature that inhibits judgment and reasoning.
Province (Vancouver) 31 Dec. 1990: 45

Duncan's complex irony makes judgements about authorial stance difficult, especially because Duncan often seems to criticize and condone the colonial viewpoint at the same time.
Essays on Canadian Writing 75 (2002): 85–117

See also CONCILIATION; SPELLING, CANADIAN.

judicial, judicious, juridical   *Judicial* usually refers to judgments in law, but it can also be applied to moral or aesthetic judgments. *Judicious* means showing good judgment, in the sense of choosing sensibly. *Juridical,* close in meaning to *judicial* but a much less common word in Canadian English, usually refers to the administration of justice.

There are doubtless self-defined limitations on judicial law-making power. . . .
Canadian Bar Review 66.3 (1987): 505

The other large division of critics may be called judicial, and their best writing is usually about what they have not liked.
Robertson Davies *A Voice from the Attic* 1960: 195

Surely there are smarter ways of enhancing security, such as the judicious placement of trees and landscaping to curtain key areas from view.
Toronto Star 28 April 2006: A18

Not infrequently verbose and repetitive, [this book] could have benefited from judicious editing.
Canadian Journal of History 14.1 (1989): 122

An Ontario proposal to give juridical standing to Islamic law in Ontario family arbitration has reverberated around the world.
Gazette (Montreal) 7 Sept. 2005: A12

He also authored numerous articles for legal journals, in which he presented his views on legal theory, juridical administration and the finer points of the law.
Telegram (St. John's) 14 March 2005: A7

judicial determination   see CONCILIATION

juncture, junction   A *juncture* is a point in time; a *junction* is a literal or figurative place of meeting. Sometimes *junction* is mistakenly substituted for *juncture* in the expression 'at this juncture'. Although a juncture need not be a particularly critical or crucial time or state of affairs, some object to the phrase 'at this juncture' if it is merely a circumlocution for 'now'.

At this critical juncture in relations between the two countries a stalemate . . . led to a situation in which by 1931 relations between Germany and France were characterized by confrontation, rather than a willingness to compromise on important issues.
Canadian Journal of History 14.1 (1989): 145

At this juncture, however, it is also useful to recall that respondents were asked two sets of questions about influence. . . .
Neil Nevitte and Roger Gibbins *New Elites in Old States* 1990: 139

It would be prudent, however, to sound a note of caution at this junction.
Queen's Quarterly 95.1 (1988): 21

(A train sounds a note of caution at a *junction*; a point in an argument is a *juncture*.)

Canada's capital, *Ottawa*, in Ontario at the juncture of the Ottawa River and the Rideau Canal, has a smalltown feel, a Parliament to watch, museums to visit, and in winter a canal skating rink that runs for miles.
Alan Tucker, ed. *The Penguin Guide to Canada* 1991: 10

(The confluence of two rivers or water systems is a *junction*.)

junior   see FIRST-YEAR STUDENT; SUPERIOR

junta   *Junta* is a Spanish word meaning 'government council' or 'committee'. In contemporary English it refers to the group that takes power after a revolution or coup. The CBC has long directed its announcers to pronounce the word *JUN ta* (so that the first syllable rhymes with *bun*) on the grounds that it was added to our English vocabulary hundreds of years ago. Today, however, the Spanish pronunciation *HOON ta* may actually be the more common one in Canada.

juror, jurist   A *juror* is a member of a jury. A *jurist* is an expert in the field of law. In Canadian and British English, a *jurist* is a noted legal scholar. In American English, judges and lawyers are also commonly called *jurists*.

Custom appears to have overcome law, or have been considered as being law in this instance—an absorbing matter for consideration by jurists, even if not for contract lawyers.
Canadian Bar Review 6.3 (1987): 613

Last February no less a jurist than Justice Bertha Wilson of the Supreme Court of Canada told an audience at Osgoode Hall that some aspects of criminal law 'cry out for change. . . .'
Ottawa Citizen 8 Nov. 1990: A13

(Here Wilson is being singled out for her knowledge of the law.)

Jurassic period   see CAPITAL LETTERS

just deserts   see DESSERT

juvenile   see CHILDISH

juvenilia   Usually *juvenilia* refers to the works that a writer, artist, or composer produced while still a child or adolescent. Occasionally it is used to refer to artistic productions aimed at young people. *Juvenilia* takes a plural verb and is usually pronounced *jew vuh NILL yuh*. The common misspelling *juvenalia* (perhaps influenced by the word *marginalia*, referring to things written in the margins of texts) and the corresponding mispronunciation *jew vuh NAIL yuh* can be avoided by remembering that juvenilia is produced by juveniles.

> Walker's Zastrozzi is supposed to have got its loose inspiration from an obscure piece of juvenilia by the poet Shelley.
> *Calgary Herald* 31 Oct. 1992: D16

> And that's the heart of the cynical film industry: juvenilia and genitalia.
> *Vancouver Sun* 2 April 1992: A 15

(Here *juvenilia* refers to productions aimed at young people.)

Early literary works, called 'juvenalia' in the rare-book world, are valuable not only because they are rare and often bear a celebrity's signature, but also because they can give scholars insights into how the author's style developed. . . .
Toronto Star 24 July 1992: C11

(The correct spelling is *juvenilia*.)

K

K   see DOLLAR AMOUNTS; APPENDIX II

kangaroos   see -OS, -OES

karat   see CARAT

karma, dharma   Avoid the misspellings *kharma* and *darma*. *Karma* and *dharma* are important concepts in Hinduism, Buddhism, and Sikhism. Karma is the sum of all your deeds, or the principle by which all the good or evil that you do comes back to you. Dharma is the inexorable moral law of the universe. From a human point of view, dharma is the knowledge required to lead a good and happy life.

Both *karma* and *dharma* are derived from Sanskrit, and, formerly, these words were often capitalized. Capitalization is becoming less frequent as the words become more familiar.

> The picaresque heroes of Kerouac are 'Dharma bums', social outcasts with serious social and even religious ideals.
> Northrop Frye *The Modern Century* 1990: 80

> You don't have to subscribe to Buddhist teachings about karma and rebirth to understand that any-one performing repetitive acts of killing must per-force insulate their minds from such positive and healing states as compassion and empathy.
> *Toronto Star* 22 April 2006: M6

keep from   The construction *keep* followed by *from* and a gerund has several slightly different meanings, including save from ('keep them from making the same mistake'), avoid ('keep from going outside the line') and resist ('keep from drinking'). In *The New Fowler's*, a contemporary British usage guide, R. W. Burchfield describes *keep from* with an explicit object ('Poetry kept *him* from losing his sanity') as normal English but labels the intransitive construction ('I tried to keep from laughing') archaic. Burchfield hastens to note that the questionable construction is flourishing in North America. Indeed, it is perfectly acceptable in Canada. British and Canadian usage diverge on this point because the English of North America has preserved a grammatical structure that is falling into disuse in Britain.

> 'I did everything I could do to keep from hitting him.'
> *CBC Magazine* CBC website 27 March 2001

> Dr. Roberts also stresses that the best way to keep from experiencing tinnitus is to protect your ears from loud noises. . . .
> *News Bulletin* Natural Sciences and Engineering Research Council of Canada website 7 October 2004

See also VERBS in Glossary.

keep your shirt on   see IDIOMS

keister   see BUTTOCKS

Kelt, Keltic   see CELT

kelvin   see APPENDIX II

kerb   see CURB; SPELLING, CANADIAN

kerosene, kerosine, coal oil, paraffin
These are all terms for the same oil, which is used to fuel lamps, stoves, heaters, etc. *Kerosene* is a Canadianism coined by the Nova Scotian who invented the distillation process for producing the oil, Dr. Abraham Gesner (1797–1864). *Kerosine*, formed by analogy with *gasoline*, is an accepted but uncommon spelling variant. *Coal oil* is another term used by some Canadians and Americans. *Paraffin* has two meanings: in Britain it is the name of the oil itself, and in Canada it refers to the oil in solid form—a wax used for making candles and sealing jars.

> The place was wired for electricity, and two or three dirty bulbs were burning over the grease pit, but kerosene lanterns were hanging from beams nearby, just in case.
> Howard Engel *Murder Sees the Light* 1984: 53

> All those long, lone nights in a dingy room, probably working by the light of a coal-oil lamp, he sat and wrote and re-wrote and re-wrote.
> Max Braithwaite *The Night We Stole the Mountie's Car* 1971: 159

> Cover with a very thin layer of melted paraffin. Let stand until wax is set and cold.
> *Vancouver Sun* 8 Aug. 1990: C3

ketchup, catsup, catchup   All three spellings are standard. The origin of the word is uncertain, though it may be related to the Cantonese word for 'tomato juice'. Canadian and British writers strongly prefer *ketchup*; Americans prefer *ketchup* but also use *catsup* and *catchup*.

key   see QUAY

khaki, caulk, cork   *Khaki*, the name given to the colour of British military uniforms, derives from the Hindi word meaning 'dust-coloured'. In the United States and Britain it is pronounced either *KAK ee* or *KAH kee*. Many Canadians, however, particularly those who served in either of the world wars, favour the pronunciation *KAR kee*. Because the English do not generally pronounce *r* before a consonant (for example, they pronounce *farm FAHM*), Canadian soldiers assumed that when the British referred to *KAH kee*, they were simply not pronouncing an *r*.

The same phenomenon occurs in the name of the boots worn by loggers, *caulk(ed) boots* (i.e., boots with spikes or caulks). *Caulk(ed) boots* are often referred to in Canada as 'cork boots'.

kibitz, kibitzer, kibbutz   *Kibitz* was borrowed from Yiddish in the 1920s to describe the act of looking on at a card game and offering unwanted advice. By extension a *kibitzer* is a busybody or meddler. In recent usage to *kibitz* means to speak or behave in a joking manner. Both the noun and the verb are colloquial.

A *kibbutz* is a communal settlement, especially a farming settlement in modern Israel.

> A good kibitzer should be able to see the cards at least from a slightly bent position.
> Max Braithwaite *The Night We Stole the Mountie's Car* 1971: 176

> 'I think it was really important for him all those years to be able to get away from politics and have a chance to laugh and kibitz.'
> *Leader-Post* (Regina) 27 Feb. 1988: A4

> At a yuppie restaurant in Granville Island, the venerable poet holds court, kibitzing with the waitress, telling stories in a loud voice. . . .
> *Vancouver Sun* 15 Dec. 1990: D17

> During the late 1960s when ideas of the so-called 'new left' were in fashion, there were two popular ways for young people to demonstrate their commitment to the ideals of socialism. One was to spend time living and working on a kibbutz in Israel; the other was to volunteer to work cutting sugar cane in Cuba.
> *Calgary Herald* 26 Aug. 1994: A5

See also JEW, JEWISH, YIDDISH.

kickoff, kick off   *Kickoff*, a word borrowed from football, is considered standard but informal when used to refer to the start of a public event. Some dictionaries and usage guides still consider it slang, although it is common in Canadian journalism. When it is used as a noun or an adjective, *kickoff* is sometimes hyphenated: 'A kick-off dinner will be held'. *Kick off* (two words) is a verb: 'A dinner will kick off the festival'.

> 'And it's obviously the unofficial kickoff to the next election campaign.'
> *Ottawa Citizen* 18 Nov. 1994: A4

> In his campaign kick-off press conference, Tory would not commit himself to bringing back either measure.
> *Toronto Star* 8 May 2004: H2

> The train was part of a campaign to kick off . . . a marketing promotion.
> *Western Grocer Magazine* June 1990: 20

See also HYPHENATION; PHRASAL VERBS.

kidnap, abduct   Both words mean to forcibly carry someone away. When a person is kidnapped, however, a ransom of some kind is usually demanded, which is not necessarily the case with abduction. A parent, therefore, *abducts* rather than *kidnaps* his or her own child, since usually no ransom is demanded in such cases. According to Canadian law, it is possible to be charged with the abduction of a child under 14 simply for harbouring him or her with the intent of depriving a parent or guardian of the child. In other words, in legal contexts, forcible carrying-off is not always part of the definition of *abduct*.

Canadian and British writers double the *p* (*kidnapped, kidnapping, kidnappers, kidnappee*). A person who kidnaps is a *kidnapper*; someone who abducts is an *abductor* (sometimes misspelled with an -*er* ending).

> Parental abduction, the unlawful taking of a child by a parent without permission of the other parent or caregiver, made up the second largest number of missing child cases.
> *Ottawa Citizen* 17 Oct. 1990: A5

> When they did not find the boy . . . she and her ex-husband had to face the fact that he had probably been abducted. And because no one demanded a ransom, they feared that he was being exploited for sexual purposes.
> *Maclean's* 10 Dec. 1990: A54

> Because kidnapping one's own child is not an offence in the U.S., A—— was arrested only because of the Canadian warrant.
> *Province* (Vancouver) 10 Dec. 1990: 16

(Here *abducting* would be more accurate.)

> A child with magical powers . . . is kidnaped, and for uncertain reasons, only Murphy can save him.
> *Ottawa Citizen* 15 Sept. 1990: TT4

(The *p* is almost always doubled in Canadian spelling.)

> The teenager was dragged into a van while a woman trying to rescue her was punched by the abducter.
> *Ottawa Citizen* 10 Dec. 1990: A5

(The correct spelling is *abductor*.)

See also -ER, -OR; DOUBLING THE FINAL CONSONANT.

KI First Nation   see KITCHENUHMAYKOOSIB INNINUWUG

kilo, kilogram, kilometre   see APPENDIX II

kind of, sort of   The phrases *kind of* and *sort of* are similar not only in the ways they are used but in the disputes they have occasioned; the recommendations that follow apply to both.

Expressions such as 'these kind of things' and 'those sort of people' have been under attack for two hundred years because the plural determiner, *these* or *those*, does not agree with the singular noun that it modifies, *kind* or *sort*. Nevertheless, such expressions are idiomatic and have a long literary pedigree; *Webster's Dictionary of English Usage* cites examples from the writings of Sidney, Shakespeare, Milton, Dryden, Pope, Austen, and Dickens. In Canada, the idiom makes its way into print only in quotations or representations of speech. In other published writing, the determiner and the noun *kind* are either both singular (*this kind* or *that kind*) or both plural (*these kinds* or *those kinds*).

In Canadian English, when *kind* is made plural before *of*, the noun that follows *of* is usually made plural too (unless the noun is uncountable, like *bread* or *gasoline*): 'What kinds of players is he planning to draft this year?' In British English, the noun that follows *of* is often left singular: 'What kinds of player is he planning to draft this year?'

Some language commentators have objected to *a* or *an* in phrases such as 'this kind of an account'. Their argument is that *account* is being used to describe a category or genre rather than a specific account, so that the particularizing *an* is illogical. While in formal writing the construction without *a* or *an* ('this kind of account') is more common, the construction that includes the indefinite article is also found. As the *Longman Guide to English Usage* points out, the presence of the article can be significant. 'What kind of job is that?' ('How would you categorize your work?') means something quite different from the insulting rhetorical question 'What kind of a job is that?'

As an adverb, *kind of* means fairly or rather: 'kind of silly'. This use is informal and should be avoided in writing except in representations of speech.

> 'This is the time to take advantage of all the opportunities they offer you because these kinds of opportunities don't come by later in life.'
> *Calgary Herald* 6 June 2006: B5

> I'll go to the postwar years, when I began to have a memory, and trace for you my own progress from wild colonial girl to the person who gives these kinds of speeches. . . .
> Margaret Atwood *Second Words* 1982: 376

> No, I'm damn careful now about booze. Some kinds of painkiller just aren't worth it.
> Constance Beresford-Howe *Night Studies* 1985: 95

> 'Those kind of horses are subject to those things happening.'
> *Canadian Thoroughbred* Jan. 1989: 29

(This sentence is a direct quotation of speech; in formal writing, *those kinds* is recommended.)

> 'I think perhaps that maybe a bit more time needs

to elapse before those kind of decisions are made.'
> *Gazette* (Montreal) 4 March 1989: F7

(In formal writing, *those kinds* is recommended.)

> 'And what kind of a mess have you gone and made this time?' Dora snapped at Nadia.
> *Canadian Fiction Magazine* 63 (1988): 82

> Treslan described her number as 'kind of wild,' adding it's 'tiring, but a lot of fun.'
> *Today's Skater* 1991: 70

(Here the adverbial *kind of* is part of a direct quotation of speech.)

kindly   see FRIENDLY

kingdom   see SPECIES

Kitchenuhmaykoosib Inninuwug, KI First Nation, Big Trout Lake First Nation
The Aboriginal people who live near Big Trout Lake in Northern Ontario, approximately 600 km north of Thunder Bay, belong to the *Kitchenuhmaykoosib Inninuwug First Nation*. For brevity's sake, the band's name is sometimes abbreviated to *KI First Nation*, but the abbreviation should be used only after the full name has been given. The *Kitchenuhmaykoosib Inninuwug First Nation* was formerly known as the *Big Trout Lake First Nation*.

> The claim is at Big Trout Lake, about 580 kilometres north of Thunder Bay, home to the Kitchenuhmaykoosib Inninuwug First Nation (KI).
> *Toronto Star* 1 April 2006: F4

See also ABORIGINAL PEOPLE(S); APPENDIX III.

kitsch   see JEW, YIDDISH

kitty-corner, cater-corner, catty-corner
Canadians prefer *kitty-corner* to describe something diagonally opposite. The equivalent terms *catercorner(ed)* and *catty-corner(ed)* are more common in British and American English. All these terms derive from the obsolete English word *cater* (from the French *quatre*), meaning four.

> Phoenicia Foods, kitty-corner to Gus's Grill on

Agricola Street at North in Halifax, sells the chestnuts for $4.95 a pound.
Daily News (Halifax) 5 Dec. 1994: n.p.

See also FOLK ETYMOLOGY.

knelt   see -T, -ED

[knit-picking]   see NITPICKING

knives   see -F, -VE-

knowledge, knowledgeable   *Knowledge* and *knowledgeable* are frequently misspelled. First, the *d* is often left out of both words. Second, the final *e* of *knowledge* in *knowledgeable* is often omitted. It is necessary, however, to signal the soft *g* sound, as in *changeable* and *manageable*.

See also -ABLE, -(E)ABLE.

koala   see BEAR

Kootenay, Kutenai, Ktunaxa-Kinbasket The *Kootenay* (or *Kutenai* or *Kootenai*) are an Aboriginal people whose traditional territories are mainly in southeastern British Columbia, Alberta, and the United States, between the Selkirk Mountains and the Rockies. They are represented by the Ktunaxa-Kinbasket Tribal Council in Cranbrook, B.C. Their language, also called *Kootenay, Kutenai,* or *Kootenai,* is an isolate—the only member of its language family. *Kootenay* is pronounced *KOO tin ay*; *Ktunaxa-Kinbasket* is pronounced *ktoo NA ha* (with an exaggerated *h* sound) *KIN bas ket.*

Two companies battled for the lucrative fur trade with the Kootenay Indians who travelled in the foothills of Alberta.
Calgary Herald 10 July 1993: D3

The town [Creston, B.C.] also boasts a fine museum (home to one of the few remaining Kutenai canoes). . . .
Calgary Herald 21 May 1994: C7

Sophie Pierre, an elected chief of the St. Mary's band of the Ktunaxa Nation in the Kootenays, said aboriginal women face some unique hurdles in becoming leaders.
Gazette (Montreal) 4 May 1993: B4

See also ABORIGINAL PEOPLE(S); APPENDIX III.

Koran   see ISLAM; SACRED WRITINGS

Ktunaxa-Kinbasket   see KOOTENAY

kudos   *Kudos,* a Greek word meaning glory or renown, looks like an English plural. People who don't realize that *kudos* has no plural (it is an uncountable noun, like *praise* or *prestige*) occasionally use *kudo* as a singular noun meaning an accolade. *Kudos* is more common in journalism than in formal writing. It is properly pronounced either *KOO doss* or *KYOO doss,* but *KOO doze* is also often heard.

He has also won kudos for, well, just being Steve Nash.
Guardian (Charlottetown) 27 Dec. 2002: B1

But the media did get a kudo from Chief Justice Charles Dubin, who complimented them for 'acting responsibly' in respecting the gag order. . . .
Toronto Star 3 Feb. 1994: A2

(The singular construction *a kudo* is non-standard; 'a word of praise' or 'kudos' would be better here.)

See also BACK-FORMATION.

Kutenai   see KOOTENAY

Kwakiutl, Haisla, Heiltsuk, Bella Bella, Oweekeno, Kwakwaka'wakw, Kwagiulth The traditional Kwakiutl territories lie both on the mainland of British Columbia and on northeast Vancouver Island. *Kwakiutl (kwa kee OOTL)* is still used with reference to the past and to shared cultural practices, though subgroups of the Kwakiutl are now generally referred to in more specific terms. The *Haisla (HY sla)* are the northern group on the mainland. Farther south are the *Heiltsuk (HALE tsuk),* some of whom were formerly called *Bella Bella,* and the *Oweekeno (oh WEE kee no).* The southernmost Kwakiutl group on the mainland is now called the *Kwakwaka'wakw (kwa KWA ka*

WA kw). Their languages—Haisla, Heiltsuk, Ow-eekeno, and Kwakwala, respectively—all belong to the Wakashan family. The Kwakiutl on Vancouver Island call themselves *Kwagiulth* (*kwa GYOOLTH*); they also speak Kwakwala. None of these names should be pluralized with *s*.

> Despite this opposition, the Kwakiutl clung to the potlatch, refusing to give it up, knowing it was essential to their social fabric.
> *Ottawa Citizen* 6 Dec. 1994: F1

> . . . following a Haisla decision not to hunt bear in the newly protected Kitlope wilderness, the B.C. government put a moratorium on grizzly hunting in the area.
> *Vancouver Sun* 18 Nov. 1994: A27

> 'I think people forget quite quickly the grievances of the past,' said David Gladstone, an artist, historian, and hereditary chief from the Heiltsuk . . . band in Bella Bella.
> *Calgary Herald* 19 Aug. 1994: A1

> Tribal differences between Haida, Kwakwa-ka'wawkw, Gitksan, Salish and Nuu-chah-nulth are at least as sharp as those that separate the French from the Germans.
> *Gazette* (Montreal) 24 Aug. 1994: C1

> Representatives of . . . the Coast Salish, the Nuu-chahnulth and the Kwagiulth . . . offered athletes, dignitaries and spectators a traditional chanted welcome. . . .
> *Ottawa Citizen* 19 Aug. 1994: D1

See also ABORIGINAL PEOPLE(S); APPENDIX III.

L

-l, -ll The spellings of several words ending in *l* vary in Britain, Canada, and the United States. The British usually end the following words with a single *l*: *appal, distil, enrol, enthral, fulfil, instil*. They double the *l* before endings beginning with a vowel (*appalling, enthralled*) but leave it single before endings beginning with a consonant (*enrolment, fulfilment*).

In American English, these same words are spelled with two *l*'s (*appall, distill,* etc.), which are retained before endings (*enrolled, enrollment, fulfillment*) beginning with vowels or consonants.

Canadians, as usual, vary their practice, but generally follow the British spellings.

See also DOUBLING THE FINAL CONSONANT; FULFIL; SKILFUL, SKILLFUL; SPELLING, CANADIAN.

laborious see -OUR, -OR

labour see BELABOUR

Labradorian see NAMES OF RESIDENTS OF CITIES AND PROVINCES

Labrador retriever see CAPITAL LETTERS; DALMATIAN

lackadaisical A *lackadaisical* person is lazy or lacking in enthusiasm. The word derives from *lackaday*, an alteration of 'Alack the day!'—an archaic exclamation of regret. Because of the influence of the synonym *lax*, *lackadaisical* is commonly mispronounced and misspelled with an extra *s*: *lacks-*.

See also FOLK ETYMOLOGY.

lack for Some usage guides condemn *lack for* outright on the grounds that it means the same as *lack*. Yet *lack for* has a particular understated use in negative constructions: 'They do not lack for money'. This negative construction occurs in Canadian writing at all levels of formality and is standard. Idioms such as *lack for* that arose in North American English were often poorly received by British language commentators.

> The writer, in his traffic with that realm in which

dream, and myth, and fairy-tale become mingled with the most ordinary circumstances of life, does not lack for rewards and very great rewards.
Robertson Davies *One Half of Robertson Davies* 1978: 133

With 100,000 bachelors on the prairies, most of them young and virile, the bawdy houses did not lack for customers.
Pierre Berton *The Promised Land* 1984: 296

laconic　*Laconic* does *not* mean lethargic—at least according to dictionaries. Yet this usage has become very common. *Laconic* is derived from the Greek word for 'Spartan'. In the ancient world the Spartans were noted for not wasting words. Thus a laconic person is one who uses few words. A concise utterance or style of writing may also be called laconic. The word is pronounced *la KON ik*.

It turns out David, usually so reserved and laconic he makes Presbyterians seem garrulous and forthcoming, becomes Chatty Carl when he laces on the shoes.
Financial Post 9 July 1991: 11

Like Whitman, Piercy must be read in chunks, not sips, and appreciated for her courage, gut energy and verbal fecundity, not for laconic polish.
Margaret Atwood *Second Words* 1982: 278

Environmental pollution has been known to cause hyperactivity and laconic behavior in children, he said.
Globe and Mail (Toronto) 8 Feb. 1985: M3

(Here *lethargic* may be the word intended.)

His Wonder Dog, Mighty Manfred, was a laconic pooch who tended to fall asleep.
Vancouver Sun 17 March 1990: D2

(Here *lethargic* is almost certainly the word intended.)

They have been criticized for the laconic pace of construction and been threatened with having their cherished Games taken away and held somewhere else.
Times-Colonist (Victoria) 3 March 2002: D4

(Here *slow* is intended.)

While both are laconic off the ice, the CH [team crest] on their chests might as well be an S [for

Superman] when they play.
Gazette (Montreal) 14 April 1990: G1

(Here *easy-going* seems to be intended.)

lactovegetarian　see VEGETARIAN

lacy, [lacey]　see -Y, -EY

lady doctor　see JOB TITLES

laissez-faire, [lazy-faire]　see MISHEARD EXPRESSIONS

lam, on the lam　*On the lam* is an informal expression meaning on the run from the law. Occasionally people write *lamb* for *lam*, perhaps thinking that the expression has something to do with stealing young sheep. In fact, the expression derives from a Standard British English verb that is rare in Canadian English: *lam*, meaning beat or hit. *Lam it* is a British slang expression meaning to go away or run for it, analogous to the North American *beat it*.

He abducts his grandmother, Armen, from the unsavoury home for the aged where his father has put her and goes on the lam.
Queen's Quarterly 95.2 (1988): 410

I advised her to go on the lam, up to the mountains.
Canadian Fiction Magazine 64 (1988): 73

Harrison Ford stars in this re-make of the TV classic about a doctor on the lamb for a crime he didn't commit.
Whig-Standard (Kingston) 28 Aug. 1993: C2

(The correct spelling is *lam*.)

lama, llama　A *lama* is a Buddhist monk from Tibet or Mongolia; the word is also used as an honorific for a spiritual leader. The word comes from Tibetan *blama* (the *b* is silent) meaning 'superior one'. The *l* is usually lower case, although it is capitalized in a title such as *Dalai Lama*.

　A *llama* is a South American animal, similar in appearance to a camel but minus the hump. Confusingly, *llamas*, along with alpacas, guanacos, and vicunas, constitute the genus *lama*, a meaning of the single-*l* spelling of the word that few dictionaries mention. While *lama* may correctly be used to refer to both llamas and alpacas collectively, referring to the individual species by the name *lama* constitutes a spelling mistake (and a sensitive one at that).

The pronunciation of the first syllable of *lama* most often rhymes with *bomb*, and the first syllable of *llama* most often rhymes with *bam*, but either can be pronounced in either manner.

> Blessed by a Tibetan lama . . . and greeted by local llama-farm denizens, the first yak born here was welcomed by islanders this week.
> *Province* (Vancouver) 26 Aug. 2005: A28

(A rare meeting of *lama* and *llama*: both words are spelled correctly here.)

landed immigrant   see CITIZEN

larceny   see BURGLARY

la rentrée   see QUEBEC ENGLISH

largesse, largess   *Largesse* means gifts or money, usually bestowed by someone in a high position on people with less standing; it is often used ironically. Canadian writers most often use the *-esse* spelling, but *largess* is also accepted. Pronunciation varies, but the *g* is always soft, pronounced either as in *jest* or as in the French *je*.

> Under the New Deal, the Fair Deal, the New Frontier and the Great Society, it was the hand of government that bestowed largesse on the people.
> *Globe and Mail* (Toronto) 1 March 1985: P51

> . . . Red Wing owner Mike Ilitch spent more than $7-million on free agents and is expecting to see something more than a large number in the loss column to justify his largess.
> *Globe and Mail* (Toronto) 19 Oct. 1985: C6

last   see LATEST

last post, taps   (*The*) *last post* is a bugle call played in the Canadian and British armed forces at the end of the day, at military funerals,

and on Remembrance Day. The American equivalent is *taps*.

> Flags flew at half-mast as the band played the Last Post and a list of 24 lost warships and nine merchant ships was read aloud.
> *Daily News* (Halifax) 3 May 1993: n.p.

(Though newspapers often capitalize *last post*, dictionaries do not.)

> Twirling one end of the hose [an improvised musical instrument], he played taps.
> *Province* (Vancouver) 19 Feb. 1990: 11

larva, larvae   see PLURALS

larynx   *Larynx* rhymes with *rinks*. The word is often misspelled *larnyx* and mispronounced accordingly. The transposition of the sounds or letters of a word is not an uncommon linguistic phenomenon (see MISPRONUNCIATIONS AND PRONUNCIATION SHIFTS).

Larynx has two plurals: *larynxes,* and *larynges,* the latter pronounced *luh RIN jeez.*

See also PLURALS, REGULAR, IRREGULAR, FOREIGN.

lashes   see PLURALS

late, the   Literally, *the late* before someone's name means 'the recently living'. The expression is used as a sign of respect for someone who has died. Some usage guides say it is appropriate to use *the late* only for ten or fifteen years after a person's death, but others maintain that the honorific is appropriate as long as the deceased person is in living memory. 'Widow (or widower) of the late So-and-so' is redundant. *Late* should not be used with job titles ('late Head of the History Department') since it's unclear whether the incumbent has died or has simply changed jobs.

> . . . many famous works of art, such as the late Michelangelo's statue of David getting ready to fight Goliath, are not wearing a stitch of clothing.
> *Province* (Vancouver) 27 Dec. 1990: 44

(Here *the late* is inappropriate, since the sculptor died over 400 years ago.)

Neither, understandably, were the late Pablo Picasso, or the long-dead Rembrandt, also represented in the new fifth-floor gallery in Simpson's downtown Toronto department store.
Vancouver Sun 22 Dec. 1990: D16

(Here the author distinguishes between the *late* Picasso, still in living memory, and the *long-dead* Rembrandt.)

. . . it was he, along with Maurice Smith, late sports editor of the *Winnipeg Free Press*, who paved the way for a national schoolboys' championship. . . .
The Beaver Dec. 1989–Jan. 1990: 51–2

(Here it would be clearer to say either *'the late Maurice Smith, then sports editor'* or 'Maurice Smith, *former* sports editor'.)

See also ADJECTIVES AND ADVERBS; BELATED, LATE.

latest, last   Both *latest* and *last* are superlatives of *late*. Thus both *latest* and *last* can mean most recent. *Last* also means final. Occasionally *last* is ambiguous: 'the last issue of the magazine' could be the most recent or the final issue. For this reason, a few language commentators have advised that *last* be used only to mean final. Following this rule, however, would produce quite unidiomatic English.

Allow me to elaborate on this last [his own previous] statement.
W.C. Lougheed, ed. *In Search of the Standard in Canadian English* 1986: 66

(Here *latest* could not be substituted for *last*, even though *last* clearly does not mean final.)

See also FORMER, LATTER.

lath, lathe   *Lath* rhymes with *bath*. Laths are strips of wood fastened across the studs in a wall, over which plaster is applied. *Lath* can be used either as a countable noun ('He used some laths to make a trellis') or as a collective noun ('The plaster is crumbling, but the lath is fine').
Lathe rhymes with *bathe*. A lathe is a machine that shapes wood or metal by turning it against a fixed cutting tool.

Then the crews for plaster and lath moved in.
Geoffrey Ursell *Perdue, or, How the West Was Lost* 1984: 48

The day may soon come at the Fisheries Museum of the Atlantic at Lunenburg, N.S., when, next to the living display of a retired fisherman planing planks for a traditional dory, there'll be another nailing lathes on to the spruce-bough frame of a wooden lobster pot.
Vancouver Sun 17 June 1992: A9

(The word required here is *laths*.)

The profusion and similarity of rope-twist table legs . . . also indicates some form of screw-thread lathe, capable of producing at least rough turned rope-twist table legs in quantity.
Canadian Collector 21.2 (1986): 35

See also BATH, BATHE; COLLECTIVE NOUNS.

Latina, Latin American, Latino   see HISPANIC

Latin phrases, foreign phrases   Expressions taken from other languages can cause difficulties for readers and writers, and many such expressions are dealt with in individual entries in this book.

Most Latin in use in English today has been passed down through the professional ranks, from one generation of doctors, lawyers, scientists, academics, or priests to the next. For this reason, some people regard the use of Latin as elitist. Others condemn such disapproval as philistine. A very good argument against using Latin phrases, or any other foreign expressions, especially in non-technical writing, is that they are often not understood. On the other hand, there are occasions when the advantages of using a Latin phrase are unmistakable. For example, a phrase such as *tempus fugit*, 'time flies', a thousand years older than our mother tongue, appeals to our sense of history, reminding us that certain aspects of human life have not changed. Like all borrowings from foreign languages, however, Latin phrases should be used judiciously. While a Latin tag such as *caveat emptor*, 'buyer beware', would be highly inappropriate, even dangerous, in a public safety announcement, it would not be out of place in something written for readers who have the time and inclination to consult a dictionary.

Even today it is possible for a Latin phrase to gain currency with a new audience. The Latin phrase *quid pro quo*, for example, which means 'something for something', was not widely known outside the field of law until recently. However, lawyers and women's rights advocates began to use the phrase as a label for that particular variety of sexual harassment in which an employer or supervisor bargains for something, in this case sexual favours, by offering an employee something in return, such as a promotion or more hours of work. When cases of sexual harassment became headline news, the media introduced *quid pro quo* to the general public.

The more familiar a foreign phrase is, the less likely it is to be italicized. Latinisms such as *status quo*, 'the current state of things', *per diem*, '(a payment made) on a daily basis', and *ad hoc*, 'to this (immediate end)' are so much a part of some people's everyday vocabulary that they are no longer perceived as foreign, nor are they marked as such. For less familiar phrases, however, italics are still required, at least in formal contexts. In this book, individual entries recommend italicization in formal writing only where two of three dictionaries (*Concise Oxford*, *Webster's New World*, and *Random House Webster's College*) use italics. (Note that not all dictionaries indicate which foreign words should be italicized.) If an entry on a foreign phrase does not recommend using italics, it can be assumed that they are not necessary.

The pronunciation of Latin in English is muddled because different systems are used. In one system the words are pronounced in a manner approximating the speech of the ancient Romans (closer to modern Italian than to English). In another tradition the words are pronounced just as if they were written in English. The most common pronunciations of the most widely used Latin expressions are hybrids of these two systems. When in doubt, check a dictionary for typical pronunciations.

In each [lesson], Diana talks about some aspect of [sexual harrassment]—for example, the two types of harrassment: 'quid pro quo' and 'hostile environment.'
Toronto Star 4 May 1995: J4.

See also FRENCH WORDS; GERMAN WORDS; NUMBER PREFIXES; PLURALS, REGULAR, IRREGULAR, FOREIGN.

latter   see FORMER

laudable, laudatory   *Laudable* means worthy of praise and usually refers to people or actions. *Laudatory* means full of praise or commendatory; it usually refers to comments, remarks, speeches, reports, and so on.

> The integration of forest and wildlife management on Canadian public lands is a laudable goal, but one which governments have not pursued with any rigour.
> *Queen's Quarterly* 94.3 (1987): 618

> In her book she dissents from the usual laudatory approach by claiming he was an incompetent observer, amateur in his laboratory techniques, a parochial philosopher, and a neurotic personality!
> *Queen's Quarterly* 92.2 (1985): 424

> In helping government arrive at this laudatory goal, there will be targeted consultations throughout the province.
> *Telegram* (St. John's) 14 Dec. 2005: A6

> (The intended meaning is 'worthy of praise': *laudable* is the required word here.)

Laurentian Shield   see CANADIAN SHIELD

lawyer, counsel(lor), barrister, solicitor, notary public, attorney, power of attorney, attorney at law   *Lawyer* is the general term for a person trained in the law, especially one who advises clients on legal matters or acts for them in court. *Counsel* and *counsellor* are also used to refer to lawyers in Canadian court proceedings. A lawyer retained by a city or an organization is often called a *solicitor*. In the Canadian system, outside Quebec, all lawyers are granted the titles *barrister* and *solicitor*, and all lawyers called to the bar may also apply to become *notaries public*. Notaries public notarize documents, attesting to their authenticity, and take affidavits.

In the British legal system, and in some former British colonies, there is an important distinction between solicitors and barristers. Solicitors deal directly with clients, handling matters that do not go to court and preparing cases for barristers to take to court. Only barristers can plead cases before superior courts.

In Quebec, notaries (*notaires*) and lawyers (*avocats*) do work roughly equivalent to solicitors and barristers, respectively, in the British legal tradition. In other words, notaries advise clients on legal matters, while lawyers plead cases in court.

Attorney is a synonym for *lawyer* in the United States. In Canada, however, the term is usually restricted to compound titles. The federal minister of justice in Canada is called the *attorney general* (plural *attorneys general*). He or she oversees all prosecutions on behalf of the Crown. Each province also has an attorney general. The federal *solicitor general* oversees the Canadian Correctional Service and the RCMP. The lawyers who prosecute for the Crown are called *Crown attorneys*. The American equivalent is *district attorneys*.

A *power of attorney* is a document by which someone grants another person the right to conduct his or her business. And, by law, any person who has the legal authority to act on someone else's behalf is an attorney; strictly speaking, a lawyer is an *attorney at law*.

See also COUNCIL.

lay   see LIE

laze   see BACK-FORMATION

lead, led   *Led*, not *lead*, is the past tense and past participle of the verb *lead*. The confusion may arise because *lead*, the metal, is pronounced the same way as *led*, the past tense, and because both the past and the present tense of the verb *read* are spelled *read*.

He led a string of young children, playing his bejewelled trumpet.
Toronto Star 1 July 1992: A1

Silver . . . had been around New York for almost four years, playing in bands lead by Stan Getz and Lester Young, among others. . . .
Jack Chambers *Milestones* 1983: 182

(The correct spelling is *led*.)

leading question, loaded question   A *leading question* is one phrased so that it contains its own answer, or strongly suggests a particular answer. In a court of law, a lawyer must not ask a leading question of his or her own witness because that would amount to coaching the witness. Such questions are permitted only in cross-examination of uncooperative witnesses.

A *loaded question* is one that is risky to answer because it is subtly incriminating, emotionally charged, or highly controversial.

After a few days in court, I began to calm down and look at him as just another lawyer in the sense that he, too, had faults. One of them was that he showed a great penchant for asking leading questions of witnesses.
Jack Batten *Robinette* 1984: 217

'Can one really distinguish between the mass media as instruments of information and entertainment, and as agents of manipulation and indoctrination?'—Herbert Marcuse. . . . Marcuse's loaded question requires a loaded answer.
Globe and Mail (Toronto) 31 Aug. 1985: E1

leant, leapt   see -T, -ED

learned, learnt   see -ED; -T, -ED

leaves   see -F, -V-

lectern   see DAIS

led   see LEAD

leer, leery   A *leer* is a lascivious or predatory look; to *leer* is to cast such a look. The original meaning of *leer*, derived from the Old English *hleor*, 'cheek', was a sidelong look; now even a direct stare is often referred to as a leer.

Leery means wary. To be *leery of* something is to be suspicious of it. In British English *leery* is slang, but in North America it is standard.

> . . . he sidled up to you, his sharp, pinched face in an obsequious leer. . . . He never actually faced anyone. . . .
> Max Braithwaite *The Night We Stole the Mountie's Car* 1971: 64

(Here Braithwaite is using the original sense.)

> . . . she has straddled him, as he still sits there on the bench. Her mouth hungrily searches his. . . . 'Excuse me,' he says to the woman on top of him. . . . But the leering hag doesn't budge.
> *Canadian Fiction Magazine* 63 (1988): 16–17

(This *leer* is definitely not sidelong.)

> . . . he was willing to allow a certain amount of Jewish colonization there, but the British were leery of repercussions in the Arab world.
> *Canadian Journal of History* 14.1 (1989): 139

left-handed compliment   see BACKHANDED COMPLIMENT

legalese   see -ESE

legalize, decriminalize   Either of these words is appropriate when a crime is made legal: 'In 1969, the Canadian government *legalized/decriminalized* many forms of gambling'. Yet each word also has special uses. When something previously unrecognized in law is given official status (e.g., midwifery or same-sex marriage), it is *legalized*. When something that was once considered morally reprehensible loses its stigma, it may be figuratively *decriminalized* ('Addiction is decriminalized in the socio-medical model').

In the debate on the legal status of marijuana, a technical distinction is maintained between *legalize* and *decriminalize*. Those who want marijuana 'legalized' usually recommend that it have the same status as alcohol. Those who want marijuana 'decriminalized' typically advocate lessening the severity of some offences associated with the drug. In this context, 'decriminalizing an offence' does not mean making the activity named in the offence legal.

Rather, it means shifting the offence out of the Criminal Code and into the statutes dealing with minor violations.

> 'Personally, I make a distinction between legalization and decriminalization,' Clark said. 'What interests me is decriminalization because I don't want to have a young person carry forever the burden of a conviction for a criminal offence,' which could, for example, eliminate some career options.
> *Calgary Herald* 23 May 2001: A5

See also INDICTABLE OFFENCE, FELONY, SUMMARY OFFENCE, MISDEMEANOR.

legendary   see MYTHOLOGICAL

legion, legionnaire, legionary, Legionnaires' disease, commissionaire   *Legion* should be capitalized when it refers to a particular group: the Royal Canadian Legion, the American Legion, the Royal British Legion, etc. Members of these associations are called *legionnaires*. *Legionnaire* may also refer to a member of the French Foreign Legion, which consists of soldiers who are not French citizens. *Legionary* most commonly refers to soldiers in ancient Rome.

The name of the strain of pneumonia identified in 1976 at a convention of the American Legion is usually capitalized: *Legionnaires' disease*. Note the position of the apostrophe, after the *s*.

In Canada a *commissionaire* is a member of the Corps of Commissionaires, a group of retired Armed Forces personnel and police officers who are employed as security guards, dispatchers, by-law enforcement officers, and so on. Note that *commissionaire* has only one *n*, while *legionnaire* has two.

> . . . among educated urbanites the 'corny' country songs emanating from the lounges, Legion halls, and car radios of Canada are all too often associated with rural backwardness, social and political conservatism, or even worse, American mass culture.
> *Queen's Quarterly* 95.2 (1988): 292

> Legionnaire Alfred Bowden, 74, said members of

Branch 24-106 don't dwell on their wartime experiences.
Gazette (Montreal) 3 June 1990: A3

Retrospective studies have demonstrated cases of Legionnaires' disease as far back as 1943, and 23 species of the bacteria have been found—only a few of which are dangerous to humans.
Vancouver Sun 2 June 1990: F6

Visitors to the building had to get a pass from the commissionaire's desk.
Daily News 31 Dec. 1994: n.p.

legislatures   see APPENDIX I

legitimate, legitimize, legitimatize   All three forms are accepted as verbs.

. . . regardless of legal determinations, politicians will read the section as legitimating unilingualist political drives.
Queen's Quarterly 94.4 (1987): 799

. . . the basis of psychoanalysis is materialistic; it strives after truth, disregarding 'authority' that is not legitimized by reason, rejecting mysticism and metaphysics.
Henry M. Rosenthal and S. Cathy Berson, eds. *Canadian Jewish Outlook Anthology* 1988: 127

Argueta says the old code, even though accepted by the industry, really legitimatized censorship, and that the same thing could happen again.
Toronto Star 12 Feb. 1992: B3

See also DECRIMINALIZE, LEGALIZE.

leisure   Note the correct spelling: *-ei-*, not *-ie-*. The word may be pronounced to rhyme either with *seizure* (the usual American pronunciation) or *pleasure* (the British pronunciation). Canadians use both.

See also -IE-, -EI-.

leitmotif   see MOTIVE

lemma, lemmata   see PLURALS

lend   see LOAN

lengthy, long   Several usage guides, including *Fowler's* (1965), suggest that *lengthy* means overly long and implies tediousness, and should not be used as a simple synonym of *long*. This recommendation is at odds with Canadian usage, in which *lengthy* sometimes implies comprehensiveness or thoroughness.

By contrast, a secured creditor need not invoke the rather lengthy judicial machinery required to obtain an execution. . . .
J.E. Smyth et al. *The Law and Business Administration in Canada* 1987: 735

(Here the words 'rather' and 'judicial machinery' suggest that the process is indeed tedious.)

Goetz took special care with this lengthy novel, wishing to make 'every sentence and every picture genuine.'
Canadian Journal of History 14.1 (1989): 75

(Here *lengthy* means long, but not tedious.)

Closed on an off-and-on basis since 1989 for a lengthy expansion and development project, the museum officially reopens this year. . . .
Alan Tucker, ed. *The Penguin Guide to Canada* 1991: 278

(Here *lengthy* means long, but not necessarily tedious.)

lesbian   see GAY

less   see COMPLETE; FEWER; TIMES LESS; WELL KNOWN

lessor, lessee, mortgagor, mortgagee   The *lessor*, the landlord, lets a house to the *lessee*, the occupant. The *mortgagor*, the impecunious housebuyer, mortgages (i.e., pledges) his or her house to a *mortgagee*, usually a bank or trust company. If the mortgagor fails to make loan payments, then the ownership of the house is transferred to the mortgagee. In short, the people who make the monthly payments are the lessee and the mortgagor.
Mortgager is an uncommon spelling variant of *mortgagor*.

This insurance protects the lender (mortgagee) rather than the borrower (mortgagor).
Globe and Mail (Toronto) 20 April 1985: H4

. . . sellers and lessors of computer products no longer would be able to place disclaimers on warranties limiting their responsibility for product performance.
Globe and Mail (Toronto) 16 Oct. 1985: B6

The relationship between Public Works, which is the largest lessor of office space in Ottawa, and Campeau, the largest renter [owner] of space, was questioned by Mr. St. Germain. . . . In his report, Mr. Dye charged that the government ended up signing a 10-year lease for $155-million, $43 million more than Campeau was originally willing to take.
Globe and Mail (Toronto) 30 Jan. 1985: P5

(Here *lessor* is used incorrectly for *lessee*. Since Public Works is leasing space owned by Mr. Campeau, Public Works is the lessee.)

See also -ER, -OR.

lest The conjunction *lest* is fairly common in Canadian prose in spite of its oratorical ring. It means 'in order that . . . not' or 'for fear that'. *Lest* is followed by *should* or by a verb in the subjunctive mood. In the latter case, the verb following *lest* takes the form of the bare infinitive: 'Lest he perish (*not* perishes)'.

In British English *lest* is commonly followed by *should*: 'Lest he should perish'.

When you are a senior, your options are closed, your [financial] situation is fixed and you can only guard it carefully lest it erode further.
United Church Observer May 1986: 33

The writer in more popular pages has only to pity, and reject, and readers who have no firm opinions of their own will acquiesce, lest their own sophistication and modernity be called in question.
Robertson Davies *A Voice from the Attic* 1960: 33

See also SUBJUNCTIVE.

letter carrier see JOB TITLES

liable, likely, apt *Liable* meaning responsible, especially fiscally responsible, is followed by *for*: 'They were liable for damages'. *Liable* meaning vulnerable is followed by *to*: 'They were liable to increased infection after surgery'.

The traditional distinctions between *liable*, *likely*, and *apt* are that *liable* indicates exposure to the risk of something undesirable ('liable to be robbed'), *likely* indicates probability ('likely to come back'), and *apt* indicates a tendency, habit, or inclination ('apt to bolt'). Some commentators add that *liable* and *apt* should be applied only to people. On the whole, however, Canadian usage is not so discriminating. For those who would still like to observe some distinction, it may be useful to remember that *likely* is the most widely applicable and least controversial of these three words.

Children as young as seven years old were liable to imprisonment in a penitentiary with hardened criminals.
Vancouver Sun 10 Dec. 1990: A2

There is in Canada, too, a traditional opposition to the two defects to which a revolutionary tradition is liable, a contempt for history and an impatience with law.
Northrop Frye *The Bush Garden* 1971: 14

A hard-hitting piece of writing by a man is liable to be thought of as merely realistic; an equivalent piece by a woman is much more likely to be labelled 'cruel' or 'tough.'
Margaret Atwood *Second Words* 1982: 197

(Here Atwood uses *liable* and *likely* as synonyms.)

Organic pollutants like PCBs are stored in fatty tissue, so high-fat species like trout, salmon, arctic char, smelt and perch are likely to have higher levels of PCBs than are other species.
Canadian Consumer Jan. 1985: 8

When these folks aren't whining about their personal misfortunes, they're apt to be yapping on about the larger adversities around them.
Vancouver Sun 23 June 1990: D22

Out of the basic research is apt to emerge the next batch of miracle drugs or an industrial breakthrough.
Vancouver Sun 28 July 1990: B6

(Here some would substitute *likely*.)

Pneumonia is more apt to occur during the fall and spring months, he explains.
Country Guide Nov. 1986: H22

(Here some would substitute *likely*.)

liaison, liaise   The word *liaison* has long referred to communications within the military and to secret sexual relations. Now it also commonly refers to the job of fostering connections between groups. Although this use has been criticized, it's well established.

The verb *liaise*—a back-formation from *liaison*—still raises the hackles of many usage commentators. It is rare in formal Canadian writing, but common in journalism.

The most common pronunciations of *liaison* are *lee AY zun* and *LEE ay ZAWN*. Occasionally these words are misspelled without the second *i*.

. . . I spent a year at the Imperial Defence College in London before taking up my new duties as chief of the defence liaison division in the Department of External Affairs.
George Ignatieff *The Making of a Peacemonger* 1987: 120–1

. . . the nameless narrator relates his liaison with the former mistress of a pro-revolutionary colleague. . . .
Ben-Z. Shek *French-Canadian & Québécois Novels* 1991: 50

When selecting workers, both for immigration and for work permits, visa officers liaise with the department of employment, which provides them with updated lists of occupations in Canada for which there is more demand than supply.
Vancouver Sun 7 Aug. 1990: A9

See also BACK-FORMATION.

Liberal   see GRIT

liberal arts   see ARTS

libertine, libertarian   Today a *libertine* is a sexually licentious person, usually a man. Historically, however, a *libertine* was a freedman, a man released from slavery in ancient Rome. A *libertarian* is either a believer in free will or a proponent of civil liberties such as freedom of the press, or the right to vote and assemble. Libertarians in this sense are wary of government—in particular, of what they see as its encroachment on the privacy, freedom of belief, or right to expression of the individual, in the name of the public good.

In the President's resentful mind Trudeau possessed the cardinal sins of intellectual arrogance, a libertine lifestyle, and a liberal inclination that bred softness on defence and in relations with the East.
Queen's Quarterly 92.1 (1985): 115

She was a woman of independent thought, a female star in a male-dominated milieu and a sexual libertine, to boot.
Ottawa Citizen 31 Oct. 1999: C9

Thus, although ideological evolution in Quebec is generally seen as positive . . . there is also the emergence of a Left, which, in the narrator's view, began by being libertarian then became authoritarian.
Ben-Z. Shek *French-Canadian & Québécois Novels* 1991: 94

Despite the libertarian and anti-etatist [anti-state] principles of much nineteenth-century statecraft, bourgeois society created the modern interventionist state. . . .
Queen's Quarterly 94.4 (1987): 976

library   Both *r*'s in *library* should be pronounced; *LIE berry* is non-standard.

See also FEBRUARY; STANDARD ENGLISH, STANDARD.

licence, license   see -CE, -SE

lichen   *Lichen*, the plant, and *liken*, the verb, are pronounced the same way. In British English *lichen* may also be pronounced to rhyme with *kitchen*.

lie, equivocate, waffle, prevaricate, misspeak oneself   *Lie* is the bluntest and most negative of these verbs. *Equivocate, waffle,* and *prevaricate* are less harsh because they admit a grey area between truth and untruth, though people who are not inclined to accept grey areas would call these words euphemisms. *Equivocate* has two meanings. The first is to use ambiguity to create the wrong impression; the second is to speak in such a vague or contradictory way that one cannot be held to account. *Waffle* is the slang word for this practice. *Prevaricate* means to speak or act evasively; it suggests either weakness or immorality. To *misspeak oneself* is to lie accidentally by saying the wrong thing without noticing; the expression was used as early as 1894 in the United States.

> Sales staff who will do anything to make a sale—who will blatantly lie or mislead a customer—are not an asset to their employers.
> *Globe and Mail* (Toronto) 8 Jan. 1985: F9

> Five per cent of five hundred million dollars . . . was enough to make any witness equivocate on his testimony.
> Jack Batten *Robinette* 1984: 148

> While such questions were at the centre of attention in Latvia, Lithuania and Estonia, most of Georgia's radical leaders waffle on the big questions.
> *Ottawa Citizen* 13 Oct. 1990: B4

> If William Vander Zalm is shown to be a clownish prevaricator (that's liar in English), then who wants to support the development of a strong provincial government?
> *Vancouver Sun* 16 May 1991: A17

> There is no margin of error, no time for reflection and certainly no possibility of pulling a Ronald Reagan and declaring afterwards you misspoke yourself.
> *Ottawa Citizen* 1 Sept. 1990: B5

See also AMBIGUOUS, AMBIVALENT, EQUIVOCAL.

lie, lay   In eighteenth century British English, the meanings and forms of *lay* and *lie* overlapped, as they often do today in North American speech. The accepted past forms of the verb to *lie* (i.e., *lay* and *lain*) have never passed the lips of many educated Canadians. Yet writing is another matter. Writers and editors in Canada and the United States make a concerted effort to adhere to contemporary Standard British English usage, where these two verbs are distinguished as follows:

	past tense	*past participle*
lie (recline)	lay	(has) lain
lay (place, set down)	laid	(has) laid

Thus, in written Canadian English, *lay* always requires an object. You have to lay *something*: 'Lay your coat over the end of the bed'; 'I just laid it somewhere'; 'She laid great emphasis on training'; 'The media has laid siege to her house for days'. The only exception to this rule is that hens can be said simply to lay. (Presumably no object is needed because it is widely known *what* they lay.)

And, in *written* Canadian English, *lie* never takes an object: 'She lies in bed for hours'; 'Since his accident, he can neither sit nor lie comfortably'; 'The fault lies with the manufacturer'; 'A folder was lying on top of it'; 'The dogs licked her face as she lay on the rug'; 'He had just lain down to rest, when the telephone rang'.

> 'I've just been laying low, staying home, being a kid.'
> *Province* (Vancouver) 26 May 2006: B5

(The common expression *laying low* appears in this quotation of speech; the written standard requires *lying low*.)

> 'We have never laid down and died,' said Clark.
> *Calgary Herald* 13 April 1998: D3

(The written standard requires 'We have never *lain* down . . .'.)

See also HYPERCORRECTION.

lieutenant   Canadians are more likely to pronounce the first syllable of this word *loo-* than *lef-* (*Modern Canadian English Usage*, 1974; 'Survey of Vancouver English', 1984). Americans use only the former pronunciation, and the British use only the latter. Yet some Canadians feel that only *lef-* is acceptable, and *lef-* is the common pronunciation in the Canadian Forces. The 1979 'Socio-dialectology Survey' of English spoken in the Ottawa region revealed that, in general, the frequency of the *lef-* pronunciation rose with the speaker's socio-economic status; however, there was a strong shift towards *loo-* in younger speakers from all socio-economic groups.

lieutenant-governor   see HEAD OF STATE; LIEUTENANT

ligature   see DIPHTHONG

light, lighted, lit   The forms *lighted* and *lit* can both serve as either the past tense or the past participle of the verb *light*. Either form may also be used before a noun.

He lighted a cigarette and grinned at Harley.
Canadian Fiction Magazine 64 (1988): 61

We lit fires in what is now Sunnybrook Park, roasted hot dogs, and boiled cans of water for our tea.
Miriam Waddington *Apartment Seven* 1989: 29

Changes in lighting at the airstrip will enable a medical helicopter to land there at night instead of at a lighted playing field in town.
Vancouver Sun 27 July 1990: B7

A lit cigarette left on a mattress is being blamed for a fire that killed a four-year-old New Brunswick boy Saturday.
Guardian (Charlottetown) 26 April 2006: A10

See also ALIGHT, ALIT.

lightning, lightening   *Lightning* is accompanied by thunder. A *lightening* is a lessening of darkness or weight. *Lightning* is often misspelled *lightening*.

Occasionally a blink of lightning cut the darkness.
Constance Beresford-Howe *Night Studies* 1985: 137

His face changed, lightening unmistakably with enthusiasm.
Robertson Davies *One Half of Robertson Davies* 1978: 108

Chatham is a very small town and word travels at lightening speed on the street.
Globe and Mail (Toronto) 12 June 1985: P7

(The correct spelling is *lightning*.)

light-year   In scientific usage a light-year is a measurement of distance, not time. It is the distance that light travels in one earth year in the vacuum of space (about 9,460,500,000,000 km). *Light-year* is often used figuratively to refer to cultural or social distance. In scientific contexts the common use of *light-year* to refer to a very great length of time should be avoided.

The nearest star, Alpha Centauri, is 4.3 light-years away, or about 25 trillion miles.
Terence Dickinson *Halley's Comet* 1985: 43

(In this example *light-years* is a measure of distance.)

This bastion of Montreal's English-speaking establishment was light-years removed from the home life I led with my mother and my brother Leonid.
George Ignatieff *The Making of a Peacemonger* 1987: 42

(Here *light-years* is used figuratively to refer to cultural difference.)

The worksheet is from a home economics course taught at John Oliver in 1960. That's 1960s, as in 34 light years ago.
Vancouver Sun 11 May 1994: A13

(Here *light-years* refers to the enormous cultural distance between the 1960s and the 1990s.)

likable, likeable   see -ABLE, (-E)ABLE

like, as   *Like* preceding a noun, noun phrase, or pronoun is accepted: 'He laughs like a hyena'; 'Karen looks like her father when he was a baby'; 'We can't all write like him'. In these examples, *like* is being used as a preposition.

However, many usage guides strongly object when *like* is used as a conjunction. Subordinate conjunctions, such as *because*, *since*, and *although*, precede more than just a noun or noun equivalent: they precede a clause with a *verb* in it ('because I *know* him'; 'since they *came*'; 'although she *dances* well'). Objections are raised when *like* is used as a subordinate conjunction meaning *as* ('Are you going to treat me like you treated him?'), *as if* ('It looks like he's in trouble again'), *(in) the way (that)* ('Put your hands on your hips like she does'), or *such as* ('She was wearing a hat like you used to see on matrons at lunch'). In each of these examples, according to the experts, *like* should be replaced by the italicized phrase preceding the parentheses. The problem with this hard distinction between preposition and conjunction is that several words can be either: *after*, for example, can be a preposition ('He went out after the dog') or a subordinate conjunction ('She went out after Harry started to tell jokes'). The *OED* lists citations for *like* as a conjunction from the 1500s on, and this usage appears to be increasing.

That said, it is true that most of the examples we have found of *like* used as a conjunction come from quoted speech, fiction, or fairly informal prose. Thus it makes sense to avoid this construction in more formal writing.

'I tell Peggy that she's like a rock star in Canada.'
Chatelaine June 1986: 100

Nothing promotes an appreciation of peace like losing.
Saturday Night March 1986: 5

The arts in Canada are not flourishing as they should be.
Saturday Night March 1986: 8

'At first it looked like I was going to win by acclamation. . . .'
Saturday Night March 1986: 30

(Here *like* is used as a conjunction in speech; in writing it should be replaced with *as if*.)

What if we waited a year like we promised and they still didn't want us to marry, then what?
Chatelaine April 1986: 153

(In a more formal context, this *like* should be replaced with *as*.)

They are thick and wet, not drawn and white like they used to be.
David Williams *Eye of the Father* 1985: 177

(In non-fiction, an editor would probably change this *like* to *the way*.)

See also GO, LIKE, SAY; LIKE, SUCH AS.

like, such as According to some conservative editors, the word *like* should be reserved for resemblance: 'Sally, like Mary Meigs, took up writing late in life'. In their view, an actual example of something should be introduced by *such as*, and never by *like*: 'Antibiotics, such as penicillin and tetracycline, are ineffective against a cold'. Many writers try to observe this rule, especially in formal writing, but many others, including some language commentators, reject it as niggling.

Since language commentators can so rarely resist a nice distinction, their balking at this one

bears closer attention. What seems to make the difference is that this rule does not take into account the idiomatic use of *like* to introduce an actual example intended to suggest a type, not merely to illustrate one: 'I'm so glad to have a friend like Paul'. The speaker is happy not just to have a friend resembling Paul but to have Paul as a friend: Paul is an example defining a type. *Such as* would not be idiomatic in this context. Even in formal writing, *like* is preferable to introduce examples that suggest rather than merely illustrate a category.

Privacy, like individualism, is a historical product; it emerges only when there is a public domain, that is, in relation to the state.
Queen's Quarterly 96.2 (1989): 303

(Here *like* indicates resemblance.)

The primary focus of Edelson's book is on the attacks made in the last decade and a half by philosophers of science such as Ernest Nagel, Karl Popper and Adolf Grünbaum.
Queen's Quarterly 92.2 (1985): 416

One way of getting around this problem is by comparing units of analysis smaller than countries, such as provinces or states.
Canadian Journal of Sociology 14.2 (1989): 167–8

Movement heroes like Noam Chomsky and Norman Mailer also praised Orwell.
Canadian Journal of History 14.1 (1989): 8

(Some conservative editors would substitute *such as* for *like* here.)

Certainly it is unwise to start with something like *The Unnamable*.
Queen's Quarterly 94.2 (1987): 294

('*The Unnamable*' is an example that defines a category; *like* is idiomatic.)

But why use terms like 'racial origin' at all when they are so inexact?
Richard Davies and Glen Kirkland, eds. *Dimensions* 1986: 123

('Racial origin' is an example that suggests a category; *like* is idiomatic.)

And, since the world that Wallace draws from is woman-centred, her poems have a female perspective—in strong contrast to the male-centred viewpoint of a Purdy poem like 'At the Quinte

Hotel' or even of a Lee poem like 'The Death of Harold Ladoo'.
Queen's Quarterly 98.1 (1991): 59

(The poems mentioned suggest types; *like* is idiomatic.)

The theory enables us to do things such as fly around the world in a heavy bulk of metal.
Queen's Quarterly 97.4 (1990): 622

(Here *like* would be preferable because the example suggests a category.)

See also GO, LIKE, SAY; LIKE, AS.

like for, want for, say for   *Like for* ('We'd like for you to come') is heard in the speech of the Ottawa Valley and the American South. *Want for* ('He wants for us to stay in school') is rare in writing and considered nonstandard. Standard Canadian English omits the *for* in both instances.

British commentators also object to *say for* meaning tell ('She said for me to wait'). Although this construction may not appear in formal Canadian writing, it is certainly unobjectionable in speech.

Just once I'd like for a game to stop. For a referee to say, 'Take your time, Ken. Ready when you are,' and with everyone fading to the side, to look up at the crowd. . . .
Ken Dryden *The Game* 1983: 199

likely   see LIABLE

like(s) of   *The likes of* is most often used either to praise or to disparage. Usually it precedes a famous name or a list of famous names, but it can also be used slightingly: 'I wouldn't be caught dead with the likes of him'. Some commentators have taken a distinct dislike to this expression, calling it non-literary and even non-standard. However, the phrase has been Standard English for over 200 years and is used in all kinds of Canadian writing. *The like of* is a rare variant. Some commentators suggest that it is preferable to *likes* before a single name, but writers do not make this distinction.

'I did five shows with the likes of Brent Carver, Peter Donat, Albert Schultz. I looked on it as acting boot camp. . . .'
Toronto Star 6 June 2006: C8

I yearned for a place at the round table in the Algonquin. . . , parrying witticisms with the likes of Robert Benchley, James Thurber, Harold Ross, Franklin Pierce Adams and the rest.
Max Braithwaite *The Night We Stole the Mountie's Car* 1971: 11

Not only did he consider himself . . . several notches above the likes of me; he also made it clear that he found my remarks offensive and inappropriate.
George Ignatieff *The Making of a Peacemonger* 1987: 172

Lillooet, Lil'wat   see STL'ATL'IMX

limit, delimit   To *limit* something is to allow it to go to a certain point and no further. To *delimit* something is not to hold it within bounds, but to define or determine its bounds. When something is delimited by an inanimate object, that inanimate object forms its natural boundary: 'The northern boundary is delimited by a creek'.

The Elmwood expects to limit its membership to 1,500 members.
Bon Vivant Nov. 1981: 18

The thrust of these works . . . is not to delimit the borders of the novel but rather to break down established boundaries [between the novel, biography, travel writing, etc.].
Queen's Quarterly Spring 1985: 198

limited to only   see WORDINESS

limpid   see TURGID

linage, lineage   see -E

lingua franca   The phrase *lingua franca* is Italian for 'Frankish tongue'. In the seventeenth century it referred to the working language of eastern Mediterranean sea ports, a hybrid of Italian, French, Spanish, Greek, Arabic, and Turkish. Now a *lingua franca* (plural *lingua francas*) is any common or hybrid language used by people who do not share a native tongue. For example, Spanish is the lingua franca of diverse Indian peoples of Central America and English is a lingua franca in India. Metaphorically, anything that allows people of different backgrounds to understand each other is a lingua franca. A lingua franca may be a fully developed language (e.g., Latin in the Middle Ages) or a pidgin (e.g., Nigerian Pidgin in the multilingual Nigeria).

> 'Between the last vestiges of empire remaining to England and the global domination of America,' Urdang told his audience, 'the English language has become established as the lingua franca.'
> *Gazette* (Montreal) 19 May 1990: K2

> It was developed back in the '70s by a publishing industry group as a lingua franca for data base operators and typesetters.
> *Business Journal* June 1991: 18

> 'Violence is a lingua franca (in prisons). I'm just surprised there isn't more of it,' said Mr. Graham, an 11-year veteran of the correctional service.
> *Globe and Mail* (Toronto) 30 March 1985: M5

> 'Even white wine has fallen into disuse; the lingua franca of the lunch set is iced tea with Sweet'n Low.'
> *Globe and Mail* (Toronto) 25 Oct. 1985: D4

(This is a dubious use of *lingua franca*, since the communicative power of tea is limited.)

See also PIDGIN, CREOLE.

linguist Multilingual people are sometimes called *linguists*, a usage that many language commentators deplore. They advise using *polyglot* for a person who speaks several languages and reserving the word *linguist* for specialists in the field of linguistics, the study of the structure and nature of language. In academic writing, this distinction is observed—as it should be—but, in journalism, *linguist* is robustly ambiguous. Journalists use the word *linguist* to describe scholars in the field of linguistics, as well as polyglots, good foreign language learners, and highly articulate speakers. *Polyglot* is not broad enough in meaning to replace the non-academic senses of the word *linguist*.

> Nikolai Iakovlevich Marr (1865–1934), archaeolo-

gist and linguist, a polyglot and an internationally recognised authority in the languages and civilisations of the Caucasus, was elected member of academy before the October Revolution, in 1912.
> *Toronto Slavic Quarterly* 13 (2005)

(In this academic context, the terms 'linguist' and 'polyglot' are contrasted.)

> The British are western Europe's worst linguists and are getting worse, a new European Commission survey reported yesterday. Fewer than one in three Britons can converse in a second language. . . .
> *Gazette* (Montreal) 24 Sept. 2005: A32

(In this newspaper account, 'linguists' are those with knowledge of more than one language.)

See also POLYGLOT.

lion's share The expression *lion's share* comes from Aesop's fable in which a lion and several smaller animals go hunting. The lion first divides the kill and then claims everything for himself. Some commentators argue that the *lion's share* of something should mean all of it, because the lion in the fable took all of the kill. However, in English usage the *lion's share* means the largest portion, and this meaning is widely accepted.

> The lion's share, more than 95 per cent, leaves the country, and the chief beneficiaries are the Hollywood majors.
> *Vancouver Sun* 27 Nov. 1990: B11

> Prescription medicines account for the lion's share, ringing in at $20.6 billion, or eight out of every $10 spent.
> *Calgary Herald* 11 May 2006: A12

liqueur see LIQUOR

liquid see FLUID

liquor, liqueur, [liquer] *Liquor* (whisky, gin, vodka, etc.) and *liqueur* (brandy, schnapps, crème de menthe, etc.) both describe alcoholic drinks, but they are not identical: a *liqueur* is flavoured, often with fruits or spices, has a strongly sweet taste and is usually consumed with dessert. These spellings are sometimes confused, and, more commonly still, one or the other of this pair is misspelled *liquer*.

Liqueur can also refer to a chocolate filled with liqueur: 'She gave me a box of liqueurs for Christmas'.

> The tropical fruit tones give way to very smooth premium vodka and cognac, leaving a slight burn that fades quickly to a subtle aftertaste that isn't sticky like sugary liquers.
> *Edmonton Journal* 23 Aug 2003: H4

(The spelling required here is *liqueur*.)

lit   see LIGHT

litany   A *litany* is a type of prayer in which the officiant recites or chants verses, and the congregation chants formulaic responses. *Litany* is also used figuratively to refer to any repetitive, monotonous recital or account. Some people, however, use *litany* simply to indicate a large number. This extended use is not recommended.

> Plamondon recited a litany of historical 'humiliations' endured by Quebecers and speculated that a new party could be formed to work for sovereignty-association.
> *Vancouver Sun* 26 June 1990: A1

> Irving also seems to know his CanLit: at one point, Wheelwright offers a litany of praise for Canadian authors . . . that reads more like a book list than a scene from a novel.
> *Maclean's* 3 April 1989: A63

> Among the litany of great songs to follow . . . were several from the band's latest album, Word of Mouth.
> *Globe and Mail* (Toronto) 21 March 1985: E4

(This writer probably did not mean to imply that the songs were boring; 'the *host* of', or simply 'the *many*', would be better here.)

literally, figuratively   *Literally* is derived from the Latin word for 'letter'. To use words literally means to use them without metaphorical or allegorical intent, adhering strictly to the 'letter'. In different contexts, 'That car is hot' can mean (literally) that the engine has overheated or the passenger area is hot, or (figuratively) that

it is either stolen or trendy. Often, however, *literally* is used loosely to mean 'almost' or 'virtually', as in 'We were literally climbing the walls'. The speaker of this sentence would not expect to be asked how they did it. In fact, *literally* here overlaps in meaning with its opposite, *figuratively*. Although this extended use of *literally* is common in speech, it is criticized and should be avoided in writing.

> The ground staff at O'Hare Airport pulled out all the stops—literally stopping Flight 831 after it left the terminal to get the surgeon aboard for the flight to Winnipeg.
> *Vancouver Sun* 29 June 1994: B1

> This type of mousse . . . not only keeps stray strands in place, but can also keep hair literally standing on end.
> *Globe and Mail* (Toronto) 22 Jan. 1985: F8

(Here, because 'to have one's hair standing on end' is usually a figurative expression denoting terror, the writer has used *literally* to qualify it.)

> That situation . . . assured that the Athenian political stew would be boiling over—literally.
> *Globe and Mail* (Toronto) 29 May 1985: P1

(Here *literally* should be omitted.)

> Just 15 years earlier he had been, literally, king of the jazz world.
> *Globe and Mail* (Toronto) 11 May 1985: E8

(Here *unquestionably* would be a better choice.)

See also VERITABLE.

literary present   see PRESENT TENSE

litre   see APPENDIX II

livable, liveable   see -ABLE, (-E)ABLE

llama   see LAMA

loaded question   see LEADING QUESTION

loan, lend   In spoken English and in financial circles, *loan* is often used as a verb: 'Loan me your coat'; 'They loaned her 4 million dollars'. In fact, *loan* has been used as a verb since at least the sixteenth century. However, it fell out of use in England after the seventeenth century, and although it has continued to be used as a verb in North America, many North American commentators disapprove of the usage. The more common verb in writing is *lend* (past tense *lent*): 'I lent her my coat last night'. To avoid criticism it's best to use *loan* only as a noun ('The picture is on loan') in general formal writing.

> They undertook to . . . lend it $75,000 at 6 per cent for nine years, and to make a second loan of the balance for fourteen years with no interest for the first nine.
> Frederick Gibson *Queen's University* 2 (1983): 65

> The board loaned him $1-million (U.S.), at three per cent interest, to purchase a house.
> *Saturday Night* July 1986: 42

(In the context of banking, the verb *loan* is not disputed.)

> . . . I remembered the camera somebody had loaned me for the trip, which I hadn't even used once.
> *Canadian Fiction Magazine* 63 (1988): 51

(Some commentators strongly prefer *lent*.)

loath, loth, loathe, loathsome The adjective meaning reluctant is usually spelled *loath*; the older form, *loth*, is becoming obsolete. Both spellings are pronounced to rhyme with *both*.

The verb *loathe*, which means to detest, always has a final *e*. The adjective *loathsome* (sometimes misspelled *loathesome*) means repulsive. The *th* sound in these two words is like that in *breathe*.

> As the fate of the Meech accord continues to hang precariously, most of the key players in the original negotiations are more loath than ever to talk on the record about their historic closed-door sessions back in 1987.
> *Gazette* (Montreal) 14 April 1990: B1

> We are probably loathe to interfere with a system [the justice system] that has such tradition behind it.
> *Ottawa Citizen* 9 Dec. 1990: A10

(The correct spelling here is *loath*.)

> Those who like the new car like it a lot; those who

hate it loathe it—there's no middle ground.
Ottawa Citizen 28 July 1990: A25

> This night he tells a story about Beowulf; how the Saxon lord crosses the sea to Denmark to rid the Danes of Grendel, a loathsome monster.
> *Vancouver Sun* 23 July 1990: B4

> Greg Kramer's Petruchio is a fairly loathesome, swaggering brute, a bellowing presence with an ugly demeanor and an underlying sickliness.
> *Ottawa Citizen* 16 July 1994: F5

(The correct spelling is *loathsome*.)

loaves see -F, -VE

local see FUNCTIONAL SHIFT

lode, lodestar, lodestone A *lode* is a vein of metal ore. A *lodestar* is a star, such as the North Star, that shows the way; *lodestar* is used figuratively to mean a guiding principle or leading light. *Lodestone* is a naturally magnetic rock; the word is used figuratively to mean a strongly attractive person or thing.

> The bite of the gold bug drove me on. Even after the Chilcoot Pass in '98, my one burning dream was to find the mother lode in the lost mine of the Sierra.
> *Atlantic Salmon Journal* Autumn 1990: 27

> The last significant group of artists nurtured in Sugar Hill were the young jazz musicians who emerged in the wake of the bebop revolution, and among them Sonny Rollins was the lodestar.
> Jack Chambers *Milestones* 1983: 123

> Besides there's a wee stumbling block; I get lost. A lot. Without the conveniently named North Shore mountains as my lodestar, I'd never get home.
> *Province* (Vancouver) 4 March 1990: 85

> . . . already she's contemplating a further trip back to Newfoundland. It has become her lodestone, her private magnet.
> *Gazette* (Montreal) 6 June 1994: C3

> Conflict of interest is not a strong suit in the Vander Zalm understanding of life. Because of the public impression that he was using his office to enhance the worth of what became known as Schlock City, the theme park became the lodestone for demonstrators.
> *Financial Post* 11 Sept. 1990: 13

It's bad enough right now that Chris Bosh, the third-year star and lodestone of the franchise, seems to be . . . undervalued.
National Post (Toronto) 4 Oct. 2005: S4

(*Lodestar*—meaning guiding light—is the word needed here.)

-log, -logue   see ANALOG; CATALOGUE; DIALOGUE

long   see LENGTHY

long-sighted   see NEAR-SIGHTED

look   see ADJECTIVES AND ADVERBS

lookism   see -ISM

look out, look up   see IDIOMS

lookout, overlook   Canadians use *lookout* as a noun meaning a place that affords a good view of a scene below. Americans use *overlook* as a noun for this sense.

. . . [we] hiked to a lookout atop Flapper Hill to watch the morning sun brighten forested islands, strewn like stepping stones across the bay.
Globe and Mail (Toronto) 4 May 1985: T11

You're a hop and a skip, then, to the top of the dam. There are scenic overlooks worth stopping at en route.
Globe and Mail (Toronto) 2 Feb. 1985: T20

(This example comes from an article about Nevada written by an American.)

loonie, toonie   The informal, popular name for what the Canadian Mint calls the one-dollar coin is the *loonie* (plural *loonies*). The two-dollar coin has been dubbed, by analogy, the *toonie* (plural *toonies*). The loonie was introduced in 1987, the toonie in 1996. The spelling of both words, now stabilized, varied for a while: *looney*, *loony*, *twonie*, and *twoonie* were all briefly tried but rejected.

In financial news, *loonie* is sometimes used as a synonym for *Canadian dollar*.

Interestingly, the loonie would have had a different name (as would the analogous toonie)

if the original design, depicting a voyageur, had not been lost, forcing the substitution of the second-choice design, a loon.

[He] will be hanging around outside the Vancouver Art Gallery this weekend, crooning for loonies and gyrating for passers-by.
Vancouver Sun 25 Aug. 1994: D1

The loonie has been drifting lower for some time, setting eight-year lows this week. However, it is still above the all-time low of 69.20 cents US. . . .
Calgary Herald 30 Dec. 1994: C7

Better yet, spend a toonie on a packet of arugula seeds, plant them in a container and give them some sun.
Edmonton Journal 6 May 2006: D2

lose, loose   *Lose* (misplace) is sometimes misspelled *loose* (not tight)—perhaps because *lose* rhymes with *choose*. This mistake is rare in published writing.

loss leader, [lost leader]   see MISHEARD EXPRESSIONS

lot, lots   see A LOT

loth   see LOATH

lounge chair   see CHAISE LONGUE

lovable, loveable   see -E

lovely   see ADJECTIVES AND ADVERBS

low-lifes   see -F, -VE-

Loyalist   see CONSERVATIVE

loyalness   see -NESS

luck into, luck out   To *luck into* something is to have the good luck to encounter or acquire it, and to *luck out* is to be lucky. These two expressions mean almost the same thing, but many people think *luck out* means just the opposite. There is, in fact, some evidence that during the Second World War *luck out* meant run out of luck, but in the 1950s the positive meaning became established. *Luck into* and *luck out* are both informal.

> It was 10 years ago that McCaffrey basically lucked into the sport.
> *Calgary Herald* 27 June 1992: C4

> There's a quiche featured most days, and I hope they're all as successful as the broccoli one I lucked into.
> *Ottawa Citizen* 29 Oct. 1992: H5

> Dillon lucked out: he got the role of Tyler, one of the Denim Blues nice guys.
> *Ottawa Citizen* 17 June 1992: C9

> Harry and Muriel O'Reilly lucked out. They had proof that their grandchildren really belonged to them when they faced a Canada Customs officer at the Canada-U.S. border. . . .
> *Vancouver Sun* 26 May 1992: A3

> 'We've lucked out the last couple of years, losing to both John Base in Medicine Hat and Al Edwards from the U.S. in Cornwall.'
> *Globe and Mail* (Toronto) 14 March 1985: M9

(Here *luck out* refers to bad luck.)

lumber   see TIMBER

luminous   see TRANSPARENT

lunch, luncheon   see DINNER

luster, lustre   see -RE, -ER

lustful, lusty   *Lustful* means desiring, usually in a sexual way. *Lusty* means vibrant, hearty, or energetic ('The carollers gave several lusty renditions despite the cold'), but confusion between these words has led some dictionaries to add lustful as a second meaning of *lusty*. Thus the use of *lusty* in ambiguous contexts should be avoided.

> Sexually suggestive conversation was banned, as were lustful looks and sexually offensive jokes.
> *Calgary Herald* 18 June 2005: A14

> There are unlikely alliances, surprising betrayals, lusty adult sexual tension and ingeniously well-placed moments of comic relief.
> *Daily News* (Halifax) 28 Aug. 2005: 8

(Here *lusty* is used as a synonym of *lustful*.)

luxuriant, luxurious   *Luxuriant* means lush, prolific, or fertile; it usually refers to vegetation, or to a head of hair or a beard. *Luxurious* means extremely comfortable, even opulent, and often has connotations of self-indulgence.

> In Brazil's portion of the luxuriant Amazon River basin alone, at least 20 per cent of the region's rain forest—covering 9.8 million acres—has already disappeared as settlers clear land for agriculture and cattle-grazing.
> *Maclean's* 5 Sept. 1988: A38

> Many a weak chin was concealed behind a luxuriant growth of hair.
> *Gazette* (Montreal) 26 Aug. 1990: D3

> There's also 'a luxurious lobby entrance that is elegantly furnished' and has a 24-hour concierge, as well as a guest suite and party room.
> *Toronto Star* 27 May 2006: P10

> For those aching to play the elegant sophisticate with traces of Grace Kelly minimalism, there is a luxuriant balmacaan-style coat in cashmere.
> *Globe and Mail* (Toronto) 27 Aug. 1985: F3

(Balmacaan coats are usually made of tweed, which is not really hairy enough to be described as *luxuriant*; perhaps *luxurious* was intended.)

> The vignettes in The Wall Street Journal Book of Chief Executive Style show vividly that the combination of luxuriant lifestyle and the distance most CEOs keep from subordinates has created a new class in North American society.
> *Financial Post* 18 Dec. 1989: 12

(Lifestyles are *luxurious*.)

M

MA   see ABBREVIATION

ma'am, madam, madame   *Ma'am* is an oral form that is written down only in representations of speech. For all its seeming folksiness, *Ma'am* remains an appropriate way to address the Queen in speech. *Ma'am* and *madam* are sometimes used by sales clerks, restaurant staff, and people on the street to address mature women they don't know by name. Some women find this usage overly deferential and some dislike the implication that their youth is behind them (young women in the same context are addressed as *Miss*).

A letter to a woman whose name is not known may begin 'Dear Madam'. *Madam* is also used as a formal title, preceding the name of a woman's rank or office: 'Madam Prime Minister', 'Madam Chair', 'Madam Justice'.

Madame, abbreviated *Mme*, without a period (plural *Mesdames*, abbreviated *Mmes*), is French for *Mrs.* or *Ms.*: in French all adult females are addressed as *Madame*, regardless of their marital status. *Madame* is sometimes used by English-speakers to refer to the wives of foreign dignitaries: 'Madame Chiang-kai-shek'. Profes-sional women in the performing arts sometimes take the title *Madame* as well.

A woman in charge of a brothel is called a *madam* (not a *madame*).

See also MISS, MR., MRS.; MS.

macabre, macaber   Some American dictionaries list *macaber* as an alternative spelling, but Canadian writers prefer the older spelling, *macabre*. The *-er* spelling probably developed to match the pronunciation used by English-speakers unaccustomed to French: *ma CAW ber*. The more common pronunciations are closer to the original French: *ma CAW bruh* and *ma CAWB*.

See also -RE, -ER.

Mach   see GERMAN WORDS, PRONUNCIATION OF

Machiavellian   Niccolò Machiavelli (1469–1527) was an Italian statesman and political theorist whose name has become synonymous with unscrupulous political manipulation. His best-known work, *Il Principe* (*The Prince*), is remembered for the assertion that, although a ruler is morally obligated to his subjects, all means and actions are justified in order to maintain power.

The *ch* is pronounced as if it were *k* and the main stress is on *vell*. Most writers and dictionaries capitalize the adjective: *Machiavellian*.

> Macdonald—previously relatively unknown to the British public—became infamous now as a Machiavellian, cunning politician conniving for profit and prejudice with slavers and manstealers.
> William Teatero *John Anderson: Fugitive Slave* 1986: 114

macho, machismo   Borrowed from Spanish in the 1960s, these words commonly describe an exaggerated, aggressive masculinity; both are generally used disapprovingly. The adjective *macho* is also sometimes used as a noun (plural *machos*) meaning a macho man.

Macho is pronounced *MAH cho*. In Spanish the noun *machismo* is pronounced with the *ch* of *church* and the *i* is sounded as a long *e*: *mah CHEEZ mo*. Some dictionaries give only this pronunciation, but the anglicized pronunciation, with the *ch* sounded as in *mechanic* and followed by a short *i* sound, is also accepted: *mah KIZ mo*.

> Asked what they would change about men, women said men should express their feelings more, be more understanding of women's needs, be more sensitive and less macho.
> *Vancouver Sun* 30 Oct. 1990: B6

Once Butler got over his macho male football inclination to slap a helmet or punch a shoulder pad in
encouragement, he's been fine.
Times-Colonist (Victoria) 13 May 2006: A20

Machos with reform on their minds can do well by
following the example of broadcaster Jim Robson,
who has maintained a sunny attitude despite two
decades of watching hockey's hapless Canuckle-
heads.
Province (Vancouver) 11 March 1990: 75

The Calgary Police Department, which has the
most restrictive chase policies in Canada, has regulations aimed at attacking the traditional machismo of such pursuits.
Globe and Mail (Toronto) 3 Jan. 1985: P1

mad, madding   In conversation and informal writing *mad* means angry, while in formal
and literary contexts it means insane.

Madding is an uncommon word meaning
frenzied. 'The madding crowd' is an allusion to
Thomas Gray's poem *Elegy Written in a Country
Churchyard* (1751) and Thomas Hardy's novel
Far from the Madding Crowd (1874). Sometimes
writers now substitute *maddening* for the unfamiliar word *madding* ('the maddening crowd'),
but the literary sources are well known and
maddening is likely to be thought an error.

'I hope you're not mad at me for going through
your wallet?'
Howard Engel *Murder Sees the Light* 1984: 181

. . . nobody could visit the patients in these places
except the persons who had committed them;
thus, once in a country asylum, a man or woman
was lost to the world, and those who were not
mad already quickly became so.
Robertson Davies *A Voice from the Attic* 1960: 118

When Langlois comes home after working long
hours at Victor Michaels, he can suspend time, for
a little while at least, in this comfortable haven, far
from the madding crowd.
Edmonton Journal 11 May 2006: F1

In expressing the pain of gay-bashing they experience, Cadell sings poetically about 'what a lovely
day on the beach it will be' when the maddening
crowd 'swooshes out to sea, leaving all of the different ones, shining and free.'
Toronto Star 11 Sept. 1993: F14

('Maddening crowd' is likely to be considered
an error.)

Madam, Madame, Mademoiselle   see
ABBREVIATION; MA'AM

maestro, maestri   see PLURALS

Magdalen(e), magdalen(e), maudlin
Magdalene and *Magdalen* are variant spellings.
The name of the former prostitute in the New
Testament is usually spelled Mary *Magdalene*.
The *Magdalen* Islands are a group of twelve
islands in the Gulf of St. Lawrence. A
magdalen(e) is a reformed prostitute or a shelter
or reformatory for prostitutes. *Magdalen(e)* is
pronounced MAG *da leen* or MAG *da lin*.

The names of *Magdalen* College at Oxford and
Magdalene College at Cambridge are pronounced MOD *lin*, preserving a former British
pronunciation of *Magdalene*. The adjective
maudlin (MOD *lin*) means overly emotional or
tearfully sentimental (Mary Magdalene is usually shown weeping dramatically in paintings of
the Crucifixion).

Luke tells us that Jesus was accompanied on an
extensive preaching tour by 'the 12' and by many
women, including Mary Magdalene, Joanna and
Susanna, 'who provided for them out of their
means.'
United Church Observer June 1986: 16

Swimming, bicycling, wind-surfing, seafood, and
scenery draw thousands of visitors to the
Magdalen Islands each year.
Alan Tucker, ed. *The Penguin Guide to Canada*
1991: 118

He remembers with great pride hearing Oxford
University's Magdalene College Chapel Choir sing
one of his compositions. . . .
Performing Arts in Canada Spring 1990: 32

(The Oxford college is spelled *Magdalen*.)

Magna Carta, Magna Charta   *Magna Carta*,
the 'Great Charter', was signed by King John at
the demand of the English barons at
Runnymede on 15 June 1215. It guaranteed personal and political liberties and limited the

power of the monarch. The term is now also used figuratively to refer to any constitution or document that guarantees civil and political rights. Canadians prefer the spelling *Magna Carta* to the alternative *Magna Charta* for both literal and figurative uses.

Magna Carta does not take the definite article *the* when it refers to the historical document.

It took me . . . from reading Magna Carta in the British Museum Library to a Headless Valley soccer match between weary firefighters. . . .
Vancouver Sun 14 Feb. 1990: A11

. . . the Act itself may be regarded as the Magna Carta of a large number of Her Majesty's subjects in Upper Canada.
William Teatero *John Anderson: Fugitive Slave* 1986: 37

maiden name, birth name, former name, née, né

Maiden name refers to the original surname of a woman who takes her husband's name at marriage. Non-sexist usage guides recommend *birth name* or *former name* as gender-neutral alternatives. These terms are broader than *maiden name*, since they can refer to anyone's original or previous name; names are also changed for professional reasons (taking a pen name or stage name) or on adoption or ennoblement.

Né and *née*, the masculine and feminine adjectives meaning 'born' in French, are also used to indicate a person's birth name. *Né*, the masculine form, is rare. Most often *née* is used in English to specify a married woman's surname at birth. Some commentators point out that since only the surname changes with marriage, *née* should apply to it alone: 'Elizabeth Myers, née Smith', not 'Elizabeth Myers, née Elizabeth Smith'. The accent on *née* is often omitted in newspapers. However, it is useful in indicating the accepted pronunciation, which is *NAY*; some dictionaries also list the anglicized pronunciation *NEE*. Since *né(e)* is another term marked by gender, some non-sexist guides suggest substituting *formerly*, which can be used for both men and women.

Sometimes *né* or *née* is used in journalism to indicate the former name of an object or place, or to introduce the real person or place behind a fictional depiction. Dictionaries do not mention these uses—which stray from the meaning 'born'—and they should be avoided in formal writing.

His wife, Bernadette, is a French immersion teacher, and he changed his name from Strom to Morin-Strom—Morin being her maiden name—to reflect their three daughters' francophone culture.
Ottawa Citizen 24 July 1990: B5

As in other Hébert works, the heroine has several names—her stage name, Flora Fontanges, her birth name, and the name that had been given her by the disagreeable Upper Town family she was adopted by to erase her Lower Town origins.
Ben-Z. Shek *French-Canadian & Québécois Novels* 1991: 104

This week we got a letter from Mrs. J.W. Rose (nee Constance Nicholl) of Dawlish Avenue, Toronto.
Globe and Mail (Toronto) 16 May 1985: E3

(Here *née* is followed by the full name before marriage, because Mrs. Rose is using her husband's initials.)

. . . the gown designed by Montreal-born designer Arnold Scaasi (ne Isaacs, which is Scaasi spelled backwards) was available at Holt Renfrew.
Gazette (Montreal) 3 Aug. 1992: C7

(The use of *né* to refer to a man's birth name is uncommon.)

. . . [he] was a mainstay at Calgary's Skyline Hotel (nee Four Seasons) for more than a decade.
Calgary Herald 7 Oct. 1994: D1

(The use of *née* to refer to the former name of some*thing* is informal.)

The 'high, fast living' is regarded by the young men with genuine horror . . . and is intended as a clear, effective antidote to the 'quaintness' of the old town of Salterton (nee Kingston).
Gazette (Montreal) 20 Oct. 1994: B2

(Robertson Davies' fictional town of Salterton is based on the real Kingston, Ontario; this use of *née* is informal.)

But Isadora (nee Erica) is now 50, and the titillation of Fear of Flying has been replaced by prurient shlock.
Calgary Herald 27 Aug. 1994: A16

(Isadora, the heroine of Erica Jong's novel *Fear of Flying*, bears some resemblance to Erica Jong herself; this use of *née* is informal.)

mail   see COMPUTER TERMS

mail carrier, mailman   see JOB TITLES

maître   see ESQUIRE; QUEBEC ENGLISH

maize   see CORN, GRAIN, MAIZE

major   see SUPERIOR

majority, plurality, minority, age of majority   According to some authorities, *majority of* should not be applied to things that cannot be counted, such as weather, time, or work: 'I spend the majority of my time at work on the phone'. While sentences of this type are clearly established and standard, they are criticized. Substituting *most of* before uncountable nouns will forestall criticism.

Majority can take a singular or a plural verb depending on whether it refers to a single unit ('The majority is unconvinced') or a group of individuals ('The majority are parents with young children'). After a prepositional phrase containing a plural noun, the verb is always plural: 'The majority of the books in the collection were donated by their authors'.

In reference to voting: when there are only two candidates, the one with more votes has the *majority*; when there are three or more candidates, however, the terminology can vary. A candidate who wins more than half the votes has a *majority* or an *absolute majority*. A candidate who receives more votes than any other candidate, yet fewer than half the total number cast, has either a *majority* or a *plurality*.

The terms *majority* and *plurality* can also be used to describe the numerical spread in a victory. If, out of 22 votes cast, Potvin received 12, Levy 7, and Smith 3, then Potvin would win 'by a majority of two votes' (Potvin received two more votes than the combined total of the opponents). If, on the other hand, Potvin received 9 votes, Levy 8, and Smith 5, Potvin would win 'by a plurality of one vote' (Potvin was one vote ahead of the nearest opponent).

In the parliamentary tradition, a 'majority government' is one with more seats than all opposition seats combined, while a 'minority government' has the most seats of all parties, but fewer than half the total seats.

In Canada the *age of majority* is the age of full legal responsibility, at which one may vote and enter into contracts. By common-law tradition, this age is twenty-one, but it has been lowered to eighteen or nineteen in several provinces and territories.

The majority of the growth over the forecast period will stem from an acceleration in upgrades and expansion of the telecommunications infrastructure by the major telephone companies.
Computer Dealer News 21 March 1991: 16

('Most growth' would be more appropriate and less wordy.)

Quebec is also the only province where Chretien does not have an absolute majority of support among those who expressed support for a new Liberal leader.
Gazette (Montreal) 5 March 1990: A2

However, a plurality of French-speaking Quebeckers—47 per cent to 41 per cent—said they'd reject a constitutional deal if Canada's rights charter took precedence. Twelve percent were unsure.
Ottawa Citizen 2 June 1991: A4

'He didn't say how it broke down, but the majority sees things your way.'
Howard Engel *Murder Sees the Light* 1984: 205

(Note the singular verb form.)

The majority of the netsmen are tenants, and do not own the fishing rights.
Atlantic Salmon Journal Summer 1990: 35

(Note the plural verb form.)

Minority governments have not worked badly in our history.
Vancouver Sun 3 April 1991: A16

See also COLLECTIVE NOUNS.

make do, [make due]   *Make do* means to manage in straitened circumstances (to *make less do* the job). It is probably mere inattention that causes writers to substitute *make due* for *make do*.

> The Toronto Maple Leafs will have to make due without Owen Nolan for the next two weeks.
> *CBC Sports Online* 5 Jan. 2004

(Here *make due* should be *make do*.)

makeover   see PHRASAL VERBS

malapropism, Goldwynism, Irish bull   A *malapropism* is a misuse of words, especially by someone trying to sound sophisticated, resulting from a confusion between words that are similar in sound and appearance. The term derives from the name of a character in Richard Brinsley Sheridan's play *The Rivals* (1775): Mrs. Malaprop. Fowler calls Mrs. Malaprop 'the matron saint of all those who go wordfowling with a blunderbuss'. Though the accidental misuse of words had been used humorously in literature by Shakespeare and others before Sheridan, the speeches of Mrs. Malaprop (from the French *mal à propos*, 'unsuitable', 'out of place') constitute classic examples: 'Sure, if I *reprehend* anything in this world, it is the use of my *oracular* tongue, and a nice *derangement* of *epitaphs*' (read *comprehend*, *vernacular*, *arrangement*, and *epithets*, respectively).

A *Goldwynism* is a verbal blooper resulting from an illogical word choice—often a word that is the opposite of what would make sense. It takes its name from Samuel Goldwyn, the movie mogul and founder of Metro-Goldwyn-Mayer (MGM), who is said to have uttered such gems as 'Include me out' and 'You've improved it worse!' *Goldwynisms* are similar to what the British call *Irish bulls*—ludicrous, self-contradictory statements. Classic examples of Irish bulls are 'The next time I take you anywhere you'll stay home' and 'It was hereditary in his family to have no children'. The origin of the term *Irish bull* is uncertain, but it is not likely to have been the Irish who coined it.

Addressing an international meeting of tugboat operators in Halifax last month, Bacon welcomed the visitors who had come, he said, 'from all the countries across Canada.'
Maclean's 22 Oct. 1990: 17

(Roger Bacon was premier of Nova Scotia in 1990–91. Politicians are perhaps no more likely than anyone else to misuse words, but, since their every public statement is on record, they are subject to greater scrutiny.)

John Robert Colombo's *Dictionary of Canadian Quotations* (1991: 318) lists two more Canadian malapropisms:

> After nine rounds of a slam-bang boxing match at Maple Leaf Gardens, radio commentator Chuck Murphy expected a strong finish: 'Believe me, folks,' he told his audience, 'this is one close fight—a real cliff-dweller.'

> Kierans: Of course I have my own ox to grind here.

See also SLIPS OF THE TONGUE.

male nurse   see JOB TITLES

malinger   To *malinger* is to pretend to be sick. The use of *malingering* as a synonym for *remaining* or *lingering*—with negative connotations suggested by the prefix *mal*—is something new, and as yet non-standard.

> But Krutov's advisers decided it was time to clear the air and answer charges that he was overweight, malingering and has lost his desire to play the game.
> *Vancouver Sun* 18 Sept. 1990: C6

> There are still a few malingering ZZ Top fans who figure the band blew its credibility when it bear-hugged the MTV ethic five years ago with the Eliminator album.
> *Gazette* (Montreal) 14 Oct. 1990: F5

(Here *remaining* would be a better choice.)

> I also believe that jaywalking, which involves malingering in the roadway, is in the traffic act.
> *Telegram* (St. John's) 24 July 2000: 6

(Here *lingering* is the word needed.)

Maliseet, Malécite, Wolastoqiyik The Aboriginal people of the St. John River Valley whose territory overlaps New Brunswick, Quebec, and Maine are usually called *Maliseet*; sometimes the French spelling *Malécite* is used, with or without the accent. *Maliseet* is also the name of their language. *Maliseet* is not a Maliseet word but a Mi'kmaq name for this group; for this reason some members of this First Nation prefer to use their own word: *Wolastoqiyik*.

See also ABENAKI; ABORIGINAL PEOPLE(S); APPENDIX III.

man see SEXIST LANGUAGE

mandarin, Putonghua, Mandarin, Cantonese The nine highest ranks of educated officials of the Chinese Empire were called *mandarins* by Portuguese explorers in the sixteenth century. In English *mandarin* now refers to a high-ranking civil servant, or any influential person, and is suggestive of closed ranks and conservative behaviour. A *mandarin* (sometimes spelled *mandarine*) is also a small orange.

The official language of mainland China is *Putonghua*, which means 'common language' and is pronounced *POO tong gwah*. Putonghua is a standardized language, based on Mandarin, the regional dialect spoken by the majority of Chinese. Putonghua is taught in the schools, used in government, and used as a lingua franca throughout the country. The system for writing Putonghua in roman letters, rather than Chinese characters, is called Pinyin. *Putonghua* is a fairly new word in English; most English speakers use *Mandarin* to refer either to the official language of the People's Republic of China or to the regional dialect that it most closely resembles.

Cantonese is the dialect of Chinese spoken in Guangdong (formerly Canton) province and Hong Kong. Until recently, it was the dialect of most Chinese immigrants to Canada.

> He took postings in Ottawa, London, and Paris, and lived the life of a government mandarin.
> *Vancouver Sun* 31 May 1990: A10

> 'Does a finance minister really run things, or is he just a captive of the mandarins?'
> *Saturday Night* March 1986: 28

> Beginning in the 1950s, the Chinese government made Mandarin the national language to bridge the dialects across the country. Since then, the government has been working to simplify the language, renamed 'Putonghua.'
> *Vancouver Sun* 16 Jan. 2006: A7

> Yeung, who speaks fluent Mandarin and Cantonese and can understand several other dialects of the Chinese language, said there are numerous benefits to having ethnic minorities in positions of power.
> *Vancouver Sun* 27 April 1994: B4

See also CHINESE NAMES; PINYIN, WADE-GILES.

manageable see -ABLE, -(E)ABLE

maneuver see MANOEUVRE

mango see -OS, -OES

mania see PHOBIA

manifestation see QUEBEC ENGLISH

manikin see MANNEQUIN

manipulable see -ABLE, (-AT)ABLE

manipulate see SEXIST LANGUAGE

Manitoba see APPENDIX I

Manitoban see NAMES OF RESIDENTS OF CITIES AND PROVINCES

manitou In the Algonquian family of languages *manitou* means mysterious being or spirit. The supreme deity is called *Gitchi Manitou*, 'Great Spirit'.

> The Ojibwa named the place Manitou Land after the great god, Gitchi Manitou.
> *Globe and Mail* (Toronto) 17 May 1985: P4

mankind, manmade see SEXIST LANGUAGE

mannequin, manikin, mannikin *Mannequin*, *manikin*, and *mannikin* are variant spellings of the same word. *Manikin*, 'little man', was borrowed from Dutch around 1600; it was used literally to describe people of very short stature, and figuratively as an epithet of contempt. These meanings are obsolete. However, *manikin* was also used very early to refer to models of the human body, such as those used by artists, tailors, and doctors-in-training, and this meaning has survived.

Around 1900, the same word was borrowed into English again, this time via French. The French spelling, *mannequin*, is now commonly used in fashion writing and recommended by most Canadian style books. Nevertheless, some writers prefer the anglicized *mannikin*.

In French and in British English, a *mannequin* is usually a person: a living, breathing fashion model. This meaning may come as a surprise to Canadians for whom a *mannequin* is a dummy.

The headphones were tested using an 'average' ear from the head of a special dummy called a Knowles Electronics Manikin for Acoustic Research. . . .
Canadian Consumer Jan. 1985: 21

In passing, Lesje glances into the windows of dress shops, department stores, appraising the cadaverous mannequins who stand with their pelvises thrust forward, hands angular on hips, legs apart, one knee bent.
Margaret Atwood *Life Before Man* 1979: 18

As she stood stone still in the window of a fashion store called Workshop, it was difficult to tell whether she was real or a mannequin.
Saturday Night May 1986: 55

In his very first collection, he startled the audience with the languorous pace of his presentation, to the sound of Bach, a speed dictated by the fact that he could afford only six mannikins.
Globe and Mail (Toronto) 5 Feb. 1985: F8

(Here the *mannikins* are live models; this spelling is unusual for this sense.)

manner (manor) born, to the 'To the manner born' is the original quotation; it comes from Shakespeare (*Hamlet* 1.4.15) and it means accustomed from birth to a certain way of life. 'To the manor born', meaning accus-

tomed to the high life, is a pun; it's widely used, though always regarded by some as an error rather than a witticism.

As if to the manner born, Quebec Liberals accept their place at the nerve centre of the party.
Gazette (Montreal) 5 May 1988: B3

Aristocratic 'Poppy' Bush of Andover and Yale may have been to the manor born, but he's going to run a Main St., down-home presidency.
Financial Post 18 Jan. 1989: 13

(Here *to the manor born* means accustomed from birth to a high position; some object to this use.)

mannikin see MANNEQUIN

manpower see SEXIST LANGUAGE

manoeuvre, maneuver *Manoeuvre* and *maneuver* are alternative spellings. *Manoeuvre* is favoured in Canada and Britain, *maneuver* in the United States. *Manoeuvre* and its derivatives are misspelled almost as often as they are spelled correctly. Note that in the correct spellings there is no *e* between the *v* and the *r*: *manoeuvred*, *manoeuvring*, *manoeuvrability*, *manoeuvrer*. However, most Canadians pronounce *manoeuvring* as four syllables, not three, and this is probably what leads people to insert the extra *e*.

Manoeuvre is a French borrowing, and in the past the *o* and the *e* were typeset, as in French, as a ligature, *oe*. In current Canadian English the ligature is not used.

The electorate, however, was unsympathetic to this manoeuvre and Coutts lost the election.
Queen's Quarterly 95.3 (1988): 664

Precision skating is a team skating sport where up to 30 girls are required to perform complicated maneuvers in unison.
Today's Skater 1991: 59

(In Canadian English *maneuver* is much less common than *manoeuvre*.)

'Nickle is certainly manoeuvering to make a place for himself,' Richardson wrote to Macdonnell in March. . . .
Frederick Gibson *Queen's University* 2 (1983): 86

(The correct spelling is *manoeuvring*.)

. . . there are six different products being offered, all with light-weight tubular steel shafts that are cranked or angled near the top to give easy manoeuverability without extra effort.
TLC . . . for plants Summer 1991: 44

(The correct spelling is *manoeuvrability*.)

See also DIPHTHONG, DIGRAPH, LIGATURE.

manor born, to the   see MANNER BORN

manqué   *Manqué* is an adjective borrowed from French; it follows the noun it modifies and indicates a frustrated or unfulfilled vocation: 'He's a successful lawyer but a poet manqué'. In formal writing the accent should be retained.

. . . Miss Feinstein, a policewoman manqué . . . listens constantly to the police radio from her mayoral limousine.
Globe and Mail (Toronto) 23 Feb. 1985: P9

. . . Houde was an actor-manque, a born ham, a delight to look at and listen to.
Gazette (Montreal) 17 Aug. 2004: A20

manse, parsonage, rectory, vicarage   The name of the house traditionally built beside a church to house the incumbent minister varies by denomination. Presbyterian ministers live in a *manse*, as do some ministers of the United Church (depending on the denomination of the congregation before 1925, when the United Church was formed). Other United Church ministers, like their Methodist forerunners, live in a *parsonage*, while Roman Catholic or Anglican priests usually live in a *rectory*. In the Anglican Church, a vicar served a parish whose tithes did not pass to him (as they did to a rector); a vicar lived in a *vicarage*.

His father was a Presbyterian minister, and Law's childhood home was in a manse close to the broad Richibucto River. . . .
Globe and Mail (Toronto) 15 June 1985: T3

The [Anglican] church was built by its members in the late 1800s, says Les, and its rectory may have been the first mission house in the area.
Canadian Heritage Feb.–Mar. 1986: 18–19

See also RECTOR, VICAR; UNITED CHURCH.

mantel, mantle   Originally these were variant spellings of the same term, but most dictionaries and commentators now distinguish them. In contemporary use a *mantel* is a shelf above a fireplace; a *mantle* is a cloak or cover. *Mantle* often means cloak in a figurative sense: 'In becoming a politician she chose to wear her father's mantle'; 'He wore the mantle of secrecy'.

In the dining room, the mantel is swagged with pine cones, holly and fruits.
Toronto Star 2 Dec. 1989: H14

(Only the fireplace *mantel* is spelled *-el*.)

Pierre Elliott Trudeau inherited the mantle, the issues and the conflicts of Wilfrid Laurier.
Maclean's 31 March 1986: 13

[The single remaining gas lamp] stands on the corner of King and Lower Union streets, with its mantle proudly glowing day and night.
Whig-Standard (Kingston) 21 Nov. 2001: 9

(*Mantle* is the spelling for the gauzy sheath around a jet of gas.)

'In a brilliant public relations stroke, Michael Wilson has stolen the mantel of earlier tax reforms, but left behind their substance.'
City Magazine Spring 1988: 8

(Here the context requires *mantle*.)

A friend of mine had hand-cut and sanded and worked the mantle with a jacknife.
Canadian Heritage Feb.–Mar. 1986: 20

(*Mantel* is the spelling needed for a fireplace shelf.)

manufacture, manuscript   see SEXIST LANGUAGE

Maple Leaf, Maple Leaves, Maple Leafs
Maple Leaf is usually capitalized when it refers to Canada's national emblem. The official name of the flag is the National Flag of Canada, but it

is often unofficially called the Maple Leaf. The Royal Canadian Mint produces a gold coin called the Maple Leaf.

Since the standard plural of *leaf* is *leaves*, using *Maple Leaves* as the plural for the emblem, flag, or coin is probably best. However, traditional usage at the mint favours *Maple Leafs* for the coins, and *Maple Leafs* is the correct name for Toronto's National Hockey League team.

Twenty-five years ago, on a cold, damp Ottawa morning, Canada's new red-and-white Maple Leaf flag unfurled from Parliament's Peace Tower.
Province (Vancouver) 15 Feb. 1990: 14

They wrapped their leader's shaky personal credibility in giant Maple Leafs and American-style rah-rah.
Gazette (Montreal) 19 Nov. 1988: B5

(Referring to the flag, *Maple Leaves* would be more widely accepted.)

A spokesman for the Royal Canadian Mint in Ottawa said sales of Maple Leafs in the U.S. market are up by almost a third from last year's pace.
Globe and Mail (Toronto) 7 June 1985: B1

(Either *Maple Leafs* or *Maple Leaves* is acceptable for the coins.)

A Toronto Maple Leafs fan, crushed by years of failure, has put his loyalty to his once-beloved team up for sale. . . .
National Post (Toronto) 20 May 2006: A12

(*Maple Leafs* is the name of the hockey team.)

An hour of picking our way along the trail . . . brought us to a 100-foot-deep rocky valley with a small stream splashing down into a dark pool with red and orange maple leafs adrift on its surface.
Financial Post 18 Oct. 1991: 46

(When a maple leaf is foliage, the standard plural is *leaves*.)

See also -F-, -V-.

maritime, Maritimes, Maritime provinces   see ATLANTIC PROVINCES

mark   see QUEBEC ENGLISH

marketwise   see -WISE

marriage, same-sex marriage, same-sex spouse   Canadian law now defines civil marriage as 'the lawful union of two persons to the exclusion of all others'. Thus the marriage of same-sex partners should be called simply *marriage*, and their status *married*. The terms *same-sex marriage* and *same-sex spouse* are useful in contexts where they are needed to avoid confusion. The adjective *same-sex* is preferred to *gay* ('gay marriage') in being gender neutral.

See also COMMON LAW; GAY, LESBIAN, HOMOSEXUAL, TRANGENDERED, QUEER.

marsh   see SWAMP

marshal   *Marshal* is the recommended spelling for both the noun ('field marshal') and the verb ('marshal your forces'). Among major dictionaries only *Merriam-Webster's* lists *marshall* as an acceptable alternative. The final *l* of *marshal* is usually doubled before *-ed* or *-ing*.

Richard McConomy will be the grand marshal of the parade.
Gazette (Montreal) 12 Feb. 1992: F6

In his ability to absorb and marshal facts, especially the strengths and vulnerabilities of fellow politicians, Nixon rivalled Lyndon Johnson.
Queen's Quarterly 95.4 (1988): 809

. . . the rationality of a belief appears to be normally a matter of factors in which it is grounded, and of how they enable the agent to respond to relevant considerations, not of [a person's] ability to marshall such factors in defending it.
Canadian Journal of Philosophy 19 (1989): 263

(The recommended spelling is *marshal*.)

Are [pressure] groups adept at marshalling public opinion?
A. Paul Pross *Group Politics and Public Policy* 2nd ed. 1992: 92

But while Sherry quickly marshaled her resources against the physical attack of AIDS, finding the emotional strength to fight was harder.
Calgary Herald 9 Aug. 1992: A9

(The single *l* before *-ed* is quite uncommon, but not unacceptable.)

See also DOUBLING THE FINAL CONSONANT.

Marxism   see -ISM

masterful, masterly   *Masterful* can mean skilful, powerful, domineering, or authoritative, whereas *masterly* almost always means skilful. In many contexts either word is appropriate.

The adverb form of *masterly* poses some problems. No one seems to use the awkward form *masterlily*, and though *masterly* can be used as an adverb, it's confusing; *masterfully* and *in a masterly manner* are less troublesome alternatives.

Guides to gender-neutral usage suggest avoiding both words in favour of synonyms, such as *skilful*, *authoritative*, and *accomplished*, that do not imply that skill and authority are primarily male ('the master's') qualities.

Scotch is such a masterful liquor that it does not take kindly to mixing with inferior potations.
Bon Vivant Aug.–Sept. 1982: 13

(Here *masterful* means powerful or domineering.)

It is a masterful piece of drumming, probably Roach's best showing until the two takes of *Ko Ko*. . . .
Jack Chambers *Milestones* 1983: 38

(Here either word is appropriate.)

The style is masterly, for it is unceasingly witty without blinding the reader by a display of fireworks—candlelight on fine silver is rather the effect.
Robertson Davies *A Voice from the Attic* 1960: 238

(Here either word is appropriate.)

Her fictions are masterfully constructed, and critics are correct in drawing our attention . . . to the intricate texture and surface polish of her narratives.
Janice Kulyk Keefer *Reading Mavis Gallant* 1989: 36

(The adverb *masterfully* means skilfully or authoritatively, or both.)

See also SEXIST LANGUAGE.

materialist, materialistic, material   A *materialist* prizes the pleasures that money can buy over spiritual or intellectual ones. The adjective form is *materialist* or *materialistic*. These words generally describe people or attitudes, and their connotations are always unfavourable. *Material* simply means concrete, physical, or real, and is neutral in its connotations. Sometimes writers use *materialist* or *materialistic* where *material* would make more sense.

Ah, Christmas; the time of year when people go running around the malls in a frenzied dash for whatever gift they can get to satisfy the rabid materialistic instinct that seems to overtake even the most pious of people at this time of year.
Sudbury Star 15 Dec. 2005: C3

'No matter what happens—whether we have a negotiated settlement or an imposition—there will be a transition period and that means there won't be a material effect for 1995.'
Gazette (Montreal) 22 Nov. 1994: C8

The truth is that, besides all his materialistic contributions, such as helping Hydro Quebec, Levesque is largely responsible for the incredible advancement of Canada's second-largest province.
Toronto Star 1 Nov. 1987: D3

(The word required here is *material*.)

See also MATÉRIEL.

matériel   *Matériel*, spelled with an accent over the first *e*, is a military term for equipment and supplies; it should not be confused with *material*. *Matériel* is usually pronounced *ma teer ee ELL*; the accent is sometimes dropped in informal writing.

They also shipped vast amounts of war materiel to Iraq.
Maclean's 13 Aug. 1990: A20

matrix, matrices   see PLURALS

maudlin   see MAGDALEN(E)

maunder, meander   To *maunder* (rhymes with *wander*) means to express oneself in a dreamy or rambling, often incoherent, manner. The connotation is strongly negative, the implication being that the speaker is not thinking clearly. To *meander* means to follow a winding course or to wander aimlessly. A river might meander through the countryside, or a walker through a neighbourhood. *Meander* is also used in reference to speech and writing. Here the connotation is usually negative—readers tend to grow impatient with a writer who will not get to the point—but it is not necessarily so: a writer's digressions may be stimulating and enjoyable.

> His own arguments for Meech Lake have been maundering sentimentalism, spiked with historical falsehoods.
> *Ottawa Citizen* 4 March 1990: A10

> Just inject the car into a giant multilevel lot. No point maundering around like a doomed soul looking for the perfect spot.
> *Globe and Mail* (Toronto) 19 June 2004: F9

> (*Meandering* is the word needed here.)

> Lewis could have been forgiven if he had meandered easily through a lazy little talk.
> *Saturday Night* May 1986: 38

> But [the playwright's] meandering journey to this climactic encounter is refreshingly witty and inventive.
> *Gazette* (Montreal) 28 May 1994: C7

maverick   see PYRRHIC

may, can   The traditional distinction between these two words is that *may* is associated with permission, *can* with ability. Children are frequently taught to use *may* when asking permission, and are told that the question 'Can I go now?' means only 'Am I physically able to leave?' The may/can distinction is a traditional feature of elementary-school education, rather like the use of 'Sir' in the military. That *can* is used to express ability ('I can speak Hebrew') is indeed accurate. Both *can* and *may*, however, are used in contemporary English to ask permission ('Can/May I come in?). *Can* is idiomatic and correct in this use, and, especially with the addition of *please* ('Can I see your passport, please?'), unquestionably polite. Nonetheless, *may* is perceived as more formal and more

refined. Thus, in answer to the question 'Can I come in?' some people will pointedly reply, 'You *may*'.

See also MAY, MIGHT.

may, might   In some contexts, *might* acts as the past tense of *may*. For example, if someone says 'That may be true', we report it to someone else this way: 'He said that it might be true'. Often, however, the two words are used similarly to express a possibility ('I may be able to help you'; 'I might be able to help you'). Although *might* is felt by some speakers to express a more tentative possibility than *may*, others perceive little difference. This perception may explain the occasional production of puzzling sentences that use *may* where only *might* is appropriate: 'More careful drug testing may have averted the tragedy'. Here 'the tragedy' did in fact occur: the possibility of averting it existed only in the past, and so *might* is required.

> U.N. Secretary-General Boutros Boutros-Ghali also told CBC . . . that quick intervention may have prevented the wave of brutal killings that followed the death of Rwandan president Juvenal Habyarimana in an April attack.
> *Toronto Star* 30 Nov. 1994: A21

> (Here, since the killings have taken place, *might* is required.)

See also MAY, CAN.

me   see MYSELF; PRESENT WRITER

mea culpa   *Mea culpa* is a Latin phrase meaning 'through my fault' or 'my mistake'. In English a *mea culpa* is a formal apology, or an acknowledgement that one has done something blameworthy. *Mea culpa* is also used facetiously to mean something like 'Go ahead and blame me'. The popularity of the humorous use of *mea culpa* in journalism may account for the rarity of the phrase in academic writing.

> Mulroney's mea culpa came when he emerged from the meeting: 'What we have done so far leaves much to be desired.'
> *Vancouver Sun* 24 Nov. 1990: B2

One outcome of the prolonged, public dispute may be the extraction of something approaching a mea culpa from Moscow for 1956, similar to the apology given to Czechoslovakia late last year for the Soviet-led invasion of 1968.
Ottawa Citizen 4 July 1990: F9

Mea culpa, mea culpa. I went home to wash out my mouth with soap.
Gazette (Montreal) 22 Sept. 1990: J2

See also APOLOGY, APOLOGIA; LATIN PHRASES, FOREIGN PHRASES.

meager, meagre   see -RE, -ER

mean   see AVERAGE

meander   see MAUNDER

meantime, meanwhile   *Meantime* is commonly used as a noun, in the phrase 'in the meantime', whereas *meanwhile* usually appears alone in a sentence, as an adverb ('Meanwhile, back at the ranch . . .'). However, one does occasionally find 'in the meanwhile' or 'meantime, back at the ranch'.

Meantime, the number of Massey dealerships in big-tractor country continues to fall slowly.
Country Guide Nov. 1986: 9

(As an adverb *meantime* is less common than *meanwhile*.)

In the meanwhile . . . Toman readily admits that the company has 'lots of work to do.'
Whig-Standard (Kingston) 14 Oct. 1986: 1

(As a noun *meanwhile* is less common than *meantime*.)

measurement   see MILE; APPENDIX II

Mecca   see ISLAM

Me Decade   see CAPITAL LETTERS

media   see MEDIUM

median   see AVERAGE

mediation   see CONCILIATION

medicine   The fourth letter in *medicine*, as in *medical*, is *i*. The word is often misspelled *medecine*. For some people, the confusion probably arises from the French spellings *médecine*, 'medicine', and *médecin*, 'doctor'.

The 12-member commission, headed by Laval University dean of medecine Jean Rochon, will have 30 months to report to the provincial Government. . . .
Globe and Mail (Toronto) 20 June 1985: P3

(The correct spelling is *medicine*.)

medieval, mediaeval   The usual spelling is *medieval*. Its pronunciation varies: *meh DEE vul*, *meh dee EE vul*, and *mee dee EE vul* are all quite common.

See also -AE-, -OE-, -E-.

mediocre   *Mediocre* means middling, average, neither good nor bad. However, this adjective appears to be on a downhill slide; more and more it is used to mean inferior or poor. Because of this second sense, now recorded in most dictionaries, *mediocre* can be ambiguous. Context should be provided to make its meaning clear.

'You get 30, 35 starts a year. Ten times you have great stuff, 10 times it's mediocre and 10 times you have poor. Tonight, I'd have to rate my stuff as poor.'
London Free Press 28 April 1988: C1

(Here *mediocre* clearly means neither good nor bad.)

'Staying focused is what separates the good teams from the great teams and great men from mediocre men.'
Winnipeg Free Press 17 Nov. 1990: 53

(Here *mediocre* means average.)

They maintain that the United States, in addition to boasting many excellent universities, also has a large number of mediocre institutions providing students with an inferior grade of education.
Maclean's 21 Oct. 1991: A28

(Here *mediocre* is used pejoratively to mean below standard.)

medium, media   A *medium* is a means by which something is conveyed or through which something acts: for example, a medium of communication or an art medium. The plural is *media* or *mediums*. A psychic *medium* is a person through whom the deceased purportedly speak; the plural for this type of *medium* is always *mediums*.

The media usually refers to the news media (radio, television, newspapers, and magazines) or to the journalists who work in this field. In this sense *media* has become a collective noun like *committee* or *team*. It can correctly be followed by either a singular or plural verb, depending on whether the media are being considered as a collection of individuals or a unit.

Occasionally *media* is mistakenly used for *medium*, as in 'That's one media we haven't tried'.

Terrorism is his medium, as language is the medium of a poet.
National Post (Toronto) 1 June 2002: A22

Movies and music are other media through which language develops specific patterns that are soon adopted by youthful minds.
W.C. Lougheed, ed. *In Search of the Standard in Canadian English* 1986: 69

The novel's structure is also determined by its perception of that most fluid of all mediums, time.
Janice Kulyk Keefer *Reading Mavis Gallant* 1989: 80

The media is responsible for so many problems with language and written expression that I have ceased to be frustrated by daily blunders.
W.C. Lougheed, ed. *In Search of the Standard in Canadian English* 1986: 66

(Here *media* is a singular collective noun.)

The media hold a mirror up to society, but do so selectively.
Richard Davies and Glen Kirkland, eds. *Dimensions* 1986: 147

(Here *media* is a plural collective noun.)

. . . in one scene, while queuing up at the cinema, the Allen character overhears a highbrow conversation about some esoteric aspects of the film media. . . .
City Magazine Spring 1988: 20

(Here the singular form '*medium* of film' would be more appropriate.)

See also COLLECTIVE NOUNS; PLURALS, REGULAR, IRREGULAR, FOREIGN.

mega   see APPENDIX II

memento, [momento]   A *memento* is something concrete that brings back a memory; often it's a souvenir, or a gift to mark an occasion. The first three letters in *memento* are the same as in the related word *memory*; *memento* is not derived from the word *moment*. Nevertheless, since a memento can be thought of as marking a special moment, the confusion is understandable. Some dictionaries now list *momento* as a variant spelling, but style guides unanimously recommend against it. The recommended spelling is *memento,* the plural either *mementos* or *mementoes*.

The booklet is valuable when visiting the exhibition and a good memento when it ends.
Ottawa Citizen 21 Feb. 1993: C2

Terry O'Reilly . . . has asked for the penalty box from the Boston Garden as a personal momento of his National Hockey League playing days.
Calgary Herald 8 Oct. 1994: C1

(The usual—and more widely accepted—spelling is *memento*.)

See also -OS, -OES.

memorandum, memoranda, memorandums, memo, memos   *Memorandum* is the singular form and *memoranda* the traditional Latin plural. *Memoranda* is occasionally misused as the singular. *Memorandums*, the anglicized plural, now appears frequently in Canadian newspapers and magazines, but *memoranda* is still preferred in formal and academic writing. The short form *memo* (plural *memos*) is informal.

In early January, Macdonald had drafted a careful memorandum on Anderson's case and dispatched it to Governor General Head. . . .
William Teatero *John Anderson: Fugitive Slave* 1986: 115

In addition there are 280 technical memoranda on different facets of the tax which are written primarily for accountants and tax lawyers.
Ottawa Citizen 21 June 1990: E2

Over the past five years, there have been studies, reports, interdepartmental memorandums. . . .
Vancouver Sun 27 April 1990: A1

As well, Andre Bissonnette, federal Minister of State for Small Business, signed a memoranda of understanding with most provinces and the territories. . . .
Globe and Mail (Toronto) 11 Oct. 1985: B8

(The word *memoranda* is plural; Bissonnette either 'signed a *memorandum*' or 'signed *memoranda*'.)

See also PLURALS, REGULAR, IRREGULAR, FOREIGN.

memory   see COMPUTER TERMS

mendacity, mendacious, mendicancy, mendicity, mendicant   *Mendacity* is the habit of lying. *Mendacious* means prone to lying. *Mendicancy* or *mendicity* is the state of being a beggar, or the action of begging. *Mendicant* can be either an adjective ('begging') or a noun ('beggar').

Milli Vanilli was a scandal fuelled, like most scandals, by ambition, greed and mendacity.
Gazette (Montreal) 22 Nov. 1990: E1

At his worst, he has been by turns mendacious, blinkered and spiteful. . . .
Globe and Mail (Toronto) 22 June 1985: P6

I am ashamed of my whining, cringing, mendicant contemporaries. Canadian seniors have never had it so good.
Globe and Mail (Toronto) 27 June 1985: P6

There's a nice use of both words in the same sentence in a statement made by Frederick Temple, a 19th-century archbishop of Canterbury . . . : 'There is a certain class of clergymen whose mendicity is equalled only by their mendacity.'
Whig-Standard (Kingston) 30 Aug. 1986: 1

menorah   see CANDELABRUM

menus   see COMPUTER TERMS

meow, miaow, mew   In Canada and the United States cats *meow*; in Britain they *miaow*. Cats on both sides of the Atlantic *mew*.

According to a cat expert with the British Museum, cats never use meows when addressing each other, only when addressing humans.
Globe and Mail (Toronto) 10 Oct. 1985: P6

See also ONOMATOPOEIA.

mercifully   see SENTENCE ADVERBS

merry-go-round, carousel   The fairground ride consisting of painted wooden horses, or other animals, revolving to music is usually called a *merry-go-round* in Canadian and British English. The common American name is *carousel*, which some Canadians think of as a fancy word for a merry-go-round, or a term for a particularly elaborate merry-go-round.
Carousel has taken on extended literal meanings: circular slide trays and revolving luggage platforms in airports are called *carousels*. *Merry-go-round* is far more common than *carousel* in figurative uses.

Visitors to the PNE's Playland may get their last chance this year to ride the 73-year-old Vancouver carousel, which is slated for the auction block. Unless $350,000 is raised to purchase the 36-horse merry-go-round . . . it will be dismantled and sold. . . .
Vancouver Sun 24 Aug. 1990: B5

After years of self-hatred and denial, I came to the conclusion that I had been riding on that particular merry-go-round for too long and I wanted off.
Vancouver Sun 14 May 1993: A2

metal, mettle   *Metal*, meaning the hard, shiny substance that conducts heat and electricity, should not be confused with *mettle*, meaning spirit or courage. The past tense of the verb *metal*, meaning to cover in metal, is spelled *metalled* in Britain and *metaled* in the United States. Canadian dictionaries list both spellings. *Metalled roads* is a chiefly British synonym for *gravel roads*.

The promised sleek International Express, 'all first class, with air conditioned berths that are modern, metalled and well appointed,' turned out to be, at least this time, six second-class cars, four with berths and none air conditioned. . . .
Globe and Mail (Toronto) 16 Feb. 1985: T20

'It doesn't look all that bad but don't let appearances fool you,' said resident Alex Kennedy as he wheeled a maroon sedan around the reserve's winding metalled roads.
Maclean's 3 July 1989: A40

The Second World War was a time when the Royal family truly showed their mettle.
Canadian Churchman Jun.–Jul. 1986: 21

The 37 km of hard-packed sand was a natural place for the early motorists to test their metal.
Toronto Star 24 Jan. 2004: G2

(This is either a pun or a misuse: the phrase is *test their mettle*.)

See also DOUBLING THE FINAL CONSONANT.

metamorphosis, metamorphoses   see PLURALS

metaphor   see DEAD METAPHOR; METONYMY; MIXED METAPHOR; entry in Glossary

metathesis   see MISPRONUNCIATION AND PRONUNCIATION SHIFTS

meter   see -RE, -ER

methinks   see ARCHAISMS

methodology, method   A *methodology* is a systematic procedure of inquiry used in a particular discipline, or any system of methods with a philosophical basis. In reference to everyday activities, *methodology* is usually overblown: *method* or *methods* will do the job ('a method for making an omelette', 'indoor training methods').

. . . it is not clear that we know enough about how English Canadian society is stratified to be confident that the methodology used in European and U.S. sociolinguistic studies is the right methodology for Canada.
W.C. Lougheed, ed. *In Search of the Standard in Canadian English* 1986: 24

Very often, the articles in this magazine attempt to reveal the similarities of motivation and methodology that unite researchers in widely divergent fields.
Perspectives: Profiles of Research at Queen's University 1986: 30

Other methods of timing fireworks to music are primitive, Jim says.
Calgary Herald 29 June 1992: C1

I have my own easy-does-it methodology which, until recently, I'd never thought to question. First of all, I prefer fat asparagus to thin: I think it has more flavour.
Times-Colonist (Victoria) 29 March 2006: D1

(Here *method* would do; *methodology* may be a humorous touch.)

Métis, half-breed   During the fur-trading era in the region that is now Manitoba and northern Ontario, the term *Métis* (from the French for 'mixed') was used to describe anyone with both Aboriginal and European ancestry; there were both anglophone and francophone Métis. The Aboriginal ancestry was usually Cree, the European usually French or Scottish. The specific application of the term *Métis* to French-speakers reflects the cultural solidarity of francophone Métis in the regions that became Manitoba and Saskatchewan. In two uprisings led by Louis Riel, francophone Métis resisted the appropriation of their lands by the Canadian government and incoming settlers.

In 1982 the Constitution Act granted the Métis and anyone of mixed ancestry, whether associated with this particular western Canadian group or not, the same constitutional protection as other Aboriginal peoples. Since then the term has once again come to be used to refer to anyone of mixed Aboriginal and European ancestry. Some English-speaking people of mixed ancestry call themselves *halfbreeds*, a term that is derogatory if used by non-Natives.

Métis is pronounced *MAY TEE*, although some people in the Prairie provinces say *MEH tiss*, as if the word were English, and some Métis and Aboriginal people say *MET chif*. In French the final *s* is pronounced: *MAY TEECE. Métis* is both the adjective and the noun form, singular and plural. The accent should be retained in formal writing.

> Attempts by governments, churches and the general population to change Indians, Metis and Inuit into just another ethnic group in the multicultural mosaic have failed.
> *The Beaver* Feb.–Mar. 1990: 58

> The term Métis originally applied to people of French and Indian descent, but now applies to any mixed-blood Native people who identify themselves as Métis.
> Geoffrey York *The Dispossessed: Life and Death in Native Canada* 1990: 58

See also ABORIGINAL PEOPLE(S); INDIAN.

metonymy, synecdoche   *Metonymy* (pronounced *meh TAWN uh mee*) is a figure of speech in which an object closely associated with something is used to name it: 'the bottle', 'the press'. 'The pen is mightier than the sword' means that rhetoric is more effective than violence.

Synecdoche (pronounced *si NEK duh kee*) is a figure in which a part stands for a whole ('All hands on deck'; 'private eye'; 'new wheels'), a whole stands for a part ('Canada [the team] brings home the gold'; 'She was family [a relative]'), or an example stands for a class ('He was no Einstein [genius]').

metre, meter   see -RE, -ER; APPENDIX II

metric, metric ton(ne)   see APPENDIX II

Metro, subway   The underground railway in Paris is *le métro* ('the Metro'), short for *chemin de fer métropolitain*, 'urban railway'. Montreal borrowed this term. In Toronto and Edmonton the underground rapid transit is the *subway*. In British English a *subway* is an underground walkway; the London underground train system is simply called 'the underground' or, informally, 'the tube'.

Metro (often capitalized) is an abbreviation of 'metropolitan area', which refers to a large urban centre and the areas immediately adjacent to it. In Canada, both greater Toronto and the Halifax-Dartmouth area are often referred to as *Metro*.

> Police are warning people who take the Metro to be extra cautious after more than 12 people were robbed during the past two weeks.
> *Gazette* (Montreal) 13 Oct. 1994: F4

> So many clubs and their families are arriving from the Toronto area that there may be no traffic in Metro this week.
> *Ottawa Citizen* 2 Jan. 2003:

(Here *Metro* means the Toronto area.)

> . . . the possibility loomed that none of metro's high school squads would advance to the playoffs at the Nova Scotia School Athletic Federation senior boys and girls high school rugby championship.
> *Daily News* (Halifax) 10 June 2006: 43

(Here *metro* means the Halifax area.)

mettle   see METAL

mew, miaow   see MEOW

Mexican American   see HISPANIC

Micmac   see MI'KMAQ

microwavable   see -ABLE, -IBLE

Middle Ages   see CAPITAL LETTERS

Middle English   see OLD ENGLISH

midnight   see TIME

Midwest   see CAPITAL LETTERS

[might of]   see [COULD OF]

mighty   The use of *mighty* to mean 'very' has a long, respectable tradition; in fact, it appears in literary writing from the fourteenth century. Exactly when it began to be considered informal or even slang is not clear, but most commentators now associate it with down-home American speech. It is considered inappropriate for formal writing.

> It was the first time I'd seen my name in print and it looked mighty good.
> Max Braithwaite *The Night We Stole the Mountie's Car* 1971: 217

> Like a gun-slinger, a trial lawyer must be mighty fast on the draw.
> *Business Journal* June 1991: 25

migrant, migrate   see EMIGRANT

Mi'kmaq, Mi'kmaw, Micmac   The Aboriginal people whose original territory was coastal Gaspé and the Maritime provinces east of the Saint John River are known as the Mi'kmaq (pronounced *MIK MAK* or *MEEG em AK*). The spelling *Mi'kmaq* reflects the Aboriginal pronunciation of the word better than the old English spelling *Micmac*. Mi'kmaq speakers use *Mi'kmaw* (pronounced *MIK MAW*) for the singular noun and adjective and *Mi'kmaq* for the plural. While *Mi'kmaw* sometimes appears in English ('a Mi'kmaw', 'Mi'kmaw nation'), many English writers simply use *Mi'kmaq* in all contexts, and this is acceptable. Today, communities of Mi'kmaq are also found in Newfoundland and New England, particularly Boston. Their language, also called *Mi'kmaq*, is part of the Algonquian group.

> Marie Battiste, a Mi'kmaw member of the Potlo'tek First Nation of Nova Scotia and a professor in the education faculty at the University of Saskatchewan, will offer a free public Lansdowne Lecture on the topic tonight at UVic.
> *Times-Colonist* (Victoria) 1 Feb. 2001: B2

> (This usage observes the distinction between *Mi'kmaw* and *Mi'kmaq*.)

> In Drumbeat, officials and chiefs of several First Nations—the Innu of Ungava, the Mi'kmaq, the Mohawks of Akwesasne . . . describe the real story of relations between Native peoples and white settlers.
> *Ottawa Citizen* 17 March 1990: J11

See also ABORIGINAL PEOPLE(S); APPENDIX III.

mile   Although distances in Canada are now usually recorded in metric units (SI), the *mile* is still current in some contexts. The land or statute mile, used to express the limits of territorial waters, is 5280 feet (1.609 km); the air mile and the traditional nautical mile are both 6080.2 feet, or one-sixtieth of a degree of longitude measured at the equator (1.853 km). The new internationally recognized nautical mile is 6076.1 feet (1.851 km).

See also APPENDIX II.

mileage   see -E

milieu, milieux   see PLURALS

militant   see QUEBEC ENGLISH

militate, mitigate   A factor that *militates against* something reduces the likelihood that it will occur, succeed, be borne out, etc. (It might help to remember that *militate* comes from the same root as *military* and *militant*: something that militates against something else threatens to defeat it.) To *mitigate* means to soften the effect of, to alleviate, or to assuage. *Mitigate against* is often mistakenly used for *militate against*.

It is rare but not incorrect to use *militate* to mean *increase* the likelihood that something will occur: in such uses the word is followed by *in favour of* or *for*.

> Also, [women who might become politicians] hesitate to leave their families for the extended periods of federal parliamentary sessions: Canada's very vastness militates against mass female participation.
> *Gazette* (Montreal) 19 Nov. 1994: I3

> Living closer together does not mean that we will be cramped as long as new communities are designed to mitigate the effects of high density living.
> *Vancouver Sun* 14 Nov. 1990: B2

> She also points out that the relatively small size of her [television] unit mitigates against having her movie nights at home.
> *Globe and Mail* (Toronto) 17 Dec. 2005: L7

(The expression wanted here is *militates against*.)

It's not logically clear, however, just how the Bruderheim accident militates in favour of B.C.'s tough rules.
National Post (Toronto) 19 Dec. 2003: A21

millennium, millenarian, millenary, millinery A *millennium* is a period of one thousand years. The word *millennium* also refers to a thousandth anniversary or the turning year of a millennium. According to the calendar in use in most of the world (the Gregorian calendar), we are now in the first years of the third millennium AD or CE. Technically, because there is no year zero, the new millennium began at the end, not the beginning, of the year 2000. The celebration of the event, however, coincided with the change in the thousands' digit on the calendar.

'The millennium', in the belief of some Christian sects, is a thousand-year period during which Christ will reign on earth and good will triumph over evil. The term is used figuratively to mean a long period of prosperity and happiness when good will prevail. *Millenarians* are people who believe literally in the doctrine of Christ's thousand-year reign and who occasionally predict the date of its commencement. Sometimes the term *millenarian* is also applied to those who believe in the possibility of perfecting human society.

It is easy to misspell either *millennium* or *millenarian* because only the former has a double *n*. The inconsistency is attributable to different etymologies. *Millennium* derives from the Latin *mille*, 'thousand', and *annus*, 'year', while *millenarian* derives from the Latin adjective *millenarius*, 'consisting of a thousand'. The plural of *millennium* is *millenniums* or *millennia*. *Millenary* (noun and adjective) is a synonym of both *millennium* and *millenarian*. *Millinery* is the designing or selling of women's hats.

Persian Iran has been a traditional foe of the Arab world for a millennium.
Ottawa Citizen 15 Aug. 1990: A1

. . . such unknowledgeable merrymakers will do their special celebrations on the night of Dec. 31, 1999–Jan. 1, 2,000—one year before the end of the decade, the century and the second millennium.
Ottawa Citizen 14 Oct. 1990: C7

We are approaching a millennium; the year 2000 draws on apace.
Robertson Davies *A Voice from the Attic* 1960: 350

(Some would argue that Davies should have written 'the year 2001 draws on'.)

Communism-Marxism may be dead and buried (good riddance) but its millenarian ideals, borrowed heavily from Judeo-Christian egalitarian fantasies, remain intact, resurrected in various guises as social democracy, social(ist) justice and its newest reincarnation, the Greens who are merely Reds in camouflage.
Financial Post 13 Oct. 1989: 10

After completing fashion design and millinery courses in Vancouver, Crowe packed up her hat boxes and moved to London, England.
Vancouver Sun 2 Aug. 1994: C1

See also AD, BC, CE, BCE, BP, CENTURY.

milliard see BILLION

millilitre see APPENDIX II

millinery see MILLENNIUM

mimicked see -C, -CK

-minded *Career-minded, closed-minded, health-minded, high-minded, right-minded, single-minded*, and a host of other *-minded* combinations are evidence of the current popularity of *-minded* as combining form. These expressions are usually hyphenated. In long-established forms, the first element tends to be an adjective, such as *fair* or *simple*, characterizing a person's mind. New combinations usually begin with a noun, such as *budget* or *outdoors*, describing a person's preoccupation or focus.

In Britain, where lack of representation was a more serious problem, the cause of political liberty underwent no decline in popularity among those who were reform-minded. . . .
J.A.W. Gunn *Beyond Liberty and Property* 1983: 257

Anyone who knows anything about Bragg Creek knows it's a paradise for sports-minded people and nature-lovers. . . .
Calgary Herald 6 May 2006: H3

mindset see MENTALITY

miner, minor A *miner*, with an *e*, is someone who works in a mine. The word *minor*, with an *o*, has several meanings, including small, under-age, and insignificant. The pronunciations are indistinguishable. Think of *mine* and *minority* for clues to the spellings.

However, a spokesman . . . said 13 miners suffered minor injuries during the tremor.
Windsor Star 10 March 2005: B2

(Both words are spelled correctly here.)

minimal Several usage guides maintain that the adjective *minimal* has only one meaning: the smallest or the least possible ('the minimal effective dose'). Dictionary definitions some-times support this view, but in practice *minimal* has a much wider range of meanings. It's used in all types of writing to mean very small or insignificant.

Maybe he had a minimal cult then, a tiny number of people starting to really love his music.
Jack Chambers *Milestones* 1983: 289

(Here *minimal* means very small.)

In 1950–51, after two decades of minimal growth, [the professoriate] was top-heavy: nearly 77 per cent occupied positions in the two senior ranks of professor and associate professor.
Frederick Gibson *Queen's University* 2 (1983): 343

(Here *minimal* means very small.)

Club fees are low and earnings from most record-ings are minimal.
Queen's Quarterly 95.2 (1988): 299

(Here *minimal* means insignificant.)

minor see MINER; SUPERIOR

minority see MAJORITY; SEXUAL MINORITIES; VISI-BLE MINORITY

minuscule *Minuscule* is spelled *miniscule* so frequently that many dictionaries list *miniscule* if only to note that it is an error. Some critics argue that it should be considered a standard variant. *Minuscule* was formerly used to refer to some medieval writing styles and to uncapital-ized letters; the first documented use in the cur-rent sense, very small, dates from 1893.

The Canadian markets ended a disappointing week with miniscule gains.
Gazette (Montreal) 21 July 1990: H5

(The correct spelling is *minuscule*.)

The problem is that the funds available for such deals are miniscule in relation to developing coun-try debt.
Financial Post 17 May 1990: 10

(The correct spelling is *minuscule*.)

minuses see -US

minute see APPENDIX II

misandry, misanthrope, misanthropy see MISOGYNY

miscellany A *miscellany* is a collection of var-ious writings or things. The word may be pro-nounced *MISS uh lain ee* or *miss SELL uh nee*. The latter pronunciation is particularly British.

West Edmonton Mall is eight city blocks long and three blocks wide, a two-level, yellow-brick struc-ture that houses a miscellany of modern recre-ation.
Saturday Night May 1986: 49

mischief see -IE, -EI-

mischievous The standard pronunciation of *mischievous* is *MIS chuh vus*. The widespread, longstanding, but still unacceptable pronuncia-tion *mis CHEE vee us* accounts for the common misspellings *mischevious* and *mischievious*.

misdemeanor see INDICTABLE OFFENCE

mishap see ACCIDENT

misheard expressions   People often misinterpret the lyrics of songs because they hear them but never see them in writing, and, likewise, they misconstrue conventional expressions that they have heard but not read. Generally, the error goes unnoticed until the recast expression is committed to writing. In writing such expressions are a source of both embarrassment and humour. The writer may well be embarrassed by an error indicating lack of exposure to the printed word, but the reader is likely to be amused: however unintentional the punning, a recast expression represents wordplay. Here are some examples.

conventional expression	recast version
beck and call	beckon call
case in point	case and point
cut off one's nose to spite one's face	cut off one's nose despite one's face
damned with faint praise	damned with feigned praise
death knell	death nail
deep-seated	deep-seeded
for all intents and purposes	for all intensive purposes
home in on	hone in on
laissez-faire	lazy-faire
loss leader	lost leader
nip it in the bud	nip it in the butt
put someone on a pedestal	put someone on a pedal/ peddle/petal stool
root of all evil	root of upheaval
take for granted	take for granite

See also FOLK ETYMOLOGY; HOME IN ON; MANNER (MANOR) BORN, TO THE.

misogyny, misogynist, misanthropy, misanthrope, misandry   Misogyny (pronounced *mi SAH jin ee*) is hatred of women. A person who hates or disdains women is called a *misogynist*. *Misanthropy* (*mi SAN throp ee*) is hatred or distrust of the whole human species, and a person so inclined is called a *misanthrope* (*MEE zan thrope*); the word is borrowed from French. *Misanthropist*, a fairly common anglicized variant of *misanthrope*, is considered non-standard by many authorities.

   Misandry is a little-used word meaning hatred of men.

As countless stage and screen adaptations attest, the fable is one of literature's most enjoyably graphic descriptions of a hard-core misanthropist, in whom the spirit of charity has vanished in a gloomy perma-frost.
Edmonton Journal 2 Dec. 1998: C4

(Some commentators recommend *misanthrope*.)

misplaced modifiers   Modifiers may be adjectives, adverbs, phrases, or clauses; misplaced modifiers are modifiers adjacent to some word other than the one they are intended to describe. A misplaced modifier can make a sentence ambiguous or unintentionally funny. Some readers cannot resist the pleasure of pointing out the literal possibilities in a sentence such as the following: 'Jones hit the first pitch off Carmichael's leg, which was fielded and thrown to first by Riley'. The normal cure for a misplaced modifier is to shift it closer to what it modifies, or, if that seems awkward or anticlimactic, to rewrite the sentence: for example, 'Jones hit the first pitch, which bounced off Carmichael's leg before it was fielded and thrown to first by Riley'.

   Some usage experts make no allowance for readers' common sense and criticize the 'misplacement' of modifiers that are highly unlikely to cause confusion. They would, for instance, recommend rewriting 'She watched the children from inside' as 'From inside, she watched the children', even though few readers would think it was the children who were 'from inside'. Rewriting the sentence is necessary only where there is genuine ambiguity, as in 'She saw the children crossing the park'. Was she crossing the park or were the children? It would be clearer to write either 'While crossing the park, she saw the children' or 'She saw the children as they were crossing the park'.

   The difference in the placement of adverb modifiers (such as *only*, *just*, *almost*, and *even*) in formal and informal styles is discussed under ONLY.

See also DANGLING MODIFIERS; ONLY.

mispronunciation and pronunciation shifts, metathesis, epenthesis, prothesis   *Metathesis* (pronounced *meh TA thuh sis*) is a grammatical term for the unintentional transposition of letters, sounds, or syllables within a word. This linguistic phenomenon, which occurs in both spoken and written English, has accounted for the creation of some common Standard English words. For instance, the Old Norse word for excrement, *drit*, was borrowed into Middle English and metathesized as *dirt*. *Brid* was the original Old English spelling for *bird*. And the Dutch verb *crul* and noun *cruller* became *curl* and *curler* in English.

Sometimes words are metathesized to produce an easier sound sequence: *curl* is easier to say in English than *crul*, and children often pronounce *spaghetti* as *puh SKET ee*. Sometimes it is the sound pattern in other words that leads to mispronunciations; for example, people often pronounce *integral* as if it were spelled *intregal*, presumably influenced by the *intr-* form of such words as *intricate* and *introduce*.

The introduction of a sound into the middle of a word is termed *epenthesis* (*e PEN thuh sis*). Epenthesis occurs in the common pronunciation of *sherbet* as *sherbert*. What linguists call the 'epenthetic schwa' accounts for the disputed two-syllable pronunciation of *film* (*FILL um*) or the three-syllable pronunciation of *athlete* (*ATH uh leet*).

The addition of an extra sound at the beginning of a word is known as *prothesis*. This phenomenon is more common in the Romance languages than in English. For example, the Latin *schola*, from which English derived *school*, became *école* in French and *escuela* in Spanish.

> A fine athelete, he was a college football hero. . . .
> *Financial Post* 9 Jan. 1990: 11

(Here the misspelling of *athlete* reflects the epenthetic pronunciation.)

See also CALVARY, CAVALRY; HYPERCORRECTION; MALAPROPISM; SLIPS OF THE TONGUE; SPOONERISMS.

Miss, Mr., Mrs., Messrs., Mmes. *Mr.* and *Mrs.* are never unabbreviated before a name. The long form *mister* sometimes appears as a term of direct address ('Mister, could you move your car?'), but the connection between *Mrs.* and its original long form, *mistress*, has been lost. 'The missus', a slang synonym for wife, reflects the current pronunciation of *Mrs.*

In British English *Mr* and *Mrs* are spelled without periods. The British convention (which some North American editors follow) is that an abbreviation that ends with the same letter as the full word takes no period.

The plural of *Miss* is *Misses*. The plural of *Mr.* is *Messrs.* (from the French *messieurs*): 'Dear Messrs. Harmond and Lyle'. The plural of *Mrs.* is *Mmes.* (from French *mesdames*). The periods may be omitted, as they are in French.

Regarding the choice between *Ms.*, *Mrs.*, and *Miss*, see MS.

See also MA'AM, MADAM, MADAME; MS.

missing see GO MISSING

mission statement see CLICHÉ

misspeak oneself see LIE

misspell The word *misspell* is often misspelled as *mispell*—an error that can be quite embarrassing to the writer intent on pointing out someone else's mistakes.

Misspelt is less common than *misspelled*, but either form is correct as the past tense or the past participle.

> Adding insult to injury, her first name was misspelt.
> *Province* (Vancouver) 5 Feb. 1990: 15

> Brasserie Creek was also misspelled in the story.
> *Ottawa Citizen* 27 April 1990: A2

mitigate see MILITATE

mixed metaphor A mixed metaphor is a sequence of distractingly incongruous figures of speech that may produce a ludicrous image in the reader's mind: 'If I were in the driver's seat, we wouldn't be barking up the wrong tree'; 'The human eye had never before set foot in such a place'.

See also DEAD METAPHOR.

Mlle, Mme   see ABBREVIATION

modality   see QUEBEC ENGLISH

model   see DOUBLING THE FINAL CONSONANT

Moderator   see RELIGIOUS TITLES

Modern English   see OLD ENGLISH

modifiers   see DANGLING MODIFIERS; MISPLACED MODIFIERS; entry in Glossary

modus operandi, modus vivendi   *Modus operandi* is a Latin phrase meaning manner or method of operating. In police jargon it is often abbreviated to *m.o.* or *MO*, and refers to the characteristic way a criminal proceeds. The plural is *modi operandi*. *Modus vivendi* means way of living. It refers far less often to a chosen lifestyle than to a way of coping or of getting along despite differences or disagreements. *Modus vivendi* should be italicized in formal English; its plural is *modi vivendi*.

> When writing fiction, Findley's modus operandi is to find his voice first, his characters second.
> *Vancouver Sun* 24 Nov. 1990: C17

> 'But I've never seen this kind of M.O. (modus operandi or operating technique) in 27 years of police work.'
> *Ottawa Citizen* 4 Dec. 1990: A12

> 'We had a large series of break and enters with very similar modus operandis.'
> *Ottawa Citizen* 17 May 1990: A16

(The accepted plural, which would be required in formal writing, is *modi operandi*. In this informal context 'with *a* very similar *modus operandi*' might be less awkward.)

> Her awareness of the *modus vivendi* forced on city children is neither sentimental nor censorious. . . .
> Janice Kulyk Keefer *Reading Mavis Gallant* 1989: 199

> The unease has spread as members of Canada's two dominant language groups look for a new modus vivendi after 21 years of official bilingualism.
> *Ottawa Citizen* 24 March 1990: B4

> In Britain, there is a ferocious cadre of reporters whose modus vivendi is eavesdropping on conversations.
> *Ottawa Citizen* 1 Dec. 2002: A14

(Here *modus operandi* would make more sense.)

See also LATIN PHRASES, FOREIGN PHRASES.

Mohammed   see ISLAM

mold   see MOULD

mole   see APPENDIX II

molly   see GAY

momentarily   *Momentarily* means briefly, for a moment, or for the moment. It is often used in speech and newspapers to mean imminently or in a moment—a usage strongly disparaged by most usage guides. The disputed sense is not commonly found in Canadian books or academic journals, and should be restricted to informal writing.

> [The airplane] recovered momentarily as it lifted up again, then finally crashed into the dirt.
> *Vancouver Sun* 22 May 1990: A13

> Luc Besson's first film, *Le Dernier Combat*, was never released in Canada, though his second picture, *Subway* . . . should be in the theatres momentarily.
> *Globe and Mail* (Toronto) 6 Sept. 1985: E9

(Here *very soon* would be a better choice.)

See also PRESENTLY.

[momento]   see MEMENTO

Monctonian   see NAMES OF RESIDENTS OF CITIES AND PROVINCES

money, monies, moneys   Both *monies* and *moneys* are listed as standard plural forms in current dictionaries. Canadian writers prefer the *-ies* plural. In most uses *money* needs no plural, but the plural form is frequently used to refer to currencies from different countries or, in business contexts, as a synonym for *funds*. In other contexts the plural is either pretentious or humorous: 'I've depleted my monies'.

> Whether or not the provincial government was set to seize $7.4 million in unspent public school board monies is now beside the point.
> *Calgary Herald* 2 Dec. 1994: A4

Monsignor   see RELIGIOUS TITLES

mont   see FRENCH WORDS, PRONUNCIATION OF

Montagnais   see INNU

Montréalais(e), Montrealer   see NAMES OF RESIDENTS OF CITIES AND PROVINCES

mood   see entry in Glossary

moose, caribou, reindeer, elk, wapiti, red deer   Some confusion is possible because the popular names for three species of large deer found in Canada are used differently in North America and Britain. What we call *moose* (Latin name, *Alces alces*) the British usually call *elk*. What we call *caribou* (*Rangifer tarandus*) they call *reindeer*. And what we call *elk*, North American *elk*, or *wapiti* (*Cervus canadensis*) they call *red deer* (*Cervus elaphus*). North American elk and European red deer are so similar that some biologists consider them the same species.

The antlers of the male moose have hand-shaped ends, and both male and female have the distinctive roman noses, wattles, knobby knees, and large hooves that make them easy to distinguish from elk and caribou. The head of a caribou is depicted on the Canadian 25-cent piece. Caribou are slightly smaller than elk, but their antlers are heavier.

> Ontario has only a small wild elk population, but a huge whitetail deer herd, as well as moose and caribou.
> *Sudbury Star* 12 Nov. 2005: B5

See also ANTLER, HORN; PLURALS, REGULAR, IRREGULAR, FOREIGN.

Moose Javian   see NAMES OF RESIDENTS OF CITIES AND PROVINCES

moot   One long-established sense of the adjective *moot* is 'debatable', and this is the usual meaning of the word in the phrases 'a moot point' and 'a moot question'. In legal parlance a 'moot court' is a practice court where law students debate hypothetical cases. Another sense has arisen from an American legal usage in which *moot* refers to an issue that has already been decided; this sense of *moot* has moved into general usage, where it means 'academic' or 'of no practical importance'. Some dictionaries and usage commentators are reluctant to acknowledge this new meaning; however, Canadian writers use the adjective *moot* in both senses. Context should be provided to make the intended sense clear.

> Whether the point has been carried far enough, and whether their forms should have been more clearly articulated in view of the civic buildings to follow later is a moot point.
> *Canadian Architect* June 1986: 34

(Here the point is debatable.)

> Rudyard Kipling would hate me for this, but it's now a moot point whether the English, the Americans, etc., can keep order in their own countries, let alone those inhabited by his 'lesser breeds without the Law.'
> *Globe and Mail* (Toronto) 17 July 1985: P6

(Here the point is debatable.)

> . . . the table may not accurately reflect the true grades of some hogs. It's perhaps a moot point for producers, since a revised table probably wouldn't change how much they receive.
> *Country Guide* Nov. 1986: 33

(Here, as the context makes clear, the *moot point* is one of no practical significance.)

> Whether or not King is a believer is a moot point. If this were a tragic representation of human sufferings in a war, he would not have drawn a cartoon and you would not have printed it.
> *Ottawa Citizen* 8 June 1994: A12

(Here the *moot point* is one of no import, irrelevant.)

moral, morals, morale, moral support
The adjective *moral* means ethical and upright, or having to do with *morals*. *Morals* meaning ethics or a standard of conduct is always plural. A *moral* is a lesson conveyed by a story.

Morale (pronounced *mor AL*) means state of mind or level of enthusiasm. *Moral support* improves morale (rather than morals). People offer it through their physical presence or their expressions of encouragement; moral support is often contrasted with financial support.

. . . the most effective restraint on Canadian military action may not be any moral qualms among political leaders, but the weakness of Canada's depleted armed forces.
Maclean's 23 Dec. 1991: A12

The moral of the story? 'Police officers are victims like anybody else,' said Bildfell.
Calgary Herald 3 Feb. 1994: A1

Managers strive to introduce robots in physically demanding and monotonous jobs because they recognize that workers' morale is higher when they work at more pleasant and challenging tasks requiring more thought and skill.
Irving M. Zeitlin and Robert J. Brym *The Social Condition of Humanity* 1991: 360

Although she said agency brass consider the camp 'a great idea' and offer moral support, they have no money to contribute to the project.
Gazette (Montreal) 19 July 1990: G1

more   see ANOTHER; COMPARISONS; COMPLETE; TIMES LESS, TIMES MORE

more importantly, more important
Many commentators dislike the adverb phrase *more importantly* and prefer *more important*, which they view as the legitimate contraction of the original expression *what is more important*. However, it is the adverb form of this sentence modifier that Canadians favour; *more importantly* is far more common in all varieties of writing.

More importantly, if he is properly prepared to accept students as students, he will certainly recognize the complexity of English.
W.C. Lougheed, ed. *In Search of the Standard in*

Canadian English 1986: 73

But we *are* all in this together, not just as citizens of our respective nation states but more importantly as inhabitants of this quickly shrinking and increasingly threatened earth.
Margaret Atwood *Second Words* 1982: 392

They still have an office at a convenient ground-level location in the city and, more importantly, they know where Wales is.
Gazette (Montreal) 10 June 1992: E1

More important, the modern religious poet is apt to confuse inspiration with a state of grace. . . .
Northrop Frye *The Bush Garden* 1971: 79–80

See also SENTENCE ADVERBS.

more often   see OFTEN

more perfect   see PERFECT

mores   *Mores*, a plural noun, meaning customs or traditional morality, has two standard pronunciations: *MOR aze* and *MOR eez*. Although *mores* is often pronounced to rhyme with *bores*, dictionaries do not list this pronunciation, which treats the word like a regular English plural rather than a borrowing from Latin (singular *mos*, plural *mores*, 'custom').

These people have folkways and mores. . . . The mores are those folkways which are believed to have a bearing upon the welfare of the group.
Royal Bank of Canada Monthly Letter 52.6 (1971): 3

See also LATIN PHRASES, FOREIGN PHRASES.

more so   In the phrase *more so, so* stands for—and makes it unnecessary to repeat—part of the preceding sentence or clause: 'His first novel was marred by poorly delineated characters; his next one was even more so'. Sometimes writers use *more so* when *more* alone will do: 'Jack does it more so than Phil'. In informal writing *more so* often begins a sentence fragment ('They are popular here. More so in Toronto'). In formal writing, the period should be replaced by *and*.
    Occasionally writers mistakenly spell *more so* as one word.

I replied that I understood perfectly, all the more so since my brother was overseas with the Calgary Highlanders. . . .
George Ignatieff *The Making of a Peacemonger* 1987: 78

'All our analyses show that Quebecois remain openminded about immigration, perhaps even more so than other Canadians.'
Gazette (Montreal) 29 June 1994: A7

Perhaps more so than any previous Rider coach, Rita separates work from play.
Ottawa Citizen 23 June 1994: E1

(Here the *so* is unnecessary.)

But the Portland game could turn out to be the most interesting of all, moreso off the ice than on, especially with Gretzky on the sidelines.
Financial Post 19 Sept. 1991: 51

(The correct spelling is *more so*.)

Well, you've got to admit that it catches the eye. Moreso perhaps than the picture offered Canadian movie goers—a young boy and a young girl at piano practice, holding hands. . . .
Ottawa Citizen 7 July 1990: G3

(Here the period after *eye* should be changed to a comma, *moreso* replaced by *more*, and *perhaps* shifted to precede *more*.)

See also SENTENCES, SENTENCE FRAGMENT.

more than   see SPLIT INFINITIVE

more . . . than   see COMMA

more than one   Logically, *more than one* is plural, but by grammatical convention it is treated as singular: 'More than one head is going to roll'. Occasionally, notional agreement motivates a plural verb after *more than one*: 'When more than one of them *are* in the same class, they cause trouble'. Some commentators label this usage non-standard.

'. . . in each instance more than one male was involved.'
Toronto Star 30 Dec. 1992: A8

More than one man Sadie knew was drowned doing things like this.

Richard Davies and Glen Kirkland, eds. *Dimensions* 1986: 118

'What the hell was that?' more than one of us asks.
Ken Dryden *The Game* 1983: 31

If any of these 'telltale signs' are present, and particularly if more than one of them are present, prosecutors and Crown attorneys should immediately worry that the case may not be a good one.
Globe and Mail (Toronto) 5 March 2005: D3

(Some editors would change *are* to *is*.)

See also AGREEMENT, GRAMMATICAL.

Mormonism   see -ISM

mortar   see CEMENT

mortgagee, mortgagor   see LESSOR

Moslem   see ISLAM

mosquito   see -OS, -OES

most, almost   *Most* meaning 'almost' is accepted when it modifies indefinite adjectives and pronouns, such as *all, any, anybody, anyone, everybody*, and *anything*, but is considered dialectal, quaint, or facetious in other contexts: for example, 'I most laughed out loud'; 'It's most empty'.

The chapter could comfortably fit in most any book on social theory.
Canadian Journal of Sociology 14.2 (1989): 267

'Most of them can do most anything.'
Queen's Quarterly 96.2 (1989): 306

Most everyone agrees that from the start people in need of quick cash would go, usually with discretion, to the small side room of her elegant colonial home.
Canadian Fiction Magazine 63 (1988): 119

However, the important point in all this was now grasped by most everyone.
Henry M. Rosenthal and S. Cathy Berson, eds. *Canadian Jewish Outlook Anthology* 1988: 317

See also see COMPARISONS; COMPLETE.

most often   see OFTEN

most perfect   see PERFECT

mother-in-law   see IN-LAWS

Mother Nature   Non-sexist usage guides suggest laying *Mother Nature* to rest. Traditionally *Mother Nature* has been used to describe both the life-giving force that brings spring flowers and the malevolent and unpredictable force that causes storms. One example of this association of nature and the feminine was that hurricanes and tropical storms were given feminine names. Now, in response to protests, they are given feminine and masculine names alternately. To avoid stereotyping women and excluding men, some guides recommend calling *Mother Nature* simply *nature*. However, the impulse to personify nature is so strong that *Mother Nature* is not likely to disappear soon.

As several hundred New Glasgow residents waited anxiously . . . for a plane to fly by and 1,500 miniature balls to fall from above, Mother Nature ruined the day. . . .
Chronicle-Herald (Halifax) 14 May 1988: 1

Mother Nature played havoc with the snow sculptures entered in the national competition, many of them melting or falling apart on Sunday, judging day.
Chronicle-Telegraph (Quebec City) 6 Feb. 1991: 1

See also SEXIST LANGUAGE.

motive, motif, leitmotif   *Motive* comes from the same root as *motivation*, and means a reason or a probable cause: 'The suspect was found to have a motive for committing the crime'.

Motif means a dominant or repeating pattern or passage: 'The dress sported a floral motif'; 'The saxophone plays the signature motif'. The plural of *motif* is *motifs*.

Because *motive* and *motif* were borrowed, in the fourteenth and nineteenth centuries respectively, from the same French word, dictionaries list *motif* as one meaning of *motive*. Spelling

motif with an *-ive* ending, however, may confuse readers.

Leitmotif refers to the direct association between a character or idea and a piece of music, and is often associated with the work of Richard Wagner. Later, it began to refer more broadly to any repeated theme in art, and thus it became a synonym of *motif*. *Leitmotif* (sometimes spelled *leitmotiv*) should not be capitalized.

The second motive for stealing a motor vehicle is to use it for the purpose of transporting the thief from one specific location to another.
Juristat: Canadian Centre for Justice Statistics 23.1 (2003)

(This is the common use of *motive*.)

For both Nabokov and Cronenberg, the insect motif acts as a symbol of imminent change or loss. . . .
Canadian Journal of Film Studies 12.1 (2003): 57–68

(Here *motif* means theme.)

In the 1920s Emily Carr produced low-tech work, decorated with native motives, for the tourist market.
Vancouver Sun 2 March 2004: C1

(This is the rare use of *motive* to mean *motif* or repeated decoration.)

P.K. Page's fascination with the unconscious world of dreams is a prominent leitmotif in her art. . . .
Journal of Canadian Studies 38.1. (2004): 118–28

(Here *leitmotif* is used with its contemporary sense: dominant theme.)

motorway   see ROAD

mould, mold   Either spelling is appropriate for all senses, including the noun meaning fungal growth and the verb meaning shape. In Canadian texts *mould* is found more often than *mold* for all senses. *Mould* is the more common British spelling; Americans prefer *mold*.

moustache, mustache   Canadian writers prefer *moustache*, although *mustache* is occasionally found. In Britain the usual spelling is *moustache*; in the United States, *mustache*.

movable, moveable   see -ABLE, (-E)ABLE

moviedom   see -DOM

mow, mowed, mown   The past tense is *mowed*: 'She mowed the lawn'. The past participle is *mowed* or, less commonly, *mown*: 'She has mowed (*or* mown) the lawn'. *Mowed* and *mown* are both used as adjectives, but here *mown* is more common: 'mown (*or* mowed) fields'.

A *hay mow* is a storage loft in a barn. In this sense only, *mow* rhymes with *cow*.

> My sense of superiority was not totally out of control as I thought of the trainloads of weeds I had pulled, the miles of lawn I had mowed . . . in my previous life as a garden-enslaved fool.
> *Vancouver Sun* 11 May 1990: 35

> 'And they talk. "Oh, the parson hasn't had his lawn mown. How horrible. . .".'
> *Gazette* (Montreal) 4 Nov. 1990: D1

> [The wind] carries the sweet scent of freshly mown alfalfa from the river bottoms below.
> *Vancouver Sun* 29 Oct. 1990: A11

> A polo field, a huge expanse of closely mowed turf, measures 274 metres by 137 metres—roughly the size of nine football fields.
> *Gazette* (Montreal) 19 July 1990: H1

> Inside the barn there were roomy stalls for the horses and cows, a hay mow, a loft where oats and barley were stored, and nooks and crannies where chickens made their nests.
> *Gazette* (Montreal) 31 July 1994: C1

Mozart   see GERMAN WORDS, PRONUNCIATION OF

MP, MPP   see ABBREVIATION; APPENDIX I

Mr., Mrs.   see MISS

Ms.   *Ms.* (pronounced *MIZ*) was first suggested in the early 1950s as a convenient way of addressing business mail to a woman whose marital status was unknown. Like *Miss* and *Mrs.*,

Ms. is an abbreviation of *Mistress*. However, *Ms.* did not become popular until the 1970s, when the women's movement recognized its usefulness as an honorific that paralleled the male honorific *Mr.* in not indicating marital status. *Ms.* is now fully established, although it has not replaced *Miss* and *Mrs.*, which some women prefer. It is only polite to address a woman using the honorific of her choice, when it is known.

In North America *Ms.* is generally spelled with a period, while *Ms* is the usual spelling in British English. The British convention (which some North American editors follow) is to omit the period when the abbreviation ends with the same letter as the complete word.

> 'Spirit of Community' is the subject of the presentation to be given by Ms. Von Tscharner and her husband Friday morning. . . .
> *Guardian* (Charlottetown) 2 Nov. 1990: 9

> When a camera crew said it had missed their greeting, Mr. Gromyko shook Mr. Clark's hand again while Mrs. Gromyko welcomed Ms McTeer a second time.
> *Globe and Mail* (Toronto) 3 April 1985: 1

(Note the spelling of *Ms* without a period. *Mr.*, *Mrs.*, and *Ms.* should be spelled consistently— either all with a period or all without.)

See also MA'AM, MADAM; MISS, MR., MRS.

much   see VERY

muck-a-muck, muckety-muck, mucky-muck   see PIDGIN

mucus, mucous   *Mucus* is the noun. *Mucous* is the adjective. These words, which usually appear in a medical context, are often confused when they are used in other types of writing.

> A raspy hack that clears mucous from your respiratory system is doing an important job.
> *Canadian Consumer* Jan. 1985: 17

(The noun should be spelled *mucus*.)

> The candida grows and then invades the mucus membranes, becoming less friendly, increasing

allergic reactions.
Globe and Mail (Toronto) 21 Feb. 1985: CL3

(The adjective should be spelled *mucous*.)

Muhammed   see ISLAM

multi-entry   see HYPHENATION

multilateral   see UNILATERAL

Mumbai, Bombay   see PLACE NAMES

munificent   see BENEFICENT

murmur   see ONOMATOPOEIA

muscle-bound   see -BOUND

musickal   see -C, -CK

muskeg   see SWAMP

Muslim   see ISLAM

mustache   see MOUSTACHE

mutatis mutandis   *Mutatis mutandis*, pronounced *myoo TAT iss myoo TAN diss* (or *myoo TAHT iss myoo TAHN diss*) is Latin for 'what needs to be changed having been changed'. The phrase is used as a qualifier in comparisons, where loosely it translates as 'making the necessary adjustments'. Since it is always the case in making comparisons that differences must be taken into account, *mutatis mutandis* has been criticized as a redundant flourish. However, it is not always so. In contexts that demand of the reader an imaginative leap or translation, the phrase lays the ground for that shift. In formal writing, *mutatis mutandis* should be italicized as a foreign expression.

'It wasn't me,' went the postwar refrain, 'it was Adolf Hitler.' Mutatis mutandis, the same denial is invoked by many again today.
Toronto Star 9 Nov. 1992: A15

(Here *mutatis mutandis* indicates the need to substitute for 'Adolf Hitler' the name of another belligerent.)

My favourite cafe in Europe is the Grand Cafe in the main square at Oslo: this is dominated by a huge mural of the place identifying regular customers of its nineteenth-century prime—Master of the Horse Sverdrup, Landowner Gjerns, Writers Olsen and Ibsen and many another—all of whom, mutatis mutandis, are to be seen to this day eating prawns and smoking at its tables.
Vancouver Sun 27 June 1998: C8

(Here *mutatis mutandis* guides the imaginative leap from the regular customers of yesteryear to their present-day counterparts.)

This is not a new worry, and indeed it first made its appearance during the interwar period, when it could credibly be argued that Canadian grand strategy was, mutatis mutandis, almost as isolationist as American grand strategy, at least until the very end of the period.
Journal of Canadian Studies 38.2 (2004): 12

(*Mutatis mutandis* could be cut from this sentence without affecting its meaning.)

See also LATIN PHRASES, FOREIGN PHRASES.

mutual, common   Some usage commentators rigidly distinguish between *mutual* and *(in) common*. In their view, *mutual* implies reciprocity or exchange: 'The feeling is mutual'. Where no exchange is involved, that is, where the meaning is simply 'pertaining to both', they insist on *common* or *in common*: 'They had interests in common (*or* common interests)'. Other usage commentators consider this firm distinction of sense between *mutual* and *common* completely artificial. Evidence in the historical *Oxford English Dictionary* supports the latter view: *mutual* has been used as a synonym of *shared* or *common* continually since the late 1500s. Nevertheless, once a usage issue has provoked enough impassioned commentary—and this one has—editors must take note: some readers will consider phrases such as 'mutual goals', 'mutual problems', and 'their mutual high regard for Robert' simply wrong.

The phrase 'our mutual friend', although it exemplifies the disputed meaning of *mutual*, has been spared criticism, perhaps because it dates from the mid-1600s, perhaps because it is the title of a Dickens' novel, or perhaps because in a class-conscious milieu 'our common friend' might have been misunderstood to mean 'our vulgar friend'.

> Two, [a novel] by Isaac Bashevis Singer, describes a pair of married men living in pre-war Poland who admit their mutual attraction and run away.
> *Gazette* (Montreal) 18 June 1994: 13

> . . . the two reveal several mutual neuroses. Both Florence and Glen had unhappy childhoods.
> *NeWest Review* Feb.–Mar. 1990: 43

(Here some critics would insist on *common* or *shared*, because the neuroses are not reciprocal.)

> Like Grant . . . he had accompanied their mutual friend the chancellor, Sandford Fleming, on a transcontinental journey before the building of the railway. . . .
> Hilda Neatby *Queen's University* 1 (1978): 247–49

(The phrase *mutual friend* is accepted, though it is at odds with the rule.)

Myanmar, Burma   see PLACE NAMES

myriad   Originally *myriad* was a noun meaning ten thousand. It is now used as both a noun and an adjective and means a vast number, or innumerable.

> There are a myriad of wines from France to seek out, to taste and to enjoy.
> *Queen's Quarterly* 94.3 (1987): 605

> Modern nails come in myriad types and sizes— North American manufacturers make more than 300 kinds. . . .
> *Harrowsmith* Oct.–Nov. 1985: 85

See also COLLECTIVE NOUNS.

myself, I, me   Many usage guides object to the substitution of *myself* for *I* or *me*. They argue that *myself* has only two acceptable uses: for emphasis ('I myself don't like Yorkshire pudding, although I make it often') and as a reflexive pronoun ('I was angry with myself').

However, the substitution of *myself* for *I* or *me* often occurs in sentences with compound sub-

jects or objects: 'Marco, Mikhail, and myself finished our group project at midnight'; 'Jack and Julia invited my mother, my father, and myself to the opera'. This use of *myself*, which is quite common in speech, may have originated in the desire to avoid writing *I* where *me* is correct, or vice versa (see CASE). *Myself* is also quite often found instead of *me*, in both speech and writing, as the object of a preposition (*for*, *including*, *to*, etc.). *Myself* is particularly likely to appear after *than* or *as*. In sentences such as 'She is bigger than I/me' and 'She reads just as well as I/me', many speakers and writers evade the dilemma of whether to use *I* or *me* by substituting *myself*. *Myself* also commonly replaces *me* after the preposition *like*: 'She looks just like myself'; 'Workaholics like myself can only dream of holidays'. Perhaps the reason is that *like* is a verb as well as a preposition, and the beginning of a sentence such as 'You like me have lost interest' could be misread.

It seems perfectly acceptable to use *myself* for *I* or *me* in all these contexts in speech and informal writing. In more formal writing, this use of *myself* is common only after prepositions.

> Becky, Linda and I met at 7 pm sharp at the Keele subway station.
> *Women and Environments* 12.1 (1990): 9

> 'The poems that Irving Layton, Louis Dudek and myself were writing at the time weren't all that fashionable with the general readership of the period.'
> Bruce Meyer and Brian O'Riordan, eds. *In Their Words* 1984: 89

(This is a transcription of speech.)

> 'All these men and many more, including myself, were drawn to nuclear physics as a result of our undergraduate contact with Gray.'
> Frederick Gibson *Queen's University* 2: 1983: 122

> It is many months since I was invited to speak to you, and in the interval several letters have passed between your club and myself.
> Robertson Davies *One Half of Robertson Davies* 1978: 14

> Even in the life of one person like myself, living in a raw provincial city like Winnipeg, you can find the presence of duality and paradox that is so

characteristic of Canadian life.
Miriam Waddington *Apartment Seven* 1989: 38

See also LIKE, AS; PRESENT WRITER; -SELF, -SELVES; THAN.

mythological, mythic, mythical, legendary, mystic

Mythological refers to the study of myths, *mythic* to their character. *Mythical* often suggests that something is non-existent or fictional: 'Hercules was a mythical figure'.

Myths and legends are similar but not identical. Myths have their roots deep in the popular imagination and often involve supernatural figures or events that explain that the world view or practices of a society. Legends may also have supernatural elements, but they have some connection to events in history. While legends remain undocumented in credible historical sources, they are thought to be embellishments of real events; the same is not true of myths.

In contemporary usage, to call something a *myth* is to say that it is not true: 'That statement is a myth and you know it'. To call something a *legend* or *legendary* is to compliment it as deservedly well known: 'He displayed his legendary talent for filing and we finished the project on time'.

Mystic has nothing to do with *mythic*: as a noun it means a person who believes in gaining access to truth beyond human understanding, and as an adjective it describes something that is symbolic or allegorical, inscrutable or occult.

This tendency to see what is not visible opens up the landscape to mythological interpretations.
Essays on Canadian Writing 73 (2001): 72–92

Human events in the novel are coordinated with geological and mythic time.
Essays on Canadian Writing 73 (2001): 72–92

(Here *myth* is distinguished from history.)

I think we need to look not at some mythical moment when interpretation first began but at the ways in which information gleaned from previous interpretations might actually be employed.
Canadian Journal of Philosophy 34.1 (2004): 107–36

(Here *mythical* is used rather than *mythic*, to emphasize that the moment never happened.)

They ended their last tour in Vancouver in October, with a sold out show at the legendary Commodore.
Times-Colonist (Victoria) 29 Jan. 2003

(Here *legendary* means famous and extraordinary.)

Based loosely but quite obviously on the mythological exploits of Beach Boy Brian Wilson . . . Quarrington's story is one of the three or four convincing rock'n'roll novels ever written.
Toronto Star 9 May 1989: D4

(*Legendary* is more appropriate here than *mythological*.)

Yet researchers who study the evolution of language and the psychology of swearing say they have no idea what mystic model of linguistic gentility the critics might have in mind.
Gazette (Montreal) 16 Oct. 2005: D6

(If *mystic* is being used to mean obscure, it is correct; if it is being used to mean non-existent, *mythical* is a better word choice.)

See also -IC, -ICAL.

N

Na-Dene   see ATHABASCAN; DENE

nadir   see APOGEE

naive, naïf, naïveté, naivety   *Naïve* is the French feminine form and *naïf* the French masculine form of the same word. In English, these two forms are distinguished not by gender but by function. The adjective form, whether it is applied to a man or a woman, is *naive*: 'He was a naive man'. The noun referring to a naive person of either gender is *naïf*: 'She was such a naïf'. In Canada the noun for the quality is usually spelled *naïveté*. *Naivety* is a predominantly British spelling.

Any of these words may appear, as in French, with a diaeresis (two points) above the *i*, which indicates that it is pronounced separately. The *Canadian Oxford Dictionary* omits the diaeresis in *naive*, the most common of these words.

Naive is pronounced *nye EVE*. *Naïf* is pronounced *nah EEF*; and *naïveté* is pronounced *nye EVE uh TAY* or *nye EVE uh tee*.

> Children sometimes demand to know who invents jokes, and often their elders think this question naïve.
> Robertson Davies *A Voice From the Attic* 1960: 214

> In Canada . . . there appears every year a fair quantity of naive or primitive verse, to use terms more familiar in the criticism of painting.
> Northrop Frye *The Bush Garden* 1971: 3

> Probing interviews reveal Dutilleux as a scam artist and Sting as at best a naif, at worst a fool.
> *Gazette* (Montreal) 22 April 1990: F2

> In my naivete, I was not prepared for petty office politics and hysterical, demanding clients.
> *Vancouver Sun* 16 June 1990: C1

> Through our naivety, we aid these companies by telling them whether we're working or retired, the ages of our children and how much money we make.
> *Vancouver Sun* 27 June 1990: C2

(This spelling is uncommon in Canada.)

See also DIACRITICAL MARKS.

naked, nude   When used of people, *naked* and *nude* both mean unclothed. However, *naked* often conveys an additional sense of vulnerability, of being stripped bare or left unprotected. *Naked* is also more likely than *nude* to be used figuratively for non-human subjects. *Nude*, sometimes called a euphemism for *naked*, most often suggests deliberate or artistic nakedness. It is the usual choice when referring to art, or activities in which people choose to go without clothing ('nude sun-bathing'), or the places where they do so ('nude beaches').

> Later that night he set fire to the bed in his hotel room and was arrested wandering around naked; he was eventually confined to Camarillo State Hospital in a rehabilitation program.
> Jack Chambers *Milestones* 1983: 50

> They reach a grubby factory, lead their man down a set of dark, slippery stairs and into an airless basement where naked light bulbs hang from smoky ceilings.
> Pierre Berton *The Promised Land* 1984: 307

> The third work in the series, *The Studio Group* (1957), has as its theme students working from a nude model.
> *Queen's Quarterly* 95.1 (1988): 152

namely   see COLON

names   see CHINESE NAMES; FIRST NAME; JOB TITLES; MAIDEN NAME, BIRTH NAME; NAMES OF RESIDENTS; PINYIN; PLACE NAMES

names of residents of cities and provinces   There is no commonly accepted general term for the proper nouns that name the residents of a place, such as *Calgarian* for a person from Calgary. A term that has been suggested is *demonym*, from the Greek roots *demos*, 'people', and *-nym*, 'name'. Although language commentators have tried to establish rules for forming these terms, it is usually the residents of a particular city, province, state, or country who have the last word about what they are called.

In Canadian usage the residents of some provinces are known by more than one name. Both *Saskatchewanian* and *Saskatchewaner* are in use, as are *New Brunswickian* and *New Brunswicker*. *Quebecker* was the English spelling preferred by René Lévesque for a resident of the province of Quebec; however, *Quebecer* is now more widely used. The term *Québécois(e)* is usually reserved for francophone Quebeckers. Although, informally, residents of British Columbia are sometimes called *BCers*, in written English the term is *British Columbians*.

Other established names for residents of Canadian provinces are *Albertan*, *Manitoban*, *Nova Scotian*, *Newfoundlander*, *Ontarian*, and *Prince Edward Islander* (or simply *Islander*). *Yukoner* and *Labradorian* are in use, but there is no common term for a resident of the Northwest Territories. Residents of Nunavut are *Nunavummiut* (see NUNAVUT).

The most distinctive name for a resident of a Canadian city is *Haligonian* for a native of Halifax, Nova Scotia. How and why this name was chosen remains a mystery. *Hambletonians* is sometimes used humorously for residents of Hamilton, Ontario (who are *Hamiltonians* in serious contexts). A person from Saint John, New Brunswick, is called a *Saint Johner*, while someone from St. John's, Newfoundland, is a *St. Johnsian*. In the English language press all citizens of Montreal are *Montrealers*. In French-language publications a citizen of Montreal is either *un Montréalais* (male) or *une Montréalaise* (female).

Other established names for citizens of Canadian cities include *Vancouverite*, *Edmontonian*, *Moose Javian*, *Winnipegger*, *Torontonian*, *Ottawan*, and *Monctonian*. A resident of Medicine Hat, Alberta, is sometimes called a *Hatter*, a resident of Winnipeg, Manitoba, a *Pegger*.

See also QUEBECER; NUNAVUT, NUNAVUMMIUT, DENENDEH; SAINT JOHN, ST. JOHN'S.

napkin, serviette   A synonym for *napkin*, *serviette* is the less common term in Canada and is almost unknown in the United States. Its use in Canada may be influenced by British English or by the fact that it is also the French term and appears on Canadian packages. For Canadians a *serviette* is usually paper, while a *napkin* is either cloth or paper.

> An American painter of this school played a joke on his bitchy wife by painting one of her best napkins so expertly that she grabbed at the canvas trying to pull it off.
> Northrop Frye *The Educated Imagination* 1963: 40

> And cloth can replace paper towels and serviettes, even facial tissue if you don't mind doing extra laundry.
> *Vancouver Sun* 13 July 1990: D10

> He'd carry a little pad in his pocket, or draw on serviettes at the Arts and Letters Club.
> *Saturday Night* March 1986: 37

Naskapi   see INNU

narcissus, narcissi   see PLURALS, REGULAR, IRREGULAR, FOREIGN

national   see CITIZEN; NATIONAL ASSEMBLY

national anthem   see O CANADA

National Assembly, nationalist   The National Assembly is the legislature of Quebec. In Quebec English the word *nationalist* means sovereignist, not federalist.

> [Johnson's] uncompromising federalist stand renewed criticism that he isn't nationalist enough to run Quebec.
> *Toronto Star* 11 Sept. 1994: A10

See also SEPARATIST.

native, Native   *Native* is etymologically connected to the Latin word for birth. Thus a native plant is one that is indigenous to an area: it originated there, and was not introduced from somewhere else. A native of Toronto is someone who was born there, though not necessarily a resident (someone who lives there now).

Native is also used to refer to the Aboriginal people of Canada. The Federal Terminology Council recommends that this word be used as an adjective only—*Native people(s)*, not *Natives*—and that it be capitalized in references to Aboriginal peoples. Now, expecially in formal and official contexts, the adjective *Aboriginal* is supplanting *Native*.

> Sanipas, a native of Big Cove, N.B., scored twice in Sunday's game.
> *Globe and Mail* (Toronto) 2 Jan. 1985: S2

> A native lawyer from Merritt is taking legal action to get her children registered as status Indians.
> *Province* (Vancouver) 23 Dec. 1990: 26

(*Native* should be capitalized here, as should *Status*, a legal term.)

> Alberta also has all-native emergency firefighting crews.
> *Calgary Herald* 7 Aug. 1994: B2

(*Native* should be capitalized.)

See also ABORIGINAL PEOPLE(S); APPENDIX III.

NATO   see ALPHABETICAL ORDER

Nat'ooten   see CARRIER

natural   see FUNCTIONAL SHIFT

naturalist, naturist   A *naturalist* is a nature lover or a professional botanist or zoologist. A *naturist* is a nudist.

> Nature walks are conducted by a resident professional naturalist, who is eager to share the wonders of this timeless land.
> *Vancouver Sun* 6 Oct. 1990: E7

> 'There's a lot of fear and misunderstanding out there,' says David Horton, a longtime nudist and a

B.C. director of the Federation of Canadian Naturists.
Province (Vancouver) 31 Oct. 1990: 3

naturally   see COMMA

naught, nought, aught   These three words rhyme in Canadian English. *Naught* and *nought* are variant spellings of an archaic word meaning zero, or nothing, which survives in phrases such as 'to bring to naught', 'to set at naught', 'to come to naught', and 'it was all for naught'. *Naught* is the more common spelling, particularly in academic writing.

Aught, also archaic, is the opposite of *naught* and means all or anything; it survives in the jocular or dialectal 'for aught I know', meaning 'for all I know'. It also survives in the expression 'the aughts', which is sometimes used to name the first decade of a new century. 'The naughts' (the zeros) would make more sense, but, in the late nineteenth century, 'a naught' was misconstrued as 'an aught', which gave *aught* an additional meaning: naught or zero.

> We can set management goals and establish preserves in Canada for our forest birds, but this will be for naught if tropical forests vanish.
> *Queen's Quarterly* 94.3 (1987): 618

> And if Cineplex fails, all the agony of the last year will be for nought.
> *Gazette* (Montreal) 6 Jan. 1990: D1

See also STANDARD ENGLISH, STANDARD.

nauseous   *Nauseous* usually means *nauseated* or *sick*: 'I was feeling nauseous'. Some commentators disapprove of this usage, arguing that *nauseous* is only properly a synonym for *nauseating* or *sickening*. In other words, if you are feeling nauseous, you are making other people sick. Dictionaries do not support this contention. According to the *Canadian Oxford Dictionary*, the *Concise Oxford Dictionary,* and the *Merriam-Webster's Collegiate Dictionary*, *nauseous* means *either* sick or sickening.

> Not everyone drank the arrack but those who did became dizzy and nauseous on Christmas Eve.
> *Gazette* (Montreal) 29 Dec. 1990: A7

They make the whole idea of reading nauseous to thousands of decent people.
Robertson Davies *A Voice from the Attic* 1960: 37

See also SICK.

naval, navel   *Naval* describes anything related to the navy. The noun *navel* refers to the place where the umbilical cord was once attached, and is often applied figuratively.

He then reviews naval and military bases and discusses political, economic, strategic and environmental factors that led to the selection of many colonial capitals.
The Canadian Geographer Spring (1989): 93

It's easy to think we can seal ourselves off from the perils of the world. We can't, of course. The general calls it 'myopic and navel-gazing' to think so.
Globe and Mail (Toronto) 3 March 2006: A14

navy   see CANADIAN ARMED FORCES

Nazi   see GERMAN WORDS, PRONUNCIATION OF

NDP   see NEW DEMOCRATIC PARTY

né   see MAIDEN NAME

near, nearly   *Near* is standard in combinations with nouns and adjectives: 'near-miss', 'near-disaster', 'near-perfect score'. 'Nowhere near', as in 'I'm nowhere near finished', is considered informal by some commentators.

Sentences in which *near* is substituted for *nearly* before a verb, as in 'I near fainted', are no longer standard. This construction should be avoided in writing except in representations of speech.

The selection of delegates to the leadership convention in Calgary next June is nowhere near complete but already it has made a mockery of fair play and party loyalty.
Vancouver Sun 19 March 1990: 48

I damn near bawled to think I could have asked him to tag along.
David Williams *Eye of the Father* 1985: 13

near-sighted, far-sighted, short-sighted, long-sighted   In Canada and the United States *near-sighted* refers to someone who sees nearby objects better than distant ones; *far-sighted* is the opposite. *Short-sighted* is most often used figuratively to describe someone who lacks foresight. *Far-sighted* is used figuratively to describe someone with good judgment about the future. Hyphenation of these words varies.

In British English *short-sighted* and *long-sighted* are the terms commonly used in reference to physical vision.

'Many of the children were so near-sighted that it was difficult for them to see clearly beyond a couple of feet.'
Vancouver Sun 12 Dec. 1994: B5

It's like being farsighted, the distant lake and its beaches and smooth-backed basking sauropods clear-edged in the moonlight, her own hand a blur.
Margaret Atwood *Life Before Man* 1979: 142

Yet, at this opportune moment, Parks Canada has announced plans to scale back its facilities at Rocky Mountain House National Historic Site, an arbitrary and short-sighted decision that scuttles the work of local preservationists and will ensure that few Canadians ever visit this historically important community.
National Post (Toronto) 19 Feb. 2006: A18

Harper should be working on a far-sighted industrial strategy to deal with a future when Canada's natural resources are exhausted.
Windsor Star 13 May 2006: A6

Short-sighted since childhood, he had to sit in the front of the class to see the blackboard.
Leader-Post (Regina) 27 Feb. 1988: C1

(*Near-sighted* is more common for the physical condition.)

Ten storeys of stone facade on this early concrete framed building culminate in a flourish of Greek ornamental detail that you've got to be long-sighted, or have binoculars, to properly see.
Vancouver Sun 29 Dec. 1990: D16

(*Far-sighted* is more common for the physical condition.)

necessary prerequisite   see WORDINESS

née   see MAIDEN NAME

needless to say   see GOES WITHOUT SAYING

negative   see DON'T THINK; DOUBLE NEGATIVE

negative-raising   see DON'T THINK

Negro   see BLACK

neighbour   see -IE-, -EI-

neither   In formal English the pronoun *neither* always takes a singular verb: 'Neither of them is (*not* are) adequate'. The conjunction *neither* should be paired with *nor*, not *or*.

Regarding agreement of the verb after a 'neither . . . nor' construction, pronunciation, and whether *neither* should be used to introduce more than two items, see EITHER.

See also AGREEMENT, GRAMMATICAL; COMMA.

ne plus ultra   see EPITOME; SINE QUA NON

nepotism   Although *nepotism* is similar in meaning to *favouritism* and *patronage*, it refers specifically to the favouring of family members.

News item: Two Tory MPs from Ontario and one from Quebec are investigated for allegedly circumventing anti-nepotism rules by hiring one another's sons and daughters.
Vancouver Sun 23 Feb. 1990: A13

It would have been acceptable if the Conservatives stuck to the Canadian tradition of political patronage, former Liberal solicitor-general Robert Kaplan says, but they strayed into the taboo territory of nepotism.
Globe and Mail (Toronto) 8 June 1985: P5

The mayoral challenger said proposed anti-nepotism rules don't go nearly far enough because politicians' close family members—spouses, parents and children—could apply for all but a few top municipal jobs.
Toronto Star 17 May 2006: B4

Magna [International] indulged in nepotism. . . . Having the only rising talent in an organization

come from one group ruins morale.
Financial Post 26 March 1990: 2

(Since the 'group' referred to isn't a family, *favouritism* would be preferable here.)

Is there a form of regional nepotism going on? Six of the top executives of the Royal are from Saskatchewan, three of the top Imperial bosses.
Maclean's 21 Oct. 1991: A108

(Here too *favouritism* would be preferable.)

-ness   Although the words *certainness, clearness, deepness, difficultness, graveness, intenseness, loyalness, sincereness,* and *warmness* can all be found in dictionaries, they almost never appear in published writing. Their preferred synonyms are *certainty, clarity, depth, difficulty, gravity, intensity, loyalty, sincerity,* and *warmth*. The suffix *-ness* is freely added to adjectives to create nouns. The noun means the state or quality of being whatever the adjective denotes. Many writers and editors object to new words ending in *-ness* that mean the same thing as established words containing the older noun suffixes *-ty* and *-th*.

See also ENORMITY, ENORMOUSNESS.

neuter, sterilize, castrate, spay, fix   A number of verbs refer to the surgical sterilization of animals. Both male and female animals can be *neutered* or *sterilized*. Male farm animals are *castrated*; but for male house pets more euphemistic terms are often preferred (*neuter, sterilize*). Female animals are *spayed* (sometimes this word is misspelled *spade*). *Fix* is slang for *neuter* or *sterilize*.

Most importantly, male dogs that are neutered run a significantly reduced risk of medical problems later on in life.
Ottawa Citizen 6 Jan. 1990: F7

Unless you've decided to enter your dog in conformation or obedience events, or have made a conscious decision to be a dog breeder . . . you should have your dog spayed or neutered.
Dogs in Canada Special Issue 1986: 66

Pigs are usually castrated within the first few weeks of life. This pig was heading helter-skelter

into puberty, uncastrated and obviously happy with his self-image.
Harrowsmith Oct.–Nov. 1985: 16

nevertheless   see COMMA

New Brunswick, New Brunswicker, New Brunswickian   see NAMES OF RESIDENTS OF CITIES AND PROVINCES; APPENDIX I

Newburgh   see -BURGH, -BURG, -BOROUGH, -BORO

Newcastle, coals to   see CLICHÉ

New Democratic Party, NDP   The New Democratic Party was founded in 1961, an amalgamation of the Co-operative Commonwealth Federation (CCF), affiliated unions of the Canadian Labour Congress (CLC), and New Party clubs. It is a democratic socialist party. The abbreviation *NDP* is much more common than the full name of the party in Canadian news reporting. Members may be called *NDP members*, *New Democrats*, or less formally, *NDPers*. The adjective is *New Democratic*, *New Democrat*, or *NDP*, as in 'an NDP policy'.

> The classic cure for the Grits would be to move left and attempt to supplant the NDP in the hearts and minds of the voters by co-opting the New Democrat policies.
> *Ottawa Citizen* 13 Dec. 1990: A3

> It's been New Democratic policy for years to protect farmland. . . .
> *Ottawa Citizen* 13 Nov. 1990: A2

> . . . some wonder . . . whether a proposed regional garbage incinerator could be trashed by NDPers who see it as an environmental hazard.
> *Ottawa Citizen* 8 Sept. 1990: A13

Newfoundland   Newfoundlanders pronounce *Newfoundland* like *understand*, with the stress on the last syllable. Many Canadians from the rest of the country say *NEW fun lund* or *new FOUND lund*, but these pronunciations mark them as 'come-fromaway' (non-Newfoundlanders).

Newfoundland used to be an ambiguous place name, referring sometimes to the island and sometimes to the whole province, which includes Labrador. That ambiguity was resolved in 2001, when the official name of the province was changed to Newfoundland and Labrador.

See also APPENDIX I.

Newfoundland dog   see DALMATIAN

newly-wed, newlywed   see HYPHENATION

newton   see APPENDIX II

New Year's Day, April Fool's Day, Thanksgiving Day, St. Jean Baptiste Day   There is an apostrophe before the *s* in *New Year's Day*. References to the *new year*, meaning the year about to begin, should be capitalized only in a holiday greeting: 'Happy New Year'. Canadians and Americans often shorten *New Year's Day* or *New Year's Eve* to *New Year's*, a usage that sounds odd (or wrong) to speakers of British English.

April Fool's Day and *April Fools' Day* are both correct, with the former preferred in Canada.

Thanksgiving Day is celebrated on the second Monday in October in Canada, and on the fourth Thursday in November in the United States.

St. Jean Baptiste Day, 24 June, is the national holiday of Quebec. *St-Jean-Baptiste* is the French spelling, with no period after *St* and two hyphens. Both spellings, French and English, are in common use, as are hybrid variants (which should be avoided).

> CP Forest can now run the mill on New Years Day, Easter and Labor Day.
> *Ottawa Citizen* 21 Dec. 1990: C7

(An apostrophe should precede the *s*: *Year's*.)

> One game was scheduled for New Year's day.
> *Saturday Night* March 1986: 23

(*Day* should be capitalized.)

> As we begin a New Year, we look both back and forward, and our attitude will make all the difference.
> *Canadian Baptist* Jan. 1986: 17

(In references to the year rather than the day, *new year* is not usually capitalized.)

During most of these years Montgomery gave Cavendish a large turkey for New Year's . . . .
J.E. Smyth et al. *The Law and Business Administration in Canada* 1987: 592

In an unrelated matter, the PQ announced that it will hold a separate parade after the St.-Jean Baptiste parade in Montreal this Sunday.
Vancouver Sun 21 June 1990: A10

(Either all-French or all-English spelling would be preferable: *St. Jean Baptiste* or *St-Jean-Baptiste*.)

See also HOLIDAY.

next, this   The expression *next Friday* is used in two ways. Sometimes it refers to the coming Friday, in which case it is synonymous with 'this Friday'; and sometimes it means Friday of next week. In other words, if on Monday you tell people about a party *next Friday*, some people will think it is happening in four days, others in eleven. *Collins COBUILD English Usage* says *next* should not be used to refer to a day in the same week, but in fact it often is. Given the potential for confusion, it's best not to use *next* with a day of the week unless you are also specifying the date. The expressions 'this Friday' and 'a week from Friday' are unambiguous alternatives to *next Friday*.

This Saturday it's shopping. Next Saturday it'll be a mom-and-daughter pottery class. . . .
Vancouver Sun 18 Feb. 1992: C1

Blue Jay first baseman John Olerud, Argonaut lineman Jim Kardash, and Maple Leaf centre Doug Gilmour will be the big wheels next Friday in the Bike Helmet Festival. . . . The festival runs from noon to 2 p.m. on June 12 and will feature events for both adults and children.
Toronto Star 7 June 1992: E2

(Here *next Friday* means this Friday; this would have been confusing had the date not been given as well.)

Later in the week, The Gazette has put together a series of lectures by specialists in many fields of financial planning, during the four-day Savings & Investment Marketplace, to be held in Place Bonaventure from next Friday, Jan. 31, through Feb. 3.
Gazette (Montreal) 27 Jan. 1992: TWIB5

(Here again *next Friday* means this Friday, which would not have been evident if the date had not been given.)

See also DATES, AHEAD, BACK.

nexus   see -US

nice, nicety   Almost anything that is not offensive can be described as *nice*, which leads some usage experts to complain that this adjective is greatly overworked. Although there is nothing grammatically incorrect about using *nice* as an all-encompassing adjective of approval, substitution of a more precise adjective, explaining why the person, object, or situation is considered 'nice', tends to produce a more interesting statement.

When it first appeared in English, in the 1300s, *nice* (from the Latin *nescius*, 'ignorant') meant foolish or ignorant. Since then its meaning has evolved through timid, fussy, fastidious, dainty, extravagant, precise, exact, and careful to the most commonly used current senses: agreeable or delightful, first recorded in 1769, and kind or thoughtful, first recorded in 1830. An older meaning of *nice* is reflected in expressions such as 'a nice distinction' (fine or subtle), as well as in the noun *nicety*, which means subtlety rather than niceness.

It is a nice prairie, covered with beautiful grass, and dotted here and there with little poplar forests which gives the whole a very romantic appearance.
NeWest Review Oct.–Nov. 1989: 13

This operation required a nice balancing of two gauges on the switchboard and the tripping of a switch.
Imperial Oil Review Spring (1988): 28

(Here *nice* means delicate or careful.)

As a working musician, Davis showed no interest in the theoretical niceties of his innovation except as a means of relieving his music of the predictable chord progressions, creating an aural effect of lightness, and challenging his melodic ingenuity.
Jack Chambers *Milestones* 1983: 309

nickel, the nickel belt, Nickel Belt   *Nickel* is the correct spelling for both the metal and the five-cent coin. *Nickle* is a common mis-spelling. The nickel belt (not capitalized) is the geographic area around Sudbury, Ontario, where much of the world's nickel is mined. Nickel Belt (capitalized) is the name of an electoral riding in the area.

> I'd never even seen a beaver, except on the back of a nickel.
> Howard Engel *Murder Sees the Light* 1984: 57

> Now, as health minister, his fate is to nickle-and-dime the provinces to death over health costs.
> *Ottawa Citizen* 19 Aug. 1990: A6

(The correct spelling is *nickel*.)

> With McLaughlin's encouragement, Barrett teamed up with the similarly aggressive Nickle Belt MP John Rodriguez to form what caucus members call 'the nasty boys.'
> *Maclean's* 13 Aug. 1990: A12

(The correct spelling is *Nickel*.)

nighttime   see HYPHENATION

ninth   see -E

nip it in the bud, [nip it in the butt]   see MISHEARD EXPRESSIONS

Nisei   see ISSEI

Nisga'a, Nishga, Niska   The First Nation whose traditional territory is Northwest British Columbia's Nass River Valley is called *Nisga'a* (singular and plural), pronounced *NIS gah*. It was formerly called *Nishga* (or *Niska*). The Nisga'a language belongs to the Tsimshian family.

> Azak is from the Nisga'a community of Gitwinksihlkw in the Nass Valley in northern B.C.
> *Province* (Vancouver) 3 Aug. 2004: A14

See also ABORIGINAL PEOPLE(S); GITXSAN; APPENDIX III.

nitpicking, [knit-picking]   Finding fault by focusing on insignificant shortcomings or minute errors is called *nitpicking*. The metaphor, removing the eggs of lice, suggests the myopic point of view associated with the activity.

Occasionally, writers misconstrue the metaphor and misspell the expression *knit-picking*.

> I would feel a lot more secure flying if I knew that, in addition to the nitpicking, delay-causing, down-to-tweezers passenger screening, there were comprehensive background checks and screenings conducted on service staff with direct access to planes. . . .
> *Calgary Herald* 21 Nov. 2001: A18

Nlaka'pamux, Thompson   The Aboriginal people whose traditional territory is in the Stein Valley in south-central British Columbia are called the *Nlaka'pamux* (pronounced *un tla KAP mooh*); this is the most common spelling and is both singular and plural. Their language, Nlaka'pamux, belongs to the Salishan family. This group was formerly known as the *Thompson Indians*.

> As in many Native North American societies, dreams and visions were considered important among the Nlaka'pamux—particularly those visions which came after days of living shelterless in the wild while fasting.
> *Toronto Star* 30 July 1994: G13

See also ABORIGINAL PEOPLE(S); APPENDIX III.

nobody   see EVERYONE

nobody else('s)   see ELSE

noes   see -OS, -OES

nohow   *Nohow* means 'in no manner'. It is most frequently used in double negatives ('I couldn't start the car nohow'), which are condemned by grammarians. It is standard in constructions without a second negative ('She could nohow write the test'), but this usage is extremely rare in Canada.

> He too is nervous but his nerves are in a state that does no good for nobody no-how.
> *Canadian Fiction Magazine* 63 (1988): 137

(The author is using non-standard dialect.)

> . . . He feels he's in a personal slugfest with Brian Mulroney, and he isn't going to back down

nohow.
Gazette (Montreal) 20 Jan. 1990: B3

(Here again the non-standard use is intentional.)

See also DOUBLE NEGATIVE.

noisome   *Noisome* is sometimes mistakenly used to mean noisy. It derives from the same Middle English word that gave us *annoy*. It means harmful, offensive, or disgusting, and often implies a foul smell.

> Most caddies have nicknames, including one known as Downwind Vic, a caddie everyone tries to keep ahead of due to a noxious and noisome anatomical defect. . . .
> *Globe and Mail* (Toronto) 26 Aug. 1985: S2

> Of all the American culture that slops over the border and is soaked up by undiscriminating Canadians, gun love is perhaps the most noisome.
> *Vancouver Sun* 31 Aug. 1994: A18

nom de guerre, nom de plume   see PSEUDONYM

nomination   see QUEBEC ENGLISH

nonchalant   see NONPLUSSED

none   *None is* and *none are* are both correct. Generally, *none* can be followed by either a singular or a plural verb: 'None of them has a car'; 'None of them have jobs'. *None* requires a singular verb only when it means 'no part of a mass or whole': 'None of it makes (*not* make) any sense'.

> Of thirty-five undersecretaries-general, none is a woman.
> *Saturday Night* May 1986: 43

> Above all, however, we hope you share our dream of a world where all dogs are loved—where none are killed because no one wants them. . . .
> *Dogs in Canada* Special Issue 1986: 4

> None of this emerges.
> *Edmonton Journal* 13 Sept. 1992: n.p.

(Here *none* means no part and the plural verb *emerge* is not possible.)

See also AGREEMENT, GRAMMATICAL.

non-flammable   see FLAMMABLE

non-human   see HUMAN

non-inflammable   see FLAMMABLE

non-moral   see IMMORAL

nonplussed, nonchalant   *Nonplussed* means puzzled or at a loss as to what to say or do. The word comes from the Latin *non plus*, meaning literally 'no further', and suggests a state in which nothing more is forthcoming. The *non-* prefix, however, appears to indicate that the word means *not* something. *Nonplussed* is so often used to mean unconcerned, indifferent, or unruffled that it seems clear people are confusing it with *nonchalant*.

Canadian writers prefer the British double-*s* spelling; *nonplused* is a chiefly American variant.

> She seems nonplussed at the idea that she might have chosen a different career. 'Art is what holds me,' she says.
> *Torch: University of Victoria Alumni Magazine* Spring 1990: 15

> 'Hey Shutty,' Lapointe taunts, 'there's your meal ticket.' Shutt, who has made a career feasting off his linemate's rebounds, is typically nonplussed. 'Ah, that's the way I like to see him,' he says, 'ready, but not too ready. There'll be rebounds tonight.'
> Ken Dryden *The Game* 1983: 174–175

(Steve Shutt is characterized in Dryden's memoir as one who always has a quick retort and is typically calm. Here *nonplussed* is used incorrectly to mean something like *unruffled* or *nonchalant*.)

> [James Murray] cast it in linguistic terms, pointing out with a nonplused ethnocentrism that for those possessing 'the language of a civilized nation', the empire offered no less than 'the subject matter of new ideas, and the theme of new discourse'.
> John Willinsky *The Empire of Words: The Reform of the OED* 1994: 202

(Here too *nonplused* seems to mean *unruffled*, *nonchalant*, or even *unselfconscious*.)

non-profit, nonprofit see HYPHENATION

non-sexist language see INCLUSIVE LANGUAGE; SEXIST LANGUAGE

non-standard see STANDARD ENGLISH, STANDARD

Non-Status Indian see ABORIGINAL PEOPLE(S)

non-stick see HYPHENATION

non-white see VISIBLE MINORITY

noon see TIME

no one, no-one, [noone] *No one* is the form commonly used by writers and listed in dictionaries. *No-one* is rarer, but is recognized by a few authorities. *Noone* appears occasionally, but is considered an error.

> When he asked how improvements could be made noone could provide any answers.
> *Financial Post* 20 March 1989: 5

(The accepted spelling is *no one*.)

See also EVERYONE.

Nootka see NUU-CHAH-NULTH

noplace see -WHERE, -PLACE

nor see COMMA; NEITHER

Nordic see SCANDINAVIAN

normality, normalcy According to some commentators, *normality* is the only standard noun form of *normal*. Warren G. Harding used *normalcy* during the 1920 campaign for the presidency of the United States. His opponents derided him; his supporters pointed out that this form had been used before in Great Britain. Fowler called it a 'spurious hybrid', presumably because the *-cy* suffix is typically used to form a noun only from an adjective ending in *t* or *te* (*pregnant, pregnancy; accurate, accuracy*). However, the word gained currency and now, long after the Harding dispute has been forgotten, *normalcy* and *normality* are both listed in

dictionaries. One is used just about as often as the other in Canadian English.

> Durkin's *The Magpie* depicts the post World-War-I struggle between those who strive for a return to prewar normality and those who want to bring in changes.
> Miriam Waddington *Apartment Seven* 1989: 101

> For all the normalcy of the situation, the tension is oppressive, almost unbearable, because we know—as they cannot—that the world's first nuclear bomb is about to explode and reduce Hiroshima to ashes.
> *Gazette* (Montreal) 20 May 1990: F3

north see EAST

northerly Generally, *northerly* means situated to the north. A northerly wind blows *from* the north.

> It is not the end of passenger rail service between Halifax and Montreal: the Ocean, a longer, more northerly route, will continue. But Saint John and other southern communities will no longer have rail service.
> *Daily News* (Halifax) 17 Dec. 1994: n.p.

> The game-time temperature was 1 C with a northerly wind at 29 m.p.h. and a wind chill of zero.
> *Ottawa Citizen* 6 April 1994: C2

See also EAST, WEST, NORTH, SOUTH.

Northern Ireland see IRELAND

Northwest Territories Though *Northwest* is written as one word (not *North West*), the traditional abbreviation contains three letters: *NWT*. The postal service uses *NT*. Residents prefer 'Northwest Territories' to '*the* Northwest Territories. The preferred usage parallels usage for the names of provinces; that is, one doesn't say 'the Alberta'.

See also APPENDIX I.

no smoke without fire see CLICHÉ

no sooner The construction *no sooner . . . than*

is standard: 'No sooner had he signed the agreement than he wanted to make changes'. However, many critics have noticed and disapproved of the variant construction *no sooner . . . when*: 'No sooner had my neighbour stopped practising her tuba when the radiators started to bang'. In fact, *no sooner . . . when* is often used, as in the example above, when the connection between two consecutive events is random rather than logical. Although it can be argued that this is a legitimate distinction, the fact remains that *no sooner . . . when* has been tainted by criticism: in formal writing it's probably best avoided.

> No sooner did the evidence appear in the press than Pedley was forced to resign.
> Pierre Berton *The Promised Land* 1984: 248

> He no sooner arrived in the village than he was requested to leave. . . .
> William Teatero *John Anderson: Fugitive Slave* 1986: 15

> He was no sooner free of them when he met up with a tall, thin, middle-aged farmer named Seneca F.P. Digges.
> William Teatero *John Anderson: Fugitive Slave* 1986: 13

(Some editors would change *when* to *than*.)

> No sooner had emergency crews fixed one problem when another would occur.
> *Province* (Vancouver) 28 Dec. 1990: 5

(Some editors would change *when* to *than*.)

nosy, nosey   see -Y, -EY

notable see NOTICEABLE

notary public   see LAWYER

noticeable, notable, noted   Not everything *noticeable* is necessarily *notable*: noticeable things are those that can be noticed, no matter how mundane; only notable things are worth noticing. Notable people or places are *noted* for their beauty, character, charm, skill, etc.

> . . . he walked with a noticeable limp, couldn't skate, and was forced to watch practice from the stands.
> *Gazette* (Montreal) 18 Dec. 1995: F3

> While [this year] there was no single breakthrough . . . there were more notable [musical] releases than ever.
> *Daily News* (Halifax) 30 Dec. 1995: 27

> Tremolo was not, of course, nearly as well known as Rigoletto, but a noted music critic has recently observed that he was quite as good.
> J.E. Smyth et al. *The Law and Business Administration in Canada* 1987: 304

notional agreement   see AGREEMENT, GRAMMATICAL

not only . . . but also   see PARALLELISM

notorious, infamous   *Notorious* means 'of ill repute'; that is, well known for something negative: 'notorious criminal', 'notorious for not returning borrowed books'. If a cook is notorious for her cookies, they are quite likely inedible. In very formal usage *notorious* sometimes means simply well known. However, this meaning is possible only in reference to facts. *Infamous* means widely known as evil or troublesome, and may apply to people or things. *Infamous* is pronounced *IN fuh muss*, not *in FAY muss*.

> In the past, major league baseball players were notorious for reporting to spring training overweight and out of shape.
> *Canadian Living* 19 April 1986: 113

> The mood was certainly upbeat, with the notorious Ottawa Fire Department Marching Band at centre-stage.
> *Ottawa Citizen* 12 Dec. 1990: D3

(Either *well-known* is intended here or the reference is humorous.)

> A further element of adverse possession is that it must be open and notorious—a person who furtively creeps into a deserted house each night and sleeps there for a period equal to the limitation period would not thereby extinguish the title of the owner.
> J.E. Smyth et al. *The Law and Business Administration in Canada* 1987: 585

(In this highly formal use, in reference to a fact, *notorious* simply means well known.)

During the 1914 war, the country had produced no weapons apart from the infamous Ross rifle and war production had been largely confined to the manufacture of shells for the always hungry guns in France.
The Beaver Dec. 1989–Jan. 1990: 59

(The Ross rifle was extremely unreliable and dangerous.)

not too, too The use of *not too* meaning 'not very' is well established in both formal and informal Canadian writing, though some usage commentators still object to it. Their objections are founded on the possible confusion with *not too* meaning 'not excessively', as in 'not too hot to cook the crepes'. This is rarely a problem, since the context usually makes clear which sense is intended. *Not too* is a useful device for making an understatement.

My principal objection is that the author is really not too informative about pressure ridges.
Arctic 41.1 (1988): 85

What children are to the eponymous heroine of 'Irina'—darling zeros—Linnet's husband is to her, and one is not too sure that the darling part was ever applicable.
Janice Kulyk Keefer *Reading Mavis Gallant* 1989: 131

Here the ideal society is associated with a not too remote future.
Northrop Frye *The Modern Century* 1990: 33

notwithstanding   see CANADIAN BILL OF RIGHTS; DESPITE

nought see NAUGHT

noun see entry in Glossary

nouns as adjectives see ATTRIBUTIVE NOUNS

Nova Scotia see APPENDIX I

nth In mathematics n is used to indicate an indefinite number. Because n could be any number, large or small, Fowler objected to the figurative use of 'the nth degree' to mean utmost, but this sense is now fully established.

Each and every actor plays his or her character to the nth degree of detail.
Rites March 1990: 16

. . . Orleans is still in every way Joan of Arc's town; and that blunt assertion is reinforced to the nth degree during the May festival, which has been going on for more than five centuries.
Globe and Mail (Toronto) 5 Jan. 1985: T13

nuclear *Nuclear* is frequently mispronounced as if it were spelled *nucular*, even by some scientists who might be expected to connect it with the noun form *nucleus* and therefore pronounce it correctly. CBC Radio receives more calls about the pronunciation of this word than almost any other (according to 'You Don't Say', the CBC's in-house language advisory guide). The disputed pronunciation occurs because people find the arrangement of consonants in *nuclear* difficult to pronounce, or have a tendency to produce the more familiar sound of words such as *muscular* and *circular*. Thus the mispronunciation is well entrenched. However, because it is also strongly stigmatized, the standard pronunciation, *NUKE lee er*, is recommended.

See also MISPRONUNCIATION AND PRONUNCIATION SHIFTS.

nucleus, nuclei see PLURALS

nude see NAKED

number of see COLLECTIVE NOUNS

number prefixes, Greek and Latin Below is a list of numbers with their equivalent prefixes as derived from Greek and Latin and an example of an English word containing each:

English	Greek	Latin	examples
one	mono-	uni-	monotone, uniform
two	di-	bi-	dilemma, bicycle
	deuter-	du-	deuteragonist, duplicate
three	tri-	tri-	triathlon, triangle
		ter-	tertiary
four	tetra-	quadr-	tetralogy, quadriplegic
five	penta-	quin-	pentagram, quintet
six	hexa-	sex-	hexagon, sextuplets
seven	hepta-	sept-	heptathlon, September
eight	octa-	octo-	octagon, October
nine	ennea-	nona-	enneagram, nonagenarian

		nove(m)-	November
ten	*deca-*	*dec(em)*-	decade, December
hundred	*hect-*	*cent-*	hectare, century
thousand	*kilo-*	*mill(i)-*	kilogram, millennium

Many Latin words derive from Greek, which explains the similarity between some of these forms. Three, for example, is *tri-* in both Latin and Greek.

Generally, Greek is more common in mathematics and sciences: the prefixes for geometric shapes (*pentagon, hexagon, heptagon, octagon, decagon*), pointed shapes (*pentagram, hexagram*, etc.), and chemical compounds (*monoxide, tetracyclics*) tend to be Greek.

Latin prevails in the humanities and general usage: groups of people, whether musicians (*duo, trio, quartet, quintet, sextet, septet, octet*, etc.) or relatives (*triplets, quadruplets, quintuplets, sextuplets*) usually take Latin names, as do wheeled vehicles (*unicycle, bicycle, tricycle*) and measurements of time—ages (*septagenarian, octagenarian, nonagenarian*), years (*century, millennium*), and months.

September, October, November, and *December* (and also *Quintius* and *Sextilis*, which became the more familiar *July* and *August* later, under Julius Caesar and Augustus Caesar) took their names from their order in the Roman *ten*-month calendar (*sept-* being seven, *octo-* being eight, etc.). The Roman year was not actually two lunar cycles shorter than our own: two dull months of winter were simply left unnamed.

In some contexts, both Greek and Latin are used contrastively: in the metric system, for example, a *millimetre*, from Latin *milli-*, is a thousandth of a metre, while a *kilometre*, from Greek, is a thousand metres (see APPENDIX II). Some commentators advise against mixing Greek prefixes with Latin stems or vice versa (a suggestion that would entail changing *biathlete* to a *diathlete*), but most view such mixing as characteristic of English.

See also BIANNUAL, BIMONTHLY, BIWEEKLY, BIENNIAL; BARBARISMS; BICEPS, TRICEPS, QUADRICEPS, FORCEPS; DIALOGUE, DIALOG; MYRIAD; PARAPLEGIC, QUADRIPLEGIC, TETRAPLEGIC.

numbers Publishers' style guides give varying answers to the question of when numbers should be written out as words and when figures are appropriate in text. A good rule of thumb is to use words for numbers up to and including ten and figures for larger numbers. However, when they are associated with figures in a sentence, numbers to ten should also be written as figures: 'Only 3 of the 357 respondents mentioned this'. Figures are always acceptable in dates and times.

See also AGREEMENT, GRAMMATICAL; ALPHABETICAL ORDER; AVERAGE; DATES; DOLLAR AMOUNTS; HYPHENATION; NUMBERS, DECIMAL POINTS AND COMMAS WITH; NUMBER PREFIXES; TIME.

numbers, decimal points and commas with Canadian practice is affected by the use in this country of both French and English conventions. In the former, the decimal marker is the comma, not the period, which instead is used to separate figures of more than three digits into smaller groups. Thus what is written 1,500,428 in the English convention is written 1.500.428 in the French, whereas what is written 1.38 in the English convention is written 1,38 in the French. In the latter case, Legal Metrology (formerly the Metric Commission Canada), the division responsible for weights and measures, recommends retaining the traditional decimal point in English-language documents, but for figures of more than four digits it splits from both conventions, English and French: instead of either commas or periods it recommends using a space: '1 500 428'. However, the government of Canada continues to use the comma in these figures in its financial documents (*The Canadian Style*). Four-digit figures may be written without the space if they are isolated examples; if they are in a context that contains other figures of four digits or more, however, the space should be retained. The figures representing years never take a space: '1997'.

A figure should never begin or end with a decimal point ('0.5', *not* '.5') except in references to the calibre of guns ('.22-calibre'), the purity of gold ('.999 fine gold'), or stock quotations (where both '.07' and '0.07' are accepted).

See also DOLLAR AMOUNTS, NUMBERS.

Nunavut, Nunavummiut, Denendeh
Nunavut, meaning 'our land' in Inuktitut and pronounced *NUH na VUHT* or *NOO na VOOT*, is the name selected by the Inuit of the eastern Arctic for the part of the Northwest Territories ceded to them by the government of Canada in 1993. The name began to appear on Canadian maps in 1999, when the residents of this territory, who are called *Nunavummiut* (pronounced *nuh na VUH mee ut*), assumed self-government.

Denendeh (pronounced *DEN en DAY*) means 'home of the people'. It was the name proposed for a self-governing territory in the western Arctic that would result from land-claims negotiations between Canada and the Dene Nation, representing all the Aboriginal groups of the Mackenzie Valley. However, agreement on this claim was not reached, and subsequently several Aboriginal groups within the Dene Nation negotiated separate claims. *Denendeh* is sometimes misspelled *Denedeh*.

> Temperatures this spring . . . have been five degrees above average in northern Saskatchewan, Manitoba, southern Nunavut, southern Northwest Territories and northern Quebec.
> *Edmonton Journal* 9 June 2006: B9

See also ABORIGINAL PEOPLE(S); DENE; INUIT; APPENDIX III.

nurse   see JOB TITLES

Nuu-chah-nulth, Ditidaht, Nootka   The First Nation whose traditional territories are on western Vancouver Island in British Columbia are referred to as *Nuu-chah-nulth* (pronounced *noo CHAH noohl*) and, in the southeastern quarter of this territory, *Ditidaht* (*DIH dih dat*). These groups were formerly called *Nootka*. Their tradi-

tional language belongs to the Wakashan family. In *Nuu-chah-nulth*, *chah* and *nulth* are usually not capitalized. *Nuu-chah-nulth* and *Ditidaht* are used for both singular and plural.

> Cook landed at the Nuu-chah-nulth village of Yuquot, home of the powerful Chief Maquinna, setting off the fur trade, colonization and the spread of European diseases that nearly wiped out the Native people.
> *Vancouver Sun* 15 Dec. 1994: SR1

> A major Madrid museum is sending a famous hat worn by Nuu-Chah-Nulth Chief Maquinna to the exhibit. Woven and adorned with a whale hunt motif, the hat was collected by Perez at Nootka Sound.
> *Province* (Vancouver) 14 Dec. 1990: 56

> (Normally only the first letter is capitalized: *Nuu-chah-nulth.*)

> The Ditidaht Indian band opened a $500,000 visitors centre on Tuesday to serve the West Coast Trail.
> *Calgary Herald* 30 July 1992: A11

See also ABORIGINAL PEOPLE(S); APPENDIX III.

Nuxalk, Bella Coola   The *Nuxalk* are an Aboriginal people of British Columbia. They have also been called the *Bella Coola*, although this term is generally less favoured now. Their language, Nuxalk, belongs to the Salishan language family. *Nuxalk*, both a singular and plural form, is pronounced *noo HALK*.

> The Nuxalk of Bella Coola tell of people fleeing to the mountains when the sea rose to drown entire villages.
> *Vancouver Sun* 15 Jan. 2005: C5

See also ABORIGINAL PEOPLE(S); APPENDIX III.

O

oasis, oases see PLURAL, REGULAR, IRREGULAR, FOREIGN

object see entry in Glossary

object, objective *Object* has been used to mean aim or goal since the sixteenth century, and *objective* has been used as a noun with the same meaning since the late nineteenth century. *Objective* is a shortened version of the military phrase 'objective point', meaning the position that a particular manoeuvre was intended to capture. Commentators try to distinguish between *object* and *objective* in various ways: for example, by having *object* refer to an ultimate goal or aim and reserving *objective* for a strategic step towards that goal. However, such distinctions are not widely maintained. Some commentators recommend *object* as the shorter, less pretentious word, but you may choose freely—both words are standard.

> But the correctional technique remained punitive: its object was to make life so miserable for the convict that he would never consider committing another crime.
> Richard Davies and Glen Kirkland, eds. *Dimensions* 1986: 67

> Clark's main objective, as department head and later as dean, was to foster a research atmosphere at Queen's.
> Frederick Gibson *Queen's University* 2 (1983): 21

> Instead of aiming at radical change, he strove for moderation in party politics as his major political objective.
> *Queen's Quarterly* 95.3 (1988): 600

See also CASE; entry in Glossary.

object complement see entry in Glossary

oblige, obligate Both these words are used by Canadian writers when referring to a person, group, or organization that is, or feels, compelled to do something by social, legal, or moral forces.

Some commentators would limit *oblige* to contexts where the sense of compulsion is internal (a moral obligation) and *obligate* to situations where the compulsion is external (a legal obligation). However, Canadian writers do not make this distinction. *Oblige* is more commonly used for both senses in all contexts except legal writing, where *obligate* is more common.

> One of the tasks of the Canadian writer is to show Canada to itself. He is not obliged to do this, but it is one of his options.
> Robertson Davies *One Half of Robertson Davies* 1978: 281

> Instead of accepting established moral dogma, he felt obliged to study and weigh positions intellectually.
> *City Magazine* Spring 1988: 3

> As in the United States, Canadian vehicle dealers are not obligated to stick to suggested retail prices.
> *Canadian Consumer* Jan. 1986: 9

> Once the offeree has performed the act, he is not obligated to do anything more.
> J.E. Smyth et al. *The Law and Business Administration in Canada* 1987: 141

(In legal usage *obligate* is the preferred term.)

> He felt obligated to offer me the choice in spite of his total lack of funds.
> Henry M. Rosenthal and S. Cathy Berson, eds. *Canadian Jewish Outlook Anthology* 1988: 280

(Here *obligated* is used even though the sense of compulsion is internal.)

obliquity, obliqueness Several usage guides suggest that the noun form *obliquity* (pronounced *oh BLICK wi tee*) should be used when referring to indirection in speech or conduct, while *obliqueness* should be used in descriptions of lines, angles, and so on. However, writers do not maintain this nice distinction, nor do dictionaries acknowledge it. Either noun is used whether the meaning is figurative or literal; *obliqueness* is used more frequently.

> Stottlemyre's problem . . . was muscular in nature and partially caused by a hip misalignment. 'Pelvic obliquity' was the way trainer Tommy Craig put it. *Toronto Star* 25 July 1994: B4

> Egoyan is a master burlesque artist himself; he pretends to reveal big things about love, sex, and alienation but forever obscures them behind his trademark obliqueness. . . . *Province* (Vancouver) 14 Oct. 1994: B6

> Authorial impersonality and the obliqueness it engenders are crucial to the very project of her fiction. Janice Kulyk Keefer *Reading Mavis Gallant* 1989: 45

obloquy An *obloquy* (pronounced *OB luh kwee*) is a strong condemnatory utterance. The plural is *obloquies*. As an uncountable noun, *obloquy* refers to abusive language generally, or to a state of disrepute.

> . . . the defendants were seen on the evening television news, their heads hung low in the airstream of the judge's obloquy. *Globe and Mail* (Toronto) 20 June 1985: P18

> . . . you may condemn their scurrile and malicious obloquies, flouts, and calumnies, and scorn them as railers and detractors. Robertson Davies *One Half of Robertson Davies* 1978: 168

See also -Y, -IES.

observation, observance The verb *observe* has two main meanings: to watch ('observe how it's done') and to remember and respect ('observe the law', 'observe a holiday'). The noun *observation* is related to the first meaning, the noun *observance* to the second. Thus *observation* involves looking and taking notice, while *observance* refers to maintaining customs, performing religious rites, marking holidays, and so on.

In contemporary English substituting one of these nouns for the other is usually regarded as a mistake. However, many dictionaries list both meanings for both words because, from the sixteenth century through the nineteenth, the words were used more or less interchangeably, with one exception: *an observation* in the sense of a remark or comment has never been called *an observance*.

> 'There are times I'm not sure what's happening at practices or what's being said before games,' he says. 'But you learn just by observation.' *Vancouver Sun* 23 June 1992: D9

> Dr. Smol counters that *all* sciences, in their early phases, are more concerned with observation than with experimentation. . . . *Perspectives: Profiles of Research at Queen's University* 1986: 20

> With the exception of London, major European markets were closed in observance of a religious holiday. *Toronto Star* 9 June 1992: B6

> A towering classic of the French theatre, it is renowned for its precise, rigid structure, and strict observance of the neoclassical rules of unity and decorum. *Queen's Quarterly* 97.4 (1990): 641

> The story revolves around the family's observance of and interaction with a wag-about-town and self-appointed protector of their favorite cafe. *Toronto Star* 30 May 1992: J15

(This use of *observance* is disputed; *observation* is preferable.)

> And when all the classes gather together to go through the Oneg Shabbat—the religious observation that marks the beginning of the Sabbath—staff members lead them through the ritual with patience and love. *Toronto Star* 5 July 1992: A6

(This use of *observation* is disputed; *observance* is preferable.)

> Finance Minister Glen Clark's observation that a new tax on non-residential parking spaces in Greater Vancouver will not be a popular move has

to be the understatement of the week.
Vancouver Sun 17 June 1992: A14

obsolete, obsolescent   *Obsolete* means no longer in use, or outdated. *Obsolescent* describes something that is becoming obsolete. 'Planned obsolescence' refers to the practice of designing and building objects so they wear out and need to be replaced.

> Scores of obsolete, polluting factories will have to be torn down, and no one knows what to do about some 15,000 dumps of hazardous toxic waste.
> Irving M. Zeitlin and Robert J. Brym *The Social Condition of Humanity* 1991: 371

> Canada's obsolescent railway service stands in sharp contrast to the rejuvenation of the European and Japanese systems.
> *Vancouver Sun* 13 Jan. 1990: B4

obtrude   see INTRUDE

obtuse   A new use of *obtuse* to mean unclear or difficult to understand is drawing criticism from language commentators. *Obtuse* has been used figuratively in English to mean dull, stupid, or insensitive for over five hundred years. This figurative use is an extension of the literal meaning of the word in geometry, where an obtuse angle is one of between 90 and 180 degrees, while an acute, or sharp, angle is one of less than 90 degrees. Someone who is obtuse, therefore, is not acute.

The new use of *obtuse* could result from confusion with *obscure* and *abstruse*, or it could be a deliberate extension of the figurative sense. In any case, using *obtuse* to mean unclear is still considered non-standard and should be avoided.

> With increasing American dependence upon coal-fired power plants, even the environmentally obtuse Reagan administration has backed research into cleaner coal-burning technology.
> *Queen's Quarterly* 95.2 (1988): 313

(This is a standard use of *obtuse*).

> Streamlining a system with so many vested interests concealed in the most obtuse legal verbiage

will not be accomplished easily.
Globe and Mail (Toronto) 21 Oct. 1985: A7

(Here *obscure* would be better.)

> If you manage to figure out the obtuse on-screen directions for moving the cursor down and getting on-line help, you will be presented with some even more obtuse help messages.
> *Gazette* (Montreal) 22 Dec. 1990: L2

(Here *incomprehensible* would be better.)

O Canada, God Save the Queen   'O Canada' was approved as Canada's national anthem in 1967; lyrics in both official languages were officially proclaimed by Parliament in 1980. 'God Save the Queen', the former national anthem, is now designated the *royal anthem*.

'O Canada' was originally written in French in 1880. The English version sung today was written in 1908 and revised in 1980. The first verse is as follows:

> O Canada!
> Our home and native land!
> True patriot love in all thy sons command.
> With glowing hearts we see thee rise,
> The True North strong and free!
> From far and wide,
> O Canada, we stand on guard for thee.
> God keep our land glorious and free!
> O Canada, we stand on guard for thee.
> O Canada, we stand on guard for thee.

> My wife and I were among the thousands of Canadians who welcomed the Queen with spirited applause and the singing of God Save the Queen in addition to our own national anthem . . . in both French and English.
> *Ottawa Citizen* 11 July 1992: A9

occasion   *Occasion* and *occasional* are correctly spelled with two *c*s and one *s*.

occurrence   *Occurred*, *occurring*, and *occurrence* are spelled with two *r*s because *-cur* is a stressed syllable. *Occurrence* is also often misspelled *-ance* instead of *-ence*.

See also DOUBLING THE FINAL CONSONANT.

[Octoberfest]   see OKTOBERFEST

octopus, octopuses   The usual and most widely accepted plural of *octopus* is *octopuses*. The Latin plural *octopi* is also fairly common and listed by many dictionaries. It is best avoided in formal writing, however, because several authorities consider it an error. In the first edition of *Modern English Usage* (1926) Fowler argued that only a Latin word from the classical period would have a regular Latin plural. Since *octopus* is late scholars' Latin, based on a Greek word, even in Latin it would have retained a Greek plural: *octopodes*. Many dictionaries list this Greco-Latin plural. But it cannot be recommended, since it seems to exist only in dictionaries and usage guides. In fact, by the 1960s even *Fowler's* (1965) recommended *octopuses*.

> Most octopuses are about the size of a grapefruit, and many are closer to the size of a golf ball.
> *Calgary Herald* 9 Feb. 1992: B8

> If there were rebounds, they were usually cleared easily by the octopi disguised as Petes defencemen, all six over six feet.
> *Ottawa Citizen* 28 March 1992: F3

(In formal writing, *octopi* should be avoided.)

See also PLURALS, REGULAR, IRREGULAR, FOREIGN.

oculist   see OPHTHALMOLOGIST

Odawa, Ottawa   The Algonquian-speaking people named the *Ottawa* by Europeans themselves prefer the name *Odawa* (singular and plural), pronounced *oh DAW wa*. Closely related to both the Ojibwa/Anishnabe and the Pota-watomi, many Odawa settled on Manitoulin Island after the War of 1812. Now many of their descendants continue to live there; other groups are found throughout Ontario, and in Michigan, Wisconsin, and Oklahoma.

> Sir Francis Bond Head, lieutenant-governor of Upper Canada, signed a treaty with the Ojibway and Odawa in 1836 that was an attempt to relocate all the native peoples of Upper Canada on Manitoulin Island.
> *Toronto Star* 5 Aug. 1994: D11

See also ABORIGINAL PEOPLE(S); APPENDIX III.

odor, odour, odoriferous   see -OUR, -OR

odyssey   An *odyssey* (pronounced *ODD uh see*) is a long, adventurous journey or an intellectual or spiritual quest. The *Odyssey*, always capitalized, is Homer's epic telling of the ten years of travel undertaken by the Greek king Odysseus (also known as Ulysses) following the sacking of Troy. An odyssey is not a long story of heroic deeds; that is an *epic*.

> It was Terry Fox who inspired wheelchair athlete Rick Hanson to undertake his two-year 'Man in Motion' odyssey around the world.
> Alan Tucker, ed. *The Penguin Guide to Canada* 1991: 447

> This approach seems a useful one for charting the intellectual odyssey of the High-Tories.
> J.A.W. Gunn *Beyond Liberty and Property* 1983: 192

> Although a quick peek at the guide might have solved the mystery—Robert Kennedy And His Times, a three-night odyssey starting tomorrow at 8 on CTV and CBS—a discerning eye would have known all along.
> *Globe and Mail* (Toronto) 26 Jan. 1985: E1

(The word intended here is *epic*.)

See also EPIC.

-oe-   see -AE-

-oes   see -OS

oesophagus, oestrogen   see -AE-, -OE-, -E-

of, 've   see [COULD OF]

of course   *Of course* is frequently used when what is being stated is considered to be common knowledge or self-evident. In these contexts the use of *of course* signals that the writer is aware that most readers are probably informed of a certain fact, but feels it needs to be mentioned in order to maintain the flow of the discussion or to draw a conclusion. When it introduces a fact that is widely known, *of course* is a courteous way of acknowledging the reader's intelligence.

However, there are two contexts in which *of course* raises the hackles of commentators: first, where it introduces an abstruse bit of information (and sounds snobbish) and, second, where it is used to prop up a premise or conclusion that is far from self-evident. Context and intended readership are important considerations when determining whether *of course* is appropriate.

> The main difference between sherry and its colleagues, port and Madeira, is that the wine is allowed to ferment out fully before fortification with grape spirit. Port, of course, undergoes an arrested fermentation while Madeira [is] a cross between the two.
> *Bon Vivant* Nov. 1981: 24

(Here the writer assumes that discriminating wine and food lovers, at whom this magazine is aimed, know the difference between sherry and port, if not between port and Madeira.)

> The problem of how to deal with colours, sounds, heat and the like, given Descartes's geometicized conception of matter, is, of course, one which Descartes inherits from Galileo, and he grapples with it throughout his scientific work.
> *Canadian Journal of Philosophy* 19 (1989): 183

(Philosophers, the writer assumes, would be aware of Descartes's debt to Galileo.)

> Of course, early V-6s were literally hacked-down versions of 90-degree V-8s.
> *Edmonton Journal* 18 Sept. 1992: n.p.

(Here *of course* might be better deleted or replaced by *in fact*, since the average newspaper reader is not likely to know this.)

See also COMMA; GOES WITHOUT SAYING.

off, off of, from   Following the verbs *buy*, *beg*, *borrow*, *take*, or *steal*, the use of *off* (*of*) plus a noun or pronoun referring to a person is regarded as uneducated in speech and is rarely found in writing. In sentences such as 'I bought the cabinet off (of) a second-hand dealer' or 'She borrowed a dollar off (of) him', Standard English requires *from* rather than *off* or *off of*.

Generally, the two-word preposition *off of* is considered informal. It is accepted in speech ('Take that hat off of your head'), but not in writing, where the single word *off* is preferred. Note, however, the danger of mechanically cutting all occurrences of *off of* from your writing. The two words are legitimately adjacent when the preposition *of* follows a verbal noun ending in *off*, as in 'the rounding off of figures'.

> The foreman seemed to like him. Borrowed smokes off him all the time, anyway.
> *NeWest Review* Feb.–Mar. 1990: 30

(In this example from fiction, *off* indicates casual or uneducated speech.)

> Cut a four-inch-wide strip off of [the] fabric. . . .
> *Vancouver Sun* 27 Dec. 1990: C3

(The *of* is unnecessary.)

> Today we need to reacquaint ourselves with the value of small talk among strangers in taking the cold edge off of mass society.
> *City Magazine* Spring 1988: 16

(The *of* is unnecessary.)

> A sense of a lonely pessimism, of the shutting off of communication, of the inevitable victories of winter and darkness, gives the poems a plaintively muted quality. . . .
> Northrop Frye *The Bush Garden* 1971: 56

(Here *of* is a simple preposition following the verbal noun *shutting off*.)

See also BORROW.

offence, indictable   see INDICTABLE OFFENCE

offence, offense, offensive   see -CE, -SE

offer   see DOUBLING THE FINAL CONSONANT

officialdom   see -DOM

officious, official   *Officious* is not a synonym for *official*; it means generally meddlesome, or domineering and petty in exercising authority. The original meaning of *officious*, ready to serve, is now obsolete.

> In the title story, a middle-aged woman . . . finds

herself admitting to a priest and to herself that she hates her arrogant, officious husband.
Vancouver Sun 28 July 1990: D20

As William Faulkner says, the writer has supreme vanity. He does not want to be influenced or taken apart; he does not want the officious help of people who cannot, as he knows intuitively, be anything but nuisances to him.
Robertson Davies *A Voice from the Attic* 1960: 309

'My government will manage our province's finances in the responsible and officious manner that the public has demanded for so long.'
Ottawa Citizen 27 May 1994: A12

(In this otherwise positive context, *officious* appears to be the wrong word; perhaps the speaker meant something like *professional*.)

offspring   Children, real or figurative, are *offspring*, not *offsprings*.

The new generation of Quebec entrepreneurs has remarkable tools at its disposal, tools which amount to a vibrant, if not unique, model of economic development in North America: Hydro-Quebec, and its offsprings Lavalin and SNC.
Financial Post 28 Feb. 1990: 12

(Here either *offspring* or *offshoots* would be better.)

often, oftener, oftenest, more often, most often, oft, oftentimes   *Oftener* and *oftenest* are correct, but *more often* and *most often* are much more common and recommended.
   The variants *oft, often,* and *oftentimes* were all used in English by the fourteenth century. In contemporary English, *oft* is literary and poetic, while *oftentimes* is a mainly spoken form, which has been criticized as redundant.
   The more widely accepted pronunciation of *often* is with the *t* unpronounced as in *soften* or *listen*.

See also ADJECTIVES AND ADVERBS; COMPARISON.

of which   see WHO'S, WHOSE

oh   see COMMA; ZERO

Ojibwa(y), Anishnabe   The *Globe and Mail Style Book* recommends *Ojibwa* for the people

(both singular and plural) and *Ojibway* for their Algonquian language. It makes an exception to this rule for the Ojibways of Onegaming First Nation. However, it seems that generally in Canadian writing *Ojibwa* and *Ojibway* are used with almost equal frequency for both the people and their language and both these words are often pluralized with *s*. Ojibway is a member of the Algonquian language family.
   Some members of this nation have adopted the name *Anishnabe* (pronounced *a nish NAW bee*; the spelling varies), as in the 'Anishnawbe Health Centre' in Toronto.

The Ojibwas of Nawash and of Saugeen filed the claim in Ontario Court . . . earlier this month and announced it yesterday in Owen Sound.
Toronto Star 15 June 1994: A12

Nowadays, no self-respecting supporter of the cultural rebirth uses the term Ojibway. Most Ojibways prefer to be known as the Annishnawbe.
Globe and Mail (Toronto) 1 June 1993: A24

'Anishnabe is our word for "people". Ojibwa is the European name for us.'
Toronto Star 6 May 1993: W04

See also ABORIGINAL PEOPLE(S); ALGONQUIN; CHIPEWYAN; ODAWA; APPENDIX III.

Okanagan   The lake and valley in south central British Columbia and names associated with this region are spelled *Okanagan*: Okanagan First Nation, Okanagan Falls, Okanagan College. Those from outside the province often misspell the name *Okanogan*. *Okanogan* is the American spelling: Okanogan County and the Okanogan National Forest are just south of Penticton, BC, in Washington State. Straddling the international border are the Okanagan/Okanogan River and the Okanagan/Okanogan Range. The spelling of these geographical features changes at the forty-ninth parallel. Okanagan rhymes with *toboggan*.

okay, OK, O.K.   *Okay* is an American slang expression now used around the world. In writing, it most often appears in quotations or representations of speech. Canadians use the spelling *okay* far more than *OK* or *O.K.* Writing the expression out as *okay* permits it to be treated as a regular noun or verb: *okays, okayed,* instead of *OK's, OK'd,* or *O.K.'s, O.K.'d.*

Fascinating but inconclusive debate rages about the origins of this expression. Allan Walker Read, cited in the *OED* under 'O.K.', argues that it derives from a club called the O.K. Club, founded in 1840 by the supporters of the Democratic president Martin Van Buren. His nickname, based on his birthplace, Kinderhook, N.Y., was Old Kinderhook, or O.K. for short. In *Pidgins and Creoles,* however, Loreto Todd notes that similar forms meaning *yes* are found in a variety of West African languages, and that the expression 'oh ki' for *yes* had been recorded from Jamaica before 1839, the date of the first American citation (*OED*).

> My Mother blew Lizzie a kiss, 'Okay, sweetheart.'
> *Room of One's Own* March 1990: 36

> The 45-year-old former social worker refused to give his name. 'Just call me Jack, OK?'
> *Gazette* (Montreal) 6 March 1989: B4

> . . . seven applications for statutory holidays opening in York Region have been okayed, although this won't include Christmas Day.
> *Toronto Star* 8 Dec. 1995: NY2

Oktoberfest The name of the festival of beer and Bavarian culture held annually in Munich as well as in North American cities such as Kitchener-Waterloo, Ontario, is spelled *Oktoberfest*—with a *k* that reflects the German origin of the word.

> The group offered three weekends worth of carriage rides in October for Octoberfest, raising $3,400 for cancer research.
> *Times-Colonist* (Victoria) 22 Jan. 2005: D4

(The proper spelling is *Oktoberfest.*)

Old English, Anglo-Saxon, Middle English, Early Modern English, Late Modern English, Modern English Scholars use the label *Old English* for a Germanic language brought to England by invaders around 450 A.D. It is sometimes called *Anglo-Saxon* after the names of two of the invading Germanic tribes. Old English displaced the local Celtic languages

and can be regarded as the ancestor of the English spoken today.

Conventionally, the history of the English language is divided into three main periods: the Old English period (450–1150), the Middle English period (1150–1500), and the Modern English period (1500–present). Some divide the Modern English period into two: from 1500 to 1700 (Early Modern English) and from 1700 to the present (Late or Later Modern English).

The most important literary work from the Old English period is an anonymous epic poem, *Beowulf* (c. AD 1000). Chaucer (c. 1342–1400) wrote his *Canterbury Tales* in Middle English. Early Modern English is familiar to us from the works of Shakespeare (1564–1616) and the King James Bible (1611). The Late Modern English period is characterized by the rise of Standard English—that is, the English taught in schools and used in most published writing—and the development of a wide range of varieties of English, more or less distinct from British English, in former colonies of Britain.

If its geographic spread once threatened to fracture the English language into mutually unintelligible varieties, its use today as a worldwide lingua franca—in science, in trade, in transport, and in telecommunications—is an impetus toward international standardization.

See also CELT, ANGLO-CELTIC; STANDARD, STANDARD ENGLISH.

older, oldest see ELDER

old hat, old hand *Old hat* refers to something (or someone) that is out of date or tediously familiar. An *old hand* is a person with a lot of experience at something.

> It was my night to be a novelty. Tomorrow I'd be old hat, like the grinning bearskins hanging on the wall.
> Howard Engel *Murder Sees the Light* 1984: 36

> 'I was a novice and he was an old hand, and I learned parliamentary manners from him.'
> *Debates of the Senate* (Hansard) 138.78 4 Oct. 2000: 1500

Party-switching on Parliament Hill is fast becoming old hand, but Ms. Desjarlais' trek from New Democrat MP to an Independent and now to aide to Greg Thompson, the Tory Veterans Affairs Minister, is surely a political first.
Globe and Mail (Toronto) 16 March 2006: A9

(Here the phrase required is *old hat*.)

oldster   see SENION CITIZEN

omelette, omelet   Canadian writers prefer the French spelling, *omelette*, but *omelet* is not uncommon. British dictionaries list *omelette* first, American dictionaries *omelet*.

omnibus   see BUS

on   see ON TO, ONTO; LAM, BEHALF

on account of   *On account of* meaning 'because *of*' (as in 'He stayed indoors on account of the cold weather') is standard. However, *on account of* meaning simply 'because' (as in 'I walked on account of my car broke down') is stigmatized and rare in writing.

Few modern writers discuss the propriety of a governor's dismissing a government on account of some scandal.
Andrew Heard *Canadian Constitutional Conventions* 1991: 29

on behalf of, on the part of   see BEHALF

one   see YOU

one another   see EACH OTHER

one of the . . . if not the . . .   Use of the construction *one of the . . . if not the . . .* leads to faulty parallelism: 'She is one of the best, if not the best, dancer in the company'. The plural *dancers* is required after 'one of the', while 'if not the' must be followed by a singular noun, *dancer*. The sentence can be corrected in several ways: 'She is one of the best, if not the best, of the dancers in the company'; 'She is one of the best dancers in the company, if not the

best'. It may be better yet to avoid the whole structure: 'She is possibly the best dancer in the company'.

Undoubtedly, language is one of the most, if not the most, important factor promoting unity or disunity.
William Norton *Human Geography* 1992: 166

(The faulty parallelism can be corrected as follows: 'Undoubtedly, language is one of the most important factors promoting unity or disunity; indeed, it may be the most important factor.')

See also PARALLELISM.

one of those things, one of those who   The problem with these phrases is deciding whether the verb that follows should be singular, to agree with *one*, or plural, to agree with *those*. Does the phrase refer to the *one* thing or person in question, or to something characteristic of *those* many things or people of which the subject is but one example? In quoted speech the verb is often singular: 'It's just one of those things that happens'. In edited prose the more widespread practice is to make the verb plural to agree with *those*. This seems logical because statements beginning with *one of those* usually proceed to describe something common to a particular group of people or set of circumstances. However, there is no hard and fast rule about this usage. In formal contexts it's best to use a plural verb, but elsewhere either plural or singular is accepted.

Freelance journalist and film-maker Brian McKenna is one of those who remember.
Maclean's 7 Nov. 1988: A66

(Here the plural form of the verb is used following *one of those*.)

Browning is certainly one of those who has made Edmonton the City of Champions.
Edmonton Journal 16 Sept. 1992: n.p.

(Here the writer has chosen to use a singular verb following *one of those*.)

See also AGREEMENT, GRAMMATICAL; COLLECTIVE NOUNS.

only   For over two hundred years language commentators have been stating that *only* should always be placed directly before the element it modifies. In fact, though, this is not a rule of grammar: it is simply a question of style. The precise placement of *only* characterizes a formal or academic style. In conversation and in literary prose that mimics conversational rhythms, *only* is usually placed between the subject and the verb, no matter which element of the sentence it modifies.

Thus, while some commentators would say that 'Experienced servers only need apply' means every applicant with experience will be hired on the spot, few English-speakers would interpret the sentence in this way. Similarly, 'Rob only wanted five dollars' is not likely to mean he was too shy to verbalize his desire. The typical position of *only* in conversational English is between the subject and the verb, but context and sentence intonation indicate what *only* modifies. In formal writing—where a precise style is valued—and whenever there is a real risk of misunderstanding, *only* should be placed directly in front of the element it modifies: 'Only experienced servers need apply'; 'The board requested only five thousand dollars'.

> When you come from the city, you can only take outdoors in small doses.
> Howard Engel *Murder Sees the Light* 1984: 117

(In formal writing *only* would come later: 'only in small doses'.)

> He was only interested in the money.
> Constance Beresford-Howe *Night Studies* 1985: 136

(In formal writing *only* would come later: 'interested only in the money'.)

> . . . there is substantial support for the notion that the governors should intrude into the democratic process only to the minimum extent absolutely required for the basic functioning of parliamentary government.
> Andrew Heard *Canadian Constitutional Conventions* 1991: 47

> By 1941, the Native population likely comprised only one-quarter of the total population.
> Robert M. Bone *The Geography of the Canadian North* 1992: 79

See also ONLY, BUT.

only, but   The use of *only* to mean 'but' ('I wanted to, only I couldn't') is standard but informal. In Canadian writing it appears most often in fiction.

> Their mother used to do this too, go blind, and deaf, only she did it over crossword puzzles and a cigarette.
> *Queen's Quarterly* 95.3 (1988): 612

> Oh yes, a true painting there somewhere, only how to paint it?
> David Williams *Eye of the Father* 1985: 79

See also ONLY.

onomatopoeia, onomatopoeic, onomatopoetic   *Onomatopoeia* (pronounced *on oh MAT uh PEE uh*) is a technical term for a word that imitates a sound; these words are also called *echoic* or *imitative*. There are hundreds of such words in English, including *hush*, *murmur*, *plop*, *sizzle*, *squish*, *whisper*, *whiz*, and *zoom*. Of the two adjective forms, *onomatopoeic* (sometimes misspelled *onomatopoeiac*) is preferred to *onomatopoetic*.

Ontario   see SAHARA; APPENDIX I

Ontarian   see NAMES OF RESIDENTS OF CITIES AND PROVINCES

on the lam   see LAM

on the part of   see BEHALF

on to, onto   Some guides recommend against the use of *onto*, preferring *on to*, and certainly *on to* is acceptable in all contexts. The two-word form is the more common one in Canadian academic writing and in British writing generally.

However, most American writers and many Canadian writers make a distinction between these spellings, using *on to* when *on* is an adverb and *onto* for the preposition meaning 'to a position on'. Thus 'We walked on to the bridge', means we walked that far, and 'We walked onto the bridge' means we stepped on the bridge itself.

> While employees . . . were getting the buses ready for loading at dockside in Vancouver, a mast supporting the tackle equipment broke. A bus fell from a great height on to the dock and was demolished.
> J.E. Smyth et al. *The Law and Business Administration in Canada* 1987: 448

(Here *onto* would also be possible.)

> The fluid lapped at his shoes, dripped down from his hands on to his suit.
> Geoffrey Ursell *Perdue, or, How the West Was Lost* 1984: 157

(Here *onto* would also be possible.)

opaque   see TRANSPARENT

op. cit.   see IBID.

opera   see PLURALS; -US

ophthalmologist, oculist, optometrist, optician   An *ophthalmologist*—the word is pronounced *off thal MAW luh jist* and often misspelled without the first *h* or *l*—is a medical doctor specializing in diseases and defects of the eye, who may perform eye surgery. *Oculist* means the same thing, but this term has fallen out of favour within the profession. An *optometrist* is licensed to test eyesight and prescribe lenses. An *optician* makes or sells optical goods, such as prescription glasses and telescopes.
  The word *optometrist* is rare in Britain. There *ophthalmic opticians* test eyesight while *dispensing opticians* make lenses or fill prescriptions.

> Did Dr. Taylor, an ophthalmologist in Cornwall, Ont., know of a new flying eye hospital committed to curing blindness and eye diseases in developing countries?
> *Globe and Mail* (Toronto) 14 Dec. 2005: S9

> [MDs'] resistance to other legally licensed health-care practitioners, notably chiropractors and in British Columbia optometrists, has had the style of a self-interested cartel. . . .
> *Saturday Night* July 1986: 6

opine   To *opine* is to express an opinion. This verb, in use since the fifteenth century, is not common in Canadian writing. As usage critics note, *opine* now seems overly formal or stilted, except where the intended effect is humorous. Today it is most often used by writers who want to indicate, in a droll manner, their disagreement with others' opinions. The suggestion is that the person who 'opines' opines wrong.

> When asked, most of us would opine that ulcers are caused by stress and improper lifestyle, especially a poor diet.
> *Province* (Vancouver) 5 Nov. 1990: 49

> Mr. Berry opined the Senate was fulfilling its proper role in performing a check on the elected government.
> *Financial Post* 18 Oct. 1990: 12

> Parti Québécois leader Jacques Parizeau was opining the other day, speaking as another spectator to the present marchpast of history, that just about any geographic and social collectivity can claim sovereignty and set up shop as a nation.
> *Toronto Star* 4 Sept. 1991: A19

opprobrium   see APPROBATION

optician   see OPHTHALMOLOGIST

optimum, optimal, best   The *optimum* is the perfect amount or degree of something. *Optimal* conditions are those most conducive to something's happening. Although *optimal* is the adjective form, *optimum* is frequently used as an adjective as well. These terms were first used in biology to describe the conditions most favourable to growth and reproduction in living organisms. They should not be used simply to mean biggest or best.

> . . . under optimal growing conditions . . . an acre of fireweed bloom could yield as much as 450 pounds of honey.
> *Harrowsmith* Oct.–Nov. 1985: 51

> If conditions are not optimum, they may grow but not multiply.
> *Harrowsmith* Aug.–Sept. 1985: 68

> Selecting the optimum observation post begins by

scouting the countryside within a reasonable driving distance of your home.
Terence Dickinson *Halley's Comet* 1985: 111

optometrist   see OPHTHALMOLOGIST

opus, opuses, opera   see PLURALS; -US

or   see AGREEMENT, GRAMMATICAL; AND/OR; -ER, -OR; -OUR, -OR

oral   see VERBAL

orate   *Orate*, a verb formed from the noun *oration*, is often used in a humorous way to describe pompous speech-making or inflated rhetoric. It's best not to use this word where no irony is intended.

The highlight of the movie for me was the continual street scene which shows inner London in perpetual disorder . . . with voice-over accompaniment by Margaret Thatcher orating on new prosperity.
City Magazine (Spring 1988): 42

. . . the convention seemed to pay not the slightest attention to the person orating from the platform.
Queen's Quarterly 97.3 (1990): 464

See also BACK-FORMATION.

orchestrate   The figurative sense of *orchestrate*—to organize or coordinate various elements to achieve a desired effect—has been established since the 1880s. This use has aroused some negative comment but is widely found in all kinds of writing.

Thus both the king's puppet-like performance and the response to it were orchestrated by the ministers.
J.A.W. Gunn *Beyond Liberty and Property* 1983: 65

Another part of their plan calls for a Canadian Mental Health Commission to orchestrate a national approach to mental health and addiction.
Vancouver Sun 11 May 2006: A19

order   see SPECIES

ordinance, ordnance   An *ordinance* is an authoritative decree, a religious rite, or a bylaw passed by a local authority. *Ordnance* means artillery, but also refers more generally to weapons and military equipment and the military division responsible for them. The maps that Canadians refer to as large-scale maps or detailed topographical maps are known in Britain as Ordnance Survey maps because they were originally produced for military purposes.

[He said] that Kamloops had not passed any ordinance or bylaw banning the use of cedar shingles. . . .
Province (Vancouver) 8 June 1990: 47

A junior ordnance officer in 1944, he was included in the plot because . . . he had a thorough knowledge of the building where the bomb was to be set off.
Globe and Mail (Toronto) 8 May 1985: 1

Sturdy hikers clutching their ordinance survey maps will find it.
Globe and Mail (Toronto) 6 July 1985: T8

(The correct spelling here is *Ordnance*.)

See also BYLAW; GUN.

organic   With the recent proliferation of terms such as 'organic farming' and 'organic foods', *organic* has come to be seen as the opposite of *synthetic*, and as a synonym for *natural* or *healthful*. In chemistry, however, all substances are classified as either organic (meaning that they contain carbon) or inorganic (meaning that they do not contain carbon). All organic (i.e., living) matter is made of chemicals that contain carbon; it does not follow that anything organic is harmless. Many pesticides shunned by 'organic' farmers are in fact organic chemicals, and hundreds of natural organic substances found in plants and animals are extremely poisonous. Thus the adjective *organic* should not be regarded as an indicator of harmlessness.

Many inorganic and organic chemicals can be removed from drinking water by a process known as reverse osmosis.
Country Guide Dec. 1986: 15

Klein said the key reason for delaying the mill was the panel's concern over the level of chlorinated organic pollutants and the effect they would have on the fish downstream. . . .
Vancouver Sun 3 March 1990: B1

organize   see -IZE, -ISE, -YZE, -YSE

orient, orientate   Canadian and American writers prefer the verb *orient*, while British writers more commonly use *orientate*. The figurative meaning of *orient(ate)* is to adjust to one's surroundings or to a new situation. In the eighteenth century, to *orient* something meant to place it so that it faced east; by the nineteenth century that meaning had broadened to include all points of the compass.

So when a service comes along that makes it easier for . . . travellers to get oriented when they hit the ground, you know it's a good thing.
Gazette (Montreal) 29 April 1994: D3

The display suite is oriented so the kitchen and breakfast nook look out to the central courtyard. . . .
Vancouver Sun 12 Oct. 1990: E8

They are orientated on the triangular lot to both maximize views to the south over the river and provide view corridors for the surrounding residential properties.
Vancouver Sun 27 Jan. 1990: E5

See also -ORIENTED.

-oriented   Compounds formed with *-oriented* are widely used, especially in journalism and academic writing, to indicate a particular emphasis, interest, or bias: for example, 'career-oriented' or 'customer-oriented'. Some commentators consider this prolific combining form overused, and often the meaning of the new compounds is vague. Where an established adjective could convey the same meaning, it is probably better to use it.

This is to be expected, he argues, because Canadians are more collectivity-oriented.
Canadian Journal of Sociology 14.2 (1989): 144

. . . acid rain is a problem which results from our

industrialized, leisure-oriented life-style.
Queen's Quarterly 94.3 (1987): 614

I have kept in mind, however, other more exclusively text-oriented critical methods. . . .
Ben-Z. Shek *French-Canadian & Québécois Novels* 1991: viii

See also ORIENT, ORIENTATE.

-os, -oes   Most words that end in *o* are pluralized in the regular way by adding *s*: *albinos, altos, cellos, hippos, infernos, kangaroos, photos, pianos, radios*. However, some fairly common words in which a final *o* is preceded by a consonant are pluralized by adding *es*: *buffaloes, echoes, embargoes, heroes, noes, potatoes, tomatoes, torpedoes, vetoes, volcanoes*.

Note that an *e* never precedes the *s* if the word is a short form (*hippos, photos*) or a proper name (*Filipinos*), or if a vowel precedes the *o* (*cameos, ratios*).

Some words can be pluralized either way: *bravo, cargo, domino, ghetto, mango, memento, mosquito, salvo, tornado, zero*.

Residents in Alberta contended with clouds of mosquitoes that swirled over the prairies like tornados.
Vancouver Sun 4 Aug. 1990: B7

(Although both *mosquito* and *tornado* can be pluralized with *s* alone or with *es*, some editors would insist on consistency here: either *mosquitoes* and *tornadoes* or *mosquitos* and *tornados*.)

The board game [Trivial Pursuit] has made its inventors, Chris Haney and Scott Abbott, national heros and multi-millionaires.
Province (Vancouver) 5 Jan. 1990: 52

(Only *heroes* is accepted.)

ostentatiously, ostensibly   When people do something *ostentatiously*, they do it in a showy manner, to attract attention. When people do something *ostensibly* for a certain reason, this reason is the one they are making public, although it may conceal their real motivation. Occasionally writers use *ostentatiously* where *ostensibly* is required: 'Ostentatiously, he only wanted to help'.

In court last week S——, ostentatiously carrying a Bible, explained that she had found God after leaving W——, and wasn't in this for the money, not at all.
Gazette (Montreal) 25 Nov. 1992: C3

I formed the habit of bringing out my hearing aid rather ostentatiously; Andrew, catching sight of it, would raise his voice to what for most people would have been normal.
Eugene Forsey *A Life on the Fringe* 1990: 141

Ostensibly, the dinner is being held in honor of the paper's 80th anniversary. In fact, its main purpose is to raise money to pay off Le Devoir's accumulated $1.5-million debt.
Gazette (Montreal) 16 Nov. 1990: A1

Now Hydro is seeking an annual three-per-cent increase in its rates for the next few years, ostensibly to promote conservation and protect the environment. As the saying goes, if you believe that, have I got some real estate for you in Florida.
Province (Vancouver) 22 Feb. 1990: 38

Military involvement of any kind, however ostentatiously peaceful in its intentions, bestows influence as well as power upon the foreign nations participating in the operation.
Ottawa Citizen 22 Dec. 1992: A6

(The word required here is *ostensibly*.)

Saddam wants . . . ostentatiously, linkage to Israel, but to humiliate the U.S. more than out of any concern for the plight of Palestinians. . . .
Vancouver Sun 19 Dec. 1990: A3

(The word required here is *ostensibly*.)

Ottawa   see ODAWA

Ottawan   see NAMES OF RESIDENTS OF CITIES AND PROVINCES

Ottawa Valley   see CAPITAL LETTERS

-our, -or   For some Canadians, the choice of *-our* spellings is a marker of Canadian writing, since American writers by far prefer *-or*. In fact, however, preferences vary across Canada, with Ontario, British Columbia, and English-speaking Quebec leaning towards *-our* and the rest of the country leaning towards *-or*. Furthermore, preferences are not consistent across the whole

set of *-our/-or* words. In Canadian writing generally, for example, *colour* and *behaviour* are more common than *color* and *behavior*, but *odor* and *favorite* are more common than *odour* and *favourite*. Most Canadian newspapers used the space-saving *-or* forms until 1998 when the *Canadian Press Stylebook* opted for *-our* spellings. The federal government also uses *-our*.

Note that words with root forms that can be spelled either *-or* or *-our* drop the *u*, even in British English, when the endings *-ation*, *-iferous*, *-ific*, *-ize*, and *-ous* are added. The following are among the words that are often misspelled by over-zealous *-our* fans: *coloration, glamorous, honorarium, honorary, honorific, humorist, humorous, laborious, odoriferous, rigorous, valorize, valorous, vigorous*.

One is left labouriously reading field notes from someone else's study. . . .
Canadian Journal of Sociology 14.2 (1989): 238

(The correct spelling is *laboriously*.)

. . . the only purpose that he could have had was to make his letter either humourous or provocative.
Canadian Baptist Jan. 1986: 38

(The correct spelling is *humorous*.)

See also SPELLING, CANADIAN.

ours   *Ours* is a possessive pronoun like *mine* or *theirs* or *his*: 'That's ours'. Correctly spelled, it has no apostrophe. It is sometimes misspelled *our's* because the apostrophe is associated with possession.

'If they won't allow us into their market, we'll have to keep them out of ours.'
Gazette (Montreal) 3 March 1989: A4

'Tonight, our's didn't do too much.'
Ottawa Citizen 24 Nov. 1990: E5

(The correct spelling is *ours*.)

See also POSSESSIVE.

ourself, ourselves   see -SELF, -SELVES

outbound   see -BOUND

outfit, outfitter   The noun *outfit* originally referred to clothing and other equipment required for a particular activity. Later it came to be used as a collective noun identifying a group of people engaged in the same task, such as a military unit, a business organization, or a sports team. This use is informal.

An *outfitter* provides guiding services and supplies for activities such as camping, fishing, hunting, and exploring in wilderness areas.

In historical Canadian usage, an *outfit* was the annual shipment of supplies from the Hudson's Bay Company to fur-trading posts; by extension, the term came to be used for the fiscal year of the HBC.

The verb to *outfit*, meaning to provide with clothing or gear, doubles its final *t* in the forms *outfitted* and *outfitting*.

> The memo . . . does not say, however, whether Canadian seamen will be put back into bell bottoms and round sailor caps, an outfit commonly known as square rig.
> *Globe and Mail* (Toronto) 4 Jan. 1985: P4

> Trophies . . . were won by Arizona Audio at competitions in Quebec and Ontario. The outfit has more than 30 awards to its credit.
> *Gazette* (Montreal) 24 March 1994: B1

(This use of *outfit* is informal.)

> Canoeing the legendary Nahanni River . . . is a two-week trip offered by Black Feather tour outfitters and instructors. . . .
> *Globe and Mail* (Toronto) 11 May 1985: T11

> Sec. 57 [of the Wildlife Act] further states that an outfitter can be licensed for only one guiding area.
> *Vancouver Sun* 26 Nov. 1990: B1

> When Defence Minister Sam Hughes decided that Canadian troops should be armed with an all-Canadian weapon, soldiers were outfitted with a rifle designed by his friend Sir Charles Ross.
> *Globe and Mail* (Toronto) 26 Jan. 1985: T6

out loud   see ALOUD

out-migrate   see EMIGRANT

outward(s)   see -WARD(S)

overlook   see LOOKOUT

overweening   *Overweening* means arrogant, presumptuous, or excessive, and is derived from the Old English words *wenan*, 'to presume', and *ofer-*, 'too much'. It is not related to the verb *wean* and is not spelled *overweaning*.

> There is also the Big Brother factor—the tendency of overweaning officials to burrow into every nook and cranny of citizens' lives.
> *Gazette* (Montreal) 6 Jan. 1994: B3

(The correct spelling is *overweening*.)

ovolactovegetarian   see VEGETARIAN

Oweekeno   see KWAKIUTL

Oxbridge   *Oxbridge* is not a real place but a blend of the words *Oxford* and *Cambridge*. This expression refers collectively to the two oldest and most prestigious universities in Britain, distinguishing them from the 'red-brick' and 'new' universities established in the late nineteenth century and after the Second World War. The word is often used as an adjective.

> Real power is exercised, informally, by a clique of businessmen and bureaucrats dominated by graduates of the University of Tokyo and its law school—a far more powerful and tightly knit Old Boys' network than even the Oxbridge elite in England.
> *Maclean's* 11 Sept. 1989: T8

> In an era when Oxbridge-educated Brits dominated universities in this country, Innis campaigned tirelessly for the hiring of Canadian faculty.
> *Gazette* (Montreal) 25 March 2006: J9

> Her interchangeable characters are Oxbridge types, who may be exquisitely educated but who live in the world of make-believe in their attempts to solve the problems of their friends and to construct elaborate justifications for the selfishness of their own behavior.
> *Ottawa Citizen* 20 Jan. 1990: 17

See also ABBREVIATION.

oxen   see PLURAL

oxymoron   An *oxymoron* is a rhetorical or literary device in which two contradictory terms are placed together: 'burning cold'. Phrases such as 'civil service', 'military intelligence', 'industrial park', and 'Toronto life' are jokingly called *oxymorons*. The plural is either *oxymora* or, more commonly, *oxymorons*.

> I can't write as an ordinary woman because such a thing does not exist: it is an oxymoron, a contra-

diction in terms. We all know that in our species the ordinary, the norm, is constituted by the male . . . against whom the female stands out as extra-ordinary, beyond the ordinary, or ordinary plus.
> *Queen's Quarterly* 96.2 (1989): 229

> If '"oxymoron" is a paradoxical utterance combining two terms that in ordinary usage are contraries' . . . then what are the 'Progressive Conservatives'?
> *Globe and Mail* (Toronto) 16 April 1985: P7

P

p.   see ABBREVIATION

pablum, pap, pabulum   Literally, *pablum* and *pap* mean baby food; figuratively, these words describe something lacking intellectual substance or artistic quality. *Pablum* is in fact a trade name for the first vitamin-enriched, prepared baby food, which was developed at Toronto's Hospital for Sick Children around 1930 and patented in the United States. However, *pablum* is rarely found with a capital letter, and in Canadian English this trade name has almost completely supplanted the non-proprietary word from which it is derived: *pabulum*. *Pabulum*, from the Latin for 'food', now also usually means insipid intellectual fare, but in the eighteenth and nineteenth centuries it had positive connotations and meant food for thought or nourishment for the soul.

> You're anti-this or anti-that unless you homogenize your opinions into a creamy concoction of useless pablum.
> *Province* (Vancouver) 23 Aug. 1990: 43

> That a woman who is offended by the word 'arts' should be in a position to mutilate the only programming on the dial that isn't musical pablum . . . is incredible.
> *Globe and Mail* (Toronto) 24 July 1985: P6

> The Liberals' vaunted social policy review, touted for months as radical, turns out to be yet another serving of bureaucratic pabulum.
> *Calgary Herald* 6 Oct. 1994: B1

pace   This Latin expression (derived from *pax*, 'peace' and pronounced *PAH chay*) typically appears in academic or literary prose. It means 'with all due respect to' and precedes a proper name. *Pace* signals that the opinion being expressed is contrary to the views of the person named: for example, '*pace* Marx' means 'despite Marx's opinion to the contrary'. Because many people are unfamiliar with this construction—and some people think it means just the opposite ('according to Marx')—it is probably best to avoid *pace* altogether. If you do use the word, note that it requires italicization as a foreign expression.

> Their book—among others—reveals that Canada has turned out, *pace* McGregor, a lot of able and effective satire. . . .
> Linda Hutcheon *Splitting Images* 1991: 14

> (Gaile McGregor has argued that Canadian writers have not produced effective satire.)

See also LATIN PHRASES.

Pacific Rim   see CAPITAL LETTERS

paddy wagon In informal contexts and even some official documents, *paddy wagon* (or, less commonly, *paddywagon*) refers to a police van used for transporting criminals and suspects. The word is derived from *paddy*, a derogatory nickname for an Irish person (after Saint Patrick, the patron saint of Ireland). There are two theories regarding how the term originated: one has Paddy in the driver's seat of the van (in the 1920s a large percentage of New York City police officers were Irish-American) and the other has him in the back. Either way, a label derived from a stereotype should be avoided, and *patrol wagon, police wagon,* and *police van* are all uncontroversial replacements.

Eight protesters from Goulds were led in hand-cuffed-pairs to a paddy wagon Monday and brought to St. John's Lockup for the night after police were called to City Hall.
Telegram (St. John's) 19 Feb. 2002: A1

(*Police wagon* would not give offense.)

paean, pean, peon A *paean* (*PEE un*) is an outpouring of praise or thanksgiving; *pean*, the spelling used by many American writers, is very uncommon in Canada. A *peon* (*PEE on*) is a Latin American farm labourer; in the past, the term was also used in British colonial society, in India, Sri Lanka, and Malaysia, to refer to orderlies, messengers, and soldiers. Now *peon* can be used figuratively to refer to anyone from a less exalted walk of life.

Sometimes *paean* is misspelled *paeon*; less often *peon* is misspelled the same way.

I guess if you've tried only the bottled variety, you're baffled by this paean of praise to horseradish's fiery benison.
Toronto Star 24 April 1992: C18

One had to see and hear Murley's incredible, passionate soloing on Bad Back Blues, a heartfelt paeon from Elmes' pen, to believe the commitment, drive and sheer joy these musicians take in their art. . . .
Spectator (Hamilton) 16 Feb. 1994: D9

(The word intended here is *paean*, although it seems odd that anyone would write a paean to a bad back.)

The peons ridicule the mighty.
Toronto Star 7 Sept. 1992: B1

'We tend to provide low pay to the person in the information booth or the clerk. They're treated like paeons.'
Spectator (Hamilton) 21 May 1994: A7

(They're treated like *peons*.)

See also -AE-; DIPHTHONG, DIGRAPH, LIGATURE.

pagan see ATHEIST

paid, payed *Paid* is both the past tense of *pay* ('He paid no attention') and the past participle ('They have all been paid'). *Payed* is an obsolete spelling, accepted only when *pay* means to let out a rope or cable.

Mullin had already payed Cowie $6,000, so the balance of the award is $43,500.
Daily News (Halifax) 10 April 1992: 7

(The correct spelling is *paid*.)

Until recently, manufacturers of industrial safety shoes payed about as much attention to the styling of their products as fashion observers did to workwear in general.
Vancouver Sun 25 June 1992: C3

(The correct spelling is *paid*.)

. . . the tethered satellite will be payed out slowly, unreeled from a drum by an electric motor [to rise] 20 kilometres above the shuttle's orbit of 298 kilometres.
Vancouver Sun 29 July 1992: A10

(Here *payed* is correct.)

pajamas see PYJAMAS

palate, palette, pallet The *palate* is the roof of the mouth and, by extension, the sense of taste. A *palette* is the board on which an artist mixes colours for painting. *Palette* is also used figuratively to refer to a range of colour, sounds, or materials. A *pallet* is a straw mattress or a wooden frame on which goods are stacked in a warehouse.

palomino see CAPITAL LETTERS

paleo-, palaeo- This prefix means ancient or prehistoric. Canadians and Americans usually spell it *paleo-*, as in *paleontology*, the study of extinct plants and animals through fossils. The British spell it *palaeo-*.

See also -AE-, -OE-, -E-.

palette, pallet see PALATE

panda see BEAR

pandemic see ENDEMIC

pander, panderer To *pander to* once meant to pimp for, but now it means to cater to. Someone who panders is a *pander* or, more commonly in Canada and the United States today, a *panderer*. *Pander* came into English from the name of a character in Chaucer's *Troilus and Criseyde*, Pandare, who acts as a go-between for the two lovers.

We pander to the ideal of Work as few Victorians did. . . .
Robertson Davies *A Voice from the Attic* 1960: 34

It makes him sound like a writer who's deliberately pandering to some kind of cheesy popular taste, though in reality nothing could be further from the truth.
Margaret Atwood *Second Words* 1982: 320

But Clinton is no panderer to the powerful.
Financial Post 27 Dec. 1991: 36

Mulroney also described Liberal Leader Jean Chretien as a flip-flopper and Reform Leader Preston Manning as a panderer of regional resentment.
Toronto Star 29 Nov. 1991: A1

(Here *panderer* should be followed by *to*, not *of*. However, it is also possible that *promoter* was meant; if so, 'promoter of' is the accepted phrase.)

His 'human' feelings are a sham, and director Robert Rooney makes this numbingly clear by having Ted Dykstra play him in extravagant style, bounding from tier to tier of the Coliseum-like set, sloppily kissing his whore, and exchanging conspiratorial glances with his pander, Amor.
Globe and Mail (Toronto) 27 Sept. 1985: E5

(The noun *pander* is uncommon in Canadian English; here it literally means *pimp*.)

Panhandle, the see CAPITAL LETTERS

pants *Pants* are outerwear in Canada and the United States, underwear in Britain. What North Americans call *pants* the British call *trousers*. What the British call *pants* North Americans call *underpants*. In British English, *pants* is also slang meaning rubbish or nonsense.

I took off my shoes and socks and rolled up my pants.
Howard Engel *Murder Sees the Light* 1984: 57

I was told my class was 'pants.' . . . 'These are pants,' I said tugging at the leg of my trousers. The offending student laughed. 'Those aren't pants, Miss,' he said. And, reaching into his own trousers, he displayed for me an alarming amount of white cotton. 'THESE are pants.'
Sara Beck *Queen's Alumni Review* Holiday Season 2002: 18

(Canadian Sara Beck took a teaching job in a British high school.)

pap see PABLUM

paparazzo, paparazzi *Paparazzi* has been recently borrowed from Italian as a name for the photographers who stalk celebrities in hopes of snapping a candid shot. The singular *paparazzo* is seldom seen; *paparazzi*, the plural form, appears frequently in newspaper and magazine writing. The pronunciations are *pah pih ROT so* and *pah pih ROT see*.

But it's just part of the job, explains Roger Karnbad, a 10-year paparazzo who's packing twin Nikons for this shoot.
Gazette (Montreal) 18 Aug. 1990: H8

The camera bugs reminded me of paparazzi from the gutter tabloids in pursuit of some unlucky movie celebrity.
Vancouver Sun 13 Jul. 1990: A13

'It's simple, really,' says paparazi Mike Erickson, 'People enjoy looking at photographs of other people.'
Province (Vancouver) 24 May 1990: P11

(A single camera-wielding celebrity hound is a *paparazzo*. The word is misspelled as well: the *z* should be doubled.)

paperboy   see JOB TITLES

papyrus, papyri   see PLURALS

para-   The prefix *para-* has three meanings. In the words *paramedic*, *paramilitary*, and *paranormal*, *para-* is derived from a Greek preposition meaning 'beside', 'beyond', or 'outside'. The second meaning of *para-* is 'guarding against', derived from the Latin verb *parare*, 'to prepare': thus a *parachute* guards against a fall and a *parasol* guards against the sun. Finally, *para-* is a clipped form of *parachute* in such words as *paratrooper*, *paraglider*, and *parasailing*. Para- compounds normally do not take a hyphen.

> Hence, Alberta and British Columbia now provide paralegal services to aboriginals who have to face the court.
> Irving M. Zeitlin and Robert J. Brym *The Social Condition of Humanity* 1991: 277

> . . . parasailing, wind surfing, snorkelling, scuba diving, deep sea fishing all vie for your attention and your pesos.
> *Leader-Post* (Regina) 27 Feb. 1988: B18

See also HYPHENATION.

paraffin   see KEROSENE

paraglider   see PARA-

paragon   see EPITOME

paragraph   A paragraph is a block of text that is distinguished typographically, by indenting the first line or by leaving an extra line space above and below, or by both means. Composition books generally describe the paragraph as a subsection of an argument in which one main idea is discussed. However, paragraphing varies in newspapers, academic books and journals, magazines, reference works, advertising copy, etc. A paragraph can be as short as a single sentence or many sentences in length. Both the look of the text on the page and the reading habits of the intended audience influence paragraph length.

parallelism   Parellelism (the repetition of a particular grammatical structure or part of speech) can be an effective rhetorical device: 'I came, I saw, I conquered'; 'short and sweet'; 'what's hot and what's not'. Once a parallel series has been set up, however, the writer should ensure that all the elements in it have the same form. For example, 'The puppy likes to sleep, to eat, and to play' is fine. But 'The puppy likes to sleep, eating, and to play' won't do, since 'eating' is not parallel to the other forms, which begin with 'to'. Similarly, in 'He came for the food, the drink, and because he is such a social animal', the first two elements are nouns, while the third is a clause and therefore not parallel. This could be rewritten in various ways: for example, 'He came because he likes good food, good drink, and good company'.

In a series of more than two elements, it is possible either to repeat the prepositions (*on*, *at*, etc.), the *to* in infinitives (as in *to eat*), or the articles (*a*, *an*, *the*) each time, or to drop them after the first use: 'The puppy likes to sleep, (to) eat, and (to) play'; 'We brought a stereo, (a) picnic lunch, and (a) beach umbrella'. In a series with only two elements, however, dropping these words for the second element creates an unbalanced effect, and many usage guides warn against it. Such problems usually occur with the following correlative conjunctions: *both . . . and*; *not only . . . but also*; *either . . . or*; *neither . . . nor*. What follows the second element in these constructions should be parallel with what follows the first: 'The book is either on the bed or on the chair' (*either* and *or* followed by a prepositional phrase) and 'The book is on either the bed or the chair' (*either* and *or* followed by a noun) are both acceptable, but 'The book is either on the bed or the chair' is not. A similar problem arises in sentences like 'Calcium is not only found in milk but also in vegetables'; this should be rewritten 'Calcium is found not only in milk but also in vegetables'.

Another form of faulty parallelism occurs

with possessives. A structure such as 'the great physicist Albert Einstein's insights' makes 'the great physicist' (a common noun phrase) parallel to 'Albert Einstein's' (a possessive noun phrase). The solution is to rewrite: 'the insights of the great physicist Albert Einstein'.

Finally, items treated as parallel in a list should be at roughly the same level of generality: for example, 'We visited Newfoundland, Nova Scotia, and New Brunswick' or 'We visited St. John's, Dartmouth, and Moncton', but not 'We visited Newfoundland, Dartmouth, and New Brunswick'.

Parallelism is the concern of the stylist, not the grammarian. Sentences containing elements that are not parallel are not necessarily wrong or ambiguous, but they are often less fluent or readable.

paralyse, paralyze see ISE, -IZE, -YSE, -YZE

paramedic, paramilitary see PARA-

paramount, tantamount *Paramount* means most important or supreme. *Tantamount,* derived from Anglo-French *tant amunter*, 'to amount to as much', means equal or equivalent to.

Leisure activities have always been of paramount importance to the Inuit, who are very social in nature.
Arctic 41.1 (1988): 76

'Sending the children back to Chernobyl is tantamount to sending them back to a Nazi gas chamber.'
Gazette (Montreal) 22 Feb. 1994: A3

But for those to whom driving a Ford would be paramount to treason, purchasing a pre-owned 1993–2002 Camaro can fill the need for brute speed.
Gazette (Montreal) 28 Feb. 2005: E1

(The expression required here is '*tantamount* to treason'.)

paranormal see PARA-

paraphernalia *Paraphernalia* is derived from a plural Latin noun referring to a woman's personal belongings, separate from her dowry. In modern English it means trivial odds and ends or equipment, and is used with either a singular or a plural verb. Note the spelling; sometimes the second *r*, which is usually not pronounced, is left out in writing.

Parenthetical hints and tips, reverse chronology, asides and footnotes, all the paraphernalia of post-modernist ambiguity is here in controlled profusion.
Globe and Mail (Toronto) 16 Feb. 1985: E17

(In this example the noun *paraphernalia* takes a singular verb, *is*.)

Official paraphernalia, including Blue Jays caps, pennants, buttons and 'No. 1 fingers'—giant gloves with the index finger raised—were being sold faster than vendors could replenish the stock.
Globe and Mail (Toronto) 7 Oct. 1985: A12

(In this example *paraphernalia* takes a plural verb, *were*.)

See also AGREEMENT, GRAMMATICAL; COLLECTIVE NOUNS.

paraplegic, quadriplegic, tetraplegic
Someone who is *paraplegic* has been injured in the back, and is paralysed in the legs and part or all of the torso. Someone who is *quadriplegic* (or more rarely *tetraplegic*) has been injured in the neck, and is paralysed in the legs, torso, and part or all of the arms. Note the *a* in *paraplegic* and *tetraplegic* and the *i* in *quadriplegic*.

Avoid using these terms as nouns, as in 'He is a paraplegic', because this implies that the person's entire identity has been subsumed by the injury. The words should only be adjectives describing a person, as in 'He is paraplegic'. Sometimes it may be appropriate to avoid the medical term altogether, and instead describe what the person can do: 'He has full use of his arms' or 'She uses an electric wheelchair with mouth controls to get around' (see DISABILITIES for more on this subject).

The terms *tetraplegic* and *tetraplegia* are more common outside North America, and may eventually gain currency in Canada too. (The

American Spinal Cord Association recommends using *tetraplegia* rather than *quadriplegia*.) For now, however, these terms are too rare in Canada to be used without an explanation.

All of these words are often mispronounced with an extra syllable, as if there were a vowel between the *p* and *l* (see MISPRONUNCIATION).

He broke his neck, became a quadraplegic and requires a wheelchair to get around.
Calgary Herald 14 April 2003: D16

(Quadriplegic is spelled with an i. The phrasing 'became quadriplegic' is preferred.)

See also DISABILITIES; INCLUSIVE LANGUAGE; MISPRONUNCIATION; NUMBER PREFIXES.

parapraxis   see SLIPS OF THE TONGUE

parasailing, parasol, paratrooper   see PARA-

parent   see FUNCTIONAL SHIFT

parentheses, brackets   Printers and editors usually differentiate between *parentheses* and *brackets*, using the former term for round brackets ( ) and the latter for square [ ]. However, *brackets* is also a generic term for round brackets, square brackets, or braces { }.

The singular of *parentheses* (pronounced *puh REN thuh seez*) is *parenthesis*. A parenthesis is a parenthetical remark—that is, an interjection or aside—or one half of a pair of parentheses: 'You forgot the closing parenthesis'.

Parentheses enclose matter that interrupts the flow of a sentence or paragraph. For example:

• digressions:

The two election pamphlets, 'A Fair Deal for Canada' and 'Meeting the Challenge' (neither of which was widely distributed), took a similar approach.
Alan Whitehorn *Canadian Socialism* 1992: 220

• particularizations:

The majority of the judges (5 of 7) had decided that Section 251 violated Canadian women's constitutional rights to the security of the person.

Janine Brodie, Shelley A. M. Gavigan, and Jane Jenson *The Politics of Abortion* 1992: 59

• examples:

. . . a province may exempt itself from the effect of an amendment derogating from its legislative powers or proprietary rights (e.g., in natural resources), by resolution of the legislature.
Queen's Quarterly 94.4 (1987): 786

• translations:

In the long run he decides to . . . offer his manuscript to the city and the world, including the *vendus* (sellouts) who have betrayed him.
Ben-Z. Shek *French-Canadian & Québécois Novels* 1991: 52

• optional elements:

1/2 cup cocoa
(1/2 cup chopped walnuts)

• alternative phrasings:

If three or more units out of 500 fail the test(s), the lot is sent back, explained Wong.
Computer Dealer News 21 March 1991: 26

• documentation of sources:

However, recent work has identified several dense and productive populations (Alliston and Patterson, 1978; Calef and Heard, 1979; Bromley, in press).
Arctic 41.1 (1988): 18

In some contexts it is possible to replace parentheses with paired commas or dashes. Parentheses usually signal a stronger disruption of syntax than paired commas, but a less dramatic break in the sentence than dashes.

Newspapers often use parentheses to enclose explanatory information inserted in a quotation:

'We hope that this (Black Sea) incident will not hinder the process of bettering Soviet-American relations.'
Calgary Herald 14 Feb. 1988: A2

In books and academic writing, the convention is different: anything added to or altered in a quotation is enclosed in *square brackets*. Parentheses are reserved for material that was in parentheses in the original:

> 'The Reichsfuhrer [Himmler] has summoned me to take up a special assignment in Russia.'
> *Canadian Journal of History* 14.1 (1989): 77

> One claims that the lyric is 'by and large, [the] least ironical' of all the literary forms.
> Linda Hutcheon *Splitting Images* 1991: 25

> 'I want to tell you myself before you hear from any other source,' he wrote to Chancellor Richardson, 'that George V (whiskers and all) has been graciously pleased to offer me the principalship of Aberdeen University and that I have been graciously pleased to accept.'
> Frederick Gibson *Queen's University* 2 (1983): 128

(Here the parenthetical element was added by the letter-writer, not the quoting author.)

The Latin word *sic* in square brackets is used to flag mistakes or peculiarities in quoted matter. *Sic* means 'thus' (i.e., 'It was thus in the original'). The use of [*sic*] prevents readers from thinking that the quoting writer has introduced a mistake into a quotation, or failed to notice something amiss. However, the device should be used judiciously. It can seem priggish and condescending, and sometimes merely reveals the ignorance of the quoting writer. *Sic* should be italicized:

> Ross, an early Canadian modernist, noted that Canada has 'quite a number of poems about diving, whereas they are lacking in US and english [*sic*] writers.'
> *Queen's Quarterly* 97.3 (1990): 426

> 'This time around we are willingly feeling our way through unchartered (sic) territory.'
> *Toronto Star* 11 June 2006: C8

(Here *sic* tells readers that the editor is aware the phrase should properly be *uncharted territory*.)

The conventions for combining parentheses with other types of punctuation are as follows. When a sentence in parentheses stands alone, its final punctuation mark goes inside the closing parenthesis:

> (The present decade began, too, with the failure of the Meech Lake Accord, and the Mohawk crisis, both of which have affected Quebec deeply.)
> Ben-Z. Shek *French-Canadian & Québécois Novels* 1991: 46

A parenthetical sentence contained within another sentence has no initial capital or final period. It may, however, end in a question mark or exclamation mark:

> My generalism (please do not confuse this with dilettantism because they are not the same) clearly led me to seek the editorship because of the scope it allows for putting this predilection into practice.
> *Queen's Quarterly* 92.2 (1985): 442

> A society-page roster of a recent Hunt Club soirée at the Ritz (what could be more anglo?) reads like a *Who's Who* of francophone high society, with a sprinkling of WASPs for old time's sake.
> Alan Tucker, ed. *The Penguin Guide to Canada* 1991: 144

> I was surprised at first and a little angry, for it seemed he hadn't understood at all (then I realized he was only doing his general manager's job).
> Ken Dryden *The Game* 1983: 15

(Note the position of the period here—outside the final parenthesis.)

A comma is never placed in front of an opening parenthesis. If a parenthetical remark occurs at a point in a sentence where a comma is normally required—for example, between a subordinate clause and a main clause—the comma is placed after the closing parenthesis:

> If she were to discover a country which had never been discovered before (and she fully intended to do this sometime), she would of course name it after herself.
> Margaret Atwood *Life Before Man* 1979: 80

One final remark on style: most writing guides caution against the overuse of parenthetical remarks in discursive writing. While conversation is full of asides and derailments, it is usually considered better form in an essay to plan the sequence of ideas and to stay on topic. Short parenthetical remarks may be helpful, but long ones should be scrutinized. They can often be transformed into notes, better integrated into the flow of the argument, or dropped altogether.

See also PARENTHETICAL ELEMENTS entry in Glossary

parkway   see ROAD

parlay, parley   *Parlay* (pronounced *PAR LAY* or *PAR lee*) has a long-standing meaning among American gamblers: to stake all the winnings from one bet on another wager. (The British term is *double up*.) The extended definition of *parlay* is to build upon a small advantage or piece of good fortune, a usage in which the element of risk is de-emphasized. The usual construction is 'to parlay *x* into *y*', *y* being something much better.

Historically, a *parley* (pronounced *PAR lee*), from the French verb *parler*, 'to speak', is an informal conference between enemies, usually to discuss terms of surrender or points of disagreement. In popular usage, however, *parley* can refer to any kind of informal discussion.

In 10 years, he had parlayed his navy training as a supply officer into the position of general manager of Refinery Engineering Ltd. . . .
Globe and Mail (Toronto) 3 Jan. 1985: E4

It required a Shultz-Gromyko parley in January to launch the arms talks.
Globe and Mail (Toronto) 15 March 1985: P6

. . . the United Steelworkers are having a big parley later this week to discuss different strategies for dealing with Cominco's changed management style.
Vancouver Sun 6 Feb. 1990: C1

(Here *parley* means conference or meeting.)

When wages went down, they parleyed a student business loan into their own one-truck outfit. . . .
CBC News [transcript] 22 May 1995

(The word needed here is *parlayed*.)

parlous   *Parlous* (pronounced *PAR lus*) is an archaic variant of *perilous*. It usually appears in stock phrases such as 'parlous conditions' and 'parlous times'.

A mother-fixation resulted from these parlous years, later expressing itself in Wagner's inordinate fondness for soft fabrics and well-upholstered women.
Queen's Quarterly 92 (1985): 215

We live in parlous times when the only political leaders speaking up for a strong and united Canada are those who failed to deliver when the chips were down.
Vancouver Sun 15 Aug. 1990: A12

parsonage   see MANSE

part   see BEHALF

Parthian shot   see PARTING SHOT

participle   see entry in Glossary

parties, political   see POLITICAL PARTIES

parting shot, Parthian shot   A cutting remark made just as one is leaving (or retreating) is sometimes called a *parting shot*. This expression appears to have been derived from *Parthian shot* (see FOLK ETYMOLOGY). *Parthian shot* alludes to the horsemen of ancient Parthia who, even while turned in flight, were able to devastate an enemy with their arrows. The unfamiliar expression *Parthian shot* developed the more transparent alternative form *parting shot*, which appears to have completely supplanted the original in Canadian English.

[She] can't resist a few parting shots at the professions of architecture and architectural criticism. Even to the innocent eye, the feisty text is bound to appear motivated . . . by revenge. . . .
Globe and Mail (Toronto) 25 May 1985: E11

A will should be your last statement of caring to those you hold dear. Unfortunately, Johnston says, many people choose to use it as their parting shot.
Vancouver Sun 26 March 1994: C7

partner   see COMMON LAW; MARRIAGE

parts of speech   see entry in Glossary

pass away   see EUPHEMISM

passersby   see PLURAL

passive voice   see DANGLING MODIFIERS; VOICE (in Glossary); WORDINESS

past history   The phrase *past history* is idiomatic and used by many established writers, even though the word *past* is, strictly speaking, redundant. *Past history* can suggest water under the bridge, or history that is not relevant to present considerations; or *past* may balance the adjective *future* in another phrase in the same sentence. In other words, there are contexts where this idiom, a favourite target of language commentators, is quite defensible.

> The three covered their tracks so well that no whisper of scandal leaked out until a royal commission . . . brought down its report in 1915. By then it was past history.
> Pierre Berton *The Promised Land* 1984: 245

> Past history is no guarantee of future performance, but it can tell you a lot about management ability.
> . . .
> *Ottawa Citizen* 17 Dec. 1990: F1

> The effect of such words is to give the impression that all past history was a kind of bad dream, which in these enlightened days we've shaken off.
> Northrop Frye *The Educated Imagination* 1963: 62

patent   see BLATANT

patient   see CUSTOMER

patio   see PORCH

patriate, repatriate, patriation   The verb *patriate* (pronounced *PAY tree ate*) is a recent Canadianism referring to the process of giving full control of the Canadian Constitution to Canadians. Until 1982, all amendments to Canada's Constitution had to be passed by the legislative body that had created it, the British parliament. As early as the 1960s, people talked about *repatriating* the Constitution; but, since *repatriate* means to bring someone or something back home, the word was inappropriate for the Constitution, which had never resided in Canada. The new coinage *patriate* is now fully

established and means to bring legislation under the constitutional authority of an autonomous country (*OED*). By extension of this meaning, *patriate* is now sometimes used of strategies for bringing or keeping wealth in a country.

> The Canadian government and nine provinces reached an agreement on a plan to patriate the British North America Act and entrench a Charter of Rights four years ago today.
> *Globe and Mail* (Toronto) 5 Nov. 1985: A14

> 'I got enthused, I got emotionally involved in what I was doing,' he says, pointing to his considerable efforts in support of former Prime Minister Pierre Trudeau's campaign to repatriate the Constitution.
> *Globe and Mail* (Toronto) 12 Oct. 1985: A10

(Here *patriate* would be more accurate.)

> The use of the word 'repatriate' in reference to Quebec is both historically inaccurate and insulting to the intelligence of all Canadians. Neither the people of Quebec nor its government had seceded from Confederation.
> *Gazette* (Montreal) 5 March 1989: B2

(The writer is objecting to *repatriate* because it means to bring 'back' to the country, and Quebec has not seceded.)

> The plan was to bring on gold options to help patriate some of the futures trading directed to U.S. exchanges and capture new business developing in Canada in precious metals.
> *Globe and Mail* (Toronto) 31 Jan. 1985: B3

See also CONSTITUTION.

patron   see CUSTOMER

patronage   see NEPOTISM

payed   see PAID

peaceful, peaceable   The usual distinction between these words is that *peaceful* means characterized by peace, and thus can describe either a person or a place, while *peaceable* means fond or desirous of peace and usually describes only people. A people's desire for peace is extended to their nation in Northrop Frye's well-known characterization of Canada as a country on a quest for 'the peaceable kingdom' (*Literary History of Canada*, 1965). Frye took the phrase from the title of a painting (c. 1830) by the American Edward Hicks, which shows William Penn working out a treaty with some Aboriginal people, while in the foreground a child sits with a group of animals including lions, tigers, and bears (an allusion to Isaiah 11:6).

Both *peacefully* and *peaceably* are used to mean in a peaceful manner.

> Although our country is one of the most peaceful and prosperous on earth, although we do not shoot artists here, although we do not execute political opponents and although this is one of the few remaining countries in which we can have a gathering like this without expecting to be arrested or blown up, we should not overlook the fact that Canada's record on civil rights issues is less than pristine.
> Margaret Atwood *Second Words* 1982: 395

> Outside, a sturdy shelter belt of poplars and spruce encircles the house protectively; the winter fields are peaceful and deserted.
> *Chatelaine* April 1986: 190

> Although strikers are entitled to picket at or near the place of the employer's business, they must do so peaceably and only for the purpose of obtaining or communicating information.
> J.E. Smyth et al. *The Law and Business Administration in Canada* 1987: 516

See also -ABLE, (-E)ABLE.

peak, peek, pique   Writers occasionally use *peak* (high point) when they mean *peek* (glance).

The verb *pique* means stimulate: 'My curiosity was piqued by the flashing lights'. Since interest can both *peak* (reach a peak) and *be piqued*, *peak* and *pique* are also occasionally confused.

> Taking into account his personal property and other assets, his real wealth at its peak was probably at least double this figure.
> *National Post* (Toronto) 27 May 2006: FW3

> And four delirious young girls from New Jersey do their darndest to sneak a peak at the Fab Four. . . .

Gazette (Montreal) 5 March 1989: T65

(The correct spelling here is *peek*.)

> Over the years a favorite way to deal with hockey intermissions has been to switch channels. Occasionally a between-periods interview can pique interest. . . .
> *Globe and Mail* (Toronto) 12 Oct. 1985: P12

> The officers' curiosity peaked even more when a computer check of the papers the motorist gave them indicated he wasn't who he alleged to be.
> *Gazette* (Montreal) 26 May 1990: A3

(Although curiosity can be said to *peak*, it cannot peak 'even more'. The sense here requires the passive verb *was piqued*.)

peal, peel   Bells and laughter *peal*; if you think that sound is *appealing*, it may help you remember the spelling. The skin of a fruit and the related verb are spelled *peel*: 'She peeled off her snowsuit'; 'The paint is peeling off the walls'.

> The principal bell-ringer this weekend was 14 years old when the war ended. . . . It was very fitting that he led Saturday's repetition of those peels.
> *Telegram* (St. John's) 28 May 2005: B1

(The word for the ringing of bells is *peals*.)

pean   see PAEAN

pearl   see PURL

peccadillo   see IMPECCABLE

pedagogue, pedant   A *pedagogue* is a teacher. A *pedant* is someone more concerned with correcting others than teaching them, and more interested in the mastery of minutiae than the broad implications of learning. When a pedagogue is also a pedant, the context must make it clear: *pedagogue* in itself is not pejorative.

The spelling *pedagog* is an alternative in the United States but is not used by Canadian writers.

> Both musicians have graduated in organ performance . . . and are now continuing their studies with

the internationally renowned concert organist and pedagogue Antoine Bouchard.
Chronicle-Telegraph (Quebec City) 24 July 1991: 4

How many times were we corrected on these two phrases alone, and how often do we say 'It is I' or 'I took only one cookie' because we suspect some pedagogue's hammer is still hovering above our cerebellum?
W.C. Lougheed, ed. *In Search of the Standard in Canadian English* 1986: 80

(Here the *pedagogue* is also a *pedant*. For the rules alluded to, see CASE and ONLY.)

Are those who dislike this trend just old-fashioned pedants, more interested in legalisms than action?
National Post (Toronto) 7 Jan. 2006: A21

pedal, peddle, pedlar, peddler   *Pedal* comes from the Latin *pedalis*, meaning 'of the foot'. A *pedal* is a lever operated by the foot, and to *pedal* is to operate a machine by pushing its pedals. Canadian writers are divided on whether to use a single or a double *l* before the endings *-ed*, *-ing*, and *-er*. British dictionaries double the final consonant; American dictionaries do not.

To *peddle* is to sell something, especially in small quantities, or to promote an idea or way of life. Canadian writers favour the noun *peddler* (the American spelling) but also use the older variant *pedlar*. In Britain the usual spelling is *pedlar*, although *peddler* is used in Britain for someone who sells drugs.

The *soft pedal* on a piano softens the notes played. Figuratively, to *soft-pedal* (usually hyphenated) something is to de-emphasize it or be restrained about it. The phrase is sometimes spelled *soft-peddling*, perhaps by those who think it means selling something without aggression (see FOLK ETYMOLOGY).

When I peddled past 25 miles an hour, the bicycle actually took off and flew. You could steer through the air by leaning to one side or the other. . . .
Vancouver Sun 5 Sept. 1990: D1

(The correct spelling is *pedalled* or *pedaled*.)

The provincial capitals are monstrosities of iron and concrete, representatives of a Soviet sub-species of urban planning inhabited by joyless

pedallers bent over the handlebars of their identical lives.
Globe and Mail (Toronto) 24 Aug. 1985: 1

Far from developing and nurturing a sturdy sense of self-reliance, he has been a peddler of pipe-dreams.
Financial Post 17 Sept. 1990: 12

He was a prosperous pedlar of gents' natty garments and ladies' whalebone corsets.
Vancouver Sun 3 Feb. 1990: B4

These were hard-nosed conclusions, but when it came to sentencing Biller, the panel—quite strangely, in my view—began to soft-peddle them.
Vancouver Sun 5 April 2005: D4

(The phrase is *soft-pedal*, meaning de-emphasize.)

See also DOUBLING THE FINAL CONSONANT; MISHEARD EXPRESSIONS.

pedant   see PEDAGOGUE

peddle, peddler   see PEDAL

pedigree   see PUREBRED

pedlar   see PEDAL

peek   see PEAK

peel   see PEAL

peer, peerless   A *peer* is equal to someone else, being in the same age or social group, or having the same level of ability. *Peerless* describes something with no equal. *Peer* is also used to refer to a member of the British nobility.

By the time Davis . . . left the Charlie Parker Quintet in December 1948, he had already laid the foundation that would make him Parker's peer in the development of jazz.
Jack Chambers *Milestones* 1983: 89

One listen reveals the double-CD set as a rich, astonishing sonic adventure. A second listen and you're almost struck dumb by Mitchell's peerless artistry.
Daily News (Halifax) 1 Dec. 2005: 28

The idea of a British peer dictating to Canadians

. . . did not sit easily in a region where, in principle at least, every man was considered the equal of every other if he was willing to work.
Pierre Berton *The Promised Land* 1984: 192

Pegger see NAMES OF RESIDENTS OF CITIES AND PROVINCES

Pekingese see CAPITAL LETTERS; DALMATIAN

pellucid see TURGID

pen name see PSEUDONYM

pensioner see SENIOR CITIZEN

penultimate, ultimate *Penultimate* means the 'last but one' or 'next to last'. Sometimes *penultimate* is mistakenly used as a synonym for *ultimate*, which means last, best possible, or unsurpassable.

Scoresby's survey of the Greenland coast was his penultimate voyage to the Arctic. His last was in 1823.
Arctic 41.1 (1988): 46

Once a week when the Liberals ran Ottawa, about 30 of the town's deputy ministers—the princes of the public service—would gather . . . for the insiders' penultimate plum, a high-level briefing on what had happened that week in the meetings of the Cabinet and its most important committees.
Globe and Mail (Toronto) 29 Nov. 1985: P32

(Here *penultimate* is incorrectly used to mean *ultimate*.)

'This will be the penultimate resort in Alberta. There isn't anything else of this stature in terms of luxury—and it will be quite exclusive.'
Calgary Herald 25 March 2006: K1

(Here *penultimate* is incorrectly used to mean *ultimate*.)

peon see PAEAN

people, peoples see PERSONS; SEXIST LANGUAGE

people of colour see VISIBLE MINORITY

Péquiste A *Péquiste* (pronounced *PAY KEEST*)

is a member or supporter of the Parti Québécois (or PQ), the provincial political party seeking the independence of Quebec. The word *Péquiste* was formed by adding the suffix *-iste* to the party initials *PQ*. In English, adjectives derived from proper names (e.g., Orwellian) are usually capitalized, but *péquiste* is often lower-case when it is an adjective ('péquiste candidate'), probably because of the influence of French (*un Français*, but *un homme français*). In formal writing the acute accent over the first *e* is required, though it seldom appears in English newspapers.

But this secured for the Péquistes only 6% of the seats in the National Assembly.
David V.J. Bell *The Roots of Disunity* 1992: 112

'They can be a good Liberal or a good Pequiste . . . but they need . . . to fit the profile,' Allaire said.
Gazette (Montreal) 8 April 2006: A11

Guitard, a former pequiste activist, draws her support from all parties.
Ottawa Citizen 5 Dec. 1992: F2

(Capitalization of the adjective is optional.)

percentage, per cent, percent *Percentage* is always one word. Canadians prefer the two-word spelling of *per cent*, although the single-word spelling is also common. British dictionaries list *per cent* first, American dictionaries *percent*.

Per cent is followed by either a single or a plural verb form, depending on the related noun: 'Fifteen per cent of the *total is* added to the bill for service' or 'Only twenty per cent of the *students are* going to pass the test'.

The per cent symbol (%) is used only with figures: '8%'.

See also NUMBERS.

per diem see LATIN PHRASES

perfect, more perfect, most perfect Some usage experts consider perfection an absolute condition; hence they argue that the adjective *perfect* should not be used in comparisons, and they object to the phrases *more* (or *less*) *perfect* and *most* (or *least*) *perfect*. However, *more perfect* and *most perfect* have long been used to suggest the varying degrees to which perfection may be approximated. *Perfect* belongs to a set of adjectives—including *complete, excellent, extreme,* and *unique*—that denote superlative qualities without being considered grammatically superlative terms. *More perfect* is enshrined in the American Constitution, which aims for 'a more perfect union' of the United States. Though some may object, the consensus is that *perfect* can be compared.

> Thus by the end of the 1950s the universities of Canada were seen not merely as the means for achieving a more perfect social justice, but also as holding the keys to economic prosperity and even national survival.
> Frederick Gibson *Queen's University* 2 (1983): 357

> The Great Cross in the churchyard is one of the world's most perfect specimens. . . .
> *Canadian Churchman* April 1986: 11

> 'You just want it to be the most perfect book that you can make it.'
> *Gazette* (Montreal) 23 March 2006: F15

See also COMPLETE; UNIQUE.

performance art, performing arts   see ARTS

perigee   see APOGEE

period of time, time period   A number of usage commentators criticize the phrase *period of time* (or *time period*) as redundant, arguing that either *period* or *time* should be used, but not both. Yet *period of time* is idiomatic and both *period* and *time* by themselves have other meanings. Alone, neither word is as easy to interpret as the disputed phrase. Canadian writers do not hesitate to use it.

> Each essay treats the development of an idea or a set of ideas over a period of time.
> J.A.W. Gunn *Beyond Liberty and Property* 1983: 1

> When . . . performance is spread over a period of time and is to be paid for on completion, a frustra-

tion of the contract before its completion may cause serious hardship for the performer or his estate.
> J.E. Smyth et al. *The Law and Business Administration in Canada* 1987: 319

> . . . tradition is a body of practice in a certain area, accumulated over a certain period of time, that for one reason or another is considered meaningful enough to be passed on from one generation to the next.
> Miriam Waddington *Apartment Seven* 1989: 84

> But brain-fever was generally invoked by novelists when they wanted to get a character out of the way for an unspecified period of time.
> Robertson Davies *One Half of Robertson Davies* 1978: 164

> The book's point of departure is the time period after the crash, after Millett has been 'trashed' by the media, the women's movement, and various friends and lovers who could not deal with her success.
> Margaret Atwood *Second Words* 1982: 210

perk, perquisite, prerequisite   A *perk* is a special privilege on top of a salary or wage, such as the right to use a company car. *Perk* is actually a short form, and most dictionaries label it informal. In formal writing the long form *perquisite* should be used.

A *perquisite* should not be confused with a *prerequisite*, which is a requirement that must be fulfilled before something else can happen.

> The perks EA lays on at the office are sweet, and include a full-size sports field, in-house drycleaning, an outsize gym, salons, deli dining and, of course, a library of every video game ever produced.
> *Province* (Vancouver) 4 June 2006: B3

> It isn't the praise, or the generous perks of celebrity; it is the implicit, unstated respect it gives.
> Ken Dryden *The Game* 1983: 13

> These 'new people' . . . did not know that gentlefolk had new candles in every stick every day, and objected to the lively trade in long candle ends which was part of cook's perquisites.
> Robertson Davies *A Voice from the Attic* 1960: 138

> An ethical society is not a prerequisite of scientific advancement. Neither is respect for ethical values

a prerequisite for scientific insight and achievement.
Canadian Journal of Philosophy 19 (1989): 294

. . . the craft unceremoniously dumped us out. . . . Even though we were both experienced flat-water canoeists, lessons and supervision with qualified white-water instructors should have been a prerequisite.
Gazette (Montreal) 20 May 1994: D4

Run down a list of perquisites for winning a Grey Cup ring—an MVP-calibre quarterback, sound defence, expert coaching and depth—and the Lions would seem to satisfy most of the them, with the exception of an exceptional offensive line.
Vancouver Sun 9 Feb. 2006: F4

(The word intended here is *prerequisites*.)

perogy, pyrohy The word for a Ukrainian dumpling filled with potato, cheese, or meat is spelled in various ways. In western Canada *pyrohy* is popular, but *perogy* is probably the most common Canadian spelling. The usual pronunciation is *puh ROH gee*.

perpetrate, perpetuate To *perpetrate* a crime or evil act is to commit it. To *perpetuate* something is to ensure that it continues.

. . . I could see with my own eyes the horrors that were being perpetrated in the name of supposedly just causes.
George Ignatieff The Making of a Peacemonger 1987: 23

When they mark their ballots, the delegates will be voting not for a mere leader but for a man they judge able to perpetuate the dynasty for another decade.
Globe and Mail (Toronto) 19 Jan. 1985: P1

Many men and some women have insisted his act represents but a single horrific incident perpetuated by a madman.
Province (Vancouver) 5 Jan. 1990: 34

(The word required here is *perpetrated*.)

Wolf 'kills' make good headlines, but I think your article missed a crucial opportunity to enlighten the public at large, rather than perpetrate polarization on an issue for which solutions must be found.
Province (Vancouver) 25 May 1990: 48

(A better choice here is *perpetuate*.)

perquisite see PERK

per se *Per se* (pronounced *per SAY* or, especially in legal circles, *per SEE*) is a Latin expression that means 'in or of itself', 'intrinsically', or 'as such': 'This drug is not a poison *per se*, but, if you drink alcohol while you are taking it, you become very sick'.

Some traditionalists counter that rising divorce rates actually have little to do with changing economic circumstances. . . . Instead, they contend, it is the liberalization of divorce laws per se that has caused divorce rates to soar.
Irving M. Zeitlin and Robert J. Brym *The Social Condition of Humanity* 1991: 194

It is not guns per se that are the problem. The problem has several aspects, including cultural conditions and a lack of application of existing law.
Vancouver Sun 2 Aug. 1990: A10

He had no commitment to freedom and democracy per se, but realized they were necessary to revitalize the economy.
Financial Post 29 Aug. 1991: 7

See also LATIN PHRASES.

persona In Latin a *persona* is an actor's mask, and this meaning is preserved in the modern English use of *persona* for an actor's stage personality or a fictional voice assumed by a writer. Another meaning became popular at the beginning of the century when the writings of the psychoanalyst Carl Jung were translated into English. Jung used *persona* to mean the externalized outer self that we use in our social dealings, as opposed to our private inner self or soul. Thus any person's public personality or façade may now also be called a *persona*. The plural is either *personae* or *personas*.

The unnamed 74-year-old nurse recounts to the main persona crucial and extraordinary, yet believable, incidents of tragic womanhood. . . .
Ben-Z. Shek *French-Canadian & Québécois Novels* 1991: 94

(Here the *persona* is a fictional character.)

On this particular trip, he played the peasant rather than worker and his persona allowed him to gather extensive information on the individuals and settlements he visited.
Canadian Journal of History 14.1 (1989): 68

(Here *persona* refers to a façade or assumed role.)

Now she's trying to find an adjective to describe her on air persona, having already rejected descriptions like bubbly, quirky and boisterous.
Globe and Mail (Toronto) 15 May 1985: S10

See also PERSONA NON GRATA, PERSONA GRATA.

personal, personally   *Personal* is often called redundant when used in combinations such as 'personal opinion' or 'personal friend', since opinions and friends are assumed to be personal. Constructions such as 'I personally think . . .' are criticized on similar grounds. However, *personal* and *personally* are not necessarily empty words in these phrases. Sometimes a distinction is being made between private and public life, and sometimes first-hand involvement is being emphasized, as in 'I personally took your order'.

Whatever personal opinions the sovereign may hold or may have expressed to her Government, she is bound to accept and act on the advice of her ministers. . . .
Andrew   Heard   *Canadian   Constitutional Conventions* 1991: 43

(Here *personal opinions* are private beliefs as opposed to public policy.)

For Milwaukee speed skater Marty Pierce there was a moving personal memory when it was all over.
Calgary Herald 14 Feb. 1988: 19

(Here *personal* indicates that the memory was important in a private way.)

Burroughs's personal reputation, like his professional status, was open to interpretation.
Gazette (Montreal) 4 March 1989: K11

(Here *personal* is used to parallel *professional*.)

He won a solid majority in the 1986 provincial election, largely on the basis of his personal charisma.
Chronicle-Herald (Halifax) 9 April 1988: 6

(Here *personal* is indeed redundant, since charisma can only be personal.)

See also PERSONNEL; SENTENCE ADVERBS.

personality   see CHARACTER

persona non grata, persona grata   *Persona non grata* is a term used to describe a person who is not welcome or wanted; *persona grata* describes one who is welcome. These Latin phrases were first used in diplomacy. A foreign representative whom a country was willing to accept was *persona grata*, while one deemed unacceptable was *persona non grata*. Of course, a chilling in the relations between two countries might quickly cause *persona grata* to become *non grata*.

The plural of *persona non grata* is *personae non gratae*, but in journalism *persona non grata* is often used as a plural. Some language commentators recommend this usage on the grounds that *persona non grata* is now being used like an adjective in English (equivalent to 'unwelcome'), and thus should be invariable. However, wordplays such as 'male persona non grata' (in reference to a man barred from a mother–infant group) and 'pachydermata non grata' (in reference to elephants on the rampage) demonstrate that at least some writers still construe *persona non grata* as a modified noun rather than a phrasal adjective. Thus the plural form of the phrase should be preserved, if not in newspaper writing, at least in formal usage.

In formal writing *persona non grata* should be italicized as a foreign phrase. *Persona* is spelled with only one *n*. Note that these expressions are used without an article.

Morel is likely persona non grata in Calgary after his call in overtime of Game 6 of the Flames Smythe Division semifinal against Los Angeles. . . .
Ottawa Citizen 18 April 1990: C3

A tiny force of 15 Native policemen, trained by Quebec and Ontario police, have some control of the Canadian side, but are persona non grata on the American side.
Province (Vancouver) 4 May 1990: 20

(In journalism, though not in formal writing, *persona non grata* may be used with a plural antecedent.)

. . . he was disqualified . . . as one who still maintained friendly if not cordial relations with those *personae non gratae* George Lawson and George Weir.
Hilda Neatby *Queen's University* 1 (1978): 109

Those expelled did not include 11 Iraqi diplomats declared personae non grata by French President Francois Mitterrand.
Ottawa Citizen 17 Sept. 1990: A6

(Formal writing would require *gratae* here.)

Fed up with being persona non gratis in Hollywood because she was overweight and not 25, the Emmy-Award winning actor decided to fight fire with fat.
Province (Vancouver) 7 March 2006: B3

(*Gratis* means free; the phrase should read *persona non grata*, or not welcome.)

See also LATIN PHRASES, FOREIGN PHRASES.

personnel   *Personnel* (*per sun ELL*) means staff. It is treated as singular when considered as a unit ('Personnel is our main concern') and as a plural when considered as a collection of individuals ('All personnel are expected to attend the meeting'). Many critics object when *personnel* is used with a number ('fifteen personnel') on the grounds that *personnel* is a collective noun. However, the use of *personnel* as a countable noun is also well established.

Sometimes *personnel* is misspelled *personel*.

Personnel were dropped, agencies reorganized, salaries reduced.
Pierre Berton *The Promised Land* 1984: 211

The Earl and his party—only three personnel—left Saskatchewan early Sunday evening after a full day in Moose Jaw.
Leader-Post (Regina) 24 June 2004: B1

It's also a popular area for military and RCMP personel.
Ottawa Citizen 21 May 1994: E1

(The correct spelling is *personnel*.)

See also COLLECTIVE NOUNS; PERSONAL.

persons, people, peoples   Some usage guides state that *persons* rather than *people* should be preferred as the plural of *person* ('We had five persons over for dinner'); these guides would reserve *people* for collective uses ('the people of India'). In Canadian writing, however, *persons* is commonly found only in legal and bureaucratic contexts. The usual and recommended plural for *person* in general contexts is *people*. *Persons* would strike most readers as odd or affected.

When *people* refers to an ethnic group or nationality, its plural is *peoples*: 'These two peoples have a longstanding enmity'.

. . . the cooperation of two persons can accomplish considerably more than can two individuals working alone.
Irving M. Zeitlin and Robert J. Brym *The Social Condition of Humanity* 1991: 62

The funnel uprooted trees, destroyed farms and houses and left eight people dead, 269 injured and 600 homeless.
Maclean's 10 Feb. 1986: 5

Caribou, musk-ox and buffalo have become integral parts of the diets of Canada's northern peoples. . . .
Vancouver Sun 18 Dec. 1990: B5

perspective, prospective   *Perspective*, meaning point of view, is often mistakenly used to mean *prospective*, meaning aspiring or potential. Note the location of the *r* in the *per*- and *pro*-prefixes, and remember the *o* in *potential* to keep their meanings straight.

Currently, 33 institutions are involved with the fair, travelling to cities across Canada to tell perspective students about their programming.
Leader-Post (Regina) 15 Oct. 2005: G7

(Here *prospective*—meaning *potential*—is the desired word.)

perspicacious, perspicuous, perspicacity, perspicuity   Someone who is *perspicacious* (*per spi KAY shus*) is discerning and perceptive; prose that is *perspicuous* (*per SPICK yoo us*) is clear and lucid. *Perspicacity* is superior discernment, a quality attributed to people, while *perspicuity*, clarity of expression, is a quality usually attributed to a style of writing, an argument, etc.

The words *perspicuous* and *perspicuity* are seldom used by Canadian writers, which may be why *perspicuity* tends to be confused with *perspicacity*.

Presumably an experienced lawyer perspicacious and prudent enough to qualify as a judge should not need a 'code of conduct to regulate behavior on and off the bench'.
Gazette (Montreal) 26 Oct. 1994: B2

With the perspicacity that hindsight bestows, however, I can now see how the elements of Tory success were present in that committee room.
Globe and Mail (Toronto) 19 June 1985: P7

U.S. forward Tony Granato took a hooking penalty in front of the net and then questioned the perspicacity of referee Mark Faucette.
Globe and Mail (Toronto) 30 April 1985: S3

(In other words, Granato questioned the referee's powers of observation, doubtless to little avail.)

Looking into the future takes perspicuity but so does looking into the past and human nature.
Vancouver Sun 27 Nov. 1993: C6

(The word required here is *perspicacity*.)

persuade   see CONVINCE

persuasion   In the nineteenth century the word *persuasion* was widely used to refer to a set of religious convictions or to the group of people holding these beliefs ('the Jewish persuasion', 'the Episcopal persuasion', 'the Catholic persuasion'), or to political parties and their followers (e.g., 'the Tory persuasion'). By the mid-nineteenth century this usage was being mocked by writers who began to use *persuasion* facetiously as a synonym for *race, sex, nationality*, and so on: in other words, to describe any category of person, whether united by conviction or by mere happenstance ('the female persuasion', 'the Irish persuasion', 'the haircutting persuasion'). Eventually, *persuasion* became a general synonym for *kind* or *sort*, applied, often facetiously, to things as well as to people.

The market area abounds in restaurants of every persuasion.
Alan Tucker, ed. *The Penguin Guide to Canada* 1991: 307

Nor will a cabbage culture suffice for us, however many persuasive political and literary people of the truck-garden and green-grocer persuasion may appear among us.
Robertson Davies *One Half of Robertson Davies* 1978: 284

True, there are a couple of fillies in there but the vast majority is of the male persuasion.
Province (Vancouver) 31 July 1990: 58

peruse, perusal   To *peruse*, meaning to read or study, has two conflicting finer senses in current English: to go over thoroughly or to skim quickly. Dictionaries have begun to record the second, newer sense, which is widely used in informal writing and in speech. Writers, however, should be aware of the word's potential ambiguity. In formal Canadian usage *peruse* almost always means to read through carefully or study in detail. The related noun is *perusal*.

. . . I had wisely invested the time required to peruse it from cover to cover.
Canadian Journal of Sociology 14.2 (1989): 230

[They] submitted two documents for the cabinet's perusal: Kennedy's judgment and a written argument from Robinette. The cabinet took five months to make up its mind.
Jack Batten *Robinette* 1984: 206

Having briefly perused your letters to the editor, I was both alarmed and outraged by the comments of one writer.
Vancouver Sun 7 July 1990: D23

(In newspaper writing *peruse* is often used in its more recent sense, to look through quickly.)

The book is arranged in two-page spreads, with drawings on one side and text on the other. Readers can plow from cover to cover or peruse randomly.
Vancouver Sun 17 Nov. 1990: D17

(Here *peruse* suggests reading in a casual manner.)

Peterborough, Peterboro   see -BURGH, -BURG, -BOROUGH, -BORO

ph   see F, PH

phantasy   see FANTASY

pharisee   The *Pharisees* were members of an ancient Jewish sect characterized as very strict and spiritually superior. Since the 1500s *pharisee* has been used to refer to any self-righteous or hypocritical person. The adjective form is *pharisaic(al)*. *Pharisee* should be capitalized when referring to the ancient sect and uncapitalized in its figurative sense.

> That religious practices could become harmful addictions might initially strike one as paradoxical. Yet the lives of the Pharisees quickly come to mind as graphic examples. . . .
> *Mennonite Brethren Herald* 7 March 1986: 29

> Political pharisees in Victoria and Ottawa still wrestle with the 'morality' of attempting to address street kids and prostitutes in their own earthy language and imagery—a decision that gave Jesus Christ no second thoughts.
> *Vancouver Sun* 3 Jan. 1990: A11

> In the mid-nineteenth century, the use of anesthetics in childbirth was denounced as impious. The then head of the Anglican Church [Queen Victoria], a forthright and fecund woman, accepted anesthesia in her deliveries and the Pharisees were routed.
> *Globe and Mail* (Toronto) 8 March 1985: P7

(Here *pharisees*, uncapitalized, would be preferable.)

phase, faze   A *phase* is a stage. Things can be *phased in*, meaning introduced by stages, or *phased out*, meaning withdrawn or taken out of production in stages.

If you are *fazed* by something, you are daunted or perturbed by it. *Faze* is an informal variant of the obsolete word *feeze*, meaning put to flight. Because the word *phase* is more common, *faze* is sometimes misspelled *phase*.

> Thirty-five millimetre projectors will eventually be phased out and replaced with digital projectors.
> *National Post* (Toronto) 10 June 2006: FP1

> Occasional power failures in the seniors' building where [she] lives don't faze her, but they're inconvenient if she wants to get down from her 17th-floor apartment.
> *Gazette* (Montreal) 13 Dec. 1990: D9

> 'Like many hopeful people, Gilbert isn't phased by bad news.'
> *Canadian Fiction Magazine* 63 (1988): 38

(The correct spelling here is *fazed*.)

phat   see F, PH

phenomenon, phenomena, phenomenons   The singular is *phenomenon*, the plural *phenomena*. However, the *OED* cites uses of *phenomena* as a singular noun as far back as 1576. In speech *phenomena* is often used as a singular ('a strange phenomena'), and it can occasionally be found in edited prose. However, unlike *agenda* and *candelabra*—formal Latin plurals whose use as singular nouns is now accepted—*phenomena* is not recognized as a singular.

Phenomenons is sometimes used as the plural, especially in reference to exceptional or remarkable people, but *phenomena* is more widely accepted.

> It would be hard to improve upon the clear logical image which Shakespeare has given us here of the unique character of language as a phenomenon among other phenomena of the world. . . .
> R. A. Wilson *The Birth of Language* 1937: 152

> 'I have never seen this phenomena emerge as strongly as it has this year.'
> *Leader-Post* (Regina) 22 July 2003: B1

('This' indicates the singular; thus *phenomenon* should be used here.)

> As space shuttle photography has made clear, political boundaries are unnatural phenomenons.
> *Financial Post* 21 June 1989: 1

(In formal writing the recommended plural is *phenomena*.)

See also AGENDA; CANDELABRUM; CRITERION.

Philippines, Philippine, Filipino, Filipina   The country is the *Philippines*. The adjective form is *Philippine* or *Filipino* (also spelled *Pilipino*). Citizens are *Filipinos*; a woman or girl from the Philippines may be called a *Filipina*. *Filipino* is the language.

The discrepancy between the spelling of the country and the nationality is confusing. The Philippines was named after Felipe II, the sixteenth-century Spanish king. The English name of the country is based on the English version of that monarch's name: Philip. The word *Filipino* is a direct borrowing from Spanish, while the alternative spelling *Pilipino* is Filipino.

philistine   The *Philistines* were a tribe in ancient Palestine characterized as barbaric by their enemies, the Israelites. In figurative use a *philistine* is any person who disdains cultural pursuits, who is materialistic and smug. *Philistine* is also used as an adjective. Both the adjective and the noun should be capitalized only in references to the ancient Philistines.

> These people are traditionally known as philistines and the only thing they collect is interest on their money.
> *Globe and Mail* (Toronto) 4 May 1985: A1

> People who don't know about art but know what they like make philistine cheap shots that pass in some circles as wit but which are really profound revelations of ignorance.
> *Vancouver Sun* 24 March 1990: A13

> If he is revolutionary, the poet in him may have to argue with a Philistine materialist also in him who does not really see the point of poetry at all.
> Northrop Frye *The Bush Garden* 1971: 133

(Here *philistine*, uncapitalized, would be preferable.)

phishing   see F, PH

phobia, mania   In medical terms, a *phobia* is a morbid, incapacitating fear and a *mania* is an excited madness. In common use, however, these meanings are somewhat attenuated: a *phobia* is an irrational fear and a *mania* is a craze or desire for something. The plurals are *phobias* and *manias*.

> Fear of motherhood. You don't have to be single to be susceptible to the new phobias surrounding

dependence and commitment.
> *Chatelaine* June 1986: 107

> What with the puritan mania for health and exercise driving all before it, the smokers' style is beginning to look corny, definitely out of the past.
> *Globe and Mail* (Toronto) 12 Jan. 1985: E22

phone, call, ring   *Phone* is the accepted clipped form of *telephone*, but *telephone* is more common and appropriate in formal writing. Canadians usually talk *on the phone*; *over the phone* is less common. *By phone* is used mainly when referring to a procedure carried out using the telephone: 'I ordered the tickets by phone'. Canadians refer to the action of contacting a person by telephone (or cellular telephone) as *calling*, *phoning*, or, especially in speech, *giving someone a call*, but they rarely use the British and Australian expressions *ring* and *ring up*. Unlike Canadians, the British do not commonly use the verb *call* to mean *telephone*.

phony, phoney   Canadian writers use these two spellings about equally. Though some dictionaries and usage guides label *phon(e)y* informal or slang, its use in formal and academic prose is incontestable. If you prefer the *phony* spelling, the plural is *phonies*; if you choose *phoney*, the plural can be either *phonies* or *phoneys*.

> But this was the phony war.
> William Teatero *John Anderson: Fugitive Slave* 1986: 47

> If our experience is limited, we can be roused to enthusiasm . . . by something that we can later see to have been second-rate or even phoney.
> Northrop Frye *The Educated Imagination* 1963: 44

> Gretzky and the entire Edmonton Oiler team . . . were called phonies and undeserving of their vaunted status.
> *Globe and Mail* (Toronto) 24 May 1985: M7

> Immigration officials say that's because phoneys have stopped applying for refugee status.
> *Gazette* (Montreal) 6 May 1989: B1

See also -Y, -EY.

photos   see -OS, -OES

phrasal verbs   A phrasal verb consists of a verb combined with one or two prepositions, which in this context are often called particles. The phrase functions as a single word with a sense distinct from the literal meaning of each word on its own. For example, the sense of *go out* is different in 'She went out the door with Sam' and 'She went out with Sam for two years'. In the second sentence, *went out (with)* is a phrasal verb meaning dated.

Occasionally writers will hyphenate phrasal verbs, presumably because they have seen the noun and adjective forms of these verbs hyphenated. Note that 'They break up often' needs no hyphen, but in 'Their break-up (*or* breakup) was final' the two words must be hyphenated or joined; similarly, 'He backs up his players', but 'The back-up group is great'.

Modifiers formed from phrasal verbs are almost always hyphenated ('I think the calibre of play is better in *play-off* season'), while nouns formed from phrasal verbs are either hyphenated or solid ('I watch the NHL *play-offs/playoffs*'). A noun compound should be written with a hyphen if its form might be confusing without one. Compounds formed with *-in* are almost always hyphenated: *break-in, cave-in, shut-in*. And noun compounds with *-on* are usually hyphenated: *carry-on, slip-on, turn-on, walk-on*. Perhaps this is because *-in* and *-on* are common word endings. Compounds formed with *-out*, on the other hand, are usually written as one word: *burnout, handout, takeout*. And nouns formed with *-over*, *-off*, and *-up* are quite often written without a hyphen: *carryover, makeover, pushoff, takeoff, breakup, setup*. A hyphen is recommended when the first word in the compound has more than one syllable: *cover-up, follow-through*.

They line-up 40 strong at the try-outs hoping to run laps if Andy doesn't like the way they threw a ball or dogged it on the way to first after popping up.
Province (Vancouver) 19 Aug. 1990: 63

(The phrasal verb is two words, *line up*; *line-up* is the noun form.)

Subsidies . . . cause overproduction of food in certain places, rip-off consumers and taxpayers, and drive farmers off the land.
Financial Post 10 April 1989: 16

(The slang phrasal verb required here is two separate words, *rip off*; *rip-off* or *ripoff* is the noun form.)

Const. Kevin O'Neil said the woman was arrested by the officer, who called for back up.
Windsor Star 23 Feb. 2006 A4

(The noun form required here is usually treated as a solid compound, *backup*, or hyphenated, *back-up*.)

He was appointed deputy director of the CIA in 1972, just a few weeks before the breakin at the Watergate Hotel that was to bring down Mr. Nixon's presidency.
Globe and Mail (Toronto) 1 April 1985: P11

(The usual form is *break-in*.)

Members . . . that could have done the translation were no doubt suffering from burn-out already.
Fuse Magazine 13.4 (1990): 11

(The usual noun form is a solid compound, *burnout*.)

When followthrough cannot be guaranteed, it is better to do more than promised rather than less than expected.
Globe and Mail (Toronto) 18 Nov. 1985: B12

(The recommended spelling is *follow-through*.)

See also IDIOMS.

phrase   see entry in Glossary

phreaking   see F, PH

phylum   see SPECIES

piano   see COLLOQUIAL; -OS, -OES

picnicker   see -C, -CK

pidgin, creole   A *pidgin*, sometimes misspelled *pigeon*, is a simple language used for communication by two or more groups who do not share a language. For example, Chinook Jargon was a pidgin spoken by the many Aboriginal groups along the Pacific coast of North America, from California to Alaska, and by the Europeans and Asians who came into contact with them—in the sea otter hunt, in logging, in trade, and in the gold rush. Chinook Jargon, which is a mixture of two Aboriginal languages, Nootka and Chinook, with English and French, was used as a lingua franca until the early twentieth century. Some of its expressions have passed into English, including *muckety-muck* (also *muckymuck*, *muck-a-muck*), 'important person', and *saltchuck*, 'ocean'.

Children who grow up hearing mainly pidgin learn it as their first language. A pidgin that becomes the first language of a generation of speakers is called a *creole*. A creole rapidly develops additional vocabulary, more complex grammatical structures, and greater stylistic flexibility. An example is Jamaican Creole English. The West Africans brought to Jamaica as slaves spoke a variety of languages and were forced to develop a pidgin to communicate with their masters and with each other. Their children transformed this pidgin language into a creole.

The speakers of a creole are often subjected to social pressure to 'decreolize', or make their language conform more closely to the standard version of the colonial language. But sometimes the speakers of a creole assert their pride in their culture by accentuating the differences between their language and the dominant one. This tendency is called 'hypercreolization'; the lyrics of rap music are an example of the hypercreolization of Black English in the United States.

> And so, as the sun sinks slowly into the saltchuck, we bid farewell to Maggie Tefler, friend of fallen womanhood.
> Margaret Laurence *The Diviners* 1974: 307

See also ACCENT, DIALECT; LINGUA FRANCA.

pièce de résistance   see COUP DE GRÂCE

piercèd   see DIACRITICAL MARKS

pigeon, dove   Pigeons and doves belong to the same family, Columbidae. The common names of individual species may contain either *pigeon* or *dove*: 'band-tailed pigeon', 'mourning dove'. *Pigeon* is the word generally chosen to describe the sometimes annoying birds that flock in public squares and roost in gables. *Dove* is the more poetic word, connoting peace and, in Christian belief, symbolizing the Holy Spirit.

> Now, St. Mark's Square is flooded about 100 times each winter, forcing the pigeons to the filigreed stone of the cathedral's spires. . . .
> *Bon Vivant* Feb.–Mar. 1983: 11

> The dove designates the pavilion as a place of peace.
> *United Church Observer* May 1986: 18

See also PIDGIN, CREOLE.

pinch-hit, pinch-hitter   In baseball, someone who *pinch-hits* goes to bat for another player. A *pinch-hitter* is a better batter than the player who is replaced. In figurative use, however, a person who pinch-hits for someone else is brought in as a substitute in an emergency. Some language commentators and baseball fans complain that the figurative use ignores the idea of the pinch-hitter's superiority. Nonetheless, the figurative sense is popular, common, and recognized by dictionaries.

Pitch-hitter is sometimes mistakenly used for *pinch-hitter*; a *pinch-hitter* goes in to bat in a *pinch*.

> I was sent to Paris in January 1962 to pinch-hit for Jules while he was convalescing in southern France. . . .
> George Ignatieff *The Making of a Peacemonger* 1987: 199

> Eftodie, who agreed to pinch-hit in an interview because the restaurant owner was away getting supplies, said high gasoline prices that discourage people from heading out on the highway are the biggest problem at Penny's.
> *Leader-Post* (Regina) 20 Feb. 2006: B2

> With the bases loaded, Richmond sent pitch-hitter Luis Lopez and his .355 to the plate.
> *Ottawa Citizen* 26 April 1994: F2

(The usual expression is *pinch-hitter*.)

pinnacle   see EPITOME

Pinyin, Wade-Giles Several attempts have been made to convert Chinese writing into the Roman alphabet. Pinyin, the system developed by the government of the People's Republic of China and officially adopted in 1958, is now the system most widely used and recognized worldwide. It should be noted, however, that for both linguistic and political reasons, Pinyin is still not fully accepted in Hong Kong and Taiwan.

Pinyin combines roman letters and accents; the accents, which distinguish tones, are often dropped in English. *Pinyin* means 'spelling by sound' in Chinese, but spoken Chinese varies greatly from region to region. Pinyin represents the sound of the official standard spoken language of mainland China (Putonghua). English speakers should note that Pinyin is a system of transliteration rather than anglicization. In other words, the relationship between letters and sounds in Pinyin is not always the same as it is in English.

Some common Chinese family names in Pinyin illustrate major differences in the English and Pinyin letter-sound correspondences:

Li is pronounced *LEE*
Qi is pronounced *CHEE*
Xu is pronounced *SHOO*
Wang is pronounced *WONG*
Zhang is pronounced *JONG*
Cai rhymes with *hi* and the initial *c* is pronounced like the *ts* in *hats*

Formerly, English speakers were more familiar with the Wade-Giles (W-G) system of transliteration. 'I Ching', for example, is a Wade-Giles conversion, whereas 'Yi Jing' is Pinyin; 'Mao Tse-tung' is a Wade-Giles conversion, whereas 'Mao Zedong' is Pinyin. Today in academic writing and library records, the Pinyin system is preferred; yet well-known, older renditions of Chinese names (Confucius, Chiang Kai-shek) and places (Peking) are still widely acknowledged.

See also CHINA; CHINESE NAMES; MANDARIN.

pique see PEAK

pistol see GUN

pitiful, pitiable, piteous   All three words can mean evoking pity. In addition, *pitiful* and *pitiable* are sometimes applied to people or things that arouse a mixture of pity and contempt. These two words also mean meagre or negligible; this last sense is related to the previous ones, because something meagre or inadequate may arouse either pity or contempt. The word *piteous* is less common; it often describes sounds such as cries or sobbing, and rarely expresses disdain.

The first thing that occurs to you as you enter the camp is that the walls and the watchtowers are lower than you had imagined—a pitiful reminder of how powerless the inmates were.
Globe and Mail (Toronto) 29 April 1985: P7

[The Tories] had become, at least last autumn, a kind of national joke, somehow transformed from triumphant conquerors into rather pitiful incompetents.
Saturday Night Feb. 1986: 5–6

According to Martin Kenny, an agricultural researcher at Cornell University who has been studying the impact of the new reproductive technologies on Third World countries, the benefits go to a pitiful few.
Harrowsmith Oct.–Nov. 1985: 46

(Here *pitiful* means meagre.)

Here Holtby and his family came upon a pitiable sight: a horse had struggled to the top only to drop dead of exhaustion, the ants and hawks already transforming the cadaver into a skeleton.
Pierre Berton *The Promised Land* 1984: 131

The colonialists imposed foreign religions and taxes on the natives, brought diseases with them, introduced forced labor at pitiable wages and destroyed family units with alcohol in one hand and the Bible in the other.
Vancouver Sun 13 Aug. 1990: A7

(Here *pitiable* means meagre.)

When no human audience ventured within earshot [of my recorder playing], I entertained dogs on the beach at David Bay, oblivious to their piteous howls.
Vancouver Sun 30 Aug. 1993: A3

Pittsburgh see -BURGH, -BURG, -BOROUGH, -BORO

placable see -ABLE, -IBLE

-place see -WHERE

place names The Canadian Permanent Committee on Geographical Names regulates place names and standardizes their spelling. It issues the *Gazetteer of Canada* series, the authoritative source for the spellings of Canadian place names, and posts this information on the Government of Canada website *Geographical Names of Canada / Toponymie du Canada* <geonames.nrcan.gc.ca>.

Even Canadians often stumble over the pronunciation of Canadian place names. Some names look French but are pronounced as if English: Bienfait, SK (*BEEN fate*). Other place names look French but are of Aboriginal origin: Shemogue, NB (*SHIM oh GWEE*); Esquimalt, BC (ess KWEYE malt). Sometimes the same place name is pronounced differently in different provinces: Dalhousie, NS (*dal HOW zee*) and Dalhousie, ON (*dal HOO zee*). A useful list of Canadian place names with pronunciations that might give a news reader pause can be found in *NewsTalk: The Definitive Guide to TV, Radio and Online Journalism* published by the Canadian Press.

Though we might like the names on our maps to stay the same, place names do change. In Canada, some Aboriginal place names have been restored: *Auyuittuq* National Park was formerly *Baffin Island* National Park. In India, *Mumbai* recently became the official name of that country's most populous city. (The former name, *Bombay*, has not been completely supplanted: it is still in use in some local institutions such as the *Bombay Stock Exchange*, and is still preferred by some groups within the country.) The country once named *Burma* by its British colonial rulers was renamed *Myanmar* by a military junta in 1989—this is the name of the country in the Burmese language. Those who oppose the rule of this junta, however, consider calling the country *Myanmar* in English to be a recognition of the junta's authority, and resist it. Thus today both English names, *Burma* and *Myanmar*, remain in use within and outside the country.

When more than one place name seems to be in use, remember that the options often reflect sensitive issues of political struggle and identity: consult widely to ascertain which name is most appropriate to your context.

See also ASIA; ATLANTIC PROVINCES; BALKANS, BALTIC; BOSNIA AND HERZEGOVINA; BRITAIN; CALGARY; CAMBODIA, KAMPUCHEA; COMMA; CAPITAL LETTERS; CARIBOO; GLOUCESTER, WORCESTER; HUDSON BAY; INCLUSIVE LANGUAGE; IRELAND; NORTHWEST TERRITORIES; NUNAVUT, NUNAVUMMIUT, DENENDEH; QUEBEC; SAHARA; SAINT JOHN, ST. JOHN'S; SAULT, THE SOO; SCANDINAVIAN; ST., STE.; SLOVAKIA, SLOVENIA; UKRAINE; WEST INDIES, CARIBBEAN; YUKON.

plaid see TARTAN

planets see EARTH

plateau, plateaux see PLURALS

platonic The adjective that refers to the philosopher Plato and his teachings is capitalized: *Platonic*. Uncapitalized, *platonic* is usually part of a phrase such as 'platonic friendship' or 'platonic relationship', where it means non-sexual. Occasionally *platonic* is used more generally to mean idealistic or visionary but impractical.

> Sceptics had previously criticized Platonic claims to know entities that lie beyond the world of sense experience. . . .
> *Queen's Quarterly* 95.3 (1988): 595

> Ackroyd parts company with previous Dickens biographers who conjecture that this was a decidedly un-Victorian sexual relationship, arguing theirs was a platonic, though no doubt, passionate, affair.
> *Vancouver Sun* 22 Dec. 1990: D19

> For the next few months, she and I became 'friends' in what, for me, was a painfully platonic relationship.
> *Chatelaine* April 1986: 150

Platonism see -ISM

platypuses   see -US

play down   see DOWNPLAY

play-off, playoff   see PHRASAL VERBS

playwright, playwriting   A person who writes plays is a *playwright*, not a *playwrite*. A *wright*, as in *wheelwright* or *shipwright*, is someone who designs or builds things; the term is now obsolete except in combinations.

Though *playwrite* is never used as a finite verb ('She playwrites'), the *-ing* form *playwriting* is common, functioning as an adjective or a noun.

> This warm and moving story won the 1988 Alberta Culture playwriting award.
> *Leisure Life* 1988: 58

> . . . PWM, widely recognized as Canada's premier play development centre, is now celebrating its 25th year in the business of encouraging and promoting Canadian playwriting.
> *Gazette* (Montreal) 4 March 1988: H4

> Playwriter/actress Denise Clarke talks about the curious bird/human love affair and the avian sanctuary on Thursday. . . .
> *Times-Colonist* (Victoria) 16 Feb. 2005: A2

> (*Playwright* is preferred.)

See also COPYRIGHT.

plead, pleaded, pled, plead   In Canadian English the past tense and past participle of *plead* are usually *pleaded* and occasionally *pled* or *plead* (pronounced PLED). *Pleaded* is the safest choice for formal use, since some commentators label *pled* regional dialect and many dictionaries do not even list the spelling *plead* for the past tense or participle.

> The Nova Scotia Judicial Council clearly stated in 1989 that Judge ——, who pleaded guilty to an assault on his wife, could not deal impartially with similar cases in his court.
> Andrew Heard *Canadian Constitutional Conventions* 1991: 124

> He pled the pup's case with every possible airline. . . .
> *Edmonton Journal* 23 July 1994: D4

> He plead not guilty at a July appearance and a trial date was set for the fall.
> *Ottawa Citizen* 27 Oct. 1990: I6

> (Few dictionaries list the past tense *plead*.)

See also PLEAD GUILTY.

plead guilty, plead not guilty, plead innocent   The established phrases in Canadian courts are *plead guilty* and *plead not guilty* or *enter a not-guilty plea*. The popular expression *plead innocent*, criticized by some usage guides, is rarely found in Canadian writing, whether legal or journalistic.

> He had earlier confessed to the crimes but pleaded not guilty.
> *Mennonite Brethren Herald* 7 March 1986: 27

> Michael O'Shaughnessy said his client . . . will plead innocent to a first-degree murder charge when he appears in provincial court in Brockville Friday.
> *Ottawa Citizen* 21 March 1990: B2

> (The technically correct expression *plead not guilty* is preferable in court reporting.)

See also PLEAD, PLEADED, PLED, PLEAD.

pled   see PLEAD; PLEAD GUILTY

plenitude   *Plenitude* means abundance. *Plentitude* is a rare variant that, although sometimes found in print, is considered an error by most authorities. *Plenitude* is labelled literary or formal by some dictionaries and guides, but it is found fairly often in Canadian journalism.

> One thing they do take advantage of is Quebec City's plenitude of eateries.
> *Financial Post* 1 Nov. 1990: 94

> The road ahead figures to be painful some nights, joyous on others while the Canucks work in a plentitude of unpredictable young talent.
> *Vancouver Sun* 24 Oct. 1990: F1

> (The usual spelling is *plenitude*.)

pleonasm   see WORDINESS

plethora   In the 1500s *plethora* (pronounced PLETH *or uh*) was a medical term for an excess of body fluid; by 1700 *plethora* referred to any excessive fullness. Dictionaries still consistently define a *plethora* as a superfluity or overabundance, but Canadians commonly use the word to mean simply a lot, or a wealth, and they use it as often with positive connotations as with negative ones.

When the phrase 'a plethora of' is followed by a plural noun ('a plethora of examples'), the verb that follows may be singular or plural, depending on whether the writer views the 'plethora' as a unit or as a collection of individual items.

> In addition to many useful maps and a chronology of events, it contains a plethora of primary source material both in the text and in a very useful 104 pages of appendices. . . .
> *Canadian Journal of History* 14.1 (1989): 144

(Here *plethora* means wealth and has a positive connotation.)

> The plethora of different rules and exemptions have . . . resulted in double taxation and excessive compliance costs at all levels of business.
> *Financial Post* 28 Nov. 1990: 17

(Here the connotations of *plethora* are negative. Also note the plural verb *have*; *has* would also be correct.)

See also AGREEMENT, GRAMMATICAL; COLLECTIVE NOUNS.

plow, plough   *Plow* is the usual spelling of both the noun and the verb in Canadian newspapers, but *plough* is common in other types of writing. *Plow* is almost non-existent in British English, and *plough* is almost non-existent in modern U.S. English.

> . . . now the plow cuts below the topsoil to expose the rocks that prevent a more luxuriant growth.
> *Vancouver Sun* 2 June 1990: D20
> Readers can plow from cover to cover or peruse randomly.
> *Vancouver Sun* 17 Nov. 1990: D17

> The chilled steel plough was ideal for turning the tough sod of the Canadian prairie.
> Pierre Berton *The Promised Land* 1984: 13

> . . . I ploughed on through the rest of the paper without a second thought.
> *NeWest Review* Oct.–Nov. 1989: 20

plexus   see -US

plop   see ONOMATOPOEIA

plurality   see MAJORITY

plurals, regular, irregular, foreign   The regular English plural simply adds *-s* to the singular noun: *apple, apples*. However, there are several general categories of exception to the rule.

If the singular form ends in *-s* (or *-x*, *-sh*, or *-ch*), *e* is added before the *s*: *buses, the Joneses, successes; foxes; lashes; benches*. But note *stomachs*: when *-ch* is pronounced as *k*, no *e* is added.

If the singular ends in *-y* preceded by a consonant, the *y* becomes *i* and *-es* is added to make the plural: *pony, ponies; spy, spies*. Proper names are exceptions to this rule: 'the three Marys', 'the Hornbys'. Words ending in a vowel plus *-y* form regular plurals: *days, pulleys*.

If the singular ends in *-f* or *-fe*, the plural ending is sometimes *-ves*: *loaf, loaves; knife, knives*. See -F, -V-.

Three nouns add *-(r)en* to form the plural: *brethren, children, oxen*.

Many nouns referring to animals and fish have the same form in the singular and plural, including *cod, deer, moose, salmon, sheep*.

Some nouns change the vowel to make the plural: *foot, feet; goose, geese; man, men; tooth, teeth; woman, women*.

If the singular ends in *-o*, usually the plural is formed by adding *-s* (*banjos*), but some words require *-es* (*heroes*). See -OS, -OES.

Compound nouns generally form the plural in the usual way by adding *-s* at the end: *babysitters, mail carriers, has-beens*. However, if a noun referring to a person forms the first element of a compound, it is usually pluralized: *passers-by, daughters-in-law, governors general, poets laureate*.

The lists below contain common words borrowed from foreign languages that often, especially in formal or technical writing, form their plurals as they would in the source language.

• *Latin plurals*

Most English words derived from Latin form their plurals in the regular way, by adding *-s* or *-es*, and this is the safest choice if you are in doubt (see also -US). However, there are some Latin borrowings that still form their plurals according to the rules of Latin, at least in formal contexts:

– singular ends in *-a*, plural in *-ae*: *alumna, alumnae; formula, formulae; larva, larvae*

– singular ends in *-ex* or *-ix*, plural in *-ices*: *appendix, appendices; cortex, cortices; index, indices; matrix, matrices*

– singular ends in *-um*, plural in *-a*: *addendum, addenda; bacterium, bacteria; compendium, compendia; cranium, crania; crematorium, crematoria; curriculum, curricula; datum, data; medium, media; memorandum, memoranda; quantum, quanta; spectrum, spectra; stratum, strata*

– singular ends in *-us*, plural in *-i*: *alumnus, alumni; bacillus, bacilli; cactus, cacti; crocus, croci; focus, foci; fungus, fungi; gladiolus, gladioli; narcissus, narcissi; nucleus, nuclei; papyrus, papyri; radius, radii; stimulus, stimuli; streptococcus, streptococci; stylus, styli; syllabus, syllabi; terminus, termini; uterus, uteri*

– singular ends in *-us*, plural in a vowel plus *-ra*: *corpus, corpora; genus, genera, opus, opera*

• *Greek plurals*

– singular ends in *-sis* (pronounced *-siss*), plural in *-ses* (pronounced *-seez*): *antithesis, antitheses; axis, axes; basis, bases; crisis, crises; ellipsis, ellipses; hypothesis, hypotheses; metamorphosis, metamorphoses; oasis, oases; parenthesis, parentheses; synopsis, synopses; thesis, theses*

– singular ends in *-a*, plural in *-ata*: *lemma, lemmata; schema, schemata; stigma, stigmata*

– singular ends in *-on*, plural in *-a*: *criterion, criteria; phenomenon, phenomena*

• *French plurals*

– singular ends in *-eau, -eu, -iau*, plural adds *-x*: *beau, beaux; bureau, bureaux; château, châteaux; fabliau, fabliaux; milieu, milieux; plateau, plateaux; tableau, tableaux*

– singular ends in *-s*, plural is unchanged: *chamois, chassis, corps, faux pas, patois*

• *Italian plurals*

– singular ends in *-o*, plural in *-i*: *concerto, concerti; graffito, graffiti; maestro, maestri; paparazzo, paparazzi; virtuoso, virtuosi*

See also ALUMNUS, ALUMNA, ALUMNI, ALUMNAE; APOSTROPHE; BACTERIUM; BASES; BEAU; BEER; BÊTE NOIRE; BICEPS; BONA FIDES; BUS; CACTUS; CANDELABRUM; CARIBOO, CARIBOU; CATASTROPHE; CONCERTO; CRITERION; CURRICULUM VITAE; DAIS; DATA; -F, -V-; -FUL; GLADIOLUS; GENIUS; GRAFFITI; HORS D'OEUVRE; INUKSHUK; LOONIE; MAPLE LEAF; MEDIUM; MEMORANDUM; MONEY; OCTOPUS; -OS, -OES; PAPARAZZO, PAPARAZZI; POSSESSIVE; REFERENDUM; RHINOCEROS; STRATUM; -US; -Y, -IES.

plus Some commentators condemn *plus* in any context other than the arithmetical. However, *plus* is standard when it means 'as well as' or 'in addition to'. Note that this usage does not affect the number of the verb: 'The rent from the basement apartment plus her pension is (*not* are) what she lives on'.

There are two common disputed usages. One is to equate *plus* with *and* and use it as a conjunction: 'She goes to school plus she has kids'. The other is the use of *plus* to mean *besides* or *besides which*: 'I don't want to invite him because his ex-girlfriend will be here; plus I just don't like him.' These two uses of *plus* are informal and should be avoided in formal writing.

Plus is also used as a noun meaning advantage ('Experience is a plus'); *pluses* is the usual plural.

. . . our games reduce almost to formula: physical readiness plus emotional readiness equals victory.
Ken Dryden *The Game* 1983: 183

The master bedroom, with en suite bathroom, plus a third bedroom are located on the third floor.
Vancouver Sun 30 Nov. 1990: E5

(Here the plural verb '*are* located' indicates that *plus* is being used as a conjunction. In formal writing, where this use is unacceptable, *and* should replace *plus*.)

. . . this one offers discount deals at retail establishments, and sells for only $10, plus it's easy to find everywhere.
Province (Vancouver) 18 Dec. 1990: 40

(*Plus* is often used to join clauses in newspaper writing. Here it allows the writer to avoid repeating *and*, but this use is avoided in formal writing.)

'It's much easier to pack and travel once, plus you don't have to pay high mileage charges,' she said.
Calgary Herald 2 July 1994: E1

(This use of *plus* to mean *besides* is informal.)

See also AGREEMENT, GRAMMATICAL; TOGETHER WITH.

p.m.   see TIME

podium   see DAIS

poets laureate   see PLURALS, REGULAR, IRREGULAR, FOREIGN

pogey, unemployment insurance, UI, UIC, employment insurance, EI   *Pogey* is a Canadian slang expression referring to welfare payments or insurance benefits for the unemployed. *Pogey* was originally used to refer to the hostels and relief centres set up for the unemployed during the Great Depression, as well as the food, clothing, shelter, or payments doled out to the needy. Unemployment benefits were also formerly referred to by the initialism *UI* (or *UIC*, after the Unemployment Insurance Commission). However, in 1996 the official name of the program was changed to *employ-*

ment insurance and *EI* became the popular short form.

Cape Bretoners are a proud people, [and] social programs like pogey and welfare are the last resort.
United Church Observer May 1986: 38

Still, Montreal has more people on pogey than any other reporting area, closely followed by Toronto.
Financial Post 2 Dec. 1991: 3

'Francois and I had a little money from other small projects . . . but we were all on UIC.'
Globe and Mail (Toronto) 15 June 1985: E7

. . . after all, EI allows plant owners to keep a skilled workforce in place for an entire year, while only paying them for periods of seasonal work.
Telegram (St. John's) 10 June 2006

See also BABY BONUS.

point in time, at this   see WORDINESS, VARIATION

poison, toxin, toxic   A *poison* is any substance that can cause death or injury to the living organism into which it is introduced, whereas a *toxin* is a poisonous substance produced by a living organism. Certain bacteria, plants, insects, shellfish, and other organisms produce toxins. For example, salmonella bacteria make a toxin responsible for food poisoning in humans. The adjective *toxic* can refer to either poisons or toxins; thus 'toxic chemicals' are always poisonous but are not necessarily toxins. Few general readers will find the use of *toxin* to mean *poison* disturbing; however, the distinction is worth maintaining in scientific contexts.

The Saguenay River is so highly polluted—partly by heavy metals and other toxins . . . —that whales and other marine life have been poisoned.
Gazette (Montreal) 6 March 1989: A4

(Since heavy metals are not produced by living organisms, it would be is more accurate to refer to them as 'toxic substances'.)

The leak of toxins from an abandoned gold mine

into a river that supplies drinking water . . . rivals the Valdez oil spill off the coast of Alaska, the area's MP says.
Province (Vancouver) 25 Oct. 1990: 31

(Here 'toxic substances' would be more accurate.)

poky, pokey   see -Y, -EY

police officer, cop, policeman, policewoman   Police forces in Canada do not make the military distinction between officers and the ranks; thus any member of a police force is a *police officer* and may be addressed as *officer*. Terms for the various ranks—constable, patrol officer, detective, sergeant, inspector, superintendent, etc.—vary from force to force. *Cop* is informal, but not generally considered offensive. *Police officer* is preferred to *policeman* or *policewoman* as non-sexist usage.

A cop who turned criminologist believes the key to university security is more students patrolling their own campuses.
Vancouver Sun 4 Dec. 1990: A2

The turning point, says Joly, came in 1974 when the Ontario Police Commission abolished the rank of 'policewoman' and required all forces to give women the same starting rank as men—constable.
Ottawa Citizen 15 Aug. 1990: D3

(In Ontario before 1974, *policewoman* designated not only the gender of the police officer, but her particular—low—rank.)

Ottawa's policemen are fitter than their counterparts in the Ontario Provincial Police, the Quebec Police Force and the RCMP.
Ottawa Citizen 15 July 1990: A10

(This statement could suggest to some readers either that there are no women officers on the Ottawa force or that the women officers were not part of the fitness study; *police officers* would be better here.)

Her mentor, who's a policewoman, couldn't make it to last night's Girls Empowerment Mentoring (GEM) workshop in north-end Halifax, but her influence was certainly there.
Daily News (Halifax) 16 May 2006: 7

(Substituting *police officer* for *policewoman* would de-emphasize the mentor's sex; here, however, this was likely just what the writer wanted to stress.)

See also COP; JOB TITLES; SWAT, EMERGENCY RESPONSE TEAM, ERT.

politic, political, polity, politics   In modern English the adjective *politic* means shrewd or prudent when applied to people, and judicious or expedient when applied to actions. *Politic* meant *political* until the eighteenth century; this sense is now found only in the phrase *body politic*, meaning nation or state. The noun *polity* refers to a political organization or government.

When *politics* means political beliefs or sympathies, it usually takes a plural verb ('His politics are different from mine'), but when it means the business of government or public life, it usually takes a singular verb ('Politics is consuming his life').

The Mick Jagger of music magazine interviews is canny and politic, yet impatient with superficial or silly questions.
Queen's Quarterly 92.2 (1985): 268

Many . . . consider it more politic to quietly fire an employee . . . than admit publicly that they have been conned, risking loss of customer confidence or even stockholder liability.
Globe and Mail (Toronto) 26 July 1985: P82

Many subsequent political theorists agreed that moderate property and economic independence are a precondition for a stable polity.
Irving M. Zeitlin and Robert J. Brym *The Social Condition of Humanity* 1991: 100

Wieland's politics in the early 1970s were clearly as nationalist as they were feminist; they were also ecological.
Linda Hutcheon *Splitting Images* 1989: 103

Even politics, although taken seriously by the inhabitants, is a laughing matter for Leacock: Smith the conman rigs the election by circulating the rumour that he has won, and Mariposa, ever sensitive to majority opinion, votes for him en bloc.
Margaret Atwood *Second Words* 1982: 187

political correctness, politically correct
see INCLUSIVE LANGUAGE

political parties see BLEU; CONSERVATIVE; GRIT;
NEW DEMOCRATIC PARTY; PÉQUISTE; SOCIAL CREDIT
PARTY

politics see POLITIC

polyglot *Polyglot*, derived from the Greek for
'many-tongued', is most often used to mean 'of
many languages': a city or a text may be
described as polyglot. An extension of this
meaning to include 'culturally or ethnically
mixed' is becoming common. Some dictionaries list this sense, which seems unobjectionable.
However, the indiscriminate use of *polyglot* to
mean mixture or mishmash is not accepted.

Mr. Vito-Finzi, described as an entrepreneurial
polyglot, was born on a British ship off Australia of
diplomatic Italian and Russian parents.
Globe and Mail (Toronto) 2 Feb. 1985: S12

A note of panic crept into the press reports when
the United States was mentioned: with its polyglot
immigrant masses, it was seen as a mongrel
nation.
Pierre Berton *The Promised Land* 1984: 139

The third in a family of 12 children, Mass was born
on Rachel Street in Montreal, in the modest, polyglot neighborhood made famous by novelist
Mordecai Richler.
Ottawa Citizen 13 Nov. 1993: B5

When Dolores Chew came to Canada from India
at age 20, she said it wasn't as much of a culture
shock because she is 'kind of a polyglot,' a mix of
Indian, Chinese, Irish and French blood.
Gazette (Montreal) 22 Nov. 1993: F1

(Here the emphasis is on cultural rather than
linguistic diversity.)

. . . the volumes of the new building are purer,
larger, and less broken up than the existing abbey,
itself an unusual polyglot of architectural styles.
Gazette (Montreal) 18 Sept. 1993: J3

(Here *polyglot* is used to mean a mixture; *pastiche* would be an acceptable substitute.)

See also LINGUIST.

pom-pom, pompon Canadians prefer the
spelling *pom-pom* (or *pompom*) although *pompon*, ending in *n*, is the older form. The *Globe
and Mail Style Book* recommends *pompon* for the
small tufts on tams and sombreros, clown suits,
and honeymoon cars, and *pom-pom* for the larger balls waved by cheerleaders, but Canadian
writers in general wave these distinctions aside.
Pom-pom is the only accepted spelling for the
anti-aircraft gun.

Among the honored was Vancouver promoter
Murray Pezim, who donned a tartan tam with a
pom-pom.
Financial Post 9 March 1989: 3

In glaring orange skirts and shirts, waving one
orange pompom and one of gold, they dance a
few unsynchronized steps and jump up and down.
Edmonton Journal 20 Feb. 2006: C2

There is a drum-beating, beer-throwing, pompon-
tossing argument in progress south of the border
about the origin of 'the wave.'
Vancouver Sun 20 Oct. 1990: D6

pond While most Canadians think of a *pond*
as a rather small body of still water, in New
England and Newfoundland dialects a pond is
a lake: Canadians who visit Walden Pond in
Massachusetts are often surprised at how big it
is.

ponies See PLURALS, REGULAR, IRREGULAR, FOREIGN

pop see SOFT DRINK

population see QUEBEC ENGLISH

porch, veranda(h), stoop, patio, deck A
porch can be large or small, covered or uncov-
ered. Thus the term *porch* can be applied to the
structures that some people call either *verandas*
or *stoops*. *Veranda* (less often, *verandah*) usually
labels a structure that is quite grand, attached to
a large, elegant house. A *stoop* is always a very
simple, small structure, usually without a roof,
belonging to a modest dwelling.
Patio and *deck* are newer terms describing
more recent additions to domestic architecture.

Unlike porches, they are generally attached to a back or side entrance; neither is normally roofed. A *patio* is usually stone or cement, while a *deck* is made of wood; both are large enough to allow several people to sit in a group.

> I turned to her, thinking she'd gone mad and brought us to a haunted house, for . . . the gabled porch running around all four sides sagged. . . .
> *Queen's Quarterly* 96.2 (Summer 1989): 393

> And then it assailed him again, those smells, [from] a house whose leaning front porch looked as though it was being allowed to rot slowly into the ground.
> *Canadian Fiction Magazine* 63 (1988): 60

> And the sweep of verandah around two or three sides of the house gave architects the opportunity to exaggerate the contrasts of dark and light on the facade, and to unite the house with its garden.
> *Canadian Collector* 21 (1986): 46

> A pot of tea simmers on his wood stove, replenished occasionally with ice water dipped from the lake, 20 metres from his door stoop.
> *Globe and Mail* (Toronto) 6 March 1985: P1

pore, pour   To *pore* over something is to study it or be absorbed in it. This verb is often misspelled *pour*.

> Hundreds of auditors would pore over as many as 10,000 randomly selected tax returns.
> *Ottawa Citizen* 29 May 1990: B8

> Anne's father, Otto Frank (the only one of the eight in hiding to survive), and his Dutch publishers pour over the two versions and decide which sections of each they will include.
> *Orbit* 34.1 (2004): 16–18

(The correct spelling is *pore.*)

port, starboard   *Port* is the left side of a boat or aircraft if one is on board and facing forward; *starboard* is the right. *Starboard* is from the Old English *steorbord*, meaning steering side. Old English boats were always steered by a paddle on the right side, and therefore were moored with the left side of the vessel facing the shore or *port*.

> It was a three-storey structure made of wood siding and had a distinct list to starboard.
> Max Braithwaite *The Night We Stole the Mountie's Car* 1971: 25

(These nautical terms are not applied only to ships; here *starboard* forms part of an extended ship metaphor.)

portable   see QUEBEC ENGLISH

portend, portent, portentous   *Portend* is a verb, usually applied to circumstances rather than people, meaning to presage or foreshadow. *Portent* is a noun referring to an omen or a sign of things to come. *Portentous* is an adjective describing something significant with respect to the future, or something gravely important or ponderous. Occasionally it is used to mean self-important, and it is often misspelled *portentious*—perhaps because of confusion with *pretentious*.

> In Winnipeg . . . the continued marginalization of the city in the national urban hierarchy does not portend a good future for the new middle class and therefore the renewal of the inner city.
> *City Magazine* Spring 1988: 39

> Police and prosecutors say there is no evidence of the childhood abuse that typically portends such adult violence.
> *Toronto Star* 2 July 1994: K6

> Recalling a portent of success, Martin tells of wandering down a Dublin street in 1982. He was confronted by a ragtag youngster who promised luck for a penny.
> *Vancouver Sun* 17 Jan. 1990: A8

> Is there cause for optimism? Ahead on the highway is as strong a portend as any, a sign marking the conclusion of our journey: The town of Hope.
> *Vancouver Sun* 13 Aug. 1994: C1

(The word required here is the noun *portent*.)

> Samuel Black Freeman, defender of Anderson, the man with the portentous name, the victorious counsel in a legal battle of immense significance, nearly evaporates from the pages of history.
> William Teatero *John Anderson: Fugitive Slave* 1986: 170

The commission on Quebec's future began its public hearings yesterday on a grave, even portentous note.
Gazette (Montreal) 7 Nov. 1990: B3

So begins a portentious, compellingly stylish series of events that raises questions that will eventually be answered in a film that meditates on the nature of heroism, faith, fate, and other weighty matters with mixed results.
Times-Colonist (Victoria) 24 Nov. 2000: D1

(The correct spelling is *portentous*.)

portmanteau word   see ABBREVIATION

possessive   The possessive case is marked either by an apostrophe or by an *of* phrase: *Brian's book, the days of the week*. The possessive case (also called the genitive case) is associated with possession in rather a loose sense; in fact, it is used to indicate a wide range of relationships, including description (*a summer's day*) and association (*a writers' club*).

An apostrophe followed by *s* forms the possessive of singular nouns and some pronouns: *the university's administrators, Martha's hat, everyone's answer, Canada's climate, one dollar's worth, a day's income, a year's results, no one's responsibility.*

Traditionally, Classical names ending in *s* are marked possessive with an apostrophe only: *Mars' anger, Herodotus' narrative, Socrates' wisdom*. Similarly, other names that end with an *iz* sound often take only an apostrophe: *Moses' tablets, Jesus' teachings, Bridges' poetry*. However, it is also always acceptable to add *'s* to a name that ends in *s*: *Charles's role, Keats's poetry, Descartes's theory* (in French names such as this, the *s* ending the name is not pronounced).

The possessive of regular plural nouns is formed by adding an apostrophe after the *s* marking the plural: *their parents' lives, the students' vote, the Browns' dog.*

The few English plurals that do not end in *s* add *'s* to indicate the possessive: *the children's party, the men's room, the women's lockers, people's needs.*

Where possession is joint, only the last noun in a series of two or more nouns needs to be marked possessive: *Gilbert and Sullivan's operas* (they wrote them jointly); *John and Mary's children* (they have the same children). Where possession is separate, each noun should be marked possessive, at least in formal writing: 'He is playing a selection of Beethoven's and Mozart's concerti'; 'John's and Mary's children are coming' (they have different children). In speech and informal writing this nicety is seldom observed.

Difficulties sometimes arise with family names, which are pluralized just like other nouns. Thus Mr. Brown, Mrs. Brown, and the Brown children are the Browns. When we visit them, we go to the Browns' house—or just to the Browns'. When the family name ends with *s*, things get a little more complicated. We try to keep up with the Joneses; if we are lucky enough to be invited there, we go to the Joneses'. Some proprietary names ending in *s* contain an apostrophe (*Bollum's Books, McDonald's*) and others don't (*Zellers*). Here the style of the company should be followed. Canadian companies with operations in Quebec dropped the English possessive form from their names in that province to comply with the Charter of the French Language (Bill 101, passed in 1977), which required that public signs be in French only; thus *Eaton's* became *Eaton* in Quebec.

Sometimes, particularly in phrases that express affiliation, such as *citizens' band, teachers' college*, or *veterans' club*, the apostrophe is dropped after a plural noun. The plural noun is treated as an adjective (see ATTRIBUTIVE NOUNS) rather than a possessive. Usage guides are divided on whether this trend should be encouraged. Newspaper style books support omitting the apostrophe here (and in expressions such as *five weeks' work*). More conservative authorities recommend retaining the apostrophe. The official names of organizations reflect the current lack of consensus on this point: *Ontario Secondary School Teachers' Federation, Nova Scotia Music Educators Association.*

In speech it is common and acceptable to add a possessive marker to the end of a clause: *the man who lives next door's dog*. In writing, this construction should be avoided by using an *of* phrase (*the dog of the man who lives next door*) or, perhaps more naturally, by using a participle (*the dog belonging to the man next door*).

Although the possessive is traditionally used with inanimate nouns, especially nouns of place and nouns closely associated with people and their work (*Mercury's orbit, Vancouver's architecture, the hospital's budget*), an *of* phrase is usually preferable in formal writing: *the erosion of the bluff* rather than *the bluff's erosion; the mysteries of economics* rather than *economics' mysteries*.

> Beaune [is] a tasters' dream: any day you can wander into the cellars at a dozen establishments. . . .
> *Bon Vivant* Aug.–Sept. 1982: 10

(The singular *taster's* is required here.)

> Most Canadian's perception of the quality of European wines is nonsense.
> *Bon Vivant* Nov. 1981: 38

(The plural *Canadians'* is required here.)

> Some womens' groups don't feel we've been giving them the kind of material they would like to have.
> *Canadian Baptist* Feb. 1986: 47

(Since *women* is plural, the correct spelling is *women's*.)

> A Saskatchewan library exhibit about Palestinian and South African childrens' art was condemned. . . .
> *Briarpatch* April 1990: 3

(Since *children* is plural, the correct spelling is *children's*.)

> 'When Eaton's, Ogilvy's and Steinberg's and the rest were asked to shed their apostrophes'—one form of Francization stipulated in the bill—'why didn't they just stand together, denounce the law as lunatic, and refuse to comply?'
> *Toronto Star* 26 Sept. 1991: A29

See also APOSTROPHE; CASE; DOUBLE POSSESSIVE; ELSE; FRANCIZATION; ITS, IT'S; PARALLELISM; POSSESSIVE BEFORE GERUND; PRONOUN WITH POSSESSIVE ANTECEDENT; OURS; THEIRS; WHO'S, WHOSE; WORTH; YOUR, YOU'RE, YOURS.

possessive before gerund   When the *-ing* form of the verb is used as a noun, it is usually called a gerund or verbal noun (e.g., '*Running* is his life'). A major usage debate centres on the use of the possessive with the gerund. Some commentators (notably Fowler, 1926 and 1965) argue that the possessive is the only correct possibility (as in 'I worry about *his* running so much on pavement'; '*Jane's* being on the committee has improved matters'). Others have no difficulty with object pronouns and common nouns preceding gerunds ('I worry about *him* running so much on pavement'; '*Jane* being on the committee has improved matters'). In these latter examples, the *-ing* forms are treated as if they were participles, like those in the somewhat clumsier sentences 'Running so much on pavement, he has made me worry' and 'Being on the committee, Jane has improved matters'.

In formal writing, Canadian writers do tend to use possessive pronouns before gerunds. And even in informal writing and speech, the possessive form of pronouns is more likely at the beginning of a sentence. Consider the difference between 'My talking to his sister made him nervous' and 'Me talking to his sister made him nervous'. The latter sentence seems odd, even ungrammatical or uneducated.

When nouns precede gerunds, however, emphasis plays a part in the decision whether to use the possessive form. In 'The committee disapproved of the researcher's collecting rare specimens', the focus is on the collecting; in 'The committee disapproved of the researcher collecting rare specimens', the focus could be on the researcher (with the sentence implying that the committee might not object to a different researcher). Long noun phrases before the gerund are rarely made possessive: 'The emergency brake release sticking was the last straw'.

It appears that writers have always varied their use of the possessive with the gerund according to considerations of formality, emphasis, and sound without much self-torment (unless they have read Fowler) and we suggest they continue to do so.

I think for them my being gay was more difficult

to deal with than my being potentially terminal-
ly ill.
Daniel Gawthrop *Affirmation* 1984: 68

I do not relish our becoming the turkey dinner on
the table of the Americans.
Now Magazine (Toronto) 3–9 Nov. 1988: 8

They seemed not to find anything odd in
Christiane's being in bed and Karen and Heinz's
anxious hovering.
Ann Davis *Somewhere Waiting* 1991: 59

Much of her fiction portrays the awfulness of children's being subjected to their parents' whims.
Janice Kulyk Keefer *Reading Mavis Gallant* 1989: 17

Plainly there was no chance of the union's getting
all it wanted, as there was no chance of the general manager's being able to get away with conceding nothing.
Eugene Forsey *A Life on the Fringe* 1990: 74

This rubbish about the British North America Act's
being 'foreign' and 'imposed' still keeps cropping
up.
Eugene Forsey *A Life on the Fringe* 1990: 156

(Forsey—or his editor—has been particular to
insert the possessive here; few people would
notice if it were dropped.)

I never heard of him going near there.
Howard Engel *Murder Sees the Light* 1984: 102

Robinette said it was okay, he'd admit whatever it
was Smythe was going to testify to without him
going in the box.
Jack Batten *Robinette* 1984: 195

I'd like to see them taking a much larger part in
public life. . . .
Maclean's 10 Feb. 1986: 8

But when did we last hear of a picture being
burned?
Robertson Davies *A Voice from the Attic* 1960: 264

I remember him being sent sprawling by a cow he
was trying to milk. . . .
George Ignatieff *The Making of a Peacemonger*
1987: 34

postal addresses Increasingly, mail is sorted
by machine. If your wedding invitations are
addressed by a calligrapher and sent out in
square rather than rectangular envelopes,
human intervention will definitely be required
at the sorting stage. Machines cannot properly
orient square envelopes, and optical character
readers cannot recognize embellished letters.
Nevertheless, these hypothetical wedding invitations would still be delivered. Recognizing the
exigencies of style, Canada Post does not *dictate*
address style. What follows are its recommendations on the matter.

Addresses should be typed using plain fonts,
or hand printed in capital letters. The postal
code should be written on the same line as the
city and province or territory (which leaves
room below the address for a machine-readable
bar code). Punctuation should be omitted:
abbreviations should be written without periods (ST, RR, APT), and the comma between the
city and the province or territory should be left
out. Diacritics and punctuation marks in proper names are the exception; these (as in ST.
JOHN'S, or TROIS-RIVIÈRES) should be
retained. Provinces and territories should be
identified only with their official two-letter
postal abbreviations (listed in Appendix I). The
standard address format for destinations within
Canada is as follows:

NANCY JONES
126 BLEECKER AVE
BELLEVILLE ON   K8N 3T7

When a street number contains a fraction,
there should be a space between the whole
number and the fraction (126 ½ BLEECKER
AVE), but, if a letter is appended to a street
number, no space intervenes (126B BLEECKER
AVE).

A unit number *precedes* a street number and is
separated from it by a hyphen: 212-1869
ROYAL OAK WAY. Thus, here the *unit* number is
212, and the *street* number is 1869. The traditional format in which a unit number follows
the street name is also acceptable: 1869 ROYAL
OAK WAY APT 212. When a street name *is* a
number, the number of the house and the number of the street should be separated by a space,
not a hyphen: 123 22ND AVE.

Internal delivery information (e.g., SALES
DIRECTOR, BIOLOGY DEPT, FIFTH FLOOR)
should be placed in the line(s) above the street
or postal box address:

JOHN JAMES
SENIOR SOFTWARE DEVELOPER
ACME DIRECT SALES
PO BOX 4001 STN A
VICTORIA BC   V8X 3X4

Street types may be translated from French to English (RUE to ST, CH[emin] to RD, AV to AVE, BOUL to BLVD, etc.) and vice versa. The names of streets, however, are not translatable. Thus, AV DES PINS may be translated to DES PINS AVE, but PINE AVE is not an acceptable alternative.

Great Britain, Australia, and the United States all share the Canadian postal address format. In an international address, the country of destination forms the last line. The postal or zip code should be placed in the line above:

MARIA TALBOT
4417 DEXTER ST NE
WASHINGTON DC   20019-4649
USA

In Continental Europe and Mexico, street numbers typically follow street names, and postal codes precede city names:

MATTHIAS SCHMIDT
MARKTPLATZ 18
97070 WÜRZBURG
GERMANY

Sample English-language address formats for many countries can be found on the Internet (search 'international address formats'). International mail sent from Canada may be addressed in the language of the destination country as long as the last line of the address consists of the name of that country written in full in English—or French.

Additional information, including official postal abbreviations and country names (cross-referenced to geographic and former political names) can be found on the Canada Post website.

postdoctoral, postgraduate   see GRADUATE

posthumous   *Posthumous* means occurring after death. Thus a book published posthumously is published after the death of the author, and a posthumous child is one born after the father has died. The word is pronounced *PAWST yoo muss*.

John Heath's *Aphrodite* . . . is a posthumous collection of poems by a writer who was killed in Korea at the age of thirty-four.
Northrop Frye *The Bush Garden* 1971: 104

postman   see JOB TITLES

potatoes   see -OS, -OES

pothole   see SWAMP

pour   see PORE

poutine   see QUEBEC ENGLISH

power of attorney   see LAWYER

practically, almost   Some usage guides say that *practically* should not be used as a synonym for *almost*, but should be reserved for the sense 'in a practical way', the opposite of 'theoretically'. However, the *OED* records that *practically* was being used to mean *almost* by the mid-1700s. Certainly this is its most common meaning in various types of Canadian writing, including journalism, literary essays, autobiography, biography, and history, as well as in fictional dialogue.

Practically every match was a mismatch.
Globe and Mail (Toronto) 17 Jan. 1985: M10

Practically everybody who habitually reads poetry habitually writes it as well.
Northrop Frye *The Bush Garden* 1971: 56–7

(Here Frye uses *practically* to mean almost.)

The simultaneous influence of two larger nations speaking the same language has been practically beneficial to English Canada, but theoretically confusing.
Northrop Frye *The Bush Garden* 1971: 218

(Here, where Frye uses *practically* to mean 'in a practical way', it stands in contrast to *theoretically*.)

practice, practise   see -CE, -SE

prairie, Prairie provinces   The word *prairie* should not be capitalized when it refers to any flat grassland: 'The sky dominates the prairie landscape'. *Prairie* is capitalized, however, when it refers to a specific region: 'The Prairie electorate sent a clear message to Ottawa'. The term *Prairie provinces* refers to Manitoba, Saskatchewan, and Alberta.

> When I was growing up in the prairies in the mid-twenties and early thirties, we were taught in school that the sunsets of Manitoba were the most spectacular in the world, and we believed it.
> Miriam Waddington *Apartment Seven* 1989: 36

(A capital *P* is recommended for the name of the region.)

> [Separation from the rest of Canada] would leave the prairie Provinces without an outlet to the Western Sea, but that could be a boost for beleaguered Churchill, Manitoba. . . .
> *Ottawa Citizen* 30 June 1994: A9

(Here *Prairie provinces* is recommended.)

Precambrian   see CAPITAL LETTERS; CANADIAN SHIELD

precede   see -CEED, -CEDE, -SEDE

precedence, precedents   *Precedence* means priority, the fact of preceding something else in time, space, or rank. A *precedent* is an earlier occurrence or case that is used as a guide or justification in subsequent cases. *Precedents*, the plural of *precedent*, is sometimes confused with *precedence* because the two words are pronounced the same way.

> The reason is based on precedence: that is, a writer has to write something before a critic can criticize it.
> Margaret Atwood *Second Words* 1982: 11

> The Supreme Court's eventual ruling could set a precedent for other cases, and may help clarify when a jury should be allowed to consider such a controversial defence strategy.
> *Windsor Star* 14 March 2006: A4

> This first panel, however, did establish some precedence for use in the future.
> *Financial Post* 23 Oct. 1989: 3

(The required word here is *precedents*.)

See also INCIDENTS, INCIDENCE.

precipitous, precipitate   *Precipitous* is related to *precipice*; thus 'a precipitous bluff' is a very steep one and 'a precipitous drop in interest rates' is a sharp decline. The adjective *precipitate,* pronounced *pruh SIP i tut,* means sudden or hasty and often implies recklessness. (The verb with the same spelling, pronounced *pruh SIP i TATE,* means to trigger, as in 'New work schedules precipitated the strike', or to condense atmospheric vapour into drops or flakes, as in 'It is definitely precipitating, although it's hard to say whether that's rain or snow'.)

Usage guides have tended to instruct writers not to confuse the adjectives *precipitous* (steep) and *precipitate* (rash), and this advice should still be heeded in formal writing. Cliff faces, however, are dangerous places, strongly associated in people's minds with rashness and drama. *Precipitous* is now so commonly used to mean rash, sudden or ill-considered that the *New Oxford Dictionary* records this meaning without comment.

> . . . the merry-go-round hardly represents cutting-edge technology. It has no sharp curves, no precipitous drops and it never raised a scream from even its youngest riders.
> *Gazette* (Montreal) 9 June 2006: A18

(This is the fully accepted use of *precipitous.*)

> . . . the Prangnell era turned out to be a time of precipitous decline.
> *Saturday Night* May 1986: 13

(Here *precipitous* is used figuratively. This use is fully accepted.)

> He had . . . shocked the Canadian government into precipitate action, and bamboozled everybody into taking part in an adventure whose outcome was uncertain and, for some, would be horrific.
> Pierre Berton *The Promised Land* 1984: 114

precondition

(Here *precipitate* means hasty or rash.)

Thus, although we find compelling both the notion of a fixed maximum life span of 115 years and the notion that the onset of infirmity due to chronic disease can be delayed, we realize that to accept either at the moment may prove to have been precipitous.
Queen's Quarterly 97.1 (1990): 13–14

(Here *precipitous* means too hasty.)

But any precipitous move to speed the withdrawal of U.S. troops could have catastrophic consequences.
National Post (Toronto) 3 June 2006: A17

(Here *precipitous* means sudden and ill-considered.)

precondition *Precondition*, coined in 1825 by Samuel Taylor Coleridge, has become a popular word, especially in the fields of social science and politics. Several usage guides declare the word redundant, arguing that *condition* means the same thing. However, it is not always clear whether a condition is something required before something else can happen or whether it is a necessary coexistent factor. The word *precondition* resolves this ambiguity.

In the tumultuous days of the English civil war, Hobbes produced his Leviathan (1651), a classic study of power as a precondition of social peace.
Irving M. Zeitlin and Robert J. Brym *The Social Condition of Humanity* 1991: 74

(Here *condition* would be ambiguous.)

. . . he argues that a background which is structured by image schemata is an important part of an utterance's meaning, not just a precondition of the utterance's having meaning.
Canadian Journal of Philosophy 19 (1989): 302

(Here *condition* would be ambiguous.)

predate, pre-date see HYPHENATION

predecessor, successor A *predecessor* precedes you; a *successor* takes your place or succeeds you.

By means of language we are also given the opportunity to acquire the socially inherited knowledge and experience of our predecessors—without having to repeat their trials and errors.
Irving M. Zeitlin and Robert J. Brym *The Social Condition of Humanity* 1991: 14

Its membership and income had both dropped, and it had to contend with finding an adequate successor to the dynamic René Lévésque.
Alan Whitehorn *Canadian Socialism* 1992: 213

'Of course, in five years it's possible that my predecessor will say that we can't afford noble sentiments such as these.'
Queen's Journal (Kingston) 14 Sept. 1993

(Here *successor* is the word required.)

predicate see entry in Glossary

predict in advance see WORDINESS

predominant, predominate *Predominant* is the adjective that corresponds to the verb *predominate*, just as *dominant* corresponds to *dominate*. However, a surprising number of writers use *predominate* as the adjective, and have done so for at least four centuries, according to the OED. *Predominate* is listed as a variant form of *predominant*—and the adverb *predominately* as a variant form of *predominantly*—in some dictionaries.

Although *predominate* and *predominately* can be found in Canadian writing, the much more common *predominant* and *predominantly* are recommended.

Nova Scotia, predominant producer of yuletide lobster, ships about 360 tonnes each December to France. . . .
Spectator (Hamilton) 23 Dec. 1994: C11

In Ontario, two grapes predominate in ice wine production: vidal and Riesling.
Spectator (Hamilton) 19 Nov. 1994: 21

(Here *predominate* is used correctly as a verb.)

The predominate fuel source of the proposals is natural gas. . . .
Ottawa Citizen 1 March 1990: E12

(Here *predominant* is recommended.)

From a varietal perspective, red wines aged in

wood and made predominately from cabernet sauvignon, pinot noir or syrah/shiraz are good bets.
Vancouver Sun 28 March 1990: C5

(Here *predominantly* is recommended.)

pre-eminent   see IMMANENT

preface   see FOREWORD

prefer   see DOUBLING THE FINAL CONSONANT

prefix, suffix   see PREFIX in Glossary

prejudice, prejudiced   Strictly speaking, a *prejudice* can be either a favourable or an unfavourable opinion, but in actual usage a prejudice is usually negative. A 'negative prejudice' is a prejudice *against* something; a 'positive prejudice' is one *for* or *in favour of*. The word is often misspelled *predjudice*, with a *d* before the *j*.

Occasionally the adjective *prejudiced* is also misspelled without its final *d*, perhaps because it is not clearly audible in speech: 'He's prejudice' instead of 'He's prejudiced'.

I must say that I am strongly prejudiced towards rear-wheel drive. I don't like that lumber wagon feel of a front-wheel-drive car.
Calgary Herald 18 Dec. 1998: F10

(Here *prejudiced towards* means in favour of.)

The protesters had gathered . . . for a rally organized by the Canadian Centre on Racism and Predjudice.
Gazette (Montreal) 10 Nov. 1992: A3

(The correct spelling is *prejudice*.)

première, début   A *première* is the first public performance or the opening of a play, film, work of music, etc. A *début* (pronounced *DAY byoo* or *day BYOO*) is the first public appearance of a performer or the formal entrance into society of a young woman. Normally, only people make débuts. The verb *première*, meaning to open or perform for the first time, is standard.

Although in journalism *début* is used as a verb meaning to make a début, this use is considered unacceptable in more formal contexts, probably because the English verb forms look awkward, cause spelling difficulties, and lead to pronunciations that are far from the original French: *débuts, débuted, débuting* (pronounced *day byoos, day byood*, and *day byoo ing*). Both words often appear without accents, and some dictionaries list the accentless forms first, indicating that they are the most common.

The Toronto Symphony subsequently premiered Alexina Louie's *The Eternal Earth*. . . .
Queen's Quarterly 94.1 (1987): 179

Now the resident ingenue at The Variety Dinner Theatre in Toronto, Shilton debuted in Variety's 1983 smash hit Pump Boys and Dinettes.
Maclean's 10 Feb. 1986: 44

(Here 'made her début' or 'made her first appearance' would be more formal.)

See also FUNCTIONAL SHIFT.

premise, premises, premiss   A *premise* (plural *premises*) is a statement, assumed to be true, that is taken as the starting point of an argument or line of reasoning. *Premiss* (plural *premisses*) is a British spelling variant used occasionally in Canadian scholarly writing. *Premises* is a plural noun referring to a building and grounds. Because *premises* looks like a plural, some people incorrectly assume that there is a singular form, *premise*, for this sense.

The Nemaiah Chilcotins filed suit in B.C. Supreme Court a year ago to stop clearcut logging on the premise that it would destroy their traplines.
Vancouver Sun 18 Dec. 1990: B2

He believes a novel demands acceptance of the writer's premises, 'so I often read the first page of a book many times.'
Vancouver Sun 26 Oct. 1990: P35

Given Descartes' distinction between intuition and deduction . . . and his claim . . . that at least in some cases conclusions can be drawn from premisses in a single 'unclouded' glance, I do not

want to press the notion of proof very hard.
Canadian Journal of Philosophy 19 (1989): 227

At Fifty-Six Gallery . . . the refurbished premises have opened with a group show. . . .
Vancouver Sun 27 Oct. 1990: D10

. . . Rose's production of Krizanc's play . . . [was] staged by Necessary Angel in the Canadian Stage Company's Berkeley Street premise.
Queen's Quarterly 97.3 (1990): 376

(The word required here is *premises*.)

prepackaged   see ANTI-, ANTE-

preposition   see entry in Glossary

preposition at end   The English poet and dramatist John Dryden (1631–1700) is to be blamed for propagating the notion that a sentence should never end with a preposition. Dryden probably got the idea from Latin, where a preposition cannot be the last word in a sentence. Critics of the structure in English call it 'inelegant'. In some cases it is just that. In other cases, however, trying to avoid a final preposition results in noticeable inelegance.

Sometimes a preposition functions as part of a phrasal verb: 'look out', 'move on', 'break up'. In sentences where a phrasal verb ends a sentence, there is no avoiding a preposition at the end: 'We're done for'; 'Come on in'; 'It must be seen to'. Questions such as 'What are you waiting for?' and 'Who is that story by?' can be rephrased as 'For what are you waiting?' and 'By whom was that story written?'; but these alternative constructions sound stilted in all but the most formal contexts.

Prepositions appeared at the end of written English sentences in Old English, and examples can be found in the works of Chaucer, Shakespeare, Milton, Swift, and other famous writers. Although Fowler called the supposed rule a 'cherished superstition', and current usage guides unanimously agree with him that a sentence ending with a preposition is good English, the usage still has its opponents. However, those who oppose this usage on the grounds that good writers have characteristically avoided it haven't a leg to stand on.

We have, then, at least three possible concepts of *standard* to deal with.
W.C. Lougheed ed. *In Search of the Standard in Canadian English* 1986: 34

The court assumes that a minor living at home is provided for.
J.E. Smyth et al. *The Law and Business Administration in Canada* 1987: 175

These are qualities which the more self-advertising poems give little hint of.
Northrop Frye *The Bush Garden* 1971: 69

In the old theatres they had smelly kennels in which to change their clothes. . . . Gentlemen, I appeal to you with all the force of which I am capable: give us back a theatre which it is a pleasure to be in!
Robertson Davies *One Half of Robertson Davies* 1978: 80

(These sentences show Davies using both constructions.)

See also PHRASAL VERBS.

prepositions after verbs   see PHRASAL VERBS

prerequisite   see PERK

prescribe, proscribe   To *prescribe* means to order or direct, or to lay down a rule; to *proscribe* means to condemn, forbid, or outlaw. Laws can both prescribe and proscribe things; this is where confusion may arise.

Zoning by-laws prescribe the use and type of buildings that may be erected in various districts of a municipality. . . .
J.E. Smyth et al. *The Law and Business Administration in Canada* 1987: 570

It was not just the Sun Dance that was proscribed. The more severe and committed Protestant sects on the frontier were opposed to all dancing.
Pierre Berton *The Promised Land* 1984: 216

Ontario natural resources officials, who are conducting the proscribed fire as part of a regular program to clear budworm-destroyed trees, said the burn is tentatively set for next Sunday. . . .
Globe and Mail (Toronto) 16 July 1985: P4

(A fire that is deliberately set by forestry officials must have been *prescribed*.)

War crimes are common law offences, the study said, because they are internationally prescribed offences and 'there is a duty imposed on individuals by international law not to commit war crimes.'
Globe and Mail (Toronto) 12 Feb. 1985: P1

(The word required here is *proscribed*, 'outlawed'.)

preseason   see ANTI-, ANTE-

presentation   see PRESENTIMENT

present incumbent   see INCUMBENT

presently   Some usage specialists maintain that the only acceptable contemporary meaning of *presently* is soon; others, that *presently* can also be used to mean at present, or now. The first group argue that accepting the second meaning may lead to ambiguity—yet all agree that 'now' was the original meaning of the word; the sense 'soon' appeared in the sixteenth century. The *OED* states that *presently* meaning at present has been obsolete in literary English since the seventeenth century, but that it has remained in use in some British dialects and has been revived in the United States in the twentieth century.

Canadian newspaper style guides list 'soon' as the only correct sense, but North American dictionaries list 'at present' as a second meaning. In Canadian usage both senses are found: the more common one is actually 'at present'. Canadian writers need not hesitate to use either sense, but should ensure that the context prevents any ambiguity.

That is a point to which we shall presently return.
Irving M. Zeitlin and Robert J. Brym *The Social Condition of Humanity* 1991: 61

And this selection is, finally, only half the show it should be, but more of that presently.
Globe and Mail (Toronto) 19 Oct. 1985: D13

The presently accepted doctrine of parliamentary privilege . . . appears to be a necessary policy to pursue.
Andrew Heard *Canadian Constitutional Conventions* 1991: 99

In fact, the tone of the book seems more contemporary now than it did in, say, 1971, when it was believed that society could change itself a good deal faster than presently appears likely.
Margaret Atwood *Second Words* 1982: 370

See also MOMENTARILY.

present tense, historical present, literary present   The present tense is often used in English to refer to events in the near future: 'I leave Friday'; 'When is your appointment?'

In both formal and informal English, the present tense is sometimes used to make the recounting of past events seem vivid and immediate: 'The fog is closing in. The children are playing in the water, oblivious. We call to them. . . .' This use is called the historical present.

A convention in literary criticism, sometimes referred to as the *literary present*, is to use the present tense to discuss the action of a story, film, or play. The reasoning is that the story is not over and done with, but may continually be experienced by readers or viewers.

present writer, this writer   Some writers refer to themselves as 'the present writer/author/reviewer' or 'this writer/author/reviewer' in an effort to avoid *I*, *me*, and *my*. Many commentators find such constructions old-fashioned, falsely modest, and overly formal. 'The present writer' and similar phrases are likely to bewilder some readers. The more direct *I* or *me* is recommended.

The present reviewer does not share the surprise, if it is there, but he fully concurs in the admiration.
Northrop Frye *The Bush Garden* 1971: 48

(This sentence sounds quite formal by today's standards, and few readers would object if Frye referred to himself as *I* rather than *the present reviewer* and *he*.)

Although this story . . . and many of my other stories about salmon fishing contain interactions between poachers and law officials, it is in no way the intention of this writer to glorify poachers or

the act of breaking the law.
Atlantic Salmon Journal Summer 1990: 45

(Having written 'my other stories', the author could continue in the first person by writing '*my* intention'. 'This writer' may indicate mock seriousness.)

president-elect see ELECT

prestigious, prestige In the seventeenth century both *prestige* (pronounced *press TEEZH* or *press TEEDJ*) and *prestigious* (pronounced *press TEEJ yus* or *press TIJ yus*) referred to deception and conjuring. In the nineteenth century the meaning of *prestige* shifted and the word came to refer to respect based on a good reputation. *Prestigious* followed a similar transformation, but was not so readily accepted by the critics. Even in the 1980s, some authorities insisted that *prestigious* implied deception and should not be used to mean having a solid reputation or imparting prestige. However, no dictionary supports this antiquated view, and *prestigious* is used with positive connotations in all types of contemporary writing.

To me 'prestigious' means, and always will mean, juggling tricks, because it derives from *praestigiae*, and when it is used in the modern way I feel as though a rusty sword had been thrust into my—well, not perhaps into my heart, but into some sensitive part of my body.
Robertson Davies *One Half of Robertson Davies* 1978: 12–13

. . . we can imagine [most societies] as pyramids: hierarchies of strata with the wealthiest, most powerful and most prestigious at the top, and the impoverished, weak and despised at the bottom.
Irving M. Zeitlin and Robert J. Brym *The Social Condition of Humanity* 1991: 112

Two Vancouver writers are in the running for a prestigious national writing award.
Province (Vancouver) 18 Nov. 1990: 78

presumptive, presumptuous *Presumptive* is almost exclusively a legal or technical term, meaning based on likelihood or reasonably presumed. For example, a 'presumptive diagnosis' is one that is based on a reasoned consideration of the available evidence.

The derogatory term *presumptuous* describes behaviour that is unduly bold or overly familiar—behaviour that presumes too much. *Presumptious* is an archaic spelling, now considered an error.

'The presumptive diagnosis is a viral diarrhea outbreak,' said Dr. Douglas Pudden. . . .
Globe and Mail (Toronto) 16 Oct. 1985: A19

Both Steiniger's and Leroy's . . . observations provide presumptive evidence of an important role of social learning. . . .
Canadian Journal of Psychology 44 (1990): 316

Because of her Algerian background, she realized it would be wrong to expect these women to change their ways abruptly, and presumptuous to interfere with their customs.
Saturday Night Feb. 1986: 66

'The problem has to be solved in Canada, by Canadians. . . . We are not being so presumptive as to tell you what to do.'
Vancouver Sun 1 Dec. 1990: B7

(The word required here is *presumptuous*.)

'It is presumptious of the commission to proceed as they are doing,' board chairman John Tolton told reporters after the hearing.
Globe and Mail (Toronto) 9 Feb. 1985: P15

(The accepted spelling is *presumptuous*.)

See also HEIR.

pretense, pretence, pretension, pretentious Canadians use the spelling *pretense* (favoured in the United States) slightly more often than *pretence* (the British spelling).
Note that *pretension* is spelled *-sion*, while *pretentious* is spelled with a *t*.

Less skilled passers . . . made no pretense of passing, instead shooting the puck ahead of them to the corners, and chasing after it.
Ken Dryden *The Game* 1983: 217

Few people have illusions that all Third World countries can pay their debts, or even service them, but many people insist on the pretence.
Globe and Mail (Toronto) 30 July 1985: P6

Murray, the quintessential Canadian pop singer, doesn't have a whiff of glitz or pretension about her.
Gazette (Montreal) 19 June 1994: F1

A pretention alarm goes off when I hear writers being elevated to the rank of hermit-like martyrs. . . .
Ottawa Citizen 19 June 1994: B6

(The correct spelling is *pretension*.)

See also -CE, -SE.

pretty   *Pretty* used as an adverb (meaning fairly or somewhat) is found in all kinds of writing. Although some critics have tried to restrict its use to informal or colloquial contexts, they have had little success.

Social man is pretty well tamed by what we call civilization, until a war or a disaster shatters the cellophane wrapping.
Robertson Davies *A Voice from the Attic* 1960: 110

These policy recommendations were . . . more economic than political, since he had concluded that the political arrangements were, on the whole, pretty good.
Queen's Quarterly 95.3 (1988): 598

By and large, anglophone Canadians look pretty much like all Canadian respondents; little if any movement towards the British norm can be detected.
Neil Nevitte and Roger Gibbins *New Elites in Old States* 1990: 129

. . . some insects make pretty fair architects, and beavers know quite a lot about engineering.
Northrop Frye *The Educated Imagination* 1963: 5

prevaricate   see LIE

preventive, preventative   Most usage guides suggest that both *preventive* and *preventative* are correct; however, some note that *preventive* is more common, and a few call it preferable. While Canadian writers use *preventive* far more commonly, either word is correct as an adjective or a noun.

Fries argues . . . that it is possible to postpone the onset of the common chronic diseases by a variety of measures, mostly preventive and mostly involving aspects of life-style. . . .
Queen's Quarterly 97.1 (1990): 7

Motorists . . . reported an average cost of $661 a year for mechanical auto repairs and preventative maintenance.
Calgary Herald 11 Feb. 1994: E2

If the daily administration of a preventative is interrupted for any reason, the blood must be checked before resuming.
Dogs in Canada Special Issue 1986: 66

(Here *preventative* is used as a noun.)

pricy, pricey   see -Y, -EY

primary colour   see COLOUR

primitive, primeval, primordial   *Primitive*, *primeval*, and *primordial* all refer to the earliest times or the earliest stages of something. *Primitive* is the most commonly used word; it usually suggests something rudimentary and undeveloped. In the past *primitive* was often used by English colonists to describe Indigenous cultures, but this usage—unless carefully qualified—is now seen as Eurocentric or racist.

Primeval (also spelled *primaeval*) and *primordial* are less common words, meaning existing from the beginning or prehistoric, and often suggesting something mysterious or unspoiled: 'primeval cave paintings', 'primordial forests'. Since *primordial* in French means essential, it occasionally appears in Quebec English with this sense.

The barn has two working toilets, few lights, and primitive cooking and washing facilities.
Vancouver Sun 28 June 1994: A3

Where townsfolk are swilling beer and swatting flies, Lindsay's independent women are draped in shimmering gauze and straw hats, swimming in primeval waters and getting in touch with their innermost physical selves.
Gazette (Montreal) 15 April 1994: C1

Before Shoemaker-Levy [a comet that shattered], most astronomers thought comets were single pieces of primordial ice left over from the formation of the solar system.
Toronto Star 29 May 1994: E7

'Our first principle is to respect the primordial mis-

sion of Belanger-Campeau,' said Spicer. . . .
Gazette (Montreal) 19 Nov. 1990: A1

(This example illustrates the Quebec English use of *primordial* to mean essential.)

See also -AE-, -OE-, -E-; QUEBEC ENGLISH.

Prince Edward Islander   see NAMES OF RESI-
DENTS OF CITIES AND PROVINCES; APPENDIX I

princely   see FRIENDLY

principal, principle   The adjective *principal* means main or most important. The noun *principal* refers to the head of a school or college, to a person playing a key role in an event, or to a sum of money on which interest is charged or paid.

Principle is always a noun and means a fundamental law or a moral standard. 'In principle' means in theory. Confusion is common especially when *principal* (major) modifies a noun such as *idea* or *rule* that brings to mind the other spelling.

BC Stena's principle asset, the passenger-car ferry Vancouver Island Princess, remains tied up in Victoria. . . .
Vancouver Sun 23 Nov. 1990: D10

(The correct spelling here is *principal*.)

The aquarium has been granted approval in principal for a federal fisheries permit to catch beluga whales. . . .
Vancouver Sun 10 July 1990: B4

(The correct spelling here is *principle*.)

The principle idea is that you plant wisely for your climate.
Edmonton Journal 8 May 2004: K1

('The *principle* is that' or 'The *principal* idea is that . . .' is correct.)

prioritize, priorize   *Prioritize*, meaning give priority to or arrange in order of priority, is labelled jargon by most usage guides, but the word is common in all types and levels of writing.

Canadians use *priorize* as an alternative form

of this verb fairly frequently. However, since dictionaries have not yet listed this form, it is not recommended.

'We need to identify and prioritize issues.'
Financial Post 28 April 1989: 18

The failure of the trustees . . . to give priority to salaries and research funds over 'new buildings and that sort of thing' made it difficult for the university to attract and hold faculty members of high calibre. . . .
Frederick Gibson *Queen's University* 2 (1983): 46

(In academic writing *prioritize* is generally avoided; here 'give priority to' is used instead.)

'This necessity to protect and priorize French in all its forms of expression is . . . absolute', wrote Masson. . . .
Gazette (Montreal) 27 July 1989: B3

See also -IZE, -ISE, -YZE, -YSE.

prison   see JAIL, GAOL

pro, pros   *Pro* is an informal short form of *professional*, but not all types of professionals are called pros: doctors, lawyers, and accountants, for example, are not. Generally 'the pros' are athletes whose job it is to play a sport; the leagues they play in are also called 'the pros'. The *pro* at a golf or tennis club is a highly skilled player, usually employed by the club to give lessons. In Britain *pro* is also slang for *prostitute*.

The expression 'to be a pro' simply means to be expert at something.

'If you make it to the pros, you're battling for a job every day and your name will get tossed around if you're not battling hard and playing well or up to the coach's standards.'
Calgary Herald 14 Dec. 2003: B5

Jill Fraser, the pro at Streetsville Glen Golf Club in Brampton, Ont., suggests the following exercises to help golfers relax and limber up before they tee off.
Canadian Living 17 May 1986: 13

No matter how friendly, frisky, and helpful your salesman is, he's a pro who wheels and deals over cars daily.
Canadian Consumer March 1986: 5

proactive   The word *proactive*, which has become popular since 1970, is sometimes criticized as a redundant synonym for *active*. However, *proactive* does have a particular meaning as the opposite of *reactive*. The prefix *pro-* in *proactive* means beforehand. The word is used to describe people, policies, or measures that anticipate problems and thus avoid them, or that anticipate new developments in order to take advantage of them. Thus a proactive healthcare system would emphasize preventing illness rather than reacting to it.

Proactive should not be used to mean energetic or active. This imprecise use of the word, especially in business writing, is what has led some commentators to claim it is meaningless.

Proactive is sometimes written with a hyphen, *pro-active*, but most dictionaries list the unhyphenated form first.

. . . Lanskail said council must begin to address the shortage of seniors' housing in a pro-active manner rather than just responding to inadequate proposals.
Vancouver Sun 26 July 1990: C2

'The traditional "reactive" mode of supervision [of banks] must give way to a "proactive" mode.'
Globe and Mail (Toronto) 7 Nov. 1985: A1

A senior executive can teach the manager to recognize the myriad signals that are part of being proactive and anticipating the market.
Globe and Mail (Toronto) 7 Jan. 1985: B5

She also needs to take pro-active measures to placate a disaffected and influential green lobby that feels stonewalled by the Socred government.
Financial Post 23 Sept. 1991: 2

(This is a loose use of *proactive*, since measures to placate a disaffected lobby are necessarily reactive; '*active* measures' would be more accurate.)

The company philosophy is described by Haycock as 'pro-active.' 'We're not interested in sitting on a problem. We want to move on it and resolve it.'
Financial Post 27 Sept. 1991: 18

(Since the speaker is talking about reacting quickly to problems, this use of *proactive* is questionable.)

See also REACTIVE.

probably   see SENTENCE ADVERBS

proceed   see -CEED, -CEDE, -SEDE

pro-choice   see ABORTION

Procrustes, Procrustean   In Greek legend Procrustes was a celebrated robber who had a macabre way of accommodating his guests. He offered them one of two beds: a very short one or a very long one. If a guest chose the short bed and was too long for it, Procrustes cut off any overhanging body parts to make him fit; if he chose the long bed, Procrustes stretched him until he filled it. Theseus put an end to Procrustes by making him lie on his own bed. Hence *Procrustean* and *Procrustes' bed* have become figures of speech for an arbitrary standard or scheme imposed rigidly or ruthlessly.

The correct pronunciation is *pro KRUH steez*. The adjective *Procrustean* is generally capitalized.

It is perhaps not his fault that he has had to snip and stretch a little to fit the past neatly into his Procrustean structure.
Margaret Atwood *Second Words* 1982: 30

. . . Americans have become more narrow-mindedly intolerant of unfettered free speech and dissent as they, like Canadians, turn more and more to procrustean censorship laws to ban what is deemed 'offensive.'
Financial Post 29 June 1990: 10

(The adjective *Procrustean* is usually capitalized.)

prodigal   The adjective *prodigal* means recklessly wasteful, as in Jesus' parable of the prodigal son (Luke 15:11–32) who left home and squandered his money on riotous living. However, today *prodigal* only rarely connotes wastefulness, riotous living, or lavishness. In contemporary Canadian usage, *prodigal* is most often associated with the return of the son, when his father welcomed him home and killed a fatted calf in his honour. While the parable teaches sinners that God will forgive their sins as the prodigal's father forgave his, most current references to someone as 'a prodigal' imply simply that the person has (literally

professor

or figuratively) left home, returned, and been welcomed back.

Since the greenhouse effect grew out of a lifestyle built around the automobile and a prodigal waste of energy, more efficient vehicles are being designed. . . .
Vancouver Sun 10 March 1990: A10

(Here *prodigal* does mean reckless.)

When he went upstairs to the office to collect his stack of leaflets, they greeted him like the prodigal son.
Margaret Atwood *Life Before Man* 1979: 281

Yet all those who now pretended to be converted were being accorded preferential treatment. They were welcomed back in the manner of prodigal children returning to the fold.
Canadian Journal of History 14.1 (1989): 32

Ann Ditchburn Dances . . . marks the first time she has performed in a professional setting since arriving back in Toronto last year. And, judging by the cheers from the capacity crowd, all are very happy to have the prodigal home again.
Globe and Mail (Toronto) 30 Jan. 1985: M7

Dent is a finback that had been identified 16 years before in the water off the Rock. He hadn't been seen in three years. The prodigal had returned.
Gazette (Montreal) 28 April 1990: I12

professor see QUEBEC ENGLISH

profitwise see -WISE

program, programme *Program* is the usual Canadian spelling, although *programme* (the British spelling) is not uncommon, especially in reference to the works to be performed at a concert or to a plan of action. *Programme* may be more frequent in federal government contexts and in Quebec because it is also the French spelling. Note that in reference to computers, Canadian and British writers use *program*, the spelling used for all meanings in American English.
    The usual verb forms in Canada are *programmed* and *programming*, although *programed* and *programing*, alternative American spellings, are also acceptable.

. . . the regional development program was not designed to handle major structural shifts in the economy.
The Canadian Geographer Spring 1989: 57

Mr. Lithgow comes to York University from the Ottawa Civic Hospital where he was . . . responsible for the Hospital Foundation's fundraising programme.
Globe and Mail (Toronto) 26 Nov. 1985: B5

. . . by means of computer programmes, we used the *Survey* results for subsets of this collection of items. . . .
W.C. Lougheed, ed. *In Search of the Standard in Canadian English* 1986: 172

(The spelling *program* is recommended when the reference is to computers.)

The number of radio stations cutting back on local news programming in the United States has increased so dramatically that local news may soon become the exception on radio. . . .
Globe and Mail (Toronto) 2 Jan. 1985: B5

(Canadians usually spell *programmed* and *programming* with two *m*'s.)

Progressive Conservative see CONSERVATIVE

proletariat see BOURGEOIS

pro-life see ABORTION

prone, -prone *Prone* means disposed to or susceptible to, usually with negative implications: 'prone to error', 'prone to headaches'. *Prone* may be followed by either an infinitive or an *-ing* form of a verb: 'He was prone to let in (*or* prone to letting in) easy goals'. Some object to the use of *prone* to indicate a liking or fancy for a particular thing, as in 'prone to chocolate and anchovies'. *Partial* is a better choice in such contexts. *Prone* is also commonly used to form hyphenated compounds: *accident-prone, erosion-prone.*

At least two chains are basing their prices on two-day rentals. For those of us who are prone to send the movie back unwatched because we've fallen asleep . . . this is a worthwhile option.
Province (Vancouver) 9 Oct. 1990: 45

Most doctors now agree that if ASA is taken by a child suffering from a viral illness such as chicken pox . . . the child becomes more prone to developing a devastating illness called Reye's Syndrome.
Province (Vancouver) 31 Dec. 1990: 45

She's personally rather prone to cottons and linens ('very crisp') for weddings. . . .
Globe and Mail (Toronto) 8 Jan. 1985: F10

(Here *partial* would be a better choice.)

See also PRONE, SUPINE, PROSTRATE, RECUMBENT.

prone, supine, prostrate, recumbent
These words for describing how someone is lying down cause confusion. Most of us manage with expressions such as 'face up (*or* down)', 'on her stomach', or 'on his back'. According to dictionaries, *prone* means lying face downwards, while *supine* means lying face upwards. In popular Canadian writing, however, *prone* is used for both positions. Likewise, though *prostrate* means stretched out full-length, face down, it is often used to mean simply lying flat. *Recumbent* means reclining or lying back; the word has become more common as *recumbent bicycles* have become more popular.

The biathlon includes cross-country ski sprints of five to 20 kilometres, with up to five standing and prone shooting intervals.
Globe and Mail (Toronto) 18 Feb. 1985: S4

Fortunately she had trained herself to sleep in the supine pose of a marble saint on a sarcophagus lid.
Globe and Mail (Toronto) 24 Sept. 1985: F13

. . . the former superintendent of financial institutions . . . seemed powerless to do much more than plead with the supine board to heed his advice.
Toronto Star 19 Nov. 1994: B2

(Here *supine* is used figuratively to mean indolent or slack.)

Along Lhasa's Free Market Street, a pair of pilgrims . . . prostrate themselves full-length on the street, forehead touching the ground.
Globe and Mail (Toronto) 27 July 1985: T9

Yet, despite taxpayers' prostrate condition, the city of Montreal actually spent 1.8 per cent more

money in the fiscal year ending last March than in the previous year.
Gazette (Montreal) 21 Sept. 1994: B3

(Here *prostrate* is used figuratively to mean overcome or weakened.)

I rounded the rear bumper and saw an old woman prone on a padded bench, straining beneath a barbell.
Canadian Fiction Magazine 64 (1988): 38

(Technically, since this woman must be lying on her back, the correct word would be *supine*; however, *supine* has connotations—slack, apathetic—that are inappropriate here; simply 'lying on a padded bench' would be better.)

He gave her a wheedling look from his almost prone position in the armchair with the broken springs.
Constance Beresford-Howe *Night Studies* 1985: 67

(Here 'almost *supine*' would fit the context better.)

The hired man tried to sit up, holding onto his shoulder. With a groan, he fell back onto the dirt floor. 'This guy is nuts,' said Rick, pointing to the prostrate man.
Canadian Fiction Magazine 64 (1988): 69

(This man is *supine*, or lying on his back.)

How strange a setting for a speed merchant whose odd-yet-beautiful recumbent bicycles repeatedly outpace high-priced and hyper-engineered vehicles from the U.S., Britain and Germany.
Province (Vancouver) 10 Nov. 2002: A26

See also PRONE, -PRONE; PROSTATE, PROSTRATE.

pronoun   see entry in Glossary

pronoun agreement   see AGREEMENT, GRAMMATICAL

pronoun reference   see THAT, WHICH

pronouns between linked verbs, case   It is sometimes not obvious whether a pronoun between two linked verbs should be in the subjective or objective case. The italicized pronouns in the sentences below have a dual function. They are the objects of the main verb that they follow and the subjects of the infinitive or gerund they precede.

'John wants you and *I/me* to handle it.'

'Morgan caught *she/her* and Sylvia reading his e-mail.'

Linguists argue abstrusely about the underlying nature of such sentences, but the form these pronouns should take is not really a point of contention. When a single pronoun stands between linked verbs, people readily agree that the objective case is required:

'John wants *me* to handle it.'

'Morgan caught *her* reading his e-mail.'

The confusion surrounds only compound objects, such as 'you and me' and 'her and Sylvia'. For a general explanation of objective vs. subjective forms as well as a discussion of the pressure speakers feel to use subjective forms, see CASE.

Farriss says *The Greatest Hits* album and interviews with journalists have allowed he and fellow band members to reflect on their 17-year history. . . . *Spectator* (Hamilton) 17 Nov. 1996: n.p.

('Allowed *him* and fellow band members to reflect' is standard.)

See also CASE; BETWEEN YOU AND ME; HYPERCORRECTION; WHO, WHOM.

pronoun with possessive antecedent A few contemporary language commentators state that the antecedent of a pronoun cannot be in the possessive case. They would consider the sentence 'I took Jim's calls while he was out' ungrammatical, because the antecedent of the pronoun *he* is *Jim*, and the word *Jim* does not appear in the sentence except as the possessive *Jim's*.

When a pronoun has a possessive antecedent, certainly there may be doubt about whether the pronoun refers to the possessive noun or to the noun that the possessive modifies: for example, 'We toned down the committee's remarks. They were quite angry'. Here *they* could refer to either the committee members or their remarks. Nevertheless, possessive antecedents should not be considered ungrammatical simply because it is possible to construct ambiguous examples around them. As the citations below show, pronouns with possessive antecedents are very common in English, even in formal writing, and the construction is usually readable and clear.

Maryon Pearson's displeasure increased by several notches the following morning when she was confronted with breakfast.
George Ignatieff *The Making of a Peacemonger* 1987: 129

In some of the interviews, Davis's distaste for the whole affair is almost palpable, and the information he surrenders is largely opaque. . . .
Jack Chambers *Milestones* 1983: ix

The educator's fourth responsibility is to get fully involved in the society around him.
W.C. Lougheed, ed. *In Search of the Standard in Canadian English* 1986: 74

Mackworth's political views were subject to considerable comment, for he had expressed himself on all the major issues of the day.
J.A.W. Gunn *Beyond Liberty and Property* 1983: 129

Shirley's job requirements were many and complex: 'she uses her judgement as well as her clerical skills.'
Carl J. Cuneo *Pay Equity* 1990: 1

. . . are there still immutable principles of justice that ought to be used to judge people's conduct, no matter where they find themselves?
J.E. Smyth et al. *The Law and Business Administration in Canada* 1987: 7

(Although *they* is not technically ambiguous in this example, since 'immutable principles of justice' do not travel, the antecedent of *they* is momentarily unclear. Here it might be better to replace 'no matter where *they* find themselves' with 'anywhere'.)

See also POSSESSIVE.

pronunciation   *Pronunciation* is often misspelled and mispronounced. Note that verbs *announce, denounce, pronounce,* and *renounce* all drop the *o* in the second syllable in forming their noun derivatives: *annunciation, denunciation, pronunciation,* and *renunciation.* The second syllable of these nouns rhymes with *dunce,* not *pounce.*

See also CANADIANISMS; ENUNCIATION, ANNUNCIATION; MISPRONUNCIATION AND PRONUNCIATION SHIFTS.

proof   see EVIDENCE; -F, -V-

prophecy, prophesy, [prophesize]   Canadians most often spell the noun *prophecy* (pronounced *PROF uh see*; plural *PROF uh sees*) with a *c*, as do the British. Americans use either spelling for the noun. In all three countries it is standard to spell the verb *prophesy* (*PROF uh sigh*). Verb forms are *prophesies* (pronounced *PROF eh sighs*), *prophesied* (*PROF uh sighed*), and *prophesying* (*PROF uh sighing*). Non-standard forms such as *prophesize, prophesized,* and *prophesizing* are often used both in speech and in writing.

The quotation from Ezekiel is part of a biblical story—many would call it a prophesy—about an evil place called 'Gog, the land of Magog.'
Globe and Mail (Toronto) 12 Jan. 1985: P10

(The more common spelling of the noun is *prophecy.*)

. . . living as an Asian man in the East End of London, England, is the one awaited by all religions and prophecied to come at the end of the age.
Globe and Mail (Toronto) 20 April 1985: P7

(The verb is always spelled with an *s*: *prophesied.*)

'He may have lost this one, but he'll win a stakes race before the season is through,' prophesized Mark Zimmer. . . .
Canadian Thoroughbred Aug. 1989: 33

(The correct word is *prophesied.*)

proscribe   see PRESCRIBE

prospective   see PERSPECTIVE

prospectus   see -US

prostate, prostrate   The *prostate* gland, situated at the base of the bladder in men, is susceptible to medical problems. *Prostate* is sometimes mispronounced and misspelled with an *r*, as if it were *prostrate,* which means lying face-down.

The area has 20 per cent more low-weight births than normal and a significantly higher incidence of liver and prostrate cancer in men.
Ottawa Citizen 22 Nov. 1994: A4

(The correct spelling is *prostate.*)

See also PRONE, SUPINE, PROSTRATE, RECUMBENT.

protagonist   see ANTAGONIST

protein   see -IE-, -EI-

prothesis   see MISPRONUNCIATION AND PRONUNCIATION SHIFTS

protocol   A *protocol* is the first draft of a diplomatic agreement, or an amendment to, or clarification of, an existing treaty. *Protocol* (no article) is the code of etiquette observed by the diplomatic corps on formal occasions.

More generally, a *protocol* is any established set of procedures. For example, a professional group may develop a protocol to be used in certain circumstances for the sake of consistency, safety, or fairness: a dental association might establish a protocol for dealing with HIV-positive patients, or the police might have a protocol for dealing with spousal assault.

In computing, a *protocol* is a set of instructions for transmitting data between the parts of a computer system or between remote computer systems that are not directly linked.

Under a protocol known as the Cullen-Couture Agreement, Quebec obtained the right to select its own immigrants.
Vancouver Sun 15 May 1990: A9

And Shea said that protocol dictates that no royal engagement can be announced while the Queen is out of the country.
Maclean's 24 Feb. 1986: 37

Meanwhile, a delicate protocol problem over speaking order was resolved last week.
Maclean's 24 Feb. 1986: 24

'We need the Criminal Code to reflect this . . . ,' said Ald. Bev Longstaff, spokeswoman for the city's prostitution policy, procedure, protocol and research committee.
Calgary Herald 24 Nov. 1994: B3

prototype   see ARCHETYPE

protuberance   *Protuberance* (from Latin *tuber,* 'a hump') is something that bulges or sticks out. The word is similar in meaning to *protrusion*, hence the common misspelling *protruberance*.

proved, proven   As an adjective used before a noun, *proven* is the only appropriate form: 'He is a proven competitor'. As the past participle of *prove*, the term *proved* is widely recommended by commentators, but in Canada *proven* is so common that the choice is certainly a matter of personal preference: in the common saying 'Innocent until proven guilty', *proved* would sound odd.

Stress has a proven effect on people's physical and mental health. . . .
Canadian Social Trends 68 (2003): 6

(As an adjective, *proven* is the only option.)

Neither treatment has been proven effective.
Family Health 20.3 (2004): 36

(*Proven* is commonly used as the past participle in Canadian English.)

See also SHOW, SHOWED, SHOWN.

provenance, provenience, providence
Provenance means place of origin and is often used to refer to the ownership history of a work of art. *Provenience* is a synonym, used mainly in the United States.
Providence, meaning God's protective care, is usually capitalized. Without a capital, *providence* may mean destiny, luck, or, occasionally, good management.

. . . in the impressive notes which detail the provenance of each song, the editor emphasizes the difficulties involved with treating the songs of the Indians as texts.
Queen's Quarterly 92.1 (1985): 177

Part of the coronation service instituted for William and Mary referred to the role of divine Providence in placing the king over his people. . . .
J.A.W. Gunn *Beyond Liberty and Property* 1983: 156

provinces and territories   see NAMES OF RESIDENTS OF CITIES AND PROVINCES; APPENDIX I

provost   In Canada a *provost* is usually a senior administrator in a college, university, or cathedral. In this sense the word is usually pronounced *PRO voast* or *PRAW vuhst*.
Provost (or *provost marshal*) is also a term designating the head of a military police unit or other police officer. In this sense it is generally pronounced *PRO vo*; both syllables rhyme with *go*.

. . . I got a phone call asking whether I would allow my name to go forward as a candidate for the position of provost of Trinity College at the University of Toronto.
George Ignatieff *The Making of a Peacemonger* 1987: 254

He won the position of civilian provost in November 1984—a key position in charge of the jail guards and matrons—which is run by the district for the RCMP.
Vancouver Sun 24 July 1990: B2

pseudonym, pen-name, nom de plume, nom de guerre, alias, a.k.a.   All these terms refer to assumed names. *Pseudonym*, from the Greek for 'false name', is the most general, and may be used for any assumed name. *Pen-name* is a direct translation of the nineteenth-century pseudo-French expression *nom de plume* (plural *noms de plume*); both terms refer to a fictitious name used by an author.
The expression actually used in French is *nom de guerre* (plural *noms de guerre*); literally it means war name, but it is used to refer to a name assumed in pursuit of any profession or goal. In formal writing *nom de guerre* should be

italicized as a foreign phrase.

An *alias* is a false name often, but not necessarily, associated with criminal activity. The term *a.k.a.* (or *aka*), pronounced as three letters, is police jargon for 'also known as'.

Smith is a pseudonym. He asked that his name not be used for the simple reason that he—like many men—doesn't want to be publicly connected to an article about the modern bachelor pad.
National Post (Toronto) 3 June 2006: WP9

They mark the birth on Nov. 30, 1835, of Samuel Langhorne Clemens [Mark Twain], the satirical writer who took his pen-name from the two-fathom depth marker call of the Mississippi River pilots.
Globe and Mail (Toronto) 8 June 1985: T11

Mr. Abbas, known under the noms de guerre of Abul Abbas or Abu Khaled, is a tall, powerfully built 38-year-old. . . .
Globe and Mail (Toronto) 14 Oct. 1985: A9

'I'm not a daredevil,' said Mr. Fitzgerald, who used the alias Nathan Boya when he rode his rubber ball over the Horseshoe Falls on July 15, 1961.
Globe and Mail (Toronto) 2 Feb. 1985: M1

Henri Charriere, aka Papillon, a petty criminal condemned for a murder he didn't commit, did escape on his ninth attempt.
Toronto Star 22 Oct. 1994: L23

'I don't know all the tunes, but Richard (Newell, AKA Biscuit) knows 'em all. . . .'
Spectator (Hamilton) 14 Dec. 1995: 10

(Because *a.k.a.* is an abbreviation for a phrase that would not be capitalized, *a.k.a.* or *aka* is preferable.)

psychologist, psychiatrist, psychology, psychiatry

Psychologists and *psychiatrists* are doctors of two different types. A psychologist has a PhD in psychology and studies the mind and behaviour within a particular field of specialization (clinical, behavioural, sports, etc.). A psychiatrist has a medical degree (MD) and usually deals more specifically with mental or behavioural disorders. When dealing with patients, a psychiatrist is licensed to prescribe medication, while a psychologist uses non-pharmaceutical methods of treatment. The word *psychology* can also refer to mental activity or thought processes more generally: 'There is a psychology to the painting that defies explanation'.

If the predictions of Masciuch (1995) hold true for the future of school psychology, school psychologists must become even better prepared to incorporate increased family involvement in schools in productive and mutually supportive ways.
Canadian Journal of School Psychology 15.1 (1999): 31

On the fifth day of his hospitalization, psychiatry was consulted because he was experiencing visual hallucinations.
Canadian Journal of Psychiatry 49.11 (2004) 787

Older literary modes, richer in memory, psychology, and interior monologue, are now deemed too slow and complicated for film.
Queen's Quarterly 110.2 (2003): 236

See also DOCTOR, DR.

publicly Adjectives of more than one syllable ending in *-ic* form adverbs by adding *-ally*: *basic, basically*; *fantastic, fantastically*; *holistic, holistically*; *realistic, realistically*. *Publicly*, the only common exception to this rule, is often misspelled *publically*.

pun A pun is specifically a joke that plays on words that sound alike but have different meanings.

. . . a chance encounter between your dog and the back end of [a skunk] can 'reek' havoc in your life.
Gazette (Montreal) 1 Oct. 1990: B7

(Here the pun is on *reek*, 'smell' and *wreak havoc*, 'reduce to chaos'.)

'She criticized my apartment so I knocked her flat.'
Richard Davies and Glen Kirkland, eds. *Dimensions* 1986: 55

(Here a double pun turns on the two senses of *knock*, 'punch' and 'criticize', and the two senses of *flat*, 'horizontal' and 'apartment'.)

See also DOUBLE ENTENDRE; HOMOPHONE; MISHEARD EXPRESSIONS.

punctuation see APOSTROPHE; COLON; COMMA; DASH; EXCLAMATION MARK; PARENTHESES, BRACKETS; QUESTION MARK; QUOTATION, QUOTATION MARKS; SEMI-COLON; SENTENCES, SENTENCE FRAGMENT, RUN-ON SENTENCE.

purebred, thoroughbred, pedigree, genealogy In North America *purebred* and *thoroughbred* can be used interchangeably for any domestic animal that has been carefully bred through several generations. For horse breeders, however, *thoroughbred* (often capitalized) refers to a specific type of race horse developed in the seventeenth and eighteenth centuries by crossing English mares with Arabian stallions. *Thoroughbred* is sometimes used metaphorically to describe someone who is refined, or 'of good breeding'.

The noun *pedigree* means the recorded line of descent of a purebred animal. The adjective form *pedigreed* describes such an animal. *Genealogy,* often misspelled *geneology,* and *family tree* are more often used of records of human descent, but *pedigree* can also apply to people and, figuratively, to ideas or products.

> . . . if she had been fertile her value as a purebred breeding cow would have been ten times the beef price.
> J.E. Smyth et al. *The Law and Business Administration in Canada* 1987: 215

> Standardbreds will often jog or 'brush' (sprint) five or six miles before a race: sturdier than their thoroughbred cousins, they need the distance to loosen up.
> *Saturday Night* July 1986: 32

> Breeders love to rattle off pedigrees—generation after generation after generation.
> *Dogs in Canada* Special Issue Aug. 1986: 30

> His first act is to stock it with prize cattle and pedigreed sheep.
> *Harrowsmith* Aug.–Sept. 1985: 52

> In Paul Martin, they have a bilingual, high-profile candidate with . . . an impeccable Liberal pedigree—and, as a bonus, he's from Quebec.
> *Vancouver Sun* 30 Jan. 1990: A9

purl, pearl The spelling of the knitting stitch is not the same as the spelling of the gem: 'Knit one, *purl* two'.

> Dana Givon is acknowledged as the top student knitter because she has not only mastered the basic stitch, but can also do pearl stitches, ribbing and moss.
> *National Post* (Toronto) 17 April 2003: PM12

(The spelling in knitting is *purl.*)

purple prose, blue language, yellow journalism In *De arte poetica,* the Roman poet Horace refers to overly flowery passages in a literary work as 'purple patches sewn on to make a fine display in the distance'. The expression *purple prose* thus describes ornate writing in which style is emphasized over substance. It is often confused with *blue language,* a term for profane or sexually explicit writing; in fact, *Random House Webster's College Dictionary* now lists 'risqué' as one of the definitions of *purple.*

Yellow journalism is sensational or unscrupulous newspaper writing: it may exploit human suffering to sell copy, or dispense with fairness and objectivity to advance a certain point of view.

> But the temptation to wallow and disport myself in the purple prose of the doting collector is strong, and it will need all my vigilance to resist it.
> Robertson Davies *A Voice from the Attic* 1960: 252

> Otherwise, information takes precedence over fine writing, which is as it should be, especially in a field long beset by purple prose and indifference to hard fact.
> *Globe and Mail* (Toronto) 23 Jan. 1985: SB1

> . . . the writer's dirty, purple prose [is] giggled, moaned, bitched and sighed by Ms Burroughs.
> *Performing Arts in Canada* July 1988: 10

(Here *purple* is used to mean 'risqué' rather than 'ornate'. Some dictionaries list this meaning.)

> The headline, some callers said, inappropriately attached political meaning to a story of personal tragedy and suffering. . . . 'I was offended, I found it totally incredible. The Citizen is isolated on this one. It's yellow journalism.'
> *Ottawa Citizen* 3 Dec. 1994: A2

purposely, purposefully *Purposely* means on purpose, and is the opposite of *accidentally.* *Purposefully* means with a sense of purpose, with determination to accomplish a goal, and is the opposite of *aimlessly*. *Purposefully* should be reserved for contexts in which the action described is performed with determination, or with a definite goal in mind. Used in this sense, *purposefully* generally follows the verb, while *purposely*, meaning on purpose, usually precedes it. In some contexts either word makes sense.

So she purposely kept news of the grant a secret.
The Beaver Feb.–Mar. 1990: 35

. . . his prominent jaw thrust ahead of him as both lance and shield, he strides purposefully to a small blue chalkboard.
Ken Dryden *The Game* 1983: 166

purposes   see INTENTS AND PURPOSES.

pushoff   see PHRASAL VERBS

puss, pus   *Puss* is the cat. *Pus*, with a single *s*, is the word for seepage from an infected wound.

put someone on a pedestal, [put someone on a pedal/peddle/petal stool]   see MISHEARD EXPRESSIONS

put up with   see IDIOMS

pyjamas, pajamas   Canadians use both spellings with about equal frequency. British dictionaries list *pyjamas* first, American dictionaries *pajamas*.

pyrohy   see PEROGY

pyrrhic   A *pyrrhic victory* is won at too great a cost. The phrase originated when Pyrrhus, king of Epirus, was victorious in a battle against the Romans, but was said to have claimed that another such battle would ruin him. In contemporary use the phrase sometimes denotes a hollow victory. While paying too dearly can make a victory seem empty, sometimes a victory seems hollow only because it was attained too easily; in such cases, the adjective *pyrrhic* is inappropriate.

The pronunciation is *PEER ik*. Some dictionaries capitalize *Pyrrhic*, while others, including the *Canadian Oxford Dictionary*, do not. Words derived from proper names, such as *philistine*, *maverick*, and *stetson* tend to lose their capital letters as they are integrated into everyday speech and the association with their namesake is lost.

[The strike] was a Pyrrhic victory for the steelworkers, many of whom aren't being recalled to work.
Gazette (Montreal) 23 Nov. 1990: D1

Instead, the government pressed on, apparently supported by public opinion, and paid a pyrrhic price.
Toronto Star 13 June 1987: B3

Surely it is a pyrrhic victory if the library is unchallenged merely because it is unchallenging.
Globe and Mail (Toronto) 5 Oct. 1985: D19

(This victory was hollow because it was obtained without effort, not because it was won at great cost: *pyrrhic* is inappropriate here.)

See also CAPITAL LETTERS; EPONYM; PHILISTINE.

Q

q-, qu-   English words containing *q* without a *u* immediately following are rare and almost always transliterated from other languages, such as Arabic (the emirate of *Qatar*), Chinese (the *Qing* dynasty), or Inuktitut (*Iqaluit*—pronounced *i KAL oo it*—the capital of Nunavut). Qantas, the name of the national airline of Australia, is an acronym derived from 'Queensland and Northern Territories aerial service'.

See also ABBREVIATION; NUNAVUT; PINYIN.

qua   *Qua*, meaning 'as', is best restricted to literary, academic, and legal writing, because it is slightly ponderous in tone and most people are not sure what it means. In most contexts *as* will do.

The most common construction with *qua* is one in which the same noun or noun phrase is used before and after *qua*. The meaning of this construction varies. For example, 'Art *qua* art has no dollar value' means 'Art in itself has no dollar value'. 'It is not a matter of efficiency; he is enamoured of routine *qua* routine' means '. . . routine for the sake of routine'. 'Animals *qua* animals cannot legislate their own safety' means 'Animals being animals . . .'. Sometimes *qua* is used merely to provide a rhetorical flourish, as in 'I don't dislike sports *qua* sports—I just think they are a waste of time'. Here, the phrase '*qua* sports' does not refine the meaning of *sports* in any way. In cases like this *qua* should be avoided.

Qua also means in the capacity or role of: 'He was a superb surgeon *qua* technician, but his dealings with the unanaesthetized left something to be desired'; 'Is the university overvaluing the professor *qua* researcher and undervaluing the professor *qua* teacher?' In this construction different nouns are used before and after *qua*, the second naming one aspect of the first.

Some critics consider this the only usage of *qua* that is appropriate. However, neither common practice nor dictionaries support this restriction of the meaning.

> The novelist *qua* novelist, as opposed to the utopian romancer, takes what is there as a point of departure.
> Margaret Atwood *Second Words* 1982: 428

> The one kind of criticism that the poet himself, *qua* poet, engages in—the technical self-criticism which leads to revision and improvement—is a criticism with which the reviewer has nothing to do.
> Northrop Frye *The Bush Garden* 1971: 124

> . . . the complainant . . . was seeking relief qua bidder, not qua shareholder.
> *Canadian Bar Review* 66.3 (1987): 633

See also LATIN PHRASES.

quadriceps   see BICEPS

quadriplegic   see PARAPLEGIC

Quaker   The formal name of the religious group commonly known as Quakers is 'The Society of Friends'. Members of the faith refer to one another as 'Friends'. But *Quaker* is an acceptable term for most references to the religion or one of its adherents. The name *Quaker* may allude to an admonition of the group's founder, George Fox, that they should 'tremble at the word of the Lord'.

> . . . the Empress Alexandra of Russia, prompted both by Tolstoy's importunings and by those of the Society of Friends of England, had persuaded the Czar that the Doukhobors might leave Russia. . . .
> Pierre Berton *The Promised Land* 1984: 69

> She was raised a Quaker, and Quakers, from what

he'd seen of them, were smilers rather than laughers.
Margaret Atwood *Life Before Man* 1979: 116–17

quality Many commentators criticize the use of *quality* as an adjective meaning 'of high quality' ('a quality product'), but all the major dictionaries list this meaning without remark. Note, however, that the adjective *quality* has become clichéd in combination with certain nouns ('quality education', 'quality time'), and that *quality* as an adjective usually appears in fairly informal writing. In formal writing *quality* is more likely to be used as a neutral term requiring a modifier: 'high-quality product', 'work of poor quality'.

. . . they simply cannot keep giving quality education without more money.
United Church Observer June 1986: 33

. . . they have found that the consumer is definitely interested in new flavours and quality products.
Western Grocer May–Jun. 1990: 48

See also FUNCTIONAL SHIFT.

quandary *Quandary* is occasionally misspelled *quandry*, probably because it is often pronounced with only two syllables, like *laundry*. Dictionaries list the pronunciation with an optional middle syllable: *KWON d(uh) ree*.

quantum, quantum leap Some usage commentators object to the use of *quantum* to mean 'large', pointing out that its Latin meaning is simply 'amount'. They also note that the expression *quantum leap* as it is commonly used distorts the meaning of this term in physics.
In physics a *quantum* is the minimum amount of energy capable of existing independently, and a *quantum leap* (the abrupt transition of an electron between one energy level and another), though an extremely significant event, is one of subatomic—infinitesimally small—proportions. Thus some commentators will allow *quantum* to be used in figurative contexts where it means 'significant', but draw the line at its use to mean 'giant'. Nevertheless, despite the inaccuracy, most major dictionaries

now list 'large' as a meaning of *quantum*. It's best to avoid this sense when writing for physicists.

Since that time there has been a quantum acceleration of forest management in the form of planting, tending, nursery capacity. . . .
Queen's Quarterly 94.3 (1987): 610-11

Tiger appeared on the Mike Douglas Show at age two, played exhibitions with Sam Snead and Jack Nicklaus, and his television appeal was solely responsible for quantum gains in PGA Tour prize money.
Calgary Herald 4 May 2006: C6

For people who can remember having to swallow 40 pills and more in a single day, that would represent a 'quantum leap in the evolution of HIV Therapy'. . . .
Vancouver Sun 17 June 2006: C7

See also PLURALS, REGULAR, IRREGULAR, FOREIGN.

quash, squash *Quash* has a special legal sense: to nullify, revoke, or set aside a decision, licence, action, etc. Either *quash* or *squash* can be used to mean suppress or quell.

The lawyers are asking the court to quash the Gomery commission report, claiming that it is biased, lacked procedural fairness and that its conclusions are not supported by the evidence.
Edmonton Journal 6 May 2006: A7

Canada's premiers, who constitutionally have enough power over trade to squash or seal the deal, recognize that fact.
Ottawa Citizen 14 June 1986: H1

(Here *squash* might be defended because it alliterates with 'seal'; however, given the context of formal negotiations, *quash* is recommended.)

When Torvill and Dean moved on after the 1984 Winter Olympics, the order came from the International Skating Union that . . . the precise laws of ice dancing would be enforced strongly and all show business routines would be squashed.
Today's Skater 1991: 26

(Here, given the context of laws and regulations, *quashed* might be better.)

Popular music routinely finds ways to quash the

oddballs, eccentrics and outlaws who provide its flavor.
Gazette (Montreal) 6 June 1990: B4

(Here *squash* would also be possible.)

'The membership is a lot more militant than the leadership at this point and the leadership tries to squash the militancy.'
Ottawa Citizen 28 Sept. 1988: A11

(Here *quash* would also be possible.)

Lu will take part in a march and candlelight vigil Sunday in Toronto to commemorate the massacre that occurred when Chinese soldiers entered the square to squash a protest involving thousands of civilians.
Edmonton Journal 3 June 2006: G8

(Here *quash* would also be possible.)

quasi   Borrowed from the Latin meaning 'as if', *quasi* is used as a prefix before nouns, adjectives, or adverbs to suggest a substitute for the real thing. When used before a noun, *quasi* can mean part-, near- or pseudo-. When it qualifies an adjective or adverb, it can convey a range of meanings, such as nearly, partly, sort of, somewhat, or virtually. Although context usually makes the meaning clear, the tone of *quasi* can be difficult to discern: in some cases it is neutral and in others it is pejorative. Compounds formed with *quasi* are usually hyphenated. *Quasi* is pronounced to rhyme with *Ozzie* or *day's eye*.

The cast of characters usually includes quasi-historical figures (King Arthur, for instance), along with supernatural beings.
Performing Arts in Canada March 1988: 14

What I wanted to hear was . . . a symphony of tolling bells, at times quasi-human in character, speaking of jubilation and also of tears.
Queen's Quarterly 92.1 (1985): 102

The United Church has become a quasi-political organization.
Globe and Mail (Toronto) 30 June 2006: A16

quay, key, cay   *Quay*, *key*, and *cay* are all pronounced *KEE*; *cay* is also pronounced *KAY*. A *quay* is a landing platform or wharf. *Key* and *cay* are both terms for a small low island or emer-

gent reef or sandbank. All three words are derived from the French word *quai*, meaning 'wharf'.

The quay was already empty of passengers from Sweden.
David Williams Eye of the Father 1985: 24

The Florida Keys is actually a collection of dozens of small coral islands that separate the Atlantic from the Gulf of Mexico.
Gazette (Montreal) 24 Nov. 1990: 16

The two most isolated islands . . . are Long Cay and North East Cay, off Belize.
Vancouver Sun 10 Nov. 1990: E3

Quebec, Québec   Most English-speaking Canadians say *kwuh BECK* or *kuh BECK*; *KWEE beck* is less acceptable. The French pronunciation *KAY BECK* is rare outside Quebec. Although the English spelling conventionally omits the accent, writers sometimes include it, especially if they are discussing French language issues.

See also QUEBEC ENGLISH; QUEBECER, QUEBECKER; APPENDIX I.

Quebec English   The French language is leaving its mark on the English of Quebec. It has long been recognized that Quebec French is influenced by English. Francophone Quebecers have interacted with unilingual English speakers for centuries, and the *anglicismes* they have thus assimilated are the subject of much study and debate. Anglophone Quebecers, however, were little influenced by French until the 1970s, when Quebec passed language laws ensuring that English speakers, particularly those in the workplace, were exposed to French. In subsequent decades, as more Quebec anglophones became bilingual, more Quebecers began to switch back and forth between English and French in their conversations (a process linguists call 'code-switching'). Code-switching facilitated the movement of words between French and English, as did the increasing use of both languages by immigrants who were native speakers of neither. Over time, more and more French words—particularly those connected to local life, linguistic politics, and provincial institutions—entered the English of Quebec until eventually 'Quebec English' constituted a distinct dialect, or regional variety, of Canadian English. For the benefit of non-Quebecers, this entry categorizes and explains some of the vocabulary peculiar to Quebec English. It also discusses problematic French-influenced usages unacceptable in Quebec English.

Unproblematic direct borrowings from French into Quebec English include the following:

calèche — a one-horse carriage, common in tourist areas

casse-croûte — a snack bar (literally, '*break crust* of bread')

cinq à sept — a party with drinks and snacks held from five to seven, right after work

garderie — a daycare centre

maître — an honorific title used by and of lawyers (See also ESQUIRE, ESQ., MAÎTRE.)

poutine — French fries served with cheese curds and gravy

la rentrée — the return to school and work from the summer holidays

tenue de ville — business attire (usually used on an invitation)

vedette — a star in the entertainment business, usually a movie star

Some French expressions in Quebec English would puzzle a francophone from Paris or Port au Prince, for they are unique to Canadian French:

allophone — a person, often an immigrant, whose first language is neither English nor French

caisse populaire — a credit union

dépanneur — a corner store

Quebec anglophones often use clipped forms of these borrowings: *allo*, *caisse pop*, and *dep*.

Many French terms and acronyms used in Quebec English relate to government. Quebec, unlike New Brunswick, is not officially bilingual; French is the only official language. Since official English-language versions of the names of provincial government institutions, services, and documents do not exist, anglophones have borrowed the French terms, including the following:

CEGEP — an acronym (pronounced *SAY zhep*) for *Collège d'enseignement général et professionnel*, also written *Cégep*. Students move from high school to *Cégep* after grade 11 and take either a two-year university preparation program or a three-year vocational or professional program.

CLSC — an initialism (pronounced letter-by-letter) for *Centre local des services communautaires*, a community health care clinic

DEC — an acronym (pronounced *DECK*) for *Diplôme d'études collégiales*, the diploma awarded students completing the two-year university preparation program at a *Cégep*

régie — a board or government office

SAQ — an acronym (pronounced either *SACK* or *ESS AY CUE*) for *Société des alcools du Québec*, that is, the liquor store

Because no official provincial guidelines on English usage exist, the City of Montreal published *The City of Montreal Style Guide: A Handbook for Translators, Writers and Editors* (2001), by Victor Trahan, to assist the many people in the city who produce English translations or edit English texts. Such texts may retain French orthographic features uncharacteristic of general Canadian English, including French spellings (francisation, modernisation), accents (Québec), and hyphenation (St-Laurent Boulevard, René-Levesque Park).

French has influenced the vocabulary of Quebec English in subtle ways. Some English words are used far more frequently in Quebec than elsewhere because they have nearly the same form as common French words. The following words—everyday vocabulary for Quebec anglophones—seem formal or rather unusual in other dialects of English:

ameliorate — used as a general synonym of *improve*

anglophone, francophone — now used not only in Quebec but across Canada as nouns to designate an English-speaker or a French-speaker or as adjectives meaning English-language and French-language

collectivity — used as a synonym of *community*: 'Aboriginal collectivities'

congress — used as a synonym of *conference* or *colloquium*

fête — used as both a noun and a verb, meaning celebration or celebrate

functionary — used without negative connotations as a synonym of *civil servant* or *official*

exposition — used in preference to *exhibition*

modality — used as a synonym of *procedure*

population — used not only in the social sciences but generally to mean 'the people' or 'the general public'

vernissage — used as a synonym of *art opening* or *opening reception*. (In other dialects of English, a *vernissage* is a private preview preceding the public opening of an exhibition.)

Pressure from French has given the words above greater currency in Quebec English, and, in some cases, breathed new life into obsolescent English meanings.

There are many more words in English that are close in form to French words but not in meaning. These deceptive look-alike pairs are called *faux amis* or 'false friends'. Francophones learning English predictably incorporate *faux amis* into their second language, extending the meaning of the English word to include the French sense. (And, of course, anglophones learning French make the same error in reverse.) The following meanings are characteristic of heavily French-influenced English or 'Frenglish'; they are *not* accepted in Quebec English and should be avoided:

actually — used like French *actuellement* to mean currently or at this time

command — used to mean place an order, e.g., for a meal

conference — used to mean lecture or presentation

delay — used to mean a deadline or period of time: 'The contract must be submitted within a delay of two weeks (*read* within two weeks)'.

inscription — used to mean registration

interrogate — used to mean ask, in other than formal or policing contexts

manifestation — used to refer to a protest or demonstration in the street

mark — used to mean brand: 'Gucci is a good mark.'

militant — used to refer to a member of an organization or supporter of a cause as opposed to a radical activist

nomination — used to mean appointment, e.g., to a board of directors

note — used to mean grade or mark (in school)

primordial — used to mean essential rather than 'existing from the earliest times'

professor — used of a teacher at the elementary or secondary level

security — used to mean safety in the context of accident prevention

syndicate — used to mean labour union

Typically Frenglish meanings are rejected by native speakers of English because they create ambiguity and cause confusion. Yet, a few *faux amis*, perhaps those whose standard English equivalent seems more cumbersome or less apt, have become accepted usage among anglophones in Quebec, among them the following:

animator — meaning group facilitator, workshop leader, or radio or TV host. Quebecers also use *animator* to mean film cartoonist.

coordinates — meaning contact information. Someone who asks 'May I have your coordinates?' isn't looking for a readout from your Global Positioning System, but would like your business card or your address and phone number, etc.

portable — meaning laptop computer

'The problem in the past was that we'd hire someone with some education, say with a CEGEP DEC, and we'd train them and they'd go elsewhere, to larger companies,' Gagliardi said.
Gazette (Montreal) 14 Jan. 2006: F3

(In Quebec English, a *CEGEP DEC* is a two-year college diploma.)

'Call the Regie and check on the worker. If the person doesn't have a permit of either kind, close the door,' Emond said.
Gazette (Montreal) 16 Oct. 2006: A6

(In Quebec English, a *régie* is a government board or office. The acute French accent has been dropped from the word in this newspaper story but would likely be retained in formal writing.)

He worked as a functionary in the forestry department until the next tide of anti-Communist protest carried Vaclev Havel to the presidency in late 1989.
Gazette (Montreal) 10 Nov. 1992: n.p.

(The word *functionary*, meaning civil servant, is used more often in Quebec than the rest of Canada.)

Police are investigating a religious counsellor after drugs were found in his suitcase. . . . The man, known as a pastoral animator, was working at the Riviere des Prairies detention centre on a temporary basis.
Gazette (Montreal) 6 Sept. 2006: A5

(In Quebec English, an *animator* is a group facilitator.)

See also BLONDE, BLONDE; ENTRÉE, APPETIZER; ESQUIRE, ESQ., MAÎTRE; FRANCIZATION; FRANCOPHONE, ANGLOPHONE, ALLOPHONE.

Quebecer, Quebecker, Québécois(e), Franco-, French Canadian

Quebecer and *Quebecker* are both common and acceptable spellings. *Quebecer* predominates in English-Canadian newspapers and seems to be gaining ascendancy; the *Canadian Oxford Dictionary* lists this form first. Yet *Quebecker* is still recommended in *Editing Canadian English* and the Canadian government manual *The Canadian Style*. Some people think *Quebecer* looks odd because most English words that end in *c* add *k* before a suffix (as in *trafficker*, or *panicky*).

The French words *Québécois* and *Québécoise* (feminine) are also frequently used in English, but generally only to refer to the French-speaking residents of Quebec. Since English word processing programs do not always successfully produce French accents, it's futile to insist on their use. However, if you can produce them,

note that *Québécois(e)* requires either two accents or none. Often Anglophone writers omit the second accent in *Québécois*, probably because *Québec* has only one accent and because in English *Québécois* is usually pronounced *KAY beck wah*, not *KAY BAY kwah*. Sometimes English writers use *Québécois*, without a final *e*, to refer to a woman; in French this *e* would be required. While it is common for words assimilated into English to lose their inflections as well as their accents, in this case it's worth making the effort to retain them.

Approximately 1.2 million francophone Canadians live outside Quebec: they are known as *Franco-Ontarians*, *Franco-Manitobans*, *Fransaskois* (singular and plural; French-speaking residents of Saskatchewan), *Franco-Albertans*, and *Franco-Columbians* (sometimes spelled as in French, *Franco-Colombiens*). Francophones living in the Atlantic provinces are generally called *Acadians*. *Franco-Americans* are francophone citizens of the United States, most of whom are of Canadian descent.

Francophone Canadians inside and outside Quebec have traditionally been referred to as *French Canadians* (the adjective form is hyphenated: 'French-Canadian writers'). While some francophones value this designation, others reject it, either because they identify themselves only as Québécois or because the label *French Canadian* implies that anglophone Canadians are the norm. Since both English and French are official languages of Canada, *French Canadian* and *English Canadian* should be used in a parallel fashion.

. . . Quebecers can hardly deny that the New Brunswick Acadians (40% of the province) and Franco-Ontarians are chiefly distinctive because of their language and culture, a heritage they share with their Quebec cousins.
Financial Post 13 Sept. 1991: 11

The Perfect Circle is a slim novel about a Quebecoise who falls in love with an older man while on vacation in Tuscany.
Gazette (Montreal) 27 May 2006: J5

(English-language newspapers don't normally use accents; in a magazine or book, this would be *Québécoise*.)

Chloe Gilbert, a Quebecois who has been in B.C. since 1981, married a unilingual anglophone and is now the mother of two children.
Vancouver Sun 17 Feb. 1990: A8

(Here French would require *Québécoise*.)

Lavoie, a Franco-Manitoban, has chosen to build his career in Montreal as has Roch Voisine, the New Brunswick Acadian who was the big winner at this year's awards gala.
Financial Post 20 Oct. 1989: 12

It is distressing to see Saskatchewan shirking its clear constitutional duty by dropping the school reform plan it had worked out so carefully with the Fransaskois.
Gazette (Montreal) 25 April 1990: B2

Stephan Cloutier gives a stunning one-man performance in Un One Way, a drama about the reality of being a francophone in Maillardville in 1909 and the choices a franco-Columbian must make between his history and language, his anglophone spouse and his need to live in French in order to find his original culture.
Vancouver Sun 2 March 2001: F7

(Usually *franco-* is capitalized.)

See also ACADIA; FRANCOPHONE, ANGLOPHONE, ALLO-PHONE.

queen see CAPITAL LETTERS; GAY

queer see GAY

question see LEADING QUESTION; RHETORICAL QUESTION

question mark Question marks are placed at the end of direct questions:

Is there any way to fix this?

How did it end?

Direct questions include tag questions, which are separated from the main sentence by a comma, and questions in declarative word order:

Sue already did that, didn't she?

You're not putting that on your credit card?

A period, not a question mark, is used at the end of an indirect question:

He asked if there was any way to fix this.

They wondered if she'd already done that.

Polite requests for action are often framed as questions, and some commentators state that they do not need question marks:

Will you turn off that light, please.

Can I squeeze in here.

However, it is unlikely that anyone will complain if you follow such requests with a question mark. In letters concerning employment, or official letters of invitation or inquiry, a request phrased as a question should be punctuated with a question mark to indicate that compliance is not being taken for granted:

Could you please respond to our proposal as soon as possible?

When a direct question is an element within a sentence, it is followed by a question mark:

Why me? is a typical first response.

The question on all our minds was why did we wait?

For some people Who can I blame? is a mantra.

When the question element begins in the middle of the sentence, you may capitalize the first word if that makes the sentence more readable.
When one sentence conflates a series of separate questions, use a series of question marks:

Have you ever had rubella? red measles? mumps? chicken pox?

Use only one question mark if a question is not complete till the end of a series:

Do you prefer milk, soy milk, or cream in your coffee?

A question mark goes inside the quotation marks if the quotation is a question and outside them if the main sentence is a question. If both are questions, only one question mark, inside the quotation marks, is needed:

We asked, 'Can we come?'

Did she really say, 'Ask Nana, my cat'?

Do they routinely say, 'And how will you be paying?'

Notice that there is no period after the question marks above, and that no comma follows the question mark in sentences like the following:

'Shall we dance?' he whispered.

A question mark in parentheses—(?)—indicates uncertainty about the accuracy of a date or fact, or about whether something should be included in a final draft. A question mark in parentheses may also be shorthand for incredulity—a graphic sign of disbelief in, or shock at, the information being passed along. This use of the question mark should be reserved for letters to friends or other semi-private writing. For a wider audience, which cannot be depended upon to share the writer's assumptions, some explanation is required.

questionnaire   *Questionnaire* is often misspelled with only one *n*.

quick, quickly   *Quick* can be used as both an adjective ('They made a quick decision') and an adverb ('Come quick'). However, *quick* is rarely used as an adverb in formal writing; it most commonly appears in reported or fictional speech, or in fixed expressions such as 'get rich quick'. Most usage guides, while acknowledging the legitimacy of *quick* as an adverb, are quick to note that writers prefer *quickly*. Certainly this is the case in Canadian English.

'Mommy, come quick,' Sarah screams again. . . .
Ken Dryden *The Game* 1983: 17

. . . the idea has taken off in Montreal and the promoter expects it to catch on quickly in the Quebec City region too.
Chronicle-Telegraph (Quebec) 3 April 1991: 2

He knew he must act quickly.
Pierre Berton *The Promised Land* 1984: 72

See also ADVERBS WITHOUT -LY; SLOW, SLOWLY.

quid pro quo   *Quid pro quo* is a Latin expression meaning 'this in return for that'. A *quid pro quo* may be an exchange, a trade-off, a covert deal, or, less commonly, an act of retaliation.

. . . when the government imposed capital gains taxation, it removed the tax on inherited wealth in Canada as a quid pro quo for the wealthy.
Globe and Mail (Toronto) 30 May 1985: P5

Canadian officials have strongly denied recent reports that Reagan wants any sort of quid pro quo on defence spending by Canada . . . for his announcement on acid rain.
Toronto Star 28 March 1987: B1

See also LATIN PHRASES, FOREIGN PHRASES.

quiet, quieten   *Quiet* and *quieten* are both accepted as verbs meaning to make quiet or to become quiet. Either may be followed by *down*.

The talk has localized and quieted.
Ken Dryden *The Game* 1983: 166

Things quietened down near midnight and I decided to go back to the office.
Gazette (Montreal) 17 Jan. 1990: A4

What followed was his standard-issue speech, warning that the deficit must be cut to quieten the fires of inflation, to calm international markets and to improve the financial legacy left to future generations.
Ottawa Citizen 2 March 1990: A4

Quiet Revolution   see CAPITAL LETTERS

quip   Usage commentators discourage the use of the verb *quip* on the grounds that it is unnecessary: a remark witty enough to qualify as a quip should not have to be identified, and a trite or dull remark cannot be made humorous with a label. However, *quip* often serves an important function by letting the reader know that a quotation that could be taken seriously was delivered facetiously.

'Before I had a child, I had no identity,' quipped Copps, who also pointed out that sexism in the media isn't the sole preserve of men.
Province (Vancouver) 25 Nov. 1990: 36

(Here *quipped* identifies the ironic tone of the remark.)

'He's my new idol,' Hayward quipped.
Gazette (Montreal) 2 Oct. 1990: F5

(Here again *quipped* conveys the ironic tone of the remark.)

quisling   see COLLABORATION

quit   *Quit* is not only the present tense but also the past tense and past participle; *quitted* is also correct for the past tense and past participle, but it is extremely rare.

In contemporary Canadian English, *quit* means give up or stop. Older meanings of *quit* have been preserved only in literary writing. These include leave ('They quit London'); be rid of ('We'll be quit of them soon'); and relinquish ('She knew she could never quit her creature comforts').

Her name was Maureen and she made me quit hockey for my teeth.
Canadian Fiction Magazine 64 (1988): 39

Yet tens of thousands of sturdy men, women, and children, who quit their tiny Carpathian farms to make a new life in a world of strangers, endured it all. . . .
Pierre Berton *The Promised Land* 1984: 49

So I told him . . . that he was making an ass of himself, that he was well quit of Gates Ajar Honeypot, and that he must positively stop trying to be Charles Dickens.
Robertson Davies *One Half of Robertson Davies* 1978: 112

She refuses to quit the conjugal apartment . . . because, as she says, 'I live here.'
Janice Kulyk Keefer *Reading Mavis Gallant* 1989: 144

quite   *Quite* has two meanings: entirely, as in 'quite dead', and to an extent, as in 'quite funny'. The first meaning dates from the fourteenth century, the second from the nineteenth. Many usage commentators have remarked on

the potential ambiguity of *quite*, and many have labelled the more recent meaning informal. However, *quite* troubles language commentators far more than it does language users.

The possibility for ambiguity is certainly present in Britain. In British English 'I was quite happy' may mean either 'I was utterly happy' or 'I was fairly happy'. 'This tea is quite cold' may mean 'This tea is stone cold', or simply 'This tea is rather cold'. Stress and intonation differentiate these meanings in British speech, and context may do the same in writing.

In contemporary Canadian English these sentences would rarely be ambiguous: only the second interpretations are likely. In Canadian English there are only two contexts in which *quite* is taken to mean entirely, exactly, or absolutely. The first is after *not*: 'I'm not quite ready'; 'That isn't quite full'. The second is before 'all-or-nothing' adjectives or adverbs (words that *fairly* could not modify): 'quite dead', 'quite alone', 'quite unsolicited', 'quite genuine'. In any other context *quite* means to a certain extent. The meaning fairly or moderately, as in 'quite good' or 'quite quickly', shades into the meaning noticeably or significantly, as in 'His ears turned quite red'; 'It's quite far away'; 'We waited quite some time'. The 'to an extent' meaning of *quite* is certainly not restricted to informal writing in Canadian English and need not be avoided.

The idiom *quite a*, as in 'quite a nice place' or 'quite a light colour', is conversational in tone and acceptable in most contexts. However, in very formal writing the order of the two words should be reversed: 'a quite light colour'. When *quite a* precedes a bare noun (without an adjective), it is sometimes appropriate to formal writing and sometimes not. When it means notable or considerable, as in 'quite a contrast' or 'quite a reduction', it is staid enough for formal writing. When it means 'an impressive specimen of a', as in 'quite a man', it is slang.

For what we witness . . . is the laceration of young lives: wounds severe enough to maim, if not quite kill.
Janice Kulyk Keefer *Reading Mavis Gallant* 1989: 90

Although difficult to define, post-modernism

exhibits one quite unmistakable trait: it revises and disputes agreed-upon notions of progress and modernity. . . .
The Canadian Geographer Spring 1989: 70

Much to his astonishment, he found it quite interesting.
Irving M. Zeitlin and Robert J. Brym *The Social Condition of Humanity* 1991: 236

Tattoos are quite popular on the men. . . .
Maclean's 16 Dec. 1991: A72

I find the music of composers of French background . . . to be frequently quite dense in texture compared to that of their Anglo-Canadian colleagues.
Queen's Quarterly 94.1 (1987): 185

I make no pretense to owning an impressive collection, but I have quite an assembly of folios, quartos, octavos, and duodecimos. . . .
Robertson Davies *A Voice from the Attic* 1960: 161

'The night Cissy took a snootful? That was quite a night.'
Howard Engel *Murder Sees the Light* 1984: 210

(Here *quite a* is slang.)

Quixote, quixotic   *Don Quixote*, the name of the hero of Cervantes' satiric novel, is usually pronounced *DON kee HO tee*. The adjective *quixotic*, meaning romantically idealistic or foolishly impractical, is pronounced *kwik ZOT ic*.

See also CAPITAL LETTERS.

quiz   To *quiz* someone is to ask him or her a lot of questions, usually in a teasing manner or simply to satisfy one's own curiosity. A *quiz* may be a short test at school, a not-so-serious self-directed test in a magazine, or a series of questions on a television game show. Some usage guides contend that *quiz* should be used only in popular writing. In fact, although *quiz* often describes an informal activity, the word itself is not slang or even informal, and is appropriate for any level of writing.

Also disputed is whether *quiz* (noun or verb) should be used for highly formal interrogations and inquiries, such as those conducted by police and government committees. This usage is rare except in newspaper writing, where the brevity of *quiz* appeals to those writing headlines. In formal writing, words with more serious connotations, such as *interrogate* and *investigate*, are preferable.

The *z* is doubled in the plural of the noun (*quizzes*) and in the verb forms (*quizzes, quizzed, quizzing*).

Mistaken by everyone for a nurse . . . I quizzed and eavesdropped my way through the evening.
Margaret Atwood *Second Words* 1982: 88

Sunday afternoons were given over to a record review programme . . . that was made 'entertaining' by quizzes, contests and spoofs by Alan MacFee.
Queen's Quarterly 92.1 (1985): 25

COUPLE QUIZZED IN ATTACK ON SHIP: A French-speaking couple has been detained for questioning in connection with last week's bombing of the Greenpeace flagship Rainbow Warrior. . . .
Globe and Mail (Toronto): 16 July 1985: P1

(Here *quizzed* replaces the more appropriate verb *questioned* in a headline.)

The opposition also quizzed Miss Fish about high lead levels in the blood of children in east-end Toronto. . . .
Globe and Mail (Toronto): 8 June 1985: P11

(Here *questioned* or *interrogated* would convey the seriousness of the investigation more clearly than *quizzed*.)

quotation, quotation marks   British publishers use single quotation marks (' ') for a first quotation and double quotation marks (" ") for a quotation within a quotation. American publishers prefer double quotation marks first, and single within. Both styles are used in Canada and either is correct—though switching back and forth is not. This book uses single quotation marks first:

'Did you memorize "In Flanders Fields" in school?'

(i) punctuating quotations of speech

Quotation marks are placed around a direct quotation, but not around indirect speech (a report of what someone said):

> She said, 'I'll see you there.'

> She said she would see us there.

The clause that identifies a speaker is set off from a quotation by commas:

> 'I don't know what I think,' he said, 'until I start to write.'

A quoted sentence that is integrated into another sentence and is not reported speech is not set off by commas:

> 'Live free' is very appealing, but I don't like 'Live free or die' quite as much.

A sentence break can be contained within a pair of quotation marks:

> 'I'll get it. You got it last time,' she said.

Question marks and exclamation marks are placed inside the quotation marks if they belong to the quotation and outside if they belong to the main sentence:

> She said, 'What can I do?'

> They actually used the word 'antiquated'!

> He said, 'That's ridiculous!'

If the quotation and the main sentence are both questions, only one question mark is needed, inside the quotation marks:

> Did you hear Larry say, 'Don't you hate that kind of thing?'

Note that a question or exclamation mark at the end of a quotation replaces the usual comma or period:

> 'Oh, no!' he said.

Colons and semicolons are always placed outside quotation marks:

> He is always disparaging 'the junk they sell

today'; meanwhile, he buys every new gadget that comes on the market.

Most Canadian publishers follow the American convention of putting all periods and commas inside closing quotation marks. This book follows the British style: periods and commas are placed outside closing quotation marks unless the punctuation is part of the passage being quoted.

> He was a 'remittance man', which means he was being paid to stay away from home.

The comma after *visit* in the example below is placed inside the closing quotation mark because it takes the place of an understood period.

> 'My brother is coming for a visit,' she said.

(ii) punctuating quotations from written sources

A quotation of prose longer than four lines is usually indented in a block rather than enclosed in quotation marks:

> Indent the whole passage five spaces from the normal left margin; the right margin does not have to be changed. Block quotations do not begin with a further indentation, even if you are quoting the beginning of a paragraph. However, if the quotation has a paragraph break *within* it, begin this paragraph on a new line and indent it five spaces from the margin of the block quotation. In a book, the block containing the quotation is often set in reduced type.

Newspapers and magazines set in columns cannot mark long quotations of speech or writing by indenting. Instead, the beginning of each paragraph in a long quotation is marked with opening quotation marks. The quotation marks are closed only at the end of the final quoted paragraph.

One or two lines of poetry may be quoted within a text in quotation marks (line breaks should be indicated by a slash), but more than two lines of poetry are set off from the text in an indented block that preserves the original format of the poem.

The spelling and punctuation of the original should be retained in a quotation. If there is an error in what you are quoting and you want to signal to your reader that you are merely reproducing what was in the original, insert *sic* (a Latin word meaning 'thus'; usually italicized) right after the error, in square brackets:

'Toronto, the capital of Canada [sic], is located on the shore of Lake Ontario.'

'We have asked for full cooperation from the medias [sic].'

If you are forced to change a verb tense or pronoun in a quotation so that it will fit into your sentence, enclose what you have changed in square brackets. For example:

In *Apartment Seven* (1989: 32) Waddington describes F.R. Scott as 'shin[ing] with an icy composure that always made [her] feel like a pre-World War I Russian immigrant fresh off the boat.'

An omission of words within a quotation should be marked with ellipsis points (. . .), although what is obviously only a fragment of a sentence may be quoted without them. In scholarly writing, ellipsis points indicating where a quotation has been trimmed are sometimes enclosed in square brackets [. . .] to differentiate them from ellipsis points appearing in the original text. Generally, in formal writing three ellipsis points are used to indicate an omission within a sentence and four to indicate an omission between sentences. The first of the four is considered to be the sentence period, so it does not need a space in front of it. It and the following three points each have one space between them. The ellipsis points between sentences can indicate that you have dropped the end of the first sentence or the beginning of the next (or both), or that you have omitted one or more sentences between these sentences. Commas, dashes, semicolons, and colons before or after ellipsis points may be dropped or preserved, depending on whether they clarify the structure of the altered sentence. Here are two versions of the same text—the first complete, the second compressed— illustrating various uses of ellipsis points:

The pages of Mayhew are a huge peepshow of Victorian London as it really was, and not as the novelists of the day were compelled by convention to represent it. It is not too much to say that the general reader who delights in Dickens, Thackeray, Surtees, Trollope, Cockton, Lever—yes, and perhaps also George Eliot—cannot squeeze the fullest flavour from his favorites unless he has some knowledge of Mayhew. He primes the pump of our imagination. To him, therefore, our homage and our thanks. He was not a novelist, but a sociological journalist. Yet after a perusal of his masterly pages, we come to the novelists who were his contemporaries fresher, better informed, and capable of a deeper understanding, a richer enjoyment.
Robertson Davies *A Voice from the Attic* 1960: 127

Here is the compressed version:

The pages of Mayhew are a huge peepshow of Victorian London as it really was, and not as the novelists of the day were compelled by convention to represent it. . . . The general reader who delights in Dickens, Thackeray, Surtees, Trollope . . . cannot squeeze the fullest flavor from his favorites unless he [sic] has some knowledge of Mayhew. . . . He was not a novelist, but a sociological journalist. Yet after a perusal of his masterly pages, we come to the novelists who were his contemporaries . . . capable of a deeper understanding. . . .

Notice that after the first ellipsis, where the beginning of a sentence has been dropped, the first letter of the resulting sentence has been capitalized. In scholarly or legal writing, where even such a slight alteration might be considered important to the interpretation of the text, this capital letter would be enclosed in square brackets.

The *sic* in the compressed version of the passage above is optional: a contemporary writer might insert it to indicate that conventions of gender-neutral language used today might support the use of *he or she* here, rather than *he* alone, to stand for the general reader.

When a quoted sentence ends with an ellipsis

and then is followed by a page number or other reference in parentheses, the sentence period migrates to follow the last parenthesis: 'Yet after a perusal of his masterly pages, we come to the novelists . . . capable of a deeper understanding. . .' (127).

In academic writing, the sources of all quotations are documented (i.e., recorded) either in parentheses in the body of the text or in footnotes or endnotes. Documentation allows the reader to verify or follow up on any material quoted. For the proper format of documentation, consult a style guide currently in use in your field.

(iii) quotation marks for titles

Quotation marks are conventionally placed around the titles of chapters, articles, essays, short poems, songs, episodes in television series, or anything else that is part of a larger work. The titles of self-contained works, such as books, newspapers, magazines, journals, compact discs, movies, and television programs, are italicized (or underlined). The title of a work that has never been published, such as a lecture or dissertation, is usually put in quotation marks. For a more thorough discussion of these conventions, see ITALICS AND QUOTATION MARKS.

(iv) referring to words

Either quotation marks or italics are used to indicate words that are being referred to as words:

'Cygnet' and 'signet' are pronounced the same way.

Quoth is an archaism.

A translation of an italicized foreign word usually appears in quotation marks:

The name derives from Latin *rufus*, 'redheaded'.

Quotation marks around a word may signal that it is likely to be unfamiliar to the reader:

Mark Jones is a 'Pakeha', a Maori word used widely in New Zealand for non-Maoris.

Once the word has been explained, the quotation marks should be dropped.

(v) indicating irony

Quotation marks may also signal irony—a quarrel with a word that others use straightforwardly:

My 'rehabilitation' consisted of being beaten up and tutored in crime.

Unless the irony is very obvious, this shorthand method of signalling dissatisfaction with a word may simply confuse the reader.

Fowler, in his 'Superiority' article, chastises writers who are eager to use vogue words or slang phrases but at the same time put them in quotation marks to signal disdain of such expressions. He recommends that they have the courage of their convictions and either use an expression straight or avoid it altogether.

See also ITALICS AND QUOTATION MARKS; QUOTE, QUOTATION.

quote, quotation   According to many usage commentators, *quote* is only a verb. It should not be used as a short form for the noun *quotation* ('quotable quotes'); nor should *quotes* be used as a short form for *quotation marks* ('Should this sentence be in quotes?'). This advice is often ignored.

The noun *quote* is fairly common in published academic writing, and in journalism and business writing the noun *quote* is used far more frequently than *quotation*. *Quotes* appears in the discussion of single and double quotation marks in some conservative style guides. In short, the nouns *quote* and *quotes* are too common in writing at every level to be considered incorrect, though it is true that *quotation* and *quotation marks* are preferred in formal and academic writing.

Any archivist or historiographer . . . will be disturbed further by the mistakes that appear in quotations from the archival record.
Arctic 41.1 (1988): 76

To appreciate the centrality of language in the production of meaning and of self (and incidentally to make sense of the language postmodernists typically employ, as in this Kristeva quote) it is useful to recall the traditions upon which postmodernism has been built.
Queen's Quarterly 97.3 (1990): 405

'Socialism'—my quotes this time—turned out to be alien and uncivilized in Russia.
Vancouver Sun 17 Feb. 1990: A4

See also QUOTATION, QUOTATION MARKS.

quoth *Quoth* is an archaism. When it appears in contemporary prose it is invariably facetious, signaling a mock elevation of style. Several commentators think *quoth* is never funny, but of course this is a matter of taste.

Quoth means 'said' and is used to identify the speaker of a direct quotation. It is the past tense form of the verb *quethe*, 'to say', which (unlike its derivative *bequeath*) did not survive to become a regular verb in contemporary English. *Quoth* takes a first- or third-person subject (never *you*), and the subject always follows the verb: 'quoth he', not 'he quoth'. Note that *quoth* does not end in *e*.

> Check out the projected $420 million 1976 Montreal Olympics, which, quoth mayor Jean Drapeau, 'could no more lose money than man could have a baby.'
> *Province* (Vancouver) 17 May 1990: 85

See also ARCHAISMS.

Qur'an see ISLAM

q.v. The Latin abbreviation *q.v.* stands for *quod vide*, 'which see', and alerts the reader to a reference or cross-reference. Though *q.v.* (plural *qq.v.*) is common in older works, more recent reference publications tend to use either the English word *see* or a special typeface, for example, small capitals, to direct the reader to related items.

See also LATIN PHRASES.

R

Rabbi see RELIGIOUS TITLES

raccoon see SPELLING, CANADIAN

race *Race* is a term weighed down by the history of European imperialism and the pseudo-scientific hierarchization of people of different skin colours that was used to rationalize it. *Race* is unquestionably an imprecise concept, and arguably an irrelevant one. At the same time, the political ramifications of visible differences among people are so real that discussions of the concept of *race* cannot be avoided. The African-American literary theorist Henry Louis Gates Jr. has suggested putting the word *race* in quotation marks to remind readers that the whole concept of racial categorization is questionable. In Canada, there is a growing tendency to resist and avoid labelling people by race; yet, as some commentators have pointed out, a physical description of a missing person or a criminal suspect that does not mention race or skin colour is ludicrous. Thus the recommendation of the Canadian Press, Canada's national news agency, is to identify people by race, colour, or national origin only if this information is truly pertinent.

See also BLACK; CAPITAL LETTERS; INDIAN; INCLUSIVE LANGUAGE; -ISM; VISIBLE MINORITY.

racist   see -IST, -ALIST

rack, wrack   A *rack* is a type of framework. One notorious rack was an instrument of torture; as a result, *rack* has connotations of extreme suffering, as in the expressions 'nerve-racking' and 'racked with pain'. *Wrack* is related to wreckage, and now is most often found in the expression 'wrack and ruin', which suggests a state of utter destruction. *Rack* and *wrack* are confused so frequently that most dictionaries now list both spellings for the verb meaning torment and the noun meaning destruction.

> . . . breeders rack their brains to come up with suitable, original, memorable names for each pup.
> *Dogs in Canada* Aug. 1986: 8

> Yes, Flora sold the place, and these new people picked it up real reasonable. Old Wayne'd let it go to wrack and ruin.
> Howard Engel *Murder Sees the Light* 1984: 192

> The short story which he was writing wracked him with tension.
> *Canadian Fiction Magazine* 63 (1988): 66

(The traditional spelling of the verb meaning torment is *rack*.)

> The luxury of studying such abundant wildlife has its own problems. For example, getting the information without disrupting your subjects can be nerve-wracking.
> *Beautiful British Columbia* Spring 1990: 37

(The traditional spelling is *nerve-racking*.)

> In fact, he had to wrack his brain to remember his toughest saves.
> *Vancouver Sun* 17 Jan. 1990: D1

(The traditional spelling in the expression meaning to strain one's brain is *rack*.)

> They were warned year after year that building a country by credit card would lead to rack and ruin.
> *Calgary Herald* 18 Oct. 1993: A4

(Here the traditional spelling is *wrack*.)

See also WREAK.

racquet, racket   In Canadian English *racquet* is the more common spelling for the item of sporting equipment and the game of *racquet-*

ball, but *racket* is not considered incorrect. *Racket* is used for all other meanings of the word, such as an uproar or a fraudulent scheme. *Raquet*, without the *c*, is a misspelling.

radiator   In Canadian English, *radiator* is pronounced either *RAID ee ay ter* or *RAD ee ay ter*. The first pronunciation matches that of the verb *radiate*; the second, which is common in Canada but considered non-standard elsewhere, may be influenced by the pronunciation of *rad*, the short form for *radiator*.

radios   see -OS, -OES

Radio-Canada, Radio Canada   *La Société Radio-Canada*, or *Radio-Canada*, is the French-language network of the Canadian Broadcasting Corporation (CBC) and the name by which the entire corporation is known in French. Like the anglophone division, *Radio-Canada* broadcasts on both radio and television. *Radio-Canada* is not to be confused with *Radio Canada International*, Canada's international short-wave, satellite, and Internet radio service.

radius, radii   see PLURALS, REGULAR, IRREGULAR, FOREIGN

railway, railroad   Canadians say both *railway* and *railroad*, but *railway* is much more common, as in the company name Canadian National Railway. *Railway* is also preferred in Britain. *Railroad* is more common in the United States.

Perhaps because of the American connection, the nineteenth-century escape route into Canada for slaves is usually known as the Underground Railroad.

Railroad has several informal senses that are not shared with *railway*. If the government forces a measure hastily through the legislature, it is said to have *railroaded* it through. To *be railroaded* is to be coerced into doing something, or to be falsely convicted of a crime.

> Because of its proximity to Detroit, [Windsor] was a terminal on the Underground Railroad.
> *The Beaver* Feb.–Mar. 1990: 34

Once again, the people of Ontario were railroaded into something they did not want. . . .
Maclean's 1 Oct. 1990: A4

raise, rise   In Canada and the United States an increase in salary is a *raise*; in Britain it is usually a *rise*. Some dictionaries also list *raise* as a noun meaning an increase in price, a higher bet, or a raised place. Other authorities insist that only *rise* is correct in these contexts.

When it functions as a verb, *raise* takes an object: 'Don't raise her hopes'; 'The landlord will raise our rent'. The verb *rise* does not take an object: 'The dough will rise'; 'The temperature rose last night'. The past tense and past participle of *raise* are both *raised*: 'The cheers raised the roof'; 'They had raised the bridge'. The past tense and past participle of *rise* are *rose* and *risen*: 'The temperature rose yesterday'; 'The sun has risen'.

But there it was for all to see: our senators voting themselves a raise. . . .
Ottawa Citizen 8 June 1990: A2

But when there is more money than there are goods, money loses its value. For some time this was taken into consideration by a raise in prices.
Our Times April 1990: 20

(Here *rise* would be more widely accepted.)

raising, negative-   see DON'T THINK

rancour, rancor   *Rancour* rhymes with *banker*. It means spite or festering ill will. *Rancor* is an alternative American spelling, uncommon in Canada. The adjective has only one spelling: *rancorous*.

See also -OUR, -OR; SPELLING, CANADIAN.

range   see COLLECTIVE NOUNS

rarefy, rarify   Both spellings are now listed in the dictionary; *rarefy* is preferred by most authorities. The -*efy* and -*ify* spellings have been in competition since this word entered the English language around 1600. The spelling with an *e* parallels the word's Latin antecedent: *rarEfacere*, 'to make rare'. The spelling with an *i*

is probably influenced by the words *rarity* and *verify*. *Rarefy* means to make scarcer, thinner, or more refined. In contemporary English, it is almost always used as a past participle meaning lofty or esoteric: 'a rarefied atmosphere', 'rarefied discourses'.

rarely ever   Some critics object to *rarely ever*, preferring *rarely if ever* or *rarely* alone. However, *rarely ever* was used as early as 1694 and is found at all levels of Canadian writing.

Supplies rarely ever meet demand.
Dogs in Canada Aug. 1996: 29

See also EVER.

rarify   see RAREFY

rascally   see FRIENDLY

rates   see TAX

rather than   In the sentence 'Why don't you write rather than call/calling?' either *call* or *calling* is grammatical. *Rather than* functions both as a conjunction, meaning 'and not', and as a preposition, meaning 'instead of'. With the conjunction, the verb forms on either side are parallel: '*felt* rather than *heard* the music', 'will *replace* rather than *renovate* the back kitchen'; after the preposition, the verb that follows is a gerund (i.e., an -*ing* form that acts as a noun): 'Internationalism means that one *acts* abroad with others rather than *acting* abroad unilaterally'. In published Canadian writing both constructions are common.

Less common in writing, but also grammatical, is the use of *rather than* followed by a bare infinitive to indicate a course of action not taken: 'Rather than slave away for another ten years, I took (*or* am taking *or* will take) early retirement'. The verb tense in the main clause can vary.

'I know writers who will send the book back rather than be critical,' says Mark Anthony Jarman, the author of the story collection *19 Knives* and an honest *Globe* reviewer.
National Post (Toronto) 31 March 2001: 242

(Here the verbs around *rather than* are parallel.)

Rather than seeing acting as an escape from self, as she originally had, she now saw it more and more as an exploration of self, a personal journey of discovery.
Queen's Quarterly 98.1 (1991): 170

(Here *rather than* means 'instead of', and the verb that follows is a gerund.)

Rather than remain in York, she resolved to spend the months that William would be away with her brother in New York.
Katherine M. J. McKenna *A Life of Propriety* 1994: 102

(Here *rather than* followed by a bare infinitive indicates a choice rejected.)

See also THAN.

rationalize, rationalization   The original meaning of *rationalize*, to make something conform to reason, or to explain it in rational terms, still appears occasionally in academic writing. In popular usage, however, this meaning has been almost completely supplanted by a psychological meaning that first became current in the 1920s: to *rationalize* is to offer excuses to oneself and others for behaviour that one is not proud of. In the context of business and administration, Canadians also use *rationalize* to mean reorganize to operate more efficiently. This use is often euphemistic, since rationalizing usually entails eliminating jobs.

Lengthy and learned treatises were written in attempts to digest and rationalize the cases into a logical pattern.
J.E. Smyth et al. *The Law and Business Administration in Canada* 1987: 374

. . . he rationalizes his obsession by pretending that he gambles only to secure a fortune and future safety for his granddaughter, Nell.
Robertson Davies *One Half of Robertson Davies* 1978: 218

For a Christian husband to use chain-of-command thinking to rationalize the physical and psychological abuse of his wife is abominable.
Mennonite Brethren Herald 7 March 1986: 15

The hospitals have agreed to more rationalization of clinical services—a turn of events that's remarkable to those who remember the turf wars between doctors protecting their departments. . . .
Whig-Standard (Kingston) 5 June 1992: 1

ratios   see -OS, -OES

ravage, ravish   To *ravage* means to destroy or cause severe damage to. The related noun is most often used in the plural to refer to the destructive effects of something, as in 'the ravages of war'. The countryside is ravaged, not ravished, by war. To *ravish* means either to rape or abduct, or to transport with emotion and fill with pleasure and delight. The use of *ravish* to mean rape is now restricted to Classical allusions. To find someone *ravishing* usually means to find that person attractive.

During late summer, the same hurricanes that ravage the Caribbean can blow themselves out weak as pussycats on the final leg through Atlantic Canada with a day or two of rain.
Alan Tucker, ed. *The Penguin Guide to Canada* 1991: 32

Apollo attempted to ravish a maiden named Daphne.
Vancouver Sun 12 May 1990: R8

(In this reference to Greek myth, *ravish* means rape.)

She was ravishingly beautiful, to begin with. His first impulse was to bring her home and feed her a good meal, but his wife would never put up with that.
Canadian Fiction Magazine 63 (1988): 11

The ravishes of drugs, broken homes, crime, suicide and a thousand other blights on our society all tell us the same message. . . .
Canadian Baptist Feb. 1986: 55

(The word required here is *ravages*.)

ravel, unravel   Both *ravel* and *unravel* mean to fray or come unknit: 'The flag was ravelled'; 'My cuffs were unravelling'. Both words also mean disentangle or elucidate ('unravel the mystery'), though *ravel* is rare in this sense.

Either verb is correctly spelled with a single or

a double *l* before *-ed* or *-ing*; Canadians prefer the double-*l* spellings.

> Paint the cord ends with FrayCheck or clear nail polish against ravelling. . . .
> *Toronto Star* 16 Dec. 1993: FA7

> She steals scenes without even trying, just by lurking about forlornly in her unravelling sweater and muttering to herself.
> *Calgary Herald* 4 March 1994: E1

> The audience knows whodunit early, so the fun comes with watching the police attempt to unravel the mystery.
> *Calgary Herald* 25 March 2006: E3

See also DOUBLING THE FINAL CONSONANT.

ravish   see RAVAGE

raze   The current meaning of *raze* is to demolish or level a structure. Thus the expression 'raze to the ground' is redundant. However, it is idiomatic and sometimes used for emphasis.

> Under Pretoria's long-range plan, black villages located in areas now designated for whites are to be razed and their residents moved to tribal homelands. . . .
> *Globe and Mail* (Toronto) 8 Jan. 1985: P11

> . . . a fire razed the Lower Town in 1845.
> *Chronicle-Telegraph* (Quebec City) 7 Aug. 1991: 5

> The scene is usually set in an older, upscale neighborhood. A small bungalow on a large lot is sold. Its new owner has it razed to the ground.
> *Ottawa Citizen* 9 April 1990: D1

RCMP   see ABBREVIATION, CONTRACTION, SUSPENSION, ACRONYM, INITIALISM

re   *Re* is a Latin word meaning 'in the matter of' or 'regarding'. It is not generally italicized, nor is it followed by a period, since it is not an abbreviation. Typically *re* is used in naming legal cases or at the head of business letters and memoranda to introduce the subject. In general use it is considered informal and thus appropriate to journalism but not to academic essays, where *in regard to*, *concerning*, and *about* are better choices.

> According to the court, the correct question was identified in the American case of Re Guardianship of Eberhardy. . . .
> *Canadian Bar Review* 66.3 (1987): 643

> Re your question: In my opinion Prozac will continue to be available.
> *Ottawa Citizen* 31 Dec. 1990: C5

> Re: Diane Francis's column. . . . I am 72, retired, but born and raised in Alberta and a fifth-generation Canadian.
> *Financial Post* 30 Dec. 1991: 5

See also LATIN PHRASES.

re-   The prefix *re-* has two basic senses: 'back', as in *rebel* (fight back), *recall* (call back), *retrace* (go back), and 'again', as in *refill*, *rekindle*, and *remake*. *Re-* in the sense of 'again' is a productive prefix, which means it is used freely to create new words such as *reborrow*, *refreeze*, and *reinvestigate*. Though many writers use hyphens in such words, style guides consistently advise against hyphenating unless the base word begins with an *e* (*re-elect*, *re-enter*), or the absence of a hyphen would lead to confusion with a homonym; for example: *re-cover* ('I'm going to have that chair re-covered') and *recover* ('They won't recover a penny of their investment'); *re-sign* ('The American Sign Language interpreter re-signed the lawyer's question') and *resign* ('He refuses to resign'); *re-form* ('Twenty years later the group re-formed and went on tour') and *reform* ('He will never reform').

Repay back is redundant because *repay* means pay back.

> It is possible that maintaining a response set from original learning to relearning is necessary to find savings in a recognition test.
> *Canadian Journal of Psychology* 44.3 (1990): 415

> The historical vineyards were re-worked to show that 'significant differences' existed, and could be traced to variations in founding traditions.
> Neil Nevitte and Roger Gibbins *New Elites in Old States* 1990: 2

(The hyphen in *re-worked* is unnecessary.)

> . . . the Goetz who re-entered the school system was not the same man who had taken leave the

year before.
Canadian Journal of History 14.1 (1989): *69*

. . . the wilfully imaginative and subjective re-cre-ation of Vancouver's voyage to the west coast of Canada undermines the echoing of the cliché of 'objective' historiography.
Linda Hutcheon *Splitting Images* 1991: 22

(The hyphen in the word *re-creation* distinguish-es it from recreation.)

The beauty of this is the money that is donated here is loaned out there, repaid back to the imple-menting partner and loaned again.
Calgary Herald 21 July 2005: N1

(Either *repaid* or *paid back* would suffice.)

See also REFER BACK; REVERT.

-re, -er Canadian writers overwhelmingly pre-fer the *-re* (i.e., British) spellings of the words *fibre, lustre, meagre, metre* (for the metric unit; the measuring device is always spelled *meter*), *sombre, spectre,* and *theatre.* However, the pre-ferred American spellings (*fiber, luster, meager, meter, somber, specter,* and *theater*) are also found in Canadian writing and dictionaries, and are perfectly acceptable. Most style guides recom-mend the consistent use of either *-re* or *-er* spellings.

See also CENTRE, CENTER; MACABRE; SPELLING, CANA-DIAN; TIMBER, TIMBRE.

reactive, reactionary Anything that reacts to or is a reaction to something else may be called *reactive.* For example, unstable chemicals are highly reactive; a psychological depression triggered by some particular event is called a 'reactive depression'.
Reactionary is less broadly applicable; it is usu-ally restricted to the sphere of politics, where it refers to extreme conservatism. A person who strongly resists (reacts against) social and politi-cal change may be called 'a reactionary'. This label, the opposite of 'a radical', is usually pejo-rative.

'I work on a very reactive basis. It is crisis manage-ment.'
Maclean's 18 July 1988: A42

Still, it was in keeping with the kind of advice that Decima has been giving Peres: to try to set the campaign agenda and avoid a strictly reactive pos-ture.
Maclean's 31 Oct. 1988: A28

'The Court is a reactionary bastion standing in the way of badly needed reform.'
J. E. Smyth et al. *The Law and Business Administra-tion in Canada* 1987: 23

'We always seem to be reactionary,' [Social Services Minister John] Efford told a news confer-ence. 'We need emphasis on prevention.'
Vancouver Sun 1 Nov. 1990: A14

(Here *reactive* would be better. The minister is deploring the timing, not the conservatism, of social programs.)

'We're thinking about the future, when in the past, especially after [the steroid scandal in] Seoul, we were in a reactionary role.'
Province (Vancouver) 18 June 1990: 24

(Here *reactive* would be better.)

See also PROACTIVE.

real estate agent   see REALTOR

realistically   see PUBLICLY

realize, realization   see -IZE, -ISE, -YZE, -YSE

really, real   *Really* can mean 'in truth' or 'unquestionably' ('He didn't really want to go'; 'We really hit it off'), or 'very' ('I was really tired'). In the phrase 'really sick', *really* is thus open to two interpretations: either 'genuinely' or 'extremely'. In context, this potential ambiguity is quickly dispelled and rarely causes confusion.
   In principle, only adverbs modify adjectives or other adverbs. Yet sometimes *real* replaces *really* and functions as an adverb meaning *very*: 'It's a real nice car; it goes real fast'. This adver-bial use of *real,* which has been noted with dis-approval for over a century, is common in North American but not in British English. Even in Canada and the United States the usage is gen-erally a spoken form, signaling a high degree of informality, and carried into published writing only as an imitation of relaxed talk.

Real and *really* have also come under attack as filler words. Some commentators claim that, in phrases such as 'real facts', 'real life', 'real dairy products', and 'real danger', the adjective *real* actually weakens the sense of the noun. Some also claim that the adverb *really* could be cut from almost any sentence with no change in meaning. In fact, whether *real* or *really* is redundant cannot be determined out of context. The phrase 'real facts' may seem irredeemable, yet it might be used to differentiate the truth from the 'facts' contained in a falsified résumé. And someone who urges you to 'really have a holiday' may be thinking of your tendency to take work along on vacation. Often *real* and *really* are used to signal a contrast, explicit or implied. On the other hand, for some speakers *real* and *really* are simply verbal tics. If *real* and *really* crop up frequently in your writing, it may be time to start cutting.

I told my parents I intended staying out until it got really cold.
Richard Davies and Glen Kirkland, eds. *Dimensions* 1986: 116

'And if we don't get some real cold weather, it could be later than that.'
Globe and Mail (Toronto) 3 Jan. 1985: M9

(The use of *real* is informal.)

'We played real well in the third period'.
Globe and Mail (Toronto) 8 Jan. 1985: S3

(The use of *real* is informal.)

But not many reasonable people today would deny that the poet is entitled to change whatever he likes when he uses a theme from history or real life.
Northrop Frye *The Educated Imagination* 1963: 24

(Here *real life* contrasts with life as a novelist or poet constructs it.)

See also ADJECTIVES AND ADVERBS.

Realtor, real estate agent Though the Canadian Real Estate Association and its American counterpart are trying to stop it, *Realtor* seems to be going the way of *Kleenex*: today it often appears without the capital indi-

cating that it is a trademark. *Realtor* was specially coined to distinguish real estate agents belonging to member companies from those in companies that did not belong to the association. However, *realtor*, without a capital, has come to refer to anyone making a living in the real estate business. This generic use of *realtor* to mean real estate agent or salesperson is now found in all types of published writing, including newspapers, even though the style books of several Canadian newspapers instruct their writers to avoid *realtor*, or to use it only with a capital letter in reference to companies belonging to the Canadian Real Estate Association.

In Britain the term *Realtor* is not used; real estate agents are called 'estate agents'.

Clerks, barbers, motormen, storekeepers all became instant realtors.
Pierre Berton *The Promised Land* 1984: 323

Homeowners, realtors and renovation experts we consulted said you should renovate to improve your enjoyment of a house. . . .
Canadian Consumer Feb. 1986: 11

Mr. James R. Gairdner, President and Chairman of Johnston & Daniel Limited, Realtor, is pleased to announce the appointment of Ms. Judith Rucinski as Vice-President. . . .
Globe and Mail (Toronto) 22 March 1985: B2

(Here *Realtor* is used as a proprietary term in the manner approved by the Canadian Real Estate Association.)

See also TRADEMARKS, BRAND NAMES.

reason being, the see COLLOQUIAL

reason is because, reason why Objections have been made to both these phrases on the grounds that they are redundant. *Because* is usually defined as meaning 'for the reason that', in which case writing *the reason is because* is the same as writing 'the reason is for the reason that'. Any sentence using the phrase can be rewritten to drop either *because* or *the reason*. For example, 'The reason he agreed is because he is her friend' can be rewritten 'He agreed because he is her friend', or 'The reason he agreed is that he is her friend'. Although examples of *the reason is because* can be found in the work of eminent writers since the seventeenth century, editors and teachers often find it objectionable; thus the safest course is to avoid it.

The reason why is similarly redundant, since *why* in this context means 'for that reason'. Nonetheless, *the reason why* is viewed more tolerantly, perhaps because, if *why* is replaced by the unobjectionable *that*, the resulting sentence may appear to have too many *that*s: 'The reason *that* he agreed was simply *that* he was in a hurry'. For whatever reason, most authorities defend *the reason why* as an idiom, and Canadian literary writers are certainly not averse to using it. Be aware, however, that some people will criticize the usage.

> Freed figures the reason for the rash of listings headaches is because of increased competition.
> *London Free Press* 28 April 1988: C3

(Here *because of* could be deleted or the sentence could be rewritten: 'Freed figures the rash of listings headaches results from increased competition.')

> Johnston said one reason why Fraser Surrey Dock got into difficulties three years ago was because Pacific Australia Direct Line moved to Lynnterm. . . .
> *Vancouver Sun* 7 Dec. 1990: D7

(This sentence could be rewritten: 'Johnston said one reason for Fraser Surrey Dock's difficulties was that Pacific Australia Direct Line moved to Lynnterm. . .'.)

> But not many reasonable people today would deny that the poet is entitled to change whatever he likes when he uses a theme from history or real life. The reason why was explained long ago by Aristotle.
> Northrop Frye *The Educated Imagination* 1963: 24

See also SIMPLE REASON; THAT, OMISSION OF

rebel   see RE-

rebellion, revolution, revolt   In history a *rebellion* is a widespread and usually armed uprising against an established ruler or government. Rebellions are usually unsuccessful; a rebellion that succeeds is called a *revolution*. A *revolution* is the actual overthrow of the government and results in significant change to the social organization. *Revolution* is often used figuratively to refer to a major change in social practice: 'sexual revolution', 'computer revolution', 'communication revolution'. A *revolt* is an uprising or an act of protest against authority that may be quickly contained, but that in retrospect is often seen as marking the beginning of a period of significant social change.

> In December 1837 authorities in Upper Canada put down an attempted rebellion.
> *The Beaver* Feb.–Mar. 1990: 28

> [Nelson Mandela] was further charged with sabotage and conspiracy to overthrow the government by revolution.
> *Chatelaine* Jun.–Jul. 1986: 103

> A national tax revolt is on the horizon unless the federal government moves quickly to ease the tax burden on Canadians. . . .
> *Calgary Herald* 15 June 1994: A8

reborrow   see RE-

rebound, redound   *Rebound* means spring back, as in 'The puck rebounded off the boards', and in this sense is usually followed by *off* or *from*. To *rebound* is also used metaphorically in Canadian English to mean to recoil or to adversely affect the originator, and in this sense it is followed by *on* or *upon*: 'Our neglect of the car rebounded on us'. In British English, the sense 'to recoil on' is filled by *redound* followed by *on* or *upon*: 'Their malicious comments redounded on them'. In Canadian use, *redound* is usually followed by *to* and then a word such as 'credit', 'advantage', or 'dishonour'. It means add or accrue to, as in 'Your children's behaviour redounds to your credit'. *Redound* is also used in this way in British English.

> Name-calling also has a way of rebounding on the perpetrator.
> *Engineering Dimensions* May–Jun. 1988: 25

> . . . the critic who feels free to avoid evaluation ignores an important reality, which may one day rebound on his own freedom.
> *Queen's Quarterly* 92.2 (1985): 374

'In all humility, we suggest a few amendments which will redound to your credit should you adopt them.'
Globe and Mail (Toronto) 14 Feb. 1985: P7

In many cases, takeovers redound to the benefit of both the purchaser and the company purchased.
Financial Post 15 Jan. 1990: 10

rebuses see -US

recall see -RE

recant, recount Heresies are *recanted*; stories are *recounted*. To *recant* is to formally retract statements one has made or disavow beliefs one has held. To *recount* means to tell or narrate.

. . . the Roman Catholic Church admitted that it had erred in its dealings with astronomer Galileo when they arrested him and forced him to recant his teachings as heresy or be burned at the stake.
Toronto Star 26 Dec. 1992: J26

R—— recounted for the court the final few minutes of P——'s life.
Toronto Star 12 Dec. 1992: A6

Four years later, with many hiking stories to recant, Jeff moved back to the 'big city'. . . .
Staff Directory, CKUA Radio Network (University of Alberta) website June 2006

(Jeff had stories to tell; the word needed here is *recount*.)

recapitulate, recap To *recapitulate* means to briefly go over the main points of something, usually a speech or discussion. It does not mean to repeat something in its entirety, as some writers mistakenly believe. The clipped form *recap* has come into use as both a verb and a noun. Most dictionaries label *recap* informal. Its use is largely restricted to speech, newspaper and magazine writing, and sports and news commentaries on radio and television.

And yet when it came time for the presiding judge to instruct the jury, he had recapitulated the evidence and the arguments in only a few words. . . .
Jack Batten *Robinette* 1984: 134

Of course, the press of the early 1770s was given to presenting shabby copy; only the intrusion of unprecedented events seems to have spared readers a wholesale recapitulation of essays penned seventy years before.
J.A.W. Gunn *Beyond Liberty and Property* 1983: 28

(A *recapitulation* is a summary; 'wholesale repetition' would be better here.)

As I look forward to my 1985 forays into the marketplace, I can't help but recap—nay, rehash—last year's triumphs and failures.
Canadian Consumer Jan. 1985: 2

recede see -CEED, -CEDE, -SEDE

receive see -IE-, -EI-

reciprocal see MUTUAL

reckon *Reckon* meaning suppose, expect, or guess is informal. Mainly restricted to speech or reported speech, it is more common in Britain, the United States, and Australia than in Canada.
Reckon in the sense of calculate or judge is standard in formal writing.

Monte Vines reckoned he couldn't win the case, so he struck a deal with Moses.
Saturday Night April 1986: 35

(This use is informal.)

. . . the social bonds that we know derive from the society we know and from the feelings that Platonists and vulgar moralists reckon to be 'lower.'
Queen's Quarterly 95.3 (1988): 598

(The use of *reckon* meaning deem or judge is accepted in any type of writing.)

recognize see -IZE, -ISE, -YZE, -YSE

reconnaissance, reconnoitre *Reconnaissance* (pronounced *reh CON uh sunse*) is a military term referring to an exploratory survey of enemy territory—a look at the lay of the land—preceding a military operation. The word is often used figuratively. A related word is *reconnoitre* (*reh con NOY ter*), which is used as both a verb and a noun. *Reconnoiter* is an alternative, chiefly American, spelling.

Note that *reconnaissance* is spelled with a double *n* and a double *s*.

> He had the mannerisms of a rodent on trap reconnaissance.
> *Vancouver Sun* 6 Dec. 1994: B1

> The shooter had apparently reconnoitered the area and picked a spot in the lane from which he could see the doctor through a patio window.
> *Vancouver Sun* 15 Nov. 1994: A3

> It was déjà vu all over again for Pyette, who was here for a pretty serious reconnoitre in the late 1980s.
> *Vancouver Sun* 28 June 1994: A13

recount see RECANT

recover, re-cover see HYPHENATION; RE-

rector, vicar In the most general terms, a *rector* is a person in charge and a *vicar* is a deputy.

In the Anglican Church of Canada a *rector* is a priest in charge of a parish or ministry; a *vicar* is a priest who ministers in a parish or within a ministry, but is not officially in charge of it. A vicar may also be an assistant to a bishop.

In the Roman Catholic Church a *rector* is a priest in charge of a parish, or at the head of a seminary, college, or university. A *vicar* is a priest serving as an administrative assistant, official delegate, or missionary for a bishop. *Vicar of Christ* is one of the pope's titles.

In the Church of England a *rector* is a priest in charge of a parish where, historically, the priest received the tithes of the parish. A *vicar* is the priest in charge of a parish where, historically, the priest was paid a stipend by the layperson, cleric, or religious house that received the tithes.

Not all rectors are clerics. At certain secular universities, colleges, and schools, the head or principal is called the rector. In a tradition that originated in Scotland, a university official elected by the student body is also called the rector.

> The preacher was Canon Robert Greene, rector of St. Bartholomew, Toronto.
> *Canadian Churchman* April 1986: 5

> There are complete plans of the building itself, a list of vicars since 1514 and chronological and scholarly research by archeological and theological experts.
> *Canadian Churchman* April 1986: 11

> Ottawa's Archbishop Marcel Gervais has named Rev. Pat Powers as episcopal vicar for administration.
> *Ottawa Citizen* 16 May 1992: F6

> The Health Department has asked Denis Gagnon, vice-rector of research at Laval University, to study new drug review and drug monitoring procedures. . . .
> *Toronto Star* 26 June 1992: C8

> [He] announced that Norman Rogers, . . . who had been elected rector by the students, had accepted appointment for the customary three-year term.
> Frederick Gibson *Queen's University* 2 (1983): 146

See also MANSE, PARSONAGE, RECTORY; RELIGIOUS TITLES.

rectory see MANSE; RECTOR

recumbent see PRONE, SUPINE

recur, recurrence, reoccur, reoccurrence
Recur and *recurrence* are the established and recommended forms. *Reoccur* rarely appears in Canadian writing, and is not found in most desk dictionaries, although it is listed in the *OED* with citations from the nineteenth century. *Re(oc)cur* means to happen again or repeatedly.

> . . . Canada's war effort would be one of limited liability . . . aimed at avoiding a recurrence of the dread conscription crisis of 1917.
> Frederick Gibson *Queen's University* 2 (1983): 179

> This is playing havoc with our federal finances as budget deficits reoccur from one year to the next. . . .
> *Financial Post* 10 April 1989: 17

(The more widely accepted form is *recur*.)

See also OCCURRENCE.

recyclable see -ABLE, -IBLE

redolent   *Redolent* is used with the prepositions *with* and *of*. When *redolent* is used in its literal sense, 'exuding a certain smell', it is usually followed by *with*. Figuratively, *redolent* means suggestive and is usually followed by *of*, but this is not a rule. Both prepositions are used in both senses.

A sugar refinery worker spent an hour leading us through the cobwebbed, Dickensian factory redolent with the sweet smell of molasses.
Vancouver Sun 8 Dec. 1990: E1

. . . Purdy recounts an incident in which he's told his poems aren't 'romantic' but are instead 'hard-boiled': a slightly archaic adjective, redolent of rock-jowled, mush-hearted 'thirties newspapermen and Humphrey Bogart private detectives.
Margaret Atwood *Second Words* 1982: 98

redound   see REBOUND

Red Tory   see CONSERVATIVE

redundancy   see WORDINESS

re-elect, re-enter   see RE-

reeve   In Ontario, Manitoba, Saskatchewan, Alberta, and British Columbia, a *reeve* is the chair of a rural municipal council whose duties are similar to those of the mayor of an urban community. This meaning is a Canadianism. Historically, in British English, a *reeve* was a magistrate or the manager of a landowner's estate. *Reeve* should be capitalized only when used as a title before a name.

The man . . . was a local contractor, William Brewer, who later became the first reeve of South Vancouver.
Province (Vancouver) 20 June 1990: 2

Westminster Reeve Dave Murray said . . . the proposal was made in the spirit of co-operation.
London Free Press 28 April 1988: B1

refer back   In this phrase *back* is not always necessary, but neither is it always redundant. Sometimes it can help to clarify the meaning, especially in cases where *back* means again or indicates a reference to the past.

When I saw that the Opposition was likely to persist, I . . . asked that the report of the committee be referred back for further study.
Queen's Quarterly 97.3 (1990): 468

(Here *back* means again.)

'In referring to those painters, I was referring back to my own education, and to when I made those Mao paintings with all this hope and idealism.'
Maclean's 22 July 1991: A39

(Here *back* means back in time.)

See also DOUBLING THE FINAL CONSONANT; RE-.

referendum, referendums, referenda   During the constitutional debates in 1991–92 on the Charlottetown Accord, major Canadian newspapers overwhelmingly preferred the regular plural *referendums* to the Latin plural *referenda*. Either is correct.

It took two referendums before a majority of only 7,000 Newfoundlanders voted to become Canadians on July 22, 1948.
Toronto Star 18 Dec. 1991: A1

Referenda should be held on important issues such as abortion, capital punishment and key constitutional questions.
Ottawa Citizen 30 March 1991: B2

See also PLURALS, REGULAR, IRREGULAR, FOREIGN.

reflexive pronouns   see -SELF, -SELVES

reform, re-form   see RE-

refugee   see ÉMIGRÉ

refute, confute, dispute   The verbs *refute* and *confute* both mean to disprove, while to *dispute* means to question or argue against.
Refute usually implies that evidence or a developed argument has proved something or someone wrong. *Refute* is sometimes used simply to mean deny or dispute. This extended sense is not widely accepted and should be avoided.
Confute is an uncommon word implying the application of overwhelming proof against a

person or case: 'Security videos confuted his claim that he had never set foot in the building'. Note that to *confute* does not mean to mix up or confuse.

> Herder's primary object was to refute this thesis by submitting evidence and argument to show that language was invented and gradually perfected by man as the natural means of developing his own reason.
> R. A. Wilson *The Birth of Language* 1937: 21

> 'I seriously refute the observations of some senior police management who are saying the increase in injuries is a direct result of our work to rule.'
> *Globe and Mail* (Toronto) 11 June 1985: M1

(Here *dispute* would be better.)

> And here is a new Mitchell novel, *Ladybug, Ladybug*. . . . The man who accused him of goofing off [and wasting his talent as a writer] is confuted by the fact that the novel was written at all.
> *Ottawa Citizen* 14 Jan. 1989: C3

> The confuted logic by which they justify the irrational policy is that the others are 'rogue' states. . . .
> *Toronto Star* 23 June 1994: A27

(The word required here is *confused*.)

regarding   see IN REGARD[S] TO

regardless, irrespective, [irregardless]
Regardless means without regard to: 'regardless of ability to pay'. *Irrespective* is a slightly more formal synonym. *Irrespective* is always followed by *of*, whereas *regardless* may appear alone, without anything after it: 'We loved her regardless'. In this position *regardless* means nonetheless.

Irregardless, presumably a blend of these two words, is heavily stigmatized as uneducated. Because it contains two negative affixes, *ir-* and *-less*, it is considered a double negative. Although it is heard in speech and occasionally appears in writing, it should be avoided in both.

> Guralnick and Marcus agree Johnson's recordings would have made him a crucial figure regardless.
> *Vancouver Sun* 18 Oct. 1990: A18

> Who should have access to technologies such as

test tube fertilization? Couples only? Single women irregardless of their sexual inclinations?
> *Gazette* (Montreal) 22 Nov. 1990: A6

(Here either *irrespective* or *regardless* is required.)

> Logic would dictate that those intractable fellows must have carefully quantified and considered the cost implications of their actions to their constituents, choosing to go ahead irregardless.
> *Financial Post* 30 Oct. 1990: 14

(The word required here is *regardless*.)

See also DOUBLE NEGATIVE.

regard(s)   see IN REGARD[S] TO

Régie   see QUEBEC ENGLISH

Registered Indian   see ABORIGINAL PEOPLE(S)

regretful, regrettable   *Regretful* is usually applied to people; it means feeling sorry or distressed: 'Now it was too late and she was regretful'. *Regrettable* usually describes events or circumstances, or other people's behaviour, and means causing or likely to cause regret (as in 'a regrettable move'); *unfortunate* and *ill-judged* are synonyms. *Regretful* is often used where *regrettable* is appropriate. The same confusion occurs with the adverbs *regretfully* and *regrettably*.

> Jean-Pierre Beaudry was laid off after 23 years with Shell Canada, but he's neither bitter nor regretful.
> *Ottawa Citizen* 15 Jan. 1994: E4

> Like performance anxiety or Scarlett Johansson, hair loss hits men hard, leading even the most urbane to regrettable decisions.
> *National Post* (Toronto) 28 July 2005: AL6

> 'It's really regretful the whole thing is off,' she said. 'It's going to disappoint a lot of people.'
> *Province* (Vancouver) 4 July 1990: 5

(The word required here is *regrettable*, meaning unfortunate.)

> 'They have a regretful attitude that lawyers interfere with the normal immigration process.'
> *Globe and Mail* (Toronto) 24 April 1985: M3

(The word required here is *regrettable*; 'they' are not feeling regret.)

'The response from the Bulgarians has been, regretfully, insults.'
Globe and Mail (Toronto) 22 May 1985: P5

(The word required here is *regrettably*.)

Reich   see GERMAN WORDS, PRONUNCIATION OF

reign   see -IE-, -EI-

rein   see FREE REIN; -IE-, -EI-

reindeer   see MOOSE

reiterate, iterate   Something that is *reiterated* is said or done again or repeatedly. *Iterate* means the same thing, but for some reason the apparently redundant *reiterate* is the more common form. Some usage commentators have attempted to distinguish between the two words, claiming that *iterate* (meaning simply repeat) is properly used when something is done or said again, whereas *reiterate* (meaning repeat again) should apply to something that has been stated or done three times or more. This is pure pedantry and has nothing to do with actual usage. In fact, *iterate* appears very rarely in Canadian writing, except in the field of computer programming.

. . . Wordsworth reiterates in poem after poem the invitation: Come forth, and bring with you a heart/ That watches and receives.
R.A. Wilson *The Birth of Language* 1937: 69

Already, Quebec voices are iterating their deep misgivings about the vortex of nationalism.
Gazette (Montreal) 9 March 1991: H8

reject   see RE-

relatively, comparatively   *Relatively* and *comparatively* both mean in relation to something else. They are also commonly used in all types of writing to mean fairly or somewhat. Although this use is standard, words such as *fairly*, *somewhat*, or *nearly* are better choices in contexts where no specific comparison is being made.

To Gassy Jack, a sailor and saloon-keeper of the early days, [urban pollution] represents a perversion of life far more sinister than his own relatively healthy vulgarity and vice.
Northrop Frye *The Bush Garden* 1971: 15

(Here an explicit comparison is being made between pollution and vulgarity.)

The trend to increasing off-farm income, even for families considered to be farming relatively full-time, is consistent with observations made elsewhere. . . .
The Canadian Geographer Spring 1989: 39

(Here *almost* would be a better choice.)

relatives, omitted   see THAT, OMISSION OF

relieve   see -IE-, -EI-

relevant   *Relevant*, meaning pertinent or bearing on the matter at hand, is often mispronounced and misspelled *revelant*.

'In our minds, we're champions,' he declared, 'because we beat all the amateurs entered here.' . . . Right or wrong, the quote becomes revelant now because Brasseur and Eisler will defend their 1993 world championships in Japan next Tuesday. . . .
Toronto Star 18 March 1994: E4

(The correct spelling is *relevant*.)

See also MISPRONUNCIATION AND PRONUNCIATION SHIFTS, METATHESIS.

religion,   spirituality,   spiritualism
Religions are moral codes and traditions of worship, usually believed to be divinely inspired, and the social institutions that their adherents form. The word *spirituality* sometimes refers to supernatural beliefs or rituals that are not endorsed by institutionalized religions, as in 'new age spirituality'. *Spirituality* also refers to matters of the spirit, as opposed to physical nature, or an emphasis on the spiritual over the worldly. *Spiritualism*, which is often used mistakenly for *spirituality*, is the belief that the spirits of the dead can communicate with the living, usually through mediums.

Buddhism remains the largest religion of South Korea.
Telegram (St. John's) 10 June 2006: D11

They clung tenaciously to their religion; indeed, the presence of Roman Catholic and Greek Orthodox churches in the rural Prairies acted as a spur to the retention of language and culture.
Pierre Berton *The Promised Land* 1984: 62

In the delicate balance he sought between sensuality and spirituality, Coltrane became a touchstone for the artistic temper of the time.
Jack Chambers *Milestones* 1983: 273

Relatives of the victims said they had previously attended healing rites in the house that were a mixture of Christianity and spiritualism, calling the spirits of the dead for consultation.
Vancouver Sun 14 Dec. 1990: A3

Judaism provides me with the faith and power to see and realize a purer spiritualism, a closer look at God and humanity than I've ever experienced before.
Vancouver Sun 11 Dec. 1990: B3

(The word required here is *spirituality*.)

See also GOD, GODS; RELIGIOUS TITLES.

religious titles Titles for clergy vary from denomination to denomination. The Roman Catholic title *Cardinal* is placed between the first name and the last: 'Marc Cardinal Ouellet'. In subsequent references the first name is omitted: 'Cardinal Ouellet'. In both the Roman Catholic and Anglican churches, *Archbishop* and *Bishop* are placed before the full name: 'Archbishop Desmond Tutu'. *Archbishop* with the surname is used in subsequent references: 'Archbishop Tutu'. Catholic priests are called *Father*. Catholic *Monsignors* are so titled only in the first reference: 'Monsignor Boyle'. Subsequent references use *Father*: 'Father Boyle'. Though a Catholic priest may be referred to as Reverend So-and-so, Catholics don't use 'the Reverend' as a noun, as in 'The Reverend dropped in for a visit'; many Protestant denominations also discourage this usage. *Reverend* is never abbreviated when used with *the*, whether as a noun or with the full name: 'the Reverend John Smith'.

In the Anglican Church deans are referred to as *Very Reverend* (which may be abbreviated *Very Rev.*), and then *Dean*. Archdeacons are called *Venerable* (*Ven.*) and then *Archdeacon*. Canons are called *Reverend* and then *Canon*. Lesser Anglican clergy are referred to as *Reverend* and in subsequent references as *Mr.*, *Mrs.*, *Miss*, *Ms.*, or *Dr.* Note that the honorifics *Very Reverend*, *Venerable*, and *Reverend* should always be followed by the first and last name.

A United Church moderator, if ordained, is *Right Reverend* on the first reference and then *Mr.*, *Mrs.*, *Ms.*, *Miss*, or *Dr.* Former moderators are *Very Reverend*. A lay moderator is called simply *Moderator*: 'Moderator Anne Squires'. All United Church ministers are called *Reverend* and, in second references, *Mr.*, *Mrs.*, *Ms.*, *Miss*, or *Dr.* Presbyterian ordained moderators and all ministers are *Reverend* in the first reference and then *Mr.*, *Mrs.*, *Miss*, *Ms.*, or *Dr.* Most other Protestant ministers can be referred to in the same way, though some denominations do not use the honorific *Reverend*; among them are the Christian Scientists, the Jehovah's Witnesses, the Mormons, and the Seventh-day Adventists.

The title *Rabbi*, applied to religious scholars, teachers, and leaders in the Judaic tradition, is used before the full name in the first reference; *Mr.*, *Mrs.*, *Miss*, *Ms.* or *Dr.* is used in subsequent references.

In Islam, religious leaders of various types, including those who lead prayers in mosques, are called *imams*. Some Muslim groups also use *Imam* as a title before a name. Sunni Muslims call a revered scholar and arbiter of Islamic law a *mufti*, while Shiites, especially in Iran, use the term *ayatollah*. The words *Mufti*, meaning 'legal expert', *Sheikh*, meaning 'revered elder' (cf. *sheik*, another spelling of the same Arabic word), and *Ayatollah* are all used as religious titles.

Within the Hindu tradition, those who conduct religious services are called *pandits* (cf. the English word *pundit*), and *Pandit* is used as a title of respect not only for religious scholars but also for acknowledged masters in other fields: 'Pandit Ravi Shankar'.

Buddhist teachers in the West are sometimes given the honorific *Rev.* or *Ven*: 'Ven. Miao Hsin'.

See also LAMA, LLAMA; MANSE, PARSONAGE, RECTORY, VICARAGE; RECTOR, VICAR; TITLES OF PEOPLE.

reluctant   see RETICENT

remarkably   see ADJECTIVES AND ADVERBS

Renaissance   see CAPITAL LETTERS

renounce, renunciation   see PRONUNCIATION

renown, renowned   *Renown*, which rhymes with *crown*, is a noun meaning fame. *Renowned* is the corresponding adjective and means famous. Sometimes *renown* is incorrectly used as the adjective; dictionaries do not recognize this usage.

Reknown and *reknowned* sometimes find their way into print (presumably writers are thinking of *well-known*), but these spellings are considered errors.

Rigoletto, an operatic singer of great renown, was engaged to give a concert in Montréal.
J.E. Smyth et al. *The Law and Business Administration in Canada* 1987: 304

The view that the numerical size of a group is highly significant in determining its forms of interaction was first systematically stated by the renowned sociologist Georg Simmel.
Irving M. Zeitlin and Robert J. Brym *The Social Condition of Humanity* 1991: 60

The two officers removed their helmets and laid down their guns in a sign of respect and trust to local elders, who are usually renown for their hospitality.
Whig-Standard (Kingston) 6 March 2006: 9

(The correct spelling is *renowned*.)

He put himself in position for a promotion by gaining some reknown as the tutor of the Flames. . . .
Province (Vancouver) 26 Jan. 1990: 59

(The correct spelling is *renown*.)

Reknowned for his robust energy, Mr. Thomson exercised daily at the Cambridge Club in downtown Toronto and could be seen walking with his wife and grandchildren around his neighborhood.
National Post (Toronto) 13 June 2006: A1

(The correct spelling is *renowned*.)

reoccur, reoccurrence   see RECUR

repairable, unrepairable, reparable, irreparable   Generally, *repairable* and *unrepairable* describe machines ('The toaster is repairable'), while *reparable* and its negative *irreparable* are used to describe such things as damage (e.g., to reputations), harm, or loss.

Repairable is pronounced *reh PAIR uh bul*, and *reparable* is pronounced *REP er uh bul*.

. . . in his address to the recycling conference, Anderson revealed that only one in 12 appliances is repairable.
Gazette (Montreal) 22 Oct. 1990: D2

Business should ask questions such as those posed in a submission to the Brundtland Commission. . . . 'Is this the best design . . . built to last . . . easily reparable or recyclable?'
Financial Post 22 May 1989: 18

(This use of *reparable* to describe an object is unusual in Canadian writing.)

All we could expect to accomplish would be to . . . cause irreparable damage to our friendship with Nigeria.
George Ignatieff *The Making of a Peacemonger* 1987: 237

repatriate   see PATRIATE

repay   see RE-

repel   see REPULSE

repertoire, repertory   *Repertoire* and *repertory* are interchangeable when they refer to the inventory of pieces that an artist, band, theatre company, etc., is prepared to perform, or, by figurative extension, the range of behaviours that a person or animal is capable of. *Repertoire* is the more common choice.

Repertory is also used as an adjective to describe a type of theatre in which a company performs short runs of many different plays, or a type of cinema presenting short runs of many previously released films rather than long runs of new films.

He had but a small repertoire: pieces by Bach, Kreisler and a handful of others.
Queen's Quarterly 92.1 (1985): 98

. . . the nightly repertory of the quintet includes surprisingly few of the compositions recorded for Dial and Savoy the previous year.
Jack Chambers *Milestones* 1983: 78

Animals possess a small repertory of sounds and gestures by which they communicate danger and the like to one another.
Irving M. Zeitlin and Robert J. Brym *The Social Condition of Humanity* 1991: 13

It had one repertory theatre, no ballet company, and hardly any decent brie.
Margaret Atwood *Second Words* 1982: 402

replace   see SUBSTITUTE

replacement worker, scab, strikebreaker
Of the terms commonly used for someone who takes over the work of a striking worker, *replacement worker* is the most neutral. In the eighteenth century, *scab* was first used to refer to someone who refused to join a trade union. Around the turn of that century it took on its contemporary meaning of *replacement worker*; it can also refer to a worker who refuses to join a strike. Because *scab* is highly partisan and pro-union, it often appears in quotation marks in print. The slightly less partisan term *strikebreaker* was in use as early as 1904 for workers brought in to do the work of strikers.

The proposals, unveiled last week, would make union-organizing easier and limit the use of replacement workers during a strike.
Ottawa Citizen 12 Nov. 1991: A4

Bousquet . . . received at least one call from a part-time employee who claimed he had been harassed and treated 'like a scab' by the unionized workers.
Gazette (Montreal) 23 Feb. 1990: A1

He joined the majors as a 'scab' during the 1979 umpires' strike. . . .
Ottawa Citizen 30 June 1990: E5

In Ottawa, an orthopedic surgeon . . . suffered a concussion after picketers, apparently mistaking him for a strikebreaker, knocked him from his bicycle.
Maclean's 23 Sept. 1991: A32

replete, complete   *Replete* in most uses means filled to abundance with something, whereas *complete* means whole, full, lacking nothing. In some contexts, either word may be used; if the writer wishes to stress abundance, *replete* is the best choice. *Replete* is often used in connection with food, meaning that the eater's appetite is satisfied, or even sated.

Thus, while the book is replete with facts and figures, it is further enhanced by direct quotes. . . .
Harry M. Rosenthal and S. Cathy Berson, eds. *Canadian Jewish Outlook Anthology* 1988: 115

(Here *replete* means abundantly filled with; *complete* would not work.)

Burlington's produced an 'Avengers' show, complete with catsuits, tattoos, bouffants, mid-parts, guns and glitter.
Gazette (Montreal) 30 Dec. 1990: F3

(Here *replete* would also fit, if the writer wished to suggest abundance.)

Andrew and Gordievsky have produced a big book, replete with a full scholarly apparatus.
Gazette (Montreal) 29 Dec. 1990: I2

(Here *complete* would be better, since presumably a scholarly apparatus is not improved by abundance.)

'When replete, the eaters washed their hands. . . .'
Gazette (Montreal) 31 March 1990: B2

replica   In fine arts a *replica* is a reproduction of a work made by, or supervised by, the original artist. Although some critics insist on preserving this specialized sense, *replica* is used generally to mean a copy or reproduction, and is now more often applied to artifacts than to works of art. The phrase 'replica copy' is redundant.

Perdue, dressed in a miniature replica of the same suit, stood beside him.
Geoffrey Ursell *Perdue, or, How the West Was Lost* 1984: 41

The fisherperson is allowed one trophy-size fish to take back home: however, a replica can be made by the taxidermist and you will not be able to tell the difference.
Up Here Jan.–Feb. 1990: 55

[They] have created an exact replica of the century-old Ontario Georgian house where Mr. MacRobbie spent his childhood and early years.
Globe and Mail (Toronto) 18 May 1985: H1

reputation   see CHARACTER

reserve, reservation, rez, res   Aboriginal peoples in Canada who signed treaties were settled on *reserves*. In the United States these areas are called *reservations*, and objections are often raised to the use of *reservation* to refer to a Canadian reserve. *Rez* (sometimes *res*) is slang for *reserve*, as in Tomson Highway's play *The Rez Sisters*.

A group of Mohawks snarled traffic yesterday on part of a highway on the Kahnawake reserve to show solidarity with Indian demonstrators in Toronto.
Gazette (Montreal) 18 Dec. 1994: A3

A particularly senseless and counterproductive policy was the official opposition to the use of farm machinery on Indian reserves.
NeWest Review Dec.–Jan. 1990: 33

By allowing the Native people to live on reservations and to exist as a kingdom within a kingdom, so to speak, we have been denying them their rights as Canadians.
Sudbury Star 5 June 2006: A11

(Here *reservations* should be replaced by *reserves*.)

Tomson's father, Joe Highway, was originally from the Pelican Narrows Indian Reserve in northeastern Saskatchewan and his ancestors came from this 'rez' and from Cumberland House, Saskatchewan.
Tomson Highway *The Rez Sisters* 1988: vi

resident   see CITIZEN

resign, re-sign   see RE-

respective, respectively   *Respective* and *respectively* are common in academic writing. Often these words have no real function in the sentence, in which case they are both wordy and pretentious. *Respective* or *respectively* should be used only when one series of particulars

must be matched with another in the same sentence—and even then the sentence can often be unambiguously worded without them.

If, respectively, geographers and anthropologists elaborate in this way, historians have any number of temporal, topical, or biographical lacunae to which they can channel their attention.
Queen's Quarterly 97.4 (1990): 567

(Here *respectively* could be omitted.)

Thus Malinowski delineated the respective spheres of magic, science, and religion and their effects on both the individual and society.
Irving M. Zeitlin and Robert J. Brym *The Social Condition of Humanity* 1991: 210

(Here *respective* could be omitted.)

The causes of the conflict between them are to be found not in their biological makeup but in their respective social organizations.
Irving M. Zeitlin and Robert J. Brym *The Social Condition of Humanity* 1991: 31

(Here *respective* could be omitted.)

The APR reputed for temperate crop plants such as tomato, wheat and peas amounts to 17, 45 and 2% of total respiration respectively.
Arctic 41.1 (1988): 1

(In this sentence *respectively* is useful.)

New and used implements are interest-deferred until November 1 and May 1 next year, respectively.
Country Guide Dec. 1986: 20

(Here too *respectively* is useful.)

respite   *Respite* means reprieve or temporary relief from a stressful situation. Sometimes it is preceded by an article ('grant a respite') and sometimes it is not ('find respite'). The standard pronunciation in Canada and the United States is *RESS pit*. Canadians also say *reh SPITE*, but this pronunciation is criticized.

. . . it is a place where visitors find a friendly welcome in idyllic surroundings, relaxation and a wonderful respite from city life.
Leisure Life 1988: 49

Another family took advantage of publicly funded respite care. The child with special needs stayed overnight on occasional weekends, giving the rest

of the family a chance to enjoy some less intense time together.
Toronto Star 15 June 2006: R5

responsible, responsibility   The correct spellings are *responsible* (ending in *-ible*), *responsibility*, and *responsibilities*. These words are frequently misspelled in various ways.

> The Canadian Radio-Television and Telecommunications Commission would close up shop in Quebec or be responsable for a few marginal technical matters.
> *Gazette* (Montreal) 7 Sept. 1991: B3

> (The correct spelling is *responsible*. Since *responsable* is French for *responsible*, this misspelling probably reflects the influence of Quebec French.)

See also -ABLE, -IBLE; QUEBEC ENGLISH.

restaurateur   The owner of a restaurant is a *restaurateur*, spelled without an *n* and pronounced *RES tuh ruh TER*. However, *restauranteur* has become so common in print that dictionaries, including the *Canadian Oxford Dictionary* and *Merriam-Webster's*, are beginning to list it as a variant spelling.

> The Polar Bear Swim Club and the yearly dip were founded in 1920 by the late Vancouver restaurateur Peter Pantages.
> *Province* (Vancouver) 29 Dec. 1994: A2

> Food service professionals, in particular—whether chefs, caterers, . . . or restauranteurs—are realizing the specialty food industry supplies quality foods to help business.
> *Western Grocer* Aug. 1990: 26

> (The more widely accepted spelling is *restaurateur*.)

restive, restless   Both words may mean fidgety or agitated, but *restive* usually implies impatience or rebelliousness in the face of restraint or authority, while *restless* is not necessarily associated with restraint. *Restive*, which comes from the Middle French *rester*, 'to remain', was once commonly applied to horses that were balky and obstinate.

> The students . . . could grow restive on bitter winter days when compelled to accompany the professor and his instruments out onto the windswept and frozen lake for what must have seemed interminable lectures.
> Hilda Neatby *Queen's University* 1 (1978): 9–10

> One of the cows is restive, shifting her weight from back hoof to back hoof as Cinnamon . . . prepares her for the milker.
> *Canadian Heritage Magazine* Aug.-Sept. 1986: 14

> [Kim Campbell] alone was in a position to keep restive Quebecers and disaffected westerners from turning to regional parties.
> *Toronto Star* 23 Oct. 1993: A1

> If you need a break from the restless, all-day scampering between live jazz sites, pop into Metro Reference Library.
> *Toronto Star* 29 June 1994: D2

restrictive and non-restrictive clauses
see COMMA; THAT, WHICH

résumé, resumé, resume   A *résumé* is any summary, though in Canadian English the word most often refers to a summary of someone's work experience written as part of a job application. In French *résumé* is pronounced *RAY ZOO MAY*. The usual English pronunciation is *REZ oo may*. This difference in pronunciation—in English the first *e* is not given a long *a* sound—may account for the tendency to drop the first accent: in Canadian writing, the most widely used form is *resumé*. Note, however, that not all dictionaries list this form. Some dictionaries list *resume* with no accents at all as a standard form but reject *resumé* as a hybrid of English and French. Other dictionaries list *résumé*, presumably because it reflects the English pronunciation and distinguishes the noun from the verb *resume*, but do not list the accentless *resume*. In formal writing *résumé* with two accents is the safest spelling. All three spellings are defensible, however.

> His exotic résumé included a B.A. in Asian studies . . . and a stint with U.S. Airforce intelligence.
> *Saturday Night* July 1986: 40

> Some professionals . . . estimate that personnel specialists spend approximately 30 seconds

reviewing a resumé.
Queen's Quarterly 94.4 (1987): 852

Philip's relationship to Janie Burroughs was something Elizabeth had forgotten during her witty, lighthearted resumé of her domestic situation at the lunch table. . . .
Margaret Atwood *Life Before Man* 1979: 198

(Here *resumé* means a brief account, or vignette.)

You may apply in confidence by forwarding a complete resume naming the position for which you are applying. . . .
Engineering Dimensions Jul.–Aug. 1988: 52

See also CURRICULUM VITAE.

retch, wretch, wrench To *retch* is to attempt to vomit. A *wretch* is an unfortunate soul. To *wrench* is to twist violently.

'The slightest thing would trigger her gagging reflex,' he says. 'I found her dry wretching.'
Ottawa Citizen 22 May 2004: D12

(The correct spelling is *retching*.)

Every few years, some ink-stained wretch scrounging for something to write on a slow day resurrects the decline of written English. . . .
Vancouver Sun 12 May 2006: A19

Andy Duvall of New York missed a gut-wretching eagle putt on the 12th hole at Roseland during June's AJGA championship.
Windsor Star 28 Dec. 2002: A21

(The correct word is *gut-wrenching*.)

reticent, reluctant *Reticent*, in its most common and widely accepted sense, is the opposite of *talkative* or *forthcoming*. Sometimes *reticent* means restrained, especially with respect to artistic productions.

In addition, *reticent* is frequently used as a synonym for *reluctant* or *hesitant*. This usage, however, is acknowledged by only a few dictionaries and is disputed by language commentators; it should be avoided in writing. *Reticent* is pronounced *RET ih sent*.

But the normally reticent . . . developer happily discusses the episode now as one that has set a precedent. . . .
Vancouver Sun 23 Aug. 1990: D12

On the subject of Shaw's unconsummated and mostly unhappy marriage . . . Holroyd is fairly reticent.
Vancouver Sun 3 Feb. 1990: C4

. . . many ventured reasons why the church seemed reticent to engage, at a local level, the pain of the economy.
United Church Observer May 1986: 37

(In this example *hesitant* or *reluctant* would be preferable.)

We must be strategic and selective, and not be reticent to switch course if required.
International Journal 59.4 (2004): 815–28

(In this example, *hesitant* or *reluctant* would be preferable.)

revenge see AVENGE

Reverend see RELIGIOUS TITLES

reverse discrimination see EQUALITY

revert To *revert* is to go back or return to a former condition, belief, or subject. In law, money or property that *reverts* to former owners (or their heirs) is returned to them. The common usage *revert back* is redundant.

No one wants to revert to the feudal systems our ancestors tried to escape.
Country Guide Nov. 1986: 42

He claims 90 per cent of people who try vegetarianism revert back to eating beef.
Vancouver Sun 17 July 1990: D6

(The word *back* is unnecessary here.)

See also RE-.

review, revue A *review* is a critical report, a periodical publication, a military inspection, a general survey of the literature in a scholarly field, or a revue. *Revue* has only one meaning: a stage show featuring sketches, dancing, and songs that parody current events and fads. Revues were a popular form of entertainment in nineteenth-century France, and the English borrowed both the idea and the word from the

French. While the English spelling *review* can be used for the stage show, *revue* is not an accepted spelling variant for the other meanings of *review*.

> Since Elias does not offer his readers a review of the literature, appropriate questions need to be raised about the place of this research within the existing knowledge.
> *NeWest Review* Dec.–Jan. 1990: 33

> Hosted by comedians Roger Abbott and Don Ferguson of CBC's *Royal Canadian Air Farce*, the 'Against Free Trade Revue' poked fun at Prime Minister Brian Mulroney's plans for a free trade agreement with the United States.
> *United Church Observer* May 1986: 51

> But there's more—theatrical comedy six nights a week . . . and noon-time musical reviews.
> *Canadian Living* 17 May 1986: 3

> Other highlights of the Sarnia Games are the colourful opening ceremonies . . . and the Ceilidh Tent featuring 'Fraser's Highlanders', a local group gaining great revues from the visitors. . . .
> *Leisure Life* May 1988: 24

(The correct spelling here is *reviews*.)

revision   see BACK-FORMATION

revolt   see REBELLION

revolution   see REBELLION; APPENDIX II

revue   see REVIEW

rez   see RESERVE

rhetoric   see entry in Glossary

rhetorical question   In oratory a rhetorical question is one posed purely for effect, not to get information. The question is phrased in such a way that there is only one possible answer, which the listeners are expected to supply for themselves. Some humorous rhetorical questions are 'Are we men or are we mice?' and 'Do fish swim?' A rhetorical question has the effect of a forceful statement and is usually delivered in a persuasive tone. However, in writ-ing, where the readers' reactions cannot be gauged, such questions can have unexpected results. Writers should make sure that their readers will answer a rhetorical question cor-rectly—even if that means supplying the answer themselves.

rhinoceros, rhinoceroses   The usual plural form is *rhinoceroses*. The singular form, *rhinocer-os*, can also be used as a plural: 'The rhinoceros are under the trees'. *Rhinoceri* is listed in some dictionaries, but this form is considered incor-rect by some commentators because it is based on the false assumption that *rhinoceros* is a Latin noun forming its plural in *-i*. In fact, the correct Latin plural of this originally Greek word is *rhinocerotes*, a form that had some currency in the nineteenth century but is now obsolete. Many writers avoid the problem of selecting the correct plural by using the informal short forms *rhino* and *rhinos*.

> Just as rhinoceroses in Africa are killed for their horns, so sheep in Quebec might be killed for their stomachs.
> *Gazette* (Montreal) 13 Dec. 1990: B2

> The vintage prints speak eloquently, filling the Special Exhibitions Hall with images of . . . rhinoceri and elephants, circus performers, an her-maphrodite, jazz musicians, statues in Rome.
> *Ottawa Citizen* 6 Oct. 1990: G3

(Either *rhinoceroses* or *rhinoceros* is recommend-ed.)

See also PLURALS, REGULAR, IRREGULAR, FOREIGN.

rhyme, rime   The earliest spelling, *rime*, was displaced by *rhyme* in the fifteenth century because scholars mistakenly believed that the word was derived from *rhythm*. *Rhyme* refers to words with similar terminal sounds, or to sim-ple verse, as in 'nursery rhymes'. Now *rime* usu-ally means frost; it can, however, be used as a variant spelling of *rhyme* (Coleridge famously used this spelling to create an archaic effect in *The Rime of the Ancient Mariner*). *Rhyme off* is an informal expression meaning to list or name a series of things.

'It works for me too, except for the place where he rhymes "spastic" with "plastic."'
Margaret Atwood *Second Words* 1982: 338

His fingers dance over the listings and he rhymes off case quantities for all the good vintages of Chateau Lafite as far back as 1868 . . . and scads more.
Bon Vivant Aug.–Sept. 1982: 14

rid, ridded   The past tense and past participle (the form used after *have*) can be either *rid* or *ridded*.

Occasionally *ridded* is mistakenly substituted for *ridden* meaning infested or afflicted, as in 'flea-ridden'.

'With its use of "free" verse, Imagism rid a lame poetry of a musty Georgian Romanticism.'
Queen's Quarterly 92.2 (1985): 310

'We've rid him of the habit,' says veteran 86ers trainer Lou Moro.
Vancouver Sun 27 April 1990: E3

. . . the Rockets ridded themselves of the Utah Jazz with a 94-83 victory in their best-of-seven Western Conference championship series.
Gazette (Montreal) 1 June 1994: F5

With slump-ridded Leo Gomez out for at least a month following wrist surgery, Baltimore Orioles are considering signing third baseman Kevin Seitzer. . . .
Toronto Star 24 July 1993: C3

(Gomez was *slump-ridden*.)

riding   In Canada, and only in Canada, a *riding* is an electoral district or constituency. The term was borrowed into English from the Old Norse word *thrithjungr*, later spelled *triding*, which meant a third part. Originally, in England, *triding* was particular to the county of Yorkshire, which was divided into three administrative divisions. Over time, *triding* lost its initial *t*, and *riding* was the form that was brought to Canada. Although the ridings in Yorkshire were abolished by the British government in 1974, and the term is now seldom used in Britain, it is an integral part of Canadian political vocabulary.

Provincial Liberals . . . nominated him as their candidate in the riding of West York in 1948.
Jack Batten *Robinette* 1984: 156

rife   see RIPE

riff, rift   Sometimes *riff* is mistakenly used in place of *rift*. In jazz a *riff* is a repeated musical phrase, especially one used as background for a soloist or improvisation; the term is probably a shortened form of *refrain*. A *rift* is a split or break.

But they have handed the opposition Parti Québécois an array of problems to use as ammunition during the daily question period: the handling of the Mohawk crisis, . . . the public riff between Environment Minister Pierre Paradis and Energy Minister Lise Bacon over future James Bay development. . . .
Gazette (Montreal) 13 Oct. 1990: B5

(The word required here is *rift*.)

The veracity of that account has been strenuously questioned, as has her role in creating a riff between her husband and his children.
National Post (Toronto) 31 May 2003: SP1

(The word required here is *rift*.)

rifle, riffle   The verb *rifle* means to ransack, rob, or steal; to *rifle through* a purse, drawer, etc., is to search it hurriedly. The verb *riffle* means to leaf through pages, or to shuffle a deck of cards.

'You're not getting off so easily,' she breathes, and rifles his pockets for change.
Canadian Fiction Magazine 63 (1988): 17

One of the great joys in life . . . is a fashion bargain, so you may see me rifling through the racks at the great Canadian designer clearance sale.
Toronto Star 19 May 1994: D5

The premier smiled and riffled through his papers.
Ottawa Citizen 30 Nov. 1994: A10

Mr. Keegstra . . . rifled through a small pamphlet as he listened to the prosecutor.
Globe and Mail (Toronto) 17 July 1985: 3

(If Keegstra was leafing through a pamphlet, the word required is *riffled*.)

rift   see RIFF

right   see ADVERBS WITHOUT -LY

right-minded   see -MINDED

rigorous   see -OUR, -OR

rime   see RHYME

ring   The past tense is *rang*: 'Before the war, the bells rang every Sunday for an hour'. The past participle (the form that follows *have*) is *rung*: 'She has rung your doorbell twice'. The use of *rung* as the past tense is considered non-standard: 'She *rung* that bell as if she wanted to break it'.

> 'I rang the handbell at 9 sharp.'
> *Gazette* (Montreal) 2 Sept. 1990: A2

> Through the centuries, church bells have rung in celebration and in warning, in victory and in defeat.
> *Province* (Vancouver) 29 June 1990: 22

> 'The last World Cup rung the alarm bells.'
> *Vancouver Sun* 2 Oct. 1990: C7

> (The standard past tense is *rang*.)

See also PHONE; STANDARD, STANDARD ENGLISH.

rip   see COMPUTER TERMS

ripe, rife   *Ripe* means at its peak: 'The peach is ripe, juicy, and ready for eating'. *Rife* means prevalent ('The weeds are rife in the fields') or containing something prevalent ('The fields are rife with weeds'). *Ripe* is sometimes mistakenly used for *rife*, especially when the thing that abounds is a good thing.

> Murray predicts that 2004 will be ripe with opportunity and that advisors need to actively pursue new clients before the markets instill complacency.
> *Advisor's Edge* Jan. 2004

> (The word needed here is *rife*.)

rise   see RAISE

road, concession road, side road, street, highway, parkway, expressway, freeway, autoroute, trail, motorway, turnpike, toll road, thruway, express toll route
Road is the most general of these words. In the past *road* referred to the main route between towns or cities, and often the road took its name from a destination. (In Kingston, for example, Bath Road leads to Bath, Sydenham Road to Sydenham, and Perth Road to Perth.) Now *road* may designate anything from a paved highway to a dirt track, depending on the context. A *concession road* is a rural road, especially in Ontario and Quebec. In these provinces the land for settlers was subdivided into parcels called concessions, and concession roads generally run east–west along the boundaries between them. *Side roads* are north–south rural roads. *Streets* are usually urban.

Highway has, at least since 1859, meant the most direct and least time-consuming route from one place to another and is still used figuratively in this sense: 'the highway to riches', 'the information highway'. Now, in North America, a *highway* is a road designed to carry fast-moving traffic. In Canada *highway* generally refers to a two-lane road connecting two major centres. *Expressway* is the common term for a multi-laned, limited access road. The term *collector lanes* for the lanes running parallel to an expressway and affording access to it is a Canadianism, now also used in the United States. *Freeway*, which originated in the United States in the 1930s, is widely used in western Canada. *Highway*, *expressway*, and *freeway* are use interchangeably by many Canadians. The French word *autoroute* sometimes finds its way into Canadian English, especially in reference to highways in Quebec. *Trail* is often used in the names of historic scenic highways in various parts of Canada. A *parkway* is an expressway bordered by beautiful scenery or well-tended trees and grass.

In Britain *motorway* is the only term for a limited access highway with at least two lanes in each direction. A *turnpike* was originally a *toll road* (which motorists paid a toll for using); now *turnpike* is used in the United States like *thruway* (an accepted spelling in the United States) for any major highway, whether or not tolls are charged. The privately owned, pay-for-use highway through the Greater Toronto Area, which has no toll booths but assesses tolls electronically, is called an *express toll route* (407 ETR).

> [Hunters] had set up at the edge of a wheat field earlier that morning and had already taken a couple of [Canada geese] when they saw yet another car stop along the concession road about three quarters of a mile away.
> *Gazette* (Montreal) 20 Oct. 1990: 65

> Seferis purchased the property . . . and two months later learned that the highway on which it was located would be superseded by the new freeway. . . .
> J.E. Smyth et al. *The Law and Business Administration in Canada* 1987: 223

> The 'new' city [of Quebec], beyond the 18th-century bastions, reaches out . . . to the shopping malls of suburbia, the provincial autoroute (highway) network, and the airport at nearby Sainte-Foy.
> Alan Tucker, ed. *The Penguin Guide to Canada* 1991: 272

> Drive the Cabot Trail, too, . . . and also try the Lighthouse Route south from Halifax along a coast that's furrowed and rocky.
> Alan Tucker, ed. *The Penguin Guide to Canada* 1991: 9

See also SKID ROAD; THRU.

rob, steal, robbery   Generally speaking, people and places are *robbed* ('The bank was robbed'; 'I was robbed'), while objects are *stolen* ('My wallet was stolen'). 'Our jewels were robbed' is considered non-standard. Some commentators also disapprove of 'Their house was robbed while they were away', insisting on 'Their house was burglarized', because the legal definition of *robbery* includes a face-to-face encounter and violence or intimidation.

See also BURGLARY.

robin   see CAPITAL LETTERS; SPECIES

rococo   see BAROQUE

role, roll   A *role* is a part to be played. *Roll* is the spelling of all other meanings: a bun, something wrapped around itself, a list of names. It is the 'list' meaning of *roll* that is most commonly misspelled.

> This was proven by the role call of the vote to defeat the government.
> *Ottawa Citizen* 30 Nov. 2005: A17

(The proper spelling is *roll call*; think of a scroll with names on it.)

romance, Romance languages, Romanticism, romantic, romancer   The word *romance* was first used to distinguish the vernacular Latin dialects used in the Roman provinces from the Latin spoken in Rome. These regional vernaculars evolved into the modern *Romance languages* including French, Spanish, Portuguese, Italian, and Romanian. The first *romances* were fanciful adventure tales written in these dialects (formal Latin was reserved for scholarly and official writings), stories told in poetry and prose dealing with the exotic, the heroic, and the passionate as opposed to the everyday or the real. This use of *romance* is close to one modern meaning: a fictional tale of extraordinary events, a fabrication. Gradually, however, *romance* took on the meaning that is more common today: a passionate love story.

Romanticism refers to an artistic movement of the late eighteenth and early nineteenth centuries that celebrated freedom of individual expression and creativity. The adjective *Romantic*, when capitalized, refers to this movement ('Keats was a Romantic poet').

Some usage guides object to the verb *romance* meaning to woo or court, but most dictionaries accept this usage. Note, however, that the noun form *romancer* is ambiguous: it may refer to a lover, or to a storyteller or liar, or now, especially in journalism, to a romantic movie.

> In romance we have a simplified and idealized world, of brave heroes, pure and beautiful heroines, and very bad villains.
> Northrop Frye *The Educated Imagination* 1963: 48

(Here *romance* means the early adventure-story genre.)

In a survey of 48 women, those who regularly read romance novels reported making love twice as often as women who said they didn't enjoy this genre.
Chatelaine April 1986: 32

(Here *romance novels* are love stories.)

John's romancing of Lois was wholesome, orderly and single-minded.
Jack Batten *Robinette* 1984: 28

(Here *romancing*, from the verb *romance*, means courtship.)

I further suggested that an anglophone romancer would never refer to the object of his affection as a 'little cabbage.'
Gazette (Montreal) 14 Dec. 2002: H5

(Here *romancer* means lover.)

romantic, Romanticism   see ROMANCE

roman type   see CAPITAL LETTERS

roofs   see -F, -V-

root-bound   see -BOUND

root of all evil, [root of upheaval]   see MISHEARD EXPRESSIONS

rostrum   see DAIS

rouge   see BLEU

round   see AROUND

route, rout   Most Canadians pronounce *route* like *root*, but a strong minority rhyme it with *pout*. Both pronunciations are accepted. British dictionaries list the *root* pronunciation first, but note that the *pout* pronunciation is frequently used by the military. Americans, like Canadians, are divided: some use the pronunciation that rhymes with *pout* for a paper route and the one that rhymes with *root* for a highway.

The pronunciation that rhymes with *pout* was popular in Britain until the nineteenth century. Early British colonists carried the older pronunciation to Canada and the United States, where it survived, while in Standard British (non-military) English it faded from use.

Rout meaning defeat decisively is pronounced to rhyme with *pout*. *Rout* meaning to cut a groove also rhymes with *pout*, although it is a metaphorical extension of *root*, the verb for what pigs do with their snouts. Canadians prefer '*root* around' (search haphazardly) and '*root* out' (find, get rid of) to the alternative spellings with *rout*. These phrasal verbs are based on *root* (pull up by the roots), and the spelling *rout* is well established in only one context: 'rout out of bed' (meaning 'force to emerge from bed').

royal anthem   see O CANADA

Royal Vingt-Deuxième Régiment   see VAN DOOS

rubric   *Rubric* is derived from the Latin for 'red ochre', a pigment used by the Romans for the titles of legal documents. Hence a *rubric* is the title of a law. It is also any title, heading, or note that is printed either in red or in some distinctive typeface. Figuratively, a *rubric* is a topic or theme: 'They discussed the embargoes under the rubric of economic development'.

Rubrics are the directions for conducting a religious service, which originally appeared in red type in prayer books. A *rubrician* (rhymes with *magician*) is an expert on ecclesiastical rites. By extension of the liturgical meaning, a *rubric* is any established rule of procedure or conduct.

The mayor and council draw up some impressive arguments in their manifesto . . . under the compelling rubric: 'Toward a New Generation of Government.'
Vancouver Sun 5 Sept. 1991: A16

It is a dereliction of responsibility . . . to defend bad scholarship under the rubric of academic freedom.
Maclean's 6 March 1989: A5

One cannot forge a nation by encouraging separateness under the rubric of multiculturalism. *Maclean's* 10 Sept. 1990: A11

runneth   see ARCHAISMS

running shoes, runners, sneakers, tennis shoes, trainers   Many Canadians call the rubber-soled shoes they use for sports, exercising, or casual wear *running shoes* or, informally,

runners; Americans usually call these *sneakers* or *tennis shoes*. In Britain the parallel term is *trainers* (which might puzzle those of us who think of trainers as absorbent underpants for toddlers).

run-on sentence   see SENTENCE

rye   see WHISKY

S

-**'s, -s'**   see APOSTROPHE; POSSESSIVE; POSSESSIVE BEFORE GERUND

saccharin, saccharine   The artificial sweetener is *saccharin* (*SACK a rin*). The adjective meaning sickeningly sweet is spelled with an *e*, *saccharine*, but usually pronounced the same way.

sacred writings   Names of sacred texts, such as the Bible, the Koran, the Talmud, the Torah, the Upanishads, and the Vedas, are capitalized; unlike the titles of other books, however, they are not italicized. Names of books and sections of the Bible (Genesis, Ezekiel, the New Testament) are capitalized but neither italicized nor put in quotation marks. The word *bible* is not capitalized when it is used metaphorically to refer to an indispensable guide: 'the birdwatcher's bible'.

The adjective *biblical* is never capitalized, and some editors recommend not capitalizing the adjectives derived from the names of other sacred texts. But this seems to be a cry in the wilderness: *Vedic* and *Koranic* are always capitalized, and *Talmudic* more often than not. Dictionaries consistently capitalize such adjectives; *biblical* remains the exception.

According to the Bible, . . . King Herod ordered the

massacre of all children two years old and under. *Ottawa Citizen* 29 Dec. 1992: B1

Rao . . . recites passages from the Vedas and the Bhagavad-Gita, ancient Hindu texts. *Calgary Herald* 24 Oct. 1992: G8

It is further believed that this will mark the beginning of a thousand years of peace, which was spoken of in the biblical Book of Revelation. *Toronto Star* 26 Dec. 1992: J21

The women . . . chant, perform healing rituals, discuss social justice and read from *Dreaming the Dark* by American witch Starhawk—the bible to many of this kind of group. *Calgary Herald* 26 Dec. 1992: H7

As regards religion, most of my friends remember Biblical stories from Sunday school and that's about it. *Ottawa Citizen* 28 Dec. 1992: B8

(The adjective *biblical* should not be capitalized.)

At this time, she works on writing reform legislation using a Koranic foundation, so it can not be attacked as un-Islamic. *Globe and Mail* (Toronto) 3 June 2006: D11

Segal is a professor of Talmudic studies at the University of Calgary. *Calgary Herald* 9 July 1992: B3

sacrilegious   *Sacrilegious* is sometimes misspelled *sacreligious*, probably because of the influence of *religious*, but the two words are not etymologically related. *Sacrilegious*, which refers to the disrespectful treatment of something sacred, is derived from the Latin *sacr-*, meaning 'sacred', and *legere*, 'to steal'. *Religious* is derived from the Latin *religio*, 'reverence'.

safes   see -F, -V-

Sahara   *Sahara* is the Arabic word for desert. Some commentators object to *Sahara desert* as redundant, and prefer *Sahara* alone. Canadian writers use both forms. Since most Canadians are not familiar with Arabic, *Sahara desert* is not recognized as a redundant usage and is perfectly acceptable. Many Canadian place names are similarly derived from non-English words. For example, although *Ontario* is probably derived from an Iroquoian word meaning 'beautiful lake', the name *Lake Ontario* is not considered redundant. And *Yukon* comes from *yu-kun-ah*, 'great river', but few English-speakers are aware that *Yukon River* means 'great river river'.

He is also planning a grand-scale movie in the Sahara.
Globe and Mail (Toronto) 20 Feb. 1985: M9

Experts claim those areas are drier than the Sahara desert.
Up Here Mar.–Apr. 1990: 42

said   see AFOREMENTIONED

Saint(e)   see ST., STE.

Saint John, St. John's   Saint John is the largest city in New Brunswick. *Saint* is usually spelled out, and abbreviating it may annoy New Brunswickers.

St. John's is the capital and largest city of Newfoundland.

In the 1930s, Messer organized the New Brunswick Lumberjacks who played dances and a Saint John radio show.
Queen's Quarterly 95.2 (1988): 296

Incidentally, St. is not a standard spelling for the city of 'Saint' John, although it is used for the

name of the river and the county.
W.C. Lougheed, ed. *In Search of the Standard in Canadian English* 1986: 18

After hitting the road for 2½ months, they wrapped up with a performance in St. John's, Newfoundland. . .
Province (Vancouver) 13 June 2006: B7

See also ST., STE.

Saint Johner   see NAMES OF RESIDENTS OF CITIES AND PROVINCES

sake   Canadian writers use possessive forms in phrases such as *for old time's sake* or *for Pete's sake*. In expressions such as *for goodness' sake* or *for convenience' sake*, where the possessive noun ends with an *s* sound, most commentators consider the apostrophe optional.

However, shifting the possessive *s* to the end of *sake* (*for god sakes* instead of *for god's sake*, or *for heaven sakes* instead of *for heaven's sake*) is considered non-standard in writing.

For goodness' sake, even a selection of cantaloupe, strawberry and watermelon ices is underlaid with a tricolor sauce for a total of six contrasting flavors.
Globe and Mail (Toronto) 14 Dec. 1985: D17

The sales were good, for goodness sake.
Globe and Mail (Toronto) 21 Dec. 1985: D1

(This spelling is accepted, but *goodness'* is more common.)

Photographers are even following Jennifer into the ladies' room, for goodness sakes.
Vancouver Sun 31 Aug. 1990: D2

(In writing *sake* should not be plural unless preceded by a plural, as in 'for their sakes'.)

salable, saleable   see -ABLE, -(E)ABLE

salad days   see HEYDAY

salesgirl, saleslady, sales representative   see JOB TITLES

Salish, Salishan   see NUXALK; SECWEPEMC; STL'ATL'IMX; NLAKA'PAMUX

salmon   see PLURALS

saltchuck   see PIDGIN

same   see EXACT SAME

same-sex marriage, same-sex spouse   see MARRIAGE

sanatorium, sanitarium, [sanitorium]
Canadian writers use both *sanatorium* and *sanitarium* to refer to a place of treatment for the physically or mentally ill or a place of rest and relaxation. Some usage guides have tried to distinguish these words on the basis of etymology. *Sanatorium*, they argue, is derived from the Latin root *sanatorius* meaning 'health-restoring', and should therefore refer to a place that treats the sick. *Sanitarium*, which is derived from the Latin *sanitas* meaning 'health', should be reserved for the 'health resort' sense. This tenuous distinction is certainly not reflected in usage.

Canadian writers use both words with equal frequency. *Sanatorium*, the older form, is preferred in Britain. *Sanitarium* is an American variant spelling that is now fully established in North America. Many Canadian writers use a hybrid spelling, *sanitorium*, but few dictionaries acknowledge this variant, and it should be avoided.

Should one Table Officer miss his bus while the other is holidaying at a sanatorium, Parliament could well stall in want of a name for a face.
Globe and Mail (Toronto) 3 April 1985: 6

(Here *sanatorium* means health resort.)

In 1876, John Harvey Kellogg tried to develop a nutritious food that feeble and often toothless patients in a sanitarium could eat.
Ottawa Citizen 14 Feb. 1990: C1

(Here *sanitarium* means place of treatment.)

Most telling perhaps was his encounter in Volgograd (formerly Stalingrad) with eight veterans of the city's defence in the Great Patriotic War, out for the day from their sanitorium.
Financial Post 16 Sept. 1991: 39

(Most dictionaries do not recognize the spelling *sanitorium*.)

sanction   To *sanction* something always means to approve of it, but as a noun *sanction* has two contradictory meanings. Sometimes a *sanction* is a sign of approval and sometimes it's a sign of disapproval (i.e., a penalty). In the negative sense *sanction* is often plural: 'economic sanctions'. When using this word, writers should ensure that the context makes it clear whether the positive or the negative sense is intended.

If political authority has sanctioned nuclear-generated power, should the individual researcher avoid involvement with it on the grounds of personal disapproval?
Perspectives: Profiles of Research at Queen's University 1986: 34

Short of a papal confirmation . . . a cardinal's blessing and encouragement is about the highest sanction Descartes could have hoped for to confirm his vocation.
Canadian Journal of Philosophy 19 (1989): 216

(Here *sanction* is used positively.)

Anthropologists have found that sanctions for criminal behaviour exist in the most primitive societies.
Richard Davies and Glen Kirkland, eds. *Dimensions* 1986: 66

(Here *sanction* is used negatively.)

sang   see SING

sanguine, sanguinary   *Sanguine* (pronounced *SANG gwin*) means cheerful, optimistic, or rosy. *Sanguinary* means bloody or delighting in violence.

Unfortunately, there are two factors which make this conclusion too sanguine.
Queen's Quarterly 94.4 (1987): 801

There are many ironies in this discussion, which takes place at the approach of the 50th anniversary of history's most sanguinary war, unleashed by Nazi Germany. . . .
Financial Post 8 March 1989: 12

Anne Parillaud portrays a woman with sanguine taste in Innocent Blood.
Vancouver Sun 25 Sept. 1992: C6

(She portrays a vampire; *sanguinary* would be more appropriate.)

sanitarium, [sanitorium]   see SANATORIUM

sank   see SINK

sans   From the French meaning 'without', *sans* is found primarily in speech and in the breezy journalistic prose of entertainment, travel, and gossip columnists. It is pronounced as in French: like *song* without the *ng*.

> . . . to accuse a middle class couple of eating at McDonald's, sans children, is akin to accusing them of putting plastic slipcovers on the couch.
> *Globe and Mail* (Toronto) 14 March 1985: CL3

See also FRENCH WORDS, PRONUNCIATION OF.

Sansei   see ISSEI

SAQ   see QUEBEC ENGLISH

Sarcee   see TSUU T'INA

Saskatchewan   see APPENDIX I

Saskatchewaner, Saskatchewanian   see NAMES OF RESIDENTS OF CITIES AND PROVINCES

Sasquatch, Bigfoot, Abominable Snowman, yeti   According to folklore, a hairy, man-like creature inhabits the mountainous regions of the Pacific Northwest and of Tibet. In British Columbia and Alberta it is called *Sasquatch*, from the Salish word for 'hairy man'. Arguments for its existence are based on Aboriginal legend, reported sightings beginning in 1850, and large footprints found in the snow and earth, which gave rise to its name in the United States, *Bigfoot*.

Abominable Snowman is the name given to the Sasquatch-like creature in the Himalayas. The Abominable Snowman is also called the *yeti*, a Tibetan term for this man-like creature.

> The most controversial presentation . . . will be evidence that the so-called 'wildman,' or Bigfoot or Sasquatch, observed in the Canadian and U.S. Rockies, could actually be a species of giant ape which supposedly became extinct more than 600,000 years ago.
> *Globe and Mail* (Toronto) 13 April 1985: P10

> Fully garbed for winter, you resemble Bigfoot or an overloaded coat-tree.
> *Up Here* Jan.–Feb. 1990: 78

> If this giant ape is still alive, it could also explain persistent reports of Asian man-like creatures, known as the Yeti (the Abominable Snowman) in the Himalayas. . . .
> *Globe and Mail* (Toronto) 13 April 1985: P10

> But the Shenzhen paper was insistent—not only was the yeti reposing comfortably in the Wuhan walk-up, it was drinking from a ladle, eating from a rice bowl and 'making sounds like an old man.'
> *Globe and Mail* (Toronto) 12 Feb. 1985: P11

sault, the Soo   *Sault* (pronounced *SOO*) is a Canadian English word dating from the seventeenth century and borrowed from the French of the early explorers. As a noun it means waterfall or rapids. In the expression 'sault the rapids', it is a verb meaning shoot. In contemporary English *sault* is rare, though it has found its way into place names such as Long Sault and Sault Ste. Marie. In French the *l* has been dropped and *saut* is pronounced *so*.

The Soo is the nickname of the city of Sault Ste. Marie and the canal system there; it should be used only in informal writing.

> Sault Ste. Marie, affectionately known as the 'Soo,' is the navigational gateway between Lake Superior and Lake Huron; the International Bridge across the St. Marys River connects the city to its Michigan sister of the same name.
> Alan Tucker, ed. *The Penguin Guide to Canada* 1991: 444

> 'A few [freighters] always run until freeze-up. Sometimes they get caught in the ice-pack through the Soo.'
> David Williams *Eye of the Father* 1985: 46

savant, idiot savant   A *savant* (pronounced *sa VONT*) is a learned person, especially a distinguished scholar. *Idiot savant* is a medical term, now considered outdated, for someone with mental deficiencies who nonetheless possesses an astonishing aptitude in areas such as music or mathematics. In current medical—though not popular—usage, *savant* alone is used for this group as well.

And so it came to pass that . . . Andrew Petter, law professor, constitutional savant and resident authority on the infamous Meech Lake accord, was acclaimed the new champion of virtue in Saanich South.
Vancouver Sun 6 Feb. 1990: B1

[Sociologists] Jim and Mary Maxwell, garage sale savants at Queen's University in Kingston, say it was the tight economy of the early seventies that first impelled us to turn our houses inside out for the neighbors' amusement.
Globe and Mail (Toronto) 27 April 1985: H1

The world's best [Scrabble] players, many from Thailand, speak no English and resemble idiot savants, in that they memorize tens of thousands of seven- and eight-letter words.
Province (Vancouver) 17 Aug. 2005: A22

See also DISABILITIES.

savvy   The noun *savvy* means know-how or street smarts; the adjective means knowing or shrewd; and the verb means understand ('Do you savvy?'). All these uses are informal; the verb form is the least common and the least acceptable in writing. *Savvy* is derived from Portuguese via pidgin English.

. . . it was clear to all who knew him that he had extraordinary ambition, tenacity, and savvy.
Saturday Night July 1986: 20

The savvy nightlife purveyor knows that the surest path to a person's wallet is not through the head but through the crotch.
Saturday Night Feb. 1986: 52

saw, seen   The past tense of *see* is *saw* ('I saw her leave for work'); the past participle is *seen* ('I have seen her leave every morning this week'). *Seen* as the past tense ('I seen her leave for work') is a common but stigmatized usage, considered unacceptable in both speech and writing. Examples of *I seen* usually appear in print only in transcribed speech or fictional dialogue.

'I seen he was going crazy and saw my chance to get away.'
Vancouver Sun 6 Dec. 1990: A20

(Here, in quoted speech, a newspaper editor has let the non-standard 'I *seen*' stand.)

I seen you looking at the snake and dagger on my forearm.
Canadian Fiction Magazine 64 (1988): 94

(Here the non-standard 'I *seen*' is put in the mouth of a fictional character.)

say for   see LIKE FOR

sc.   see VIZ., SC.

scab   see REPLACEMENT WORKER

scald, scold   To *scald* means to burn with hot liquid, and to *scold* means to berate. Some writers mistakenly spell *scald* with an *-o-*. Remembering that *sc<u>a</u>ld* rhymes with *b<u>a</u>ld* may help.

The Arena Service Worker is exposed to burns to his body from scolding water.
'Job Demands Analysis, Arena Service Worker' Greater Vancouver Regional District website 1999

(The correct spelling is *scalding*.)

Scandinavian, Nordic, Alpine   Scandinavia is a region in northwestern Europe that includes Sweden, Norway, Denmark, and parts of Finland. Culturally, Greenland, Iceland and the Faroe Islands can also be considered part of Scandinavia, while some parts of Finland are culturally and linguistically distinct.

Nordic is an anthropological term used to describe the physical characteristics of the Scandinavian and Finnish peoples. It is now also used more generally as a synonym for *Scandinavian*. In the sporting world *Nordic* refers to cross-country skiing and ski jumping, while *Alpine*, which means 'from the mountains', refers to downhill skiing. *Nordic* and *Alpine* are usually capitalized.

Parliament made beer legal in May, but gave the island country of 251,000 until March 1 to prepare for the change that ended Iceland's isolation from its ale-loving Scandinavian cousins.
Gazette (Montreal) 2 March 1989: A10

A group including Canada, the United States, the Nordic nations, Switzerland and Australia have already started. . . .
Globe and Mail (Toronto) 23 March 1985: P1

The 22-year-old started out in Nordic skiing, which he called 'our country's most popular sport,' but after five years, he switched to Alpine skiing. . . .
Gazette (Montreal) 6 March 1989: C5

scapegoat   see FUNCTIONAL SHIFT

Scarborough   see -BURGH, -BURG, -BOROUGH, -BORO

scarcely   see HARDLY

scared of   Some authorities maintain that the idiom is either *scared by* or *afraid of*. Canadian writers avoid *scared of* in academic and serious writing, but use it freely in journalism and fiction.

It's enough to make you scared of flying. . . .
Gazette (Montreal) 4 March 1989: K3

The police said we were heroes, but we were more scared of what the editor would say if we came back without our story.
Province (Vancouver) 6 Dec. 1990: 3

scarf   see -F, -V-

scarify, scarification   *Scarify* is a blend of the words *scare* and *horrify*, and has senses related to both *scar* (cut physically or wound with harsh criticism) and *scare* (terrify or horrify). *Scarification* is the practice of scarring the body for aesthetic or ritual purposes, or of scoring seeds to assist in germination.

This scarifying thriller is tough to shake: there is an image of a little girl in a nightgown, shuffling toward you on a TV screen, that may keep you from sleeping for a night or two.
Ottawa Citizen 4 March 2003: C3

In African cultures, they have things like tattoos and scarification, where you go from boyhood to manhood.
Ottawa Citizen 22 July 1990: E1

Scarification means scraping a hard seed, nicking it or treating it with heat or boiling water—making germination easier by physically changing the seed.
Harrowsmith Aug.–Sept. 1986: 63

scary, [scarey]   see -Y, -EY

scenario   A *scenario* is the outline of a play, film, or television program. Over the last few decades the theatrical meaning has been extended so that a situation unfolding in real life or a hypothetical situation can be called a *scenario*. *Scenario* can also refer to a proposal, a plan, or a setting. Although several critics call the extended uses of *scenario* trite, they are standard in all types of writing.
Scenario is sometimes misspelled *scenerio*.

With . . . a rough scenario in his head, he then set to work with the dancers and musicians.
Performing Arts in Canada March 1988: 9

Consider the following scenario, recently sketched by one Harvard economist.
Irving M. Zeitlin and Robert J. Brym *The Social Condition of Humanity* 1991: 252

In Quebec . . . a much more disturbing scenario was unfolding.
Janine Brodie, Shelley A. M. Gavigan, and Jane Jenson *The Politics of Abortion* 1992: 93

Miller's WEFA Group . . . has developed a scenerio in which the deficit could be reduced by $9 billion by the end of 1992 without unduly harming the economy.
Financial Post 17 April 1989: 8

(The correct spelling is *scenario*.)

sceptic   see SKEPTIC

schedule   The competing pronunciations for this word are *SKEH jool*, *SKEH joo ul* (favoured by Americans) and *SHEH jool* (favoured by the British). Sociolinguistic studies indicate that the *sk* pronunciations are by far preferred by Canadian speakers of all ages and backgrounds, and that *SHEH jool* is on the decline.

schema, schemata   see PLURALS

scientific English   The level of technicality in a given piece of writing should reflect the background knowledge of the likely reader, not the expertise of the author. Because technical terms and phrasings defeat communication if a reader doesn't fully understand them, it is preferable to use non-scientific terms for non-specialist readers (e.g., *bruises* rather than *contusions*). When it is necessary to use a technical term, a concise explanation can be worked into the sentence in which the term first appears. Writing can clearly communicate scientific information to general readers without being technically daunting. Even a scientist writing for other scientists should try to keep scientific jargon to a minimum.

> It is possible that individual variations in the three-dimensional context resulting from positionings of to-be-detected target lines within the context are more dissimilar than is the case when the same target lines appear within unconnected contexts or alone.
> *Canadian Journal of Psychology* 44.3 (1990): 389

(Here even a research psychologist would probably appreciate less complicated phrasing.)

See also COLLOQUIAL, INFORMAL, SLANG, JARGON; SPECIES, GENUS.

Schiller, schnapps, schnitzel   see GERMAN WORDS, PRONUNCIATION OF

scholarly   see ADJECTIVES AND ADVERBS; FRIENDLY

science   see -IE-, -EI-

scold   see SCALD

score   In one of its senses *score* means twenty or a set of twenty. For example, the phrase 'threescore and ten' means seventy: three times twenty, plus ten. The plural form *scores* is often used loosely to mean many, but usually implies less than a hundred.

> . . . I found myself scribbling lists of words and idioms ranging from a dozen to a score or more of items I wanted to remind myself of for one reason or another.
> W.C. Lougheed, ed. *In Search of the Standard in Canadian English* 1986: 49

> The loneliness of the long-distance runner is nothing compared with the loneliness of working at home, especially if you once worked among scores of people.
> *Toronto Star* 21 June 1993: B3

Scottish, Scots, Scotch   The *OED* describes the use of the adjectives *Scotch*, *Scots*, and *Scottish* as 'somewhat unsettled'. *Scottish* is the original adjective, which was contracted to *Scots* in Scotland and to *Scotch* in England. The Scottish writers Robert Burns (1759–96) and Walter Scott (1771–1832) often used the 'English' form, *Scotch*. Since their time, however, the adjective *Scotch* has fallen out of favour in Scotland, and *Scots* has also become less common. In contemporary Scotland the preferred adjective form is *Scottish*. Canadians tend to use *Scottish* or *Scots*, reserving *Scotch* for certain fixed expressions including 'Scotch whisky', 'Scotch pine', 'Scotch plaid', 'Scotch broth', and 'Scotch egg'.

The people are *Scots* or *the Scottish*. The dialect of English spoken in Scotland (particularly in the Lowlands) is called *Scots*.

> Mrs. Marchenko maintained . . . a genuine Scottish reserve. . . .
> *Canadian Fiction Magazine* 63 (1988): 84

> [Alice] Munro, counterpointing the story with an ancient Scots ballad about faeries and an enchanted boy, weaves in and out of the past with confidence.
> *Vancouver Sun* 14 April 1990: C4

> 'If it weren't for the Irish and the French and the Scottish in Canada, there would be no folklore here.'
> *Performing Arts in Canada* March 1988: 15

> The two men were . . . rivals for the leadership of the Kingston Scots community.
> William Teatero *John Anderson: Fugitive Slave* 1986: 174

> We referred to ourselves as Scotch and not Scots. When, years later, I learned that the usage in

Scotland was different it seemed to me rather an affectation.
John Kenneth Galbraith *The Scotch* 1966: 12

scrolled   see COMPUTER TERMS

sculpture, sculpt   The verb forms *sculpture* and *sculpt* are found in most Canadian, British, and American dictionaries. Some critics prefer the older verb *sculpture* to the back-formation *sculpt*, but Canadian writers use *sculpt* more often.

More consideration is being given to sculpturing of interiors, Riley says. . . .
Vancouver Sun 24 March 1990: G4

. . . there is virtually no form of expression in the visual arts that she can't master, whether it be printmaking, installations, sculpting or her mainstay—drawing.
Gazette (Montreal) 5 May 1990: I5

See also BACK-FORMATION.

Scylla and Charybdis   To be *between Scylla and Charybdis* means to be faced with two choices, each of which involves hardship. The phrase comes from Homer's epic *The Odyssey*, in which Odysseus must sail between two rocky shores. On one side is a multi-headed monster named Scylla (*SILL uh*) and on the other is a violent whirlpool named Charybdis (*kuh RIB dis*). Avoiding one peril means moving closer to the other. To 'steer a mid-course between Scylla and Charybdis' means to find a way of avoiding both difficulties.
Between a rock and a hard place is a more common metaphor for the same situation, but it is not appropriate in formal writing.

Guiding the screw through the channel, with only 1.5-millimetre clearance on either side, Tredwell felt as if he were navigating between Scylla and Charybdis. . . . 'If we put the screw too far to the left, we'll put it through his spinal cord and he'll be paralysed. If we put it too far to the right, it'll go into one of his arteries and he might bleed to death.'
Vancouver Sun 11 Sept. 1992: A1

[Unions] know they have farmers and other shippers caught between a rock and a hard place.
Country Guide Nov. 1986: 12

-se   see -CE

sear, sere   To *sear* is to scorch, cauterize, or brand. A *sear* is the mark that results from being burned. The adjective *sere* means dried up or withered. Shakespeare's character Macbeth compares old age to 'the sere and yellow leaf' (*Macbeth* 5.3.23).

When the pan is very hot, place the steaks in it and sear the meat for 4 minutes.
Globe and Mail (Toronto) 9 Jan. 1985: SB2

In no time, the sere forest floor was sodden and silent.
Gazette (Montreal) 13 Nov. 1990: D16

Both plays deal with the crises of middle-aged protagonists beginning to glimpse the sere leaf of old age beyond the fading dreams and glories of youth.
NeWest Review Oct.–Nov. 1989: 46

search   see COMPUTER TERMS

seasonable, seasonal   *Seasonable* means appropriate to the time of year, or timely: 'seasonable advice'. *Seasonable* weather is normal for the season. *Seasonal* means controlled by the season of the year or limited to a season. *Seasonal* employment (for example, fruit picking) occurs only during a particular season.

Temperatures soared to 11.6 Thursday and Friday. Early next week, however, they will plummet to more seasonable lows of -8 to -11. . . .
Ottawa Citizen 17 March 1990: A20

In the factory . . . the women are lucky to be working, and live in fear of seasonal layoffs.
Henry M. Rosenthal and S. Cathy Berson, eds. *Canadian Jewish Outlook Anthology* 1988: 294

Granted, the loch was covered with heavy haze, for it was still morning and unseasonally mild for early May.
Globe and Mail (Toronto) 27 April 1985: T7

(The word required here is *unseasonably*.)

secession, secede, succession, succeed
Secession is a formal act of withdrawal, usually from a political federation or religious organization; thus to *secede* (pronounced suh SEED) means to resign allegiance and break away.

Succession is the process of one thing following another. To *succeed* (pronounced suk SEED) to a throne is to take it up when the previous monarch has died.

> In the northwest, there is talk of secession from Ontario to join neighbouring Manitoba.
> *Toronto Star* 8 Aug. 2005: A17

> The farm was acquired via succession from the male farmer's family in 1977.
> *The Canadian Geographer* 48.2 (2004): 191–208

> In rapid secession, Northrop went on to buy the electronic systems division of Westinghouse in 1996; Logicon Inc., a leading supplier of defence information technology in 1997; and the Ryan Aeronautical unit of Allegheny Teledyne Inc., makers of unmanned surveillance aircraft, in 1999.
> *Ottawa Citizen* 27 Oct. 2001: D4

> ('In rapid succession' is the phrase wanted here.)

See also CEED, -CEDE, -SEDE; PREDECESSOR, SUCCESSOR; SUCCESS.

second When it means next after the first, or is used as a verb meaning to support and endorse, *second* is pronounced with the stress on the first syllable: *SECK und.*

A military sense of *second*, to shift someone temporarily to another unit, has moved into general usage, particularly in large organizations. This verb is stressed on the second syllable: *se KOND.*

> The motion was duly seconded and unanimously approved by the meeting. . . .
> J.E. Smyth et al. *The Law and Business Administration in Canada* 1987: 172

> Lunan, an officer in the Canadian Army, had been seconded in 1944 to the Wartime Information Board where he was employed as editor of a military journal, *Canadian Affairs.*
> Frederick Gibson *Queen's University* 2 (1983): 278

> One institute staff member is co-ordinating the project through which 10 instructors, seconded from Canada's petroleum industry, are teaching 1,920 employees. . . .
> *Edmonton Journal* 23 Oct. 2002: G3

secondary colour see COLOUR

Second World War see FIRST WORLD WAR

secular, sectarian *Secular* means having to do with this world rather than the next, worldly or temporal as opposed to religious or spiritual. In the Catholic Church a secular priest is one who does not belong to a religious order. *Sectarian* means having to do with religious or political sects.

> . . . the division of reality into secular and sacred worlds that was at the very centre of this culture provided the justification for separating women from men and assigning distinct roles to each sex.
> *Queen's Quarterly* 98.1 (1991): 284

> For many years a feature of the Winnipeg bonspiel was its annual church service; but, in an increasingly secular society, the church service has been done away with along with the one-time reverence for Sunday.
> *The Beaver* Dec. 1989–Jan. 1990: 52

> On the one hand, there is much understanding and genuine goodwill among pilgrims, while on the other, there are the cliques that form around race, culture and sectarian distinctions at every stop.
> *Gazette* (Montreal) 20 May 2006: J4

security see QUEBEC ENGLISH

Secwepemc, Shuswap Both *Secwepemc* (*SHWEP muh*; singular and plural) and *Shuswap* (*SHOO swop*) are in use to refer to this Aboriginal group whose traditional territory is in the south-central interior of British Columbia; the Secwepemc Nation prefers the former. Their language belongs to the Salishan family.

> About 60 natives, from the Chilcotin, Shushwap, Nuxalk, and Carrier peoples, gathered for the

opening of the judicial hearings . . . at the Ulkatcho reserve, 330 km west of Williams Lake.
Vancouver Sun 8 Dec. 1992: A4

(The correct spelling is *Shuswap*. Note that *Native(s)* should be capitalized when it refers to Aboriginal people; note too that this word is more acceptable when used as an adjective, as in *Native people*.)

He challenged the Reform MP to take a program at the Secwepemc Cultural Education Society for a year.
Gazette (Montreal) 12 June 1994: A6

See also ABORIGINAL PEOPLE(S); NATIVE; APPENDIX III.

-sede   see -CEED

see   see SAW, SEEN

seeing as, seeing as how   When *seeing* is used to mean 'in view of the fact', it is usually followed by *that*: 'Seeing that I had the day off, I slept in'. *Seeing as* and *seeing as how* are constructions that, to some, have a quaint or rural flavour, and are rarely found in formal writing.

That requires a tremendous leap of imagination as well as faith, seeing that the halcyon days come only at this time of year and last only for a couple of weeks.
Vancouver Sun 17 Dec. 1990: A10

But the people of the hamlet were polite at first, seeing as they hadn't had a visitor of Rambo's species before.
Up Here Jan.–Feb. 1990: 14

See also BEING AS.

seem   see ADJECTIVES AND ADVERBS; DON'T THINK; DUE TO

seen   see SAW

see where   Constructions that use *where* to mean *that* ('I see where it's time to go'; 'I read where they are going to take down the steeple') are now considered unsuitable for writing and informal in speech. This use of *where* is rare in Canadian writing.

'I can see where it will take more of my time . . . but not more than I figured before I agreed to run for the office.'
Canadian Rodeo News March 1990: 15

segue, [segueway], Segway   *Segue* comes from the Italian word for 'follow'; the *-ue* ending is pronounced in a manner approximating the Italian: *seg WAY*. When borrowed into English, *segue* was originally a musical instruction, meaning to proceed without pause into a second piece or perform a second piece in the same manner as the first. In the early twentieth century, the meaning shifted and generalized. Although *segue* still means that there is no pause, it usually now refers to the transitional, often improvised, material intended to create a smooth transition between two songs, two stage acts, one topic of conversation and another, etc.

The atypical spelling of *segue* leads to two problems. On the example of words like *tongue* and *catalogue*, some believe that the *-ue* is silent, and pronounce the word *SEG*. Others who know the proper pronunciation spell the word *segway* or *segueway*. Those who have heard the word often spell it wrong, while those who are familiar with the word in print often say it wrong.

The misspelling is probably reinforced by *Segway*, the brand name of a motorized scooter that one rides standing up. Even the name of the scooter is sometimes misspelled *Segueway*.

seize   see -IE-, -EI-

Sekani   see CARRIER

seldom ever, seldom if ever   *Seldom ever* is sometimes criticized as redundant because 'We seldom ever go out' can be written 'We seldom go out' without changing the sense. But *seldom ever* is a respectable idiom with a long history in English. Today it is mainly restricted to informal writing, such as journalism. In formal writing the more logical version of the expression, *seldom if ever*, is strongly preferred.

In Britain, the government seldom ever changes and the underlings are so unhappy they travel thousands of miles abroad to smash up other people.
Maclean's 23 July 1990: A44

The vast majority of people who call themselves skiers will seldom ever venture beyond the security of the ski area boundaries. . . .
Vancouver Sun 2 Jan. 1992: B10

Myths are seldom if ever actual hypotheses that can be verified or refuted; that is not their function: they are coordinating or integrating ideas.
Northrop Frye *The Modern Century* 1990: 115

See also EVER.

-self, -selves The pronouns that end with *-self* or *-selves* are called reflexive pronouns because they normally refer back to the subject of the sentence or clause in which they appear: 'I will do it myself'; 'Henry thinks for himself'; 'They take themselves very seriously'. If the pronoun form is singular, it is followed by *-self*: 'Did you do that by yourself?' If plural, it is followed by *-selves*: 'You were squabbling among yourselves'. Since *we* and *they* are plural pronouns, the corresponding reflexive pronouns are traditionally also plural: *ourselves* and *themselves*, not *ourself* and *themself*.

Writers sometimes use the non-standard form *ourself* when they are referring to themselves formally or in mock elevated style as 'we': 'We satisfied ourself that indeed these exquisite desserts were made on the premises'. However, *ourselves* is standard even when the reference is to only one person.

People also use *themself*, especially in speech, when it is clear that the pronoun, though plural in form, actually refers to a single person: 'Someone could really hurt themself'. This word has long been considered unacceptable, especially in formal language. Now, however, *themself* is increasingly used in the very formal language of Canadian federal and provincial legislation, the reason being that English has no indefinite reflexive form corresponding to the gender-neutral indefinite pronouns. Canadian writers who strive to be both formal and non-

sexist have sometimes relied on rather awkward constructions such as 'Everyone must determine this for him- or herself'. Even mentioning both sexes, however, does not satisfy the requirements of legislation, which deals with 'persons' as legal entities, including corporate bodies. Thus, when a law mentions 'a person' and a reflexive pronoun follows, the choices are: *themselves*, which is the wrong number; *himself or herself or itself*, which is cumbersome; or *themself*, which already exists at the informal level of the language. (*Oneself* is conventionally linked only to *one*: 'One must look out for oneself', not 'Everyone must look out for oneself'.) Many usage commentators believe the time has come to legitimize the use of *they* to mean 'he or she' (see EVERYONE) as well as the use of *themself* to mean 'himself or herself (or itself)', and these uses of *they* and *themself* may gradually become common in all types of formal writing. Until then, however, writers in the gender-neutral vanguard must brace themselves for criticism.

We can't separate ourself completely from our past.
Daily News (Halifax) 3 Feb. 1993: 20

(The accepted form is *ourselves*.)

We can appreciate what they're doing . . . but we'd just as soon do it ourself.
Ottawa Citizen 6 June 1990: E11

(The accepted form is *ourselves*.)

'I just hope the person who did this has the decency to give themself up.'
Vancouver Sun 9 March 1990: A8

(Though not uncommon in speech, *themself* is disputed in writing.)

'This is particularly a problem for someone who finds themself attracted to members of the same sex.'
Daniel Gawthorp *Affirmation* 1994: 122

(Though not uncommon in speech, *themself* is disputed in writing.)

No person shall directly or indirectly do any of the following things unless the person is authorized to do it by an Act of the Assembly or by the Minister under this Act: 1. Operate or maintain a universi-

ty. . . . 3. Hold themself out to be a university.
Post-secondary Education Choice and Excellence Act,
2000, Ontario Statutes and Regulations

(*Themself* is now used as a gender-neutral reflexive pronoun in Canadian legislation.)

See also EVERYONE; [HISSELF], [THEIRSELVES]; MYSELF;
SEXIST LANGUAGE; YOU, ONE.

self-deprecating, self-depreciating   see
DEPRECIATE

selves   see -F, -V-

semantic drift   see entry in Glossary

semi-, demi-, hemi-   All three of these prefixes mean half: *semi-monthly, demitasse, hemisphere. Semi-* is derived from Latin, *demi-* from
French, and *hemi-* from Greek. Often the sense
of the prefix is 'partly', as in *semi-automatic* and
demigod. Only *semi-* is used freely to form new
combinations (which are usually hyphenated
until they become familiar words): *semi-retired,
semi-detached, semi-serious.*

semi-automatic   see SEMI-, DEMI-, HEMI-

semicolon   Semicolons are used to link closely related independent clauses. Sometimes the
semicolon takes the place of a coordinating
conjunction (e.g., *and, but, for*) or a conjunctive
adverb (e.g., *instead*):

> Nobody talked about it on the street; they just
> shook their heads and bit their lips.
> Max Braithwaite *The Night We Stole the Mountie's
> Car* 1971: 57

> Personally, I mistrust the notion of thinking on
> one's feet; I have known many speakers who prid-
> ed themselves on that ability, and I am sorry to say
> that many of them were blatherers; they did not
> know when to stop.
> Robertson Davies *One Half of Robertson Davies*
> 1978: 9

A sentence introduced by a conjunctive
adverb, such as *however, nevertheless,* or *thus,*
may be joined to the previous sentence using a
semicolon:

> Rock outcrops in the study area are oriented
> along a northwest-southeast axis; consequently,
> cliff faces most often face either southwest or
> northeast.
> *Arctic* 41.1 (1988): 27

It is a common error to use a comma rather
than a semicolon to make the linkages
described above, resulting in a run-on sentence
(see SENTENCES, SENTENCE FRAGMENT, RUN-ON SEN-
TENCE).

Usually a comma separates items listed in a
text, but when the elements listed are complex,
or contain commas, semicolons are used to separate them:

> The proposed cut-offs by the CHRC were as fol-
> lows: fewer than 100 employees, 70 per cent; 100
> to 500 employees, 60 per cent; and more than
> 500 employees, 55 per cent.
> Carl J. Cuneo *Pay Equity* 1990: 30

Note that semicolons are always placed outside
any quotation marks:

> However, this did not mean 'simply the transfer of
> title of large enterprises to the state'; rather, it
> called for 'decentralized ownership and control'.
> Alan Whitehorn *Canadian Socialism* 1992: 63

**semi-detached, semi-monthly, semi-
retired, semi-serious**   see SEMI-, DEMI-, HEMI-

senior   see SENIOR CITIZEN; SUPERIOR

**senior citizen, senior, aged, elderly, pen-
sioner, oldster**   Some commentators, particularly British ones, consider the North
American expressions *senior citizen* and *senior*
euphemistic. They argue that *old people, the
aged, the elderly,* and *pensioners* are perfectly
good terms to describe people who are old or
retired. However, it is difficult to imagine a
North American journalist who would replace
'Martha is a senior, active in several community organizations' with 'Martha is an old person,
active in . . .'. Though they should be neutral
terms, *old, elderly,* and *aged* often carry negative
connotations of frailty, dependence, and dimin-
ished capability. *Senior* and *senior citizen,* on the

other hand, are terms of respect; there seems to be no good reason to avoid using them.

Oldster is a humorous coinage modelled on *youngster*; it should be used only in a lighthearted context.

See also INCLUSIVE LANGUAGE.

senior (student)   see FIRST-YEAR STUDENT

sensational   In contemporary writing, *sensational* tends to be used in one of two ways: to describe something that piques in the general public an intense, often prurient, curiosity ('sensational evidence at the murder trial') or to describe something felt to be excellent or superb ('The movie was sensational'). Some critics object to the second sense, but it is widespread in informal use and standard in informal writing. *Sensational* originally meant pertaining to the senses, a meaning now conveyed by the word *sensory*.

> Increased supplies of newsprint accentuate an emphasis on sensational news.
> Wallace Clement and Glen Williams, eds. *The New Canadian Political Economy* 1989: 120

> Tourism has been a mainstay, with some fluctuations, since the mid-1940s, but this past year was sensational.
> *Beautiful British Columbia* Spring 1990: 38

sensible, sensibleness, sensibility, sensitive, sensitivity, sensitiveness   The most common meaning of *sensible* is having sound judgment. The related noun is *sensibleness*. An old-fashioned, now literary, meaning of the phrase *sensible of* is aware of: 'I am sensible of your predicament'. This older meaning of *sensible* is related to the noun *sensibility*, meaning the capacity for subtle feeling. A person of 'delicate sensibility' has subtle emotional, aesthetic, or intellectual responses. When a particular sensibility is ascribed to a sex, a nationality, an occupation, a period, a place, etc., the term refers to a set of ideas, attitudes, and preferences believed to characterize that group, occupation, etc. The adjective *sensitive* and its related noun

forms, *sensitivity* and *sensitiveness*, have to do with the capacity to respond to stimuli: 'The human ear is not sensitive to these frequencies'. *Sensitive* can mean finely tuned or accurate ('a sensitive measure') attuned to others ('a sensitive listener'), or easily hurt ('sensitive about his hairline'). To be *sensitive to* something means to be aware of and concerned about it; the sense is similar to that of the old-fashioned expression *sensible of*.

In a political context, a 'sensitive issue' is one that could cause a strong public reaction. Thus it is one that is handled carefully, often evasively.

> Sensible planning also demands that you reserve your accommodations in advance.
> *Dogs in Canada* Special Issue 1986: 14

> The sensibleness of his judgments gave readers everywhere much of what they needed to know about opera in general in order to appreciate other productions of other works in their own towns. . . .
> *Queen's Quarterly* 94.2 (1987): 352

> 'We are, at the same time, sensible of the inconvenience that may result from the exercise of such a jurisdiction.'
> William Teatero *John Anderson: Fugitive Slave* 1986: 127

> (This quotation dates from 1861, when *sensible* was commonly used to mean *aware*.)

> As a critical approach to works of art, [psychoanalysis] has been productive of much that is interesting and revealing, though it is by no means a substitute for a cultured mind, or for delicate sensibility and intuition. . . .
> Robertson Davies *A Voice from the Attic* 1960: 68–9

> The title of the book has been pilfered from Margaret Atwood's *Journals of Susanna Moodie*, a book unusually rich in suggestive phrases defining a Canadian sensibility.
> Northrop Frye *The Bush Garden* 1971: x

> Despite his stern demeanour Draper was a sensitive man, patient, humane and with a warm sense of humour.
> William Teatero *John Anderson: Fugitive Slave* 1986: 162

> 'This is a very sensitive matter that unfortunately

has already received unduly extensive publicity.'
Maclean's 24 Feb. 1986: 21

sensory, sensual, sensuous   *Sensory, sensual,*
and *sensuous* all refer to what we apprehend
through our five senses. *Sensory* is neutral, referring to the senses in a purely physical way:
'Sensory input is relayed to the brain'. *Sensual*
usually refers to the indulgence or gratification
of carnal desires. *Sensuous* was apparently
coined by Milton in 1641 to avoid any hint of
the lewdness implied by *sensual*. *Sensuous* is the
broader term, applied to any type of aesthetic,
intellectual, or physical pleasure derived from
the senses. However, many writers use *sensual*
and *sensuous* interchangeably.

> The sensory processes include visual, auditory,
> olfactory, and tactile.
> *Queen's Quarterly* 92.2 (1985): 419

> The cult of the Maenads . . . worshipped Dionysus
> . . . in a ritualized frenzied celebration of sensual
> and sexual existence. . . .
> *NeWest Review* Oct.–Nov. 1990: 44

> . . . poetry, according to Milton, who ought to
> have known, is 'more simple, sensuous and pas-
> sionate' than philosophy or science.
> Northrop Frye *The Educated Imagination* 1963: 9

> There was tremendous pressure . . . to have a real-
> ly hot, sensuous, passionate scene between Daisy
> and Max. . . .
> *NeWest Review* Feb.–Mar. 1990: 18

sentence adverbs   A sentence adverb differs
from a simple adverb in that it relates to the
whole sentence, or to a whole clause within a
sentence, rather than to a single word or phrase:
'*Fortunately*, they got home before their guests
arrived'. This particular construction, meaning
'It is fortunate that . . .', is not disputed.
However, the use of certain words as sentence
adverbs is criticized. An example is *hopefully*. In
the sentence 'They waited hopefully for the surgeon's report', *hopefully* acts as a simple adverb
describing the manner in which they waited:
'full of hope'. By contrast, in the sentence
'Hopefully, he won't need an operation', *hopefully* does not modify a particular word or
phrase but the sentence as a whole; it's a sen-

tence adverb meaning 'It is to be hoped that
. . .'. Those who object to this use of *hopefully*
maintain that, since the same word can also be
used as a simple manner adverb, it may be
ambiguous. Other dual-purpose adverbs, such
as *thankfully* and *mercifully*, have also been criticized as sentence adverbs, though not so vocif-
erously. There is no grammatical justification
for condemning the use of particular words as
sentence adverbs while considering others
acceptable; nonetheless, it is only particular
words that are criticized, and *hopefully* attracts
criticism like a lightning rod.

The sentence adverb flourishes despite critics'
objections because it is a concise way of expressing an attitude towards a statement. In the sentence 'Thankfully, she escaped without injury',
the single word *thankfully* conveys the sense of
the phrase 'I am thankful that'; in 'Bluntly, they
are not up to the task', the sentence adverb
bluntly condenses the sense of 'If I may be
blunt'.

Sentence adverbs can appear in a number of
positions in a sentence, though the most common position is at the beginning. Common
sentence adverbs include *bluntly, briefly, candidly, confidentially, frankly, generally, honestly, personally*, and *seriously*. Note the placement of the
sentence adverbs in the following examples:
'They are probably out for the evening'; 'You
may join us, certainly'; 'Despite their unappe-
tizing appearance, surprisingly, they are quite
delicious'.

Writers do need to be careful not to use
adverbs that might be either sentence adverbs
or regular adverbs of manner: for example,
'They left thankfully' could mean 'They left
with a feeling of gratitude' or 'Thank goodness
they're gone'. When an adverb is intended as a
sentence adverb in an ambiguous context, setting it off from the rest of the sentence with a
comma or commas is advised.

> He then thankfully accepted a gift of $2,000 from
> the grateful trustees. . . .
> Hilda Neatby *Queen's University* 1 (1978): 167

(Here *thankfully* is a regular adverb modifying
the verb *accepted*.)

Copy protection is thankfully not a problem in the CDROM arena and that alone should spur development.
Computer Dealer News 21 March 1991: 51

(Here *thankfully* is a sentence adverb.)

Mercifully the hall chime announced the end of the hour.
Constance Beresford-Howe *Night Studies* 1985: 24

(Here *mercifully* is a sentence adverb.)

Hopefully she looked up for their elevator to arrive.
Constance Beresford-Howe *Night Studies* 1985: 35

(Here *hopefully* is a regular adverb modifying the verb looked.)

Hopefully Albert Einstein's views will help to . . . restore the cynics to a more healthy view of the need to continue the campaign for human rights. . . .
Henry M. Rosenthal and S. Cathy Berson, eds. *Canadian Jewish Outlook Anthology* 1988: 330

(Here *hopefully* is a sentence adverb; this is the disputed usage.)

sentences, sentence fragment, run-on sentence, comma splice The boundaries of a sentence in writing are the capital letter of the first word and the period, exclamation mark, or question mark that follows the last word. To be complete in grammatical terms, a sentence must have a subject and a predicate. Inexperienced writers occasionally produce sentence fragments: strings of words that lack a subject or a predicate, even though they are punctuated as if they were sentences. Sentence fragments are common and accepted in speech, or in writing that represents speech, and skilled writers occasionally use them for effect. Some types of fragments, however, are not acceptable. Examples of the most common types of fragments follow.

A complete sentence, such as 'The issues were different', has a subject ('The issues') and a predicate ('were different'). However, when *because* (or any other subordinate conjunction, such as *although* or *when*) is placed in front of such a sentence it is transformed into a subordinate clause, which, as its name suggests, requires something to complete it. 'Because the issues were different' is a sentence fragment. To make a complete sentence, the fragment must be attached to an independent clause: 'I didn't agree with you then, because the issues were different'.

Similarly, relative clauses beginning with *who(m)*, *which*, *whose*, or *that* are not sentences; as their name suggests, they relate to something else in the same sentence. 'Which I don't like' is a fragment; 'He came in late, which I don't like' is a complete sentence.

Being cannot be used as a predicate, nor can other *-ing* verb forms. Thus 'My candidate being of the same party as Pierre Trudeau' is a fragment: simply substituting *was* for *being* would produce a sentence.

Run-on sentences (sometimes called run-together sentences) are not just long sentences but two sentences punctuated as one. Usually such sentences are closely connected in meaning. Sometimes the writer puts a comma between the two sentences, an error called a comma splice or a comma fault. Often adverbs such as *however* or *therefore* will trigger a comma splice because writers assume that these words have the force of conjunctions when in fact they do not. Usually the simplest way to correct a run-on sentence or a comma splice is to insert a semicolon between the sentences (see SEMICOLON).

Only if sentences are very short and parallel in structure can they be connected with commas in formal writing. Julius Caesar's comment on the conquest of Britain—'I came, I saw, I conquered'—needs only commas (although semicolons would also be acceptable).

He doesn't know what 'love' means between them any more, though they always say it. For the sake of the children.
Margaret Atwood *Life Before Man* 1979: 6

(Here the fragment 'For the sake of the children' is punctuated as a sentence, although it has neither subject nor verb and could have been attached to the preceding sentence. Atwood has purposely used a sentence fragment to highlight the cliché.)

Few will ever see this timeless land. Its rivers go unnamed, its animals roam without fear.
Up Here Mar.–Apr. (1990): 27

(Although the second sentence in this passage is actually two sentences joined with a comma, this is acceptable because they are short and parallel in structure.)

But while the place isn't perfect, I can work to make this the co-op I want. I can lobby, I have a vote.
Women and Environments Spring (1990): 5

(Although the second sentence in this passage is actually two sentences joined with a comma, this is acceptable because they are short and parallel in structure.)

See also COMMA.

separate   *Separate*, *separately*, and *separation* are often misspelled with *-per-* instead of *-par-*.

separatist, sovereignist, independantiste, sovereigntist, independentist   All these terms describe supporters of an independent Quebec. *Separatist* is the term commonly used by those who dislike the idea of Quebec's breaking away. *Sovereignist* and *independantiste* are favoured by those who espouse a sovereign Quebec. *Sovereignist* and *independantiste* are Canadianisms (you won't find them listed in British or American dictionaries) adapted from the French words *souverainiste* and *indépendantiste*. The variants *sovereigntist* and *independentist* also appear in Canadian journalism, but much less frequently.

He was whisked into cabinet by Brian Mulroney, only to turn on the Tories and found the separatist Bloc Quebecois two years later.
Ottawa Citizen 24 Dec. 1994: A4

To understand why Quebec will never give up its sovereignist aspiration, one will have to take a look at history.
Gazette (Montreal) 14 Dec. 1994: B2

Although independantiste sentiment was much in evidence, some who joined in the parade described themselves as federalist.
Gazette (Montreal) 25 June 1993: A1

Dumont, straddling the fence as both a sovereigntist and a confederalist, needs platforms from which to promote his views.
Ottawa Citizen 27 Dec. 1994: A12

. . . he was sure Quebecers would re-elect the Liberal government instead of an independentist Parti Quebecois.
Gazette (Montreal) 13 May 1994: B2

See also NATIONAL ASSEMBLY; QUEBEC ENGLISH; QUEBECER.

seppuku   see HARA-KIRI

sepsis, septicemia, septic, aseptic, antiseptic   *Sepsis* is infection of the body by toxin-producing bacteria. *Septicemia* (occasionally spelled *septicaemia*) is sepsis of the blood, commonly known as blood poisoning. *Septic* usually means causing infection or infected; however, a *septic tank* is a disposal system in which waste is decomposed and purified by bacterial activity. *Aseptic* (the *a* is stressed and rhymes with *pay*) means free from bacteria and viruses—a desirable state for a wound or an operating room, but not for a septic tank. *Antiseptics* are substances that kill germs; in metaphorical contexts *antiseptic* means sterile.

All these words are derived from the Greek root *sep-*, meaning rot. People sometimes mistakenly insert a *c* into that root, writing *sceptic*, for example, instead of *septic*.

In newborn care, for example, about eight in a thousand babies get an infection called neonatal sepsis. . . .
Calgary Herald 28 Dec. 1992: B1

The [germ] creates a condition called septicemia, which causes the breakdown of all internal organs. . . .
Calgary Herald 3 June 1992: A1

But if all doctors were hacking off legs with septic instruments in barber shops and losing sponges inside people's lungs because they're drunk during the operation, we would not think of medicine as an honourable profession. . . .
Margaret Atwood *Second Words* 1982: 347

. . . a regulation septic system [was] installed where there had been only a holding tank before.
Harrowsmith Oct.–Nov. 1985: 62

Using aseptic techniques in handling the milk, I thought we were safe.
Harrowsmith Oct.–Nov. 1985: 10

It has antiseptic properties that will keep the disease organisms at bay until the seedling has time to harden off.
TLC . . . for plants Spring 1991: 14

But there's a balance to be found between too much reality and an antiseptic museum with fish photos on the wall.
Vancouver Sun 30 June 1992: B1

Cottagers are being forced to check their sceptic tanks for leaks.
Ottawa Citizen 19 Sept. 1992: F1

(The correct spelling is *septic*.)

Showing more convenience than invention is a new, small, asceptic package of shelf-stable 2 per cent milk labelled Caf-O-Lait.
Gazette (Montreal) 27 May 1992: C6

(The correct spelling is *aseptic*.)

See also -AE-, -OE-, -E-; SKEPTIC, SCEPTIC.

sere   see SEAR

seriously   see SENTENCE ADVERBS

serve   see SERVICE

server   see WAITER

service, serve   Many usage commentators have objected to the use of *service* as a verb, as in 'This hospital services a population of 100,000'. Most of these commentators explicitly endorse only one use for the verb *service*: to do maintenance and repair work on cars or other machines. Their advice is to avoid *service* where the older and perfectly adequate verb *serve* is possible.

But there are now many contexts where *service* has acquired a special meaning and *serve* is not possible. For example, to service land is to provide it with utilities such as electricity and sewers. To service a debt is to make periodic payments on it. To service a region is to provide a specific service within it. Male animals service female animals.

The real point of contention is whether it is proper to say people are *serviced* rather than *served*. In business and administration this usage is extremely common; outside that sphere, however, it should be avoided.

The municipalities must pass on the costs of buying and servicing industrial land to end users.
Financial Post 2 Dec. 1991: U3

. . . many African countries find themselves forced to borrow not for development purposes but to service their debts.
Globe and Mail (Toronto) 15 July 1985: B12

Izvestia's former stablemate With Approval . . . was servicing 'as good a book [selection] of mares in relation to his stud fee as any freshman stallion in North America this year.'
Financial Post 24 Oct. 1991: 51

Granada Canada now operates 55 stores and service centres, servicing about 200,000 customers.
Financial Post 16 Oct. 1991: 17

(Here *serve* would also work.)

Trailer fees are annual service fees paid by fund managers to brokers for initiating the relationship and servicing the client over time.
Financial Post 13 Aug. 1991: 15

(Here *serve* would also work.)

'We're not servicing that 13-17 age group,' says Morena Mazzara, community recreation coordinator. . . .
Province (Vancouver) 23 Oct. 1990: 57

(Here *serve* would also work.)

serviette   see NAPKIN

settee, settle   see CHESTERFIELD

setup   see PHRASAL VERBS

sew, sewed, sewn   The past tense of the verb is *sewed*: 'Leo sewed the buttons on his coat yesterday'. The past participle is either *sewn* or *sewed*.

I had sewn since I was 6—for my dolls.
Gazette (Montreal) 28 Aug. 1990: D2

'The doctors told my husband . . . that they had just sewed me up with sponges and were expecting me to die.'
Province (Vancouver) 28 June 1990: 65

see GENDER

sexism, chauvinism   *Sexism* is the attitude, or a manifestation of the attitude, that one sex is superior to or more important than the other. Usually *sexism* refers to a bias against women, but logically the term can also refer to discrimination against or stereotyping of men.

Chauvinism is not the same thing as *sexism*. *Chauvinist* is derived from the name of Nicolas Chauvin, a French soldier who served under Napoleon and who became famous for his aggressive loyalty to the Empire and his devotion to his leader. *Chauvinism* originally referred to unreasoning devotion to one's country; then its meaning was broadened to include proud and blinkered partiality to any place, group, or cause. *Male chauvinism*, a phrase that became popular in the 1970s, means overweening pride in the male gender. Thus in the phrase *male chauvinist* the adjective *male* identifies not the sex of the biased person but the nature of the bias. It's best to avoid using *chauvinism* by itself to mean *male chauvinism* unless the context makes the meaning clear.

> Finally, we should actively support those feminists struggling to combat sexism and inequality in sport.
> *Queen's Quarterly* 94.1 (1987): 129

> . . . we were going to hear a fine concert and—this was what gave a special edge to the occasion—we were going to hear a Canadian, one of our own, who had beyond all question achieved world celebrity. There was a spice of chauvinism in our enthusiasm, and who would say that we were unjustified, or wrong?
> Robertson Davies *One Half of Robertson Davies* 1978: 23

> Huck, it is claimed, is a white chauvinist and Jim is a stereotyped, chuckleheaded Black.
> Henry M. Rosenthal and S. Cathy Berson, eds. *Canadian Jewish Outlook Anthology* 1988: 259

> A suicide pact by four girls who took rat poison so their parents could lavish everything on their brother has shocked South Koreans and raised questions about male chauvinism and the plight of the poor.
> *Gazette* (Montreal) 6 March 1989: E7

> 'Dad,' Wilson jokes, 'was responsible for the men, who all turned out to be chauvinists, and Mom was responsible for the women, who all turned out independent.'
> *Chatelaine* June 1986: 97

(Here the context makes it clear that these *chauvinists* are sexist rather than nationalist.)

See also -ISM; SEXIST LANGUAGE.

sexist   see -IST, -ALIST

sexist language   Most writers' handbooks, style guides, and composition texts now contain a section on sexist language. Avoiding sexist language means describing women and men in ways that do not stereotype them on the basis of their sex and omitting irrelevant references to such things as appearance and marital status. The terms used to describe the two sexes should be parallel (e.g., not 'man and wife' but 'husband and wife') and gender-neutral (e.g., 'police officer', not 'policeman').

In the past *man* and *mankind* were used as 'generic' terms to refer to both sexes; now *people*, *individuals*, *humankind*, and *human beings* are all considered better alternatives. Similarly, the 'generic' pronoun *he* is replaced in several ways: by rewriting the sentence to avoid pronouns altogether; by using plural forms; or, when no alternative is available, by using *his or her*, *he or she*, or *her and him*. Some writers alternate between masculine and feminine pronouns; others routinely use *she* where *he* was used in the past, and still others use *s/he*; however, these choices are less conventional than those above, and are quite likely to distract the reader.

Following the indefinite pronouns (*anyone*, *none*, *one*, *each*, *either*, *everyone*, *someone*, etc.), most usage guides accept the common use of the plural pronoun *they* in speech: 'Anyone who hasn't handed in their assignment should see the teacher'. Many commentators feel that the use of the plural pronoun should now also be accepted in writing; for a detailed discussion of this point, see EVERYONE and -SELF, SELVES.

Non-sexist usage guides also recommend avoiding the verbs *master*, meaning learn thoroughly (as in 'master French'), and *man*, meaning staff (as in 'man the booth'). Words in which *man* is a prefix or suffix, such as *manpower*, *manmade*, *foreman*, and *cameraman*, are eschewed in favour of phrases like *work force*, *synthetic*, *supervisor*, and *camera operator*. Note, however, that many words with the letters *man* in them do not in fact derive from *man*, but from the Latin root *man(u)*, 'hand', including *manufacture*, *manipulate*, and *manuscript*.

See also ALUMNUS; BLOND; BRUNETTE; CHAIR; CO-ED; INCLUSIVE LANGUAGE; JOB TITLES; MASTERFUL; MOTHER NATURE; -SELF, -SELVES; SEXISM; WAITER.

sexual harassment   see HARASS

sexual minorities   Sexual minorities are groups whose sexual orientation or gender identity sets them apart from the majority of the population: *lesbians*, *gay men*, *bisexuals*, *transsexuals*, and *transgendered people*.

> Like judges and all links in the justice system, they should always be rigorously neutral—not just to the media but to ethnic groups, political groups, sexual minorities and everyone else.
> *Gazette* (Montreal) 25 Oct. 1990: B2

> . . . it is no longer possible to make jokes about disempowered groups such as ethnic or religious minorities, and it is becoming increasingly unacceptable to joke about sexual minorities. . . .
> *Queen's Quarterly* 96.2 (1989): 232

See also GAY, LESBIAN, HOMOSEXUAL, TRANSGENDERED, TRANSSEXUAL, TRANS, QUEER, LGBTQ; SEXUAL ORIENTATION; VISIBLE MINORITY.

sexual orientation, sexual preference
Both terms are in common use. Those heterosexuals, bisexuals, lesbians, and gays who don't feel that they 'chose' their sexuality may prefer the term *sexual orientation* to *sexual preference*.

> For some time, groups have been lobbying to have the Human Rights Act amended to include protection against discrimination on the basis of age, family status and sexual orientation.
> *Vancouver Sun* 26 July 1990: A15

> 'Why do people feel it necessary to tell you they've come out of the closet? I don't go around telling the world my sexual preference.'
> *Canadian Churchman* April 1986: 14

See also GAY; SEXUAL MINORITIES.

shade   see COLOUR

Shakespeareana, Shakespeariana   see -(I)ANA

shall, will   Many Canadians have been taught a rule for *shall* and *will* that they do not use in speech and ignore in all but the most formal writing. The first part of the rule requires one to express the simple future in the first person with *shall* ('I/we shall') and in the second or third person with *will* ('you will'; 'he/she/they will'). Canadians usually express the simple future in the first person with *will* ('I will come tomorrow'), as do most speakers of Scottish, Irish, and American English.

The second part of the rule requires the use of *will* with the first person to indicate a clear intention or resolve on the part of the speaker(s): 'I (*or* we) will do it' amounts to a promise, whereas 'I (*or* we) shall do it' simply indicates what is expected to happen. *Shall* with the second and third persons, according to this rule, indicates necessity: 'They shall be captured'; 'Britons never shall be slaves'.

This 'rule', which was derived from the practice of educated speakers in southern England, is no longer reflected in usage even in that variety of English. H.W. Fowler and F.G. Fowler's *The King's English* (3rd ed. 1931) comments: 'It is unfortunate that the idiomatic use [of the shall-will distinction], while it comes by nature to southern Englishmen . . . is so complicated that those who are not to the manner born can hardly acquire it' (142). *Fowler's* (1965) notes that the idiom of North America, Scotland, and Ireland 'has made formidable inroads; and insistence on the rules laid down in the OED . . . may before long have to be classed as insular pedantry.'

In Canadian English *shall* is now reserved mainly for asking polite questions with the first person: 'Shall we play cards now?'; 'Shall we meet tomorrow?'; 'Where shall I put my coat?' In academic prose *shall* persists with the first person to indicate the simple future in fixed expressions like 'as we shall see'. In Canadian legal English *shall* is still often used with the second and third persons to emphasize the binding nature of an agreement.

> Perhaps you would like to know about the day John wakes up and notices that Mary has turned into a great white shark, in which case we will quickly realize that we are in the middle of a modern psychological novel and change the subject at once.
> Margaret Atwood *Second Words* 1982: 335

(Here *will* is used with the first person to indicate the simple future.)

> If the price of oil and gas skyrockets in the future . . . we shall have to continue to supply the U.S. at the same price charged to Canadians.
> *Engineering Dimensions* 1988: 34

(Here *shall* is used to indicate the simple future; a promise or resolve would have required the phrasing 'we *will* have to continue'.)

> We shall see that political language at the election of 1734 already included a number of terms for the voice of the people on political matters. . . .
> J.A.W. Gunn *Beyond Liberty and Property* 1983: 262

(Here *shall* indicates the simple future; 'we *shall* see' is a fixed expression in academic contexts.)

> But he is a veritable gourmet compared to his friend, who shall remain nameless for the sake of his mother. The friend opens a can of Duncan Hines vanilla icing when he's hungry, and eats it off his index finger.
> *Globe and Mail* (Toronto) 21 March 1985: CL3

(Although here the context is informal, 'who *shall* remain nameless' is a fixed expression.)

> 'Canada is and shall remain a haven for those fleeing oppression and we want that clearly understood,' Miss Macdonald said. . . .
> *Globe and Mail* (Toronto) 12 Jan. 1985: P3

(Here *shall* is used with the force of *must*.)

> Company's auditors shall prepare and deliver a statement of operating profits to you and to us as promptly as possible after 31st December each year, which statement shall be binding upon the company and you.
> J.E. Smyth et al. *The Law and Business Administration in Canada* 1987: 281

(Here *shall* emphasizes that the terms of this agreement are legally binding.)

See also SHAN'T.

shambles   The most common sense of *shambles* is general confusion or mess. Originally, a *shambles* was a butcher's slaughterhouse. This sense was subsequently extended to refer to any scene of destruction and bloodshed. A few usage commentators still dispute the legitimacy of a *shambles* without blood, but Canadian writers use the word in all types of writing simply to mean great disorder; a writer trying to preserve the older sense of *shambles* would almost certainly be misunderstood.

> So the discipline of the school was a shambles. Big kids bullied little kids. At noon they played rugby in the halls or set up folding chairs and had hurdle races.
> Max Braithwaite *The Night We Stole the Mountie's Car* 1971: 60

shammy   see CHAMOIS

shan't   *Shan't* is the contraction of *shall not*: 'I shan't be attending'. It is seldom used in Canadian or American writing. *Won't*, the contraction of *will not*, is used much more often: 'I won't be attending'.

> Stephen Stills was, with Neil Young (whom we shan't discuss any longer in this piece), a founding member of Buffalo Springfield.
> *Vancouver Sun* 30 Aug. 1990: F2

> And even if I live to be a very old person, I shan't know the answer.
> Robertson Davies *One Half of Robertson Davies* 1978: 60

See also CONTRACTIONS; SHALL, WILL.

she, her   see CASE; GENDER

shear, sheared, shorn, shears, sheer, sheers To *shear* means to cut. The past tense is *sheared*. The past participle (the form used after *have* or as an adjective) is either *sheared* or *shorn*. *Shears* are used to shear sheep, clip hedges, cut heavy cloth, and so on.

Sheer means nearly transparent. Very thin fabric is *sheer*, and curtains made of such fabric are *sheers*. *Sheer* also means steep ('a sheer drop') and utter or complete ('sheer luck'). The verb to *sheer*, meaning to swerve, is rarely used in Canadian writing.

'Grass can't grow well if it's underfed, but the bizarre American syndrome of force-feeding it only to sheer off all its luxuriant locks contributes nothing to its health and is wasteful to boot'.
Province (Vancouver) 14 June 1990: 112

(The correct spelling is *shear*.)

Shears hung on swing arm rods cosy up the windows.
Calgary Herald 18 Nov. 2000: D1

(The spelling of the curtains is *sheers*.)

sheaves see -F, -V-

sheep see PLURALS

sheik see -IE-, -EI-

shelves see -F, -V-

sherbet, sherbert, sorbet The usual and most widely accepted spelling is *sherbet*, but *sherbert* reflects a common pronunciation and appears in several recently published American dictionaries. The word is derived from the Turkish *serbet* and has recently been reborrowed in its French form, *sorbet* (pronounced *sor BAY* or *SOR bet*). Both sherbet and sorbet are frozen fruity desserts; only sherbet contains milk.

It was there we tried the best hand-made sherbert we have ever had.
Leader-Post (Regina) 26 Nov. 2004: F1

(The usual spelling is *sherbet*.)

Between the salmon and venison courses, Stadtlander plans to serve a prune, plum and apple sorbet.
Ottawa Citizen 19 Oct. 1994: E5

sheriff *Sheriff* is often misspelled *sherrif*. In Canada a sheriff executes orders of the court, serving writs, seizing chattels, evicting tenants, escorting people to jail, and so on. Assistants to the sheriff are called sheriff's officers or bailiffs. In the United States a sheriff is the chief law-enforcement officer of a county.

At the courthouse, the sheriff addresses potential jurors to determine if any changes have occurred since they filled out the form, such as financial disability or illness.
Toronto Star 23 June 1992: A1

The other day he turned up in Dodge City, Kan., where they gave him an honorary sherrif's badge.
Gazette (Montreal) 2 July 1992: C9

(The correct spelling is *sheriff*.)

shibboleth *Shibboleth* is most often used to mean a firmly established but mistaken belief, especially one connected to ethnic difference. A shibboleth is also a peculiarity of speech, dress, or behaviour that identifies someone as part of a particular group, race, or social class. In the biblical story (Judges 12: 4–6) the word *shibboleth* was used by Jephthah to distinguish his own Gileadite men from the defeated Ephraimites, who could not pronounce the *sh* sound. All men were asked to pronounce *shibboleth*, and anyone replying *sibboleth* was executed.

I was dismayed to see The Globe and Mail repeating the old shibboleth that whites 'have lived on the tip of the continent for three centuries, longer than the Bantu people, who migrated south after the Cape Dutch settlers arrived'.
Globe and Mail (Toronto) 4 March 1985: 6

His 78 years have not slowed him down exactly: indeed, instead of being a firecracker trying to explode every social shibboleth within range, he has become a cannon, aiming big shots at big targets.
Maclean's 19 Nov. 1990: A45

For them *joual* is a shibboleth: those who speak it pass, those who don't fail.
Margaret Atwood *Second Words* 1982: 265

shine, shined, shone   In Canada *shone* (which rhymes with *gone*, or less often with *stone*) is the usual past tense and past participle of *shine* except in the 'polish' sense, where *shined* is the usual choice: 'The sun shone while we shined our shoes'. Speakers of British English also tend to maintain this distinction, but in the United States usage is more mixed. There *shined* often refers to light: 'They shined the light in his face'.

The balance of the soloists performed to the standard that was expected, though none shone with exceptional sparkle.
Province (Vancouver) 2 April 1990: 42

During the course of the trip he has his suit pressed and shoes shined.
Financial Post 10 July 1991: 12

'It was dark and when my lights suddenly shined on it, I . . . tried to swerve out of the way,' says Efford, who wasn't injured when the huge animal collapsed on his left front fender.
Province (Vancouver) 9 Nov. 1990: 64

(The more common form is *shone*, but *shined* is correct.)

See also SHINNY, SHINY.

shinny, shiny   The informal hockey game is *shinny*, often misspelled *shiny*. The surface of the ice is *shiny*.

Not only did the CBC have 14 hours of coverage from rinks across the country . . . but the Rideau Canal also postponed the leisurely skates of thousands for the excitement of shiny hockey.
Ottawa Citizen 22 Feb. 2004: B1

(The proper spelling for informal hockey is *shinny*.)

See also SHINE, SHINED; WHINNY, WHINY.

ship   see BOAT

shire   see GLOUCESTER

shocking   see AWFUL

[shoe-in]   see SHOO-IN

shoeing   see -E

shone   see SHINE

shoo-in, [shoe-in]   The proper spelling for the expression meaning a sure bet is *shoo-in*: 'He's a shoo-in for the award'. To *shoo* usually means to drive something away, but *shoo-in* derives from the practice of fixing horse races: the horse that is pushed to the front of the pack by complicit jockeys is shooed *in* to victory. Today *shoo-in* does not connote wrongdoing. A common misspelling, perhaps influenced by 'foot in the door', is *shoe-in*.

He's ranked ninth in the world standings this season . . . and looks like a shoe-in for another National Finals Rodeo in Las Vegas.
Star-Phoenix (Saskatoon) 1 Oct. 2005: B2

(The proper expression is *shoo-in*.)

shorn   see SHEAR

short   see FUNCTIONAL SHIFT

shortfall, shortcoming   A *shortfall* is a situation in which—or the amount by which—actual income falls short of anticipated income, or what one has falls short of what one needs. *Shortfall* has strong economic connotations. A better choice for human failings and defects of design is *shortcoming*.

In 1985 the conference received only 94.4% of expected congregational donations, a shortfall of $127,000.
Mennonite Brethren Herald 7 March 1986: 25

In 1986, the crop shortfall is predicted to be between 900,000 and 1.2 million tonnes, with 5.8 million [people] continuing to need assistance.
Canadian Baptist Feb. 1986: 6

The main shortcoming of Durkheim's theory is its onesidedness.
Irving M. Zeitlin and Robert J. Brym *The Social Condition of Humanity* 1991: 207

They did admit to some minor shortcomings, such as gossiping, cheating on diets and being lazy about cleaning up.
Chatelaine June 1986: 28

The sports centre, which offers activities ranging from gymnastics to roller blading, is Galperin's way of addressing what he believes is a serious shortfall in the Canadian sports system.
Toronto Star 1 Oct. 1992: NY6

(Here *shortcoming* would be more appropriate.)

Despite its shortfalls, however, the encyclopedia offers much new information that would not otherwise be readily available.
Canadian Heritage Magazine Feb.–Mar. 1986: 43

(Here *shortcomings* would be more appropriate.)

short shrift   To give someone *short shrift* means to pay little or insufficient attention to him or her. On the crowded scaffolds of Elizabethan England, busy executioners often limited Roman Catholic priests to a shortened version of the Catholic sacrament known then as *shriving*, in which a penitent confesses sins and receives absolution. This practice became known as giving *short shrift*. Now occasionally the expression is mistakenly rendered as *short shift*. The confusion of *shift* and *shrift* probably reflects the infrequent use of the archaic word *shrift* in modern English.

A common error in dealing with prescribed topics is to emphasize one portion while giving short shrift to another.
Margot Northey and David B. Knight *Making Sense in Geography and Environmental Studies* 1992: 66

The Genies' poor schedule placement drew criticism from filmmaker Atom Egoyan, who said Canadian cinema had been given short shift by the country's broadcasters.
Daily News (Halifax) 8 Dec. 1998: 38

(The conventional expression is *short shrift*.)

See also FOLK ETYMOLOGY.

short-sighted   see NEAR-SIGHTED

shot   see GUN

[should of]   see [COULD OF]

should've   see CONTRACTIONS

show, showed, shown   The past tense is *showed*: 'She showed me her pictures of Iceland'. The past participle can be either *shown* or *showed*: 'She had shown the pictures to the class'; 'The cinema has showed this film before'. However, *shown* is the usual choice.

And, she says, experience has shown there is a festival audience for roots, reggae and ska music.
Ottawa Citizen 17 June 2006: F1

None of the horses in the Daffodil had showed the slightest inclination to set the pace in an earlier race.
Province (Vancouver) 27 May 1990: 68

shrift   see SHORT SHRIFT

shrink, shrank, shrunk, shrunken
Although the usual past tense of *shrink* is *shrank*, some authorities also allow *shrunk*: 'My T-shirt shrank (or shrunk) in the dryer'. *Shrunk* is more common in speech, but is never used in formal writing. The past participle is either *shrunk* or *shrunken*. *Shrunk* is more common when the past participle is part of a verb ('The market has shrunk'), *shrunken* when it functions as an adjective ('shrunken hopes').

Herman shrank into the seat of his cutter like a turtle withdrawing its exposed, vulnerable skin into the cavern of its shell.
Queen's Quarterly 92.3 (1985): 493

Yet on the subject of academic freedom, as on all others, he shrank from professions of piety.
Frederick Gibson *Queen's University* 2 (1983): 343

The Canadian Football League shrunk its distinctive ball a few years ago, the result, some say, of complaints from transplanted American quarterbacks.
Vancouver Sun 1 Dec. 1990: D6

(In formal writing, *shrank* would be used.)

She looks surprisingly old, like a woman shrunken by age to the size of a ten-year-old. . . .
Margaret Atwood *Life Before Man* 1979: 30

Shuswap   see SECWEPEMC, SHUSWAP

shut   see CLOSE

shut-in   see PHRASAL VERBS

SI   see APPENDIX II

Siamese cat   see CAPITAL LETTERS

Siamese twins   see CONJOINED TWINS

sic   see PARENTHESES; QUOTATION

sick, ill, vomit   In Canadian English the expression *to be sick* covers a wide range of meaning, including most forms of ill health as well as nausea, so that *to be sick* and *to be ill* are very nearly synonyms. In Standard Southern British English, however, *to be sick* usually means to vomit, as it does in Australian English. In Britain someone is *ill*, not *sick*, with a bad cold. When the adjective *sick* is used before a noun, as in 'a sick child' or 'sick time', the meaning is the same in North American and British English.

In Canadian English, to be nauseated or vomiting is to be 'sick to (*or* at) one's stomach'. Newfoundlanders say 'stomach-sick'. Of the dozens of informal expressions meaning to vomit, *to throw up* is perhaps the most commonplace.

See also NAUSEOUS, NAUSEATING, NAUSEATED.

sideroad   see ROAD

sidle   see BACK-FORMATION

sight   see CITE

signal   see DOUBLING THE FINAL CONSONANT

Sikh   The Hindi word *sikh* means disciple and is traditionally pronounced *SICK*. Because this pronunciation is an unfortunate homophone of the English word *sick*, *Sikh* is commonly pronounced *SEEK* in Canada and the United States, even though Sikh Canadians prefer the *SICK* pronunciation. British dictionaries list both pronunciations. *Sikh* should always be capitalized; Sikhs, like Jews, are distinguished as both an ethnic and a religious group.

The Sikh religion emerged in the Punjab region of the Indian subcontinent in the sixteenth century. Sikhism requires that all Sikh men vow to observe what are called the 'five K's': to carry a ceremonial dagger (*kirpan*), to wear a beard and not cut their hair (*kes*), and to wear a comb (*kanga*), soldier's shorts (*kach*), and an iron bracelet (*kara*). The common titles *Singh* ('Lion') and *Kaur* ('Princess') are often adopted by male and female Sikhs respectively, usually as last names. To avoid confusion, it is best to write Sikh names out in full. Note that not all those with the last name Singh are Sikh.

Richard Popplewell tells the fascinating . . . history of British efforts to monitor the Sikh diaspora before World War I, especially on the West coast of Canada.
Canadian Journal of History 14.1 (1989): 87

See also CHINESE NAMES, FAMILY NAMES.

Siksika   see BLACKFOOT

silicon, silicone, silica   *Silicon* and *silicone* are different substances; these terms are not interchangeable. *Silicon*, the earth's second most abundant element, is widely used in electronic devices in the form of 'chips' of pure silicon. *Silicones*, a group of compounds containing silicon, carbon, hydrogen, and oxygen, are resistant to water, heat, and electric currents; they are used in plastic surgery and the manufacture of lubricants and waterproof polishes and sealants.

Silicon combines with oxygen to make *silica*, which occurs as quartz, mica, opal, and clay, and is the main component of sand.

Other cultures offer decorative tattooing . . . while ours offers silicon injections. . . .
Globe and Mail (Toronto) 16 Feb. 1985: E17

(Plastic surgeons inject *silicone*, not *silicon*.)

similar   see ANALOGOUS

simile   see CATASTROPHE, CATASTROPHES; entry in Glossary.

simple, simplistic   *Simple* means plain, easy, straightforward, or uncomplicated: a simple solution to a problem is a good one. *Simplistic* is a negative word, usually applied to ideas and arguments, that means lacking in depth, complexity, or subtlety. *Simplistic* should not be used as a high-flown substitute for *simple*.

Of all the . . . gifts sent to the students, one very simple present made the biggest impression: A maple tree from Acton.
Calgary Herald 2 July 1992: N1

While . . . the mind can be seen as analogous to a computer . . . to regard ourselves as nothing more than sophisticated computers is simplistic and dangerous.
Saturday Night Jan. 1986: 10

'Units are becoming more complicated rather than more simplistic,' admits Orla Johnston, assistant marketing manager for Panasonic's personal communications division. . . .
Canadian Living Nov. 1990: 208

(Here *simpler* should replace *more simplistic*.)

simple reason   A number of usage commentators object strongly to the expression *for the simple reason that*, since the reason given may not seem as simple to the reader as it does to the writer; instead they recommend *because*. However, the tone of *for the simple reason* is not always patronizing. Often *simple* means something like sole, and substituting *because* would eliminate a nuance of the meaning.

Despite finishing last or near last in most of her races, she usually wins the masters women [title] for the simple reason that she is the only masters woman.
Daily News (Halifax) 22 Dec. 1994: 48

He could find no fault with the legislation for the simple reason that he authored it. . . .
Toronto Star 24 Oct. 1994: A16

simulacrum   Usually an image or shadowy representation of something, a *simulacrum* may also be a deceptive substitute, a sham. *Simulacra* is the preferred plural form, but *simulacrums* is also correct. *Simulacrum* is pronounced *sim uh LAY crum*.

. . . the Mexican actress Ofelia Medina is an eerie simulacrum of Frida—she appears on screen next to the real self-portraits, and the feeling that she is Frida intensifies.
Globe and Mail (Toronto) 2 Sept. 1985: S11

. . . tourists impose their own reality on that place, a 'simulacrum' that approximates the past but distorts the very reality they seek.
Vancouver Sun 26 May 1990: D1

See also PLURALS, REGULAR, IRREGULAR, FOREIGN.

simultaneous, simultaneously   The adjective *simultaneous* ('simultaneous translation') is quite often used mistakenly in place of the adverb *simultaneously* ('The two will run simultaneously').

Ferchat said the Koreans would get the next two at a better price, as construction would take place simultaneous with last year's sale.
Financial Post (Toronto) 14 Nov. 1991: 4

(Here the adverb *simultaneously* is required.)

See also ADJECTIVES AND ADVERBS; SYNCHRONOUS.

sincereness   see -NESS

sine qua non, ne plus ultra   In Latin *sine qua non* means 'without which not'. In English the phrase is used as a noun for a thing or condition that is essential or indispensable. The usual pronunciation is *SIN e KWA NAWN*. Several usage guides suggest using a more familiar phrase, such as 'indispensable condition', 'absolute prerequisite', or 'essential ingredient', because *sine qua non* may not be widely understood. This concern is legitimate. In fact, *sine* *qua non* is sometimes confused with another Latin phrase, *ne plus ultra*, meaning the acme, the ultimate.

> Editorial independence is the sine qua non of any worthy professional or scientific journal.
> *Globe and Mail* (Toronto) 3 April 2006: A12

> Apricot nectar, the sine qua non of the recipe, is not always available on grocery store shelves.
> *Daily News* (Halifax) 3 March 1993: 23

> The networks can count on an audience [for the 1986 Grey Cup game] of upwards of five million. By comparison, the National Football League's Super Bowl, supposedly the ne plus ultra of professional football, has never pulled an audience that big in Canada.
> *Gazette* (Montreal) 29 Nov. 1986: D1

> The psychologists . . . should explore what dark side of the human psyche posits aging mothers as either disgusting or funny while aging fathers are regarded as the sine qua non of virility.
> *Ottawa Citizen* 9 Jan. 1994: B2

(The phrase required here is *ne plus ultra*, referring to 'the height' of virility.)

See also EPITOME; LATIN PHRASES.

sing, sang, sung   The usual past tense of *sing* is *sang*: 'We sang happily'. The past participle is *sung*: 'We have sung carols every year'. In the nineteenth century *sung* was commonly used as the past tense, but this form is now considered non-standard.

> At 25, he sung We Are the World—doing each of the song's 18 distinct voices. . . .
> *Vancouver Sun* 11 Oct. 1990: F5

(The standard past tense is *sang*.)

singeing   see -E

single-minded   see -MINDED

singular and plural   see AGREEMENT, GRAMMATICAL; PLURALS

sink, sank, sunk, sunken   The usual past tense of *sink* is *sank* and the past participle is *sunk*: 'The ship sank'; 'The ship has sunk'. *Sunk*

is sometimes used as the past tense, but rarely in writing. *Sunken* is usually an adjective: 'sunken treasure', 'sunken eyes', 'a sunken living room'. *Sunken* is obsolescent in Canadian writing as a variant of the past participle.

> In 1991, drilling activity in Canada sunk to its lowest level since 1975.
> *Financial Post* 23 Dec. 1991: 28

(The past tense *sunk* is not wrong, but *sank* is far more common in Canadian writing.)

> . . . it is still too early to know whether Bourassa's proposal will present Mulroney with a plank on which to walk out of the political hole in which his party has sunken following the failure of the Meech Lake talks. . . .
> *Gazette* (Montreal) 2 Feb. 1991: B4

(The usual past participle is *sunk*.)

sinus   see -US

sirup   see SYRUP

sister-in-law   see IN-LAWS

site   see CITE

situation   *Situation* is criticized as redundant in phrases such as 'emergency situation', 'crisis situation', and 'in the classroom situation'. *Emergency*, *crisis*, and *in the classroom* alone are more direct and effective.

> The media have an important role to play in any crisis situation but it is imperative that they do not jeopardize a safe resolution.
> *Ottawa Citizen* 3 Dec. 1990: A9

(Here *crisis* alone would convey the nature of the situation.)

> The Anti-lock Braking System (ABS) allows any driver to handle emergency situations like a professional.
> *Canadian Consumer* March 1986: 10

(The single word *emergencies* would describe the situation adequately.)

See also WORDINESS.

Six Nations see IROQUOIS

sizable, sizeable see -ABLE, (-E)ABLE

sizzle see ONOMATOPOEIA

skeptic, sceptic Canadian newspapers over-whelmingly use *skeptic* and its related forms, but *sceptic* and *skeptic* are used with equal frequency in other types of writing. British dictionaries list *sceptic* first, American dictionaries *skeptic*. Both spellings are pronounced *SKEP tic*. Many authorities argue that the *sk* spelling more accurately reflects this pronunciation and avoids confusion with *septic*. They may have a point: see SEPSIS, SEPTICEMIA, SEPTIC.

skewer, skew Writers sometimes use *skewer* when they mean *skew*. To *skew* means to twist or distort, while to *skewer* means to pierce, as with a skewer. *Skewer* is also used figuratively at all levels of writing to mean ridicule or satirize.

> Don't run with the stick in your mouth, he'd tell the kids, already seeing them fall, seeing the pointed stick skewering up through the roof of the mouth.
> Margaret Atwood *Life Before Man* 1979: 24

> The police have managed to skew the law in ways that produce the results they want, namely, a relatively certain conviction against certain kinds of individuals.
> *Globe and Mail* (Toronto) 23 March 1985: 10

(Here *skew* means distort.)

> There's a deliciously tangy literary spat abrewing, pitting . . . Margaret Atwood against portly Robert Fulford, a sort of high priest of Canadian arts and letters who says he was skewered in a recent Atwood work.
> *Ottawa Citizen* 30 June 1990: C12

(Here *skewer* means ridicule.)

> But one thing [drugs] all do the same is to skewer the way things normally work inside your head.
> *Gazette* (Montreal) 29 April 1990: C4

(The word required here is *skew*.)

> The Phillipses are big on Do's and Don'ts lists—and they're guaranteed to induce major chuckles from folks with a skewered sense of reality.
> *Gazette* (Montreal) 1 Oct. 1990: B11

(The word required here is *skewed*.)

skid road, skid row Some critics prefer *skid road* on the grounds of historical accuracy; however, most Canadian writers use *skid row*. Dictionaries list both forms.

Skid road was originally a logging term for a road made of greased logs, or skids, over which lumber was dragged by teams of mules or oxen. The term was first applied to a slum area—the loggers' part of town—in Seattle, Washington, in 1852; Vancouverites began using the phrase in the same way before 1900. Gradually the term *skid row* came into use as well to refer to a slum or an area frequented by drifters and alcoholics, even in cities with no lumber industry.

Both terms should be capitalized only in reference to a specific place.

> The street's off at an angle, a curious little hiccup in the orderly progression of arrow-straight thoroughfares on either side. . . . That odd lean to Gore is a reminder that it was once a 'skid road,' the genuine article, a wide swath cut through the forest down which loggers skidded their trees with the assistance of yoked oxen.
> *Province* (Vancouver) 19 Aug. 1990: 27

> Mere decades ago, Hastings Street, around Main—today's Skid Road, home to the poor and socially disenfranchised—was Vancouver's bustling downtown.
> *Vancouver Sun* 12 Jan. 1990: B6

> By . . . 1974, the longtime working class neighborhood had deteriorated into flophouses and a Skid Road.
> *Toronto Star* 23 Aug. 1987: E1

(The capitals are unnecessary: 'a *skid road*'.)

skiffs see -F, -V-

skilful, skillful Canadians use both of these spelling variants, and neither is clearly preferred. *Skilful* is the contemporary British spelling, *skillful* the American.

skim milk, skimmed milk, whip cream, whipped cream, whipping cream   The form *skim milk* is more common in Canadian English than *skimmed milk*, except in the phrase 'partly skimmed milk'. *Whip cream* is common in speech but almost never appears in writing. In writing, *whipped cream* and *whipping cream* are used to distinguish the beaten dessert topping from the heavy cream from which it is made.

See also ICE CREAM.

slain   see SLAY

slang   see COLLOQUIAL

slant   see SLASH

slash, slash mark, stroke, virgule, slant, diagonal, solidus, backslash   A *slash* or *slash mark*, also called a *stroke*, a *virgule*, a *slant*, a *diagonal*, or a *solidus*, is used to separate alternatives ('a strictly objective/quantified research method', 'a German industrialist/investor'), the elements of a date ('1998/7/14'), and the numerator and denominator of a fraction ('5/8'). It is also used to replace *per* in measurements ('100 km/h') and *to* in ratios ('new/returning customers'; 'male/female parity'). A slash is sometimes used instead of a hyphen to indicate a period spanning two calendar years ('1962/63'). Note that there is no space before or after the slash in any of these uses.

A slash is also used to separate lines of poetry run on in a prose text; in this use, a space should be inserted before and after the slash.

The *backslash* or *reverse solidus* (\) , which leans in the opposite direction, is used in computer programming.

> The law, however, 'oldest of the hierarchs / Composed of electronic sparks', . . . ultimately denies the significance of man in the scheme of things.
> *Queen's Quarterly* 97.3 (1990): 423

See also AND/OR; DATES; HYPHENATION; QUOTATION.

slate   In Canada and the United States, to *be slated* means to be scheduled or designated, as in 'slated for surgery' or 'slated for publication'. In British English, to *slate* is a colloquialism meaning to criticize severely. The two expressions have different roots. The North American verb *slate* is related to the noun *slate* meaning chalkboard and its figurative extension meaning a list of candidates proposed for election or nomination. The British verb *slate* is thought to be a modern variation on the verb *slat*, which dates from the thirteenth century and means to slap or to knock down. *Slate* meaning criticize is unfamiliar in North America, as is a political *slate* in Britain.

> They were slated to arrive in mid-January.
> Pierre Berton *The Promised Land* 1984: 75

> Alderman John Bannister . . . took pains to deny rumours that property on Barrie Street, one block east of the university, 'was slated for expropriation'.
> Frederick Gibson *Queen's University* 2 (1983): 386

> An alliance of about 800 artists, artist-run centres and art critics . . . have proposed a slate of 11 candidates to stand for election at the VAG annual general meeting on March 28.
> *Globe and Mail* (Toronto) 28 Feb. 1985: E1

slaughter   see MASSACRE

Slavey, Dene-Tha(h), Slavey Dene   Both *Slavey* and *Dene-Tha* or *Dene-Thah* (pronounced DEN ay THAH) are in use for this Aboriginal group, whose language, Slavey, is a member of the Athapaskan language family (sometimes called Na-Dene). The group occasionally identify themselves as *Slavey Dene*. Most of their traditional territory is in the Northwest Territories, although it extends into northern British Columbia and Alberta. All three names can be used as singular and plural.

> Characters [on the television program *North of 60*] will sometimes speak the Slavey language, and a Northwest Territories cultural advisor is on hand to

help keep things authentic.
Calgary Herald 6 Oct. 1992: D1

'I don't think we can resurrect anything before the next election,' [Western Arctic MP Ethel] Blondin, a Slavey Dene and strong Yes campaigner, said as the reality of Monday's referendum results began to sink in.
Calgary Herald 28 Oct. 1992: A8

With the abuse finally surfacing, the Dene Tha band is starting a time of healing and recovery. . . .
Calgary Herald 21 Dec. 1992: A15

See also ABORIGINAL PEOPLE(S); ATHABASKAN; DENE; NUNAVUT, NUNAVUMMIUT, DENENDAH; APPENDIX III.

slay, slew, slain, slayed   The past tense of *slay* meaning kill is *slew* and the past participle is *slain*. *Slay* has a second, informal sense: an act or performer that slays an audience is a huge hit. In this sense the past tense can be *slayed*.

Fortunately, the young hero Perseus spotted the charming princess, slew the beast and claimed the hand of Andromeda.
Gazette (Montreal) 12 Oct. 2002: G7

. . . legend says that demigod Maui chased and slayed the dragon Moo Kuna for trying to drown his mother, the goddess Hina.
Vancouver Sun 8 Dec. 1990: E1

(The usual past tense for this sense is *slew*.)

In a recent five-week period in Quebec, 13 women were slain by a husband or lover.
Province (Vancouver) 11 Oct. 1990: 38

Monday night, before a near-capacity house at the Centrepointe Theatre, Crowell . . . slayed the audience with a high-energy, two-hour set.
Ottawa Citizen 1 May 1990: D5

See also SLOUGH, SLOUGH OF DESPOND, SLEW.

sled, sleigh, toboggan, cutter, sledge, cariole, carryall   In Canada the children's toy on runners used for coasting down snowy hills is called either a *sled* or a *sleigh*. A *toboggan*, used for the same purpose, is curved up at one end and has no runners. Larger sleighs, now primarily used for winter parties, are pulled by horses. *Cutter* is a Canadianism for a light horse-drawn

sleigh. The small, low cargo vehicle used in the north, pulled by dog teams and occasionally by people, is called a *sled* or a *sledge*. *Cariole* is a Canadianism derived from Canadian French; it refers to a light sleigh pulled by horses or occasionally dogs. In English Canada *carryall* was once a common spelling, influenced by folk etymology.

Parents pulled their children on sleds past the Pantheon and skiers glided through the Spanish Steps area.
Globe and Mail (Toronto) 7 Jan. 1985: C10

Off he went on a tour of all the villages, seated in a six-horse sleigh, with a choir of maidens chanting psalms.
Pierre Berton *The Promised Land* 1984: 95

Outside the door the sleigh and horses awaited. No, not prancing steeds pulling a fancy cutter. Just a large farm sleigh piled high with fragrant hay. . . .
Vancouver Sun 24 Dec. 1993: A3

So when Doug Hannah hooked the harness onto the sled, the big Malamute was howling and leaping with the rest of the sled team.
Globe and Mail (Toronto) 4 Dec. 1985: C4

Bring your camera to capture the age-old arts of traveling by dog team and sledge and of traditional Inuit seal hunting.
Up Here Mar.–Apr. 1990: 38

In temperatures of -52C, the men travelled an average of 14 kilometres daily, each carrying 60 kilograms . . . of supplies divided between a backpack and sledge each man pulled behind.
Province (Vancouver) 4 Oct. 1990: 19

. . . these shaggy ponies hauled logs out of the bush and pulled the family to Sunday mass; released from their labours, they drew daredevil carioles over frozen rivers.
Saturday Night July 1986: 33

See also FOLK ETYMOLOGY.

slew   see SLAY; SLOUGH

slips of the tongue   A slip of the tongue is an unintentional error in speech, either in pronunciation or in word choice. Such verbal gaffes often provide amusement; they are also of particular interest in the field of psycholinguistics because they shed some light on how language is produced in the brain.

Slips of the tongue fall into a number of patterns. One of the most frequent errors is the transposition of initial letters between two terms, as in 'You have hissed my mystery lecture'. William Archibald Spooner, an Oxford don, produced so many funny examples of such slips that they are now called 'spoonerisms'. English-speakers often transpose sounds within particular words, a phenomenon known as *metathesis*: for example, saying *intregal* instead of *integral*. A consonant may be shifted from one word to another: *pinch hit* comes out as *pitch hint*. Or an initial or final consonant may carry over to another word, as in this slip in a commentary by Don Cherry (on *Hockey Night in Canada*, 24 Oct. 1992): 'Cream rises to the crop' (instead of 'to the top'; or perhaps Cherry was thinking of the phrase 'cream of the crop').

Words are sometimes unintentionally blended in speech, producing 'boibbling' instead of *boiling and bubbling*. Sometimes words that are 'close' are introduced into phrases that sound plausible but don't quite make sense: 'a *reclining* hairline', '*unravelling* a plaque', 'the basic *tenants* of an argument'. This sort of slip of the tongue, choosing the wrong word, is commonly called a *malapropism*. The celebrated *Freudian slip*, technically a *parapraxis*, is the unintentional substitution of a word in speech or writing that supposedly reveals an unconscious thought or desire, usually construed as sexual: 'She bakes the breast bed I've ever had'.

See also MALAPROPISM; MISPRONUNCIATION; SPOONERISM.

slough, slough of despond, slew   The definition of *slough* varies across Canada: on the Pacific coast it is a shallow saltwater estuary or a backwater channel of a river; in the interior of British Columbia it is a marsh; and across the prairies it is a hollow that fills with water in the wet season and often produces good-quality hay called 'slough grass'. Some prairie sloughs are round areas of sinking soil also known as potholes. In this sense Canadians usually pro-

nounce *slough* to rhyme with *slew* (which is also an alternative, though uncommon, spelling). However, in the expression *slough of despond*, meaning a fit of depression and despair, they often use the British pronunciation, which rhymes *slough* with *cow*; the phrase comes from the name of a bog that blocks the path of the hero of John Bunyan's *Pilgrim's Progress* (1678).

Slough (pronounced SLUFF) is the old, shed skin of a snake or other animal. To *slough* (usually followed by *off*) is to shed something or to cast it off: 'He sloughed off their critical comments'.

The sun shone, the snow melted, the frogs sang in the sloughs.
Max Braithwaite *The Night We Stole the Mountie's Car* 1971: 182

John Turner admits to no dark night of doubt during his slog through the slough of Liberal despond.
Saturday Night March 1986: 17

The same tendency to slough over the consequences was present in efforts by Mandeville and others to identify luxury with happier circumstances.
J.A.W. Gunn *Beyond Liberty and Property* 1983: 98

(Here the writer seems to have confused two idiomatic expressions: *slough off* and *gloss over*.)

I looked at my watch at the side of the bed, where I'd left it behind as I sloughed all my city clothes nearly a week ago.
Howard Engel *Murder Sees the Light* 1984: 150

However tempting it may be . . . to try to slough responsibility off on the provinces, abortion law is not traffic law.
Vancouver Sun 21 July 1989: A14

See also SLAY; SWAMP.

Slovakia, Slovenia   Slovakia and Slovenia, two relatively new countries of central Europe, are frequently confused. Czechoslovakia split into two countries, the Czech Republic and Slovakia, in 1993. Slovakia borders the Czech Republic as well as Poland, Ukraine, Hungary and Austria. Slovenia, formerly a part of Yugoslavia, has been an independent country since 1991. Slovenia is bounded by Italy,

Croatia, Austria, Hungary, and the Adriatic Sea. The longer names of these countries are the Slovak Republic and the Republic of Slovenia.

> . . . business travellers should avoid tactless comparisons with the Czech Republic, or worse, confusing Slovakia with Slovenia. . . .
> 'Tips for Business Travellers—Slovak Republic' International Trade Canada website March 2005

See also BALTIC, BALKANS.

Slovenia   see SLOVAKIA, SLOVENIA

slow, slowly   The use of *slow* as an adverb, as in 'go slow', 'driving too slow', and 'talk slower', has often been subjected to criticism on the grounds that *slowly* is the correct adverb form. However, there are a few adverbs in English, called 'flat adverbs' or 'zero adverbs', that have the same form as the corresponding adjective. These include *fast, slow, quick, wide,* and *deep*: 'Come quick'; 'Turn wide'. Most zero adverbs also have an adverb form that ends in *-ly*. Often these forms are used in different contexts. For example, *slow* is used directly after a verb, while *slowly* can be placed elsewhere in the sentence: 'Slowly he opened his mouth to speak'.

See also ADVERBS WITHOUT -LY.

small arms   see GUN

smelt   see -T, -ED

smoke without fire, no   see CLICHÉ

smoky, smokey   see -Y, -EY

smoulder, smolder   Both spellings are common in Canadian writing. The British use *smoulder*; Americans strongly prefer *smolder*.

See also SPELLING, CANADIAN.

sneaked, snuck   In Canadian writing the usual past tense or past participle of *sneak* is *sneaked*. The form *snuck* is sometimes used in fiction and journalism, and is very common in speech. *Snuck* was first recorded in the dialect of

the American South at the end of the nineteenth century. This form has made rapid progress towards acceptability in the United States and Canada; it may even sneak into formal Canadian writing in the next few years.

> While George took care of family business, somebody sneaked into his backyard and made off with two prize boars.
> *Vancouver Sun* 9 April 1990: A9

> 'He'd been hoping for a crime that at best would be apprehended, snuck up on, come across.'
> Howard Engel *Murder Sees the Light* 1984: 219

> In a dramatic escape, they dodged government spies within the choir, as well as their vigilant manager, and snuck out of their Toronto hotel.
> *Globe and Mail* (Toronto) 24 December 2006: A1

sneakers   see RUNNING SHOES

snicker, snigger   Both *snicker* and *snigger* describe a half-suppressed laugh. Americans prefer *snicker*, but the English consider the word obsolete and use only *snigger*. For Canadians *snigger* may imply more malice than *snicker*, but they use both words with about equal frequency.

> The very computer I have used for the past 8 years now has an antiquated look about it. My own children snicker when I defend it.
> *Daily News* (Halifax) 4 Aug. 1994: n.p.

> She thought the man would be offended—she was intending to be offensive—but she was almost sure she heard a snicker at the other end of the line.
> Margaret Atwood *Life Before Man* 1979: 274

> Spiteful, sniggering, conceited, infantine Mozart!
> *Queen's Quarterly* 92.2 (1985): 331

> I have never thought of myself as a satirist: I do not sit down to my work sniggering with malice and muttering, 'Here goes with the acid!'
> Robertson Davies *One Half of Robertson Davies* 1978: 281

snowbound   see -BOUND

snuck   see SNEAKED

snuggly, snugly, Snugli   *Snuggly* is an informal adjective. *Snuggly* things are warm and cosy, and *snuggly* people invite cuddling. *Snugly*, with a single *g*, is the adverb form of *snug*: 'Bandages should be applied snugly.' This adverb is often misspelled *snuggly*.

Snugli is a proprietary term for a soft, pack-sack-like baby carrier. *Snuggly* is sometimes used as a generic term for this type of item.

> There's no better way to get snuggly on the sofa than by adding some plump, plush pillows. . . .
> *Daily News* (Halifax) 17 Sept. 2004: 9

> A helmet should fit snugly, level and square, with the front covering the forehead.
> *Calgary Herald* 13 Oct. 2005: E6

> Slowly, the 'wish list' for the hospital grew to include lightweight strollers, diapers, baby intercoms, snugglies, nursing pads, small stuffed toys for babies, assorted baby toiletries and, most importantly, infant and newborn clothing.
> *Jewish Independent* (Vancouver) 21 May 2004: n.p.

so see COMMA

so . . . as see AS . . . AS

so-called The expression *so-called* signals irony. Its use indicates the writer's skepticism about the accuracy of a title, name, or label, as in 'this so-called expert'. *So-called* should not be used simply to give the usual name for something, as in 'The so-called home page is the entry point to the website'.

Although some language guides recommend that what follows *so-called* not be put in quotation marks, on the grounds that a double indication of irony is unnecessary, other commentators consider the use of quotation marks a matter of preference or tone.

> [Wollstonecraft] believed that physical exercise was essential and that doll-playing and other so-called feminine games would quickly be relegated to rainy afternoons if girls were allowed to romp in the fields along with their brothers.
> Miriam Waddington *Apartment Seven* 1989: 173

> 'Women are already flooding the so-called traditional jobs by the millions.'
> Carl J. Cuneo *Pay Equity* 1990: 115

> Clearly Englishmen had long been familiar with the notion that individual liberty did not necessarily flourish in a so-called 'free-state.'
> J.A.W. Gunn *Beyond Liberty and Property* 1983: 239

(Some editors would remove the quotation marks around 'free-state'.)

> Associated with the Urban Revolution is the introduction of copper and bronze—the so-called Bronze Age.
> Irving M. Zeitlin and Robert J. Brym *The Social Condition of Humanity* 1991: 303

(Here *so-called* is not necessary unless the writer has an objection to the term *Bronze Age*.)

See also QUOTATION, QUOTATION MARKS.

soccer, football What Canadians and Americans call *soccer* is what the rest of the English-speaking world calls *football*. Canadians and Americans reserve the term *football* for the contact sport, developed in the United States, in which heavily padded players throw, kick, or run with an oval ball. Internationally, this game is known as American football. Most North American sports fans know that Americans and Canadians play the game by slightly different rules, and call the Canadian version 'Canadian football'.

> Strangely, Quinn, a native of Quebec City, has never played a game of soccer in his life. 'Football was always my game,' said Quinn. . . .
> *Gazette* (Montreal) 18 June 1992: H1

> 'If we don't grant clubs a license, they can play their football—but without spectators.'
> *Gazette* (Montreal) 20 Jan. 1992: C5

(Here a British speaker is referring to the game known in Canada as *soccer*.)

> [In] American or Canadian football . . . a team must advance the ball 10 yards to get a first down.
> *Vancouver Sun* 20 June 1992: D3

Social Credit Party, funny money, Créditiste, Socred Social Credit principles were developed in the 1920s by an English engineer named C.H. Douglas. Douglas believed that a strong economy depended on the purchasing power of the people, and that the government should distribute 'credit' to consumers. His ideas were seized upon by an evangelist named William Aberhart, who led the Social Credit Party to victory in Alberta in 1935. The Aberhart government's monetary reforms and issuing of scrip known as *funny money* gave rise to the nickname *funny-money party*.

However, over the next few decades Social Credit policy diverged significantly from Douglas's original ideas, and the party gained prominence in several provinces by following conservative financial policies and promoting development. Social Credit members in Quebec formed their own group in 1963 and adopted the name *Ralliement des Créditistes*, or simply *Créditistes*. Members of the Social Credit Party or the Ralliement des Créditistes held seats in the House of Commons between 1935 and 1980. By the end of the 1980s the Social Credit Party was active only in the West. Members of the Social Credit Party are informally known as *Socreds*.

Similarly, even today, in Western Canadian elections, a protest vote may go Social Credit or NDP without much regard to the difference in political philosophy between these parties.
Northrop Frye *The Bush Garden* 1971: 229

. . . Mr. Bourassa's Liberals thrashed the Union Nationale, the Créditistes and the Parti Quebecois at the polls, and Mr. Bourassa became the youngest premier in Quebec's history.
Globe and Mail (Toronto) 28 Nov. 1985: A4

The Socred government had been plagued by a series of mini-scandals ranging from vote juggling to cabinet ministers guzzling expensive French wine on the taxpayers' tab.
Henry M. Rosenthal and S. Cathy Berson, eds. *Canadian Jewish Outlook Anthology* 1988: 316

soda see SOFT DRINK

sofa see CHESTERFIELD

soft drink, pop, soda, float All these words refer to a drink of sweetened, carbonated water. *Soft drink* is the term that most Canadians use in writing and formal speech. In casual speech Canadians, like the British, often say *pop*; but in writing *pop* is considered slang. The compound *soda pop* is now rare. While some Americans use *soda* instead of *pop*, in Canada *soda* usually means club soda; however, a *soda* may also refer to a drink made with ice cream in a soft drink, also called a *float*.

. . . he stood at the soft drink and hot-dog stand, hands in his pockets fingering pennies, keys, feeling out of place, a scavenger.
Margaret Atwood *Life Before Man* 1979: 288

Since 1980, the $3-billion soft drink market has been growing at around five percent per year.
Western Grocer May–Jun. 1990: 20

The Grade 8 students left the chamber and paced the foyer outside the meeting, listlessly sipping pop while the fights continued.
Globe and Mail (Toronto) 16 Jan. 1985: M4

solder In Canadian and American English *solder* (both the noun meaning the metal alloy and the verb meaning to fuse) rhymes with *fodder*. In British English the *l* is pronounced.

solicitor see LAWYER

solid, stolid *Solid* things are heavy, firm, sturdy, or strong; *solid* people are physically strong and big or figuratively staunch or reliable (as in the cliché 'a solid citizen'). *Stolid* people are phlegmatic, slow, unemotional, and undemonstrative. Once applied only to people, *stolid* is now occasionally used to describe places and institutions, and is perhaps being confused with *solid*.

He was dignified, a devout Presbyterian, true to its puritanical tradition of stolid self-development and public duty. . . .
William Teatero *John Anderson: Fugitive Slave* 1986: 78

The first black American expert in modern dance to work with one of Europe's most stolid cultural institutions, he spent three years as assistant director of the Opera Ballet's experimental arm.
Globe and Mail (Toronto) 16 Feb. 1985: E9

(Here *stolid* appears to mean *conservative* or *traditional*, in contrast to 'experimental'.)

Dr. Savage's popularity will get its truest test only when his candidate faces the electorate in one of the traditional swing seats, or a stolid Liberal riding.
Daily News (Halifax) 4 Nov. 1993: 20

(Here *stolid* could be argued to apply to a personified riding, meaning one that is unlikely to prove volatile or to change its loyalties. However, *solid* would convey the same meaning without puzzling readers.)

solidus   see SLASH

soliloquies   see -Y, -IES

solstice   see EQUINOX

soluble, solvable, insoluble, unsolvable, dissolvable   A problem for which a solution can be found is *soluble* or *solvable*; a problem that cannot be solved is *insoluble* or *unsolvable*. Substances that can be dissolved in a liquid are *soluble* or *dissolvable*; those that do not dissolve are *insoluble*.

This seems to indicate that the problem is soluble.
Globe and Mail (Toronto) 7 Feb. 1985: M12

The Canadian Institute for Advanced Research [is] setting its sights on the kinds of big questions not normally solvable in Canada.
Globe and Mail (Toronto) 28 Jan. 1985: P13

Spokesmen for the Ottawa and Carleton boards of education asked a provincial education commission . . . to help them find solutions to problems that they feel are insolvable without provincial guidelines or arbitration.
Globe and Mail (Toronto) 15 Feb. 1985: M3

(The word required here is either *insoluble* or *unsolvable*.)

A cleanup was not possible . . . because the chemicals are water soluble and were dispersed in the river.
Globe and Mail (Toronto) 23 Dec. 1985: A17

somber, sombre   see -RE, -ER

somebody   see EVERYONE

somebody else('s)   see ELSE

someone   see EVERYONE

someplace   see -WHERE, -PLACE

something, somewhat   *Something* and *somewhat* are sometimes used interchangeably as adverbs: 'Nova Scotia is something/somewhat like her home in Maine'; 'The visit was something/somewhat less than perfect'. In these phrases either word suggests an undetermined portion or extent. Some commentators prefer *somewhat* to *something* in descriptions of people ('She is somewhat [*not* something] like her mother') but allow that *something* and *somewhat* are both acceptable in the fixed expression 'something/ somewhat of a': 'He's something/ somewhat of a snob'.

More often in speech than in writing, *something* intensifies an adjective, creating an adverb phrase: 'The dog howled something terrible'; 'She smokes something fierce when she's working'. This construction is listed in dictionaries as informal, and in writing it is appropriate only for representations of very casual speech. The more widely accepted construction replaces the *something* phrase with an adverb: 'The dog howled terribly'. Also considered inappropriate for formal writing is the use of *something* to describe a remarkable person, event, or thing, as in 'That storm was really something!' or 'She's something else!'

The somewhat rigid but manifestly decent Clyde Wells remains immensely popular. . . .
Province (Vancouver) 31 Dec. 1990: 20

He was a young, handsome farm-implement dealer in a windbreaker, whose interest in school matters was somewhat less than nothing.
Max Braithwaite *The Night We Stole the Mountie's Car* 1971: 20

Isn't he somewhat of a bohemian?
NeWest Review Dec. 1989–Jan. 1990: 29

This makes Inga and Gertrude something less than friends and something more than strangers.
Queen's Quarterly 92.1 (1985): 51

Productivity in these cattle ranches is ridiculously low, something like 30 to 50 kilograms per hectare, annually.

Irving M. Zeitlin and Robert J. Brym *The Social Condition of Humanity* 1991: 366

The process is something of a vicious circle.
J.E. Smyth et al. *The Law and Business Administration in Canada* 1987: 100

'Cat's panting something terrible!'
Queen's Quarterly 95.3 (1988): 612

(This use is acceptable only in informal dialogue.)

someway   *Someway* is a variant of *somehow* or *in some way* ('I'll do it someway'; 'Someway he got out'). *Someway* is less formal than *somehow* and rarely appears in Canadian writing except in transcribed speech. It is listed in American but not English dictionaries.

'I find when people are really getting serious about something, whether it's a union or whether it's dying, they want God involved someway or somehow.'
Ottawa Citizen 18 Nov. 1990: F3

'We're going to have to look for runs someway.'
Ottawa Citizen 31 July 1994: E1

somewhat   see SOMETHING

somewhere   see -WHERE, -PLACE

Soo, the   see SAULT

sophist, sophistry, sophistication   In the fifth century B.C., in ancient Greece, *sophists* were men admired for their wisdom and knowledge. A century later a group of travelling teachers in Greece called themselves the *Sophists*. They received payment for providing an education designed to enhance success in public life. Because they were criticized for valuing success in debates more than truth and knowledge, the Greek root *sophos*, 'wise', took on connotations of cleverness and deceit. Thus *sophistry* became a term for subtle but deceptive argumentation.

Sophistication, which originally meant the use of sophistries, or disingenuousness, by 1850 was beginning to mean worldliness, or a lessening of naturalness or simplicity. The word's connotations have since changed from negative to positive, or at least neutral. Now sophistication is often something to be admired: for example, 'sophisticated new technology' is complex and highly evolved.

That the ethical point of view need not be accepted by the individual as overriding was the message of the Sophist.
Canadian Journal of Philosophy 19 (1989): 298

(Here *Sophist* is capitalized because the reference is to the historical Sophists.)

What is a good book, says the sophist, smiling like a wolf trap. Any book is a good book which feeds the mind something which may enlarge it, or move it to action. A book is good in relation to its reader.
Robertson Davies *A Voice from the Attic* 1960: 293

(Here 'the *sophist*' represents any tricky debater.)

Our national antipathy to mental skill may be due in part to religious and literary traditions that often equate such accomplishment with sophistry and the devil, in contrast with the simpler virtues of plain, honest folk.
Globe and Mail (Toronto) 7 Sept. 1985: P6

I longed for the wit and sophistication of New York City.
Max Braithwaite *The Night We Stole the Mountie's Car* 1971: 11

(Unlike *sophistry*, *sophistication* often has positive connotations.)

. . . improvement in the quality of medical records and the sophistication of medical diagnosis has facilitated the connecting of certain diseases with certain occupations.
J.E. Smyth et al. *The Law and Business Administration in Canada* 1987: 513

sophomore   see FIRST-YEAR STUDENT

sorbet   see SHERBET

sort of   see KIND OF

so . . . that   see COMMA

sound   see ADJECTIVES AND ADVERBS

sound out   According to most dictionaries and usage guides, *sound out* is now an accepted idiom referring to questioning carried out in order to discover someone's opinion or attitude. At election time, for example, politicians sound out voters. The verb *sound* by itself used to have this meaning; in fact, some commentators maintain that it still should, and that *out* is redundant. In contemporary Canadian English, however, only depths are *sounded*: people are *sounded out*.

> Munro attracted support from several trustees and especially from J.M. Macdonnell who went to Halifax to sound him out.
> Frederick Gibson *Queen's University* 2 (1983): 85

> H.R. Halpin, the Moose Mountain farm instructor, was told to sound out the Indians.
> Pierre Berton *The Promised Land* 1984: 246

source   see INFORMER

sour grapes   see CLICHÉ

south   see EAST

South Asia(n)   see ASIA; INDIAN

southbound   see -BOUND

Southeast Asia   see ASIA

sovereign, sovereignist, sovereigntist   see -IE-, -EI-; SEPARATIST

sow, sowed, sown   The past tense is *sowed*: 'The president sowed the seeds of her own downfall'. The past participle is either *sown* or *sowed*: 'The farmer has sown the field'; 'The mistake has sowed suspicion'. *Sown* is far more common.

> But it won't be too many years before you're going to reap what you've sown.
> *Toronto Star* 12 Nov. 1994: K9

> In essence, Canada is reaping the military incapacity it has sowed.
> *Calgary Herald* 3 June 2006: A26

spacy, spacey   see -Y, -EY

spam   see COMPUTER TERMS

span   see SPIN

spat   see SPIT

spay   see NEUTER

Speaker, deputy speaker   Some editors capitalize *Speaker* when it refers to the presiding officer of a legislative assembly; others don't. However, since legislatures are full of small-*s* speakers, capitalization is recommended to avoid ambiguity. Since *deputy speaker* is not ambiguous, the name of this position is often not capitalized. The name of either position is capitalized if it's used as a title directly before a person's name.

> He soon became a leading Manitoba politician, rising to Speaker of the legislature.
> Pierre Berton *The Promised Land* 1984: 21-22

> Still, Mulroney succeeded in winning a prediction from Thomas (Tip) O'Neill, the powerful speaker of the House of Representatives, that Congress was unlikely to stall trade negotiations.
> *Maclean's* 31 March 1986: 23

> (Here a capital *S* would make *speaker* unambiguous.)

> Steve Paproski speaks English, as well as Ukrainian and Polish, and is now struggling with a fourth tongue—French—for his role as deputy speaker of the House of Commons.
> *Saturday Night* Feb. 1986: 17

> Charbonneau remained out of the chamber yesterday, leaving Deputy Speaker Nathan Nurgitz to handle his duties.
> *Gazette* (Montreal) 6 Oct. 1990: A1

See also CAPITAL LETTERS.

special, specially, especial, especially   Some critics would reserve *special* and *specially* for things that are exceptional in that they are meant for a specific purpose: 'She is a special agent working overseas'; 'I made dinner specially for him'. *Especial* and *especially* then would be used to describe things that are exceptional by virtue of degree: 'There's an especial closeness between them'; 'The dinner was especially tasty'. However, in contemporary Canadian writing *special* has largely replaced the rarely used adjective *especial*, while the adverb *especially* is used far more often than *specially*. *Especial* and *specially* are uncommon and may strike some readers as formal or even literary. *Specially* is still recommended in expressions where it means for a specific purpose: 'These cases were made specially for his antique camera equipment'.

Some commentators feel that *special* is becoming less special with overuse.

Among the issues on the Paris summit agenda, two took on a special urgency.
Maclean's 24 Feb. 1986: 26

While most new managers assume positions of responsibility with little or no formal preparation . . . women are often at an especial disadvantage as new managers.
Ottawa Citizen 4 Nov. 1990: C7

(This use is uncommon.)

The Hague is home to what's billed as the world's largest panoramic painting, in a building erected especially to house the huge work.
Calgary Herald 2 July 1994: B12

(Here some commentators would prefer *specially*.)

Regrettably, it is perfectly possible to be an effective writer and a boob as well; writers are not, by definition, intellectual or even specially literate.
Davies *A Voice from the Attic* 1960: 345

(Some commentators would prefer *especially* here.)

specialize, specialization see -IZE, -ISE, -YZE, -YSE

specialty, speciality Canadians are far more likely to use *specialty* than the chiefly British form *speciality* (pronounced *spesh ee AL i tee*) but either form is acceptable.

specie, species *Specie* (pronounced *SPEE shee*) is a rare word for money in the form of coins. *Species* is both singular and plural for a biological category of plants and animals: 'a rare species of plant'; 'many endangered species of wildlife'. By extension, in general writing *species*

is used to mean sort or kind: 'That species of politician is unaware of these issues'.

The *c* in *species* is usually pronounced as *sh* outside Canada, but *SPEE seez* is a common and accepted Canadian pronunciation.

. . . Beck provides considerable detail as to the manner in which Howe, as a believer in specie, tried to stem the flow of paper money. . . .
Queen's Quarterly 92.2 (1985): 386

In order to ensure the survival of a species, its natural habitat must be preserved.
Chronicle-Herald (Halifax) 14 May 1988: 3

. . . gulls are taking over nesting areas previously used by other species, especially the common tern.
Globe and Mail (Toronto) 4 Jan. 1985: M1

Dream a Little Dream, latest of this tired species, stars heavyweight actor Jason Robards. . . .
Gazette (Montreal) 5 March 1989: F6

She keeps a record of every [bird] specie she encounters in a given year by placing a check mark beside 'Peterson's Systematic Checklist' in the handy book just described.
Ottawa Citizen 9 June 1990: B7

(The correct form is *species*, even in the singular.)

See also -IE-, -EI-; SPECIES, GENUS.

species, genus, family, order, class, phylum, division, kingdom *Species* is at the bottom of the hierarchy used by biologists to categorize living beings: species, genus, family, order, class, phylum, division, kingdom. Members of the same species can interbreed; those of different species cannot. The system of binomial (two-term) nomenclature followed in biology uses the species and genus designation together to distinguish particular plants, animals, and micro-organisms from one another.

Robin, for example, is a sufficiently accurate term to use when a large red-breasted bird shows up on your lawn or your child has a project about spring. In Britain, however, *robin* names a much different, smaller bird. Both have red breasts and both belong to the family

Turdidae, but that's where the similarity ends. The North American robin's scientific name is *Turdus migratorius*, while the European robin is *Erithacus rubecula*.

The first term in these Latin names designates the genus and is capitalized; the second designates the species and is not capitalized. Both terms are italicized. Often a popular name is given first, with the scientific name following in parentheses. By convention, categories above the rank of genus are printed in roman rather than italic type.

See also SCIENTIFIC ENGLISH; SPECIE, SPECIES.

speciesism   see -IST, -ISM

spectators   see AUDIENCE

specter, spectre   see -RE, -ER

spectrum, spectra   see COLOUR; PLURAL

speedometer   see BARBARISMS

spellbound   see -BOUND

spelling, Canadian   Spelling, like punctuation, is ultimately governed by convention. In contemporary English, creative, freestyle spelling is not tolerated. Accepted spellings are codified in dictionaries, and spelling difficulties are generally the same for all writers of English, wherever in the English-speaking world they may live. Established variants do exist, however, especially between British and American conventions, and it is here that Canadian writers tend to show a distinctive pattern of preferences.

British and American spelling initially diverged because of the influence of Samuel Johnson's dictionary (1755) in Britain and of Noah Webster's (1828) in the United States. Canadian spelling preferences have varied over time, and vary today from region to region, as the result of settlement history; the choice of spellers, dictionaries, and textbooks by school boards; and the influence of newspaper spelling. Generally, Ontarians are the most British in their spelling choices, with British

Columbians and Newfoundlanders close behind, while Albertans, followed by other Prairie Canadians, are the most American.

Most Canadians, whatever they think or say they do, use a mixture of British and American spellings. The major Canadian newspapers carry stories from both British and American wire services; these may or may not be rewritten to conform with the local style before publication. Thus Canadian readers take in variant spellings every day, often without really thinking about it. And if they do think about it, they may think they are using the British spelling when they are using the American, or vice versa. Further, Canadians never use the British spellings for some words (like *gaol*, *kerb*, and *tyre*) and very rarely use the American spellings for others (like *check* for bank draft, or *maneuver*). Although Canadians do not use either British or American spelling consistently, they tend to be consistent within some major categories. For example, most Canadians choose the *ize/yze* endings (also favoured by Americans) over the *-ise/yse* endings more common in Britain. Like the British, Canadians tend to double the *l* at the ends of words when adding suffixes: *equalled*, *modelling*, *traveller*. Canadians, like the British, prefer *-ce* endings on nouns like *defence* and *offence*. Most Canadians choose the British spellings of *axe*, *catalogue*, *centre*, *cheque*, *fulfil*, *grey*, and *manoeuvre*, but follow American spelling with *analyze*, *carburetor*, *criticize*, *encyclopedia*, *judgment*, *medieval*, *movable*, *peddler*, *plow*, *program*, *raccoon*, and *woollen*. Canadians are divided over whether to use *-our* or *-or* endings. The authors of *Editing Canadian English* conclude that although it makes sense to advise against mixing spellings within the major categories (such as *-our*, *-or*), 'mixing *between* categories not only is acceptable, but may well constitute the "Canadian style."'

See also -ABLE, -EABLE; -ABLE, -IBLE; -AE-, -OE-, -E-; AQ-, ACQ-; -C, -CK; CAPITAL LETTERS; -CE, -SE; -CEED, -CEDE, -SEDE; CENTRE, CENTER; DOUBLING THE FINAL CONSONANT; -E; -ER, -OR; EXH-, EX-; -IE-, -EI-; -IZE, -ISE, -YZE, -YSE; -L, -LL; -LOG, -LOGUE; -OUR, -OR; PLURALS; Q-, QU-; QUEBEC ENGLISH; -RE, -ER; -Y; -EY.

spendthrift   Since *thrift* now means good money management, one might think a *spendthrift* a frugal sort. In fact, a spendthrift is a person who spends money recklessly and wastefully. An early meaning of *thrift* was accumulated wealth or, more specifically, an inheritance: thus a spendthrift was someone who squandered an inheritance.

A hard drinker and spendthrift, he borrowed heavily to supplement the small amounts that he earned. . . .
Maclean's 24 Feb. 1986: 60

spicy, [spicey]   see -Y, -EY

spies   see PLURAL

spigot   see TAP

spiky, [spikey]   see -Y, -EY

spilt   see -T, -ED

spin, span   For the verb *spin*, the past tense and the past participle (the form used after *have*) are both *spun*. *Span* in this sense is an archaic past tense. To *span*, meaning to extend over, is a regular verb with the past tense and past participle *spanned*.

Knitters spun the hair of various animals for yarn. . . .
Vancouver Sun 13 Dec. 1990: F10

A success in Calgary's 1988 Winter Olympics has spun off some extra gold—in the form of a contract for a city firm to work on the 1994 edition of the Games in Norway.
Province (Vancouver) 14 Nov. 1990: 42

Langley . . . focuses his inquiry on US foreign policy in Central America and the Caribbean during the three decades spanned by the two Roosevelts.
Queen's Quarterly 92.2 (1985): 397

spinney   see FOREST

spiral   The verb *spiral* means to move upwards or downwards in a circular motion. Some critics object when the direction of the spiral is not specified, but normally the context makes the direction clear.

Davis's artistic course in the last half of the 1950s has the appearance of a steady upward spiral at the head of the cohesive quintet. . . .
Jack Chambers *Milestones* 1983: 216

In public housing especially, the maxim 'everybody's property is nobody's property' [helps explain] the all too frequent downward spiral of neglect.
Queen's Quarterly 94.4 (1987): 979

Professionalization, specialization, inflation, and the rapid growth of an elderly Jewish population will spiral service costs over the next decade.
Henry M. Rosenthal and S. Cathy Berson, eds. *Canadian Jewish Outlook Anthology* 1988: 45

(Clearly costs are expected to *spiral upward*.)

See also FUNCTIONAL SHIFT.

spiritualism, spirituality   see RELIGION

spit, spat, spitted   The past tense and past participle of *spit* can be either *spat* or *spit*. *Spat* is the preferred past tense and past participle in Canada and Britain, but in the United States *spit* is preferred for both forms.

Spitted is the past tense and past participle of the verb *spit* meaning to pierce with a stick.

[He] cursed and struggled with the arresting officer, then spat at him. . . .
Vancouver Sun 15 Nov. 1990: A8

My salmon turned down river, went over the bar and into the rapids, leaped and spit out the tiny fly all in a matter of seconds.
Atlantic Salmon Journal Summer (1990): 28

. . . Brian started thumping on Stephen. Ordered to stop, he said: 'Somebody spitted on me.'
Ottawa Citizen 23 April 1990: B1

(The standard past tense is either *spit* or *spat*.)

She was impatient . . . with these stories which were so foreign and which, like their endless stories about wars and suffering and horror, children spitted on swords, had nothing to do with her.
Margaret Atwood *Life Before Man* 1979: 249

(Here *spitted* is the past tense of the verb meaning to impale.)

split infinitive   The infinitive form of the English verb is preceded by *to*: 'to run', 'to think', 'to write', and so on. It is one form of the verb that can be used like a noun: 'To err is human'. Some usage experts have argued that the two-word infinitive phrase should be treated as a unit; thus, if a word is inserted between *to* and the base verb, they name the structure that results a 'split infinitive'. A well-known example of a split infinitive is the motto from *Star Trek*: 'To boldly go where no man has gone before' (*boldly* 'splits' the infinitive). Split infinitives are very common in speech and quite common in writing. They are least common in scholarly writing in the humanities. Because of a widespread prejudice against split infinitives, it might be best to avoid them in letters of application or academic essays, even if you find the argument for avoiding them unconvincing.

The rule against splitting the infinitive is one of the few that are more firmly adhered to by teachers than by usage guides. Most guides admit, with varying degrees of reluctance, that in the interests of clarity or smoothness it is sometimes better to split the infinitive than to avoid doing so.

English writers started splitting the infinitive at least as early as 1380; condemnation of such constructions did not begin until the nineteenth century. And certainly it seems rather arbitrary that the split infinitive in the sentence 'To carefully revise this will take time' is vehemently opposed when no one objects to the interjection of the adverb in quite similar structures, such as 'This needs to be carefully revised' or 'This appears to have been carefully revised'. Fowler notes that the rule against the split infinitive (which prohibits 'to really understand') has led some people to overcorrect (see HYPERCORRECTION) and pluck adverbs out of all verb phrases, producing structures like 'really to be understood' or 'to be understood really', even though no authority objects to '*to be* really understood'.

Various structures in English suggest that there is no indissoluble bond between the *to* and the base verb in an infinitive. In the sentence 'We were going to but we decided not to', the base verb has been dropped altogether. In the informal expression 'Gotta go', the *to* of the infinitive has been assimilated to the preceding word, *got*.

Theoretical arguments aside, it is not difficult to produce examples of sentences that require a split infinitive: 'They gave her enough to *more than* satisfy her needs'; 'They gave her enough to *all but* satisfy her needs'; 'His most regrettable decision was to *not* hire a supervisor'. In this last example, if *not* were placed in front of *to*, readers might still understand that failing to hire a supervisor was his most regrettable decision, but they might also read the sentence an entirely different way: hiring the supervisor, while regrettable, was not his most regrettable decision.

Trying to avoid a split infinitive can lead to ambiguous or awkward writing. If 'She wanted to really help him' is rewritten 'She wanted really to help him', the reader may wonder whether *really* modifies *want* or *help*. If it is rewritten 'She wanted to help him really', the implication is that her intentions were good, but she didn't succeed. Neither revision is equivalent to the sentence with the split infinitive. To avoid splitting an infinitive, then, simply shifting the adverb will not always work; frequently the entire sentence must be reworked.

Only the moon and a handful of asteroids are known to ever approach closer.
Terence Dickinson *Halley's Comet* 1985: 2

. . . the university was prepared to ask a professional editor to teach their [students] how to deal with written material, how to correctly cite references, and to do general copy editing.
W.C. Lougheed, ed. *In Search of the Standard in Canadian English* 1986: 133

. . . recent political liberation makes it possible for women to publicly discuss their dissatisfactions.
Canadian Journal of History 14.1 (1989): 153

It is indeed difficult to systematically plan and implement legal and social reforms.
J.E. Smyth et al. *The Law and Business Administration in Canada* 1987: 18

The Association resolved . . . to strongly encourage all airlines licensed in Canada to voluntarily ban smoking on all flights of three hours or less scheduled flying time.
Canadian Consumer Jan. 1985: 49

spoilt   see -T, -ED

spoonerism   Reverend William Archibald Spooner was warden of New College at Oxford from 1903 to 1924. Spooner had a habit of transposing the initial sounds of words in a sentence. Although he certainly did not produce all the slips of the tongue that are attributed to him, he is known to have said 'through a dark glassly' and to have told a nervous bridegroom that 'It is kisstomery to cuss the bride'. He is also reported to have once called Queen Victoria 'our queer old dean'. In honour of Spooner, funny slips of this sort came to be called *spoonerisms*.

See also MISPRONUNCIATION; SLIPS OF THE TONGUE.

spoonful   see -FUL

spouse   see COMMON LAW; MARRIAGE

spring, sprang, sprung   The usual past tense is *sprang*: 'The cat sprang after the bird'. *Sprung* is less common but not wrong. The past participle is always *sprung*: 'The cat had sprung after the bird'.

Some school boards decided to bend the rules for the year, but many didn't and a coalition of anti-dual-entry parents sprang into being.
Vancouver Sun 15 Nov. 1990: C2

The Toronto offence, dormant in the opening 15 minutes, sprung to life for 13 second-quarter points. . . .
Province (Vancouver) 23 Aug. 1990: 75

(The usual past tense is *sprang*, but *sprung* is not wrong.)

square brackets   see PARENTHESES; QUOTATION

squash   see QUASH

squish   see ONOMATOPOEIA

St., Ste., Saint(e)   In English Canada, abbreviations of the title *Saint* (or its French feminine form, *Sainte*) usually take a period (*St.*, *Ste.*; plurals *Sts.*, *Stes.*), although a no-period style is also acceptable (see ABBREVIATION). In Quebec place names with *Saint(e)* always include a hyphen ('Saint-Ambroise'); when the title is abbreviated it does not take a period ('St-Ambroise', 'Ste-Agathe'). The French style is also used for many Canadian place names outside Quebec. All these abbreviations are sometimes alphabetized under *sa-* rather than *st-*.

See also ALPHABETICAL ORDER.

stadium, stadiums, stadia   Both plural forms of *stadium* are in use in Canadian writing, though the Latin plural *stadia* is much less common than the English plural *stadiums*.

There are domed stadiums in Montreal, Toronto and Vancouver.
Vancouver Sun 14 Sept. 1990: D4

Additionally, Canada now is equipped with two of the most magnificent indoor stadia on the entire continent.
Province (Vancouver) 29 Jan. 1990: 29

See also PLURALS, REGULAR, IRREGULAR, FOREIGN.

staffs   see -F, -V-

stalactite, stalagmite   Both are mineral formations found in caves: *stalactites* point down and *stalagmites* point up. Some people avoid confusion of these terms by thinking of the *c* in *stalactite* as standing for the ceiling from which stalactites hang and the *g* in *stalagmite* as standing for the ground from which they rise. Others think of stalac*tites* as hanging on tight.

Tiny dribbles of water often form icicle-like stalactites that hang from the ceiling, or stalagmites that rise up from the floor like graceful pillars.
Globe and Mail (Toronto) 12 Dec. 1985: A2

stamp, stomp   *Stomp* is a variant of *stamp* meaning bring one's foot down heavily. A few sources label *stomp* non-standard, but it is standard in Canadian English.

The Indian government and the World Health Organization are both predicting the plague will

be stomped out by mid-October.
Gazette (Montreal) 8 Oct. 1994: H8

The country station . . . has put Corb Lund's rendition of Stompin' Tom Connors' The Hockey Song into regular rotation.
Edmonton Journal 6 May 2006: E1

See also CHOMP, CHAMP AT THE BIT.

stanch, staunch In Canadian journalism, the verb meaning to stop the flow (of blood, tears, etc.) is more often spelled *stanch* than *staunch*; however, it is more often pronounced to rhyme with *paunch* than *ranch*. The adjective meaning firm, strong, or steadfast is almost always spelled *staunch* and pronounced to rhyme with *paunch*. Canadian, British, and American dictionaries give both spellings for both the verb and the adjective.

They also wanted to stanch the losses at the government's landholding corporation, B.C. Place, which was so debt-ridden that it was borrowing money just to pay interest on previous borrowings.
Vancouver Sun 6 March 1990: A16

The best that can be hoped for if Meech Lake does pass is relief—relief that the present ordeal is over, the flood of words stanched for a time.
Gazette (Montreal) 21 June 1990: B3

It is true that Via Rail was costing taxpayers more than $600 million a year, and that the drain had to be staunched.
Gazette (Montreal) 12 Jan. 1990: B2

He was a staunch supporter of his patron and former employer, John A. Macdonald.
William Teatero *John Anderson: Fugitive Slave* 1986: 172

stand see FOREST

Standard English, standard Standard English is used in the media, taught in the education system, and understood from region to region. Broadly speaking, it is the English spoken by educated people in cities.

A particular word, meaning, spelling, pronunciation, or grammatical construction is called standard if it is widely used by educated

people, and non-standard if it is not. Non-standard usages fall into two categories: regionalisms, which are confined to a particular area within a country ('I'm after doing that' means 'I've just done that' in Newfoundland dialect but not in the rest of Canada) and usages that are considered uneducated, such as the double negative ('Nobody said nothing').

Usage commentators do not always agree on whether particular usages are standard. One reason is that the usages they tend to discuss are in transition. As individuals, we judge the acceptability of usage on the basis of our knowledge and experience of the language. For example, if we think people are starting to confuse two words, we resist the change. Ultimately, though, Standard English is defined collectively and socially. Once enough influential people have made a mistake, the 'mistake' becomes standard. For example, over the course of the sixteenth century, 'a napron' became 'an apron' because most people thought the initial *n* of *napron* (which is related to the word *napkin*) belonged to the indefinite article. While Standard English is conservative—which contributes to its intelligibility over long periods of time—it is not unchanging.

As well as evolving over time, Standard English varies from country to country in the English speaking world. 'I am having a cat [I own a cat]' is a standard construction in Indian English, but nonstandard in Canadian, British, and American English. 'I could have done' is a standard sentence in British English, but it would need to be either shortened ('I could have') or lengthened ('I could have done it') to conform to the rules of Canadian English. One distinctive aspect of Standard Canadian English is its pattern of blending British and American pronunciations and spellings (see SPELLING, CANADIAN); another is its uniformity across a great geographic expanse. Unlike the British, the French, or even Americans, Canadians often cannot tell by their accents what region or city their fellow Canadians hail from.

In many cases, the recommendations made in this book do not hinge on whether a particular usage is standard; instead, they have to do with its formality or informality. The word *booze*, for example, is used by most educated speakers and appears frequently in newspapers. It is undoubtedly a standard word, and yet it would be out of place in the title of an article in a medical journal. For a discussion of levels of formality, see FORMAL, INFORMAL WRITING.

See also ACCENT, DIALECT; COLLOQUIAL; FORMAL, INFORMAL WRITING; VERNACULAR.

standard time, daylight time, daylight saving(s) time, British Summer Time There are six time zones in Canada: Newfoundland, Atlantic, Eastern, Central, Mountain and Pacific.

Name	abbrev.	time variance
Newfoundland Standard Time	NST	12:30 p.m.
Atlantic Standard Time	AST	12:00 noon
Eastern Standard Time	EST	11:00 a.m.
Central Standard Time	CST	10:00 a.m.
Mountain Standard Time	MST	9:00 a.m.
Pacific Standard Time	PST	8:00 a.m.

Abbreviations for the time zones should be used only with specific times: '8 a.m. NST'.

Both the *Globe and Mail Style Book* and the *Canadian Press Stylebook* recommend *daylight time* rather than *daylight saving time*: 'Pacific Daylight Time', Eastern Daylight Time', '8 a.m. NDT'. However, most Canadians refer to the general phenomenon as either *daylight saving time* or *daylight savings time*. The British refer to daylight saving time as British Summer Time, or BST.

Daylight saving time for all of Canada except Saskatchewan, which remains on standard time year round, runs from 2 a.m. on a designated Sunday in the spring to 2 a.m. on a designated Sunday in the fall. In March the clock is put ahead one hour, and in November it is put back, as in the popular saying 'Spring forward, fall back'. The names of specific zones are capital-

ized ('Eastern Standard Time'), but general references ('switch from standard time to daylight time') are not.

> Trapping, education spending, sex education, daylight saving time, metric, free trade—name the cause and you can find someone organized against it.
> *Ottawa Citizen* 8 April 1990: A9

> It contains most of the same features as the original, but adds slow-motion playback . . . and a world clock onscreen menu with a Daylight Savings Time feature that automatically changes the time.
> *Toronto Star* 21 July 1994: G2

(The capital letters are unnecessary, and *saving* is preferred to *savings*.)

See also DATES, AHEAD, BACK; TIME.

stank   see STINK

starboard   see PORT

state, head of   see HEAD OF STATE

States, the   see AMERICAN

stationary, stationery   *Stationary* meaning 'standing still' ends in -*ary*. *Stationery* meaning paper, cards, envelopes, etc., ends in -*ery*. *Stationary* is often misused for *stationery*; the opposite error is seldom made.

> While the Ticats' play last season suggested the need for some housecleaning, Beckman said he isn't ready to order pink slips from the local stationary store.
> *Vancouver Sun* 19 Dec. 1990: D12

(The word required here is *stationery*.)

stationary engineer   see JOB TITLES

status   see -US

Status Indian   see ABORIGINAL PEOPLE(S)

status quo   see LATIN PHRASES

staunch   see STANCH

stave, stave off, stove   The verb *stave* is rare except in the phrase *stave off*, which means to fend off. The past tense and past participle of this phrase are the same: *staved off*. The variant past tense and past participle *stove* is usually used in reference to boats. In this context, *stove* means smashed, with either an active or a passive sense.

> Dartmouth staved off elimination by defeating Smith Falls in Hardy Cup Eastern Canadian final play. . . .
> *Ottawa Citizen* 17 April 1990: C6

> . . . they were almost swamped in a tangle of jammed driftwood, almost stove in on a snag. . . .
> Robert Kroetsch *Badlands* 1975: 121

steal   see ROB

stein   see GERMAN WORDS, PRONUNCIATION OF

stem   The verb *stem* is now occasionally used to mean stimulate or spur: 'It was my grandfather who stemmed my interest in baseball'. This use is at odds with the accepted transitive meaning of the verb *to stem*, to stop or to stanch. The newer meaning creates radical ambiguity. Without context, it is not at all clear whether the grandfather in the example sentence above piqued the writer's interest in baseball or successfully redirected it.

Stem meaning to stop the flow is etymologically related to *stammer*. *Stem* meaning to arise or spring is derived from the noun *stem* ('flower stem'). Traditionally, *stem* meaning stop has been used only transitively, i.e., with a direct object: 'Politicians vowed to stem the tide of violence'. *Stem* meaning arise has been used only intransitively, typically with the preposition *from*: 'The charges stem from a year-long police investigation'.

It is not unusual for a verb that is used only intransitively ('Birds *fly*') to later develop transitive meanings ('*fly* a helicopter') and for these new meanings to gain quick acceptance. The new transitive use of *stem* to mean stimulate, however, will be strenuously resisted because of the ambiguity it creates.

We saw the same public attention given to our recent decision in the *Latimer* case. Indeed, that case has stemmed a rich debate in the pages of countless Canadian newspapers. . . .
'The Role of Judges in Modern Society' Supreme Court of Canada website 5 May 2001

(This use of *stemmed* is nonstandard. *Stimulated* or *generated* would be better here.)

See also HOMOPHONE, HOMOGRAPH, HOMONYM.

step-, half-   You acquire a *stepsister* or *stepbrother* if your father or mother marries someone who already has a son or daughter. A *half-sister* or *half-brother* is related to you by blood ties: you share the same biological father or mother. The *step-* prefix is usually used without a hyphen: *stepmother*, *stepfather*, *stepchild*; however, the hyphen is preferred in *step-parent*. Most commonly *half* is combined with a hyphen, but it may also appear simply as an adjective: *half brother*.

> 'Does that mean Mum could get married again, too, and we'd have a stepfather?'
> Constance Bereford-Howe *Night Studies* 1985: 130

> The group will focus on problems and concerns that step-parents face on a daily basis.
> *Gazette* (Montreal) 13 April 1990: B8

> Her half-sister Micki tells how . . . Christiane would lower peanut-butter sandwiches on a string from the balcony.
> Ann Davis *Somewhere Waiting* 1991: 218

> She eventually got to know her half brothers and sisters who lived in Trail.
> *Vancouver Sun* 10 Feb. 2003: B5

stereotype   see ARCHETYPE

sterilize   see NEUTER

stiff upper lip   see CLICHÉ

stifling   see STULTIFYING

stigma, stigmatize, stigmata   A *stigma* was the owner's mark burned into the skin of a slave in ancient Rome. *Stigma* later came to be used figuratively to mean disgrace or shame. To *stigmatize* is to reproach or to set a mark of disgrace upon. *Stigmata*, the marks left on the hands and feet of Christ by the crucifixion, are also said to occur on the bodies of certain holy people by divine favour. The plural of *stigma* is usually *stigmas*, but the Greek plural *stigmata* is favoured for this religious sense.

> Coal also faces the stigma of being the most environmentally unfriendly of the fossil fuels.
> *Financial Post* 14 June 1990: 18

> Western culture tends to over-value high intelligence and stigmatize low intelligence.
> *Globe and Mail* (Toronto) 29 July 1985: P7

> Only 20 kilometres distant is St. Giovanni Rotondo, site of the Capuchin monastery where Padre Pio is said to have received the Stigmata—the wounds of crucifixion.
> *Globe and Mail* (Toronto) 24 Aug. 1985: T9

(Here *Stigmata* is capitalized to indicate reverence.)

See also PLURALS, REGULAR, IRREGULAR, FOREIGN.

still lifes   see -F, -V-

stimulant, stimulus, stimuli   In scientific writing a *stimulant* is a drug or other agent that temporarily increases the activity in a part of the body, while a *stimulus* is any agent causing a psychological or bodily change: 'Caffeine and nicotine are common stimulants'; 'The stimulus of hot, humid weather causes an overheated body to perspire'. Dictionaries list both terms as standard for 'an incentive to action or thought'. In Canadian writing *stimulus* (plural *stimuli*) is more often chosen for this general sense: 'Money was insufficient stimulus; she would not work overtime'.

> Caffeine acts as a stimulant, and sugar causes the blood sugar level to shoot up. . . .
> *Chatelaine* April 1986: 30

> The truly dedicated, omnivorous reader is almost physically sick when deprived of his innocent stimulant.
> *Ottawa Citizen* 15 March 1986: B3

(Here books are humorously compared to a *stimulant* such as caffeine.)

The past three decades have seen a flowering and variegated enrichment of the novel as both an echo of, and a stimulus for, the changes of the Quiet Revolution.
Ben-Z. Shek *French-Canadian & Québécois Novels* 1991: 45

> The press had absorbed the political functions of the pulpit and, as the necessary stimulant to public opinion and vehicle of it, increasingly dominated the political system.
> J.A.W. Gunn *Beyond Liberty and Property* 1983: 287

(In this sense *stimulus* is more common.)

> We should care because the bombardment of visual stimuli (including the average viewer's annual exposure to 32,000 TV commercials) is transforming the way we learn, speak and interact.
> *Gazette* (Montreal) 8 Nov. 1989: C1

See also PLURALS, REGULAR, IRREGULAR, FOREIGN.

stink, stank, stunk   *Stank* and *stunk* are both accepted for the past tense of *stink*. Generally, writers prefer *stank*, but *stunk* is common in speech. *Stunk* is the only accepted past participle: 'It has stunk in here for days'.

> The cities stank of horse manure.
> Pierre Berton *The Promised Land* 1984: 293

> The place stunk and occasionally someone would get their arm or hand pecked.
> *Canadian Fiction Magazine* 64 (1988): 63

St. Jean Baptiste Day   see NEW YEAR'S DAY

St. John's, St. Johnsian   see SAINT JOHN; NAMES OF RESIDENTS OF CITIES AND PROVINCES

Stl'atl'imx, Lil'wat, Lillooet   The Aboriginal people whose traditional lands are around Lillooet, British Columbia, are the *Stl'atl'imx* (*STLAT lee um*); their language is also *Stl'atl'imx*. Those whose traditional lands are around Mount Currie, B.C., are the *Lil'wat* (*LILL wat*). These groups were formerly called *Lillooet*.

> Williams, 43, is a non-status Stl'atl'imx Indian raised in Lillooet and knows a thing or two about rednecks.
> *Daily News* (Halifax) 12 July 1992: 15

He has been working full-time with the Stl'atl'imx Nation Tribal Police since January.
Vancouver Sun 18 Nov. 1994: A2

. . . land claims have been made on the Stein by the Nlaka'pamux (Lytton) and the Lil'wat (Mt. Currie) peoples.
Vancouver Sun 15 July 1994: B4

See also ABORIGINAL PEOPLE(S); APPENDIX III.

stoic, stoical   *Stoic* and *stoical* both mean unmoved by emotions or indifferent to pain. Capitalized, *Stoic* refers to a school of Greek philosophers or their intellectual heirs. Zeno founded this school around 300 B.C.; it got its name from the portico, or *stoa*, where he taught in Athens. Stoic philosophy held that it was virtuous to be wise and wise to be unmoved by the vicissitudes of fortune, whether they brought pleasure or pain.

Some usage guides suggest that *stoic* should be reserved for this school of philosophy: however, *stoic* is used more often than *stoical* to mean impassive or uncomplaining. This general use is widespread and accepted.

Some writers use *stoic* where *steadfast, determined*, or *restrained* would be more precise.

. . . the waning days of the pagan Roman Empire . . . saw a swing to the anti-sex Stoic philosophy that also called into question all non-procreative sexual acts.
Edmonton Journal 24 July 1994: D8

She was independent, self-sufficient, stoic, and imbued with the Protestant work ethic.
Edmonton Journal 10 Jan. 1994: B3

Most of the women wept, the men were stoical.
Vancouver Sun 9 Nov. 1992: A1

On the other side are the stoic royalist faithful. The Royal Family, they insist, has been in tight places before. . . .
Spectator (Hamilton) 22 Dec. 1994: A9

(Here *steadfast* might be better than *stoic*, since these royalists clearly demonstrate passion for the monarchy.)

Artworks don't get much more austere or stoic than those of Ryoji Ikeda.
Edmonton Journal 3 Dec. 1994: D2

(Here *restrained* might be better.)

stolid   see SOLID

stomach   see BELLY

stomp   see STAMP

stone   A *stone* (plural *stone*) is a British measure of weight equivalent to 6.35 kilograms, or 14 pounds. *Stone* is generally used to give the weights of people or hefty pets: 'He weighed 12 stone'.

stony, stoney   see -Y, -EY

stoop   see PORCH

store-bought   see [BOUGHTEN]

stormbound   see -BOUND

story, storey, floor   The word meaning a narrative is always spelled *story*, and its plural is *stories*. In Canada and in Britain, the floor of a building is usually spelled *storey* (plural *storeys*). *Story* and *stories* are less common variant spellings for this sense, favoured in the United States.

In North America, the ground level of a building is the first floor or the first storey; a building of ten floors has ten storeys. In Britain the ground level (the first storey) is called the ground floor and the next level up (the second storey) is called the first floor, the level after that the second floor, and so on.

By 1910, Eaton's had completed an eight-storey building and was planning to go to twelve storeys.
Pierre Berton *The Promised Land* 1984: 322

The building's upper story was completely gutted and the ground floor suffered extensive smoke and water damage.
News North (Yellowknife) 19 Feb. 1990: 2

straight-, strait-, straightened, straitened   *Straight-* is used in combinations to mean directly, as in *straightaway* or *straightfor-*

ward. Strait- is used in combinations to mean restricting or rigid, as in *straitjacket*, a device that restricts the arms, or *strait-laced*, describing someone whose conduct is restricted by prudish morals.

Something that has been *straightened*, such as a bent nail, has been made straight; someone in *straitened* circumstances is restricted by poverty and hardship.

> I remember watching a TV movie where Houdini is in a straitjacket immersed upside down in a tank of water.
> *Room of One's Own* March 1990: 97

> But if the Canadian mining industry has had little to cheer about during the past three or four years, it has shown a capacity to adapt to more strait-ened circumstances.
> *Globe and Mail* (Toronto) 14 March 1985: B2

> There's nothing mysterious about the way our [pulp and paper] industry reacts to straightened circumstances.
> *Vancouver Sun* 27 March 1990: C1

(The correct spelling is *straitened*.)

> [The] Social Services Minister . . . wants to be a 66-year-old Socred sex symbol—not a straight-laced prude.
> *Province* (Vancouver) 15 March 1990: 3

(The correct spelling is *strait-laced*.)

> Jim Mills looked about as uncomfortable as any 6'8", 280-pound free spirit could tucked into a tuxedo that felt like a black straightjacket.
> *Vancouver Sun* 23 Nov. 1990: D1

(The correct spelling is *straitjacket*.)

stratagem, strategy A *stratagem* is a military manoeuvre to deceive or surprise an enemy, or more generally a clever scheme seen as under-handed or a deliberate trick to achieve an objective. *Strategy* is the art of using available resources to achieve a goal.

> . . . I tried to spill some of the drink over my shoulder as I drained each glassful but Khrushchev immediately spotted my stratagem and announced that the Count ('or should I say ex-Count?') was trying to cheat.
> George Ignatieff *The Making of a Peacemonger* 1987: 143

This will force lower-ranked teams to rethink their strategy of playing for a tie in order to hope for a win via penalty shots.
Ottawa Citizen 18 June 2006: A13

stratum, strata *Stratum* is the singular form, *strata* the plural. Though American and Canadian dictionaries accept *stratums* as an alternative English plural, it rarely appears in Canadian writing.

Sometimes *strata* is mistakenly used as if it were singular to refer to a single layer of something; this use is uncommon and is not accepted. Usage commentators flatly condemn the double plural *stratas*.

Pronunciation varies: *STRAY tum, STRA tum,* or *STRAW tum.*

> The Mounted Police subscribed to the commonly held belief that criminality was a phenomenon largely confined to inferior people at the lowest stratum of the social order.
> Pierre Berton *The Promised Land* 1984: 221

> He tries to burrow under its blacktop and find out what really makes it beat by talking to people from all strata of society, and exploring the areas the city tourist bureaus would rather he didn't see.
> *Vancouver Sun* 4 Aug. 1990: D13

> It is brought back up to its 'natural' level by adding carbon dioxide pumped out of the ground from below the pocket, or strata of water.
> *Ottawa Citizen* 26 April 1990: D15

(Here *strata* is mistakenly used as a singular noun.)

> No social strata eludes the broad expanse of her gaze, from the humble lives of superstitious Swiss peasants, to the structured culture of Chinese mandarins, or the tragic intransigence of Thai emperors.
> *Globe and Mail* (Toronto) 15 June 1985: B9

(Here again *strata* is mistakenly used as a singular noun.)

> A minimum of an hour is required to view the complex didactic materials that build layer upon layer, association upon association like stratas of a rich, multinational archeological dig.
> *Vancouver Sun* 21 April 1990: E9

(*Strata* is already plural; here either *strata* or *stratums* would be correct.)

See also PLURALS, REGULAR, IRREGULAR, FOREIGN.

streak   see FUNCTIONAL SHIFT

street   see ROAD

streetwise   see -WISE

streptococcus, streptococci   see PLURALS

stress   see entry in Glossary

strike, struck, stricken   *Struck* is the usual past participle of the verb *strike* ('struck by a car', 'struck by the resemblance'); *stricken* is an archaic past participle that survives in the expression 'stricken from the record' and is used in figurative contexts to mean afflicted ('drought-stricken', 'panic-stricken').

> . . . should a player compete in five consecutive games without having a major for fighting or roughing, one of his prior offences shall be stricken from the record.
> *Daily News* (Halifax) 7 Sept. 1994: 37

> Could the medical profession do more for Terry if he were alive today than they were able to do when he was first stricken with cancer?
> *Queen's Quarterly* 97.2 (1990): 253

> I remember how stricken she looked that morning Mother was asleep in her chair by the wood-stove.
> David Williams *Eye of the Father* 1985: 110

strikebreaker   see REPLACEMENT WORKER

string, strung, stringed   The past tense and past participle of the verb *string* are both *strung*. *Stringed* is an adjective used of musical instruments.

> [They] painstakingly strung garlands of purple, pink and green cellophane-wrapped candy and hung them on a six-foot blue cascade fir.
> *Ottawa Citizen* 1 Dec. 1990: E1

> The Warriors had strung a large sheet of nylon across the entrance to the compound to shield their eyes from the glare of the powerful spotlights the soldiers use.
> *Ottawa Citizen* 11 Sept. 1990: A2

strive, strove, strived, striven   The past tense is either *strove* or *strived*. The past participle (the form used after *have*) is either *strived* or *striven*.

> Both strove to upgrade playing standards.
> *Gazette* (Montreal) 22 Dec. 1990: F2

> Here we strived to put on a show that we hoped would impress our neighbors and all who came to visit.
> *Vancouver Sun* 21 July 1990: F4

> Branch, who has strived to rid junior hockey of its blood-and-guts image, said the public perception of the OHL will suffer.
> *Province* (Vancouver) 7 Feb. 1990: 64

> Such an outcome could destroy everything the two reformers have striven to achieve in foreign and domestic policy.
> *Gazette* (Montreal) 21 Dec. 1990: A10

strophe   see CATASTROPHE, CATASTROPHES

struck   see STRIKE

strung   see STRING

stunk   see STINK

stylus, styli   see PLURALS

subconscious   see CONSCIOUS

subject   see CASE; CITIZEN; entry in Glossary

subject complement   see VERB

subject–verb agreement   see AGREEMENT, GRAMMATICAL

subjunctive   The English verb is described in traditional grammar as being in one of three moods (or modes): the imperative, the indicative, or the subjunctive. A verb in the imperative mood is an order: 'Slow down!' A verb in the indicative mood describes a real action (or a fictional action intended to imitate a real one) in the past, present, or future. A verb in the subjunctive mood refers to an action hoped for, thought probable, recommended, imagined, and so on, as opposed to one being reported as fact. In contemporary English the subjunctive mood is usually indicated by special auxiliary verbs, such as *should*, *may*, *might*, and *would*, which are called modals:

It might be serious.

I wish he would see the doctor.

Though the modal auxiliaries serve a subjunctive function in contemporary English, they are not what is traditionally called the subjunctive, which is marked by distinctive verb forms that predate the modal auxiliaries. These forms survive in contemporary English in a few situations. First, phrases that use the subjunctive to express a wish persist as 'fossils' or fixed expressions: 'God save the Queen'; 'God bless you'; 'Heaven forbid'. Today sentences like these are often interpreted as orders because their verbs lack the -*(e)s* ending they would have in statements. But to issue orders to God would be presumptuous; in fact, these sentences express wishes: 'May God bless you', etc. Sometimes these phrases invert the subject and verb: 'perish the thought', 'suffice it to say', 'be that as it may', 'far be it from me'. People do not make new sentences of this type. We do not say, for example, 'Last my new car until it is paid for'. Instead we use *may* or *let*: 'May you do well' or 'Let the best candidate win'. In North America the subjunctive is also regularly used in *that*-clauses expressing a recommendation, intention, demand, etc.:

They insist that she *study* piano.

We thought it best that he *take* a holiday.

My recommendation will be that it *stay*.

The subjunctive in these phrases is easy to spot because it is used with third-person singular subjects (*he*, *she*, *it*) where the indicative form of regular verbs would end in *s*. This subjunctive can be replaced either by *should* ('They insist that she should study piano'), which is common in British English, or by the indicative

('They insist that she studies piano').

Finally, the subjunctive is commonly used in clauses expressing conditions in the present or future that are impossible, improbable, or hypothetical; these clauses are usually introduced by *if*, *as if*, *though*, or *as though*, or triggered by verbs like *wish* or *suppose* in the main clause. In this form, the subjunctive is usually marked by the use of the verb *were* instead of the usual indicative *was*:

He talks as if he were the boss.

I wish he were here.

Suppose he were able to go after all.

Again, the subjunctive in these sorts of sentences may be replaced by the indicative.

Standard Canadian English does require the subjunctive in the common phrase 'if I were you', even though the indicative 'if I was you' is common in Standard British English. (British and Australian writers usually avoid the subjunctive in all but the most formal prose.) In all other hypothetical *if*-clauses in the present or future, including those referring to conditions that are clearly impossible, either the subjunctive or the indicative mood is grammatically correct.

Because the use of this subjunctive structure has become optional, language commentators have been speculating for over a century that it will disappear. In fact, it is still quite common, especially in formal usage. The subjunctive mood is now a stylistic choice. For example, it can make a suggestion seem more polite—purely hypothetical rather than directive:

If you came to our next meeting . . .
(*indicative*)
If you were to come to our next meeting . . .
(*subjunctive*)

Or it can be a sign of cynicism, the equivalent of adding the disclaimer 'not that that would ever happen' to a hypothetical clause:

If the government was serious about reform
. . . (*indicative*)

If the government were serious about reform . . . (*subjunctive*)

If I lost twenty pounds . . . (*indicative*)

If I were to lose twenty pounds . . . (*subjunctive*)

Even in formal writing, however, the subjunctive is not an option in every *if*-clause. Where *if* means 'whether', it should not be followed by the subjunctive: 'He wondered if it was (*not* were) time to go'. Nor is the subjunctive appropriate in reference to real and repeated possibility in the past, where *if* could be replaced by *when*: 'If she was (not *were*) faced with a deadline, she procrastinated.'

Our pilot program was successful and independent evaluators recommended that it be continued.
Province (Vancouver) 30 Dec. 1990: 24

(Canadians use the subjunctive—*be*, in this case—in *that*-clauses containing recommendations or demands.)

There, Bourassa quickly came under heavy pressure to insist that Quebec receive an expanded constitutional veto. . . .
Maclean's 7 Oct. 1991: A22

(Here *receive* is a subjunctive used in the context of a demand.)

Furthermore, I also suggest that Mr. Cote accept complete medical, ethical and legal responsibility for those who suffer increased morbidity and mortality from delayed attention.
Gazette (Montreal) 27 Dec. 1990: B2

(Here *accept* is a subjunctive used in the context of a recommendation.)

All the while she hummed or sang and moved slowly and gently as if she were warming up for a dance instead of a drawing session.
Arctic 41.1 (1988): 74

(Here the subjunctive is used in an *if*-clause presenting an imagined condition.)

I am quite sure that if it were available in an inexpensive but rugged paperback edition, English-language newspapers across the nation would buy it.
W.C. Lougheed, ed. *In Search of the Standard in Canadian English* 1986: 124

Also, a government would have no choice but to resign or call an election if it were defeated on an issue it had previously declared to be a matter of confidence.
Andrew Heard *Canadian Constitutional Conventions* 1991: 69–70

(The subjunctive mood is most common in formal writing.)

'If I were you I wouldn't put up with me.'
Howard Engel *Murder Sees the Light* 1984: 157

'Only if I was you, miss, I'd keep a sharp eye on my belongings.'
Constance Beresford-Howe *Night Studies* 1985: 72

(Standard Canadian English requires 'if I *were* you'. The fictional speaker here is a British immigrant.)

At that moment, without warning, the elevator gave a sudden lurch as if it was about to drop.
Constance Beresford-Howe *Night Studies* 1985: 210

(The indicative mood is used in this hypothetical *if*-clause. The subjunctive *were* would also be correct.)

. . . indeed, he wondered if it were really desirable.
W.C. Lougheed, ed. *In Search of the Standard in Canadian English* 1986: 39

(When *if* means whether, it should not be followed by the subjunctive. The form required here is the indicative *was*.)

Perhaps you are reminded of the story of the traveller in Ireland who stopped a native on a country road and asked him if he were going in the right direction for Ballyragget.
Robertson Davies *One Half of Robertson Davies* 1978: 199

(When *if* means whether, it should not be followed by the subjunctive. The form required here is the indicative *was*.)

See also COME; IF I WERE YOU; LEST.

subpoena, summons A *subpoena* and a *summons* are both calls to appear in court, but their legal applications differ. *Subpoenas* are usually issued to witnesses or to obtain records; *summonses* are issued to people accused of minor offences, requiring them to appear in court and answer the charges.

Subpoena, from the Latin for 'under penalty' (in other words, appear or else), is pronounced *suh PEE na*. Verb forms include *subpoenaed* and *subpoenaing*, and the plural *subpoenas* is more common than the Latin plural *subpoenae*. A variation in spelling found occasionally in American usage is *subpena*.

> The committee issued subpoenas earlier this month demanding documents from the Office of Economic Development.
> *Daily News* (Halifax) 26 April 2006: 12

> A police officer arrived on the scene and presented her with a summons for dangerous driving.
> J.E. Smyth et. al *The Law and Business Administration in Canada* 1987: 2

> She is going to try to have the child subpoenaed as a witness.
> *Ottawa Citizen* 5 Oct. 1994: B3

See also -AE-, -OE-, -E-; INDICTABLE OFFENCE.

subsist, exist   *Subsist* shares with *exist* the idea of continuing to have life, being, or animation. However, *subsist* suggests that life is barely maintained; it is often used in the context of inadequate nourishment.

> Most Nepalese subsist by eking out a living on farms in the valleys and terraced hillsides south of the Himalayan range, areas accessible only by foot.
> *Globe and Mail* (Toronto) 17 May 1985: B6

> Nutrition is culturally determined and poor people are likely to subsist on what comes in packages; fast-food outlets cluster like scavengers in low-income areas.
> *Globe and Mail* (Toronto) 18 Dec. 1985: A2

> Plant life has been found to exist on the sea floor at much greater depths than previously predicted.
> *Globe and Mail* (Toronto) 7 Jan. 1985: M6

substantial, substantive   Both words mean 'of substance'. However, *substantial* usually refers to things of real physical substance ('a substantial meal', 'substantial holdings; 'a substantial piece of furniture'). *Substantive* usually refers to matters of intellectual, theoretical, or political significance. A *substantive* is a noun.

> The profits that will be generated when this is reversed will be substantial.
> *Calgary Herald* 31 Dec. 1994: C3

> Doubtless we owe an immense intellectual debt to those extraordinary thinkers, for we have acquired from them a large body of substantive knowledge about a wide range of human societies and cultures.
> Irving M. Zeitlin and Robert J. Brym *The Social Condition of Humanity* 1991: 328

> Although Twigg offers a self-deprecating assessment of B.C. Bookworld as an 'intentionally superficial publication,' . . . its pages nonetheless carry some substantial content.
> *Vancouver Sun* 29 Sept. 1990: D2

(Here *substantive* would work as well or better, since the reference is to intellectual content.)

substitute, replace   No one will object if you say or write 'I substituted margarine for butter', or 'I replaced the butter with margarine'. But many commentators do object to the use of *substitute* to mean replace or make do, as in 'I substituted butter with margarine', or 'I had no currants so I substituted with raisins'. The disputed structures are not new; they have been used in informal English for about 300 years. Nevertheless, some people find them confusing, and they are rarely found in edited writing.

> Brian Topp, forest products analyst . . . , said the downtime strategy has forced customers to substitute with lower quality pulps, such as U.S.-produced southern softwood, where price drops have been substantial.
> *Financial Post* 31 Oct. 1990: 19

(Here 'make do with' or *substitute* alone, without *with*, would be better.)

> 'You don't eat excessive amounts of protein and fat, but they could be lowered,' she says, adding that I can substitute with more carbohydrates.
> *Vancouver Sun* 23 Jan. 1990: B3

(The word *with* should be dropped.)

subtle   The *b* is silent. *Subtle* rhymes with *shuttle*.

subway   see METRO

succeed One succeeds *in doing* something or *at* something. One succeeds *to* a position. The construction *succeed* plus the infinitive (e.g., 'succeed to do') is unidiomatic.

> At the last U.S. Open . . . a microcomputer succeeded in defeating several players rated higher than 2000, which would put it into the Expert category.
> *Globe and Mail* (Toronto) 12 Jan. 1985: H6

> I have two boys and I want them to succeed at soccer.
> *Province* (Vancouver) 21 June 2001: A37

> 'I am convinced that we will succeed to emerge from this deep crisis.'
> *Gazette* (Montreal) 19 Nov. 1990: B1

(Here 'succeed to emerge' is unidiomatic; 'succeed in emerging' would be better.)

See also -CEED, -CEDE, -SEDE; PREDECESSOR, SUCCESSOR; SECESSION, SECEDE, SUCCESSION, SUCCEED.

successor see PREDECESSOR

succinct see CONCISE

such as see COLON; LIKE, SUCH AS

suffrage, sufferance, suffering, suffer *Suffrage* means the right to vote, and sometimes more specifically the extension of voting rights to include women. *Sufferance* means tolerance, usually in the sense of not objecting, rather than giving approval. Neither should be confused with *suffering*, although the verb *suffer* can mean either feel pain or tolerate without objection.

> Obviously this new political sovereignty—universal male suffrage—had not solved the immense economic inequalities in French society. . . .
> *Canadian Journal of Sociology* 29.3 (2004): 333–57

(Here *suffrage* refers to voting rights.)

> I wanted students to know about an extraordinary organizing effort that was maintained for over a century before suffrage was achieved.
> *Canadian Dimension* 37.5 (2003): 23

(Here it is understood that *suffrage* refers to the extension of voting rights to women.)

> This is the second time Brownstone has played Albertine at 70, a woman whose inner rage and sense of sufferance has sabotaged her life.
> *National Post* (Toronto) 25 Jan. 2005: AL1

(*Sufferance* means tolerance: *suffering* is more appropriate here.)

sufficient see -IE-, -EI-

suite, apartment, flat A *suite* is a set of connecting rooms. For most Canadians the term suggests commercial space or rooms in a hotel, but some, particularly British Columbians, use *suite* as a synonym for *apartment*. The equivalent British term, used occasionally in Canadian English, is *flat*.

> Within each triplex are two three-level suites and one single-level suite, each with two bedrooms and two bathrooms.
> *Vancouver Sun* 17 Feb. 1990: C4

> Me, I fled for a while to one of Vancouver's few Women's Shelters; then found a basement suite and a job.
> *Room of One's Own* June 1990: 8

> . . . Tony Bradbury packed up his family and boarded a plane back to England where they'll live in a one-bedroom flat with relatives.
> *Vancouver Sun* 12 Dec. 1990: A13

sulphur, sulfur Canadian writers prefer the spelling *sulphur* (*sulphate, sulphuric*, etc.) to *sulfur*. The British use *sulphur*; Americans prefer *sulfur*.

summary offence see INDICTABLE OFFENCE

summer time see STANDARD TIME

summons see SUBPOENA

sung see SING

sunk, sunken see SINK

Sunshine Coast see CAPITAL LETTERS

[supercede] see SUPERSEDE

superior, senior, inferior, junior, major, minor *Superior* and *senior* are comparative adjectives borrowed from Latin. In comparisons, *superior* means higher or better, and *senior* means more advanced or older. In explicit comparisons it is generally considered unacceptable to precede these words with *more*, for the same reason that one would not precede an English comparative like *higher* with *more*. *Superior* and *senior* and their opposites *inferior* and *junior* are followed by *to* rather than *than*: 'John's work is superior to (*not* superior than) Jane's'; 'Jill is senior to (*not* senior than) Jack.'

Superior and *senior* have also developed non-comparative senses. *Superior* means high-quality, and *senior* means high-ranking or experienced, as in 'superior artistry' or 'senior academics'. Strictly speaking, if these non-comparative senses are admitted, it should be possible to write 'His artistry was more superior than mine', but such constructions are still unacceptable. *Senior* and *junior*, however, are so widely used in their non-comparative senses that some commentators do accept structures like 'Gail is more senior than Jack'. Similarly, the phrase 'our more senior managers' is accepted because it means 'our more experienced managers' or 'our managers with more seniority'.

Major and *minor* have gone further along the path from Latin comparative to English adjective, in that they are not used in comparisons with *to*. However, commentators still argue that they are comparative, meaning greater and lesser. Thus these critics condemn the use of *major* and *minor* as ordinary adjectives. They would change 'My operation was more major than yours' to 'My operation was more serious than yours', and amend 'It's not as minor a problem as you think' by substituting *trivial* or *insignificant* for *minor*. Eventually, *major* and *minor* may lose any connotation of comparison, but for now it is safest to treat these words as if they meant 'relatively large or important' and 'relatively small or unimportant'.

We feel superior to him, but we do not scorn him.
Robertson Davies *A Voice from the Attic* 1960: 231
It is more superior to anything likely to be con-

cocted in the constitutional pressure cooker this month.
Gazette (Montreal) 7 Aug. 1992: B3

(Here *more* should be dropped.)

Not only was this very much more than any previous Queen's principal had received, it was also three times the salary of the most senior professor.
Frederick Gibson *Queen's University* 2 (1983): 88–9

(Here *senior* is used as a non-comparative adjective meaning highly ranked. Thus 'the *most senior* professor' is the most highly ranked.)

The bacteria is not as major a problem in Nova Scotia as it is in Alberta, said Sullivan. . . .
Cape Breton Post (Sydney, N.S.) 27 June 1990: 17

(Here *major* should be replaced with *serious*; 'as major as' is non-standard because *major* means *relatively* important.)

United, which had made previous repairs to the plane's plumbing system, made a more major repair before putting the plane back in service.
Gazette (Montreal) 6 Nov. 1992: E7

(Since *major* is already comparative, *more major* is nonstandard. The sentence could be rewritten: 'United, which previously had made minor repairs . . . made a major repair before putting the plane back in service.')

See also INFERIOR TO.

superlative see entry in Glossary

supersede, [supercede] *Supersede* is the only spelling recognized by Canadian, British, and American dictionaries with the exception of *Merriam-Webster's*, which has begun to list the very common misspelling *supercede* as a variant. The word is often misspelled because it deviates from the common spelling pattern in *precede*, *recede*, *intercede*, and so on.

. . . the Supreme Court decided that the provinces may no longer supercede the priorities set out in the Federal Bankruptcy Act.
Financial Post 9 Oct. 1989: 15

(The most widely accepted spelling is *supersede*.)

See also -CEED, -CEDE, -SEDE.

supervise   see -IZE, -ISE, -YZE, -YSE

supervisor   see SEXIST LANGUAGE

supine   see PRONE

supper   see DINNER

supplement   see COMPLIMENT

suppose   see DON'T THINK

supposed to   The expression *supposed to* meaning 'expected to' or 'should' is sometimes misspelled *suppose to*, probably because the *d* is not always clearly pronounced.

> So, it is different from other forms of communication in that it is not suppose to have a purpose or aim apart from the success of the sociable moment. . . .
> *City Magazine* Spring 1988: 19

(The correct spelling is *supposed*.)

See also USED TO.

surf   see COMPUTER TERMS

surprise   see -IZE, -ISE, -YZE, -YSE

surprisingly   see SENTENCE ADVERBS

surrounded   Some consider the phrases 'completely surrounded' and 'surrounded on all sides' redundant, since *surrounded* alone means encircled or enclosed on all sides. The same critics find 'surrounded on three sides' illogical. However, these phrases are idiomatic and seem perfectly natural to most people. In formal writing, to avoid what some consider to be a misuse of *surrounded*, words such as *bordered*, *bounded*, or *flanked* may be used to describe an object or person that is not completely encircled.

> The fortress is completely surrounded by water.
> *Globe and Mail* (Toronto) 2 Feb. 1985: T3

> To Torontonians, Ontario is a wealthy, self-assured metropolis, surrounded on three sides by a hinter-

land of farms and towns, and beyond, wilderness.
> *Ottawa Citizen* 23 Sept. 1989: B3

> The reconstructed City of Refuge is bounded on three sides by sea and on the fourth by a high wall, so a fugitive faced a marathon swim to reach the safety of its confines.
> *Globe and Mail* (Toronto) 17 April 1985: M7

surveil   see BACK-FORMATION

suspect, suspicious   Both words are regularly used to describe something that is viewed with suspicion, or that arouses suspicion. However, *suspect* is a better choice in contexts where *suspicious* could also mean 'feeling suspicion'. For example, 'The neighbours are rather suspicious' is ambiguous, since it could mean either that they act as if they suspect something odd is going on or that they are up to something odd themselves. To make it clear, one could write either 'The neighbours are getting suspicious' or 'The neighbours are rather suspect', depending on which meaning is intended.

> . . . cast and crew eat lunch, joking about the take-out sandwiches filled with meat of highly suspect origin.
> *Globe and Mail* (Toronto) 4 Jan. 1985: E3

> Biopsies of suspicious areas are taken and analyzed.
> *Globe and Mail* (Toronto) 3 Jan. 1985: P18

> . . . if, in order to attain such a result, a court has to go to the lengths of overturning settled principles, the methodology and policy of the court become even more suspect and open to criticism.
> *Canadian Bar Review* 66.3 (1987): 610

(Here *suspicious* would be confusing.)

See also SUSPECT, SUPPOSE; SUSPECTED.

suspected   Many commentators object to phrases like 'the suspected murderer' because the person referred to is being given the label *murderer* before this has been established by a court of law. Phrases like 'the murder suspect', 'the suspect', or 'the man suspected of murder' are more considerate and more accurate.

See also ALLEGED.

suspension   see ABBREVIATION

suspicious   see SUSPECT

sustain   To *sustain* can mean to support ('sustain life') or to suffer ('sustain injuries'). Some commentators have criticized its use in the second sense on the grounds that it is logically inconsistent with the first. Critics of the second sense usually regard it as a recent corruption. In fact, the verb *sustain* has had these two meanings since the 1400s and both are accepted.

> . . . the Cree and Inuit appear determined to defend the values that have helped to sustain them in their harsh environment over thousands of years.
> *Maclean's* 12 Aug. 1991: A10

> And in January, his wife . . . died as a result of injuries sustained in a car accident.
> *Maclean's* 8 July 1991: A42

> In fact, it took 25 years to recoup the losses sustained in the market's tumble.
> *Globe and Mail* (Toronto) 29 Oct. 2004: B11

swale   see SWAMP

swam   see SWIM

swamp, marsh, bog, muskeg, slough, pothole, coulee, swale, wetlands   *Swamp* and *marsh* are both used to describe an area of wet, spongy land periodically or permanently covered with water. The vegetation of marshes differs from that of swamps: a *marsh* contains mostly grasses and sedges, whereas a *swamp* also has trees and shrubs. A *bog* is an area of wet, spongy, usually peaty ground that forms over thousands of years as vegetation slowly invades a lake. In Canada, bogs cover large areas in the northern parts of the Prairie provinces and consist of acidic water covered by a deep mat of vegetation that includes moss and black spruce trees. This terrain is called *muskeg*.

Slough is pronounced to rhyme with *slew* or sometimes, in Atlantic Canada, with *cow*. The definition of a slough varies across Canada (see

SLOUGH). Some prairie sloughs are round areas of sinking soil also known as *potholes*. A *coulee* is a deep ravine or gully that is usually dry in the summer. A *swale* is a shallow depression in the land that often collects water. *Wetlands* is a general term for areas that are wet for much or all of the year.

> The entire country in spring was a heaving bog, dotted by sloughs, little streams, and ponds left by the rapidly melting snow.
> Pierre Berton *The Promised Land* 1984: 129

> Each had to find his own way, work out his own salvation in slough or muskeg, and care for his family at nightfall.
> Pierre Berton *The Promised Land* 1984: 128

> Perhaps it came from the grassy banks of old meltwater coulees and stream valleys, Willow Creek and the Old-man River, that we explored as children.
> *NeWest Review* Dec. 1989–Jan. 1990: 15

> Grass that had been 10 inches high the year before went up to 20, and in the swales where it had been high to begin with, it looked something like a bamboo grove.
> *Harrowsmith* Aug.–Sept. 1985: 56

> The Waterfowl Gardens depict eight different wetland habitats in Manitoba, ranging from prairie potholes to the tundra of the far north. . . .
> Alan Tucker, ed. *The Penguin Guide to Canada* 1991: 476

See also TUNDRA.

swap, swop   *Swap*, meaning exchange, functions as both a noun and a verb. It's an informal word, largely restricted to magazine and newspaper writing. *Swop* is a British spelling variant, rarely used by Canadians.

> . . . participants enjoyed an afternoon of rodeo games, followed by a . . . great evening of tunes, with tall tales being swapped around the campfire till the wee hours.
> *Canadian Biker Magazine* Feb. 1990: 10

> . . . the city attained ownership of most of the land there through a series of land swaps in the 1960s with a railway and the B.C. government.
> *Gazette* (Montreal) 5 March 1989: I4

SWAT Team, Emergency Response Team, ERT   The acronym *SWAT*, coined in the Los Angeles Police Department in the 1960s, originally stood for Special Weapons Assault Team and punned on *swat* meaning strike. Later *SWAT* was recast as Special Weapons *And* Tactics, a name change that downplayed violence (and, at the same time, allowed editors to stop worrying about whether 'SWAT *Team*' was redundant). The Canadian public uses 'SWAT team' generically, for any specially trained, military-style unit within a police force, and metaphorically, for rapid responders in other domains: 'environmental SWAT team'. Note, however, that the official name of the special police units varies from force to force. *Emergency Response Team* or *ERT* (pronounced EE ARE TEE) is a more common designation in Canada than SWAT. Also note that the acronym *ERT* does double duty in Canada, for it also stands for 'estrogen replacement therapy'.

> There are even reality shows with names like *Clean Sweep* that send SWAT teams of neatniks into the lairs of the messy to reform us. . . .
> *Gazette* (Montreal) 25 June 2005: A6

> ERT members discovered the body while clearing the house for fellow officers.
> *Star-Phoenix* (Saskatoon) 25 Aug. 2005: A3

(Here *ERT* stands for Emergency Response Team.)

> Recent technological developments have made it even simpler for women to take ERT once a week by using an estrogen patch. . . .
> *Daily News* (Halifax) 17 Oct. 2000: 28

(Here *ERT* stands for estrogen replacement therapy.)

swell, swelled, swollen   The past tense of *swell* is *swelled*: 'Her ankles swelled in the heat'. The past participle may be *swollen* ('The wood had swollen after the rainstorm') or *swelled* ('The river had swelled after the thaw'). Both forms are used as adjectives: 'swollen head' *or* 'swelled head'.

> My heart had swollen to three times normal size from the strain of working too hard.
> *Ottawa Citizen* 12 Oct. 1990: F1

> . . . by the time police had searched all the cars and the convoy reached LaSalle, the crowd in LaSalle had swelled to 400.
> *Gazette* (Montreal) 8 Nov. 1990: A3

> They sought refuge in the tree overnight to escape the freezing waters of a swollen creek below.
> *Ottawa Citizen* 2 May 1990: B6

> 'We can't afford to go into the game with swelled heads because we're unbeaten and ranked second in the country.'
> *Gazette* (Montreal) 5 Oct. 1990: B6

(Here *swelled* is an adjective.)

swim, swam, swum   The past tense of *swim* is *swam*. The past participle is *swum*: 'She has swum it before'.

> 'We've never swam a big meet like this before in January.'
> *Province* (Vancouver) 26 Jan. 1990: 60

(The past participle *swum* is required here.)

swinging   see EUPHEMISM

swollen   see SWELL

swop   see SWAP

syllable   see entry in Glossary

syllabus, syllabi   see PLURALS

sympathy   see EMPATHY

synchronous, in sync(h), simultaneous, coincident, concurrent   These modifiers all mean existing or occurring at the same time. The adjective *synchronous* is common only in technical and scientific writing, while *sync(h)*, pronounced SINK, a clipped form of *synchrony*, used in the phrases *in sync(h)* (synchronized, in accord) or *out of sync(h)* (disjointed, disconnected) is informal and often non-technical. The spelling *sync*, without *h*, is more common.

Simultaneous usually refers to activities proceeding at the same time. Literally, *coincident* means occupying the same time or space, but it is also applied metaphorically to people or things that are in exact agreement. *Concurrent* often refers to prison terms, especially life sentences, to be served simultaneously rather than consecutively (since the power of human justice does not extend beyond the grave).

> Alternatively, climatic change may have been synchronous across the southern Canadian Cordillera. . . .
> *Canadian Journal of Earth Sciences* 26 (1989): 263

> Back in the arena, a full-throated crowd sang The Star-Spangled Banner beautifully, and got a little out of sync on O Canada, and laughed at itself.
> *National Post* (Toronto) 12 June 2006: S4

> The provincial government is considering allowing off-track wagering in 'teletheatres,' where simultaneous telecasts of live horse races are played.
> *Vancouver Sun* 18 Oct. 1990: A17

> Their coincident time in office spanned only 27 months, from Kennedy's inauguration on Jan. 20, 1961, until Diefenbaker's departure on April 22, 1963.
> *Maclean's* 10 Dec. 1990: T6

> For at the end of this intellectual trail is the reality that B.C.'s real interests are coincident with Quebec's real interests.
> *Vancouver Sun* 9 Nov. 1991: B5

> Running on a $1.5 million Stratus mainframe computer, SUZY can currently handle up to 200 concurrent users. . . .
> *Vancouver Sun* 9 May 1990: D1

> He was sentenced to 11 concurrent life terms with no eligibility for parole for at least 25 years.
> *Vancouver Sun* 7 Dec. 1990: A14

See also SIMULTANEOUS, SIMULTANEOUSLY.

syndicate   see QUEBEC ENGLISH

syndrome   In medicine, *syndrome* refers to a set of distinct symptoms that usually appear together and indicate a disease or condition. Most authorities now accept the figurative, often jocular, use of *syndrome* to refer to a characteristic attitude or pattern of behaviour, but many consider the word to be overused in this sense.

> When I was five years old we didn't know what DNA did . . . or the causes of Down's syndrome.
> *Queen's Quarterly* 93.1 (1986): 86–7

> To avoid the deluge-and-dearth harvest syndrome—having too much of one vegetable at one time and none at another—plan before you plant.
> *Canadian Living* 17 May 1986: 98

> Entertainment Liberation Frustration Syndrome: If you've ever tried to get a CD or DVD removed from its packaging, you've probably suffered from this to at least some degree.
> *Toronto Star* 19 June 2006: E1

See also DOWN SYNDROME.

synecdoche   see METONYMY

synonym, antonym, thesaurus   *Synonyms* are words with similar meanings (e.g., *thin, svelte, slim,* and *skinny*), while *antonyms* have opposite meanings (*hot* and *cold, tall* and *short, high* and *low*). While they are similar, synonyms can't always be used interchangeably. For example, water can be called either *clear* or *colourless,* but a *clear* red liquid could not be called *colourless.* Because of the connotations of the words, most people would rather be called *slim* or *slender* than *skinny.*

Peter Mark Roget published the first book-length collection of words categorized according to meaning in 1852. *Roget's Thesaurus,* or word treasury, was modelled on the scientific classification of plant and animal species. It gathers and groups all the words that convey a certain general meaning, but offers no definitions. Roget's book has been followed by a succession of synonym finders. These books are useful tools for the writer struggling to find the *mot juste* or to recall a word that has slipped the memory, but they can have a very peculiar effect on the style of writers hoping to inject some elegance and variety into their vocabularies. Because synonyms aren't equivalent words, a thesaurus should be used only in conjunction with a good dictionary. Even better, perhaps, is to write in your own idiom and to avoid words you haven't encountered before.

See also CONNOTATION(S); HOMOPHONE, HOMOGRAPH, HOMONYM.

synopsis, synopses   see PLURALS

synthetic   see ARTIFICIAL; SEXIST LANGUAGE

syrup, sirup   Canadian, British, and American dictionaries all list *syrup* first. *Sirup* is an American variant, rare in Canadian usage.

systematize, systemize   Both forms of this verb entered the language in the late 1700s, and both are listed in many current dictionaries. However, *systematize* dominates in contemporary English and is the only form found in formal Canadian writing.

> Atwood seems compelled to classify and systematize, to make patterns, in one part of her mind, while an alternative self glimpses a more fluid reality, a creative surreality.
> *Saturday Night* Jan. 1986: 41

systemic, systematic   *Systemic* was originally a medical term describing a condition that affected a whole organism or biological system. A virus that wreaks havoc with your whole body is having a *systemic* effect. Now *systemic* is often used metaphorically to describe problems infecting or pervading social systems and institutions. This is the sense of *systemic* in the common phrases 'systemic racism' and 'systemic discrimination'. 'Systemic discrimination' has to do with inequities and prejudices within the operation of a system (the education system, etc.) that are not overt or easy to locate, but that are present nonetheless. For example, a requirement that all firefighters be over six feet tall could be seen as evidence of systemic discrimination against most women and, in some minority groups, most men as well. (Today, most such physical requirements have been replaced by standards of strength and fitness, so that no one is automatically excluded.)

The phrase 'systemic discrimination' is quite often confused with 'systematic discrimination'. To be *systematic* in your approach to a task is to make a plan and carry it out in a thorough and orderly way. Thus 'systematic discrimination' and 'systematic racism' involve not unconscious prejudice but deliberate acts of repression. The Nazis' treatment of the Jews during the Second World War was an extreme example of 'systematic racism'. Apartheid in South Africa—an explicit government policy of exclusion on the basis of race—was another.

> Employers do not have to work at discriminating against these groups; it comes naturally. This massive and systemic discrimination cannot be eradicated by dealing with its manifestations on a one by one, case by case basis, as our human rights system demands.
> *Maclean's* 15 Oct. 1990: A44

> Communist China invaded its tiny neighbor in 1950 and began a process of systematic repression, torture and—according to Tibetans—genocide.
> *Maclean's* 15 Oct. 1990: A44

> Contrary to the claims by the immigration ministry, the facts seem to indicate that delay is caused by a policy of systemic discrimination against visible minorities.
> *Gazette* (Montreal) 13 Dec. 1990: B2

(A policy of deliberate exclusion of visible minorities would be 'systematic discrimination'. Given the sense of the sentence, either 'caused by a policy of discrimination' or 'caused by *systematic* discrimination' would be better.)

T

-t, -ed *Leant, learnt, smelt, spelt, spilt,* and *spoilt* are chiefly British forms of the past tense and past participle forms. Canadians, like Americans, are far more likely to use the *-ed* forms of these verbs. However, Canadians do use *burnt, dreamt, knelt,* and *leapt* quite often.

See also BEREAVED, BEREFT; CLEAVE; -ED.

table In Britain, to *table* a resolution, motion, or bill is to put it on the table, to bring it forward for consideration. In the United States, the opposite is meant: to *table* an item on the agenda is to postpone it. In Parliament, Canadians employ the British meaning. However, confusion may arise in other settings, where Canadians use the same word for both meanings.

> The legislation must be tabled and passed in the House of Commons before January 1, 1989, when the agreement comes into effect.
> *Engineering Dimensions* Mar.–Apr. 1988: 31

(Here *table* means bring forward.)

> 'If it's not settled by Monday, we will have to make a decision, whether we table legislation or we give more time to negotiate.'
> *Gazette* (Montreal) 26 April 1990: A7

(The speaker here is wondering whether or not a strike should be ended immediately by bringing forward legislation.)

> Aldermen on city council's land use, planning and transportation committee tabled the report until Feb. 18 while they await more detail on the proposal, which suggests nearly half of the money be raised through a local improvement bylaw.
> *Calgary Herald* 22 Jan. 2004: B7

(Here *table* means postpone.)

tableau, tableaux see PLURALS

table d'hôte see À LA CARTE

tack, take a different tack, tact, track The expression *take a different* (or *another*) *tack* comes from sailing. A boat sailing against the wind must run at an oblique angle, zig-zagging to make headway. It is time to take another tack (sail at a different angle to the wind) when the boat made some progress upwind but is getting too far off course. Figuratively, the phrase means to take another approach.

Since not everyone is a sailor, and taking a different tack often involves exercising *tact*, some people confuse *tack* and *tact* in this expression. Others have made sense of an unfamiliar metaphor by substituting rail for sail: 'taking a different track'.

> However, Canadair is taking its competition seriously, and officials have decided to take a new tack in marketing the CL-215T.
> *Maclean's* 12 Sept. 1988: A26

> Elizabeth Anderson of the B.C. Green Party took a slightly different tact in her presentation, lashing out at the very roots of representative democracy.
> *Vancouver Sun* 18 April 1990: NS3

(The idiom calls for *tack*.)

> The Odyssey, an imaginative series that spent its first two seasons following a 12-year-old coma victim's imaginary struggles in a fantasy world, has taken a different track this third season.
> *Vancouver Sun* 21 Nov. 1994: C1

(The idiom calls for *tack*.)

See also FOLK ETYMOLOGY.

taiga see TUNDRA

take see BRING

take for granted, [take for granite] see MISHEARD EXPRESSIONS

take off, takeoff, takeout   see IDIOMS;
PHRASAL VERBS

takeover   see FUNCTIONAL SHIFT

Talmud   see SACRED WRITINGS

tantamount   see PARAMOUNT

tap, faucet, valve, spigot   Canadians use
tap more frequently than *faucet*, though many
use either word. *Tap* is the usual term in Britain,
while *faucet* is common in the United States.
Some Canadians make a distinction of sense,
reserving *faucet* for the fixture that uses one tap
to control the flow of both hot and cold water.
While kitchens and bathrooms have either
faucets or taps, *tap* is the broader term. Only *tap*
is used in industrial settings for devices controlling the flow of liquids. A British-style pub may
be called a 'taproom', while many bars sell 'beer
on tap' or 'draft beer'. Water that is piped into
homes is called 'tap water', never 'faucet water'
(even in the United States).

Some Canadians, especially in Newfoundland
and Quebec, distinguish between indoor taps
and outdoor *valves* used for hoses and sprin-
klers. *Spigot* is an uncommon word in Canadian
English, most often used figuratively.

> I took the hand and ran it under the cold tap.
> Howard Engel *Murder Sees the Light* 1984: 92

> When a bathroom hot water faucet is quickly
> turned off, sometimes a 'bang' is heard in the
> pipes behind the wall.
> *Toronto Star* 16 Dec. 1994: A1

> A pipeline that supplies the Ontario Hockey
> League with high-octane talent is slowly having its
> spigot closed.
> *Daily News* (Halifax) 24 Oct. 1994: 30

tap (telephone)   see BUG

Tapiriit Kanatami   see INUIT

taps   see LAST POST

target   The use of *target* to mean quota, objective, or goal has been criticized because, according to some, a target is something 'aimed at',
'hit', or 'missed', not something 'reached',
'achieved', or 'exceeded'. Nonetheless, many
writers do use *target* as a synonym for *objective*
or *goal*, and dictionaries record this meaning.

Critics of the metaphorical use of *target* could
just as well take aim at the word *goal*, but no
one suggests that the literal sense of *goal* (winning post or net) should govern the verbs with
which it can be used. This is probably because
goal has been used as a metaphor since the early
seventeenth century, while the figurative sense
of *target* dates only from the 1940s.

> But Drew was as determined as any Soviet com-
> missar to fulfil his self-imposed export quota, and
> the fuse to his temper began smouldering when-
> ever anyone suggested the fifteen per cent target
> might be overly ambitious.
> George Ignatieff *The Making of a Peacemonger*
> 1987: 177

> Initially, industry participation will be voluntary
> but if the first target of reduction . . . is not met,
> the federal government intends to enforce the
> guidelines with legislation.
> *Western Grocer* May–Jun. 1990: 94

tartan, plaid   In Scotland, *tartan* is the distinctive design on the fabric used to make kilts
and other garments. Specific tartans are traditionally associated with specific clans. A *plaid* is
a length of woollen cloth worn over one shoulder as part of traditional Scottish Highland
dress. However, Canadians generally use *plaid*
for the pattern ('a plaid shirt'), and occasionally
refer to the garment that the Scots call a *plaid* as
a *tartan*.

> [The man] was last seen wearing a green cotton
> plaid shirt, beige pants and plaid bedroom slippers.
> *Globe and Mail* (Toronto) 4 June 1985: M4

(The Scots would say *tartan*.)

> He was . . . strikingly attired in winter in the Royal
> Stuart tartan which he preferred to an overcoat,
> and apparently occasionally substituting a high-
> land bonnet for the conventional mortarboard.
> Hilda Neatby *Queen's University* 1 (1978): 89

(The Scots would call the garment a *plaid*.)

tautology   see WORDINESS

tax, excise, duty, customs, rates   *Tax* is a general word for a compulsory payment levied by government to support state expenditures. *Excise* is tax paid on goods manufactured or produced within the country. *Duty*, or *customs*, is tax paid on goods brought into Canada from another country. In Canada and the United States, local taxes paid on the assessed value of property are called *property taxes*; the equivalent British term is *rates*. In Canada a *ratepayers' association* is a municipal taxpayers' group.

> The municipalities don't think their ratepayers should pay higher taxes for Victoria's decision to buy the most expensive technology available.
> *Globe and Mail* (Toronto) 9 March 1985: 6

See also EXCISE.

tax evasion, tax avoidance   *Tax evasion* refers to an illegal act whereby a person or company underpays or fails to pay income tax. *Tax avoidance* refers to arranging one's financial affairs in order to pay as little tax as possible.

> A Kemptville man has been found guilty of tax evasion and fined $42,000 for not reporting the proceeds of an illegal drug trafficking business.
> *Ottawa Citizen* 28 Feb. 2006: B3

> Let's be clear: There's no investigation into the legality of trusts. They are a perfectly legal (if immoral) form of tax avoidance for investors.
> *Globe and Mail* (Toronto) 24 April 2006: A17

tea   see DINNER

team, teem   *Team* is certainly the more common word, but some people mistakenly use it for all meanings of these two homophones.

A group of people working or playing together is a *team*; animals harnessed together are a *team*. To *team up* means to join forces.

To *teem* is to be plentiful, to swarm. If something is *teeming* with something, it abounds in it. In reference to rain, to *teem* means to pour.

> Anybody out there interested in teaming up with

me to open a consulting firm?
> *Ottawa Citizen* 24 May 1992: A6

> Paris in the 1960s was teeming with Quebec students, virtually all of them ardent separatists.
> George Ignatieff *The Making of a Peacemonger* 1987: 215

> I am 77 and walk a mile and a half to the store to pick up my Gazette, unless there is teeming rain or a blizzard, at which time I take the car.
> *Gazette* (Montreal) 27 Jan. 1990: A7

> Montreal's Old Port . . . is teaming with activity this summer.
> *Gazette* (Montreal) 13 June 1992: K4

(The correct spelling is *teeming*.)

See also COLLECTIVE NOUNS.

teaspoonful   see -FUL

teem   see TEAM

teeth, teethe   see BATH

televise   see BACK-FORMATION

television   see BARBARISMS

temblor   see TREMOR

temporary   see FUNCTIONAL SHIFT

temporize   see EXTEMPORIZE

temps   see FRENCH WORDS, PRONUNCIATION OF

tempus fugit   see LATIN PHRASES

tenant, tenet   A *tenant* is a renter. A *tenet* is a fundamental principle or belief. *Tenent* is a common misspelling for both these words.

> . . . when a unit is vacated, the doorknobs are changed and new keys are issued to the new tenant.
> *Calgary Herald* 3 June 1992: B1

> It is a basic tenet of business that you profit from your competitor's misfortune.
> *Calgary Herald* 29 Dec. 1992: A7

The Pharmasave will move into the former grocery, and other mall tenents will move into the old
drug store space.
Guardian (Charlottetown) 30 March 2000: A5

(The word required here is *tenants*.)

This week, it was one of football's basic tenents—
hang onto the ball.
Vancouver Sun 19 July 1990: C1

(The word required is *tenets*.)

[tenderhooks]   see TENTERHOOKS

tendinitis, tendonitis   The term for inflam-
mation of a tendon is spelled either *tendinitis* or
tendonitis. Both spellings are common and
accepted; *tendinitis* is more common in
Canadian writing.

tenet   see TENANT

tennis shoes   see RUNNING SHOES

tense   see entry in Glossary

tenterhooks   The word *tenterhooks* dates from
the late fifteenth century: a *tenter* was a
machine used for stretching cloth, and a *tenter-
hook* was what held the cloth taut. The
metaphorical expression *on tenterhooks* refers to
being on edge, nervous, or in suspense—
stretched taut, as if by a tenter. Knowing the
word *tenter* may help you avoid the common
misspelling *tenderhooks*.

Carter is once again waiting on tenderhooks for
word from the Raptors' medical staff he can return
to the lineup Sunday. . . .
National Post (Toronto) 24 Jan. 2003: S2

(The word should be spelled *tenterhooks*.)

tenue de ville   see QUEBEC ENGLISH

terminate   Critics find this word pretentious
and overused: anything today—from marriages, to people, to conversations—may be
said to be terminated. While *terminate* is common and appropriate in legal and quasi-legal

contexts, there are many preferable synonyms
for general use, including *end*, *stop*, *bring to an
end*, and *fire*.

A buyer may terminate the contract during this
period by giving written notice to the seller.
J.E. Smyth et al. *The Law and Business Administration in Canada* 1987: 411

Unhappy marriages were usually tolerated in previous generations; today they are usually terminated.
Irving M. Zeitlin and Robert J. Brym *The Social
Condition of Humanity* 1991: 195

(Here *terminated* fits the context, since marriage
is being discussed as an economic arrangement.)

Again, at this point the conversation was terminated.
City Magazine Spring 1988: 19

(Here *ended abruptly* or *ceased* would be preferable.)

Michael had discussed terminating Brian with the
President of the Company and the Director of
Human Resources a number of times. . . .
Queen's Quarterly 94.4 (1987): 843

(Simply *firing* him would be kinder.)

terminus, termini   see PLURALS

terrible   see AWFUL

terrorist   see GUERRILLA

terrorize   see -IZE, -ISE, -YZE, -YSE

testimony   see EVIDENCE

tetraplegic   see PARAPLEGIC

Tex-Mex   see HISPANIC

than   For centuries, language commentators
have debated whether the pronouns that follow
than should be subjective (*I*, *she*, *he*, *we*, and
they) or objective (*me*, *her*, *him*, *us*, and *them*). At
present, usage varies with the level of formality.
In informal speech and writing, the objective
pronouns are used: 'She is taller than *him*'; 'He
trusted Michael more than *me*'. In formal

speech and writing, either subjective or objective pronouns are used, depending on which would be appropriate if the verb were repeated after *than*: 'She is taller than he [is]'; 'He trusted Michael more than [he trusted] me'. 'He trusted Michael more than I' would mean 'more than I did'. Note that this distinction can't be made in informal usage.

Many people balk at using a subjective pronoun after *than* ('They were more fortunate than we') because they think it sounds pedantic. The pedantic ring can always be avoided by repeating the verb: 'They were more fortunate than we were'.

A comparison that starts with *as* must be completed with *as* ('It's *as* good *as* new'), never with *than* (as in 'There were twice *as* many *than* before').

Than is often misspelled *then*, though the error is more likely to reflect haste than genuine confusion.

> . . . there were younger men around the clubs, men such as Sonny Rollins, a tenor saxophonist from Harlem who was three years younger than he.
> Jack Chambers *Milestones* 1983: 122

> I don't think they know any better than me.
> *Canadian Fiction Magazine* 64 (1988): 106

(Here *than me* is appropriate, since the tone is conversational; *than I* would be required in a formal context.)

> . . . I learned inadvertently that a male hired later than I was being paid significantly more than me.
> *Women and Environments* 12.2 (1989–90): 26

(Given the formal tone of the sentence, *me* should be replaced by *I*.)

> And twice as many civilians were hurt in those chases than in 1987.
> *Gazette* (Montreal) 3 March 1989: A3

(Here *than* should be changed to *as*.)

See also CASE; DIFFERENT FROM; SUPERIOR, SENIOR.

thankfully   see SENTENCE ADVERBS

Thanksgiving Day   see NEW YEAR'S DAY

that, omission of   Especially in spoken English, *that* is often omitted: 'the gloves [that] you thought [that] I'd left behind'. *That*-less constructions are referred to by grammarians as 'omitted relatives' or 'contact clauses'. In the eighteenth century, usage writers condemned the omission of *that* in written English. Now some usage guides maintain just the opposite, that it is better to omit *that* whenever possible. Since both structures are grammatically correct, rhythm and clarity should guide your choice. The omission of *that* is more common in informal writing than in formal prose.

See also REASON IS BECAUSE; THAT, WHICH; THAT, WHO, WHOM.

that, which   Most writers use *that* and *which* without any difficulty. However, they may well be troubled by a sense that there is some rule about these words that they are breaking. Even Robertson Davies felt this unease: 'To this day I cannot be sure when I should use "that" and when I should use "which", but my secretary knows, and between us we keep up some sort of pretence' (*One Half of Robertson Davies*, 1978: 13). In fact, the problem is with the 'rule', not the writers. It can be traced to Fowler, who suggested that 'if writers would agree to regard *that* as the defining [restrictive] relative pronoun, and *which* as the non-defining, there would be much gain in both lucidity and ease.' Most book editors follow Fowler's advice, particularly in scholarly and reference books. Yet even Fowler admitted 'it would be idle to pretend that it is the practice either of most or of the best writers.'

Later usage guides elevated this suggestion to a rule. Now, however, most writers ignore it, and literary writers are the most likely to use both *which* and *that* to introduce restrictive clauses.

If you are still interested in following the 'rule', you need to understand the difference between a restrictive and a non-restrictive clause. A restrictive (or defining) clause identifies the noun it modifies, and cannot be deleted without interfering with the meaning of the whole sentence (see also COMMA). In the sentence 'The book that (*or* which) John lent me last week is fascinating', the clause *that* (or *which*) *John lent me* is necessary to make it clear which book we are talking about. Obeying Fowler's recommendation, a writer would only use *that* in this sort of sentence, though, as noted above, either *that* or *which* is grammatical. The sentence above can easily be changed so that it contains a non-restrictive (or non-defining) clause: '*Wuthering Heights*, which John lent me last week, is fascinating'. The clause *which John lent me last week* is not needed to specify which book we are discussing; it simply adds more information. The rest of the sentence ('*Wuthering Heights* is fascinating') can be properly interpreted without the non-restrictive clause. Most writers naturally follow Fowler's recommendation to use *which* to introduce non-restrictive clauses.

Occasionally, *that* is used to introduce a non-restrictive clause: '*Wuthering Heights*, that you say is your favourite novel, is on the reading list'. Only *which*, however, is acceptable. The use of *which* to refer not to one noun (as in the examples above) but to a whole preceding sentence or idea ('Ray chews gum almost constantly, which I don't like') has been condemned as an incorrect pronoun reference, as has the similar use of *this*. However, both usages are common in Standard English, and usage guides have begun to relent.

> By no means did the Tory Creed consist only of ideas that had outlived their time.
> J.A.W. Gunn *Beyond Liberty and Property* 1983: 136

(Here *that* is used with a restrictive clause.)

> Death occurs today on the same general principle which governed it a century ago; for every living creature there is a death apiece.
> Robertson Davies *A Voice from the Attic* 1960: 129

(Here *which* is used with a restrictive clause.)

> Sam Pollock, then general manager of the Canadiens, offered me a generous extension to my contract, which had one year left to run.
> Ken Dryden *The Game* 1983: 13

(Here *which* is used with a non-restrictive clause.)

> . . . Guangzhou's White Swan, located on Shamian Island that was once headquarters for the opium trade, remains one of the most opulent.
> *Vancouver Sun* 1 June 1990: G1

(Since Shamian Island is clearly identified by name, the information provided in the restrictive *that* clause is not essential: *which*—preceded by a comma—should replace *that*.)

See also COMMA; THAT, OMISSION OF; THAT, WHO, WHOM.

that, who, whom   Some people think it inappropriate to use the relative pronoun *that* to refer to a person, as in 'the man that just spoke to me'. They think only *who* (or *whom*) should refer to people: 'the man who spoke to me'. But dictionaries and usage guides do not support this idea: they agree unanimously that *that* can refer to people.

However, *that* and *who* or *whom* are not freely interchangeable. When *that* refers to a person, the clause it introduces is almost always restrictive. In other words, the *that*-clause identifies the person, or the type of person, being referred to: 'the girl that just jogged by', 'anybody that thinks so'. *That* is not acceptable in formal writing when it links a nonrestrictive clause to a person: in other words, when it introduces a clause adding information about a person whose identity has already been specified: 'The previous owner, who (*not* that) told us the roof was new, must have been mistaken'.

> But now she found herself sitting with the very man that Lastivka had just talked about.
> *Canadian Fiction Magazine* 63 (1988): 73

> 'Do you have anybody that you consider to be your poetic father?'
> Bruce Meyer and Brian O'Riordan, eds. *In Their Words* 1984: 109

> There are many disturbing examples of this, from the continued gender gap in wages to the growing proportion of households headed by women that are poor.
> *Women and Environments* 12.1 (1990): 15

> 'And what about the night watchman that uses this—'
> Constance Beresford-Howe *Night Studies* 1985: 214

(Since the phrase 'the night watchman' identifies a particular person, formal English would require *who* instead of *that*.)

My friend that helped me manoeuvre about the big city wouldn't even buy into the magazine for a 50% ownership.
Canadian Biker Magazine Feb. 1990: 4

(Either '*The* friend *that* helped me . . .' or '*My* friend, *who* helped me. . .' would be required in formal writing.)

See also COMMA; THAT, WHICH; WHO, WHOM.

Thatcherism   see -ISM

that is   *That is* is a connecting phrase often used in formal prose to introduce a rewording or explanation of what has just been said. When the elements equated by *that is* are not complete sentences, a comma precedes and follows *that is*: 'Photosensitive pigments, that is, pigments that fade when exposed to strong light, are not recommended'. When a whole sentence precedes and follows *that is,* the construction should be punctuated as two separate sentences: 'These pigments are photosensitive. That is, they will fade if exposed to strong light.' Alternatively, the sentences may be linked with a semicolon or colon: 'These pigments are photosensitive; that is, they will fade. . .'.

> If the term is broken, that is, if the seller delivers a substantially different quantity, the buyer is free to reject the goods.
> J.E. Smyth et al. *The Law and Business Administration in Canada* 1987: 383

> . . . in the early years of North American economic development, Canada's frontier was 'harder' than that of the United States. That is, Canada was a vast and inhospitable country compared to the U.S., and its natural resources were less accessible.
> *Canadian Journal of Sociology* 14.2 (1989): 164

> The four greatest historians of the post-Roman period are often thought of as national historians; that is, there is a general assumption that Jordanes was concerned to record the history of the Goths, Gregory of Tours that of the Franks, Bede the history of the English Church, and Paul the Deacon the deeds of the Lombards.
> *Canadian Journal of History* 14.1 (1989): 92

> The other reason is based on precedence: that is, a writer has to write something before a critic can criticize it.
> Margaret Atwood *Second Words* 1982: 11

See also COLON; I.E., E.G.

the, a, an   An initial definite or indefinite article (*the*, *a*, or *an*) is ignored in the alphabetizing of titles in indexes or library catalogues. In other words, *The Progress of Love* can be found under *P*, not *T*.

When a title beginning with *the*, *a*, or *an* is mentioned in a text, the initial article is normally retained, with a capital and in italics. But there are exceptions. When the title of a book is preceded by a possessive or an adjective, the initial article may be omitted: 'We read Dickens' *Christmas Carol* every year' (*A Christmas Carol*); 'The much-maligned *Fire-Dwellers* depicted an extramarital affair in a sympathetic light' (*The Fire-Dwellers*). The word *the* at the beginning of the title of a handbook, almanac, atlas, encyclopedia, or dictionary is rarely capitalized and italicized except in scholarly writing: 'There is a picture of Howie Morenz in the *Canadian Encyclopedia*' (*The Canadian Encyclopedia*). Scholars, however, often refer to a title exactly as it appears on its title page. According to the practice of many editors, the word *the* before the name of a newspaper is never capitalized and italicized, regardless of whether *The* appears on the newspaper's masthead. But again, scholars may make a point of reproducing the exact title of the newspaper as it appears on the masthead of the issue(s) they are citing. The French definite article is never dropped from the name of French-language newspapers such as *Le Soleil* and *Le Devoir*.

The should not be capitalized before the name of a company, a publisher, or an organization—the Hudson's Bay Company, the University of Toronto Press, the Institute for Research on Public Policy—unless *the* is part of the legal name of the organization and the context requires the legal name.

When *The* is part of a place name (as it would appear on a map), it is capitalized: 'The Hague',

'The Pas'. For informal terms and nicknames, *the* is lowercase: 'the South', 'the Prairies', 'the Soo' (the nickname of Sault Ste. Marie).

> Not even the *Canada Year Book* or Mel Hurtig's *Canadian Encyclopedia* had room for it.
> *United Church Observer* May 1986: 43

> It is attested to by an average of one letter per week in the correspondence columns of *The Globe and Mail*.
> W.C. Lougheed, ed. *In Search of the Standard in Canadian English* 1986: 26

> Why should the Hudson's Bay Company publish a history magazine? Most Canadians already know the answer to that question. . . . it is also The Governor and Company of Adventurers of England Trading Into Hudson's Bay.
> *The Beaver* Feb.–Mar. 1990: 4

> 'French-English battle creeps into the N.W.T.,' declared the weekend Globe and Mail, wrapping us neatly up with a story on the Soo, a column from Quebec and an editorial.
> *News North* (Yellowknife) 19 Feb. 1990: 6

theater, theatre   see -RE, -ER

theft   see BURGLARY

thee   see ARCHAISMS

their, they're, there   People often mix up *their* ('their things'), *they're* ('They're here'), and *there* ('There aren't any'). These substitutions usually result from inattention rather than genuine confusion.

> 'All their doing is putting out our records.'
> *Gazette* (Montreal) 3 Dec. 1992: F1

(The correct spelling here is *they're*.)

> . . . his reading rewarded his solitude and extended it, for their were few children his own age who could match his devotion to the printed word.
> *Calgary Herald* 8 Aug. 1992: B9

(The correct spelling here is *there*.)

> Big projects can acquire a life force of there own.
> *Queen's Quarterly* 92.2 (1985): 368

(The correct spelling here is *their*.)

theirs   *Theirs* is a possessive pronoun like *mine, ours, yours, his, hers,* and *its.* Like them, it has no apostrophe. However, because in many other contexts possession is indicated with an apostrophe, sometimes *theirs* is incorrectly written *their's*.

> For Canadians who want a united country, the best strategy is to stay cool, optimistic and flexible, and support those leaders who keep their heads while many about them are losing their's.
> *Ottawa Citizen* 3 Jan. 1991: A13

(The correct spelling is *theirs*.)

See also ITS, IT'S; POSSESSIVE.

[theirselves]   see [HISSELF]

them, those   'Do you like them?' is Standard English, but 'Do you like them shoes?' is not. In Standard English, *them* never functions as an adjective. The accepted adjective form is *those*: 'Do you like those shoes?' The use of *them* as an adjective, though not uncommon, is stigmatized as an uneducated usage.

> 'Tell them kids to keep the hell outa the furnace room.'
> Max Braithwaite *The Night We Stole the Mountie's Car* 1971: 69

(The standard form is *those*.)

> . . . I even wrote the President, I scrawled out them words and took the letters to Miss Payne, my old school teacher and asked her would she fix the grammar.
> *Queen's Quarterly* 94.1 (1987): 92

(The standard form is *those*.)

[themself]   see -SELF, -SELVES

there   see THEIR

therefor   Once a variant of *therefore, therefor* now has a distinct meaning and pronunciation. Pronounced with the emphasis on the last syllable, the word means 'for that (*or* those)'. *Therefor* is rare; some dictionaries label it archaic, and its use is now confined mostly to legal and business writing.

The frigate program will be abandoned and replaced with icebreaker building, designs therefor having already been completed.
Ottawa Citizen 22 March 1986: B3

Sections 40 to 42 of the Constitution Act, 1982, are repealed and the following substituted therefor. . . .
Province (Vancouver) 10 June 1990: 40

The Inter-Church Committee for Refugees, a group comprised of representatives of most Canadian faiths, charged that the bill violates Canada's human rights guarantees and is therefor illegal.
Toronto Star 6 May 1987: A1

(The intended meaning here is 'as a result'; the correct spelling is *therefore*.)

therefore   see SENTENCES

there is, there are   *There is* or *there's* before a plural, as in 'There's more glasses somewhere,' is very informal. In writing, *there are* is required before a plural noun.

Before a collective noun, either *there is* or *there are* is correct: 'There is a whole group of people on your porch' or 'There are a host of options'. *There is* is more common.

A list of two or more things that begins with a singular noun is usually introduced by *there is*: 'There is time and money at stake'. *There are* is also correct.

'The day is gone when the league can rely on its hardcore fans—there's not enough hard-core fans to pay the bills.'
Leader-Post (Regina) 27 Feb. 1988: C5

(This is a quotation of informal speech. Even in semiformal writing, *there are* should replace *there's*.)

'If there's problems with residence life we'll just have to look at it and see if we can fix it.'
News North (Yellowknife) 26 Feb. 1990: 2

(To agree with the plural noun 'problems', *there's* should be *there are* and both *it's* should be *them*.)

We're talking travel accessories, of which there is a mind-boggling assortment available.
Chronicle-Herald (Halifax) 14 May 1988: 9

And where there are fitness programs, there is also above-average productivity, morale, motivation and loyalty among workers. . . .
London Free Press 28 April 1988: B8

(Here *there is* introduces a list that begins with a singular noun; *there are* would also be correct, but rarely introduces a list unless the first item mentioned is plural.)

See also AGREEMENT, GRAMMATICAL; COLLECTIVE NOUNS.

thesaurus   see SYNONYM

thesis, theses   see PLURALS

they   see EVERYONE

they're   see CONTRACTIONS; THEIR

thieves   see -F, -V-

think   see DON'T THINK

this week   see NEXT

this writer   see PRESENT WRITER

thither   see HITHER

Thompson   see NLAKA'PAMUX

thoroughbred   see PUREBRED

those   see ONE OF THOSE THINGS; THEM

though   see ALTHOUGH; COMMA

thrash, thresh   In rural Canada, the verb *thrash* is commonly used as a variant of *thresh*, meaning to separate grain from husks and stems. However, in standard urban dialects the two words are usually distinguished. *Thresh* refers to the farm operation (*threshing*), while *thrash* is almost always reserved for other meanings: to administer a beating, to flail one's limbs, to go over something repeatedly. To 'thrash something out' is to discuss it thoroughly in the hope of reaching a resolution or consensus.

> His triumph as he tracks down each part of his trouble has the quality of a man who has chased a burglar and given him a sound thrashing.
> Robertson Davies *A Voice from the Attic* 1960: 64

> He thrashes, moans; his elbow flails the window.
> Margaret Atwood *Life Before Man* 1979: 209

> The purpose of the conference was to bring all the leftwing elements of the party together to thrash out a common programme. . . .
> *Canadian Journal of History* 14.1 (1989): 24

> Fava beans can be shelled by hand or threshed by foot in a box or on a tarp.
> *TLC . . . for plants* Spring 1991: 57

> She does not want to line up and learn to throw grenades, she doesn't want to work a threshing machine. . . .
> Margaret Atwood *Life Before Man* 1979: 291

thru, thro', thruway   *Thru* is a chiefly American spelling variant of *through*. In Canada it is mainly restricted to journalism (usually in entertainment notices, etc., giving dates: 'Monday thru Thursday'). *Thru* was introduced by the American spelling-reform movement of the late nineteenth and early twentieth centuries. Major Canadian dictionaries label *thru* informal, and it should be avoided in formal writing. The poetic short form of *through* is *thro'* or *thro*.

Thruway, a common word for an expressway or toll highway in the United States, is fully established.

> It runs Tuesday thru Saturday for the next three weeks.
> *Province* (Vancouver) 10 July 1990: 2

> The easiest way is via Interstate 81 and the New York Thruway to the Massachusetts Turnpike.
> *Ottawa Citizen* 9 June 1990: G2

See also ROAD.

thunderous   see DISASTROUS

thus, [thusly]   Some people are tempted to add *-ly* to *thus* in order to make it an adverb (as *quick* is turned into *quickly*). In fact, *thus* is itself an adverb and hence does not require an *-ly* ending. Though *thusly* is listed in some dictionaries, many people consider it pompous or even ridiculous.

> She dedicates the novel thusly: 'To my Ryerson colleagues, not one of whom is depicted in these pages.'
> *Globe and Mail* 28 Nov. 1985: D1

(Here *as follows*, *in this way*, or *thus* would be a better choice.)

tidal wave, tsunami   Strictly speaking, *tidal waves* are not tidal. These enormous, destructive ocean waves are usually caused by seismic activity. Geographers and oceanographers use the borrowed Japanese term *tsunami* (from *tsu*, 'harbour', and *nami*, 'wave'). In technical use, *tsunami* (pronounced *tsoo NAM ee*) is the appropriate term; however, *tidal wave* is well-established and unobjectionable in general use.

> Underwater seismic activity off Mexico's southern coast produced a tidal wave that swept away 300 homes in the fishing village of Cuajinicuilapa.
> *Vancouver Sun* 30 June 1990: B7

> The Japanese have discovered that low-lying bushes or hedges dissipate the effects of tsunamis—the giant waves which are generated by undersea earthquakes and volcanic eruptions.
> *Globe and Mail* (Toronto) 29 May 1985: P13

> Even before Los Angeles rapper Ice-T opened his mouth Wednesday night at the Commodore, the anticipation of what he might say had already sent out enough tsunamis of outrage. . . .
> *Vancouver Sun* 16 Aug. 1990: B7

(Here *tsunamis* is used figuratively.)

tight   see ADVERBS WITHOUT -LY

'til, till   see UNTIL

timber, lumber   Many Canadian and American writers distinguish between *timber*, wood to be cut, and *lumber*, the processed product ready for use in building. Thus Canadians refer to a 'stand of timber' but a 'lumberyard', though they may refer to a single piece of finished wood, such as a beam in a house, as a *timber*.

The primary meaning of *lumber* in British English is what North Americans call *junk*: useless and cumbersome objects. The North American *lumberyard* is a *timberyard* in Britain.

> Peeking his head out from the branches more than 25 metres above ground, Victoria resident Paul Winstanley said he took up residence in the tree to protest logging old-growth timber.
> *Province* (Vancouver) 9 Dec. 1990: 14

> Hazelwood said Northwood's sawmills can produce 680 million board feet of lumber annually.
> *Province* (Vancouver) 30 Nov. 1990: 64

> . . . here was a crudely squared-off four-inch by four-inch timber almost six feet long, exactly like the kind used to shore up a mine shaft.
> *Atlantic Salmon Journal* Autumn (1990): 28

See also TIMBER, TIMBRE.

timber, timbre *Timber* is wood. *Timbre* is a musical term for the tonal quality that identifies a particular musical instrument or singing voice. Although Canadians are used to seeing either *-re* or *-er* at the ends of words such as *theatre* and *centre*, the spelling of *timber* and *timbre* is invariable. Both words can be pronounced to rhyme with *limber*. *Timbre* is more often pronounced to rhyme with *amber*, or, in a closer approximation of its original French pronunciation, *TAHM bruh*.

> Her rich, strong voice has the timbre that characterizes great Strauss interpreters. . . .
> *Globe and Mail* (Toronto) 28 Feb. 1985: E6

See also -RE, -ER; TIMBER, LUMBER.

time, a.m., p.m., midnight, noon A colon separates the hours and minutes of the time of day in Canadian and American English ('8:15'), while in British English a period is used ('8.15'). The abbreviations *a.m.* and *p.m.*—also correctly but less commonly written without periods, with capital letters, etc.—stand for the Latin words *ante meridiem* and *post meridiem*, 'before noon' and 'after noon'.

'Five in the afternoon', 'five o'clock in the afternoon', '5:00 in the afternoon', '5:00 p.m.', and '5 p.m.' are all acceptable ways of writing the time. However, '5 p.m. in the afternoon' is redundant, and style guides also reject 'five p.m.', on the grounds that *a.m* and *p.m.* should be used only with figures.

A.m. and *p.m.* should not be used to distinguish midnight from noon. Even usage guides do not agree on which abbreviation belongs to which twelve o'clock. It's best to write '12 midnight' or '12 noon'.

The twenty-four-hour clock eliminates the confusion inherent in having a twelve-hour cycle occur twice each day: noon is 12:00; midnight is 24:00 or 00:00; 12:45 a.m. is 00:45; 6 p.m. is 18:00, and so on. This system is used internationally and is familiar to francophone Canadians. Most English Canadians, on the other hand, grapple with it only in bus and train schedules and do not have an idiom ('Come about 19:30') to use the system conversationally.

The convention for presenting an elapsed time, such as the winning time in a race, is to separate the hours, minutes, and seconds by colons and to separate the seconds from the tenths or hundredths of a second by a decimal point. Thus '2:18:49.89' means 'two hours, eighteen minutes, and 49.89 seconds'.

> We had been warned that we had to be on board before 4.00 p.m. . . .
> George Ignatieff *The Making of a Peacemonger* 1987: 26

> (The use of a period instead of a colon in the time is not common in Canada.)

> In Ottawa he had the reputation of staying all night at his desk, leaving behind a pile of work for his clerks at 6 a.m. and returning at ten o'clock looking as fresh as ever.
> Pierre Berton *The Promised Land* 1984: 19

> Then, a minute or two before 12 noon, Lemaire moves.
> Ken Dryden *The Game* 1983: 108

> Summerland's Linda Stenseth topped the women in 2:55.17.
> *Vancouver Sun* 9 Oct. 1990: C4

(This race was a marathon. The winning time was nearly three hours—2:55:17, with two colons—not two minutes and 55.17 seconds.)

See also DATES, AHEAD, BACK; STANDARD TIME.

time period　see PERIOD OF TIME

times less, times more　Many language commentators maintain that the phrase *times less* ('costs five times less') is illogical because 'times' suggests multiplication, not division. They prefer 'One-tenth as much rain this summer' to 'Ten times less rain this summer'. On the other hand, these expressions are idiomatic, and many reputable writers have used them.

Commentators also prefer '*x* times as many/much' to '*x* times more' in comparisons, because '*x* times more' is ambiguous. If Sanjay has three apples, then saying that Lee has 'five times more' could mean either that Lee has three apples and then fifteen *more* (on top of that), or simply that Lee has fifteen apples. In contexts where precision matters, it is clearer to say '*x* times as many' or '*x* times as much'.

> . . . worse still, she does not perform the function parents insistently demand of their children: extending their egos . . . making them feel authoritative and important to someone, even if that someone is six times smaller than he or she.
> Janice Kulyk Keefer *Reading Mavis Gallant* 1989: 114

> Keep the engine in tune because a badly tuned car may emit ten times more pollution than one that's well maintained.
> *Vancouver Sun* 9 Oct. 1990: 13

(In a scientific context, 'ten times *as much* pollution *as* one . . .' would be more precise.)

time zones　see STANDARD TIME

tingly, [tingley]　see -Y, -EY

tint　see COLOUR

tip of the iceberg　see CLICHÉ

titillate, titivate　To *titillate*, derived from the Latin word for 'tickle', means to amuse or excite. *Titivate* is an old-fashioned, humorous word meaning to spruce up or adorn something, often oneself. Sometimes *titillate* is misspelled *titilate*, and sometimes it is confused with *titivate*.

> It's a judgment call, but one based on the highest sense of professionalism, not on prurient curiosity intended to titillate.
> Richard Davies and Glen Kirkland, eds. *Dimensions* 1986: 147

> A driver applies mascara to her eyelashes in the rearview mirror as she zips along in the passing lane of the 401. . . . Surely these movers and sprucers worry about safety. 'Definitely,' states one traffic light titivator, 'but beauty comes first.'
> *Toronto Star* 21 Nov. 1992: H1

> It would be the easiest thing in the world for me to write a rhapsodic tribute that would titivate the jaded tastebuds of Stratford or Charlottetown. . . .
> *Globe and Mail* (Toronto) 13 April 1986: E1

(The word required here is *titillate*.)

title　see ENTITLE

titles of people　A good general Canadian reference to titles, honours, and forms of address is the *Canadian Almanac and Directory*, published annually (Toronto: Canadian Almanac & Directory Publishing Co.). The *Canadian Press Stylebook* contains a useful section on military ranks, titles, and abbreviations.

See also ATTRIBUTIVE NOUNS, FALSE TITLES; DOCTOR; HONOURABLE; MISS, MRS., MR.; MS.; RELIGIOUS TITLES.

titles of works　see ITALICS AND QUOTATION MARKS; THE, A, AN

toboggan　see SLED

toe the line, toe the mark　The first word in this idiom is *toe*, not *tow*. This expression, meaning to do what is expected of one, to conform to the rules, is a figurative use of a term once used literally in sports such as foot racing and boxing, where contestants began the event by positioning themselves with a toe touching a line or mark. Contemporary writers often appear to have a tug-of-war, rather than a foot race, in mind.

> Lolita makes him toe the mark by threats of exposure and prison; Humbert keeps her somewhat in check by counterthreats that if he goes to jail, she goes to reform school.
> Robertson Davies *A Voice from the Attic* 1960: 244

> I believe the station is sending a message to broadcasters to tow the line or face the consequences.
> *Province* (Vancouver) 11 June 2003: A21

(The correct spelling is *toe*.)

See also FOLK ETYMOLOGY.

together   The adverb *together* is often criticized as redundant after the verbs *assemble, connect, join,* and *gather;* yet usage guides do not suggest that *together* should never follow these verbs. Sometimes it is used effectively for emphasis or balance: 'For where two or three are gathered together in my name, I am there in the midst of them' (Matthew 18:20).

See also ALL TOGETHER; TOGETHER WITH.

together with, as well as, in addition to
Together with, in addition to, and *as well as* are compound prepositions introducing phrases that—at least in grammatical terms—are parenthetical, and thus do not affect the verb. When *together with, as well as,* or *in addition to* is used to link a singular noun to another noun, the verb that follows must be singular: 'A strong theoretical background, together with some practical experience, is what we are looking for'. All these expressions are different from the linking word *and. And* links two singular nouns to create a compound subject requiring a plural verb: 'A college diploma *and* some practical experience *are* what we are looking for'. Overall, Canadian writers follow the recommended usage.

The other, Arsino de las Casas, together with his wife Elena, provides me with a link to the outside world.
Canadian Fiction Magazine 63 (1988): 122

The modest increase, together with Thursday's report of a 0.6-per-cent drop in retail sales in April, was likely to allay some of the fears in financial markets. . . .
Chronicle-Herald (Halifax) 14 May 1988: 31

See also AGREEMENT, GRAMMATICAL; TOGETHER.

toilet   see EUPHEMISMS

tomatoes   see -OS, -OES

tome   Although it originally referred to a volume in a set, *tome* can now refer to any large, heavy book. *Tome* is often used facetiously in light writing and journalism.

> This tome was a monumental contribution to law and became known as Justinian's Code.
> J.E. Smyth et al. *The Law and Business Administration in Canada* 1987: 46

> . . . [Middlemarch] will be serialized on PBS over the next six weeks. . . . The sound you hear is the mass exhalation of students with this weighty tome on their reading list.
> *Ottawa Citizen* 9 April 1994: F5

ton, tonne (metric)   see APPENDIX II

tone   see COLOUR

too   see ADJECTIVES AND ADVERBS; NOT TOO

toonie   see LOONIE

toothsome, toothy   *Toothsome* means pleasant to the taste or palatable, as in 'a toothsome piece of cheesecake'. It is also used figuratively and often jocularly to mean sexually attractive. *Toothsome* does not mean *toothy*, as in 'He flashed a toothy grin'.

> A plateful of the obscure wild vegetable purslane—cooked or raw—is surprisingly toothsome. . . .
> *Province* (Vancouver) 1 June 1990: 52

Like Playboy of 30 years ago, Scope Magazine surrounds its essential content, pictures of toothsome girls, with heavy articles on issues of the day.
Ottawa Citizen 10 May 1990: I1

As a stage personality, he has a distinct affinity with our national animal; like the beaver, he's toothy, genial and insanely busy. . . .
Globe and Mail (Toronto) 18 Sept. 1985: T10

top of, be on   see IDIOMS

toque   see TUQUE

Torah   see SACRED WRITINGS

tornado   see CYCLONE

Torontonian   see NAMES OF RESIDENTS OF CITIES AND PROVINCES

torpedoes   see -OS, -OES

tortuous, torturous   *Tortuous* means full of twists and turns, circuitous, as in 'tortuous roads' or 'tortuous conversation'. It can also mean devious: 'a tortuous mind'. *Torturous* means excruciatingly painful: 'torturous medical tests'. The senses of these words often overlap: for example, a 'tortuous negotiation' can also be 'torturous' to the participants.

The tortuous streets narrowed and climbed in steps, but cobbles had been replaced like missing teeth, and the centuries sand-blasted from the rough stone exteriors of houses.
Queen's Quarterly 96.2 (1989): 354

During a decade of tortuous negotiations . . . the Crees managed, if not to stop the project, to exact a multimillion dollar price.
Gazette (Montreal) 12 May 1990: K3

For almost half a century, efforts to develop a less archaic and torturous method of trapping animals have been made by assorted interests. . . .
Gazette (Montreal) 18 June 1990: B2

'Repeatedly beating and mutilating someone else can only be described as tortuous conduct.'
Calgary Herald 30 June 1994: A24

(Here the word needed is *torturous*.)

Tory   see CONSERVATIVE

total, totally   *Total* and *totally* are overused modifiers that can often be omitted with no loss of meaning or emphasis. In fact, phrases such as 'total fiasco', 'totally annihilated', and 'totally eradicated' are probably more emphatic without the modifiers.

See also DOUBLING THE FINAL CONSONANT.

tow   see TOE THE LINE

toward(s)   see -WARD(S)

to wit   *To wit* is criticized as an old-fashioned and legalistic phrase meaning namely or that is (to say). It is rare in contemporary Canadian usage and is most often used humorously.

Back in 1066, a chap by the name of William the Conqueror invaded England and, as conquerors will, demanded that his new subjects speak his language—to wit: Norman French.
Province (Vancouver) 1 Nov. 1990: 40

toxic, toxin   see POISON

toy poodle   see DALMATIAN

traceable   see -ABLE, (-E)ABLE

track   see TACK

trademarks, brand names   A *trademark* is a distinctive name or logo, registered in law, that identifies products or services in the marketplace as those of a particular company. A company can lose exclusive rights to a registered name if it can be proven that the name is no longer associated with a particular brand in people's minds. Brand names for new products, especially products for which there is no established term, are often used generically. In addition, brand names are sometimes used figuratively to suggest something quite different from the original sense (as in the phrase 'a Band-Aid solution', where 'Band-Aid' means inadequate).

In both these cases, brand names sometimes appear in writing without the capital letters that distinguish them as trademarks. This usage is strongly discouraged by trademark-owners who risk losing sole rights to brand names they have marketed. Sometimes, when a usage that infringes on a trademark appears in a publication that is widely circulated and influential, such as a dictionary or large-circulation newspaper, the owners of the trademark take legal action against the publisher. For this reason it is standard practice in certain kinds of writing, particularly journalism, to capitalize all trademarks ('Kleenex', 'Aspirin', 'Band-Aid') or to use their generic equivalents ('tissue', 'painkiller', 'adhesive bandage').

The *Canadian Trade Index*, a database maintained online by the association of Canadian Manufacturers and Exporters, lists trademarks registered in Canada. A long list of generic equivalents for common trademarks can be found in the *Canadian Press Stylebook*.

Note that the common-noun elements in brand names are usually not capitalized: 'Bic pen'.

'They also used to have a trademark on the term "jumbo" but they lost too many legal battles and it became accepted as part of the vernacular.'
Calgary Herald 7 Nov. 1993: C1

Royal Bank's trademark lion is now migrating to Royal Trust's logo, a discreet symbol of its $1.6 billion takeover that combines the country's biggest bank with its second-biggest trust company.
Vancouver Sun 27 Dec. 1993: D9

Ticket prices are kept low, shows are usually benefits, and promotion consists of cheaply Xeroxed posters plastered all over town.
Ottawa Citizen 25 Sept. 1993: F1

trafficking   see -C-, -CK-

tragedy   In literature a *tragedy* is the story of the downfall of a heroic figure; a modern tragedy may feature a more ordinary figure who suffers (and usually dies) as a result of psychological or social conflicts. These literary definitions have led some critics to object to the use of *tragedy* to describe minor misfortunes and mishaps. To avoid being accused of lacking a sense of proportion, it's probably best to reserve *tragedy* for events that involve loss of human life or potential.

The death of seven American astronauts was a tragedy.
Maclean's 24 Feb. 1986: 2

It would be a tragedy to do away with the zoo altogether.
Vancouver Sun 9 Nov. 1990: B6

(Here *tragedy* is rather strong; *regrettable* might be better.)

The tragedy is that to most youngsters in primary school, science is perceived as a formal, mechanistic, passionless activity.
Queen's Quarterly 93.1 (1986): 89

(That science is perceived in this way is a sad fact, but not irreversible, not a *tragedy*.)

trail   see ROAD

trainers   see RUNNING SHOES

traipse, trapes   *Traipse* is an informal verb of unknown origin meaning to walk, wander, or trudge. *Trapes* is a rare alternative spelling.

Mary Had a Little Lamb . . . was based on Mary Sawyer, whose lamb would traipse after her like a pet dog.
Vancouver Sun 3 July 1990: 20

transferable, [transferrable]   The standard spelling is *transferable*. Among major dictionaries, only *Merriam-Webster's* lists *transferrable* as an acceptable alternative. Most authorities consider the double *r* an error, even though it follows the common spelling rule to double the final consonant of a *stressed* syllable before adding an ending. (*Transferable*, unlike *preferable*, is usually stressed on the second syllable.)

Such subscription rights are transferrable.
J.E. Smyth et al. *The Law and Business Administration in Canada* 1987: 710

(The more widely accepted spelling is *transferable*.)

See also DOUBLING THE FINAL CONSONANT.

transgendered people   see SEXUAL MINORITIES

translatable   see -ABLE, (-AT)ABLE

transparent, opaque, translucent, luminous, clear, colourless   Ordinary window glass is *transparent*: you can see everything through it. Wood is *opaque*: you can't see through it. Most white paper is *translucent*, or semi-transparent: only shadowy forms can be seen through it. *Transparent* and *opaque* are also used figuratively, the first to mean easily seen through and the second to mean obscure or difficult to understand.

A *translucent* material does not emit light; it only lets light through. The word *luminous* refers to something that emits light. Nevertheless, these words are used interchangeably in figurative contexts, especially in reference to skin or complexions.

Transparent and *clear* are synonyms; note, however, that these terms do not necessarily mean colourless. A piece of stained glass or a tinted lens can be described as transparent or clear.

. . . they realized that translucent glass doors would admit light into a dark entry from a windowed kitchen.
Globe and Mail (Toronto) 7 Dec. 1985: G3

This week's tour by senior federal cabinet ministers in Alberta is a transparent effort to win back Tory party supporters, opposition MPs said. . . .
Ottawa Citizen 6 Sept. 1990: A5

She is opaque as a rock.
Margaret Atwood *Life Before Man* 1979: 199

The same features that can make Pfeiffer look gorgeous in another movie—the translucent skin, the large lopsided mouth—make her look interesting in Frankie & Johnny.
Maclean's 21 Oct. 1991: A98

While her latest heroine is obsessed with the physical ravages of middle age, Atwood seems to be holding up well: she is physically striking, with luminous skin and penetrating blue eyes.
Maclean's 3 Oct. 1988: A56

Glass on all windows facing the Cardinal's house would be opaque.
Globe and Mail (Toronto) 15 May 1985: M4

(Presumably windows let in some light: perhaps *translucent* or *frosted* was intended here.)

'I think it's a translucent opera. You can see the motives clearly.'
Globe and Mail (Toronto) 5 Oct. 1985: D5

(The word required here is *transparent*: *translucent* suggests that things can't be seen clearly.)

Another tapered-waist vase in rich red, emerald green, blue and clear glass, fetched a little less— $1,840.
Canadian Collector 21.4 (1986): 30

(Here *clear* means colourless.)

The filigrana technique embeds threads of glass in opaque white or colours within clear glass of another colour.
Canadian Collector 21.4 (1986): 30

(Here *clear* glass is coloured.)

See also IRIDESCENT.

transpire   Plants *transpire*, which means that they release water vapour. More generally, *transpire* means to leak out or to be emitted. In the eighteenth century *transpire* began to be used figuratively of secrets that had leaked out or become known. Used in this figurative way, sometimes 'It transpired that . . .' seemed to mean 'It came about that . . .', and by the early 1800s *transpire* was being used as a synonym for *happen* or *occur*.

Because this newest sense of *transpire* was based on a misunderstanding, it has been bitterly disputed. Some people still regard it as incorrect, even though reputable writers have used *transpire* in this sense for well over a century. Most dictionaries now list 'happen' as a standard meaning, and Canadian writers commonly use the word in this way. However, if you are sensitive to criticism you may want to restrict *transpire* to contexts where 'come to be known' would also fit.

. . . trees transpire—that is, they breathe in dry, carbon-dioxide-laden air and breathe out moisture

and oxygen.
Harrowsmith Jun.–Jul. 1985: 27

Shock gripped neighbours and friends, who could only wonder what had transpired inside the white bungalow that had served as the family home for many decades.
Daily News (Halifax) 23 Dec. 2005: 3

(This is the disputed use.)

transsexual   see SEXUAL MINORITIES

trapes   see TRAIPSE

travel   see DOUBLING THE FINAL CONSONANT

travelwise   see -WISE

truly   see -E

trawler, troller   *Trawler* and *troller* (pronounced *TRAW ler* or *TROLE er*) both refer to a boat that drags a fish-catching contraption through the water, or to a person who fishes from such a boat. *Trawling* is a type of commercial fishing: a *trawler* is a large boat equipped to catch fish, either by dragging a bag-shaped net (trawl net) along the ocean floor or by trailing a long buoyed line (trawl line) to which are attached short lines with baited hooks. *Trolling* generally refers to a type of sport fishing in which a fishing line, often rotating, is dragged behind a slowly moving boat.

In British Columbia, a distinction is made in the commercial fishery between *trollers*, which fish with baited hooks, and *trawlers*, which fish with a trawl net.

. . . a small dock sheltered a beamy rowboat with a small battery-powered motor for trolling. . . .
Howard Engel *Murder Sees the Light* 1984: 67

They were trolling with downriggers and using a Cisco Kid red-and-white artificial bait when the trophy fish struck.
Whig-Standard (Kingston) 14 Oct. 1986: 1

Maritime National Fish Ltd. operated five trawlers, each of which was fitted with an otter trawl for catching fish. . . .
J.E. Smyth et al. *The Law and Business Administration in Canada* 1987: 327

Mr. Fraser offered last week to allocate 35,000 chinook . . . to commercial trollers, with the rest for anglers.
Globe and Mail (Toronto) 19 April 1985: P8

(In British Columbia *trollers* are commercial vessels.)

tread, trod, trodden   *Tread* is an irregular verb, with the past tense *trod* and the past participle *trod* or *trodden*:

Don't tread any more mud into the living room.

Yesterday, the whole soccer team trod mud into the carpet.

You've trod(den) on my petunias.

Occasionally, in Canadian and American English, *tread* is treated as a regular verb with the past tense and past participle *treaded*: 'He treaded water for thirty minutes'. *Treaded* is unlikely to arouse much controversy if it is limited to this one aquatic context.

However, a surprisingly large number of writers treat *trod* as the present tense of the verb ('Every time I tango, I trod on my partner's feet'), with the past tense and past participle *trod* or *tread*. This usage, probably influenced by the verb *trot*, is definitely non-standard.

But if judicial attention were turned to the operation of the legislative branch of government, it would have to tread lightly.
Andrew Heard *Canadian Constitutional Conventions* 1991: 99

On their first date, the St. Andrew's Ball, Wilson wore a kilt and trod on her feet on the dance floor.
Saturday Night March 1986: 23

The way ahead led through the bush on a path that had been well trodden at one time, but which was beginning to allow new growth through the packed earth.
Howard Engel *Murder Sees the Light* 1984: 115

He looked at the crystal-dark heavens and treaded water slowly, throbbing up and down as his head circled the sky.
Queen's Quarterly 93.2 (1989): 320

Football observers have long thought that the CFL has treaded on the NFL's toes by expanding into the U.S. with four franchises.
Province (Vancouver) 25 July 1994: A36

(The usual past participle is *trod* or *trodden*.)

Fillion learned to trod the boards here starting with high school plays. . . .
Edmonton Journal 28 April 1994: D3

(The correct form here is *to tread*.)

It's not news that the traditional family is trodding down the dinosaur path.
Vancouver Sun 20 Nov. 1990: B3

(Either 'treading the dinosaur path' or 'trotting down the dinosaur path' would do here.)

Treaty Indian   see ABORIGINAL PEOPLE(S)

treble   see TRIPLE

trek   A *trek* is a long, slow journey, especially one made over land. English borrowed *trek* from the Afrikaans verb *trekken*, meaning to travel or make an organized migration. The word was used to describe the northward migrations of the Boers of South Africa during the eighteenth and nineteenth centuries. Even when it is used humorously, *trek* should connote an arduous journey.

He and the other Klondikers faced a 64 kilometre trek over the notoriously steep White Pass.
Up Here Jan.–Feb. 1990: 33

. . . there was the long journey across Europe from their home villages, then the stormy ocean voyage in the holds of immigrant ships, and finally the trek first by rail and then by ox cart to their prairie homesteads.
Pierre Berton *The Promised Land* 1984: 45

It was a Saturday night near the end of my first rickshaw season when a co-runner and I were making our usual trek back from Hull.
Ottawa Citizen 10 Dec. 1993: C5

tremor, earth tremor, temblor   Canadians use *tremor* and *earth tremor* as synonyms for *earthquake*. Americans also use *temblor*, a word borrowed from Spanish. *Tremblor* is a misspelling of the Spanish borrowing; some authorities also consider *trembler* a misspelling,

but others accept it as a colloquial term for an earthquake, derived from the verb *tremble*. In formal writing *tremor* is a better choice.

Every few months, many residents of Victoria hear dishes rattling because of barely perceptible earth tremors.
Maclean's 1 May 1989: A59

Meanwhile, the U.S. National Earthquake Information Centre . . . said in a news release that the official magnitude for the first temblor on the Richter scale of earthquake intensity had been revised up to 8.1.
Globe and Mail (Toronto) 26 Sept. 1985: P14

(This report is from an American press agency.)

. . . the Arctic trembler was nearly as strong as the horrifying San Francisco quake last October.
Up Here Mar.–Apr. 1990: 11

(This usage is informal; in formal writing *tremor* is preferred.)

triceps   see BICEPS

trillion   see BILLION

triple, treble   *Triple* and *treble* are interchangeable both as verbs meaning to make or become three times greater and as adjectives meaning threefold or three-part. *Triple* has also acquired specific associations having to do with sports: 'triples' in baseball, the 'Triple Crown' in horse racing, the 'triple axel' in skating, and the 'triple jump' in track and field, to name but a few. In addition, *treble* has a special musical sense: high-pitched or above middle C. In Canadian English *treble* is used far less commonly than *triple*, but it is sometimes favoured by business writers.

To root them out, the Montreal immigration office plans to more than triple its inspectors to 20.
Gazette (Montreal) 4 March 1988: B1

The company will treble Canadian purchases and plans to build a $25-million parts plant north of Toronto.
Globe and Mail (Toronto) 31 May 1985: B6

triumphant, triumphal   *Triumphant* refers to people—specifically, those who are victorious and exultant. Objects that commemorate a victory and activities contingent on victory or success are *triumphal*: 'triumphal arch', 'triumphal parade', 'triumphal tour'. People are never *triumphal*, though a mood can be either *triumphant* or *triumphal*.

> We reached London in July 1919 just in time to see a triumphant Lord Haig ride through the city at the head of a parade which marked the victory of British forces over their World War I enemies.
> George Ignatieff *The Making of a Peacemonger* 1987: 31

> The triumphal gates were typical of exhibition architecture while the statue was modelled on the Winged Goddess of Samothrace in the Louvre.
> *Toronto Star* 17 June 1987: A6

trivial, trivia   *Trivial* means insignificant or trifling. The noun form *trivia* is derived from a Latin plural meaning 'unimportant matters'. In English *trivia* is usually treated as a plural form, but few object to its use as a singular.

> In a free society the dull stuff of politics is often the important stuff, but the exciting trivia command the most attention.
> *Vancouver Sun* 23 June 1990: B4

> (Here *trivia* is treated as a plural noun.)

> In the end, such trivia is about all we have to work with.
> *Province* (Vancouver) 10 Oct. 1990: 63

> (Here *trivia* is treated as a singular noun.)

See also COLLECTIVE NOUNS.

trod, trodden   see TREAD

troller   see TRAWLER

troop, troupe, trooper, trouper, troops
Both *troop* and *troupe* come from the Middle French word *troupe*, 'group' or 'herd'. In modern English *troop* and its variants usually refer to military or uniformed groups of some kind, while *troupe* is reserved for groups of actors or entertainers. Thus a *trooper* is a cavalry soldier or an American state police officer, while a *trouper* is an actor, usually an experienced one who can

be counted on to perform well under difficult circumstances. It is this kind of theatrical trouper that the expression *old* (or *real*) *trouper* refers to—someone who carries on through good and bad. Traditionally associated with *troopers* is an aptitude for swearing: 'swears like a trooper'.

Although a *troop* is a military unit, the plural form *troops* usually refers to individuals: for example, '10,000 troops' means 10,000 soldiers, not 10,000 groups of soldiers.

> That . . . is what the old trooper hopes as he prepares to play one of his most important roles.
> *Globe and Mail* (Toronto) 27 May 1985: P12

> (The correct spelling is *trouper*.)

truculent, truculence   The first meaning of *truculent* (pronounced TRUK yu lunt) was fierce or savage, as in 'truculent wars', but now *truculent* means defiant or belligerent. The noun form is *truculence* or, rarely, *truculency*.

> The view of public spirit promoted by Thomas Gordon in *Cato's Letters* suggested a more active and truculent citizenship than had been advocated by many others.
> J.A.W. Gunn *Beyond Liberty and Property* 1983: 269

> 'He was quiet, reflective, a little drunk, maybe, a little truculent, but nothing wild.'
> Howard Engel *Murder Sees the Light* 1984: 103

> Tiger was a fighter but his public truculence has been over-emphasized.
> *Province* (Vancouver) 26 Feb. 1990: 27

true facts   Facts are true by definition. The phrase *true facts* is redundant except where there is an explicit contrast between alleged facts and true ones.

> I watched this episode and was in no way offended, but rather glad that at last the true facts of this campaign were being openly aired.
> *Ottawa Citizen* 14 Nov. 1992: A11

> If George Bush wanted to help his old friend Brian Mulroney, he might direct his ambassador in Ottawa to make a few pointed remarks about these true facts of American political life.
> *Financial Post* 16 April 1991: 13

> (Here *true* is redundant.)

trust company   see BANK

trustee, trusty   A *trustee* (pronounced *trus TEE*) is a member of a board that administers a corporation or institution, or a person appointed to administer property in trust. A *trusty* (pronounced *TRUS tee*; plural *trusties*) is a prison inmate who has been granted special privileges in recognition of good behaviour. The adjective *trusty* is an old-fashioned word meaning trustworthy; it may have a slightly comic effect in modern usage.

> Since she requires someone to administer the fund and to pay the money out for his care, she appoints a trustee.
> J. E. Smyth et al. *The Law and Business Administration in Canada* 1987: 288

> He said he initially asked for the assignment . . . because he knew it carried with it a highly prized trusty status within the prison system.
> *Winnipeg Free Press* 17 Nov. 1990: 20

> Red Green (Steve Smith) covers a chair with his trusty duct tape during a promotional appearance at a hardware store in Edmonton for his new film, Duct Tape Forever.
> *Gazette* (Montreal) 6 April 2006: D10

Tsilhqot'in   see CARRIER

tsunami   see TIDAL WAVE

Tsuu T'ina, Sarcee   Members of the Alberta First Nation living just south-west of Calgary are called *Tsuu T'ina* (singular and plural), pronounced *tsoo TEEN ah*. Their language, also called *Tsuu T'ina*, is a member of the Athapaskan family. Both the people and the language were formerly called Sarcee.

> . . . Roy Whitney, chief of the Tsuu T'ina Nation west of Calgary, formerly known as the Sarcee reserve, became the first Native appointed to the board.
> *Calgary Herald* 26 Nov. 1992: B1

> The [Treaty 7 Tribal Council] represents the Tsuu T'ina, Siksika, Peigan, Blood and Stoney Nations.
> *Calgary Herald* 3 Sept 1992: A3

See also ABORIGINAL PEOPLE(S); APPENDIX III.

tuff, tuft   *Tuff* is a porous rock formed from volcanic ash. A *tuft* is a bunch of hair, feathers, threads, or the like, joined together at one end.

> Molokini has Maui's only 'tuff' volcano cone, formed when molten rock superheats water inside the lava, exploding it into ash and dust. When cooled, it hardens into 'tuff,' a spongy, buff-colored rock.
> *Vancouver Sun* 3 Nov. 1990: E6

> Another guide [to distinguish the male panda from the female] . . . is the tuffs of fur, which are almost like whiskers, on Qing Qing's face.
> *Globe and Mail* (Toronto) 18 July 1985: M1

(The correct spelling is *tufts*. See the example that follows.)

> 'Tuffs'? Poor little Qing Qing. Imagine having to lug around chunks of volcanic detritus on his whiskers.
> *Globe and Mail* (Toronto) 29 July 1985: P6

(A reader caught the mistake.)

tummy   see BELLY

tundra, Barrens, Barrenlands, taiga   The *tundra*, in Canada also called the *Barrens*, the *Barrenlands*, or the *Barren Grounds*, is a huge region of the northern hemisphere characterized by permafrost, low-lying vegetation, muskeg, low annual precipitation, long dark winters, and short summers of almost continuous sunlight. In Canada the tundra extends from the Mackenzie Delta to James Bay and east to Labrador.

The Canadian *taiga* is the arc of forest just south of the tundra, consisting of spruce, fir, pine, and tamarack trees, as well as birch and poplar in the more southerly areas.

> You can revel in the colorful mosses, lichens and tiny wildflowers of the tundra, the stunted spruce and tamarack forest of the taiga. . . .
> *Globe and Mail* (Toronto) 15 June 1985: T7

> But fall is a time of abundance on the Barrens, so

we feast on the profusion of ripe berries at our feet.
Up Here Mar.–Apr. 1990: 26

All my reading had not prepared me for one strange thing about the Barrenlands: you always have the feeling that the land is somehow sentient, watching you.
Up Here Jan.–Feb. 1990: 43

And now the provincial government has just opened the Parc des Grand Jardins, a tract of mountains, forest and taiga that supports a caribou herd and is home to dozens of rare species of plants and flowers.
Gazette (Montreal) 14 July 1990: 13

See also SWAMP, MARSH, BOG, MUSKEG.

tuque, toque *Tuque* (the vowel pronounced as in *too* or *few*) is a Quebec French variant of the French word *toque*; originally it referred specifically to the long knitted hat worn by voyageurs and habitants. Adopted into English, it came to refer not only to these hats but also to any knitted woollen winter cap. Many, perhaps most, Canadian writers now spell this word *toque*. Either spelling is correct for the winter hat, but note that *toque* (when pronounced *TOKE*) has several other senses, including a chef's hat and a close-fitting brimless woman's hat.

'When she noticed I didn't have any hats, she went right to her house and gave me some of hers. She would give you the tuque off her head.'
Daily News (Halifax) 19 May 2006: 12

An ordinary toque and small earmuffs have been adequate when I am moving.
Up Here Mar.–Apr. 1990: 16

[The] chef, Shamash Brooks, is a Rastafarian. (His toque has an extra big balloon top to hold the dreadlocks.)
Calgary Herald 3 Aug. 1994: B7

turgid, turbid *Turgid* means swollen or distended; it is generally used figuratively to describe writing that is pompous or bombastic. *Turbid* means muddy or cloudy; it is a less common word than *turgid* and is most often used literally. The two words can appear in similar contexts, literal and figurative. A river in flood can be both turbid (muddy-coloured) and turgid (swollen beyond its banks). A poor piece of prose may be both turbid (unclear or obscure) and turgid (stuffy and overwritten). However, these words are not synonyms.

We all know of refereed journals that publish articles of inferior quality, that are dry as dust, turgid and predictable, and of unrefereed journals that are outstanding and have sparkle.
Queen's Quarterly 92.2 (1985): 442

Water in the Capilano and Seymour reservoirs is also turbid, which means Vancouverites will see cloudy water coming from their taps for the next while.
Vancouver Sun 27 Nov. 1990: A1

Turkish bath   see CAPITAL LETTERS

turn off, turn out   see CLOSE

turn-on   see PHRASAL VERBS

turnpike   see ROAD

'twas   see ARCHAISMS

twister   see CYCLONE

type   see WORDINESS

typhoid fever   see TYPHUS

typhoon   see CYCLONE

typhus, typhoid fever *Typhus* and *typhoid fever* are sometimes confused. In fact, typhoid fever was once thought to be a form of typhus, but now it is understood that the two diseases are caused by completely different micro-organisms.

Typhus is caused by various bacteria of the genus *Rickettsia* and spread by three kinds of insects: lice, fleas, and ticks. Ticks spread the variety of typhus known as Rocky Mountain Spotted Fever.

Typhoid fever, also known as enteric fever, is caused by the bacterium *Salmonella typhi*. It is spread by infected food, water, or food-prepara-tion workers; the most notorious of the latter was 'Typhoid Mary', a cook who was the source of an outbreak of typhoid in the U.S. in the 1930s.

tyre   see SPELLING, CANADIAN

U

ugly   see ADJECTIVES AND ADVERBS

ukelele   see UKULELE

Ukrainian, Ukraine   *Ukrainian* is often mis-spelled *Ukranian*. *Ukraine* has been preferred to *the Ukraine* since the country became independ-ent, in 1990, because the definite article sug-gests a geographic area ('the Caribbean', 'the Arctic', 'the Maritimes') rather than a political entity ('Scotland','Angola').

Independence has also created a burst of self-con-fidence that has spurred Ukranian officials to chal-lenge Moscow on the most fundamental issues.
Calgary Herald 28 Jan. 1992: A4

(The correct spelling is *Ukrainian*.)

Russian separatists in the Crimean peninsula of Ukraine have said delineation of the border with Russia could trigger armed resistance.
Vancouver Sun 24 June 1992: A8

In the spring of 1944, the Red Army came crash-ing into the Ukraine and the lands bordering the Black Sea.
Canadian Journal of History 14.1 (1989): 79

(In this historical reference *the Ukraine* is appro-priate.)

See also YUKON.

ukulele, ukelele   The Portuguese brought a small, four-string guitar to Hawaii in 1869, and the Hawaiians, who delighted in it and adapted it to their own musical style, called it a *uku lele*, purportedly, a 'flea leaping'. Because the second syllable of *ukulele* is unstressed in English, the second vowel is reduced to an indeterminate sound (schwa), reflected in an alternative spelling: *ukelele*. Both English spellings date from the nineteenth century, but the more common and more widely accepted spelling today is the one that parallels the Hawaiian: *ukulele*.

Ulster   see IRELAND

ultimate   see PENULTIMATE

ultimatum, ultimatums, ultimata   The usual plural of *ultimatum* is *ultimatums*. *Ultimata*, the Latin plural, is also correct but rare.

Ultimatums are sometimes used as a bully tactic to force a distraction from the problems at hand.
Toronto Star 22 July 2004: C2

. . . the forthcoming campaign . . . would, after all, have been launched with or without ultimata by the Liberal Senate.
Toronto Star 31 July 1988: B3

See also PLURALS, REGULAR, IRREGULAR, FOREIGN.

umlaut   see DIACRITICAL MARKS

un-   see IN-, UN-

unaffected   see DISAFFECTED

unaware, unawares   *Unaware* and *unawares* both date from the sixteenth century, and these words used to function interchangeably as both adjectives and adverbs. Now *unaware* is usually the adjective, often followed by *of* or *that* ('She is unaware of our visit'; 'He is unaware that she is here'), while *unawares* is the usual choice for adverbial use, as in 'stumble on something unawares' or 'be caught unawares'.

. . . three different specialists had been prescribing drugs for her, each unaware of what the other was doing.
Gazette (Montreal) 4 March 1989: A1

Many companies are developing policies on sexual harassment and those who aren't may find they are caught unawares.
Province (Vancouver) 22 May 1990: 49

unbeknownst, unbeknown   Usage commentators variously maintain that these words are dialectal, slang, humorous, or pretentious. Since *unbeknownst* and *unbeknown* are widely used in neutral contexts, you may ignore the controversy.

The trade can also be revoked if the player is seriously ill or injured, unbeknownst to the team acquiring him.
Financial Post 19 Oct. 1989: 51

That teen, the defence argued, was trying to impress the girl—who, unbeknown to the trio, was taping the phone call—with his dark and melodramatic boasts. . . .
Globe and Mail (Toronto) 11 Feb. 2005: A9

un-Canadian   see HYPHENATION

uncharted, unchartered   *Uncharted* means unmapped, unknown. *Unchartered* is a rare word meaning not furnished with a charter, unauthorized. People often mistakenly substitute *unchartered* for *uncharted* in such expressions as 'uncharted territory' and 'uncharted waters'.

. . . the American ship of state drifted irrevocably toward the rocks and threatened to drag other nations into the uncharted waters of political uncertainty.
William Teatero John Anderson: Fugitive Slave 1986: 111

Long before [the charter was issued], however, the board of the still unchartered university at Kingston had been constituted under the Act of Incorporation.
Hilda Neatby Queen's University 1 (1978): 28

Those are unchartered waters for the Blue Jays, their fans and Canada.
Daily News (Halifax) 5 Oct. 1992: 44

(The word required here is *uncharted*.)

uncomfortable   see -ABLE, -IBLE

unconscious   see CONSCIOUS

uncountable noun   see COUNTABLE entry in Glossary

undiscriminating   see INDISCRIMINATE

undoubtedly, undoubtably   *Undoubtedly* is an idiomatic expression meaning certainly or very likely. *Undoubtably* is a rare word meaning in a way that precludes doubt ('tests showed undoubtably . . .'). Sometimes *undoubtably* is used where idiom calls for *undoubtedly*.

. . . Dryden was arguably hockey's greatest goalie and undoubtedly its greatest pontificator.
Vancouver Sun 29 June 1993: D8

Other great greys include Spectacular Bid, undoubtably one of the best race horses of all time. . . .
Canadian Thoroughbred Aug. 1989: 15

(The word required here is *undoubtedly*.)

A tax of $100 for every tonne of carbon dioxide released into the atmosphere would undoubtably hit hard in Alberta. . . .
Vancouver Sun 23 March 1990: B2

(The word required here is *undoubtedly*.)

uneatable   see EDIBLE

uneducated   see entry in Glossary

unequivocal, unequivocally, [unequivocable], [unequivocably] *Unequivocal* means unmistakable, unambiguous. The adverb form is *unequivocally*. *Unequivocable* and *unequivocably* are nonstandard variant forms of these words.

> A resolution will go before the UN Security Council in the next few weeks, but it is still unclear whether it gives an unequivocable green light to the use of force against Iraq.
> *Ottawa Citizen* 21 Nov. 1991: A1

(The standard spelling is *unequivocal*.)

> We Canadians are far too polite but need to say unequivocably that we will not tolerate such repulsive behaviour.
> *Times-Colonist* (Victoria) 13 April 2004: A11

(The standard spelling is *unequivocally*.)

See also AMBIGUOUS, AMBIVALENT, EQUIVOCAL.

unexceptionable, unexceptional, exceptionable *Unexceptionable* means not open to criticism or objection; *unexceptional* means ordinary. An unexceptionable speech is irreproachable, while an unexceptional speech is lacklustre. The rare word *exceptionable* means giving cause for objection.

> Although the cleaning of the Sistine Chapel ceiling is complete, controversy still goes on about the project. . . . By now, most art historians and conservators have found the restoration procedures unexceptionable. . . .
> *Vancouver Sun* 11 Jan. 1992: D10

> The Bootle Freemans were similarly unremarkable, leading lives as unexceptional as those of any of their neighbors.
> *Calgary Herald* 13 Feb. 1994: B7

> The statement that an exotic dancer's 'profession is to promote lust' is not, on its own, exceptionable; that is indeed why such dancers are hired.
> *Globe and Mail* (Toronto) 13 Feb. 1985: P6

> Manning's support for free-market economics is unexceptional; his preference for balanced budgets is an admirable goal, difficult for any government to accomplish.
> *Financial Post* 26 June 1991: 11

(The intended sense appears to be *unexceptionable*, beyond reproach.)

unfriendly see FRIENDLY

unhuman see HUMAN

UNICEF, Unicef see ABBREVIATION; ALPHABETICAL ORDER

unilateral, bilateral, multilateral An action that is undertaken by one party is *unilateral*; by two parties, *bilateral*; and by three or more, *multilateral*. Generally these terms are applied to the acts of institutions or states rather than of people: 'unilateral declaration of independence', 'bilateral agreement'. But lately people as well as institutions have been accused of making 'unilateral (i.e., unnegotiated) decisions'.

> We should deal with the United States more often in multilateral forums to 'blunt (American) unilateral policies,' the foreign policy report recommends.
> *Toronto Star* 15 Nov. 1994: A1

> 'I don't need a motion,' he declared unilaterally, announcing one of his initiatives. 'I'll just fire that off.'
> *National Post* (Toronto) 20 Nov. 1999: B9

uninterested see DISINTERESTED

unique *Unique* means one of a kind or different from all others. Hence some critics maintain that it should not be used with modifiers such as *very*, *most*, or *more*, since nothing can be 'very' or 'more' one of a kind. Note, however, that something or someone can be almost or nearly one of a kind, and that *unique* has also been used as a synonym for terms such as *unusual*, *distinctive*, *exceptional*, *outstanding*, and *remarkable* since the early seventeenth century (*OED*). In this sense, *unique* can be modified. Although Canadian writers use *unique* in both ways, in formal writing the safest course is to use it only in the first sense.

> The rate at which these coastal, old-growth trees are being cut means that this unique forest is dis-

appearing just as the tropical forests are.
Irving M. Zeitlin and Robert J. Brym *The Social Condition of Humanity* 1991: 369

(Here *unique* means one of a kind.)

She is almost unique among Quebec writers in that her work has been translated into twelve languages.
Margaret Atwood *Second Words* 1982: 259

(Here *unique* means one of a kind.)

Perhaps the most unique attribute of this volume is the coverage given to the history of Japanese intelligence by Ian Nish and John Chapman.
Canadian Journal of History 14.1 (1989): 87

(Here *remarkable* or *outstanding* would be a better choice.)

See also COMPLETE; PERFECT.

United Church   The United Church is Canada's largest Protestant denomination. It was formed in 1925 through the union of the country's Methodists and Congregationalists with most of its Presbyterians. This denomination exists only in Canada. *United* (or *United Church*) is often used as an adjective: 'We're United; they're Catholic'.

In worship, Sunday-school classes and conferences, United Church members will soon be dissecting television and newspapers while exploring the church's 1990–91 mission theme: Gospel, Culture & Media: Where Do We Get Our Values?
Vancouver Sun 14 July 1990: A11

'[My mother] was United Church.'
Bruce Meyer and Brian O'Riordan, eds. *In Their Words* 1984: 138

See also MANSE.

United Empire Loyalist   see CONSERVATIVE

United Kingdom   see BRITAIN

United States   see AMERICAN

university, school, faculty, college, collegiate, community college, CEGEP   A *university* provides post-secondary education lead-

ing to degrees in a range of subjects; at the core of the university curriculum are the liberal arts and general sciences. Most Canadian universities grant graduate degrees and carry out advanced research. Within a university, a *school* focuses on a particular area of study: 'school of business', 'school of urban planning'. A *faculty* is a group of departments focused on a particular branch of knowledge: 'faculty of medicine', 'of law', 'of engineering'. The teaching staff of a university is referred to as the *faculty*, or *faculty members*.

In Canada, a *college* is either a private high school, part of a university, or a community college. Within a university, a college usually has its own teaching staff, classrooms, and residence. Unlike Americans, Canadians seldom use *college* as a synonym for *university*. Since many high schools in Ontario are called *collegiate institutes*, the term *collegiate* is as likely to refer to secondary as to post-secondary education.

Community colleges, found in all provinces and territories, were first established in the 1960s to provide post-secondary education, including vocational and technical courses, relevant to the needs of the community. Community college programs usually grant diplomas, but some colleges offer a limited range of first- and second-year university courses, and a few grant university degrees. The trend is toward increasing integration of college and university programs. In Quebec a community college is called a *CEGEP* (pronounced *SAY zhep*), an acronym for 'Collège d'enseignement général et professionel'; most university-bound students in Quebec first attend CEGEP (see QUEBEC ENGLISH) for two years.

unkempt, unkept   An untidy personal appearance is *unkempt*, from the Middle English word 'uncombed'. The word's meaning has broadened to the extent that even kitchen counters and landscapes are described as *unkempt*.

Promises broken are promises *unkept*. The use of *unkept* to mean untidy or not kept up is not wrong but rare in contemporary edited prose.

Looking unkempt and a tad dishevelled at 20 can look quite adorable. It gets less and less adorable with every passing decade.
Ottawa Citizen 14 Jan. 2006: I9

But they did have a certain stamina and resourcefulness engendered by the climate, terrain, and ruggedness of the unkempt Laurentian slopes.
The Beaver Dec. 2001–Jan. 2002: 21

Left-wing supporters, on the other hand, say the unrest has been fueled by government cutbacks, decades of unkept promises and a culture of despair fed by persistent unemployment.
National Post (Toronto) 8 Nov. 2005: A10

'We end up paying higher taxes and our land value is going to go down because of unkept roads and no benefits.'
Calgary Herald 13 Feb. 2006: B6

(*Unkept* meaning 'not kept up' is not common in edited prose. Here it appears in quoted speech.)

unlawful   see ILLEGAL

unmoral   see IMMORAL

unorganized   see DISORGANIZED

unpractical   see IMPRACTICAL

unravel   see RAVEL

unreadable, illegible   Both words can refer to a text that cannot be read because the person who wrote it had bad handwriting, because the ink on the page has faded, etc. However, only *unreadable* can be used to describe material that is legible but so dull or poorly organized that no one can bear to read it.

The price for a pound is large, the price for a kilogram is small, sometimes so tiny it is almost illegible.
Globe and Mail (Toronto) 24 Oct. 1985: A1

. . . his plays were performed only in living rooms or read, like the covert samizdat works of banned Russian artists, on secretly-circulated typescripts that became fainter and fainter with every photo-

copying so that by the sixth or seventh edition of these 'un-books' on onion-skin, the text was practically unreadable.
Vancouver Sun 6 Jan. 1990: E3

Theal and other historians of southern Africa who wrote long and detailed narratives were often unreadable.
Queen's Quarterly 92.1 (1985): 225

(Here *unreadable* means that no one can read these historians with any pleasure.)

unrepairable   see REPAIRABLE

unsanitary, insanitary   *Unsanitary* is preferred in Canadian English; *insanitary* is rare. Both forms of this word are common in American English. In Britain *insanitary* is the usual form.

See also IN-, UN-.

unsatisfied, dissatisfied   Both terms imply that someone or something is left unfulfilled. *Unsatisfied* is more often applied to things (hunger, debt, curiosity, etc.), to suggest that a demand remains unfulfilled or a condition unappeased. *Dissatisfied* almost always describes people and implies a personal or emotional response of discontent. At a restaurant, John's dinner may leave his hunger unsatisfied (or unappeased), but that does not necessarily mean that he is dissatisfied with his meal. At art school, Mary may be personally dissatisfied with her drawings, even though they do not leave the requirements of her course unsatisfied. *Dissatisfied* is the more common word, and its connotations of disgruntlement are stronger.

The reader cannot help thinking that Sachs could not have been unaware of Violette's painful desire for him, or without pleasure in leaving it unsatisfied.
Miriam Waddington *Apartment Seven* 1989: 185

. . . the FDA could refuse to allow Canadian blood into the United States for processing if it remains unsatisfied with the Canadian Red Cross's handling of the blood it collects.
Ottawa Citizen 7 Sept. 1994: A3

Sometimes, then, both parents will be dissatisfied with the psychologist's conclusions.
Ottawa Citizen 18 Nov. 1994: B6

But it was not long before more militant feminists . . . became dissatisfied with mere legislative fairness.
Queen's Quarterly 94.1 (1987): 3

'I see a lot of subcontractors who are unsatisfied because they're not going to get the business,' committee chairman Gay Helmsing said, referring to three businesses that have lodged verbal complaints and a stack of written complaints.
Leader-Post (Regina) 27 Feb. 1988: A3

(Discontented people are usually described as *dissatisfied*.)

unsociable   see ANTISOCIAL

unsolvable   see SOLUBLE

until, till, 'til, up until, until such time
In current usage *until* is by far the most common form in all varieties of writing. *Till*, however, is just as respectable, and is not the short form that some people believe it to be; in fact, *till* was the earliest form of the word. *Until* is almost always preferred as the first word in a sentence. An abbreviated form of *until*, the poetic *'til* is sometimes found in advertising copy and breezy, tongue-in-cheek writing. It should not be used in serious contexts. Both *til*, without an apostrophe, and *'till*, with one, are spelling errors.

The phrase *up until* is objected to by some critics who judge the *up* unnecessary. As well, *until such time as* is considered verbiage, since *until* itself means up to the time of. But shorter is not always better; sometimes these longer expressions can improve the rhythm of a sentence.

Until recently, there was reason for cautious optimism.
Business Journal June 1991: 1

Till recently, I too held this myth dear to my heart. Henry M. Rosenthal and S. Cathy Berson, eds.
Canadian Jewish Outlook Anthology 1988: 282

(*Till* is unusual at the beginning of a sentence.)

So shop 'til you drop; your country's economy is counting on you.
Financial Post 8 Dec. 1989: 9

'If you think sales are bad now, wait 'til you see the beginning of next year because they are going to get a lot worse.'
Vancouver Sun 9 Nov. 1990: C5

We had a lazy lunch and didn't fish again 'till evening.
Atlantic Salmon Journal Autumn 1990: 24

(Since it is not a short form, *till* does not require an apostrophe.)

Up until quite recently, the creative person, say in literature, was typically one who 'wanted to write', and what he wanted to write was usually poetry or fiction.
Northrop Frye *The Modern Century* 1990: 99–100

(Some critics object to *up until*.)

Until such time as we can pluck the fetus from a woman's body and give it life, should we not entrust the destiny of that fetus to the person whose body holds it and allow that person to be responsible to God?
Calgary Herald 21 Feb. 1988: D4

(Some critics object to *until such time as*.)

See also WORDINESS, VARIATION.

unwieldy, [unwieldly]   *Unwieldy* is the accepted and common form of the word meaning cumbersome or awkward. *Unwieldly* is sometimes used in speech and newspaper writing, but is not listed in contemporary dictionaries. The *OED* conjectures that *unwieldly* originated as a typographical error.

The tax specialist owes much of his worth to his clients to the enormous complexity of tax laws; the lawyer is similarly indebted to a cumbersome and unwieldly legal system as is the accountant to an equally cumbersome and unwieldly set of accounting rules. . . .
Financial Post 4 Jan. 1990: 9

(The accepted spelling is *unwieldy*.)

up   Some usage guides object to the use of *up* as a verb meaning increase ('They upped their prices overnight'), but dictionaries list this sense without comment. It is more common in newspapers and magazines than in formal or academic prose. The expression *up and* ('They just up and left') is very informal and rare in print.

> When Louis Riel touched off the Saskatchewan rebellion in 1885, White began to churn out extras, hiring gangs of boys to turn the press and upping the price to a quarter.
> Pierre Berton *The Promised Land* 1984: 171

> Well, the old VCR just up and died recently.
> *Globe and Mail* (Toronto) 7 May 2005: 1

See also UNTIL.

Upanishads   see SACRED WRITINGS

upcoming   see DOWNPLAY

upmost, uppermost   see UTMOST

up until   see UNTIL

upward(s)   see -WARD(S)

urban, urbane   *Urban* means having to do with cities or towns. *Urbane* describes manners that are smooth, refined, and courteous—qualities that were once associated with city-dwellers.

> I was urbane, witty, cocky, capable of the greatest heights.
> Max Braithwaite *The Night We Stole the Mountie's Car* 1971: 13

Urdu   see HINDU

-us   Some people mistakenly assume that all nouns borrowed from Latin that end with *-us* should form their plurals with *-i*, along the pattern of *stimulus, stimuli* (see also PLURALS, REGULAR, IRREGULAR, FOREIGN). In fact, the Latin words *apparatus, census, conspectus, hiatus, impetus, nexus, plexus, prospectus, sinus,* and *status* do not change to form their plurals. Thus the Latin plural of *impetus* is simply *impetus* (not *impeti*); the English plural is *impetuses*. All these words

are best pluralized with *-es*: 'My sinuses are killing me'.

Another group of Latin nouns ending in *-us* form their plurals by changing a vowel and adding *-ra*: *corpus, corpora; genus, genera;* and *opus, opera*. These words can also be made plural by adding *-es*: *corpuses, genuses, opuses*.

A third group of nouns with the *-us* ending are either pseudo-Latin or Latin expressions other than nouns in their base form. The only way these words can be made plural is by adding *-es*: *ignoramus, ignoramuses; minus, minuses; omnibus, omnibuses; rebus, rebuses*.

A fourth group of nouns derived from Latin simply never take Latin plurals: *bonus, bonuses; chorus, choruses; campus, campuses; circus, circuses; virus, viruses*.

Finally, some *-us* nouns are late Latin renderings of Greek words and are made plural by adding *-es*: *hippopotamus, hippopotamuses; octopus, octopuses; platypus, platypuses; rhinoceros, rhinoceroses*.

use, usage   The definitions of the nouns *use* and *usage* overlap to some extent, but *use* applies to any act of using or being used, whereas *usage* suggests a pattern of habitual use by a number of people. To use *usage* when *use* will do ('his usage of my driveway') is to risk sounding pompous. With respect to language, *usage* refers to established or customary patterns of language use; in law a *usage* is a customary practice—for example, a standard business practice—that may be taken into consideration in a judicial decision.

> Lum Bim yesterday became the latest and the biggest name among China's record-setting women swimmers to be suspended for drug use.
> *Toronto Star* 8 Dec. 1994: D6

> In 1989 and 1992, the Seniors Drug Action Program studied drug-usage patterns of 2,000 B.C. long-term care residents. . . .
> *Vancouver Sun* 1 Nov. 1994: A12

> So the word has been turned on its head in American usage and now a 'liberal' is regarded by many Americans as being close to socialist, if not communist.
> *Ottawa Citizen* 30 Dec. 1994: A8

. . . the traditional distinctions between usage, binding convention, and positive law may seem over-simplified and inadequate to describe the many informal rules that give substance to constitutional structures and processes.
Andrew Heard *Canadian Constitutional Conventions* 1991: 15

[The book's] herculean usage of primary sources and relevant statistics is truly impressive.
Canadian Journal of History 14.1: 122

(Here *use* would be a better choice than *usage*, since no group behaviour is implied.)

See also UTILIZE, USE.

used to   In speech it is difficult to distinguish between *used to* and *use to* in expressions such as 'The water level used to be higher' and 'She used to walk to work' because the *d* is not pronounced. Consequently, the *d* is sometimes forgotten in writing.

Complications arise when *used* is combined with *did* or *didn't*. In these cases some usage guides prefer *use to*, noting that just as we would write 'She didn't want to swim', and not 'She didn't wanted to swim', so we should write 'She didn't use to swim' rather than 'She didn't used to swim'. Others argue that *used to* is now an invariant form. *Webster's Dictionary of English Usage* suggests that *didn't use to* is the more common form in American writing. The British *Longman Guide to English Usage* suggests that *didn't used to* is preferable. In Canadian writing *didn't used to* appears to be more common than *didn't use to*, but neither form of the expression is common in writing except in representations of speech. *Never used to* is always an acceptable way of sidestepping the controversy.

She used to recall with nostalgia the natural beauty which surrounded her during her happy childhood.
George Ignatieff *The Making of a Peacemonger* 1987: 9

'I use to pretend I was Canadian skater Lynne Nightengale.'
Gazette (Montreal) 4 March 1989: T10

(Only *used to* is standard.)

Senators didn't used to be embarrassed by their office.
Ottawa Citizen 3 Oct. 1990: A2

Fort Washington, Penn., didn't use to be a household name but through the magic of television advertising it is becoming well known, too much so.
Ottawa Citizen 11 May 1990: C16

[Writing essays is] all too much like homework, which I never used to get done on time either. . . .
Margaret Atwood *Second Words* 1982: 11

See also SUPPOSED TO.

UTC   see GREENWICH MEAN TIME

uterus, uteri   see PLURALS

utilize, use   The verb *utilize* usually suggests an especially clever or effective use of something. Where the meaning is merely 'make use of', *use* is recommended. *Utilise* is a British spelling seldom seen in Canadian writing.

The upgraded ground station will utilize remote sensing technology to improve management of natural resources and monitoring of the environment.
Province (Vancouver) 22 Nov. 1990: 51

Foot traffic utilizes pathways through rank growth.
Vancouver Sun 7 July 1990: E1

(Here a simple 'walkers *use*' or 'pedestrians *use*' might be clearer than 'foot traffic *utilizes*'.)

See also -IZE, -ISE.

utmost, uppermost, upmost   'Your *utmost*' is your best effort. *Utmost,* derived from Old English 'outmost', means furthest, greatest, or maximal.

Uppermost means highest, or most prominent: 'the uppermost reaches of the mountain', 'uppermost in her mind'.

Upmost is a rare variant of *uppermost*, which some contemporary dictionaries do not list. Usually *upmost* is considered an error when it appears in contexts where *utmost* is established.

She accompanied me to the radiation room where I lay, alone and still, willing the machines to do their utmost.
Canadian Women's Health Network 4.3 (2001): 10

Lack of charcoal layers in the uppermost metre of the peat was considered evidence that the site had not been burned for at least five centuries.
Canadian Journal of Forest Research 34.7 (2004): 1400

Construction, a major job creation sector, is of the upmost importance under the current administration's economic plan.
Industry Canada website 31 Aug. 2005

(The conventional phrase is 'of the utmost importance': most editors would change *upmost* to *utmost* here.)

See also MISHEARD EXPRESSIONS.

V

vacation   see HOLIDAY

vaccination   see IMMUNIZATION

vacillation   see AMBIVALENCE

vagary, vagaries   A *vagary* (the plural form, *vagaries*, is more common) is an unpredictable action or an eccentric whim. The usual pronunciation in Canada and Britain is *VAY guh ree*; *va GAIR ee* is common in the United States.

 . . . it was at least as hard a century ago as it is now for people of conventional mind to recognize that a man can be interested in the vagaries of sexual behavior without wishing to practise them himself.
Robertson Davies *A Voice from the Attic* 1960: 270

vale, veil   A *vale* is a valley, although this old-fashioned term is now seldom used except in place names such as 'River Vale'.

Something that conceals or obscures, like the gauzy fabric that may hang from a woman's hat, is a *veil*: 'bridal veil'. To 'take the veil' is to become a nun.

See also VALE OF TEARS, VEIL OF TEARS.

vale of tears, veil of tears   *Vale* is a synonym of *valley*. The *Oxford English Dictionary* records the world-weary metaphor 'vale of tears'

as early as the sixteenth century, and variants such as 'vale of misery' and 'vale of woe' a century earlier. In this century, however, a spelling confusion has spawned a competing metaphor. '*Veil* of tears' is the spelling seen in contemporary Canadian newspapers approximately a third of the time, and this expression often refers, not to our mortal existence, but to a welling of tears. Some conservative language commentators reject the newer metaphor as a benighted reinterpretation of the original (see FOLK ETYMOLOGY), but '*veil* of tears' is clearly well established in journalism. A spelling distinction should be maintained between the traditional and newer metaphors: *vale* for life on this earth and *veil* for tears filming the eyes.

The great novelist [Margaret Laurence] departed this vale of tears in 1987, cigarette still dangling defiantly from her mouth, still blazing against the small-minded.
Daily News (Halifax) 12 Aug. 2004: 15

'People say to me, time and time again—and sometimes through a veil of tears—"You know, Mary Jane, the reason we didn't get formally married was that we wanted to keep it simple".'
Globe and Mail (Toronto) 18 Feb. 2004: F5

They follow the rules, embody obedience and in that discipline discover a life above this veil of tears.
Sudbury Star 9 March 2002: D10

(Here the appropriate spelling is *vale*.)

valorize, valorous see -OUR, -OR

valve see TAP

Vancouverite see NAMES OF RESIDENTS OF CITIES AND PROVINCES

Van Doos, Vandoos, Royal Vingt-Deuxième Régiment The esteemed Royal 22e Régiment of the Canadian Forces is Canada's largest regiment and the only one consisting almost solely of francophones. While the *Royal 22e Régiment* (*Royal Vingt-Deuxième Régiment* in full) is its official title, in English it is sometimes called the *Royal 22nd Regiment*. The French name is preferable in most contexts.

Van Doos is the regiment's unofficial name. In the First World War, English-speaking soldiers thought they heard *Van Doos* instead of *vingt-deux*, and referred to the regiment as such. Although originally a confusion, *Van Doos* is not considered derogatory, but is a proud nickname. Sometimes quotation marks are used to indicate its informal status, but they are not necessary.

Vandoos (one word) is sometimes used, and *Van Doo* (a back-formation with no *s*) sometimes acts as a singular ('He is a Van Doo') and more rarely as the name of the unit as a whole ('The Van Doo Regiment'), but *Van Doos* is the form recommended by the *Canadian Press Stylebook* and listed in the *Canadian Oxford Dictionary*.

> He served with the storied Royal 22nd Regiment, the Van Doos, before being posted to Cyprus. . . .
> *Gazette* (Montreal) 9 Nov. 2005: A7

(*Van Doos* is correct, though the preferred form for the official name is *Royal 22e Régiment* even in English writing.)

See also BACK-FORMATION; FOLK ETYMOLOGY.

vanguard see AVANT-GARDE

van, von see ALPHABETICAL ORDER

variant see entry in Glossary

variation see WORDINESS

various Some usage commentators object to the use of *various* as a pronoun, as in 'I spoke with various of the delegates'. They argue that *various* is an adjective, only. While comparable terms such as *several*, *some*, *many*, and *few* have shifted to pronoun use and are now undisputed in that capacity, *various* is still rarely used as a pronoun in Canadian writing, and most dictionaries do not list it as one.

> Meanwhile he called on various of his friends in Toronto who were also friends of Queen's. . . .
> Hilda Neatby *Queen's University* 1 (1978): 273

(Some would omit the *of his* and use *various* as an adjective: 'He called on *various* friends'.)

See also FUNCTIONAL SHIFT; VARIOUS DIFFERENT.

various different *Various different* is an idiom meaning 'several different'. However, the phrase grates on many people's ears because the primary meaning of *various* is different or diverse. In formal writing *several different*, or *various* or *different* alone, is recommended.

> The view is consistent with treating the various different correct descriptions of reality as complementary rather than competitive.
> *Canadian Journal of Philosophy* 19 (1989): 307

(Here *several different*, or *various* alone, would be better.)

See also WORDINESS, VARIATION.

vase Canadians pronounce this word *VAHZ*, *VAYZ*, or *VACE*. The first is the usual British pronunciation; the second is primarily Canadian; and the third is chiefly American.

Vedas see SACRED WRITINGS

vedette see QUEBEC ENGLISH

vegetarian, ovolactovegetarian, lactovegetarian, vegan *Vegetarian* is the broadest term for a person who does not eat meat.

Vegetarians who do eat eggs and dairy products are sometimes called *ovolactovegetarians*. *Lactovegetarians* drink milk but will not eat eggs. Someone who refuses to eat or use any animal products (including leather and fur clothing) is called a *vegan* (pronounced *VEJ un* or *VEE gun*).

vehicular   see H-

veil   see -IE-, -EI-; VALE; VALE OF TEARS

veil of tears   see VALE OF TEARS

vein   see -IE-, -EI-

venal, venial   A *venal* person can be bribed; a *venal* system is corrupt. *Venial* faults are trivial and easily excused; *venial* sins—unlike mortal sins—are not punishable by damnation. Unlike *venal*, *venial* is never applied to people.

> . . . anyone who wanted to get rid of a tiresome relative (perhaps to gain access to his money) had but to bribe a couple of venal apothecaries, and the deed was done. . . .
> Robertson Davies *A Voice From the Attic* 1960: 116–17

> . . . most of the faux pas are the venial sins of omission.
> *Globe and Mail* (Toronto) 7 Dec. 1985: D3

Venerable   see RELIGIOUS TITLES

venetian blinds   see CAPITAL LETTERS

venue   *Venue* (pronounced *VEN yoo*) has been used for centuries in legal parlance to refer to a location. A judge may order a change of venue for a trial, fearing the defendant cannot be fairly tried in the locale where the crime was committed; or *venue* may refer to the scene of a crime. Recently the use of the term has broadened so that concerts, special events, and public meetings can be said to take place in a certain venue. Some commentators disapprove of this use, probably because it is new. Interestingly, although *venue* is borrowed from French,

in that language it doesn't refer to a location; rather, it means arrival or coming.

> An Ontario Supreme Court judge has ordered a change of venue for the trial of two youths who were charged as juveniles in October, 1982, with first-degree murder. . . .
> *Globe and Mail* (Toronto) 30 Jan. 1985: M3

(This is an example of common legal usage.)

> When city people buy an old farm, not just as a venue for lawn parties but because they're converts to country life, they usually get carried away.
> *Harrowsmith* Aug.–Sept. 1985: 52

> The bottom has dropped out of Nova Scotia's only arts centre, the province's sole full-time venue for entertainment of a national or international calibre.
> *Gazette* (Montreal) 1 March 1989: C11

veranda(h)   see PORCH

verb   see entry in Glossary

verbal, oral   *Verbal* usually means spoken, as in the legal expressions 'verbal contract' and 'verbal order'. But *verbal* does not necessarily mean spoken. Any communication in words—whether spoken or written—can in fact be described as *verbal*, and 'verbal ability', or language ability, is often contrasted with 'mathematical ability'. To eliminate the ambiguity, some editors insist that only *oral* be used to distinguish spoken from written communication, and that *verbal* be used to mean 'in words'. Although this recommendation isn't widely followed, it does make sense to refrain from using *verbal* to mean *oral* in literary criticism or in discussions about language itself.
Oral, besides meaning spoken ('oral tradition'), can refer to anything to do with the mouth ('oral surgery', 'oral hygiene').

> Verbal proposals were permissible, but a letter was much to be preferred because it could be kept for future reference.
> Robertson Davies *A Voice from the Attic* 1960: 85

> Yet nowhere in all of the correspondence or in the contractual agreements . . . was a pledge of secre-

cy asked for or given. Preston insisted he'd made a verbal commitment to the directors. . . .
Pierre Berton *The Promised Land* 1984: 233

Reality, in this fifteen-chapter novel, becomes a species of verbal confetti.
Janice Kulyk Keefer *Reading Mavis Gallant* 1989: 83

(Here *verbal* means having to do with words, in this case written.)

Nabokov writes with style, and style—as distinguished from verbal and syntactical foppery, which is sometimes mistaken for it—gives a dimension to a book which can be disquieting when exercised on such a theme as this.
Robertson Davies *A Voice from the Attic* 1960: 245

(Here *verbal* means having to do with words, in this case written.)

The written prose . . . doesn't have the excitement of the verbal version, and so, it is argued, the journalist, particularly if he is writing for TV or radio, should try for more of that, by using the patterns of ordinary speech.
W.C. Lougheed, ed. *In Search of the Standard in Canadian English* 1986: 91

(Here *spoken* or *oral* might be more precise than *verbal*.)

verbal phrases, verbs with prepositions
see PHRASAL VERBS

verbals   see entry in Glossary

verb–subject agreement   see AGREEMENT, GRAMMATICAL

verily   see ARCHAISMS

veritable
Although *veritable* literally means real or true, it usually modifies metaphors rather than statements of literal fact. Its function is to assure readers that no matter how exaggerated the metaphor may seem, it is appropriate.

The explosion of literary output in Quebec in the 1960s was followed by a veritable flood of translations.
Ben-Z. Shek *French-Canadian & Québécois Novels* 1991: 136

One had a raffia bag on her lap, a veritable cornucopia from which she drew mandarins, biscuits, and candy to bribe her two small boys on the seat behind.
Queen's Quarterly 96.2 (1989): 353

See also LITERALLY, FIGURATIVELY.

vermin
Vermin is a collective noun for offensive or injurious insects, animals, or, figuratively, persons. Occasionally it refers to a single creature.

In the backyard of this same building, a deserted mother and two children shared a woodshed with rats and other vermin.
Pierre Berton *The Promised Land* 1981: 294

It seems [he] found a rat in his garden and dispatched the vermin with a broom handle.
Toronto Star 16 Nov. 1994: E6

See also COLLECTIVE NOUNS.

vernacular
The *vernacular* is everyday language as it is spoken in a particular place, as opposed to formal, literary usage. To use the vernacular, therefore, means to use natural, unstuffy, conversational language. Perhaps because a good deal of slang makes its way into everyday language, writers sometimes use a phrase such as 'in the vernacular', or 'to use the vernacular', to apologize for introducing slang into their writing.

In the Renaissance the term *vernacular* referred to the language spoken in a particular country—English, French, German, etc.—as opposed to Latin, the universal language of scholars and the church.

In the stories in this issue of CFM, I see the vernacular is still alive. The colloquial voice which speaks for the human condition is loud in Saskatchewan.
Canadian Fiction Magazine 64 (1988): 6

In their early years they had been sodbusters, to use the vernacular, and she had hated it.
Pierre Berton *The Promised Land* 1984: 161

Marcel's paranoid ravings about being chased by policemen (dogs, in the Quebec vernacular) . . .

vernissage

are far more dramatic. . . .
Gazette (Montreal) 13 June 1992: D10

'In the vernacular, cut the crap in future issues.'
Catholic Register 23 Aug. 1986: 4

Yiddish has always been the vernacular, everyday language spoken by the Jews of Eastern Europe. Hebrew was the language of learning, prayer, and ritual.
Miriam Waddington *Apartment Seven* 1989: 74

See also COLLOQUIAL; FORMAL, INFORMAL WRITING; STANDARD ENGLISH, STANDARD.

vernissage   see QUEBEC ENGLISH

vertigo, vertiginous   *Vertigo* is pronounced with the stress on the first syllable (*VER ti go*) and refers either to physical dizziness or to a dizzy, confused state of mind. The adjective *vertiginous* (pronounced *ver TIJ in us*) means suffering from dizziness ('vertiginous sight-seers'), or dizzying ('vertiginous cliffs').

very   see ADJECTIVES AND ADVERBS

very, much   Most adjectives can be intensified with *very* ('very pretty', 'very large', etc.), but often past participles (the verb form that follows *has*, *have*, and *had*, as in 'has *teased*', 'have *eaten*', or 'had *discussed*') cannot. Some past participles are used before nouns as modifiers: 'the teased puppy', 'the half-eaten cookie'. And some of these participial modifiers, including such common words as *excited*, *interested*, *pleased*, *surprised*, and *tired*, have become fully established as adjectives and are regularly modified by *very*. Others, though, retain some of their verbal quality and are customarily modified by a different adverb, such as *much*, *greatly*, *highly*, or *thoroughly*: 'much debated', 'much loved', 'much travelled', 'greatly appreciated', 'highly admired', 'thoroughly disliked'. If you think that *very* sounds odd in front of a particular participial modifier, try substituting one of these adverbs; if it fits, it is almost certainly a better choice.

vest   To *vest* means to confer on or charge with. Financial control, authority, property

rights, etc., are vested *in* a person or group. For example, the chancellor of a university awards degrees by virtue of the authority vested *in* him or her. A person or group is vested *with* these rights or powers: 'The government is vested with budgetary control'. A 'vested interest' is the legal right to the present or future enjoyment of a property or benefit, or, metaphorically, a personal stake or selfish interest in a particular arrangement or system.

Thus the Lieutenant Governor is vested with the prerogatives of the Crown for all aspects relevant to the governing of the province.
Andrew Heard *Canadian Constitutional Conventions* 1991: 17

The fact is, present politicians have such an enormous vested interest in the status quo it is ridiculous to expect them to even consider fundamental change.
Financial Post 13 May 1991: 11

vetoes   see -OS, -OES

vicar   see RECTOR

vicarage   see MANSE

vice, vise   *Vice* and *vise* both rhyme with *mice*. Most North American writers distinguish between depravity, *vice*, and a clamp, *vise*, but the British use *vice* for both meanings.

Truly, this is an instance where vice loses half its evil by losing all its grossness.
Robertson Davies *A Voice From the Attic* 1960: 281–2

She gripped my arm as if in a vise and led me to the bus stop.
Canadian Fiction Magazine 63 (1988): 92

. . . he held us off with one hand while the other clamped a vice around our pet's muzzle, twisting it upside down. . . .
Room of One's Own June 1990: 4

(Most Canadians use *vise* for this sense.)

vicious circle, vicious cycle, virtuous cycle, vicious spiral   One meaning of *vicious circle* is a fault of logic in which a proposition is used to establish a conclusion, which is in turn used to prove the original proposition (see also BEG THE QUESTION, another term for circular reasoning). Since the early nineteenth century, *vicious circle* has also been used to describe situations in which the short-term solutions to problems only aggravate the original problems. *Vicious cycle* is also used to describe this pattern of self-perpetuating ill effects. In the mid-twentieth century, the parallel expression *virtuous cycle* (or *circle*) was coined for a recurrent beneficial cycle of cause and effect. Although the adjective *virtuous* suggests a spiritual interpretation, this expression seldom refers to 'kindness repaid in kind'. Typically it is used in financial contexts to describe buoyant economies and business practices that pay off.

Vicious spiral sometimes describes a faltering economy.

> Awards of damages for professional negligence have led to extensive use of liability insurance; because of uncertainty concerning liability and the risk of heavy damages, insurance premiums are steadily increasing. Professional fees, in turn, must increase to cover insurance costs. As fees increase, clients expect more for their money, and when they are disappointed are much more likely to sue. The process is something of a vicious circle.
> J.E. Smyth et al. *The Law and Business Administration in Canada* 1987: 99–100

> 'I have no appetite in the morning.' It's a vicious circle. A person who has long abandoned the breakfast habit isn't going to be hungry in the morning.
> *Chatelaine* April 1986: 30

> Once out of prison, a heroin addict had to begin the vicious cycle of crime all over again to feed his or her habit. . . .
> *Province* (Vancouver) 6 July 1990: 3

> In other parts of the Maritimes, it meant subsidizing industries in small urban centres in the hope of attracting more industry and more labour and setting up a virtuous cycle.
> *Subury Star* 13 Oct. 2002: A7

> That in turn could pull Japan out of the vicious spiral of declining profits, shrinking business investment and souring loans it has been trapped in for much of the past decade, many economists argue.
> *Globe and Mail* (Toronto) 19 Sept. 2002: B12

See also BEG THE QUESTION; SPIRAL.

Victoriana   see -(I)ANA

victuals, vittles   *Victuals*—the term is almost always pluralized—means food and provisions. It is pronounced *VIT uls*, which accounts for the informal variant spelling *vittles*. The discrepancy between the standard spelling and the pronunciation dates from the sixteenth century, when scholars altered the Old French borrowing *vitaille* to make it resemble its Latin root, *victualia*. The new spelling included a *c*, but the pronunciation remained unchanged. Infrequently, *victual* functions as a verb: 'The army was victualled for a long expedition'.

> Records at Moose Factory show that on Christmas Day, 1705, each four-man mess had been doled out enough victuals to make the York Factory rations look like a snack.
> *Globe and Mail* (Toronto) 19 Oct. 1985: A10

> On the way out, patrons can purchase vittles they just can't live without from a food boutique.
> *Globe and Mail* (Toronto) 26 Sept. 1985: E9

(Here this spelling adds a humorous effect.)

> . . . clerks in the victualling office were ordered to burn Byng in effigy. . . .
> J.A.W. Gunn *Beyond Liberty and Property* 1983: 274

videographer   see FILMMAKER

vigorous   see -OUR, -OR

vilify   *Vilify* is correctly spelled with a single *l*. The common spelling error *villify* is perhaps influenced by *villain*.

villain, villein   A *villain* is a scoundrel, someone of depraved or criminal character. *Villein* is a historical term for a peasant in medieval England. Villeins were bound in servitude to their feudal lords but were free in their relations with all others. *Villain* is sometimes misspelled *villian*, perhaps because of the influence of *ruffian*, or perhaps because -*ian* is such a common word ending ('Kantian', 'Canadian'). *Villain* is pronounced *VILL un*; *villein* may be pronounced *VILL un*, *VILL ane*, or *vill ANE*.

violin   see FIDDLE

virgin birth   see IMMACULATE CONCEPTION

virgule   see SLASH

virtuoso, virtuosic, virtuosity   *Virtuoso* is a term that has always teetered between high praise and disparagement. From the seventeenth century to the nineteenth, *virtuoso* meant both scholar and dilettante, connoisseur of the fine arts and frivolous collector of arty objects. The meaning most familiar today dates from the eighteenth century: someone with outstanding technical skill in playing a musical instrument or singing. This meaning is equivocal, however, because technical excellence may be considered either the basis of the highest musical achievement or the prop of a sterile performance. The domain of the word *virtuoso* has broadened in the twentieth century: a contemporary Canadian virtuoso is as likely to wield a hockey stick as a violin bow.

The plural of *virtuoso* is either *virtuosos* or *virtuosi*. The adjective form of the noun, *virtuosic*, is uncommon; more often writers use the noun as an adjective: 'virtuoso performance'. *Virtuosity* is the talent of the virtuoso, not moral goodness or virtue.

'Everybody tried to be a virtuoso. The drummer who played the fastest, the trumpeter who blew the highest—they were the best.'
Jack Chambers *Milestones* 1983: 131

The musicians who earn Davis's highest praise are always those who articulate melodies by a few carefully placed notes rather than by virtuoso runs at great speed.
Jack Chambers *Milestones* 1983: 33

Without virtuoso individual skills, team play becomes both virtue and necessity, and what others understand as unselfishness is really cold-eyed realism.
Ken Dryden *The Game* 1983: 85

Liszt's Piano Concerto No. 1 has never been regarded as one of his finest works . . . and is far too often treated as a mere vehicle for empty virtuosic display.
Times-Colonist (Victoria) 15 April 1996: 1

virus   see COMPUTER TERMS; FLU; -US

vis-à-vis   *Vis-à-vis* is pronounced *VEEZ a VEE*. The accent over the *a* is sometimes omitted from English-language texts, but the hyphens should be used. Literally, this French borrowing means 'face to face with', but in contemporary use it more often means in relation to, in comparison with, or concerning.

The intensity of the sectarian divisiveness in Canadian towns, both religious and political, is an example: what such groups represent, of course, vis-à-vis one another, is 'two solitudes,' the death of communication and dialogue.
Northrop Frye *The Bush Garden* 1971: 226

The Great Ape Project is controversial largely because it demands a huge leap in our thinking about ourselves vis-a-vis the rest of the living world.
Toronto Star 6 Nov. 1994: C8

vise   see VICE

visible minority, people of colour, non-white   Some writers use the term *visible minority* very broadly to include any group whose appearance may be used as a basis for discrimination, including people with disabilities, members of racial minorities, and women. Others use the term only for those who do not belong to the majority racial group. However, *minority* is a misleading and unsatisfactory term, for it implies that the group it designates matters less than the majority. Further, many populations who are labelled in this way are in fact the majority. For example, First Nations peoples constitute the majority of the population in the north. However, those belonging to such groups are treated as if they were a 'minority', so the term has a certain metaphorical aptness.

People of colour refers to those who do not fall into the category *white*, and is preferred to *non-white*, which implies that white is the norm. *Women of colour* is a term used by feminists in particular to characterize women struggling against both racism and sexism.

Another striking limitation in the university system

is its accessibility for people of colour.
Rites March 1990: 9

Canadian employers feel 'quite free' to discriminate against non-white people, a federal New Democratic Party task force was told. . . .
Globe and Mail (Toronto) 7 March 1985: M5

(Here *non-white* should be replaced with *people of colour*.)

I think that many women today, including poor women, and women of colour, poor or not, are able to tap into a collective reclamation of at least some of the components that make home.
Room of One's Own June 1990: 36

See also BLACK; INDIAN; RACE; SEXUAL MINORITIES.

visionary   In Canadian English *visionary* is most often used as a complimentary term for someone far-sighted and imaginative. Yet most dictionaries and usage guides define a *visionary* negatively as a dreamer whose plans and ideas are unrealistic and impractical; and commentators suggest that a person with unusual foresight be called 'a person of vision' rather than 'a visionary'. Nevertheless, *visionary* and 'person of vision' are often used interchangeably. Similarly, while the dictionary definition of the adjective *visionary* is 'impractical and unrealistic' or 'seen in a vision', the adjective too is now most often used to mean far-sighted and imaginative.

Bruce Firestone was called a visionary and a maverick, an impulsive dreamer with out-of-this-world ideas.
Province (Vancouver) 11 Dec. 1990: 37

(Here *visionary* is used in a negative sense.)

There is a need for people who are visionary, energetic, outgoing and who are willing to knock on doors.
Canadian Baptist Feb. 1986: 9

(Here *visionary* has favourable connotations.)

visit, visit with   British usage guides criticize the phrase *visit with* as a wordy variant of *visit*. However, in North America the phrase *visit with* has a slightly different meaning from *visit*. It means to chat or talk with, and is occa-

sionally used even in reference to telephone conversations.

They've visited all 10 dealerships in town, searching for the best price.
Calgary Herald 31 Dec. 1994: E3

Current club and federation leaders should visit with their predecessors, to delve into the historical perspective. . . .
Snowmobile Canada 1991 Buyer's Guide: 4

(Here *visit with* means 'talk to'.)

See also COMPUTER TERMS; VISITATION.

visitation, visit   *Visitation* is a formal word for a formal visit. It may be used in reference to pastoral calls made by members of the clergy, to official visits such as ship inspections, or to the visits made to a funeral home to pay last respects to a deceased person. In North America 'visitation rights' are court orders allowing parents without custody to visit their children.

The Visitation (capitalized) refers to the visit that the Virgin Mary paid to Elizabeth before the birth of Jesus (Luke 1: 39–56). A *visitation* can also be an affliction 'visited' upon someone by God, or a divine inspiration.

Visitation should not be used as a fancy synonym of *visit*, though it is sometimes used humorously to describe an unwelcome visit.

U.S. courts are coming up with tortured solutions like awarding divorced parents 'joint custody' of their frozen embryos (nothing so far about visitation rights).
Winnipeg Free Press 17 Nov. 1990: 58

Will its purported visitation from the Holy Spirit manifest itself in ways other than ecstatic physical surrender?
Toronto Star 4 Dec. 1994: A1

'Maybe we will [move] one day, but we like our Oxfordshire home so much, and would miss terribly the perpetual visitations from our sons and their wives and the grandchildren.'
Globe and Mail (Toronto) 16 Nov. 1985: E6

(The writer is perhaps being humorous about these 'perpetual visitations' but, if not, *visits* is the better word choice.)

visual arts   see ARTS

vittles   see VICTUALS

viz., sc.   The obsolescent Latin abbreviations *viz.* and *sc.* are not widely understood. They are used like the English words *namely, that is,* or *specifically* to introduce a more precise rewording or amplification of what precedes. *Viz.* is an abbreviation of Latin *videlicet,* 'it is permitted to see'. The final *z* in *viz.* is a medieval Latin symbol for *et.* There is no traditional pronunciation for this short form; rather, it is read aloud as the English word *namely. Sc.,* also *scil.,* an abbreviation of *scilicet,* means 'it is permitted to know' and is pronounced *SILL i set, SIGH li set,* or *SKEE li ket.*

[Eighteen items] were retained to tap five aspects of negative feelings for a friend (viz., detachment, conflict, submission, worry, and jealousy).
Canadian Journal of Behavioural Science 35.1 (2003): 242

(*Specifically* or *namely* would be more widely understood than *viz.*)

Accordingly, it may be claimed that 'it is true that' has semantic features similar to 'it is not the case that'; sc., it operates on a sentence or proposition and returns a different sentence or proposition. . . .
Canadian Journal of Philosophy 34.1 (2004): 82

(In prose for a general audience, *in other words* could replace *sc.*)

See also LATIN PHRASES; I.E., E.G.; AMPERSAND.

vizsla   see DALMATIAN

vocal, voluble   *Vocal* means produced by the voice, as in 'vocal music'. It also means expressive, unguarded in speech, or outspoken. *Voluble,* from the Latin for 'rolling', means characterized by a rapid or steady flow of speech. Although *voluble* can overlap with *vocal* in this sense, it does not necessarily suggest outspokenness, nor does it mean loud.

The most vocal conservatives were the Fascist parties of Italy, Germany, Spain, France, and England.
Queen's Quarterly 96.3 (1989): 601

Roosevelt had made enemies and his critics were vocal.
Gazette (Montreal) 31 Dec. 1994: H3

Galley, affable as well as voluble, has had a lot to talk and yip and be high-tempo about this season. . . .
Ottawa Citizen 19 May 1990: E1

On issue after issue the government's critics . . . are voluble on what they are against but silent or vague about what they are for.
Gazette (Montreal) 18 Oct. 1990: C1

vocation, avocation   Taken from the Latin for 'calling', a *vocation* is a primary occupation, job, or profession. The prefix *a-* means 'away from' in Latin; thus an *avocation* is a diversion from one's calling—an occupation pursued for enjoyment, or a hobby.

His introduction to law (his vocation) and politics (his avocation) came in the legal offices of John Sandfield Macdonald, Ontario's first premier.
Globe and Mail (Toronto) 16 Nov. 1985: E17

I should like to think of myself as a writer in a country where a writer is recognized as a man with a vocation and not merely as a man with a hobby.
Robertson Davies *One Half of Robertson Davies* 1978: 138

. . . gardening is one of the few careers where it's possible to combine an avocation with a vocation.
Globe and Mail (Toronto) 22 June 1985: H7

voice   see entry in Glossary

volcanoes   see -OS, -OES

voluble   see VOCAL

vomit   see SICK

vouch, avow, vouchsafe   To *vouch* for a statement is to stand behind its truth. To *vouch* for a person is to confirm his or her integrity. To *avow* means to admit, acknowledge, or declare openly. Thus to *avow* that someone is honest and true is to *vouch* for that person's character.

Vouchsafe is a formal word meaning to give or to grant, as one would a favour. Sometimes it is misused to mean say, attest, or confirm.

The books mentioned . . . are vouched for by Miss Hackett as having attained this sale, though in some cases their success was not immediate.
Robertson Davies *A Voice from the Attic* 1960: 360

Hoadly was quite conspicuous as a Whig who clearly and frankly avowed that the king and the two houses of Parliament were 'co-ordinate.'
J.A.W. Gunn *Beyond Life and Property* 1983: 133

Such truth as we are vouchsafed is a truth of dis-connections and lacunae.
Janice Kulyk Keefer *Reading Mavis Gallant* 1989: 160

To read *Hurly-Burly* is to be vouchsafed an entry into the otherwise closed universe of big-league journalism.
Gazette (Montreal) 17 Feb. 1990: K2

What these ideas were, Peres would not vouch-safe—although they appeared to involve the composition of the Palestinian delegation to peace talks.
Vancouver Sun 25 Jan. 1990: A3

(Here *vouchsafe* is misused to mean divulge.)

. . . the people who are victims of long lenses, bugging and taped telephone calls are rarely ordi-nary citizens asleep in small flats. As Diana, Charles et al. can vouchsafe.
Maclean's 1 Feb. 1993: 13

(Here *attest* or *confirm* would be more appropri-ate.)

voyageur   see COUREUR DE BOIS

vulnerable   The standard pronunciation is *VUL nur a bul*—with an audible *l* in the first syl-lable.

W

Wabanaki   see ABENAKI

Wade-Giles   see PINYIN

waffle   see LIE

Wagner   see GERMAN WORDS, PRONUNCIATION OF

waiter, waitress, server, wait staff
Restaurants today are making less use of the gender-marked terms *waiter* and *waitress*, per-haps because they are required to use a gender-neutral term when they advertise such posi-tions (see JOB TITLES). The preferred term for food-service staff in major Canadian restaurant and hotel chains is *server*. *Wait staff* is also used as a collective noun. *Waiter* is only very occa-sionally applied to female staff.

Francine Lachapelle, a server in a tiny coffee shop in Old Montreal, said women are discriminated against even in some of their more traditional jobs. . . .
Gazette (Montreal) 11 June 1990: A9

Part of it is the genuine friendliness of the wait-staff, the apparently unforced delight that they take in the fact that of all restaurants, you have chosen this one.
Vancouver Sun 11 Oct. 1990: F21

Caesar's Palace and Restaurant manager . . . want-ed only female waiters.
Province (Vancouver) 25 May 1990: 21

See also COLLECTIVE NOUNS; JOB TITLES; SEXIST LAN-GUAGE.

wait on, wait for   To most Canadians the verb *wait on* means to serve, but in some region-al dialects *wait on* also means wait for. This sec-ond sense of *wait on* should probably be avoid-ed in formal writing, although fiction writers do use it in representations of speech. Curiously, there is a highly formal use of *wait on* meaning 'wait for' that has escaped censure: to wait on a board or governing body is to await its official decision or action.

An obsolescent meaning of *wait on* is to call on or pay a respectful visit to.

I'm waiting on UIC benefits and keep hoping Orville, who owns this place, will get an opening so he can give me a job.
Canadian Fiction Magazine 64 (1988): 106

. . . three separate and independent agencies . . . had to wait on the unpredictable movements by the benevolent but often apparently somnolent monster at Whitehall.
Hilda Neatby *Queen's University* 1 (1978): 33

(This is the formal use of *wait on*.)

In 1881, when there were only two women under-graduates, one Mr. Anderson was appointed 'a committee' to wait on the ladies and ask them to attend the meetings of the society.
Hilda Neatby *Queen's University* 1 (1978): 209

(This is the obsolescent meaning of *wait on*.)

waitress, wait staff see WAITER

waive, wave, waivers To *waive* means to relinquish ('waived our right to sue') or to refrain from enforcing ('waived the dress code for the day'). To *wave* something aside is to dismiss it, as with a wave of the hand. In professional sports, to be *waived* or put on *waivers* is to have your contract offered to other clubs.

The gallery admission fee is waived for the afternoon, and refreshments will be served.
Guardian (Charlottetown) 19 March 2006: C1

But Judge McFarlane waved aside his objections, saying that 'he was listening and noting carefully' what was taking place.
Globe and Mail (Toronto) 31 May 1985: P13

(Here *waved aside* means dismissed perfunctorily.)

Parrott didn't say so in the House, but the project would also be waived past the Environmental Protection Act, which meant that it would be built with virtually no legislative or public scrutiny.
Harrowsmith Aug.–Sept. 1985: 32

(Here *waived past* appears to be a confusion with *waved past*. Alternatively, the author could have written that proper procedures would be *waived*—put aside or not enforced.)

He picked up winger Martin Gelinas on waivers from the Quebec Nordiques. . . .
Vancouver Sun 16 June 1994: F3

walk-on see PHRASAL VERBS

Walpoliana see -(I)ANA

wangle see WRANGLE

want for see LIKE FOR

wapiti see MOOSE

-ward(s) When directional words such as *downward(s)*, *inward(s)*, *outward(s)*, *toward(s)* and *upward(s)* function as adjectives, they do not end in *s*: 'a downward glance'. When they function as adverbs, they may or may not end in *s*: 'She looked downward(s)'. Canadians do not strongly favour one form of the adverb over the other. The British generally prefer the *-s* adverbs, Americans the shorter forms.

Backward(s) is a special case. Canadians use both *backward* and *backwards* as adjectives. *Backward* means shy ('a backward child'), or slow to develop, or towards the back ('a backward pass'). The adjective *backwards* means back-to-front: 'I think that's backwards'; 'He went about it in his usual backwards way'.

Wind shear is a sudden shift in wind speed and direction due to a rapid downward rush of cooled air.
Calgary Herald 30 Dec. 1992: B1

(Here *downward* is an adjective.)

Over the last few weeks rates across the board have trickled downward—again.
Toronto Star 26 Dec. 1992: F1

(Here *downward* is an adverb; *downwards* would be equally acceptable.)

According to the Conference Board survey, increases to base pay are moving downwards.
Ottawa Citizen 12 Dec. 1992: J1

(Here *downwards* is an adverb; *downward* would be equally acceptable.)

Where she used to be backward and shy, she now asserts herself as a full shareholder in the collaboration with Eisler.
Toronto Star 7 Feb. 1992: C5

Well, time for another of our backwards critiques. (This column was always slightly cockeyed.)
Gazette (Montreal) 25 June 1992: D1

Old Backwards Knees [the ostrich] isn't the most attractive of God's creatures.
Gazette (Montreal) 28 June 1992: B6

See also AFTERWARD(S).

warmness   see -NESS

warp, weft, woof   On a loom, the *warp* threads are the ones that run lengthwise and are repeatedly crossed by the *weft* (or *woof*) threads. *Warp and weft* (or *warp and woof*) is often used figuratively with the same sense as *fabric*.

Bias garments are cut . . . with the grain arrows aligned to the fabric's true bias, the 45-degree angle mid-way between warp and weft.
Toronto Star 24 March 1994: C4

'Canadian Pacific is part of the warp and woof of Canadian history.'
Maclean's 24 Feb. 1986: 47

warranty   see GUARANTEE

washroom   see EUPHEMISM

WASP   *WASP*, an acronym for 'White Anglo-Saxon Protestant', is pronounced *wasp* but normally written in capitals to avoid confusion with the insect. This acronym is often used as a shorthand reference to the Canadian elite. Some have objected that it is inaccurate when applied to white Canadians in general or the elite in particular, since many are neither Anglo-Saxon nor Protestant. Although it is frequently found in contexts where it is not derogatory, some consider the term a slight. The objections to this term are perhaps beginning to outweigh its usefulness.

It is about WASP migrants almost exclusively, virtually ignoring the large number of ethnic pioneers. . . .
The Beaver Dec. 1989–Jan. 1990: 44

William Wasp, she used to call him, fondly enough, before she realized that he found it a racial slur.
Margaret Atwood *Life Before Man* 1979: 20

Would the editors of The Gazette kindly consider a moratorium on the use of the term 'WASP'—especially in the context of the 'anglo-Canadian business establishment'. . . ?
Gazette (Montreal) 2 Sept. 1990: B3

See also ABBREVIATION; CELT, ANGLO-CELTIC.

wastage, waste   *Wastage* is loss caused by wear and tear, leakage, evaporation, decay, illness, and so on. The word does not imply human mismanagement and should not be used as a fancy synonym for *waste*—which is the reckless use of resources.

The result is that MAP packaged products have a much longer shelf life resulting in less food wastage and easier inventory control.
Daily News (Halifax) 7 March 1994: 15

(Here *wastage* means spoilage.)

Britain's poor health performance and its poor economic performance 'have common roots in the social divisions and wastage of human skills and abilities among a substantial proportion of the population,' Wilkinson maintains.
Toronto Star 14 May 1994: B2

(Here *waste* would be better: poor use is being made of people's skills.)

watershed, divide   Canadians use *watershed* to refer to the region drained by a single river system, or to a slope that drains in one direction. In this they differ from Fowler, who maintained that a watershed is the line of high land from which water flows into two different river systems or oceans. Canadians, like Americans, usually call this line of high land a *divide*. However, Canadians use *watershed* figuratively in all kinds of writing to mean a turning point or critical turn of events, a sense derived from the one that Fowler preferred.

The focus could shift almost immediately to the Stein watershed, an 1,160-square-kilometre wilderness region the province has slated for development.
Globe and Mail (Toronto) 4 Nov. 1985: N4

Just north of Sunwapta Pass lie the Columbia Icefields, a continental divide that separates waters heading to the Pacific and Arctic Oceans from those heading to Hudson Bay.
Gazette (Montreal) 5 May 1990: J1

The Franklin expedition of 1845 was the watershed of Britain's arctic epic.
Arctic 41.1 (1988): 46

It was a watershed in the child-welfare system, and a victory for the native people of Manitoba.
Saturday Night April 1986: 35

waterspout   see CYCLONE

watt   see APPENDIX II

wave   see WAIVE

wax   One sense of the verb *wax* is to grow or become. Things that 'wax and wane' grow and shrink. Perhaps because the phrases 'to wax poetic' and 'to wax eloquent' are common, some people incorrectly assume that to *wax* means to speak; this assumption is made obvious when they modify the word with an adverb such as *eloquently*, even though no one would write 'become eloquently' or 'grow eloquently'.

Attendance in the public galleries, mostly senatorial aides, waxed and waned. . . .
Province (Vancouver) 6 Dec. 1990: 13

Our consumer panelists didn't wax poetic, though, as they ran the five stirrers through their paces.
Canadian Consumer Jan. 1986: 21

. . . foreign residents wax eloquently about having to pay $13 for a bunch of asparagus at one of the currency grocery stores.
Ottawa Citizen 21 Oct. 1990: W3

(The word required here is the adjective *eloquent*.)

It is true that many *philosophes* . . . waxed enthusiastically about the virtues of the Chinese empire which they perceived to be a rationally disciplined

and ordered society run by mandarin intellectuals.
Canadian Journal of Sociology 14.2 (1989): 263–64

(The word required here is the adjective *enthusiastic*.)

we, us, our   see CASE

weathergirl,   weatherman,   weather reporter   see JOB TITLES

Web, web page, website   see COMPUTER TERMS

we'd   see CONTRACTIONS

weft   see WARP

weigh   see -EI-, -IE-

weird   *Weird* means supernatural or unearthly, or, by extension, unusual or strange. Some critics object to the extended sense, but it is now standard. *Weird* is derived from the Old English noun *wyrd*, meaning 'fate' or 'destiny'. In *Macbeth* Shakespeare used the noun as an adjective, calling the three witches the 'weird sisters'; hence the modern use of *weird*. *Weird* is commonly misspelled *wierd*, because it does not follow the *i* before *e* spelling rule.

The blaze began in earnest then, with flickering fingers of flame lighting up the room and throwing weird, dancing shadows on the wall.
Dogs in Canada Special Issue 1986: 90

Honey Harbour to the south and Go Home Bay (weird names but great country) to the north also have summer churches.
United Church Observer June 1986: 22

See also -IE-, -EI-.

well   see ADJECTIVES AND ADVERBS

well known   *Well known* is usually hyphenated when it precedes the noun it modifies ('well-known works') and written as two words when it does not ('These works are well known').

The comparative and superlative forms *better known* and *best known* are far more common in published writing than *more well known* and *most well known.* The latter pair, which treat *well* as part of a two-word adjective rather than as an adverb, are cumbersome but not incorrect.

The negative forms *less well known, lesser known,* and *less known* are all common and acceptable.

> To this day, the Regina Manifesto is probably better known and more frequently cited than any other CCF-NDP manifesto, and for many Canadians it is the touchstone of Canadian socialism.
> Alan Whitehorn *Canadian Socialism* 1992: 38

> If P.K. Page's visual art has suffered unjust neglect, it may be because she has not been situated in the tradition of more well-known painters such as Lawren Harris, Emily Carr, Bertram Brooker and Jock Macdonald, whose philosophy and aesthetic she in part shares.
> *Journal of Canadian Studies* 38.1 (2004): 194

> (Some editors would replace 'more well-known' with 'better known'.)

See also HYPHENATION.

Welsh, Welch   The current spelling for someone or something from Wales is *Welsh*; the older spelling *Welch* now survives in the name of the Royal Welch Fusiliers. The slang verb *welsh* or *welch*, meaning to fail to pay a debt or to go back on a promise, is now considered a slur against people of Welsh descent.

> Opera lovers may see the Welsh National Opera Company perform Bellini's Norma. . . .
> *Globe and Mail* (Toronto) 5 Jan. 1985: T2

> . . . Mr. Graves went to France to fight as an infantry captain with the Royal Welch Fusiliers during the First World War.
> *Globe and Mail* (Toronto) 9 Dec. 1985: D14

> Edwards was 'a four flusher,' 'a tin horn,' and 'a welcher on poker debts.'
> Pierre Berton *The Promised Land* 1984: 271

> (Here 'welcher' suggests now-dated dialect.)

> He accused the federal Government of trying to 'fuzzify and welsh out' on the negotiation roles that it agreed to at the first ministers' meeting in

Halifax last week.
> *Globe and Mail* (Toronto) 5 Dec. 1985: A3

> (This writer has marked the offensive expression 'welsh out' as a direct quotation.)

See also GYPSY, GIPSY

Weltanschauung   see GERMAN WORDS, PRONUNCIATION OF

went   see GO

were   see IF I WERE YOU; SUBJUNCTIVE

west   see EAST, WEST, NORTH, SOUTH

West Indian   see INDIAN; WEST INDIES

West Indies, Caribbean   There is no established distinction between the terms 'the West Indies' and 'the Caribbean'. In the strict geographical sense, they refer only to those islands within or bordering on the Caribbean Sea, namely the Greater Antilles—Cuba, Jamaica, and Hispaniola, containing Haiti and the Dominican Republic—and the Lesser Antilles, the chain of islands extending from the Virgin Islands to Curacao.

However, cultural and political discussions of the West Indies or the Caribbean, particularly those associated with the British colonial heritage, sometimes include the Bahamas and Bermuda and the mainland countries of Belize (formerly British Honduras) and Guyana (formerly British Guiana).

Caribbean is frequently misspelled; remembering that it is derived from the name of the Carib Indians, who inhabited the West Indies when Columbus arrived, may help with the spelling. The usual pronunciation of *Caribbean* is *kair i BEE un*, but *kuh RIB ee un* is equally acceptable.

> But the two young men were basking in an unmistakably Caribbean atmosphere. The town house was filled with the pungent smell of a West Indian fish fry. . . .
> *Maclean's* 29 April 1991: T8

> The meeting was aimed at strengthening century-old trade ties between Canada and Caribbean

nations such as Barbados, Belize, Guyana, Trinidad and Tobago, Jamaica and Grenada.
Financial Post 20 March 1990: 3

(Here Belize and Guyana are included in the Caribbean.)

Although Florida, Bermuda, Mexico and Venezuela are not technically part of the Caribbean, they are considered as Caribbean destinations by many travel agents and tour operators.
Gazette (Montreal) 19 Dec. 1992: C1

The Commonwealth Best First Book award, worth $4,000, went to Bahamian author Robert Antoni, also from the Carribean and Canada region.
Toronto Star 5 Nov. 1992: A2

(The correct spelling is *Caribbean*.)

See also INDIAN, EAST INDIAN, INDO-CANADIAN, SOUTH ASIAN, WEST INDIAN.

wetlands   see SWAMP

Wet'suwet'en   see CARRIER

wharf   see -F, -V-

when   see IS WHEN

where   see IS WHEN, IS WHERE; -WHERE

-where, -place   The adverbs *anywhere*, *everywhere*, *somewhere*, and *nowhere* are used on both sides of the Atlantic, but the variants *anyplace* and *someplace* (especially 'someplace else', 'anyplace else') are common only in Canada and the United States. British authorities label the *-place* variants unacceptable, while the Americans defend them. In Canada *anyplace* and *someplace* are common in speech, but they are decidedly less formal than *anywhere* and *somewhere*, the only forms to appear in formal writing. *Anyplace* and *someplace* appear occasionally in fiction and the press. *Noplace* and *everyplace* are rarely used.

You're not going to find this much entertainment value anyplace else.
Toronto Star 13 June 1994: A2

I hear sirens far away urgently going someplace.
Queen's Quarterly 93.1 (1986): 70

And it will happen again next year, someplace else, for the same reasons. . . .
Daily News (Halifax) 18 June 1994: 19

whereas   The conjunction *whereas* has two different meanings. In the preamble of a formal proclamation or resolution it means 'in view of the fact that'. The Canadian Constitution Act, 1982, begins 'Whereas Canada is founded upon principles that recognize the supremacy of God and the rule of law' and goes on to list the freedoms and rights that every Canadian is entitled to. Much more commonly *whereas* is used like *while* to suggest contrast, and it is particularly useful in contexts where *while* might simply mean 'during the time'. Consider the difference between 'She went to chef school while he did an MBA' and 'She went to chef school, whereas he did an MBA'.

WHEREAS $900,000 of a $1.4 million fund for the elimination of wage discrimination is being shuffled into the mill rate stabilization fund; and WHEREAS the remaining $500,000 allotted to pay equity will only be disbursed after union negotiations with the city have been completed; therefore BE IT RESOLVED that the female members of city council . . . accept an annual salary of $30,276.18, which is calculated as 66 per cent of what the male members of city council [will receive]. . . .
Calgary Herald 6 Feb. 1994: A6

(In this pseudo-proclamation, *whereas* means 'in view of the fact that'.)

. . . the bands were trained to the new lively tempo of the piece, whereas the crowds, though full of fervor, leaned toward the old dirge-like version.
Ottawa Citizen 23 June 1994: A11

See also WHEREFORE.

wherefore   *Wherefore* is an archaic adverb meaning to what end or why. Thus, the oft-quoted lament of Shakespeare's Juliet, 'Wherefore art thou Romeo?', does not mean 'Romeo, where are you?' but 'Why are you Romeo [an enemy of my family]?'

In contemporary legal language, *wherefore* is a conjunction meaning for this reason, which is often used to introduce the resolution clause of a petition.

. . . WHEREAS . . . children are finding their daily trips over the road very difficult; WHEREFORE your petitioners urge the Government of Newfoundland and Labrador to upgrade and pave the approximately four kilometres of Route 235 from Birchy Cove to Bonavista.
House of Assembly Newfoundland and Labrador Hansard 21 May 2002

See also WHEREAS.

whet the appetite   *Whet* derives from an Old English word meaning sharpen. To *whet the appetite* is to sharpen or stimulate it—not, as some writers think, to satiate it. Occasionally *whet* is misspelled *wet*, perhaps by writers who plan on whetting their appetites with an aperitif, or perhaps through confusion with the expression *wet one's whistle*, meaning take a drink.

Anne of Green Gables, a 1985 mini-series . . . whetted viewer appetites for more Montgomery.
Gazette (Montreal) 7 Jan. 1990: F1

Even success in the replacement market, however, isn't really enough to whet the appetites of TV manufacturers. Nor will it satisfy PC makers.
Computer Dealer News 21 March 1991: 32

(Given the context and the parallel second sentence, it appears that this writer is mistakenly using *whet* to mean satisfy.)

Domestic accounts appear now to have fully whetted their appetite with new supply.
Financial Post 22 Nov. 1990: 27

(Here again it appears that the writer is mistakenly using *whetted* to mean satisfied.)

. . . you may only find a few tantalizing details to wet your appetite in the book's 246 pages.
Edmonton Journal 13 Sept. 1992: D6

(The correct word is *whet*.)

See also FOLK ETYMOLOGY.

whether   see IF; WHETHER OR NOT

whether or not   Many usage guides recommend omitting *or not* after *whether*. However, there are contexts where this is not possible:

'We are going ahead whether they like it or not'. It is possible to omit the *or not* when the sense of the phrase is roughly equivalent to 'if'. For example, 'I don't know whether or not I did the right thing' may be rewritten 'I don't know whether I did the right thing', which is more concise. In formal writing, where conciseness is highly valued, an optional *or not* is usually omitted. In fiction and journalism, where the writing is usually more idiomatic, *or not* is often retained. This is a point of style. Sometimes *whether* alone is more elegant; sometimes including *or not* is more rhetorically effective. Let your ear guide your choice, and keep in mind the level of formality required.

Whether is often misspelled *wether* (which, incidentally, is the term for a castrated ram).

. . . fifty-seven per cent favoured it whether it created jobs or not.
Saturday Night Jan. 1986: 13

(Here it is not possible to omit *or not*.)

As a result there is some debate about whether the Charter of Rights applies to the internal workings of the legislatures and to the operation of political parties.
Andrew Heard *Canadian Constitutional Conventions* 1991: 84–85

(In formal writing, *or not* is usually omitted if possible.)

Those who have made this argument have questioned whether a distinctively Japanese pattern actually exists.
Irving M. Zeitlin and Robert J. Brym *The Social Condition of Humanity* 1991: 360

(In formal writing, *or not* is usually omitted if possible.)

The real question is: Does she care whether the human race survives or not?
Margaret Atwood *Life Before Man* 1979: 19

(In fiction and journalism, an optional *or not* is often retained.)

. . . her client will also await the RCMP's conclusions before deciding whether or not to pursue charges.
Maclean's 11 Nov. 1991: A29

(In fiction and journalism, an optional *or not* is often retained.)

'I don't know yet—in the minds of the committee—wether we should be there in more than observer status.'
Financial Post 13 Aug. 1990: 3

(The correct spelling is *whether*.)

See also IF, WHETHER.

which   see THAT, WHICH

Whig   see GRIT

while   see AS, WHILE, BECAUSE; AWHILE; WHEREAS

whinny, whiny   A *whinny* is the sound a horse makes. To *whinny* is to make such a sound. *Whiny*, sometimes spelled *whiney*, is the adjective related to *whine*.

The horses whinnied their greeting, and the cows contentedly chewed their cud.
Edmonton Journal 24 Dec. 1998: G3

Also, young children often behave beautifully for hours while their mother is away and then turn into whinny, demanding, unpleasant children upon her return.
Sudbury Star 20 Feb. 2006: B6

(The word needed here is *whiny*.)

See also SHINNY, SHINY; -Y, -EY.

whip cream, whipped cream   see SKIM MILK

whisky, whiskey   Almost all dictionaries and usage guides suggest that *whisky* is the British and Canadian spelling, while *whiskey* is the Irish and American spelling. However, some Canadian writers maintain the distinction between Scotch *whisky* and Irish *whiskey*, and in general Canadians use the two variants about equally. What Canadians refer to as *rye* or *rye whisk(e)y* is called 'Canadian whisky' outside the country. The usual plural of *whisky* is *whiskies*; of *whiskey*, *whiskeys*.

Harry invited me out to his car for a drink of fairly good rye whiskey.
Max Braithwaite *The Night We Stole the Mountie's Car* 1971: 108

We even tried, God help us, to sell rye whisky to the Scots.
George Ignatieff *The Making of a Peacemonger* 1987: 177

whisky jack, whisky-john   see FOLK ETYMOLOGY

whisper   see ONOMATOPOEIA

white   see BLACK

white paper   see GREEN PAPER

whiz   see ONOMATOPOEIA

whither   see HITHER

who, whom   Traditionally, *who* is used as the subject of a sentence or clause and *whom* is used as the object of a verb or preposition. In spoken Canadian English, however, *who* has largely displaced *whom*—which is not to say that *whom* is moribund. Often the same people who find *whom* overly fastidious in casual conversation take pains to use it correctly in their formal writing.

• *Informal usage*
In informal spoken Canadian English, *who* tends to be the form of the interrogative pronoun at the beginning of a sentence, whether it is a subject or an object:

'Who is asking?'
(*Who* is the subject.)

'Who are they interviewing?'
(*Who* is the object; *they* is the subject.)

'Who do I send it to?'
(*Who* is the object; *I* is the subject.)

Whom is used consistently only in constructions such as 'some of whom', 'none of whom', or 'seven of whom'.

• *Formal usage*
In formal writing 'Whom are they interviewing?' and 'To whom do I send it?' are still

required. When *who* or *whom* is used as a relative pronoun, the correct form is determined by its function *within* the relative clause:

'She chose someone whom they knew.'
('they knew him'—*whom* is the object of the relative clause)

'She chose someone who would entertain them.'
('he would entertain them'—*who* is the subject of the relative clause)

The objective form is always required directly after a preposition: 'by whom she had a child', 'with whom they had much in common'.

• *Overuse of whom*
Because *whom* sounds more refined than *who*, it tends to be overused in formal speech and writing. People sometimes insert it in sentences where *who* is the appropriate form: 'Whom do you think you are?'; 'I cannot say whom it will be' (see also HYPERCORRECTION). This erroneous substitution is particularly common when *who* is a relative pronoun directly followed by a parenthetical phrase such as 'I think' or 'we imagine':

'Chris is someone whom we think will go far.'
('who will go far'—*who* is correct)

'Here at last was someone whom he hoped could love him.'
('who could love him'—*who* is correct)

'Whom shall I say is calling?'
('who is calling?'—*who* is correct)

This error is very common in literary writing and has been since the Renaissance—so common, in fact, that some commentators refuse to regard it as an error at all. They label the whole structure grammatically ambiguous and accept either *who* or *whom* in the context. While these commentators may be more realistic about English grammar, they also tend to be less adamant than those who consider *whom* wrong

in the examples above. It's probably best, therefore, to avoid *whom* in such contexts.

. . . in order to get the coveted degrees or (real baseness, this) to gain favor with people whom I temporarily believed knew better about such things than myself, I have pretended to love the drama only.
Robertson Davies *A Voice from the Attic* 1960: 158

(Some editors would correct 'whom I temporarily believed knew better' to 'who I temporarily . . .'.)

See also CASE; PRONOUNS BETWEEN LINKED VERBS.

who else('s)   see ELSE

who's, whose   *Who's* is a contraction of *who is* or *who has*: 'Guess who's here!'; 'Who's been using my computer?'. *Whose* is the possessive form of *who*: 'Whose coat is that?'; 'Whose are these?' Because *who's* ends with an apostrophe followed by *s*, it looks like a possessive form, and people mistakenly substitute it for *whose*: 'Who's card is this?' And occasionally people make the opposite mistake, using *whose* where the contraction is required: 'Whose on the phone?'

Whose is also a possessive adjective: 'the woman whose house we bought'. Some people are ill at ease using *whose* with things: 'a car whose wheels are out of alignment'. They feel obliged to write 'a car the wheels of which are out of alignment', even though that sounds stiff. Grammarians in the late eighteenth century invented the rule that the relative pronoun *whose* should be reserved for people. At that time the rule was a departure from established usage, and it never did catch on in either popular or literary writing. However, the rule has been a bugbear for generations of conscientious writers. Happily for the contemporary writer, usage guides are now unanimous in approving the use of *whose* with a non-human antecedent. In fact, many guides express a preference for *whose* as less clumsy than *of which*.

They meet at a reception attended by everybody who's anybody in Hong Kong.
Financial Post 16 Dec. 1990: 7

'I'm a big guy whose going to work the corners, drive for the net and help my teammates.'
Daily News (Halifax) 18 March 1992: 43

(Here *who's*, the contraction of *who is*, is required.)

For weeks he talked about the little girl he'd played with all day and who's name sounded something like 'Maggie.'
Province (Vancouver) 7 Oct. 1990: 6

(Here *whose* is required.)

The mosses include species whose distribution is widespread in Canada.
Canadian Journal of Earth Sciences 26 (1989): 261

(Often *whose* is more readable than *of which*.)

He also assumes . . . that we are in the midst of a profound . . . environmental crisis whose solution might require a theory of its origins.
Queen's Quarterly 92.1 (1985): 208–9

See also CONTRACTIONS; THEIRS.

wholly see -E

whosoever see ARCHAISMS

why see REASON IS BECAUSE

wide see ADJECTIVES AND ADVERBS; ADVERBS WITHOUT -LY; SLOW, SLOWLY

widow, widower *Widow* is perhaps the only word in the English language that is feminine in its basic form and adds a suffix to form a masculine: *widower*. In figurative use, a *widow* is a hand of cards dealt to the table, or, in printing, a single line of type carried over to the top of a new page.

Many commentators object to the phrase 'widow of the late', since if a woman is a widow, her husband must be dead. 'Widow of so-and-so' and 'wife of the late' are both unobjectionable.

Last year, Ms. Miller became a widow when her husband succumbed to cancer, leaving her to raise the four children.
National Post (Toronto) 26 April 2005: A10

We read . . . of the growing affection of Mina for Angéline's father, the widower M. de Montbrun.
Ben-Z. Shek *French-Canadian & Québécois Novels* 1991: 10

See also LATE, THE.

wifedom see -DOM

will see SHALL

wind-up see FUNCTIONAL SHIFT

Winnipegger see NAMES OF RESIDENTS OF CITIES AND PROVINCES

-wise The suffix *-wise* is standard in compounds such as *streetwise* and *travelwise*, where it means knowledgeable about. It is also long established as meaning in the position or direction of, as in *crosswise* and *clockwise*. Since the 1930s *-wise* has also come to be used to mean 'in terms of', or 'with regard to'. This sense is common in business jargon (*careerwise*, *marketwise*, *profitwise*, *salarywise*, *saleswise*) and has begun to proliferate, but there is still strong resistance to it in serious general writing. New words formed with *-wise* are usually considered slangy or inelegant.

What a religious attitude will not give you is a shrewd, worldly-wise novel by Trollope or Thackeray.
Robertson Davies *One Half of Robertson Davies* 1978: 207

'The focus that our social conditioning places upon us (and I say even from before we're born—class-wise, gender-wise, race-wise, culturally) fragments everything.'
Room of One's Own June 1990: 37

(The phrase after the dash could be rewritten: 'with respect to class, gender, race and culture'.)

'We have a great board. Everybody on there is easy to talk to and they're all level-headed. And there's a good mix personality-wise.'
Canadian Rodeo News March 1990: 15

(Here the *-wise* suffix is unnecessary: 'And there's a good mix of personalities' would do.)

See also HYPHENATION.

wit   see TO WIT

withdrawal   *Withdrawal* is widely misspelled *withdrawl*, perhaps because it is often pronounced with only two syllables, and because *drawl* is a recognizable (albeit unrelated) word. Both the three- and two-syllable pronunciations are standard: *with DRAW ul* or *with DRAWL*.

> The decision . . . has since led to the dismissal or withdrawl of about 50,000 charges. . . .
> *Financial Post* 9 July 1991: F7

(The correct spelling is *withdrawal*.)

with regard[s] to   see IN REGARD[S] TO

witness box, witness stand   In Canadian and British courtrooms, witnesses testify from a *witness box*. Because American legal dramas are common fare on Canadian television, American legal terminology creeps into Canadian usage. American courtrooms have a *witness stand*, and witnesses 'take the stand'. Some Canadians strongly object to the use of American terminology in Canadian contexts.

> As the mother sobbed, her son leaned forward in the witness box and began to weep quietly, causing Judge Gove to order a brief adjournment.
> *Vancouver Sun* 13 Oct. 1990: A1

> But when Jackson took the witness stand, he was giving in to waves of belligerence.
> Jack Batten *Robinette* 1984: 16

(Some prefer *witness box* in reference to a Canadian courtroom.)

wives   see -F, -V-

Wolastoqiyik   see MALISEET

wolves   see -F, -V-

woman doctor   see JOB TITLES

wonder   To state that one is wondering something is not to ask a question, and thus no question mark is required:

I wonder when they'll finish.

She wondered why they did that.

On the other hand, if the word *wonder* introduces a direct question, a question mark is required:

I wonder, 'Will they ever finish?'

Why did they do that? she wondered.

Some writers put the direct question (Will they ever finish? or Why did they do that?) in quotation marks, while others reserve quotation marks for things that are actually spoken, not merely thought. Either style is acceptable.

> It makes one wonder if the Newfoundlanders will seek the same kind of status.
> W.C. Lougheed, ed. *In Search of the Standard in Canadian English* 1986: 70

> I often wondered what he was doing, where he was going.
> Jack Chambers *Milestones* 1983: 124

> I wonder what my uncle would recommend?
> *Queen's Quarterly* 96.1 (1989): 44

(This is a statement and should end with a period, not a question mark.)

> 'What will wicked boys do now?' he wondered.
> *Queen's Quarterly* 92.3 (1985): 494

> Why didn't he know that? Adam wondered.
> *Canadian Fiction Magazine* 64 (1988): 56

(This writer does not use quotation marks around thoughts.)

> What part did she play in her mother's life, I wondered.
> Max Braithwaite *The Night We Stole the Mountie's Car* 1971: 165

(The first part of this sentence is a direct question: a question mark should replace the comma after 'life'.)

See also QUOTATION, QUOTATION MARKS.

wondrous   see DISASTROUS

wont, wonted   *Wont* is used as an adjective after the verb *be* to mean apt, or likely, or accustomed: 'They are wont to complain'. The noun *wont* normally occurs in the expression 'as is my (your, his, etc.) wont', where *wont* means habit or custom. The adjective *wonted* is placed before the noun it modifies and means usual or customary. Pronunciation of *wont* varies: it may rhyme with *won't*, *want*, or, occasionally, *punt*.

. . . the Coliseum crowds are wont to boo the Rangers. . . .
Globe and Mail (Toronto) 28 Nov. 1985: C5

Instead, as has been his wont for almost 30 years, Dylan weathered the storm and delivered the ultimate in idiosyncratic performances. . . .
Gazette (Montreal) 30 May 1990: E9

We have to be ready when Hollywood rolls out its red carpet and wallows in its wonted spectacular excess.
Ottawa Citizen 22 Feb. 2004: C2

wood, woods   see FOREST

woof   see WARP

woollen   see SPELLING, CANADIAN

Worcester, Worcestershire   see GLOUCESTER

wordiness, variation   The rallying cry of William F. Strunk Jr. and E.B. White in their widely known *Elements of Style* was 'omit needless words'. Attempting to cut the number of words in a piece of writing is certainly a good way to focus revision. However, not everyone likes a consistently plain style. The point of cutting words is not to reduce all prose to sameness, but to ensure that the writer's points are made engagingly and convincingly by cutting out unnecessary phrases and repetition.

A pleonasm is a phrase in which one or more words are superfluous because they express a meaning already expressed in another word. Some pleonasms have entered the language. The phrase 'I saw it with my own eyes' was perhaps first used for comic emphasis, but now it is an idiom. Others in the same category are 'gather together', 'mental telepathy', and 'the reason why'. The pleonasms below are commonly criticized and should always be avoided in writing:

audible to the ear	limited to only
combine together	most favourite
consecutive days in a row	necessary prerequisite
free gift	predict in advance
	revert back

Sometimes writers repeat an idea in different words without clarifying or amplifying the original idea: 'Shakespeare's historically inaccurate picture of Richard III is no longer believed to be true to the facts of the monarch's life'. This sort of circular statement, called a tautology, should definitely be pruned.

Language commentators have also criticized as wordy the following multi-word phrases that have one-word equivalents.

wordy	*alternative*
as far as x is concerned	concerning x, with respect to x
at this point in time	now, today
by means of	by
due to the fact that	because
during the course of	during
in the event that	if
in the near future	soon
in spite of the fact that	although
on a temporary basis	temporarily
until such time as	until
with the exception of	except

The shorter alternative is often better and should always be considered. Sometimes, however, the longer phrase answers to the requirements of rhythm, balance, or emphasis.

In an earnest attempt to avoid boring the reader with repetition, some writers fall into a trap that Fowler, in his *Dictionary of Modern English Usage*, calls 'elegant variation'. Fowler points out that if we vary a key word, readers may well wonder if the varied term should be read as equivalent to the key word or different from it. Here is one of his many examples: 'There are 466 cases; they consist of 366 matrimonial suits, 56 Admiralty actions, and 44

Probate cases'. He recommends omitting *suits* and *actions* so that the reader will not have to wonder how a suit, an action, and a case might differ. Repeating a key phrase is often necessary to maintain the cohesion of a paragraph.

One of the most common and confusing forms of elegant variation is the attempt to avoid repeating *say* by using words such as *admit, advise, affirm, allege, argue, assert, claim, concede, contend, declare, disclose, opine, reveal,* and *state*. These words all have different connotations (of guilt, concealment, assuredness, and so on) and should not be used simply to avoid repeating *say*.

The passive voice (see VOICE in the Glossary) is always wordier than the active voice and many language commentators suggest avoiding it altogether. However, the passive voice is conventional and acceptable in scientific and legal writing. In other types of writing, the danger lies in using the passive voice merely to sound lofty. If the passive voice is used consistently, the effect is deadening, for every action seems to take place at one remove. 'A decision was reached by the board of trustees, and a committee has been established so that the question can be examined further' is probably better rewritten 'The board of trustees has decided to establish a committee to study the question further'. When used judiciously, however, the passive voice can highlight a significant point: 'The case was televised worldwide'. The active voice ('Television networks broadcast the case around the world') would not be an improvement here.

Speech is often more redundant than writing—and it should be, because listeners, unlike readers, have no chance to go back and reread something they didn't understand the first time. Even in writing, the discussion of complex or unfamiliar concepts may also require a somewhat repetitive style.

However, no cure has been found for writing that is produced to fill a page rather than to pursue an argument or entertain or inform. Sometimes writers are expected to produce prose that sounds impressive while conveying little in the way of detail. Advertising copywriters and bureaucrats often fall victim to the demand for prose that does not commit them (or their employers) to anything specific. Here is an example (from *Background Paper on Regional Planning and Development in Ontario,* Ontario Regional Trilevel Conference, 1973):

> In our modern society a government cannot govern effectively without planning ahead. The great and often competing demands made upon all levels of government today mean that government must have a clear and realistic idea of how these demands can be met. To do this is to plan. Any other approach is irresponsible.
>
> The act of planning and developing policies for program implementation can take many forms and operate at many levels. Within the framework of provincial responsibilities the process of planning covers a multitude of programs and interests. For example, as part of our continuing concern for individual wellbeing the province has developed a coherent set of policies and implementation programs in the field of social development.

Apart from conveying the vague sense that the government has plans intended to promote 'individual wellbeing', this passage is filler—which may well have been all it was intended to be.

See also BEING AS; COMPARISONS; CONSENSUS; DESPITE; FOR FREE; GOES WITHOUT SAYING; IN REGARD(S) TO; INTENTS AND PURPOSES; INVITED GUEST; PAST HISTORY; PERSONAL; RE-; REASON IS BECAUSE; REFER BACK; REVERT; TOGETHER; TOTAL; UNTIL.

wore   see WEAR

worked   see WROUGHT

worker   see JOB TITLES

work force, workman   see JOB TITLES; SEXIST LANGUAGE

World War I, World War II   see FIRST WORLD WAR

World Wide Web   see COMPUTER TERMS

worn   see WEAR

worse, [worser]   *Worser* is non-standard. *Worse* is correct as an adjective ('a worse result'), an adverb ('We played worse than the beginners'), and a noun ('definitely the worse of the two'). Until the eighteenth century, *worser* and *worse* were both common in literary writing, but today *worser* is considered uneducated.

> Worser still, it was utterly delicious and, in our weakened state, irresistible.
> *Gazette* (Montreal) 23 Feb. 1990: B7

(The correct word is *worse*.)

See also COMPARISONS.

worship   see DOUBLING THE FINAL CONSONANT

worth   'Twenty dollars' worth' means the worth of twenty dollars in kind. It is a possessive construction that has traditionally required an apostrophe. However, usage on this point is shifting. Where other dictionaries list 'two cents' worth', *Merriam-Webster's* now lists 'two cents worth'. Increasingly, the apostrophe is being dropped from plural possessives that specify amounts: 'two million dollars worth of business', 'three weeks holidays'. Books and scholarly journals tend to retain the apostrophe in these expressions, and this book is no exception. However, either style—with or without the apostrophe—is acceptable, as long as it is used consistently. Note that the apostrophe is always required when the amount is singular: 'a day's pay'.

> If the stairs are well proportioned, a few dollars' worth of paint may be all that's needed to brighten them.
> *Chatelaine* April 1986: 114

> Robinette gave Eagleson an appointment and thirty minutes' worth of advice.
> Jack Batten *Robinette* 1984: 222

> . . . while the proceedings cost him forty thousand dollars in lost work, he gained a million dollars worth of publicity for his cause. . . .
> *Queen's Quarterly* 95.4 (1988): 838

> But, as a scattering of words to buttress the display of 15 seconds worth of film, it is effective, and even laudable.

> W.C. Lougheed, ed. *In Search of the Standard in Canadian English* 1986: 96

> The Michigan Press Association was so eager that it offered to give two or three dollars worth of ads for every dollar Canada expended. . . . Factoria, it was said, would attract a million dollars' worth of industries and would have a population of two hundred in its first year.
> Pierre Berton *The Promised Land* 1984: 172–73, 340

(For the sake of consistency, an apostrophe should follow *dollars* in both of these sentences or in neither.)

> That means you have to put 1,000 snow crystals in a row to get one centimetre's worth.
> *Toronto Star* 3 May 1992: G6

(When the possessive is singular, the apostrophe is required.)

See also POSSESSIVE.

would have   see [HAD HAVE]

[would of]   see [COULD OF]

wrack   see RACK

wrangle, wangle   In British English, to *wrangle* is to argue or quarrel, while to *wangle* is to obtain something through persuasion or manipulation. Canadians and Americans share these meanings but also use *wrangle* as a synonym of *wangle*: '*wangle* concert tickets' *or* '*wrangle* concert tickets'. Some writers make a slight distinction of sense using *wangle* to describe getting something by fawning or scheming and *wrangle* by struggling or arguing.

In Canadian and American—though not British—English, there is yet another verb to *wrangle*, which means to work as a *wrangler* or ranch hand, wrestling with cows and rounding up the herd. This is the verb Canadians are using metaphorically when they '*wrangle* (wrestle) with a math assignment' or '*wrangle* (round up) an audience'.

> The ship sat in harbor for two months while officials wrangled over the passengers' fate.
> *Vancouver Sun* 14 Feb. 1990: B8

(*Wrangle* means argue in both Britain and North America.)

For the past two years, I've been trying to wangle an interview with Stephen Harper. I've smiled cheerily at him in airplanes. I've grinned at him in hallways. . . . I've asked his friends to put in a good word for me. I've done everything but send him flowers, but no dice.
Globe and Mail (Toronto) 27 May 2006: A19

(*Wangle* means obtain something by fawning or scheming in both Britain and North America.)

Both the Defence Agency and the Foreign Ministry successfully wrangled more money out of the tightfisted Finance Ministry in negotiations. . . .
Financial Post 24 Jan. 1989: 9

(*Wrangle* is used as a synonym of *wangle* only in North America.)

She recently wrangled nearly 1,000 volunteers for the Calgary International Children's Festival. . . .
Calgary Herald 21 July 2006: SW23

(*Wrangle* meaning round up is unfamiliar in Britain.)

wrath, wrathful, wroth   *Wrath* is intense anger or great indignation. *Wrathful* is the adjective form meaning deeply angry or moved to vengeance. *Wroth*, an archaic variant of *wrathful*, is used only as a predicate adjective, as in 'God was wroth'. Generally, Canadians pronounce *wrath* to rhyme with *path* and *wroth* to rhyme with *moth*. For some British speakers, *wrath* rhymes with *moth* and *wroth* with *both*.

'While I would not give vent to my wrath so overtly, I understand his point.'
Queen's Quarterly 92.2 (1985): 442

It made you think of Church words like the wrath of God. . . .
Constance Beresford-Howe *Night Studies* 1985: 142–43

. . . Chunky, in a wrathful temper reminiscent of his grandfather, quit after 25 years as a director of the Royal Bank of Canada.
Globe and Mail (Toronto) 29 Nov. 1985: P68

wreak   *Wreak* (pronounced *REEK*) is used most often in the expression *wreak havoc*, meaning to cause destruction. But one can also wreak

(i.e., inflict) such things as mayhem, evil, anger, and vengeance. 'Wreck havoc' is a mistaken form of 'wreak havoc', influenced no doubt by the fact that wreaking havoc amounts to wrecking things.

The past tense of *wreak* is *wreaked*: 'wreaked havoc'. 'Wrought havoc' is often seen but, strictly speaking, is not idiomatic. *Wrought* is an archaic past form of the verb *work* ('What hath God wrought?'). The confusion is hardly surprising, given that both *wreaked* and *wrought* are nearly obsolete and mostly confined to fixed expressions.

But when men took it upon themselves to wreak the wrath of God on transgressors, they assumed the right to wreak some of their own wrath in the process.
Richard Davies and Glen Kirkland, eds. *Dimensions* 1986: 66

Equally absent is . . . any mention of the havoc wreaked on the urban landscape by the freeway.
Canadian Heritage Magazine Feb.–Mar. 1986: 43

In other matches, the eerily unpopulated Sky-Dome continued to wreck havoc on seeded players.
Ottawa Citizen 14 Feb. 1990: F2

(The idiom is *wreak havoc*.)

As in the ill-fated Meech Lake amendment, changes in provincial governments could again wreck havoc by reversing ratifications.
Ottawa Citizen 2 Feb. 1991: A3

(The idiom is *wreak havoc*.)

The greenish-yellow cloud wrought havoc among unprotected Canadian and French North African troops huddled in their trenches.
Maclean's 18 Feb. 1991: A34

(The idiom is *wreaked havoc*.)

See also FOLK ETYMOLOGY; WROUGHT, WORKED.

wreath, wreathe   see BATH

wreck   see WREAK

wrench   see RETCH

wretch   see RETCH

wright   see PLAYWRIGHT

writer, present   see PRESENT WRITER

wrong   see ADVERBS WITHOUT -LY

wroth   see WRATH

wrought, worked   In Early Modern English, *wrought* was the usual past tense and past participle of *work*. Although *worked* is the past participle used generally today, *wrought* is preserved in several distinct usages. For example, things that are well crafted are often called 'finely wrought'. A person whose emotions are all worked up may be described as 'overwrought'. *Wrought* is sometimes used to mean brought about, as in 'changes wrought by revolution'. Finally, *wrought iron* is decorative ironwork often used for furnishings and railings.

They appreciate the beauty of top-quality

turquoise beads and the intrinsic worth of . . . a finely wrought silver bracelet.
Globe and Mail (Toronto) 5 March 1985: F9

In 1844, inventor Samuel Morse sent the first public message—'What God hath wrought'—over his electric telegraph between Washington, D.C., and Baltimore.
Globe and Mail (Toronto) 24 May 1985: M2

So one should acknowledge that improvements have taken place, . . . but I am not sure Davis can be said to have wrought them himself.
Queen's Quarterly 94.2 (1987): 347

It's helped the congregation focus on the community outside those big wooden doors and wrought-iron gate at the foot of George Street West.
Telegram (St. John's) 14 June 2006: B1

See also WREAK.

www   see COMPUTER TERMS

X

X   When X-rays were discovered in 1895, their nature was a mystery: hence the name *X*-rays. In every domain from mathematics to game shows, *x* represents something or someone unknown or unidentified.

The British often call an X-shaped mark a 'cross'. Canadians use this pronunciation only in combinations, such as *X-country* or *X-C* meaning cross-country ('X-country team', 'X-C skiing') or *X-references* meaning cross-references. In the combinations *X-ray*, *X-treme* ('X-treme sports') and *Xpresspost* (the Canada Post express mail service), the letter is pronounced *ecks*.

Mr. X is a lawyer and the nexus of a $400-million merchandising fortune.
Globe and Mail (Toronto) 21 Dec. 1985: A10

Xmas   *Xmas* (pronounced *KRIS mus* or, more

informally, *EX mus*) is not another deplorable manifestation of the commercialization of Christmas. However, since that is what this abbreviation is widely believed to be, it is best reserved for advertising copy and informal writing. In fact, *Xmas* has been in use since the 1500s, and *Xianity* was used before 1100. The *X* represents *chi*, the first letter of the Greek word for Christ; thus *X* is an abbreviation of *Christ*.

The toys are distributed at Xmas by the Salvation Army to needy children in the area.
Canadian Biker Magazine Feb. 1990: 12

. . . the Websters' annual Xmas bash is usually held at their home in Westmount. . . .
Gazette (Montreal) 27 Jan. 1990: K3

Y

-y, -ey If you sometimes hesitate over whether an adjective ends in *-y* or *-ey* (*stony* or *stoney*?), you are not alone. Variant spellings often appear in print because there is no hard and fast rule about whether to drop the *e* before adding *y* (cf. *pricey* and *spicy*). Dictionaries sometimes list two spellings for such adjectives, placing the majority usage first.

Below is a list of *-y/-ey* variants that occur in published Canadian writing, with the majority usage in bold type. Less acceptable variants— i.e., those that some dictionaries do not list— are bracketed. Note that the questionable spellings invariably end in *-ey*. Clearly, it is always acceptable to drop the *-e-*, although it is not always the norm.

> **achy**, [achey]
> **bony**, [boney]
> cagy, **cagey**
> gamy, **gamey**
> homy, **homey**
> **lacy**, [lacey]
> **nosy**, nosey
> **phony**, phoney
> poky, **pokey**
> pricy, **pricey**
> **scary**, [scarey]
> **smoky**, smokey
> spacy, **spacey**
> **spicy**, [spicey]
> **spiky**, [spikey]
> **stony**, stoney
> **tingly**, [tingley]
> **whiny**, whiney

See also -E; PHONY, PHONEY; SCARIFY, SCARY, SCARIFI-CATION; WHINNY, WHINY; WHISKY, WHISKEY; -Y, -IES.

-y, -ies Nouns that end in *-y* preceded by a consonant form their plurals by changing the *y* to *i* and adding *-es*: *lady, ladies; spy, spies; sty, sties.* Nouns that end in *-quy*, like *colloquy, obloquy,* and *soliloquy,* are pluralized the same way: *colloquies,* *obloquies, soliloquies.* Most nouns that end in *-ey* are pluralized *-eys,* but some have an alternative *-ies* plural: *moneys* or *monies.* Proper names retain the *y* when made plural: 'three Marys'.

See also PLURALS; MONEY.

yacht *Yacht* (pronounced *YAHT*) is often misspelled *yatch,* on the pattern of more familiar words such as *catch* and *hatch.*

yang see YIN

Yankee, Yank Today *Yankee* and the short form *Yank* can refer to any inhabitant of the United States, but originally only inhabitants of New England were called *Yankees.* Thus these terms are still sometimes used to refer specifically to New Englanders or, especially in the American South, to inhabitants of the states that fought against the Confederacy in the American Civil War. *Yankee* or *Yank* is sometimes used to convey a stereotype of Americans as brash, egocentric, and materialistic, but these words are not necessarily pejorative. Americans themselves have used *Yankee* with pride: 'Yankee ingenuity', 'New York Yankees'.

> The Canadian likes to be objective about Americans, and likes to feel that he can see a bit of Sam Slick in every Yankee: as a North American, therefore, he has a good seat on the revolutionary sidelines. . . .
> Northrop Frye *The Bush Garden* 1971: 137

> Only New Englanders and their progeny are Yankees, and the division between them and southerners has been and is the defining feature of American cultural and political history.
> *Guardian* (Charlottetown) 16 March 2000: A6

> (Here *Yankee* means New Englander.)

> Every other head in the place turns slowly, sizing him up, with wordless malevolence, as yet

another Yank with too much money.
Globe and Mail (Toronto) 5 Jan. 1985: M7

The Brits and the Yanks are part of a contingent of some 75 aircraft currently in Cold Lake for . . . tactical air exercises.
Globe and Mail (Toronto) 1 June 1985: P10

See also CANUCK.

yay   see YEA

ye   *Ye* is an archaic or dialectal form of *you*. In Middle English it was the plural of *thou*, and in some current dialects it can replace *you* as either subject or object, singular or plural.

Ye is also an archaic spelling of *the*—now always facetious or intentionally quaint. Authorities are divided over whether *ye*, as in 'Ye Olde Gifte Shoppe', should be pronounced *YEE* or *the*. Certainly the historically correct pronunciation is the same as *the*. In Middle English writing, the symbol þ represented the sound *th*, and *the* was spelt þe. Early printers, who had only the Roman alphabet at their disposal, could not reproduce þe, so they substituted the letter *y* for it. However, this printer's convention was never intended to reflect pronunciation. In reading historical documents, therefore, the definite article *ye* should be pronounced *the*. Contemporary usage is another matter. In contemporary contexts the 'mispronunciation' *YEE* is actually preferable, because it cues the listener to the quaint spelling and the mock-archaic style.

'Be ye salmon fishermen?'
Atlantic Salmon Journal Autumn 1990: 23

'Well, Mr Shaw, I'll tell ye: Latin is the only language that myshtifies [sic] the Devil.'
Eugene Forsey *A Life on the Fringe* 1990: 5

'This Philosophy is not of that kind which tendeth to vanity & deceipt but rather to profit & to edification inducing first ye knowledge of God & secondly ye way to find out true medicines in ye creaters. . . .'
Queen's Quarterly 95.1 (1988): 34

(In this historical quotation, the definite article *ye* should be pronounced as *the*.)

Model versions of the British originals, local snuggeries are springing up all over town, purveying imported ales and Ye Olde England conviviality. . . .
Alan Tucker, ed. *The Penguin Guide to Canada* 1991: 292

(Here the pronunciation *YEE* is acceptable, even preferable.)

See also ARCHAISMS.

yea, yay, yeah   A vote of approval may be called a *yea*; a dissenting vote is a *nay*. Both words rhyme with *say*.

Yea means 'indeed' in constructions such as 'difficult, yea impossible'. It means 'so' in the slang expression *yea big*, which is usually accompanied by a hand gesture. The cheer is spelled *yea*, or *yay*, or, occasionally, *yeah*; all these words rhyme with *say*.

The casual pronunciation of *yes* (*YA*) is almost always spelled *yeah*.

[The] new council . . . will want to hear the results of a two-year environmental study . . . before saying yea or nay to residential development on the property.
Vancouver Sun 10 May 1990: B1

What is false, what is legitimate, what is right, yea, what is moral in a free society can be determined only by the constant play of unfettered debate.
Globe and Mail (Toronto) 27 March 1985: P6

'Yea,' shouted a covey of school kids, spotting Mr. Buzzer and waving.
Vancouver Sun 28 June 1990: B1

'Yay, yay, yay, yay!!!' Everyone cheered, jumping up and down.
Gazette (Montreal) 23 Dec. 1990: D1

Curious onlookers cheered, shouting 'Yeah!' at every sound of shattered glass as cars sped through.
Gazette (Montreal) 29 Aug. 1990: A1

'Yeah, I guess.'
Queen's Quarterly 95.2 (1988): 403

year   see APPENDIX II

yellow journalism   see PURPLE PROSE

yet   see COMMA

yeti see SASQUATCH

Yiddish see JEW

yin, yang In Chinese Taoist philosophy, *yin* and *yang* are the two opposite but complementary principles of the universe, thought to coexist in most things and to operate cyclically to produce change. *Yin* is the passive principle; *yang* is the active principle. The spread of Eastern philosophy to North America has brought these words into popular use here. Allusions to *yin* and *yang* in Canadian writing usually suggest a harmonious blending of opposites.

Sometimes writers take the principle of complementarity too far, spelling *yin* incorrectly as *ying*. The expression *yin-yang* is slang.

It also means we can experience, in one, the yin and the yang of New York live entertainment from the bright lights of Broadway to the basements of Greenwich Village.
Globe and Mail (Toronto) 18 May 1985: T2

But there is a yang to the ying of this celestial cruise.
Gazette (Montreal) 23 July 1990: A1

(The correct spelling is *yin*.)

As choreographer, he is well aware of the yin-yang balance of his creative energy—the need to alternate very theatrical pieces with more straightforward but equally challenging dance invention.
Performing Arts in Canada March 1988: 7

'I had yin-yang feelings for my new son. I loved him dearly. But then I would wonder if I made a real mistake having him.'
Vancouver Sun 27 Dec. 1990: B3

yogurt, yogourt, yoghurt, yoghourt *Yogurt* is the most common spelling in published Canadian writing, but *yogourt*, a bilingual spelling, is favoured by Canadian dairy producers, who must satisfy bilingual food labelling requirements. *Yogourt* is in fact the French spelling, used in English only in Canada. The alternatives *yoghurt* and *yoghourt* are correct but uncommon.

In North America the first syllable, *yog-*, is pronounced to rhyme with *vogue*; in Britain it rhymes with *log*.

. . . frozen yogurt is healthier than ice cream because it has less cholesterol, less fat and fewer calories.
Province (Vancouver) 29 July 1990: 69

. . . her small stationwagon is so filled with yogourt containers, clattering cans and plastic bottles, it looks like a travelling depot.
Gazette (Montreal) 22 April 1990: A1

Nichol stocks . . . yoghurt and cheese.
Province (Vancouver) 7 Feb. 1990: 45

Smoked salmon and avocado roulade with cucumber and yoghourt salad.
Bon Vivant Aug. 1981: 7

yoke, yolk A *yoke* is a wooden crosspiece fastened over the necks of a pair of draft animals to allow them to pull together. *Yoke* has many other senses that are extensions of this literal sense.

A *yolk* is the yellow part of an egg. *Merriam-Webster's* lists *yoke* as an alternative spelling for this meaning, but all other authorities consider it an error.

[The Canadian West] was like an emerging nation that has shaken off the Imperial yoke and is determined to rally under one united political force.
Pierre Berton *The Promised Land* 1984: 276

. . . sometimes the birds would actually lay an egg while being lifted. These would land on the floor, their yokes bleeding into the mud.
Canadian Fiction Magazine 64 (1988): 63

(The correct spelling is *yolks*.)

Yonsei see ISSEI

you, one In all but the most formal styles of writing, the pronoun *you* is now commonly used both in direct address to the reader ('You can avoid this problem by . . .') and as an indefinite pronoun ('You can't balance the budget without cuts to services'). In the past, usage guides suggested that *one* replace these uses of *you* in writing. However, *one* is not common in Canadian English, and can sound stilted unless the whole passage is quite formal. Slightly more informal than *you* but less stuffy than *one* are constructions with *those who, anyone, everyone, people*, etc.: 'Those who insist on lower taxes should expect reduced services'. Ultimately, this is a question of style and tone, and the writer must decide which pronoun is most appropriate in a particular context. Switching back and forth between *you* and *one* in the same passage is considered a stylistic fault.

See also FORMAL, INFORMAL WRITING; PRESENT WRITER; -SELF; [YOUS].

younger   see ELDER, ELDEST, OLDER, OLDEST

young offenders   The section of Canadian law dealing with young people who commit crimes was known as the *Juvenile Delinquents Act* from 1908 until 1984, when it was replaced by the *Young Offenders Act*, itself replaced in 2003 by the *Youth Criminal Justice Act*. Although the phrase *young offender* does not appear in that latest act, it is still the common term in Canada for a person between his or her twelfth and eighteenth birthdays who is found guilty of a crime.

Like all labels implying guilt, the term *young offender* should be applied only after a person has been found guilty. Young people may be *found guilty* of a crime, but the terms *convicted* and *conviction* are not applied to their legal proceedings.

> One of the two in custody was 17 and a young offender on the night of the crime.
> *Calgary Herald* 22 Nov. 2005: A6

(Regardless of the evidence, a suspect should not be called a young offender before being found guilty: 'and will be tried under the Youth Criminal Justice Act' would be an appropriate way to indicate the suspect's status.)

your, you're, yours   *Your* is a possessive adjective: 'Bring your bathing suit'. *You're* is a contraction of *you* and *are* that is common in speech but rare in writing except in representations of speech: 'If you're not here by nine, we won't expect you'.

Yours is a possessive pronoun like *mine, hers, his,* and *theirs*: 'I forgot my copy. Did you bring yours?' Though it is a possessive form, *yours* is never written with an apostrophe.

> 'You have to change your game if your going to be successful against them.'

Leader-Post (Regina) 29 April 2003: C3

(Here the second *your* should be *you're*—a contraction of *you are*.)

See also CONTRACTIONS; POSSESSIVE; THEIRS.

[yous], [youse], you all, you guys   In Standard English *you* is both singular and plural. The use of *yous* (also spelled *youse*) to refer to more than one person is considered uneducated or dialectal. (In some dialects *youse* has been generalized so that it also applies to an individual.) *Youse* is common in Ireland and in areas of Irish settlement in Canada, the United States, and Australia. In the American South, *you all* or *y'all* functions similarly. Many Canadians use *you guys* in informal speech to address a group, regardless of gender. These informal variants of *you* never appear in writing, except in representations of speech.

> 'Why doan youse come and sit with me?'
> *Canadian Fiction Magazine* 64 (1988): 129

> 'At this rate it'll take you guys a week.'
> *Canadian Fiction Magazine* 64 (1988): 63

-yse   see -IZE

Yukon   Though other Canadians often say *the Yukon*, residents of this territory prefer that the definite article be dropped, indicating that Yukon is not just a geographic area like 'the North' but a political entity like Alberta or Canada.

> He has worked as a high school teacher in Ontario, British Columbia, Yukon and Northwest Territories.
> *Ottawa Citizen* 28 Aug. 1990: E3

See also NORTHWEST TERRITORIES; SAHARA; UKRAINE; APPENDIX I.

Yukoner   see NAMES OF RESIDENTS OF CITIES AND PROVINCES

yuppiedom   see -DOM

-yze   see -IZE

Z

zed, zee Canadians usually pronounce the name of the last letter of the alphabet *ZED*, as do the British. Although most Canadians are aware of the American pronunciation, *ZEE*, few use it—except in Newfoundland, where *ZEE* is more common. There has been some speculation that American children's television would make inroads on the *ZED* pronunciation in Canada. Surveys in southern Ontario indicate that very young children there do say *ZEE*, but later (perhaps reflecting the influence of formal education) shift to *ZED*.

zenith see APOGEE

zero see -OS, -OES

zero, oh Canadians often say *oh* for *zero* when giving telephone numbers; however, *zero* should not be read as *oh* in any context that combines letters and numbers, such as a postal code. The Canadian postal code K0H 1M0, for example, should be read aloud as 'kay zero aitch one em zero'.

zero adverbs see ADVERBS WITHOUT -LY

zigzag see DOUBLING THE FINAL CONSONANT

zip see COMPUTER TERMS

zoology According to some authorities, the only acceptable pronunciation of *zoology* is *zoh ALL uh jee* (the first syllable rhyming with *go*). However, most Canadians, including zoologists, say *zoo ALL uh jee*, influenced, no doubt, by the word *zoo*. Recent dictionaries give both pronunciations.

zoom see ONOMATOPOEIA

Appendix I
Provinces and Territories

province or territor	abbreviation *common* *postal*		legislature	legislative memaber
Newfoundland and Labrador	N.L.	NL	House of Assembly	MHA
Nova Scotia	N.S.	NS	House of Assembly	MLA
Prince Edward Island	P.E.I.	PE	Legislative Assembly	MLA
New Brunswick	N.B.	NB	Legislative Assembly	MLA
Quebec	Que.	QC *or* P.Q.	National Assembly	MNA *or* deputy (député)
Ontario	Ont.	ON	Legislative Assembly	MPP
Manitoba	Man.	MB	Legislative Assembly	MLA
Saskatchewan	Sask.	SK	Legislative Assembly	MLA
Alberta	Alta.	AB	Legislative Assembly	MLA
British Columbia	B.C.	BC	Legislative Assembly	MLA
Nunavut	Nvt.	NU	Legislative Assembly	MLA
Northwest Territories	N.W.T.	NT	Legislative Assembly	MLA
Yukon	Y.T.	YT	Legislative Assembly	MLA

See also NAMES OF RESIDENTS.

Appendix II
A Note on Measurement

measurement, SI, metric system   In 1970, the Canadian government adopted SI units as Canada's official measurement. SI is short for *Système international d'unités*, commonly known in English as the metric system.

The list on the following page gives information on the most commonly used SI units, with the seven base units listed in italics. The one- and two-letter short forms listed for SI units are called letter symbols, not abbreviations. Some commonly used expressions involving SI letter symbols include:

> kilometres per hour: km/h
> grams per millilitre: g/mL
> kilowatt-hours: kwh
> revolutions per minute: rpm

Letter symbols are not italicized, followed by periods, or made plural: 'a distance of 17 km'. A space is left between the number of units and the letter symbol—'The dog is 2 kg overweight'—except when writing temperatures: '15°C' (fifteen degrees Celsius). In SI the numbers and the unit names are either both written as words ('fifteen kilograms') or given as a numeral with a symbol ('15 kg').

Units derived from proper names are written without capital letters, with the exception of *Celsius*, though the first letter of their letter symbols is capitalized: *ampere*, A; *joule*, J; *kelvin*, K; *newton*, N; *pascal*, Pa; *watt*, W. Prefixes up to *kilo-* are also written as letter symbols without capital letters (*1 kw* for one kilowatt); those above, such as *mega* (10^6) and *giga* (10^9), are capitalized when written as symbols (*10 MW* for ten megawatts). See two pages following for a list of metric prefixes.

The pronunciation of kilometre varies: both *KILL o mee ter* and *kill AW muh ter* are accepted.

Most of the world uses metric. Great Britain retains the Imperial system of units (feet, yards, miles, pounds, gallons, acres, etc.) for some uses even as the country officially adopts metric measurements. In the United States, where concessions to metric are happening more slowly, most measurements are made in a system called *United States customary*, which shares the terms of the Imperial system but defines some differently (most significantly measures of volume).

Some Canadians still use some Imperial measurements: people usually state their height in feet and inches and weight in pounds, though in official documents these would be recorded in centimetres and kilograms. In Canada, ovens indicate the temperature in *degrees Fahrenheit*, though weather forecasts report *degrees Celsius*. Beer is sold by the *pint* in bars, though soft drinks are bought in grocery stores by the *litre*. While highway signs are in kilometres, most real estate measurements of length and area are Imperial: 'The dining room is 60 square *feet*'. The true Canadian style is thus a blend of SI and Imperial terms, not merely both or entirely either. For detailed guidelines about metric, see the *Canadian Metric Practice Guide* and other publications of the Canadian Standards Association, or consult Canada's Weights and Measures Act, 1985, at http://laws.justice.gc.ca/en/W-6/.

See also CELSIUS.

SI Base Units and Some Common Metric Measurement

unit	letter symbol	measures	relationship to base
metre	m	length	
hectare	ha	area	= 10 000 square metres
litre*	L	volume	= cubic decimetre (dm³)
millilitre**	mL	volume	= 1/1 000 of a litre *or* one cubic centimetre
nautical mile	M *or* n.m.	marine/aerial distance	= 1 852 metres
knot	kn	marine/aerial speed	= nautical mile per hour
kilogram	kg	mass	
tonne †		mass	= 1 000 kilograms
newton	N	force	= metre kilogram per second squared
pascal	Pa	pressure	= newton per square metre
second	s	time	
minute	min	time	= 60 seconds
hour	h	time	= 60 minutes
day	d	time	= 24 hours
year ††	a	time	= 365 days
kelvin	K	temperature (scientific use)	
degree Celsius	°C	temperature (common use)	= K –273.15
ampere	A	electric current	
candela	cd	intensity of light	
mole	mol	pure substance	

* The letter symbol for *litre*, L, is capitalized to avoid confusion with the numeral 1.

** Although a millilitre is equivalent to a cubic centimetre, the abbreviation *cc* should never be used in SI.

† A tonne can be called a *metric ton* or a *metric tonne*, but in French *tonne* could mean *tonne* (meaning a *metric ton(ne)*) or *ton*, which is an Imperial measure and an entirely different quantity.

†† The letter symbol for *year*, a, is derived from *annum*, the Latin word for year

Metric Prefixes

tera	T	one trillion	1 000 000 000 000	10^{12}
giga	G	one billion	1 000 000 000	10^{9}
mega	M	one million	1 000 000	10^{6}
kilo	k	one thousand	1 000	10^{3}
hecto	h	one hundred	100	10^{2}
deca	da	ten	10	10^{1}
deci	d	one-tenth	0.1	10^{-1}
centi	c	one-hundredth	0.01	10^{-2}
milli	m	one-thousandth	0.001	10^{-3}
micro	μ	one-millionth	0.000 001	10^{-6}
nano	n	one-billionth	0.000 000 001	10^{-9}
pico	p	one-trillionth	0.000 000 000 001	10^{-12}

See also BILLION, TRILLION, MILLIARD; NUMBER PREFIXES, GREEK AND LATIN.

Appendix III
Aboriginal Groups Mentioned in the Guide

Aboriginal group	Relevant entry in guide
Algonquin	ALGONQUIN, ALGONKIN, ALGONQUIAN, ALGONKIAN
Atikamekw	INNU, MONTAGNAIS, NASKAPI, ATIKAMEKW
Blackfoot	BLACKFOOT, SIKSIKA
Chipewyan	CHIPEWYAN, CHIPPEWA
Dakelh	CARRIER, NAT'OOTEN, WET'SUWET'EN, DAKELH, SEKANI, TSILHQOT'IN, CHILCOTIN
Dene	DENE, NA-DENE
Ditidaht	NUU-CHAH-NULTH, DITIDAHT, NOOTKA
Gitxsan	GITXSAN, GITKSAN
Haida	HAIDA
Haisla	KWAKIUTL, HAISLA, HEILTSUK, BELLA BELLA, OWEEKENO, KWAKWAKA'WAKW, KWAGIULTH
Heiltsuk	KWAKIUTL, HAISLA, HEILTSUK, BELLA BELLA, OWEEKENO, KWAKWAKA'WAKW, KWAGIULTH
Innu	INNU, MONTAGNAIS, NASKAPI, ATIKAMEKW
Inuit	INUIT, INUK, INUKTITUT, INUVIALUIT, ESKIMO, INUPIAT, INUPIAQ
Inuvialuit	INUIT, INUK, INUKTITUT, INUVIALUIT, ESKIMO, INUPIAT, INUPIAQ
Kitchenuhmaykoosib Inninuwug	KITCHENUHMAYKOOSIB INNINUWUG, KI FIRST NATION, BIG TROUT LAKE FIRST NATION
Kootenay	KOOTENAY, KUTENAI, KTUNAXA-KINBASKET
Kwagiulth	KWAKIUTL, HAISLA, HEILTSUK, BELLA BELLA, OWEEKENO, KWAKWAKA'WAKW, KWAGIULTH
Kwakwaka'wakw	KWAKIUTL, HAISLA, HEILTSUK, BELLA BELLA, OWEEKENO, KWAKWAKA'WAKW, KWAGIULTH
Lil'wat	STL'ATL'IMX, LIL'WAT, LILLOOET
Maliseet	MALISEET, MALÉCITE, WOLASTOQIYIK
Mi'kmaq	MI'KMAQ, MI'KMAW, MICMAC
Montagnais	INNU, MONTAGNAIS, NASKAPI, ATIKAMEKW
Naskapi	INNU, MONTAGNAIS, NASKAPI, ATIKAMEKW
Nat'ooten	CARRIER, NAT'OOTEN, WET'SUWET'EN, DAKELH, SEKANI, TSILHQOT'IN, CHILCOTIN
Nisga'a	NISGA'A, NISHGA, NISKA
Nlaka'pamux	NLAKA'PAMUX, THOMPSON
Nuu-chah-nulth	NUU-CHAH-NULTH, DITIDAHT, NOOTKA
Nuxalk	NUXALK, BELLA COOLA
Odawa	ODAWA, OTTAWA
Ojibwa	OJIBWA(Y), ANISHNABE
Oweekeno	KWAKIUTL, HAISLA, HEILTSUK, BELLA BELLA, OWEEKENO, KWAKWAKA'WAKW, KWAGIULTH
Passamaquoddy	ABENAKI, WABANAKI

Plains Cree	CREE
Potawatomi	ODAWA, OTTAWA
Secwepemc	SECWEPEMC, SHUSWAP
Sekani	CARRIER, NAT'OOTEN, WET'SUWET'EN, DAKELH, SEKANI, TSILHQOT'IN, CHILCOTIN
Six Nations	IROQUOIS, SIX NATIONS, IROQUOIAN
Slavey	SLAVEY, DENE-THA(H), SLAVEY DENE
Stl'atl'imx	STL'ATL'IMX, LIL'WAT, LILLOOET
Swampy Cree	CREE
Tsilhqot'in	CARRIER, NAT'OOTEN, WET'SUWET'EN, DAKELH, SEKANI, TSILHQOT'IN, CHILCOTIN
Tsuu T'ina	TSUU T'INA, SARCEE
Wet'suwet'en	CARRIER, NAT'OOTEN, WET'SUWET'EN, DAKELH, SEKANI, TSILHQOT'IN, CHILCOTIN
Woodlands Cree	CREE

See also ABORIGINAL PEOPLE(S).

Glossary

article   The definite article (*the*) and the indefinite article (*a/an*) both precede nouns; the former usually indicates that the noun to come has been mentioned before, while the latter indicates either that the noun is being introduced into the discourse or that the reference is not specific ('indefinite'). (See A, AN.)

Canadianism   A Canadianism is a word or expression that is used only in Canada (*Mountie, EI*) or a sense of a word that is exclusively or nearly exclusively restricted to Canada (*acclamation, allophone, dépanneur, loonie, pogey*).

clause   A clause contains, as a minimum, a subject and a predicate: 'Birds sing'. An independent clause can stand alone as a complete sentence. Independent clauses can also be joined by coordinate conjunctions: 'Birds sing, fish swim, and we dance the tango'. (See **conjunctions** below.)

A subordinate clause cannot stand alone as a sentence. It is preceded by a subordinate conjunction, which links the clause to the main clause in the sentence: 'Because I like singing, I joined the choir'. Noun clauses ('I didn't like *what I saw*'), adjective clauses ('The book, *which was shoved under the couch*, finally turned up'), and adverb clauses ('His eyes rolled *as if he were going to faint*') perform the same functions in sentences as nouns, adjectives, and adverbs.

Adjective clauses are also called 'relative clauses'. A relative clause may be introduced by a relative pronoun (*who, whom, which*, or *that*): 'She looked around for the umbrella *that he had lent her*'. A relative pronoun acts both as a pronoun, in that it refers to a noun, and as a subordinate conjunction, in that it heads a clause that is dependent on a main clause. Relative clauses may also be introduced by rel-

ative adverbs such as *where, why*, and *when*: 'The locker *where he stored his clothes* is empty'. For restrictive and nonrestrictive clauses, see THAT, WHICH.

coin   To coin a word is to make it up: 'The residents of Banff coined the term *go-bys* to refer to the tourists'.

comparative   The comparative form of an adjective or adverb—used in making comparisons—is usually marked by an *-er* ending (*taller, further*) or by the use of *more* (*more beautiful; more wildly*). (See COMPARISONS.)

compound subject   A compound subject is a subject formed from two nouns or noun equivalents joined by a coordinate conjunction: '*Boys* and *girls* come out to play'; '*What I like* and *what I get* are two different things'.

conditional   A conditional clause expresses the idea that one thing will happen on condition that another one happens; conditional clauses usually begin with *if, unless*, or *provided that*: 'If he comes, we can get started'. (See [HAD HAVE].)

conjunction   A conjunction is a word that joins other words, phrases, or clauses. The main coordinate conjunctions—*and, but, or, nor*—join items that are considered equal in importance or parallel. Correlative conjunctions come in pairs: *either . . . or; neither . . . nor; both . . . and; not only . . . but also*. Subordinate conjunctions, such as *because, while, even though*, and *as soon as*, join items that are considered unequal in importance.

conjunctive adverbs   These words form links between sentences. Some common conjunctive adverbs are *however, therefore, nevertheless, further*, and *for example*. (See SENTENCES.)

convention In the field of language study, a convention is a writing practice that has evolved or been worked out over time by editors, lexicographers, and educators. Most conventions relate to matters of spelling, punctuation, and style.

countable noun, uncountable noun A countable noun (sometimes called a count noun) refers to things that can be counted and thus can be singular or plural (*word*, *words*), whereas an uncountable noun (sometimes called a mass noun) refers to things without clear boundaries and is generally found in the singular (*flour*, *wine*). Note that when an uncountable noun is pluralized, it means 'kinds of': *flours* (e.g., whole wheat, graham, rice); *wines* (e.g., red, white, sparkling). When an uncountable noun is treated as a countable noun ('I'll have a coffee'), the reference is to some understood quantity: 'a (cup of) coffee'. (See FEWER, LESS.)

figure of speech A figure of speech at its most general is a use of language that departs from the ordinary in structure, sound, rhythm, or content to achieve a special effect. For example, metaphors and similes (see below) are figures of speech, as are puns. Figures of speech sometimes include what are usually called rhetorical figures, such as the rhetorical question (see RHETORICAL QUESTION).

gerund, verbal noun see **verbals** below

infinitive An infinitive is the base form of the verb preceded by *to*: *to run*, *to be*. It can be used as a noun ('To err is human'), an adjective ('I need something to read'), or an adverb ('They were anxious to see me'). In some formulations, the *to* can be dropped, as in 'The children helped us (to) carry the packages', or does not occur, as in 'They made him do it' (*to* is not possible before *do*). In other formulations, the *to* may be expanded: 'He came *in order to* help me'; 'They laid out their clothes *so as to* be ready in the morning'.

inflection, inflected form Nouns, pronouns, adjectives, adverbs, and verbs have inflections (suffixes), or inflected forms marked by changes in vowels (e.g., *sing*, *sang*), etc. that indicate such things as number (*cat*, *cats*), gender (*she*, *he*), case (*his*, *him*), degree of comparison (*big*, *bigger*, *biggest*), tense (*do*, *did*), mood (see below), and so on.

intensifier, intensify An intensifier is an adverb that either heightens or tones down the impact of the meaning of an adjective or adverb: '*very* good', '*somewhat* badly', '*highly* motivated', '*slightly* interested'.

intonation This term refers to the patterns of falling and rising pitch that indicate sentence types. Usually, in English, intonation rises at the end of a question and falls at the end of a statement.

metaphor A metaphor is a figure of speech that draws an analogy between two things by equating them: 'He is a rock'. (See DEAD METAPHOR; MIXED METAPHOR.)

modifier, modify Words and phrases that modify the meaning of other words, phrases, or clauses are called modifiers. For example, adjectives modify nouns, and sentence adverbs modify whole sentences. (See ADJECTIVES AND ADVERBS; MISPLACED MODIFIER; SENTENCE ADVERB.)

mood English has three moods: indicative (a factual statement, such as 'He runs daily'), imperative (an order, such as 'Run for your lives!'), and subjunctive (a wish or hypothetical statement, such as 'God be praised!'; 'If I were you . . .'; see SUBJUNCTIVE).

noun Nouns name persons, places, things, or ideas. Proper nouns are the names of specific people, institutions, places, etc., and are capitalized; common nouns—all the others—are not capitalized. Abstract nouns (*liberty*, *democracy*, *insight*, etc.) are contrasted with concrete ones (*wood*, *applesauce*). Individual nouns (*cow*, *insight*) are contrasted with collective nouns (*team*, *herd*). (See COLLECTIVE NOUNS; and **countable nouns**, above.)

object The person or thing that receives the action of the verb is its object. Any sentence that contains a transitive verb has a direct object: 'The truck hit the *pillar*'. Some verbs (for example, *give, offer, pay, send*) routinely take both a direct and an indirect object: 'The government paid my cousin a pension'. Here *cousin* is the indirect object, that is, the person or thing indirectly affected by the action. In most sentences of this kind, the indirect object can also appear in a phrase beginning with *to* or *for*: 'The government paid a pension to my cousin'.

Prepositions also take objects: 'on the *desk*'. Pronouns that are objects of verbs or of prepositions are in the objective case: 'I love *him*'; 'Between you and *me*, he's lovable'. (See CASE.)

object complement The object complement is an adjective or noun that qualifies the direct object while complementing the verb: 'They painted the kitchen *green*'; 'We thought him *a fool*'. The verbs *believe, call, consider, find, make,* and *think* often precede this structure.

parenthetical elements These are elements that are not essential to the meaning of a sentence. To set them off from the main body of the sentence, they are often enclosed in commas, parentheses, or dashes: 'My nephew, *who is nine*, loves baseball'; 'We had a great deal of trouble at Customs *(don't even ask)*, but finally we found our way outside to the sunlight again'.

participle This is the general term for two verb forms: the present participle, formed with *-ing,* and the past participle, formed in various ways—most often with *-ed,* and occasionally with *-t* (*knelt*), *-en* (*proven*), or *-n* (*known*), or irregularly (*sung, thought*). The present participle is used to form the present and past continuous tenses ('He is running for mayor'; 'They were hoping for victory'), as a noun (here a gerund, or verbal noun: 'Running is my life'), as an adjective ('running water'), or as an adjectival or adverbial participial phrase ('Running desperately, they caught the train'). The past participle is used to form the present or past perfect tense with forms of *have* (*have lived, had run*) and the passive voice with forms of *be* (*has been depressed, was stolen*). It is also used in adjectival or adverbial participial phrases ('Aged five, he entered kindergarten'). (See **verbals**, below.)

parts of speech The parts of speech are the different classes, or types, of words. The traditional parts of speech are noun, pronoun, verb, adverb, adjective, preposition, interjection ('Oh!'), and conjunction.

phrase A phrase is a sequence of grammatically related words that can be distinguished from a clause in that it has no finite verb (i.e., no verb that is marked for tense; see **tense**, below). Phrases often include verbals (see **verbals**, below), but these act as nouns, adjectives, or adverbs, rather than verbs.

predicate In traditional grammar, the predicate is one of the two major constituents of a sentence: the other is the subject. The predicate contains a verb (i.e., a verb marked for tense; see **tense**, below) and can be thought of as asserting something about the subject.

prefix, suffix A prefix is an element such as *dis-, non-, over-,* and *re-* that when added to the beginning of a word changes its meaning (e.g., *non-* added to a word makes it negative: *non-smoker*). A suffix is an element attached to the end of a word that changes its grammatical or lexical meaning or function. For example, the suffix *-s* indicates that a noun is plural, and *-ed* marks the past tense of regular verbs, while the suffixes *-ness* and *-ity* are used to make nouns from adjectives: *goodness, generosity*. The addition of prefixes or suffixes often raises questions of spelling (e.g., *likeable* vs. *likable*) or hyphenation (*non-profit* vs. *nonprofit*).

preposition A preposition is a word that is placed before a noun or noun equivalent to show the relation between that noun and something elsewhere in the sentence: 'I put the book *on* the desk'; 'She ran *towards* the entrance'. Some common prepositions are *about, above, at, below, down, during, except, past,* and *within*. The preposition with its noun object is called a prepositional phrase.

pronoun   A pronoun is a word that is used instead of a noun. Normally, it refers to a particular noun or noun equivalent that has already been mentioned; this noun is called its antecedent. Some pronouns do not have antecedents (for example, the *it* in 'It is raining') and others use the speech situation to form the link ('Which book?' *'That* one'.) The eight kinds of pronoun are personal (e.g., *I, you, them*), reflexive (e.g., *himself, themselves*), indefinite (e.g., *some, each, any*), reciprocal (e.g., *one another, each other*), demonstrative (e.g., *this, that, these, those*), interrogative (e.g., *who, which, what*); relative (e.g., *who, which, that*), and intensive (e.g., I *myself*, they *themselves*).

rhetoric   This term is often used to refer to wordy or ideologically charged speech ('empty rhetoric', 'right-wing rhetoric'). However, rhetoric is also the art and study of persuasion. Courses that are called composition courses in Canada are often called rhetoric courses in the United States. (See RHETORICAL QUESTION.)

semantic drift   Over time, many word senses shift, sometimes slowly, sometimes quickly. For example, *Canadian* first referred to Aboriginal peoples, then to French-speaking settlers, then to inhabitants of Upper and Lower Canada, and now sometimes to English-speaking Canadians only. (See EFFETE.)

simile   A simile is a figure of speech that draws attention to a comparison by using *like* or *as*: 'She sings like a bird'.

stress   In English, some syllables are emphasized more strongly than others. Stress can differentiate meaning. For example, the verb *permit* is stressed on the second syllable ('Do *per MIT* me to come'), while the noun is stressed on the first ('I need a building *PER mit'*). Most contemporary dictionaries indicate the stress with a mark preceding the stressed syllable, so that the verb is written *per'mit,* and the noun

'permit. Every word spoken in isolation has at least one stressed syllable, but in sentences only certain words are stressed.

subject   Grammar conventionally divides the sentence into the subject and the predicate. The subject in a statement—a noun phrase—usually precedes the verb: 'The cat chased the mouse'. Pronouns that are in subject position take the subjective case: 'I am going'. (See CASE.)

subject complement   see **verb**, below

superlative   The superlative form of adjectives and adverbs is typically formed by adding -est (*biggest, fastest*) or *most* (*most beautiful, most efficiently*). (See COMPARISONS.)

syllable   A syllable in English is either a vowel alone or a vowel with one or more consonants before or after it. Words are made up of one or more syllables. Dictionaries often mark syllable breaks.

tense   Verbs that are marked for tense indicate the time at which something took place. The present and past tenses are marked by inflections of the verb (I *walk*, he *walks*; I *walked*, he *walked*), while the future is formed most often by combining *will* with the infinitive (I *will walk*). Other tenses are formed by combining *be* and *have* with the infinitive, present participle, or past participle (I *am walking*; I *have walked*; I *had walked*). Sometimes verbs that are marked for tense are called finite verbs, to distinguish them from verb forms such as infinitives and verbals, which are not marked for tense and are called non-finite.

uneducated   Although few people in Canada have no education, there are forms of speech that are associated with a lack of education. These are usually criticized when they appear in writing and often elicit disapproval when they appear in speech. Thus the label 'uneducated' marks stigmatized usages and pronunciations.

variant   Often there are two (or more) ways of spelling or pronouncing a word, or of combining words in structures, that are acceptable. These forms are called variants.

verb A verb describes an action (*run*, *scrub*), a happening (*fall*, *flow*), or a state of being (*be*, *exist*, *feel*). Verbs that describe actions are classified as transitive (those that require a direct object) or intransitive (those that don't). Some verbs can be either transitive or intransitive. For example, in 'I hurried the children out the door', *hurried* is transitive, with *children* as the object. In 'We hurried', the verb is intransitive.

Copula (or linking) verbs describe a state of being; they link the subject to its complement: 'I am bored'; 'She seems an excellent speaker'; 'He remained Dean'. This complement—the subject complement—describes or identifies the subject. The most common copula verb is *be*; others are *appear*, *feel*, *remain*, *seem*, and *sound*. Some regular verbs are also used as copula verbs:

go (bad), get (married), run (wild), turn (bitter).

verbals This is the collective term for gerunds (sometimes called verbal nouns) and participles, past and present. They do not have tense, and act as nouns, adjectives, and adverbs rather than as verbs. (See DANGLING MODIFIER and POSSESSIVE WITH GERUND.)

voice Sentences with transitive verbs can be in the active voice or the passive voice: 'I ate the cake'; 'The cake was eaten by me'. In an active sentence, the subject is the agent of the action; in a passive sentence, the subject is the object of the action. Some argue that the passive voice is wordier and more formal than the active, but often it is useful (when the agent is not known, for example) or conventional (in scientific and legal writing, for example). (See WORDINESS, VARIATION.)

Sources

The Strathy Corpus is a large (approximately 50 million words), authentic sample of mostly written Canadian English ranging across a variety of subjects and representing different levels of formality. The corpus, which contains fiction and non-fiction books, popular magazines, newspapers, Internet news, academic journals and theses, transcripts of university lectures, parliamentary transcripts, and so on, is a tool that allows us to take a broad look at patterns of Canadian usage. Below is a list of the sources for the example sentences illustrating the entries in this guide. Not every text in the Strathy Corpus is listed among the sources below, and not every text listed below is a Strathy Corpus text. Some electronic texts have been accessed through subscription databases such as Canadian Newsstand and Canadian Business and Current Affairs.

Books

Atwood, Margaret. *Life Before Man*. Toronto: McClelland and Stewart, 1979.

———. *Second Words: Selected Critical Prose*. Toronto: Anansi, 1982.

———. *The Blind Assassin*. Toronto: McClelland and Stewart, 2000.

Ballstadt, Carl, ed. *The Search for English Canadian Literature*. Toronto: University of Toronto Press, 1975.

Batten, Jack. *Robinette: The Dean of Canadian Lawyers*. Toronto: Macmillan, 1984.

Bell, David V.J. *The Roots of Disunity: A Study of Canadian Political Culture*. Rev. edn. Toronto: Oxford University Press, 1992.

Beresford-Howe, Constance. *Night Studies*. Toronto: Macmillan, 1985.

Berton, Pierre. *The Promised Land: Settling the West, 1914–1986*. Toronto: McClelland and Stewart, 1992.

Bone, Robert M. *The Geography of the Canadian North*. Toronto: Oxford University Press, 1992.

Braithwaite, Max. *The Night We Stole the Mountie's Car*. Toronto: McClelland and Stewart, 1971.

Brodie, Janine, Shelley A.M. Gavigan, and Jane Jenson. *The Politics of Abortion*. Toronto: Oxford University Press, 1992.

Chambers, Jack. *Milestones I: The Music and Times of Miles Davis to 1960*. Toronto: University of Toronto Press, 1983.

Cheetham, Mark A., with Linda Hutcheon. *Remembering Postmodernism: Trends in Recent Canadian Art*. Toronto: Oxford University Press, 1991.

Clarke, George Elliott. *Fire on the Water: An Anthology of Black Nova Scotian Writing*. Potter's Lane, NS: Pottersfield, 1991.

Clement, Wallace, and Glen Williams, eds. *The New Canadian Political Economy*. Kingston, ON: McGill–Queen's University Press, 1989.

Colombo, John Robert. *Dictionary of Canadian Quotations*. Don Mills, ON: Stoddart, 1991.

Crisp, Quentin, and John Hofsess. *Manners from Heaven: A Divine Guide to Good Behaviour*. Toronto: HarperCollins, 1985.

Cuneo, Carl J. *Pay Equity: The Labour-Feminist Challenge*. Toronto: Oxford University

Press, 1990.

Davies, Richard, and Glen Kirkland, eds. *Dimensions*. Toronto: Gage, 1986.

———. *A Voice from the Attic*. Toronto: McClelland and Stewart, 1960.

———. *One Half of Robertson Davies*. New York: Penguin, 1960.

Davis, Ann. *Somewhere Waiting: The Life and Art of Christiane Pflug*. Toronto: Oxford University Press, 1991.

Dickenson, Terence. *Halley's Comet: A Mysterious Visitor from Outer Space*. Barrington, NJ: Edmund Scientific, 1985.

Dryden, Ken. *The Game*. Toronto: Macmillan, 1983.

Engel, Howard. *Murder Sees the Light*. New York: Penguin, 1984.

Forsey, Eugene. *A Life on the Fringe: The Memoirs of Eugene Forsey*. Toronto: Oxford University Press, 1990.

Frye, Northrop. *The Bush Garden: Essays on the Canadian Imagination*. Toronto: Anansi, 1971.

———. *The Educated Imagination*. Toronto: CBC, 1963.

———. *The Modern Century*. New edn. Toronto: Oxford University Press, 1990.

Galbraith, John Kenneth. *The Scotch*. Baltimore, MD: Penguin, 1966.

Gawthrop, Daniel. *Affirmation: The AIDS Odyssey of Dr Peter*. Vancouver: New Star, 1994.

Gibson, Frederick. *Queen's University, Volume II, 1917–1961, To Serve and Yet Be Free*. Kingston, ON: McGill–Queen's University Press, 1983.

Gunn, J.A.W. *Beyond Liberty and Property: The Process of Self-Recognition in Eighteenth-Century Political Thought*. Kingston, ON: McGill–Queen's University Press, 1983.

Heard, Andrew. *Canadian Constitutional Conventions: The Marriage of Law and Politics*. Toronto: Oxford University Press, 1991.

Highway, Tomson. *The Rez Sisters*. Saskatoon: Fifth House, 1988.

Hutcheon, Linda. *Splitting Images: Contemporary Canadian Ironies*. Toronto: Oxford University Press, 1991.

Ignatieff, George. *The Making of a Peacemonger*. Toronto: Penguin, 1987.

Jones, Jennifer. *Making the Links: A Book for Young Women about Sexual Violence, Drugs and Alcohol*. Kingston, ON: AWARE, 1992.

Keefer, Janice Kulyk. *Reading Mavis Gallant*. Toronto: Oxford University Press, 1989.

Klinck, Carl F., gen. ed. *Literary History of Canada: Canadian Literature in English*. 2nd edn. 3 vols. Toronto: University of Toronto Press, 1976.

Kroetsch, Robert. *Badlands*. Toronto: General, 1975.

Laurence, Margaret. *The Diviners*. McClelland and Stewart, Bantam, 1975.

Lougheed, W.C., ed. *In Search of the Standard in Canadian English*. Occasional Paper Number 1. Kingston: Strathy Language Unit (Queen's University), 1986.

McKenna, Katherine M.J. *A Life of Propriety: Anne Murray Powell and Her Family, 1755–1849*. Kingston, ON: McGill–Queen's University Press, 1994.

Meyer, Bruce, and Brian O'Riordan, eds. *In Their Words: Interviews with Fourteen Canadian Writers*. Toronto: Anansi, 1984.

Neatby, Hilda. *Queen's University, Volume I, 1841–1917: And Not to Yield*. Kingston, ON: McGill–Queen's University Press, 1978.

Nevitte, Neil, and Roger Gibbins. *New Elites in Old States: Ideologies in the Anglo-American Democracies*. Toronto: Oxford University Press, 1990.

Northey, Margot, and David B. Knight. *Making Sense in Geography and Environmental Studies: A Student's Guide to Research, Writing, and Style*. Toronto: Oxford University Press, 1992.

Norton, William. *Human Geography*. Toronto: Oxford University Press, 1992.

Pross, Paul A. *Group Politics and Public Policy*. 2nd edn. Toronto: Oxford University Press, 1992.

Purdy, A.W., ed. *The New Romans: Candid Canadian Opinions of the United States*. Edmonton: Hurtig [1968].

Reynolds, Wendy, and Vera Madden. *Drug Wise: A Book for Older Women about Safe Drug Use*. Kingston, ON: AWARE, 1992.

Rosenthal, Henry M., and S. Cathy Berson, eds. *Canadian Jewish Outlook Anthology*. Vancouver: New Star, 1988.

Shek, Ben-Z. *French Canadian & Québécois Novels*. Toronto: Oxford University Press, 1991.

Shields, Carol. *The Stone Diaries*. Toronto: Random House, 1993.

Smyth, J.E., et al. *The Law and Business Administration in Canada*. Scarborough, ON: Prentice Hall, 1987.

Story, G.M., W.J. Kirwin, and J.D.A. Widdowson, eds. *Dictionary of Newfoundland English*. 2nd edn. Toronto: University of Toronto Press, 1990.

Sutherland, Fraser. *The Monthly Epic: A History of Canadian Magazines*. Toronto: Fitzhenry and Whiteside, 1989.

Teatero, William. *John Anderson: Fugitive Slave*. Kingston, ON: Treasure Island Books, 1986.

Tucker, Alan, ed. *The Penguin Guide to Canada*. New York: Penguin, 1991.

Ursell, Geoffrey. *Perdue: And How the West Was Lost*. Toronto: Macmillan, 1984.

Waddington, Miriam. *Apartment Seven: Essays Selected and New*. Toronto: Oxford University Press, 1989.

Whitehorn, Alan. *Canadian Socialism: Essays on the CCF-NDP*. Toronto: Oxford University Press, 1992.

Williams, David. *Eye of the Father*. Toronto: Anansi, 1985.

Willinsky, John. *The Empire of Words: The Reign of the OED*. Princeton, NJ: Princeton University Press, 1994.

Wilson, Richard Albert. *The Birth of Language*. London: Dent, 1937.

Geoffrey, York. *The Dispossessed: Life and Death in Native Canada*. Toronto: Lester and Orpen Dennys, 1989.

Zeitlin, Irving M., and Robert J. Brym. *The Social Conditions of Humanity*. Toronto: Oxford University Press, 1991.

Magazines

Advisor's Edge Jan. 2004

Arctic 41.1 (1988), 57.2 (2004), 57.3 (2004)

Atlantic Salmon Journal Summer 1990, Autumn 1990

Beautiful British Columbia Spring 1990

BC Business April 2004

The Beaver Dec. 1989–Jan. 1990, Feb.–Mar. 1990, Dec. 2001–Jan. 2002

Bon Vivant Aug. 1981, Nov. 1981, Aug.–Sept. 1982, Feb.–Mar. 1983

Border Crossings 23.3 (2004)

Briarpatch Dec. 1989–Jan. 1990, April 1990

Business Journal June 1991

Canadian Appraiser 47.3 (2003)

Canadian Architect June 1986

Canadian Baptist Jan. 1986, Feb. 1986

Canadian Biker Magazine Feb. 1990

Canadian Business 27 Oct. 2003, 1 March 2004

Sources

Canadian Churchman April 1986, June–July 1986

Canadian Collector 21.1 (1986), 21.2 (1986), 21.4 (1986)

Canadian Consumer Jan. 1985, Jan. 1986, Feb. 1986, March 1986

Canadian Dimension 37.4 (2003), 37.5 (2003)

Canadian Fiction Magazine 63 (1988), 64 (1988), 89 (1994), 97/98 (2000)

Canadian Grocer Dec. 2003–Jan. 2004

Canadian Heritage Feb.–Mar. 1986, Aug.–Sept. 1986

Canadian Issues March 2004

Canadian Living 19 April 1986, 17 May 1986, Nov. 1990

Canadian Rodeo News March 1990

Canadian Social Trends 68 (2003)

Canadian Thoroughbred Jan. 1989, Aug. 1989

Canadian Women's Health Network 4.3 (2001)

Canadian Yachting Feb. 2005

Catholic Register 16 Aug. 1986, 23 Aug. 1986

Chatelaine April 1986, June–July 1986, 78.3 (2005)

City Magazine 10.1 (Spring 1988)

Computer Dealer News 7 March 1991, 21 March 1991

Computing Canada 1 March 1991

Country Guide Nov. 1986, Dec. 1986

Dogs in Canada Special Issue Aug. 1996

Engineering Dimension Mar.–Apr. 1988, May–June 1988, July–Aug. 1988

Fuse Magazine 13.4 (1990)

Harrowsmith June–July 1985, Aug.–Sept. 1985, June–July 1986, Aug.–Sept. 1986, Oct.–Nov. 1985

Imperial Oil Review Spring (1988)

Kingston Life Magazine Fall 2003

Legion Magazine Jan.–Feb. 2005

Leisure Life May 1988

Maclean's 10 Feb. 1986, 24 Feb. 1986, 31 March 1986, 28 July 1986, 8 Sept. 1986, 28 March 1988, 23 May 1988, 27 June 1988, 11 July 1988, 18 July 1988, 29 Aug. 1988, 5 Sept. 1988, 12 Sept. 1988, 19 Sept. 1988, 3 Oct. 1988, 31 Oct. 1988, 7 Nov. 1988, 14 Nov. 1988, 21 Nov. 1988, 6 March 1989, 3 April 1989, 1 May 1989, 12 June 1989, 3 July 1989, 11 Sept. 1989, 2 Oct. 1989, 16 April 1990, 23 July 1990, 13 Aug. 1990, 10 Sept. 1990, 1 Oct. 1990, 15 Oct. 1990, 22 Oct. 1990, 19 Nov. 1990, 10 Dec. 1990, 17 Dec. 1990, 18 Feb. 1991, 4 March 1991, 22 April 1991, 29 April 1991, 3 June 1991, 1 July 1991, 8 July 1991, 22 July 1991, 12 Aug. 1991, 19 Aug. 1991, 26 Aug. 1991, 23 Sept. 1991, 7 Oct. 1991, 14 Oct. 1991, 21 Oct. 1991, 11 Nov. 1991, 9 Dec. 1991, 16 Dec. 1991, 23 Dec. 1991, 24 Feb. 1996, 30 Aug. 2004, 117.36–37 (2004)

Manitoba Business 25.7 (2003)

Mennonite Brethren Herald 7 March 1986, 4 April 1986

NeWest Review Oct.–Nov. 1989, Dec. 1989–Jan. 1990, Feb.–Mar. 1990, Oct.–Nov. 1990

Now Magazine 3–9 Nov. 1988, 18–24 April 1996, 17–23 May 2001

Orbit 34.1 (2004), 34.2 (2004)

Our Times March 1990, April 1990

Outdoor Canada Summer 2002

Performing Arts in Canada March 1988, July 1988, Spring 1990

Photo Life July–Aug. 1991

Perspectives: Profiles of Research at Queen's University 1986

Queen's Alumni Review Holiday Season 2002
Rites March 1990, Feb. 1990
Royal Bank of Canada Monthly Letter 52.6 (1971)
Saturday Night Jan. 1986, Feb. 1986, March 1986, April 1986, May 1986, July 1986
Snowmobile Canada 1991 Buyers Guide
TLC . . . for plants Spring 1991, Summer 1991
Today's Skater 1991
Torch: University of Victoria Alumni Magazine Spring 1990
United Church Observer May 1986, June 1986
Up Here Jan.–Feb. 1990, Mar.–Apr. 1990
Western Grocer May–June 1990, Aug. 1990
Women and Environments 12.1 (1990), 12.2 (1990)

Journals

The Aboriginal Nurse 18.1 (2003)
Alberta Counsellor 28.1 (2003)
Alberta Journal of Educational Research 50.2 (2004)
Alternatives Journal 27.4 (2001), (2002)
BC Studies 140 (Winter 2003–4)
BC Historical News 37.1 (2004)
Bank of Canada Review (Ottawa) Winter 2002–3
Beyond Numbers Feb./March 2004
Canadian–American Public Policy 52 (2002)
Canadian Bar Review 66.3 (1987)
The Canadian Geographer Spring 1989, 48.2 (2004)
Canadian Journal for the Study of Adult Education 16.2 (2002)
Canadian Journal of Behavioural Science 35.1 (2003)
Canadian Journal of Botany 67.4 (1989)
Canadian Journal of Communication 29.1 (2004)
Canadian Journal of Earth Sciences 26 (1989)
Canadian Journal of Film Studies 12.1 (2003)
Canadian Journal of Forest Research 34.7 (2004)
Canadian Journal of Higher Education 34.1 (2004)
Canadian Journal of History 14.1 (1989)
Canadian Journal of Philosophy 19 (1989), 34.1 (2004), 34.4 (2004)
Canadian Journal of Physiology and Pharmacology 82.8/9 (2004)
Canadian Journal of Psychiatry 44.3 (1990), 49.11 (2004)
Canadian Journal of School Psychology 15.1 (1999)
Canadian Journal of Sociology 14.2 (1989), 29.3 (2004)
Canadian Journal of Zoology 67.4 (1989)
Canadian Medical Association Journal 172.2 (2005)
Canadian Speeches April 1994
CAUT Bulletin 51.5 (May 2004)
Clinical and Investigative Medicine 24.1 (2004)
Convergence 36.3–4 (2003)
Education Canada Summer 1989, Spring 1995, 44.2 (2004)
English Quarterly 34.1–2 (2002)
Environmental Reviews 12.3 (2004)
Essays on Canadian Writing 73 (2001), 75 (2002)

Sources

Family Health 20.3 (2004)

Hansard. Debates of the Senate 138.78 4 Oct. 2000

Hansard. House of Assembly Newfoundland and Labrador 21 May 2002

Health Law Journal 10 (2002)

Herizons 17.3 (2004)

International Journal 59.4 (2004)

Ivey Business Journal 68.2 (2003)

Journal of Canadian Studies 38.1 (2004), 38.2 (2004)

Journal of Eastern Townships Studies 23 (2003)

Journal of Nutrition Education 33.1 (2001)

Journal of Palliative Care 20.3 (2004)

Journal of Travel Medicine 8.6 (2001)

Journal of Ukrainian Studies 28.1 (2003)

Juristat: Canadian Centre for Justice Statistics 22.10 (2002)

Juristat: Canadian Centre for Justice Statistics 23.1 (2003)

Law Now 29.3 (2004–5)

Plant 63.10 (2004)

Queen's Quarterly 92.1 (1985), 92.2 (1985), 92.3 (1985), 93.1 (1986), 93.2 (1989), 93.3 (1986), 93.4 (1986), 94.1 (1987), 94.2 (1987), 94.3 (1987), 94.3 (1987), 94.4 (1987), 95.1 (1988), 95.2 (1988), 95.3 (1988), 95.4 (1988), 96.1 (1989), 96.2 (1989), 96.3 (1989), 97.1 (1990), 97.2 (1990), 97.3 (1990), 97.4 (1990), 98.1 (1991), 101.4 (1994), 107.4 (2000), 108.3 (2001), 110.2 (2003), 110.4 (2003), 111.1 (2004)

Room of One's Own March 1990, June 1990

Toronto Slavic Quarterly 13 (2005)

Truck News 24.9 (2004)

Newspapers

Cape Breton Post (Sydney, N.S.) 27 June 1990

Calgary Herald 14 Feb. 1988, 21 Feb. 1988, 19 June 1990, 2 Jan. 1992, 3 Jan. 1992, 28 Jan. 1992, 9 Feb. 1992, 16 May 1992, 1 June 1992, 3 June 1992, 7 June 1992, 18 June 1992, 27 June 1992, 29 June 1992, 2 July 1992, 4 July 1992, 9 July 1992, 23 July 1992, 30 July 1992, 8 Aug. 1992, 9 Aug. 1992, 3 Sept. 1992, 11 Sept. 1992, 12 Sept. 1992, 20 Sept. 1992, 26 Sept. 1992, 6 Oct. 1992, 24 Oct. 1992, 28 Oct. 1992, 31 Oct. 1992, 12 Nov. 1992, 19 Nov. 1992, 26 Nov 1992, 2 Dec. 1992, 5 Dec. 1992, 20 Dec. 1992, 21 Dec. 1992, 26 Dec. 1992, 28 Dec. 1992, 29 Dec. 1992, 30 Dec. 1992, 6 Feb. 1993, 23 Feb. 1993, 26 Feb. 1993, 18 March 1993, 28 April 1993, 28 May 1993, 29 May 1993, 19 June 1993, 30 June 1993, 10 July 1993, 30 Sept. 1993, 18 Oct. 1993, 30 Oct. 1993, 7 Nov. 1993, 10 Nov. 1993, 14 Dec. 1993, 17 Dec. 1993, 19 Dec. 1993, 21 Dec. 1993, 26 Dec. 1993, 29 Dec. 1993, 2 Jan. 1994, 4 Jan. 1994, 3 Feb. 1994, 6 Feb. 1994, 8 Feb. 1994, 11 Feb. 1994, 13 Feb. 1994, 4 March 1994, 16 April 1994, 21 April 1994, 16 May 1994, 21 May 1994, 25 May 1994, 26 May 1994, 28 May 1994, 4 June 1994, 8 June 1994, 11 June 1994, 14 June 1994, 15 June 1994, 18 June 1994, 19 June 1994, 26 June 1994, 30 June 1994, 2 July 1994, 18 July 1994, 23 July 1994, 3 Aug. 1994, 7 Aug. 1994, 18 Aug. 1994, 19 Aug. 1994, 26 Aug. 1994, 27 Aug. 1994, 15 Sept. 1994, 22 Sept. 1994, 6 Oct. 1994, 7 Oct. 1994, 8 Oct. 1994, 21 Oct. 1994, 5 Nov. 1994, 7 Nov. 1994, 12 Nov. 1994, 14 Nov. 1994, 24 Nov. 1994, 26 Nov. 1994, 27 Nov. 1994, 2 Dec. 1994, 4 Dec. 1994, 20 Dec. 1994, 30 Dec. 1994, 31 Dec. 1994, 14 Jan. 1995, 21 July 1995, 13 Dec. 1995, 17 Dec. 1995, 13 April 1998, 18 Dec. 1998, 18 Nov. 2000, 23 May 2001, 21 Nov. 2001, 31 Jan. 2002, 27 Oct. 2002, 28 Jan. 2003,

14 April 2003, 13 Sept. 2003, 23 Nov. 2003, 14 Dec. 2003, 2 Jan. 2004, 22 Jan. 2004, 4 Oct. 2004, 12 Oct. 2004, 17 Dec. 2004, 7 Jan. 2005, 22 March 2005, 18 June 2005, 21 July 2005, 2 Aug. 2005, 18 Aug. 2005, 9 Sept. 2005, 8 Oct. 2005: A31, 13 Oct. 2005, 14 Oct. 2005, 22 Nov. 2005, 2 Dec. 2005, 10 Dec. 2005, 13 Jan. 2006, 10 Feb. 2006, 10 Feb. 2006, 13 Feb. 2006, 27 Feb. 2006, 11 March 2006, 19 March 2006, 25 March 2006, 30 March 2006, 5 April 2006, 20 April 2006, 28 April 2006, 29 April 2006, 30 April 2006, 1 May 2006, 4 May 2006, 6 May 2006, 11 May 2006, 20 May 2006, 24 May 2006, 3 June 2006, 6 June 2006

Catholic New Times (Toronto) 16 Jan. 2005

Chronicle–Herald (Halifax) 9 April 1988, 14 May 1988, 12 Jan. 1990

Chronicle–Telegraph (Quebec City) 6 Feb. 1991, 27 March 1991, 3 April 1991, 22 May 1991, 5 June 1991, 6 June 1991, 3 July 1991, 24 July 1991, 7 Aug. 1991, 14 Aug. 1991, 7 Oct. 1991

Daily Gleaner (Fredericton) 26 April 1988

Daily News (Halifax) 17 Feb. 1992, 8 March 1992, 15 March 1992, 18 March 1992, 28 March 1992, 10 April 1992, 23 June 1992, 24 June 1992, 12 July 1992, 21 Sept. 1992, 5 Oct. 1992, 16 Oct. 1992, 6 Nov. 1992, 7 Nov. 1992, 19 Nov. 1992, 21 Nov. 1992, 25 Nov. 1992, 30 Dec. 1992, 3 Feb. 1993, 13 Feb. 1993, 3 March 1993, 3 May 1993, 22 May 1993, 27 June 1993, 1 July 1993, 1 Aug. 1993, 19 Sept. 1993, 4 Nov. 1993, 13 Nov. 1993, 8 Dec. 1993, 12 Dec. 1993, 7 March 1994, 10 March 1994, 19 April 1994, 3 May 1994, 12 May 1994, 16 June 1994, 18 June 1994, 23 June 1994, 29 June 1994, 27 July 1994, 4 Aug. 1994, 17 Aug. 1994, 7 Sept. 1994, 28 Sept. 1994, 24 Oct. 1994, 17 Nov. 1994, 4 Dec. 1994, 5 Dec. 1994, 17 Dec. 1994, 19 Dec. 1994, 22 Dec. 1994, 31 Dec. 1994, 30 Dec. 1995, 20 Oct. 1996, 8 Dec. 1998, 17 Oct. 2000, 20 Jan. 2002, 20 April 2002, 23 Aug. 2002, 5 Oct. 2002, 23 June 2003, 22 Oct. 2003, 12 Aug. 2004, 17 Sept. 2004, 20 Feb. 2005, 9 May 2005, 28 Aug. 2005, 1 Dec. 2005, 23 Dec. 2005, 17 Jan. 2006, 1 April 2006, 19 April 2006, 26 April 2006, 16 May 2006, 19 May 2006, 28 May 2006, 10 June 2006

Dominion (Montreal) 12 Sept. 2003

Edmonton Journal 24 Dec. 1988, 8 Sept. 1992, 13 Sept. 1992, 16 Sept. 1992, 18 Sept. 1992, 19 Sept. 1992, 20 Sept. 1992, 10 Jan. 1994, 13 April 1994, 16 April 1994, 28 April 1994, 19 May 1994, 31 May 1994, 23 July 1994, 24 July 1994, 22 Aug. 1994, 1 Oct. 1994, 17 Oct. 1994, 28 Nov. 1994, 3 Dec. 1994, 11 Feb. 1995, 11 Sept. 1995, 2 Dec. 1998, 10 Dec. 2000, 2 June 2001, 23 Oct. 2002, 31 Jan. 2003, 19 Aug. 2003, 23 Aug. 2003, 19 Feb. 2004, 14 June 2004, 13 July 2004, 2 March 2005, 20 March 2005, 21 Aug. 2005, 10 Nov. 2005, 23 Nov. 2005, 8 Jan. 2006, 20 Feb. 2006, 28 Feb. 2006, 3 March 2006, 23 March 2006, 29 March 2006, 1 April 2006, 9 April 2006, 20 April 2006, 25 April 2006, 2 May 2006, 4 May 2006, 6 May 2006, 11 May 2006, 13 May 2006, 3 June 2006, 9 June 2006

Evening Telegram (St. John's) 25 May 1993, 23 May 1993

Financial Post 18 Jan. 1989, 24 Jan. 1989, 30 Jan. 1989, 23 Feb. 1989, 8 March 1989, 9 March 1989, 17 March 1989, 20 March 1989, 10 April 1989, 17 April 1989, 24 April 1989, 28 April 1989, 22 May 1989, 21 June 1989, 9 Oct. 1989, 13 Oct. 1989, 19 Oct. 1989, 20 Oct. 1989, 23 Oct. 1989, 14 Nov. 1989, 8 Dec. 1989, 18 Dec. 1989, 19 Dec. 1989, 4 Jan. 1990, 9 Jan. 1990, 12 Jan. 1990, 15 Jan. 1990, 23 Feb. 1990, 28 Feb. 1990, 20 March 1990, 22 March 1990, 26 March 1990, 17 May 1990, 14 June 1990, 29 June 1990, 13 Aug. 1990, 11 Sept. 1990, 17 Sept. 1990, 21 Sept. 1990, 1 Oct. 1990, 18 Oct. 1990, 30 Oct. 1990, 31 Oct. 1990, 1 Nov. 1990, 22 Nov. 1990, 28 Nov. 1990, 16 Dec. 1990, 4 March 1991, 25 March 1991, 12 April 1991, 16 April 1991, 24 April

1991, 1 May 1991, 13 May 1991, 7 June 1991, 26 June 1991, 9 July 1991, 10 July 1991, 13 Aug. 1991, 20 Aug. 1991, 13 Sept. 1991, 16 Sept. 1991, 19 Sept. 1991, 23 Sept. 1991, 27 Sept. 1991, 4 Oct. 1991, 10 Oct. 1991, 16 Oct. 1991, 18 Oct. 1991, 23 Oct. 1991, 24 Oct. 1991, 31 Oct. 1991, 14 Nov. 1991, 15 Nov. 1991, 2 Dec. 1991, 9 Dec. 1991, 10 Dec. 1991, 23 Dec. 1991, 27 Dec. 1991, 30 Dec. 1991, 20 April 1994

Gazette (Montreal) 17 June 1985, 17 Aug. 1985, 29 Nov. 1986, 14 Nov. 1987, 4 March 1988, 5 May 1988, 19 Nov. 1988, 1 March 1989, 2 March 1989, 3 March 1989, 4 March 1989, 5 March 1989, 6 March 1989, 7 March 1989, 6 May 1989, 27 July 1989, 8 Nov. 1989, 6 Jan. 1990, 7 Jan. 1990, 12 Jan. 1990, 17 Jan. 1990, 20 Jan. 1990, 27 Jan. 1990, 7 Feb. 1990, 11 Feb. 1990, 12 Feb. 1990, 17 Feb. 1990, 18 Feb. 1990, 23 Feb. 1990, 5 March 1990, 8 March 1990, 10 March 1990, 14 March 1990, 31 March 1990, 13 April 1990, 14 April 1990, 18 April 1990, 20 April 1990, 22 April 1990, 25 April 1990, 26 April 1990, 28 April 1990, 29 April 1990, 5 May 1990, 12 May 1990, 17 May 1990, 19 May 1990, 20 May 1990, 26 May 1990, 30 May 1990, 2 June 1990, 3 June 1990, 6 June 1990, 11 June 1990, 16 June 1990, 18 June 1990, 21 June 1990, 22 June 1990, 28 June 1990, 7 July 1990, 13 July 1990, 14 July 1990, 18 July 1990, 19 July 1990, 21 July 1990, 23 July 1990, 26 July 1990, 18 Aug. 1990, 26 Aug. 1990, 28 Aug. 1990, 29 Aug. 1990, 1 Sept. 1990, 2 Sept. 1990, 5 Sept. 1990, 8 Sept. 1990, 13 Sept. 1990, 14 Sept. 1990, 22 Sept. 1990, 23 Sept. 1990, 1 Oct. 1990, 2 Oct. 1990, 4 Oct. 1990, 5 Oct. 1990, 6 Oct. 1990, 10 Oct. 1990, 13 Oct. 1990, 14 Oct. 1990, 18 Oct. 1990, 20 Oct. 1990, 22 Oct. 1990, 25 Oct. 1990, 27 Oct. 1990, 29 Oct. 1990, 30 Oct. 1990, 31 Oct. 1990, 4 Nov. 1990, 7 Nov. 1990, 8 Nov. 1990, 13 Nov. 1990, 15 Nov. 1990, 16 Nov. 1990, 19 Nov. 1990, 22 Nov. 1990, 23 Nov. 1990, 24 Nov. 1990, 4 Dec. 1990, 6 Dec. 1990, 8 Dec. 1990, 12 Dec. 1990, 13 Dec. 1990, 14 Dec. 1990, 16 Dec. 1990, 18 Dec. 1990, 21 Dec. 1990, 22 Dec. 1990, 23 Dec. 1990, 27 Dec. 1990, 28 Dec. 1990, 29 Dec. 1990, 30 Dec. 1990, 2 Feb. 1991, 9 March 1991, 2 May 1991, 7 Sept. 1991, 27 Jan. 1992, 8 Feb. 1992, 12 Feb. 1992, 27 Feb. 1992, 18 March 1992, 21 March 1992, 28 March 1992, 9 April 1992, 27 May 1992, 2 June 1992, 4 June 1992, 6 June 1992, 7 June 1992, 9 June 1992, 10 June 1992, 13 June 1992, 14 June 1992, 17 June 1992, 18 June 1992, 25 June 1992, 28 June 1992, 2 July 1992, 9 July 1992, 28 July 1992, 1 Aug. 1992, 3 Aug. 1992, 7 Aug. 1992, 31 Aug. 1992, 2 Sept. 1992, 22 Oct. 1992, 4 Nov. 1992, 6 Nov. 1992, 10 Nov. 1992, 22 Nov. 1992, 24 Nov. 1992, 25 Nov. 1992, 26 Nov. 1992, 3 Dec. 1992, 5 Dec. 1992, 10 Dec. 1992, 17 Dec. 1992, 19 Dec. 1992, 27 Dec. 1992, 28 Dec. 1992, 29 Dec. 1992, 2 Jan. 1993, 30 Jan. 1993, 19 Feb. 1993, 20 Feb. 1993, 16 March 1993, 21 March 1993, 25 April 1993, 4 May 1993, 26 May 1993, 10 June 1993, 13 June 1993, 21 June 1993, 25 June 1993, 27 June 1993, 30 June 1993, 24 July 1993, 18 Sept. 1993, 25 Sept. 1993, 1 Oct. 1993, 3 Oct. 1993, 4 Oct. 1993, 3 Nov. 1993, 5 Nov. 1993, 12 Nov. 1993, 14 Nov. 1993, 22 Nov. 1993, 13 Dec. 1993, 16 Dec. 1993, 19 Dec. 1993, 21 Dec. 1993, 22 Dec. 1993, 28 Dec. 1993, 6 Jan. 1994, 15 Jan. 1994 , 12 Feb. 1994, 22 Feb. 1994, 26 Feb. 1994, 1 March 1994, 24 March 1994, 15 April 1994, 29 April 1994, 30 April 1994, 7 May 1994, 12 May 1994, 13 May 1994, 15 May 1994, 20 May 1994, 28 May 1994, 1 June 1994, 2 June 1994, 3 June 1994, 4 June 1994, 5 June 1994, 6 June 1994, 10 June 1994, 11 June 1994, 12 June 1994, 13 June 1994, 14 June 1994, 18 June 1994, 19 June 1994, 21 June 1994, 25 June 1994, 29 June 1994, 30 June 1994, 1 July 1994, 2 July 1994, 31 July 1994, 24 Aug. 1994, 10 Sept. 1994, 18 Sept. 1994, 21 Sept. 1994, 8 Oct. 1994, 13 Oct. 1994, 15 Oct. 1994, 20 Oct. 1994, 21 Oct. 1994, 26 Oct. 1994, 10 Nov. 1994, 12 Nov. 1994, 18 Nov. 1994, 19 Nov. 1994, 22 Nov. 1994, 26 Nov. 1994, 6 Dec. 1994, 7 Dec. 1994, 9 Dec. 1994, 14 Dec. 1994, 18 Dec. 1994, 20 Dec.

1994, 22 Dec. 1994, 24 Dec. 1994, 26 Dec. 1994, 30 Dec. 1994, 31 Dec. 1994, 5 July 1995, 28 Sept. 1995, 18 Dec. 1995, 28 Dec. 2000, 12 Oct. 2002, 14 Dec. 2002, 24 May 2003, 24 Jan. 2004, 18 April 2004, 28 April 2004, 17 Aug. 2004, 21 Aug. 2004, 27 Sept. 2004, 1 Nov. 2004, 23 Dec. 2004, 28 Feb. 2005, 8 May 2005, 13 June 2005, 25 June 2005, 7 Sept. 2005, 24 Sept. 2005, 16 Oct. 2005, 2 Nov. 2005, 9 Nov. 2005, 5 Dec. 2005, 5 March 2006, 19 March 2006, 23 March 2006, 25 March 2006, 6 April 2006, 8 April 2006, 12 April 2006, 15 April 2006, 20 April 2006, 22 April 2006, 7 May 2006, 9 May 2006, 13 May 2006, 20 May 2006, 22 May 2006, 24 May 2006, 25 May 2006, 27 May 2006, 9 June 2006, 10 June 2006

Globe and Mail (Toronto) 1 Jan. 1985, 2 Jan. 1985, 3 Jan. 1985, 4 Jan. 1985, 5 Jan. 1985, 7 Jan. 1985, 8 Jan. 1985, 9 Jan. 1985, 10 Jan. 1985, 11 Jan. 1985, 12 Jan. 1985, 14 Jan. 1985, 15 Jan. 1985, 16 Jan. 1985, 17 Jan. 1985, 18 Jan 1985, 19 Jan. 1985, 21 Jan. 1985, 22 Jan. 1985, 23 Jan. 1985, 24 Jan. 1985, 25 Jan. 1985, 26 Jan. 1985, 28 Jan. 1985, 29 Jan. 1985, 30 Jan. 1985, 31 Jan. 1985, 1 Feb. 1985, 2 Feb. 1985, 4 Feb. 1985, 5 Feb. 1985, 7 Feb. 1985, 8 Feb. 1985, 9 Feb. 1985, 12 Feb. 1985, 13 Feb. 1985, 14 Feb. 1985, 15 Feb. 1985, 16 Feb. 1985, 18 Feb. 1985, 19 Feb. 1985, 20 Feb. 1985, 21 Feb. 1985, 22 Feb. 1985, 23 Feb. 1985, 26 Feb. 1985, 27 Feb. 1985, 28 Feb. 1985, 1 March 1985, 2 March 1985, 4 March 1985, 5 March 1985, 6 March 1985, 7 March 1985, 8 March 1985, 9 March 1985, 11 March 1985, 14 March 1985, 16 March 1985, 18 March 1985, 19 March 1985, 20 March 1985, 21 March 1985, 22 March 1985, 23 March 1985, 25 March 1985, 27 March 1985, 28 March 1985, 29 March 1985, 30 March 1985, 1 April 1985, 3 April 1985, 4 April 1985, 6 April 1985, 13 April 1985, 16 April 1985, 17 April 1985, 19 April 1985, 20 April 1985, 23 April 1985, 24 April 1985, 26 April 1985, 27 April 1985, 29 April 1985, 30 April 1985, 2 May 1985, 4 May 1985, 8 May 1985, 9 May 1985, 11 May 1985, 14 May 1985, 15 May 1985, 16 May 1985, 17 May 1985, 18 May 1985, 22 May 1985, 23 May 1985, 24 May 1985, 25 May 1985, 27 May 1985, 28 May 1985, 29 May 1985, 30 May 1985, 31 May 1985, 1 June 1985, 3 June 1985, 4 June 1985, 7 June 1985, 8 June 1985, 11 June 1985, 12 June 1985, 15 June 1985, 18 June 1985, 19 June 1985, 20 June 1985, 22 June 1985, 24 June 1985, 25 June 1985, 27 June 1985, 6 July 1985, 10 July 1985, 11 July 1985, 13 July 1985, 15 July 1985, 16 July 1985, 17 July 1985, 18 July 1985, 24 July 1985, 25 July 1985, 26 July 1985, 27 July 1985, 29 July 1985, 29 July 1985, 30 July 1985, 20 Aug. 1985, 24 Aug. 1985, 26 Aug. 1985, 27 Aug. 1985, 28 Aug. 1985, 29 Aug. 1985, 30 Aug. 1985, 31 Aug. 1985, 2 Sept. 1985, 4 Sept. 1985, 5 Sept. 1985, 6 Sept. 1985, 7 Sept. 1985, 9 Sept. 1985, 11 Sept. 1985, 18 Sept. 1985, 23 Sept. 1985, 24 Sept. 1985, 26 Sept 1985, 27 Sept. 1985, 4 Oct. 1985, 5 Oct. 1985, 7 Oct. 1985, 10 Oct. 1985, 11 Oct. 1985, 12 Oct. 1985, 14 Oct. 1985, 16 Oct. 1985, 17 Oct. 1985, 19 Oct. 1985, 21 Oct. 1985, 22 Oct. 1985, 23 Oct. 1985, 24 Oct. 1985, 25 Oct. 1985, 26 Oct. 1985, 28 Oct. 1985, 31 Oct. 1985, 2 Nov. 1985, 4 Nov. 1985, 5 Nov. 1985, 7 Nov. 1985, 9 Nov. 1985, 15 Nov. 1985, 16 Nov. 1985, 18 Nov. 1985, 20 Nov. 1985, 21 Nov. 1985, 23 Nov. 1985, 24 Nov. 1985, 26 Nov. 1985, 28 Nov. 1985, 29 Nov. 1985, 30 Nov 1985, 4 Dec. 1985, 5 Dec. 1985, 7 Dec. 1985, 9 Dec. 1985, 11 Dec. 1985, 12 Dec. 1985, 14 Dec. 1985, 16 Dec. 1985, 18 Dec. 1985, 20 Dec. 1985, 21 Dec. 1985, 23 Dec. 1985, 26 Dec. 1985, 30 Dec. 1985, 13 April 1986, 1 Nov. 1986, 28 May 1991, 2 Oct. 1991, 23 Oct. 1992, 1 June 1993, 19 Sept. 2002, 18 Feb. 2004, 1 May 2004, 19 June 2004, 29 Oct. 2004, 11 Feb. 2005, 5 March 2005, 7 May 2005, 14 Dec. 2005, 17 Dec. 2005, 24 Dec. 2005, 3 March 2006, 16 March 2006, 3 April 2006, 24 April 2006, 27 May 2006, 3 June 2006, 30 June 2006

Guardian (Charlottetown) 2 Nov. 1990, 12 Dec. 1998, 16 March 2000, 30 March 2000, 24

April 2001, 27 Dec. 2002, 30 Aug. 2003, 18 Oct. 2004, 3 Sept. 2005, 7 Jan. 2006, 8 March 2006, 19 March 2006, 19 April 2006, 26 April 2006, 2 May 2006, 16 May 2006, 24 May 2006

Independent Voice (Kingston) July/August 2005

Jewish Independent (Vancouver) 21 May 2004

Kingston This Week 10 May 2006

Leader–Post (Regina) 27 Feb. 1988, 6 Oct. 2000, 21 Nov. 2002, 14 March 2003, 17 April 2003, 29 April 2003, 22 July 2003, 19 Aug. 2003, 24 June 2004, 26 Nov. 2004, 14 Dec. 2004, 20 July 2005, 3 Sept. 2005, 25 Oct. 2005, 16 Dec. 2005, 14 Feb. 2006, 20 Feb. 2006, 11 April 2006, 24 April 2006, 6 May 2006, 19 May 2006, 29 May 2006

London Free Press 6 May 1986, 28 April 1988, 6 May 1988

National Post (Toronto) 20 Nov. 1999, 31 March 2001, 1 Dec. 2001, 8 Dec. 2001, 31 Dec. 2001, 1 June 2002, 23 Nov. 2002, 24 Jan. 2003, 17 April 2003, 31 May 2003, 2 July 2003, 3 Oct. 2003, 22 Nov. 2003, 19 Dec. 2003, 30 Jan. 2004, 17 June 2004, 14 Aug. 2004, 21 Sept. 2004, 1 Oct. 2004, 25 Jan. 2005, 27 Jan. 2005, 1 March 2005, 4 April 2005, 23 April 2005, 26 April 2005, 10 May 2005, 13 June 2005, 28 July 2005, 30 July 2005, 2 Aug. 2005, 1 Sept. 2005, 15 Sept. 2005, 4 Oct. 2005, 12 Oct. 2005, 8 Nov. 2005, 7 Jan. 2006, 4 Feb. 2006, 19 Feb. 2006, 13 March 2006, 17 March 2006, 21 March 2006, 24 March 2006, 8 April 2006, 22 April 2006, 9 May 2006, 20 May 2006, 24 May 2006, 27 May 2006, 3 June 2006, 10 June 2006, 12 June 2006, 13 June 2006, 22 June 2006

News North (Yellowknife) 19 Feb. 1990; 26 Feb. 1990

Ottawa Citizen 17 Sept. 1985, 12 Dec. 1985, 14 Dec. 1985, 15 March 1986, 22 March 1986, 14 June 1986, 21 Feb. 1987, 10 April 1987, 22 July 1988, 28 Sept. 1988, 14 Jan. 1989, 11 June 1989, 23 Sept. 1989, 6 Jan. 1990, 15 Jan. 1990, 20 Jan. 1990, 20 Jan. 1990, 22 Jan. 1990, 10 Feb. 1990, 14 Feb. 1990, 24 Feb. 1990, 1 March 1990, 2 March 1990, 4 March 1990, 10 March 1990, 17 March 1990, 21 March 1990, 24 March 1990, 25 March 1990, 7 April 1990, 8 April 1990, 9 April 1990, 17 April 1990, 18 April 1990, 23 April 1990, 26 April 1990, 27 April 1990, 29 April 1990, 1 May 1990, 2 May 1990, 10 May 1990, 11 May 1990, 12 May 1990, 14 May 1990, 17 May 1990, 19 May 1990, 29 May 1990, 6 June 1990, 8 June 1990, 9 June 1990, 21 June 1990, 29 June 1990, 30 June 1990, 4 July 1990, 7 July 1990, 8 July 1990, 11 July 1990, 15 July 1990, 22 July 1990, 24 July 1990, 28 July 1990, 9 Aug. 1990, 15 Aug. 1990, 19 Aug. 1990, 28 Aug. 1990, 1 Sept. 1990, 2 Sept. 1990, 6 Sept 1990, 8 Sept. 1990, 9 Sept. 1990, 11 Sept. 1990, 14 Sept. 1990, 15 Sept. 1990, 17 Sept. 1990, 19 Sept. 1990, 27 Sept. 1990, 1 Oct. 1990, 3 Oct. 1990, 6 Oct. 1990, 7 Oct. 1990, 12 Oct. 1990, 13 Oct. 1990, 14 Oct. 1990, 16 Oct. 1990, 17 Oct. 1990, 19 Oct. 1990, 20 Oct. 1990, 21 Oct. 1990, 24 Oct. 1990, 27 Oct. 1990, 29 Oct. 1990, 1 Nov. 1990, 2 Nov. 1990, 4 Nov. 1990, 8 Nov. 1990, 13 Nov. 1990, 16 Nov. 1990, 18 Nov. 1990, 24 Nov. 1990, 29 Nov. 1990, 30 Nov. 1990, 1 Dec. 1990, 3 Dec. 1990, 4 Dec. 1990, 6 Dec. 1990, 7 Dec. 1990, 9 Dec. 1990, 10 Dec. 1990, 12 Dec. 1990, 13 Dec. 1990, 16 Dec. 1990, 17 Dec. 1990, 20 Dec. 1990, 21 Dec. 1990, 23 Dec. 1990, 24 Dec. 1990, 29 Dec. 1990, 31 Dec. 1990, 3 Jan. 1991, 23 Feb. 1991, 30 March 1991, 2 June 1991, 27 June 1991, 4 Nov. 1991, 12 Nov. 1991, 21 Nov. 1991, 27 Nov. 1991, 26 Jan. 1992, 6 Feb. 1992, 8 March 1992, 19 March 1992, 28 March 1992, 12 April 1992, 30 April 1992, 2 May 1992, 5 May 1992, 16 May 1992, 24 May 1992, 3 June 1992, 17 June 1992, 24 June 1992, 27 June 1992, 29 June 1992, 4 July 1992, 11 July 1992, 2 Aug. 1992, 4 Aug. 1992, 29 Aug. 1992, 19 Sept. 1992, 29 Oct. 1992, 31 Oct. 1992, 9 Nov. 1992, 14 Nov. 1992, 17 Nov. 1992, 28 Nov. 1992, 5 Dec. 1992, 12 Dec. 1992, 13 Dec. 1992, 22 Dec.

1992, 24 Dec. 1992, 28 Dec. 1992, 28 Dec. 1992, 29 Dec. 1992, 30 Dec. 1992, 14 Jan. 1993, 18 Feb. 1993, 21 Feb. 1993, 28 Feb. 1993, 23 March 1993, 24 March 1993, 21 April 1993, 20 May 1993, 10 June 1993, 25 Sept. 1993, 31 Oct. 1993, 13 Nov. 1993, 18 Nov. 1993, 10 Dec. 1993, 11 Dec. 1993, 15 Dec. 1993, 30 Dec. 1993, 9 Jan. 1994, 14 Jan. 1994, 4 March 1994, 26 March 1994, 30 March 1994, 6 April 1994, 9 April 1994, 18 April 1994, 26 April 1994, 5 May 1994, 12 May 1994, 21 May 1994, 27 May 1994, 29 May 1994, 31 May 1994, 1 June 1994, 8 June 1994, 19 June 1994, 21 June 1994, 23 June 1994, 25 June 1994, 28 June 1994, 30 June 1994, 3 July 1994, 12 July 1994, 13 July 1994, 16 July 1994, 20 July 1994, 24 July 1994, 31 July 1994, 7 Aug. 1994, 19 Aug. 1994, 1 Sept. 1994, 3 Sept. 1994, 7 Sept. 1994, 11 Sept. 1994, 13 Sept. 1994, 30 Sept. 1994, 3 Oct. 1994, 5 Oct. 1994, 7 Oct. 1994, 15 Oct. 1994, 18 Oct. 1994, 19 Oct. 1994, 23 Oct. 1994, 1 Nov. 1994, 3 Nov. 1994, 18 Nov. 1994, 22 Nov. 1994, 25 Nov. 1994, 26 Nov. 1994, 27 Nov. 1994, 30 Nov. 1994, 1 Dec. 1994, 3 Dec. 1994, 4 Dec. 1994, 6 Dec. 1994, 17 Dec. 1994, 22 Dec. 1994, 23 Dec. 1994, 24 Dec. 1994, 27 Dec. 1994, 28 Dec. 1994, 30 Dec. 1994, 30 July 1995, 16 Sept. 1995, 26 Nov. 1995, 10 Aug. 1999, 31 Oct. 1999, 11 Nov. 1999, 25 Jan. 2000, 29 May 2000, 10 July 2000, 27 Oct. 2001, 1 Dec. 2002, 2 Jan. 2003, 4 March 2003, 22 Feb. 2004, 22 May 2004, 8 July 2004, 20 Nov. 2004, 24 Dec. 2004, 30 April 2005, 5 June 2005, 10 Sept. 2005, 11 Sept. 2005, 17 Oct. 2005, 30 Nov. 2005, 15 Dec. 2005, 7 Jan. 2006, 11 Jan. 2006, 14 Jan. 2006, 17 Jan. 2006, 26 Jan. 2006, 30 Jan. 2006, 4 Feb. 2006, 28 Feb. 2006, 4 March 2006, 19 March 2006, 5 April 2006, 8 April 2006, 21 April 2006, 23 April 2006, 25 April 2006, 30 April 2006, 1 May 2006, 3 May 2006, 14 May 2006, 17 June 2006, 18 June 2006

Province (Vancouver) 4 Jan. 1990, 5 Jan. 1990, 7 Jan. 1990, 26 Jan. 1990, 29 Jan. 1990, 5 Feb. 1990, 7 Feb. 1990, 15 Feb. 1990, 19 Feb. 1990, 22 Feb. 1990, 23 Feb. 1990, 26 Feb. 1990, 4 March 1990, 7 March 1990, 11 March 1990, 15 March 1990, 16 March 1990, 20 March 1990, 21 March 1990, 26 March 1990, 2 April 1990, 3 April 1990, 19 April 1990, 29 April 1990, 4 May 1990, 6 May 1990, 17 May 1990, 22 May 1990, 24 May 1990, 25 May 1990, 27 May 1990, 1 June 1990, 8 June 1990, 10 June 1990, 13 June 1990, 14 June 1990, 18 June 1990, 20 June 1990, 24 June 1990, 28 June 1990, 29 June 1990, 4 July 1990, 6 July 1990, 10 July 1990, 29 July 1990, 31 July 1990, 7 Aug. 1990, 12 Aug. 1990, 19 Aug. 1990, 22 Aug. 1990, 23 Aug. 1990, 6 Sept. 1990, 14 Sept. 1990, 4 Oct. 1990, 7 Oct. 1990, 9 Oct. 1990, 10 Oct. 1990, 11 Oct. 1990, 18 Oct. 1990, 19 Oct. 1990, 23 Oct. 1990, 25 Oct. 1990, 29 Oct. 1990, 31 Oct. 1990, 1 Nov. 1990, 5 Nov. 1990, 8 Nov. 1990, 9 Nov. 1990, 13 Nov. 1990, 14 Nov. 1990, 18 Nov. 1990, 22 Nov. 1990, 25 Nov. 1990, 26 Nov. 1990, 29 Nov. 1990, 30 Nov. 1990, 6 Dec. 1990, 7 Dec. 1990, 9 Dec. 1990, 10 Dec. 1990, 11 Dec. 1990, 13 Dec. 1990, 14 Dec. 1990, 18 Dec. 1990, 23 Dec. 1990, 27 Dec. 1990, 28 Dec. 1990, 29 Dec. 1990, 30 Dec. 1990, 31 Dec. 1990, 25 July 1994, 14 Oct. 1994, 29 Dec. 1994, 19 July 1995, 21 June 2001, 18 Sept. 2002, 10 Nov. 2002, 7 May 2003, 11 June 2003, 3 Aug. 2004, 12 Sept. 2004, 17 Aug. 2005, 26 Aug. 2005, 23 Nov. 2005, 22 Jan. 2006, 17 Feb. 2006, 7 March 2006, 7 May 2006, 25 May 2006, 26 May 2006, 1 June 2006, 4 June 2006, 13 June 2006

Queen's Journal (Kingston) 2 Feb. 1993, 14 Sept. 1993, 8 Feb. 1994, 21 Sept. 2004

Spectator (Hamilton) 16 Feb. 1994, 21 May 1994, 13 June 1994, 14 July 1994, 22 Aug. 1994, 8 Sept. 1994, 28 Sept. 1994, 30 Sept. 1994, 19 Nov. 1994, 22 Dec. 1994, 23 Dec. 1994, 6 Oct. 1995, 13 Dec. 1995, 22 Dec. 1995, 17 Nov. 1996

Star–Phoenix (Saskatoon) 12 April 2002, 17 Oct. 2002, 10 Feb. 2003, 4 July 2003, 24 Oct. 2003, 19 Aug. 2004, 15 Nov. 2004, 10 March 2005, 28 April 2005, 19 July 2005, 22

July 2005, 25 Aug. 2005, 1 Oct. 2005, 16 Feb. 2006, 22 March 2006, 8 April 2006, 18 April 2006, 20 April 2006, 19 May 2006

Sudbury Star 10 Nov. 1999, 29 Sept. 2000, 9 March 2002, 27 Sept. 2003, 1 May 2004, 6 Aug. 2005, 12 Nov. 2005, 15 Dec. 2005, 18 Jan. 2006, 20 Feb. 2006, 27 Feb. 2006, 28 Feb. 2006, 8 May 2006, 5 June 2006

Telegram (St. John's) 24 July 2000, 16 Feb. 2001, 24 Aug. 2001, 28 Oct. 2001, 19 Feb. 2002, 12 June 2003, 12 March 2004, 8 Nov. 2004, 28 Nov. 2004, 10 March 2005, 14 March 2005, 28 May 2005, 6 June 2005, 29 July 2005, 14 Dec. 2005, 11 Jan. 2006, 13 Jan. 2006, 26 March 2006, 9 April 2006, 15 April 2006, 1 May 2006, 10 June 2006, 10 June 2006, 14 June 2006

Times–Colonist (Victoria) 20 June 1995, 15 April 1996, 28 June 1996, 8 Jan. 1999, 29 June 1999, 24 Nov. 2000, 1 Feb. 2001, 19 Jan. 2002, 3 March 2002, 29 Jan. 2003, 23 April 2003, 13 April 2004, 22 Jan. 2005, 16 Feb. 2005, 15 May 2005, 12 Sept. 2005, 1 Oct. 2005, 22 Dec. 2005, 29 March 2006, 16 April 2006, 13 May 2006, 20 May 2006

Toronto Star 28 March 1987, 6 May 1987, 13 June 1987, 17 June 1987, 23 Aug. 1987, 1 Nov. 1987, 5 Nov. 1987, 31 July 1988, 21 Nov. 1988, 31 Dec. 1988, 2 Dec. 1989, 28 March 1990, 2 June 1990, 14 Aug. 1990, 28 Oct. 1990, 20 Nov. 1990, 4 Sept. 1991, 26 Sept. 1991, 12 Oct. 1991, 17 Oct. 1991, 29 Nov. 1991, 5 Dec. 1991, 18 Dec. 1991, 23 Dec. 1991, 5 Jan. 1992, 11 Jan. 1992, 1 Feb. 1992, 7 Feb. 1992, 12 Feb. 1992, 10 April 1992, 21 April 1992, 24 April 1992, 26 April 1992, 3 May 1992, 13 May 1992, 20 May 1992, 23 May 1992, 25 May 1992, 30 May 1992, 7 June 1992, 9 June 1992, 23 June 1992, 26 June 1992, 1 July 1992, 5 July 1992, 24 July 1992, 3 Aug. 1992, 8 Aug. 1992, 29 Aug. 1992, 1 Sept. 1992, 7 Sept. 1992, 13 Sept. 1992, 1 Oct. 1992, 11 Oct. 1992, 14 Oct. 1992, 18 Oct. 1992, 23 Oct. 1992, 30 Oct. 1992, 31 Oct. 1992, 5 Nov. 1992, 9 Nov. 1992, 14 Nov. 1992, 21 Nov. 1992, 24 Nov. 1992, 30 Nov. 1992, 7 Dec. 1992, 12 Dec. 1992, 26 Dec. 1992, 28 Dec. 1992, 30 Dec. 1992, 31 Dec. 1992, 1 Jan. 1993, 15 Jan. 1993, 22 Jan. 1993, 22 Feb. 1993, 25 Feb. 1993, 23 March 1993, 10 April 1993, 3 May 1993, 6 May 1993, 23 May 1993, 25 May 1993, 15 June 1993, 19 June 1993, 21 June 1993, 2 July 1993, 18 July 1993, 24 July 1993, 11 Sept. 1993, 23 Oct. 1993, 30 Oct. 1993, 5 Nov. 1993, 13 Nov. 1993, 25 Nov. 1993, 26 Nov. 1993, 4 Dec. 1993, 8 Dec. 1993, 9 Dec. 1993, 16 Dec. 1993, 20 Dec. 1993, 1 Jan. 1994, 20 Jan. 1994, 3 Feb. 1994, 14 Feb. 1994, 26 Feb. 1994, 5 March 1994, 18 March 1994, 24 March 1994, 30 March 1994, 6 April 1994, 9 April 1994, 11 April 1994, 13 April 1994, 17 April 1994, 21 April 1994, 3 May 1994, 14 May 1994, 19 May 1994, 26 May 1994, 29 May 1994, 4 June 1994, 5 June 1994, 6 June 1994, 13 June 1994, 15 June 1994, 17 June 1994, 18 June 1994, 20 June 1994, 23 June 1994, 28 June 1994, 29 June 1994, 30 June 1994, 2 July 1994, 12 July 1994, 21 July 1994, 25 July 1994, 30 July 1994, 31 July 1994, 5 Aug. 1994, 11 Sept. 1994, 26 Sept. 1994, 30 Sept. 1994, 2 Oct. 1994, 10 Oct. 1994, 22 Oct. 1994, 23 Oct. 1994, 24 Oct. 1994, 4 Nov. 1994, 6 Nov. 1994, 12 Nov. 1994, 13 Nov. 1994, 15 Nov. 1994, 16 Nov. 1994, 19 Nov. 1994, 20 Nov. 1994, 21 Nov. 1994, 22 Nov. 1994, 23 Nov. 1994, 30 Nov. 1994, 1 Dec. 1994, 3 Dec. 1994, 4 Dec. 1994, 8 Dec. 1994, 11 Dec. 1994, 16 Dec. 1994, 22 Dec. 1994, 24 Dec. 1994, 27 Dec. 1994, 31 Dec. 1994, 4 May 1995, 11 May 1995, 16 May 1995, 1 Oct. 1995, 5 Oct. 1995, 8 Dec. 1995, 12 Jan. 2000, 29 Oct. 2000, 25 Feb. 2001, 20 May 2001, 2 March 2002, 25 March 2002, 9 Nov. 2002, 4 Jan. 2003, 26 Jan. 2003, 20 Nov. 2003, 24 Jan. 2004, 22 Feb. 2004, 8 May 2004, 24 May 2004, 22 July 2004, 11 Dec. 2004, 26 Dec. 2004, 17 Jan. 2005, 23 Jan. 2005, 18 March 2005, 4 June 2005, 23 June 2005, 26 June 2005, 6 Aug. 2005, 7 Aug. 2005, 8 Aug. 2005, 21 Oct. 2005, 9 Jan. 2006, 25 Feb. 2006, 1 April 2006, 2 April 2006, 15 April 2006, 16 April 2006, 21

April 2006, 22 April 2006, 28 April 2006, 2 May 2006, 4 May 2006, 7 May 2006, 17 May 2006, 21 May 2006, 25 May 2006, 27 May 2006, 28 May 2006, 6 June 2006, 8 June 2006, 11 June 2006, 15 June 2006, 19 June 2006

Toronto Sun 26 Oct. 1992, 16 Feb. 1994, 24 Feb. 1994, 15 Sept. 1994, 16 Oct. 1994

Vancouver Sun 21 July 1989, 2 Jan. 1990, 3 Jan. 1990, 6 Jan. 1990, 12 Jan. 1990, 13 Jan.1990, 17 Jan. 1990, 20 Jan. 1990, 23 Jan. 1990, 25 Jan. 1990, 27 Jan. 1990, 30 Jan. 1990, 3 Feb. 1990, 6 Feb. 1990, 12 Feb. 1990, 14 Feb. 1990, 17 Feb. 1990, 19 Feb. 1990, 21 Feb. 1990, 23 Feb. 1990, 24 Feb. 1990, 3 March 1990, 6 March 1990, 9 March 1990, 10 March 1990, 12 March 1990, 17 March 1990, 19 March 1990, 20 March 1990, 22 March 1990, 23 March 1990, 24 March 1990, 27 March 1990, 28 March 1990, 4 April 1990, 9 April 1990, 14 April 1990, 16 April 1990, 17 April 1990, 18 April 1990, 21 April 1990, 22 April 1990, 27 April 1990, 3 May 1990, 5 May 1990, 6 May 1990, 9 May 1990, 10 May 1990, 11 May 1990, 12 May 1990, 15 May 1990, 17 May 1990, 19 May 1990, 22 May 1990, 26 May 1990, 31 May 1990, 1 June 1990, 2 June 1990, 9 June 1990, 16 June 1990, 17 June 1990, 21 June 1990, 23 June 1990, 26 June 1990, 27 June 1990, 28 June 1990, 30 June 1990, 3 July 1990, 7 July 1990, 9 July 1990, 10 July 1990, 13 July 1990, 14 July 1990, 17 July 1990, 19 July 1990, 20 July 1990, 21 July 1990, 23 July 1990, 24 July 1990, 26 July 1990, 27 July 1990, 28 July 1990, 2 Aug. 1990, 4 Aug. 1990, 7 Aug. 1990, 8 Aug. 1990, 10 Aug. 1990, 11 Aug. 1990, 13 Aug. 1990, 15 Aug. 1990, 16 Aug. 1990, 21 Aug. 1990, 23 Aug. 1990, 23 Aug. 1990, 24 Aug. 1990, 25 Aug. 1990, 30 Aug. 1990, 31 Aug. 1990, 5 Sept. 1990, 7 Sept. 1990, 8 Sept. 1990, 14 Sept. 1990, 15 Sept. 1990, 18 Sept. 1990, 19 Sept. 1990, 21 Sept. 1990, 29 Sept. 1990, 2 Oct. 1990, 5 Oct. 1990, 6 Oct. 1990, 9 Oct. 1990, 11 Oct. 1990, 12 Oct. 1990, 13 Oct. 1990, 17 Oct. 1990, 18 Oct. 1990, 19 Oct. 1990, 20 Oct. 1990, 23 Oct. 1990, 24 Oct. 1990, 26 Oct. 1990, 27 Oct. 1990, 29 Oct. 1990, 30 Oct. 1990, 1 Nov. 1990, 3 Nov. 1990, 5 Nov. 1990, 9 Nov. 1990, 10 Nov. 1990, 13 Nov. 1990, 14 Nov. 1990, 15 Nov. 1990, 16 Nov. 1990, 17 Nov. 1990, 20 Nov. 1990, 23 Nov. 1990, 24 Nov. 1990, 26 Nov. 1990, 27 Nov. 1990, 30 Nov. 1990, 1 Dec. 1990, 4 Dec. 1990, 5 Dec. 1990, 6 Dec. 1990, 7 Dec. 1990, 8 Dec. 1990, 10 Dec. 1990, 11 Dec. 1990, 12 Dec. 1990, 13 Dec. 1990, 14 Dec. 1990, 15 Dec. 1990, 17 Dec. 1990, 18 Dec. 1990, 19 Dec. 1990, 20 Dec. 1990, 21 Dec. 1990, 22 Dec. 1990, 27 Dec. 1990, 28 Dec. 1990, 29 Dec. 1990, 2 March 1991, 3 April 1991, 16 May 1991, 5 Sept. 1991, 9 Nov. 1991, 2 Jan. 1992, 11 Jan. 1992, 13 Jan. 1992, 1 Feb. 1992, 18 Feb. 1992, 20 Feb. 1992, 19 March 1992, 2 April 1992, 3 April 1992, 8 April 1992, 14 April 1992, 18 April 1992, 20 April 1992, 24 April 1992, 26 May 1992, 10 June 1992, 11 June 1992, 17 June 1992, 20 June 1992, 23 June 1992, 24 June 1992, 25 June 1992, 30 June 1992, 18 July 1992, 29 July 1992, 7 Aug. 1992, 11 Sept. 1992, 12 Sept. 1992, 25 Sept. 1992, 26 Oct. 1992, 7 Nov. 1992, 9 Nov. 1992, 8 Dec. 1992, 9 Dec. 1992, 11 Dec. 1992, 16 Dec. 1992, 28 Dec. 1992, 29 Dec. 1992, 5 April 1993, 14 May 1993, 27 May 1993, 5 June 1993, 18 June 1993, 26 June 1993, 29 June 1993, 8 July 1993, 30 Aug. 1993, 12 Nov. 1993, 13 Nov. 1993, 20 Nov. 1993, 27 Nov. 1993, 29 Nov. 1993, 15 Dec. 1993, 16 Dec. 1993, 18 Dec. 1993, 24 Dec. 1993, 27 Dec. 1993, 29 Jan. 1994, 5 Feb. 1994, 12 Feb. 1994, 21 March 1994, 25 March 1994, 26 March 1994, 31 March 1994, 7 April 1994, 9 April 1994, 12 April 1994, 27 April 1994, 7 May 1994, 9 May 1994, 11 May 1994, 16 May 1994, 28 May 1994, 11 June 1994, 16 June 1994, 18 June 1994, 23 June 1994, 24 June 1994, 25 June 1994, 27 June 1994, 28 June 1994, 29 June 1994, 15 July 1994, 23 July 1994, 25 July 1994, 2 Aug. 1994, 13 Aug. 1994, 25 Aug. 1994, 30 Aug. 1994, 31 Aug. 1994, 15 Sept. 1994, 4 Oct. 1994, 8 Oct. 1994, 14 Oct. 1994, 22 Oct. 1994, 1 Nov. 1994, 15 Nov. 1994, 17 Nov. 1994, 18 Nov. 1994, 18

Nov. 1994, 21 Nov. 1994, 24 Nov. 1994, 2 Dec. 1994, 3 Dec. 1994, 6 Dec. 1994, 8 Dec. 1994, 12 Dec. 1994, 14 Dec. 1994, 15 Dec. 1994, 17 Dec. 1994, 22 Dec. 1994, 31 Dec. 1994, 11 Feb. 1995, 1 April 1995, 14 May 1995, 10 June 1998, 27 June 1998, 9 March 2000, 22 Sept. 2000, 2 March 2001, 31 Oct. 2001, 3 May 2002, 10 Feb. 2003, 3 May 2003, 8 May 2003, 14 July 2003, 2 March 2004, 15 Jan. 2005, 18 Jan. 2005, 5 April 2005, 18 April 2005, 29 June 2005, 27 Aug. 2005, 15 Nov. 2005, 6 Jan. 2006, 16 Jan. 2006, 30 Jan. 2006, 9 Feb. 2006, 18 March 2006, 25 March 2006, 10 April 2006, 14 April 2006, 22 April 2006, 29 April 2006, 5 May 2006, 6 May 2006, 12 May 2006, 23 May 2006, 3 June 2006, 9 June 2006, 17 June 2006

Whig–Standard (Kingston) 29 June 1985, 30 Aug. 1986, 14 Oct. 1986, 24 June 1991, 5 June 1992, 28 Aug. 1993, 10 May 1994, 13 Oct. 1995, 30 May 2000, 27 June 2000, 11 April 2001, 21 Nov. 2001, 20 Feb. 2002, 27 Dec. 2002, 30 June 2003, 14 June 2005, 23 Sept. 2005, 28 Oct. 2005, 17 Dec. 2005, 6 March 2006, 28 March 2006, 29 March 2006, 1 April 2006, 4 April 2006, 15 April 2006, 24 April 2006, 29 April 2006, 19 May 2006, 23 May 2006, 26 May 2006

Windsor Star 28 Dec. 2002, 23 Aug. 2003, 10 March 2005, 29 Oct. 2005, 23 Nov. 2005, 25 Jan. 2006, 23 Feb. 2006, 14 March 2006, 1 April 2006, 11 April 2006, 2 May 2006, 6 May 2006, 13 May 2006, 18 May 2006, 23 May 2006

Winnipeg Free Press 17 Nov. 1990

Conference Proceedings

Background Paper on Regional Planning and Development in Ontario, Ontario Regional Trilevel Conference 1973

Television

CBC News [transcript], 20 Sept. 1994
CBC News [transcript], 23 Nov. 1994
CBC News [transcript], 30 Dec. 1994
CBC News [transcript], 22 May 1995
CTV News [transcript], 1 Oct. 1994
CTV News [transcript], 14 Dec. 1994
CTV News [transcript], 24 Dec. 1994
Hockey Night in Canada CBC Television Broadcast, 24 Oct. 1992

Websites

'2004 Property Tax Deferral Program'. City of Toronto website, 2004
Admissions, University of Calgary website, May 2006
Admissions, University of Waterloo website, May 2006
'Alberta Initiative for School Improvement'. Alberta Government website, 2006
Athletics Canada website, 20 Dec. 2005
AudioWorld Online website, 19 Aug. 2003
'British Columbia'. CBC News website, 25 Feb. 2000
CBC Magazine CBC website, 20 Oct. 2004
CBC Magazine CBC website, 27 March 2001
CBC News Online website, 18 Feb. 2003
CBC News Online website, 21 Sept. 2004
CBC News Online website, 3 May 2005
CBC Sports CBC website, 16 April 2003
CBC Sports Online website, 5 Jan. 2004

Citizenship and Immigration Canada website, 27 Sept. 2005

Concordia University Online Study Skills Help website, 1998

CTV Forums Online website, 8 Nov. 2005

Department of French, Simon Fraser University website, 2004–5

'Fact Sheet'. Ontario Ministry of the Environment website, June 2006

Final Agreement on the Quebec Parental Insurance Plan. *Régime québécois d'assurance parentale* website, June 2006

Industry Canada website, 31 Aug. 2005

'Job Demands Analysis, Arena Service Worker'. Greater Vancouver Regional District website, 1999

Living with Bengals: a personal weblog website, 1 Oct. 2005

McGill University website, June 2006

Media Release, Canadian Judicial Council website, 22 July 2002

News Bulletin, Natural Sciences and Engineering Research Council of Canada website, 7 Oct. 2004

Ontario Ministry of Child and Youth Services website, 25 Nov. 2005

'Our History'. Theatre Kingston website, 2002

Palys, Ted S. *Background Report for BC Supreme Court Little Sister's Book and Art Emporium v. The Queen 7 Oct. 1994*, posted on author's webpage

Post-secondary Education Choice and Excellence Act, 2000, Ontario Statutes and Regulations website

Proceedings of the Standing Senate Committee on National Security and Defence Issue 10:2, Parliament of Canada website, Feb. 2005

Régie de l'assurance maladie website, June 2006

'School-Aged Children Across Canada'. Canadian Policy Research Network website, 2001

Staff Directory, CKUA Radio Network (University of Alberta) website, June 2006

'Standing Orders 222 Shuswap'. Department of National Defence website, 1 Sept. 2005

'Support the ROM'. Royal Ontario Museum website, 19 Oct. 2006

'T-cell count (CD4 count)'. *Plain and Simple Fact Sheets* Canadian AIDS Treatment Information Exchange website, April 2003

'That We May Know Each Other'. United Church of Canada website, 2004

'The Role of Judges in Modern Society'. Supreme Court of Canada website, 5 May 2001

'Tips for Business Travellers—Slovak Republic'. International Trade Canada website, March 2005

Vancouver Liquor Licensing Commission report. City of Vancouver website, 3 Nov. 1995

'What is La Francophonie?' Canadian International Development Agency website, 20 Dec. 2005

'What's happened to left-wing Liberalism?' CBC News Analysis and Viewpoint, CBC website, 26 Jan. 2004

Works Consulted

Following are the works we most frequently consulted in the course of writing the guide. Most citations of these works in the entries refer to the title (or a short form of it), with these exceptions: OED (*Oxford English Dictionary*), 3rd edition, online; Fowler (the original *Dictionary of Modern English Usage*, 1926); *Fowler's* (the second edition, 1965, revised by Sir Ernest Gowers); and 'Survey of Vancouver English' ('Final report to the Social Sciences Research Council on An Urban Dialect Survey of Vancouver English').

General Dictionaries

American Heritage Dictionary of the English Language. 3rd edn. Executive ed. Anne H. Soukhanov. Boston: Houghton Mifflin, 1992.

Canadian Oxford Dictionary. 2nd edn. Ed. Katherine Barber. Toronto: Oxford University Press, 2004.

Collins Canadian English Dictionary and Thesaurus. Ed. Elspeth Summers and Andrew Holmes. Toronto: HarperCollins, 2004.

Collins COBUILD English Language Dictionary. Ed.-in-chief John Sinclair. London: Collins, 1987.

Collins English Dictionary. 6th edn. Ed. Jeremy Butterfield. Glasgow: HarperCollins, 2003.

Concise Oxford English Dictionary. 11th edn. Ed. Catherine Soanes and Angus Stevenson. Oxford: Oxford University Press, 2004.

Concise Oxford Dictionary of Current English. 9th edn. Ed. Della Thompson. Oxford: Clarendon Press, 1995.

Dictionary of Canadianisms on Historical Principles. Ed.-in-chief Walter S. Avis. Toronto: Gage, 1967.

Encarta World English Dictionary. Ed.-in-Chief Kathy Rooney. London: Bloomsbury Publishing, 1999.

Funk and Wagnalls Canadian College Dictionary. Ed. Walter S. Avis. Toronto: Fitzhenry and Whiteside, 1989.

Gage Canadian Dictionary. Ed. Gaelan Dodds de Wolf et al. Toronto: Gage, 1997.

Gage Canadian Dictionary. Co-ordinating ed. Patrick D. Drysdale. Toronto: Gage, 1983.

ITP Nelson Canadian Dictionary of the English Language. Executive ed. Susan Green. Toronto: ITP Nelson, 1997.

Merriam-Webster's Collegiate Dictionary. 11th edn. Ed.-in-chief Frederick C. Mish. Springfield, Massachusetts: Merriam-Webster, 2003

New Oxford American Dictionary. Ed. Elizabeth J. Jewell and Frank Abate. New York: Oxford University Press, 2001.

New Oxford Dictionary of English. Ed. Judy Pearsall. Oxford: Oxford University Press, 1998.

New Shorter Oxford English Dictionary. Ed. Lesley Brown. 2 vols. Oxford: Clarendon Press, 1993.

Oxford Encyclopedic English Dictionary. Ed. Joyce M. Hawkins and Robert Allen. Oxford: Clarendon Press, 1991.

Oxford English Dictionary. 3rd edn. Chief Ed. John Simpson. Oxford University Press, 2006. http://dictionary.oed.com/ (requires subscription)

Oxford English Dictionary. 2nd edn. Ed. J.A. Simpson and E.S.C. Weiner. 20 vols. Oxford: Clarendon Press, 1989. (Compact edition, one volume, 1991.)

Oxford English Dictionary Additions Series. Ed. John Simpson and Edmund Weiner. Oxford: Clarendon Press, 1993–.

Random House Webster's College Dictionary. Ed.-in-chief Robert B. Costello. New York: Random House, 1991.

Random House Webster's Unabridged Dictionary. 2nd edn. Ed. Wendalyn R. Nichols. New York: Random House, 2001.

Reader's Digest Webster's Canadian Dictionary and Thesaurus. New Lanark, Scotland: Geddes & Grosset, 2004.

Webster's American Dictionary: College Edition. 2nd edn. New York: Random House, 2000.

Webster's New World College Dictionary. 4th edn. Ed. Michael Agnes. Cleveland, Ohio: Wiley Publishing, 2002.

Usage Guides, Style Guides, and Specialized Dictionaries

American Heritage Book of English Usage. Boston: Houghton Mifflin, 1996.

American Usage and Style: The Consensus. Roy Copperud. New York: Van Nostrand Reinhold, 1980.

Cambridge Australian English Style Guide. Pam Peters. Cambridge: Cambridge University Press, 1995.

Cambridge Grammar of the English Language. Rodney Huddleston and Geoffrey K. Pullum. Cambridge: Cambridge University Press, 2002.

Cambridge Guide to English Usage. Pam Peters. Cambridge: Cambridge University Press, 2004.

Canadian Law Dictionary. 5th edn. John A. Yogis. New York: Barron's Educational Series, 2003.

Canadian Oxford High School Dictionary. Ed. Katherine Barber et al. Toronto: Oxford University Press, 2001.

The Canadian Press Stylebook: A Guide for Writers and Editors. 13th edn. Ed. Patti Tasko. Toronto: Canadian Press, 2004.

The CP Stylebook: A Guide for Writers and Editors. Rev. edn. Ed. Peter Buckley. Toronto: Canadian Press, 1993.

The Canadian Style: A Guide to Writing and Editing. Public Works and Government Services Canada. Toronto: Dundurn Press, 1997.

Chicago Manual of Style. 15th edn. Chicago: University of Chicago Press, 2003.

City of Montréal Style Guide. Victor Trahan. Montreal: Service du greffe, 2001.

Columbia Guide to Standard American English. Kenneth G. Wilson. New York: Columbia University Press, 1993.

Concise Dictionary of Medical-Legal Terms. Joseph A. Bailey. New York: Parthenon Publishing Group, 1998

Dictionary of Canadian Law. Daphne A. Dukelow and Betsy Nuse. Scarborough, ON: Carswell, 1991.

Dictionary of Contemporary American Usage. Bergen Evans and Cornelia Evans. New York: Random House, 1957.

Dictionary of Modern Legal Usage. Bryan A. Garner. New York: Oxford University Press, 1987.

Eats, Shoots & Leaves. Lynne Truss. New York: Penguin, 2003.

Editing Canadian English. 2nd edn. Catherine Cragg et al. Toronto: Macfarlane Walter & Ross, for the Editors' Association of Canada, 2000.

Editing Canadian English. Lydia Burton et al. Vancouver: Douglas and McIntyre, for the

Freelance Editors' Association of Canada, 1987.

Garner's Modern American Usage. Bryan A. Garner. Oxford: Oxford University Press, 2003.

The Gazette Style. Rev. edn. Joseph N. Gelmon. Montreal: Gazette, 1995.

The Globe and Mail Style Book: A Guide to Language and Usage. Rev. edn. J.A. (Sandy) McFarlane and Warren Clements. Toronto: Penguin, 1995.

Good English Guide: English Usage in the 1990s. Geoffrey Howard. London: Pan Macmillan, 1993.

Harper Dictionary of Contemporary Usage. 2nd edn. William and Mary Morris. New York: Harper and Row, 1985.

The King's English. 3rd edn. Ed. H.W. Fowler and F.G. Fowler. Oxford: Clarendon Press, 1931.

Lapsing Into a Comma. Bill Walsh. Chicago: Contemporary Books, 2000.

List of Names for Countries, Capitals and Inhabitants. André Racicot. Ottawa: Goverment of Canada, 2000.

Longman Guide to English Usage. Sidney Greenbaum and Janet Whitcut. Harlow, Essex: Longman, 1988.

MLA Manual and Guide to Scholarly Publishing. 2nd edn. Ed. Joseph Gibaldi. New York: Modern Language Association of America, 1998.

Modern American Usage. 1st edn. Wilson Follett 1966. 2nd edn. Rev. by Erik Wensberg. New York: Hill and Wang, 1998.

New Fowler's Modern English Usage. 3rd edn. Ed. R.W. Burchfield. Oxford: Clarendon Press, 1996.

Dictionary of Modern English Usage. 1st edn. H.W. Fowler, 1926; 2nd edn. Rev. by Ernest Gowers. Oxford: Clarendon Press, 1965.

NewsTalk. Ed. Georgette McCulloch and Mike Omelus. Toronto: Broadcast News, 2003.

The New York Public Library Writer's Guide to Style and Usage. Ed. Andrea J. Sutcliffe. New York: HarperCollins, 1994.

The New York Times Manual of Style and Usage. Allan M. Siegal and William G. Connolly. New York: Three Rivers Press, 1999.

No Uncertain Terms. William Safire. New York: Simon and Schuster, 2003.

Oxford Guide to English Usage. 2nd edn. E.S.C. Weiner and Andrew Delahunty. Oxford: Clarendon Press, 1993.

Oxford Style Manual. Ed. R.M. Ritter. Oxford: Oxford University Press, 2003.

The Penguin Dictionary of American English Usage and Style. Paul W. Lovinger. New York: Penguin Books, 2001.

Reader's Digest Success with Words: A North American Guide to the English Language. New York: Reader's Digest, 1983.

Talking Gender: A Guide to Nonsexist Communication. Ruth King et al. Toronto: Copp Clark Pitman, 1991.

Webster's Dictionary of English Usage. New York: Merriam-Webster, 1989.

Word Court. Barbara Wallraff. New York: Harcourt, 2000.

Your Own Words. Barbara Wallraff. New York: Counterpoint, 2004.

Databases
'The CBC Language Guide'. CBC, 1995. (Not commercially available.)

TERMIUM Plus®: The Government of Canada's terminology and linguistics database

Surveys
The English Language as Used in Quebec: A Survey. Tom McArthur. Occasional Paper Number 3. Kingston, ON: Strathy Language Unit (Queen's University), 1989.

'Final Report to the Social Sciences and Humanities Research Council of Canada on An Urban Dialect Survey of the English Spoken in Vancouver'. R.J. Gregg. April 1984. (Ms.)

Modern Canadian English Usage: Linguistic Change and Reconstruction. M.H. Scargill. Toronto: McClelland and Stewart with the Canadian Council of Teachers of English, 1974.

'Socio-dialectology Survey of the English Spoken in Ottawa: A Study of Sociological Variation in Canadian English'. H.B. Woods. Ph.D. dissertation. University of British Columbia, 1979.

General Works on Canadian English and Usage in Canada

Focus on Canada. Varieties of English around the World, G11. Ed. Sandra Clarke. Amsterdam: John Benjamins, 1993.

In Defence of Plain English: The Decline and Fall of Literacy in Canada. Victoria Branden. Willowdale, ON: Hounslow, 1992.

In Search of the Standard in Canadian English. Ed. W.C. Lougheed. Occasional Paper Number 1. Kingston, ON: Strathy Language Unit (Queen's University), 1986.

Our Own Voice: Canadian English and How It Is Studied. R.E. McConnell. Toronto: Gage, 1979.

Social and Regional Factors in Canadian English: A Study of Phonological Variables and Grammatical Items in Ottawa and Vancouver. Gaelan Dodds de Wolf. Toronto: Canadian Scholars' Press, 1992.

Speaking Canadian English: An Informal Account of the English Language in Canada. Mark M. Orkin. New York: David McKay, 1970.

Words Fail Us: Good English and Other Lost Causes. Bob Blackburn. Toronto: McClelland and Stewart, 1993.

Writing on Canadian English 1792–1975: An Annotated Bibliography. Walter S. Avis and A.M. Kinloch. Toronto: Fitzhenry and Whiteside [1977].

Writings on Canadian English 1976–1987: A Selective, Annotated Bibliography. Occasional Paper Number 2. W.C. Lougheed. Kingston, ON: Strathy Language Unit (Queen's University), 1988.

Words: Wonder and Woe. Blair Shewchuk. CBC website http://www.cbc.ca/news/indepth/words/.

You Don't Say. Ed. George Rich. CBC office of Broadcast Language. Vols 4.1–6.4, Dec. 1979–July 1981. (An in-house newsletter on usage and pronunciation for CBC announcers.)

Regional Dictionaries and Phrasebooks

Cold as a Bay Street Banker's Heart: The Ultimate Prairie Phrase Book. Chris Thain. Saskatoon: Western Producer, 1987.

Dictionary of Newfoundland English. 2nd edn with supplement. Ed. G.M. Story, W.J. Kirwin, and J.D.A. Widdowson. Toronto: University of Toronto Press, 1990.

Dictionary of Prince Edward Island English. Ed. T.K. Pratt. Toronto: University of Toronto Press, 1988.

South Shore Phrase Book: A New, Revised and Expanded Nova Scotia Dictionary. Comp. Lewis J. Poteet. Hantsport, NS: Lancelot, 1988.

Wet Coast Words: A Dictionary of British Columbia Words and Phrases. Tom Parkin. Victoria: Orca, 1989.

Other

Cambridge Encyclopedia of Language. David Crystal. Cambridge: Cambridge University Press, 1987.

Works Consulted

Canadian Encyclopedia. 2nd edn. Ed.-in-chief James H. Marsh. Edmonton: Hurtig, 1988. (Now available at http://www.thecanadianencyclopedia.com/.)

The Collins Dictionary of Canadian History: 1867 to the Present. David J. Bercuson and J.L. Granatstein. Toronto: Collins, 1988.

Comprehensive Grammar of the English Language. Randolph Quirk et al. London: Longman, 1985.

Oxford Companion to the English Language. Ed. Tom McArthur. Oxford: Oxford University Press, 1992.

Pidgins and Creoles. 2nd edn. Loreto Todd. London, Routledge, 1991.